lonely planet

The World

A Traveller's Guide to the Planet

THE WORLD

Contents

KEY
. . . .

- Africa
- America
- Antarctica
- Asia
- Australia/Oceania
- Europe

Welcome to the World

Third Rock from the Sun. Mother Earth. The Blue Marble. The spinning ball of rock that is the world goes by many names, but it is also the place that each and every one of us calls home. And wherever it is that you call home, you can be sure that if you travel – near or far – the world will exhibit its overwhelming beauty and diversity. Adventure and inspirational experiences await around every corner, so what's stopping you? Go forth and explore.

Natural Wonders

Comedian Steven Wright once quipped, 'You can't have everything – where would you put it?' Weighing in at 5.97219×1024 kg, and with 149 million sq km of landmass (and another 361 million sq km of ocean), the world has room enough to fit 'everything'. Amidst all of that 'everything' there is so much to discover, from rivers deep, like the Nile (snaking 6850km from central Africa to the Mediterranean), and the sunken shores of the Dead Sea (427m below sea level), to mountains high, like the Himalayas (more than 100 peaks over 7200m, including Everest at 8848m), the Andes and the Alps.

Across seven continents and 221 countries, 'everything' takes plenty of wondrous forms. There are mighty expanses of greenery, like the Amazon basin (7 million sq km of jungle), while beneath the crystal-clear Pacific Ocean lies the Great Barrier Reef (stretching 2300km), and the scarred hide of the Grand Canyon is a repository of 2 billion years of geological history.

Not all the world's wonders are inanimate, however. Wildlife spectacles include the annual wildebeest migration (two million strong) across the Serengeti, the stoic emperor penguins of Antarctica, and the diverse menagerie on the Galapagos Islands, where people seem out of place.

Spectacular Cities

It is people, not animals, who have colonised the entire planet. Since foregoing stone tools, inventing the wheel (3300BC) and first smelting iron (1200BC), humankind has embarked on a big production number that features countless cultures, civilisations and empires. History suggests that humans were naturally inclined to warfare but also –more positively – to congregating and cohabiting, thus, over time the city was born.

More than half of the world's population now live in cities. They are the pulsating beacons that attract us, with their bright lights and human interaction, epicentres of culture, industry and endeavour. And each has its own distinctive character: New York with its skyscrapers and taxicabs, London with its parks, pubs and palaces, Sydney with its bridge and Cape Town set against the rugged panorama of Table Mountain. A tour of urban conurbations will take you to geographical oddities (İstanbul straddling the border of Europe and Asia), and cities of faith (Jerusalem, holy to Judaism, Islam and Christianity), cities with thousands of years of history (Athens, Damascus, Varanasi) and booming new cities mushrooming across Asia, Africa and South America.

Heron Island, Great Barrier Reef, Australia

Man-Made Marvels

Cities may be the hubs that you pass through as you roam, but they are not necessarily humankind's greatest achievements. These are many and dispersed, assuming myriad physical forms.

Mystery clings to many, such as the Great Pyramid of Giza built in 2560BC, the Terracotta Warriors in Xī'ān and the mighty stone *moai* of Easter Island. Others no less awe inspiring were built for specific purposes, like St Basil's Cathedral in the Kremlin, the Great Wall of China, and the Taj Mahal, a monument to love. More modern spectacles like the architectural extravaganzas of Dubai and the Shanghai skyline may lack the gravity of history but if anything are more dazzling.

All of these monuments contribute to the ways of life that go on around them, which reminds us that not all of humankind's achievements are tangible. Just as intoxicating and just as worth getting out and seeing are cultures, festivals and events, from Viennese coffeehouse culture to Cuban jazz, from full moon parties on Koh Samui to Maasai warrior dances under an African sunset.

There is all this and plenty more besides to be encountered as you venture into the world. This book can act as inspiration and as a first step on your own voyage of discovery. Listed here is every country; each includes enough of a taste of its top sites and experiences to get your feet itchy, basic practical information to help you start planning, and a map to help you plot a rough itinerary. Where exactly you want to go and how you proceed from here is entirely up to you, but we encourage you to get out there and do it!

Need to Know

Most widely spoken languages

If you can speak one or more of the following languages, you can communicate with these percentages of the world's population.

%

▲ Mandarin 14.4%   △ Arabic 4.4%   ▲ Russian 2.3%

▲ Spanish 6.2%   △ Portuguese 3.3%   ▲ Japanese 1.9%

△ English 5.4%   ▲ Bengali 3.1%   ▲ French 1.1%

△ Hindi/Urdu 5.7%

Languages

It's the babble of Babel out there! There are almost 7000 languages spoken in the world today. These are divided into six major language families, and around 130 smaller ones. The distribution of languages across the globe reflects movements of people through history, and language families include some unlikely relatives: for example, Albanian is related to English, Hindi, Persian and Russian. The size of countries and populations don't necessarily account for numbers of languages, either: in New Guinea almost 450 languages are spoken by a population of only 3.5 million people.

It's estimated that half of the world's population speaks more than one language. Fear not if you don't: a smile can go a long way, even amongst people you share no language with. That said, learning a few words of the language spoken at your destination can open a lot of doors.

Time

We all know that as the world orbits the sun, the planet is also spinning, meaning that for some of us the sun is setting, and for others it is rising. So, when it is bedtime in Sydney, locals will be reaching for a late-afternoon chai in Mumbai, lunching in London or getting ready to rise in New York. To make life easier, the world is divided into time zones.

Time zones

The clever fellows at London's Royal Observatory saw to it that from the 1880s Greenwich Mean Time (GMT) was adopted as the global reference time. Each time zone is designated as either being + or − whole numbers of hours (or half hours) from GMT. In 1972, Coordinated Universal Time (UTC) replaced GMT (it works the same way, but UTC accounts for stray 'leap seconds').

Websites

Lonely Planet (www.lonelyplanet.com) Travel portal

Time and date (www.timeanddate.com) Time differences

XE (www.xe.com) Currency conversion

world time zones

	VANCOUVER SAN FRANCISCO LOS ANGELES				WASHINGTON NEW YORK BOSTON							

-12	-11	-10	-9	-8	-7	-6	-5	-4	-3	-2	-1	0 GMT

| | | | | | MEXICO CITY
DALLAS | SÃO PAULO
RIO DE JANEIRO | | | | | DUBLIN
LONDON |

So you want to be a millionaire?
US $100 buys you...

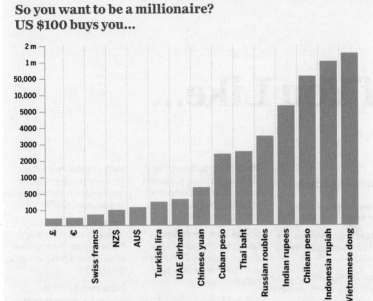

* Exchange rates correct at time of printing

Money

Wherever you go in the world you'll need a fistful of cash (or a credit card). There are around 180 different currencies circulating in the world today. So-called hard currencies – think the US$, the British £, the European €, the Yen and the Swiss Franc – are widely accepted, so can be handy to carry.

Depending on where you go, and where you come from, you will need to exchange your own currency into that of your destination. How far your money will go depends on exchange rates: they may make you feel like a pauper, or a millionaire.

Money-saving tips

➡ Consider low-season travel

➡ Look for favourable exchange rates; when one currency rises against yours, another may fall

➡ Book ahead for the best deals

Travel documents

Back in the day, explorers and conquerors left home without so much as a note from mother and crossed borders with impunity. You can't get away with that nowadays. To leave your own country and to enter any other, you need a passport, a travel document certifying your identity and issued by your govern-

ment. To visit many countries you also may need a visa, a stamp in your passport that allows you to temporarily enter said country.

Rules & regulations

Regulations and rules regarding visas are many and complex, and vary from country to country. Some countries allow visa-free travel to passport holders of other countries (such as in the EU), while others may allow certain visitors to obtain a visa upon arrival. Still others require aspiring visitors to get a visa before they leave home. Bottom line: investigate visa requirements before you book your next trip.

	CAPE TOWN BERLIN PARIS		DUBAI MOSCOW	MUMBAI DELHI		SINGAPORE BEIJING HONG KONG		SYDNEY MELBOURNE			
0 GMT	+1	+2	+3	+4	+5	+6	+7	+8	+9	+10	+11	+12

DUBLIN
LONDON

If You Like...

Beach Paradise

Australia Plunging waterfalls, pristine beaches and reefs. (p53)

Maldives Whiter-than-white powder sand and luminous cyan-blue water. (p527)

Portugal The Algarve has a varied coastline; sandy islands, dramatic cliffbacked shores and rarely-visited beaches. (p688)

Puerto Rico Backed by low scrub rather than craning palms, Playa Flamenco is the only public beach on the island. (p690)

Seychelles White-sand beaches lapped by luxuriously warm waters and trees leaning over the shore. (p740)

Spain According to one count, the emerald-green northern Spanish region of Asturias boasts more than 600 beaches. (p784)

Tahiti & French Polynesia Bora Bora: a perfect Morse-code ring of small islets. (p828)

Thailand The soaring limestone karsts of Railay are one of Thailand's most famous natural features. (p850)

Cultural Festivals

Carnaval, Brazil Carnaval is nonstop revelry, with nearly 500 street parties happening in every corner of town. (p128)

Día de Muertos, Mexico Day of the Dead; the happy-sad remembrance of departed loved ones at the beginning of November. (p554)

Goroka Show, Papua New Guinea Massive feather headdresses, rustling grass skirts and evocative face and body paint. (p658)

Holi, India Hindus celebrate the beginning of spring by throwing coloured water and *gulal* (powder) at anyone within range. (p391)

Naadam, Mongolia Two or three days of serious wrestling, horse racing and archery action. (p564)

New Orleans, United States of America New Orleans' riotous annual Mardi Gras and Jazz Fest are famous the world over. (p901)

History

Brú na Bóinne, Ireland Ireland's finest Stone Age passage tomb, predating the pyramids by some six centuries. (p414)

Flanders Fields, Belgium Manicured graveyards with white memorial crosses bear silent witness in seemingly endless rows. (p87)

Gallipoli, Turkey Memorials and cemeteries mark the spots where young men from far away fought and died in gruelling conditions. (p878)

Machu Picchu, Peru A ruin among ruins with emerald terraces, backed by steep peaks and Andean ridges. (p665)

Persepolis, Iran The artistic harmony leaves you in little doubt that in its prime Persepolis was at the centre of the known world. (p404)

Petra, Jordan Petra has been drawing the crowds since Jean Louis Burckhardt rediscovered this spectacular site in 1812. (p447)

Pompeii, Italy A once-thriving Roman town frozen in time 2000 years ago in the midst of its death throes. (p425)

Tikal, Guatemala The remarkably restored temples are a testament to the cultural and artistic heights scaled by this jungle civilization. (p351)

Food & Drink

Beer, Czech Republic Czechs claim to have the best *pivo* (beer) in the world and who are we to argue? (p228)

Champagne, France Celebrated around the world for the sparkling wines that have been produced here since the days of Dom Pérignon. (p298)

Copenhagen, Denmark One of the hottest culinary destinations in Europe, with more Michelin stars than any other Scandinavian city. (p232)

Japan Attention to detail, genius for presentation and insistence on the finest ingredients results in memorable cuisine. (p442)

Malaysia Start with Chinese-Malay 'Nonya' fare, move on to Indian curries, Chinese buffets and Malay food stalls. (p524)

San Sebastián, Spain Chefs here have turned *pintxos* (Basque tapas) into an art form. (p782)

Turkey Mezes aren't just a type of dish, they're a whole eating experience. (p876)

Vietnam Essentially it's all about the freshness of the ingredients. The result? Incomparable texture and flavour combinations. (p928)

Whisky, Scotland Scotland's national drink has been distilled here for more than 500 years. (p730)

Adventure

Blue Hole, Belize The sheer walls of the Blue Hole Natural Monument drop more than 400ft into the ocean. (p90)

Diving, Red Sea, Egypt Underwater world of coral cliffs, colourful fish and spookily beautiful wrecks. (p257)

Hiking, Dolomites, Italy This tiny pocket of northern Italy takes seductiveness to dizzying heights. (p428)

Hiking, New Zealand The sublime forests, mountains, lakes, beaches and fiords have made NZ one of the best hiking destinations on the planet. (p611)

Outdoor Adventure, Switzerland This country begs outdoor escapades with its larger-than-life canvas of hallucinatory landscapes. (p819)

Rafting, Slovenia Slovenia is an outdoor destination and fast rivers like the Soča cry out to be rafted. (p756)

Safari, Botswana Chobe National Park ranks among the elite of African safari destinations. (p117)

Skiing, Andorra 193km of runs and a combined lift system that can shift over 100,000 skiers per hour. (p24)

Zip Lining, Costa Rica Few things are more purely joyful than clipping into a high-speed cable, laced above and through the seething jungle canopy. (p204)

Natural Wonders

Cappadocia, Turkey The hard-set honeycomb landscape looks sculpted by a swarm of genius bees. (p875)

Dead Sea, Israel & the Palestinian Territories Cobalt-blue waters, outlined by snow-white salt deposits, reddish-tan cliffs and tufts of dark-green vegetation. (p419)

Grand Canyon, United States of America It took 6 million years for the canyon to form and some rocks exposed along its walls are 2 billion years old. (p902)

Great Barrier Reef, Australia Stretching more than 2000km along the Queensland coastline, with dazzling coral, languid sea turtles and tropical fish of every colour and size. (p53)

Iguazú Falls, Argentina The roar, the spray and the sheer volume of water live forever in the memory. (p39)

Lake Baikal, Russia Baikal's gob-smacking vistas and the tough going will leave you breathless. (p706)

Mt Everest, Nepal Tibet has easily the best views of the world's most famous mountain. (p597)

Ngorongoro Crater, Tanzania The magic starts while you're still up on the rim, with the chill air and sublime views over the enormous crater. (p842)

Northern Lights, Iceland Celestial kaleidoscope known for transforming long winter nights into natural lava lamps. (p381)

Salto Ángel (Angel Falls), Venezuela Witness the cascade of the world's tallest waterfall, as it thunders 979m from the plateau of Auyantepui. (p921)

Man-Made Wonders

Acropolis, Greece Embodies a harmony, power and beauty that speak to all generations. (p329)

Stonehenge, England People have been drawn to this myth-rich ring of boulders for more than 5000 years. (p263)

Pyramids of Giza, Egypt Witness the extraordinary shape, impeccable geometry and sheer bulk of the pyramids. (p255)

Taj Mahal, India The marble mausoleum is the world's most poetic parting. (p389)

Great Wall, China Perfectly chiselled bricks, overrun with saplings, coil splendidly into the hills. (p177)

Eiffel Tower, France Pedal beneath it, skip the lift and hike up, buy a crêpe from a stand here or visit it at night. (p295)

La Sagrada Família, Spain Barcelona's quirky temple soars skyward with an almost playful majesty. (p779)

Temples of Angkor, Cambodia The Cambodian 'god-kings' of old each strove to better their ancestors in size, scale and symmetry. (p143)

For other **themes & activities**, see the index p949

Itineraries

A map showing a route through Asia with the following labeled locations: JAPAN, TOKYO, Mt Fuji, CHINA, Shanghai, Luang Prabang, Macau, HANOI, Halong Bay, HONG KONG, Mekong River, Chiang Mai, LAOS, THAILAND, VIETNAM, Siem Reap (Angkor Wat), CAMBODIA, Phuket, Krabi, PACIFIC OCEAN, SINGAPORE.

3 MONTHS A Mighty Asian Junket

This is the "Asian century", so a jaunt through the great cities and landscapes of Asia is definitely in order!

Start your trip in booming **Tokyo**, a city combining tradition and ultra-modernity, from where you can visit the solemn majesty of **Mt Fuji**. Crossing to the continental landmass of Asia, head for **Shanghai**, the most dynamic city in the world's fastest changing nation. Then turn your gaze southward to **Hong Kong**, for fantastic shopping and leisurely ferry trips, or lap up the Portuguese ambience in nearby **Macau**. Zip across to historic **Hanoi** to savour its graceful architecture en route to the surreal-looking limestone islands of **Halong Bay**. Returning via Hanoi, hop across to **Luang Prabang**, glistening with temples and on the banks of the **Mekong River**. Move on to the moated old city of **Chiang Mai** to enjoy a meditation retreat, before heading for the awe-inspiring ruins of **Siem Reap** and **Angkor**. Skipping south it's time for a beachside idyll on the Andaman Sea, either at **Phuket** or **Krabi**. Move on to **Singapore** for shopping and for planning your next moves.

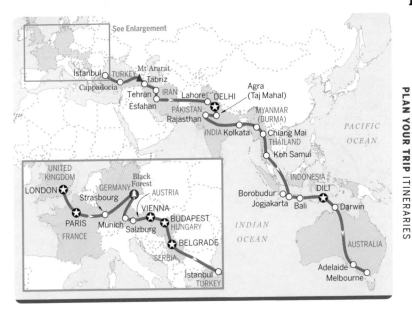

6 MONTHS The Hippy Trail: London to Melbourne

A rite of passage for many, the overland trail from Europe and across Asia has inspired generations of travellers, including Maureen and Tony Wheeler, the founders of Lonely Planet.

Starting from **London**, head to **Paris** for a view of the Eiffel Tower and the Louvre. Motor eastwards to view the half-timbered houses of **Strasbourg**, then trundle through the **Black Forest** en route to the provincial charms of **Munich**. Take in the musical atmosphere and charming architecture of **Salzburg** then head for the operas and coffeehouses of **Vienna**. Stately **Budapest** and buzzing **Belgrade** provide spa treatments and throbbing nightlife en route to **İstanbul**, the mighty Turkish city astride two continents. Catch a Bosphorus ferry, then make a bee-line for the otherworldly landscapes of **Cappadocia**. Passing the foothills of **Mt Ararat**, aim for **Tabriz** across the Iranian border. Enjoy the teahouses of **Tehran** before revelling in the breathtaking architecture of **Esfahan** and hitting the desert road. Head to the old city of **Lahore** for its arts scene and serene Mughal gardens.

Cross the Indian frontier and head to thunderous **Delhi**, with its Red Fort and fragrant bazaars, and continue to **Agra** to swoon before the sublime architecture of the **Taj Mahal**. Zip westward to the deserts and dreamy fortresses of **Rajasthan**. Then, passing through the clamour of **Kolkata**, move on to **Myanmar**, now opening up to tourism. From there it's a short hop to a spa retreat in **Chiang Mai**, before zipping in to throbbing Bangkok. **Koh Samui** provides an island idyll in the Gulf of Thailand before you move on to Indonesia. **Jogjakarta** is a centre for Javanese art, and puppetry and is the gateway to the Buddhist monuments at **Borobudur**. Next, hit **Bali** for some sun 'n' surf before skipping to rapidly changing **Dili**. From there it's a short hop to **Darwin**, Australia's most Asian-flavoured city, from where you can drive across the desert to **Adelaide**, before hitting **Melbourne**, the artistic and cultural capital of Australia.

A Mediterranean Odyssey

The Mediterranean has been the scene of countless cultures, empires and civilisations throughout history – come here for a dizzying array of art, culture and natural beauty on show.

Venice, seaboard city of art and maritime endeavour, has been the embarkation point for many an odyssey. Follow in the footsteps of Lord Byron, that swashbuckling romantic, and head towards **Ravenna**, with its Byzantine mosaics, before moving on to the Renaissance time capsule that is **Florence**, then to **Rome**, to gawk at the **Colosseum**. Ferrying across the Adriatic brings you to Croatia's idyllic **Dalmatian coast**, dropping in at **Split** and **Dubrovnik**, described by Byron as the 'pearl of the Adriatic'. From here cross into Bosnia-Hercegovina to the achingly slim bridge in Mostar. Back on the coast, savour the breathtaking scenery of the **Bay of Kotor**, then push on to gorgeous beachside **Sveti Stefan** and **Bar**. Heading into Albania you'll encounter post-communist **Tirana** with its colourful buildings and the hilltop citadel of **Gjirokastra**. Down on the Ionian coast lie idyllic Corfu, Ithaka, the island home that Homer long sought, and **Cephalonia**, where Lord Byron fetched up. From here you can reach **Athens** to see the **Acropolis**, or catch a ferry onward throughout the Greek islands, or back to Italy.

Naples is Italy's pulsing southern metropolis and is the transit point for **Sicily**, home to Greek temples and slumbering **Mt Etna**. From here aim for Sardinia's crystalline **Emerald Coast** then the quiet fishing villages and rugged interior of **Corsica**. The Corniche at **Nice**, and **Monaco** are sun-splashed places to linger. **Marseille** then beckons, with its castle and gritty port ambience. Inland is **Aix en Provence**, and the Provençale landscapes of **Arles** that inspired Van Gogh. Beyond lies **Barcelona**, city of art and architecture and gateway to the **Balearic Islands**. Head south for the nightlife in the Spanish capital, **Madrid**, then onward for the Moorish delights of **Córdoba**, **Seville** and **Granada**. Finish in **Gibraltar**, gateway to the Atlantic, and the westernmost point of Hercules' travels.

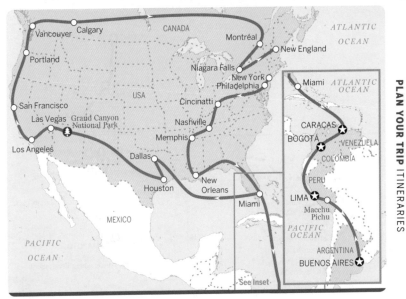

2 MONTHS Road Trippin' the Americas

Considering the wide open spaces of the American landmass, it stands to reason that this was the birthplace of the road trip. You can tailor your own odyssey, following in the footsteps (or tyre treads) of Jack Kerouac, and many more besides.

Start in **New York**, the city that never sleeps, then ramble down to historic **Philadelphia** for a picture of what colonial American cities looked like, then press on to **Cincinatti** on the banks of the Ohio River, where Jack Kerouac once passed. From there head south to **Nashville**, country music Mecca and home to historic buildings and big-name sports. Continuing the musical theme, roll on to **Memphis** to pay respects to Elvis and Johnny Cash, then follow the Mississippi down to steamy **New Orleans** for southern cooking, ornate architecture and the jazz clubs that Kerouac haunted. Then, if you're inclined, you could head to Latin-flavoured **Miami**, and roll on to reverse the tracks of Che Guevara by heading south to **Caracas**, **Bogotá** and **Lima**, en route to the lofty heights of **Macchu Picchu**, before fetching up in **Buenos Aires**, a slice of Europe in the southern hemisphere.

Alternatively, go west, young man, hitting **Dallas** for cowboys and cheerleaders, then mozy on down to sprawling, boot-scootin' **Houston**. For awesome desert views and iconic landscapes the **Grand Canyon** is a must, before getting a dose of glitz and striking it rich in **Las Vegas**. Cruise on to **Los Angeles** to spot a star in **Hollywood**, then follow Kerouac's footsteps again to **San Francisco**. Head north to counter-culture **Portland**, before crossing the Canadian border and hitting the hip neighbourhoods of **Vancouver**. Don your spurs to drop in at 'cowtown' **Calgary**, then cruise over the seemingly endless prairie and above the Great Lakes to **Montréal** for diverse cuisines and European-style architecture. Complete your loop to New York either via Lake Ontario and the muscular shoals of water plummeting over **Niagara Falls** or through the picturesque landscapes of **New England**.

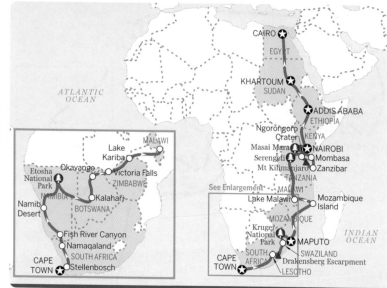

4 MONTHS   Safari of a Lifetime

Africa offers vast landscapes, an opportunity to see wildlife on a scale unrivalled anywhere else in the world, and more cultural diversity than you can poke a rhino's horn at.

From **Cape Town**, after climbing Table Mountain, and sampling the wineries of **Stellenbosch**, you can choose either of two routes. Enjoy the floral bounty of **Namaqaland**, as you proceed to **Fish River Canyon** for fantastic hiking. Continue through the **Namib Desert** and the desolate Skeleton Coast, as you aim for **Etosha National Park**. If you don't spot a lonely rhino there, head east towards the **Kalahari**, where you can walk with bushmen, and then the lush **Okavango** delta, realm of wallowing hippos. Onward in the footsteps of Dr Livingstone to **Victoria Falls**, to spy the endlessly rushing waters of the 'smoke that thunders'. Continue via **Lake Kariba** to **Malawi** to enjoy chilling out on the 'lake of stars', as Livingstone did back in the day.

The alternative route from Cape Town is through the rugged **Drakensberg Escarpment**, to the mountainous kingdom of **Lesotho**, the perfect spot for a pony trek, and then **Swaziland**. Press on to **Kruger National Park**, for a chance to spot the Big Five. Slide into Mozambique to hit **Maputo** for its Portuguese atmosphere and beachside caipirinhas, then proceed up the coast in the wake of Ferdinand Magellan, diving with whale sharks, then stopping in at the faded architectural grandeur of **Mozambique Island**. From there proceed to **Lake Malawi** and north into Tanzania, being sure to visit the premier wildlife areas of the **Serengeti** and **Ngorongoro Crater**. Then strike out for the peak of **Mt Kilimanjaro** and on to the Indian Ocean and enjoy the spice gardens and beaches of **Zanzibar**, where Livingstone once holed up. Sultry **Mombasa** is an entrepôt of Swahili culture and the gateway to Kenya. Proceed via the **Masai Mara** to **Nairobi**. From there you can head via **Addis Ababa**, **Khartoum** and **Cairo** to the Mediterranean, to complete a mighty trans-continental journey.

Band-e-Amir lakes, Bamiyan

CAPITAL
Kabul

POPULATION
31.1 million

AREA
652,230 sq km

OFFICIAL LANGUAGES
Dari, Pashto

Afghanistan

A battered, but beautiful and proud country, Afghanistan's road to recovery remains uncertain, yet the resilience of its people and beauty of its landscapes endures.

Throughout its history, Afghanistan has been a country united against invaders but divided against itself. In another world, Afghanistan would be near the top of any list of must-see tourist destinations. Its allure, spread by Great Game romantics and travel literature alike, has only been heightened by its inaccessibility over the last 30 years.

At the crossroads of Asia, Afghanistan has blended cultural ingredients from the Indian subcontinent, Central Asia and Persia into something distinctive and enticing. Old Silk Road oases recall a rich history of Buddhist

and Islamic empires, while the mightily rugged Hindu Kush Mountains that bisect the country are as beautiful as Afghan hospitality is famously warm.

Before its recent travails, Afghanistan was a vital stage on the overland hippy trail, beguiling visitors with its rugged landscapes, thriving bazaars, heady mix of cultures, and the Afghan people themselves, who greeted all with charm and ready gregariousness. For hardy travellers with a taste for adventures, these charms still beckon.

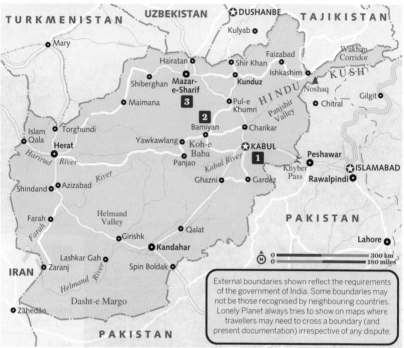

External boundaries shown reflect the requirements of the government of India. Some boundaries may not be those recognised by neighbouring countries. Lonely Planet always tries to show on maps where travellers may need to cross a boundary (and present documentation) irrespective of any dispute.

Afghanistan's
Top Experiences

Kabul

1 Kabul is exciting, frustrating, inspiring and shocking in equal measure. Once a stop on the hippy trail, and then ruined by civil war, Kabul's path to reconstruction remains rocky. In recent years it has boomed with new buildings, fancy restaurants and busy bazaars.

Food & Drink

Pulao Steamed rice with meat (topped with almonds, raisins and grated carrot) is eaten everywhere from communal plates.

Steamed dumplings Served with yoghurt sauce, stuffed with meat (*mantu*) or leeks (*ashak*).

Tea Green tea (*chai sabz*) or black tea (*chai siah*) are both served highly sweetened and scalding hot.

Bamiyan

2 Once a place of Buddhist pilgrimage, Bamiyan is now more closely associated with the destruction visited on Afghanistan's culture. The two giant statues of the Buddha that once dominated the valley lie in rubble, victims of the Taliban's iconoclastic rage. Yet the Bamiyan Valley remains one of the most beautiful places in Afghanistan, and a must-see for any visitor.

Mazar-e Sharif

3 North Afghanistan's biggest city, Mazar-e Sharif was long overshadowed by the power of its neighbour Balkh. It took a 12th-century mullah to change that. He claimed to have found the hidden tomb of Ali, the Prophet Mohammed's son-in-law, buried in a local village. Its shrine today is the focus of the national Nawroz (Navrus) celebrations.

When to Go

MAR–MAY

➡ In spring there's fine weather, but rain and snowmelt can make many roads difficult to traverse.

JUN–AUG

➡ Summer can be blisteringly hot, although Kabul enjoys pleasantly cool nights.

SEP–NOV

➡ Autumn is warm and dry, with plenty of delicious Afghan fruit.

Berat

CAPITAL
Tirana

POPULATION
3 million

AREA
28,748 sq km

OFFICIAL LANGUAGE
Albanian

Albania

With stunning mountain scenery, a thriving, multicoloured capital city and beaches to rival anywhere else in the Mediterranean, Albania has become the sleeper hit of the Balkans.

Albania has natural beauty in such abundance that you might wonder why it's taken 20 years for the country to take off as a tourist destination since the demise of a particularly insular strain of communism in 1991. So backward was Albania when it emerged blinking into the bright light of freedom that it needed two decades just to catch up with the rest of Eastern Europe. Albania may have been largely ignored by the rest of the world, but that doesn't seem to have bothered the Albanians. They've just got on with embracing life in a languid and chaotically post-communist way.

Albania offers a remarkable array of unique attractions, largely due to this very isolation: ancient mountain codes of behaviours, forgotten archaeological sites and villages where time seems to have stood still are all on the menu. Lively, colourful Tirana is the beating heart of Albania, where this tiny nation's hopes and dreams coalesce into a vibrant whirl of traffic, brash consumerism and unfettered fun.

Albania's
Top Experiences

Lake Koman Ferry

1 Catch the Lake Koman Ferry through stunning mountain scenery, then continue to Valbonë and trek the 'Accursed Mountains'. One of Albania's undisputed highlights is this superb three-hour ferry ride on the vast Lake Koman, connect-ing the towns of Koman and Fierzë. Lake Koman was created in 1978 when the River Drin was dammed, with the result that you can cruise through spectacular mountain scenery where many incredibly hardy peasants still live as they have for centuries, tucked away in tiny mountain villages.

Berat

2 Explore the Unesco World Heritage–listed museum towns of dramatic Berat, the so-called 'city of a thousand windows'. Its most striking feature is the collection of white Ottoman houses climbing up the hill to its castle. Its rugged mountain setting is particularly evocative when the clouds swirl around the tops of the minarets, or break up to show the icy top of Mt Tomorri. The old quarters are lovely ensembles of whitewashed walls, tiled roofs and cobble-stone roads. Surrounding olive and cherry trees decorate the gentle slopes.

Ionian Coast

3 Catch some sun at Drymades or one of the many beaches along the south's dramatic Ionian Coast. As you zigzag down the mountain from the Llogaraja Pass National Park, the white crescent-shaped beaches and azure waters call out with positively siren-like appeal. Drymades, boasting a laid-back charm, is surrounded by orange orchards and pine copses, while nearby Dhërmi caters to the party crowd.

Ruins of Butrint

4 Travel back in time to the ruins of Butrint, hidden in the depths of a forest in a serene lakeside setting, part of a 29-sq-km national park. Greeks from Corfu settled on the hill in Butrint (Buthrotum) in the 6th century BC. As you enter the site the path leads to Butrint's 3rd-century-BC Greek theatre, secluded in the forest below the acropolis. Close by are the small public baths. Deeper in the forest is a wall covered with crisp

ALVARO LEIVA / GETTY IMAGES ©

Greek inscriptions, and the 6th-century palaeo-Christian baptistry.

Tirana

5 Feast your eyes on the wild colour schemes and experience the hip Blloku cafe culture in Tirana. Having undergone a transformation of extraordinary proportions since it awoke from its communist slumber in the early 1990s, Tirana is now unrecognisable, with its buildings painted in horizontal primary colours, and public squares and pedestrianised streets a pleasure to wander. Trendy Blloku buzzes with well-dressed nouvelle bourgeoisie hanging out in bars or zipping between boutiques. Tirana's traffic does daily battle with both itself and pedestrians in a constant scene of chaos.

Loud, crazy, colourful and dusty – Tirana is never dull.

Gjirokastra

6 Take a trip into the traditional Southern Albanian mountain town of Gjirokastra, with its spectacular Ottoman-era mansions and impressive hilltop fortress. Defined by its castle, roads paved with chunky limestone and shale, imposing slate-roofed houses and views out to the Drina Valley, Gjirokastra is an intriguing hillside town described beautifully by Albania's most famous literary export and local-born author, Ismail Kadare (b 1936), in *Chronicles of Stone*. These days it's the 600 'monumental' houses, a blend of Ottoman and local architectural influences, that attract visitors.

if Albania were 100 people

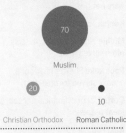

95 would be Albanian
3 would be Greek
2 would be other

belief systems
(% of population)

70
Muslim

20
Christian Orthodox

10
Roman Catholic

population per sq km

ALBANIA GREECE USA

≈ 15 people

When to Go

JUN
➡ Enjoy the perfect Mediterranean climate and deserted beaches.

AUG
➡ Albania's beaches may be packed, but this is a great time to explore the mountains.

DEC
➡ See features and shorts at the Tirana Film Festival, while the intrepid can snowshoe to Theth.

Bunker Love

On the hillsides, beaches and generally most surfaces in Albania, you will notice small concrete domes (often in groups of three) with rectangular slits. Meet the bunkers: Enver Hoxha's concrete legacy, built from 1950 to 1985. Weighing in at 5 tonnes of concrete and iron, these little mushrooms are almost impossible to destroy. They were built to repel an invasion and can resist full tank assault – a fact proved by their chief engineer, who vouched for his creation's strength by standing inside one while it was bombarded by a tank. The shell-shocked engineer emerged unscathed, and tens of thousands were built. Today, some are creatively painted, one houses a tattoo artist, and some even house makeshift hostels.

Food & Drink

Byrek Pastry with cheese or meat.

Fergesë Baked peppers, egg and cheese, and occasionally meat.

Fërgesë Tiranë A traditional Tirana dish of offal, eggs and tomatoes cooked in an earthenware pot.

Konjak Local brandy.

Midhje Wild or farmed mussels, often served fried.

Paçë koke Sheep's head soup, usually served for breakfast.

Qofta Flat or cylindrical minced-meat rissoles.

Raki Popular spirit made from grapes.

Raki mani Spirit made from mulberries.

Sufllaqë Doner kebab.

Tavë Meat baked with cheese and egg.

Skanderbeg Museum

Kruja

7 Kruja was the birthplace of Skanderbeg, Albania's national hero. Although it was over 500 years ago, there's still a great deal of pride in the fact that he and his forces defended Kruja from the Ottomans until his death. As soon as you get off the *furgon* (minibus), you're face to knee with a statue of Skanderbeg wielding his mighty sword with one hand, and it just gets more Skanderdelic after that. An ancient castle juts out to one side, and the massive Skanderbeg Museum juts out of the castle itself.

Llogaraja Pass National Park

8 Reaching this pine-tree-clad realm (1025m) is a highlight of travels in Albania. If you've been soaking up the sun on the southern coast's beaches, it seems impossible that after a steep hairpin-bend climb you'll be up in the mountains. There's great scenery up here, including the *pisha flamur* (flag pine) – a tree resembling the eagle design on the Albanian flag. Watch clouds descending onto the mountain, shepherds on the plains guiding their herds, and thick forests where deer, wild boar and wolves roam.

Getting Around

Bus The first bus/*furgon* departure is often at 5am and things slow down around lunchtime. Fares are low, and you either pay the conductor on board or when you hop off.

Car & Motorcycle The road infrastructure is improving; there's an excellent highway from Tirana to Kosovo, and the coastal route from the Montenegro border to Butrint, near Saranda, is in good condition.

Train Albanians prefer bus and *furgon* travel, and when you see the speed and the state of the (barely) existing trains, you'll know why. However, the trains are dirt cheap and travelling on them is an adventure

Sahara Desert

CAPITAL
Algiers

POPULATION
38 million

AREA
2.4 million sq km

OFFICIAL LANGUAGE
Arabic

Algeria

Stretching from the Mediterranean to the Sahara, Algeria is the colossus of North Africa, a distinctively Maghrebian destination revealing little-visited attractions to the adventurous traveller.

Africa's largest country lies just a short hop from Europe and, with tourists still a novelty, offers attractions as unpeopled as they are varied.

The capital, Algiers, is one of the Maghreb's most urbane and charismatic cities, with a heady, nostalgic mix of colonial and modernist architecture, and a traditional medina at its vertiginous heart. Across the north are stunning coastlines, lush rural hinterland and a number of well-preserved Roman cities.

Algeria's trump card, though, is its extraordinary Saharan region. Whether it's a glimpse of the sand seas and dunes that surround Timimoun, or a plunge headlong into the far south from Tamanrasset, these are the desert landscapes of dream and legend.

Perhaps best of all, Algerians welcome visitors with warmth and a genuine curiosity. For accessible adventure and a complex, enthralling cultural odyssey, head for Algeria now.

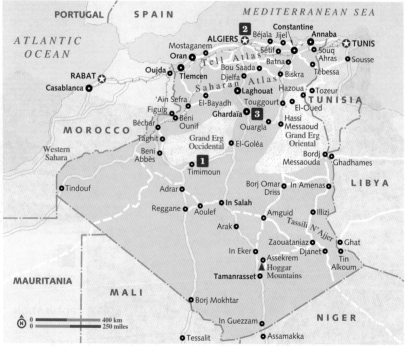

Algeria's
Top Experiences

Timimoun

1 The largest oasis in the Grand Erg Occidental, this desert city is enchanting. Its characteristic architecture, red mud buildings studded with spikes, hints at sub-Saharan Africa. Its location, at the edge of an escarpment, makes for breathtaking views across a salt lake and out to the dunes beyond.

Algiers

2 Experience the country's fascinating capital, where modern, traditional and colonial Algeria meet. The heart of the city is a steep and narrow maze of streets and there are several magnificent Ottoman palaces to explore. Above the medina is the city's Citadel. Labyrinthine streets spill down to the big blue of the Bay of Algiers, sea and sky and green ravines glimpsed at every step.

Ghardaïa

3 In the river valley of the Oued M'Zab, on the edge of the Sahara, is a cluster of five towns: Ghardaïa, Melika, Beni Isguen, Bou Noura and El-Ateuf. Often referred to collectively as Ghardaïa, the capital, the once distinct villages are gradually sprawling together, but retain separate identities. Bargain for a boldly patterned carpet, peek at a pristine medieval town and swim in the shade of date palms.

Food & Drink

Couscous Slow-steamed hand-rolled semolina.

Tajine Slow-cooked stew in a conical-topped earthenware dish, often prepared with lamb.

Tea Served strong tea around a Tuareg campfire.

When to Go

NOV–APR

➧ Less fierce temperatures. High season in the Sahara (the autumn date harvest is a bonus).

MAR–JUL

➧ The north literally blooms in spring; warm, dry days for exploring sprawling Roman sites.

AUG

➧ Oran's annual Raï festival and Ramadan.

Ski lift, Pyrenees

CAPITAL
Andorra la Vella

POPULATION
85,458

AREA
468 sq km

OFFICIAL LANGUAGE
Catalan

Andorra

The Thumbelina, Catalan-speaking principality of Andorra, a dramatic realm of mountain scenery amid the Pyrenees, is one of Western Europe's most intriguing corners.

Some say Andorra's nothing but skiing and shopping. Racing down snow-packed pistes, molly-coddling après-ski mulled wine and sleeping snug between boutique-hotel ice walls is how most think of this tiny principality in Europe, neatly wedged between France and Spain in the mountainous eastern Pyrenees.

Shake yourself free of Andorra la Vella's tawdry embrace, take one of the state's three secondary roads and you're very soon amid dramatic mountain scenery. This minicountry offers by far the best ski slopes and resort facilities in all the Pyrenees, as well as secret hoard of thermal spas that soothe skied-out limbs.

Once the snows melt, there's an abundance of great walking, ranging from easy strolls to demanding day hikes in the principality's higher, more remote reaches. Strike out above the tight valleys and you can walk for hours, almost alone.

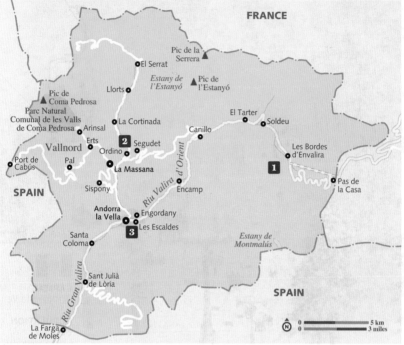

Andorra's
Top Experiences

Skiing

1 Shush your way over the snowfields of Grandvalira. With 193km of runs and a combined lift system that can shift over 100,000 skiers per hour, it's the largest ski area in the Pyrenees.

Walking Trails

2 Ordino is Andorra's most attractive village and at an elevation of 1300m, it's a good starting point for summer activity holidays. From mid-July to mid-September, the Canillo and Soldeu gondolas whisk you up to the higher reaches, from where you can walk or hire a mountain bike to whizz back down.

La Caldea

3 Steep yourself in the warm mineral waters of space-age La Caldea. All glass and gleaming like some futuristic cathedral, Europe's largest spa complex offers lagoons, giant jacuzzis, vapour baths and saunas, fed by warm thermal springs. It is a blissful experience after a day of high-speed fun on the ski slopes or invigorating summer time walks.

Food and Drink

Cabrito con picadillo de frutos secos Goat roasted with almonds and pine nuts.

Escudella A thick soup of *albondigas* (meat balls), perhaps with chicken and a lump or two of sausage, chick peas, carrots, and potatoes. Almost the national dish.

Pato con pera de invierno Roast duck with pears.

When to Go

MID-JAN–MID-FEB

➡ Ski slopes at their quietest after New Year and before French school holidays.

MID-JUN–MID-JUL & SEP

➡ Camp and hike either side of summer's holiday peak, before new snow falls.

SEP

➡ On the 8th September every hamlet and village celebrates Fiesta de Meritxell, which also marks Andorra's national day.

Serra da Leba, near Lubango

CAPITAL
Luanda

POPULATION
18.6 million

AREA
1.2 million sq km

OFFICIAL LANGUAGE
Portuguese

Angola

Fronting the Atlantic and stretching into the interior of the mighty continent, Angola is nothing if not diverse, a land of traumatic history and startling natural treasures.

Angola is an eye-opener – in more ways than one. Scarred painfully by years of debilitating warfare and practically untouched by foreign visitors since the early 1970s, the country remains remote, with few observers privy to its geographic highlights and vast cultural riches.

Despite advancements in infrastructure and a dramatically improved security situation, travel in Angola remains the preserve of adventurers, or those on flexible budgets. But with the transport network gradually recovering and wildlife being shipped in to repopulate decimated national parks, the signs of recovery are more than just a mirage.

For outsiders, the attractions are manifold. Chill out on expansive beaches, sample the solitude in virgin wildlife parks or sift through the ruins of Portuguese colonialism.

The Angolans themselves are a part of the country's appeal. They are resilient after years of war and hardship, yet still exhibiting a rock-solid Christian faith, and harbouring an unwavering desire to dance like there is no tomorrow.

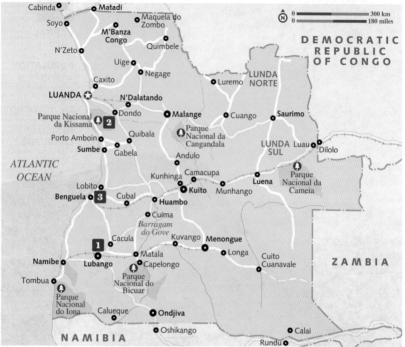

Angola's
Top Experiences

Lubango

1 Almost untouched by the war, breezy Lubango offers cascading waterfalls, spectacular volcanic fissures and a vibrant small-city ambience, all surrounded by mountains and nestled in a cool central valley

Food & Drink

Alãos (white coffee) Historically one of the world's largest producers of the bean; locals love it with milk.

Pastelerias These pastry and coffee shops have a distinctly European flavour thanks to the legacy of the Portuguese.

Street food Easy to find from the women who sell fruit and baguette-like sandwiches from washing bowls across the city centre.

Parque Nacional da Kissama

2 One of Africa's largest, emptiest and most surreal wildlife parks, Kissama is also Angola's most accessible and well-stocked wildlife park. This 990,000-hectare swath of coastal savannah punctuated by gnarly baobab trees is home to elephants, water buffaloes, indigenous palanca antelopes and a population of nesting sea turtles.

Benguela

3 Chill out on the blissfully empty beaches of Angola's most laid-back town. Coastal Benguela is Angola's second city and self-proclaimed cultural capital. Nestled on the shores of the Atlantic, the city is surrounded by fine beaches and bisected by the lush Cavaco River valley; a veritable oasis of green in an otherwise dry and arid desert.

When to Go

JUN–SEP

➡ The cooler dry season is the best time to visit.

NOV–APR

➡ Hot and rainy in the tropical northern jungle.

YEAR-ROUND

➡ The southern belt's arid conditions are influenced by its proximity to the Kalahari Desert.

CAPITAL
The Valley
....
POPULATION
15,754
....
AREA
91 sq km
....
**OFFICIAL
LANGUAGE**
English

Anguilla

Something old, something new, something borrowed, something blue – wedding bells immediately come to mind, but what about Anguilla?

As rabid consumerism devours many Caribbean hot spots, this little limestone bump in the sea has, thus far, maintained its charming menagerie of clapboard shacks (something old) while quietly weaving stunning vacation properties (something new) into the mix. Visitors will discover a melting pot of cultures (something borrowed) set alongside mind-blowing Caribbean Sea beaches (something very, very blue).

Anguilla is, however, not the place for a vacation 'on a shoestring' – authenticity comes at a premium here. Although the island has garnered somewhat of a reputation as St-Barth's stunt-double, it really is anything but. From its village capital, the Valley, to its offshore island cays, Anguilla flaunts its down-to-earth charms to the jetset subset who crave a vacation off the travel radar.

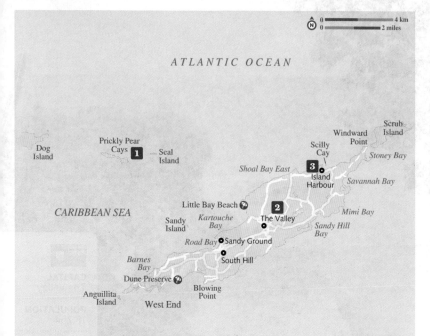

ATLANTIC OCEAN

CARIBBEAN SEA

Dog Island

Prickly Pear Cays **1**

Seal Island

Scrub Island

Windward Point

Scilly Cay

Stoney Bay

Shoal Bay East **3**

Savannah Bay

Island Harbour

Little Bay Beach

Sandy Island

Kartouche Bay

The Valley **2**

Mimi Bay

Sandy Hill Bay

Road Bay   Sandy Ground

South Hill

Barnes Bay

Dune Preserve

Anguillita Island

Blowing Point

West End

Anguilla's
Top Experiences

Prickly Pear

1 This windswept limestone bump above the waves has excellent snorkelling opportunities and features nothing but creamy beige sand ambushed by curls of rolling turquoise waves. Hop on a sailboat or catamaran and make your way over to this supersecluded mini-Anguilla.

Food & Drink

BBQ tents Popular weekend tents serving smoky ribs spring up on the side of the road.

Lobster & crayfish These are two of Anguilla's locally caught specialties. Crayfish are reasonable sized creatures that have sweet, tender meat, and are commonly served three to an order.

The Valley

2 Escape from your resort and check out the Valley to see what makes the island tick. Although no part of Anguilla feels particularly urban, the Valley has the island's conglomeration of government buildings, which gives it more of a village vibe. Get a double dose of Caribbean history and check out the interior of the adjacent St Gerard's church, which has a unique design incorporating a decorative stone front, open-air side walls and a ceiling shaped like the hull of a ship.

Island Harbour

3 This working fishing village is not a resort area, and its beach is lined with brightly colored fishing boats rather than chaise longues. There are another half-dozen semisecluded beaches in the area, of which Junk's Hole is tops.

When to Go

DEC–APR	JUL–AUG	OCT–DEC
➡ High season ➡ Inflated rates	➡ Prices drop to reasonable levels – capitalize on breezy weather before the humidity kicks in.	➡ Heaviest rainfall ➡ Many hotels shut down in September and often October.

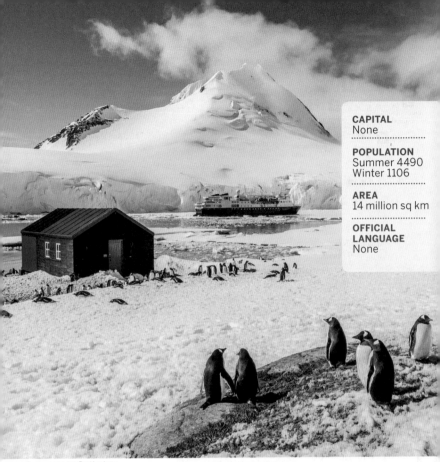

Gentoo penguins, Port Lockroy

Antarctica

No place on Earth compares to this vast white wilderness of elemental forces: snow, ice, water, rock. Antarctica is simply stunning.

Antarctica's surreal remoteness, extreme cold, enormous ice shelves and mountain ranges, and myriad exotic life forms invariably challenge you to embrace life fully. Ice and weather, not clocks and calendars, determine the itinerary and the timetable of all travel here.

This continent is home to some of the world's most extraordinary species. Some migrate far and wide, like the enormous whales, others remain close to the continent, like the Weddell seal and the emperor penguin. Millions of seabirds skim the Southern Ocean, the world's most abundant ocean – species such as far-flung albatrosses and petrels circle these waters.

Antarctica possesses an unnamable quality, which is simply the indescribable feeling of being a small speck in a vast, harshly beautiful land. A land where striated ice towers float among geometric pancake ice, literally untouched mountains rear from marine mist, and wildlife lives, year in and year out, to its own rhythms, quite apart from human concerns.

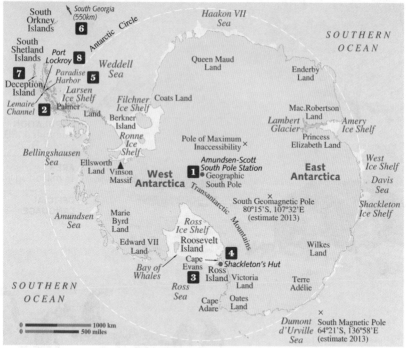

Antarctica's
Top Experiences

Amundsen-Scott South Pole Station

1 First reached just 100 years ago by the valiant explorer Roald Amundsen during the Heroic Age of Antarctic exploration, the South Pole still embodies myth, hardship and glory. Today it is topped by a new high-tech station surrounded by cutting-edge astrophysical observation equipment (including a neutrino detector array buried approximately 1.9 km below the ice).

Cruising the Lemaire Channel

2 The sheer-sided Lemaire Channel is a perennial favorite for photography buffs and naturalists.

Under pale-pink skies, glaciers tumble slow-motion to the sea from the mountains overhead. Your Zodiac glides past a floe topped by basking Weddell seals, another crowded by a noisy group of gentoo penguins. Nearby, an enormous female leopard seal sleeps off a recent meal.

Cape Evans

3 Reaching Ross Island's Cape Evans isn't easy – but then again, it never was. Dog skeletons bleach on the sand in the Antarctic sun, chiding *memento mori* of Captain Robert Scott's death march from the Pole. Inside Scott's hut from that ill-fated *Terra Nova* expedition a collection of sledging pennants, rustling pony harnesses and a sighing wind evoke the

doomed men who left here with high hopes of reaching the pole.

Shackleton's Hut

4 Step inside Ernest Shackleton's *Nimrod* expedition hut at Cape Royds on Ross Island and enter an eerily preserved world from a century ago. Amazingly intact despite 100 years of blasting Antarctic storms, the wooden house is surprisingly homey. Colored glass medicine bottles line shelves, a fur sleeping bag rests on one of the bunks and tins of food with unappetizing names (boiled mutton, lunch tongue, pea powder) are stacked on the floor, awaiting diners who will never return. Adélie penguins fill the cape now, breeding in summer.

PAUL SOUDERS / GETTY IMAGES ©

Lemaire Channel

Paradise Harbor

5 The pragmatic whalers who worked in the waters of the Antarctic Peninsula at the beginning of the 20th century were hardly sentimental. Yet they named this harbor Paradise, obviously quite taken with the stunning icebergs and reflections of the surrounding mountains. Gentoos and shags call the area home. A climb up the hill here offers magnificent glacier views – if you're lucky you might see one calving into the Southern Ocean.

Grytviken, South Georgia

6 A tall granite headstone marking the last resting place of British explorer Ernest Shackleton, known to his loyal men as 'the Boss,' stands at the rear of the whalers' cemetery at Grytviken. This old whaling station is still strewn with evidence of its past industry, and its museum gives insight into whaling life, and into South Georgia's history and wildlife. Meanwhile, seals wriggle outside the station's white-clapboard whalers' church.

if Antarctica were 100 people

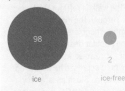

58 would be tourists
34 would be staff and crew
8 would be scientists

continental makeup
(% of land)

98
ice

2
ice-free

scientists in Antarctica

SUMMER   WINTER

= 500 people

When to Go

HIGH SEASON
(Dec & Jan)

➡ Expect up to 20 hours of sunlight each day, and the main influx of Antarctic visitors.

➡ Days are as warm as they get here.

➡ Penguins hatch eggs and feed chicks; seabirds soar.

SHOULDER
(Nov & Feb–Mar)

➡ November: the ice breaks up and penguins court.

➡ February and March: prime time for whale-watching, and penguin chicks are fledging.

LOW SEASON
(Apr–Oct)

➡ Continuous sunrise and sunset bring fantastic skies, bracketing midwinter, when 24-hour darkness reigns.

➡ Winterovers find aurora australis, isolation and extreme temperatures.

Green Icebergs

Every once in a great while, visitors to Antarctica are treated to an exceptional wonder: a green iceberg. These beautiful jade or bottle-green icebergs are colored for the same reason that seawater is: they contain organic material from the degradation of marine plants and animals. The more organic material, the greener the ice or the seawater.

Under very special conditions the organic matter in seawater freezes onto the underside of ice shelves floating on the ocean, forming 'marine ice.' Under rare conditions an iceberg becomes unstable due to uneven melting and turns over, exposing its vibrant green marine underside.

Even rarer are striped icebergs, which form when seawater fills up and freezes in crevasses on the bottom of ice shelves.

Food & Drink

Frozen, dried and canned food form the majority of meals for those stationed at the South Pole. Cooking is challenging: the risk of fire means that all stoves are electric, which take longer than gas ranges. Most food is stored outdoors, where it freezes solid, and it can take up to two weeks for meat to defrost in the walk-in refrigerator!

Through the long dark winter, chocolate is a favorite. One popular dessert is 'buzz bars,' brownies with chocolate-covered espresso beans baked into them. 'Slushies' are very fresh snow with Coke or liquor added. Ice cream is also a local favorite, but since it's stored outdoors, it has to be microwaved before it can be eaten.

Interestingly, the station gets its water from a well, an improvement over the former inefficient system of melting clean snow, which required large amounts of fuel and time.

GEOFF RENNER / GETTY IMAGES ©

Deception Island

7 Deceptive in more ways than one, with its secret harbor, slopes of ash-covered snow and hidden chinstrap penguin rookery at Baily Head, Deception Island offers the rare opportunity to sail inside a volcano. Now classified as having 'a significant volcanic risk,' Deception remains a favorite for the industrial archaeology of its abandoned whaling station, half-destroyed by an eruption-induced mudflow and flood. Some will stop for a quick dip in the island's heated geothermal currents.

Antarctic Museum

8 Each year, tens of thousands of visitors flock to Britain's beautifully restored Bransfield House, the main building of Base A, built at Port Lockroy during WWII. Not only does it offer the chance to spend up big at the well-stocked souvenir shop and to mail postcards at the busy post office, the museum's old wooden skis, clandestine 1944 radio transmitter and wind-up HMV gramophone are evocative artifacts of the explorers who once lived for years at this wilderness outpost.

Getting Around

Tours All cruises/packages are guided tours. You can also book through third-party organizations, such as universities, to have particular expert guides.

Zodiacs Generically known as RIBs (rigid inflatable boats; other name-brands are Naiad, Avon and Polarcirkel), these are the backbone of tourist travel in the Antarctic. These small (nine to 16 passengers), inflatable boats powered by outboard engines have a shallow draft which is ideal for cruising among icebergs and landing in otherwise inaccessible areas. Zodiacs are very stable in the water, and are designed to stay afloat even if one or more of their six separate air-filled compartments are punctured.

English Harbour

Antigua & Barbuda

Frolic on the beach, play golf, indulge in a fancy meal or explore Britain's naval history in Antigua. Or escape to remote, unspoiled Barbuda, where winged creatures outnumber people.

On Antigua, life is a beach. It may seem like a cliché, but this improbably shaped splotch of land is ringed with beaches of the finest white sand, made all the more dramatic by the azure waters, which are so clear they'll bring a tear to your eye or a giggle to your holiday-hungry throat.

If life on Antigua is a beach, its isolated neighbor Barbuda *is* a beach: one smooth, sandy low-rise amid the reef-filled waters. Birds, especially the huffing and puffing frigates, greatly outnumber people. Meanwhile, back on Antigua, there are lots of people, many famous. Guitar-picker Eric Clapton, rag-trader Giorgio Armani and tastemaker for the masses Oprah all have winter homes here. Some of the Caribbean's most exclusive resorts shelter in the myriad bays and inlets.

But don't worry; mere mortals thrive here as well. No matter your budget, you will find a beach with your name on it.

CAPITAL
St John's

POPULATION
90,156

AREA
443 sq km

OFFICIAL LANGUAGE
English

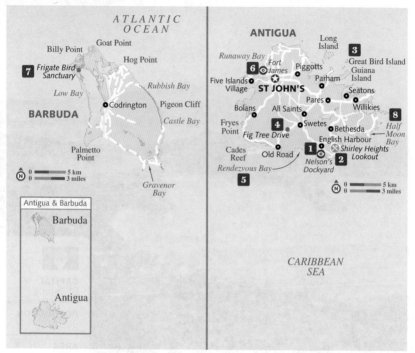

Antigua & Barbuda's
Top Experiences

Nelson's Dockyard

1 At the far southern tip of Antigua, the village of English Harbour sits atop two bays, separated by a peninsula that is the site of Nelson's Dockyard, considered the one must-see historical attraction on Antigua (and one of the preeminent historic sites in the Caribbean). A restored 18th-century British naval base, it was named for English captain Lord Horatio Nelson, who spent the early years of his career here. Travel back to the 18th century as you wander along cobbled lanes and past meticulously restored old buildings. Still a working marina, it's also one of the world's key yachting centers and attracts an international flotilla to its regattas.

Shirley Heights Lookout

2 For nearly three decades, locals and clued-in visitors have made the pilgrimage to Shirley Heights Lookout on Sunday afternoons. That's when this dazzlingly located hilltop restaurant-bar hosts wildly popular barbecues that vibrate with a steel-drum band in the afternoon and live reggae and calypso after 7pm. Come for romantic sunsets and dancing under the stars, all fuelled by wicked rum punches. Views of English Harbour are truly breathtaking. On other days it's quieter but still worth the trek for lunch and sunset drinks. The other party night is Thursday, when a steel band plays.

Great Bird Island

3 From Antigua's northern reaches, in the distance beckons the unspoiled nature of Great Bird Island. Part of the North Sound National Park, this uninhabited, aptly named island is a bird-watcher's delight and teems with frigate birds, laughing gulls, purple martins, red-billed tropic birds and other winged creatures. Mangroves lure a bevy of marine life, making this a great snorkeling destination, as well. You'll need to take a guided tour to the island.

Fig Tree Drive

4 Old Road marks the start of Fig Tree Drive. One of the most picturesque routes on the island, this narrow 5-mile-long road ser-

NICO TONDINI / GETTY IMAGES ©

Dockyard Museum, Nelson's Dockyard

pentines through patches of rainforest past bananas (called 'figs' in Antigua), coconut palms and big old mango trees. Roadside stands sell fruit and fresh juices. Fig Tree Drive ends at the village of Swetes. En route, pop into Fig Tree Studio Art Gallery to see what the local art scene is up to.

Rendezvous Bay

5 One of Antigua's most attractive beaches is also among its remotest, reachable only by high-clearance 4WD, by boat or after a 90-minute walk through the rainforest. Make the effort, though, and you'll be rewarded with dreamy golden sand and footprint-free solitude.

Fort James

6 Fort James, a small stronghold at the north side of St John's Harbour, dates back to 1706, but most of what you see today was built in 1739. The site drips with atmosphere: it's moodily run-down and is rarely the scene of crowds. In the fort's reconstructed officers' quarters, bluff-top Russell's offers drinks and seafood with

if Antigua & Barbuda were 100 people

91 would be black
4 would be mixed
2 would be white
3 would be other

belief systems
(% of population)

76 Protestant
10 Roman Catholic
5 other Christian
9 other/none

population per sq km

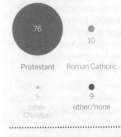

ANTIGUA AND BARBUDA | PUERTO RICO | USA

≈ 30 people

When to Go

HIGH SEASON
(Dec–Apr)

➡ People fleeing the northern winter arrive in droves and prices peak.

➡ Driest period is February to April.

➡ Antigua Sailing Week (April) is the largest regatta in the Caribbean.

SHOULDER
(May–Jun & Nov)

➡ The weather is good, rains are moderate.

➡ Warm temperatures elsewhere reduce visitor numbers.

➡ Best mix of affordable rates and good weather.

LOW SEASON
(Jul–Oct)

➡ Hurricane season; the odds of being caught are small, but tropical storms are like clockwork.

➡ Room prices can be up to 50% less than in high season.

➡ Antigua's 10-day Carnival is held in July–August.

JOHN CANCALOSI / GETTY IMAGES ©

Crazy for Cricket

To Antiguans, cricket is not a sport but a religion. The tiny island state has produced some of the world's best cricketers, including Andy Roberts, Curtly Ambrose and, most famously, Sir Vivian Richards, aka King Viv or the 'Master-Blaster.' Known for his aggressive style of batting, he became captain of the West Indies team between 1980 and 1991.

Not surprisingly, when it came time to build a new stadium for the 2007 World Cup (with major financing courtesy of mainland China), it was named after Antigua's famous son. About 4 miles east of St John's, the 10,000-seat Sir Vivian Richards Cricket Ground ranks among the region's top cricket facilities.

Food & Drink

Black pineapple The local pineapple was first introduced by the Arawaks and is smaller than your garden variety. It's known as 'black' because it's at its sweetest when a kind of dark green. It grows primarily on the southwest coast, near Cades Bay

Pepperpot Antigua's national dish is a hearty stew blending meat and vegetables, such as okra, spinach, eggplant, squash and potatoes. It's often served with fungi, which are not mushrooms but cornmeal patties or dumplings.

Rock lobster This hulking crustacean has a succulent tail but no claws and is best served grilled.

Rum Cavalier and English Harbour are the locally produced rums and best mixed with fruit juice for a refreshing – if potentially lethal – punch.

Wadadli Antigua Brewery makes this local brew, a fresh pale lager, with desalinated seawater.

awesome eyefuls of the ocean and passing boats from its wide verandas. Sunsets can be achingly beautiful.

Frigate Bird Sanctuary

7 The expansive, shallow Codrington Lagoon National Park, which runs along Barbuda's west coast, supports one of the world's largest colonies of frigate birds. More than 5000 of these black-feathered critters nest in sections of the lagoon's scrubby mangroves – with as many as a dozen birds roosting on a single bush. Because of this density, the birds' nesting sites are abuzz with

squawking, and the sight of all those blood-red inflating throat pouches is mesmerizing. The most popular time to visit the rookery is during the mating season, from September to April (December is peak time).

Half Moon Bay

8 Half Moon Bay, in the southeast of the island, is an undeveloped crescent-shaped bay with yet another beautiful white-sand beach lapped by water the color of Blue Curacao. There's usually pretty good bodysurfing along the northern end, while the calmer waters to the south offer decent snorkeling conditions.

Getting Around

Bicycle Check with your hotel, as many rent out a bike or two to guests. A couple of places on Antigua rent bikes.

Boat Barbuda Express runs bumpy 1¾-hour rides aboard a catamaran from St John's (Antigua). Take precautions if you're prone to seasickness.

Bus There is no public transportation on Barbuda, but Antigua has a decent system of private minivans and small buses.

Taxi On both Antigua and Barbuda, fares are regulated by the government, but it's best to confirm this with the driver before riding away.

Iguazú Falls

CAPITAL
Buenos Aires

POPULATION
42.6 million

AREA
2.8 million sq km

OFFICIAL LANGUAGE
Spanish

Argentina

Start free associating on the word 'Argentina,' and it's apparent why the country holds travelers in awe: tango, gauchos, fútbol, the Andes. The classics alone make a wanderlust cocktail.

While Argentina's big cities have a lot of urban pleasures to offer (think cafes, purple jacaranda flowers draped over sidewalks, stylish residents of Buenos Aires, and handsome stone facades), their real purpose is to springboard travelers into the country's greatest attraction: the natural world. From mighty Iguazú Falls in the subtropical north to the thunderous, crackling advance of the Perito Moreno Glacier in the south, Argentina is a vast natural wonderland. The country boasts some of the Andes' highest peaks, several of which top 6000m near Mendoza and San Juan. It's home to rich wetlands that rival Brazil's famous Pantanal, mountains painted in rustic colors, deserts dotted with cacti, massive ice fields and arid steppes in Patagonia, cool lichen-clad Valdivian forests, glacial lakes, Andean salt flats, a spectacular Lake District, penguins, flamingos, caimans, capybaras and more. All unforgettable sights and adventures waiting for you to experience and be amazed by – and you will be, bet on that!

Argentina's
Top Experiences

Iguazú Falls

1 The peaceful Iguazú river, flowing through the jungle between Argentina and Brazil, plunges suddenly over a basalt cliff in a spectacular display of sound and fury that is one of the planet's most awe-inspiring sights. The Iguazú Falls are a primal experience for the senses: the roar, the spray and the sheer volume of water live forever in the memory. But it's not just the waterfalls; the jungly national parks that contain them offer a romantic backdrop and fine wildlife-watching opportunities.

Quebrada de Humahuaca

2 You're a long way from Buenos Aires up here in Argentina's northwestern corner, and it feels a whole world away. This spectacular valley of scoured rock in Jujuy province impresses visually with its tortured formations and artist's palette of mineral colors, but is also of great cultural interest. The Quebrada's settlements are traditional and indigenous in character, with typical Andean dishes supplanting steaks on the restaurant menus, and llamas, not herds of cattle, grazing the sparse highland grass.

Purmamarca, Jujuy province

TAMIEKARAN / GETTY IMAGES ©

Glaciar Perito Moreno

3 As glaciers go, Perito Moreno is one of the most dynamic and accessible on the planet, but what makes it exceptional is its constant advance – up to 2m per day. Visitors can get very close to the action via a complex network of steel boardwalks. Its slow but constant motion creates an audio-visual sensation as building-sized icebergs calve from the face and crash into Lago Argentino. A typical way to cap off the day is with a huge steak dinner back in El Calafate.

Cementerio de la Recoleta

4 A veritable city of the dead, Buenos Aires' top tourist attraction is not to be missed. Lined up along small 'streets' are hundreds of old crypts, each uniquely carved from marble, granite and concrete, and decorated with stained glass, stone angels and religious icons. Small plants and trees grow in fissures while feral cats slink between tombs, some of which lie in various stages of decay. It's a photogenic wonderland, and if there's strange beauty in death you'll find it in spades here.

if Argentina were 100 people

97 would be white
1 would be mestizo
1 would be Asian
1 would be other

....

ethnicity
(% of population)

92
2
Roman Catholic   Jewish

2   4
Protestant   other

....

population per sq km

ARGENTINA   USA   UK

🚶 ≈ 15 people

Hiking the Fitz Roy Range

5 With rugged wilderness and shark-tooth summits, the Fitz Roy Range is the trekking capital of Argentina. Climbers may suffer on its windswept, world-class routes, but hiking trails are surprisingly easy and accessible. Park rangers help orient every traveler who comes into El Chaltén. Once on the trail, the most stunning views are just a day hike from town. Not bad for those who want to reward their sweat equity with a craft beer at the brewery.

Wine Tasting Around Mendoza

6 With so much fantastic wine on offer, it's tempting just to pull up a bar stool and work your way through it, but getting out there and seeing how the grapes are grown and processed is almost as enjoyable as sampling the finished product. The best news is that wine tasting in Argentina isn't just for wine snobs – there's a tour to meet every budget, from DIY bike tours for backpackers to tasting-and-accommodation packages at exclusive wineries.

Ushuaia

7 Location, location, location. Shimmed between the Beagle Channel and the snow-capped Martial Range, the bustling port of Ushuaia is the final scrap of civilization seen by Antarctica-bound boats. But more than the end of the earth, Ushuaia is a crossroads for big commerce and adventure. Snow sports brighten the frozen winters and long summer days mean hiking and

Gardel & the Tango

In June 1935 a Cuban woman committed suicide in Havana; meanwhile, in New York and in Puerto Rico two other women tried to poison themselves. It was all over the same man: tango singer Carlos Gardel, who had just died in a plane crash in Colombia.

Gardel was born in France (a claim contested by both Argentina and Uruguay), and when he was three his destitute single mother brought him to Buenos Aires. In his youth he entertained neighbors with his rapturous singing, then went on to establish a successful performing career.

Gardel played an enormous role in creating the tango *canción* (song) and almost single-handedly took the style out of Buenos Aires' tenements and brought it to Paris and New York. His crooning voice, suaveness and overall charisma made him an immediate success in Latin American countries.

Food & Drink

Beef Argentines have perfected grilling beef, instilling a smoky, salty outer layer to their delectable steaks.

Dulce de leche Argentina has turned milk and sugar into the world's best caramel sauce; find it in most of the country's sweetest concoctions.

Ice cream Argentina makes some of the world's best helado, swirled into a miniature peaked mountain with a spoon stuck in the side.

Italian food You'll find pizza and pasta at so many restaurants, it's a wonder the locals can consume it all.

Maté Although most first-time maté drinkers can barely choke the stuff down, this bitter, grassy tea is an important social bonding experience.

Wine Exploring Argentina by the glass will take you from the malbecs of Mendoza to the torrontés of Cafayate to the syrahs of San Juan.

Vineyard in Lujan de Cuyo, Mendoza

biking until the wee hours. Happening restaurants, the boisterous bars and welcoming B&Bs mean you'll want to call this port home for at least a few days.

Península Valdés

8 Once a tawny, dusty peninsula with remote sheep ranches, today Península Valdés is a hub for some of the best wildlife-watching on the continent. The main attraction is seeing endangered southern right whales get acrobatic and up-close; whale-watching tours actually attract these huge mammals. But the cast of wild characters also includes killer whales, Magellanic penguins, sea lions, elephant seals, rheas, guanaco and numerous sea birds. There's a ton to be seen on shore walks, but diving and kayak tours take you even deeper into the ambience.

Los Esteros del Iberá

9 These protected wetlands offer astonishing wildlife-watching opportunities around shallow

When to Go

HIGH SEASON
(Nov–Feb)

➡ Patagonia is best (and most expensive) December to February.

➡ Crowds throng to the beaches from late December through January.

➡ For ski resorts, busiest times are June to August.

SHOULDER
(Sep–Nov & Mar–May)

➡ Temperature-wise the best times to visit Buenos Aires.

➡ The Lake District is pleasant; leaves are spectacular in March.

➡ The Mendoza region has its grape harvests and wine festival.

LOW SEASON
(Jun–Aug)

➡ Good time to visit the North.

➡ Many services close at beach resorts, and mountain passes can be blocked by snow.

➡ July is a winter vacation month, so things get busy.

vegetation-rich lagoons. Head out in a boat and you'll spot numerous alligators, exotic bird species, monkeys, swamp deer, and possibly the world's cutest rodent, the capybara – but no, you can't take one home.

Colonial Salta

10 Argentina's northwest holds its most venerable colonial settlements, and none is more lovely than Salta, set in a fertile valley. Postcard-pretty churches, a sociable plaza and a wealth of noble buildings give it a laid-back historic ambience that endears it to all who visit. Add in great museums, a lively folkloric music scene, and a fistful of attractions: that's one impressive place.

Best on Film

El secreto de sus ojos (The Secret in Their Eyes; 2009) Thriller that won the 2010 Oscar for best foreign-language film.

Historias mínimas (Intimate Stories, 2002) Three separate people traveling in Patagonia.

La historia oficial (The Official Story, 1985) Oscar-winning film on the Dirty War.

Un novio para mi mujer (A Boyfriend for My Wife; 2008) Comedy about a husband plotting his divorce.

Best in Print

And the Money Kept Rolling In (and Out) (Paul Blustein, 2005) How the IMF helped bankrupt Argentina.

In Patagonia (Bruce Chatwin, 1977) Evocative writing on Patagonia's history and mystique.

The Motorcycle Diaries (1993, Ernesto Che Guevara et al) Based on the travel diary of the Argentine-born revolutionary.

Uttermost Part of the Earth (E. Lucas Bridges, 1947) Classic book about Tierra del Fuego's now-extinct indígenas.

Getting Around

Air Argentina is a huge country, so flights are good for saving time. Delays happen occasionally, however.

Bus Generally the best way to get around Argentina. Buses are fast, frequent, comfortable, reasonably priced and cover the country extensively.

Car Renting a car is useful for those who want the most travel independence in remote regions like Patagonia.

Train A few train lines can be useful for travelers but generally this is not the most efficient method of transportation.

Mar del Plata

11 Argentina's premier beach resort is a heaving human zoo in summer – but that's what makes it such fun. Compete with *porteños* (Buenos Aires residents) for a patch of open sand, then lay back and enjoy watching thousands of near-naked bodies worship the sun, play sand games or splash around in the surf. When the sun goes down it's time for steak or seafood dinners, followed by late-night theater shows and nightclubs.

San Telmo

12 One of Buenos Aires' most charming neighborhoods is San Telmo, lined with cobblestone streets, colonial buildings and a classic atmosphere that will transport you back to the mid-19th century. Be sure to take in the Sunday *feria* (street fair), where dozens of booths sell antiques and knickknacks, while buskers perform for loose change. Tango is big here, and you can watch a fancy, spectacular show or catch a casual street performance – both will wow you with their smooth style and amazing feats of athleticism.

Iglesia San Francisco, Salta

JUAN MABROMATA / GETTY IMAGES ©

Tatev monastery, Syunik

CAPITAL
Yerevan

POPULATION
3.1 million

AREA
29,743 sq km

OFFICIAL LANGUAGE
Armenian

Armenia

Armenia is said to have its head in the west and its heart in the east: here you can experience a Mediterranean lifestyle beneath the Caucasus mountains.

Although Armenians carry a lot of psychological baggage from a traumatic 20th century, you'd hardly notice it from a quick tour around the country. The rapidly modernising capital, the boutique tourism industry and the warm welcome you'll receive everywhere seem to belie the country's reputation for tragedy. Rather than letting past woes weigh it down, Armenia has built its memorials, dusted itself off and moved on. For travellers, easily visited highlights include ancient monasteries, candlelit churches and high-walled forts – but lasting impressions lie more with the Armenians themselves.

You'll easily find friends among these gracious, humble and easy-going people, even without a common language. The travel experience is wide-ranging – you can have a four-star holiday in Yerevan and Sevan or a much simpler experience in rural towns like Dilijan and Goris. Many travellers only spend a week or less as they shuttle around the region but those with more time get to experience the best spots in crowd-free bliss.

Armenia's
Top Experiences

Yerevan

1 Immerse yourself in the lively cultural life, buzzing cafe scene and wealth of museums in the capital Yerevan. While it's the undeniable cultural, economic and political heart of the nation, Yerevan can at times feel like a city on permanent holiday. All summer long, Yerevanites saunter up and down the main boulevards, preening in high fashion and fast cars while occasionally popping into a cafe to schmooze over a drink or two.

Tatev Monastery

2 Armenia's rich collection of ancient churches and monasteries is a world treasure that has developed over thousands of years. The general layout and design are almost universal and you'll soon become accustomed to seeing the ubiquitous conical roof, resembling Mt Ararat. Closer inspection reveals that each monastery has its own unique character and design variation. Tatev's mountaintop perch is on the edge of the Vorotan Canyon, and is a jaw-dropping World Heritage–listed church. The views down the gorge reach to the peaks of Karabakh.

Yeghegis Valley

3 Go exploring in the idyllic Yeghegis Valley, peppered with quaint villages, old churches and even a mysterious Jewish cemetery. The beautiful valley is surrounded by towering peaks and contains a rare concentration of churches, including Tsakhatskar Monastery, a crumbling agglomeration of churches and old *khatchkars*. It has a couple of churches, including the very unusual Surp Zorats, where worshippers gathered before an outdoor altar, where once horses and soldiers were blessed before going off to battle.

Dilijan

4 Break for a few days in Dilijan for some fine mountain scenery, hiking trails and its historic old town. It's billed as the 'Switzerland of Armenia', and although that may be a bit of a stretch, alpine Dilijan is still one of the

Water Day, Yerevan

most pleasant regions in the country. During Soviet times this was the peaceful retreat for cinematographers, composers, artists and writers to come and be creative; today it's a centre for tourism with a number of fine B&Bs and a revitalised historic district.

Echmiadzin

5 Step back in time at holy Echmiadzin, the Vatican of the Armenian Apostolic Church, the place where St Gregory the Illuminator saw a beam of light fall to the earth in a divine vision, and where he built the first Mother Church of Armenia. For Armenian Christians, Echmiadzin has unparalleled importance. It was the capital of Armenia from

180 to 340, during which time Christianity was first adopted by the Armenian nation.

Debed Canyon

6 Marvel at the World Heritage–listed monasteries Haghpat and Sanahin in the steep-sided Debed Canyon. This canyon manages to pack in more history and culture than just about anywhere else in the country. Nearly every village along the Debed River has a church, a chapel, an old fort and a sprinkling of *khatchkars* somewhere nearby. Two World Heritage–listed monasteries, Haghpat and Sanahin, justly draw most visitors, but there are plenty more to scramble around.

if Armenia were 100 people

98 would be Armenian
1 would be Yezidi
1 would be other

belief systems
(% of population)

95 — Armenian Apostolic
4 — other Christian
1 — Yezidi

population per sq km

ARMENIA · UK · TURKEY

🯅 = 35 people

When to Go

MAR–MAY

➡ Spring brings a riot of flowers but also a lot of rain.

LATE SEP–EARLY NOV

➡ Autumn has long, warm days and more stable weather.

JUN–AUG

➡ In summer Yerevan can be 40°C for days at a time. Conditions in the north are mild.

Punch Drunk

Oghee (pronounced something like 'orh-ee') are delicious fruit vodkas, sometimes called *vatsun* or aragh, made in village orchards everywhere. Around 60% alcohol, *oghee* is made from apples, pears, apricots, pomegranates, grapes, cherries, Cornelian cherries or cornels, mulberries and figs. The best mulberry (*t'te*) and Cornelian cherry (*hone*) *oghee* are intense, lingering liqueurs. Vedi Alco makes some *oghee* commercially, weaker than the village stuff. You won't need to go far to try some; it's a usual accompaniment to a *khoravats* dinner. The drink tastes best in autumn, when homes turn into distilleries after the harvest.

Food & Drink

Cognac The country's national liquor, around 40% alcohol.

Dolma Rice wrapped in vine leaves.

Ishkhan khoravats Grilled trout from Lake Sevan

Jajik Dip made from yoghurt with cucumbers and fennel.

Kartofel atari graki mej Baked potatoes cooked in cow dung (which is said to boost flavour).

Khash A thick winter stew made from animal parts.

Khoravats Barbecued food; pork is the favourite, though lamb, beef and sometimes chicken are usually available.

Kilikia A typical middle-European lager; very good when fresh

Siga A popular grilled fish dish.

Soorch A potent, finely ground cup of lusciously rich coffee, with thick sediment at the bottom. It goes well with honeyed pastries such as baklava.

CHRISTOPHE CERISIER / GETTY IMAGES ©

Sevan Monastery, Lake Sevan

Lake Sevan

7 Relax by the clear waters of Lake Sevan, a refreshing break when temperatures soar in summer. Perched at 1900m above sea level, the great blue eye of Lake Sevan covers 940 sq km and is 80km long by 30km at its widest. Its colours and shades change with the weather and by its own mysterious processes, from a dazzling azure to dark blue and a thousand shades in between. The freshwater lake supports a healthy fish population.

Mount Aragats

8 Stretch your legs on Mt Aragats, a 4000m snow-covered mountain that offers views of famed Mt Ararat. Snow covers the top of the highest mountain in modern Armenia almost year-round, so climbing is best in July, August or September. The southernmost of its four peaks (3893m) is easy enough for inexperienced climbers, but the northern peak (4090m) is more challenging and requires crossing a snowfield (experienced hikers only).

Getting Around

Bicycle Take plenty of care on the roads – local driving styles are somewhat less predictable than in Western countries, and some road surfaces are awful (though there is a gradual overall improvement).

Car If you can get used to the way locals overtake, weave around potholes and like to go fast, driving here is quite possible. It is often no more expensive, and quite common practice, to hire a local driver for intercity trips or excursions.

Minibus The minibus (marshrutka) is king of public transport in Armenia. One or other of these forms of transport reaches almost every village in the region, and there are frequent services between larger towns and cities.

Willemstad, Curaçao

CAPITAL
Oranjestad (A)
Kralendijk (B)
Willemstad (C)

POPULATION
110,663 (A)
15,800 (B)
146,836 (C)

AREA
180 sq km (A)
294 sq km (B)
444 sq km (C)

OFFICIAL LANGUAGES
Dutch, Spanish, English, Papiamentu

Aruba, Bonaire & Curaçao

The ABCs of the Caribbean, Aruba, Bonaire and Curaçao boast white-sand beaches, world-class diving and an intriguing mix of Dutch culture in the food, language and colonial architecture.

These three tiny islands once formed the Netherlands Antilles and are still independent territories within the Kingdom of the Netherlands, so Dutch culture is very much in evidence.

East coast Americans fleeing winter make Aruba the most touristed island in the southern Caribbean – not surprising given that it has miles of the best beaches, sociable rum shops, plenty of upmarket package resorts and a compact and cute main town, Oranjestad.

Bonaire's appeal is its amazing reef-lined coast. Entirely designated a national park, the beautiful waters lure divers from across the globe.

Go-go Curaçao balances commerce with Unesco-recognized old Willemstad and an accessible beauty, thanks to hidden beaches along a lush coast. It's a wild mix of urban madness, remote vistas and a lust for life.

Flights between Aruba, Bonaire and Curaçao are frequent so you can hop between them or choose one and soak up the sun.

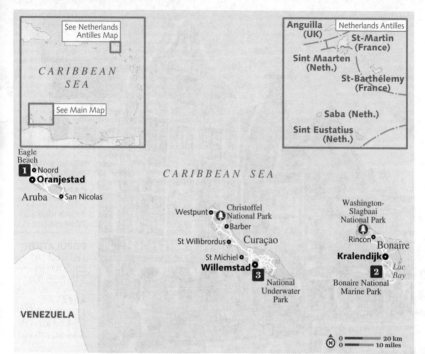

Aruba, Bonaire & Curaçao's
Top Experiences

Eagle Beach

1 Frolic on a long ribbon of powdery sand at Aruba's Eagle Beach, northwest of the capital Oranjestad. This is the island's best beach and frequently makes the list of best beaches in the world. Vendors, loungers and shade trees mean you can relax.

Bonaire National Marine Park

2 This Unesco World Heritage marine park covers the entire coast of Bonaire island to a depth of 200ft (60m) and is a diver's paradise with more than 90 named dive sites. The closeness of the reefs and the clarity of the waters make for unparalleled access – you can reach more than half of the identified dive sites from shore.

Willemstad

3 Curaçao's capital is both a big city and a small town. The heart and soul is Willemstad's old town, where the island's colonial Dutch heritage sets a genteel tone amid markets, museums and even a nascent cafe culture. Wandering the Unesco World Heritage–recognized old town and absorbing its rhythms makes a cultural contrast to the island's fine beaches.

Food & Drink

Frikandel Classic Dutch deep-fried meaty snack.

Funchi Based on cornmeal, it is formed into cakes and fried.

Goat stew A classic dish that most Arubans will say is made best by their own mother.

Keshi yena Cheese casserole with chicken, okra and a few raisins for seasoning.

When to Go

DEC–APR	SEP–MAY	JUL & AUG
➜ High season with pleasant temperatures and low humidity.	➜ Rainfall is highest at this time though the island is fairly dry, averaging 25mm per month.	➜ The hottest months but temperatures are still pleasant and dry.

Twelve Apostles, Great Ocean Road

CAPITAL
Canberra

POPULATION
22.3 million

AREA
7.7 million sq km

**OFFICIAL
LANGUAGE**
English

Australia

Australia – the sixth-largest country on this lonely planet – is dazzlingly diverse: a sing-along medley of mountains, deserts, reefs, forests, beaches and multicultural melting-pot cities.

Most Australians live along the coast, and most of these folks live in cities. In fact, Australia is the 18th-most urbanised country in the world. Sydney is a glamorous collusion of beaches, boutiques and bars. Melbourne is all arts, alleyways and Australian Rules football. Brisbane is a subtropical town on the way up; Adelaide has festive grace and pubby poise. Boomtown Perth breathes west-coast optimism; Canberra transcends political agendas. And the tropical northern frontier town of Darwin and chilly southern sandstone city of Hobart couldn't be more different. No matter which city you're wheeling into, you'll never go wanting for an offbeat theatre production, a rockin' live band or a lofty art-gallery opening.

There's a heckuva lot of tarmac across this wide brown land. From Margaret River to Cooktown, Jabiru to Dover, the best way to appreciate Australia is to hit the road: Australia's national parks and secluded corners are custommade for camping trips down the dirt road.

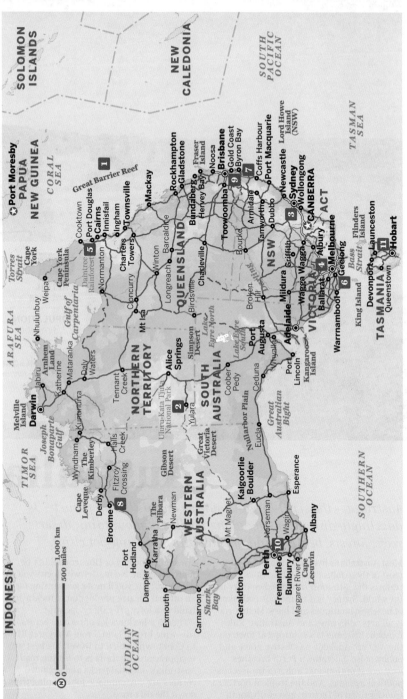

Australia's

Australia's
Top Experiences

Great Barrier Reef

1 Unesco World Heritage–listed? Check. Oprah Winfrey–endorsed? Check. The Great Barrier Reef is jaw-droppingly beautiful. Stretching more than 2000km along the Queensland coastline, it's a complex ecosystem populated with dazzling coral, languid sea turtles, gliding rays, timid reef sharks and tropical fish of every colour and size. Whether you dive on it, snorkel over it or explore it via scenic flight or glass-bottomed boat, this vivid undersea kingdom and its coral-fringed islands are unforgettable.

Uluru-Kata Tjuta National Park

2 No matter how many times you've seen it on postcards, nothing truly prepares you for the grandeur of the Rock as it first appears on the outback horizon. With its remote desert location, deep cultural significance and spectacular natural beauty, Uluru is a special pilgrimage. But Uluru-Kata Tjuta National Park offers much more. Along with the equally captivating Kata Tjuta (the Olgas), there are mystical walks, sublime sunsets, sparkling night skies, luxury hotels and ancient desert cultures to encounter.

Sydney Opera House

3 Magnificent Sydney Opera House on Sydney Harbour is a headline act in itself. An exercise in architectural lyricism like no other, Jørn Utzon's building on Circular Quay's Bennelong Point more than holds its own amidst the visual feast of the harbour's attention-grabbing bridge, shimmering blue waters and jaunty green ferries. Best of all, everyone can experience the magic on offer here – a stunningly sited waterside bar, acclaimed French restaurant, guided tours and star-studded performance schedule make sure of that.

Melbourne

4 Why the queue? Oh, that's just the line to get into the latest hot 'no bookings' restaurant in Melbourne. The next best restaurant/chef/cafe/food truck may be the talk of the town, but there are things locals would never change: the leafy parks and gardens in the inner city 'burbs; the clunky trams that whisk the creative northerners to sea-breezy St Kilda; and the allegiances that living in such a sports-mad city brings. The city's world-renowned street-art scene expresses Melbourne's fears, frustrations and joys.

if Australia were 100 people

79 would speak English at home
3 would speak Chinese at home
2 would speak Italian at home
1 would speak Vietnamese at home
15 would speak another language at home

belief systems
(% of population)

64	19	2
Christian	Agnostic	Buddhist
2	1	12
Muslim	Hindu	other

population per sq km

AUSTRALIA   NEW ZEALAND   USA

≈ 3 people

Daintree Rainforest

5 Lush green rainforest replete with fan palms, prehistoric-looking ferns and twisted mangroves tumble down towards a brilliant white-sand coastline in the ancient, World Heritage–listed Daintree Rainforest. Enveloped in a cacophony of birdsong, frog croaking and the buzz of insects, you can explore the area via wildlife-spotting night tours, mountain treks, canopy walks, 4WD trips, horse riding, kayaking, croc-spotting cruises, tropical-fruit orchard tours...Whew! If you're lucky, you might even spot an elusive cassowary.

Great Ocean Road

6 The Twelve Apostles (rock formations jutting out of wild waters) are one of Victoria's most vivid sights, but it's the 'getting there' road trip that doubles their impact. Take it slow while driving along roads that curl beside spectacular Bass Strait beaches, then whip slightly inland through rainforests alive with small towns and big trees. The secrets of the Great Ocean Road don't stop here; further along is maritime treasure Port Fairy and hidden Cape Bridgewater. For the ultimate in slow travel, walk the Great Ocean Walk from Apollo Bay to the Apostles.

Byron Bay

7 Up there with kangaroos and Akubra hats, big-hearted Byron Bay (just Byron to its mates) is one of the enduring icons of Australian culture. Families on school holidays, surfers and sun-seekers

Aboriginal Storytelling

Aboriginal people had an oral culture so storytelling was an important way to learn. Stories gave meaning to life and were used to teach the messages of the spirit ancestors.

Although beliefs and cultural practices vary according to region and language groups, there is a common world-view that these ancestors created the land, the sea and all living things. This is often referred to as the Dreaming and Aboriginal people attribute their origins and existence to these ancestors.

Through these stories, the knowledge and beliefs are passed on from one generation to another and set out morals to live by.

Food & Drink

Australia is huge, and it varies so much in climate, that at any time of the year there's an enormous array of produce on offer. In summer, kitchen bowls overflow with fresh fruit, including nectarines, peaches, cherries and mangoes. Seafood is always freshest close to the source; on this big island it's plentiful.

Bugs Shovel-nosed lobsters without a lobster's price tag (try the Balmain and Moreton Bay varieties).

Fish You can sample countless wild fish species but even snapper, trevally and whiting taste fabulous barbecued.

Marron A prehistoric-looking freshwater crayfish from Western Australia.

Oysters Connoisseurs prize Sydney rock oysters and Tasmania is known for its Pacific oysters.

Prawns Prawns in Australia are incredible, particularly sweet school prawns or the eastern king (Yamba) prawns found along the northern New South Wales coast.

TIM BARKER / GETTY IMAGES ©

Bar in Chinatown, Melbourne

from across the globe gather by the foreshore at sunset, drawn to this spot on the world map by fabulous restaurants, a chilled pace of life, endless beaches and an astonishing range of activities on offer. More than that, they're here because this is one of the most beautiful stretches of coast in the country.

Broome & Northwest Western Australia

8 Harsh, remote and stunningly beautiful, Australia's final frontier promises unparalleled adventure. Scorched spinifex and boab plains hide plunging waterfalls, while pristine beaches and reefs fringe an inhospitable coast. Explore three World Heritage sites: Shark Bay, Ningaloo and Purnululu, and Broome, one of the world's great travellers' crossroads, where every evening, from your vantage point on beautiful Cable Beach, a searing crimson sun slips past camels and tourists into the turquoise Indian Ocean.

When to Go

HIGH SEASON
(Dec–Feb)

➜ Summertime: local holidays, busy beaches and cricket.

➜ Prices rise for big-city accommodation.

➜ Central and northern Australia high season is June to August due to mild days and low humidity.

SHOULDER
(Sep–Nov)

➜ Warm sun, clear skies, shorter queues.

➜ Local business people are relaxed, not yet stressed by summer crowds.

➜ Autumn (March to May) is also shoulder season

LOW SEASON
(Jun–Aug)

➜ Cool rainy days down south; mild sunny skies up north.

➜ Low tourist numbers; attractions keep slightly shorter hours.

➜ Head for the desert, the tropical north or the snow.

Gold Coast

9 Brash, trashy, hedonistic, over-hyped...Queensland's Gold Coast is all of these things, but if you're looking for a party, bring it on! Beyond the fray is the beach – an improbably gorgeous coastline of clean sand, warm water and peeling surf breaks. The bronzed gods of the surf, Australia's surf life-savers, patrol the sand and pit their skills against one another in surf carnivals. Also here are Australia's biggest theme parks – a rollercoaster, movie buff and waterworld nirvana!

Best on Film

Gallipoli (director Peter Weir; 1981) Nationhood in the crucible of WWI.

Lantana (director Ray Lawrence; 2001) Mystery for grown-ups: a meditation on love, truth and grief.

Mad Max (director George Miller; 1979) Mel Gibson gets angry.

Ten Canoes (directors Rolf de Heer and Peter Djigirr; 2006) The first Australian film scripted entirely in Aboriginal language.

Two Hands (director Gregor Jordan; 1999) Vicious humour in Sydney's criminal underworld.

Best in Print

Dirt Music (Tim Winton; 2002) Guitar-strung Western Australian page-turner.

Montebello (Robert Drewe; 2012) Part memoir, part exposé of British nuclear tests in WA.

Oscar & Lucinda (Peter Carey; 1988) Man Booker Prize winner. How to relocate a glass church.

The Secret River (Kate Grenville; 2005) Tales of 19th-century convict life around Sydney.

Getting Around

Air Fast-track your holiday with affordable, frequent, fast flights between majo centres. Carbon offset your flights if you're feeling guilty.

Bus Australia's extensive bus network is a reliable way to get around, though i isn't always cheaper than flying and it can be tedious over huge distances.

Car The best way to explore Australia is by car and having a 4WD is essential t off-the-beaten-track driving into the outback. Larger car-rental companies ha drop-offs in major towns and cities.

Train Trains are more comfortable than buses, and there's a certain long-dista 'romance of the rails' that's alive and kicking. Shorter-distance rail services w most states are run by state rail bodies, either government or private.

Perth & Fremantle

10 Perth may be isolated, but it's far from being a backwater. Sophisticated restaurants fly the flag for Mod Oz cuisine – some in restored heritage buildings in the CBD – and chic cocktail bars linger in laneways. Contrasting with the flashy front the city presents to the Swan River, Perth's more bohemian inner suburbs echo with the thrum of guitars and the sizzle of woks. Just down the river, the pubs of Fremantle serve some of Western Australia's finest craft beers, and colonial buildings punctuate a glorious Victorian townscape.

MONA, Tasmania

11 Occupying a riverside location a ferry ride from Hobart's harbourfront, Moorilla Estate's Museum of Old & New Art (MONA) is a world-class institution. Described by its owner, Hobart philanthropist David Walsh, as a 'subversive adult Disneyland', three levels of underground galleries showcase more than 400 often controversial works of art. Visitors may not like everything they see, but it's guaranteed that intense debate and conversation will be on the agenda after viewing one of Australia's unique arts experiences.

Market square, Hallstatt

CAPITAL
Vienna

POPULATION
8.42 million

AREA
83,871 sq km

**OFFICIAL
LANGUAGE**
German

Austria

Austria is a contrast of spectacular natural landscapes and elegant urban sleeves. One day you're plunging into an alpine lake, the next you're exploring a narrow backstreet of Vienna.

For such a small country, Austria has made it big. This is, after all, the land where Mozart was born, Strauss taught the world to waltz and Julie Andrews grabbed the spotlight with her twirling entrance in *The Sound of Music*. This is where the Habsburgs built their 600-year empire, and where past glories still shine in the resplendent baroque palaces and chandelier-lit coffee houses of Vienna, Innsbruck and Salzburg. This is a perfectionist of a country and whatever it does – mountains, classical music, new media, castles, cake, you name it – Austria does it exceedingly well.

Beyond its grandiose cities, Austria's allure lies outdoors. And whether you're schussing down the legendary slopes of Kitzbühel, climbing high in the Alps of Tyrol or pedalling along the banks of the sprightly Danube (Donau), you'll find the kind of inspiring landscapes that no well-orchestrated symphony, camera lens or singing nun could ever quite do justice.

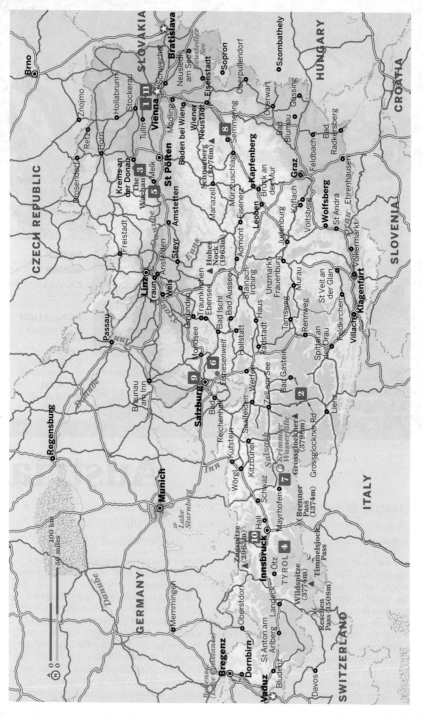

Austria's
Top Experiences

Imperial Palaces of Vienna

1 Imagine what you could do with unlimited riches and Austria's top architects at hand for 640 years and you'll have the Vienna of the Habsburgs. The monumental Hofburg whisks you back to the age of empires; marvel at the treasury's imperial crowns, the equine ballet of the Spanische Hofreitschule and the chandelier-lit apartments fit for Empress Elisa-beth. The palace is rivalled in grandeur only by the 1441-room Schloss Schönbrunn, a Unesco World Heritage site, and baroque Schloss Belvedere both set in exquisite gardens.

Grossglockner Road

2 Hairpin bends: 36. Length: 48km. Average slope gradient: 9%. Highest viewpoint: Edelweiss Spitze (2571m). Grossglockner Rd is one of Europe's greatest drives and the showpiece of Hohe Tauern National Park. The scenery unfolds as you climb higher on this serpentine road. And what scenery! Snowcapped mountains, plunging waterfalls and lakes scattered like gemstones are just the build-up to Grossglockner (3798m), Austria's highest peak. Start early and allow enough time, there's an outstanding view on every bend.

Schloss Schönbrunn, Vienna

BARRY WINIKER / GETTY IMAGES ©

The Wachau

3 When Strauss composed 'The Blue Danube', he surely had the Wachau in mind. Granted Unesco World Heritage status for its natural and cultural beauty, this stretch of the Danube Valley waltzes you through landscapes of terraced slopes, forested slopes and apricot orchards. Beyond the Stift Melk, Dürnstein's Kuenringerburg begs exploration. This hilltop castle is where the troubadour Blondel attempted to rescue Richard the Lionheart from the clutches of Duke Leopold V.

if Austria were 100 people

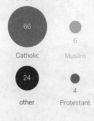

77 would be Austrian
23 would be foreign citizens

belief systems
(% of population)

66 Catholic
6 Muslim
24 other
4 Protestant

population per sq km

AUSTRIA   USA   GERMANY

🯅 ≈ 30 people

Outdoor Adventure in Tyrol

4 If there's foaming water, a tall mountain or a sheer ravine, there are heart-pumping outdoor escapades in Austria. For a summertime buzz, you can't beat throwing yourself down raging rivers such as the Inn and Sanna in Tyrol, Austria's rafting mecca. Or strap into your harness and be blown away by the Alpine scenery paragliding in the Zillertal. Cyclists use the cable-car network to access the many high-altitude and downhill routes.

Stift Melk

5 Austria's greatest works of art are those wrought for God, some say. Gazing up at the golden glory of Stift Melk, Austria's must-see Benedictine abbey-fortress, you can't help but agree. The twin-spired monastery church is a baroque tour de force, swirling with prancing angels, gilt flourishes and Johann Michael Rottmayr's ceiling paintings. Such opulence continues in the library and marble hall, both embellished with illusionary *trompe l'oeil* tiers by Paul Troger.

Eisriesenwelt

6 The twinkling chambers and passageways of Eisriesenwelt are like something out of Narnia under the White Witch. Sculpted drip by drip over millennia, the icy underworld of the limestone Tennengebirge range is billed as the world's largest accessible ice cave. Otherworldly sculptures, shimmering lakes and a cavernous *Eispalast* (ice palace) appear as you venture deep into the frozen heart of the mountain, with your carbide lamp in hand.

The Sound of Music

Salzburg is a celebrity for those who have never even set foot in the city, thanks to its star appearance in The Sound of Music. The sculpture-dotted Mirabellgarten of 'Do-Re-Mi' fame, the Benedictine nunnery Stift Nonnberg, the 'Sixteen Going on Seventeen' pavilion in Hellbrunn Park – it's enough to make you yodel out loud.

Did you know that there were 10, not seven von Trapp children, the eldest of whom was Rupert (so long, Liesl)? Or that the captain was a gentle, family-loving man and Maria no soft touch? Or, that in 1938 the von Trapp family left quietly for the US instead of climbing every mountain to Switzerland? For the truth behind the Hollywood legend, stay the night at the original Villa Trapp, a 19th-century mansion in the Aigen district.

Food & Drink

Cheese Dig into gooey *Käsnudeln* (cheese noodles) in Carinthia, *Kaspressknodel* (fried cheese dumplings) in Tyrol and *Käsekrainer* (cheesy sausages) in Vienna.

Kaffee und Kuchen Coffee and cake is Austria's sweetest tradition. Must-tries: flaky apple strudel, chocolatey *Sacher Torte* and *Kaiserschmarrn* (sweet pancakes with raisins).

Meat Go for a classic Wiener schnitzel, *Tafelspitz* (boiled beef with horseradish sauce) or *Schweinebraten* (pork roast). The humble wurst (sausage) comes in various guises.

Potatoes Lashings of potatoes, either fried (*Pommes*), roasted (*Bratkartoffeln*), in a salad (*Erdapfelsalat*) or boiled in their skins (*Quellmänner*).

Wine Jovial locals gather in rustic *Heurigen* (wine taverns) identified by an evergreen branch above the door. Sip crisp grüner veltliner whites and spicy blaufränkisch wines.

MARIO EDER / GETTY IMAGES ©

Paragliding, Tyrol

Krimmler Wasserfälle

7 No doubt you'll hear the thunderous roar of the 380m-high Krimmler Wasserfälle, Europe's highest waterfall, before you see it. You can't help but feel insignificant when confronted with the sheer force and scale of this cataract, which thrashes immense boulders and produces the most photogenic of rainbows. It looks best from certain angles, namely from the Wasserfallweg (Waterfall Trail). The path zigzags up through moist, misty forest to viewpoints that afford close-ups of the three-tiered falls and a shower in its fine spray.

When to Go

HIGH SEASON
(Apr–Oct)

➡ High season peaks from July to August.

➡ In lake areas the peak is June to September.

➡ Prices rise over Christmas and Easter.

➡ Salzburg is busiest in July and August for the Salzburg Festival.

SHOULDER
(Apr–May & late Sep–Oct)

➡ The weather's changeable, the lakes are chilly and the hiking's excellent.

➡ Sights are open and less crowded.

LOW SEASON
(Nov–Mar)

➡ Many sights are closed at this time of year.

➡ There's a cultural focus in Vienna and the regional capitals.

➡ Ski resorts open from mid-December.

Semmeringbahn

8 The monumental Semmeringbahn (Semmering Railway) is a panoramic journey through the eastern Alps, as well as a nostalgic trip back to early rail travel. Some 20,000 workers toiled to create the railway, an Alpine first, in a feat of 19th-century engineering that is now a Unesco World Heritage site. Though steam has been replaced by electricity, you can still imagine the wonder of the first passengers as the train curves around 16 viaducts, burrows through 15 tunnels and glides across 100 stone bridges. The grandeur of the railway and landscapes is timeless.

Festung Hohensalzburg

9 Work up a sweat on the steep walk or step into the funicular and sway up to Salzburg's glorious fortress, Festung Hohensalzburg, beckoning on a forested peak above the city. Glide through the Golden Hall, with its celestial ceiling capturing the starlit heavens. After all this beauty, you will find yourself cast among a chilling array of medieval

Best on Film

Metropolis (1927) Industry and prescient futuristic grunge by director Fritz Lang.

The Counterfeiters (2007) A Jew whose remarkable skill in counterfeiting puts him in the service of Nazis.

The Piano Teacher (2001) Masterpiece directed by Michael Hanecke about a masochistic piano teacher.

The Third Man (1949) Classic film noir set in Vienna.

Best in Print

Danube (Claudio Magris; 1986) Mid-1980s Italian travel journal covering the river's length.

Last Waltz in Vienna: The Destruction of a Family 1842–1942 (George Clare; 1982) Autobiographical account of a Jewish family's fate.

Vienna: The Image of a Culture in Decline (Edward Crankshaw; 1938) Travel description and history.

Getting Around

Bicycle Most regional tourist boards have brochures on cycling facilities and routes within their region. It's possible to take bicycles on trains with a bicycle symbol at the top of its timetable.

Bus Services operate in most cities and are complemented by a few night bus lines. In remote regions plan head and travel on a weekday.

Car Small towns and even small cities often have limited or no car-hire services, so reserve ahead from major cities.

Train Austria's national railway system is integrated with the bus services. Trains are good by any standard, and with a discount card it's inexpensive.

torture instruments in the Fortress Museum. Don't miss the 360-degree views from the tower.

Innsbruck

10 Set against an impressive backdrop of the Nordkette Alps, Tyrol's capital is the kind of place where one moment you are celebrating cultural achievement in elegant state apartments or the Gothic Hofkirche, and the next you are whizzing up into the Alps inside Zaha Zadid's futuristic funicular or heading out for the ski pistes. If clinging to a fixed rope while you make your way across seven

peaks sounds too head-swirling, try the mountain-bike track.

MuseumsQuartier

11 Once the imperial stables, now one of the world's biggest exhibition spaces, Vienna's 60,000-sq-m MuseumsQuartier contains more art than some small countries. Emotive works by Klimt and Schiele hang out in the Leopold Museum, while the basalt MUMOK highlights provocative Viennese Actionists, and the Kunsthalle new media. Progressive boutiques, workshops and cafes take creativity beyond the canvas.

FRANZ PRITZ / GETTY IMAGES ©

Palace of the Shirvanshahs, Baku

CAPITAL
Baku

POPULATION
9.6 million

AREA
86,600 sq km

OFFICIAL LANGUAGE
Azerbaijani

Azerbaijan

Marrying timeless tradition and ultra-modernity, Azerbaijan reveals a melange of cultural influences and outstanding attractions at the meeting point between Europe and Asia.

Azerbaijan (Azərbaycan) is a tangle of contradictions and contrasts. Tucked beneath the Caucasus Mountains and facing the Caspian Sea, it is where Central Asia edges into Europe, with a melange of Turkic, Persian and Russian influences contributing to its fabric. A nexus of ancient historical empires, it was, according to some, the site of the Garden of Eden.

Surrounded by semi-desert on the oil-rich Caspian Sea, the cosmopolitan capital, Baku, rings its Unesco-listed ancient core with mushrooming new skyscrapers. Yet barely three hours' drive away are timeless rural villages, clad in lush orchards and backed by the soaring Great Caucasus mountains

The modern Azerbaijanis, well versed in Turkic legend and Persian poetry, are a passionate and overwhelmingly hospitable people, who enjoy the timeless pleasures of a glass of *çay* (tea) with friends and the lyrical intensity of local bards singing *muğam* (traditional musical style).

Azerbaijan's
Top Experiences

Modern Baku

1 With an elegant centre, pedestrianised, tree-lined streets filled with exclusive boutiques and a skyline of modernist towers, Azerbaijan's capital is a dynamic boom town. Baku is the South Caucasus' largest and most cosmopolitan metropolis. Few cities in the world are changing as quickly and nowhere else in Eurasia do East and West blend as seamlessly or as chaotically. And romantic couples defy Islamic stereotypes by canoodling their way around wooded parks and handholding on the Caspian-front Bulvar (promenade), whose greens and opal blues make a mockery of Baku's desert-ringed location.

Baku's Old City (İçəri Şəhər)

2 Unesco World Heritage status has helped kerb the corporate gentrification of this fascinating area hemmed in by an exotically crenellated arc of fortress wall. The Old City contains some of Baku's most accessible sights, and its quieter back alleyways are minor attractions in their own right, as are the tree-lined streets of 'oil-boom' mansions just beyond. The Palace of the Shirvanshahs, mostly dating to the 15th century and painstakingly (over)restored in 2003, is a focal point. The tapering 29m Maiden's Tower is Baku's foremost architectural icon.

Şəki

3 Snoozing amid green pillows of beautifully forested mountains, Şəki (Sheki) is Azerbaijan's loveliest town, dappled with tiled-roof old houses and topped off with a glittering little khan's palace. The sturdy stone perimeter wall of Hacı Çələbi's Nukha Fortress today encloses an 18th-century palace, tourist office, craft workshops, several museums and a decent café-restaurant, all set in patches of sheep-mown grass. Beyond the walls there are two 19th century mosques, numerous shops stocking *halva* (a delicious sweet popular in Central Asia and the Middle East) and an historic caravanserai.

Quba

Mountain Villages in the Quba hinterlands

4 Venture into high-altitude shepherd villages with unique languages and dramatic canyonland scenery. Amid the sheepy Caucasian foothills and canyons lie Azerbaijan's grandest mountain panoramas and its most fascinating villages. Perhaps the most memorable are mysterious, white-washed Buduq and crag-top Qrız, whose name means 'dagger' and whose central feature is an ancient graveyard. Easier to reach are the fabled ancient village of Xınalıq and Laza whose jaw-dropping setting counterpoints emerald meadows, high green crags and long mountain waterfalls.

Lahıc

5 Copper beaters' and carpet weavers' workshops line the cobbled main street of this mountain hideaway. Azerbaijan has many delightful mountain villages, but tourist-savvy Lahıc is quainter and more accessible than most. It is locally famous for its Persian-based dialect and its traditional coppersmiths. Hiking and regional scenery is inspiring and, at least in summer, there's an unusually good smattering of English speakers to help you get a feel for rural life.

The Caspian littoral

6 Lining the coast south from Baku is a fascinating collage of beaches, oil workings, seascapes, Soviet

if Azerbaijan were 100 people

91 would be Azeri
2 would be Dagestani
2 would be Russian
1 would be Armenian
4 would be other

belief systems
(% of population)

93
Muslim

3 — Russian Orthodox
2 — Armenian Orthodox
2 — other

When to Go

JAN

➡ January is bitingly cold; remote Caucasian villages can be cut off for months by snow.

APR–JUN

➡ Showers interspersed by clear skies enliven flower-dappled fields in lower Azerbaijan.

OCT

➡ Baku is particularly pleasant though much of the rural countryside is parched brown.

population per sq km

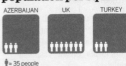

AZERBAIJAN   UK   TURKEY

👤 = 35 people

IZZET KERIBAR / GETTY IMAGES ©

Blessed Bread

If you look carefully behind any apartment block you're likely to see bags of discarded stale bread hanging on trees or hooks, separate from the domestic trash. That's because bread is considered holy and can't simply be binned or even placed on the ground, leaving superstitious Azeris with a disposal problem.

Eating bread with someone is considered to seal a bond of friendship, while it's necessary to share sweets or pastries with strangers (or give it to a mosque) when a wish-prayer has been granted.

Food & Drink

Çay The national drink is tea, usually served in pear-shaped armudi glasses and sucked through a sugar lump for sweetness, or accompanied by jams and candies.

Dolma Various vegetables, kələm (cabbage leaves) or yarpaq (vine leaves) are stuffed with a mixture of rice and minced lamb, ideally infused with fresh mint, fennel and cinnamon.

Ləvəngi Talysh-style toyuq (chicken) or baliq (fish) stuffed with a paste of herbs and crushed walnuts.

Piti A popular two-part stew. To eat, start by tearing up pieces of bread into a separate bowl. Sprinkle with sumac and then pour the piti broth over the top. Eat the resultant soup as a first course. Then transfer the remaining piti solids to the dish and mush together using spoon and fork, and add another sprinkling of sumac.

Tikə Flame-grilled kebabs that consist of meaty chunks, often including a cube of tail-fat that locals consider a special delicacy.

Mud volcanoes

townships and desolate semi-deserts. At Baku's southern limits, the James Bond Oil Field was so nicknamed after featuring in the movie *The World is Not Enough*. The area has been considerably tidied up since then but there are still plenty of nodding-donkey oil pumps at work. The scene is best surveyed from near Bibi Heybət Mosque, which was for centuries the region's holiest shrine.

Qobustan

7 Explore Stone- and Bronze Age petroglyphs, then move on to a nearby 'family' of wonderfully weird mud volcanoes. High above the Caspian shore, Stone Age hunter-gatherers once came together at these sites, leaving their mark on cave walls, which still bear their engravings. The caves have crumbled into a craggy chaos of boulders but the ancient etchings are protected in the Unesco-listed Qobustan Petroglyph Reserve. Some 10km south is a weird collection of baby mud volcanoes, a gaggle of 'geologically flatulent' little conical mounds that gurgle, ooze and spit thick, cold, grey mud.

Getting Around

Air From Baku there are flights to Gəncə, Lənkəran and Zaqatala three or four times weekly.

Bus & Minibus Almost all but the most remote villages can be reached by bus or minibus.

Car & Taxi Long-distance taxis can be surprisingly inexpensive, especially if shared. To reach remote mountain villages you may need to rent a 4WD.

Train Trains are slower and less frequent than road transport, but they're also cheap. The main railway line through Central Asia runs from Batumi in the west and on to Gəncə and Baku in Azerbaijan.

JANE SWEENEY / GETTY IMAGES ©

Elbow Cay, Cay Sal Bank

CAPITAL
Nassau

POPULATION
319,031

AREA
13,880 sq km

OFFICIAL LANGUAGE
English

The Bahamas

Scattered like a handful of pirate's gold across 100,000 sq miles of turquoise ocean, the islands of the Bahamas could practically patent the word 'paradise.'

Dotted like dabs of silver and green paint on an artist's palette, the Bahamas are ready-made for exploration. Just ask Christopher Columbus – he bumped against these limestone landscapes in 1492 and changed the course of history. But the adventure didn't end with the *Niña*, the *Pinta* and the *Santa Maria*. From pirates and blockade dodgers to rum smugglers, wily go-getters have converged and caroused on the country's 700 islands and 2400 cays for centuries.

So what's in it for travelers? There's sailing around the Abacos' history-filled Loyalist Cays. Partying til dawn at Paradise Island's over-the-top Atlantis resort. Diving the spooky blue holes of Andros. Kayaking the 365 Exuma Cays. Lounging on Eleuthera's pink-sand beaches. Pondering pirates in Nassau. There's a Bahamian island to match most every water-and-sand-based compulsion, each framed by a backdrop of gorgeous, mesmerizing blue.

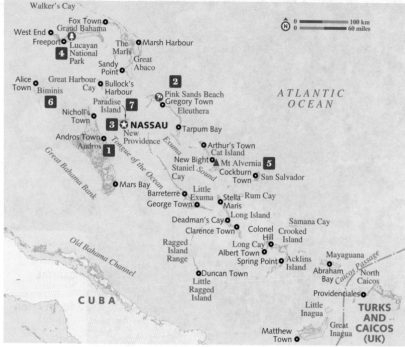

The Bahamas'
Top Experiences

Andros Reef

1 Just off the east coast of Andros lies the world's third-largest barrier reef, a 140-mile stretch of otherworldly coral forest, psychedelic sponge grottoes and eerie hidden caverns. The reef teems with sea life – schools of parrotfish, spotted moray eels, giant eagle rays, even the odd sea turtle or shark. The island's bizarre blue holes – water-filled vertical caves occurring both inland and off shore – attract advanced divers and National Geographic crews. On the far side of the reef, the bottom drops dizzyingly into a 6000ft abyss known as the Tongue of the Ocean. A free-fall into its depths is often described as the 'dive of a lifetime.'

Pink Sands Beach

2 Celebs like Mick Jagger, Elle Macpherson and Harrison Ford have all been snapped frolicking on the rosy shores of Harbour Island's Pink Sands Beach. Why not join them? The powdery sand shimmers with a pink glow – a result of finely pulverized coral – that's a faint blush by day and a rosy red when fired by the dawn or sunset. It's been called the world's most beautiful beach by a slew of international glossies, and we won't argue. If you do spot a star, just follow the locals' lead and say 'good afternoon.' Harbour Islanders treat everyone – A-listers and mere commoners alike – with the same laid-back friendliness.

Colonial Nassau

3 Many visitors to Nassau never make it past the duty-free shops of Bay St. Their loss. Downtown Nassau is a pink-and-white colonial jewel, with government buildings as ornate as wedding cakes, 18th-century forts complete with canons and dungeons, and crumbling graveyards full of pirates and those who hunted them. Surveying the city from the top of Fort Fincastle, you can almost hear the 'arrrg!' of notorious scourges like Blackbeard and Calico Jack. Several interesting history museums illuminate the city's past and provide helpful walking maps.

GREG JOHNSTON / GETTY IMAGES ©

Lucayan National Park

4 This 40-acre national park is Grand Bahama's finest treasure. It's known for its underwater cave system, one of the longest in the world. Visitors can easily check out two of the caves via a short footpath. The park is also unique because it's home to all six of the Bahamas' vegetation zones. Mangrove trails spill out onto the secluded and beautiful Gold Rock Beach, definitely worth a stop if you're out this way.

Mt Alvernia Hermitage

5 Sitting atop the highest peak in the Bahamas (a not-quite-Himalayan 206ft above sea level), this atmospherically crumbling monastery, on Cat Island, graces many a postcard. Built by Father Jerome, an itinerant priest and architect, it resembles a miniature version of the medieval churches of the father's native England. The trek to the hermitage is truly awe-inspiring, as are the panoramic views from the peak (especially at sunset).

if the Bahamas were 100 people

85 would be black
12 would be white
3 would be Asian or Hispanic

belief systems
(% of population)

35 Baptist

15 Anglican

14 Roman Catholic

8 Pentecostal

5 Church of God

23 other

population per sq km

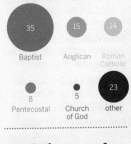

BAHAMAS   CUBA   UK

♦ = 35 people

When to Go

HIGH SEASON
(Dec–Feb)

➡ Winter in the US and Europe drives crowds to the Bahamas, and prices skyrocket.

➡ Expect sunny, warm days and slightly chilly nights.

SHOULDER
(Mar–Aug)

➡ In March and April, Spring Breakers turn Nassau and Grand Bahama into party central.

➡ Spring is balmy, summer is steamy.

➡ Destinations such as Andros and the Biminis have their high season in spring, when fishing is best.

LOW SEASON
(Sep–Nov)

➡ Fall hurricane season means few crowds and rock-bottom prices, but it can also mean... hurricanes.

➡ Days are mild, through sometimes rainy.

Fish Fry

From Nassau to the tiniest Out Islands, local social life revolves around the Fish Fry. A Fish Fry is both a place and an event. As a place, it's usually a collection of brightly painted wooden shacks in a central location, either downtown or by the harbor. During the day it's empty, but at night it lights up as an outdoor food market, each shack serving plates of fried seafood – conch, turbot, lobster – and hearty sides like peas 'n' rice. Everybody gathers at the Fish Fry to eat, drink, gossip and dance, fueled by homemade wine and rake 'n' scrape beats. It's one part church picnic, one part neighborhood party, one part food court, one part nightclub. On some islands, the Fish Fry only happens on Friday or Saturday night, while on others it's a nightly event.

Food & Drink

Boil fish A breakfast dish of grouper stewed with lime juice, onions and potatoes. Usually served with johnnycake, a type of flat cornbread.

Conch Roasted, cracked (fried), chopped into salads or dipped in dough and fried into fritters, this chewy sea snail is the most ubiquitous food in the Bahamas. Think calamari.

Guava duff Boiled pastry filled with sweet guava paste and topped off with rum or cream sauce.

Peas 'n' rice A humble combination of rice and red beans is the island's top starch.

Rum cocktails Try Goombay Smash or a Bahama Mama.

Souse A thick stew of lamb, sheep's head, pig's trotter or other 'leftover' meats.

Spiny Caribbean lobster The Bahamas' native lobster, often served sauteed with onions and pepper.

GREG JOHNSTON / GETTY IMAGES ©

Sea kayaking through mangroves, Bimini Island

The Biminis

6 Itty-bitty Bimini has an outsized reputation. Its proximity to the Gulf Stream makes it one of the world's premier big-game fishing spots, attracting heavyweights like Ernest Hemingway and Howard Hughes since the early 20th century. During Prohibition, Bimini was a base for rum-runners heading to Florida, only 53 miles east. The combination of macho fishermen and lawless bootleggers gave Bimini a gritty, slightly Wild West feel, which it retains to this day.

Atlantis Revelry

7 If Disneyland, Vegas and Sea World birthed a lovechild, the gargantuan Atlantis resort would be the overpriced but irresistible spawn. Paradise Island's Atlantis is a full-immersion, 24/7 vacation bacchanalia, and many visitors never leave the resort grounds. Why would you? You can plunge down 200ft waterslides at the on-site water park, explore faux archaeological ruins, eat live conch at a celebrity-chef-run sushi bar, test your luck at the vast casino. And more. Way more.

Getting Around

Air Interisland flights offer the only quick and convenient way to travel within the Bahamas; islanders ride airplanes like Londoners use buses.

Boat The only major interisland ferry operator in the Bahamas is Bahamas Ferries (www.bahamasferries.com), which runs a high-speed ferry linking Nassau, Andros, the Abacos, Eleuthera and the Exumas. Mail boats and water taxis provide other waterborne options.

Bus Nassau and Freeport have dozens of *jitneys* (private minibuses) licensed to operate on established routes. There's not much public transportation on the Out Islands.

Taxi Licensed taxis are plentiful in Nassau and Freeport. Taxis are also the main local transportation in the Out Islands.

Al-Fatih Mosque, Manama

CAPITAL	Manama
POPULATION	1.3 million
AREA	760 sq km
OFFICIAL LANGUAGE	Arabic

Bahrain

This tiny island state is the smallest of all Arab countries, and is one of the most easygoing of the Gulf states.

Like an oyster, Bahrain's rough exterior takes some prising open, but it is worth the effort. From the excellent National Museum in Manama to the extraordinary burial mounds at Sar, there are many fine sites to visit.

The country has long been defined by its relationship with water. Meaning 'Two Seas' in Arabic, Bahrain maintains its gaze not on the island's minimal land mass, but on the shallow waters that lap its shores. The sweet-water springs that bubble offshore helped bring about 4000 years of settlement, the layers of which are exposed in rich archaeological sites around the island. The springs also encouraged lustrous pearls – the trade that helped to build the island's early fortunes.

Much of Manama's modern wealth, illustrated in high-profile building projects, rises proudly from land 'reclaimed' from the sea. With the projected effects of climate change, however, the sea may yet have the last laugh.

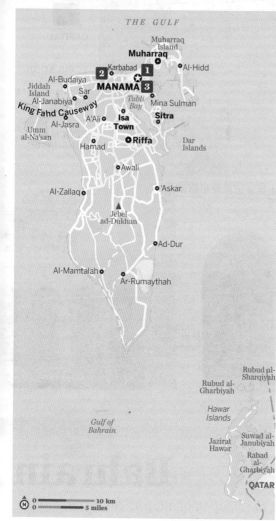

THE GULF

Muharraq Island

Muharraq

Karbabad **2** **1**

Al-Hidd

Al-Budaiya

Jiddah Island

Sar

MANAMA **3**

Al-Janabiya

Tubli Bay

Mina Sulman

King Fahd Causeway

A'Ali

Al-Jasra

Isa Town

Sitra

Umm al-Na'san

Al-Jasra

Hamad

Riffa

Dar Islands

Awali

Al-Zallaq

'Askar

Jebel ad-Dukhan

Ad-Dur

Al-Mamtalah

Ar-Rumaythah

Rubud al-Sharqiyah

Rubud al-Gharbiyah

Hawar Islands

Gulf of Bahrain

Jazirat Hawar

Suwad al-Janubiyah

Rabad al-Gharbiyah

QATAR

0 ——— 10 km
0 ——— 5 miles

Bahrain's
Top Experiences

Bahrain National Museum

1 Open the door on ancient Dilmun at Bahrain National Museum in Manama. The museum, housed in a postmodern building with landscaping that brings the waterfront up to the windows, showcases archaeological finds from ancient Dilmun. Among these are beautiful agate and carnelian beads and earthenware burial jars.

Bahrain Fort

2 Take a 16th-century view of the sea from Bahrain Fort. The fort was built by the Portuguese as part of a string of defences along the Gulf. The moated fort is particularly attractive at night, when the surrounding history of the site seems to rise out of the excavations and linger between the floodlights.

Al-Fatih Mosque

3 A visitor wanting to learn more about Islam could not do better than to visit this grand mosque, with its informative guides. Built on reclaimed land in 1984, Al-Fatih Mosque is the largest building in the country and is capable of holding up to 7000 worshippers. The mosque was built with marble from Italy, glass from Austria and teak wood from India, carved by Bahraini craftspeople, and has some fine examples of interior design.

When to Go

NOV–MAR

➡ Bask in the relative cool of a Gulf winter with daily blue skies.

APR

➡ Join life in the fast lane during the Formula One Grand Prix.

APR

➡ Enjoy traditional dancing at the annual Heritage Festival.

Food & Drink

Khabees Dates in a variety of sizes, colours and states of ripeness.

Makbus Rice and spices with chicken, lamb or fish in sauce.

Rangena Coconut cake.

CAPITAL
Dhaka

POPULATION
163.7 million

AREA
143,998 sq km

OFFICIAL LANGUAGE
Bangla (Bengali)

Bangladesh

Gorgeously green yet swamped with people, Bangladesh is a rural wonderland laden with waterways, peppered with villages and bursting with humanity.

Bangladeshis are famously friendly, and you are almost certain to receive a warm welcome everywhere you go. The tourism industry is in its infancy and foreign visitors are still an unusual sight outside Dhaka. If you enjoy making friends, mixing with the locals and having the opportunity to travel around a country without bumping into too many other foreign faces, then Bangladesh is probably just the place you've been looking for.

More than 700 rivers flow through this small country and the result is a deliciously lush landscape with more shades of green than you ever imagined. There are almost as many kilometres of rivers in Bangladesh as there are roads, and travelling by boat is a way of life here. This provides a fabulous opportunity to see the country from a more unusual angle. Even if you're going nowhere in particular, travelling by boat is one of the most rewarding things you can do during your visit. Bangladesh isn't a tick-the-sights-off-the-list type of country, so slow down, relax and discover new ideas and ways of life.

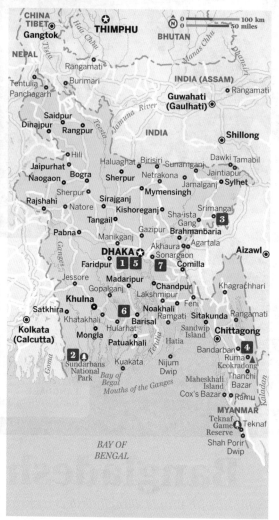

Bangladesh's
Top Experiences

River Trips

1 Rivers are the lifeblood of Bangladesh. More than 700 of them criss-cross the country, and travelling along them is an experience not to be missed. From cross-river car ferries or creaking old paddle-wheel steamers to traditional wooden yachts or the humble rowboat (try the Buriganga River crossing in Dhaka from the main ferry port at Sadarghat), it is said that there are more types of boats in Bangladesh than in any other country. So whether you fancy a multi-day adventure deep into the countryside or just a quick jaunt around a city dock, get yourself down to a river ghat, and get involved.

Tracking Tigers in the Sundarbans

2 The mangrove forests of the Sundarbans National Park are home to the largest single population of tigers found anywhere in the world. There are around 400 Royal Bengal tigers roaming the region, and boarding a boat in search of them is an undisputed highlight of a trip to Bangladesh. It's possible to dip into the forest on a self-organised day trip from Mongla, but for a true adventure, and to increase your admittedly slim chances of seeing a tiger, book yourself onto a four-day boat tour from Khulna.

Cycling Srimangal

3 Much of Bangladesh is perfect terrain for cycling, but it's only in Srimangal – the tea-growing capital of Bangladesh – that travellers can easily rent bikes to go exploring. The landscape here is a casual cyclist's dream: hilly enough to be interesting, but not too steep to be exhausting. There are lakes to visit, villages to swing by and forests to free-wheel through – and the gently rolling hills of the surrounding tea estates ensure the scenery is always top notch.

Hiking off the Beaten Track

4 The country's eastern regions of Sylhet and Chittagong contain forested hills and small, rugged mountains. This is no Himalaya, but the landscape offers plenty of opportunity to stretch your legs with a

SABBIR PHOTOGRAPHY / GETTY IMAGES ©

number of worthwhile hikes. There are relatively simple day hikes you can take from places like Srimangal, but for something more off the beaten track, base yourself in Bandarban, find yourself a good guide and head off in the direction of one of the forested peaks of the Chittagong Hill Tracts.

Old Dhaka

5 For some, the assault on the senses is too much to handle, but for others, the unrivalled chaos that is squeezed into the narrow streets of Old Dhaka is the main attraction of a stay in the capital. No matter where you've come from, or what big cities you've visited before, Old Dhaka will knock you for six with its manic streets, its crazy traffic and its nonstop noise and commotion. But the food is fabulous, the historical narrative fascinating and the sheer weight of humanity absolutely unforgettable.

if Bangladesh were 100 people

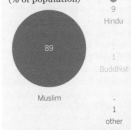

33 would be aged 0-14
19 would be aged 15-24
38 would be aged 25-54
5 would be aged 55-64
5 would be aged 65+

belief systems
(% of population)

● 9 Hindu

89 Muslim

1 Buddhist

1 other

population per sq km

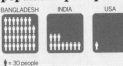

BANGLADESH   INDIA   USA

⬤ ≈ 30 people

When to Go

HIGH SEASON
(Oct–Mar)

➡ Cooler temperatures; almost chilly in January and February.

➡ Dry; the worst of the monsoon has gone; some late rains in October.

➡ Prices in Cox's Bazar may be inflated.

SHOULDER
(Apr–May)

➡ Almost unbearably hot, without the cooling monsoon rains.

➡ Join honey harvesters for the honey-collecting season in the Sundarbans.

➡ Mangos start ripening in May.

LOW SEASON
(Jun–Sep)

➡ Monsoon season disrupts plans and sees much of Bangladesh under water.

➡ Hot, but the rains cool the air.

➡ Tea-picking season in full swing in Sylhet.

Rickshaw Art

One of your first, and perhaps strongest, impressions of Bangladesh is likely to be the rainbow colours of a cycle-rickshaw. More than just a cheap form of transport, the humble rickshaw is a work of art in Bangladesh. Rickshaw artists aim to decorate the vehicles with as much drama and colour as possible, and paint images that are both simple and memorable. This is street art for the ordinary man or woman, and it is unashamedly commercial.

Common themes include idealised rural scenes; wealthy cities crammed with cars, aeroplanes and high-rise buildings; unsullied natural environments; and dream homes with sports cars parked outside. Images of Bangladeshi and Indian film and pop stars are by far the most popular designs.

Food & Drink

The fiery curries and delicately flavoured biryanis that make up so much of Bangladeshi cuisine will keep you drooling throughout your adventures in this country. Bengalis (both in Bangladesh and India's West Bengal) consider their food to be the most refined in the subcontinent and though this causes debate, everyone is in agreement that Bengali sweets truly are the finest you can dip your sticky fingers into.

A typical Bangladeshi meal includes a curry made with vegetables and either beef, mutton, chicken, fish or egg, cooked in a hot spicy sauce with mustard oil and served with dhal (cooked yellow lentils) and plain rice.

Fish is every Bangladeshi's favourite meal. The fish you are most likely to eat – boiled, smoked or fried – are *hilsa* and *bhetki*. These are virtually the national dishes of Bangladesh and it's said they can be prepared in around 50 different ways.

Painam Nagar mansion, Sonargaon

Riding the Rocket

6 Steeped in almost 100 years of history, Bangladesh's famous paddle-wheel steamer may not be the fastest thing on the waterways these days, but it gets more and more romantic each passing year. There are four remaining Rockets – all built in the early part of the 20th century – and although you can no longer ride them all the way from Dhaka to Khulna, you can still take long overnight trips on them. Book yourself a cabin, put your feet up and watch Bangladesh float by.

Hidden Treasures

7 Modest, unassuming Bangladesh isn't blessed with any of the world-famous, top-drawer sights of some of its neighbours, but it does contain a number of lesser-known gems, and hunting them down is half the fun. Whether it's the ruined monastery of Paharpur, the dilapidated hundred-year-old mansions in Sonargaon or the scattered ruins of Sona Masjid (Gaud), plotting a route to these hidden treasures is part of what makes visiting Bangladesh such an adventure.

Getting Around

Boat Given that there are some 8433km of navigable inland waterways, boats are a common means of getting around. Public ferries are always worth inquiring about if you're at a town with a river ghat.

Bus Local bus travel is cheap and extremely convenient. Buses to main towns leave frequently, and tickets don't need to be booked in advance. The downside, though, is the often extreme lack of comfort and worryingly poor safety. The most comfortable bus options are private coaches.

Car Driving gives you the freedom to quickly and easily go where you please, when you please, but it does insulate you somewhat from Bangladesh and it is far more expensive than public transport. Driving in Bangladesh takes nerves of steel and a lot of patience.

Bathsheba Beach

CAPITAL
Bridgetown

POPULATION
288,725

AREA
430 sq km

OFFICIAL LANGUAGE
English

Barbados

From surfing the waves to windsurfing the shallows to snorkeling the reefs, you may never dry off. But if you do, this genteel island's verdant interior might lure you for a tropical hike.

Barbados is ringed by azure water and white-sand visions that fuel the fantasies of those stuck in chilly winter climes.

No matter your budget or style, you'll find a place to stay, especially on the popular south and west coasts. Elsewhere, however, is where you'll find what makes the island special. Barbados has lush scenery among rolling hills dotted with fascinating survivors of the colonial past. Vast plantation homes show the wealth of European

settlers, while several botanical gardens exploit the beauty possible from the perfect growing conditions.

The wild Atlantic-battered east coast is a legend with surfers; those looking for action will also find windsurfing, hiking, diving and more. Away from the glitz, it's still a civilized place (with a 98% literacy rate) of classic calypso rhythms, an island-time vibe and world-famous rums.

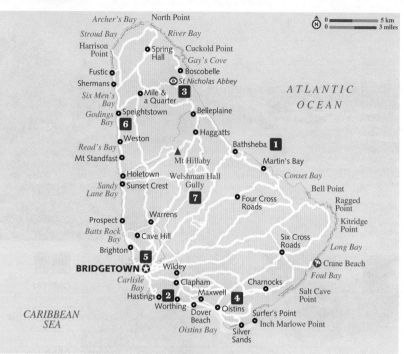

Archer's Bay · North Point
Stroud Bay · River Bay
Harrison Point · Spring Hall · Cuckold Point
Fustic · Boscobele · Gay's Cove
Shermans · St Nicholas Abbey
Six Men's Bay · Mile & a Quarter **3**
Godings Bay · Speightstown · Belleplaine
6
Weston · Haggatts
Read's Bay · Bathsheba **1**
Mt Standfast · Mt Hillaby · Martin's Bay
Holetown · Welshman Hall · Conset Bay
Sandy Lane Bay · Sunset Crest · Gully · Bell Point
7 · Four Cross Roads · Ragged Point
Prospect · Warrens · Kitridge Point
Batts Rock Bay · Cave Hill · Six Cross Roads · Long Bay
Brighton · **5** · Wildey · Crane Beach **7**
BRIDGETOWN · Foul Bay
Carlisle Bay · Clapham · Charnocks
Hastings **2** · Maxwell · Salt Cave Point
Worthing · **4**
Dover Beach · Oistins · Surfer's Point
Oistins Bay · Silver Sands · Inch Marlowe Point

ATLANTIC OCEAN

CARIBBEAN SEA

Barbados'
Top Experiences

Surfing the Soup Bowl

1 The world-famous reef break known as the Soup Bowl is right off the beach in northern Bathsheba. It is one of the best waves in the Caribbean islands. Don't underestimate the break just because the region is not known for powerful surf – Soup Bowl gets big. Moreover, the reef is shallow and covered in parts by spiny sea urchins. It's a strong right-handed break which has three take-off points that can be surfed point to point if you are fast and can read the wave. Overall, the best months are August to March. For good surfers, it's September to November during hurricane season and the start of cold

fronts. Famed surfer Kelly Slater calls it a 9+ on a scale of one to 10. For beginners March to May is best.

Accra Beach

2 Accra Beach is a picture-perfect crescent of sand that you'll want to immediately photograph and post on Facebook to irritate those left at home. Backed by shade trees, there's surf to make things interesting but nothing too dramatic. A new boardwalk allows you to walk west for more than 3km to Hastings. Stop for a glass of champagne at longtime favorite Champers, with a dreamy location off the main road right on the water overlooking Accra Beach.

St Nicholas Abbey

3 St Nicholas is one of the oldest plantation houses in the Caribbean and a must-see stop on any island itinerary. Owner and local architect Larry Warren has undertaken a massive improvement program. The grounds are now simply gorgeous, with guinea fowl wandering among the flowers. The interior re-creates the mansion's 17th-century look, right down to the furniture. An old steam engine has been restored and the plantation is again bottling its own rum and molasses; you can taste some and enjoy a snack at the serene cafe. Be sure to read the lurid history of the plantation's founders: murder, intrigue, sex!

Oistins Fish Fry

4 Revel in one of the Caribbean's great parties, the weekly Oistins Fish Fry. With soca (an energetic off spring of calypso), reggae, pop and country music, vendors selling barbecued fish, and plenty of rum drinking, the legendary Fish Fry is *the* weekly social event on the island. It's roughly 60% locals, 40% tourists and there's a joyous electricity in the air on Friday night, which is just a tad more fun than the fish fry's other night, Saturday. It's held in a complex of low-rise modern buildings right on the sand next to the fish market in the town of Oistins; food is served from 6pm to 10.30pm. Buy an icy bottle of Banks beer and wander the scene.

Cricket at Kensington Oval

5 The national sport, if not national obsession, is cricket. Per capita, Bajans boast more world-class cricket players than any other nation. One of the world's top all-rounders, Bajan native Sir Garfield Sobers, was knighted by Queen Elizabeth II during her 1975 visit to Barbados, while another cricket hero, Sir Frank Worrell, appears on the face of the B$5 bill. In Barbados you can catch an international test match or just a friendly game on the beach or grassy field. Thousands of Bajans and other West Indians pour into the world-class matches at Kensington Oval, in Garrison near Bridgetown.

if Barbados were 100 people

93 would be black
3 would be white
3 would be mixed
1 would be East Indian

belief systems
(% of population)

63 Protestant

5 Roman Catholic

7 other Christian

25 other

population per sq km

BARBADOS USA UK

† ≈ 15 people

When to Go

DEC–APR

➡ The tourist high season, with people fleeing the northern winter.

➡ Prices peak.

MAY–JUN & NOV

➡ The shoulder season has the best mix of affordable rates and good weather.

JUL–OCT

➡ Rainy; hurricane season – although many years see none.

➡ Good for surfing holidays.

Bajan Culture

Bajan culture displays some trappings of English life: cricket, polo and horse racing are popular pastimes, business is performed in a highly organized fashion, gardens are lovingly tended, older women often wear prim little hats and special events are carried out with a great deal of pomp and ceremony.

However, on closer examination, Barbados is very deeply rooted in Afro-Caribbean tradition. Family life, art, food, music, architecture, religion and dress have more in common with the nearby Windward Islands than with London. The African and East Indian influences are especially apparent in the spicy cuisine, rhythmic music and pulsating festivals.

Food & Drink

Bananas Local varieties are green even when ripe.

Banks The island's crisp lager is refreshing after a day in the sun.

Barbadian rum Considered some of the finest in the Caribbean, with Mount Gay being the best-known label.

Conkies A mixture of cornmeal, coconut, pumpkin, sweet potato, raisins and spices, steamed in a plantain leaf.

Cou-cou A creamy cornmeal and okra mash.

Cutters Meat or fish sandwiches in a salt-bread roll.

Fish cakes There are myriad Bajan recipes, made from salt cod and deep-fried.

Flying fish Served fried in delicious sandwiches all over the country. It's a mild white fish that is great sautéed or deep-fried.

Jug-jug A mixture of cornmeal, green peas and salted meat.

Roti A curry filling rolled inside flat bread.

RICHARD CUMMINS / GETTY IMAGES ©

Speightstown

6 Easily the most evocative small town on Barbados, Speightstown combines old colonial charms with a vibe that has more rough edges than the endlessly upscale precincts to the south. The town is a good place for a wander. Since the main road was moved east, traffic is modest, so take time to look up at the battered old wooden facades, many with overhanging galleries. A radiant vision in white stucco, Arlington House is an 18th-century colonial house that now houses an engaging museum run by the National Trust.

Welchman Hall Gully

7 Welchman Hall Gully is a thickly wooded ravine with a walking track that leads you through nearly 200 species of plants, including spices like nutmeg. Such gullies were too difficult for growing crops and as a result preserve some of the tropical forests that once covered the island. Look for bearded fig trees, which gave their old Portuguese name *Los Barbados* (the bearded ones) to the island.

Getting Around

Bicycle Barbados offers good riding for the adventurous. It's hilly but roads are not usually steep (excepting parts of the east). However, most roads are quite narrow, so traffic is a constant bother in the west and south.

Bus It's possible to get to virtually any place on the island by public bus. There are three kinds: government-operated public buses are large and blue with a yellow stripe. Privately operated minibuses are intermediate-sized buses painted yellow with a blue stripe. Route taxis are individually owned minivans that have 'ZR' on their license plates and are painted white. All types of bus charge the same fare.

Taxi Taxis have a 'Z' on the license plate and usually a 'taxi' sign on the roof. They're easy to find and often wait at the side of the road in tourist areas.

CAPITAL
Minsk

POPULATION
9.6 million

AREA
207,600 sq km

OFFICIAL LANGUAGES
Belarusian, Russian

St Peter & Paul Church, Minsk

Belarus

Belarus allows the chance to visit a Europe with minimal advertising, no litter or graffiti and a generous people who relish life's simple pleasures.

Eastern Europe's outcast, Belarus (Беларусь) lies at the edge of the region and seems determined to avoid integration with the rest of the continent at all costs. Belarus, widely billed as 'the last dictatorship in Europe', is to the uninitiated a country deeply in thrall to the USSR circa 1974. This is the land of Soviet-style architecture, state-run media and a centralised economy that ensures every supermarket carries the same bland assortment of goods. Despite the hardships, Belarusians still find reasons to be cheerful:

traditional folk singing and dancing features prominently on the calendar.

Outside the monumental Stalinist capital of Minsk, Belarus offers a simple yet pleasing landscape of cornflower fields, thick forests and picturesque villages. The country also offers two excellent national parks and is home to Europe's largest mammal, the *zoobr* (or European bison). While travellers will always be subject to curiosity, they'll also be on the receiving end of warm hospitality and genuine welcome.

Belarus'
Top Experiences

Brest

1 This prosperous, cosmopolitan border town looks more to the EU than to Minsk. It has plenty of charm and has performed a massive DIY job on itself in recent years. The main sight is the Brest Fortress, a WWII memorial where Soviet troops held out against the Nazi onslaught.

Minsk

2 The capital of Belarus is a progressive and modern place at odds with its own reputation. Fashionable cafes, restaurants and nightclubs vie for your attention, while sushi bars and art galleries have sprouted in a city centre constructed to the tastes of Stalin. Despite the strong police presence and obedient citizenry, you'll find that there's more than a whiff of rebellion in the air.

Belavezhskaya Pushcha National Park

3 A Unesco World Heritage site, this is the oldest wildlife refuge in Europe. Some 1300 sq km of primeval forest is all that remains of a canopy that eight centuries ago covered northern Europe. At least 55 mammal species call this park home, but it is most celebrated for its 300 European bison, the continent's largest land mammal.

Food & Drink

Belavezhskaya A bitter herbal alcoholic drink.

Draniki Potato pancakes, usually served with sour cream.

Kletsky Dumplings stuffed with mushrooms, cheese or potato.

Kvas A mildly alcoholic drink made from black or rye bread, commonly sold in Belarus.

When to Go

JUN–AUG
➡ Don't worry about coming here in the high season: come to escape the crowds elsewhere.

MID-JUL
➡ Join in Vitsebk's superb Slavyansky Bazaar festival and celebrate all things Slavic.

JUL
➡ On 6 July watch the locals celebrate Kupalye, a fortune-telling festival with pagan roots.

Grand Place, Brussels

CAPITAL
Brussels

POPULATION
10.4 million

AREA
30,528 sq km

OFFICIAL LANGUAGES
Dutch,
French,
German

Belgium

Fabulously historic and deliciously tasty, bursting with cutting-edge art yet never really showy, gently humorous and decidedly multilingual – Belgium is a little country full of big surprises.

Stereotypes of comic books, chips and sublime chocolates are just the start in eccentric little Belgium; its self-deprecating people have quietly spent centuries producing some of Europe's finest art and architecture. Bilingual Brussels is the dynamic yet personable EU capital, but also sports what's arguably the world's most beautiful city square. Flat, Dutch-speaking Flanders has many other alluring medieval cities, all easily linked by regular train hops. In hilly, French-speaking Wallonia, the attractions are contrastingly rural – castle villages, outdoor activities and extensive cave systems.

Pack a spare stomach. Belgians create a remarkable range of edible specialities including some of the planet's most mouth-watering chocolates. Jumbo wine-soaked mussels are served up with crispy, twice-fried *frites* (chips). And then of course there's the beer. Brewing is an almost mystical art in Belgium, where some of the finest ales are still created in working monasteries to age-old recipes. To be sipped, slowly!

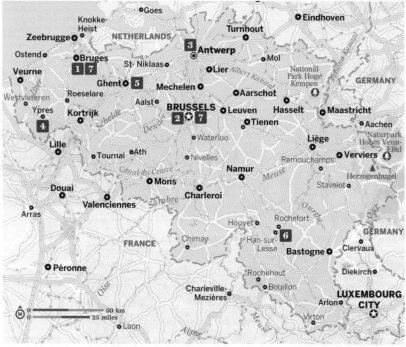

Belgium's
Top Experiences

Bruges

1 Cobblestone lanes, dreamy canals, soaring spires and whitewashed old almshouses combine to make central Bruges (Brugge in Dutch) one of Europe's most picture-perfect historic cities. The only problem is that everyone knows, so it does get very busy. But come midweek in February and you'll have it largely to yourself. Or escape the crowds and carriage rides by dipping into some of Bruges' majestic art collections. The Groeningemuseum is hard to beat, offering a potted history of Belgian art, with an outstanding selection of works by the Flemish Primitives.

Brussels' Grand Place

2 The magnificent Grand Place is one of the world's most unforgettable urban ensembles. Oddly hidden, the enclosed cobblestone square is only revealed as you enter on foot from one of six narrow side alleys. The focal point is the magnificently spired 15th-century town hall, but each of the fabulous antique guildhalls has a charm of its own. The cobblestones were laid in the 12th century, when it was used as a marketplace; indeed the square still plays host to a flower market, as well as hosting Christmas stalls, concerts and – every two years – a dazzlingly colourful 'carpet' of flower petals.

Antwerp Art & Fashion

3 Cosmopolitan and confident, Antwerp is a city that has everything. Its skyline is still dominated by one of the lowlands' most magnificent stone steeples and its medieval house-museums are stuffed with works by its most famous 17th-century resident, Pieter Paul Rubens. Today it attracts art lovers and mode moguls, club queens and diamond dealers, with state-of-the-art museums, vibrant nightlife and a reputation as one of Europe's capitals of haute couture. It's hard to think of anywhere else in the world with so many designer fashion boutiques huddled so close together.

MAS (Museum aan de Stroom), Antwerp

Flanders Fields

4 For much of the 20th century, Flanders Fields were synonymous not with potato and hop production but with poppies and death in the wake of the mindless battles of WWI. The area around Ypres remains dotted with manicured graveyards where white memorial crosses bear silent witness in seemingly endless rows. Museums improve every year at explaining the battles' context and helping visualise conditions. And the incredible rebuilt central squares of Diksmuide and Ypres are wonders in themselves.

Ghent

5 If you love the medieval charm of Bruges but want to be a little more original, a great choice is Ghent. Known as Gent in Dutch and Gand in French, Ghent is Flanders' unsung historic city. Like a grittier Bruges without the crush of tourists, it sports photogenic canals, medieval towers, great cafes and some of Belgium's most inspired museums. Always a lively student city, it's small enough to feel cosy but big enough to stay vibrant and dynamic.

if Belgium were 100 people

60 would speak Dutch
39 would be speak French
1 would speak German

belief systems
(% of population)

75

25

Roman Catholic   other

When to Go

HIGH SEASON
(Jul & Aug)

➡ Warm weather, many outdoor activities and festivals.

➡ Hotels get overloaded in the Ardennes, Bruges and coastal towns, but are cheaper in Brussels.

SHOULDER
(May, Jun, Sep)

➡ Pleasant weather reasonably likely.

➡ Crowds thinner, prices might fall slightly but most tourist facilities still open.

➡ Rush-hour traffic jams return.

LOW SEASON
(Nov, Feb, Mar)

➡ Weather often cold and wet.

➡ Hotels cheaper but some attractions close.

➡ From the start of Lent there are numerous superbly colourful carnivals.

population per sq km

= 30 people

Cartoon Culture

Belgium has a consuming passion for comic strips, which are considered the 'Ninth Art'. Foreigners might know the boy-reporter Tintin, Belgium's most iconic comic-strip character for decades. Tintin's adventures involve a beloved and humorous team of misfits, including dog Snowy, crusty companion Captain Haddock and half-deaf Professor Calculus, fan of a malaprop or two.

Despite some criticism of racial stereotyping, the Tintin comic books have been translated into more than 50 languages and still sell more than two million copies a year. Blistering barnacles! And that's more than two decades after the death of creator Georges Remi, whose pen name, Hergé, comes from his reversed initials, RG, pronounced in French.

Food & Drink

Chicons au gratin Endive rolled in ham and cooked in cheese/béchamel sauce.

Chocolates The essentials are pralines and creamy *manons*, filled bite-sized chocolates sold from an astonishing range of specialist *chocolaterie* shops.

Filet Américain A blob of raw minced beef, typically topped with equally raw egg yolk.

Mosselen/moules In-the-shell mussels, typically cooked in white wine and served with a mountain of *frites* (chips).

Paling in 't groen Eel in a sorrel or spinach sauce.

Stoemp A home-cooking classic: mashed veg-and-potato dish.

Vlaamse stoverij/carbonade flamande Semi-sweet beer-based meat casserole.

Waterzooi A cream-based chicken or fish stew. .

DENNIS K. JOHNSON / GETTY IMAGES ©

Caves of the Ardennes

6 You don't need to be a daring speleologist to explore some of northern Europe's most awesome cave systems, hollowed out beneath the rolling country-side of the Belgian Ardennes. The best known at Han-sur-Lesse even starts with a train ride, while at Remouchamps you float part of the way on an underground river. Once you're caved out, the sur-rounding areas have oppor-tunities for gentle kayaking and are set amid pretty val-leys with grey-stone villages and plenty more castles.

Belgian Beer

7 Ordering in a Belgian beer pub requires you to trawl through a menu that might have 200 choices. Incredibly, each brew comes served in its own special, oc-casionally outlandish, glass. Exports of Hoegaarden, Leffe and Stella Artois have introduced mainstream Belgian brewing into bars worldwide. Many breweries offer visits by arrangement for groups. Drop-in oppor-tunities are possible at De Halve Maan in Bruges and the brilliantly old-fashioned Cantillon lambic-works in Brussels.

Getting Around

Bicycle Cycling is a great way to get around in flat Flanders, less so in chaotic Brussels or undulating Wallonia.

Bus Bus frequency is highest on school days. Fewer operate on Saturdays; Sunday services are often non-existent. Rural journeys are often slow.

Car In Bruges, Ghent, Antwerp and/or Brussels, you'll spend more time finding parking than actually driving anywhere. However, in rural Belgium having a car will transform your experience.

Train There is an extensive rail network, with more regular services in Flanders than in more-rural Wallonia. Belgian Railways offers discounted packages to certain mainstream destinations, known as B-Excursions.

Jaguar

CAPITAL
Belmopan

POPULATION
334,297

AREA
22,966 sq km

OFFICIAL LANGUAGE
English

Belize

With one foot planted in the Central American jungles and the other dipped in the Caribbean Sea, Belize combines the best of both worlds.

Sitting smack dab between Spanish-speaking Central America and the Caribbean (geographically and culturally), Central America's youngest nation definitely dances to its own beat. Belize's 240 miles of coastline and uncountable islands offer amazing swimming and beachcombing, and its barrier reef (the northern hemisphere's largest) is a diver's paradise. Belize's jungles are dotted with ancient structures built in the days when Belize was but a small part of the greater Maya kingdom, offering much for the intrepid to explore. Culturally, Belize is surprisingly diverse. Though officially an English-speaking nation, expect to hear Spanish, Kriol, Garifuna and Maya, with perhaps a bit of Cantonese and Mennonite German thrown in for good measure.

Though among the pricier destinations in Central America, for cuisine, diversity and culture, Belize still offers more than enough bang for your buck to make it worth the trip. So what's not to love?

Sergio Butrón Casas
Santa Elena
Chetumal
Corozal
Bahía de Chetumal
MEXICO
San Pablo
Sarteneja
San Estevan
Shipstern
Orange Walk
La Unión
Indian Church
Crooked Tree
Maskall
San Pedro
Shark Ray Alley **3**
Caye Caulker **4**
Ambergris Caye **7**
Bermudian Landing
Ladyville
Rancho Dolores
Belize City
Hattieville
Turneffe Islands
La Democracia
☆ BELMOPAN
Gales Point Manatee
Blue Hole Natural Monument ● **2**
Barrier Reef
Lighthouse Reef
San Ignacio (Cayo)
Benque Viejo del Carmen
Hummingbird Hwy **5**
Douglas da Silva
6
Hopkins
Dangriga
Maya Centre
Sittee River
Tobacco Caye
South Water Caye
Glover's Reef **1**
Caracol **8**
Victoria Peak (3675ft)
Red Bank
Seine Bight
Independence
Lark Caye
Placencia
San Miguel
Monkey River
CARIBBEAN SEA
San Antonio
San Felipe
Pueblo Viejo
Sapodilla Cayes
Punta Gorda
Hunting Caye
Barranco
Bahía de Amatique
Gulf of Honduras
Puerto Cortés
Modesto Méndez
Livingston
Puerto Barrios
HONDURAS
GUATEMALA
Cuyamel
Morales

MEXICO
MEXICO
Rio Bravo

0 ___ 40 km
0 ___ 20 miles

Belize's
Top Experiences

Kayaking Glover's Reef Atoll

1 Lying like a string of white-sand pearls, Glover's Reef Atoll consists of half a dozen small islands surrounded by blue sea as far as the eye can see. Its unique position, atop a submerged mountain ridge on the edge of the continental shelf, makes it an ideal place for sea kayaking, both between the islands and around the shallow central lagoon. Get a kayak with a clear bottom and you're likely to see spotted eagle rays, southern stingrays, turtles and countless tropical fish swimming beneath as you paddle.

Diving the Blue Hole

2 The sheer walls of the Blue Hole Natural Monument drop more than 400ft into the ocean. Although it is half filled with silt and natural debris, the depth still creates a perfect circle of startling azure that is visible from above. The wall of the Blue Hole is decorated with a dense forest of stalactites and stalagmites from times past. A school of reef sharks – as well as plenty of sponges and invertebrates – keeps divers company as they descend into the mysterious ocean depths.

Snorkeling Shark Ray Alley

3 Local fisherfolk used to come to Shark Ray Alley to clean their catch, and their discards would attract hungry nurse sharks and southern stingrays. As a result these predators have long become accustomed to boats, which nowadays bring snorkelers instead of fishers. Shark Ray Alley is the top snorkeling destination in Hol Chan Marine Reserve, a protected part of the Belize Barrier Reef that harbors an amazing diversity of colorful coral and other marine life.

Caye Caulker

4 A brisk breeze is almost always blowing (especially between January and June), creating optimal conditions to cruise across the water on sailboat, windsurfer or kiteboard. The world's second-largest barrier reef is just a few miles off shore, beckoning snorkelers and divers to frolic with the fish. The mangroves teem with life, inviting exploration by kayak. All these adventures

HENRY GEORGI / GETTY IMAGES ©

await, yet the number-one activity on Caye Caulker is still swinging in a hammock, reading a book and sipping a fresh-squeezed fruit juice. Paradise.

The Hummingbird Highway

5 Arguably Belize's most beautiful stretch of road, the Hummingbird Highway offers unparalleled views of the Maya Mountains as it winds through jungles, orchards and tiny villages. Heading southeast from Belmopan, the highway stretches 49 miles (79km) to the junction of the Southern Highway and the turnoff to Dangriga. It also offers plenty of reasons to stop for a few hours (besides a near constant procession of postcard-perfect vistas).

Explore St Herman's Cave, hike the jungle loop trail, or have a dip in the crystal-clear Blue Hole. If you prefer showering with a view, the Barquedier Waterfall is down the road.

Hopkins

6 Halfway between the hustle of Dangriga and the tourist vibe of Placencia lies slacked-out Hopkins, a low-key Garifuna town where life hasn't changed much in decades. Children walk the town's one street selling their mothers' freshly baked coconut pies and chocolate brownies; local men catch fish by day and play drums at night; and the pace of life is pleasantly slow. Best of all is the beach, which is as pretty as any in Southern Belize, but it is never crowded.

if Belize were 100 people

34 would be mestizo
25 would be Creole
15 would be Spanish
6 would be Garifuna
11 would be Maya
9 would be other

belief systems
(% of population)

39 Roman Catholic
8 Pentacostal
5 Seventh Day Adventist
5 Anglican
28 other
15 none

population per sq km

BELIZE   MEXICO   USA

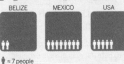

👤 ≈ 7 people

When to Go

DEC–APR
➡ Higher prices and drier weather; ideal for beachside days, diving and wildlife spotting.

MAY–NOV
➡ Discounts abound for those willing to brave the heat and heavy rains of the low season.

SEP
➡ National holidays spark two festive weeks of music, dancing and parades.

Bileez Kriol

Although English is the official language of Belize, when speaking among themselves most locals use Kriol (Creole). According to one local journalist, Kriol is *'di stiki stiki paat,'* or 'the glue that holds Belize together.' While this patois sounds like English, most anglophones will have a hard time understanding it. It is a language that 'teases but just escapes the comprehension of a native English speaker,' as one frustrated American traveler so aptly stated.

Kriol derives mainly from English, with influences from Mayan and West African languages, as well as Spanish. Linguists claim that it has its own grammatical rules and a small body of literature, as well as speaking populations in different countries – criteria that determine the difference between a dialect and a language.

Food & Drink

Hudut Possibly the most beloved Garifuna dish is made from plantain, cooked until tender, mashed with a big mortar and pestle, then cooked with local fish like snapper and coconut milk.

Rice & beans A staple of Belizean cuisine, rice and beans comes in two varieties: 'rice and beans,' where the two are cooked together; and 'beans and rice,' where beans in a soupy stew are served separately in a bowl. Both variations are prepared with coconut milk and red beans, which distinguishes them from other countries' rice and beans. Both variants are usually served with chicken or beef (and sometimes more exotic items like gibnut; a type of rodent found in South and Central America) – plus some spices and condiments, such as coconut milk.

Seafood Seasonal lobster (June to February) is always excellent, and conch fritters are a must-try.

Caana, Caracol

Ambergris Caye

7 Also known as La Isla Bonita, Ambergris Caye is the ultimate tropical paradise vacation destination (and that's what Madonna thought, too). Spend your days snorkeling the reef, kayaking the lagoon or windsurfing the straits; pamper yourself at a day spa or challenge yourself at a yoga class; ride a bike up the beach or take a nap at the end of your dock. After the sun sets, spend your evenings enjoying the country's most delectable dining and most happening nightlife.

Caracol

8 Step out of the modern world and into the ancient world at Belize's largest Maya site, where you'll spend the day wandering through a city that once rivaled Tikal in political influence. Standing in the central area of temples, palaces, craft workshops and markets, you'll feel the power and glory of ancient Caracol. At 141ft, Caana (meaning Sky Place) is still the tallest building in Belize. In addition to being the country's preeminent archaeological site, Caracol also teems with jungle wildlife.

Getting Around

Boat Fast motor launches zoom between Belize City, Caye Caulker and Ambergris Caye frequently every day. Even faster boats run between Corozal and Ambergris Caye, and a handy ferry service runs between Placencia and Mango Creek.

Bus The bad news: the dizzying array of companies offering bus services throughout Belize can be intimidating to those used to consistent scheduling. The good news: most Belizeans get around by bus, and though it may seem chaotic, it's fairly simple. Most of the bus companies often congregate around central terminals or market areas. A great website keeping tabs on the ever-changing companies, schedules and bus stops (and more) in Belize is www.guidetobelize.info.

Floating market, Lake Nokoué, Ganvié

CAPITAL
Porto-Novo

POPULATION
9.9 million

AREA
112,622 sq km

OFFICIAL LANGUAGE
French

Benin

For all its tumultuous past, Benin is an African success story, a beacon of stability in a tough neighbourhood and its people amongst Africa's friendliest.

The birthplace of voodoo and a pivotal platform of the slave trade for nearly three centuries, Benin is steeped in a rich and complex history still very much in evidence across the country.

A visit to this small, club-shaped nation could therefore not be complete without exploring the Afro-Brazilian heritage of Ouidah, Abomey and Porto Novo, learning about spirits and fetishes. But Benin will also wow visitors with its natural beauty, from the palm-fringed beach idyll of the Atlantic coast to the rugged scenery of the north. The Parc National de la Pendjari is one of the best wildlife parks in West Africa. Lions, cheetahs, leopards, elephants and hundreds of other species thrive here.

In fact, Benin is wonderfully tourist-friendly. There are good roads, a wide range of accommodation options and ecotourism initiatives that offer travellers the chance to delve deeper into Beninese life. Now is an ideal time to go because the country sits on the cusp of discovery.

BURKINA FASO

NIGER

Parc Regional du W

Gaya

Malanville

Tindangou

Parc National de la Pendjari **1**

Nadiagou

Banikoara

Porga

Batia

Kandi

Ségbana

Tanguiéta

Tanougou Falls

Boukoumbé

Natitingou

Koussoukoingou

Nadoba

Ndali

Nikki

Kémérida

Kétao

Djougou

Kara

Parakou

Bassila

TOGO

NIGERIA

Savalou

Savé

Oyo

Dassa Zoumé

Atakpamé

Kétou

Ouaké

Ibadan

Abomey

Bohicon

Tohoun

Bopa Lake Ahémé

Possotomé

Ganvié **2** PORTO NOVO

Comé **3**

Hilakondji

LOMÉ

Grand Popo

Ouidah

Cotonou

Abomey-Calavi

Lagos

Lake Nokoué

Gulf of Guinea

Atakora Mountains

Pendjari River

Ouémé River

Mono R.

Niger River

Benin's
Top Experiences

Parc National de la Pendjari

1 Amid the majestic landscape of the Atakora's rugged cliffs and wooded savannah live lions, cheetahs, leopards, elephants, baboons, hippos, myriad birds and countless antelopes. The 275,000-hectare

Parc National de la Pendjari, is one of the best in West Africa.

Ganvié

2 Spend a night at the lacustrine stilt village of Ganvié, where 30,000 Tofinu people live in bamboo huts on stilts several kilometres out on Lake Nokoué.

When to Go

NOV–FEB

➡ Warm, dry weather. Prime wildlife watching. Harmattan can produce hazy skies.

MAR–MAY

➡ The hottest period, after the harmattan lifts. Clear skies and some rain in the south.

JUN–OCT

➡ Usually downright wet and humid; a dry spell mid-July to mid-September in the south.

Food & Drink

Fish A highlight of local cuisine in southern Benin. Usually barracuda, dorado or grouper, served grilled or fried.

La Béninoise Local beer and a passable drop.

Tchoukoutou Millet-based brew.

They live almost exclusively from fishing. Despite the fact that the town has become a tourist magnet, it's a terrific place to explore and sample village life.

Lake Ahémé

3 The fertile shores of this body of water are a wonderful place to spend a few days, particularly around Possotomé, the area's biggest village. There's good swimming in the lake and various trips and excursions are possible in the surrounding area. Learn traditional fishing techniques, meet craftspeople at work or go on a fascinating two-hour botanic journey to hear about local plants and their medicinal properties.

Flatts Inlet

CAPITAL
Hamilton

POPULATION
69,839

AREA
54 sq km

OFFICIAL LANGUAGE
English

Bermuda

Playground of the rich and famous, this little British Overseas Territory in the North Atlantic shines as an island holiday destination with a great mix of luxury life and colonial cool.

Bermuda's promise of sun, sea and pink sand lures vacationers to its shores. Celebs like to call it home, and millionaire executives pop over for a little R&R. If you're looking for peace and quiet, Bermuda has pampering resorts to soothe your soul. Romantics will find atmospheric inns with four-poster beds and candlelight dining. The island is surrounded by a fantastic coral reef that harbors colorful fish and has ensnared scores of shipwrecks, making for memorable diving and snorkeling at spots like El-bow Beach in Paget Parish. Elsewhere, the crystal-clear waters of Southampton Parish provide perfect conditions for kayaking and yachting.

On land you can play a round at a world-class golf course, hike peaceful trails and sunbathe on glorious pink-sand beaches. Or stroll the crooked streets of the colonial settlement of the Town of St George, Britain's oldest surviving town in the New World, which is so well preserved it's been made a World Heritage site.

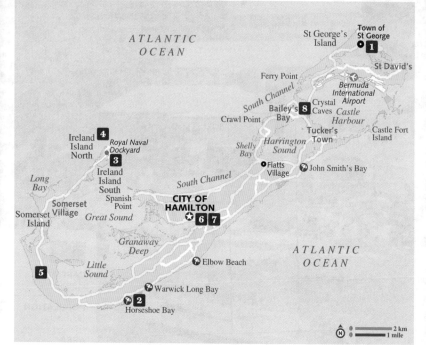

Bermuda's
Top Experiences

Town of St George

1 Bermuda's heritage-listed colonial town exudes a real historic charm. Some of its centuries-old buildings have been set aside as museums, but others continue to function as public meeting places, churches and shops. King's Square, the historic heart of town, has quaint 18th-century features like the original pillory and stocks used to publicly chastise rowdy locals, and (for gossipy ladies) a ducking stool. Light-hearted re-enactments of this punishment are performed by costumed actors. There are several interesting museums to explore, the 1612 St Peter's Church and cruises out on St George's Harbour.

Horseshoe Bay

2 With its turquoise waters lapping onto pink sands, Horseshoe Bay is as gorgeous as it gets. On an island with many pink-sand beaches (so many that most resorts have their own little private patch of sand), you'll soon see why this is widely regarded as Bermuda's most beautiful. Not surprisingly, it can get quite packed with locals and tourists on a hot summer's day. The Beach House here offers water sports rentals, snacks and a changing facility.

Royal Naval Dockyard

3 Take the ferry from Hamilton across to these Dockyards established

by the British navy when they chose this site as their 'Gibraltar of the West'. In addition to the Bermuda Maritime Museum, you can pass a pleasant hour or two strolling about the Dockyard grounds, stop in at the pub, craft markets and the Bermuda Snorkel Park.

Diving Bermuda

4 Bermuda abounds with shipwrecks, but many people are surprised to discover the waters here also harbor splendid coral. Despite its northerly location, the combination of shallow water and warm ocean currents support a thriving reef system. Bermuda boasts 24 species of hard coral and another two dozen species of soft coral, including

wavering sea fans and sea whips. Although hundreds of miles of cool water separate Bermuda from the Caribbean, many species of tropical fish common to the Caribbean can also be found feeding among the corals in Bermuda. Great wreck dives include the *Constellation* and the *Cristobel Colon*, a 500ft Spanish luxury liner that ran aground in 1936.

Hit the Greens

5 With its English heritage and resort lifestyle, Bermuda lends itself nicely to a round of golf. You'll get scenic ocean vistas from the greens and all eight of the island courses have a distinctly Bermudian character. Port Royal is a jewel with stunning views, challenging tees and cliff-side holes that help rank it among the best public golf courses in the world. St George's, one of the few golf courses that can boast being within the boundaries of a World Heritage site, offers panoramic views of old Fort St Catherine and the turquoise seas beyond.

City of Hamilton

6 Bermuda's capital is the island hub and a place you'll likely visit numerous times. It manages to look quaint and traditional on one hand and cosmopolitan on the other. With panoramic views and winding dungeons, hilltop Fort Hamilton is a star attraction, but take some time to visit the historical museum and national gallery. In the evening have a bowl of fish chowder and a rum swizzle at the Hog Penny Pub.

if Bermuda were 100 people

54 would be black
31 would be white
8 would be mixed
7 would be other

belief systems
(% of population)

49 Protestant
14 Roman Catholic
19 other
18 none

population per sq km

BERMUDA   USA   UK

† ≈ 30 people

When to Go

APR–OCT
➡ The warmest season with high humidity and also the busiest. Book ahead for hotels.

NOV–MAR
➡ Winter season is cooler. Fewer visitors so hotels and resorts drop their prices.

AUG–OCT
➡ This period of summer is also hurricane season, though it is outside the main zone.

Bermuda's Pink Sand Beaches

Bermuda's fabulous pink-tinged sand is made up of particles of coral, marine invertebrates and various shells, but it takes its distinctive light pink hue from the bodies of one particular sea creature, a member of the order *Foraminifera*. A marine proto-zoan abundant on Bermudian reefs, *Foraminifers* have hard, tiny shells that wash up on shore after the animal within the shell dies. These pink shell fragments provide the dominant color in what would otherwise be a less-distinctive confetti of bleached white coral and ivory-colored calcium carbonate shells.

Food & Drink

Bermuda fish chowder Tangy concoction of fresh fish, typically rockfish or snapper, flavoured with local black rum and sherry peppers sauce.

Black Seal Rum Bermuda's very own dark rum, which is also the main ingredient in the popular Bermuda swizzle.

Codfish cakes Savoury grilled patty made of mashed codfish, potatoes and a pinch of curry.

Ginger beer Locally brewed soft drink and often mixed with Black Seal rum and known as 'dark 'n stormy'.

Portuguese bean soup Popular staple of spicy *liguicia* and red beans introduced by Portuguese immigrants.

Shark hash Chopped-up shark bits mixed with potatoes and pan fried.

Sunday codfish breakfast Tra-ditional meal of of codfish, eggs, boiled Irish potatoes, bananas and avocado, with a sauce of onions and tomatoes.

Bermuda Underwater Exploration Institute

7 Before heading out div-ing or snorkeling, check out this institute, which unravels the mysteries of the underwater world via an amazing array of exhibits and interactive displays. These include diving bells and submersibles, a simulated 12,000ft dive in a bathysphere, and an incred-ible gold coin and jewellery collection recovered from wrecked Spanish galleons.

Crystal Caves

8 The most spectacular of Bermuda's numer-ous cave systems, Crystal Cave has thousands of crystal-like stalactites hanging above a greenish-blue pond. Despite its enormous size, this huge subterranean cavern wasn't even discovered until 1907 when two boys dropped a rope through a hole in the ground, shimmied down and found themselves inside. Today a series of 82 steps leads 120ft below the sur-face to a crystal-clear pond that fills the cave floor.

Getting Around

Bicycle Bikes (known as pedal cycles here) are a pleasant way to get around the island and can be rented at numerous shops.

Boat Public ferries, which operate daily in the Great Sound and Hamilton Harbour, offer a scenic alternative to the bus. As the distances across water are often shorter, the ferries can also be quicker.

Bus Bermuda has a good island-wide public bus system that you can use to reach most sights and beaches. Most services originate in Hamilton.

Scooter Strict restrictions mean there is no car rental in Bermuda, but the popular alternative is a motor scooter which can be rented at numer-ous cycle shops. No license is required.

Monks in ceremonial robes at Gangte Goemba, Phobjikha Valley

CAPITAL
Thimphu

POPULATION
725,296

AREA
38,394 sq km

OFFICIAL LANGUAGE
Dzongkha

Bhutan

Bhutan is no ordinary place. It is a Himalayan kingdom with a reputation for mystery and magic, where a traditional Buddhist culture carefully embraces global developments.

Bhutan holds many surprises. It's a country where the rice is red and where chillies aren't just a seasoning but the main ingredient. It's also a deeply Buddhist land, where monasteries are part of the mainstream, and where giant protective penises are painted beside the entrance to many houses. While it visibly maintains its Buddhist traditions, Bhutan is not a museum. You will find the Bhutanese well educated, fun loving and vibrant.

So why come here? Firstly there is the amazing Himalayan landscape, where snowcapped peaks rise above shadowy gorges cloaked in primeval forests. Taking up prime positions in this picture-book landscape are the majestic, fortress-like dzongs and monasteries. This unique architecture embodies Buddhist culture and sets the scene for spectacular tsechus (dance festivals). Then there are the textiles and handicrafts, outrageous archery competitions, high-altitude trekking trails, and stunning flora and fauna. If it's not Shangri-La, it's as close as it gets.

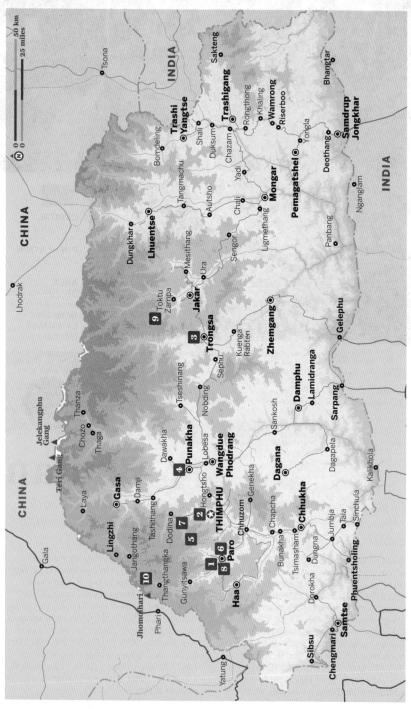

50 km
25 miles

CHINA

INDIA

CHINA

INDIA

Tsona

Lhodrak

Gala

Yatung

Jelekangphu
Gang ▲

Teri Gang ▲

Jhomolhari ▲

Thanza

Chozo

Thaga

Laya

Lingzhi

Jangothang

Tashithang

Damji

● **Gasa**

Dodina

Thangthangka

Gunyitsawa

Phari

Phari

Dungkhar

Lhuentse ●

Toktu
Zampa

Bomdeling

Trashi
Yangtse ●

Shali

Dungsum

Trashigang

Chazam

Rongthong

Khaling

Wamrong ●
Riserboo

Bhangtar

**Samdrup
Jongkhar** ●

Sakteng

Tangmachu

Autsho

Yadi

Mesithang

Ura

Jakar ●

Chali

Sengor

Ligmethang

Mongar ●

Pemagatshel ●

Yongla

Nganglam

Deothang

Panbang

Trongsa ●

Kuenga
Rabten

Sephu

Zhemgang ●

Tseshinang

Nobding

Damphu ●
Lamidranga

Dawakha

Punakha ●
Lobesa

**Wangdue
Phodrang** ●

Hongtsho

Sankosh

Dagana ●

Dagapela

Sarpang ●

Kalikhola

Thimphu ●

Genekha

Chapcha

Chhukha

Jumbja

Tala

Dagana

Sinchula

Gelephu ●

Thanza

Paro ●

Chhuzom

Bunakha

Tsimasham

Dungna

Dorokha

Phuentsholing ●

Haa ●

Tashithang

Dodina

Sibsu

Chengmari ●

Samtse ●

① ② ③ ④ ⑤ ⑥ ⑦ ⑧ ⑨ ⑩

Bhutan's
Top Experiences

Taktshang Goemba

1 Bhutan's most famous monastery, Taktshang Goemba (Tiger's Nest Monastery) is one of its most venerated religious sites. Legend says that Guru Rinpoche flew to this site on the back of a tigress to subdue a local demon; afterwards he meditated here for three months. This beautiful building clings to the sheer cliffs soaring above a whispering pine forest. The steep walk to the monastery is well worthwhile, providing tantalising glimpses of the monastery, views of the Paro valley and splashes of red-blossom rhododendrons.

Thimphu Weekend Market

2 Thimphu's bustling weekend market is the biggest and brightest in the country. The food section is an olfactory overload with dried fish competing with soft cheese, betel nut and dried chilli to assault your nostrils. Curly fern fronds (*nakey*) and red rice are just some of the exotic offerings. Cross the fast-flowing Wang Chhu on the traditional cantilever footbridge to get to the handicraft and textile stalls where you can barter for 'antiques', rolls of prayer flags, reams of material or even a human thigh-bone trumpet.

Trongsa Dzong & the Tower of Trongsa Museum

3 Sprawling down a ridge towards a gorge, Trongsa Dzong sits in a central position in Bhutan's geography. Both the first and second kings ruled from this strategic position and inside is a labyrinth of many levels, narrow corridors and courtyards. Overlooking the dzong, the Tower of Trongsa Royal Heritage Museum is housed in the watchtower. It is dedicated to the history of the dzong and the royal Wangchuck dynasty and has exhibits ranging from personal effects of the royals to Buddhist statues.

if Bhutan were 100 people

50 would be Bhote
35 would be Nepali
15 would be tribal

belief systems

(% of population)

75 Buddhist
25 Hindu

population per sq km

BHUTAN   USA   INDIA

☖ ≈ 20 people

Punakha Dzong

4 Superbly situated where two rivers converge, Punakha Dzong is postcard perfect and serenely monastic. Built by the Zhabdrung in 1637, it is the winter home of the Je Khenpo and the venue for the coronation of kings of Bhutan. Visit in spring to see the jacaranda trees splash lilac flowers down the whitewashed walls and red-robed monks wandering on a sea of purple petals. The fortress-thick walls are cold and silent one moment, then warmed with the echoes of giggles in another as a horde of young monks head off for a meal.

Druk Path Trek

5 The Druk Path is the most popular trek in Bhutan. The main draws are monasteries, alpine scenery, a convenient length, and a compelling sense of journey that comes from walking between Paro and Thimphu, Bhutan's most popular destinations. On all treks you'll be expertly guided and your pack will be carried by ponies. Trekking takes you beyond the roads and reach of modernisation. Meeting traditionally dressed locals tending their crops and animals according to century-old traditions will be a highlight of your trip.

Rinpung Dzong & National Museum

6 Paro's Rinpung Dzong is a hulking example of the fortress-like dzong architecture that glowers protectively over the valley and town. The colourful Paro tsechu is held here in spring; the festival culminates with a *thondrol* (huge religious picture) depicting Guru

The Blue Poppy

The blue poppy, Bhutan's national flower, is a delicate blue- or purple-tinged bloom with a white filament. It takes several years to grow, then it eventually flowers for the first and last time, produces seeds, and dies.

At one time the blue poppy was considered a Himalayan myth, along with the *migoi* (yeti). In 1933 a British botanist, George Sherriff, found the plant in the remote mountain region of Sakteng in eastern Bhutan. Despite this proof, few people have seen one.

Food & Drink

The Bhutanese love chillies. So much in fact that some dishes consist entirely of chillies, accompanied by chilli-infused condiments.

Bhutan's national dish is *ema datse*, large green (sometimes red, but always very hot) chillies, prepared as a vegetable not as a seasoning, in a cheese sauce. Hotel and trekking cooks make some excellent nonspicy dishes, such as *kewa datse* (potatoes with cheese sauce) and *shamu datse* (mushrooms with cheese sauce). More seasonal are the delicious asparagus and unusual *nakey* (fern fronds), the latter typically smothered in the ever-present *datse*.

Beef and fish come from India or Thailand, usually flown in frozen and safe. During the summer you may be limited to chicken, or a vegetarian diet in remote parts of the country. Yak meat is available, but only in winter.

Foremost among Tibetan-influenced snacks are *momos*, small steamed dumplings that may be filled with meat or cheese. Fried cheese momos are a speciality of several Thimphu restaurants.

Look for the strings of rock-hard, dried yak cheese, called chugo, hanging from shop rafters, but be careful of your teeth.

Dancers in traditional costume at Trashi Chhoe Dzong, Thimphu valley

Rinpoche being unfurled. Above the dzong is an old, round watchtower, the *ta dzong*, home to the excellent National Museum, which has an informative and eclectic collection.

Thimphu Valley

7 Thimphu valley delights with its cultural attractions, including the Trashi Chhoe Dzong, which celebrates its tsechu in autumn. Bhutan's capital also provides many out-of-town sights. There are good walks not far from the capital, taking in a handful of perfectly positioned monasteries with excellent views down the valley. And just west of Thimphu's centre at Motithang Takin Preserve is your best bet for spotting Bhutan's national animal, the takin.

Kyichu Lhakhang

8 Kyichu Lhakhang is one of Bhutan's oldest, most venerated and most beautiful temples and it sits just a short distance from the gateway town of Paro. The oldest temple in

When to Go

HIGH SEASON
(Mar–May, Sep–Nov)

➡ The weather is ideal in spring and autumn. Book flights well in advance.

➡ Views are best in October. Rhododendron blooms peak in March and April.

SHOULDER
(Dec–Feb)

➡ Bhutan has seasonal tariffs so, along with fewer tourists, there are savings to be made by travelling now.

➡ The weather is still pleasant. It can be cold in December and January.

LOW SEASON
(Jun–Aug)

➡ Monsoon rains and leeches put an end to most treks.

➡ High-altitude flowers are at their peak.

this twin-temple complex is believed to have been built in AD 659 by King Songtsen Gampo of Tibet. The outside grounds hum with prayers and spinning prayer wheels, while inside a treasured 7th-century statue of Jowo Sakyamuni sits in the sanctuary. Easy day walks can be commenced in the vicinity of this serene lhakhang.

Bumthang

9 The valleys comprising Bumthang make up the cultural heartland of Bhutan and are ideal for day hikes to monasteries.

Getting Around

Air Bhutan has ambitious plans for domestic air services. Check with your tour company to see the current status.

Bus Public buses are crowded and rattly, and Bhutan's winding roads make them doubly uncomfortable. Private operators such as Dhug, Metho and Sernya use more comfortable Toyota Coasters that cost about 50% more than the minibus fare.

Car & Motorcycle Since all transport is provided by tour operators, you normally do not have to concern yourself with driving. If you are arranging your own transport, you are still far better off using the services of a hired car and driver or a taxi.

Bumthang's ancient monasteries and temples figure prominently in Bhutan's early development as well as in the foundation of the unique aspects of Bhutanese Buddhism. Witness the imprint of Guru Rinpoche, hoist Pema Lingpa's 25kg chainmail, and stare into the churning waters of Membartsho, where Pema Lingpa uncovered hidden treasures.

Jhomolhari Trek

10 Bhutan's treks are physically demanding but hugely rewarding. They generally reach high altitudes and remote regions, and several are justifiably renowned in international trekking circles. The Jhomolhari trek is to Bhutan what the Everest Base Camp route is to Nepal: a trekking pilgrimage. The trek takes you within an arm's reach of Jhomolhari and Jichu Drakye, two of Bhutan's most beautiful summits. It crosses a high pass and visits the remote village of Lingzhi, then crosses another pass before making its way towards Thimphu. It also affords an excellent opportunity to see yaks.

Jhomolhari base camp, Thimpu region

DUCON DAVID / GETTY IMAGES ©

Aymará woman near Huayna Potosí

CAPITAL
La Paz

POPULATION
10.5 million

AREA
1.1 million sq km

OFFICIAL LANGUAGES
Spanish, Quechua, Aymara

Bolivia

Rough around the edges, superlative in its natural beauty, rugged, vexing, complex and slightly nerve-racking, Bolivia is one of South America's most diverse and perplexing nations.

Every second of every day is an adventure in Bolivia. Plunging from the Andes down to the edge of the Amazon, multiday journeys follow ancient Inca paving, while trips along rivers deep in the heart of the Amazon take you past the riotous barks of monkeys and a thriving mass of biodiversity that will leave you awestruck.

Bolivia is a wild place and nature lovers, aesthetes and poets alike will find landscapes, views, and nature-born experiences not seen in many other places on the planet.

The cultural, historical and spiritual depths and richness of Latin America's most indigenous nation are astounding. Officially a Plurinational State, Bolivia is an amazing place to learn from and experience a diverse mix of peoples. It is home to at-risk cultures and languages that could disappear within our lifetime, and its people maintain traditions and beliefs that reach back to the days of the Inca kings and Tiwanaku cosmologist priests.

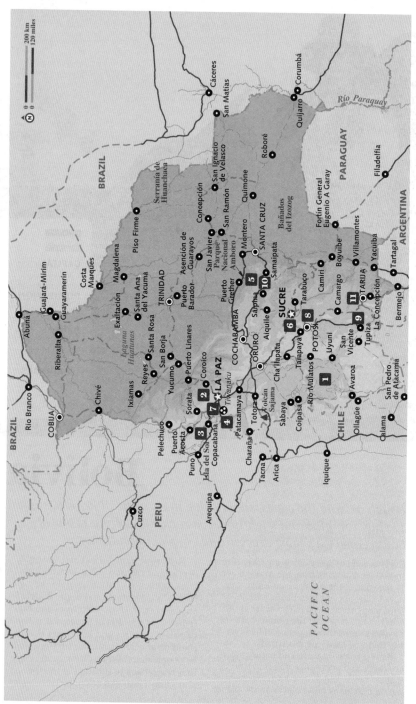

Bolivia's
Top Experiences

Salar de Uyuni

1 Who knew feeling this cold could feel so good? While a three- to four-day jeep tour through the world's largest salt flat will leave your bones chattering, it could quite possibly be the defining experience of your Bolivian adventure. The vastness, austerity and crystalline perfection of the salt flat will inspire you. An early morning exploration of rock gardens, geyser fields and piping hot springs along with the camaraderie of three days on the road with your fellow 'Salterians' will create a lasting memory.

Trekking in the Cordillera Real

2 Walk in the path of the Inca along the many trekking routes that weave their way from the Andes into the Amazon Basin, through the remarkable skyward-bound wilderness of the Cordillera Real, north of La Paz. These four- to 14-day treks are no small undertaking, but it will be worth every step, every drop of sweat and every blister. Along the way, you'll have the chance to dine with indigenous families, cool off beside cascading waterfalls and connect with Pachamama (Mother Earth) deep within her potent green realm.

CUAN HANSEN / GETTY IMAGES ©

Isla del Sol, Lake Titicaca

3 Plopped onto sprawling Lake Titicaca like the cherry on top of an ice-cream sundae, Isla del Sol is considered to be the birthplace of Andean civilization. You can follow forgotten Inca roads to small archaeological sites, isolated coves and intact indigenous communities. After exploring you can take in the sunset with a *cerveza* (beer) from your ridge-top lodge. The lake itself has a magnetism, power and energy unique in this world – no wonder many claim the ancient civilization of Atlantis was found here.

if Bolivia were 100 people

30 would be Quechua
30 would be mestizo
25 would be Aymará
15 would be white

belief systems
(% of population)

95 Roman Catholic
5 Protestant

population per sq km

BOLIVIA   US   UK

🚶 ≈ 9 people

Tiwanaku

4 Bolivia's hallmark archaeological site sets your imagination on fire. Despite lacking the power and prestige of other ruins in Latin America – those who have visited Machu Picchu or Tikal will be hard-pressed not to strike comparisons – this pre-Inca site has a lot to offer. A massive celebration is held on the winter solstice, with smaller ones taking place for the other solstice and equinoxes. The on-site museum provides a thought-provoking glimpse into life in this religious and astronomical center. An easy day-trip from La Paz, Tiwanaku is a good place to start your Andean odyssey.

Parque Nacional & Área de Uso Múltiple Amboró

5 Sandwiched between the old and new roads to Cochabamba is one of Bolivia's most biodiverse, and fortunately most accessible, protected areas – the breathtaking Parque Nacional Amboró. Here the lush, leafy Amazon kisses the thorny, dusty Chaco, and the sweaty lowlands greet the refreshing highlands. Stunning scenery, wonderful wildlife and the assistance of professional tour agencies make this a wilderness just begging to be explored.

Sucre

6 Glistening in the Andean sun, the white city of Sucre is the birthplace of the nation and a must-see for any visitor to Bolivia. It's an eclectic mix of the old and the new, where you can while away your days perusing historic buildings and museums, and spend your nights enjoying the city's famous nightlife.

Chullpa Tombs

A *chullpa* is a funerary tower or mausoleum that various Aymará groups built to house the mummified remains of some members of their society, presumably people of high rank or esteem within the community. The Oruro department is particularly rich in *chullpas*, especially along the shores of Lago Poopó and around the Sajama area.

A *chullpa* was constructed of stone or adobe, and typically had a beehive-shaped opening, which nearly always faced east toward the rising sun. The body was placed in the fetal position along with various possessions. Some communities would ritually open the *chullpas* on feast days and make offerings to their mummified ancestors; the Chipaya still do.

Most tombs, however, have been looted (apart from some bones here and there), and the mummies can now be found in museums, such as the Museo Antropológico Eduardo López Rivas in Oruro. The biggest concentration of *chullpas* is found along the road from Patacamaya to Chile. There are also *chullpas* along the Lauca circuit.

Food & Drink

Api A yummy drink made from a ground purple corn.

Carne Beef – typically *asado* (barbecued) or *parrillada* (grilled).

Mate de coca An infusion of water and dried coca leaves.

Pollo Chicken, either *frito* (fried), *a la broaster* (cooked on a spit), *asado* or *dorado* (broiled).

Salteñas, tucumanas, empanadas Pastry shells stuffed with vegetable and meat goodness.

Singani Grape brandy.

Sopa Soup starts every meal; for those with nut allergies, note that *maní* means peanut.

Visitors to Sucre invariably fall in love with the place.

La Paz Markets

7 The whirling engine that feeds and fuels a nation, the markets of La Paz are so crazy, so disjointed, so colorful and mad and remarkable that you'll end up spending at least a few afternoons wandering from stall to stall. There are sections for food, sections for sorcery, sections where you can buy back your stolen camera, sections for pipes and Styrofoam – in every shape and form imaginable – and sections packed with fruits, flowers and smelly fish that will push you to olfactory overload.

Potosí

8 Said to be the highest city in the world, Potosí once sat upon a land laden with silver that funded the Spanish empire for centuries. Though the mines are now all but barren and the city has long been in economic decline, the remnants of the wealthy

When to Go

HIGH SEASON
(May–Oct)

➡ Mostly sunny days, but cooler in the Altiplano.

➡ Reliable weather good for easy transit, and climbing, trekking and mountain biking.

➡ Prices are higher. August is the most popular month.

SHOULDER
(Oct & Feb–Apr)

➡ August to October is a great time to visit the Salar de Uyuni.

➡ This is a good period for budget hunters.

➡ Festivals across the nation put a smiley face on the rainy season.

LOW SEASON
(Nov–Apr)

➡ The rainy season; it can be miserable in the lowlands.

➡ Overland transit is hard or impossible in some areas.

➡ Climbing is dangerous, trekking and biking tedious.

past can still be seen in the cracked brickwork of the ornate colonial-era buildings and churches. Potosí's most famous museum, the Casa de la Moneda, was once the national mint and offers a fascinating insight into the rise and fall of a city that once described itself as 'the envy of kings.'

Tupiza

9 Cut from the pages of a Wild West novel, the canyon country around Tupiza is an awesome place for heading off into the sunset (in a saddle, atop a mountain bike, on foot or by 4WD). From town you can ramble out into the polychromatic desert and canyons, visiting hard-cut mining villages and the town where Butch Cassidy and the Sundance Kid met their end. The pleasant weather and lyrical feel of the town make it a welcome retreat after a bit of hardship in the highlands.

Best on Film

Amargo Mar (Bitter Sea; 1984) A look at the loss of Bolivia's coastline to Chile.

Cocalero (2007) Documentary on Morales' run for the presidency.

The Devil's Miner (2005) Documentary on a young boy working in Potosí's silver mine.

Best in Print

Fat Man from La Paz: Contemporary Fiction from Bolivia (2003, Santos) Modern fiction.

Whispering in the Giant's Ear: A Frontline Chronicle from Bolivia's War on Globalization (2006, Powers) A look at battles over natural resources.

Getting Around

Air Flights will save you days of travel, but can add to your overall budget. In the Amazon, flying is now much preferred to boat travel. Cancellations are common so call ahead to make sure you are still booked.

Boat Less common in the lowlands than they used to be, boat services can still be organised by the adventurous. Keep bags padlocked.

Bus Direct *cama* (reclining seat), semi-*cama* (partially reclining seat) and tourist-class services cost more but can save several hours. Keep valuables with you on the bus (not in the overhead bin). Bring water, warm clothes and even a sleeping bag if going anywhere in the Altiplano. Stay safe – if your driver is drunk, don't get on, or get down. Daytime driving is the safest.

Samaipata

10 Cosmopolitan Samaipata manages to retain the air of a relaxing mountain village, despite becoming an increasingly unmissable stop on the Bolivian tourist trail. But it's not just the great-value accommodations and top-class restaurants that bring in the visitors. Samaipata's proximity to the mystical El Fuerte ruins and a series of worthy day trips to nearby areas of outstanding natural beauty mean that many visitors find themselves staying for a lot longer than they planned.

Wine-Tasting, Tarija

11 Take a deep breath of the thin mountain air and prepare to sample wine from the world's highest vineyards. Though rarely sold outside Bolivia, Tarija wines, produced in a Mediterranean-like climate at altitudes of up to 2400m, are sold throughout Bolivia and have received international plaudits for their fresh, aromatic taste. Whether you prefer *tinto* (red), *rosado* (rosé) or *blanco* (white), you are likely to be pleasantly surprised by the quality on offer and may find yourself taking a bottle or two home.

JUERGEN RITTERBACH / GETTY IMAGES ©

Kravice waterfalls, near Ljubuški

Bosnia & Hercegovina

This craggily beautiful land retains scars from the 1990s civil war, but today visitors will remember Bosnia and Hercegovina for its spontaneous welcome and its intriguing cultural melange.

The Bosnians described their country as a 'heart-shaped land' and looking at a map reveals that such a description is not too wide of the mark geographically. Over centuries this rugged domain at the centre of the Balkans has been the scene of intense commingling of peoples, traditions and cultures, a fact belied by the factional strife of the 1990s. Political tensions still linger after those fratricidal wars, but Bosnians of all stripes look to a brighter and better future.

Major drawcards for travellers are the reincarnated antique centres of Sarajevo and Mostar, where rebuilt historical buildings counterpoint fashionable bars and cafes. Elsewhere Socialist-era architectural monstrosities are surprisingly rare blots on predominantly rural landscapes. Many Bosnian towns are lovably small, wrapped around medieval castles and surrounded by mountain ridges or cascading river canyons. Few places in Europe offer better rafting or such accessible, inexpensive skiing.

CAPITAL
Sarajevo

POPULATION
3.9 million

AREA
51,197 sq km

OFFICIAL LANGUAGES
Bosnian,
Croatian,
Serbian

Bosnia & Hercegovina's
Top Experiences

Mostar's Old Town

1 Nose about Mostar's atmospheric Old Town and admire the magnificently rebuilt Stari Most. At dusk the lights of numerous millhouse restaurants twinkle across gushing streamlets. Narrow Kujundžiluk 'gold alley' bustles joyously with trinket sellers. And in between, the Balkans' most celebrated bridge forms a majestic stone arc between reincarnated medieval towers. It's an enchanting scene. Stay longer to enjoy memorable attractions in the surrounding area as well as seeing young daredevils plunging from the bridge's slender arch into the racing green waters below.

Rafting the Una River Valley

2 Raft down one of Bosnia & Hercegovina's fast-flowing rivers from Bihać. The adorable Una River goes through varying moods: in the lush green gorges northwest of Bihać, some sections are as calm as mirrored opal while others gush over widely fanned rapids. There are lovely watermill restaurants at Bosanska Krupa and near Otoka Bosanska. Southwest of Bihać there's a complex of cascades at Martin Brod while the river's single most dramatic falls are at glorious Štrbački Buk, which forms the centrepiece of the new Una National Park.

Počitelj

3 The stepped Ottoman-era village of Počitelj is one of the most picture-perfect architectural ensembles in the country. Cupped in a rocky amphitheatre, it's a warren of stairways climbing between ramshackle stone-roofed houses and pomegranate bushes. The 1563 Hadži Alijna Mosque has been restored since the 1990s' destructions while the 16m clock tower (Sahat Kula) remains bell-less as it has been since 1917. The most iconic building is the octagonal Gavrakapetan Tower in the part-ruined fort. For even better panoramas climb to the uppermost rampart bastions.

Stari Most (Old Bridge), Mostar

RICHARD I'ANSON / GETTY IMAGES ©

Mehmet Paša Sokolović Bridge, Višegrad

4 The 10-arch, Unesco-listed Mehmet Paša Sokolović Bridge was built in 1571 and was immortalised in Ivo Andrić's Nobel Prize–winning classic *Bridge on the Drina*. To build on the connection, Višegrad is constructing Andrićgrad – a stone-walled mini 'old' town that's a historical fantasy cum cultural museum. The town is otherwise architecturally unexciting but it's set between a series of impressive river canyons.

Skiing

5 Ski the 1984 Olympic pistes at Jahorina or Bjelašnica or explore the wild uplands behind them.

Multi-piste Jahorina has by far the widest range of hotels, each within 300m of one of Jahorina's seven main ski lifts. At Bjelašnica, an attraction here is the floodlit night skiing and, in summer, the possibilities of exploring the magical mountain villages behind.

Trebinje

6 Wine and dine in historic little Trebinje and wander the low-key, stone-flagged Old Town. It's just 28km from Dubrovnik, but in tourist terms a whole world away. Trebinje's small, walled Old Town (Stari Grad) is attractive but very much 'lived in', its unpretentious cafes offering an opportunity to meet friendly local residents and hear Serb viewpoints on recent history.

if Bosnia & Hercegovina were 100 people

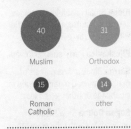

48 would be Bosniak
37 would be Serb
14 would be Croat
1 would be other

belief systems
(% of population)

40 Muslim
31 Orthodox
15 Roman Catholic
14 other

population per sq km

BOSNIA & HERCEGOVINA | CROATIA | ITALY

† ≈ 25 people

When to Go

APR–JUN

➡ Beat the heat in Hercegovina; blooming flowers in Bosnia; peak-flowing rivers.

JUL

➡ Accommodation fills up in Mostar and Sarajevo but for beginners the rafting is best now.

MID-JAN–MID-MAR

➡ Skiing gets cheaper after the New Year holidays.

Ivo Andrić

Bosnia's best-known writer, Ivo Andrić (1892–1975), won the 1961 Nobel Prize for Literature. With extraordinary psychological agility, his epic novel, the classic *Bridge on the Drina*, retells 350 years of Bosnian history as seen through the eyes of unsophisticated townsfolk in Višegrad. His *Travnik Chronicles* (aka Bosnian Chronicle) is also rich with human insight, portraying Bosnia through the eyes of jaded 19th-century foreign consuls in Travnik.

Food & Drink

Bosanski Lonac Slow-cooked meat-and-veg hotpot.

Burek Cylindrical lengths of filo-pastry filled with minced meat, often wound into spirals. *Burečdici* is the same served with kajmak and garlic, *sirnica* is filled instead with cheese, *krompiruša* with potato and zeljanica with spinach.

Ćevapi (Ćevapčići) Minced meat formed into cylindrical pellets and served in fresh bread with melting *kajmak* (thick semi-soured cream).

Hurmastica Syrup-soaked sponge fingers.

Klepe Small ravioli-like triangles served in a butter-pepper drizzle with grated raw garlic.

Pljeskavica Patty-shaped Ćevapi.

Sarma Small *dolma* parcels of rice and minced meat wrapped in a cabbage or other green leaf.

Sogan Dolma Slow roasted onions filled with minced meat.

Tufahija Whole stewed apple with walnut-filling and topped with whipped cream.

Uštipci Bready fried dough-balls often eaten with sour cream, cheese or jam.

Coloured lanterns on Kundurdžiluk, old Turkish Quarter, Sarajevo

Sarajevo

7 Potter around the timeless pedestrian lanes of Sarajevo, and sample its fashionable cafes and eclectic nightlife. Baščaršija, the bustling old Turkish Quarter, is a warren of marble-flagged pedestrian courtyards and lanes full of mosques, copper workshops, jewellery shops and inviting restaurants. The riverbanks and avenues Ferhadija and Maršala Tita are well endowed with Austro-Hungarian architecture. And attesting to Sarajevo's traditional religious tolerance, you'll find within a couple of blocks several mosques, a synagogue, the artfully flood-lit 1872 Orthodox Cathedral and the Catholic Cathedral.

Dervish House, Blagaj

8 The signature sight in pretty Blagaj village is the half-timbered Tekija (Dervish House) standing beside the surreally blue-green Buna River where it gushes out of a cliff cave. Upstairs the Tekija's wobbly wooden interior entombs two 15th-century Tajik dervishes and attracts pious pilgrims. The best views are from across the river on a footpath leading behind an attractive riverside restaurant.

Getting Around

Bus Bus stations pre-sell tickets. Between towns it's normally easy enough to wave down any bus en route. Advance reservations are sometimes necessary for overnight routes or at peak holiday times.

Car & Motorcycle There's minimal public transport to the most spectacular remote areas so having wheels can really transform your trip. Bosnia's winding roads are lightly trafficked and a delight for driving if you aren't in a hurry.

Train Trains are slower and less frequent than buses but generally around 30% cheaper.

Lion, Okavango Delta

CAPITAL
Gaborone

POPULATION
2.1 million

AREA
581,730 sq km

OFFICIAL LANGUAGE
English

Botswana

Blessed with some of the greatest wildlife spectacles on earth, Botswana is one of the great safari destinations in Africa.

There are more elephants in Botswana than any other country on earth, the big cats roam free and there's everything from endangered African wild dogs to aquatic antelopes, and from rhinos making a comeback to abundant birdlife at every turn.

This is also the land of the Okavango Delta and the Kalahari Desert, at once iconic African landscapes and vast stretches of wilderness. Put these landscapes together with the wildlife that inhabits them, and it's difficult to escape the conclusion that

this is wild Africa at its best. Botswana may rank among Africa's most exclusive destinations – accommodation prices at most lodges are once-in-a-lifetime propositions – but self-drive expeditions are also possible. And whichever way you visit, Botswana is a truly extraordinary place.

The ancestors of the San left behind extraordinary records in the form of rock paintings dotted throughout the region. The Tsodilo Hills showcase the pictorial record of this prehistoric culture.

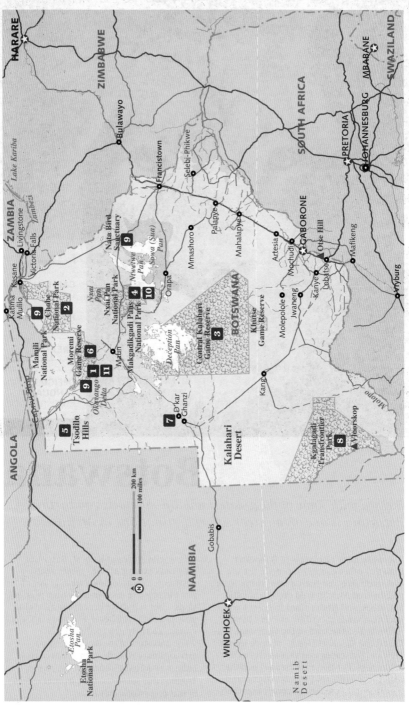

Botswana's
Top Experiences

Okavango Delta

1 The Okavango is an astonishing, beautiful, wild place. Home to wildlife spectacles of rare power and drama, the delta changes with the seasons as flood waters ebb and flow, creating islands, river channels and pathways for animals that move this way and that at the waters' behest. Exclusive and remote lodges are an Okavango speciality but self-drivers can find outstanding campsites in the heart of the Okavango's Moremi Game Reserve. No visit to the delta is complete without drifting through the water in a traditional *mokoro* (dugout canoe).

Chobe National Park

2 Chobe boasts more elephants – tens of thousands of them – than anywhere else on earth. And these are big elephants, really big. Then there are the iconic landscapes of Savuti, with its elephant-eating lions; or Linyanti, one of the best places on the continent to see the endangered African wild dog; or the Chobe Riverfront, where most of Africa's charismatic megafauna comes to drink. Put all of this together and it's easy to see why Chobe National Park ranks among the elite of African safari destinations.

MINT IMAGES · FRANS LANTING / GETTY IMAGES ©

1

Central Kalahari Game Reserve

3 There is something about the Kalahari, a name that carries more than a whiff of African magic. Perhaps it is the sheer vastness of this desert, Africa's largest protected wilderness area. The presence of black-maned Kalahari lions doesn't hurt either. Whatever the reason, this is not your average desert, home instead to ancient river valleys, light woodland and surprising concentrations of wildlife around its extensive network of salt pans.

Makgadikgadi Pans National Park

4 Part of the world's largest network of salt pans, the endless horizons of Makgadikgadi are one of the Kalahari's least-known treasures. Here the country takes on a different hue, forsaking the blues and greens of the delta for burnished oranges, shimmering whites and golden grasslands. During the rainy season zebras migrate en masse, in one of the great wildlife migrations in a continent of many. During the dry season wildlife draws near to the rejuvenated Boteti River in similarly epic numbers. And across the pans, remote islands of baobabs rise up from the salt like an ancient African oasis.

San Rock Art

5 The Tsodilo Hills, Botswana's only Unesco World Heritage site, are sometimes referred to as the 'Louvre of the Desert'. More than 4000 ancient paintings, many dating back thousands of years, adorn the caves and cliffs of these picturesque mountains, which remain a sacred site for the San people. Expertly rendered in ochre-hued natural pigments, the paintings are at once beautiful and an invaluable chronology of the evolving relationship between human beings and the natural world. And such is their remoteness that you might just have them all to yourself.

Moremi Game Reserve

6 Moremi Game Reserve, which covers one-third of the Okavango Delta, is home to some of the densest concentrations of wildlife in all of Africa. Best of all, it's one of the most accessible corners of the Okavango, with well-maintained trails and accommodation that ranges from luxury lodges to public campsites for self-drivers. Moremi has a distinctly dual personality, with large areas of dry land rising between vast wetlands. The most prominent 'islands' are Chief's Island, accessible by *mokoro* from the Inner Delta lodges, and Moremi Tongue at the eastern end of the reserve, which is mostly accessible by 4WD.

The Mokoro Experience

One of the best (and also cheapest) ways to experience the Okavango Delta is to glide across the waters in a *mokoro* (plural *mekoro*), a shallow-draft dugout canoe traditionally hewn from an ebony or a sausage-tree log. A *mokoro* may appear precarious at first, but it is amazingly stable, surprisingly swift and ideally suited to the shallow delta waters.

A *mokoro* can typically accommodate two passengers and some limited luggage, and is propelled by a poler who stands at the back of the canoe with a *ngashi*, a long pole made from the mogonono tree.

Food & Drink

Local Batswana cooking is, for the most part, aimed more at sustenance than exciting tastes. Forming the centre of most Batswana meals nowadays is *mabele* (sorghum) or *bogobe* (porridge made from sorghum), but these staples are rapidly being replaced by imported maize mealies, sometimes known by the Afrikaans name mealie pap, or just plain pap. This provides the base for an array of meat and vegetable sauces like *seswaa* (shredded goat or lamb), *morogo* (wild spinach) or *leputshe* (wild pumpkin). For breakfast, you might be able to try *pathata* (sort of like an English muffin) or *megunya*, also known as fat cakes. These are little balls of fried dough that are kind of like doughnuts minus the hole and, depending on your taste, the flavour.

Oh, and don't forget mopane worms. These fat suckers are pulled off mopane trees and fried into little delicacies – they're tasty and a good source of protein. You might be able to buy some from ladies selling them by the bag in the Main Mall in Gaborone or in Francistown.

if Botswana were 100 people

79 would be Tswana
11 would be Kalanga
3 would be Basarwa
7 would be other

belief systems
(% of population)

72 Christian
6 Badimo
2 other

population per sq km

BOTSWANA   SOUTH AFRICA   USA

≈ 4 people

San men, Makgadikgadi Pans National Park

The San People

7 In Botswana opportunities exist to meet the San people – the original inhabitants of Southern Africa, whose presence stretches back as much as 20,000 years. Chances to interact with these modern-day descendants of all our ancestors – in a way that can benefit the local community – exist in villages such as D'kar.

Kgalagadi Transfrontier Park

8 This 28,400-sq-km binational park is one of the largest and most pristine arid wilderness areas on the continent. The park is also the only place in Botswana where you'll see the shifting sand dunes that many mistakenly believe to be typical of the Kalahari. This is true desert; in the summer it can reach 45°C, and at night it can drop to -10°C. Kgalagadi is home to large herds of springboks, eland and wildebeest, as well as a full complement of predators, including lions (one estimate puts the lion population of the park at around 450), cheetahs, leopards, wild dogs, jackals and hyenas. Over 250 bird species are present, including several endemic species of larks and bustards.

Birdwatching

9 Botswana is a birding utopia with almost 600 species recorded. Species include the delta's famous African skimmers, bee-eaters, lilac-breasted rollers, pygmy geese, goshawks,

When to Go

MAY–AUG

➡ Dry season: wildlife concentrated around waterholes and generally fine weather.

SEP–OCT

➡ Extremely hot temperatures and good dry-season wildlife watching.

DEC–APR

➡ The rainy season when many tracks are impassable but tourist numbers fewer.

several species of vultures and African fish eagles. In the Okavango Panhandle, a narrow strip of swampland extending for about 100km, the waters spread across the valley to form vast reed beds and papyrus-choked lagoons that offer superb conditions for birdwatching. At Chobe Riverfront there is extraordinary variety in the birdlife along the riverfront and overhead there's a good chance of spotting African fish eagles. During the rains, Nata Bird Sanctuary is a sea of pink flamingos and other migratory birds. The rest of the year, one quarter of Botswana's birds call the sanctuary home.

Best on Film

Eye of the Leopard (2006) A remarkable chronicle of two years in the life of a leopard mother and her cub in the delta.

The Last Lions (2011) Follows a lioness and her cubs as they struggle to survive in the heart of the Okavango Delta.

Ultimate Enemies (2003–06) Three-part series documenting the enduring rivalry of lions with buffaloes, hyenas and elephants.

Best in Print

Jamestown Blues (Caitlin Davies) Set in a poor salt-mining town, it explores the disparities between expatriate and local life through the eyes of a young Motswana girl.

No.1 Ladies' Detective Agency (Alexander McCall Smith) The book that created a phenomenon.

Place of Reeds (Caitlin Davies) Fascinating story of life as a Motswana wife and mother.

Serowe: Village of the Rain Wind (Bessie Head) An intriguing cultural study of life in Serowe in eastern Botswana.

Getting Around

Air Domestic air services are fairly frequent and usually reliable, Air Botswana (and charter flights) is not cheap and only a handful of towns are regularly served.

Bus & Combi Buses and combis regularly travel to all major towns and villages throughout Botswana but are less frequent in sparsely populated areas such as western Botswana and the Kalahari. Public transport to smaller villages is often nonexistent, unless it's is along a major route.

Car The best way to travel around Botswana is to hire a vehicle. Remember, however, that distances are long and we generally recommend that you rent a vehicle outside the country (preferably South Africa), where the range of choice is greater and prices are generally lower.

Off-Road Driving

10 There's plenty to challenge 4WD enthusiasts who like to get off-road. In many remote places age-old tracks (in perilous condition after the rains) are the only way to navigate through the African wilderness. If the notion of exploring 12,000 sq km of disorientating salt pans is your idea of a holiday adventure, then calibrate your GPS and head straight for the Makgadikgadi Pans.

Fly-In Safaris

11 If the world is your oyster, then the sheer sexiness of taking off in a little six-seater aircraft to nip across to the next remote safari camp or designer lodge is a must. It also means you'll be able to maximise your time and cover a selection of parks and reserves to give yourself an idea of the fantastic variety of landscapes on offer. Fly-in safaris are particularly popular, and sometimes a necessity, in the delta region of Botswana.

On safari, Makgadikgadi Pans National Park

MARC ROMANELLI / GETTY IMAGES ©

Cristo Redentor, Corcovado

CAPITAL
Brasilia

POPULATION
201 million

AREA
8.5 million sq km

OFFICIAL LANGUAGE
Portuguese

Brazil

Tropical islands, lush rainforests, marvelous cities and picture-perfect beaches set the scene for the great Brazilian adventure.

One of the world's most captivating places, Brazil is a country of powdery white-sand beaches, verdant rainforests and wild, rhythm-filled metropolises. Brazil's attractions extend from frozen-in-time colonial towns to otherworldly landscapes of red-rock canyons, thundering waterfalls and coral-fringed tropical islands. Add to that Brazil's biodiversity: legendary in scope, its diverse ecosystems boast the greatest collection of plant and animal species found on earth. There are countless places where you can spot iconic species in Brazil, including toucans, scarlet macaws, howler monkeys, capybara, pink dolphins and sea turtles.

Brazil offers big adventures for travel. There's horseback riding and wildlife watching in the Pantanal, kayaking flooded forests in the Amazon, ascending rocky cliff tops to panoramic views, whale watching off the coast, surfing stellar breaks off palm-fringed beaches and snorkeling crystal-clear rivers or coastal reefs: it's all part of the great Brazilian experience.

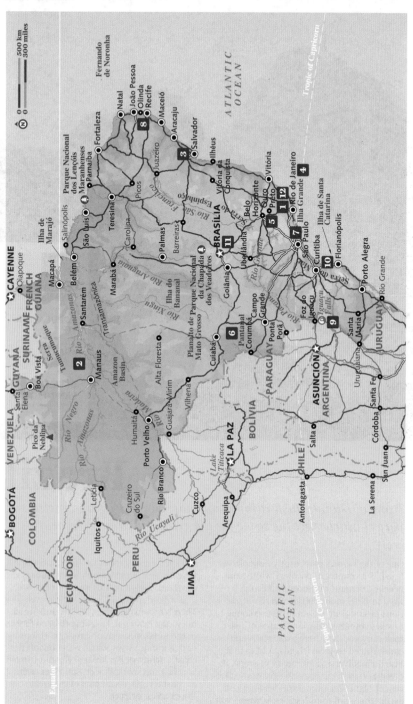

Brazil's
Top Experiences

Pão de Açúcar, Rio de Janeiro

1 Some say to come around sunset for the best views from that absurd confection of a mountain. But in truth, it doesn't matter when you come; you're unlikely to look at Rio (or your own comparatively lackluster city) in the same way. From here the landscape is pure undulating green hills and golden beaches lapped by blue sea, with rows of skyscrapers sprouting along the shore. The ride up is good fun: all-glass aerial trams that whisk you up to the top. The adventurous can rock-climb their way to the summit.

The Amazon

2 Needless to say, the best reason to visit the Amazon is to get out into the jungle: to ply the winding waterways in a canoe, to hike lush leafy trails, to scan the canopy for monkeys, sloths and other creatures. The world's biggest and best-known rainforest has outdoor excursions of all sorts, and for all types of travelers: from easy nature hikes to scaling 50m trees, from luxury lodges to makeshift camps in the forest. Whatever your interest, experience, ability or budget, there's a jungle trip in the Amazon waiting to blow your mind.

Canoeing on the Amazon, Pará

JAQUES JANGOUX / GETTY IMAGES ©

Salvador

3 The capital of Afro-Brazil, Salvador is famous for capoeira, Candomblé, Olodum, colonial Portuguese architecture, African street food and one of the oldest lighthouses in the Americas. Today's lively Bahian capital offers a unique fusion of two vibrant cultures. The festive music and nightlife scene culminates in February with one of Brazil's best Carnavals.

Ilha Grande

4 Thanks to its isolation, Ilha Grande served for decades as a prison and leper's colony.

if Brazil were 100 people

54 would be white
38 would be mulatto (mixed white and black)
6 would be black
2 would be other

belief systems
(% of population)

74 Roman Catholic
15 Protestant
7 none
3 other
1 Spiritualist

population per sq km

BRAZIL   USA   UK

↑ ≈ 24 people

Spared from development by this unusual history, its jungle-clad slopes and dozens of beaches are some of the best preserved in all of Brazil. Days are spent hiking through lush Atlantic rainforest, snorkeling amid aquamarine seas and basking in crisp waterfalls. With no motor vehicles to spoil the party, this is one clean, green island – a true nature lover's paradise. It's also an easy day's journey from Rio.

Ouro Preto

5 The 18th-century streets of Ouro Preto veer between one baroque masterpiece and the next. You can admire the sculpted masterpieces of Aleijadinho, discover the 18th-century African tribal king turned folk hero Chico-Rei and gaze upon opulent gilded churches. The Holy Week processions are among the country's most spectacular.

The Pantanal

6 Few places can match the wildlife-watching experience provided by the Pantanal, a remote wetland in the heart of Mato Grosso. From cute capybaras to stately storks, the animal life abounds and is easy to see in the open marshy surroundings. There's also no better place in South America to see the elusive jaguar!

São Paulo

7 Rivaling the frenetic pace of New York, the modernism of Tokyo and the prices of Moscow, São Paulo is home to a pool of 20 million potential foodies, clubbers and cocktail connoisseurs and nearly 30,000 restaurants, bars and clubs to satiate them. From contemporary gourmet

---

Rhythms of Brazil

Shaped by the mixing of varied influences from three continents, Brazilian popular music has always been characterized by great diversity. The *samba canção* (samba song), for example, is a mixture of Spanish bolero with the cadences and rhythms of African music. Bossa nova was influenced by samba and North American music, particularly jazz. Tropicália mixed influences ranging from bossa nova and Italian ballads to blues and North American rock. Brazil is still creating new and original musical forms today.

Food & Drink

Barreado A mixture of meats and spices cooked in a sealed clay pot for 24 hours and served with banana and farofa; the state dish of Paraná.

Carne de sol Tasty, salted meat, grilled and served with beans, rice and vegetables.

Cozido A meat stew heavy on vegetables.

Feijoada Bean-and-meat stew served with rice and orange slices, traditionally eaten for Saturday lunch.

Moqueca Bahian fish stew cooked in a clay pot with *dendê* (palm) oil, coconut milk and spicy peppers.

Pão de queijo Balls of cheese-stuffed tapioca bread.

Pastel Thin square of dough stuffed with meat, cheese or fish, then fried.

Pato no tucupí Roast duck flavored with garlic, juice of the manioc plant and jambú; a favorite in Pará.

Pirarucu ao forno Delicious Amazonian fish, oven cooked with lemon and other seasonings.

Vatapá Seafood dish of African origins with a thick sauce of manioc paste, coconut and *dendê* oil.

Pelourinho, Salvador

haunts to edgy offerings of Baixo Augusta and bohemian bars in Vila Madalena, it's an avalanche of bolinhos, booze and beats that outruns the sunrise on most nights.

When to Go

HIGH SEASON
(Dec–Mar)

➡ The high season coincides with the northern hemisphere winter.

➡ It's a hot, festive time, though expect higher prices and minimum stays (typically four nights) during Carnaval.

SHOULDER
(Apr & Oct)

➡ The weather is warm and dry along the coast, though it can be chilly in the south.

➡ Prices and crowds are average, though Easter week draws crowds and high prices.

LOW SEASON
(May–Sep)

➡ Aside from July, which is a school-holiday month, you'll find lower prices and cold temperatures in the south.

➡ July to September are good months to visit the Amazon or Pantanal.

Recife & Olinda

8 These two contrasting Northeastern neighbors with an intertwined history and shared culture make a heady double act.

Recife is the big-city big sister with skyscrapers and traffic, but also a fascinating historic center becoming more appealing through renovations and new museums and restaurants. Cute, tree-covered Olinda has tranquil winding lanes, colonial churches and artists' galleries. Their vibrant shared heritage comes together at Carnaval with riotous street festivities.

Iguaçu Falls

9 No matter the number of waterfalls you've checked off your bucket list, no matter how many times you have thought to yourself you'd be just fine never seeing another waterfall again,

Iguaçu Falls will stomp all over your idea of water trickling over the edge of a cliff. The thunderous roar of 275 falls crashing across the Brazil and Argentina border floors even the most jaded traveler. Loud, angry, unstoppable and impossibly gorgeous, Iguaçu will leave you stunned.

Santa Catarina

10 Santa Catarina is synonymous with the good life and that has a whole lot to do with its sun-toasted shores. Whether you hang out in Florianópolis, where an easy path to paradise boasts 42 idyllic beaches sitting within an hour's drive, or head south of the capital to Guarda do Embaú, one of Brazil's best surfing spots, or Praia do Rosa, the state's most sophisticated beach resort, a powerful punch of wow will greet you the first time you dig your toes into the state's unspoiled sands.

Brasilia

11 What the city of the future really needed to back up its claim to be the harbinger of Brazil's 'new dawn' was an architect capable of designing buildings that looked the part. In Oscar Niemeyer they found the right man for the job. The 'crown of thorns' Catedral Metropolitana is a religious masterwork and the interplanetary Teatro Nacional is out of this world! Brasília is a city overloaded with architectural gems, designed by a genius inspired by the concept of a better future.

Getting Around

Air Useful for crossing Brazil's immense distances; can save days of travel; prices are generally high, but airfare promotions are frequent.

Boat Slow, uncomfortable, but brag-worthy transport between towns in the Amazon, with trips measured in days rather than hours. You'll need a hammock, snacks and drinking water.

Bus Extensive services from *comun* (conventional) to *leito* (overnight sleepers) throughout the country, except for the Amazon.

Carnaval in Rio

12 Get plenty of sleep before you board the plane, because once you land, it's nonstop revelry. With nearly 500 street parties happening in every corner of town, you will not lack for options partying during Carnaval in Rio. For the full experience, join a samba school and parade amid pounding drum corps and mechanized smoke-breathing dragons in the Sambódromo. Or assemble a costume and hit one of the Carnaval balls around town.

Best on Film

Central do Brasil (Central Station, 1998) Walter Salles' moving tale of a homeless boy and an older woman on a road trip across Brazil.

Cidade de Deus (City of God, 2002) Brutality and hope in a Rio favela by award-winning director Fernando Meirelles.

Orfeu Negro (Black Orpheus, 1959) Retelling of a classic myth, set during Carnaval with a bossa nova soundtrack.

Best in Print

Brazil on the Rise (Larry Rohter, 2010) Insightful portrait of the politics, culture and challenges of the South American nation.

Gabriela, Clove and Cinnamon (Jorge Amado, 1958) Hilarious story of seduction and betrayal set in 1920s Bahia, written by one of Brazil's best writers.

The Lost City of Z (David Grann, 2009) Gripping journey into the Amazon to retrace the steps of lost explorer Colonel Fawcett..

Samba school parade at Carnaval

Omar Ali Saifuddien Mosque, Bandar Seri Begawan

CAPITAL
Bandar Seri Begawan

POPULATION
415,717

AREA
5,765 sq km

OFFICIAL LANGUAGE
Malay

Brunei

Blessed with picturesque water villages, glorious rainforests, stunning mosques and some outstanding cuisine, Brunei is as polite and unassuming as its people.

The small sultanate of Brunei almost looks like a geographic comma plunked between Sarawak and Sabah. It certainly forms a conceptual one, because unless you're a petroleum engineer, when folks ask 'Why go to Brunei?' the answer is usually the travelling equivalent of a pause: transfer or stopover.

But there's more here than passport queues. This quiet *darussalam* (Arabic for 'abode of peace') has the largest oilfields in Southeast Asia, and because oil generates money, Brunei hasn't turned its rainforests into palm plantations. Old-growth greenery abounds, especially in verdant Ulu Temburong National Park. Because booze is banned, the citizens of the capital, Bandar Seri Begawan (BSB), are mad for food and shopping.

This tranquil (sometimes somnolent) nation is the realisation of a particular vision: a strict, socially controlled religious state where happiness is found in pious worship and mass consumption. Visit and judge the results for yourself.

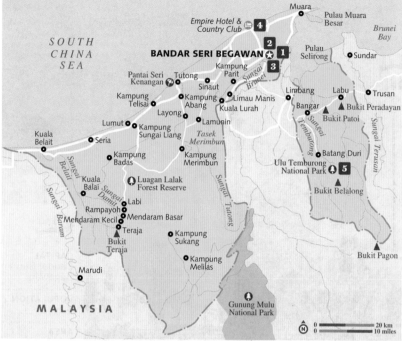

Brunei's
Top Experiences

Kampung Ayer (Water Village)

1 Borneo is modernising quickly, but even the most tech-savvy entrepreneur is only a generation removed from the kampung ayer, or water village. Some only grow up in these waterbound communities, yet many live out their days in them. That's the case in the water village that hugs Brunei's capital, Bandar Seri Begawan, the largest of its kind in the world. Some residents live humbly, while others park sports cars before catching a water taxi home, a fascinating juxtaposition of nostalgia and development all set on stilts.

Bandar Seri Begawan

2 Cities built on oil money tend to be flashy places, but with the exception of a palace you usually can't enter, a couple of enormous mosques and one wedding cake of a hotel, Bandar (as the capital is known, or just BSB) is a pretty understated place. Urban life pretty much revolves around good shopping, great restaurants and, depending on your level of piety, illicit parties or Islam (and sometimes both). BSB also has a few museums and the biggest water village in the world, a little slice of vintage that speaks to the Bruneian love of cosiness and nostalgia. There is a pleasant promenade along the waterfront, which is a nice spot for an evening stroll.

Omar Ali Saifuddien Mosque

3 Built from 1954 to 1958, Masjid Omar Ali Saifuddien – named after the 28th sultan of Brunei (the late father of the current sultan) – is surrounded by an artificial lagoon that serves as a reflecting pool. The mosque is the happening centre of city life in Bandar come evenings; folks come for prayer, then leave to eat or shop, which is sort of Brunei in a nutshell. The 44m minaret makes it the tallest building in central BSB. This being Brunei, the interior is lav-

Water village stilt houses, Bandar Seri Begawan

ish. The floor and walls are made from the finest Italian marble, the stained-glass windows and chandeliers were crafted in England, and the luxurious carpets were flown in from Saudi Arabia and Belgium. Jigsaw enthusiasts can admire the 3.5-million-piece Venetian mosaic inside the main dome and a ceremonial stone boat sitting in the lagoon is a replica of a 16th-century *mahligai* (royal barge).

Empire Hotel & Country Club

4 Pharaonic in its proportions and opulence, this 523-room extravaganza was commissioned by Prince Jefri as lodgings for guests of the royal family. To recoup some of the US$1.1 billion investment, it was quickly transformed into an upscale resort. So, now anyone with a thing for Las Vegas–style bling can wander past, check out the enormous pool complex outside (popular with expats and the wealthy), grab a tea in the lounge or hang out in the lobby and sit beside one of the Empire's US$500,000 gold and Baccarat crystal lamps. The hotel has two of these – the other one resides in the Emperor Suite and can be appreciated privately for around B$17,000 per night. But hey, it's worth a visit here for the gilded spectacle.

if Brunei were 100 people

66 would be Malay
10 would be Chinese
3 would be indigenous
21 would be other

belief systems
(% of population)

79 Muslim
8 Buddhist

9 Christian
4 other

population per sq km

BRUNEI   MALAYSIA   INDONESIA

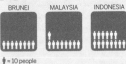

👤 ≈ 10 people

When to Go

OCT–DEC

➡ The rainiest, if coolest, months of the year.

JAN–MAY

➡ February and March are the driest months. National Day is celebrated on 23 February.

JUN–AUG

➡ It's hot. The sultan's birthday (15 July) is marked with festivities around the country.

Brunei's Big Guns

One of the more interesting exhibits in the Brunei Museum – partly because it's one of the few pieces native solely to Brunei – is a series of *bedil*, or cannons. It was not oil but these bronze-cast weapons that were once the source of the sultanate's wealth and power.

The cannons of Brunei subjugated many of the smaller kingdoms of Borneo and extended the sultanate's power all the way to the Philippines. They were so common they became an expected dowry gift; perhaps rightly so – *bedil* are beautiful.

All are decorated in a baroque fashion, and some are carved to resemble dragons and crocodiles, because let's face it: what's more terrifying than a cannon ball erupting from a crocodile's mouth?

Food & Drink

Ambuyat Brunei's unofficial national dish is a gelatinous porridge-like goo that's eaten with a variety of flavourful sauces.

Bumbu A pounded chilli-based paste containing, at its most basic, garlic and shallots, which forms the foundation of curries, soups and stews.

Drinks The sale and public consumption of alcohol is officially banned in Brunei, but some places (often hotels and high-end restaurants) do discreetly serve it at times.

Meat Fish and seafood are common, whereas chicken, beef and buffalo, though available, are more special occasion meats in Brunei.

Sago flour A primary starch for Bruneians, sago flour is laboriously extracted from the trunk of a variety of palm tree. It's mixed with water and cooked to make *ambuyat*.

Ulu Temburong National Park

5 It's odd that in a country as manicured and regulated as Brunei, there's still a sizable chunk of true untamed wilderness. Therein lies the appeal of Ulu Temburong National Park, located in the heart of a 500-sq-km area of pristine rainforest. It's so untouched that only about 1 sq km of the park is accessible to tourists. To protect it for future generations, the rest is off-limits to everyone except scientists, who flock here from around the world. The forests are teeming with life, including as many as 400 kinds of butterfly, but don't count on seeing many vertebrates if you come here. The best times to spot birds and animals, in the rainforest and along river banks, are around sunrise and sunset, but visitors are much more likely to hear hornbills and Bornean gibbons than to see them.

Getting Around

Bus Brunei's bus system is rather chaotic, at least to the uninitiated, however buses do service many destinations in and out of BSB.

Car Brunei has Southeast Asia's cheapest petrol. If you're driving a rental car with Malaysian plates and are not a Brunei resident, you'll be taken to a special pump to pay more (this is to prevent smuggling).

Taxis A convenient way of exploring – if you can find one. There is no centralised taxi dispatcher and it's next to impossible to flag one down on the street, but hotels can often recommend drivers and provide you with their phone numbers.

Water taxi If your destination is near the river, water taxis – little motorboats – are a good way of getting there.

CAPITAL
Sofia

POPULATION
7 million

AREA
110,879 sq km

OFFICIAL LANGUAGE
Bulgarian

Rila Monastery

Bulgaria

From wild, wooded mountain ranges speckled with remote villages and enchanting monasteries to vibrant modern cities and long sandy beaches hugging the Black Sea coast, Bulgaria rewards exploration.

Bulgaria may attract the majority of its visitors with its long, sandy Black Sea beaches, but there's much more to see than that. Bulgaria boasts no fewer than seven mountain ranges and varied landscapes ideal for hiking, cycling, climbing and wildlife-watching. And you'll find some of Europe's most modern and reasonably priced ski resorts.

The depth of Bulgaria's history and culture are immediately evident. There are countless churches and a full measure of Orthodox monasteries full of vibrant icons,

picturesque villages of timber-framed houses 19th-century revival-era architecture and cobbled lanes, and dramatic reminders of the country's heritage, from Thracian tombs and Roman ruins to medieval fortresses, Ottoman mosques and communist monuments slowly crumbling away into history.

Bulgaria's cities reward visitors, with treasure-filled museums and galleries, and parks sprinkled with cafes and restaurants where the coffee is strong, the cuisine hearty and the conversation always animated.

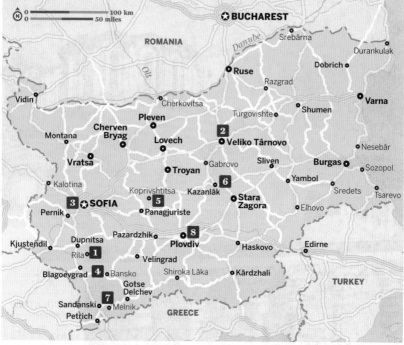

N 0 ___ 100 km
0 ___ 50 miles

☉ **BUCHAREST**

ROMANIA

Danube

Srebârna

Durankulak

Dobrich

Ruse

Razgrad

Varna

Vidin

Cherkovitsa

Turgovishte

Shumen

Nesebâr

Pleven

Cherven Bryag

Montana

Lovech

2

Veliko Târnovo

Gabrovo

Sliven

Burgas

Sozopol

Vratsa

Troyan

6

Sredets

Tsarevo

Kalotina

Koprivshtitsa

Kazanlâk

Yambol

3 ☉ **SOFIA**

5

Stara Zagora

Pernik

Panagjuriste

Elhovo

Kjustendil

Dupnitsa

Pazardzhik

8

Rila **1**

Plovdiv

Haskovo

Edirne

Velingrad

Blagoevgrad

4 Bansko

Shiroka Lâka

Kârdzhali

TURKEY

Gotse Delchev

Sandanski

7

Melnik

GREECE

Petrich

Bulgaria's
Top Experiences

Rila Monastery

1 Set peacefully in a forested valley south of Sofia, Rila Monastery is Bulgaria's biggest and most storied spiritual treasure; a former centre of learning and culture that kept national spirits up during the Ottoman occupation. A Unesco World Heritage site since 1983, the monastery grew from a 10th-century hermit's hut, and has been rebuilt many times since. Its elaborate arches and precious frescoes and icons create a sublime and sumptuous atmosphere.

Veliko Târnovo

2 The unquestioned highlight of Bulgaria's central heartland, the grand old city of the tsars – Bulgaria's capital in medieval times – offers a mix of antiquity, boutique bliss and nightlife. This university town, set high above the ribboning Yantra River, is popular with visitors both local and foreign, who marvel at the oddly endearing 'Sound and Light Show' held nightly at the impressive Tsarevets Fortress, a still-robust medieval citadel.

Aleksander Nevski Memorial Church, Sofia

3 Rising majestically over the rooftops of the Bulgarian capital, this beautiful Orthodox church, dedicated to the memory of the 200,000 Russian soldiers who died in the Russo-Turkish War (1877–78), took 30 years to construct, and was completed in 1912. The shimmering golden domes are visible several streets away, while the vast, candlelit interior is decorated with Italian marble, alabaster and fading murals. Daily services are led by robed, white-bearded priests, accompanied by chanting choirs.

Skiing in the Pirin Mountains

4 High in the Pirin Mountains are Bulgaria's most famous ski areas: Bansko and Borovets. With the highest pistes starting from 2500m, Bansko is known for its long, steep runs and extended ski seasons. It's also an international party scene, offering everything from

Bansko ski area

refined restaurants and spa treatments to crowded bars and clubs. The slopes at Borovets, north beyond Mt Musala, also top 2500m. While the trails at this long-established favourite are less challenging, there is plenty of trickier, open terrain for thrill seekers.

Koprivshtitsa

5 This unique museum village, nestled between Karlovo and Sofia, is a perfectly preserved hamlet filled with Bulgarian National Revival-period architecture, cobblestone streets, and bridges over a lovely brook. Nearly 400 buildings of architectural and historical significance are protected by government decree, among them churches and house museums containing decor and implements from yesteryear.

Thracian Tombs

6 Bulgarians are rightly proud of their Thracian heritage, and the ancient tribes who produced slave leader Spartacus and the semidivine, lyre-playing Orpheus were fantastically skilled artists and crafts-people. Today, the most obvious reminders of their culture are the elaborate tombs that have been unearthed across southern and central Bulgaria. The best of these is the amazing beehive tomb in Kazanlâk, erected for a 4th-century-BC king, and adorned with remarkably well-preserved murals of chariot racing and feasting. It is now a Unesco World Heritage site.

if Bulgaria were 100 people

77 would be Bulgarian
8 would be Turk
4 would be Roma
11 would be other

belief systems
(% of population)

60 — Eastern Orthodox

7 — Muslim (Sunni)

1 — Muslim (Shia)

28 — other

4 — none

population per sq km

BULGARIA   GREECE   ROMANIA

♦ ≈ 15 people

When to Go

JAN

➡ This is a great time to go skiing in Bansko or down Mt Vitosha.

MAR–MAY

➡ Fine spring weather welcomes folk and festivals across the country.

JUN–SEP

➡ Spend lazy days on the Black Sea beaches and nights at Bulgaria's best clubs.

Vasil Levski

It's a name you'll see on street signs and public buildings in every Bulgarian town, and the matinee idol looks will soon become familiar. It's Vasil Levski, the 'Apostle of Freedom' and Bulgaria's undisputed national hero.

Born Vasil Ivanov Kunchev in Karlovo in 1837, Levski (a nickname meaning 'Lion') originally trained as a monk, but in 1862 fled to Belgrade to join the revolutionary fight against the Turks, led by Georgi Rakovski. A few years later he was back, travelling incognito around Bulgaria, setting up a network of revolutionary committees. Levski, who believed in the ideals of the French Revolution, was a charismatic and able leader of the independence movement, but he was captured in Lovech in December 1872 and hanged in Sofia in February 1873; the Levski Monument marks the spot where he died.

Food & Drink

Banitsa Flaky cheese pasty, often served fresh and hot.

Beer Zagorka, Kamenitza and Shumensko are the most popular nationwide brands.

Kavarma This 'claypot meal', or meat stew, is normally made with either chicken or pork.

Kebabche Thin, grilled pork sausage, a staple of every *mehana* (tavern) in the country.

Shishcheta Shish kebab, consisting of chunks of chicken or pork on wooden skewers with mushrooms and peppers.

Shkembe chorba Traditional tripe soup.

Tarator Chilled cucumber and yoghurt soup, served with garlic, dill and crushed walnuts.

Wine Many excellent varieties.

Bulgarian Wine

7 Bulgaria's winemaking tradition dates to ancient Thracian times, and fine wine has been enjoyed here by everyone from Roman writers and French crusaders to former British Prime Minister Winston Churchill, who used to order barrels of the local red from Melnik. Distinct wine-growing regions exist from the Danube to the Black Sea to the Thracian Plain, and numerous wineries offer tastings that are usually complemented by meats, cheeses and memorable rustic views.

Plovdiv

8 Arty, fun-loving Plovdiv makes a great alternative to Sofia for travellers. It's an eminently walkable and safe student city, loaded with great restaurants, bars and galleries, and boasting a dynamic cultural scene. The evocative Old Town features National Revival–era homes clinging to cobblestoned lanes, museums and galleries, and a magnificent Roman amphitheatre; while the hip Kapana district is home to unpretentious indie cafes and bars, perfect for a night out on the town.

Getting Around

Air The only scheduled domestic flights within Bulgaria are between Sofia and Varna and Sofia and Burgas.

Bus There are several frequent modern, comfortable buses between the larger towns, while older, often cramped minibuses also run on routes between smaller towns.

Car Bulgaria's roads are among the most dangerous in Europe and the level of fatalities each year is high.

Train The Bulgarian State Railways boasts an impressive 4278km of track across the country, linking most towns and cities.

Market, Bobo-Dioulasso

CAPITAL	Ouagadougou
POPULATION	18.3 million
AREA	274,200 sq km
OFFICIAL LANGUAGE	French

Burkina Faso

Previously called Upper Volta and little noticed in the wider world, Burkina Faso nonetheless ends up being many travellers' favourite West African country.

Land-locked Burkina Faso (Burkina to locals) may not have many big-ticket attractions, yet it invariably wins the hearts of travellers for the warmth of its welcome. The vibrant cities, thriving arts milieu, stunning traditional architecture, surprising wildlife-watching opportunities and stirring landscapes will all turn your head. The country's other big draws are its enchanting landscapes – from atmospheric Sahelian plains, to rolling savannah and surprising geology – and the lively cultural scene.

Ouagadougou and Bobo-Dioulasso, Burkina's two largest and gloriously named cities, are famous for their long-standing musical traditions and beautiful handicrafts. In Bobo, *griots* (a traditional caste of musicians or praise singers), blacksmiths and 'nobles' (farmers) still live in their respective quarters but happily trade services and drink at the same *chopolo* (millet beer) bars. Throw in Fespaco, Africa's premier film festival, held in the capital every odd-numbered year, and there's enough to engage your mind and senses for a couple of weeks or so.

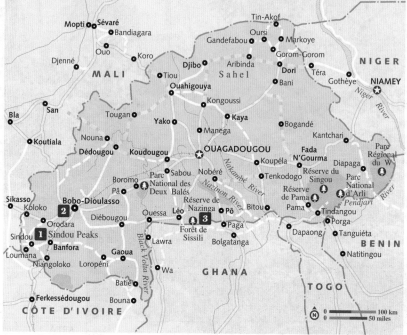

Burkina Faso's
Top Experiences

Sindou Peaks

1 One of Burkina Faso's most spectacular landscapes, the Sindou Peaks (Pics de Sindou) are a narrow, craggy chain featuring a fantastic array of tortuous cones sculpted by the elements. The geological fantasyland is ideal for hiking.

Bobo-Dioulasso

2 Bobo, as Bobo-Dioulasso is widely known, may be Burkina Faso's second-largest city, but it has a small-town charm and its tree-lined streets exude a languid, semi-tropical atmosphere. You'll have plenty to do during the day in and around the city, but save some energy for night-time to enjoy Bobo's thriving music scene and excellent restaurants.

Réserve de Nazinga

3 Come face to face with elephants at Réserve de Nazinga. The park also has antelopes, monkeys, warthogs, crocodiles and plenty of birds, but the mighty wandering elephants are the stars of the show. The best time to see them is December to April, although the chances of sightings are pretty good year-round.

Food & Drink

Aloco Plantain fried with chilli in palm oil.

Attiéké Grated cassava.

Graine A hot sauce made with oil-palm nuts.

Kedjenou Simmered chicken or fish with vegetables.

Riz Sauce Rice with sauce.

When to Go

JAN–FEB

➡ Perfect wildlife-viewing time; dusty harmattan winds can produce hazy skies.

APR–SEP

➡ Hot season (Apr–May) best avoided; rainy season (Jun–Sep) challenging for transport.

OCT–DEC

➡ A lovely time of year, with green landscapes and pleasant temperatures.

CAPITAL
Bujumbura

POPULATION
1.3 million

AREA
27,830 sq km

OFFICIAL LANGUAGE
Kirundi, French

Burundi

A pint-sized country with a traumatic past but a forward-looking and welcoming people, Burundi is emerging from the fog of its civil war.

Tiny Burundi is an incongruous mix of soaring mountains, languid lakeside communities and a tragic past blighted by ethnic conflict. While similar Hutu-Tutsi conflicts have been soothed in Rwanda by removing historical tribal labels, Burundi has chosen a different path, one of open dialogue and good-hearted debate.

Now the word is out that the war is over, Burundi is receiving a trickle of travellers and the country is safer now than it has been for years. Its steamy capital, Bujumbura, has a lovely location on the shores of Lake Tanganyika, and just outside the city are some of the finest inland beaches on the continent. For those inclined to adventure, its jungle-clad volcanoes offer lung-busting escapades tracking chimpanzees.

Burundians also have an irrepressible joie de vivre, and their smiles are as infectious as a rhythm laid down by any of the Les Tambourinaires drummers for which the country is famous.

Burundi's
Top Experiences

Saga Beach

1 Down a cold one under the shade of a palm tree on Saga Beach (pronounced Sagga), one of Africa's finest inland beaches. Bujumbura's Lake Tanganyika beaches are some of the best of any landlocked country in Africa, and the sand is white and powdery.

Bujumbura

2 Dine out in style and dance into the wee hours in Burundi's vibrant capital Bujumbura. Frozen in time after a decade of conflict, there has been almost no development in Bujumbura since the 1980s. It retains much of its grandiose colonial boulevards and public buildings. 'Buj' has a freewheelin' reputation for its dining, drinking and dancing scene.

Chutes de la Karera

3 Take a cold shower under one of four waterfalls at the Chutes de la Karera. The prettiest of the four is the cascade Nyakai I. Upstream from this is the smallest of the four falls, Nyakai II, an ideal spot for an impromptu shower. This watercourse is joined by that of Mwaro Falls before creating the namesake and tallest waterfall in the area, Karera Falls.

Food & Drink

Brochettes (kebabs) and *frites* (fries) are a legacy of the Belgian colonial period, but there are also succulent fish from Lake Tanganyika and serious steaks.

When it comes to drink, Burundi is blessed with a national brewery churning out huge bottles of Primus.

When to Go

YEAR-ROUND	OCT–MAY	JUN & AUG
➡ Altitude affects regional temperature. Bujumbura is warmer than elsewhere.	➡ Mild rainy season with a brief dry spell in December and January.	➡ Locals flock to Lake Tanganyika beaches during the 'long dry' season.

Khmer dancers in traditional dress

CAPITAL	Phnom Penh
POPULATION	15.2 million
AREA	181,035 sq km
OFFICIAL LANGUAGE	Khmer

Cambodia

With a history both inspiring and depressing, Cambodia delivers an intoxicating present for adventurous visitors, from the glory of Angkor to the simplicity of village life.

Ascend to the realm of the gods at Angkor Wat, a spectacular fusion of spirituality, symbolism and symmetry. Descend into the darkness of Tuol Sleng to witness the crimes of the Khmer Rouge. This is Cambodia, a country with a history both inspiring and depressing, a captivating destination that casts a spell on all those who visit.

Fringed by beautiful beaches and tropical islands, sustained by the mother waters of the Mekong River and cloaked in some of the region's few remaining emerald wildernesses, Cambodia is an adventure as much as a holiday. This is the warm heart of Southeast Asia, with everything the region has to offer packed into one bite-sized chunk.

Despite the headline attractions, Cambodia's greatest treasure is its people. The Khmers have been to hell and back, but thanks to an unbreakable spirit and infectious optimism they have prevailed with their smiles and spirits largely intact.

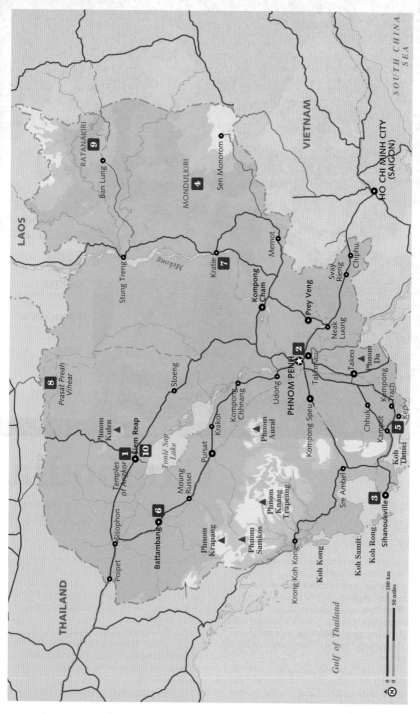

Cambodia's
Top Experiences

Temples of Angkor

1 One of the world's most magnificent sights, the temples of Angkor are so much better than the superlatives. Choose from Angkor Wat, the world's largest religious building; Bayon, one of the world's weirdest, with its immense stone faces; and Ta Prohm, where nature runs amok. The temples are the perfect fusion of creative ambition and spiritual devotion. The Cambodian 'god-kings' of old each strove to better their ancestors in size, scale and symmetry. Today, the temples are a point of pilgrimage for all Cambodians, and no traveller to the region will want to miss their extravagant beauty.

Phnom Penh

2 The Cambodian capital is a chaotic yet charming city that has thrown off the shadows of the past to embrace a brighter future. Boasting one of the most beautiful riverfronts in the region, Phnom Penh is in the midst of a boom, with hip hotels, designer restaurants and funky bars ready to welcome urban explorers. Experience emotional extremes at the inspiring National Museum and the depressing Tuol Sleng prison, showcasing the best and worst of Cambodian history. Once the 'Pearl of Asia', Phnom Penh is fast regaining its shine.

Angkor Thom

CULTURA TRAVEL / GARY LATHAM / GETTY IMAGES ©

Sihanoukville

3 Despite a reputation for backpacker hedonism, Sihanoukville's real appeal lies in its beaches. On nearby islands like Koh Rong and Koh Rong Samloem, resorts are creating a laid-back beach vibe. On the mainland, it's only 5km from the grittier central beach, Occheuteal, to Otres Beach, still mellow and sublime despite the long-looming threat of development. More central Victory Beach, Independence Beach, Sokha Beach, and even backpacker favourite Serendipity Beach all have their charms and unique personalities.

if Cambodia were 100 people

90 would be Khmer
5 would be Vietnamese
3 would be Cham
1 would be Chinese
1 would be other ethnic minorities

belief systems

(% of population)

96
Buddhist

2
Muslim

2
other

population per sq km

CAMBODIA   LAOS   UK

🚶 ≈ 30 people

Mondulkiri

4 Eventually the endless rice fields and sugar palms that characterise the Cambodian landscape give way to rolling hills. Mondulkiri is the wild east, home to the hardy Bunong people, who still practise animism and ancestor worship. Elephants are used here, but better than riding them is visiting them at the Elephant Valley Project, where you can experience 'walking with the herd'. Add thunderous waterfalls, jungle treks and black-shanked douc spotting to the mix and you have just the right recipe for adventure.

Kampot & Kep

5 These south coast retreats form the perfect combination for those looking to get beyond the beaches of Sihanoukville. In laid-back Kampot, take in the wonderful colonial architecture, explore the pretty river by paddleboard or kayak, and day-trip to wild Bokor National Park. Sleepier Kep offers its famous Crab Market, hiking in Kep National Park and hidden resorts to escape from it all. Crumbling half-century-old villas in both towns offer glimpses of a time when these were prime destinations for Phnom Penh's privileged few.

Battambang

6 This is the real Cambodia, far from the jet-set destinations of Phnom Penh and Siem Reap. Unfurling along the banks of the Sangker River, Battambang is one of the country's best-preserved colonial-era towns. Streets of French shophouses host everything from fair-trade

Cambodian Fight Club

The whole world knows about *muay Thai* (Thai boxing) and the sport of kickboxing, but what is not so well known is that this contact sport probably originated in Cambodia. *Pradal serey* (literally 'free fighting') is Cambodia's very own version of kickboxing.

An even older martial art is *bokator*, or *labokatao*, which some say dates back to the time of Angkor. It translates as 'pounding a lion' and was originally conceived for battlefield confrontations. Weapons include bamboo staffs and short sticks, as well as the *krama* (scarf) in certain situations.

Food & Drink

Fruit Cambodia is blessed with many tropical fruits and sampling these is an integral part of a visit to the country. The fruits most popular with visitors include the *mongkut* (mangosteen) and *sao mao* (rambutan).

Prahoc Fermented fish paste forms the backbone of Khmer cuisine. Built around this are the flavours that give the cuisine its kick: the secret roots, the welcome herbs and the aromatic tubers.

Rice Rice from Cambodia's lush fields is the principal staple, enshrined in the Khmer word for 'eating' or 'to eat', *nyam bai* – literally 'eat rice'. Many a Cambodian, particularly drivers, will run out of steam if they run out of rice. It doesn't matter that the same carbohydrates are available in other foods, it is rice and rice alone that counts.

Salads Cambodian salad dishes are popular and delicious, although they're quite different from the Western idea of a cold salad. *Phlea sait kow* is a beef and vegetable salad, flavoured with coriander, mint and lemongrass. These three herbs find their way into many Cambodian dishes.

PETER PTSCHELINZEW / GETTY IMAGES ©

Temple interior, Kampot

cafes to bike excursions. Beyond the town lies the Cambodian countryside and a cluster of ancient temples – while they're not exactly Angkor Wat, they do, mercifully, lack the crowds. Further afield is Prek Toal Bird Sanctuary, a world-class bird sanctuary. Battambang in a word? Charming.

When to Go

HIGH SEASON
(Nov–Mar)

➡ Cool and windy; the best all-round time to be here.

➡ Book accommodation in advance during the peak Christmas and New Year period.

SHOULDER
(Jul–Aug)

➡ Wet in most parts of Cambodia, with high humidity, but the landscapes are emerald green.

➡ South coast can be busy as Western visitors escape for summer holidays while school is out.

LOW SEASON
(Apr–Jun & Sep–Oct)

➡ April and May spells hot season, when the mercury hits 40°C and visitors melt.

➡ September and October can be wet.

Kratie

7 Gateway to the rare freshwater Irrawaddy dolphins of the Mekong River, Kratie is emerging as a busy crossroads on the overland route between Phnom Penh and northeastern Cambodia or southern Laos. The town has a certain decaying colonial grandeur and boasts some of the country's best Mekong sunsets. Nearby Koh Trong is a relaxing place to experience a homestay or explore on two wheels. North of Kratie lies the Mekong Discovery Trail, with adventures and experiences themed around the mother river, including community-based homestays, bicycle rides and boat trips.

Prasat Preah Vihear

8 The mother of all mountain temples, Prasat Preah Vihear stands majestically atop the Dangkrek Mountains, forming a controversial border post between Cambodia and Thailand. The foundation stones of the temple stretch to the edge of the cliff as it falls precipitously away to the plains below, and the views across northern Cambodia are incredible. The 300-year chronology of its construction also offers an insight into the metamorphosis of carving and sculp-

Best on Film

Apocalypse Now (1979) In Francis Ford Coppola's masterpiece, a renegade colonel, played by Marlon Brando, goes AWOL in Cambodia. Martin Sheen plays a young soldier sent to bring him back, and the ensuing encounter makes for one of the most powerful indictments of war ever made.

The Killing Fields (1984) This definitive film on the Khmer Rouge period in Cambodia tells the story of American journalist Sydney Schanberg and his Cambodian assistant Dith Pran during and after the war.

Best in Print

Cambodia's Curse (Joel Brinkley; 2011) Pulitzer Prize–winning journalist pulls no punches in his criticism of the government and donors alike.

Cambodia Now (Karen Coates; 2005) A no-holds-barred look at contemporary Cambodia through the eyes of its diverse population.

The Gate (François Bizot; 2004) Bizot was kidnapped by the Khmer Rouge, and later held by them in the French embassy.

Getting Around

Air Relatively expensive domestic flights link Phnom Penh and Siem Reap.

Bicycle Cambodia is a great country for adventurous cyclists.

Boat Less common than in the old days of bad roads, but Siem Reap to either Battambang or Phnom Penh remain popular routes.

Bus The most popular form of transport for most travellers, connecting all major towns and cities.

Car & Motorcycle Private car or 4WD is an affordable option for those who value time above money. Exploring Cambodia by motorcycle is an amazing way to travel for experienced riders.

ture during the Angkorian period. It's all about location, though, and it doesn't get better than this.

Ratanakiri

9 The setting for Colonel Kurtz's jungle camp in *Apocalypse Now*, Ratanakiri is one of Cambodia's most remote and pretty provinces. Home to Virachey National Park, one of the largest protected areas in the country, this is serious trekking country. Possible animal encounters here include elephants and gibbons. Swimming is popular too, with jungle waterfalls

and a beautiful crater lake within striking distance of provincial capital Ban Lung. Home to a diverse mosaic of ethnic-minority people, Ratanakiri is a world away from lowland Cambodia.

Siem Reap

10 Buzzing Siem Reap, with a superb selection of restaurants and bars, is the base for temple exploration. Beyond town lie floating villages on the Tonlé Sap lake, adrenaline-fuelled activities like quad biking and ziplining, and such cultured pursuits as cooking classes and birdwatching.

Floating house, Tonlé Sap lake

FELIX HUG / GETTY IMAGES ©

Traditional huts, Mandara Mountains

CAPITAL
Yaoundé

POPULATION
23.1 million

AREA
475,440 sq km

OFFICIAL
LANGUAGES
English, French

Cameroon

Here at the crossroads of West and Central Africa, Cameroon, home to diverse peoples and cultures, spans the spectrum of signature African landscapes,

Cameroon is Africa's throbbing heart, a crazed, sultry mosaic of active volcanoes, white-sand beaches, thick rainforest and magnificent parched landscapes broken up by the bizarre rock formations of the Sahel. With both Francophone and Anglophone regions, not to mention some 263 ethnic groups, (speaking around 230 local languages), the country is a vast ethnic and linguistic jigsaw, yet one that, in contrast to so many of its neighbours, enjoys a great deal of stability.

Cameroon's coast is lapped by the languid waters of the Gulf of Guinea and its landscape extends from the steamy tropical beaches of the south and even steamier rainforests of the interior to the semi-deserts of the Sahelian north.

With good infrastructure, travel is a lot easier here than in many parts of Africa. Still, you'll miss none of those indicators that you're in the middle of this fascinating continent: everyone seems to be carrying something on their heads, makossa music sets the rhythm, the streets smell like roasting plantains and African bliss is just a piece of grilled fish and a frosty beer away.

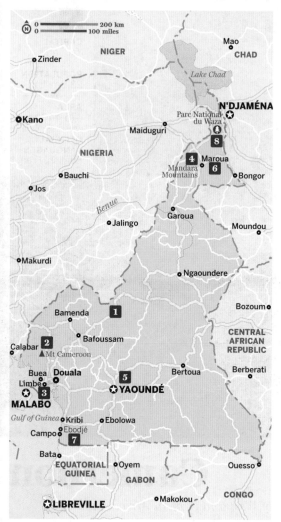

Mount Cameroon

2 Most hikes to the summit of West Africa's highest peak take two or three days, but it's no stroll in the park. The difficulty stems not only from its height (4095m), but from the fact that you start from near sea level, making a big change in altitude in a relatively short distance. November to April is the main climbing season, although it's possible to climb the mountain year-round.

Limbe

3 Limbe is a charming place, blessed with a fabulous natural position between the rainforest-swathed foothills of Mt Cameroon and the dramatic Atlantic coastline. Popular with both foreign and Cameroonian tourists, this is a great spot to chill on the beach for a few days. The Limbe Wildlife Centre contains rescued chimpanzees, gorillas, drills and other primates, all housed in large enclosures, with lots of interesting information about local conservation issues.

Mandara Mountains

4 Basalt cliffs dot a volcanic plain, dust storms conceived on the Nigerian border sweep out of the sunset onto thorn trees, red rock cairns and herds of brindle cattle...and frankly, you wouldn't be half surprised to see a cowboy or a dragon or both pass across this awesome, evocative landscape. The Mandara Mountains run west from Maroua to the Nigerian border and have become very popular – justifiably so – with Africa hikers.

Cameroon's
Top Experiences

Ring Road

1 The northwest highlands bear the pretty name 'Grassfields', an appellation too pleasant to really encapsulate this landscape. These aren't gentle fields; they're green and yellow valleys, tall grass, red earth and sharp mountains. Clouds of mist rise with wood smoke from villages speckled on this deceptively inviting terrain. The 367km Ring Road runs around the Grassfields, and if it were in better shape, it'd be one of Cameroon's great scenic drives.

President's Palace, Yaoundé

Yaoundé

5 Let's be brutally honest: West Africa is famous for many things, but pleasant cities – especially capitals – are not among them. Then Yaoundé comes along: green and spread over seven hills, though not exactly a garden city, it's planned, thoughtfully laid out and self-contained. While it is nowhere near as vibrant (or chaotic) as its coastal rival Douala, it enjoys a temperate climate, relatively clean and well-maintained streets and even boasts a host of 1970s government buildings in various exuberant styles that will keep architecture fans happy.

Sahel at Maroua

6 Wander the surreal streets of the crossroads of the Sahel at Maroua. If you've seen *Star Wars* and remember Mos Eisley, spaceport in the desert, you know exactly what Maroua looks like: low, brown streets running like dry riverbeds between squat beige buildings, all of it overtaken day and night by a colourful cast – Fulani, Chadians, etc – in robes of sky blue, electric purple and blood red, as if their clothes contain all the colours that have been leeched out of the surrounding sun-swept semi-desert.

Ebodjé

7 Ebodjé, a small fishing village 25km north of Campo, is home to a sea turtle conservation project and ecotourism site run by

if Cameroon were 100 people

31 would be Cameroon Highlanders
19 would be Equatorial Bantu
11 would be Kirdi
10 would be Fulani
29 would be other

belief systems
(% of population)

40 indigenous beliefs

40 Christian

20 Muslim

population per sq km

CAMEROON   USA   NIGERIA

👤 ≈ 15 people

When to Go

NOV–FEB

➡ It's dry but not too hot, though you can usually expect a harmattan haze.

FEB

➡ Join athletes running to the summit of Mt Cameroon in the Race of Hope.

OCT

➡ Cameroon's biggest festival, Tabaski, takes place, most impressively in Foumban.

National Football Team

Cameroon exploded onto the world's sporting consciousness at the 1990 World Cup when the national football team, the Indomitable Lions, became the first African side to reach the quarter-finals.

Football is truly the national obsession. Every other Cameroonian male seems to possess the team's strip; go into any bar and there'll be a match playing on the TV.

When Cameroon narrowly failed to qualify for the 2006 World Cup, the country's grief was almost tangible.

In contrast, when Cameroon qualified for the 2010 World Cup, the nation exploded into wild celebration. This qualification marked the sixth time Cameroon had entered the tournament, setting a record for any African nation.

Food & Drink

Cameroonian cuisine is more functional than flavourful. The staple dish is some variety of peppery sauce served with starch – usually rice, pasta or *fufu* (mashed yam, corn, plantain or couscous).

One of the most popular sauces is *ndole*, made with bitter leaves similar to spinach and flavoured with smoked fish.

Grilled meat and fish are eaten in huge quantities. Street snacks include fish or *brochettes* (kebabs).

Beer is incredibly popular and widely available, even in the Muslim north.

Street snacks are generally very cheap, but prices for a main meal increase dramatically in sit-down restaurants and business hotels outside of the major cities.

PETER PERRY / GETTY IMAGES ©

Giraffes, Parc National du Waza

KUDU Cameroun. Visitors are taken out at night to spot egg-laying turtles, although there's no guarantee you'll see any. Even if you don't see any turtles, the beach is gorgeous, pristine and better than anything you'll see in Kribi. Plus the sense of silence and starry-skyness as night falls in the village, which lacks electricity, is magical.

Parc National du Waza

8 The most accessible of Cameroon's national parks, Parc National du Waza is also the best for viewing wildlife. While it can't compare with East African parks, you're likely to see elephants, hippos, giraffes, antelopes and – with luck – lions. Late March to April is the best time for viewing, as the animals congregate at water holes before the rains. Waza is also notable for its particularly rich birdlife. The park is closed during the rainy season. A guide is obligatory in each vehicle. Walking isn't permitted.

Getting Around

Air Internal flights connect Douala and Yaoundé to Maroua and Garoua.

Bus *Agences de voyages* (agency buses) run along all major and many minor routes in Cameroon. Prices are low and fixed, and on some bus lines you can even reserve a seat.

Car Driving in Cameroon is perfectly feasible, with decent roads and no police harassment. You can hire cars in all large towns but it is very expensive, partly because you'll need a 4x4 for most itineraries and this becomes essential in the rainy season.

Train Cameroon's rail system operates three main lines. Yaoundé to N'Gaoundéré is of most interest to travellers, as it's the main way to get between the southern and northern halves of the country.

Emerald Lake, Yoho National Park, British Columbia

Canada

Canada is more than its hulking mountain, craggy-coast good looks: it also cooks extraordinary meals, rocks cool culture and unfurls wild, moosespotting road trips.

The globe's second-biggest country has an endless variety of landscapes. Sky-high mountains, glinting glaciers, spectral rainforests and remote beaches are all here, spread across six times zones. It's the backdrop for plenty of ah-inspiring moments – and for a big provincial menagerie. That's big as in polar bears, grizzly bears, whales and, everyone's favorite, moose.

The arts are an integral part of Canada's cultural landscape, from the International Fringe Theater Festival in Edmonton to mega museums such as Ottawa's National Gallery. Montreal's Jazz Festival and Toronto's starstudded Film Festival draw global crowds.

Sip a *café au lait* and tear into a flaky croissant at a sidewalk bistro in Montréal; head to an Asian night market and slurp noodles in Vancouver; join a wild-fiddling Celtic party on Cape Breton Island; kayak between rainforest-cloaked aboriginal villages on Haida Gwaii: Canada is incredibly diverse across its breadth and within its cities. You'll hear it in the music, see it in the arts and taste it in the cuisine.

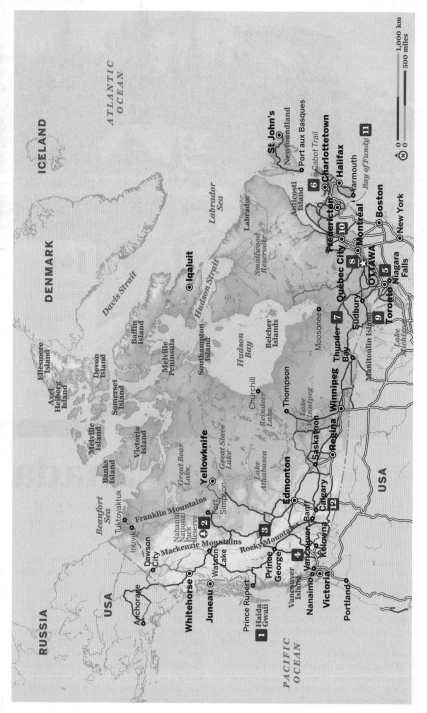

Canada's
Top Experiences

Haida Gwaii

1 Once known as the Queen Charlotte Islands, this dagger-shaped archipelago 80km off British Columbia's coast is a magical trip for those who make it. Colossal spruce and cedars cloak the wild, rain-sodden landscape. Bald eagles and bears inhabit the ancient forest, while sea lions and orcas patrol the waters. But the islands' real soul is the resurgent Haida people, best known for their war canoe and totem pole carvings. See the lot at Gwaii Haanas National Park Reserve, which combines lost Haida villages, burial caves and hot springs with some of the continent's best kayaking.

Nahanni National Park Reserve

2 Gorgeous hot springs, haunted gorges and gorging grizzlies fill this remote park near the Yukon border, and you'll have to fly in to reach them. Only about 1000 visitors per year make the trek, half of them paddlers trying to conquer the South Nahanni River. Untamed and spectacular, it churns 500km through the Mackenzie Mountains. Thirty-story waterfalls, towering canyons and legends of giants and lost gold round out the journey north.

Totem poles, Gwaii Haanas National Park Reserve, Haida Gwaii

PETER RYAN / GETTY IMAGES ©

The Rockies

3 The sawtooth of white-topped mountains straddling the BC/Alberta border inspires both awe and action. Four national parks – Banff, Yoho, Kootenay and Jasper – offer opportunities for hiking, kayaking and skiing. The train provides another popular way to experience the grandeur: luminous lakes, jumbles of wildflowers and glistening glaciers glide by as the steel cars chug up mountain passes and down river valleys en route to points east or west. View of Mt Robson, Mt Robson Provincial Park, British Columbia

Vancouver

4 Vancouver always lands atop the 'best places to live' lists, and who's to argue? Sea-to-sky beauty surrounds the laid-back, cocktail-lovin' metropolis. With skiable mountains on the outskirts, 11 beaches fringing the core and Stanley Park's thick rainforest just blocks from downtown's glass skyscrapers, it's a harmonic convergence of city and nature. It also mixes Hollywood chic (many movies are filmed here) with a freewheeling counterculture (a popular nude beach and the Marijuana Party political headquarters) and buzzing multicultural communities.

if Canada were 100 people

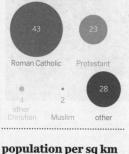

28 would be of British Isles origin
23 would be of French origin
15 would be of other European origin
34 would be of other origin

belief systems

(% of population)

43 Roman Catholic
23 Protestant
4 other Christian
2 Muslim
28 other

population per sq km

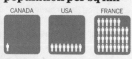

CANADA   USA   FRANCE

👤 ≈ 4 people

Niagara Falls

5 Crowded? Cheesy? Well, yes. Niagara is short, too – it barely cracks the top 500 worldwide for height. But come on, when those great muscular bands of water arc over the precipice like liquid glass, roaring into the void below, and when you sail toward it in a mist-shrouded little boat, Niagara Falls impresses big time. In terms of sheer volume, nowhere in North America beats its thundering cascade, with more than one million bathtubs of water plummeting over the edge every second.

Cabot Trail

6 The 300km Cabot Trail winds and climbs over coastal mountains, with heart-stopping sea views at every turn, breaching whales just offshore, moose nibbling roadside and plenty of trails to stop and hike. Be sure to tote your dancing shoes – Celtic and Acadian communities dot the area, and their foot-stompin', crazy-fiddlin' music vibrates through local pubs.

Trans-Canada Highway

7 Canada's main vein stretches 7800km from St John's, Newfoundland to Victoria, BC and takes in the country's greatest hits along the way. Gros Morne National Park, Cape Breton Island, Québec City, Banff National Park and Yoho National Park are part of the path, as are major cities including Montréal, Ottawa, Calgary and Vancouver. It takes most road-trippers a good month to drive coast to coast, so what are you waiting for? Fuel up, cue the tunes, and put the pedal to the metal.

Hockey

Canadians aren't fooling around when it comes to hockey. They play hard and well. Grassroots hockey, aka pond hockey, takes place in communities across the country every night on a frozen surface. All you need is a puck, a hockey stick and a few friends to live the dream.

Hockey is Canada's national passion and if you're visiting between October and April taking in a game is mandatory (as is giving a shout-out to the nation's 2010 Olympic gold medal-winning team).

Vancouver, Edmonton, Calgary, Toronto, Ottawa, Winnipeg and Montréal all have NHL teams who skate hard and lose the odd tooth. Minor pro teams and junior hockey clubs fill many more arenas with rabid fans.

Food & Drink

Beavertails Fried, sugared dough.

Beef Alberta is the nation's beef capital and you'll find top-notch Alberta steak on menus at leading restaurants across the country.

Lobster The main dish of the east, boiled in the pot and served with a little butter. Dip into some chunky potato salad and hearty seafood chowder while waiting for your crustacean to arrive.

Maktaaq Whale skin cut into small pieces and swallowed whole.

Maple Syrup Québec is the world's largest maple-syrup producer, processing around 6.5 million gallons of the sweet pancake accompaniment every year.

Prairie Oysters Bull's testicles prepared in a variety of ways designed to take your mind off their origin.

Poutine French fries topped with gravy and cheese curds.

Seal Northern speciality served boiled.

Stanley Park, Vancouver

Montréal Jazz Festival

8 Where else can you join more than two million calm, respectful music lovers (no slam dancing or drunken slobs) and watch the best jazz-influenced musicians in the world, choosing from 500 shows, many of which are free? Only in Montréal, Canada's second-largest city and its cultural heart. The good times roll 24/7.

Manitoulin Island

9 The largest freshwater island in the world and floating right smack in Lake Huron's midst, Manitoulin is a slowpoke place of beaches and summery cottages. Jagged expanses of white quartzite and granite outcroppings edge the shoreline and lead to shimmering vistas. First Nations culture pervades, and the island's eight communities collaborate to offer local foods (wild rice, corn soup) and eco-adventures (canoeing, horseback riding, hiking). Powwows add drumming, dancing and stories to the mix.

When to Go

HIGH SEASON (Jun–Aug)

➡ Sunshine and warm weather prevail; far northern regions briefly thaw Accommodation prices peak.

➡ December through March is equally busy and expensive in ski resort towns.

SHOULDER (May, Sep & Oct)

➡ Crowds and prices drop off.

➡ Temperatures are cool but comfortable.

➡ Attractions keep shorter hours.

➡ Fall foliage areas (ie Cape Breton, Québec) remain busy.

LOW SEASON (Nov–Apr)

➡ Places outside the big cities and ski resorts close.

➡ Darkness and cold take over.

➡ April and November are particularly good for bargains.

Old Québec City

10 Québec's capital is more than 400 years old, and its stone walls, glinting-spired cathedrals and jazz-soaked corner cafes suffuse it with atmosphere, romance, melancholy, eccentricity and intrigue on par with any European city. The best way to soak it up is to walk the Old Town's labyrinth of lanes and get lost amid the street performers and cozy inns, stopping every so often for a *café au lait*, flaky pastry or heaped plate of poutine (fries smothered in cheese curds and gravy) to refuel.

Best on Film

Away from Her (directed by Sarah Polley; 2006) Alzheimer's breaks apart a rural Ontario couple.

Bon Cop, Bad Cop (directed by Eric Canuel; 2006) An Anglophone and Francophone join forces; one of Canada's top-grossing films.

C.R.A.Z.Y. (directed by Jean-Marc Vallée; 2005) A teen misfit in 1970s Montréal dreams of a brighter future.

Incendies (directed by Denis Villeneuve; 2010) Québec siblings travel to the Middle East and uncover their immigrant mother's tortured history.

Best in Print

Beautiful Losers (Leonard Cohen; 1966) Experimental oddity involving love, sex and Aboriginals.

Indian Horse (R Wagamese; 2012) A culturally displaced Ojibway boy grows up to become a hockey star.

The View from Castle Rock (Alice Munro; 2006) Short stories that merge fiction and family history by the 2013 Nobel Prize winner for Literature.

Getting Around

Air Air Canada operates the largest domestic-flight network, serving some 150 destinations.

Boat Public ferry systems operate extensively in British Columbia, Québec and the Maritime provinces.

Bus Buses are generally clean, comfortable and reliable.

Car An extensive highway system links most towns. The Trans-Canada Hwy stretches from Newfoundland to Vancouver Island. Distances can be deceivingly long and travel times slow due to single-lane highways. All major rental-car companies are readily available.

Train Outside the Toronto– Montréal corridor, train travel is mostly for scenic journeys.

Bay of Fundy

11 This ain't your average bay, though light houses, fishing villages and other maritime scenery surround it. The unique geography of Fundy results in the most extreme tides in the world. And they stir up serious whale food. Fin whales, humpbacks, endangered North Atlantic right whales and blue whales swim in to feast, making whale watching here extraordinary. Tidal bore rafting, where outfitters harness the blasting force of Fundy's waters, is another unique activity.

Calgary Stampede

12 You can always find a few cowboys kicking up dust in booming, oil-rich Calgary. But when you look down and everyone is wearing pointy-toe boots, it must be mid-July, time for the Stampede. Bucking broncos, raging bulls and lasso-wielding guys in Stetsons converge for the 'Greatest Outdoor Show on Earth,' which highlights western rodeo events and chuckwagon racing. A huge midway of rides and games makes the event a family affair.

Ponto do Sol, Santo Antão

CAPITAL
Praia

POPULATION
531,046

AREA
4,033 sq km

OFFICIAL LANGUAGE
Portuguese

Cape Verde

Rising from the Atlantic 500km off the coast of West Africa, the islands of Cape Verde are at once unmistakeably African and a world away from the continent

Set sail with the Saharan trade winds and rock and roll across stormy Atlantic seas for days. Then, just before you're halfway to Brazil, an island rises into view. You have reached Cape Verde, an arrow-shaped archipelago that is the region's most Westernised country, where the people are richer and better educated than almost anywhere on the continent.

Though it may appear as a set of flyspecks poking out of the eastern Atlantic, this 10-island archipelago packs a punch. On Santo Antão, craggy peaks hide piercing green valleys of flowers and sugar cane, ideal for epic hikes. São Vicente is home to the cultural capital of the islands, Mindelo, which throbs with bars and music clubs. On Boa Vista, Sal and Maio, wispy white dunes merge with indigo-blue seas on unspoiled beaches of soft sand. Throw in the constant beat of music that Cape Verde is famed for and the renowned *morabeza* (Creole for hospitality) of its people and you'll see why many have come – and never left

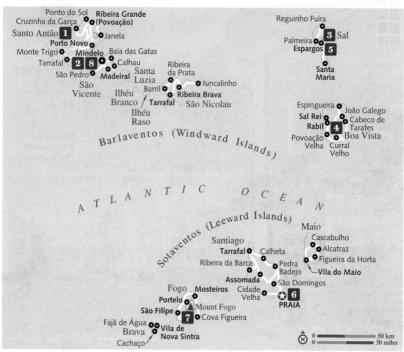

Cape Verde's
Top Experiences

Santo Antão

1 Dramatic canyons, cloud-soaked peaks and vertigo-inspiring drops all help to make Santo Antão a hiker's paradise. Walks here cover all ranges of abilities, from gentle hour-long valley hikes to strenuous ascents only for the fittest. The classic hike is from the Cova crater (1170m), with its fascinating patchwork of farms, down to the stunning Valé do Paúl.

Mardi Gras

2 There's nothing like it anywhere else in Africa. Taking the best African beats and mixing it up with a healthy dose of Latin style and Brazilian sex appeal, the result is one sultry, raunchy party you'll never forget. Preparations begin several months in advance and on Sunday you can see the various groups practising for the procession. The saucy costumes are worn only on Mardi Gras Tuesday.

Sal

3 The good news is the beach on Sal is the beach of Santa Maria. A sublime strip of gentle sand and ever-so-blue waters with world-class windsurfing and lots of fun-in-the-sun activities. But avert your eyes from this view and you're in for a shock. Santa Maria, the king of Cape Verdean resorts, is a grim, wind-battered building site that in places resembles a war zone more than an international holiday resort.

Boa Vista

4 With its feathery lines of peachy dunes, stark plains and scanty oases, Boa Vista looks as if a chunk of the Sahara somehow broke off the side of Africa and floated out to the middle of the Atlantic. Though the island offers some fantastic if wind-blown beaches, incredible windsurfing, the pretty little town of Sal Rei, and an ever-increasing number of resorts and hotels, it's the desert interior that is the best reason for venturing out here. Be ready for some rough off-roading, as most of Boa Vista's roads are treacherous.

Pedra do Lume

5 On Espargos a great attraction is the surreal,

Fontainhas village, Santo Antão

lunarlike Pedra do Lume, the crater of an ancient volcano where seawater is transformed into shimmering salt beds. You can see the old salt-extraction machinery of the 1805 plant; float in the medicinal salt water; have a massage, salt scrub or mud treatment at the small Salinas Relax spa; and have a meal at the restaurant. Other points of interest include the fish market in Palmeira, the gorgeous Igrejinha beach at the far-eastern end of Santa Maria and the Buracona natural swimming pool.

Praia

6 Cape Verde's capital and largest city, Praia, has the sprawling suburbs of any developing city. In the centre, standing on a large fortresslike plateau (hence the name Platô) and overlooking the ocean, is an attractive old quarter with enough to keep you occupied for a day. During your ambles around the multihued streets of the old Platô quarter, be sure to spend some time ferreting around the small food market.

Mount Fogo

7 The conical volcano, shrouded in black cinder, rises dramatically out of the floor of an ancient crater known as Chã das Caldeiras ('Chã'). Bound by a half-circle of precipitous cliffs, Chã was born when, sometime in the last 100,000 years, some 300 cu km of the island collapsed and slid

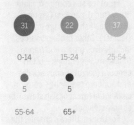

if Cape Verde were 100 people

71 would be Creole
28 would be African
1 would be European

....

age structure (years)
(% of population)

31	22	37
0-14	15-24	25-54

5	5
55-64	65+

....

population per sq km

CAPE VERDE   PORTUGAL   SENEGAL

♦ ≈ 25 people

When to Go

AUG–OCT
➡ During the so-called rainy, but very hot, season, weeks can go by without a downpour.

DEC–APR
➡ Strong winds blow in dust all the way from the Sahara and make it the best time for surfing.

JUN–OCT
➡ Turtle-watching season (February to May is whale-watching time).

Cesária Évora

Undisputed queen of the *morna* and Cape Verde's most famous citizen, Cesária Évora wowed the world with a voice at once densely textured and disarmingly direct.

Cesária vaulted to stardom in 1997 when, at the second annual all-African music awards, she ran away with three of the top gongs. Suddenly people around the world were swaying to the rhythms of Cape Verde's music, even if they couldn't point the country out on a map.

Évora left her native Mindelo in favour of Paris, but the 'barefoot diva' never put on airs; she was known to appear onstage accompanied by a bottle of booze and a pack of ciggies. When she died at 70 in 2011, after a bout of illness, Cape Verde declared two days of national mourning and the Mindelo airport was renamed in her honour. Her music legacy very much lives on.

Food & Drink

While Cape Verdean cuisine may include Portuguese niceties it's built on a firm African base, with *milho* (corn) and *feijão* (beans) the ubiquitous staples. To these the locals add *arroz* (rice), *batatas fritas* (fried potatoes) and *mandioca* (cassava).

From the sea come excellent *atum* (tuna), *garoupa* (grouper), *serra* (sawfish) and *lagosta* (lobster). Other protein sources include *ovos* (eggs) and *frango* (chicken). Vegetables – often *cenoura* (carrots), *couve* (kale) and *abóbora* (squash) – come in *caldeirada* (meat or fish stews), or simply steamed.

For drinks, there's *grogue*, the local sugar cane spirit; *ponch* (rum, lemonade and honey); some reasonable wines from Fogo; Strela, a decent bottled local beer; and, of course, Portuguese beers and wines. A decent caffeine fix is available everywhere, but tea is harder to find.

Music shop, Mindelo, São Vicente

into the sea to the east. The main cone has been inactive for more than 200 years, though there have been regular eruptions in Chã.

Mindelo

8 Set around a moon-shaped port and ringed by barren mountains, Mindelo is Cape Verde's answer to the Riviera, complete with cobblestone streets, candy-coloured colonial buildings and yachts bobbing in a peaceful harbour. Around a bend is the country's deepest industrial port, which in the late 19th century was a key coaling station for British ships and remains the source of the city's relative prosperity. Mindelo has long been the country's cultural centre, producing more than its share of poets and musicians, including the late Cesária Évora and it's still a fine place to hear *morna* while downing some *grogue*. Savvy locals, plus a steady flow of travellers, support a number of cool bistros and bars.

Getting Around

Air TACV serves all the inhabited islands except Brava and Santo Antão.

Boat The only reliable scheduled services are between Praia, Brava and Fogo, and between Mindelo (São Vicente) and Santo Antão. Seas can be rough and the crossings rocky, especially during winter months. It's always a good idea to bring a reserve of water and snacks.

Car You can rent cars on many islands, but the only three that make the expense worth it are Santiago, Boa Vista and possibly Fogo.

Minibus & Taxi Ranging from comfortable vans to pick-up trucks with narrow wooden benches, *aluguers* provide connections between even relatively small towns on most islands. They pick up people at unmarked points around town, set off when they're more or less full, and drop passengers off anywhere on the way, on request.

Diving off Little Cayman island

CAPITAL
George Town

POPULATION
53,737

AREA
264 sq km

OFFICIAL LANGUAGE
English

Cayman Islands

Laze on stunning beaches, scuba dive at world class sites and spot Grand Cayman's brilliant blue iguanas – the Cayman Islands are much more than just a tax haven.

What's so surprising about the three Cayman Islands at first is how un-British they are for a British territory – Grand Cayman seems straight from the US, with ubiquitous SUVs jostling for space at upscale malls and US dollars changing hands as if they were the national currency. Think of it as a much more orderly version of South Florida.

For many Grand Cayman *is* the Cayman Islands, with its glitzy shops, five-star hotels and lovely white-sand Seven Mile Beach. But go beyond its long western coastline and explore the low-key rest of the island to discover a Caribbean lifestyle. Or visit tiny Cayman Brac and Little Cayman, where life runs at a slow pace and the natural delights that see people coming back again and again – from birdwatching and hiking to diving and snorkeling – are never far away.

While synonymous worldwide with tax havens and beach holidays, the Cayman Islands appeal to those who want to avoid gaudy diversions and stop worrying after applying their sunscreen.

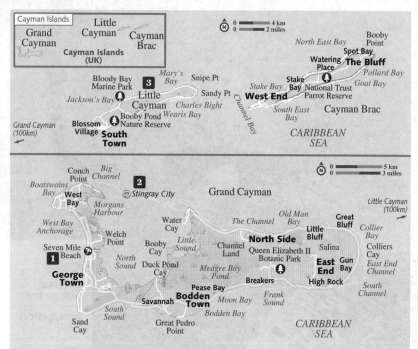

Cayman Islands'
Top Experiences

Seven Mile Beach

1 Although only 5½ miles long, this gorgeous strand of flawless white sand stretches north from George Town and anchors Grand Cayman's tourist industry. It's perfectly maintained and perennially popular.

Stingray City

2 This stretch of sandy seafloor in Grand Cayman's North Sound is the meeting place for southern stingrays hungry for a meal. As soon as you enter the water, several of the beautiful prehistoric-looking creatures will glide up to you to suck morsels of squid from your tentative fingers. Local boat tours include snorkeling gear and stops at other sites.

Little Cayman

3 While most visitors head for Grand Cayman, tiny Little Cayman is a joy. With more resident iguanas than humans, this delightful island is the place to head for solitude, tranquility and the odd spot of extraordinary diving. The world renowned Bloody Bay Marine Park, with its plummeting vertical wall, is a must for divers. Beach bums should try Owen Island.

Food & Drink

Conch This large pink mollusk is cooked with onion and spices in a stew, fried up as fritters, or sliced raw with a lime marinade.

Mannish water Stewy mixture of yams plus the head and foot of a goat; may cure impotency.

Tortuga rum cake A heavy, moist cake available in a number of addictive flavors.

When to Go

DEC–APR

➡ The best and busiest season with pleasant temperatures and low humidity.

MAY–OCT

➡ Rainfall is highest at this time with frequent afternoon showers that clear quickly.

JUL & AUG

➡ The hottest and most humid months when crowds dissipate and lodging rates fall.

Gorilla, Dzanga-Sangha National Park

CAPITAL
Bangui

POPULATION
5.2 million

AREA
622,984 sq km

OFFICIAL LANGUAGE
French

Central African Republic

Central African Republic is Africa at its most raw, where travellers can float along wild rivers into an Africa that the world thought no longer existed.

Central African Republic (CAR) is a country with staggeringly rare and untouched natural beauty and some of the world's most amazing wildlife. It's one of the best places in Africa for encounters with forest elephants and lowland gorillas, and perhaps the best place in the world to see butterflies.

It's also one of the most impoverished and least developed countries on the continent. For centuries CAR was worked over and ruthlessly exploited by colonisers; independence only brought more of the same from homegrown leaders. Yet the people of this plundered nation are open and friendly; just as rich life looms in its darkest jungles, warmth, generosity and pride steadfastly survive in the hearts of its people.

CAR's border crossings can be difficult and dangerous, and flights are expensive and infrequent. It is a country not for the faint of heart. At the time of writing most of the country was not considered stable or safe enough to travel through. Check the situation with your embassy before attempting to visit.

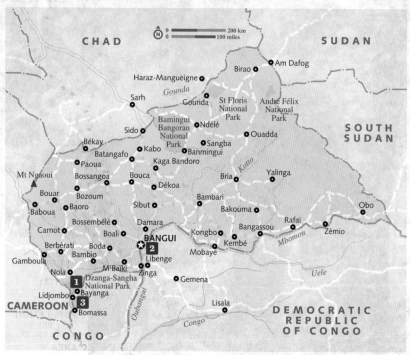

Central African Republic's
Top Experiences

Dzanga-Sangha National Park

1 Dzanga-Sangha National Park is even better than you dared hope it could be. This massive forest reserve sits at the heart of the Unesco World Heritage–listed Sangha Trinational Reserve. Get up close to lowland gorillas and elephants in this little-visited pocket of virgin rainforest.

Bangui

2 Bangui stretches along the Oubangui River with a row of lush green hills behind it. The French founded it in 1889, and by the 1970s it was known as La Coquette (The Beautiful). The moniker, still featured prominently around town, is a little ironic these days, though finally signs of rebirth are far more common than remnants of war.

Bayanga

3 Go out on an unforgettable hunting trip with the BaAka (a pygmy tribe) from Bayanga, a village outside the Dzanga-Sangha National Park. You can also join the BaAka in cultural activities, such as gathering medicinal plants, and the local Bantu residents take visitors out in pirogues to collect raffia palm wine.

Food & Drink

Manioc (also called cassava) is a staple in the Central African Republic; *ngunza* (manioc leaf salad) and *gozo* (manioc paste) are particular local favourites. You should also be sure to try locally brewed banana or palm wine.

When to Go

NOV–APR
➡ Warm weather and plenty of sunshine.

JUL–SEP
➡ The wettest months; roads get bad at this time, but the waterfalls are at their scenic peaks.

DEC–MAR
➡ The hottest time of year, with many days over 30°C.

Toubou tribesman, Ennedi

CAPITAL
N'Djamena

POPULATION
11.2 million

AREA
1.3 million sq km

OFFICIAL LANGUAGES
French, Arabic

Chad

Wave goodbye to your comfort zone and say hello to Chad, a rugged, arid, wind-blasted place and an experience that you'll never forget!

If Ghana and Gambia are Africa for beginners, Chad is Africa for the hard core. Travel here is tough. Many of the roads are broken due to years of conflict and lack of maintenance. There are few comfortable hotels and there is plenty of bureaucracy and demands for *cadeaux* (gifts) to negotiate. Added to that, the summer heat is mind-melting, travel costs can be astronomical and the security situation remains unpredictable.

So why bother, you may ask? Well, we could list the sublime oases lost in the northern deserts, tell you about the stampeding herds of wildlife in the national parks or the deep blue lure of a boat trip on Lake Chad. You may partake in the nation's feel good story as you strike out into the wild or you may find elegant, perfectly preserved shells of aquatic molluscs poking from the powdery sands of the Sahara.

Chad offers an opportunity to break with a comfortable Western world and come to a place that promises experiences, good and bad, that you'll be recalling forever.

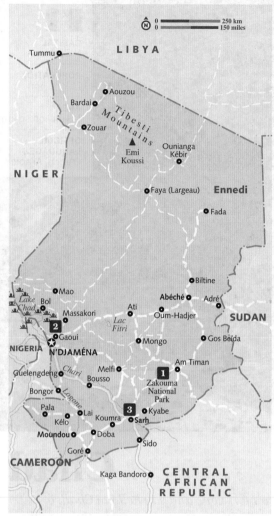

N
0 — 250 km
0 — 150 miles

LIBYA

Tummu

Aouzou

Bardai

Tibesti Mountains

Zouar

Emi Koussi

Ounianga Kébir

NIGER

Faya (Largeau)   Ennedi

Fada

Biltine

Mao   Abéché   Adré

Lake Chad   Bol   Massakori   Ati   Oum-Hadjer   SUDAN

2 Gaoui   *Lac Fitri*

NIGERIA   N'DJAMÉNA   Mongo   Gos Beïda

Melfi   Am Timan

Guelengdeng   *Chari*   Bousso   **1**

Bongor   *Logone*   Zakouma National Park

Pala   Lai   Koumra   **3** Sarh   Kyabe

Kélo   Moundou   Doba

Goré   Sido

CAMEROON   Kaga Bandoro   CENTRAL AFRICAN REPUBLIC

When to Go

NOV–JAN

➡ The coolest and thus best time for general travel.

MAR–APR

➡ The hottest months and best time to visit Zakouma National Park.

JUL–AUG

➡ The capital becomes waterlogged and road travel elsewhere slows dramatically.

Food & Drink

Tiny street stalls dish up rice, beans and soup or stew, while indoor restaurants offer omelettes, liver, salads, *brochettes* (kebabs), fish and *nachif* (minced meat in sauce).

To drink you have the usual range of *sucreries* (soft drinks), and fresh *jus*, fruit concoctions with more resemblance to smoothies. Beer is the favoured poison in bars, with a choice of local brews. Also popular is *bili-bili*, a millet beer; *cochette* is a low-alcohol version.

Chad's
Top Experiences

Zakouma National Park

1 Track herds of elephants and ogle dazzling birds in this sublime national park. Years of poaching and civil war ravaged local wildlife in this 305,000-hectare park, however, the government with the help of the EU has restocked the park and begun to implement anti-poaching measures.

Gaoui

2 Sigh over the beautiful painted houses of Gaoui, a fascinating village just minutes from N'Djaména. In a landscape of dusky browns, the brightly painted mud houses of the village of Gaoui bring colour to this otherwise drab world.

Sarh

3 See the green and pleasant side of sandy Chad and chill out along the Chari River. An agreeably sleepy town shaded by enormous trees, Sarh – the cotton capital of Chad – is little more than a provincial backwater. The Museé Regional de Sarh sold weapons, musical instruments and masks. Most nights at dusk, hippos feed on the banks of the Chari River.

Colchagua Valley

CAPITAL
Santiago

POPULATION
17.2 million

AREA
756,102 sq km

OFFICIAL LANGUAGE
Spanish

Chile

Chile is nature on a colossal scale, but travel here is surprisingly easy. Your trip can be as hard-core or as pampered as you like, but you'll always feel welcome.

Spindly Chile stretches 4300km – over half the continent – from the driest desert in the world to massive glacial fields. In between the Andes and the Pacific, the landscape is dotted with volcanoes, geysers, beaches, lakes, rivers, steppe and countless islands. What's on offer? Everything. In Chile, adventure is what happens on the way to having an adventure: explore sweeping desert solitude, craggy Andean summits, the lush forests of the fjords, first-class wine regions, up-and-coming surfing hot spots, even the exotic getaway of Rapa Nui (Easter Island). Of course, Chile is more than its striking geography: its far-flung location has fired the imagination of literary heavyweights and has been known to make poets out of bartenders and dreamers out of presidents. Closer borders have fostered intimacy with the Chilean people and rituals such as the sharing of maté tea and the welcoming attitude of *buena onda* (good vibes) are integral to the fabric of local life.

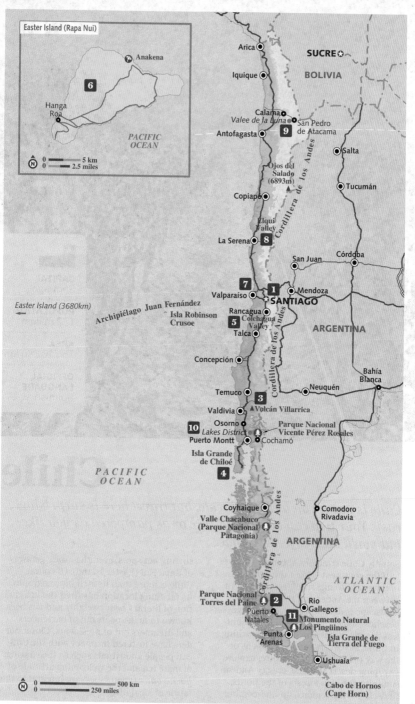

Easter Island (Rapa Nui)

Anakena

6

Hanga
Roa

*PACIFIC
OCEAN*

N   0   5 km
    0   2.5 miles

Arica

SUCRE

Iquique

BOLIVIA

Calama
Valee de la Luna   San Pedro
                    de Atacama
9

Antofagasta

Salta

Ojos del
Salado
(6893m)

Tucumán

Copiapó

Elqui
Valley

La Serena   **8**

Córdoba

San Juan

Valparaíso   **7**   **1**   Mendoza
            SANTIAGO

Rancagua
5   Colchagua
        Valley
Talca

Archipiélago Juan Fernández
Isla Robinson
Crusoe

ARGENTINA

Easter Island (3680km)

Concepción

Bahía
Blanca

Temuco   **3**

Neuquén

Valdivia   ▲ Volcán Villarrica

Osorno   Parque Nacional
10 *Lakes District*   Vicente Pérez Rosales
Puerto Montt   Cochamó

Isla Grande
de Chiloé
4

*PACIFIC
OCEAN*

Coyhaique

Comodoro
Rivadavia

Valle Chacabuco
(Parque Nacional
Patagonia)

ARGENTINA

*ATLANTIC
OCEAN*

Parque Nacional
Torres del Paine   **2**
        Puerto   Rio
        Natales   Gallegos
        11 Monumento Natural
                Los Pingüinos
        Punta
        Arenas   Isla Grande de
                Tierra del Fuego

Ushuaïa

Cordillera de los Andes

N   0   500 km
    0   250 miles

Cabo de Hornos
(Cape Horn)

Chile's
Top Experiences

Santiago's Barrio Bellas Artes

1 The name of this riverside neighborhood in central Santiago – Barrio Bellas Artes (Beautiful Art) – says it all. Fans of the fine arts can spend the day admiring Chilean works at the Museo Nacional de Bellas Artes and the Museo de Arte Contemporáneo, both housed in the stately Palacio de Bellas Artes, before checking out edgy modern photography and sculpture at the nearby Museo de Artes Visuales. Along the way, take a break at one of several sidewalk cafes along the cobblestoned pedestrian streets.

Parque Nacional Torres del Paine

2 Soaring almost vertically more than 2000m above the Patagonian steppe, the granite pillars of Torres del Paine (Towers of Paine) dominate the landscape of what may be South America's finest national park. Hike through howling steppe and winding forests to behold these holiest-of-holy granite spires. Las Torres may be the main attraction, but this vast wilderness has much more to offer. Ice trek the sculpted surface of Glacier Grey, kayak the calm Río Serrano or ascend John Gardner Pass for gaping views of the southern ice field.

Guanaco backdropped by the Torres del Paine

2

Climbing Volcán Villarrica

3 Few things are as menacing as a growling volcano, especially an eye-to-eye encounter from the crater's edge. That's exactly the sort of spectacular confrontation you volunteer for on the rewarding climb to the summit of Volcán Villarrica. Nothing quite prepares you for rounding the snow-capped edge of a 2847m sulfur-spewing menace. Then the snow-toboggan slide back down the mountain ensures heart rates remain on overdrive. But don't worry – it hasn't erupted since 1984!

if Chile were 100 people

95 would be white and white-Amerindian
4 would be Mapuche
1 would be other

belief systems
(% of population)

70 Roman Catholic

15 Evangelical

1 Jehovah's Witnesses

14 other

population per sq km

CHILE   CANADA   USA

⬆ ≈ 4 people

Churches of Chiloé

4 No matter how many European cathedrals, Buddhist monasteries or Islamic mosques you've seen, the cluster of 17th- and 18th-century wooden churches that make up Chiloé's Unesco World Heritage site will be unlike any previously encountered. Each an architectural marvel marrying European and indigenous design, boasting unorthodox colours and construction, these cathedrals were built by Jesuit missionaries working to convert pagans to the papacy. Their survival mirrors the Chilote people's own uncanny resilience.

Colchagua Valley Wine Tasting

5 Anyone who's tasted Chilean wine is already familiar with the charms of the Colchagua Valley, whether or not they're aware of it. The bright sunshine and rich soil of Chile's best-established wine region, located several hours south of Santiago, is responsible for some of the richest Cabernet Sauvignon in South America. Taste this famous vino straight from the barrels at wineries like the posh Lapostolle, the old-fashioned Viu Manent, or the up-and-coming Emiliana, an organic vineyard employing innovative biodynamic growing techniques.

Easter Island

6 The strikingly enigmatic *moai* (statues) are the most pervasive image of Easter Island (Rapa Nui). Dotted all around the island, these massive carved figures stand on stone platforms, like colossal puppets on a supernatural stage. Anakena Beach, Easter

The Chilean Mine Miracle

After suffering one of the largest earthquakes ever recorded in 2010, the world was watching again on October 13, 2010 when 33 Chilean miners who had been trapped for 69 days in the San José mine were hauled up one by one from 700m down in the earth. They emerged stumbling, blind as moles in the desert glare and the world sighed in collective relief for a small miracle.

Their survival was only possible because of a borehole that had penetrated their chamber 17 days into their ordeal. After the hole came a tube and what the Chileans called *palomas* – messenger doves. In these capsules, videos and love letters went up, baked pies and medication went down. It was the line that connected the surface to the depths, life to a world devoid of it, and billions of viewers to 33 anxious souls. Chile, no stranger to struggle, had something else. Solidarity.

Food & Drink

Maté A type of tea popular in Patagonia and made from the dried leaves of the yerba maté.

Pasteles Find these hearty baked casseroles, a traditional specialty made with *choclo* (corn), *carne* (meat), *jaiva* (crab) or *papas* (potatoes), in small towns and at family tables.

Pisco The grape brandy is mixed with fresh lemon juice and sugar to make the famous pisco sour cocktail.

Seafood Chile's long coastline means a bounty of fabulously fresh *pescados* (fish) and *mariscos* (shellfish) used in soups, stews and *ceviche* (marinated raw seafood).

Wine Chile's wine regions are rightfully world-famous; one varietal to try is Carmenere, a rich red that originated in Bordeaux but is now produced only here.

Island's stunning white-sand playground sandwiched between sparkling turquoise sea and cococunt groves is a special place to see these unqiue archaeological sites.

Valparaíso's Hills

7 It's the busy port that put Valparaíso on the map, but it's the city's steep *cerros* (hills) that have inspired generations of poets, artists, and philosophers. A maze of winding paths, colorfully painted cottages, antique elevators and glowing streetlamps climb up the hills, offering ever more dramatic views of the sea below.

Elqui Valley

8 Spend a few languid days in the lush Elqui Valley and you'll start to wax lyrical, or even channel Nobel Prize–winning poet Gabriela Mistral who grew up in these parts. Infused by poetry, pisco, pretty villages and star-sprinkled night skies, this is a wholesome land of spiritual retreats, ecofriendly inns, hilltop observatories and artisanal

When to Go

HIGH SEASON
(Nov–Feb)

➡ Patagonia is best December to February.

➡ Beaches throng with crowds from late December through January.

➡ Best time for ski resorts is June to August.

SHOULDER
(Sep–Nov & Mar–May)

➡ Good times to visit Santiago.

➡ The Lakes District is pleasant; April's fall foliage in the south.

➡ Wine country has its grape harvests and wine festivals (March).

LOW SEASON
(Jun–Aug)

➡ A good time to visit the north.

➡ Services are few on Carretera Austral, and mountain passes can be blocked by snow.

➡ Accommodation busy in July during winter vacation.

distilleries of the potent little grape. Sample food cooked solely by the sun's rays, get your aura cleaned, feast on herb-infused Andean fusion fare and ride the valley's mystic wave.

Valle de la Luna

9 See the desert don its surrealist cloak in Valle de la Luna as you stand atop a giant sand dune, with the sun slipping below the horizon and multicolored hues bathing the sands, all with a backdrop of distant volcanoes and the rippling Cordillera de la Sal.

The Lakes District

10 Don't judge a district by its name. The Lakes District, known as

Best on Film

The Maid (2009) A maid questions her lifelong loyalty.

Violeta Went to Heaven (2012) Emotional, unflinching biopic of rebel icon Violeta Parra.

Mi Mejor Enemigo (2005) Lost Argentine and Chilean soldiers cobble out a truce.

Best in Print

Voyage of the Beagle (Charles Darwin; 1839) Observes native fauna and volcanoes.

Motorcycle Diaries (Che Guevera; 1993) The road trip that made a revolutionary.

In Patagonia (Bruce Chatwin; 1977) Iconic work on Patagonian ethos.

Liberators: South America's Struggle for Independence (Robert Harvey; 2002) This very readable book tells the history of colonial Latin America through larger-than-life heroes and swashbucklers such as O'Higgins, San Martín and Lord Cochrane.

Getting Around

Air Time-saving flights have become more affordable in Chile and are sometimes cheaper than a comfortable long-distance bus. LAN and Sky are the main domestic carriers.

Boat Passenger/car ferries and catamarans connect Puerto Montt with points along the Carretera Austral, including Caleta Gonzalo (Chaitén) and Coyhaique. Ferries and catamarans also connect Quellón and Castro, Chiloé to Chaitén. A highlight is the trip from Puerto Montt to Puerto Natales on board Navimag's *Evangelistas*, a cargo ship outfitted for tourism.

Bus The Chilean bus system is fabulous. Tons of companies vie for customers with *ofertas* (seasonal promotions), discounts and added luxuries such as movies. Long-distance buses are comfortable, fast and punctual, and have safe luggage holds and toilets.

Car & Motorcycle Having wheels gets you to remote national parks and most places off the beaten track. This is especially true in the Atacama Desert, Carretera Austral and Rapa Nui (Easter Island).

Los Lagos in Spanish, only tells a part of the story of this ethereal landscape. While turquoise glacial lakes dominate, they're hardly the only attraction. Towering, perfectly conal, snowcapped volcanoes, charming lakeside hamlets, spectacular national parks, a long list of outdoor adventures and a unique, German-influenced Latin culture make for a cinematic region far beyond the *agua* (water).

Monumento Natural Los Pingüinos

11 Every year, 60,000 Magellanic penguin couples convene just off the coast of Punta Arenas on Isla Magdalena. Watching them waddle around, guard their nests, and feed their fluffy and oversized offspring makes for a superb wildlife-watching experience. The penguins reside on the island between October and March.

9

IGUR ALEKSANDER / GETTY IMAGES ©

Terracotta warriors, Xī'ān

CAPITAL
Beijing

POPULATION
1.3 billion

AREA
9.6 million sq km

OFFICIAL LANGUAGES
Mandarin, Cantonese

China

Antique yet up-to-the-minute, outwardly urban but quintessentially rural, conservative yet path-breaking, space-age but old-fashioned, China is a land of mesmerising contradictions.

China is modernising at a head-spinning pace, but slick skyscrapers and Lamborghini showrooms are little more than dazzling baubles. Let's face it: the world's oldest continuous civilisation is bound to pull an artefact or two out of its hat. After three decades of full-throttle development and socialist iconoclasm, you won't find history at every turn, but travel selectively in China and rich seams of antiquity pop into view amid tumble-down chunks of the Great Wall, temple-topped mountains, quaint villages and water towns.

Culinary exploration is also an enticing aspect of Middle Kingdom travel: wolf down Peking duck, size up a sizzling lamb kebab in Kāifēng or gobble down Lánzhōu noodles on the Silk Road. And don't forget about what's cooking along China's frontier lands – always an excellent reason to get off the beaten path.

And China is vast. Off-the-scale massive. You simply have to get outside: island-hop in Hong Kong, gaze over the epic grasslands of Inner Mongolia or squint up at the mind-blowing peaks of the Himalayas.

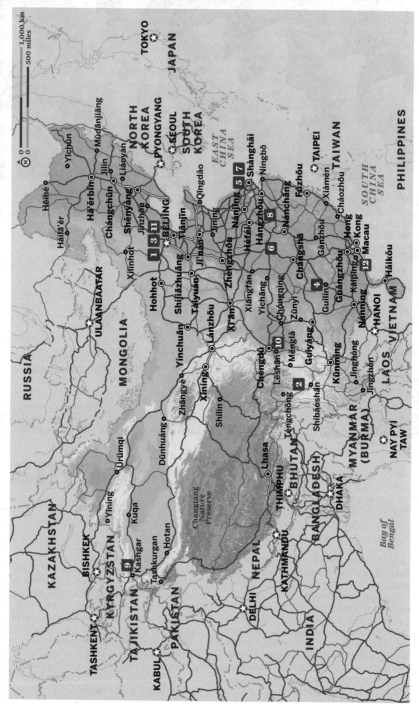

China's
Top Experiences

Great Wall

1 Spotting it from space is both tough and pointless: the only place you can truly put the Great Wall under your feet is in China. The most renowned examples undulate majestically over the peaks of Běijīng municipality but the Great Wall can be realistically visited in many north China provinces. Select the Great Wall according to taste: perfectly chiselled, dilapidated, stripped of its bricks, overrun with saplings, coiling splendidly into the hills or returning to dust. The fortification is a fitting symbol of those perennial Chinese traits: diligence, mass manpower, ambitious vision and engineering skill (coupled with a distrust of the neighbours).

Tiger Leaping Gorge

2 Picture snowcapped mountains rising on either side of a gorge so deep that you can be 2km above the river, rushing across the rocks far below. Then imagine winding up and down trails that pass through tiny farming villages, where you can rest while enjoying views so glorious they defy superlatives. Cutting through remote northwest Yúnnán for 16 spectacular kilometres, Tiger Leaping Gorge is a simply unmissable experience. Hikers returning from the gorge invariably give it glowing reviews.

CARACTERDESIGN / GETTY IMAGES ©

Forbidden City

3 Not a city and no longer forbidden, Běijīng's enormous palace is the be-all-and-end-all of dynastic grandeur, with its vast halls and splendid gates. No other place in China teems with so much history, legend and good old-fashioned imperial intrigue. You may get totally lost here but you'll always find something to write about on the first postcard you can lay your hands on.

Dragon's Backbone Rice Terraces

4 After a bumpy bus ride to northern Guǎngxī, you'll be dazzled by one of China's most archetypal and photographed landscapes: the splendidly named Dragon's Backbone Rice Terraces. The region is a patchwork of minority villages, with layers of waterlogged terraces climbing the hillsides. You'll be enticed into a game of village-hopping. The invigorating walk between Píng'ān and Dàzhài villages offers the most spine-tingling views. Visit after the summer rains when the fields are glistening with reflections.

if China were 100 people

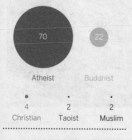

92 would be Han Chinese
8 would be ethnic minorities

belief systems
(% of population)

70　Atheist
22　Buddhist
4　Christian
2　Taoist
2　Muslim

population per sq km

CHINA　　NEPAL　　USA

≈ 35 people

The Bund, Shànghǎi

5 Shànghǎi is the country's neon-lit beacon of change and opportunity. It offers a taste of all the superlatives China can dare to dream up, from the world's highest observation deck to its largest underground theatre. Whether you're just pulling in after an epic 40-hour train trip from Xīnjiāng or it's your first stop, you'll find plenty to indulge in. Start with the Bund, Shànghǎi's iconic riverfront area where it all began.

Yangzi River Cruise

6 Snow melting from the world's 'third pole' – the high-altitude Tibet–Qīnghǎi plateau – is the source of China's mighty, life-giving Yangzi. The country's longest river, the Yangzi surges west–east across the nation. It reaches a crescendo with the Three Gorges, carved out over millennia by the inexorable persistence of the powerful waters. The gorges are a magnificent spectacle and a Yangzi River cruise is a rare chance to hang up your travelling hat, take a seat and watch the drama unfold.

French Concession, Shànghǎi

7 Once home to the bulk of Shànghǎi's adventurers, revolutionaries, gangsters, prostitutes and writers, the former French Concession is the most graceful part of Pǔxī. The Paris of the East turns on its European charms to maximum effect here, where leafy streets and 1920s villas meet art deco apartment blocks, elegant restaurants and chic bars. This is Shànghǎi at its hippest and most alluring.

Taichi

An ethereal form of moving meditation to some, an awesome arsenal of martial-arts techniques to others, taichi is quintessentially Chinese.

Zhang San Feng, a semi-legendary Wǔdāng Shān monk from the 10th or 13th century (depending on the source), is reputed to be the founder of taichi. Sitting on his porch one day, Zhang became inspired by a battle between a huge bird and a snake. The sinuous snake used flowing movements to evade the bird's attacks. The bird, exhausted, finally gave up and flew away.

Practicing taichi daily could add a decade or more to your lifespan or give you some handy moves for getting on crowded buses. And it's not all slow-going: Chen style has snappy elements of Shàolín boxing and it'll give you a leg-busting workout. Find a teacher and put some magic and mystery into your China adventure.

Food & Drink

Dim Sum Dim sum is steamed up across China, but Hong Kong, Macau and Guǎngzhōu set the benchmark.

Dumplings Head north and northeast for the best *jiǎozi* (dumplings) – leek, pork, lamb or crabmeat wrapped in an envelope of dough. If you like them crispy, get them *guōtiē* (fried). Shànghǎi's interpretation is *xiǎolóngbāo* – scrummy and steamed.

Hotpot Hotpots are ideal for banishing the bitter cold of a northern winter – though in steaming Chóngqìng old folk devour the spiciest variety in the height of summer.

Noodles Noodles offer an exciting spectrum of taste, from the wincingly spicy *dàndan miàn* (spicy noodles) through to the supersalty *zhájiàng miàn* (fried sauce noodles).

Peking Duck Purists insist you must be in Běijīng for true Peking duck, roasted to an amber hue over fruit tree wood.

NISA AND ULLI MAIER PHOTOGRAPHY / GETTY IMAGES ©

Huángshān & Hui Villages

8 Shrouded in mist and light rain more than 200 days a year, and maddeningly crowded most of the time, Huángshān has an appeal that attracts millions of annual visitors. Perhaps it's the barren landscape, or an otherworldly vibe on the mountain. Mist rolls in and out at will; spindly bent pines stick out like lone pins across sheer craggy granite faces. Not far from the base are the perfectly preserved Hui villages including Xīdì and Hóngcūn. Unesco, Ang Lee and Zhang Yimou were captivated – you will be too.

The Silk Road

9 There are other Silk Road cities in countries such as Uzbekistan and Turkmenistan, but it's in China where you get the feeling of stepping on the actual 'Silk Road', with its pervasive Muslim heritage and fragments from ancient Buddhist civilisations. Travel by bus and experience the route as ancient traders

When to Go

HIGH SEASON
(May–Aug)

➡ Prepare for crowds at traveller hotspots and summer downpours.

➡ Accommodation prices peak during the first week of the May holiday period.

SHOULDER
(Feb–Apr, Sep & Oct)

➡ In the north this is the optimum season, with fresh weather and clear skies.

➡ Accommodation prices peak during holidays in early October.

LOW SEASON
(Nov–Feb)

➡ Domestic tourism is at a low ebb, but things are busy and expensive for Chinese New Year.

➡ Weather is bitterly cold in the north and at altitude, and only warm in the far south.

once did. Kashgar is the ultimate Silk Road town and remains a unique melting pot of peoples, but Hotan is equally special: a rough-and-tumble town still clinging to bygone days.

Grand Buddha, Lèshān

10 You can read all the stats you like about Lèshān's Grand Buddha statue – yes, its ears really are 7m long! – but until you descend the steps alongside the world's tallest Buddha statue and stand beside its feet, with its toenails at the same level as your eyes, you can't really comprehend just how massive it is. Still not impressed? Consider then that this wonderful, riverside stone statue was carved painstakingly into the cliff face above you more than 1200 years ago.

Best on Film

Raise the Red Lantern (Zhang Yimou; 1991) The exquisitely fashioned tragedy from the sumptuous palette of the Fifth Generation.

Still Life (Jia Zhangke; 2005) Bleak and hauntingly beautiful portrayal of a family devastated by the construction of the Three Gorges Dam.

Best in Print

Diary of a Madman & Other Stories (Lu Xun) Astonishing tales from the father of modern Chinese fiction.

Dreaming in Chinese (Deborah Fallows) Insightful observations of living among Chinese people and learning Mandarin in China.

The Rape of Nanking (Iris Chang) Puts into perspective China's deep-rooted ambivalence towards its island neighbour, Japan.

Getting Around

Air Despite being a land of vast distances, it's quite straightforward to navigate your way terrestrially around China by rail and bus if you have time.

Bicycle Cycling through China allows you to go when you want, to see what you want and at your own pace. You will have virtually unlimited freedom of movement but, considering the size, terrain and infrastructure of China, you will need to combine your cycling days with trips by train, bus, boat, taxi or even planes.

Bus Long-distance bus services are extensive and reach places you cannot get to by train; with the increasing number of intercity highways, journeys are getting quicker.

Běijīng's Hútòng

11 To get under the skin of the capital, you need to get lost at least once in its enchanting, ancient alleyways. Hútòng are Běijīng's heart and soul; it's in these alleys that crisscross the centre of the city that you'll discover the capital's unique street life. Despite its march into the 21st century, Běijīng's true charms – heavenly courtyard architecture, pinched lanes and a strong sense of community – are not high-rise. It's easy to find that out; just check into a courtyard hotel and true Běijīng will be right on your doorstep.

Diāolóu in Kāipíng

12 If you only have time for one attraction in Guǎngdōng, Kāipíng's diāolóu should be it. Around 1800 outlandishly designed watchtowers and fortified residences scatter higgledy-piggledy in the farmland around Kāipíng, a town near Guǎngzhōu. These sturdy bastions built in the early 20th century may not be what you'd typically expect in the Middle Kingdom, but they inspire awe with their eccentric fusion of foreign and domestic architectural styles: Greek, Roman, Gothic, Byzantine and baroque.

10

FELIX HUG / GETTY IMAGES ©

Independence festivities, Cartagena

CAPITAL
Bogotá

POPULATION
45.7 million

AREA
1.1 million sq km

OFFICIAL LANGUAGE
Spanish

Colombia

File under Colombia: soaring Andean summits, unspoiled Caribbean coast, Amazon jungle, archaeological ruins and colonial communities. Colombia boasts all of South America's allure and more.

Forget everything you've ever heard about Colombia – for decades demonized, today Colombia is a safe, affordable, accessible and utterly thrilling destination.

Whatever you want, you'll find it here. Whether that's floating down Amazonian backwaters, wandering through perfectly preserved colonial towns, diving pristine Caribbean reefs or galloping on horseback along mountain ridges overlooking ancient indigenous burial sites, it's all in Colombia. Just to seal the deal, Colombians are friendly, welcoming and helpful people – they receive tourists like long-lost brothers and sisters.

Security improvements have driven the continent's longest-running civil conflict into all but the most remote and inaccessible areas of the country, where travelers have no reason to visit. And best of all many Colombians, for years caged in their cities, can now enjoy their beautiful country, too.

Yet still some people think it's all just cocaine and coffee. They couldn't be more wrong. Spend some real time here and fall head over heels for this intoxicating country.

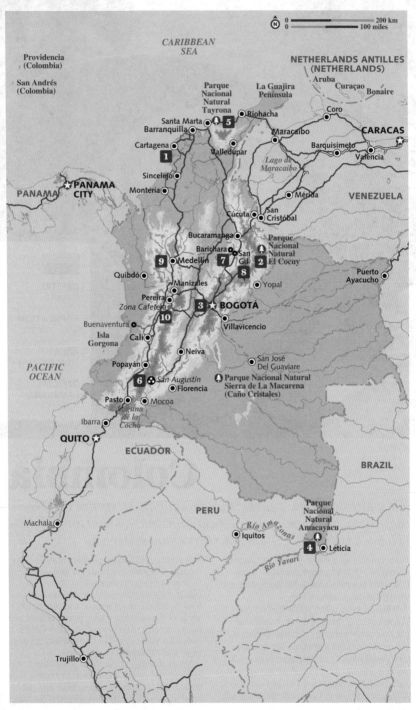

Colombia's
Top Experiences

Cartagena's
Old Town

1 The hands of the clock of the Puerta del Reloj wind back 400 years in an instant as visitors enter Cartagena's walled old town. Strolling the streets here is to step into the pages of a novel by Gabriel García Márquez. The pastel-toned balconies overflow with bougainvillea and the streets are abuzz with food stalls around magnificent, Spanish-built churches, squares and historic sites. This is a living, working town that just happens to look a lot like it did centuries ago.

Trekking in
El Cocuy

2 The weeklong Güicán–El Cocuy trek in Parque Nacional Natural (PNN) El Cocuy is one of Colombia's most coveted – and for good reason. In season (December to February), everything throughout the Sierra Nevada del Cocuy region is characterized by burnt-auburn sunrises that bounce off craggy peaks, and the páramo ecosystem of glacial valleys, mountain plains and high-altitude lakes. On clear days, the entire gorgeous swath of Los Llanos can be seen before you from the surrounding 4650m-high peak viewpoints.

Iglesia de San Pedro Claver, Old Town, Cartagena

Bogotá's Museo del Oros

3 There are few places in the world where one can get a sense of what finding a long-lost buried treasure might be like, but Bogotá's Museo del Oro – one of South America's most astonishing museums – will floor you with a sensation of Indiana Jones proportions. Over 55,000 pieces of spit-shined gold and other materials from all the major pre-Hispanic cultures in Colombia are exhibited thematically over three floors, culminating in the astonishing and intricate Balsa Muisca, found in 1969.

if Colombia were 100 people

58 would be mestizo   1 would be Amerindian
20 would be white
14 would be mulatto
4 would be black
3 would be mixed black-Amerindian

belief systems
(% of population)

90 Roman Catholic
2 No religious beliefs
8 Protestant

population per sq km

COLOMBIA   US   UK

👤 ≈ 32 people

Wildlife Lodges on the Río Yavarí

4 The sheer size of the Amazon is nearly incalculable to the average person (Colombia's portion alone is bigger than Germany), so it goes without saying there are many places to bed down on a once-in-a-lifetime trip. But the protected Río Yavarí, which forms the border between Brazil and Peru for over 800km, is one of the only spots to access all three Amazonian ecosystems: *terra firme* (dry), *várzea* (semi-flooded) and *igapó* (flooded). A mob of wildlife awaits.

Beaches of PNN Tayrona

5 The beaches at Parque Nacional Natural (PNN) Tayrona near Santa Marta on the Caribbean coast are among the country's most beautiful. Tayrona's limpid waters heave against a backdrop of jungle that sweeps like a leafy avalanche down from the soaring Sierra Nevada de Santa Marta, the world's highest coastal mountain range. The picturesque white-sand beaches are lined with palm trees and strewn with vast boulders, some cleaved in half, looking as if a giant has had a geological temper tantrum.

Ancient Statues of San Agustín

6 Scattered throughout rolling green hills, the statues of San Agustín are a magnificent window into pre-Columbian culture and one of the most important archaeological sights on the continent. More than 500 of the monuments, carved from volcanic rock and depicting sacred animals and anthropomorphic figures,

Bussing About, *Chiva*-Style

The *chiva* – a piece of popular art on wheels – is a Disneyland-style vehicle that was Colombia's principal means of road transportation several decades ago. The body is made almost entirely of wood and is painted with colorful decorative patterns, each different, with a main painting on the back.

Today, *chivas* have almost disappeared from main roads, but they still play an important role on back roads between small towns and villages. *Chivas* take both passengers and any kind of cargo, animals included. If the interior is already packed, the roof is used for everything and everybody that doesn't fit inside. *Chivas* usually gather around markets, from where they depart for their journeys along bumpy roads.

Food & Drink

Colombian cuisine is referred to as *comida criolla* (Creole food). There are two distinct regional variations of *comida criolla* – the mountain highlands, where most of the population lives, and the Caribbean and Pacific coasts. They differ primarily in availability of ingredients (more fish and plantain on the coast, for example). The quality of the natural ingredients here is high (as is the high standard of hygiene in its preparation), meaning even those with the most jaded taste buds will find something unique to tempt their palate.

When it comes to Colombian cuisine, simplicity is key. Rice, beans, some meat or fish, a salad and fresh tropical fruit juice, and your average Colombian is content.

Coffee is Colombia's number-one drink, and its biggest (legal) export. Vendors amble the streets with thermoses of coffee and milk and for a few coins will pour you a small plastic cup of *tinto* (black coffee, called *perico* in Bogotá), *pintado* ('painted' with a little milk), or *cafe con leche* (with more milk).

Cabo San Juan de la Guía, Parque Nacional Natural (PNN) Tayrona

have been unearthed. Many statues are grouped together in an archaeological park, but many more are in situ, and can be explored on foot or by horseback.

Colonial Barichara

7 There is something immediately transcendent about stepping foot in stunning Barichara, arguably Colombia's most picturesque and pristinely preserved colonial village: its rust-orange rooftops, large, symmetrically cobbled streets, whitewashed walls and potted-plant balconies all contrast against a backdrop of postcard-perfect Andean green. Barichara is a slow-paced marvel – its name means 'place of relaxation' in the regional Guane dialect – and finding oneself wandering its streets in a sleepwalker's daze, blindsided by its beauty, wouldn't be unusual.

Outdoor Adventures in San Gil

8 As far as Colombian cities go, San Gil isn't

When to Go

HIGH SEASON
(Dec–Feb)

➡ Sunny skies and warmish days throughout the Andes.

➡ Stays dry everywhere but the Amazon.

➡ San Andrés and Providencia are gorgeous, as usual.

SHOULDER
(Mar–Sep)

➡ Bogotá, Medellín and Cali experience a secondary rainy season in April/May.

➡ Best whale-watching is July to October on the Pacific coast.

➡ Cartagena shines through April, hard rains begin in May.

LOW SEASON
(Oct–Nov)

➡ Flash floods often wash out roads in the Andean region.

➡ Cartagena is disproportionally wet in October.

➡ Low water levels in the Amazon mean excellent hiking and white-sand beaches.

much to look at, but what it lacks in natural beauty, it more than makes up in high-octane amusements. Peddle, paddle, rappel, spelunk, bungee or paraglide – whatever your passion – San Gil is Colombia's go-to outdoor adventure playground, most famous for heart-stopping Classes IV and V rapids on the Río Suárez, but boasting a résumé far beyond whitewater rafting. Get wet, get airborne, get your courage boots on and get your adrenaline pumping – San Gil is certainly not for the faint of heart.

Best on Film

Apaporis (2010) Incisive documentary about indigenous Amazonian life.

Maria Eres Llena de Gracia (2008) Moving tale of teen pregnancy and drug-trafficking.

Perro Come Perro (2008) Tarantino-esque gangster flick.

Rosario Tijeras (2004) Vengeful hit-woman's thrilling tale.

Todos Sus Muertos (2011) Devastating critique of corruption and apathy in Colombia.
....

Best in Print

Beyond Bogota – Diary of a Drug War Journalist in Colombia (Garry Leech) Essential reading for news that's not in the papers.

Calamari (Emilio Ruiz Barrachina) Cartagena-set historical romance.

Delirium (Laura Restrepo) Explores personal and political madness in mid-80s Bogotá.

One Hundred Years of Solitude (Gabriel García Márquez) Magic realist masterpiece.

Getting Around

Air Colombia's domestic air network is extensive and the country has more than half a dozen main passenger airlines and another dozen smaller carriers. Charter airlines also compete on some of the more popular routes.

Bus Buses are the principal means of intercity travel, and go just about everywhere. Most long-distance intercity buses are more comfortable than your average coach-class airplane seat, and the overnight buses sometimes have business class–sized seats.

Car Vehicle rental is expensive and, considering how cheap and extensive bu transportation is in Colombia, there is little reason to self-drive.

Medellín Nights

9 After sunset, Medellín really comes into its own, with stylish restaurants and buzzing nightlife that goes on until the early hours. El Poblado in particular is crammed with classy eateries, many of which turn into lively bars when the plates are cleared away. Later on, attention turns to the sweaty discos of Barrio Colombia, and later still to the neon-lit mega clubs of Autopista Sur. And don't leave town without visiting the elite bars of La Strada, which offer great people-watching among the city's rich and surgically enhanced.

Coffee Fincas in the Zona Cafetera

10 Jump in a classic WWII jeep and go on a caffeine-fueled, coffee-tasting adventure. Many of Zona Cafetera's best coffee farms have thrown open their gates and embraced tourism – eager to show visitors what sets Colombian coffee apart and share a little of their hardworking culture. Strap on a basket and head into the plantation to pick your own beans before heading back to the traditional farmhouse to enjoy the end product, accompanied by the sounds of flowing rivers and birdsong.

Coffee beans

PICTUREGARDEN / GETTY IMAGES ©

Mayotte Island

CAPITALS
Moroni (C)
Mamoudzou (M)

POPULATION
752,288 (C)
223,765 (M)

AREA
2,235 sq km (C)
374 sq km (M)

OFFICIAL LANGUAGES
Arabic & French (C
French (M)

Comoros & Mayotte

Scattered across the Indian Ocean, the enchanting Comoros islands are the kind of place you go to drop off the planet for a while.

The Comoros are so remote even an international fugitive could hide out here. Rich in Swahili culture, and devoutly Muslim, the charming inhabitants come from a legendary stock of Arab traders, Persian sultans, African slaves and Portuguese pirates. Nicknamed 'Cloud Coup-Coup' land because of their crazy politics, the three independent islands have experienced almost 20 coups since gaining independence in 1975. In the last decade, however, the quarrelsome independent islands agreed to put their dif-

ferences aside and fly under the joint banner of the Union des Comores. The fourth island, Mayotte, is an overseas territory of France, and differs from the other Comorian islands politically in that its people are French citizens governed by French law.

Holidaying in the Comoros isn't for everyone. Everything moves slowly and tourism facilities are far from plush. But if your idea of the perfect holiday is lazy days sipping tea and talking with the locals, then the Comoros will be the kind of unpredictable adventure you've been craving.

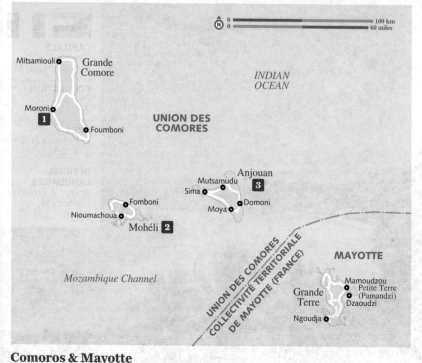

Comoros & Mayotte
Top Experiences

Moroni

1 Moroni is a timeless place where the air is redolent of the Arabian Nights. Wandering the narrow streets, you'll pass women in colourful wraps chatting on crumbling stone doorsteps, and grave groups of white-robed men whiling away the hours with games of dominoes. At sunset Moroni harbour must be one of the most beautiful sights in the Indian Ocean.

Mohéli

2 Explore the smallest, wildest and most interesting Comore, Mohéli, with fabulous beaches and turquoise seas. It's wild, undeveloped and sparsely populated. There is no question about Mohéli's backwater status: this island hasn't caught up with the 20th century yet, let alone the 21st. But this is a very good thing.

Anjouan

3 Called the 'pearl of the Comoros' by its residents, Anjouan is no doubt the most scenic of the Comoros and fulfils any lifelong fantasies of playing Robinson Crusoe on a deserted island. Known by the locals as Ndzouani or Nzwani, this is also the Comorian island that most closely resembles the image most people conjure up when daydreaming of kissing a lover in an exotic far-flung destination.

Food & Drink

Lobster Eat your first ever inexpensive lobster, and you'll remember more than the petite price tag – *langouste à la vanille* is particularly divine.

Tea Drink tea spiced with lemon grass and ginger.

When to Go

MAY–OCT
➜ Dry season.
➜ Best time to visit.

OCT–APRIL
➜ Temperatures extremely hot even during the wet season.

DEC–APR
➜ Heaviest rainfall, can reach as high as 390mm.

Parc National de la Garamba

CAPITAL
Kinshasa

POPULATION
75.5 million

AREA
2.3 million sq km

**OFFICIAL
LANGUAGE**
French

Congo, Democratic Republic of the

Compelling conversations with locals; exhilarating interactions in impenetrable forests and beckoning rivers are all on show in the Democratic Republic of the Congo.

As much a geographical concept as a fully fledged nation, the Democratic Republic of the Congo (DRC; formerly Zaïre) has one of the saddest chapters in modern history: from the brazen political folly of King Leopold of Belgium to the hideously corrupt kleptocracy of maverick leader Mobutu Sese Seko and the blood-stained battlegrounds of Africa's first 'world war'.

But after a decades-long decline in which much of the country descended into anarchy, Africa's second-largest nation is headed in the right direction. It still has a long way to go, but new roads, enormous untapped mineral wealth and the world's largest UN peace-keeping force have bred optimism among its tormented but resilient population.

Carpeted by huge swaths of rain forest and punctuated by gushing rivers and smoking volcanoes, DRC is the ultimate African adventure. There is absolutely nothing soft nor easy about it but for an African immersion you'll never forget, this is the place to be.

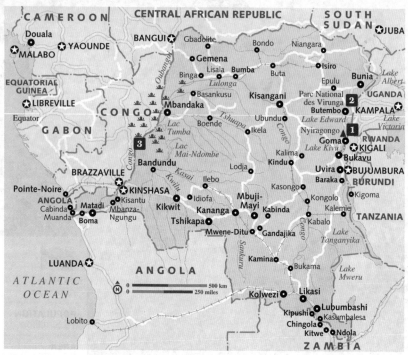

Democratic Republic of the Congo's
Top Experiences

Nyiragongo

1 Though locals fear and respect the beautiful, brooding power of the world's largest lava lake that destroyed half their city in 2002, that isn't to say you shouldn't climb it if you're feeling fit. Those who complete the five-hour climb are rewarded with views into the earth's heart. Wrapped in a sleeping bag, watching the glow of the lava light up the night sky is surreal.

Parc National des Virungas

2 There are few experiences in the world more memorable than coming face to face with a wild eastern mountain gorilla. There are six habituated families in Parc National des Virungas and you will be assigned a group to visit by the rangers. The ideal time to meet a gorilla family is when they have finished foraging and are settling for a mid-morning rest.

Congo River

3 Take the legendary boat trip down the still-wild Congo River. The classic path requires a two-week, 1730km boat ride down the river through still-untamed jungle. Unlike the old days, there are no longer steamers with passenger cabins – you'll be living out on the deck of the barges with hundreds of other people, plus all their cargo and livestock.

Food & Drink

Beer Try a Primus beer, or Turbo King if you prefer darker brews.

Fufu Manioc porridge.

Liboke Fish stewed in manioc leaves.

When to Go

DEC–MAR
➡ Dry season for the north means slightly easier travel conditions.

JAN
➡ A good month to have the mountain gorillas totally to yourself.

APR–OCT
➡ Dry season for the south and best time to attempt Kinshasa to Lubumbashi route.

Congo River

CAPITAL	Brazzaville
POPULATION	4.6 million
AREA	342,000 sq km
OFFICIAL LANGUAGE	French

Congo, Republic of the

The mighty river which gives the Congo its name snakes through a lush land of untouched jungle, wild animals and difficult history.

A land of steamy jungles hiding half the world's lowland gorillas, masses of forest elephants, and hooting, swinging troops of chimpanzees, the Congo (not to be confused with the Democratic Republic of the Congo across the Congo River) most certainly has the potential to become one of the finest ecotourism destinations in Africa. Parc National Nouabalé-Ndoki and Parc National d'Odzala are two of the most pristine for-est reserves on the continent and between them they are arguably the highlight of the whole of Central Africa.

Despite its impressive natural wonders and warm-hearted peoples, the Congo remains an unknown quantity to most outsiders and currently receives very few visitors. But for those ready to heed the call of the wild, and who are not afraid of adventure, the Congo awaits.

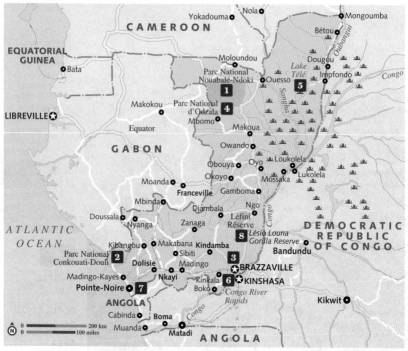

Republic of the Congo's
Top Experiences

Parc National Nouabalé-Ndoki

1 A team from *National Geographic* magazine, who visited the fledgling park in the mid-1990s, called this northern corner of Congo the world's 'Last Eden'. It is truly the world before the chainsaw. This vast region of swampy forest is home to populations of western lowland gorillas, elephants, chimpanzees and others. For the visitor what makes this park so enthralling is the ease with which the creatures are seen. The forest is known for its natural clearings in which masses of elephants and gorillas gather.

Parc National Conkouati-Douli

2 Congo's most diverse national park stretches from the Atlantic Ocean through a band of coastal savannah up into jungle-clad mountains. Poaching problems mean the wildlife-watching has for a long time been somewhat limited, but recent investment in the park infrastructure and security means that the elephants, gorillas and buffalo that live here are becoming more common, and more easily seen. The main activities are boat rides up the Ngongo River and forest walks.

Brazzaville

3 Relax in Brazzaville, a big city with a small-town feel. Founded in 1880 on the Stanley Pool (called Malebo Pool in the DRC) area of the Congo River, 'Brazza' has always been the junior partner economically with Kinshasa (DRC), which tempts and taunts from the other shore; though for travellers it's the more laid-back, and safer, town. Low-key and unassuming, with most evidence of the war years washed away, Brazzaville has a lot of charm and many visitors claim that it's the most pleasant city in Central Africa.

Shells used by fortune tellers, Brazzaville

Parc National d'Odzala

4 One of the oldest national parks in Africa, it has had a turbulent past. Once celebrated for having around 20,000 gorillas, the population was decimated about a decade ago by several outbreaks of the ebola virus, which wiped out between 70% and 95% of the gorilla population. Today the situation is much improved, gorilla numbers are growing and the park itself has received a much-needed boost with the arrival of African Parks.

Lake Télé

5 In a country like the Congo, getting off the beaten track is easy. For those who really want to immerse themselves in the deepest of jungle adventures, a journey to circular Lake Télé, in the unimaginably remote northeast of Congo, is the kind of journey people write books about. If rumours are to be believed Lake Télé is also the home of the Mokèlé-mbèmbé, a large semiaquatic creature that many describe as a sauropod, a long extinct dinosaur.

Congo River Rapids

6 These wide and powerful rapids on the Congo River at the outskirts of Brazzaville are where the Congo River gets nasty. Take a minibus to Pont Djoué from next to Centre Culturel Français. Most people observe the rapids from the nearby bar Site Touristique Les Rapides, but the best viewing is at

if the Republic of the Congo were 100 people

48 would be Kongo
20 would be Sangha
12 would be M'Bochi
17 would be Teke
3 would be other

belief systems
(% of population)

50 Christian   **48** Animist

2 Muslim

When to Go

JUN–DEC
➡ The best overall time to travel in Congo.

OCT–JAN
➡ The easiest time to see wildlife in the northern forest parks.

DEC–FEB
➡ Sea turtles nest on beaches of Parc National Conkouati-Douli.

population per sq km

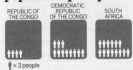

| REPUBLIC OF THE CONGO | DEMOCRATIC REPUBLIC OF THE CONGO | SOUTH AFRICA |

♦ ≈ 3 people

Travel by Barge or Pirogue

Journey for the sake of the journey and travel by barge. Between June and December, when river levels are high enough, barges run up the Congo and Oubangui River from Brazzaville. Some go to Bangui and Impfondo and others veer left at Mossaka, taking the even wilder Sangha River to Ouesso.

There are more or less weekly departures, but no schedule; boats go when they're ready. Ideally the journey between Brazza and Impfondo can be done in five days downstream and nine upstream.

If you're visiting Parc National Nouabalé-Ndoki then it's easy, and a lot of fun, to travel by boat between the park and Central African Republic's Dzanga-Sangha Reserve, from where you could continue up to Bangui by road. You can hire a speedboat from either park authority. The alternative is to rent a very leaky *pirogue* (traditional canoe) with a small engine for which you'll pay half but take at least twice as long.

Crossing the border on this route is memorable, but generally painless. Putter for hours along the stately brown Sangha River under the guard of what seems to be millions of big trees and then, quite suddenly, you come to a small clearing on the riverbank with a single wooden building staffed by a handful of soldiers, immigration officials and their families from the CAR.

Food & Drink

Northern Congolese are meat eaters (very often bushmeat) while southern Congolese love their fish. Both eat their protein almost exclusively with cassava, though you will sometimes find yams or rice in restaurants.

the other end, down the sandy track after the bridge. The main rapids themselves are well out into the middle of the river and quite hard to see, but it's still impressive even from this distance.

Pointe-Noire

7 Congo's outlet to the sea is something of a resort town. Down by the beach enjoy breezy ocean views and decent seafood – try the spicy pile of squid, prawns and lobster. For something more down to earth visit the stalls at the southern end of La Côte Sauvage for a sunset beer and plate of spicy fried fish.

Lésio Louna Gorilla Reserve

8 The Lésio Louna Gorilla Reserve, 140km north of Brazzaville, is a home for orphaned and confiscated gorillas. During a visit you can see the babies in the nursery and watch the adults living wild on an island get fed. You can also swim or just enjoy the peace and quiet at lovely Lac Bleu. If you leave Brazzaville by 5am it can all be done as a long day trip.

Getting Around

Air There are airports in Brazzaville and Pointe-Noire. Except for the Pointe-Noire to Brazzaville route, flight schedules are rarely followed and cancellations are common. Travel agencies can often get seats when airlines say their planes are full.

Bus A few proper buses now run to the north, but it's still mostly bush taxis and lorries.

Car Europcar offers expensive car and 4WD hire, but it's about half the price to just charter a taxi with driver for travelling around Brazzaville.

Train Train carriages themselves have recently been upgraded but sadly neither the track nor the engines were and it still takes 15 to 24 hours between Brazzaville and Pointe-Noire.

CAPITAL
Avarua

POPULATION
10,447

AREA
236 sq km

OFFICIAL LANGUAGES
English, Cook Islands Maori (Rarotongan)

Muri Beach, Rarotonga

Cook Islands

Fifteen droplets of land cast across 2 million sq km of wild Pacific blue, the Cook Islands are simultaneously remote and accessible, modern and traditional.

With a hip cafe culture, fine restaurants and funky nightlife, Rarotonga lives confidently in the 21st century. But beyond the island's tourist buzz and contemporary appearance is a robust culture, firmly anchored by traditional Polynesian values and steeped in oral history.

North of 'Raro', the sublime lagoon of Aitutaki is ringed with tiny deserted islands and is one of the Pacific's most improbably scenic jewels. Venture further and robust Polynesian traditions emerge nearer the surface. Drink home brew at a traditional 'Atiuan *tumunu* (bush-beer drinking club), explore the ancient *makatea* (raised coral cliffs) and taro fields of Mangaia, or swim in the underground cave pools of Mitiaro and Ma'uke. The even more remote Northern Group is a sublime South Seas idyll experienced only by a lucky few.

Penrhyn

Rakahanga
Manihiki

Pukapuka

Nassau

NORTHERN GROUP

Suwarrow

SOUTH PACIFIC OCEAN

Palmerston Atoll

3
Aitutaki   Manuae

SOUTHERN GROUP
Takutea
2 'Atiu   Ma'uke

0 ___ 200 km
0 ___ 120 miles

Rarotonga ✪ AVARUA **1** **4** **6**

Islands not to scale

Mangaia **5**

Cook Islands'
Top Experiences

Punanga Nui Market

1 Saturday morning in Avarua, Raratonga, is the time to jettison your hotel buffet and make tracks to one of the Pacific's best markets. Amid the colourful *pareu* (sarongs), handcrafted ukuleles, and performances from local musicians, is an entire morning of tasty discoveries for travelling foodies. Kick off with organic island coffee and a still-warm coconut bun, before moving on to fresh-fruit smoothies and crepes crammed with tropical fruit. Leave room for a few local specialities such as *rukau* (steamed taro leaves) or *ika mata* (marinated raw fish).

'Atiu's Caves

2 One of the Cooks' smallest – and rockiest – outer islands, 'Atiu is emerging as a hotspot for active and eco-aware travellers. Join a bird-watching tour with 'Birdman George' to seek out the endangered *kakerori* (Rarotongan flycatcher), before descending into the historical and spiritual depths of Anatakitaki Cave. Within the cave's cathedral-like arches, the avian attraction is the fascinating *kopeka* ('Atiuan swiftlet) – listen for its distinctive echolocating clicks. Take time to enjoy Anatakitaki's other attraction – a flickering candlelit dip in the cave's secluded subterranean pool.

Aitutaki

3 The Cooks' second-most visited island curls gently around one of the South Pacific's most stunning lagoons. The aqua water, foaming breakers around the perimeter reef and broad sandy beaches of its many small deserted islets make for a glorious scene: Aitutaki will take your breath away. Sunday is solemnly observed as the day of prayer and rest. Take the opportunity to see a local church service, as the singing is spine-tingling.

Loving the Lagoons

4 Snorkel, dive, kayak or paddleboard in the pristine azure waters of Rarotonga's Muri Lagoon or

Anatakitaki cave, 'Atiu

find your own deserted *motu* (island) in Aitutaki's stunning lagoon. Diving in Rarotonga is fantastic outside the reef, especially around the passages along the island's southern side. There are canyons, caves and tunnels to explore, and outside the lagoon the island drops off to around 4000m, although most diving is between 3m and 30m. Rarotonga has several well-preserved shipwrecks, including *SS Maitai* off the northern shore. Other well-known diving spots include Black Rock in the north; Sandriver and Matav-

era Wall on the island's east side; and the Avaavaroa, Papua and Rutaki passages in the south. In Aitutaki the visibility is great, and features include drop-offs, multilevels, wall dives and cave systems. Many divers ask to dive on the wreck of the *Alexander*, but it sits in a mere metre of water and is just as suitable for snorkellers.

Mangaia

5 Next to Rarotonga, Mangaia is the Cooks' most geographically dramatic island, with a towering circlet of black two-tiered

if the Cook Islands were 100 people

81 would be Cook Island Maori (Polynesian)
7 would be part Cook Island Maori
12 would be other

belief systems
(% of population)

56	**14**	**17**
Cook Islands Christian Church	other Protestant	Roman Catholic
4	**6**	**3**
Mormon	other	none

population per sq km

COOK ISLANDS   NEW ZEALAND   AUSTRALIA

👤 ≈ 3 people

When to Go

HIGH SEASON (Jun–Sep)

➡ The dry season with pleasant temperatures, lower humidity and little rain.

➡ Yachties head across the South Pacific.

➡ Whales are in the region.

SHOULDER (Apr–May & Oct–Nov)

➡ This is the period between the dry and wet seasons.

➡ Everything is open but not so many visitors around.

➡ Yachties start to arrive in May, mostly gone by late October.

LOW SEASON (Dec–Mar)

➡ Expect hot temperatures and high humidity.

➡ It's cyclone season.

➡ Planes are packed December to January as overseas-based islanders return to see their families.

The Divided Church

Ma'uke's CICC was built by two villages, Areora and Ngatiarua, in 1882. When the outside was completed, there was disagreement between the villages about how the inside should be decorated so they built a wall down the middle. The wall has since been removed, though the interior is decorated in markedly different styles. Each village has its own entrance, sits at its own side and takes turns singing the hymns. The minister stands astride the dividing line down the middle of the pulpit.

Look for the Chilean coins that are set into the wooden altar. Chilean currency was frequently traded throughout the South Pacific in the 19th century.

Food & Drink

Drinking with the guys Look forward to a few laughs with the friendly locals at an 'Atiuan *tumunu* (bush beer) session. It's a refreshing, slightly effervescent concoction, and you'll be required to introduce yourself to the group before drinking. Don't be surprised also if your local drinking buddies regale you with stories of relatives living in Auckland or Sydney.

Go local Head to Avarua's excellent Punanga Nui Market and hunt down local delicacies including *ika mata* (raw fish marinated in lime and coconut), *rukau* (steamed taro leaves), *poke* (banana with arrowroot and coconut) and *mitiore* (fermented coconut with onion and seafood).

Refresh with nature Quickly gain an appreciation of quite possibly the most refreshing drink on the planet, a chilled *nu* (young green coconut).

Te Rua Manga (The Needle), Rarotonga

raised-coral makatea (three-tiered in the island's north) concealing a huge sunken volcanic caldera that falls away on each side of the 169m Rangimotia ridge, the island's central spine. Mangaia is the Pacific's oldest island – at once craggy and lushly vegetated – and riddled with limestone caves that once served as sacred burial grounds and havens during tribal fighting.

Hiking the Cross-Island Track

6 A Cook Islands sojourn usually involves lots of good eating and drinking, and lazy days on the beach. The perfect balance to this tropical relaxation is to challenge yourself on Rarotonga's Cross-Island Track. The three- to four-hour hike via the 413m-high Te Rua Manga (The Needle) immerses walkers in some of the island's most spectacular scenery. Starting from Rarotonga's northern coast, the terrain includes tangled tree roots amid tropical forest, and meandering, rocky streams. Cool off under Wigmore's Waterfall at the trail's end, a lovely cascade dropping into a cool pool.

Getting Around

Air Flights to the Northern Group islands are expensive, and only Manihiki, Penrhyn and Pukapuka have airstrips.

Boat Shipping schedules are notoriously unpredictable – weather, breakdowns and unexpected route changes can all put a kink in your travel plans. Ships stop off at each island for just a few hours, and only Rarotonga and Penrhyn have decent harbours. At all the other islands you go ashore by lighter or barge.

Local Transport Rarotonga has a regular circle-island bus service. The larger islands have taxis and you can rent bicycles, scooters or cars.

CAPITAL
San José

POPULATION
4.7 million

AREA
51,100 sq km

OFFICIAL LANGUAGE
Spanish

Volcán Arenal

Costa Rica

In Costa Rica trails lead to rushing waterfalls, mist-covered volcanoes and deserted beaches. Regardless of which you choose, this tropical playland is a feast for the senses.

Whether you're following the shimmer of a blue butterfly from palm to palm, staring into the yawning mouth of a deep purple orchid or watching wisps of fog roll in to soften the jagged edge of mountains, Costa Rica's vivid colors last a lifetime. The canopies rustle with riotous troupes of monkeys, hillsides echo with the squawks of macaws and you can reach up to the trees and pick your day's lunch. It might seem at times like some kind of wondrous tropical fantasy land, but this is Costa Rica.

As the preeminent eco- and adventure-tourism capital of Central America, Costa Rica has earned a rightful place in the cubicle daydreams of travelers around the world. With a world-class infrastructure, visionary sustainability initiatives and no standing army, Costa Rica is a green, peaceful jewel. Considering more than a third of the country enjoys some form of environmental protection and there's greater biodiversity than the USA and Europe combined, it's a country that earns the superlative descriptions.

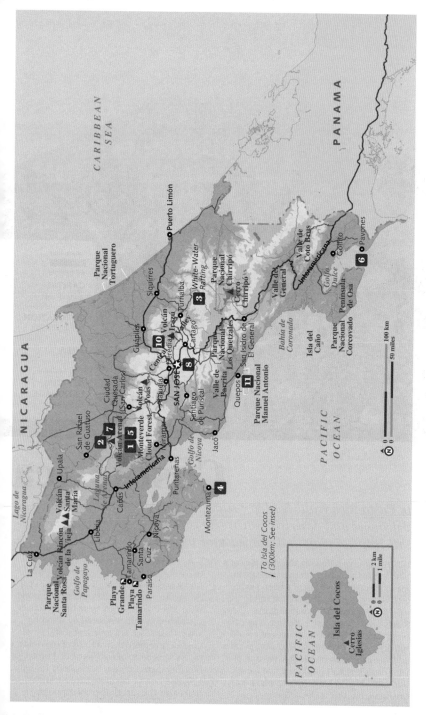

Costa Rica's
Top Experiences

Monteverde Cloud Forest

1 A pristine expanse of virginal forest totaling 105 sq km, Monteverde Cloud Forest owes much of its impressive natural beauty to Quaker expats, who left the US in the 1950s to protest the Korean War and helped foster conservationist principles with Ticos of the region. But as fascinating as the history is, the real romance of Monteverde is in nature itself: a mysterious Neverland dripping with mist, dangling with mossy vines, sprouting with ferns and bromeliads, gushing with creeks, blooming with life and nurturing rivulets of evolution.

Volcán Arenal

2 While the molten night views are gone and the volcano lies dormant, this mighty, perfectly conical giant is still worthy of a pilgrimage. There are several beautiful trails to explore, especially the magnificent climb to Cerro Chato. And although Volcán Arenal is considered by scientists to be active, you'd never know it from the serene, mist-covered vistas. Even when clouds gather, and there is a chill in the air, you are just a short drive away from relaxing in its many hot springs.

Canopy walkway, Monteverde Cloud Forest

White-Water Rafting

3 So many rivers, so little time. But the dedicated adrenaline junkie can cover some heart-pounding river miles in the span of a few days in this compact little country. For those without the drive to do them all, pick a river, any river: Pacuare, Reventazón, Sarapiquí. Any of the three are fun runs (though we're partial to the Pacuare), with rapids ranging from Class II to Class V, and all have stretches of smooth water that allow rafters to take in the luscious jungle scenery surrounding these river gorges.

if Costa Rica were 100 people

94 would be white and mestizo
3 would be black
1 would be Chinese
1 would be Amerindian
1 would be other

belief systems
(% of population)

Roman Catholic	Evangelical	other
76	14	3

none	Jehovah's Witnesses
6	1

population per sq km

COSTA RICA	UNITED STATES	CANADA

👤 ≈ 4 people

Montezuma

4 If you dig artsy-rootsy beach culture, enjoy rubbing shoulders with neo-Rastas and yoga freaks or have always wanted to spin fire, study Spanish or lounge on sugar-white coves, you'll find your way to Montezuma. Strolling this intoxicating town and rugged coastline, you're never far from the rhythm and sound of the sea. From here you'll have easy access to the famed Cabo Blanco reserve, and can take the tremendous hike to a triple-tiered waterfall.

Zip Lining in the Rainforest Canopy

5 The wild-eyed, frizzy-haired happiness of a canopy tour is self-evident. Few things are more purely joyful than clipping into a high-speed cable, laced above and through the seething jungle canopy. The best place to sample the lines is Monteverde, where the forest is alive, the mist fine and swirling, and the afterglow worth savoring.

Pacific Coast

6 Costa Rica's east coast may move to the laid-back groove of Caribbean reggae, but the country's best year-round surfing is on the Pacific coast. It's home to a number of seaside villages where the day's agenda rarely gets more complicated than a scrupulous study of the surf report, a healthy application of sunblock and a few cold Imperial beers. There are good breaks for beginners, and plenty of reliable rides (including perhaps the world's second-longest left-hand break, in Pavones).

Hot Springs

7 It may no longer creep down the mountainside,

Pura Vida

'Pura vida' – pure life – is more than just a slogan that rolls off the tongues of Ticos and emblazons souvenirs; this phrase is a bona fide mantra for the Costa Rican way of life. Hearing 'pura vida' again and again while traveling across this beautiful country – as a greeting, a stand-in for goodbye and an acknowledgement of thanks – makes it evident that the concept is deep within the DNA of this country.

The living seems particularly pure when Costa Rica is compared with its Central American neighbors: there's little poverty, illiteracy or political tumult; the country is crowded with ecological jewels and has high standards of living.

The sum of the parts makes for a country that's an oasis of calm in a corner of the world that has been continuously degraded by warfare. And although the Costa Rican people are justifiably proud, a compliment to the country is likely to be met simply with a warm smile and a two-word reply: pura vida.

Food & Drink

The Tico diet consists largely of rice and beans and – when it's time to change things up – beans and rice.

Breakfast for Ticos is usually *gallo pinto* (literally 'spotted rooster'), a stir-fry of rice and beans, usually served with eggs, cheese or *natilla* (sour cream).

Most restaurants offer a set meal at lunch and dinner called a *casado*, or a 'married man's' lunch, featuring meat, beans, rice and salad. An extremely popular *casado* is the ubiquitous *arroz con pollo*, or chicken and rice.

Seafood is plentiful, fresh and delicious. While it's not traditional Tico fare, you'll find *ceviche* on most menus (raw fish or shrimp, marinated in lime juice and served chilled). On the Caribbean coast, don't miss a chance to sample *rondón*, a spicy seafood gumbo.

KEVIN SCHAFER / GETTY IMAGES ©

Rafting, Río Sarapiquí

but beneath La Fortuna lava heats dozens of bubbling springs. Some of these springs are free, and any local can point the way. Others are, shall we say, embellished, dressed up, luxuriated. Take Tabacón Hot Springs, set in the path of Volcán Arenal's 1975 eruption. It's a cheesy but still appealing set piece, with its faux cliffs, Garden of Eden motif, and pools at a steaming 40°C (104°F).

San José

8 The heart of Tico culture and identity lives in San José, as do university students, intellectuals, artists and politicians. While not the most attractive capital in Central America, it does have some graceful neoclassical and Spanish-colonial architecture, leafy neighborhoods, museums housing pre-Columbian jade and gold, nightlife that goes on until dawn and some of the most sophisticated restaurants in the country. Street art – of both officially sanctioned and guerrilla varieties – add unexpected pops of color and public discourse to the cityscape.

When to Go

HIGH SEASON
(Dec–Apr)

➡ 'Dry' season still sees some rain, but beach towns fill with domestic tourists.

➡ Accommodation should be booked well in advance; some places enforce two- or three-day minimum stays.

SHOULDER
(May–Jul, Nov)

➡ Rain picks up and the stream of tourists starts to taper off.

➡ Roads are muddy, making off-the-beaten-track travel more challenging.

LOW SEASON
(Aug–Oct)

➡ Rainfall is highest, but heavy rains bring swells to the Pacific, and the best surfing conditions.

➡ Rural roads can be impassable due to river crossings.

Wildlife-Watching

9 Monkeys and crocs, toucans and iguanas – Costa Rica is a thrill for wildlife enthusiasts. World-class parks, long-standing dedication to environmental protection, and mind-boggling biodiversity enable Costa Rica to harbor scores of rare and endangered species. Simply put, it's one of the best wildlife-watching destinations on the globe. No matter where you travel in the country, the branches overhead are alive with critters galore.

Coffee Plantations

10 Take a little country drive on the scenic, curvy back roads of the Central Valley, where the hillsides are a patchwork of varied agriculture and coffee shrubbery. If you're curious about that magical brew that for many makes life worth living, tour one of the coffee plantations and learn all about how Costa Rica's golden bean goes from plant to cup.

Parque Nacional Manuel Antonio

11 Although droves of visitors pack Parque Nacional Manuel Antonio, it remains an absolute gem. Capuchin monkeys scurry across its idyllic beaches, brown pelicans dive-bomb its clear waters and sloths watch over its accessible trails. It's a perfect place to introduce youngsters to the wonders of the rainforest. There's not much by way of privacy, but it's so lovely that you won't mind sharing.

Getting Around

Air The domestic airlines fly small passenger planes, and you're allocated a baggage allowance of no more than 12kg. Space is limited and demand is high in the dry season, so reserve and pay for tickets in advance. Schedules change constantly and delays are frequent because of inclement weather.

Bus Local buses are a safe, cheap and reliable way of getting around Costa Rica. The longest domestic journey out of San José costs less than US$20.

Car Although car-rental agencies are ubiquitous, deceptively cheap daily rates come with the unpleasant surprise of a mandatory insurance policy, which can double the price. Most off-the-beaten-track places require a pricier 4WD vehicle for river crossings and rough roads.

Southern Caribbean

12 By day, lounge in a hammock, cruise by bike to snorkel off uncrowded beaches, hike to waterfall-fed pools and visit the remote indigenous territories of the Bribrí and Kèköldi. By night, dip into zesty Caribbean cooking and sway to reggaetón at open-air bars cooled by ocean breezes. The villages of Cahuita and Puerto Viejo de Talamanca are the perfect, laid-back home bases for such adventures.

Best on Film

Agua fría de mar (Cold Water of the Sea; 2010) A story of a young couple and a seven-year-old girl from contrasting social backgrounds who spend Christmas together along the Pacific coast. Director Paz Fabrega won the coveted VPRO Tiger award in 2010 at the Rotterdam Film Festival.

Best in Print

Around the Edge (Peter Ford) A story of traveling the Caribbean coast.

Green Dreams: Travels in Central America (Stephen Benz) An astute analysis questioning the impact of visitors on the region.

Green Phoenix (William Allen) An absorbing account about conserving the Guanacaste rainforest.

Squirrel monkey, Parque Nacional Manuel Antonio

HOLGER LEUE / GETTY IMAGES ©

Cathedrale St Paul, Abidjan

Côte d'Ivoire

Côte d'Ivoire is on the rebound, emerging from a difficult decade, revelling in a melange of modernity and a tradition with a penchant for partying.

CAPITAL
Yamoussoukro

POPULATION
22.4 million

AREA
322,463 sq km

OFFICIAL LANGUAGE
French

Côte d'Ivoire is a stunner, shingled with starfish-studded sands, and forest roads so orange they resemble strips of bronzing powder. After almost a decade of making headlines for all the wrong reasons, it is making a tentative comeback.

Once lauded as West Africa's success story – the country was a magnet for workers from across the region, and travellers drawn by idyllic beaches and intriguing cultural traditions – Côte d'Ivoire's descent into civil war in the early years of the millennium was especially tragic.

With a fragile peace holding, the outlook is more positive and travellers are beginning to return, albeit at a trickle. In the south, the Parc National de Taï hides secrets, species and nut-cracking chimps amidst its trees, while the peaks and valleys of Man offer a highland climate, fresh air and local art. Beach resorts of Assinie and arty Grand Bassam were made for weekend retreats from Abidjan, the capital in all but name, where lagoons linger between skyscrapers and cathedral spires pierce the blue heavens.

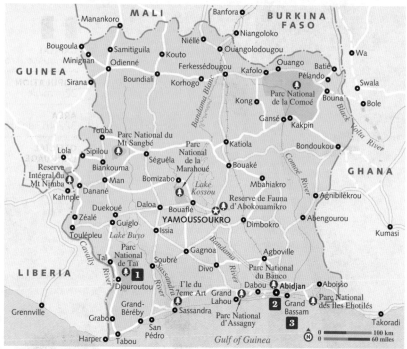

Côte d'Ivoire's
Top Experiences

Parc National de Taï

1 This 5000-sq-km reserve of rainforest is home to a colony of nutcracking chimps. It is so dense that scientists are only just beginning to discover the wealth of flora and fauna that lies within.

Abidjan

2 Côte d'Ivoire's economic engine is strapped between lagoons and waterways, overlooking the crested waves of the Atlantic. Although Abidjan took a beating during the 2011 crisis, the engine rattled on, and new bars, bistros and hotels are opening regularly; this is, after all, one of Africa's sleekest party cities.

Grand Bassam

3 Arty and bathed in faded glory, beachside Bassam was once Côte d'Ivoire's French capital. It is laid out on a long spit of land with a quiet lagoon on one side and the turbulent Atlantic on the other. A walk through town will take you past the colonial buildings the city is known for; some have been restored, while others are slowly falling apart.

Food & Drink

Aloco A dish of ripe bananas fried with chilli in palm oil.

Attiéké Grated cassava

Beer Flag is the standard beer, try locally brewed Tuborg or a Beaufort for a premium lager.

Fufu A dough of boiled yam, cassava or plantain, pounded into a sticky paste.

Poisson braisé Grilled fish with tomatoes, onions and ginger

When to Go

MAY–JUL

➡ Storms to rival those in Oct–Nov; be prepared for buckets of rain and lightning.

JUN–OCT

➡ Wet in the north but humid with bursts of rain in the south. Temperatures about 28°C.

DEC–FEB

➡ Prime beach season, with temperatures hitting 30°C and not a cloud in the sky.

Old town, Dubrovnik

CAPITAL
Zagreb

POPULATION
4.4 million

AREA
56,538 sq km

**OFFICIAL
LANGUAGE**
Croatian

Croatia

*Croatia's rare blend of glamour and authenticity make it Europe's
'it' destination, where beaches vie for attention with cultural
treasures, ancient architecture and time-tested folk traditions.*

Croatia has been touted as the 'new this' and the 'new that' for years since its re-emergence on the tourism scene, but it's now clear that it's a unique destination that holds its own and then some: this is a country with a glorious 1778km-long coast and a staggering 1244 islands. The Adriatic coast is a knockout: its sapphire waters draw visitors to remote islands, hidden coves and traditional fishing villages, all while touting the glitzy beach and yacht scene. Istria captivates with its gastronomic delights and wines, and the bars, clubs and festivals of Zagreb, Zadar and Split remain little-explored gems. Eight national parks show-case primeval beauty with their forests, mountains, rivers, lakes and waterfalls. You can end your journey in dazzling, historic Dubrovnik in the south – just the right conclusion to any trip. Best of all, Croatia hasn't given in to mass tourism: there are pockets of unique culture and plenty to discover off the grid.

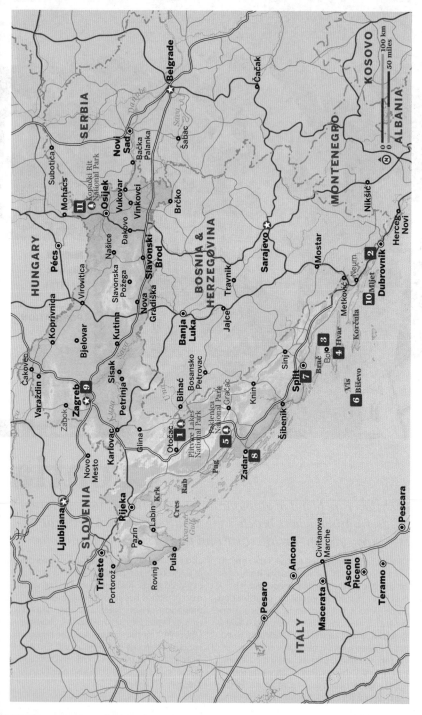

Croatia's
Top Experiences

Plitvice Lakes National Park

1 A turquoise ribbon of crystal water and gushing waterfalls in the forested heart of continental Croatia, Plitvice Lakes National Park is an awesome sight. There are dozens of lakes – from 4km-long Kozjak to reed-fringed ponds – all in an incredible hue that's a product of the karst terrain. Travertine expanses covered with mossy plants divide the lakes, while boardwalks allow you to step right over this exquisite water world. Follow hiking trails through beech, spruce, fir and pine trees to escape the crowds on the lake shore.

Dubrovnik

2 Croatia's most popular attraction, Dubrovnik is a Unesco World Heritage site for very good reason. This immense walled city was relentlessly shelled during Croatia's 1990s Homeland War. Now, its mighty walls, monasteries, medieval churches, graceful squares and fascinating residential quarters all look magnificent again. For an unrivalled perspective of this Adriatic pearl, we recommend you first take the cable car up to Mount Srd, then get up close to the city by walking Dubrovnik's walls, as history unfolds from the battlements.

KELLY CHENG TRAVEL PHOTOGRAPHY / GETTY IMAGES ©

Windsurfing in Bol

3 Bol is home to the illustrious Zlatni Rat beach, with its tongue-like shape and golden pebbles. The town is a favourite among windsurfers: the channel between the islands of Brač and Hvar provides ideal wind conditions, thanks to the westerly maestral that typically blows between May and late September. The wind picks up slowly in the morning, an excellent time for beginners to hit the waves. By afternoon, the winds are very strong, perfect for those looking to get a real-deal adrenalin kick.

if Croatia were 100 people

90 would be Croat
4 would be Serb
6 would be other

religious groups
(% of population)

- 88 Roman Catholic
- 6 other
- 4 Orthodox
- 1 Muslim
- 1 other Christian

population per sq km

CROATIA   USA   UK

= 30 people

Party-Happy Hvar

4 Come high summer, there's no better place to get your groove on than Hvar Town. Gorgeous tanned people descend from their yachts in droves for round-the-clock fun on this glam isle. With beach parties as the sun drops below the horizon far out in the Adriatic, designer cocktails sipped seaside to fresh house tunes spun by DJs, and full-moon beach parties, Hvar caters to a well-dressed, party-happy crowd. Plus there's Hvar beyond the party scene, with its gorgeous interior largely uncharted by tourist crowds.

Hiking & Climbing Paklenica

5 It's some sight. The extraordinary Paklenica National Park is best viewed from the northern coast of Pag Island, giving you an appreciation of how steeply the Velebit mountains rear up from the shore. Two great canyons cut into these majestic mountains, forming a natural trail for hikers up to the high alpine peaks of Vaganski vrh and Babin vrh. For those craving more adventure, Paklenica is also Croatia's premier rock-climbing centre, with hundreds of spectacular routes criss-crossing the park.

Biševo's Caves

6 Of the numerous caves around the remote limestone island of Biševo, the Blue Grotto (Modra Špilja) is the most spectacular. The light show produced by this rare natural phenomenon will amaze you. On a clear morning, the sun's rays penetrate through an underwater hole in this coastal cave, bathing the interior in a mesmerising silvery-blue light. Beneath

Klapa Your Hands!

There won't be a visitor to Croatia who hasn't heard the dulcet tones of a *klapa* song. This music involves a bunch of hunky men in a circle, singing tear-jerkers about love, betrayal, patriotism, death, beauty and other life-affirming subjects in honeyed multitonal harmonies.

First tenor Branko Tomić, a man whose high-toned voice complements the basses and baritones that accompany him, says of the music: 'I've sung with the Filip Dević *klapa* for 35 years. It's a passion of mine. I started singing in high school and I loved it. We sing about so many different things: we serenade, we sing traditional songs, sentimental songs about missing your family or your home town. It's a gentler, more companionship-based experience, though the new generations are starting to prefer our covers of pop songs. That's a really big thing in Croatia nowadays.'

Food & Drink

Beer Two top types of Croatian *pivo* (beer) are Zagreb's Ožujsko and Karlovačko from Karlovac.

Burek Pastry stuffed with ground meat, spinach or cheese.

Ćevapčići Small spicy sausages of minced beef, lamb or pork.

Kava A strongly brewed espresso-style coffee that is served in tiny cups.

Maneštra A thick vegetable-and-bean soup similar to minestrone.

Pljeskavica An ex-Yugo version of a hamburger.

Rakija Strong Croatian brandy comes in different flavours, from plum to honey.

Ražnjići Small chunks of pork grilled on a skewer.

the turquoise water, rocks glimmer silver and pink, creating an unearthly effect. Swimming inside is a surreal must-do experience.

Diocletian's Palace, Split

7 Experience life as it's been lived for thousands of years in Diocletian's Palace, one of the world's most imposing Roman ruins. The maze-like streets of this buzzing quarter are chock-full of bars, shops and restaurants. Getting lost in the labyrinth of narrow streets, passageways and courtyards is one of Croatia's most enchanting experiences – and you'll always find your way out easily.

Zadar

8 Fast becoming one of Croatia's top destinations, the city of Zadar boasts history and culture in spades yet retains a down-to-earth ambience. Its must-see sights include two extraordinary artistic installations created by architect Nikola Bašić. Zadar's musical festivals are

When to Go

HIGH SEASON
(Jul & Aug)

➡ Peak season brings the best weather. Hvar Island gets the most sun, followed by Split, Korčula Island and Dubrovnik.

➡ Prices are at their highest and coastal destinations at their busiest.

SHOULDER
(May–Jun & Sep)

➡ The coast is gorgeous, the Adriatic is warm enough for swimming, the crowds are sparse and prices are lower.

➡ In spring and early summer, the steady maestral wind makes sailing great.

LOW SEASON
(Oct–Apr)

➡ Winters in continental Croatia are cold and prices are low.

➡ Southeasterly winds produce heavy cloud cover; northeasterly gusts of dry air blow clouds away.

equally compelling. Held on the nearby island of Murter, the Garden Festival offers a great opportunity to catch some of the globe's most creative electronic talent.

Zagreb Cafes

9 Elevated to the status of ritual, having coffee in one of Zagreb's outdoor cafes is a must, involving hours of people-watching, gossiping and soul-searching, unhurried by waiters. To experience the truly European and vibrant cafe culture, grab a table along the pedestrian cobbled Tkalčićeva, or one of the pavement tables on Trg Petra Preradovića. Don't miss the Saturday morning *špica*, the coffee-drinking and people-watching ritual in the city centre that forms the peak of Zagreb's weekly social calendar.

Mljet

10 Cloaked in dense pine forests, pristine Mljet is an island paradise. Legend has it that Odysseus was marooned here for seven years, and it's easy to appreciate why he'd take his time leaving. The entire western section is a national park, where you'll find two sublime, cobalt-coloured lakes, an island monastery and the sleepy little port of Pomena, which is as pretty as a picture. Don't neglect eastern Mljet, home to great cove beaches and the gastronomic heaven that is Stermasi restaurant.

Kopački Rit Nature Park

11 A flood plain of the Danube and Drava Rivers, Kopački Rit – part of a brand-new Unesco biosphere reserve – offers breathtaking scenery and some of Europe's best birdwatching.

Getting Around

Air Croatia Airlines is the only carrier for flights within Croatia. There are daily flights between Zagreb and Dubrovnik, Pula, Split and Zadar.

Boat Local ferries connect the bigger offshore islands with each other and with the mainland. Service is often less frequent between October and April.

Bus Services are excellent and relatively inexpensive. There are often a number of companies handling each route so prices can vary substantially.

Car & Motorcycle Croatia's motorway connecting Zagreb with Split is only a few years old and makes some routes much faster. Zagreb and Rijeka are now also connected by motorway. However, there are stretches where service stations and facilities are few and far between.

Best on Film

Occupation in 26 Pictures (Okupacija u 26 slika; Lordan Zafranović; 1978)

You Only Love Once (Samo jednom se ljubi; Rajko Grlić; 1981)

Cyclops (Kiklop; Antun Vrdoljak; 1982)

How the War on My Island Started (Kako je počeo rat na mom otoku; Vinko Brešan; 1997)

A Wonderful Night in Split (Ta divna splitska noć; Arsen A Ostojić; 2004)

Best in Print

Black Lamb and Grey Falcon (Rebecca West; 1941) Recounts the writer's journeys through the Balkans in 1937.

Another Fool in the Balkans (Tony White; 2006) White retraces Rebecca West's journey, juxtaposing the region's modern life with its political history.

Cafe Europa – Life After Communism (Slavenka Drakulić; 1996) Wittily details the infiltration of Western culture in Eastern Europe.

9

RICHARD I'ANSON / GETTY IMAGES ©

Havana

CAPITAL
Havana

POPULATION
11.1 million

AREA
109,820 sq km

**OFFICIAL
LANGUAGE**
Spanish

Cuba

Trapped in a time-warp, Cuba is like a prince in a poor man's coat. Behind the sometimes shabby facades of communist but culturally rich Cuba, gold dust lingers.

Cuba is a country with no historical precedents: economically poor, but culturally rich; visibly mildewed, but architecturally magnificent; infuriating, yet at the same time, strangely uplifting.

Halfway between the US in the north and Latin America in the south, Cuba has long struggled to work out where it fits in. Yet, as a former Spanish colony liberally colored with French, African, American, Jamaican, and indigenous Taíno influences, there's no denying the breadth of its historical heritage. When Castro pressed the pause button on economic development in the 1960s, he inadvertently saved many endangered traditions and important historical heirlooms.

It is the Cubans themselves who have kept the country alive as the infrastructure crumbled: survivors and improvisers, poets and dreamers, cynics and sages. It is also they who have ensured that Cuba continues to be the fascinating, perplexing, paradoxical nation it is.

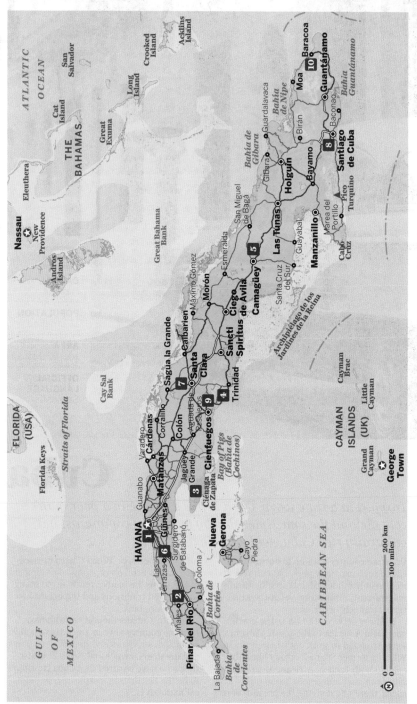

Cuba's
Top Experiences

Havana's Malecón

1 Only a fool comes to Havana and misses out on the Malecón sea drive, 8km of shabby magnificence that stretches the breadth of the city from Habana Vieja to Miramar and acts as a substitute living room for tens of thousands of cavorting, canoodling, romance-seeking *habaneros*. Traverse it during a storm, when giant waves breach the wall, or tackle it at sunset with Benny Moré on your mp3 player, a bottle of Havana Club in your hand and the notion that anything is possible come 10pm.

Cycling through the Valle de Viñales

2 Cuba is ideal for cycling and there's no better place to do it than the quintessentially rural Valle de Viñales. The valley offers all the ingredients of a tropical Tour de France: craggy *mogotes* (flat-topped hills), impossibly green tobacco fields, bucolic *campesino* huts and spirit-lifting viewpoints at every gear change. The terrain is relatively flat and, if you can procure a decent bike, your biggest dilemma will be where to stop for your sunset-toasting mojito.

Tobacco field, Valle de Viñales

2

Ciénaga de Zapata's Wildlife

3 One of the few parts of Cuba that has never been truly tamed, the Zapata Swamp is as close to pure wilderness as the country gets. This is the home of the endangered Cuban crocodile, various amphibians, the bee hummingbird and over a dozen different plant habitats. It also qualifies as the Caribbean's largest wetlands, protected in numerous ways, most importantly as a Unesco Biosphere Reserve and Ramsar Convention Site. Come here to fish, bird-watch, hike and see nature at its purest.

if Cuba were 100 people

65 would be white
25 would be mixed
10 would be black

belief systems

(% of population)

85
12   3

Nominally Catholic   other   Protestant

population per sq km

CUBA   USA   UK

= 30 people

Time-Warped Trinidad

4 Soporific Trinidad went to sleep in 1850 and never really woke up. This strange twist of fate is good news for modern travelers who can explore the perfectly preserved mid-19th-century sugar town. Though it's no secret these days, the time-warped streets still have the power to enchant with their grand colonial homestays, easily accessible countryside and exciting live music scene. But this is also a real working town loaded with all the foibles and fun of 21st-century Cuba.

Labyrinthine Streets of Camagüey

5 Get lost! No, that's not an abrupt put-down; rather it's a recommendation for any traveler passing through the city of *tinajones* (clay pots), churches and erstwhile pirates – aka Camagüey. A perennial rule-breaker, Camagüey was founded on a street grid unlike almost any other Spanish colonial city in Latin America. Here the lanes are as labyrinthine as a Moroccan medina, hiding Catholic churches and triangular plazas, and revealing left-field artistic secrets at every turn.

Las Terrazas' Eco-Village

6 Back in 1968, when the fledgling environmental movement was a bolshie protest group for long-haired students in duffel coats, the prophetic Cubans – concerned about the ecological cost of island-wide deforestation – came up with rather a good idea. After saving hectares of

Cuban Music

Rich, vibrant, layered and soulful, Cuban music has long acted as a standard-bearer for the sounds and rhythms emanating out of Latin America. This is the land where salsa has its roots, and where the African drum first fell in love with the Spanish guitar. From the down-at-heel docks of Matanzas to the bucolic villages of the Sierra Maestra, the amorous musical fusion went on to fuel everything from *son*, rumba, mambo, *chachachá, charanga, changüí, danzón* and more.

Mixed into an already exotic melting pot are genres from France, the US, Haiti and Jamaica. Cuban music has also played a key role in developing various melodic styles and movements in other parts of the world, including a style of Spanish flamenco called *guajira*, New Orleans jazz, New York salsa and West African Afrobeat.

Cuban dancing is famous for its libidinous rhythms and sensuous close-ups. Inheriting a love for dancing from birth, most Cubans are natural performers who approach dance with a complete lack of self-consciousness.

Food & Drink

Traditional Cuban food is called *comida criolla*, though after 50 years of on–off rationing, it is usually a leaner, pared-down version of what you might find on neighboring islands. Staples include rice, beans, pork and root vegetables.

Rice & beans Known variously as *moros y cristianos* or *congrí*, these ingredients anchor nearly all Cuban dishes.

Ropa vieja Shredded beef in a tomato-based sauce.

Rum Usually drunk neat by the locals, but also popular in cocktails such as mojitos, daiquiris and Cuba libres.

Tostones Unripe green plantain, sliced and fried in a shallow pan.

8

Street musicians, Santiago de Cuba

denuded forest from an ecological disaster, a group of industrious workers built their own eco-village, Las Terrazas, and set about colonizing it with artists, musicians, coffee grow-

ers and the architecturally unique Hotel Moka.

Youthful Energy of Santa Clara

7 Check your preconceived ideas about this

country at the city limits. Santa Clara is everything you thought Cuba wasn't: erudite students, spontaneous nightlife, daring creativity and private homestays in abodes stuffed with more antiques than the local decorative-arts museum. Pop into the drag show at Club Mejunje or hang out for a while with the enthusiastic students in La Casa de la Ciudad.

Folklórico Dance in Santiago de Cuba

8 There's nothing quite as transcendental as the hypnotic beat of the Santería drums summoning up the spirits of the *orishas* (African deities). But, while

When to Go

HIGH SEASON
(Nov–Mar & Jul–Aug)

➡ Prices are 30% higher and hotels may require advance bookings. Prices are higher still around Christmas

➡ Weather is cooler and drier November to March.

SHOULDER
(Apr & Oct)

➡ Look out for special deals outside of peak season.

➡ Watch out for Easter vacation, when prices and crowds increase.

LOW SEASON
(May, Jun & Sep)

➡ Some resort hotels offer fewer facilities or shut altogether.

➡ There's a hurricane risk between June and November and higher chance of rain.

most Afro-Cuban religious rites are only for initiates, the drumming and dances of Cuba's *folklórico* troupes are open to all, especially in Santiago de Cuba. Formed in the 1960s to keep the ancient slave culture of Cuba alive, *folklórico* groups enjoy strong government patronage, and their energetic and colorful shows remain spontaneous and grittily authentic.

Cienfuegos' Classical French Architecture

9 There's a certain *je ne sais quoi* about bayside Cienfuegos, Cuba's

Best on Film

Before Night Falls (Julian Schnabel; 2000) The life and struggles of Cuban writer Reinaldo Arenas.

Che: The Argentine (Steven Soderbergh; 2008) Focuses on Che's Cuban years.

El Ojo del Canario (Fernando Pérez; 2010) Award-winning biopic of José Martí.

Fresa y Chocolate (Tomás Gutiérrez Alea; 1993) Marries the improbable themes of homosexuality and communism.

Best in Print

Che Guevara: A Revolutionary Life (Jon Lee Anderson; 1997) Meticulously researched biography.

Cuba and the Night (Pico Iyer; 1996) Perhaps the most evocative book about Cuba ever written by a foreigner.

Dirty Havana Trilogy (Pedro Juan Gutiérrez; 2002) Life in Havana during the Special Period.

Our Man in Havana (Graham Greene; 1958) Greene pokes fun at both the British Secret Service and Batista's corrupt regime.

Getting Around

Bicycle Cuba is a cyclist's paradise, with bike lanes, bike workshops and drivers accustomed to sharing the road countrywide. *Poncheros* (puncture-repair stalls) fix flat tires and provide air. Throughout the country, the 1m-wide strip of road to the extreme right is reserved for bicycles, even on highways.

Car Car rental in Cuba is easy, but once you've factored in gas, insurance, hire fees etc, it isn't cheap. It's cheaper to hire a taxi for distances of under 150km.

Train Public railways serve all of the provincial capitals and are a great way to experience Cuba, if you have time and patience. While train travel is safe, the departure information provided is purely theoretical. Getting a ticket is usually no problem, as there's a quota for tourists paying in convertibles.

self-proclaimed 'Pearl of the South.' Through hell, high water and an economically debilitating Special Period, this city has retained its poise. The elegance is best seen in the architecture, a cityscape laid out in the early 19th century by settlers from France and the US. Dip into the cultural life around the center and adjacent Punta Gorda to absorb the Gallic refinement.

Baracoa's Spicy Food & Culture

10 Over the hills and far away on the eastern-most limb of Guantánamo province lies isolated Baracoa, Cuba's oldest city, found by Diego Velázquez de Cuéllar in 1511. The small yet historically significant settlement is weird even by Cuban standards for its fickle Atlantic weather, eccentric local populace and unrelenting desire to be, well, different. Watch locals scale coconut palms, listen to bands play *kiribá*, the local take on *son*, and – above all – enjoy Baracoa's infinitely spicier, richer and more inventive food, starting with the sweet treat *cucuruchu*.

Palacio de Valle, Cienfuegos

Kyrenia

CAPITAL
Nicosia (Lefkosia)

POPULATION
1.2 million

AREA
9251 sq km

OFFICIAL LANGUAGES
Greek, Turkish

Cyprus

This island country possesses a fractured identity, a passionate people, and a culture, landscape and lifestyle that capture the imagination and produce plenty of surprises.

This is not your standard Mediterranean island cliché; Cyprus reflects its proximity to Asia and the Middle East in its culture, cuisine and history. Similarly evocative is the contrast between old and new, particularly evident in the capital, Nicosia (Lefkosia), where dilapidated buildings sit round the corner from smart boutiques and arty bars.

And yet with a stunning landscape and overall mild climate outside is where it's at. From the varied beaches to the pine-clad interior, you can swim, dive, hike, bike, wine and dine, and, in winter, even ski.

Digging into the island's past has unearthed extraordinary relics, including Neolithic dwellings, Bronze Age and Phoenician tombs and exquisite Roman mosaics. And while on the streets, keep your eyes peeled for Venetian walls, Byzantine castles and churches, Roman monasteries and Islamic mosques.

Experiencing the intrinsically different Greek and Turkish societies of the island's present is increasingly easy for visitors – and will give a fuller picture of the complex and fractured Cypriot identity.

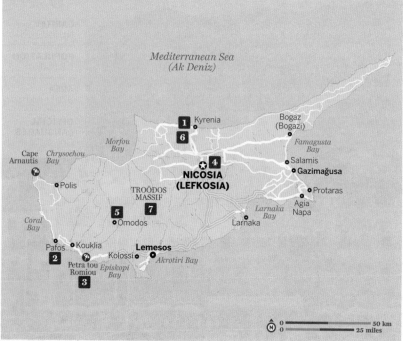

Mediterranean Sea
(Ak Deniz)

Cyprus'
Top Experiences

Kyrenia's Old Harbour

1 With the romantic silhouette of the mountains providing the backdrop, the slow pace of modern life in Northern Cyprus doesn't get any more idyllic than by Kyrenia's U-shaped Old Harbour. Its charming elevated buildings and well-kept storehouses once stockpiled tonnes of raw carob, then considered black gold by the locals. Now these edifices proffer trendy cafes and restaurants, where you can sit for hours with a Cypriot coffee or experience the *nargileh* (water pipes) as Turkish *gulets* (traditional wooden ships) bob sporadically, moored around the harbour's landing and castle.

Pafos Archaeological Site

2 One of the island's most mesmerising archaeological sites is located in the southerly resort of Pafos. A vast, sprawling site (take a hat in summer), the ancient city dates back to the late 4th century BC and what you see now is believed to be only a modest part of what remains to be excavated. Highlights include the intricate and colourful Roman floor mosaics at the heart of the original complex, first unearthed by a farmer ploughing his field in 1962.

Petra tou Romiou

3 Also known as Aphrodite's Rock & Beach, this is possibly the most famous and mythical beach in Cyprus and it's certainly one of its most unusual and impressive. It's said that waves break over Aphrodite's Rock to form a pillar of foam with an almost human shape. For the best shot to impress the folks at home, come to the strategically positioned tourist pavilion at sunset.

North Nicosia's Old City

4 Crossing the Green Line from Lefkosia into North Nicosia, the Turkish area north of the city, is an extraordinary experience. Extending like a tangled web from the Republic's smart Ledra St, old-fashioned shops selling faded jeans

and frilly shirts are flanked by kebab kiosks, coffee shops and sweet stalls, their counters piled high with freshly made halva. Visit the extraordinary mosque, a tranquil hammam and the various museums, or just wander the streets, staying until the evening, when the minarets' crescent moons are silhouetted against a backdrop of twinkling stars.

Wine Villages Around Omodos

5 The far-reaching vineyards of the *krasohoria* (wine villages) dominate Omodos' surrounding slopes. Navigating this region, where every house was once said to have its own wine-making tools, is an adventure that requires discipline and good use of the spittoon. Boutique wineries now number over 50 here, across six or seven traditional villages, with a vast array of wines and grapes. The most famous indigenous varieties derive from the *mavro* (dark-red grape) and *xynisteri* (white grape) vines, along with another 10 varieties.

if Cyprus were 100 people

77 would be Greek
18 would be Turkish
5 would be other

belief systems
(% of population)

78   18   4

Greek Orthodox   Muslim   other

population per sq km

CYPRUS   USA   UK

♦ ≈ 30 people

When to Go

HIGH SEASON
(Jul & Aug)

➡ Accommodation books out; prices increase up to 30%.

➡ Beach resorts are crowded, especially with families.

➡ Marked increase in local tourism.

➡ Temperatures can reach up to 40°C.

SHOULDER
(Mar–Jun, Sep & Oct)

➡ Ideal time to travel; pleasant weather and fewer crowds.

➡ Perfect for outdoor activities, particularly hiking and cycling in the Troödos.

➡ April and May are a dazzle of wildflowers inland.

LOW SEASON
(Nov–Feb)

➡ Skiing in the Troödos.

➡ Can be wet and cool or pleasantly mild.

➡ Some hotels and restaurants in the main resorts are closed.

The Kafeneio

In the villages, the local *kafeneio* (coffee shop) is the central meeting point. Most have two such places, distinguished by their political alignment (socialist or nationalist). They are filled with men of all generations, sitting, serving, or flipping beads. The older men sit quietly, spread across chairs, waiting out the days like oracles, eating haloumi and olives or drinking coffee and *zivania*. Good friends sit in pairs, smoking cigarettes and playing *tavli* (backgammon) in the shade of the vine leaves. Their dice rattle, while moves are counted and strategies are shaped in whispers. And come lunchtime, only the lingering smoke remains, as the men stampede home for their midday meal and siesta, returning in the evening to do it all again.

Food & Drink

It would be limiting to say that Cypriot food is only a combination of Greek and Turkish cuisine (although these are its pillars); Middle Eastern influences are also powerful here, with the flavours of Syria and Lebanon hard to miss. For a picnic, grab some bread, haloumi, olives, juicy Cypriot tomatoes and fresh figs.

Dolmades Stuffed vine leaves

Kleftiko Oven-baked lamb.

Lahmacun A kind of pizza equivalent.

Louvia me lahana Greens cooked with black-eyed beans.

Souvla Barbecued skewered lamb.

Stifado Beef and onion stew.

Wine From the Troödos Massif mountain range: sweet *komandaria* is the traditional wine, while *zivania* (a strong spirit distilled from grape pressings) is the local firewater.

St Hilarion Castle

6 Legend has it that this dreamy fortress was the inspiration for the spectacularly animated palace of the wicked queen in Walt Disney's *Snow White*. Its ruins now form a jagged outline across the rocky landscape, exuding the Gothic charm of the Lusignan court that once convened here during the summer. The castle's precipitous staircases and overrun gardens and paths form an arduous climb to its tower. From here, though, the spectacular views across the sea to the Anatolian coast only add to its magical quality.

Hiking in the Troödos

7 These mountains offer an expanse of flora, fauna and geology across a range of pine forests, waterfalls, rocky crags and babbling brooks. The massif and summit of Mt Olympus, at an altitude of 1952m, provide spectacular views of the southern coastline and welcome respite from the summer heat. Ramblers, campers, flower spotters and birdwatchers alike will be absorbed by the ridges, peaks and valleys that make up the lushest and most diverse hiking and nature trails on the island.

Getting Around

Bus Buses in the South are frequent and run from Monday to Saturday, with no services on Sunday. Buses in the North are a varied mix of old and newer privately owned buses. Costs are surprisingly reasonable.

Car First, and most important: drive defensively. Cyprus has one of the highest accident rates in Europe, despite the overall good state of its roads. If you're planning to rent a car in high season, book well in advance.

Taxi In the South, taxis are available on a 24-hour basis; they are generally modern vehicles and, apart from outside the major centres, are equipped with meters. In the North, taxis do not have meters, so agree on the fare with the driver beforehand.

Český Krumlov

CAPITAL
Prague

POPULATION
10.6 million

AREA
78,864 sq km

OFFICIAL
LANGUAGES
Czech, Slovak

Czech Republic

Prague is the equal of Paris in terms of beauty, while its history goes back a millennium. And as for Czech beer – it's the best in Europe.

Since the fall of communism in 1989 and the opening of Central and Eastern Europe, Prague has evolved into one of Europe's most popular travel destinations. The city offers an intact medieval core that transports you back 500 years in time. The 14th-century Charles Bridge, traversing two historic riverside neighbourhoods, is one of the continent's most beautiful sights. But the city is not just about history. It has a vital urban centre with a rich array of cultural offerings.

Outside the capital, castles and palaces abound – including the audacious hilltop chateau at Český Krumlov – which illuminate the stories of powerful families and individuals whose influence was felt throughout Europe. Beautifully preserved Renaissance towns that withstood the ravages of the communist era link the centuries, and idiosyncratic landscapes provide a stage for active adventures.

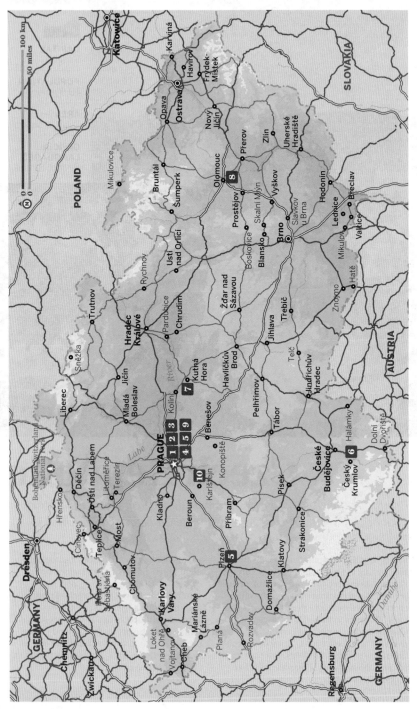

Czech Republic's
Top Experiences

Charles Bridge

1 Whether you visit alone in the morning mist or shoulder your way through the afternoon crowds, crossing Charles Bridge is the quintessential Prague experience. Built in 1357, it withstood wheeled traffic for 500-odd years – thanks, legend claims, to eggs mixed into the mortar – until it was made pedestrian-only after WWII. By day, the baroque statues stare with indifference at a fascinating parade of buskers, jazz bands and postcard sellers; at dawn, they regain some of the mystery and magic their creators sought to capture.

Prague Castle

2 A thousand years of history is cradled within the walls of Prague's hilltop castle, a complex of churches, towers, halls and palaces that is almost a village in its own right. This is the cultural and historical heart of the Czech Republic, comprising not only collections of physical treasures, such as the golden reliquaries of St Vitus Treasury and the Bohemian crown jewels, but also the sites of great historic events such as the murder of St Wenceslas and the Second Defenestration of Prague.

Amazing Architecture

3 One of Prague's prime attractions is its physical appearance. Prague Castle and the city centre are a textbook display of around 900 years of architectural evolution – bluff Romanesque, sublime Gothic, elegant Renaissance and dazzling baroque, plus 19th-century revivals of all of these – all amazingly undisturbed by the modern world and folded into a compact network of lanes, passages and culs-de-sac. And that's before you get started on the 20th century's sleek and sensual art nouveau, and Prague's uniquely Czech cubist and rondo-cubist buildings

Prague Jewish Museum

4 This museum encompasses half a dozen ancient synagogues, a ceremonial hall and former mortuary, and the powerful melancholy of the Old Jewish Cemetery. These monuments are clustered together in Josefov, a small corner of the Old Town that was home to Prague's Jews for some 800 years before it was brought to an end by an urban renewal project at the start of the 20th century and the Nazi occupation during WWII. The exhibits tell the moving story of Prague's Jewish community, from the 16th-century creator of the Golem, Rabbi Loew, to the horrors of Nazi persecution.

Czech beer

5 'Where beer is brewed, life is good', according to an old Czech proverb. Which means that life in Prague must be very good indeed, as the city is awash in breweries both large and small. Czech beer has been famous for its quality and flavour since the invention of Pilsner Urquell in 1842, but recently there has been a renaissance of microbreweries and craft beers, and you can now enjoy everything from classic *ležák* (pale lager) to *kvasnicové* (yeast beer) and *kávové pivo* (coffee-flavoured beer). Tour the Pilsner Urquell Brewery in Plzeň to see where it all started; highlights include a trip to the old cellars (dress warmly) and a glass of unpasteurised nectar.

Spanish Birds & Moravian Sparrows

Many Czech dishes have names that don't offer a clue as to what's in them, but certain words will give you a hint: *šavle* (sabre; something on a skewer); *tajemství* (secret; cheese inside rolled meat); *překvapení* (surprise; meat, capsicum and tomato paste rolled into a potato pancake); *kapsa* (pocket; a filling inside rolled meat); and *bašta* (bastion; meat in spicy sauce with a potato pancake).

Two strangely named dishes that are familiar to all Czechs are *Španělský ptáčky* (Spanish birds; sausage and gherkin wrapped in a slice of veal, served with rice and sauce) and *Moravský vrabec* (Moravian sparrow; a fist-sized piece of roast pork). But even Czechs may have to ask about *Tajemství Petra Voka* (Peter Vok's mystery; carp with sauce) and *Dech kopáče Ondřeje* (the breath of grave-digger Andrew; fillet of pork filled with extremely smelly Olomouc cheese).

Food & Drink

Becherovka A shot of this sweetish herbal liqueur from Karlovy Vary is a popular way to start (or end) a big meal. Drink it cold.

Beer Czechs claim to have the best *pivo* (beer) in the world and who are we to argue?

Carp This lowly river fish, known locally as *kapr*, is given pride of place every Christmas at the centre of the family meal.

Dumplings Every culture has its starchy side dish; for Czechs it's *knedliky* – big bread or potato balls sliced like bread and meant to mop up gravy.

Pork Move over beef, *vepřové maso* (pork) is king here. Highlights include roast pork, pork *guláš* (goulash) or pork *vepřový řízek* (schnitzel).

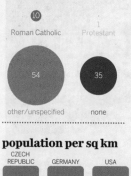

if the Czech Republic were 100 people

64 would be Czech
5 would be Moravian
1 would be Slovak
30 would be other

belief systems
(% of population)

10
Roman Catholic

1
Protestant

54

35

other/unspecified

population per sq km

CZECH REPUBLIC

GERMANY

USA

† ≈ 30 people

Sedlec Ossuary, near Kutná Hora

Český Krumlov

6 Outside of Prague, Český Krumlov is arguably the Czech Republic's only other world-class sight and must-see. From a distance, the town looks like any other in the Czech countryside, but once you get closer and see the Renaissance castle towering over the undisturbed 17th-century townscape, you'll feel the appeal; this really is that fairy-tale town the tourist brochures promised.

Kutná Hora

7 A medieval townscape, the magnificent Gothic Cathedral of St Barbara and a 'bone church' combine to make this Unesco World Heritage–listed town a popular day trip from Prague. Hang on, a *what* church? The eerie 19th-century ossuary at Sedlec monastery, near Kutná Hora, defies easy architectural description. When the Schwarzenbergs bought the monastery in 1870 they let a local woodcarver get creative with the bones piled in the crypt (the remains of around 40,000 people), resulting in the 'bone church' of Sedlec Ossuary. Garlands of skulls hang around a chandelier containing at least one of each bone in the human body; there's even a Schwarzenberg coat of arms made from bones.

Olomouc

8 Although it's practically unknown outside the Czech Republic and underappreciated at home, Olomouc is surprisingly

When to Go

MAY

➡ Prague comes alive with festivals from classical music and beer to fringe arts.

JULY

➡ Karlovy Vary shows off its arty side at the sleepy spa town's annual film fesival.

DECEMBER

➡ Prague's Christmas Market draws visitors from around the world.

majestic. The main square is among the country's nicest, surrounded by historic buildings and blessed with a Unesco-protected trinity column. The evocative central streets are dotted with beautiful churches, testifying to the city's long history as a bastion of the Catholic Church. Explore the foundations of ancient Olomouc Castle at the must-see Archdiocesan Museum, then head for one of the city's many pubs or microbreweries. Don't forget to try the cheese, *Olomoucký sýr*, reputedly the smelliest in the country.

Best on Film

Amadeus (1985) Mozart's love affair with Prague gets brilliant treatment.

Kolya (1996) Velvet Revolution-era Prague never looked lovelier.

Loves of a Blonde (1965) Miloš Forman's 'New Wave' classic.

Mission Impossible (1996) Prague was the setting for the first instalment of Tom Cruise's blockbuster trilogy.

Best in Print

The Unbearable Lightness of Being (Milan Kundera; 1984) Prague before the 1968 Warsaw Pact invasion.

I Served the King of England (Bohumil Hrabal; 1990) The Hotel Paříž is the backdrop to this humorous classic.

The Castle (Franz Kafka; 1926) We wonder which castle Kafka was thinking about?

The Good Soldier Švejk (Jaroslav Hašek; 1923) Hašek's absurdist novel is set throughout the Czech Republic.

My Merry Mornings (Ivan Klima; 1986) The sweeter side of life in communist Prague.

Getting Around

Bus Within the Czech Republic, long-distance buses are often faster, cheaper and more convenient than trains, though many bus routes have reduced frequency (or none) at weekends.

Public Transport Public transport is affordable, well organised and runs from around 4.30am to midnight daily. Purchase tickets in advance from newsstands and vending machines. Prague has an integrated metro, tram and bus network – tickets are valid on all types of transport, and for transfer between them.

Train Czech Railways provides efficient train services to almost every part of the country.

Astronomical Clock

9 Every hour, on the hour, crowds gather beneath Prague's Old Town Hall Tower to watch the Astronomical Clock in action. Despite the medieval marionette show lasting only 45 seconds, the clock is one of the Czech Republic's best-known tourist attractions. After all, it's historic, photogenic and – if you take time to study it – rich in intriguing symbolism. It's among the many attractions in the Old Town Square, one of Europe's most beautiful urban spaces.

Karlštejn Castle

10 Rising majestically above the village of Karlštejn, Karlštejn castle is rightly one of the top attractions in the Czech Republic. This fairy-tale medieval fortress is in such good shape that it wouldn't look out of place on Disneyworld's main street. The crowds come in theme-park proportions as well, but the peaceful surrounding countryside offers views of Karlštejn's stunning exterior that rival anything you'll see on the inside.

9

LUKICH / GETTY IMAGES ©

Nyhavn, Copenhagen.

CAPITAL
Copenhagen

POPULATION
5.6 million

AREA
43,094 sq km

OFFICIAL LANGUAGE
Danish

Denmark

Vikings, Hans Christian Andersen, Lego and now New Nordic cuisine – this is a small country with some big claims. It's a place that's perfected the art of living well.

Denmark is the bridge between Scandinavia and northern Europe. To the rest of Scandinavia, the Danes are fun-loving, frivolous party animals, with relatively liberal, progressive attitudes. Their culture, food, architecture and appetite for conspicuous consumption owe as much, if not more, to their German neighbours to the south as to their former colonies – Sweden, Norway and Iceland – to the north.

Packed with intriguing museums, shops, bars, nightlife and award-winning restaurants, Denmark's capital, Copenhagen, is one of the hippest, most accessible cities in Europe. And while Danish cities such as Odense and Aarhus harbour their own cultural gems, Denmark's other chief appeal lies in its photogenic countryside, sweeping coastline and historic sights such as neolithic burial chambers, the bodies of well-preserved Iron Age people exhumed from their slumber in peat bogs, and atmospheric Viking ruins and treasures from Denmark's conquering sea-going days.

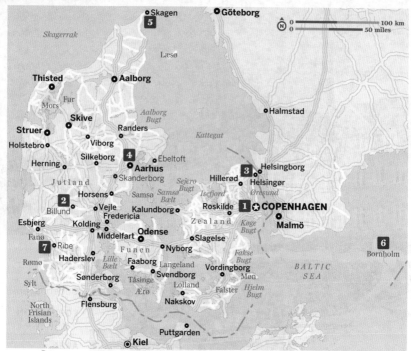

Denmark's
Top Experiences

Copenhagen

1 You may find it hard to suppress your envy for residents of Scandinavia's coolest capital. While this 850-year-old harbour town retains much of its historic good looks (think copper spires, cobbled squares and pastel-coloured gabled abodes), the focus here is on the city's design scene, a futuristic metro system, and clean, green developments. Its streets are awash with effortlessly hip shops, cafes and bars; world-class museums and art collections; brave new architecture; and a decent helping of Michelin-starred restaurants.

Legoland

2 'The Happiest Place on Earth'? Disneyland may lay claim to the slogan, but Legoland, though considerably smaller, could be a contender. This is, after all, a theme park celebrating the 'toy of the century' (as adjudged by *Fortune* magazine in 2000) in the country in which it was invented: Denmark, 'the world's happiest nation' (according to a Gallup World Poll). So you've got to believe Legoland will be something special – and it is. It's Denmark's most-visited tourist attraction (beyond Copenhagen), and it's just one of dozens of family-friendly amusement parks dotted around the country.

Kronborg Slot

3 Something rotten in the state of Denmark? Not at this fabulous 16th-century castle in Helsingør, made famous as the Elsinore Castle of Shakespeare's *Hamlet*. Kronborg's primary function was not as a royal residence, but rather as a grandiose toll house, wresting taxes from ships passing through the narrow Øresund between Denmark and Sweden. The fact that Hamlet, Prince of Denmark, was a fictional character hasn't deterred legions of sightseers from visiting the site.

Aarhus

4 Always the bridesmaid, never the bride, Aarhus labours in the shadows of

AROS Aarhus Kunstmuseum, Aarhus

Copenhagen in terms of tourist appeal, but this is a terrific city in which to spend a couple of days. It has a superb dining scene, thriving nightlife (much of it catering to the large student population), picturesque woodland trails and beaches along the city outskirts, and one of the country's finest art museums, turning heads thanks to the whimsical multicoloured walkway on its roof.

Skagen

5 Skagen is an enchanting place, both bracing and beautiful. It lies at Denmark's northern tip and acts as a magnet for much of the population each summer, when the town is full to capacity yet still manages to provide plenty of charm. In the late 19th century artists flocked here, infatuated with the impact of the radiant light on the rugged landscape. Now tourists flock to enjoy the output of the 'Skagen school' artists, soak up that luminous light, devour the plentiful seafood and laze on the fine sandy beaches.

When to Go

HIGH SEASON
(Jul–Aug)

➡ Long daylight hours, with A-list concerts, festivals and theme parks in full swing.

➡ Busy camping grounds, beaches, sights and transport.

➡ Accommodation prices peak.

SHOULDER
(May–Jun & Sep)

➡ A good time to travel, with generally mild weather and fewer crowds.

➡ Spring offers local produce, flowers and a few festivals.

➡ Autumn has golden landscapes and cosy nights.

LOW SEASON
(Oct–Apr)

➡ Cool and wet with short daylight hours but plenty of *hygge* (cosiness).

➡ Big cities have Christmas lights and ice-skating rinks.

➡ Reduced hours for sights; outdoor attractions closed.

if Denmark were 100 people

87 would live in urban areas
13 would live in rural areas

belief systems
(% of population)

95
Evangelical Lutheran

3
other Christian

2
Muslim

population per sq km

DENMARK   USA   UK

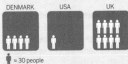

👤 ≈ 30 people

Danish Design

Along with its Scandinavian neighbours, Denmark has had a massive influence on the way the world builds its public and private spaces, and on the way it designs interiors, furniture and homewares. Since the 1950s Danish designers have blazed trails in these fields, much of their output defined by cool clean lines, graceful shapes and streamlined functionality.

These design concepts have been applied to everything from concert halls to coffee pots to Lego blocks. The result has not just been great artistic acclaim but also big business. Iconic brands include Bang & Olufsen (sleek stereos), Bodum (kitchenware), Georg Jensen (silverware and jewellery) and Royal Copenhagen Porcelain. Then there's the furniture designers and fashion houses.

Food & Drink

Akvavit Denmark's best-loved spirit is caraway-spiced akvavit, drunk straight down as a shot, followed by a chaser of øl (beer).

Beer Carlsberg may dominate, but there's an expanding battalion of microbreweries.

Kanelsnegl A calorific delight, the 'cinnamon snail' is a sweet, buttery pastry, sometimes laced with chocolate.

New Nordic flavours The celebrated culinary movement that passionately embraces local and seasonal produce.

Sild Smoked, cured, pickled or fried, herring is a local staple and best washed down with generous serves of akvavit.

Smørrebrød Rye bread topped with anything from beef tartar to egg and shrimp, the open sandwich is Denmark's most famous culinary export.

Round church, Bornholm

Bornholm

6 Bornholm is a Baltic beauty, a Danish island lying some 200km east of the mainland (located closer to Germany and Sweden than to the rest of Denmark). This magical island holds a special place in the hearts of most Danes, and is beloved for its plentiful sunshine, glorious sandy beaches, endless cycle paths, iconic *rundkirker* (round churches), artistic communities, fish smokehouses and idyllic thatched villages. If that's not enough to lure you, the island is developing a reputation for outstanding restaurants and local edibles.

Ribe

7 Compact, postcard-perfect Ribe is Denmark's oldest town, and it encapsulates the country's golden past in style, complete with an imposing 12th-century cathedral, quaint cobblestone streets, skewed half-timbered houses and lush water meadows. Stay overnight in atmospheric lodgings that exude history, and take a free walking tour narrated by the town's nightwatchman – the perfect way to soak up the streetscapes as well as tall tales of local characters.

Getting Around

Bicycle Cycling is a practical way to get around. There are extensive bike paths linking towns throughout Denmark, and bike lanes through most city centres.

Boat Ferries link virtually all of Denmark's populated islands.

Train The rail network is super-reliable, with reasonable fares and frequent services. The network extends to most corners of the country, with the exception of the southern islands and a pocket of northwestern Jutland. In these areas, a good network of local buses connects towns.

Salt flats, Lac Assal

CAPITAL
Djibouti City

POPULATION
792,198

AREA
23,200 sq km

**OFFICIAL
LANGUAGES**
French
Arabic

Djibouti

*Djibouti, a tiny speck of a country, packs a big punch, making
up for its diminutive size with austere beauty, other wordly
landscapes and geological oddities.*

Few countries in the world offer such weird
landscapes as Djibouti. Think salt lakes,
extinct volcanoes, sunken plains, limestone
chimneys belching out puffs of steam, ba-
saltic plateaus and majestic canyons. This
comes courtesy of Djibouti's location, straddling the intersection of three diverging
tectonic plates, on the edge of the Red Sea.

Outdoor adventure comes in many forms
here, with superb and challenging hiking
opportunities. Then, after extending yourself
in the rugged beauty of the interior, there is
diving and kitesurfing on the Red Sea – not
to mention snorkelling alongside mighty
whale sharks in the Gulf of Tadjoura.

Barring Djibouti City, the country is refreshingly devoid of large-scale development.
It's all about ecotravel, with some great sustainable stays in the hinterland that provide
a fascinating glimpse into rural life. Travelling independently around Djibouti may
not come cheap, but despite the high cost of
living you'll leave this corner of Africa with
new experiences and wonderful memories.

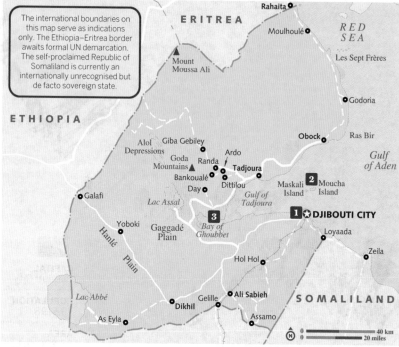

The international boundaries on this map serve as indications only. The Ethiopia–Eritrea border awaits formal UN demarcation. The self-proclaimed Republic of Somaliland is currently an internationally unrecognised but de facto sovereign state.

Djibouti's
Top Experiences

Djibouti City

1 There's a palpable sense of change in the air in Djibouti City. Under its veneer of urban bustle, the city remains down-to-earth, with jarring cultural and social combinations. Traditionally robed Afar tribesmen, stalwart GIs, sensuous Somali ladies and frazzled businessmen jostle side by side.

Red Sea

2 The glassy and pleasantly warm waters of the Red Sea are ideal for scuba diving or snorkelling. Most diving takes place off the islands of Maskali and Moucha in the Gulf of Tadjoura, which rewards divers with a host of scenic sites for all levels. Wreck enthusiasts will be spoiled, and reef dives also beckon. Djibouti is diveable year-round but November to March is best.

Bay of Ghoubbet

3 Get up close and personal with whale sharks in the Bay of Ghoubbet, at the western end of the Gulf of Tadjoura, from November to January. This spot is one of only a few places in the world where these giant yet gentle creatures appear regularly in near-shore waters, easily accessible to observers. Give the sharks a berth of at least four metres.

Food & Drink

You'll find excellent seafood, rice, pasta, local meat dishes such as stuffed lamb, and other treats imported from France in Djibouti City. In the countryside, choice is more limited, with goat meat and rice as the main staples. Alcohol is widely available in the capital.

When to Go

NOV–JAN
➡ Ideal time to visit. Perfect for outdoor activities. Whale sharks make their annual appearance.

OCT & FEB–APR
➡ The shoulder seasons are not a bad time to visit, especially in the Goda Mountains.

MAY–SEP
➡ You'll swelter under average daily temperatures of about 40°C.

Roseau

CAPITAL	Roseau
POPULATION	73,286
AREA	751 sq km
OFFICIAL LANGUAGE	English

Dominica

With waterfalls, jungle, sulfur springs, secret swimming holes, rivers, reefs and coastline, this untamed and mass-tourism-free 'nature island' promises unusual experiences and adventures.

On Dominica, nature has been as creative and prolific as Picasso in his prime. Much of this volcanic island is blanketed by untamed rainforest that embraces you with the loft and grandeur of a Gothic cathedral. Experiences await that will forever etch themselves into your memory: an intense trek to a bubbling lake, soothing your muscles in hot sulfur springs, getting pummeled by a waterfall, snorkeling in a glass of 'champagne,' swimming up a narrow gorge – the list of possible ecoadventures goes on.

In many ways, Dominica is the 'anti-Caribbean' island. It has been spared the mass tourism, in large part because there are very few sandy beaches, no flashy resorts and no direct international flights. The locals are so friendly that they often stop visitors just to wish them a good visit. Just as uniquely, Dominica is also home to about 2200 Caribs, the only pre-Columbian population remaining in the eastern Caribbean.

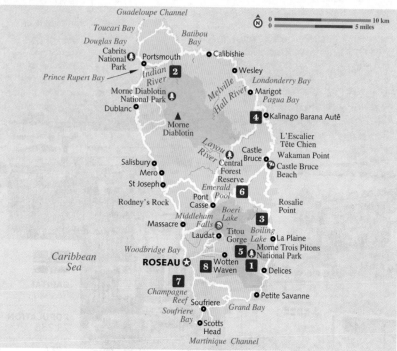

Dominica's
Top Experiences

Morne Trois Pitons National Park

1 Count the shades of green amid the breathtaking scenery of the Unesco-protected Morne Trois Pitons National Park, a stunning pastiche of lakes, fumaroles, volcanoes, hot springs and dense forest. This park stretches across 17,000 acres of Dominica's mountainous volcanic interior. Most of it is primordial rainforest, varying from jungles thick with tall, pillarlike gommier trees to the stunted cloudforest cover on the upper slopes of Morne Trois Pitons (4550ft), Dominica's second-highest mountain. The park embraces such top wilderness sites as Boiling Lake, Boeri Lake, Freshwater Lake and Middleham Falls.

Indian River

2 The slow and silent boat trip along the shady, mangrove-lined Indian River is memorable, as you glide past buttressed bwa mang trees whose trunks rise out of the shallows, their roots stretching out laterally along the riverbanks. Enjoy close-up views of egrets, crabs, iguanas, hummingbirds and other creatures that live in the air and in the jungle. Ask your guide to point out where scenes from *Pirates of the Caribbean* were filmed. Rowers are waiting at the mouth of the river; the 1½-hour trips include a stop at the Indian River Bush Bar. The 'Dynamite' rum punch is the bar's signature drink, a mixture of fruits, herbs and 'local atmosphere.'

Hike to Boiling Lake

3 Dominica's pre-eminent trek, and one of the hardest, is the six-hour roundtrip to the world's second-largest actively boiling lake (the largest is in New Zealand). Geologists believe the 207ft-wide lake is a flooded fumarole – a crack in the earth that allows hot gases to vent from the molten lava below. The fizzing, eerie-looking lake sits inside a deep cauldron, its grayish waters veiled in steam, its center emitting bubbly burps. It's a spectacular sight. The hike traverses the aptly named Valley of Desolation, whose sulfur rivers, belching steam vents and geysers evoke post-atomic grace.

KIM WALKER / GETTY IMAGES ©

Kalinago Barana Autê

4 The 3700-acre Carib Territory, which begins around the village of Bataka, is home to most of Dominica's 2200 Caribs – properly known as Kalinago. Find out about Kalinago history and culture at the Kalinago Barana Autê heritage village. The 30- to 45-minute tour of the recreated traditional village includes stops at a 'karbet', or 'men's house', a 10ft-long dugout canoe carved from a single tree, and a waterfall. Tours conclude at a snack bar and gift shop where Kalinago women weave their ornate baskets.

Swimming in Titou Gorge

5 Inside the Morne Trois Pitons National Park, a swimming hole gives way to this narrow gorge ending at a torrential waterfall. The eerily quiet, short swim through the crystal-clear water is a spooky experience. It's dark down there, with steep vine-clad lava walls no more than 5ft or 7ft apart, hence the name, which is Creole for 'small throat'. If you're not a swimmer, you can just take a refreshing dip in the swimming hole, which is fed by a hot mineral spring.

if Dominica were 100 people

86 would be black
9 would be mixed
3 would be Carib Amerindian
1 would be white
1 would be other

belief systems
(% of population)

61 Roman Catholic

21 Protestant

1 Jehovah's Witnesses

8 other Christian

1 Rastafarian

8 other

population per sq km

DOMINICA   USA   UK

👤 ≈ 30 people

When to Go

FEB–JUN

➜ The island's driest months are the most popular.

➜ Carnival runs for two weeks prior to Ash Wednesday.

JUL–OCT

➜ The rainy season, coinciding with hurricane season (peaks in August and September).

OCT–NOV

➜ World Creole Music Festival is held in October.

➜ The week leading up to Independence Day (November 3), or Creole Day, is a vibrant celebration of local heritage.

Hollywood's Treasure Island

With its wild coast, thick jungle and hidden coves, Dominica has always been a popular haunt of pirates between pillages, so it was only natural that Hollywood came calling when location scouting for the *Pirates of the Caribbean* films.

In 2005, hundreds of cast and crew, led by Johnny Depp, Orlando Bloom and Keira Knightley, invaded the island to shoot scenes of films two and three in locations such as Titou Gorge, Soufriere, the Indian River and Batibou Beach.

And if that wasn't enough, two years later, CBS filmed the reality show *Pirate Master* all around Dominica. Arrgh, mateys!

Food & Drink

Callaloo A creamy thick soup or stew blending a variety of vegetables (eg dasheen, spinach, kale, onions, carrots, eggplant, garlic, okra) with coconut milk and sometimes crab or ham.

Fresh fruit Bananas, coconuts, papayas, guavas, pineapples, and mangoes grow so plentifully they litter the roadside in places.

Kubuli Dominica uses the island's natural spring water for its home-grown beer label; you'll see red-and-white signs all over the island with Kubuli's concise slogan – 'The Beer We Drink.'

Macoucherie Rum connoisseurs crave this local concoction. Don't be fooled by the plastic bottles or cheap-looking label, it's an undiscovered gem.

Sea moss Nonalcoholic beverage made from seaweed mixed with sugar and spices and sometimes with evaporated milk. It's sold in supermarkets and at snackettes (snack bars).

ALVARO LEIVA / GETTY IMAGES ©

Emerald Pool

6 Emerald Pool takes its name from the lush green setting and crystal-clear water. At the base of a 40ft waterfall, the pool is deep enough for a refreshing dip. The short path to get here winds through a rainforest of massive ferns and tall trees. On the way back there are two viewpoints – one is a panorama of the Atlantic Coast and the other is a great view of Dominica's second-highest mountain.

Champagne Reef

7 This is one of Dominica's most unusual underwater playgrounds. Volcanic bubbles emerge from vents beneath the sea floor, rising up as drops of liquid crystal and making it feel like you're swimming in a giant glass of champagne. Best of all, you can snorkel right off the (rocky) beach. Technicolor fish and coral abound.

Wotten Waven

8 Wotten Waven is famous for its natural hot sulfur springs and, thanks to some enterprising locals, has become a low-key 'spa' destination. The biggest spa is Screw's Sulfur Spa, owned by a charismatic Rasta. It has six stonewalled pools of varying temperatures, and sulfur mud wraps and lava scrubs are available.

Getting Around

Bus Bus travel is the most economical way of getting around Dominica. Private minibuses run between major cities from 6am to 7pm Monday to Saturday, stopping as needed along the way. Fares are set by the government.

Car A 4WD is recommended for exploring in the mountains – even some of the main roads at higher altitudes are in bad condition. Drivers need a local license issued by a car-rental agency.

Punta Cana

Dominican Republic

Much more than beach resorts, the Dominican Republic is one of the Caribbean's most geographically diverse countries, with an evocative colonial history and warm welcoming people.

CAPITAL
Santo Domingo

POPULATION
10.3 million

AREA
48,670 sq km

OFFICIAL LANGUAGE
Spanish

The Dominican Republic (DR) is defined by its hundreds of miles of coastline – some with picturesque white-sand beaches shaded by rows of palm trees, other parts lined dramatically with rocky cliffs. Symbolizing both limits and escapes, the sea is the common denominator across fishing villages, where the shoreline is used for mooring boats, indulgent tourist playgrounds, small towns, and cities like Santo Domingo – the Caribbean's largest and the site of New World firsts.

Beyond the capital, much of the DR is distinctly rural. Further inland are vistas reminiscent of the European alps: four of the Caribbean's five highest peaks rise above the fertile lowlands surrounding Santiago. Remote deserts extend through the southwest, giving the DR a complexity not found on other islands. The country's roller-coaster past is writ large in the diversity of its ethnicities, not to mention the physical design of its towns and cities.

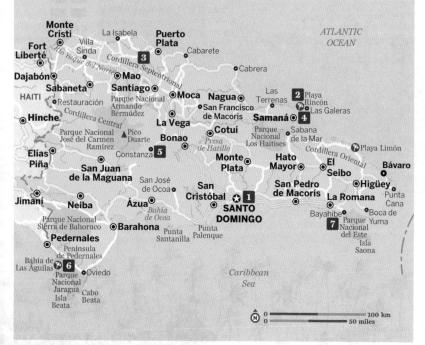

Dominican Republic's
Top Experiences

Santo Domingo's Zona Colonial

1 For those fascinated by the origin of the 'New World,' by the dramatic and complicated story of the first encounter between native people of the Americas and Europeans, the Zona Colonial, listed as a Unesco World Heritage site, is a fascinating place to explore. With its cobblestone streets and beautifully restored mansions, it's easy to imagine Santo Domingo's landmark quarter as the seat of Spain's 16th-century empire. But the past and present coexist rather gracefully here; follow in the footsteps of pirates and conquistadors one moment, the next pop into a shop selling CDs from the latest Dominican merengue star.

Playa Rincón

2 Consistently rated one of the top beaches in the Caribbean by those in the know – people who courageously brave heatstroke and sunburn in a quest for the ideal tan – Rincón is pitch-perfect. Stretching uninterrupted for almost 3km of nearly-white soft sand and multihued water, the beach even has a small stream at its far western end, great for a quick freshwater dip at the end of a long, sunny day. It's large enough for every daytripper to claim their own piece of real estate without nosy neighbors peeking over the seaweed and driftwood. A thick palm forest provides the backdrop and fresh seafood can be served upon request.

The 27 Waterfalls of Damajagua

3 Travelers routinely describe the tour of the waterfalls at Damajagua as the coolest thing they did in the DR. We agree. A short drive from Puerto Plata, a hard-won slosh to the far side of the river and a trek through the lush forest lead to these falls. Experiencing this spectacular series of cascades involves wading through clear pools, swimming through narrow, smoothwalled canyons, hiking through forest, and climbing rocks, ropes and ladders through the roaring falls themselves. And yet the real fun is on the return trip, when you can leap and slide back down the falls, some jumps as high as 10m.

5

CARDEL BERTRAND / HEMIS.FR / GETTY IMAGES ©

Las Galeras

4 This sleepy fishing village at the far eastern end of the Península de Samaná is an escape from your getaway. Fewer tourists and therefore less development means that the area around Las Galeras includes some of the more scenic locales in all the DR. Swaying palm trees back beaches ready-made for a movie set, and waves crash over hard-to-get-to cliffs. For at least one sunset, venture out to Restaurant El Cabito, where you might glimpse migrating whales and a dolphin or two.

Mountain Vistas in Constanza

5 The scenery found in the central highlands of the DR is a surprise to most visitors. Cloud-covered peaks whose slopes are a patchwork of well-tended agricultural plots and galloping forest growth rising from the valley floor are vistas not often associated with Caribbean islands. A stay on the outskirts of Constanza, truly a world away from the developing coastline, provides a front-row seat to often spectacular sunsets.

if the Dominican Republic were 100 people

73 would be mixed
16 would be white
11 would be black

belief systems
(% of population)

95 — Roman Catholic
5 — other

population per sq km

DOMINICAN REPUBLIC · USA · HAITI

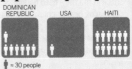

= 30 people

When to Go

HIGH SEASON
(mid-Dec–Feb &
Jul–Aug)

➡ The week before Easter is also high season (and water sports are prohibited during this week).

➡ Expect significantly higher hotel prices and beaches.

SHOULDER
(Mar–Jul)

➡ You may see short but strong daily rains in Santo Domingo (through October).

➡ March is generally one of the drier months in Samaná.

LOW SEASON
(Aug–early Dec)

➡ Hurricane season, but if there are no storms it's still an excellent time to travel.

➡ Temperatures don't vary much (except in the mountains).

➡ Room rates are deeply discounted.

Baseball

Not just the USA's game, *beísbol* is part of the Dominican social and cultural landscape – so much so that ball players who have made good in the US major leagues are without doubt the most popular and revered figures in the country. More than 400 Dominicans have played in the major leagues. Two dozen major-league teams have training facilities here.

The Dominican professional baseball league's season runs from October to January. Because the US and Dominican seasons don't overlap, many Dominican players in the US major leagues and quite a few non-Dominicans play in the winter league in the DR as well.

GREG JOHNSTON / GETTY IMAGES ©

Food & Drink

Dominican ron (rum) Known for its smoothness and hearty taste. Dozens of local brands are available, but the big three are Brugal, Barceló and Bermudez.

Fish Central to the Dominican diet – usually served in one of four ways: *al ajillo* (with garlic), *al coco* (in coconut sauce), *al criolla* (with a mild tomato sauce) or *a la diabla* (with a spicy tomato sauce).

Guineos (bananas) A staple served stewed, candied or boiled and mashed. With plantains, the dish is called *mangú*; with pork rinds mixed in it is called *mofongo*.

La Bandera (the flag) The most typically Dominican meal. Consists of white rice, *habichuela* (red beans), stewed meat, salad and fried green plantains.

Pastelitos The most common snack in the DR – fried dough containing beef or chicken, which has been stewed with onions, olives and tomatoes and then chopped and mixed with peas, nuts and raisins.

Bahía de Las Águilas

6 If you believe in fairy-tale utopian beaches, pristine Bahía de Las Águilas fits the bill. Located in the extremely remote southwestern corner of the DR, it's not on the way to anything else, but those who do make it are rewarded with 10km of nearly deserted beach forming a slow arc between two prominent capes. That you have to take a boat to get there – and that there won't be any tourists there except for you – transform it into one of the most beautiful beaches in the country.

Bayahibe

7 Clear Caribbean water, healthy reefs and plenty of fish and other sea life make this coastal village, near La Romana in the southeast, the country's best scuba-diving destination bar none. You'll find boat services to the islands of Saona and Catalina, and the island's best wreck dive, the *St George*, is out here, too. Snorkelers will find themselves equally well catered to, and there's the unique opportunity to spend a few hours cruising the shoreline in a traditional fishing vessel.

Getting Around

Air The DR's inadequate road network means travelers with limited time should consider flying.

Bus Fares are low, and reservations aren't usually necessary, on first-class buses. *Gua-guas*, rarely with air-con, range from minivans to midsize buses. They stop all along the route to pick up and drop off passengers.

Car If you're driving outside major cities, a 4WD is recommended.

Taxis Dominican taxis wait at designated *sitios* (stops), located at hotels, bus terminals, tourist areas and main public parks. Cheaper and easier to find than taxis, *motoconchos* (motorcycle taxis) are the best and sometimes only way to get around in many towns.

CAPITAL
Dili

POPULATION
1.2 million

AREA
14,874 sq km

OFFICIAL LANGUAGES
Tetun, Portugese

East Timor

With mountains to climb and untouched reefs to dive, Asia's newest country, Timor-Leste, is a winner.

It's home to a youthful population and a diverse international presence that adds just the right amount of spice. Its capital, Dili, has all the bright lights, but venture out for wild cultural experiences. Stay in a grand Portugese *pousada* on a misty hilltop, or at a quiet island ecolodge. Get rowdy dancing the night away, journey down roads alongside herds of buffalo, then wind up through rainforests dotted with coffee plants. Keep an eye out for whales as you hug the cliffs along the north-coast road. Photogenic white-sand beaches with aqua waters tempt swimmers and for those who want to delve deeper, Dili-based dive companies have spent the past decade discovering world-class dive sites.

Timor-Leste richly rewards those who venture to its mountainous interior for trekking, hot springs, dense jungles and raging rivers. Getting there is a major part of the adventure, whether by vehicle, mountain bike, foot or even Timor pony – however, it is well worth the effort. Trailblaze your way through this amazing country: it's adventure with a smile.

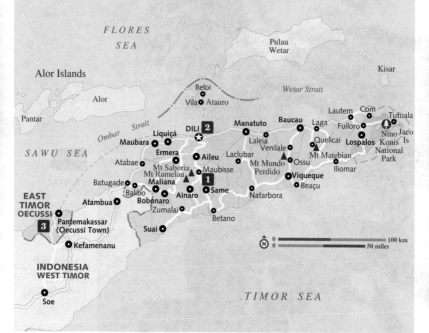

East Timor's
Top Experiences

Maubisse

1 Wake up in chilly Maubisse, 70km from Dili, and watch clouds rising, uncovering the village below, with coffee plantations and misty valleys giving way to views of the coast.

Food & Drink

Dili's fresh fish, lobster and prawns will make your mouth water.

Sure, there are a few fine-dining places that serve up amazing seafood in Asian, Portuguese and African flavours, but nothing beats the nightly charcoal-grill food stalls on the Av de Portugal beachfront, where the seafood is simple and fresh.

Go Diving in Dili

2 Enjoy being in one of the few cities in the world where the reef is just steps away from the urban centre. The reef fringing the entire north coast of Timor-Leste provides spectacular diving and snorkelling. Many sites, including the legendary K41 east of town, are easily accessed by walking in from the beach, with dramatic drop-offs just 10m offshore in parts.

Oecussi

3 The remote enclave of Oecussi is a Cinderella-in-waiting. Surrounded on all sides by Indonesian West Timor, Oecussi can be tricky to get to. But if you make the journey, you'll be rewarded with long stretches of beach and reef, some of the most beautiful *tais* (woven cloth) in the country and pools of hot mud bubbling in its southernmost region. Relax into the slow pace of this beautiful and secluded district.

When to Go

YEAR ROUND
➡ Temperatures are equatorial hot year round.

MAY–NOV
➡ Good weather and great for diving with no silt-laden rivers flowing into the sea.

DEC–APR
➡ Very wet, so travel can be difficult, with unsealed roads impassable.

Giant tortoise, Volcán Alcedo, Isla Isabela, Galápagos

CAPITAL
Quito

POPULATION
15.4 million

AREA
283,561 sq km

OFFICIAL LANGUAGE
Spanish

Ecuador

Picturesque colonial centers, Kichwa villages, Amazonian rainforest and the breathtaking heights of the Andes – Ecuador may be small, but it has a dazzling array of wonders.

Wandering the cobblestone streets of Ecuador's historic centers of Quito and Cuenca is a fine way to delve into the past. But beyond its cities, the Ecuadorian landscape unfolds in startling variety.

The Andes can seem like a fairy tale place, with a patchwork of small villages, gurgling brooks and rolling fields. As the mists clear, a view of towering snow-covered peaks comes into view.

The famed Galápagos Islands are a magnet for wildlife lovers. See massive lumbering tortoises, marine iguanas (the world's only seagoing lizard), doe-eyed sea lions, blue-footed boobies and a host of unusual species.

The Amazon rainforest offers a vastly different wildlife-watching experience. Set out on rivers and trails snaking through the undergrowth in search of monkeys, sloths, toucans, river dolphins and anacondas.

Premontane cloud forest is yet another biologically rich area, and home to a fantastic array of avian life, with some of the best bird-watching in South America.

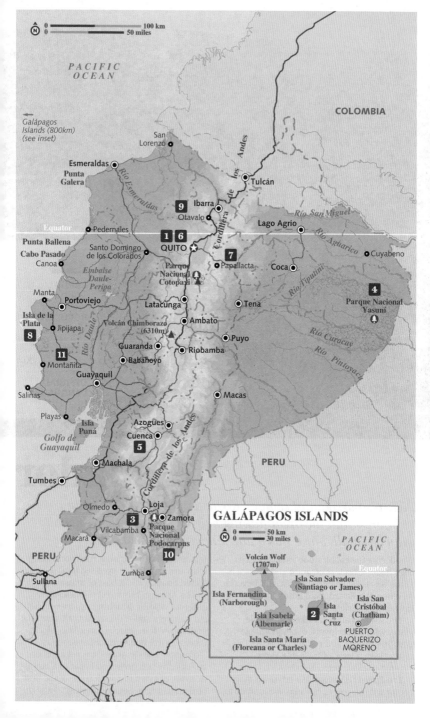

PACIFIC OCEAN

COLOMBIA

Galápagos Islands (800km) (see inset)

San Lorenzo

Esmeraldas
Punta Galera

Tulcán

9 Ibarra
Otavalo

Cordillera de los Andes

Río San Miguel
Río Aguarico

Equator

Pedernales

Lago Agrio

Cuyabeno

Punta Ballena
Cabo Pasado
Canoa

Santo Domingo de los Colorados

1 6
QUITO

7 Papallacta

Coca

Parque Nacional
Yasuní **4**

Embalse Daule-Peripa

Parque Nacional Cotopaxi

Río Tiputini

Manta

Portoviejo

Latacunga

Ambato
Tena

Río Curaray

Isla de la Plata **8**
Jipijapa

Volcán Chimborazo (6310m)

Puyo

Río Pintoyaco

11
Montañita

Guaranda
Babahoyo

Riobamba

Guayaquil

Salinas

Macas

Playas

Isla Puná

Azogues
Cuenca **5**

Golfo de Guayaquil

Cordillera de los Andes

PERU

Machala

Tumbes

Olmedo

Loja

Zamora

3
Vilcabamba

Parque Nacional Podocarpus

10

Macará

PERU

Zumba

Sullana

GALÁPAGOS ISLANDS

0   50 km
0   30 miles

PACIFIC OCEAN

Volcán Wolf (1707m)

Equator

Isla San Salvador (Santiago or James)

Isla Fernandina (Narborough)

2 Isla Santa Cruz

Isla San Cristóbal (Chatham)

Isla Isabela (Albemarle)

PUERTO BAQUERIZO MORENO

Isla Santa María (Floreana or Charles)

Ecuador's
Top Experiences

Quito Old Town

1 A Spanish-colonial stunner, Quito's vibrant Centro Histórico is packed with elaborate churches and mournful monasteries (some centuries in the making), people-packed plazas and looming bell towers. History lurks around every corner of this well-preserved center. Delve into the past by stepping off the cobblestones and entering beautifully maintained museums, historic mansions and jaw-dropping sanctuaries. Afterwards, have a meal in one of El Centro's old-world restaurants or join the festivities on lively La Ronda street before retiring to one of the many charming guesthouses in the neighborhood.

Iguana Spotting in the Galápagos

2 There aren't many places that can beat the Galápagos Islands for close encounters of the prehistoric kind. Rather than scurrying away when approached, the unique species of iguanas found throughout the archipelago go about their slow-moving business with little concern for the clicking cameras. The dark gray or black marine iguanas pile on top of one another and bask in the sun, whereas the imposing yellow land iguanas nibble on cactus plants for sustenance.

JOHN COLETTI / GETTY IMAGES ©

Vilcabamba

3 The air in Vilcabamba just feels right – not too hot, not too cold; mountain fresh with just a hint of incense – giving this southern highland draw a mystical quality. Perhaps that's why you'll find more foreigner-owned businesses here than almost anywhere else in Ecuador. And who can blame them? The hiking is great, there's a national park nearby for backwoods adventures on horseback and mountain bike, and the pitch-perfect spa resorts will cater to your every need, whim and desire.

if Ecuador were 100 people

65 would be mestizo
25 would be Amerindian
7 would be white
3 would be black

belief systems
(% of population)

95 Roman Catholic
5 other

population per sq km

ECUADOR   USA   UK

≈ 30 people

Parque Nacional Yasuní

4 This vast tract of protected rainforest contains a simply dazzling biodiversity matched almost nowhere else on earth. Excitement-filled canoe trips through tiny overgrown creeks and hikes across the jungle floor with experienced guides reveal all manner of flowers, plants and creatures, many of which you'll not even have heard of before, let alone seen in real life, while several populations of indigenous peoples continue to resist contact with the outside world here. This natural wonder remains, at present, unspoiled.

Cuenca

5 The colonial center of Cuenca has been charming visitors since the 16th century. And while the cobblestone streets, polychrome facades and remarkably well-preserved cathedral will have you snapping a photo on nearly every corner, it's the town's laid-back feel, friendly locals and bohemian spirit that will truly fill your heart and soul. Top that off with great nightlife, plenty of museums and galleries, and some of Ecuador's best eateries, and there's no doubt this is a top highlight of southern Ecuador.

Riding the TelefériQo

6 Proving there's more than one way to summit the Andean peaks, the TelefériQo whisks you up by aerial tram to breathtaking heights (4100m) over Quito. In a city of sublime views, Cruz Loma offers the finest if you go on a clear day. Here, Quito spreads out across the Andean valley, with majestic

Indigenous Tribes

Humbling, fascinating and unforgettable: just a few words to describe a visit to an indigenous village in the Oriente.

The Huaorani are an Amazonian tribe living between the Río Napo and the Río Curaray. They number no more than 4000 and remain one of Ecuador's most isolated indigenous groups. They have a reputation for being warriors. They make no distinction between the physical and spiritual worlds and have an intimate understanding of the rainforest.

Visitors will be introduced to customs that have remained unchanged for centuries, learn about indigenous trapping, hunting and cooking techniques, see how *chicha* (a fermented corn drink) is made, watch local dancing and singing and perhaps witness a shamanistic soul-cleansing ritual.

Food & Drink

Arroz con pollo Rice with small bits of chicken mixed in.

Ceviche Marinated raw seafood.

Churrasco Fried beef, eggs and potatoes, a few veggies, slices of avocado and tomato, and rice.

Cuy Roasted guinea pig.

Encebollado A brothy seafood and onion soup poured over yuca and served with fried banana chips and popcorn.

Encocado Shrimp or fish cooked in a rich coconut sauce.

Hornado Whole roasted pig.

Llapingachos Fried potato-and-cheese pancakes.

Locro de papa Potato soup served with avocado and cheese.

Maito Fish or chicken grilled in palm leaves.

Pollo a la brasa Roast chicken, often served with fries.

Seco de chivo Goat stew.

3

peaks (including Cotopaxi) visible in the distance. At the top, extend the adventure by hiking (or by horseback) to the 4680m summit of Rucu Pichincha.

The Steaming Waters of Papallacta

7 The beautifully maintained public baths just outside the Andean village of Papallacta offer one of

Ecuador's best natural highs: move between baths of thermally heated water surrounded by mountains, swim in the fantastic pool, enjoy a bracing jump into the icy plunge pool and then get right back into those steaming baths. It's even more magical at night, when you can lie back and watch the stars come out in the giant black sky above.

Whale-Watching off Isla de la Plata

8 In terms of sheer awe-inspiring natural power, experiencing the breaching of a humpback whale is hard to equal. From June to September every year nearly 1000 of these majestic creatures

When to Go

HIGH SEASON
(Jun–Sep)

➡ Sunny, clear days in the highlands; less rain in the Oriente.

➡ December to April is high season on the coast: warm temperatures and periodic showers.

➡ January to May is high season in the Galápagos.

SHOULDER SEASON
(Oct–Nov)

➡ Cooler temperatures, more showers (usually sun in the morning and rain in the afternoon) in the highlands.

LOW SEASON
(Dec–May)

➡ Cooler, rainier days in the highlands.

➡ June to December is low season in the Galápagos with cooler, drier weather and rougher seas.

➡ Low season is April to July in the Oriente; heavy rain is common.

migrate to the waters off the coast of Ecuador. The prime base for organizing boat trips, during which you might also spot dolphins and killer, pilot and beaked whales, is the fishing town of Puerto López.

Local Crafts, Otavalo Market

9 Every Saturday the world seems to converge on the bustling indigenous town of Otavalo in the Andes, where a huge market (which goes on in a rather redacted form every other day of the week, too) spreads out from the Plaza de Ponchos throughout the town. The choice is enormous, the quality immensely changeable and the crowds can be a drag, but you'll find some incredible bargains here among the brightly colored rugs, traditional crafts, clothing, striking folk art and quality straw hats.

Best on Film

Entre Marx y una Mujer Desnuda (1996) Portrays a group of young intellectuals in Quito.

Qué tan lejos (2006) Road movie about two young women on a journey of self-discovery in the Andean highlands.

Best in Print

Floreana (1961) Recounting of eccentrics and colorful episodes on the Galápagos by Margret Wittmer.

The Farm on the River of Emeralds (1978) Moritz Thomsen's compelling memoir about living on the Ecuadorian coast.

The Villagers (1934) Jorge Icaza's portrait of the hardships of Andean indigenous life.

Savages (1995) Hilarious, eye-opening account of the Huaorani vs the oil industry by Joe Kane.

Getting Around

Canoe The most common boat travel is by motorized canoe, which acts as a water taxi or bus along the major rivers of the Oriente and parts of the northern coast. Motorized canoes are often the only way to a rainforest lodge.

Bus In terms of scope and affordability, Ecuador's bus system is impressive to say the least. Buses are the primary means of transport for most Ecuadorians, guaranteed to go just about anywhere. They can be exciting, cramped, fun, scary, sociable and grueling, depending on where you're going and who's drivin'

Truck In remote areas, trucks often double as buses. Sometimes these are large flatbed trucks with a tin roof, open wooden sides and uncomfortable wooden-plank seats. These curious-looking 'buses' are called *rancheras* or *chivas*.

Parque Nacional Podocarpus

10 Down by the Peruvian border is one of the southern highland's least-visited reserves. With elevations from 900m to 3600m, Podocarpus is home to an amazing array of plant and animal life. There are an estimated 3000 plant species here (many of which are endemic). For bird lovers, an astounding 600 unique types of feathered friends await. Top that off with trails, highland lakes and sweeping views and you have one of Ecuador's most unique offbeat attractions.

Surfing, Montañita

11 A dependable year-round beach break and a welcoming community of experienced surfers and mellow dreadlocked travelers make this coastal village an ideal stop for those looking to ride some waves. Beginners unafraid to take a little pounding and swallow some salt water can find willing locals for lessons and there are smaller breaks north of here in Olón. Even if you're not looking to get air on gnarly overheads, watching the exploits while stunning sunsets provide the backdrop is not a bad alternative.

Pyramids of Giza

CAPITAL
Cairo

POPULATION
85.3 million

AREA
1 million sq km

OFFICIAL LANGUAGE
Arabic

Egypt

Perhaps no other people in the world say 'Welcome' so frequently – and mean it every time. Egypt's ancient civilisation still awes, but today's Egyptians are pretty amazing, too.

With sand-covered tombs, austere pyramids and towering Pharaonic temples, Egypt brings out the explorer in all of us. Visit the Valley of the Kings in Luxor, where Tutankhamun's tomb was unearthed, and see the glittering finds in the Egyptian Museum in Cairo. Hop off a Nile boat to visit a waterside temple, or trek into the desert to find the traces of Roman trading outposts. You never know – your donkey might stumble across yet another find, just as many previous discoveries were made.

Egypt is the most traveller-friendly country in the Middle East. This means you'll enjoy decent places to sleep and English spoken to some degree everywhere. It also means that if you ever get into a jam, an Egyptian will likely be there to help you out. Then again, an Egyptian will also be there to sell you some papyrus or perfume – an undeniable reality of travel here. But the souvenir sales are a minor irritant when compared with the chance to connect with some of the world's most generous people.

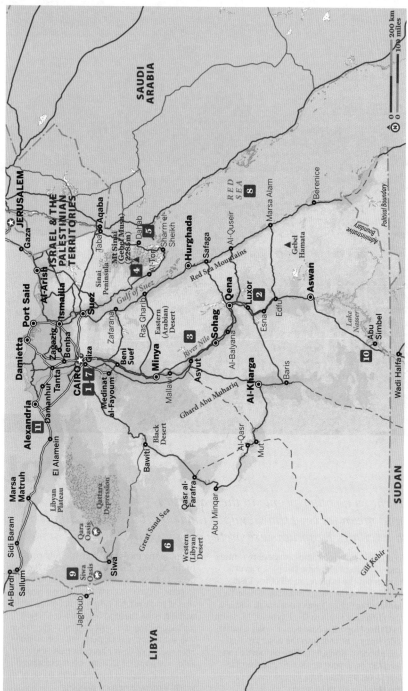

Egypt's
Top Experiences

Pyramids of Giza

1 Towering over the urban sprawl of Cairo and the desert plains beyond, the Pyramids of Giza and the Sphinx are at the top of every traveller's itinerary. For nearly 4000 years, the extraordinary shape, impeccable geometry and sheer bulk of the Giza Pyramids have invited the obvious question: 'How were we built, and why?' Centuries of research have given us parts of the answer.

We know they were massive tombs constructed on the orders of the pharaohs by teams of workers tens-of-thousands strong. No trip to Egypt is complete without a photo of you in front of the last surviving ancient wonder of the world.

Luxor

2 With the greatest concentration of ancient Egyptian monuments anywhere in Egypt, Luxor

rewards time spent here. You can spend days or weeks around this town, walking through the columned halls of the great temples on the east bank of the Nile, such as the Ramesseum, or climbing down into the tombs of pharaohs in the Valley of the Kings on the west bank. Time spent watching the sun rise over the Nile or set behind the Theban hills are some of Egypt's unforgettable moments.

Memorial Temple of Hatshepsut, Deir al-Bahri

Cruising the Nile

3 A cruise on the Nile River has always ranked among the world's most exciting and most romantic travel experiences. The Nile is Egypt's lifeline, the artery that runs through the entire country, from south to north. Only by setting adrift on it can you appreciate its importance and its beauty, and more practically, only by boat can you see some archaeological sites as they were meant to be seen. Sailing is the slowest and most relaxing way to go, but even from the deck of a multistorey floating hotel you're likely to glimpse the magic.

if Egypt were 100 people

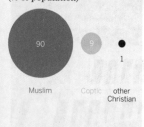

45 would live in urban centres
55 would live outside urban centres

belief systems
(% of population)

90 Muslim
9 Coptic Christian
1 other

population per sq km

EGYPT KENYA UK

♦ ≈ 15 people

Mt Sinai

4 It may not be the highest of Sinai's craggy peaks, but Mt Sinai is the peninsula's most sacred. A place of pilgrimage for Jews, Christians and Muslims alike, the summit affords the magnificent spectacle of light washing over the sea of surrounding mountaintops. Down below, tucked into the mountain's base, is St Katherine's Monastery. Its sturdy Byzantine fortifications are built over the spot where Moses is believed to have witnessed the burning bush.

Dahab

5 Laid-back Dahab, a midsized town near the southern tip of the Sinai, is Egypt's version of a chill pill, the place for ruin-fatigued travellers to cast off the history lessons and recuperate in one of the small-scale beachfront hotels. Once your batteries have recharged, dive into Dahab's famous underwater world or organise some desert adventure fun. Though you may find you're also seduced by the joy of doing nothing for a few more days.

Desert Safaris

6 Whether you travel by 4WD, camel or foot, for a couple of hours or a couple of weeks, you'll be able to taste the simple beauty and isolation of wildest Egypt. The highlights of an excursion in Egypt's Western Desert include camping among the surreal formations of the White Desert, crossing the mesmerising dunes of the Great Sand Sea and heading deep into the desert to live out English Patient fantasies at the remote Gilf Kebir.

Find Your Own Ahwa

Cairo's *ahwas* – traditional coffeehouses – are essential places to unwind, chat and breathe deeply over a sheesha. Dusty floors, rickety tables and the clatter of dominoes and *towla* (backgammon) define the traditional ones. But newer, shinier places – where women smoke as well – have expanded the concept, not to mention the array of sheesha flavours, which now include everything from mango to bubblegum.

Most *ahwas* are open from 8am to 2am or so, and you can order a lot more than tea and coffee: try karkadai (hibiscus, hot or cold), irfa (cinnamon), kamun (cumin, good for colds), yansun (anise) and, in winter, hot, milky sahlab.

Food & Drink

Fuul The national dish is an unassuming peasant dish of slow-cooked fava beans with garlic, parsley, olive oil, lemon, salt, black pepper and cumin.

Fiteer The Egyptian pizza has a thin, flaky pastry base, and is topped with salty haloumi cheese and olives, or comes sweet with jam, coconut and raisins.

Kushari A vegetarian's best friend: noodles, rice, black lentils, chickpeas and fried onions, with a tangy tomato sauce. Many kushari shops also sell *makaroneh bi-lahm*, a baked pasta-and-lamb casserole.

Shwarma Strips of lamb or chicken sliced from a vertical spit, sizzled on a hot plate with chopped tomatoes and garnish, and then stuffed into shammy bread.

Ta'amiyya (also known as felafel) Ground broad beans and spices rolled into patties and deep fried, often stuffed in shammy bread as a sandwich.

Jackson Reef, Red Sea

Egyptian Museum

7 The scale of the Egyptian Museum is simply overwhelming. More than a hundred rooms are packed to the rafters with some of the most fascinating treasures excavated in Egypt: glittering gold jewellery, King Tut's socks and mummies of the greatest pharaohs, plus their favourite pets. Don't push yourself to see it all, and do hire a guide for an hour or two to unlock some of the storehouse's secrets.

Red Sea Diving

8 Egypt's Sinai and Red Sea coastlines are the doorstep to a wonderland that hides below the surface. Whether you're a seasoned diving pro or a first-timer, Egypt's underwater world of coral cliffs, colourful fish and spookily beautiful wrecks is just as staggeringly impressive as the sights above. Bring out your inner Jacques Cousteau by exploring the enigmatic wreck of WWII cargo ship the Thistlegorm, a fascinating museum spread across the sea bed.

When to Go

HIGH SEASON
(Oct–Feb)

➡ Egypt's 'winter' is largely sunny and warm, with very occasional rain (more frequent on the Mediterranean).

➡ Be prepared for real chill in unheated hotels, especially in damp Alexandria.

SHOULDER
(Mar–May, Sep–Oct)

➡ Spring can have dust storms disrupting flights.

➡ Heat can extend into October, when crowds are lighter.

➡ Warm seas and no crowds at Mediterranean spots.

LOW SEASON
(Jun–Aug)

➡ Scorching summer sun means only the hardiest sightseers visit Upper Egypt.

➡ Avoid the Western Desert.

➡ High season on the Mediterranean coast.

Oasis Life

9 It's impossible not to relax in an oasis – here, with the endless desert shimmering on the horizon, you can float in hot springs or explore the remains of ancient Roman outposts and tribal villages. In Siwa, the Dahab of the desert, cold springs and palm groves keep you cool during the day. In Dakhla, the restored mud-brick town of Al-Qasr gives a glimpse of centuries-old oasis living. It's easy to spend enough time out here to make the long drive worth it.

Best on Film

Death on the Nile (1978) Agatha Christie's whodunit has Poirot investigating the murder of an heiress on board a Nile cruiser.

Sphinx (1980) Adapted from a bestselling novel by Robin Cook (Coma), this is a tale about antiquities smuggling shot entirely in Cairo and Luxor, but from which no one emerges with any credit, except the location scout.

The Spy Who Loved Me (1977) The Pyramids, Islamic Cairo and Karnak provide glamorous backdrops for the campy, smirking antics of Roger Moore as James Bond.

Best in Print

Maryam's Maze (Mansoura Ez-Eldin; 2004) One of the brightest new talents to come out of Egypt.

The Cairo Trilogy (Naguib Mahfouz; 1957) Nobel prizewinner, Mahfouz's three novels are, in order: Palace Walk; Palace of Desire; Sugar Street.

The Yacoubian Building (Alaa Al Aswany; 2002) Best-selling exposé of contemporary Egyptian society.

Getting Around

Air EgyptAir (www.egyptair.com) is the only domestic carrier, and fares can be surprisingly cheap, though they vary considerably depending on season.

Bus You can get to just about every city, town and village in Egypt on a bus, at a very reasonable price. For many long-distance routes beyond the Nile Valley, it's the best option, and sometimes the only one.

Train Egypt's rail system comprises more than 5000km of track to almost every major city and town. Aside from two main routes (Cairo–Alexandria, Cairo–Aswan), you have to be fond of trains to prefer them to a deluxe bus. But for destinations near Cairo, trains win because they don't get stuck in traffic.

Abu Simbel

10 Ramses II built Abu Simbel a long way south of Aswan, along his furthest frontier and just beyond the Tropic of Cancer. But these two enormous temples are a marvel of modern engineering as well: in the 1960s they were relocated, block by block, to their current site to protect them from the flooding of Lake Nasser. To appreciate the isolation, spend the night at Abu Simbel, either on a boat on the lake or at Nubian cultural centre and ecolodge Eskaleh.

Alexandria

11 Flaunting the pedigree of Alexander the Great and the powerful queen Cleopatra, Egypt's second-largest city is rich in history, both ancient and modern. Visit the Bibliotheca Alexandrina, the new incarnation of the ancient Great Library, or any number of great small museums around town. Walk the souqs of atmospheric Anfushi, the oldest part of the city, and be sure to feast on fresh seafood with a Mediterranean view along the grand waterfront corniche.

Al-Qasr, Dakhla

DANIELA DIRSCHERL / GETTY IMAGES ©

Playa El Zonte, La Libertad

CAPITAL
San Salvador

POPULATION
6.1 million

AREA
21,040 sq km

OFFICIAL LANGUAGES
Spanish, Nahuat

El Salvador

Surf's up in El Salvador, a tiny Central American nation finally emerging as a hot travel destination after a not-so-distant civil war and internal hardships kept it off the tourist radar.

El Salvador is Central America's smallest, most densely populated country, with the region's largest economy and its fewest foreign tourists. Once only a trickle of headstrong surfers and foreign correspondents passed through its rigorous border posts, but now a new breed of traveler is pushing through in search of an authentic experience in an undervisited land.

El Salvador is a perennial tease. Glimpses of tropical paradise, lush tracts of pre-industrial national park lands, colonial splendor astride pristine volcanic lakes, searing colors and a fierce creative vision sit quietly in the shadows of an indomitable local pride. Here you'll find a glorious coastline, a buzzing culture-clad capital, hard-core war tourism and small-town charm by the plaza-load.

Salvadorans themselves are increasingly content to return home from prolonged stints abroad, the once enviable rite of passage now cut short by global economics and a growing sentiment that home might just be where the fresh start is.

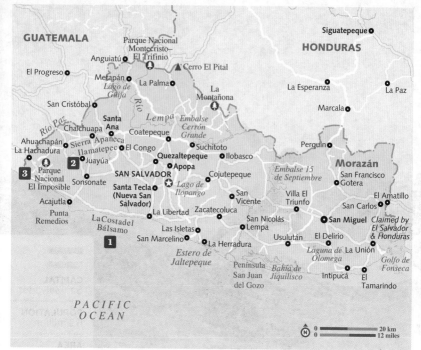

El Salvador's
Top Experiences

Surfing the South Coast

1 Catch a wave at some of Central America's best surf spots along Costa del Balsamo, including Punta Roca (scenes from the classic surf flick *Big Wednesday* were filmed here), Playa El Sunzal and Playa El Tunco.

Juayúa's feria

2 Juayúa is famed for its weekend *feria gastronómica* (food fair) where crowds from across the country sample the region's best cuisine, including barbecued iguana, guinea pig and frog skewers. During the week, Juayúa returns to its relaxed roots, as travelers stroll the warm, cobblestone streets or venture into the surrounding hills to explore hot springs and waterfalls.

Parque Nacional El Imposible

3 In the Apaneca llamatepec mountain range, this forest – the remains of a threatened ecosystem – is home to an extraordinary variety of plant and animal life, including pumas, tigrillos, wild boars, king hawks and black-crested eagles. Hiking can get muddy and steep but offers grand vistas of misty peaks and the gleaming Pacific Ocean.

Food & Drink

Casamiento A mixture of rice and beans often eaten at breakfast.

Pane French bread stuffed with chicken, salsa, salad and pickled vegetables.

Pupusa Popular street food consisting of round cornmeal dough stuffed with cheese, refried beans and pork rinds, grilled and topped with pickled cabbage.

When to Go

DEC–MAR

➡ The busiest season is *verona* (dry).Climate is hot between Christmas and Easter.

NOV & APR

➡ Either side of peak season the weather is still warm and dry; beaches less crowded.

MAY–OCT

➡ The *invierno* (wet season) is low season, though it usually only rains at night.

Broadway village, Cotswolds

CAPITAL
London

POPULATION
53 million

AREA
130,395 sq km

**OFFICIAL
LANGUAGE**
English

England

*Tower Bridge, Buckingham Palace, Manchester United, The Beatles.
England does icons like no other place on earth, and travel here is
a fascinating mix of famous names and hidden gems.*

From the Roman remains of Hadrian's Wall
to the medieval architecture of Canterbury
Cathedral, England is full of astounding
variety. In the cities, the streets buzz day
and night, filled with tempting shops and
restaurants, and some of the finest museums
in the world. After dark, cutting-edge clubs,
top-class theatre and formidable live music
provide nights to remember. Next day, you're
deep in the English countryside admiring
quaint villages or enjoying a classic seaside
resort. There really is something for every-

one, whether you're eight or 80, going solo
or travelling with your friends, your kids or
your grandma.

Travel here is a breeze, and although the
locals may grumble (in fact, it's a national
pastime) public transport is very good, and a
train ride through the English landscape can
be a highlight in itself. Whichever way you
get around, in this compact country you're
never far from the next town, pub, restaurant, national park or the next impressive
castle on your hit list of highlights.

England's
Top Experiences

Stonehenge

1 Mysterious and compelling, Stonehenge is England's most iconic ancient site. People have been drawn to this myth-rich ring of boulders for more than 5000 years, and we still don't know quite why it was built. Most visitors gaze at the 50-tonne stones from behind the perimeter fence, but with enough planning you can arrange an early morning or evening tour and gain access to the inner ring itself. In the slanting sunlight, away from the crowds, it's an ethereal place. This is an experience that stays with you.

London

2 You could spend a lifetime exploring London and find that the slippery thing's gone and changed on you. One thing is constant: that great serpent of a river enfolding the city in its sinuous loops, linking London both to the green heart of England and the world. There is no place on earth that is more multicultural and the narrow streets are steeped in fascinating history, magnificent art, imposing architecture and popular culture. When you add an endless reserve of cool to this mix, it's hard not to conclude that London is one of the world's great cities, if not the greatest.

1

Oxford

3 A visit to Oxford is as close as most of us will get to the brilliant minds and august institutions that have made this city famous across the globe. But you'll catch a glimpse of this rarefied world in the cobbled lanes and ancient quads where student cyclists and dusty academics roam. The beautiful college buildings, archaic traditions and stunning architecture have changed little over the centuries, leaving the city centre much as Einstein or Tolkien would have found it.

Hadrian's Wall

4 Hadrian's Wall is one of the country's most revealing and dramatic Roman ruins, its 2000-year-old procession of abandoned forts, garrisons, towers and milecastles marching across the wild and lonely landscape of northern England. The wall was about defence and control, but this edge-of-empire barrier also symbolised the boundary of civilised order – to the north lay the unruly land of the marauding Celts, while to the south was the Roman world of orderly taxpaying, underfloor heating and bathrooms.

if England were 100 people

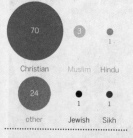

85 would be British
4 would be South Asian
2 would be African & Afro Caribbean
9 would be other

belief systems
(% of population)

70 Christian
3 Muslim
1 Hindu
24 other
1 Jewish
1 Sikh

population per sq km

ENGLAND	SCOTLAND	USA

👤 ≈ 35 people

The Lake District

5 William Wordsworth and his Romantic friends were the first to champion the charms of the Lake District and it's not hard to see what stirred them. The dramatic landscape of whale-backed hills, deep valleys, misty mountain lakes and high peaks makes this craggy corner of the country the spiritual home of English hiking. Strap on the boots, stock up on mint cake and drink in the views: inspiration is sure to follow.

York

6 With its Roman and Viking heritage, ancient city walls and maze of cobbled streets, York is a living showcase for the highlights of English history. Join one of the city's many walking tours and plunge into the network of snickelways (narrow alleys), each one the focus of a ghost story or historical character. Explore the intricacies of York Minster, the biggest medieval cathedral in all of northern Europe, or admire the exhibits from more recent times at the National Railway Museum, the world's largest collection of historic locomotives.

Cornwall

7 You can't get further west than the ancient Celtic kingdom of Cornwall. Blessed with the wildest coastline and most breathtakingly beautiful beaches in England, this proudly independent land has always been determined to march to its own tune. While the staple industries of old – mining, fishing and farming – have all but disappeared, Cornwall has since reinvented itself as one of the nation's creative corners. Explore the space-age domes of the Eden Project, sample culinary creations or chill out on the

Cricket

Along with Big Ben and cups of tea, cricket is an icon of England. Dating from the 18th century – although its roots are much older – this quintessentially English sport spread through the Commonwealth during Britain's colonial era. Australia, the Caribbean and the Indian subcontinent took to the game with gusto, and today the former colonies delight in giving the old country a good spanking on the cricket pitch.

While many English people follow cricket like a religion, to the uninitiated it's an impenetrable spectacle. Spread over one-day games or five-day 'test matches', progress seems so slow, and dominated by arcane terminology like 'innings, overs, googlies, outswinger, leg-bye and silly-mid-off'. If you're patient and learn the intricacies, you might find cricket as enriching and enticing as all the Brits who remain glued to their radio or computer all summer 'just to see how England's getting on'.

Food & Drink

Christmas Pudding A dome-shaped cake with fruit, nuts and brandy or rum, traditionally eaten at Christmas.

Cornish Pasty Savoury pastry, southwest speciality, now available countrywide.

Fish and Chips Long-standing favourite, best sampled in coastal towns.

Full English Breakfast This usually consists of bacon, sausages, eggs, tomatoes, mushrooms, baked beans and fried bread.

Ploughman's Lunch Bread and cheese – pub menu regular, perfect with a pint. Sometimes also includes salad, pickle, pickled onion and dressings.

Roast Beef & Yorkshire Pudding Traditional lunch on Sunday.

Leicester Square, West End

faraway Isles of Scilly for inspiration.

The Cotswolds

8 The most wonderful thing about the Cotswolds is that no matter where you go or how lost you get, you'll still end up in an impossibly quaint village of rose-clad cottages and honey-coloured stone. There'll be a charming village green, a pub with sloping floors and fine ales, and a view of the lush green hills.

London's Theatre Scene

9 However you budget your time and money in London, make sure you take in a show. For big names, head for the West End (the London equivalent of New York's Broadway), where famous spots include the National Theatre, Old Vic, Shaftesbury and Theatre Royal at Drury Lane. For new and experiental works, try the Donmar Warehouse and Royal Court. Either way, you'll soon see that London's theatre scene easily lives up to its reputation as one of the finest in the world – whatever New Yorkers say.

When to Go

HIGH SEASON (Jun–Aug)

➡ Weather at its best. Accommodation rates high, particularly in August.

➡ Roads busy, especially in seaside areas, national parks and popular cities.

SHOULDER (Easter–May & mid-Sep–Oct)

➡ Crowds reduce. Prices drop.

➡ March to May sun mixes with sudden rain; September and October can feature balmy 'Indian summers'.

LOW SEASON (Dec–Feb)

➡ Wet and cold is the norm. Snow can fall, especially up north.

➡ Opening hours reduced October to Easter; some places shut for the winter. Big-city sights operate all year.

Liverpool Museums

10 After a decade of development, the reborn waterfront is once again the heart of Liverpool. The focal point is Albert Dock, a World Heritage Site of iconic and protected buildings, including a batch of top museums: the Merseyside Maritime Museum and International Slavery Museum ensure the good and bad sides of Liverpool's history are not forgotten, while the Tate Liverpool and the Beatles Story museum celebrate popular culture and the city's most famous musical sons (still).

Stratford-upon-Avon

11 The pretty town of Stratford-upon-Avon is where William Shakespeare, the world's most famous playwright, was born and later shuffled off this

Best on Film

Billy Elliott (2000) The story of an aspiring young ballet dancer striving to escape the slag-heaps and boarded-up factories of the industrial north.

Brief Encounter (1945) A classic tale of buttoned-up English passion.

The Full Monty (1997) A troupe of laid-off steel workers become male strippers.

Best in Print

I Never Knew That About England (Christopher Winn) A treasure trove of bizarre facts.

Notes from a Small Island (Bill Bryson) It's dated, but this American's fond take on British behaviour is still spot-on today.

Watching the English (Kate Fox) A fascinating field guide to the nation's peculiar habits.

Getting Around

Air Flights aren't really necessary for tourists; even if you're going from one end of the country to the other, trains compare favourably with planes, once airport down-time is factored in.

Bus & Coach If you're on a tight budget, long-distance buses (called coaches in England) are nearly always the cheapest way to get around, although they're also the slowest – sometimes by a considerable margin.

Car & Motorcycle The downsides for drivers include traffic jams and high parking costs in cities.

Train For long-distance travel around England, trains are generally faster and more comfortable than coaches but can be more expensive, although with discount tickets they're competitive – and often take you through beautiful countryside.

mortal coil. Today, its tight knot of Tudor streets form a living map of Shakespeare's life and times. Huge crowds of thespians and theatre lovers come to take in a play at the famous theatre. Visit the five historic houses owned by Shakespeare and his relatives, then take a respectful detour to the old stone church where the Bard was laid to rest.

Peak District

12 Curiously, you won't find many peaks in the Peak District, but you will find blissful miles of tumbling moorland, plunging valleys, eroded gritstone crags, lush farmland and ancient pocket-sized villages. This beautiful landscape attracts a veritable army of outdoor enthusiasts – cyclists, hikers, cavers and rock climbers – on summer weekends, while those seeking more relaxing enjoyment can admire the rural market and famous puddings of Bakewell, the Victorian pavilions of spa-town Buxton and stunning Chatsworth House – the 'Palace of the Peak'.

View from Froggatt Edge, Peak District National Park

DAVID ELSE / GETTY IMAGES ©

Red-eared guenon, Bioko Island

Equatorial Guinea

A country of two distinct halves, Equatorial Guinea is a nation divided not only by the sea but also by oil wealth and its attendant issues.

Equatorial Guinea's large reserves of black gold were discovered beneath the ocean's floor off the coast of Bioko Island in the mid-1990s, and the subsequent industrial development forever changed the island's landscape, economy and culture. The country's mainland (Rio Muni), however, is much the same as it has been for centuries.

With oil wealth came problems: failed coups, danger money, bushmeat and buckets of oil – you could say Equatorial Guinea has something of a reputation.

However, this is also the land of primates with painted faces, soft clouds of butterflies and insects so colourful they belong in the realm of fiction. On the mainland, white beaches, forest paths and junglescapes await. And if the excited beats of Equatorial-Guinea hip hop don't get you dancing, the architecture will – Gothic cathedrals, ancient wooden churches and butter-coloured homes.

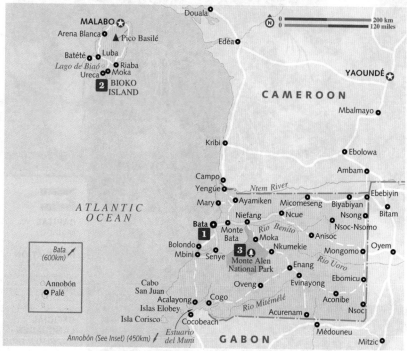

Equatorial Guinea's
Top Experiences

Bata

1 Watch the city of Bata grow vertically with oil money; it's undergoing the kind of makeover that would make for good reality TV. Until recently, the largest town on the mainland was a pleasant enough stop that didn't really warrant a raised eyebrow, but now it's positively gleaming, with wide California boulevards.

Bioko Island

2 Go wide-eyed over the strange combination of dense rain forest, rare wildlife and oil platforms. Little highland town Moka, wedged between charcoal peaks, mahogany giants and glossy lakes, is a breath of fresh air. Rise with the sun and hike through slices of evergreen forest. Fans of the TV series *Lost* reckon Bioko served as inspiration for the fictional island.

Monte Alen
National Park

3 Gorillas? In Equatorial Guinea? Too right there are. Monte Alen is one of the least known national parks in Africa and therefore one of the cheapest places to see a gorilla family picnic. The park's lush velvety jungle is also home to chimpanzees, forest elephants, mandrills, crocs and burping frogs the size of footballs.

Food & Drink

Malamba A liquor brewed from sugar cane.

Osang Local tea.

Seafood Eat seafood that has been plucked from the ocean that very day.

When to Go

DEC–FEB

➡ The dry season on Bioko Island.

JUN–AUG

➡ The best time for travel on the mainland.

**MAR–MAY &
SEP–NOV**

➡ Temperatures fall; roads are less easily navigated during the wet season.

Rocky path below Asmara

CAPITAL
Asmara

POPULATION
6.2 million

AREA
117,600 sq km

**OFFICIAL
LANGUAGES**
Tigrinya,
Arabic,
English

Eritrea

Eritrea, a mere sliver on the Horn of Africa, boasts a wealth of culture, history and natural beauty for travellers to experience.

Historically intriguing, culturally compelling and scenically magical, Eritrea is one of the most secretive countries in Africa. For those who have a hankering for off-the-beaten-track places, it offers challenges and excitement aplenty, with a unique blend of natural and cultural highlights. The country wows visitors with its awesome scenery, from the quintessentially Abyssinian landscapes – escarpments, plateaus and soaring peaks – to the deserted beaches of the Red Sea coast.

Culturally, Eritrea is a melting pot. It might be a tiddler of a country by Africa's standards, but it hosts a kaleidoscopic range of ethnic groups who have contributed to a cultural fabric that ranges from rock-cut monasteries and Ottoman-era harbour towns, to the evening *passeggiata* on Asmara's main thoroughfare.

Despite its human and natural riches, Eritrea endures the tough political and economic landscape and travellers are severely restricted. Nonetheless, this country remains one of the most inspiring destinations in Africa.

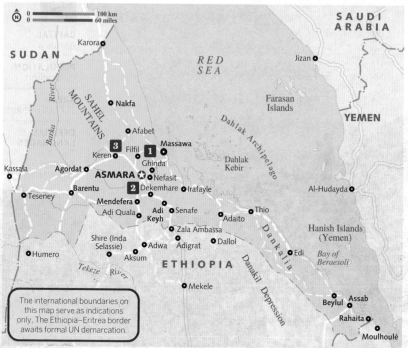

N
0 — 100 km
0 — 60 miles

SAUDI ARABIA

SUDAN

RED SEA

Karora

SAHEL MOUNTAINS

Barka River

Nakfa

Afabet

Jizan

Farasan Islands

YEMEN

Kassala

Agordat

Keren · Filfil **1** Massawa

Ghinda

ASMARA ✪ Nefasit

Dahlak Archipelago

Dahlak Kebir

Teseney

Barentu

2 Dekemhare

Irafayle

Al-Hudayda

Mendefera

Adi Quala

Adi Keyh · Senafe

Zala Ambassa

Adaito

Thio

Hanish Islands (Yemen)

Humero

Shire (Inda Selassie)

Adwa

Aksum

Adigrat

Dallol

Danakalia

Edi

Bay of Beraesoli

Tekeze River

ETHIOPIA

Danakil Depression

Mekele

Beylul · Assab

Rahaita

Moulhoulé

The international boundaries on this map serve as indications only. The Ethiopia–Eritrea border awaits formal UN demarcation.

Eritrea's
Top Experiences

Massawa

1 Explore the alleyways and streets of this historic coastal town. Entering the old town, you could be forgiven for thinking you're in Zanzibar or Yemen. Sadly, Massawa was all but flattened during the struggle for independence, and a number of historical buildings are derelict.

Asmara

2 Asmara is a surprisingly slick city crammed with architectural gems – including art deco, international, cubist, expressionist, functionalist, futurist, rationalist and neoclassical styles – harking back to the city's heyday as the 'Piccolo Roma' (small Rome). Isolated for nearly 30 years during its war with Ethiopia, Asmara has kept its heritage buildings almost intact.

Keren

3 Keren is perhaps the most remarkable of all of Eritrea's provincial towns. Hemmed in by a range of rugged, good-looking mountains, it boasts an attractive setting, as well as an appealing melange of architectural styles. It's also an active market town with an agreeable multiethnic buzz – the Tigré, the Tigrinya and the Bilen have all made Keren home.

Food & Drink

Injera Large Ethiopian pancake-style bread.

Tibsi Sliced lamb, pan-fried in butter, garlic, onion and sometimes tomato.

Zigni Lamb, goat or beef cooked in a hot sauce.

When to Go

FEB–APR & SEP–NOV

➡ It's possible to visit any time of year, but this is the ideal time to visit.

DEC–JAN

➡ The lows can approach freezing point.

JUN–AUG

➡ Rainy season in the highlands and hot and torrid in the eastern lowlands.

Tallinn Old Town

CAPITAL
Tallinn

POPULATION
1.2 million

AREA
45,228 sq km

OFFICIAL LANGUAGE
Estonian

Estonia

Embracing change with gusto, Estonia is a country of understated charms, an irresistible mix of Baltic earthiness and Nordic flavours.

Estonia doesn't have to struggle to find a point of difference in Eastern Europe; it's completely unique. It shares a similar geography and history with Latvia and Lithuania. Its closest ethnic and linguistic buddy is Finland, yet they were separated by 50 years of Soviet rule. For the past 300 years Estonia has been linked to Russia, but the two states have as much in common as a barn swallow and a bear (their respective national symbols).

In recent decades, and with a new-found confidence, Estonia has crept from under the Soviet blanket and leapt into the arms of Europe. The love affair is mutual: Europe has fallen for the chocolate-box allure of Tallinn, while travellers seeking something different are tapping into Estonia's captivating blend of Eastern European and Nordic appeal.

National parks provide plenty of elbow room and quaint villages evoke a timeless sense of history. You can experience unspoilt seaside or windswept island solitude, while still enjoying the comforts of a thoroughly modern, e-savvy country that's hell-bent on catching up with its Nordic neighbours in the quality-of-life stakes.

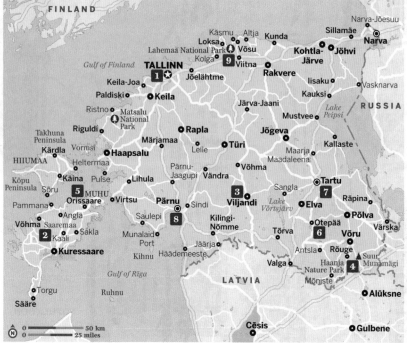

Estonia's
Top Experiences

Tallinn

1 Tallinn fuses modern and medieval to come up with a vibrant mood all its own. It's an intoxicating mix of ancient church spires, glass skyscrapers, baroque palaces, cafes set on sunny squares and bike paths to beaches and forests – with a few Soviet throwbacks in the mix for added spice. The jewel in Tallinn's crown remains its two-tiered Old Town, a 14th- and 15th-century jumble of turrets, spires and winding streets

Saaremaa

2 Escape to the island of Saaremaa for castles, coastlines and spas. For Estonians, Saaremaa (literally 'Island Land') is synonymous with space, spruce, peace and fresh air – and killer beer (there's a long history of beer home-brewing). Estonia's largest island (roughly the size of Luxembourg) still lies covered in pine and spruce forests and juniper groves, while old windmills, lighthouses and tiny villages appear unchanged by the passage of time. During the Soviet era, the island was off limits. This unwittingly resulted in the protection of the island's rural charm.

Viljandi

3 One of Estonia's most charming towns, Viljandi, 90km east of Pärnu, is a relaxed place to visit. It's a good base for exploring the country's largest flood plain and bog area (no laughing!) and the town itself has a gentle 19th-century flow to it. Easily the biggest event on the calendar is the hugely popular four-day Viljandi Folk Music Festival, held in late July and renowned for its friendly relaxed vibe and impressive international line-up (incorporating traditional folk, folk rock and world music).

Haanja
Nature Park

4 With 169 sq km of thick forests, rolling hills, picturesque villages, sparkling lakes and meandering rivers, this protected area south of Võru encompasses some of the nicest scenery in the country. Stock up on maps and information about the park's multifarious hiking and cross-country skiing opportunities from the park's visitor centres.

MARGUS MUTS / GETTY IMAGES ©

Muhu

5 Connected to Saaremaa by a 2.5km causeway, the island of Muhu has the undeserved reputation as the 'doormat' for the bigger island – lots of people passing through, but few stopping. In fact, Estonia's third-biggest island offers plenty of excuses to hang around, not least the country's best restaurant and some excellent accommodation options. A true gem is Koguva in the island's west, a step-back-in-time, fairy-tale fishing village dating from at least the mid-16th century. It's still mainly inhabited by descendents of the original settlers.

Otepää

6 Get back to nature, even if the snow's a no-show, at the 'winter capital'.

This small hilltop town is the centre of a scenic area beloved by Estonians for its forests, hills and lakes, and its nature-frolicking activities – hiking, cycling and swimming in summer and cross-country skiing in winter. A 12km nature trail and bike path encircle the 3.5km-long 'holy lake', which is rich in pagan legend. It was blessed by the Dalai Lama; a small monument commemorates his visit.

Tartu

7 Further your local education among the bars and cafes of Tartu, Estonia's premier university town and second city. If Tallinn is Estonia's head, Tartu may well be its heart (and possibly its university-educated brains, too). It lays claim to being Estonia's spiritual capital –

if Estonia were 100 people

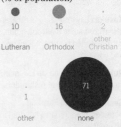

69 would be Estonian
25 would be Russian
2 would be Ukrainian
1 would be Belarusian
3 would be other

belief systems
(% of population)

10 Lutheran
16 Orthodox
2 other Christian
1 other
71 none

population per sq km

ESTONIA   FINLAND   RUSSIA

♦ ≈ 3 people

When to Go

APR–MAY

➡ See the country shake off winter's gloom.

JUN–AUG

➡ White nights, beach parties and loads of summer festivals.

DEC

➡ Christmas markets, mulled wine and long cosy nights.

Kiiking – what the...?

From the weird and wacky world of Estonian sport comes kiiking. Invented in 1997, Kiiking sees competitors stand on a swing and attempt to complete a 360-degree loop around the top bar, with their feet fastened to the swing base and their hands to the swing arms.

The inventor of kiiking, Ado Kosk, observed that the longer the swing arms, the more difficult it is to complete a 360-degree loop. Kosk then designed swing arms that can gradually extend, for an increased challenge. In competition, the winner is the person who completes a loop with the longest swing arms – the current record stands at a fraction over 7m! Go to www.kiiking.ee to get a more visual idea of the whole thing.

Food & Drink

Berries and mushrooms Seasonal delights freshly picked from the forests in summer and autumn respectively.

Kama Light meal or drink made from buttermilk combined with a mixture of boiled, roasted and ground peas, rye, barley and wheat.

Kana ja kartul Chicken and potatoes, for when you're porked out.

Kasukas Layered salad of Russian origin containing beetroot, potato, carrots, salted herring, boiled egg and yoghurt.

Rukkileib Rye bread, an Estonian staple, usually free at restaurants.

Sealiha ja kartul Pork and potatoes, prepared in a hundred different ways.

Suitsukala Smoked fish; usually trout or salmon.

Vana Tallinn A syrupy, sweet liqueur of indeterminate origin, best served over ice, in coffee or to disguise bad Russian sparkling wine. There's also a cream version.

Lifeguard station, Pärnu

DANITA DELIMONT / GETTY IMAGES ©

locals talk about a special Tartu *vaim* (spirit), created by the 19th-century feel of many of its wooden-house-lined streets, and the beauty of its parks and riverfront.

Pärnu

8 Get sand in your shorts in Pärnu, Estonia's summertime drawcard. Local families, young party-goers and holidaymakers join in a collective prayer for sunny weather while strolling the golden-sand beaches, parks and historic centre of Pärnu, Estonia's premier seaside resort. In truth, most of Pärnu is quite docile, with leafy streets and parks intermingling with turn-of-the-century villas

that reflect the town's past as a resort capital of the Baltic region.

Lahemaa National Park

9 The perfect country retreat from the capital, Lahemaa takes in a stretch of coast deeply indented with peninsulas and bays, plus 475 sq km of pine-fresh forested hinterland. Visitors are well looked after, with cosy guesthouses, manor houses, camping grounds and an extensive network of pine-scented forest trails. There is an abundance of sightseeing, hiking, cycling and boating to be done here; remote islands can also be explored.

Getting Around

Bicycle Touring cyclists will find Estonia mercifully flat.

Bus The national bus network is extensive, linking all the major cities to each other and the smaller towns to their regional hubs.

Car & Motorcycle Estonian roads are generally very good and driving is easy. Car and bike hire is offered in all the major cities.

Train Most people prefer the buses to the trains, for convenience of services and for comfort.

Hamer woman

CAPITAL
Addis Ababa

POPULATION
93.9 million

AREA
1.1 million sq km

OFFICIAL LANGUAGES
Oromo, Amharic, Somali, Tigrayan, Arabic, English

Ethiopia

In Ethiopia you'd be hard-pressed to find a better combination of nature and culture. The best part: there'll be no crowds to hinder the experience.

Ethiopia's landscape impresses in both scale and beauty. Travellers will be thrilled by the amazing backdrop of canyons, chasms, lakes, savannah plains and high plateaus, not to mention the mesmerisingly desolate Danakil Depression, peppered with an astonishing 25% of Africa's active volcanoes.

Ethiopia is one of the few African countries to have escaped European colonialism, so it has also retained much of its cultural identity. A highlight of any trip to the Horn is witnessing some of the many ceremonies and festivals that are an integral part of traditional culture in the region. They may be Christian, Islamic or animist festivals, or village events, such as a wedding, a rite-of-passage celebration or a local market day.

Its wide-ranging and fertile highlands are laden with historical treasures ranging from ancient Aksumite tombs and obelisks to 17th-century castles. It's not dubbed the Cradle of Humanity for nothing: archaeologically speaking, Ethiopia is to sub-Saharan Africa what Egypt is to North Africa.

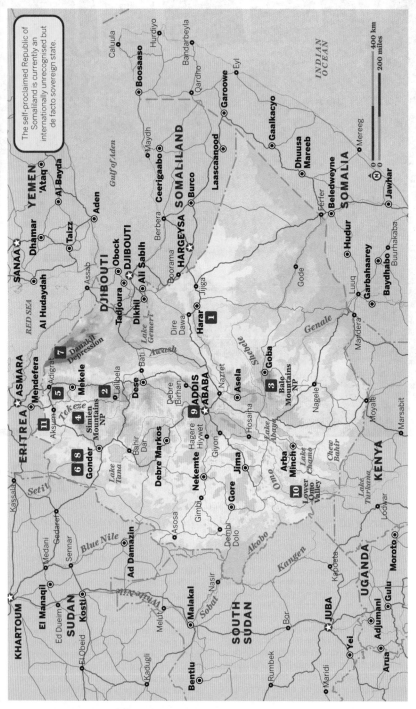

The self-proclaimed Republic of Somaliland is currently an internationally unrecognised but de facto sovereign state.

Ethiopia's
Top Experiences

Harar

1 By far the most intriguing city in Ethiopia, Harar is a joy to explore. Getting lost in its crooked alleyways is just as fascinating as visiting the many museums, markets and traditional homes packed inside the old city walls. And then there are the hyenas. Two families feed them by hand, and let you do it, too, but these large carnivores wander throughout the city and you may just bump into one while walking about at night. Thankfully, they find enough scraps of meat so that they have no interest in people.

Lalibela

2 Seeing the rock-hewn churches of Lalibela on TV and in books is not enough to prepare you for the experience of walking inside them for real. Carved entirely out of rock, the still-functioning churches are large, artistically refined and mostly in excellent states of preservation. One of the many local legends about the site's origin states that the king wanted to make a new Jerusalem so pilgrims didn't have to make the long, dangerous journey to the real one. An early morning visit, when locals come to seek blessings and inspiration, shows their mystical side.

Bet Giyorgis (St George's Church), Lalibela

CAVAN IMAGES / GETTY IMAGES ©

Bale Mountains

3 The Ethiopian wolf is the rarest canid in the world, but on the 4000m-high Sanetti Plateau in the Bale Mountains you are almost guaranteed to see them. And when you're not watching wolves hunt giant mole-rats, your eyes will be drawn to the fairy-tale forests draped in 'old man's beard' and the sheer drop of the Harenna Escarpment. Though the mountains are prime trekking territory there's no need to step out of your car to enjoy them since you can drive right through on the highest all-weather road in Africa.

if Ethiopia were 100 people

35 would be Oromo
27 would be Amara
6 would be Somali

6 would be Tigraway
4 would be Sidama
22 would be other

belief systems
(% of population)

43 Ethiopian Orthodox Christian

34 Muslim

19 Protestant

3 traditional

1 other

population per sq km

ETHIOPIA   UK   USA

≈ 30 people

Simien Mountains

4 With deep canyons and bizarrely jagged mountains sculpting scenery so awesome that if you saw it in a painting you might question whether it was real or not, the Simien Mountains are one of the wonders of the natural world. They're an important preserve for some of Ethiopia's endemic wildlife, and sitting amid a troop of tame gelada monkeys at Sankaber is an experience you'll never forget. This is terrific trekking territory, but also easily accessible by car.

Rock-Hewn Churches of Tigray

5 Hidden like jewels in the arid Tigrayan countryside, the old rock-hewn churches of Tigray will wow you. Partially carved and partially constructed, most sit on remote cliffsides requiring long walks (and sometimes steep climbs) and the sense of discovery upon arrival is a big part of their appeal. But they also delight on their artistic and historic merits alone.

Gonder

6 Gonder preserves a treasure trove of history. The walls of the Royal Enclosure contain a half-dozen medieval palaces and a host of legends; you can easily imagine the grand feasts they held here as you walk among them. Further out are peaceful and atmospheric sites, including Fasiladas' Bath, the Kuskuam complex and Debre Berhan Selassie Church, saved from the marauding Sudanese Dervishes by a swarm of bees.

Hair-Raising Beliefs

Hairstyles in all societies form an important part of tribal identification. Reflecting the large number of ethnic groups, Ethiopian hairstyles are particularly diverse and colourful. Hair is cut, shaved, trimmed, plaited, braided, sculpted with clay, rubbed with mud, put in buns and tied in countless different fashions. In the Omo Valley, hairstyles are sometimes so elaborate and valued that special wooden headrests are used as pillows to preserve them.

In rural areas, the heads of children are often shaved to discourage lice. Sometimes a single topknot or tail plait is left so that 'God should have a handle with which to lift them unto Heaven', should he decide to call them.

Food & Drink

Ethiopian food and the myriad ways in which it's prepared is not only some of the most diverse on the continent, but also totally different to any other cuisine you may have encountered.

Plates, bowls and even utensils are replaced by *injera*, a one-of-a-kind pancake of countrywide proportions. Atop its rubbery confines sit delicious multicoloured mounds of spicy *kai wat* (meat stews), tasty *wat* (vegetable curry) and even cubes of *tere sega* (raw meat). Eat up, but remember to leave some leftovers on the plate after a meal. Failing to do so is sometimes seen as inviting famine.

Ethiopia also has a well-founded claim to be the original home of coffee, and it continues to be ubiquitous across the country. An invitation to attend a coffee ceremony is a mark of friendship or respect, though it's not an event for those in a hurry! At least three cups must be accepted, the third in particular is considered to bestow a blessing – it's the *berekha* (blessing) cup.

Danakil Depression

7 The actively volcanic Danakil Depression features a permanent lava lake and a vast field of yellow and orange sulphuric rocks. Just as interesting are the hearty Afar people who eke out a living from the baking, cracked plains. Though there are regular tours into its depths, travel here is not easy due to the lack of roads, services and normal temperatures. The Danakil Depression may feel inhospitable, but the sense of exploration is real. The best way to visit this territory is with a well-established tour operator.

Timkat

8 Timkat, the feast of Epiphany, celebrates the baptism of Christ with a three-day festival starting on 19 January. Join the procession behind regalia-draped priests as the church *tabots* (replicas of the Ark of the Covenant) are taken to a nearby body of water on the afternoon of the eve of Timkat. Next morning, the *tabots* are paraded back to the church accompanied by much singing and dancing. In Gonder, the historic Fasiladas' Bath is filled with water just once a year for this colourful celebration.

When to Go

HIGH SEASON
(Jan–Mar)

➡ Expect sunny skies and warm days.

➡ These months are good for wildlife watching.

➡ Ethiopia's most colourful festivals, including Timkat and Leddet.

SHOULDER SEASON
(Oct–Dec)

➡ The country is green, skies are sunny and there are fewer visitors. Trekking during this time is particularly sublime.

➡ Good for birding.

LOW SEASON
(Apr–Sep)

➡ The rainy season in southern Ethiopia and the scorching hot temperatures in the lowlands can make travel difficult.

Addis Ababa

9 Addis Ababa is evolving at a fast pace. The noisy, bustling capital of Ethiopia is blessed with a balmy climate, with cloudless blue skies for about eight months of the year. It offers plenty of cultural highlights, including the Ethnological Museum and the National Museum. Addis is also famed for its buzzing restaurant scene and nightlife, with lots of eateries, bars, galleries and clubs.

Lower Omo Valley

10 The Lower Omo Valley is a remarkable

Best on Film

In Search of Myths and Heroes The first in Michael Wood's sumptuously filmed series seeks the truth behind the Sheba legend.

Lost Kingdoms of Africa Dr Gus Casely-Hayford explores ancient Ethiopian cultures and legends.

The Great Rift: Africa's Wild Heart A finely crafted portrait of the Rift Valley and its wildlife.

Origins of Us Exploring who we are and where we came from, this BBC series starts where it all began – Ethiopia.

Best in Print

The Chains of Heaven (Philip Marsden) If you read one book on Ethiopia, make it this one; the author walks across the north Ethiopian plateau and in the process reveals much about Ethiopian culture and history.

Sheba: Through the Desert in Search of the Legendary Queen (Nicholas Clapp) Successfully blending personal travel accounts through Ethiopia, Yemen and elsewhere with thorough academic research to shed light on one of history's most famous characters.

Getting Around

Air Internal flights can be huge time savers. The national carrier has an extensive domestic route service and a solid safety record. It's cheaper to book your flight once in Ethiopia.

Bus If travelling by bus, opt for the newer companies, which offer better service and more comfortable buses.

Car Though expensive, it's not a bad idea to hire a 4WD with a driver, especiall[y] for southern and western Ethiopia. Having your own car allows you to stop wherever you want and saves time. The driver can also act as a guide-cum-interpreter. Note also that some national parks can only be entered with a 4W[D]. Shop around and hire through a reputable agency.

cultural crossroads. From the Mursi people and their lip plates to the Banna with their calabash hats to the body painting Karo, tradition runs deep here. While the commonly held notion that the more than a dozen ethnic groups residing here live completely outside modern society is wrong, walking through the markets and villages or attending one of the many ceremonies really is a bit like stepping back in time.

Aksumite Tombs

11 For as long as 5000 years, monoliths have been used in northeast Africa as tombstones and monuments to local rulers. In Aksum, this tradition reached its apogee. Like Egypt's pyramids, Aksum's stelae were like great billboards announcing to the world the authority power and greatness of the ruling families. Aksum's astonishing stelae are striking for their huge size, their incredible state of preservation, and their curiously modern look. Sculpted from single pieces of granite, the later ones come complete with little windows, doors and even door handles and locks.

Gentoo penguin nesting colony

CAPITAL	
Stanley	
POPULATION	
3140	
AREA	
12,173 sq km	
OFFICIAL LANGUAGE	
English	

Falkland Islands

Controversially fought over but still staunchly British, the Falkland Islands sit isolated in the wild Southern Ocean, home to penguins, waterbirds, a few humans and lots of sheep.

Most people associate the Falklands (known as Isla Malvinas in Argentina) with the 1982 war, which saw Britain regain control after an invasion by the Argentine military. These days the islands are a popular stopover for Southern Ocean cruise ships and intrepid wildlife watchers. Bays, inlets, estuaries and beaches create an attractive and tortuous coastline boasting abundant wildlife. These sea islands attract striated and crested caracaras, cormorants, oystercatchers, snowy sheathbills and a plethora of penguins –

Magellanic, rockhopper, macaroni, gentoo and king – who share top billing with sea lions, elephant seals, fur seals, five species of dolphin and killer whales.

Stanley, the islands' capital on East Falkland, is an assemblage of brightly painted metal-clad houses and a good place to throw down a few pints and listen to island lore. Elsewhere in 'Camp' – as the rest of the islands are known – you're more likely to bump into a sheep or a penguin than a person.

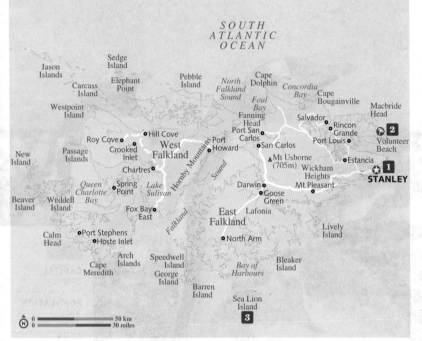

Falkland Islands'
Top Experiences

Stanley

1 The Falklands' capital is little more than a village, but still holds two-thirds of the total population. Admire the local architecture of recycled shipwrecks, chat with locals at one of the British-style pubs, visit the fascinating Falkland Islands Museum and inspect the poignant war memorials.

Volunteer Beach

2 You don't have to go to Antarctica to see king penguins – Volunteer Beach boasts the largest king penguin colony in the Falklands, where they are at the northern limit of their range. Large colonies of gentoo and Magellanic penguins also inhabit the beach, which is named after the *Volunteer*, an American whaling ship which visited nearby Port Louis is 1815.

Sea Lion Island

3 The Falklands' southern-most inhabited island has more wildlife in a smaller area than almost anywhere in the islands. It features all five species of Falklands' penguins, enormous colonies of cormorants, and is an important breeding ground for southern elephant seals. The sea lions that give the island its name are far less numerous, however, with fewer than 100 of them.

Food & Drink

Falkland Islands' cuisine is most obviously influenced by British food and drink. Fish and chips is a popular staple, as is lamb. Other fish and seafood dishes take advantage of the abundance of fresh fish available. Pubs in Stanley serve pints of English beer and bar meals.

When to Go

OCT–MAR

➔ Antarctic cruise ship season. Migratory birds return to beaches and headlands.

DEC & FEB

➔ Annual sports meetings between Christmas and New Year and after shearing in February.

APR–SEP

➔ Winter season. Cold and windy but rarely below freezing.

CAPITAL
Suva

POPULATION
903,207

AREA
18,274 sq km

OFFICIAL LANGUAGES
Fijian, English

Fiji

Fiji is surely every beach bum's vision of nirvana. Palm-fringed beaches, fish-packed reefs and smiling locals: pack your swimsuit and sunscreen, these sunny isles are so warm they sizzle.

With alabaster beaches, cloudless skies and kaleidoscopic reefs, Fiji is the embodiment of the South Pacific dream. Most who head here want little more than to fall into a sun-induced coma under a shady palm, and with over 300 islands to choose from, the decision on where to unfurl your beach towel isn't easy. While some may find that anything more than two snorkelling excursions a day and half an hour on the volleyball court is not in keeping with Fiji's famously languid sense of time, there is more to these isles than can ever be seen from a deckchair or swim-up bar.

To get to grips with the national psyche, though, you have to spend some time on the mainland. Two-thirds of the population live in urban centres and it is on Viti Levu that you'll find the country's two cities: Suva, the capital, and Lautoka, a working port town reliant on the sugar-cane farms that surround it. Suva's nightlife and large student population give it a youthful if slightly unexpected vibe.

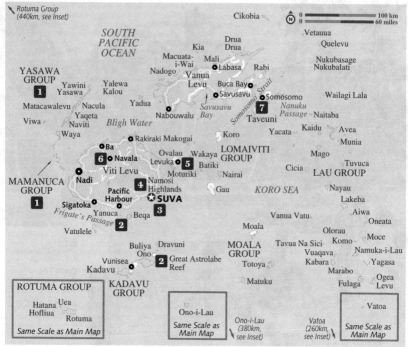

Map labels: Rotuma Group (440km, see Inset) · Cikobia · Vetauua · SOUTH PACIFIC OCEAN · Drua Drua · Quelevu · Kia · Macuata-i-Wai · Mali · Nukubasage · Nukubalati · YASAWA GROUP 1 · Nadogo · Labasa · Rabi · Yawini Yasawa · Yalewa Kalou · Vanua Levu · Buca Bay · Savusavu · Somosomo · Wailagi Lala · Matacawalevu · Nacula · Yadua · Nabouwalu · Savusavu Bay · 7 · Nanuku Passage · Naitaba · Viwa · Yaqeta Naviti · Bligh Water · Taveuni · Avea · Waya · Koro · Yacata · Kaidu · Munia · Rakiraki · Makogai · LOMAIVITI GROUP · Mago · Ba 6 · Ovalau · Wakaya · Tuvuca · Navala · Levuka 5 · Batiki · Cicia · LAU GROUP · Viti Levu · Moturiki · Nairai · MAMANUCA GROUP 1 · Nadi · Namosi Highlands 4 · Gau · KORO SEA · Nayau · Pacific Harbour · SUVA 3 · Lakeba · Sigatoka · Yanuca · Aiwa · Frigate's Passage · Beqa 2 · Vanua Vatu · Oneata · Vatulele · Moala · Olorau · Komo · Moce · Buliya · Dravuni · MOALA GROUP · Tavua Na Sici · Vuaqava · Namuka-i-Lau · Ono · 2 Great Astrolabe Reef · Totoya · Kabara · Yagasa · Vunisea · Kadavu · Matuku · Marabo · Fulaga · Ogea Levu · ROTUMA GROUP · KADAVU GROUP · Hatana Uea · Hofliua · Rotuma · Same Scale as Main Map · Ono-i-Lau · Same Scale as Main Map · Ono-i-Lau (380km, see Inset) · Vatoa (260km, see Inset) · Vatoa · Same Scale as Main Map · 0 100 km · 0 60 miles

Fiji's
Top Experiences

Mamanucas & Yasawas

1 Hot sun, tepid turquoise sea and cold refreshments are the order of the day in the Mamanuca and Yasawa island groups, off Fiji's west coast. Close to Viti Levu, the Mamanucas offer water sports of all sorts at island resorts for all budgets and all demographics, along with action-packed day tours from the mainland for the time-poor. Lacing their way northwards, the lower-key Yasawas – a string of 20 remote volcanic islands – beckon with crystal-clear lagoons, ruggedly handsome landscapes, remote villages and heavenly beaches to get stranded on.

Underwater Fiji

2 Even seasoned snorkellers are impressed by the water clarity, which can extend to 30m and beyond, and top facilities ensure that divers keep their logbooks full. From thrilling encounters with massive bull sharks in Beqa Lagoon to sedate drifts over the Great Astrolabe Reef off Kadavu, Fiji has a diverse selection of dives to choose from. No matter if you are the 'hard-core' or the 'soft-coral' type, Fijian dive-masters will know just the spot to thrill.

Suva

3 Steamy Suva offers a multicultural mix of colonial and contemporary Fiji. Gracious old buildings and monuments sketch the city's early history along a lively waterfront and harbour. Downtown boasts both air-con shopping malls and crowded handicraft stalls. Open-air eateries and fine dining restaurants get their supplies from the colourful chaos of the don't-miss municipal market. Night owls can sip sunset cocktails at modern bars then dance to the beat of a different drum at loud and lively local nightclubs.

Namosi Highlands

4 Geology looms large in the humid Namosi Highlands. Sheer canyon walls crowd the Wainikoroiluva River, forming dramatic curtains of rock as the backdrop to Fiji's

most scenic river-rafting trip taken aboard a *bilibili* (bamboo raft). The lower, longer, wider reaches of the palm-fringed waterway are usually covered in speedier style, in canoes with outboard motors, alongside villagers making their way up and down the river on slower local boats heading to or from market.

Colonial Levuka

5 The Wild West meets the South Seas at Levuka, the country's one-time colonial capital turned half-asleep backwater. You can almost imagine scabby sailors rowdily bursting out from the frayed but colourful timber shopfronts. Back then they may have been saloons but nowadays the buildings hold mainly stores of odds and ends. Women from the villages sell *dalo* and produce on the roadside, a church rises faded and cracked-white against the sky and the only sounds come from the occasional car chugging through town.

if Fiji were 100 people

57 would be Fijian
38 would be Indo-Fijian
1 would be Rotuman
4 would be other

---

belief systems
(% of population)

| 64 Christian | 1 Sikh | 6 Muslim |
| 28 Hindu | 1 other | |

---

population per sq km

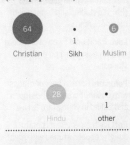

FIJI   AUSTRALIA   USA

≈ 3 people

When to Go

HIGH SEASON
(Jun–Aug & Dec–Jan)

➡ Many islanders living abroad come home to visit family.

➡ Book flights well in advance.

➡ June to August is dry, December and January are wet. Cyclone season is November to April.

SHOULDER
(May & Sep)

➡ Trade winds wick the humidity and keep temperatures pleasant.

➡ Flights are cheaper and less likely to be booked.

➡ Travel with less crowds.

LOW SEASON
(Feb–Apr & Oct–Nov)

➡ Expect hot temperatures and high humidity.

➡ Search the web for deals on resorts looking to fill empty rooms.

➡ Diving visibility can be reduced due to heavy rains.

Fijian Culture

Fiji's population is the most multiracial in the South Pacific.

Most indigenous Fijians live in villages in *mataqali* (extended family, or kinship, groups) and acknowledge a hereditary chief. Village life is supportive but also conservative, and traditional gender roles are still very much in evidence. Concepts such as *kerekere* (obligatory sharing) and *sevusevu* (a gift in exchange for an obligatory favour) are still strong, and the consumption of *yaqona*, or kava, remains an important social ritual.

Indo-Fijians are mostly fourth- or fifth-generation descendants of indentured plantation labourers. The cultural changes these labourers were forced to undergo created a relatively unrestricted, enterprising society distinct from the Indian cultures they left behind. For a taste of Indo-Fijian life you need go no further than the local curry house, or visit one of the brightly painted Hindu temples or shrines on the mainland.

Food & Drink

Kokoda A raw-fish salad marinated in lime juice, mixed with vegetables and topped with coconut cream.

Lovo Traditional Fijian oven where food is cooked in a pit on hot stones.

Palusami Corned beef or onions with coconut cream, all wrapped and baked in young taro leaves.

Roti Try the *cepelinai* (potato-dough zeppelin stuffed with meat, mushrooms or cheese).

Thali Set Indian meals with several curries.

Yaqona Also called kava or grog, this mildly narcotic drink is a muddy tea made from a root.

Traditional thatched *bure*, Navala Village

Navala Village

6 The drive up to Navala, nestled in a valley high in the Nausori Highlands, is a treat in itself. Navala is Fiji's most striking village and the country's last bastion of traditional architecture. From the chief's house to the outhouses, all buildings are constructed using age-old techniques that make use of woven bamboo walls, thatched roofs and ropes made of fibre from the surrounding bush. Cooking on an open fire, village women serve up a serious local lunch that's been caught, picked and harvested from the gardens.

Waitavala Water Slide

7 Hang ten or better, just use your bum, to cavort, slip and get a few bruises down this natural cascade of rock slides. Start by watching the local kids to get an idea of what you're in for. They make it look easy, tackling the falls surfer-style, each showing off more than the last in the hope of making it into your top holiday snaps.

Getting Around

Air Pacific Sun runs most of the regular interisland flights by light plane, and there are serveral charter operators.

Boat With the exception of the upmarket resort islands, often the only means of transport between islands is by small local boats. If the weather looks ominous or the boat is overcrowded, seriously consider postponing the trip! High-speed, comfortable catamarans link Viti Levu to the Yasawas and Mamanucas.

Bus Catching a local bus on Fiji's larger islands is an inexpensive and fun way of getting around.

Car & Motorcycle Ninety per cent of Fiji's 5100km of roads are on Viti Levu and Vanua Levu (about 20% are sealed). Both islands are fun to explore by car, which you rent from numerous hire companies..

Winter landscape, Lapland

CAPITAL
Helsinki

POPULATION
5.3 million

AREA
338,145 sq km

OFFICIAL LANGUAGES
Finnish, Swedish

Finland

Finland is the deep north, with forests and lakes as far as the eye can see, and revitalising crisp air. Choose between summer's endless light or winter's eerie frozen magic.

There's something pure in the Finnish air and a spirit that's incredibly vital and exciting. It's an invitation to get out and active year-round. A post-sauna dip in an ice hole under the majestic aurora borealis (Northern Lights), after whooshing across the snow behind a team of huskies, isn't a typical winter's day just anywhere. And canoeing or hiking under the midnight sun through pine forests populated by wolves and bears isn't your typical tanning-oil summer either.

Although socially and economically in the vanguard of nations, large parts of Finland remain gloriously remote; trendsetting modern Helsinki is counterbalanced by vast forested wildernesses elsewhere.

Nordic peace in lakeside cottages, summer sunshine on beer terraces, avant-garde design, and cafes warm with baking aromas are other facets of Suomi (Finnish) seduction. As are the independent, loyal, warm and welcoming Finns, who tend to do their own thing and are much the better for it.

Sledding & Snowmobiling, Lapland

2 Fizzing over the snow behind a team of huskies under the low winter sun is tough to beat. Short jaunts are great, but overnight safaris give you time to feed and bond with your lovable dogs and try out a wood-fired sauna in the middle of the winter wilderness. It's no fairy-tale ride though; expect to eat some snow before you learn to control your team. You can enjoy similar trips on a snowmobile or behind reindeer.

Sámi Culture, Inari

3 Finland's indigenous northerners have used technology to ease the arduous side of reindeer herding while maintaining an intimate knowledge of Lapland's natural world. Their capital, Inari, and the nearby Lemmenjoki National Park are the best places to begin to learn about Sámi culture and traditions, starting at the marvellous Siida museum.

Traditional Sauna, Kuopio

4 These days most Finns have saunas at home, but there are still a few of the old public ones left. They smell of old pine, tar shampoo and long tradition, with birch whisks and no-nonsense scrubdowns available as extras. Weathered Finnish faces cool down on the street outside, loins wrapped in a towel and hand wrapped around a cold beer. Kuopio's old-style smoke sauna takes a day to prepare and offers a memorable rural experience, with a cooling-off lake to jump into right alongside.

Finland's
Top Experiences

Helsinki

1 Though Helsinki can seem like a younger sibling compared to other Nordic capitals, it's the one that went to art school, scorns pop music, is working in a cutting-edge design studio and hangs out with friends who like black and plenty of piercings. The city's design shops are legendary and its music and pub scene kicking. On the other hand, much of what is lovable in Helsinki is older: its understated yet glorious art nouveau buildings, the spacious elegance of its centenarian cafes, and the careful preservation of Finnish heritage in its dozens of museums.

Helsinki Central railway station

Lakeland

5 This part of Finland seems to have more water than land, so it'd be a crime not to get out on it. You can take three days to paddle the family-friendly Oravareitti (Squirrel Route) or head out into Kolovesi and Linnansaari national parks to meet freshwater seals. Tired arms? Historic lake boats still ply what were once important transport arteries; head out from any town on short cruises, or make a day of it and head from Savonlinna right up to Kuopio or across Finland's largest lake, Saimaa.

Cycling, Åland Archipelago

6 Charming Åland is best explored by bicycle: you'll appreciate its understated attractions all the more if you've used pedal-power to reach them. Bridges and ferries link many of its 6000 islands, and well-signposted routes take you off 'main roads' down winding lanes and forestry tracks. Set aside your bicycle whenever the mood takes you, to pick wild strawberries, wander castle ruins, sunbathe on a slab of red granite, visit a medieval church,

if Finland were 100 people

91 would speak Finnish
6 would speak Swedish
1 would speak Russian
3 would speak other languages

belief systems
(% of population)

78 Lutheran
1 Orthodox
1 other Christian
20 none

population per sq km

FINLAND   SWEDEN   USA

= 6 people

When to Go

HIGH SEASON (Jul)

➜ Everlasting daylight and countless festivals.

➜ Attractions and lodgings are open.

➜ Hotels are cheaper.

SHOULDER (Jun & Aug)

➜ Long days with decent temperatures.

➜ Most attractions are open, but not as crowded as in July.

➜ Fewer insects up north.

LOW SEASON (Sep–May)

➜ Short, cool or cold days.

➜ Outside the cities, most attractions are closed.

➜ December to April is busy for winter sports; September is busy in northern hiking areas.

The Mökki

Tucked away in Finland's forests and lakelands are half a million *kesämökkejä*, or summer cottages. Part holiday house, part sacred place, the *mökki* is the spiritual home of the Finn and you don't know the country until you've spent time in one. The average Finn spends less than two days in a hotel per year, but several weeks in a cottage.

These are places where people get back to nature. Amenities are often basic – the gloriously genuine ones have no electricity or running water – but even the highest-flying Nokia executives are in their element, chopping wood, DIY-ing, picking chanterelles and blueberries, rowing, and selecting young birch twigs for the *vihta*, or sauna whisk.

Food & Drink

Alcoholic drinks Beer is a staple. Finns also love dissolving things in vodka; try a shot of *salmiakkikossu* (salty-liquorice flavoured) or *fisu* (Fisherman's Friend–flavoured).

Coffee To fit in, eight or nine cups a day is about right, best accompanied with a cardamom-flavoured pastry.

Fish Salmon is ubiquitous; tasty lake fish include arctic char, pike-perch and scrumptious fried *muikku* (vendace).

Meat Reindeer is a staple up north, elk is commonly eaten, and bear is also seasonally available.

Markets The *kauppahalli* (market hall) is where to go for a stunning array of produce. In summer, stalls at the *kauppatori* (market square) sell delicious fresh vegetables and fruit.

Seasonal berries Look out for cloudberries and lingonberries from Lapland, and market stalls selling blueberries, strawberries and raspberries.

quench your thirst at a cider orchard, or climb a lookout tower to gaze at the sea.

Bear-Watching, Eastern Finland

7 The brown bear (*Ursus arctos*) is the national animal of Finland. About a thousand of these powerful creatures live in the northeast, coming and going with impunity across the Finnish–Russian border. Several operators run bear hides close to the frontier, where you can sit a silent night's vigil as bruins snuffle out elk carcasses and carefully hidden chunks of salmon. The best

time to see them is between mid-April and August – with a slight gap in July when the bears have mating rather than meals in mind.

Rauma Old Town

8 The largest wooden Old Town in the Nordic countries, Vanha Rauma deserves its Unesco World Heritage status. Its 600 houses might be museum pieces, but they also form a living centre: residents tend their flower boxes and chat to neighbours, while visitors meander in and out of the low-key cafes, shops, museums and artisans' workshops.

Getting Around

Bicycle Finland is largely flat and as bicycle-friendly as any country you'll find, with many kilometres of bike paths. Distances may be a drawback, but bikes can be taken on most trains, buses and ferries.

Bus This is the main form of long-distance transport, especially in remote areas. There are two types of intercity bus service: *vakiovuoro* (regular), which stops frequently at towns and villages; and *pikavuoro* (express).

Train Finnish trains are run by Valtion Rautatiet (VR; www.vr.fi) and offer a fast, efficient service, with prices roughly equivalent to buses on the same route.

Landscaped gardens, Château de Villandry, Loire Valley

CAPITAL
Paris

POPULATION
66 million

AREA
643,801 sq km

OFFICIAL LANGUAGE
French

France

France seduces travellers with its unfalteringly familiar culture woven around cafe terraces, village-square markets and lace-curtained bistros with their plat du jour chalked on the board.

Few countries provoke such passion as La Belle France. Love it or loathe it, everyone has their own opinion about this Gallic Goliath. Snooty, sexy, superior, chic, infuriating, arrogant, officious and inspired in equal measures, the French have long lived according to their own idiosyncratic rules, and if the rest of the world doesn't always see eye-to-eye with them, well, *tant pis* (too bad) – it's the price you pay for being a culinary trendsetter, artistic pioneer and cultural icon.

If ever there was a country of contradictions, this is it. France is a deeply traditional place: castles, chateaux and ancient churches litter the landscape, while centuries-old principles of rich food, fine wine and *joie de vivre* underpin everyday life. Yet it is also a country that has one of Western Europe's most multicultural make-ups, not to mention a well-deserved reputation for artistic experimentation and architectural invention. Enjoy!

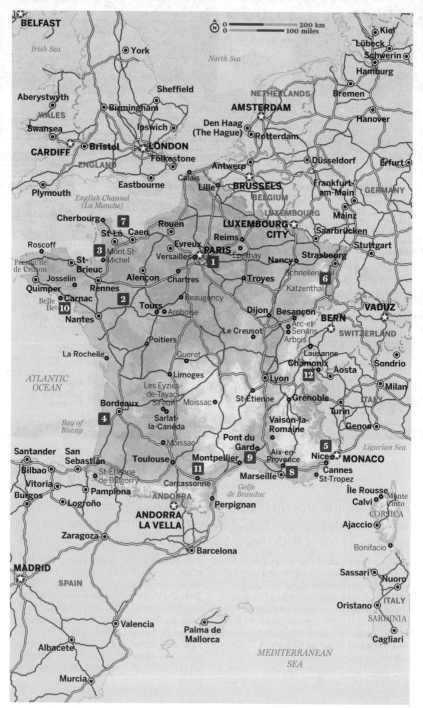

France's
Top Experiences

Eiffel Tower

1 Seven million people visit the Eiffel Tower annually but few disagree that each visit is unique. From an evening ascent amid twinkling lights to lunch at 58 Tour Eiffel in the company of a staggering city panorama, there are 101 ways to 'do' it. Pedal beneath it, skip the lift and hike up, buy a crêpe from a stand here or a key ring from the street, snap yourself in front of it, visit it at night or – our favourite – on the odd special occasion when all 324m of the tower glows a different colour.

Loire Valley Châteaux

2 If it's aristocratic pomp and architectural splendour you're after, this regal valley is the place to linger. Flowing for more than 1000km into the Atlantic Ocean, the Loire is one of France's last *fleuves sauvages* (wild rivers) and its banks provide a 1000-year snapshot of French high society. The valley is riddled with beautiful châteaux sporting glittering turrets and ballrooms, lavish cupolas and chapels. If you're a hopeless romantic seeking the perfect fairy-tale castle, head for moat-ringed Azay-le-Rideau, Villandry and its gardens, and less-visited Beauregard.

F HMOLINA / GETTY IMAGES ©

Mont St-Michel

3 The dramatic play of tides on this abbey-island in Normandy is magical and mysterious. Said by Celtic mythology to be a sea tomb to which souls of the dead were sent, Mont St-Michel is rich in legend and history, keenly felt as you make your way barefoot across rippled sand to the stunning architectural ensemble. Walk around it alone or, better still, hook up with a guide in nearby Genêts for a dramatic day hike across the bay.

Dune du Pilat

4 The Dune du Pilat is a 'mountain' that just has to be climbed. Not only is the coastal panorama from the top of Europe's largest sand dune a stunner – it takes in the Banc d'Arguin bird reserve and Cap Ferret across the bay – but also the nearby beaches have some of the Atlantic Coast's best surf. Cycle here from Arcachon and top off the heady trip with a dozen oysters, shucked before your very eyes and accompanied by *crepinettes* (local sausages).

if France were 100 people

77 would live in urban areas
23 would live in rural areas

belief systems
(% of population)

87 Roman Catholic

2 Jewish

10 Muslim

1 Protestant

population per sq km

FRANCE   USA   UK

≈ 30 people

Three Corniches, Nice

5 It's impossible to drive this dramatic trio of coastal roads, each one higher and with more hairpin bends than the next, without conjuring up cinematic images of Grace Kelly, Hitchcock, the glitz of Monaco high life, and the glamour of the royal family – all while absorbing big view after big view of sweeping blue sea fringing Europe's most mythical coastline. To make a perfect day out of it, shop for a picnic at the Cours Saleya morning market before leaving Nice.

Alsatian Wine Route

6 It is one of France's most popular drives – and for good reason. Motoring in this far northeast corner of France takes you through a kaleidoscope of lush green vines, perched castles and gentle mist-covered mountains. The only pit stops en route are half-timbered villages and roadside wine cellars, where fruity Alsace vintages can be swirled, tasted and bought. To be truly wooed, drive the Route des Vins d'Alsace in autumn, when vines are heavy with grapes waiting to be harvested and colours are at their vibrant best.

D-Day Beaches

7 This is one of France's most emotional journeys. The broad stretches of fine sand and breeze-blown bluffs are quiet now, but early on 6 June 1944 the beaches of northern Normandy were a cacophony of gunfire and explosions, the bodies of Allied soldiers lying in the sand as their comrades-in-arms charged inland. Just up the

Tour de France

No race gets the wheels of the cycling world spinning quite like the Tour de France, or 'Le Tour' as it is known here. It's the big one: one prologue, 20 stages, some 3500km clocked in three weeks by 180 riders, an entire country covered by bicycle. Broadcast in 190 countries and watched by 15 million every July, it is a spectacle of die-hard passion and epic endurance, of thigh-breaking mountain passes and hell-for-leather sprints, of tears and triumph.

The brainchild of journalist Géo Lefèvre, the race was first held in 1903 to boost sales of *L'Auto* newspaper, with 60 trailblazers pedalling through the night to complete the 2500km route in 19 days. Since then, the Tour has become *the* cycling event. And despite the headlines of skulduggery and doping scandals, it's the success stories that really grab you.

Food & Drink

Bouillabaisse Marseille's signature hearty fish stew, eaten with croutons and rouille (garlic-and-chilli mayonnaise).

Champagne Tasting in century-old cellars is an essential part of Champagne's bubbly experience.

Crêpes Large, round, thin pancakes cooked at street-corner stands while you wait.

Croque monsieur Grilled ham and toasted cheese sandwich; cheesey 'madames' are egg-topped.

Flammekueche Alsatian thin-crust pizza dough topped with sour cream, onions and bacon.

Pan Bagnat Crusty Niçois tuna sandwich dripping in fruity green olive oil.

Pâté de Foie Gras Duck- or goose-liver pâté.

Socca Chickpea-flour pancake typical to the French Riviera.

Cours Saleya market, Vieux Nice, Nice

hill from Omaha Beach, the long rows of symmetrical gravestones at the Normandy American Cemetery & Memorial bear solemn, silent testimony to the horrible price paid for France's liberation from Nazi tyranny.

Provençal Markets

8 No region is more of a market-must than this one. Be it fresh fish by the port in seafaring Marseille, early summer's strings of pink garlic, melons from Cavaillon all summer long or wintertime's earthy 'black diamond' truffles, Provence thrives on a bounty of fresh produce – grown locally and piled high each morning at the market. Every town and village has one, but those in Carpentras and Aix-en-Provence are the best known. While you're here, stock up on dried herbs, green and black olives marinated a dozen different ways, courgette flowers and oils.

When to Go

HIGH SEASON
(Jul & Aug)

➡ Queues at big sights and on the road, especially August.

➡ Christmas, New Year and Easter equally busy.

➡ Late December to March is high season in Alpine ski resorts.

SHOULDER
(Apr–Jun & Sep)

➡ Accommodation rates drop in southern France and other hot spots.

➡ Spring: warm weather, flowers, local produce.

➡ The *vendange* (grape harvest) is reason to visit.

LOW SEASON
(Oct–Mar)

➡ Prices up to 50% less than high season.

➡ Sights, attractions and restaurants open fewer days and shorter hours.

Pont du Gard

9 This Unesco World Heritage site near Nîmes in

southern France is gargantuan: 35 arches straddle the Roman aqueduct's 275m-long upper tier, containing a watercourse that was designed to carry 20,000 cubic metres of water per day. View it from afloat a canoe on the River Gard or pay extra to jig across its top tier. Oh, and don't forget your swimming gear for a spot of post-Pont daredevil diving and high jumping from the rocks nearby – a plunge that will entice the most reluctant of young historians.

Carnac Megaliths

10 Pedalling past open fields dotted with the world's greatest concentration of mysterious megaliths gives a poignant reminder of Brittany's ancient human inhabitants. No one knows for sure what inspired these gigantic menhirs, dolmens, cromlechs, tumuli and cairns to be built. A sun god? Some phallic fertility cult? It's a mystery.

Carcassonne

11 That first glimpse of La Cité's sturdy, stone, witch's-hat turrets above Carcassonne is enough to make your hair stand on end. To properly savour this fairy-tale walled city, linger at dusk after the crowds have left, when the old town belongs to its 100 or so inhabitants and the few visitors staying at the handful of hotels within its ramparts.

Best on Film

La Môme (La Vie en Rose; 2007) Story of singer Edith Piaf.

Les Choristes (The Chorus; 2004) A new teacher arrives at a school for troublesome boys.

Midnight in Paris (2011) Woody Allen tale, with standout dream scenes set in 1920s Paris.

Best in Print

Me Talk Pretty One Day (David Sedaris) Caustic take on moving to France and learning the lingo.

Paris in Color (Nichole Robertson) No photographic title better captures the extraordinary colours and hues of the French capital.

Stuff Parisians Like (Olivier Magny) Witty vignettes by a Parisian sommelier.

The Death of French Culture (Donald Morrison) Thought-provoking look at France's past and present.

Getting Around

Bicycle France is great for cycling. Much of the countryside is drop-dead gorgeous and the country has a growing number of urban and rural *pistes cyclables* (bike paths and lanes).

Bus Widely used for short-distance travel within *départements*, especially in rural areas. Services in some regions are infrequent and slow.

Car Driving can be expensive, and finding a place to park in the cities is frequently a major headache.

Train Travelling by train in France is comfortable, classy and environmentally sustainable. The jewel in the crown of France's public-transport system – alongside the Paris métro – is its extensive rail network.

Adrenalin Kick, Chamonix

12 Sure, 007 did it, but so can you: skiing the Vallée Blanche is a once-in-a-lifetime experience. You won't regret the €75-odd it costs to do the 20km off-piste descent from the spike of the Aiguille du Midi to mountaineering mecca Chamonix – every minute of the five hours it takes to get down will pump more adrenalin in your body than anything else you've ever done. Craving more? Hurl yourself down Europe's longest black run, La Sarenne, at Alpe d'Huez.

La Flégère, Chamonix

JULIAN LOVE / GETTY IMAGES ©

CAPITAL
Cayenne

POPULATION
221,500

AREA
91,000 sq km

OFFICIAL LANGUAGES
French, Creole

French Guiana

A small slice of France in South America, French Guiana is an intriguing colonial outpost with Gallic flavours in a Caribbean climate and tales of hardship from prisons of the past.

French Guiana is a tiny country of cleaned-up colonial architecture, eerie prison-camp history and some of the world's most diverse plant and animal life. It's a strange mix of French law and rainforest humidity, where only a few destinations along the coast are easily accessed and travel can be frustratingly difficult as well as expensive. As a department of France, it's one of South America's wealthiest corners, with funds pouring in to ensure a stable base for the satellite launcher. The capital Cayenne is a crossroads of the Caribbean, South America and Europe, in its architecture and its excellent food from croissants and Creolo dishes to Vietnamese pho.

But not even a European superpower can tame the vast, pristine jungle away from the city – you'll find potholes in newly paved roads, and ferns sprouting between bricks while Amerindians, Maroons and Hmong refugees live traditional lifestyles so far from *la vie Metropole* that it's hard to believe they're connected at all.

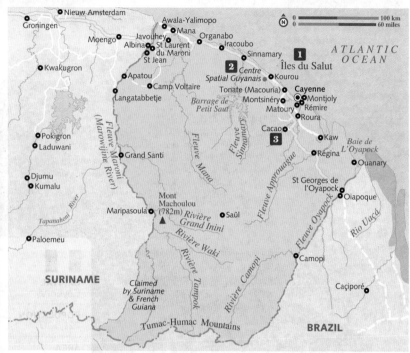

French Guiana's
Top Experiences

Îles du Salut

1 Cast away to Îles du Salut for sand, palms and a creepy, defunct penal colony. It was from 'Devil's Island' here that Henry Charrière – better known as Papillon – supposedly escaped on a bag of coconuts. These days people are escaping *to* the islands.

Satellite Spotting

2 Here's your chance to see one of the world's busiest satellite launchers at the Centre Spatial Guyanais in Kourou. The launch site is the only one in the world this close to the equator, where the earth's spin is faster than further north or south, resulting in a 'slingshot effect'. Since 1980 two-thirds of the world's commercial satellites have been launched from French Guiana.

Cacao

3 A slice of Laos in the hills of Guiana, Cacao is a village of sparkling clear rivers, vegetable plantations and no-nonsense wooden houses on stilts. The Hmong refugees, who left Laos in the 1970s, keep their town a safe, peaceful haven. Sunday, market day, is the best time for a visit if you want to shop for Hmong embroidery and weaving, and feast on Laotian treats.

Food & Drink

Fricassee Rice, beans and sauteed meat stewed in gravy – Caribbean style has a brown or red sauce with a kick of Cayenne pepper.

Gibier Bush meat like capybara, wild boar and agouti is legally hunted and found widely on menus.

Ti'punch Literally a 'small punch' made with local rum, lime juice and sugar-cane syrup.

When to Go

JAN–JUN
➡ Expect sogginess during these months, with the heaviest rains in May.

LATE JAN–MAR
➡ You can always expect Cayenne to throw a wild and exciting Carnival.

JUL–SEP
➡ It rains less during the dry season although it's hot and humid year round.

Ivindo National Park

Gabon

Gabon is Africa's last Eden, a realm of largely untouched natural riches; with its wealth of national parks it may just be, for the traveller, ecotourism heaven.

Unlike many of its neighbours, this slab of equatorial Africa enjoys both peace and stability, while its superb wildlife makes it an increasingly popular place to safari away from the crowds of East Africa. With its seemingly endless rainforest now safeguarded by the 2003 decision to turn an incredible 10% of the country into protected national parkland, Gabon is Central Africa's most progressive and traveller-friendly destination, although the competition is admittedly not too fierce.

Despite being far ahead of its unstable, war-torn neighbours, tourism in Gabon remains DIY – you either put yourself in the hands of a travel agency, or negotiate the poor roads, infrequent transport and almost total lack of reliable infrastructure yourself. Outside cosmopolitan Libreville, the country's only real city, Gabon is an undiscovered wonderland of thick jungle, white-sand beaches, rushing rivers and ethereal landscapes. Bring either plenty of money or plenty of patience, but don't miss out on this Eden-like travel experience.

CAPITAL
Libreville

POPULATION
1.6 million

AREA
267,667 sq km

OFFICIAL LANGUAGE
French

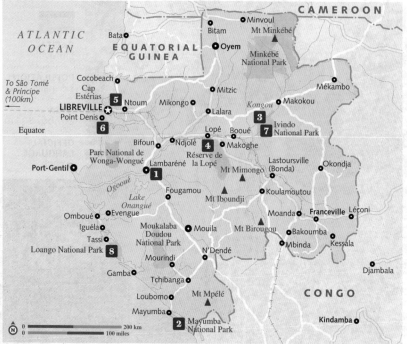

Gabon's
Top Experiences

Lambaréné

1 Explore Lambaréné, the charming and laid-back town made famous by the Nobel Peace Prize–winner Albert Schweitzer. With its glossy lakes, fast-flowing rivers, thick green foliage and ingrained sweetness. The town is somehow kinder and gentler than the rest of Gabon, as if the profound humanitarian efforts of Schweitzer changed the character of the land. The town is divided into three areas spanning the river, quite close to each other.

Mayumba National Park

2 Bodysurf the waves while watching humpback whales breach in the distance at Mayumba National Park. Closer to Congo than to Libreville, Mayumba feels like the edge of the earth. No wonder expats whisper about it – the national park is the domain of barnacled whales and shy sea turtles, and the land, if you listen to the locals, is hushed by the spirits of ancestors. Flights to Mayumba's airstrip are intermittent. It is possible to travel overland the entire way, but it's an extremely long journey.

Kongou

3 Head to Gabon's most spectacular falls at Kongou and take a trip by *pirogue* (traditional canoe) through the jungle. Gabon's answer to Niagara is the gushing falls at Kongou, and Makokou – the small capital of the Ogooué-Ivindo region – is the gateway to the falls. You can organise camping trips into the rainforest and to the falls, *pirogue* excursions and a long list of other activities, all at fairly reasonable prices. You can also negotiate a bed for the night.

Réserve de la Lopé

4 Explore beautiful Réserve de la Lopé, see wild elephants and enjoy spectacular scenery. Smack bang on the equator, Gabon's calling card doesn't disappoint. Undulating hills meet scrubby patches of savannah and enclaves of rain forest where elephants,

Pongara National Park, Point Denis

buffaloes, gorillas and some of the biggest mandrill troupes in the world can be found. There are vehicle safaris on offer, but foot safaris allow you to feel a part of the jungle, experiencing – and encountering – everything at close quarters.

Libreville

5 The muscular heart of Gabon, Libreville is its only real city and home to over a third of its population. It's also a city awash in oil money and almost totally unrecognisable as an African capital. Pavements, clean streets, smart restaurants and vast gated villas are the first impressions of the town, but stay a little longer and you'll easily discover Libreville's vibrant African heart beating away in the crowded street markets and busy residential areas.

Point Denis

6 Take a day trip to Point Denis, Libreville's weekend bolt hole. It's a quick boat ride and yet a world away from the capital. The superb stretch of sand here runs for miles along the peninsula, backing onto the Pongara National Park, and lined with fancy weekend houses. Stick to the beaten track and you'll find boutique hotels, lazy restaurants and watersports; walk to the Atlantic side of the point and you'll discover miles of empty white sand where sea turtles nest from November to January.

if Gabon were 100 people

42 would be aged 0-14
20 would be aged 15-24
30 would be aged 25-54
4 would be aged 55-64
4 would be 65+

belief systems
(% of population)

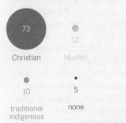

73 Christian
12 Muslim
10 traditional indigenous
5 none

When to Go

MAY–SEP

➡ The dry season makes overland transport faster and wildlife easier to see.

JUL–SEP

➡ Have a close encounter with a whale swimming off Gabon's coastline.

NOV–JAN

➡ Spot turtles coming ashore to lay their eggs on the beaches.

population per sq km

GABON   SOUTH AFRICA   USA

🚹 ≈ 6 people

Surfing Hippos

Though it hardly seems credible – a fantasy that belongs in the realm of children's novels, unicorns and flying carpets – Gabon's surfing hippos have been making waves around the world since their hobby was outed by conservationist Mike Fay in the 1990s.

Unlike human surfers, the two-ton creatures are hardly a picture of grace as they frolic among the waves, but surf they do: wading into the ocean and opening their legs to catch the swell.

Despite the hype, however, it's extremely unlikely you'll see hippos partaking – after all, their name comes from the Greek for 'river horse' and in general they prefer fresh water to seawater. Still, who can blame them for seeking a bit of extra excitement?

Food & Drink

If you don't like *fufu*, don't sweat. The heat-inducing cassava staple is a long-time favourite in Gabon, but the cuisine is just as heavy in other Central and West African staples, such as fried plantains and rice and fish dishes.

Okra, spinach and palm oil are widely eaten here, and in a country coated with such thick forest, the lure of bushmeat – notably bush hogs, antelopes, primates (including chimpanzees and to a lesser extent gorillas) and crocodiles – has been hard to shake.

Try smoked fish with rice and *nyembwe* (a sauce of pulped palm nuts).

Beer is the drink of choice – most common among those available is Castel. Régab, a beer from the Sobraga brewery in Libreville, is also popular

Hippopotamus

ROBIN SMITH / GETTY IMAGES ©

Ivindo National Park

7 Langoué Bai, in the dense, tropical 3000-sq-metre Ivindo National Park, is perhaps the pièce de résistance of all the Gabonese ecodestinations, presenting the rare opportunity to view forest animals undisturbed in their own environment. The Bai, a local word for a marshy clearing in the forest, serves as a source of minerals for the animals and acts as a magnet for large numbers of forest elephants, western lowland gorillas, sitatungas, buffaloes, monkeys and rare bird species. A Wildlife Conservation Society–built research station allows visitors to easily view the wildlife.

Loango National Park

8 Here, warm streams criss-cross pockets of thick forest and salty savannah, while vast island-dotted lagoons and miles of white-sand beach provide habitat for all manner of creatures. It's perhaps best known for its legendary surfing hippos, but you'll also find the largest concentration and variety of whales and dolphins in its waters, elephants wandering the beaches and an assortment of rare land mammals cavorting in the savannah.

Getting Around

Air This is by far the easiest way to move around in Gabon, as the roads are terrible, distances long and buses slow. However, flights aren't cheap or regular and it's common for flights to leave before their scheduled departure time, so take those two-hour check-ins seriously.

Boat There are passenger boats between Lambaréné and Port-Gentil in both directions on Thursday and Sunday.

Train Taking the Transgabonaise train line that crosses the country is a cheaper, faster and far more comfortable option than taking a *taxi-brousse*.

CAPITAL
Banjul

POPULATION
1.9 million

AREA
11,295 sq km

OFFICIAL LANGUAGE
English

The Gambia

The Gambia, the smallest country in mainland Africa, contains a lot within its compact frame, attracting sun-seekers and birdwatchers and displaying a wealth of natural riches.

This tiny sliver of land is wedged into surrounding Senegal, and is seen as a splinter in its side, or the tongue that makes it speak, depending on who you talk to. For many, The Gambia is a country with beaches that invite visitors to laze and linger on package tours. Its beaches and the adjacent resorts long ago became famous among sun-starved Europeans. But there's more here than just sun and surf.

Small fishing villages, nature reserves and historic slaving stations are all within easy reach of the clamorous Atlantic resorts. Star-studded ecolodges and small wildlife parks dot the inland like a green belt around the coast, and among birdwatchers The Gambia is revered as one of Africa's best and most accessible birding destinations – it lies on the main migratory path between Europe and Africa. On a leisurely river cruise, you'll easily spot more than 100 species while your *pirogue* (traditional canoe) charts an unhurried course through mangrove-lined wetlands and lush gallery forests.

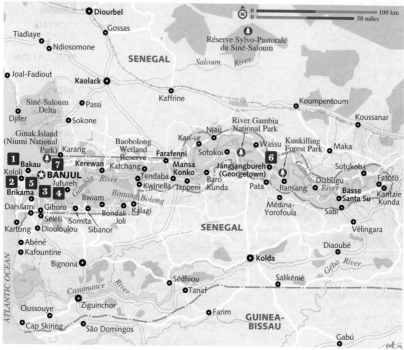

The Gambia's
Top Experiences

Atlantic Coast

1 For many tourists, the 10km stretch from Bakau to Kololi is The Gambia. Here you can indulge in fabulous food, then party the night away in the staggering selection of resorts and restaurants. Chaotic, splitting-at-the-seams Serekunda is the nation's largest urban centre, and appears to consist of one big, bustling market. The nearby coastal resorts of Bakau, Fajara, Kotu Strand and Kololi are where the sun 'n' sea tourists flock. If you can manage to dodge the persistent ganja peddlers and bumsters (touts), this is a great place to spend long days on the beach and late nights on the dance floor.

Bijilo Forest Park

2 Be teased by monkeys on the nature trail in this small reserve and community forest. A 4.5km walk takes you along a well-maintained series of trails that pass through lush vegetation, gallery forest, low bush and grass, towards the dunes. You'll see green vervet, red colobus and patas monkeys, though feeding by visitors has turned them into cheeky little things that might come close and even steal items. Monitor lizards will likely come and stare you down, too. Birds are best watched on the coastal side – more than 100 species have been counted here.

Makasutu Culture Forest

3 Tour the country in miniature, squeezed into 1000 hectares of abundant nature at Makasutu Culture Forest. Like a snapshot of The Gambia, Makasutu bundles the country's array of landscapes into a dazzling package. The setting is stunning, comprising palm groves, wetlands, mangroves and savannah plains, all inhabited by plenty of animals, including baboons, monitor lizards and hundreds of bird species. A day in the forest includes a mangrove tour by *pirogue* and guided walks through a range of habitats, including a palm forest where you can watch palm sap being tapped.

Beach resort, Kololi

Jufureh

4 Contemplate history in the town where American writer Alex Haley traced his origins. Ever since Haley's 1976 book *Roots* traced the author's ancestral lineage back to the Kinte family of Jufureh, the village has turned into a symbolic destination for those in search of answers to their past. There's little to see, although the museum, which traces slavery in The Gambia and includes a replica slave ship, is worth a visit. Across the river, the crumbling walls of the ancient slaving station on James Island remain a stark reminder of the cruel trade in humans that once took place here. Fort James was an important British trading post and the departure point of vessels packed with ivory, gold and slaves.

Abuko Nature Reserve

5 Look out for rare birds and giant crocodiles in tiny Abuko Nature Reserve, possibly the finest of Gambia's national parks. Rare among African wildlife reserves, Abuko is easy to reach, you don't need a car to go in, and it's well managed, with an amazing diversity of vegetation and animals. More than 250 bird species have been recorded in Abuko's compact area, making it one of the region's best birdwatching haunts (early morning is the best time to spot activity). The reserve is particularly famous for its Nile crocodiles and other slithering types such as pythons, puff adders, green mambas and forest cobras.

if the Gambia were 100 people

42 would be Mandinka
18 would be Fula
16 would be Wolof
23 would be other African
1 would be non-African

belief systems
(% of population)

90 Muslim   8 Christian   2 indigenous beliefs

When to Go

NOV–FEB
➡ The dry season and the best time to watch wildlife and birds.

LATE JUN–SEP
➡ Rainy season. Many places close, but you'll avoid the crowds.

OCT & MAR–MAY
➡ Decent weather and ideal for bagging a shoulder-season discount.

population per sq km

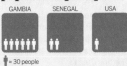

GAMBIA   SENEGAL   USA

♀ ≈ 30 people

Birdwatching

At only 11,295 sq km, The Gambia is mainland Africa's smallest country. It's also the most absurdly shaped one. Its 300km-long territory is almost entirely surrounded by Senegal and dominated by the Gambia River that runs through it. The country is flat, and vegetation consists mainly of savannah woodlands, gallery forests and saline marshes.

The bird diversity of The Gambia reaches a concentration that seems out of all proportion to its tiny size. More than 560 species have been recorded – just 80 fewer than in Senegal, which is almost 20 times larger – and the country's unique shape makes many good birdwatching sites easily accessible.

Thanks to a well-organised network of birdwatching tours and guides, The Gambia attracts large number of birdwatchers, particularly between November and February.

Food & Drink

Ataaya West Africa's classic afternoon pick-me-up. This is a punchy, bittersweet brew made from fistfuls of green tea leaves and a generous amount of sugar.

Benachin Rice cooked in tomato, fish and vegetable sauce.

Bissap A purple drink made of water, sugar and hibiscus leaves.

Bouyi Sweet, thick juice made from the fruits of the baobab tree.

Domodah Platter of rice covered with a thick, smooth groundnut (peanut) sauce with fried meat and vegetables.

Niebbe Spicy red beans, served with bread on street corners.

Palm wine Frothy, white palm wine is a much-loved drink that gets sold by the canister. The strong, yeasty flavour takes some getting used to.

Albert Market, Banjul

GALLO IMAGES / GETTY IMAGES ©

Janjangbureh

6 Follow the call of the birds in the forest around Janjangbureh (Georgetown). This sleepy, former colonial administrative centre is situated on the northern edge of MacCarthy Island in the Gambia River, and is reached via ferry links from either bank. There is little in terms of infrastructure, but a walk around town reveals a few historic buildings. The main reason to come, however, is to stay in a local lodge and take advantage of the superb birdwatching opportunities.

Banjul

7 It's hard to imagine a more consistently ignored capital city than Banjul. It sits on an island crossed by sand-blown streets and dotted with fading colonial structures. And yet, it tempts with a sense of history that the plush seaside resorts lack, and is home to a busy harbour and market that show urban Africa at its best. Since its creation in the mid-19th century the Albert Market, an area of frenzied buying, bartering and bargaining, has been Banjul's hub of activity.

Getting Around

Boat There are no scheduled passenger boats, but several tour operators offer tailor-made trips up the river that gives The Gambia its name.

Bus The southbank road from the coast eastward is in a perennial state of construction; the northbank road is a good alternative option for journeys upcountry. *Sept-place* (shared seven-seater) taxis are by no means a comfy way of travelling; however, they are infinitely better than the battered *gelli-gelli* minibuses. A few green, government-owned 'express' buses also ply the major roads.

Taxi Shared taxis called *six-six* operate on several routes around coastal resorts.

Nariqala Fortress, Old Town, Tbilisi

Georgia

A proud, richly cultured nation, boasting architectural delights and breathtaking landscapes, Georgia is a treasure awaiting discovery in the Caucasus Mountains.

CAPITAL
Tbilisi

POPULATION
4.9 million

AREA
69,700 sq km

OFFICIAL LANGUAGE
Georgian

With sublimely perched old churches and watchtowers dotting fantastic mountain scenery and green valleys spread with vineyards, Georgia is one of the most beautiful countries on earth. It offers limitless opportunities for walkers, horse riders, skiers, rafters and paragliders. Dramatic peaks rise, wolves, bears and hyenas lurk, rivers race through steep gorges and mountain folk bedeck stone shrines with sacrificed goats' heads.

The Georgians themselves are earnestly pious, high-spirited and warmly hospitable.

Georgia claims to be the birthplace of wine, and this is a place where guests are considered blessings and convivial feasting is the very stuff of life.

A deeply complicated history has given Georgia a melange of cultural influences a wonderful heritage of architecture and art, from cave cities to the inimitable canvases of Pirosmani. But this is also a country striving for a place in the 21st-century Western world, with eye-catching new buildings and facilities for the tourists who are a big part of its future.

Georgia's
Top Experiences

Tbilisi Old Town

1 Nowhere better blends the romance of Georgia's past with its striving for a new future than Tbilisi's Old Town. Winding lanes lined by rakishly leaning houses lead past tranquil old stone churches to shady squares and glimpses of the ultracontemporary Peace Bridge spanning the Mtkvari River. Casual cafes and bohemian bars rub shoulders with trendy lounge-clubs, folksy carpet shops, new travellers' hostels and small, quirky hotels. The aeons-old silhouette of Nariqala Fortress supervises everything, while Georgia's 21st-century Presidential Palace, with its egg-shaped glass dome, looks on from over the river.

Kazbegi Area

2 Just a couple of hours' drive from Tbilisi, the small town of Kazbegi is the hub of one of the region's most spectacular, yet easily accessed, high-mountain zones. The sight of Tsminda Sameba Church silhouetted on its hilltop against the massive snow-covered cone of Mt Kazbek is Georgia's most iconic image. Numerous walking, horse and mountain-bike routes lead along steep-sided valleys and up to glaciers, waterfalls, mountain passes and isolated villages – just ideal for getting a taste of the high Caucasus.

Davit Gareja

3 With a spectacular setting in remote, arid lands near Georgia's border with Azerbaijan, these much revered cave monasteries were carved out of the hillsides long, long ago. They became a cradle of medieval monastic culture and fresco painting. Saints' tombs, vivid 1000-year-old murals, an otherworldly landscape and the very idea that people voluntarily chose – and still choose – to live in desert caves, all combine to make visiting Davit Gareja (an easy day trip from Tbilisi, Telavi or Sighnaghi) a startling experience today.

Svaneti

4 Beautiful, wild and mysterious, Svaneti is an ancient land locked in the Caucasus, so remote that it was never tamed by any

Mt Chaukhi

ruler. Uniquely picturesque villages and snow-covered peaks rising over 4000m above flower-strewn alpine meadows provide a superb backdrop to the many walking trails. Svaneti's emblem is the defensive stone tower (koshki), designed to house villagers at times of invasion and local strife.

Vardzia

5 Vardzia, an entire medieval city carved out of a cliff face, is a cultural symbol with a special place in the hearts of Georgians. King Giorgi III built a fortification here in the 12th century, and his daughter, Queen Tamar, established a monastery that grew into a virtual holy city, renowned as a spiritual bastion of Georgia and of Christendom's eastern frontier. Today Vardzia is again a working monastery, with some caves inhabited by monks.

Batumi

6 Soak up the party atmosphere in Batumi, Georgia's lovable Black Sea 'summer capital'. With a backdrop of mist-wrapped hills, Batumi has sprouted new hotels and attractions like mushrooms in recent years, but it still owes much of its charm to the fin-de-siècle elegance of its original boom time a century ago. One of the first decisions of the post-Abashidze administration in 2004 was to make Batumi an attractive place to visit, something in which it has happily succeeded.

if Georgia were 100 people

84 would be Georgian
7 would be Azeri
6 would be Armenian
1 would be Russian
2 would be other

belief systems
(% of population)

84 Orthodox Christian
10 Muslim
4 Armenian-Gregorian

1 Catholic
1 other

population per sq km

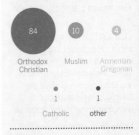

GEORGIA   RUSSIA   ARMENIA

👤 ≈ 9 people

When to Go

MAY–JUN & SEP–OCT

➡ Ideal travel season, with warm and sunny weather.

JUL–AUG

➡ Hot and humid in the lowlands, but an excellent time to be in the mountains.

DEC–FEB

➡ Temperature is often below freezing in Georgia's eastern half.

Stalin & Georgia

Iosif Jughashvili (aka Stalin), ruler of the largest country on earth for a quarter of a century and one of the key figures of 20th-century history, started life as a cobbler's son in poor, small-town Georgia.

Few would question his impact on world events: were it not for the Soviet role in WWII, Nazi Germany may well have won, and in the space of a decade Stalin turned the USSR from a peasant economy into an industrial powerhouse. Yet Stalin's Gulag camps were responsible for the deaths of many millions, he is widely blamed for the 1932 Ukraine famine in which an estimated seven million died, and his ruthless secret police terrorised the Soviet population.

He still has some admirers in Georgia. When the government finally decided to remove the large Stalin statue from Gori's central square in 2010 they did it at night, with police sealing off the square.

Food & Drink

Badrijani nigvzit Aubergine slices with walnut-and-garlic paste

Churchkhela A string of walnuts coated in a sort of pinkish caramel made from grape juice.

Khachapuri Essentially a cheese pie.

Khin-kali Spicy dumplings, usually with a minced-meat filling, although potato and/or mushroom fillings are quite widely available. You're not supposed to eat the doughy nexus at the top of the dumpling, though a few people do.

Lobio Bean paste or stew with herbs and spices.

Mkhali/pkhali Pastes combining vegetables such as aubergine, spinach or beetroot with walnuts, garlic and herbs.

Mtsvadi Shish kebab.

Wine production and storage, Nekresi Monastery, Kakheti

SEAN CAFFREY / GETTY IMAGES ©

Tusheti

7 Hike the spectacular, remote, pristine high-mountain region of Tusheti. Tucked into Georgia's far northeast corner, Tusheti has become a very popular summer hiking and horse-trekking area, but remains one of the country's most fascinating and pristine high-mountain regions. The single road to Tusheti, over the nerve-jangling 2900m Abano Pass from Kakheti, is 4WD-only and passable only from early June to early October. Evidence of Tusheti's old animist religion is plentiful in the form of stone shrines called khatebi, decked with the horns of sacrificed goats or sheep.

Kakheti

8 Spend your days sipping the wines of Kakheti in the home of Georgian wine. Evidence of winemaking in Kakheti goes back about 7000 years, and with 225 sq km of vineyards today, this is a region where wine plays a big part in daily life even by Georgian standards. Meanwhile, the age-old local method of fermenting wine in *qvevri* (large clay pots buried in the ground) continues.

Getting Around

Car Driving styles in the South Caucasus are less regimented than in Western countries (or more anarchic). It is quite common practice to hire a local driver for intercity trips or excursions.

Minibus The minibus (marshrutka; short for the Russian marshrutnoe taxi) is king of public transport in Georgia, and reaches almost every village in the region; there are frequent services between larger towns and cities.

Train Trains in the South Caucasus are slower and much less frequent than road transport. But they're also cheap, and many intercity trains run overnight so you can save money on accommodation.

Semperoper, Dresden

Germany

Prepare for a roller coaster of feasts, treats and temptations as you take in Germany's soul-stirring scenery, spirit-lifting culture, big-city beauties, romantic palaces and half-timbered towns.

Beer or wine? That sums up the German conundrum. One is at the heart of a pilsner-swilling culture, is the very reason for one of the world's great parties (Oktoberfest) and is consumed with pleasure across the land. The other is responsible for gorgeous vine-covered valleys, comes in myriad forms and is enjoyed everywhere, often from cute little green-stemmed glasses.

And the questions about Germany continue. Berlin or Munich? Castle or club? Ski or hike? East or west? BMW or Mercedes? In fact, the answers are simple: both. Why decide? The beauty of Germany is that rather than choosing, you can revel in the contrasts.

Berlin, edgy and vibrant, is a grand capital in a constant state of reinvention. Munich rules Bavaria, the centre of national traditions. Half-timbered villages bring smiles as you wander the cobblestoned and castle-shadowed lanes. Exploring this country and all its facets keeps visitors happy for weeks.

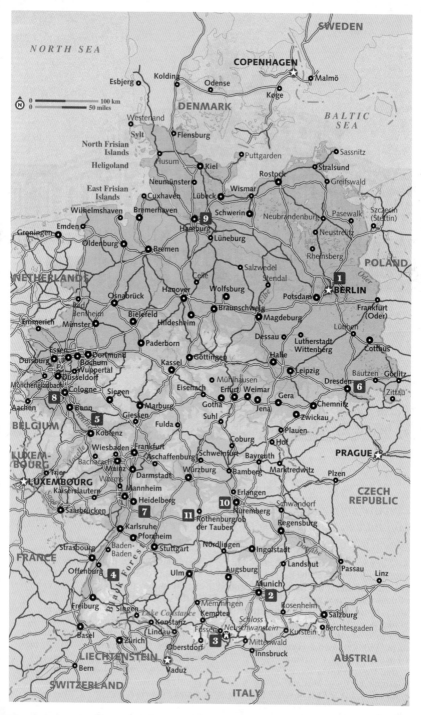

Germany's
Top Experiences

Berlin Wall

1 Few events in history have the power to move the entire world. The Kennedy assassination; landing on the moon; 9/11... And, of course, the fall of the Berlin Wall in 1989. If you were alive back then and old enough, you will probably remember the crowds of euphoric revellers cheering and dancing at the Brandenburg Gate. Although little is left of the physical barrier, its legacy lives on in the imagination and in places such as Checkpoint Charlie, the Gedenkstätte Berliner Mauer and the East Side Gallery, with its colourful murals.

Oktoberfest

2 Anyone with a taste for hop-scented froth knows that the daddy of all beer festivals, Oktoberfest, takes place annually in Munich. The world's favourite sud fest actually begins mid-September and runs for 16 ethanol-fuelled days on the Theresienwiese (Theresa's Meadow), with troops of crimson-faced oompah bands entertaining revellers; armies of traditionally garbed locals and foreigners guzzling their way through seven million litres of lager; and entire farms of chickens hitting the grill. So find your favourite tent and raise your 1L stein. 'Ozapft ist!' (It is tapped!).

HIROSHI HIGUCHI / GETTY IMAGES ©

Schloss Neuschwanstein

3 Commissioned by Bavaria's most celebrated (and loopiest) 19th-century monarch, King Ludwig II, Neuschwanstein Palace rises from the mysterious Alpine forests like a bedtime storybook illustration. Inside the make-believe continues, with chambers and halls reflecting Ludwig's obsession with the mythical Teutonic past and his admiration for composer Wagner, in a composition that puts even the flashiest oligarch's palazzo in the shade. This sugary folly is said to have inspired Walt's castle at Disneyland.

The Black Forest

4 Mist, snow or shine, this sylvan slice of southwest Germany is just beautiful. If it's back-to-nature moments you're after, the deep, dark Black Forest is the place to linger. Every valley reveals new surprises: half-timbered villages looking every inch the fairy-tale fantasy, thunderous waterfalls and cuckoo clocks the size of houses. Breathe in the cold sappy air, drive roller-coaster roads to middle-of-nowhere lakes, have your cake, walk it off on trail after gorgeously wooded trail, then hide away in a heavy-lidded farmhouse. Hear that? Silence. What a wonderful thing.

if Germany were 100 people

92 would be German
2 would be Turkish
6 would be other

....

belief systems

(% of population)

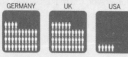

68 · 4 28

Christian   Muslim   other

....

population per sq km

GERMANY   UK   USA

† ≈ 7 people

The Romantic Rhine

5 As the mighty Rhine flows from Rüdesheim to Koblenz, the landscape's unique face-off between rock and water creates a magical mix of the wild (churning whirlpools, dramatic cliffs), the agricultural (near-vertical vineyards), the medieval (hilltop castles, half-timbered hamlets), the legendary (Loreley) and the modern (in the 19th-century sense – we're talking barges, ferries, passenger steamers and trains). From every riverside village, trails take you through vineyards and forests, up to panoramic viewpoints and massive stone fortresses.

Dresden

6 The apocalypse came on a cold February night in 1945. Hours of carpet bombing reduced Germany's 'Florence on the Elbe' into a pile of bricks. The comeback of Dresden is nothing short of a miracle. Reconstructed architectural jewels mix with stunning art collections that justify the city's place in the pantheon of European cultural capitals. Add a contagiously energetic pub quarter, Daniel Libeskind's dramatically redesigned Military History Museum and a tiara of palaces along the Elbe and you've got one enticing package.

Heidelberg

7 The 19th-century romantics found sublime beauty and spiritual inspiration in Germany's oldest university town and so, in his way, did Mark Twain, who was beguiled by the ruins of the hillside castle. Generations of students have attended lectures, sung lustily with beer

Gutenberg's Press

Johannes Gutenberg, the inventor of printing with moveable type, is one of those rare epochal figures whose achievements truly changed the course of human history.

Little is known about Gutenberg the man, who was born in Mainz in the very late 1300s, trained as a goldsmith and then, in the late 1420s, left for Strasbourg (now in France), where he first experimented with printing technology.

By 1448 he was back in Mainz, still working on his top-secret project and in debt to some rather impatient 'venture capitalists'. By 1455 Gutenberg had produced his masterpiece, the now-legendary Forty-Two-Line Bible, so-named because each page has 42 lines.

Thus began a new era in human history, one in which the printed word was to become almost universally accessible. In all of human history, arguably only two other inventions have come close to having the same impact on the availability of information: the alphabet and the internet.

Food & Drink

Beer (Bier) For most Germans, intensely hoppy pilsner is the poison of choice, although wheat beer is popular in summer.

Bread (Brot) Get Germans talking about bread and often their eyes will water as they describe their favourite type.

Sausage (Wurst) More than 1500 types are made countrywide. From sweet, smoky and tiny Nürnbergers, to that fast-food remedy for the munchies, the sliced and tomato-sauce-drowned currywurst.

Wine (Wein) Winning competitions and critics' praises, German wine in the 21st century is leagues removed from that cloyingly sweet stuff.

Schiltach, The Black Forest

steins in hand, carved their names into tavern tables and, occasionally, been sent to the student jail. All of this has left its mark on the modern-day city, where age-old traditions endure alongside world-class research, innovative cultural events and a sometimes raucous nightlife scene.

Cologne Cathedral

8 At unexpected moments you see it: Kölner Dom, the twin-towered icon of the city towering over an urban vista, dominating the view up a road. And why shouldn't it? This perfectly formed testament to faith and conviction was started in 1248 and consecrated a 'mere' six centuries later. You can feel the echoes of the passage of time as you sit in its cavernous, stained-glass-lit interior. Climb a tower for views of the surrounding city that are like no others.

Hamburg

9 Anyone who thinks Germany doesn't have round-the-clock delights hasn't been to Hamburg. This ancient, wealthy city on the Elbe River traces its roots back to the Hanseatic League

When to Go

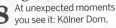

HIGH SEASON
(Jul & Aug)

➡ Busy roads and long lines at key sights.

➡ Vacancies at a premium and higher prices in seaside and mountain resorts.

➡ Festivals celebrate everything from music to wine.

SHOULDER
(Apr–Jun, Sep & Oct)

➡ Smaller crowds and lower prices, except on public holidays.

➡ Blooming flowers in spring; radiant foliage in autumn.

➡ Sunny, temperate weather ideal for outdoor pursuits.

LOW SEASON
(Nov–Mar)

➡ No lines but shorter hours at key sights; some may close for the season.

➡ Theatre, concert, opera season in full swing.

➡ Ski resorts busiest in January and February.

and beyond. By day you can tour its magnificent port, explore its history in restored quarters and discover shops selling goods you didn't think were sold. By night, some of Europe's best music clubs pull in the punters, and other diversions for virtually every taste are plentiful as well. And then, another Hamburg day begins.

Nuremberg

10 Capital of Franconia and an independent

Getting Around

Air Most large and many smaller German cities have their own airports. Unless you're flying from one end of the country to the other, planes are only marginally quicker than trains.

Bus Basically, wherever there is a train, take it. Buses are generally slower, less dependable and more polluting than trains.

Car German roads are excellent and motoring around the country can be a lot of fun. The country's pride and joy is its 11,000km network of autobahns (motorways, freeways).

Train Trains are operated almost entirely by Deutsche Bahn, with a variety of train types serving just about every corner in the country.

Best on Film

Metropolis (1927) Seminal silent flick about a subterranean proletarian subclass – it's the first film to use back projection.

Run Lola Run (1998) Energetic drama set in Berlin.

The Downfall (2004) Hitler's demise.

The Lives of Others (2006) Stasi unmasked.

The Wonderful, Horrible Life of Leni Riefenstahl (1993) Directed by Ray Muller, is a stunning three-hour epic about the controversial film-maker who rose to prominence during the Third Reich.

Best in Print

Berlin Alexanderplatz (Alfred Döblin; 1929) Berlin in the 1920s.

Complete Fairy Tales (Jacob & Wilhelm Grimm; 1812) A beautiful collection of 210 yarns, passed orally between generations and collected by German literature's most magical brothers.

Ein weites Feld (Too Far Afield; 1992) Günter Grass addresses 'unification without unity' after the fall of the wall.

The Rise & Fall of the Third Reich (William Shirer; 1960) Seminal account.

region until 1806, Nuremberg may be synonymous with Nazi rallies and grisly war trials, but there's so much more to this energetic city. Dürer hailed from the Altstadt, his house now a museum; Germany's first railway trundled from here to neighbouring Fürth, leaving a trail of choo-choo heritage; and Germany's toy capital has heaps of treasures for kids to enjoy. When you're done with sightseeing, the local beer is as dark as the coffee and best employed to chase down Nuremberg's finger-sized bratwurst.

Rothenburg ob der Tauber

11 With its jumble of neatly restored half-timbered houses enclosed by sturdy ramparts, Rothenburg ob der Tauber lays on the medieval cuteness with a trowel. One might even say it's too cute for its own good, if the inevitable deluges of day-trippers are any indication. The trick is to experience this historic wonderland at its most magical: early or late in the day when you can soak up the romance all by yourself on gentle strolls along moonlit cobbled lanes.

Nutcrackers at Christmas Market, Nuremberg

SACK / GETTY IMAGES ©

Bushbuck, Mole National Park

Ghana

Hailed as West Africa's golden child, Ghana, a historic land boasting a depth of culture and diverse natural attractions, deserves its place in the sun.

One of Africa's great success stories, Ghana is reaping the benefits of a stable democracy in the form of fast-paced development. And it shows: Ghana is suffused with the most incredible energy.

Ghana has the signature African attractions of beautiful beaches and herds of elephants in its fine national parks, plus drawcards like hiking, partying and cultural tours. With its welcoming beaches, gorgeous hinterland, rich culture, vibrant cities, diverse wildlife, easy transport and affable inhabitants, it's no wonder Ghana is sometimes labelled 'Africa for beginners'.

But this is only half the story. No trip can be complete without a visit to Ghana's coastal slave forts, poignant reminders of a page of history that defined our modern world.

Travel north and you'll feel like you've arrived in a different country, with a different religion, geography and cultural practices. The beauty is that this diversity exists so harmoniously, a joy to experience and a wonder to behold in uncertain times.

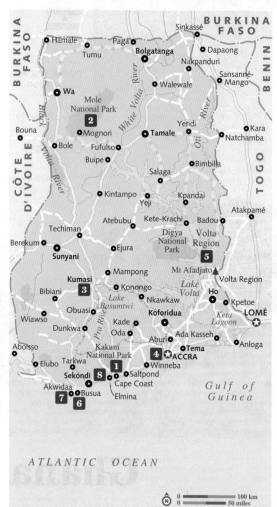

Ghana's
Top Experiences

Cape Coast

1 Tour the castles of Cape Coast to learn about the history of slavery. Forever haunted by the ghosts of the past, Cape Coast is one of the most culturally significant spots in Africa. Originally named Cabo Corso by the Portuguese, this was once the largest slave-trading centre in West Africa. At the height of the slave trade it received a workforce from locations as far away as Niger and Burkina Faso, and slaves were herded onto vessels like cattle, irrevocably altering the lives of generations to come.

Mole National Park

2 Join Africa's most inexpensive safari at Mole National Park, with its swaths of saffron-coloured savannah. There are at least 300 species of bird and 94 species of mammal, including African elephants, kob antelopes, buffaloes, baboons and warthogs. The park organises walking and driving safaris. If you don't have your own vehicle, you can rent the park's for the two-hour safari. The safaris are excellent and sightings of elephants are common from December to April.

Kejetia Market

3 Shop till you drop (and get very lost) in West Africa's biggest market, the exhilarating Kejetia Market in Kumasi. This huge market throbs like a traditional talking drum and its wares spill into the city so that no matter where you are in the town, it sometimes feels like one enormous marketplace. From afar, the market looks like an alien mothership landed in the centre of Kumasi, Closer up, the rusting tin roofs look like a circular shantytown. Inside, there are 11,000 stalls, making the market quite disorienting but utterly captivating.

Accra

4 Sample Accra's lively nightlife and join a tour for a behind-the-scenes look at what everyday life is like in the capital. Ghana's beating heart probably won't inspire love letters, but you might just grow to like it. The hot streets are perfumed with sweat, fumes and yesterday's cooking oil. Like balloons set to burst, clouds of humidity linger above stalls selling mangoes, *banku* (fermented maize

Volta River

meal) and rice. The city's tendrils reach out towards the beach, the centre and the west, each one a different Ghanaian experience.

Volta Region

5 Go hiking, climb waterfalls and swim in the former German Togoland, Ghana's Volta region in the east. The Volta region has to be the country's most underrated gem: the area is covered in lush, fertile farmland flanked by rocks, and mountains offering beautiful vistas. It is prime hiking territory and has great ecotourism ventures. Having your own car to explore pays off here as the main points of interest are relatively scattered; charter taxis will get you everywhere – just not as quickly.

Busua

6 Surf, chill and hike around Busua. Some 30km west of Takoradi, this small village is a magnet for volunteers and backpackers, who love coming here to chill on the beach for a few days. The surf here is some of the best in Ghana and there are lovely excursions to do from the village. The stunning village of Butre is worth the 3km walk. The walk itself is half the attraction: head east along the beach then veer left along a path up a hill. The views of Butre when you reach the summit are a sight to behold.

Akwidaa

7 Akwidaa's unique selling point is its long, pristine white sandy beach, by far one of the best in Ghana. The

if Ghana were 100 people

48 would be Akan
17 would be Mole-Dagbon
14 would be Ewe
7 would be Ga-Dangme
14 would be other

belief systems
(% of population)

28	43	18
Pentecostal/ Charismatic	other Christian	Muslim

5	1	5
traditional	other	none

population per sq km

GHANA   SOUTH AFRICA   UK

 ≈ 8 people

When to Go

APR–JUN
➡ The heaviest of the two rainy seasons (autumn can also be wet).

NOV–MAR
➡ The dry. The easiest season to travel in.

DEC–APR
➡ Best for wildlife viewing, with good visibility and animals congregating at water holes.

Music in Ghana

There's no doubt about it: Ghana's got rhythm.

Traditional music doesn't have the popular following that it has in countries such as Burkina. It tends to be reserved for special occasions and is associated with royalty. Contemporary music, on the other hand, is thriving. Highlife, a mellow mix of big-band jazz, Christian hymns, brass band and sailor sonnets, hit Ghana in the 1920s. WWII brought American swing to Ghana's shores, prompting the first complex fusion of Western and African music. Hiplife, a hybrid of rhythmic African lyrics poured over imported American hip-hop beats, has now been ruling Ghana since the early 1990s.

Imported American hip-hop and Nigerian music closely compete for the number two spot after highlife. Gospel music is also big, as is reggae.

Food & Drink

Fiery sauces and oily soups are the mainstay of Ghanaian cuisine and are usually served with a starchy staple like rice, *fufu* (cooked and mashed cassava, plantain or yam) or *banku* (fermented maize meal). About the most common dish you'll find is groundnut stew, a warming, spicy dish cooked with liquefied groundnut paste, ginger and either fish or meat. Palm-nut soup (fashioned from tomatoes, ginger, garlic and chilli pepper, as well as palm nut) takes its bright red colour from palm oil. *Red-red* is a delicous bean stew normally served with fried plantain.

Fresh fruit juices are, oddly, rather hard to find. Beer, on the other hand, isn't: popular brands include Star, Club, Gulder and Guinness. For something stronger, look no further than *akpeteshie*, the fiery local spirit made from palm wine.

Chapel, Elmina Castle

village itself isn't as interesting as other settlements on the coast, but you can explore cocoa plantations and forests, organise canoe trips or visit the windswept Cape Three Points, Ghana's most southern point. The walk to the cape follows the local track for a while, which is monotonous landscapewise but fascinating for local encounters (charcoal makers, *akpeteshie* – palm wine – distilleries etc).

Elmina

8 The enchanting town of Elmina lies on a narrow finger of land between the Atlantic Ocean and Benya Lagoon. Here, the air is salty and the architecture is a charming mix of colonial remnants, elderly *posubans*, (the shrines of the city's Asafo companies, ancient fraternities meant to defend the city) and a mournful historical legacy in the shape of St George's Castle. The castle, a Unesco heritage site, was built by the Portuguese in 1482 and captured by the Dutch in 1637. Ceded to the British in 1872, it was expanded when slaves replaced gold as the major object of commerce, and the storerooms were converted into dungeons.

Getting Around

Air Internal flights tend to be relatively cheap and a huge time-saver when travelling north.

Bus Buses are preferable to *tro-tros* for long journeys as they tend to be more comfortable and reliable. *Tro-tro* is a catch-all category that embraces any form of public transport that's not a bus or taxi (generally they're minibuses). It's wise to book bus tickets in advance as tickets get snapped up fast on the more popular routes. Note: there is always a charge for luggage.

Car Hiring a car with a driver is a good option if you're short on time; travel agencies can usually arrange this.

Mykonos

🇬🇷

CAPITAL
Athens

POPULATION
10.8 million

AREA
131,957 sq km

**OFFICIAL
LANGUAGE**
Greek

Greece

Experience miles of aquamarine coastline, sun-bleached ruins, strong feta and stronger ouzo. The Greek landscape thrills, and the people are passionate about politics, coffee, art and gossiping.

Don't let headline-grabbing financial woes put you off going to Greece. The alluring combination of history and hedonism, which has made Greece one of the most popular destinations on the planet, continues to beckon, and now is as good a time as ever to turn up for some fun in the sun.

Within easy reach of magnificent archaeological sites are breathtaking beaches and relaxed tavernas serving everything from ouzo to octopus.

Wanderers can island-hop to their heart's content, while party types can enjoy pulsating nightlife in Greece's vibrant modern cities and on islands such as Mykonos, Ios and Santorini. Add welcoming locals with an enticing culture to the mix and it's easy to see why most visitors head home vowing to come back. Travellers to Greece inevitably end up with a favourite site they long to return to – so get out there and find yours.

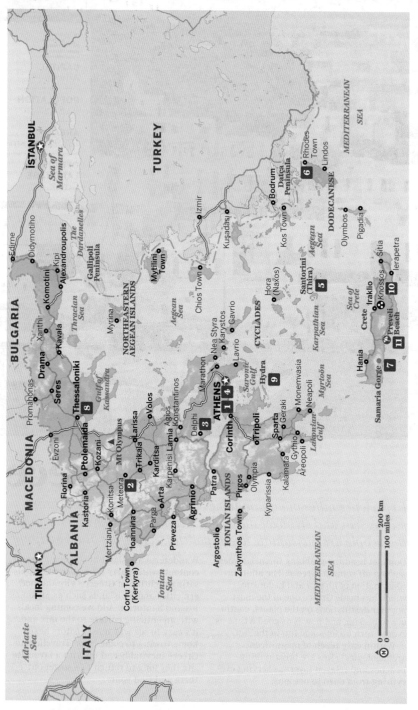

Greece's
Top Experiences

The Acropolis, Athens

1 There's a reason the Acropolis remains the quintessential landmark of Western civilisation – it is spectacular. Whether experienced during an early morning stroll up its flanks or from a dinnertime terrace with the Parthenon all lit up and glorious, the Acropolis embodies a harmony, power and beauty that speak to all generations. Look beyond the Parthenon and you'll find more intimate spots such as the exquisite, tiny Temple of Athena Nike, while the Acropolis Museum cleverly showcases the ethereal grace of the Acropolis' surviving treasures.

Meteora

2 You're not likely to forget the first moment the magnificent Meteora comes into view – soaring pillars of rock that jut heavenward, and a handful of monasteries at the summit (some dating from the 14th century). The rope ladders that once enabled the monks to reach the top have long been replaced by steps carved into the rock. Today, these spectacular stone towers beckon adventurous rock climbers from around the world

VEGA / GETTY IMAGES ©

Ancient Delphi

3 Arrive early to catch the magic of the sun's rays pouring over the Sanctuary of Athena Pronea at Delphi, the centre of the ancient Greek world. Only three columns remain of the magnificent sanctuary, but that's enough to let your imagination soar. Nearby, the Sacred Way meanders past the Temple of Apollo where the Delphic Oracle uttered prophecies that sent armies to battle and made lovers swoon.

Athens

4 Life in Athens is a magnificent mash-up of the ancient and the modern. Beneath the majestic facades of venerable landmarks, the city teems with life and creativity. And Athenians love to get out and enjoy it all. Galleries and clubs hold the exhibitions, performances and installations of the city's booming arts scene. Trendy restaurants and humble tavernas rustle up fine, fine fare. Ubiquitous cafes fill with stylin' locals, and moods run from punk rock to haute couture. Discos and bars abound and swing deep into the night.

Santorini Sunsets

5 There's more to Santorini than sunsets, but this remarkable island, shaped by the fire of prehistoric eruptions, has made the celebratory sunset its own. On summer evenings the clifftop towns of Fira and Oia are packed with visitors awed by the vast blood-red canvas of the cliff face as the sun struts its stuff. You can catch the sunset without the crowds from almost anywhere along the cliff edge. And if you miss sundown, you can always face east at first light for some fairly stunning sunrises too...

Rhodes' Old Town

6 Getting lost in Rhodes' Old Town is a must. Away from the crowds, meander down twisting, cobbled alleyways with archways above and squares opening up ahead. In these hidden corners the imagination takes off with flights of medieval fancy. Explore the ancient Knights' Quarter, the old Jewish neighbourhood or the Turkish Quarter. Hear traditional live music in tiny tavernas or dine on fresh seafood at atmospheric outdoor restaurants. Wander along the top of the city walls, with the sea on one side and a bird's-eye view into this living museum.

Samaria Gorge

7 The gaping gorge of Samaria, starting at Omalos and running down through an ancient riverbed to the Libyan Sea, is the most-trod canyon in Crete – and with good reason. The magnificent gorge is home to varied wildlife, soaring birds of prey and a dazzling array of wildflowers in spring. It's a full day's walk

The Myths, the Myths!

Some of the greatest stories of all time – and some say the wellspring of story itself – are to be found in the ancient Greek myths. For many of us, the fantastical stories of Heracles and Odysseus we heard as kids still linger in our imagination, and contemporary writers continue to reinterpret these stories and characters for books and films. Standing in the ancient ruins of an acropolis and peering across the watery horizon, it's not difficult to picture the Kraken (Poseidon's pet monster) rising from the Aegean, nor to imagine that fishing boat you see heading into the sunset as Jason's Argo en route to Colchis for the Golden Fleece. The average Greek is fiercely proud of their myths and will love entertaining you with a list of the gods.

Food & Drink

Greek coffee A legacy of Ottoman rule, Greek coffee should be tried at least once.

Greek salad Tomatoes, cucumber, onion, feta and olives.

Grilled octopus All the better with a glass of ouzo.

Gyros pitta The ultimate in cheap eats. Pork or chicken shaved from a revolving stack of sizzling meat is wrapped in pitta bread with tomato, onion, fried potatoes and lashings of tzatziki (yoghurt, cucumber and garlic).

Ouzo Sipped slowly, this legendary aniseed-flavoured tipple turns a cloudy white when ice and water are added.

Raki Cretan fire water produced from grape skins.

Souvlaki Skewered meat, usually pork.

if Greece were 100 people

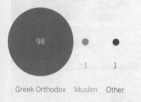

93 would be Greek
7 would be other

belief systems
(% of population)

98 1 1

Greek Orthodox   Muslim   Other

population per sq km

GREECE   USA   UK

= 30 people

Oia, Santorini

(about six hours down), and you'll have to start early, but it certainly builds character. To get more solitude, try lesser-known gorges such as Imbros Gorge, which runs roughly parallel to Samaria.

Colourful Thessaloniki

8 Stylish Thessaloniki remains northern Greece's liveliest town, thanks to its universities,

cultural scene, arts and nightlife. There's little hassle and getting about by foot is easy. Take the city in at dusk from the viewing station up by the Byzantine walls in the old quarter, known as Ano Poli (Upper Town). It's a neighbourhood full of colourful, winding little streets marked by white-plastered houses, lazy cats and Byzantine churches.

Hydra

9 Everyone approaches Hydra by sea. There is no airport, there are no cars. As you sail in, you find, simply, a stunningly preserved stone village with white-gold houses filling a natural cove and hugging the edges of

When to Go

HIGH SEASON (May–Aug)

➡ Everything is in full swing and transport is plentiful.

➡ Accommodation sometimes costs twice as much.

➡ Crowds and temperatures soar.

SHOULDER (Apr & Sep)

➡ Accommodation prices can drop by 20%.

➡ Temperatures are milder.

➡ Internal flights and ferries have reduced schedules.

➡ Few crowds.

LOW SEASON (Oct–Mar)

➡ Many hotels, sights and restaurants shut, especially on islands.

➡ Accommodation costs up to 50% less than during high season.

➡ Ferry schedules are skeletal.

surrounding mountains. Then you join the ballet of port life. Sailboats, caïques and mega-yachts fill Hydra's quays and a people-watching potpourri fills the ubiquitous harbourside cafes. Here, a mere hour and a half from Athens, you'll find a great cappuccino, rich naval and architectural history, and the raw seacoast beckoning you for a swim.

Knossos

10 Rub shoulders with the ghosts of the Minoans, a Bronze Age people that attained an astonishingly high level of civilisation and ruled large parts of the Aegean from their capital

Best on Film

300 (2007) Testosterone-fuelled retelling of the Spartans' epic stand against the might of the Persian army in the Battle of Thermopylae, 480 BC.

Captain Corelli's Mandolin (2001) Lavish retelling of Louis de Bernières' novel, awash with romance in occupied Greece.

Mamma Mia (2008) The island of Skopelos shines to the soundtrack of Abba.

Shirley Valentine (1989) Classic Greek island romance on Mykonos.

Best in Print

The Magus (John Fowles; 1966) Creepy mind games set on fictional island Phraxos.

The Odyssey (Homer; 8th century BC) Plagued by Poseidon, Odysseus struggles to return home to Ithaca.

Zorba the Greek (Nikos Kazantzakis; 1946) A spiritual bible to many; one man's unquenchable lust for life.

Getting Around

Air Domestic air travel has been very price competitive of late, and it's sometimes cheaper to fly than take the ferry, especially if you book ahead.

Boat Greece has an extensive network of ferries which are the only means of reaching many of the islands. Schedules are often subject to delays due to poor weather and prices fluctuate regularly. In summer, ferries are regular between all but the most out-of-the-way destinations.

Bus Buses are comfortable, generally run on time and are reasonably priced. There are frequent services on all major routes.

Car & Motorcycle Driving yourself is a great way to explore areas in Greece that are off the beaten track, but be careful – Greece has the highest road-fatality rate in Europe. Freeway tolls are fairly hefty.

in Knossos some 4000 years ago. Until the site's excavation in the early 20th century, an extraordinary wealth of frescoes, sculptures, jewellery, seals and other remnants lay buried under the Cretan soil. Despite a controversial partial reconstruction, Knossos remains one of the most important archaeological sites in the Mediterranean and is Crete's most visited tourist attraction.

Preveli Beach

11 Crete's Preveli Beach comprises one of Greece's most instantly recognisable stretches of sand. Bisected by a fresh-water river and flanked by cliffs concealing sea caves, Preveli is lapped by the Libyan Sea, with clear pools of water along its palm-lined riverbank that are perfect for cool dips. The beach lies under the sacred gaze of a magnificent monastery perched high above. Once the centre of anti-Ottoman resistance and later a shelter for Allied soldiers, this tranquil building offers magnificent views.

Ilulissat

CAPITAL
Nuuk (Godthab)

POPULATION
57,714

AREA
2.2 million sq km

**OFFICIAL
LANGUAGES**
Greenlandic
(East Inuit),
Danish

Greenland

Stone Age traditions collide with modern technology to create a complex society where children eat whale blubber while watching satellite TV and hunters learn first-aid skills to qualify as guides.

It's said that once a traveller has seen the rest of the world, there's always Greenland. But with climate change undoubtedly stirring things up in this part of the world, we don't think you should wait that long. Nature, at its most raw and powerful, calls the shots here: the world's biggest noncontinental island is actually more than 80% icecap, leading to the world's sparsest population.

Few places combine such magnificent scenery, clarity of light and raw power of nature. Vast swaths of beautiful wilderness and very few roads, give adventurers the freedom to wander at will, whether on foot, by ski or dogsled.

However you travel, schedule a safety margin for unpredictable weather and leave ample time in each destination to unwind, soak up the midnight sun, watch icebergs explode, be dazzled by the magic of the aurora borealis or to try some world-beating but charmingly uncommercialised opportunities for sea kayaking, rock climbing and salmon fishing.

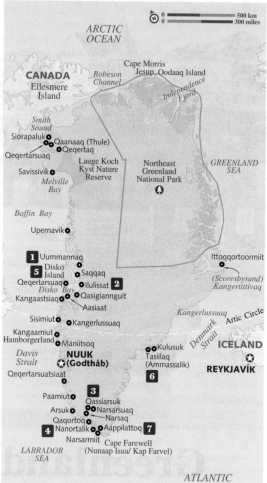

Greenland's
Top Experiences

Uummannaq

1 The towering red peak that dominates Uummannaq (Heart-shaped) Island, lords over the colourful village. Houses cling to the steep shore and wooden steps play snakes and ladders with winding roads. In winter, darkness descends for two months, but spring ushers excellent conditions for dogsledding. Many families still depend on hunting as their main source of income, and a ban on hunting and fishing by snowmobile or motorboat means that the sled and the kayak are still the primary means of transport for hunters. The authenticity of it all hits you with the smell of dogs, drying fish and stretched skins wafting through the air.

Ilulissat Kangerlua

2 This is why you spent all that money and came to Greenland: the awesome force and beauty of Unesco World Heritage–listed Ilulissat Kangerlua, one of the most active glaciers on the planet. It is one of those places so spectacular that it makes everything else pale in comparison. Just outside Ilulissat town you will be confronted with gargantuan icebergs, some the size of small towns, which lie at the mouth of the fjord. Measuring 5km wide, the glacier annually calves more than 35 cubic kilometres of ice – that's about 20 million tonnes per day (enough to supply New York with water for a year) and about a tenth of all icebergs floating in Greenlandic waters.

Qassiarsuk

3 This pretty fjordside village is widely accepted to be the site of Brattahlíð, where Erik the Red (Eiríkur Rauðe) built his farm in the 10th century. An easy-to-miss horseshoe-shaped section of turf is where it is believed the New World's first Christian church was built in 1000 AD. Legend has it that Eric the Red's wife Þjóðhildur tried to convert him to Christianity by refusing him sex, until he was baptised. While Erik never relented, he did compromise by allowing a church to be built. A number of Norse ruins, including a longhouse and church, and the recreation of an Inuit turf hut from the 19th century are also available to visit.

Nanortalik

4 The picture-perfect town of Nanortalik is like a filmset of a New England fishing village. It is Greenland's southernmost town, and its name means place of polar bears, referring to the bear population that ocassionally pass through. It is worth strolling around the town during different tides and times of the day to enjoy it in a variety of light conditions. Climb the stairs to the curious egg-shaped flagmast rock for a bird's-eye view of the town, or walk out to one of the town's landmarks – a natural stone, which at a particular angle resembles the profile of Artic explorer and national hero Knud Rasmussen.

Dogsleds & Disko

5 Dogsled under the midnight sun on the fabulously named Disko Island, Greenland's largest island. One of the best ways to get around is as the locals do; by dogsled. Greenlandic mushers harness their dogs in a fan formation as opposed to the more complicated and tangle-prone inline formation used by their counterparts in Alaska and Canada. Generally the best season to go dogsledding is March to May, when the days are longer and temperatures not so extreme, but summer sledding is available on the island, which remains the only location south of the Arctic Circle where sled dogs are permitted to be kept.

if Greenland were 100 people

89 would be Inuit
11 would be Danish and other

age structure (years)
(% of population)

21 — 0-14
17 — 15-24
43 — 25-54
11 — 55-64
8 — 65+

When to Go

LATE MAR–EARLY MAY
➔ Best time for dog sledding, skiing and tours to the North Pole.

JUL & AUG
➔ Main holiday season: long days and warmer temperatures, but it's also mosquito season.

AUG–MID-DEC & MID-FEB–APR
➔ For the most spectacular displays of the aurora borealis.

population per sq km

GREENLAND — • ≈ 0.03 people
RUSSIA
ICELAND
♦ = 1 person

Doing Time

While the most dangerous criminals are exported to Denmark's 'real jails', most other offenders are generally locked up only at night. By day many hold down jobs, make unescorted shopping trips and – most remarkably – even go on the annual reindeer hunt. That's right: they're given a gun. Well, as long as they're not drunk. This apparently lenient system makes more sense in Greenland, where there's effectively nowhere to run and so little incentive to escape. However, some provincial businesses dread Christmas, when prisoners come home for the holidays. Festive raids to steal alcohol can cost store owners much more in repairing the structural damage than in losing the value of the stolen booze.

Food & Drink

Traditional Greenlandic fare is dominated by meat, especially whale and seal.

Caribou In September virtually everyone takes time off work to hunt caribou (*tuttu*), which yield superb steaks and very tasty leg-meat, which is rarely sold.

Dovekies North Greenlanders once survived by eating these penguin-like small birds. When stuffed in hollowed-out seal carcasses and left to rot, they form the unappetising *kivioq*.

Seal Cooked by boiling chunks in water for an hour or more. The cooked meat has a deep, chocolate-brown colour. Cuts edged with a centimetre of blubber taste rather like lamb chops.

Whale The best raw whaleskin (*mattak*) comes from beluga or narwhal, taking on a slightly nutty, mushroom-like flavour when cooked.

TYLER STABLEFORD / GETTY IMAGES ©

Kayaking near Tasiilaq

Kayaking the Fjords

6 Greenlandic *qajaq* are the precursors of modern kayaks, so if you don't sea kayak in Greenland, where else would you? One of the best places to get up close to ice-choked fjords is around the village of Tasiilaq, only 100km south of the Arctic Circle. The town is an outdoor adventurer's dream landscape, surrounded by high mountains, green valleys.and water. Lots of water. A paddle from Tasiilaq across the fjord is an easy (!) 4km, while a trip around the fjord is a more challenging 20 to 30km. Paddle up!

Sailing Greenland

7 Sail through south Greenland's most magnificent fjordland scenery from Aappilattoq, a tiny fishing village sitting on a natural inland harbour. Practically inaccessible via land, it offers some of the most spectacular water travel anywhere in the world, including the weekly *Ketil*, sailing between Nanortalik and Aappilattoq from mid-November and April, returning the same day. This unmissable voyage is full of exceptional scenic wonders, but weather and ice conditions mean it is often cancelled.

Getting Around

Air Considering its climate, huge size and tiny population, Greenland is well served by air links, while public helicopters offer a unique way of seeing the scenery. Be flexible – weather conditions mean you can't assume that a service will leave on time (or even on the scheduled day).

Boat Meet the locals while weaving between icebergs, past soaring peaks and through magnificent icescapes on the ferries. Ice permitting, summer services link west-coast villages, but there are no ferries on the east coast. In winter ferries go no further north than Ilulissat.

Dogsled Many people still get around by dogsled, and visitors can arrange trips ranging from one day to a two-week expedition. The best season is from March to May.

CAPITAL
Saint George's

POPULATION
109,590

AREA
344 sq km

OFFICIAL LANGUAGE
English

Constantine, St George's

Grenada

White sand, turquoise sea, palm trees and no crowds make Grenada's beaches truly sublime. And if the mainland's too much fun, island-hop to Carriacou and Petit Martinique.

The most southerly islands in the Windward chain, Grenada and Carriacou (plus little Petit Martinique) are best known for having been invaded by the US in the 1980s and pummeled by Hurricane Ivan in the 2000s. But the storm damage is long gone and the American occupation a distant memory, and today the islands are some of the Caribbean's most appealing.

From palm-backed white sand and translucent water to gray-black dunes and rolling breakers, the beaches are gorgeous.

Grenada's corrugated coastline rises up to mist-swathed rainforest laced with hiking trails and swimmable waterfalls. St George's, with its market, forts and postcard-perfect Carenage harbor, makes for a picturesque and friendly capital, and is the departure point for ferries to the laid-back sister isles of Carriacou and Petit Martinique. And though cruise ships inject a regular flow of short-stay visitors to Grenada, you'll find all three islands refreshingly quiet and uncrowded.

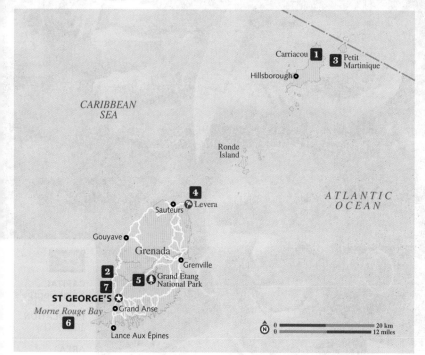

Grenada's
Top Experiences

Carriacou

1 The fact that most people don't realize there are *three* islands in the nation of Grenada is a fitting introduction to Carriacou. Like its minor island sibling (Petit Martinique), this humble isle is often forgotten. Where the island of Grenada can feel touristy and busy, you'll struggle to ever feel that way here. You won't find cruise ships, big resorts or souvenir shops – this is Caribbean life the way it was 50 years ago: quiet, laid-back and relaxed. Carriacou is off the radar of most travelers, with green hills that offer some tremendous hiking and beaches that are destined to make your all-time best-of list.

Underwater Sculpture Park

2 Think art galleries are all the same – white walls, wood floors, pretentious patrons? Well, not Grenada's Underwater Sculpture Park. For a start, it's almost 7ft beneath the surface of the sea, just north of St George's in Molinière Bay. The life-size sculptures include a circle of women clasping hands, a man at a desk and a solitary mountain biker, all slowly becoming encrusted with coral growth. The 65 original pieces, by Jason deCaires Taylor, were joined in 2010 by 14 new sculptures by local sculptor Troy Lewis, including a depiction of an Amerindian zemi idol. To

see them, you'll have to get in the water – and it's well worth the effort. Local scuba companies offer diving or snorkel excursions to the sculpture park, and some coastal cruises stop there, too.

Petit Martinique

3 They don't call it Petit for nothing – this little island is a scant 1 mile in diameter. Small, charismatic and infrequently visited, Petit Martinique is an ideal spot to get away from everything. With a steep volcanic core rising a stout 740ft at its center, there is little room on the island for much else. The solitary road runs up the west coast, but it is rarely used – locals prefer to walk. Nothing is very far and

what's the hurry? The population subsists on the fruits of the sea, either as fishermen or boat-taxi operators. With barely a thousand inhabitants, most of whom are related to each other, this is a place to find peace, quiet – and precious little else.

Levera

4 Backed by eroding sea cliffs, Levera Beach is a wild, beautiful sweep of sand. Just offshore is the high, pointed Sugar Loaf Island, while the Grenadine islands dot the horizon to the north. The beach, the mangrove swamp and the nearby pond have been incorporated into Grenada's national-park system and are an important waterfowl habitat and sea turtle nesting site.

Grand Etang National Park

5 Overhung with rainforest and snaking uphill in a series of switchback turns, the Grand Etang Road is the antithesis of the sand and surf on the coast. The mountainous center of the island is often awash with misty clouds, and looks like a lost primordial world, its tangle of rainforest brimming with life – including monkeys that often get a bit too friendly. A series of hiking trails through the protected Grand Etang National Park provide access into the fertile forest.

Morne Rouge Bay

6 Sink your toes into the soft white sand and super-blue water of Morne Rouge Bay. This stretch of

if Grenada were 100 people

82 would be black
13 would be mixed black and European
5 would be European and East Indian

belief systems
(% of population)

53 Roman Catholic   33 other Protestant   14 Anglican

When to Go

JAN–APR

➡ The driest months see measurable rainfall for 12 days a month; this is the best time to visit.

JUN–NOV

➡ The rainy season sees an average 22 days of rainfall per month in St George's.

AUG

➡ If you like to party, the raucous Carnival is a brilliant time to be in Grenada.

population per sq km

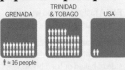

GRENADA   TRINIDAD & TOBAGO   USA

♀ ≈ 16 people

A Phoenix Rises

On September 7, 2004, Hurricane Ivan made landfall on Grenada. The first major storm to hit the island in 50 years, Ivan struck with huge force, leaving a wave of destruction that saw 90% of buildings damaged or destroyed, towns decimated and staple crops like nutmeg obliterated.

The following months and years were a dark chapter for Grenada, whose economy was left in ruins. Nonetheless, new crops were sown (with fast-growing cocoa replacing nutmeg as the nation's main agricultural export), and homes, shops and offices rebuilt, with Caribbean neighbors lending support to help restore the damage. But within this period of rebirth, instead of simply rebuilding what was once there, opportunity was found.

Hotels, schools, churches and restaurants have been rebuilt bigger and better, incorporating sustainable practices and larger floor plans. Structures that were long overdue to be upgraded were leveled and the new buildings are a massive improvement on what was once there. Today, the only real evidence of Ivan's path is the odd roofless building – and a certain wariness among locals come hurricane season.

Carenage harbor, St George's

beach is a shining example of the snow-white sand and crystal-clear blue water that the Caribbean is known for. It's mercifully quiet and pristine, there are only a handful of buildings housing hotels and restaurants, and lots of shade toward the far end.

St George's

7 St George's ticks all the boxes for a small island capital: overlooked by the requisite quota of handsome old buildings, the Carenage harbor is one of the prettiest in the Caribbean. Above the water, a jumble of streets cling to the hill that splits the city in two, lined by a picturesque mishmash of colorful post-hurricane rooftops, crumbling warehouses, grand old stone churches and an imposing fort. The main commercial centre is on the other side of the hill. South of the Carenage, on its way to the resorts at Grand Anse, the road sweeps around the Lagoon, where a forest of masts and megayacht hulls mark the upmarket Port Louis marina.

Food & Drink

Carib beer Brewed in Grenada, and always served ice-cold.

Jack Iron rum Ice sinks in this lethal local bellywash.

Lambi The local name for conch.

Oil down Beef and salt pork stewed with coconut milk.

Roti A tasty flat bread wrapped around curried meat and veggies.

Saltfish and bake Seasoned saltfish with onion and veg, and a side of baked or fried bread.

Getting Around

Air SVG Air has flights between Grenada and Carriacou.

Boat The *Osprey* is a large motorized catamaran connecting Grenada, Carriacou and Petit Martinique in less than two hours. Alternatively, consider island-hopping on the cargo boats that sail between the three islands. Departure times and dates are unscheduled and the best way to find out what's available is to ask around at the docks.

Bus Buses are a great way to get around Grenada and Carriacou. These privately run minivans operate a series of set, numbered routes crisscrossing the islands, and are inexpensive and fun.

Car To drive a vehicle you need to purchase a Grenadian driving license, which all car-rental companies can issue on the government's behalf.

Taxi You'll find taxis on Grenada and Carriacou.

CAPITAL
Basse-Terre

POPULATION
458,000

AREA
1780 sq km

OFFICIAL LANGUAGES
French, Creole

Guadeloupe

Guadeloupe offers world-class hiking, superb beaches, some of the Caribbean's best diving, and a selction of remote and virtually pristine islands.

Guadeloupe is a fascinating archipelago of islands, with each island offering travelers something different while retaining its rich Franco-Caribbean culture and identity.

Guadeloupe's two main islands look like the wings of a butterfly and are joined together by a mangrove swamp. Grande-Terre, the eastern of the two islands, has a string of beach towns that offer visitors marvelous stretches of sand to laze on and plenty of activities, while mountainous Basse-Terre, the western of the two, is home to the wonderful Guadeloupe National Park, which is crowned by the spectacular La Soufrière volcano.

South of the 'mainland' of Guadeloupe are a number of small islands that give a taste of Guadeloupe's yesteryear. Ranging from sheer relaxation on La Désirade to the charmingly village-like atmosphere of Les Saintes, the smaller islands each have their own character and round out the long list of ingredients that make Guadeloupe such a unique destination.

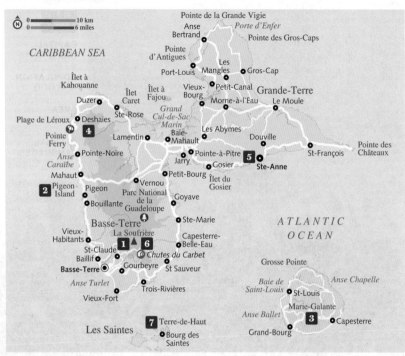

Guadeloupe's
Top Experiences

La Soufrière

1 Hike through the rainforest to the misty summit of this brooding 1467m-high active volcano. For an adventurous 1½-hour hike to La Soufrière's sulfurous, moonscapelike summit, a well-beaten trail starts at the end of the parking lot. It travels along a gravel bed and continues steeply up the mountain through a cover of low shrubs and thick ferns. In addition to a close-up view of the steaming volcano, the hike offers some fine vistas of the island. If it's fogged in, proceed slowly, as visibility can drop to just a few meters.

Réserve Cousteau

2 This marine park surrounding Pigeon Island was named after Jacques Cousteau, who declared it to be one of the world's best dive sites. There's a subaquatic statue of Cousteau near one of the dive sites: divers touch the statue's head for luck. The diving itself is world-class, with big schools of fish, coral walls and coral reefs, which are often shallow enough for snokeling. It's only a 10- to 15-minute boat ride to the dive sites, and almost all the dive shops have morning, noon and mid-afternoon outings.

Marie-Galante

3 The largest of Guadeloupe's outer islands, Marie-Galante is a rural and agricultural haven beloved by those who enjoy the quieter pleasures in life, and particularly by beach lovers who want to escape the crowds. Compared with the archipelago's other islands, Marie-Galante is relatively flat, its dual limestone plateaus rising only 150m. It is roughly round in shape, with a total land area of 158 sq km. Despite its small size, you're nonetheless sure to be able to find your very own slice of beach heaven on its unspoilt sands.

Deshaies

4 This charmingly sleepy spot has just the right blend of traditional fishing village and good selection of eating and drinking options to keep visitors happy. There's a sweet little beach framed by green hills all

around, but as Deshaies is a working fishing port, the best beach for swimming and sunbathing is at nearby Grande Anse. Thanks to its sheltered bay, the village is a popular stop with yachters and sailors and has an international feel. The local seafaring traditions have carried on into the tourist trade, with several dive shops and deep-sea fishing boats operating from the pier.

Ste-Anne

5 The busy town of Ste-Anne sees a lot of tourists, but the big resorts are well hidden and there's a good balance of amenities for tourists and authentic modern village life. It has a seaside promenade along the west side of town, a lively market and a fine white-sand beach stretching along the east side. The beach, which offers good swimming and is shaded by sea-grape trees, is particularly popular with islanders.

Chutes du Carbet

6 Unless it's overcast, the drive up to the Chutes du Carbet lookout gives a view of two magnificent waterfalls plunging down a sheer mountain face. Starting from St-Sauveur on the N1, the road runs 8.5km inland, making for a nice 15-minute drive up through a rainforest. It's a good hard-surfaced road all the way, although it's a bit narrow and twisting. Nearly 3km before the end of the road is a marked stop at the trailhead to Grand Étang, a placid lake

if Guadeloupe were 100 people

71 would be of African descent
15 would be of Indian descent
9 would be of White European descent
2 would be of Lebanese/Syrian descent
2 would be of Chinese descent
1 would be of other descent

belief systems
(% of population)

86	5	2
Roman Catholic	Protestant	Hindu
2	2	3
African Voodoo	Jehovah's Witnesses	other

population per sq km

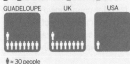

| GUADELOUPE | UK | USA |

♦ ≈ 30 people

When to Go

DEC–MAY
➡ The dry season; most people visit now, to take advantage of the perfect warm, dry weather.

JUL–NOV
➡ The wettest and most humid time, with an average of seven rainy days per month.

JUL & AUG
➡ Avoid if you can, or book well in advance; prices are sky-high and rooms scarce.

What's in a Name?

At first glance, the names given to the twin islands that make up Guadeloupe are perplexing. The eastern island, which is smaller and flatter, is named Grande-Terre, which means 'big land,' while the larger, more mountainous western island is named Basse-Terre, meaning 'flat land'.

The names were not meant to describe the terrain, however, but the winds that blow over them. The trade winds, which come from the northeast, blow *grande* (big) over the flat plains of Grande-Terre but are stopped by the mountains to the west, ending up *basse* (flat) on Basse-Terre.

Food & Drink

Acras A universally popular hors d'oeuvre in Guadeloupe, *acras* are fried fish, seafood or vegetables fritters in tempura. *Acras de morue* (cod) and *crevettes* (shrimp) are the most common and are both delicious.

Blaff This is the local term for white fish marinated in lime juice, garlic and peppers and then poached. It's a favorite dish in many of Guadeloupe's restaurants.

Colombo cabri Curried goat.

Crabes farcis Stuffed crabs are a typical local dish. Normally they're stuffed with a spicy mixture of crabmeat, garlic, shallots and parsley that is then cooked in the shell.

Ti-punch Short for petit punch, this ubiquitous and strong cocktail is the normal *apéro* (aperitif) in Guadeloupe: a mix of rum, lime and cane syrup, but mainly rum, mixed to your own proportions.

circled by a loop trail. It's just a five-minute walk from the roadside parking area down to the edge of the lake, and it takes about an hour more to stroll the lake's perimeter.

Terre-de-Haut

7 Lying 10km off Guadeloupe is Terre-de-Haut, the largest of the eight small islands that make up Les Saintes. Since the island was too hilly and dry for sugar plantations, slavery never took hold here. Conse-

quently, the older islanders still trace their roots to the early seafaring Norman and Breton colonists and many of the locals have light skin and blond or red hair. Terre-de-Haut is unhurried and feels like a small slice of southern France transported to the Caribbean. Lots of English is spoken here thanks to a big international sailing scene, and it's definitely the most cosmopolitan of Guadeloupe's outlying islands.

Getting Around

Air There are several flights per week between Pointe-à-Pitre and Marie-Galante.

Bicycle Bicycles are an adventurous, somewhat strenuous way to see Terre-de-Haut and Marie-Galante.

Boat Ferries are the principal way to get around between the islands of Guadeloupe. Multiple ferry operators run services between Grande-Terre and Terre-de-Haut, Marie-Galante and La Désirade.

Bus Guadeloupe has a good public bus system that operates from about 5:30am to 6:30pm, with fairly frequent service on main routes. Destinations are written on the buses. Bus stops have blue signs picturing a bus.

Car A driver's license from your home country is necessary to drive here.

Taxi Taxis are plentiful but expensive. There are taxi stands at the airport in Pointe-à-Pitre.

Waterfall

CAPITAL
Hagåtña
....
POPULATION
180,000
....
AREA
541 sq km
....
**OFFICIAL
LANGUAGES**
English,
Chamorro

Guam

*Northern Guam is mainly taken up by the US military's Andersen
Base but the south is a must-see, with its rural kaleidoscope of
historical villages, stunning waterfalls and pristine beaches.*

As Micronesia's most populous island, Guam is about as 'cosmopolitan' as it gets, so it cops a lot of attitude from Pacific snobs who reckon it lacks 'real island culture'. Sure, American accents are everywhere (it's an unincorporated US territory and many Guamanian homes fly the US flag) and the Chamorro language isn't spoken quite as widely as it used to be. And if you never stray from Tumon Bay – the island's glitzy duty-free shopping and accommodation hub – then undeniably you'll be over- (or under-) whelmed.

But the island is currently in the throes of retooling itself. The tourism authorities talk of how 'Product Guam' (there's that American influence) needs a complete overhaul from its current status as a Pacific theme park for Japanese tourists. There may come a day soon when Chamorro culture (long subsumed by various invasions and occupations) is promoted above all else, with an increased focus on local food and the fascinating stories underlying many of the villages.

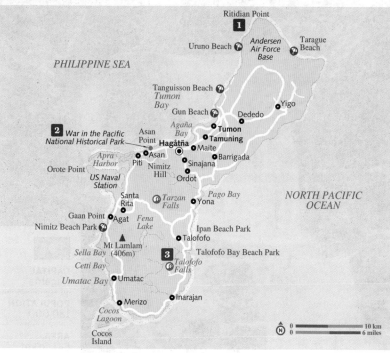

Guam's
Top Experiences

Ritidian Point

1 This national wildlife refuge, at the northernmost tip of Guam, is administered by the Fish and Wildlife Service. The star attraction is the inviting, pristine sandy beach. Azure waters, golden beaches, swaying palms – these are the paradisiacal trappings of Ritidian Point. On weekdays the beach is gloriously empty; at weekends, families and picnicking groups pick up the slack.

War in the Pacific National Historical Park

2 Reflect on Guam's turbulent WWII occupation. A number of former WWII battlefield sites are part of the park's historical holdings. The Asan Beach unit includes Asan Point, a big, peaceful and grassy beach park 1.6km further south, with guns, torpedoes and monuments.

Talofofo Falls

3 This popular swimming and picnic spot is set around a lovely two-tier cascade, with pools beneath each waterfall. At the bottom is a wooden swinging bridge with a splendid view of the falls. There's a 9m drop on the top fall, though it's usually gentle enough to stand beneath.

Food & Drink

Guam has a fixation with Spam – the Hormel company has even developed a special 'Guam Spam' with a hot-and-spicy flavouring that mimics Tabasco.

The island has the best restaurant scene in Micronesia, featuring a wide range of styles and nationalities. Most of the action is centred in Tumon Bay.

The best Chamorro food is generally found at the Chamorro Village Night Market.

When to Go

YEAR ROUND	JAN–MAY	JULY–NOV
➡ Average 81°F (28°C).	➡ Best time to visit.	➡ The rainy season.
➡ Annual average rainfall 80 inches.	➡ The dry season, with slightly lower humidity.	

Lago de Atitlán

CAPITAL	Guatemala City
POPULATION	14.4 million
AREA	108,889 sq km
OFFICIAL LANGUAGE	Spanish

Guatemala

Fascinating history, diverse culture, intriguing people, natural beauty, majestic ruins and gorgeous colonial landscapes: Guatemala has been captivating travelers for centuries.

Guatemala is a magical place. If you're into the Maya, the mountains, the markets, kicking back lakeside or exploring atmospheric pre-Columbian ruins and gorgeous colonial villages, you're bound to be captivated.

Want to surf in the morning and learn Spanish in the afternoon? No problem. Descend a volcano, grab a shower and hit the sushi bar for dinner? You can do that. Check out a Maya temple and be swinging in a beachside hammock by sunset? Easy.

Guatemala's got its problems, but they mainly keep to themselves. Travel here – once fraught with danger and discomfort – is now characterized by ease; you can do pretty much whatever you want, and your experience will only be limited by your imagination and time.

While many ask whatever happened to the Maya, the simple answer is nothing – they're still here, and some traditions continue to thrive. Living Maya culture can be witnessed in its 'pure' form in towns like Rabinal and sacred sites such as Laguna Chicabal. And the Maya themselves? Well, they're everywhere.

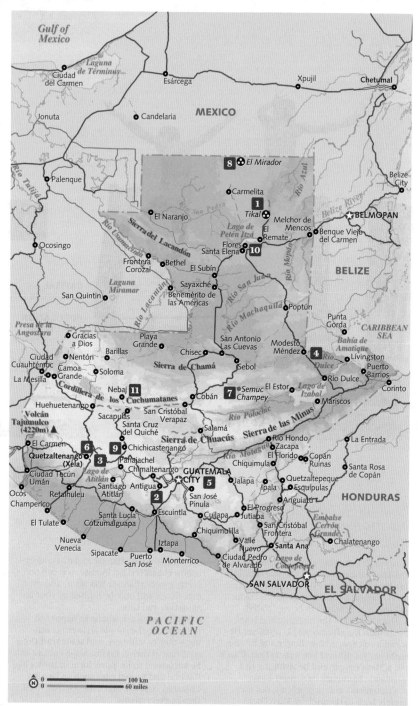

Gulf of Mexico

Laguna de Términos

Ciudad del Carmen

Jonuta

Esárcega

Xpujil

Chetumal

Candelaria

MEXICO

Palenque

Río Azul

Belize City

8 *El Mirador*

Carmelita

Ocosingo

El Naranjo

Sierra del Lacandón

Río San Pedro

1

Tikal

Lago de Petén Itzá

El Remate

Melchor de Mencos

BELMOPAN

Benque Viejo del Carmen

Frontera Corozal

Bethel

Río Usumacinta

El Subín

Flores

Santa Elena

10

Río Mopán

Belize River

BELIZE

San Quintin

Benemérito de las Américas

Sayaxché

Río San Juan

Laguna Miramar

Río Lacantún

Río Machaquilá

Poptún

Punta Gorda

Presa de la Angostura

Gracias a Dios

Playa Grande

San Antonio Las Cuevas

Modesto Méndez

4

CARIBBEAN SEA

Bahía de Amatique

Livingston

Barillas

Chisec

Río Dulce

Puerto Barrios

Ciudad Cuauhtémoc

Nentón

Soloma

Sierra de Chamá

Sebol

Río Dulce

Corinto

Camoa Grande

El Estor

Lago de Izabal

La Mesilla

Cordillera de los Cuchumatanes

Nebaj **11**

San Cristóbal Verapaz

Cobán

7 *Semuc Champey*

Río Polochic

Mariscos

Huehuetenango

Sacapulas

Salamá

Sierra de las Minas

Volcán Tajumulco (4220m) ▲

Santa Cruz del Quiché

Sierra de Chuacús

Río Hondo

Río Motagua

Zacapa

La Entrada

El Carmen **6**

Chichicastenango

9

El Florido

Copán Ruinas

Santa Rosa de Copán

Quetzaltenango (Xela)

3

Panajachel

Chimaltenango

Chiquimula

Esquipulas

Ciudad Tecún Umán

Lago de Atitlán

GUATEMALA CITY

5

Jalapa

Quetzaltepeque

HONDURAS

Ocós

Retalhuleu

Santiago Atitlán

Antigua

2

San José Pinula

Ipala

Anguiatú

Champerico

El Tulate

Santa Lucía Cotzumalguápa

Escuintla

Cuilapa

Jutiapa

El Progreso

San Cristóbal Frontera

Embalse Cerrón Grande

Chalatenango

Nueva Venecia

Sipacate

Puerto San José

Iztapa

Monterrico

Chiquimulilla

Valle Nuevo

Ciudad Pedro de Alvarado

Santa Ana

Lago de Coatepeque

SAN SALVADOR

EL SALVADOR

PACIFIC OCEAN

N

0 — 100 km
0 — 60 miles

Guatemala's
Top Experiences

Tikal

1 The remarkably restored temples that stand in this partially cleared corner of the jungle astonish for both their monumental size and architectural brilliance, as an early morning arrival at the Gran Plaza proves. Occupied for some 16 centuries, it's an amazing testament to the cultural and artistic heights scaled by this jungle civilization. A highlight is the helicopter-like vantage from towering Temple IV on the west edge of the precinct. Equally compelling is the abundance of wildlife, which can be appreciated strolling ancient causeways between ceremonial centers; tread softly so you're more likely to spot spider monkeys, agoutis, foxes and ocellated turkeys.

Antigua

2 With mammoth volcanic peaks and coffee-covered slopes as a backdrop for the scattered remnants of Spanish occupation, the former capital of Guatemala is a place of rare beauty, historical significance and vibrant culture. Consequently, it makes an appealing setting for learning Spanish and year on year a globally varied population come here to study at the city's quality institutes. This influx fuels a surprisingly sophisticated culinary panorama and bubbly nightlife scene.

Lago de Atitlán

3 Possibly the single worthiest destination in Guatemala, Atitlán elicits poetic outbursts from even the most seasoned traveler. Of volcanic origin, the alternately placid and turbulent lake is ringed by volcanoes and villages like Santiago Atitlán, with a thriving indigenous culture, and San Marcos, a haven for seekers who plug into the lake's cosmic energy. And there are enough activities – paragliding from Santa Catarina Palopó, kayaking around Santa Cruz La Laguna or hiking the glorious lakeshore trails – to make a longer stay viable.

Río Dulce

4 The Río Dulce (literally, sweet river) connects Guatemala's largest lake with the Caribbean coast, and winding along it, through a steep-walled valley, surrounded by lush vegetation, bird calls and the (very occasional) manatee is Guatemala's classic, don't-miss boat ride. This is no tourist cruise – the river is a way of life and a means of transportation around here – but you get to stop at a couple of places to visit river-dwelling communities and natural hot springs, making for a magical, unforgettable experience.

Guatemala City

5 Vibrant and raw, often confronting and occasionally surprising, the nation's capital is very much a love it or leave it proposition. Many choose the latter – and as fast as they can – but those who hang around and look behind the drab architecture and scruffy edges find a city teeming with life. For culture vultures, fine diners, mall rats and live-music lovers, the capital has a buzz that's unmatched in the rest of the country.

Quetzaltenango

6 Quetzaltenango is a kinder, gentler urban experience than the capital, and its blend of mountain scenery, highlands indigenous life, handsome architecture and urban sophistication attracts outsiders after an authentic slice of city life in Guatemala. Come here to study Spanish at the numerous language institutes, such as the well-regarded Celas Maya, or make it a base for excursions to high-altitude

Guatemala's Ancient Ruins

Stretching at its peak from northern El Salvador to the Gulf of Mexico, the Maya empire during its Classic period was arguably pre-Hispanic America's most brilliant civilization. The great ceremonial and cultural centers in Guatemala included Quiriguá, Kaminaljuyú, Tikal, Uaxactún, Río Azul, El Perú, Yaxhá, Dos Pilas and Piedras Negras. Copán in Honduras also gained and lost importance as the empire and its individual kingdoms ebbed and waned.

Visiting a Maya ruin can be a powerful experience, a true step back in time. While some sites are little more than a pile of rubble or some grassy mounds, others (such as Tikal and Copán) have been extensively restored, and the temples, plazas and ballcourts give an excellent insight into what life must have been like in these places.

Food & Drink

Atole A hot gruel made with maize, milk, cinnamon and sugar

Chile relleno Bell pepper stuffed with cheese, meat, rice or other foods, dipped in egg whites, fried and baked in sauce.

Jocón Green stew of chicken or pork with green vegetables and herbs.

Licuado Milkshake made with fresh fruit, sugar, and milk or water.

Pepián Chicken and vegetables in a piquant sesame and pumpkin seed sauce.

Tamal Corn dough stuffed with meat, beans, chilies or nothing at all, wrapped in banana leaf or corn husks and steamed.

Tapado A seafood, coconut milk and plantain casserole.

Tostada Flat, crisp tortilla topped with meat or cheese, tomatoes, beans and lettuce.

if Guatemala were 100 people

59 would be mestizo
40 would be Maya
1 would be other

Guatemalan diaspora

(% of migrating population)

84 USA
10 Mexico
2 Canada
4 other

population per sq km

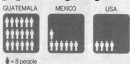

GUATEMALA   MEXICO   USA

= 8 people

PAUL KENNEDY / GETTY IMAGES ©

7

destinations such as Laguna Chicabal, a crater lake/Maya pilgrimage site, or Fuentes Georginas, a hot-springs resort ensconced in a verdant valley.

Semuc Champey

7 Guatemala doesn't have that many freshwater swimming holes that you'd really want to dive into, but the jungle-shrouded oasis of Semuc Champey is definitely an exception. Turquoise-colored water cascades down a series of limestone pools, creating an idyllic setting that many call the most beautiful place in the country.

El Mirador

8 For true adventurers, the trek to El Mirador is a thrilling chance to explore the origins of Maya history; it is still being uncovered by archaeologists whom you're likely to meet at the site. Among the hundreds of vegetation-shrouded temples is the tallest pyramid in the Maya world, La Danta, which can be climbed for panoramic views of the

When to Go

HIGH SEASON
(Dec–May)

➡ Around key times (Christmas, New Year, Easter) hotel prices are at their highest.

➡ Accommodation should be booked well in advance for Easter in Antigua.

SHOULDER
(Oct–Nov)

➡ Rains begin to ease up, but October is peak hurricane season.

➡ Mild temperatures and clear days make this a good time to be traveling and hiking in the highlands.

LOW SEASON
(Apr–Sep)

➡ Prices drop, crowds thin out at archaeological sites, and booking accommodation is rarely necessary.

➡ Daily afternoon rains can make traveling chilly in the highlands and muddy in the jungle.

jungle canopy. It's at least a six-day hike unless you hop a chopper to the site.

Chichicastenango

9 More than a place to shop, the twice-weekly market here is a vivid window on indigenous tradition, an ancient crossroads for the area's K'iche' Maya–speaking inhabitants and a spiritually charged site. At Santo Tomás church in the center of town and the hill of Pascual Abaj on its southern edge, shamans overlay Maya rituals upon Christian iconography. It's a good place to shop too, especially if you're after finely woven textiles.

Best on Film

Aquí me Quedo (2010; Rodolfo Espinoza) Subtle political commentary, black comedy and satire abound in this story of a kidnapping, shot in Quetzaltenango.

Capsulas (2011; Verónica Riedel) A look at greed, corruption and the drug trade from one of Guatemala's few female directors.

When the Mountains Tremble (1983; Pamela Yates & Newton Thomas Sigel) Documentary featuring Susan Sarandon and Rigoberta Menchú, telling the story of the civil war.

Best in Print

A Mayan Life (Gaspar Pedro Gonzáles; 1995) An excellent study of rural Guatemalan life.

The Art of Political Murder (Francisco Goldman; 2008) Meticulously-researched account of the assassination of Bishop Gerardi.

The President (Miguel Ángel Asturias; 1946) Nobel Prize–winning Guatemalan author takes some not-too-subtle jabs at the country's long line of dictators.

Getting Around

Chicken Bus Recycled US school buses, these ones are cheap, go everywhere, stop for everybody and have no maximum capacity.

Pickup Truck In rural areas where there is no bus service this is a common way to get around. Flag one down wherever, climb in the back and hang on. Fares are equivalent to chicken buses.

Pullman Bus Running only on major highways, these are the most comfortable choice, although quality ranges from recycled Greyhounds to brand-new Mercedes. You get your own numbered seat and they run semidirect or direct.

Shuttle Bus Booked through travel agents, hotels etc, these nonstop minibuses run between major tourist destinations offering door-to-door service.

Flores

10 An isle of calm at the threshold of a vast jungle reserve, Flores is both a base for exploring El Petén and a stunning spot to recharge your rambling batteries. Unwinding at the numerous dining and drinking terraces that look across Lago de Petén Ixtá, or cruising in a weathered long boat to even smaller islets, you're likely to find companions for forays to Tikal or more remote places. But the picturesqueness of the town, with its captivating tableau of distant villages, is reason enough to head here.

Nebaj & the Ixil Triangle

11 A pocket of indigenous culture in a remote (though easily accessed) alpine setting, Nebaj is little visited, yet it's essential Guatemala. Homeland of the Ixil Maya people, with their own language and vivid clothing, it's also a crossroads for hikes through the spectacular Cuchumatanes mountain range, with dozens of intensely traditional villages such as Cocop and Chajul, where community-run lodging and meals are amiably provided.

K'iche Maya local and child, Chichicastenango market

DIEGO LEZAMA / GETTY IMAGES ©

Balafon player, Conakry

CAPITAL
Conakry

POPULATION
11.2 million

AREA
245,857 sq km

OFFICIAL LANGUAGE
French

Guinea

Neglected infrastructure makes travelling here a challenge, but Guinea is a country of untapped potential, both for the traveller and for its resilient inhabitants.

Imagine you're travelling on a smooth highway, and then get tempted by a tiny, dusty turn-off into rugged terrain, where surprising beauty and treacherous vistas define the route. Guinea is that turn-off.

Guinea could be a West African paradise. With a strong self-reliant streak and with almost half of the world's bauxite reserves, post-colonial Guinea had all the ingredients for success. As a traveller destination, its future looked similarly assured with a vibrant capital, world-class musical scene and beautiful scenery in the interior. Sadly it hasn't quite worked out that way. Decades of dictatorial rule have left Guinea's long-suffering people still dreaming of a prosperous future that should have begun decades ago.

Yet, this is a country blessed with amazing landscapes. Nature lovers can lose themselves on long hikes past plunging waterfalls, proud hills and tiny villages, or track elephants through virgin rainforest. And while Guinea is not famed for its beaches, those it does have are stunning, and often deserted.

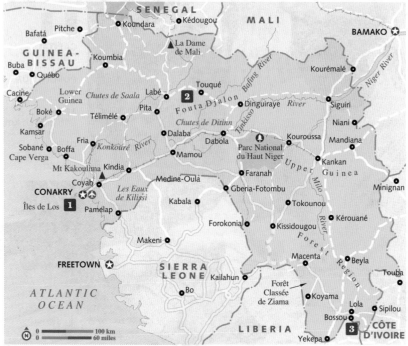

Guinea's
Top Experiences

Îles de Los

1 There's little here to tell you that the Îles de Los were once used as prisons and slave-trading stations. Today the islands are popular for weekenders escaping Conakry's fumes and are tranquil stretches of palm-fringed sands. Stretch out and sip fresh coconut juice.

Fouta Djalon

2 Not only the scenery changes as you wind your way up the serpentine curves of the Mamou route: the population changes too. You'll pass elegant old men in indigo *boubous* and striking ladies as they walk to the mosque. This impressive plateau is also an old centre of Islamic learning. Temperatures are cool and the landscape is simply stunning and perfect for treks.

Bossou Environmental Research Institute

3 Researchers from around the world come to the Bossou Environmental Research Institute to study the famous chimpanzees in the surrounding hills. There's not much primary forest left, though the area remains scenic and is a great place to come face to face with chattering chimps.

Food & Drink

Beer Try the local varieties: Skol, Guiluxe and Flag.

Café noir An espresso-like coffee.

Kulikuli Peanut balls cooked with onion and cayenne pepper.

Riz gras Rice fried in oil and tomato paste and served with fried fish, meat or vegetables.

When to Go

NOV–DEC

➜ The best time to visit as rains have swollen rivers and waterfalls, and the landscape is green.

JUL–AUG

➜ The rainy season; many roads become inaccessible, and Conakry turns into a giant mud bath.

JAN

➜ Temperatures can fall to 6°C and below at night in the highland areas.

CAPITAL
Bissau

POPULATION
1.7 million

AREA
36,125 sq km

OFFICIAL
LANGUAGE
Portuguese

Guinea-Bissau

One of Africa's most forgotten corners, Guinea-Bissau is one of its most beautiful and diverse, infused with Portuguese influence and home to little visited island idylls.

For a country that consistently elicits frowns from heads of state and news reporters, Guinea-Bissau will pull a smile from even the most world-weary traveller. The jokes here, like the music, are loud but tender. The bowls of grilled oysters are served with a lime sauce spicy enough to give a kick, but not so strong as to mask the bitterness. The buildings are battered and the faded colonial houses bowed by sagging balconies, but you'll see beauty alongside the decay.

Here, bare silver trees spring up like antler horns between swathes of elephant grass, and cashew sellers tease each other with an unmistakably Latin spirit. Board a boat for the Bijagós, where you can watch hippos lumber through lagoons full of fish and spot turtles nesting. Despite painful wars, coups and cocaine hauls, Guinea-Bissau buzzes with joy, even when daily life is tough and the future bleak. There must be magic in that cashew juice.

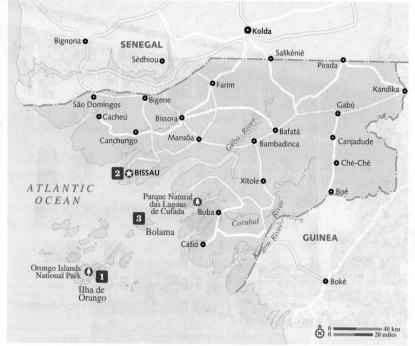

Guinea-Bissau's
Top Experiences

Ilha de Orango

1 The heart of Orango Islands National Park is home to rare saltwater hippos and the island is also the burial site of the Bijagós kings and queens. Guides can take you hippo spotting

Food & Drink

Seafood is the highlight, including shrimp, oysters and meaty *bica* (sea bream), best served sautéed with onion and lime.

A national favourite is *chabeu*: deep-fried fish served in a thick palm-oil sauce with rice.

Local brews include palm wine and the very potent liquors *caña* (rum) and *cajeu* (cashew liquor). The best beers are the imported Portuguese brands.

Bissau Velho

2 This stretch of narrow alleyways and derelict buildings, is 'guarded' by the Fortaleza d'Amura. With its bombed-out roof and shrapnel-riddled neoclassical facade, the former presidential palace is a powerful reminder of simmering conflicts. The rebuilt Assembleia Ministério da Justiça , by contrast, is an architectural expression of democratic hopes.

Bolama

3 Geographically closer to Bissau than any other island in the Bijagós, eerily beautiful Bolama feels worlds away. The Portuguese capital of Guinea-Bissau until 1943, Bolama's shores are awash with crumbling relics that were abandoned after independence. Tree-lined boulevards are mapped out by lamp posts that no longer shine, and the colonial barracks have been recast as a hospital.

When to Go

DEC–FEB

➡ The year's coolest months, when sea turtles emerge from their nests.

MAR–JUL

➡ Hot, humid and sweaty; travel with plenty of water and sunscreen.

AUG–OCT

➡ Batten down the hatches or dance in the rain; the rainwater will just keep fallin'.

Kaieteur Falls

CAPITAL
Georgetown

POPULATION
739,903

AREA
215,000 sq km

OFFICIAL LANGUAGE
English

Guyana

From towering waterfalls and tropical jungle to caiman-filled rivers, few places on the planet offer raw adventure as authentic as densely forested Guyana.

Although the country has a troubled history of political instability and interethnic tension, underneath the headlines of corruption and economic mismanagement is a joyful and motivated mix of people who are turning the country into one of the continent's premier ecotourism destinations.

Georgetown, the country's crumbling colonial capital, is distinctly Caribbean with a rocking nightlife, great places to eat and an edgy market. The interior of the country is more Amazonian with its Amerindian communities and unparalleled wildlife-viewing opportunities tucked quietly away from the capital's hoopla. Meanwhile, the coast is some of the wildest and least developed on the continent. From sea-turtle nesting grounds along the country's north coast to riding with *vaqueros* at a ranch in the south or standing in awe watching one of the world's highest single-drop waterfalls, Guyana is well worth the mud, bumps and sweat it takes to experience it. If you love nature, this promises to be the trip of a lifetime.

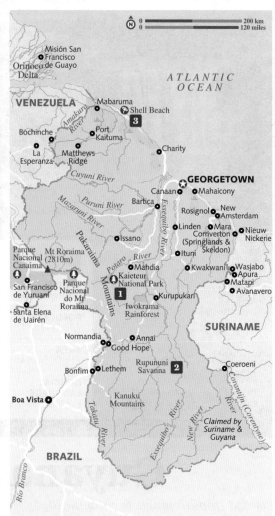

NOV–MID-JAN

➡ Coastal rainy season and the height of tourism for expats returning for Christmas.

MAY–AUG

➡ Interior and second coastal rainy season. Road travel becomes difficult.

LATE DEC

➡ 'Cashew rains' in the interior, light showers provide a welcome temperature drop.

Food & Drink

Bake and saltfish Fried bread and salted cod.

Cow heel soup Caribbean soup made with split peas, vegetables, dumplings and cow heels.

Farine Tasty cassava meal served as an accompaniment like rice.

Pepper pot A savory Amerindian game-and-cassava stew.

Guyana's
Top Experiences

Kaieteur Falls

1 Stand on the ledge of one of the world's highest single-drop fall at Kaieteur Falls. Watching 30,000 gallons of water shooting over a 250m cliff in the middle of a misty, ancient jungle without another tourist in sight is a once-in-a-lifetime experience.

Rupununi Savanna

2 Paddle though thriving populations of giant river otters and black caimans in these Africa-like plains scattered with Amerindian villages, small 'islands' of jungle and an exceptional diversity of wildlife. Rivers full of huge caimans and the world's largest water lilies cut through plains of golden grasses and termite mounds, while a mind-boggling array of birds fly across the sky.

Shell Beach

3 Take a boat ride through bird-filled rivers, mangrove swamps and savannas to Shell Beach, which extends for about 140km along the north coast toward the Venezuelan border. It's a nesting site for four of Guyana's eight sea turtle species and one of the least developed areas of the entire South American coastline with only temporary fishing huts and small settlements.

Market, Port-au-Prince

Haiti

Haiti is still struggling with the aftermath of the devastating 2010 earthquake. But this is a proud country, born of revolution, and its people are determined to rebuild for a better future.

Forget for a moment the rubble that still clogs parts of the capital. In actual fact, Haiti was once at the forefront of Caribbean tourism. In the 1950s, Port-au-Prince was rivaled only by Havana as a destination for the rich and famous; its jazz clubs and casinos a favored getaway for the Hollywood elite.

With a modicum of stability, Haiti could yet become the Caribbean's alternative travel destination par excellence: it has palm-fringed beaches to rival any of its neighbors. But lazing on the sand isn't really the point of Haiti (although you can do that, too). The richness of the country lies in its history and culture, closer to its African roots than any other Caribbean nation and ever present in its vibrant art and music scenes.

Haiti isn't the easiest country to travel in. You frequently need to keep an ear out for the news, and it can be more expensive than you'd expect. However, once you're there, travel is not only possible, but also incredibly rewarding. It's an addictive country to visit.

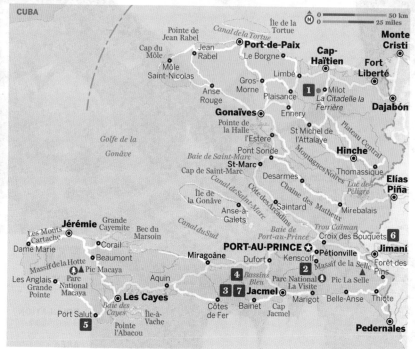

Haiti's
Top Experiences

La Citadelle la Ferrière

1 If ever a country settled on making a statement of intent on winning its independence, Haiti found it in the mighty Citadelle la Ferrière. Haitians call the Citadelle the eighth wonder of the world and, having slogged to the 900m summit of Pic la Ferrière, you may be inclined to agree. A giant battleship of a fortress sitting atop a mountain crag, with a Versailles-like ruined palace at its base, it commands its landscape as a proud symbol of the world's first black republic. Epic in concept and execution and largely hidden from the world's gaze, it easily holds its own against the best historical sites the Americas can offer.

Hiking in Parc National la Visite

2 Haiti is such a mountainous country that it would be a shame to only experience them while whizzing by in traffic. Kenscoff, above Pétionville, is the entry point for Parc National La Visite. A hike from here across the western section of Massif de la Selle to Seguin, takes six to eight hours and is one of the most spectacular walks in the country. The park still has plenty of Haiti's original pine forest, weird broken rock formations and, as the scenery opens up, great views out to the Caribbean Sea. A long day's walk on a path shared with local farmers, it's the perfect leg-stretching antidote to the buzz of the big city.

Carnival in Jacmel

3 You want shiny sequins and sanitized carnival bling? Plenty of places will serve that up for you. Jacmel's street theater is another game altogether, close to the surreal, where individuals and troupes parade and act in homemade costumes and papier-mâché masks from local artisans. Vodou, sex, death and revolution all play their part, mixed with street music and wild antics, in a parade where both crowd and performers mix as participants. Music is everywhere, from bands on organized floats to *rara* (one of the most popular forms of Haitian music) outfits on foot. And where else will you see a donkey dressed in sneakers and hat?

Kenscoff, an entry point to Parc National La Visite

Bassins Bleu

4 Bassins Bleu is tucked into the mountains 12km northwest of Jacmel, a series of three cobalt-blue pools linked by waterfalls that make up one of the prettiest swimming holes in the country. Bassin Clair is the most beautiful of the three, set deep into the mountain at the bottom of the waterfall, sheltered and surrounded by smooth rocks draped with maidenhair and creeper ferns. Local kids may delight you by lunging into the pool from the higher rocks. You're sadly less likely to see the nymphs that according to legend live in the grottoes.

Port Salut

5 Haiti is a rare Caribbean country in that it isn't really thought of as a beach destination, but that doesn't mean its beaches should be ignored. While the north coast has dramatic cliffs and crashing Atlantic breakers, the south coast – particularly at Port Salut – has great stretches of beautiful white sand fringed with palm trees. The water is warm. There's grilled fish and rum. Oh, and remember

When to Go

HIGH SEASON
(Nov–Mar)

➡ Hot and dry (the north is frequently rainy).

➡ Carnival in Port-au-Prince and Jacmel (February), the countrywide Fet Gédé Vodou festival (November).

SHOULDER
(Apr–Jul)

➡ Rain in the south.

➡ The important Vodou festival and pilgrimage of Soukri is held near Gonaïves in July.

LOW SEASON
(Aug–Oct)

➡ Hurricane season (August and September), but travel is perfectly feasible if there are no storms.

➡ Often heavy daily rainfall; humid.

if Haiti were 100 people

35 would be aged 0-14
22 would be aged 15-24
34 would be aged 25-54
5 would be aged 55-64
4 would be aged 65+

belief systems
(% of population)

80 Roman Catholic

16 Protestant

3 other

1 none

population per sq km

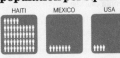

HAITI   MEXICO   USA

🧍 ≈ 8 people

Vodou

It's hard to think of a more maligned and misunderstood religion than Vodou. If you're thinking zombies and dolls with pins in them, you need to disconnect from Hollywood.

Vodou is the wellspring of the Haitian character, a sophisticated belief system with roots in the country's African past and the slave rebellion that brought Haiti to independence in 1804. For three centuries, slaves were shipped to Haiti from the Dahomey and Kongo kingdoms in West and Central Africa. As well as their labor, the slaves brought with them their traditional religions; Vodou is a synthesis of these, mixed with residual Taíno rituals and colonial Catholic iconography.

Food & Drink

Bannan Fried plantain.

Barbancourt The best locally produced brand of rum.

Diri Rice

Fritay Street snack of fried meat, fish or plantain.

Fruit Fresh fruit abounds – mangoes and avocados are particularly good.

Griyo Pork

Kabrit Goat

Lambi Conch

Pate Savoury pastries; a good street snack.

Plat complet A dish with the key elements of Haitian food – rice, beans and fried plantain – and meat, accompanied by a sauce.

Poule Chicken

Prestige The best locally produced brand of beer.

Pwa Beans

Tasso Beef

Art and craft shop, Rue du Commerce, Jacmel

that line about no tourists in Haiti? You get the beaches almost entirely to yourself.

Crois des Bouquets

6 Croix des Bouquets is the setting for one of Haiti's most vibrant art scenes. Its Noialles district is home to the *boss fé* (ironworkers), who hammer out incredible decorative art from flattened oil drums and vehicle bodies. It's great fun to wander around watching the artisans and looking for souvenirs. Popular designs include the Tree of Life, the Vodou *Iwa La Siren* (the mermaid), birds, fish, musicians and angels.

Jacmel Handicrafts

7 The charming, tranquil old port town of Jacmel is a souvenir-buyer's paradise. Its most famous output is the papier-mâché Carnival masks, unique to the town. More portable handicrafts include hand-painted placemats and boxes, wooden flowers, and models of *taptaps*, jungle animals and boats. Prices are cheap, and there's a complete absence of hard sell. Most of the shops can be found on Rue St-Anne near the Hôtel la Jacmelienne sur Plage, along with a number of galleries showcasing Jacmel's art scene.

Getting Around

Air Haiti's small size means that flights are short, saving hours on bad roads.

Boat There are a few islands and remote areas around Haiti accessible only by ferry. Boats are rarely comfortable and often dangerously overcrowded. In some areas, small boats operate as water taxis.

Bus Haiti's buses are big, cheap and seemingly indestructible affairs. There are no timetables; buses leave when full. A *taptap* is more likely to be a minibus or pickup truck, used for travel within cities, or hopping between towns.

Taxi Port-au-Prince and Cap-Haïtien have collective taxis, called *publiques*, running along set routes. There are motorcycle taxis everywhere.

Copán Ruinas

Honduras

With glorious diving around the Bay Islands, ancient Maya ruins, historic colonial towns, Caribbean beaches and steamy mountain jungles, Honduras is waiting to be rediscovered.

You've probably heard about the bad boy in the Central American 'hood. Even if you've just glanced at a headline, Honduras and trouble seem inextricably linked. In late 2009 when former President Manuel Zelaya was exiled to Costa Rica, all of the tourists went with him. But what's the reality on the ground now? Well, despite the country's rep, the vast majority of travelers actually love their time here, for the nation is simply loaded with attractions: the fabled Bay Islands (a dive and party mecca), the magical Maya ruins of Copán, the seductive beauty of the Lenca highlands and the wildlife-rich jungle reserves in La Moskitia.

It's also superb value for money: all the adventure sports that have put Costa Rica on the map are available here at backpacking rates. Honduran landscapes are extraordinary, its cultural sights compelling and its people waiting. Sure, take a little extra care, especially in the big cities... but make the move and discover Honduras for yourself.

CAPITAL
Tegucigalpa

POPULATION
8.4 million

AREA
112,090 sq km

OFFICIAL LANGUAGE
Spanish

Honduras'
Top Experiences

Bay Islands

1 Spectacular diving and snorkeling draws visitors from around the world to the three Bay Islands – Roatán, Utila and Guanaja – about 50km off the north coast of Honduras. Their reefs are part of the second-largest barrier reef in the world after Australia's Great Barrier Reef.

Copán Ruinas

2 One of the most important of all Maya civilizations lived, prospered then mysteriously crumbled around the Copán archaeological site, now a Unesco World Heritage site and a short walk from the charming town of Copán Ruinas. Today you can marvel at intricate stone carvings and epic ancient structures tracing back to an extraordinary Maya empire.

Gracias

3 Gracias was founded in 1526 by Spanish Captain Juan de Chavez and for a brief time in the 16th century, it was the capital of all Spanish-conquered Central America. Traces of its former grandeur remain in its centuries-old buildings and various colonial churches. The pace of life along the village's cobblestone streets rarely moves much faster than walking speed.

Food & Drink

Anafres Bean and *quesillo* cheese dip served in a heated clay pot and eaten like nachos.

Baleadas Breakfast staple of beans and *quesillo* wrapped in a flour tortilla.

Casabe A crispy flatbread commonly found in Garifuna communities.

When to Go

OCT–FEB
➡ Rainy season on the north coast and islands, but dry in the interior.

MAR–MAY
➡ Hot and dry everywhere, with temperatures soaring inland.

JUN–SEP
➡ Peak season for viewing whale sharks in Utila.

CAPITAL
Hong Kong

POPULATION
7.1 million

AREA
1,104 sq km

OFFICIAL LANGUAGES
Cantonese
English

Hong Kong

This enigmatic city of soaring towers, ancient rituals and action movies is safe, friendly and wonderfully well organised.

The tantalising neighbourhoods and curious islands that make up Hong Kong are a sensory delight awaiting exploration. You can find yourself swaying along on a double-decker tramcar one moment, then cheering with the hordes at the city-centre horse races, or simply gazing out at the magnificent harbour.

But over 70% of Hong Kong is mountains and sprawling country parks so escape the city limits on one of the world's best transport systems and spend your day wandering in a Song-dynasty village or hiking surf-beaten beaches. Whatever your gastronomic preferences you will be sated in Hong Kong – over a bowl of noodles with beef brisket, a basket of vegetarian dim sum, your first-ever stinky tofu or a plate of freshly steamed prawns fragrant with garlic.

Shopaholics rejoice: from ready-to-wear Chinese jackets to bespoke kitchen knives, the sheer range and variety of products on Hong Kong's shelves is mind-bending.

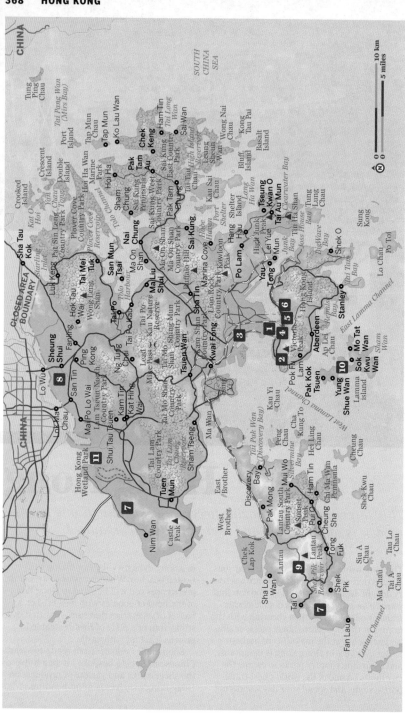

Hong Kong's
Top Experiences

Star Ferry from Kowloon to Hong Kong Island

1 A floating piece of Hong Kong heritage and a sightseeing bargain, the legendary Star Ferry was founded in 1880 and plies the calm waters of Victoria Harbour in the service of families, students, office workers, boat buffs and tourists. At only $2.50, the 15-minute ride with views of skyscrapers marching up jungle-clad hills must be one of the world's best-value cruises. While the vista is more dramatic when you're Island-bound, the art deco Kowloon pier, resembling a finger pointing at the Island, is arguably more charming.

The Peak

2 Rising above the financial heart of Hong Kong Island, Victoria Peak offers superlative views of the city and the mountainous countryside beyond. Ride the hair-raising Peak Tram (in operation since 1888) to the cooler climes at the top as a teeming mass of moneyed skyscrapers and choked apartment blocks unfolds below. At dusk Victoria Harbour glitters like the Milky Way in a sci-fi movie poster as the lights come on in this astonishing metropolis. A view to die for!

Viewing platform, Victoria Peak

JOHN SONES SINGING BOWL MEDIA / GETTY IMAGES ©

Markets

3 Mong Kok with its speciality markets is your best bet for a rewarding sprawl crawl. The mile-long Tung Choi St Market/Ladies' Market has clothes ranging from 'I Love HK' tees to granny swimwear and sexy lingerie; the flower market sells exotic seeds and gardening tools alongside fragrant florals; and the goldfish market showcases these exotic creatures in softly humming, UV-lit tanks. Complementing these are vertical markets such as a multistorey computer mall, and a mobile phone and gadget lover's heaven.

if Hong Kong were 100 people

93 would be Chinese
2 would be Indonesian
2 would be Filipino
3 would be other

occupations
(% of population)

41 wholesale and retail trade, restaurants and hotels

17 community and social services

12 financing, insurance and real estate

7 manufacturing and construction

10 transport and communications

13 other

population per sq km

HONG KONG   CHINA   SINGAPORE

 ≈ 150 people

Man Mo Temple

4 Ditch the Soho watering holes and experience Chinese folk religiosity in this atmospheric 19th-century institution. Forever wreathed in thick sandalwood smoke from the slow-burning incense coils, the popular temple is dedicated to Man and Mo, the gods of literature and war. Formerly a cultural and political focal point for the Chinese community, the dimly lit space now commands a much bigger following beyond obedient students and assorted street fighters, as the public come to perform age-old rites and have their fortunes told.

Wan Chai Dining

5 If you were to hurl yourself, eyes closed, into a random neighbourhood eatery and expect to emerge smacking your lips, you'd stand the best chance if you were in Wan Chai. The district is home to a great many restaurants suiting a range of pocket sizes. Regional Chinese cooking, European cuisines, Asian kitchens, East-West fusion, classy, midrange, hole in the wall... Just name your craving and head on down to the Wanch; you're certain to find it there.

Happy Valley Races

6 Every Wednesday night the city horseracing track in Happy Valley comes alive, with eight electrifying races and an accompanying carnival of food and beer. You can try your luck at betting or simply enjoy the collective exhilaration and the thunder of hooves. Races were first held here in the 19th century by

Rent-a-Curse Grannies

Under the Canal Road Flyover between Wan Chai and Causeway Bay, you can hire little old ladies to beat up your enemy. From their perch on plastic stools, these rent-a-curse grannies will pound paper cut-outs of your romantic rival, office bully or whiny celeb with a shoe (their orthopaedic flat or your stilettos – your call) while rapping rhythmic curses. All for only $50. Hung Shing Temple has a 'master' who performs the same with a symbolic 'precious' sword for the exorbitant sum of $100.

Food & Drink

Cha Chaan Tang Tea cafes are perhaps best known for their Hong Kong–style 'pantyhose' milk tea – a strong brew made from a blend of several types of black tea with crushed egg shells thrown in for silkiness. It's filtered through a fabric that hangs like a stocking, hence the name, and drunk with evaporated milk. 'Pantyhose' milk tea is sometimes mixed with three parts coffee to create the quintessential Hong Kong drink, tea-coffee

Dai Pai Dongs A dai pai dong is a food stall, hawker-style or built into a rickety hut crammed with tables and stools that sometimes spill out onto the pavement.

Dim Sum Dim sum are Cantonese tidbits consumed with tea for breakfast or lunch. The term literally means 'to touch the heart' and the act of eating dim sum is referred to as yum cha, meaning 'to drink tea'. Each dish, often containing two to four morsels steamed in a bamboo basket, is meant to be shared. In old-style dim sum places, just stop the waiter and choose something from the cart. Modern venues give you an order slip, but it's almost always in Chinese only.

Incense coils, Man Mo Temple

European merchants who imported stocky stallions from Mongolia, which they rode themselves. Now there are races every week except in the sweltering months of July and August.

Hiking the Hong Kong Trail

7 Right on the city's doorstep, the Hong Kong Trail transports you into emerald hills, secluded woodland and lofty paths that afford sumptuous views of the rugged south and (eventually) glimpses of its wavy shore once you've tackled the formidable Dragon's Back ridge. Starting from the Peak, the 50km route snakes across the entire length of Hong Kong Island, past picturesque reservoirs, WWII battlefields and cobalt bays. Spread over five country parks, this delightful trail invites both easy perambulations and harder hikes.

Walled Villages

8 Let Yuen Long's walled villages take you back over half a millennium, to a time when piracy was rife along the South China coast. Isolated from China's administrative heart, Hong Kong, with its treacherous shores and mountainous terrain, was an excellent hideout for pirates. Its earliest inhabitants built villages with high walls, some guarded by cannons, to protect themselves. Inside these walls today you'll see ancestral halls, courtyards, pagodas, temples,

When to Go

OCT–EARLY DEC

➡ With moderate temperatures and clear skies, this is the best time to visit.

JUN–AUG

➡ Hot, humid and rainy.

SEPT

➡ Beware of typhoons.

wells and ancient farming implements – vestiges of Hong Kong's precolonial history, all carefully restored.

Tian Tan Buddha

9 A favourite with local day trippers and foreign visitors alike, the biggest bronze outdoor seated Buddha in the world lords over the western hills of Lantau. Visit this serenely mammoth statue via the scenic Ngong Ping 360 cable-car ride. Tuck into some monk food at the popular vegetarian restaurant in the Po Lin Monastery below. Buddha's Birthday in May is a lively time to visit this important pilgrimage site.

Best on Film

In the Mood for Love (2000) Wong Kar-wai's masterpiece of smouldering love in 1960s Hong Kong.

Little Cheung (1999) A gritty take on the realities of post-1997 Hong Kong.

Love in a Puff (2010) A chain-smoking tribute to contemporary Hong Kong life.

My Life as McDull (2001) A heart-warming animation about an indigenous pig character.

Best in Print

Gweilo: Memories of a Hong Kong Childhood (Martin Booth; 2004) A much-acclaimed memoir of life in 1950s Hong Kong.

Hong Kong: A Cultural History (Michael Ingham; 2007) The definitive title in this category.

Hong Kong State of Mind (Jason Ng; 2011) A crash course on the city's idiosyncrasies.

The Hungry Ghosts (Anne Berry; 2009) Restless spirits haunt this expertly crafted tale.

Getting Around

Bus Extensive network and ideal for short rides. Most bus lines run from 6am to midnight.

Ferry Star Ferry connects Hong Kong Island and Kowloon through the scenic harbour from 7.30am to 10.20pm. More modern ferry fleets run between Central and outlying islands.

MTR Hong Kong's subway and train system covers most of the city and is the easiest way to get around. Most lines run 6am to midnight.

Tram Runs on the northern strip of Hong Kong Island. Slow, but great views. Runs from 6am to midnight.

Exploring Lamma

10 If there were a soundtrack for the island of Lamma, it would be reggae. The island has a laid-back vibe that attracts herb-growers, musicians and New Age therapists from a rainbow of cultures. Soak up the vibes in the village, and hike to the nearest beach, your unlikely compass three coal-fired plants against the skyline, looking more trippy than grim. Spend the afternoon chilling by the beach, and then, in the glow of the day's final rays, head back for steamed prawns, fried calamari and beer by the pier.

Hong Kong Wetland Park

11 Surreally nestled under an imposing arc of apartment towers, this 61-hectare ecological park in crowded Tin Shui Wai is a swampy haven of biodiversity. This is urban/nature juxtaposition at its curiously most harmonious. Precious ecosystems in this far-flung yet easily accessible part of the New Territories provide tranquil habitats for a range of waterfowl and other wildlife. Forget the man-made world for a moment and delve into a landscape of mangroves, rivers and fish-filled ponds.

KEN WELSH / GETTY IMAGES ©

Széchenyi Baths, Budapest

CAPITAL
Budapest

POPULATION
9.9 million

AREA
93,028 sq km

OFFICIAL LANGUAGE
Hungarian

Hungary

Hungary has always marched to a different drummer – speaking a language, preparing dishes and drinking wines like no others. It's Europe at its most exotic.

A short hop from Vienna, this land of Franz Liszt and Béla Bartók, paprika-lashed dishes and the romantic Danube River continues to enchant visitors. The allure of Budapest, once an imperial city, is obvious at first sight, and it also boasts the hottest nightlife in the region. Other cities, too, like Pécs, the warm heart of the south, and Eger, the wine capital of the north, have much to offer travellers, as does the sprawling countryside, particularly the Great Plain, where cowboys ride and cattle roam.

And where else can you laze about in an open-air thermal spa while snow patches glisten around you? In Hungary you'll find all the glamour, excitement and fun of Western Europe – at half the cost.

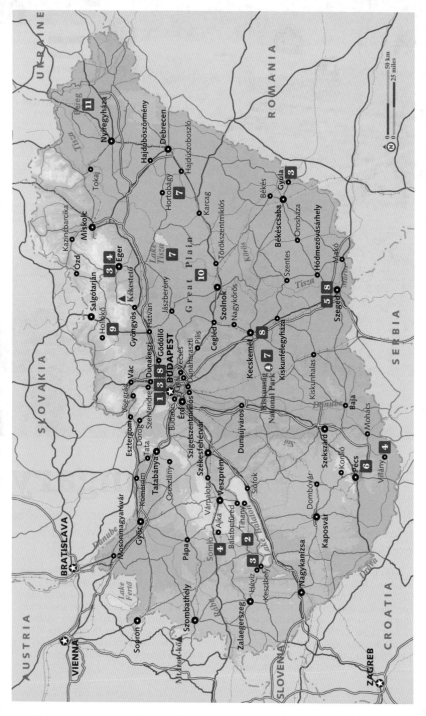

Hungary's
Top Experiences

Budapest's Castle Hill

1 Budapest boasts architectural gems in spades, but the limestone plateau towering over the Danube River's west bank is the Hungarian capital's most spectacular sight. Enclosed within the medieval castle walls, numerous attractions vie for your attention, from the splendid Great Throne Room and the treasures of the Budapest History Museum, to the claustrophobic Castle Labyrinth and the show-stopping view of Parliament across the river in Pest from Fishermen's Bastion.

Lake Balaton's Northern Shore

2 Hungary's 'sea' (and Continental Europe's largest lake) is where the populace comes to sun and swim in summertime. The quieter side of Lake Balaton mixes sizzling beaches and oodles of fun on the water with historic waterside towns like Keszthely and Balatonfüred. Tihany, a 30m-high peninsula jutting 4km into the lake, is home to a stunning abbey church, and Badacsony draws the crowds with its lakeside location, cultivated slopes and robust white wines.

Fishermen's Bastion

SYLVAIN SONNET / GETTY IMAGES ©

Thermal Baths

3 With more than 300 thermal hot springs in public use across Hungary, it's not hard to find a place to take the waters. Some of the thermal baths, like the Rudas and Király in Budapest and part of the Turkish Bath in Eger, date back to the 16th century. Increasingly popular are waterparks catering to a larger audience. Among the most unusual spa experiences in Hungary are floating on a thermal lake at Hévíz and getting into hot water at a castle at Gyula.

Wine & Pálinka

4 Hungarian wines, made here for millennia, are celebrated the world over. Honey-gold sweet Tokaj and crimson-red Bull's Blood from Eger are the best known. Don't overlook the big-bodied reds of Villány or Somló's flinty whites. Beyond the fruit of the vine is pálinka, a fruit-flavoured brandy (think apricots, plums, even raspberries) that kicks like a mule. And then there's the increasingly popular aperitif Unicum, chocolate-brown in colour and as bitter as a loser's tears.

Szeged

5 The cultural capital of the Great Plain and Hungary's third-largest city, Szeged is filled with eye-popping Art Nouveau masterpieces, students, open-air cafes and green spaces, straddling the ever-present Tisza River. Theatre, opera and all types of classical and popular music performances abound, culminating in the Szeged Open-Air Festival in summer. Szeged is also justly famed for its edibles, including the distinctive fish soup made with local paprika and Pick, Hungary's finest salami.

Pécs

6 This gem of a city is blessed with rarities of Turkish architecture and early Christian and Roman tombs. Its Mosque Church is the largest Ottoman structure still standing in Hungary, while the Hassan Jakovali Mosque has survived the centuries in excellent condition. Pécs is exceptionally rich in art and museums. What's more, the climate is mild – almost Mediterranean – and you can't help noticing all the almond trees in bloom or in fruit here.

Paprika

Paprika, the *sine qua non* of Hungarian cuisine, may not be exactly what you expect. All in all, it's pretty mild stuff and a taco with salsa or a chicken vindaloo from the corner takeaway tastes more fiery. But the fact remains that many Hungarian dishes such as *pörkölt* (stew of beef, pork or most commonly veal) and *halászlé* (fish soup) wouldn't be, well, Hungarian dishes without the addition of the 'red gold' spice grown around Szeged and Kalocsa. It comes in varying degrees of piquancy and is a culinary and culturally Magyar essential.

Food & Drink

Gulyás (goulash) Hungary's signature dish, though here it's more like a soup than a stew and made with beef, onions and tomatoes.

Gundel palacsinta Flambéed pancake with chocolate and nuts.

Halászlé Fish soup made from poached freshwater fish, tomatoes, green peppers and paprika.

Lángos Snack of deep-fried dough with various toppings (usually cheese and sour cream).

Pálinka Fruit-flavoured brandy.

Pörkölt Paprika-infused stew; closer to what we would call goulash.

Rétes (strudel) Filled with poppy seeds, cherry preserves or *túró* (curd or cottage cheese).

Savanyúság Literally 'sourness'; anything from mildly sour-sweet cucumbers to almost acidic sauerkraut, eaten with a main course.

Somlói galuska Sponge cake with chocolate and whipped cream.

Unicum A bitter aperitif nicknamed the 'Hungarian national accelerator'.

if Hungary were 100 people

92 would be Hungarian
2 would be Roma
6 would be other

belief systems
(% of population)

52 Roman Catholic
16 Calvinist
3 Lutheran
3 Greek Catholic
12 other
14 unaffiliated

population per sq km

HUNGARY GERMANY USA

👤 ≈ 11 people

Dome of Gellért Baths, Budapest

Birdwatching

7 With 250 resident species, several of them endangered and many rare, birds are plentiful in Hungary and you don't have to go out of your way to observe our feathered friends. Head to the Hortobágy on the Great Plain to see autumn migrations, or to one of the many lakes, such as Tisza, to see aquatic birdlife. Bustards proliferate in Kiskunság National Park near Kecskemét, while white storks nesting atop chimneys in eastern Hungary are quite a sight from May to October.

When to Go

HIGH SEASON
(Jul–Aug)

➡ Summer is warm, sunny and long.

➡ Resorts at Lake Balaton and Mátra Hills book out; expect long queues at attractions and high prices everywhere.

➡ Many cities grind to a halt in August.

SHOULDER
(Apr–Jun, Sep–Oct)

➡ Spring is glorious, though it can be wet in May and early June.

➡ Autumn is particularly special in the hills; festivals mark the *szüret* (grape harvest).

LOW SEASON
(Nov–Mar)

➡ November is rainy, and winter is cold and often bleak.

➡ Many sights reduce their hours sharply or close altogether.

➡ Prices are rock-bottom.

Art Nouveau

8 Art nouveau architecture and its Viennese variant, Secessionism, abound in Hungary. Superb examples, built largely during the country's 'Golden Age' in the late 19th and early 20th centuries, can be seen in cities like Budapest, Szeged and Kecskemét. The style's sinuous curves and flowing, asymmetrical forms, colourful tiles and other decorative elements stand out like beacons in a sea of refined and elegant baroque and mannered, geometric neoclassical buildings – it will have you gasping with delight.

Hollókő

9 It may consist of a mere two streets, but Hollókő is the most beautiful of Hungary's villages. Its 65 whitewashed houses, little changed since their construction in the 17th and 18th centuries, are pure examples of traditional folk architecture and have been on Unesco's World Heritage list for 25 years. Most importantly, it is a bastion of traditional Hungarian culture, holding fast to the folk art of the ethnic Palóc people and some of their ancient customs.

The Puszta

10 Hungarians tend to view the *puszta* – the Great Plain – romantically, as a region full of hardy shep-

Best on Film

Children of Glory (Szabadság, Szerelem; 2006) About the 'blood in the water' water-polo match in 1956.

Moszkva tér (2006) End-of-communism comedy with kids.

Zimmer Feri (1998) Jokes about German tourists on the Balaton.

Best in Print

Prague (Arthur Phillips; 2002) Mixed-up young American does Budapest.

Twelve Days: The Story of the 1956 Hungarian Revolution (Victor Sebestyen; 2007) Day-by-day account of the Uprising.

Getting Around

Menetrend (www.menetrendek.hu) has links to all transport timetables – bus, train, public transport and boat

Bus Buses are the mainstay of public transport in most villages, towns and cities in Hungary. They are a cheap and efficient way of getting to further-flung places. The Volánbusz (www.volanbusz.hu) network comprehensively covers the whole country.

Train MÁV (www.elvira.hu) operates clean, punctual and relatively comfortable (if not ultra-modern) train services. Budapest has a suburban railway known as the HÉV.

Tram Hungary's larger cities – Budapest, Szeged, Miskolc and Debrecen – have a tram system.

herds fighting the wind and snow in winter and trying not to go stir-crazy in summer as the notorious *délibabok* (mirages) rise off the baking soil. It's a romantic notion, but the endless plains can be explored in Kiskunság National Park and Hortobágy. Mount a mighty steed yourself or watch as Hungarian cowboys ride with five horses in hand in a spectacular show of skill and horsemanship.

Folkloric Northeast

11 Preserved through generations, Hungary's folk art traditions bring everyday objects to life. Differences in colours and styles easily identify the art's originating region. You'll find exquisite detailed embroidery, pottery, hand-painted or carved wood, dyed Easter eggs and graphic woven cloth right across the country, but the epicentre is in Bereg. The culture of the tiny villages of this region in the far northeast of Hungary has much to do with their neighbours to the east, including the brightly dyed Easter eggs.

JOHN ELK / GETTY IMAGES ©

Látrabjarg Peninsula, Westfjords

CAPITAL
Reykjavík

POPULATION
315,281

AREA
103,000 sq km

OFFICIAL LANGUAGE
Icelandic

Iceland

A mythical kingdom ruled by elves and Arctic energy, Iceland is where the past meets the future in an elemental symphony of wind, stone, fire and ice.

Iceland is, literally, a country in the making – the natural elements work in harmony to power its veritable volcanic laboratory: geysers gush, mudpots gloop, Arctic gales swish along fjords, stone towers rise from the depths of an indigo sea, and glaciers grind their way through lava fields and the merciless tundra. The sublime power of Icelandic nature turns the prosaic into the extraordinary. A dip in the pool becomes a soothing soak in a geothermal lagoon, a casual stroll can transform into a trek across a glittering ice cap, and a quiet night of camping means front-row seats to either the aurora borealis' curtains of fire, or the soft, pinkish hue of the midnight sun.

It's hard not to be deeply touched by the island's beauty – few leave without a pang. Iceland has that effect on people. Perhaps it's the landscape's austere bleakness, or maybe it has something to do with the island's tiny population, but a visit here is as much about the people you meet as it is about the ethereal landscape.

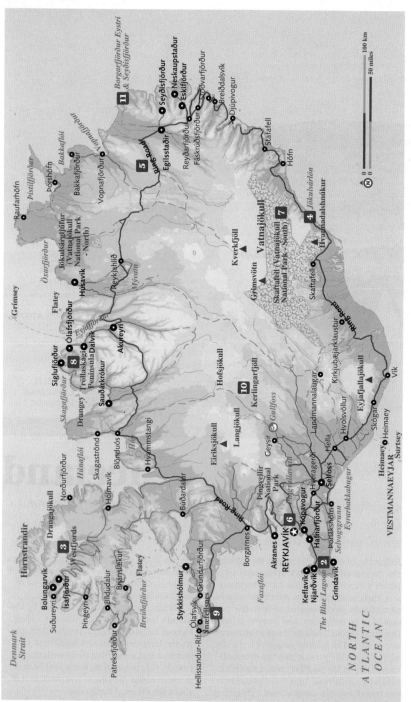

Iceland's
Top Experiences

Northern Lights

1 Everyone longs to glimpse the Northern Lights, the celestial kaleidoscope known for transforming long winter nights into natural lava lamps. The lights, also known as aurora borealis, form when solar flares are drawn by the earth's magnetic field towards the North Pole. What results are ethereal veils of green, white, violet or red light, shimmering and dancing in a display not unlike silent fireworks. Peak aurora sightings occur in the depths of winter, but look for the lights in clear, dark skies anytime between October and April.

The Blue Lagoon

2 Iceland's unofficial pastime is splashing around its surplus of geothermal water. There are 'hot-pots' everywhere – from downtown Reykjavík to the isolated peninsular tips of the Westfjords – and not only are they incredibly relaxing, they're a great way to meet the locals (and cure a mean hangover!). Everyone knows that Blue Lagoon is the big cheese; its steaming pale-blue lagoon full of silica deposits sits conveniently close to Keflavík International Airport, making it the perfect send-off before flying home, but for most it's an easy day trip from Reykjavík.

DAVE MOORHOUSE / GETTY IMAGES ©

Westfjords

3 Iceland's sweeping spectrum of superlative nature comes to a dramatic climax in the Westfjords. Sweeping beaches flank the southern coast, bird colonies abound, fjordheads tower above and then plunge into the deep, and a network of ruddy roads twists throughout, adding an extra sense of adventure. The region's uppermost peninsula, Hornstrandir, is the final frontier; the sea cliffs are perilous, the foxes are foxier, and hiking trails amble through pristine patches of wilderness that practically kiss the Arctic Circle.

Jökulsárlón

4 A ghostly procession of luminous-blue icebergs drifts serenely through the 18-sq-km Jökulsárlón lagoon before floating out to sea. This surreal scene (handily, right next to the Ring Road) is a natural film set: in fact, you might have seen it in *Batman Begins* and the James Bond film *Die Another Day*. The ice breaks off from Breiðamerkurjökull glacier, an offshoot of the mighty Vatnajökull ice cap. Boat trips among the 'bergs are popular, or you can simply wander the lakeshore, scout for seals, and exhaust your camera's memory card.

Driving the Ring Road

5 There's no better way to explore Iceland than to hire your own set of wheels and loop around Rte 1 – affectionately known as the Ring Road. The ovular strip of cement loops around the island in a clock-like fashion, passing through verdant dales decked with tumbling chutes, haunting glacial lagoons with popcorn-like icebergs, desolate strands of sea coast and arid plains of parched lava fields. Don't forget to take some of the detours – use the Ring Road as your main artery and then follow the veins as they splinter off into the wilderness.

Reykjavík

6 The world's most northerly capital combines colourful buildings, quirky people, eye-popping design, wild nightlife and a capricious soul to devastating effect. Add a backdrop of snowtopped mountains, churning seas, air as cold and clean as frozen diamonds, and fiery nights under the midnight sun, and

---

if Iceland were 100 people

89 would be Icelandic
3 would be Polish
1 would be German
2 would be Asian
2 would be other Nordic
3 would be other

belief systems
(% of population)

77 Evangelical Lutheran
5 Free Lutheran
3 Catholic
1 independent congregation
9 other
5 no religion

population per sq km

ICELAND   CANADA   USA

≈ 3 people

Food & Drink

Hangikjöt Hung meat, usually smoked lamb, served in thin slices.

Harðfiskur Brittle pieces of wind-dried haddock, usually eaten with butter.

Hverabrauð Rich, dark rye bread baked underground using geothermal heat; try it in Mývatn.

Jólaglögg Mulled wine beefed up with vodka – a popular Yuletide tipple.

Liquorice Salt liquorice and chocolate-covered varieties fill the supermarket sweets aisles.

Pönnukökur Icelandic pancakes, which are thin, sweet and cinnamon flavoured.

Pýlsur Icelandic hot dogs, made from lamb and topped with raw and deep-fried onion, ketchup, mustard and tangy remoulade (ask for 'ein með öllu' – one with everything).

Skyr Rich and creamy yoghurt-like staple, sometimes sweetened with sugar and berries.

Hallgrímskirkja church, Reykjavík

CHRISTIAN KOBER / GETTY IMAGES © | ARCHITECT: GUÐJÓN SAMÚELSSON

you'll agree that there's no better city in the world.

Vatnajökull National Park

7 Europe's largest national park covers 13% of Iceland and safeguards mighty Vatnajökull, the largest ice cap outside the poles (three times the size of Luxembourg). Scores of outlet glaciers flow down from its frosty bulk, while underneath it are active volcanoes and mountain peaks. Yes, this is ground zero for those 'fire and ice' clichés. You'll be spellbound by the diversity of landscapes, walking trails and activities inside this super-sized park. Given its dimensions, access points are numerous – start at Skaftafell in the south or Ásbyrgi in the north.

Tröllaskagi Peninsula

8 Touring Tröllaskagi is a joy, especially now that road tunnels link the spectacularly sited townships of Siglufjörður and Ólafsfjörður, once end-of-the-road settlements. The peninsula's dramatic scenery

When to Go

HIGH SEASON
(Jun–Aug)

➡ Visitors descend en masse to all corners of the country – especially Reykjavík.

➡ Endless daylight and midnight merriment abounds.

➡ The arid interior welcomes hikers.

SHOULDER
(May & Sep)

➡ Breezier weather and occasional snows in the interior.

➡ Optimal visiting conditions for those who prefer crowdless vistas to cloudless days.

LOW SEASON
(Oct–Apr)

➡ Most minor roads shut down due to severe weather conditions.

➡ Northern Lights shimmer in the sky.

➡ Brief spurts of daylight betwixt endless stretches of night.

is more reminiscent of the Westfjords than the gentle hills that roll through most of northern Iceland. As well as top-notch scenery and hiking, pit stops with pulling power include Hofsós' perfect fjordside swimming pool, Lónkot's fine local produce and Siglufjörður's outstanding herring museum, plus ski fields, whale-watching tours, and ferries to offshore islands.

Snæfellsnes Peninsula

9 With its cache of wild sand-strewn beaches and crackling sulphur lava fields, the Snæfellsnes Peninsula is one of Iceland's best escapes. Jules Verne was definitely onto something when he used the area as his magical doorway to the centre of the earth. New Age types have flocked to the region to harness its natural power and energy, and even if you don't believe in 'earth chakras', you'll undoubtedly find greater forces at play along the stunning shores.

Best on Film

101 Reykjavík (2000) Comedy with a generous twist of romance.

Heima (2007) Documentary film following Sigur Rós as they perform throughout Iceland.

Jar City (2006) Carefully crafted detective thriller set in a windswept small town.

Best in Print

The Draining Lake (Arnaldur Indriðason; 2004) A local favourite.

The Sagas of Islanders (Jane Smiley et al; 2001) Essential historical reading.

Under the Glacier (Halldór Laxness; 1968) One of the finer works by the Nobel Laureate.

Getting Around

Air Iceland has an extensive network of domestic flights, which locals use almost like buses, but weather can play havoc with schedules.

Bicycle Cycling through Iceland's dramatic landscapes is a fantastic way to see the country. However, be prepared for some harsh conditions.

Bus Iceland has an extensive network of long-distance bus routes with services operated by a number of bus companies.

Car Driving gives you unparalleled freedom and, thanks to good roads and light traffic, it's all fairly straightforward. The Ring Road (Rte 1) circles the country and is mostly paved.

Kerlingarfjöll

10 Accessible for only a handful of months each year, this pristine mountain range lies deep in Iceland's highlands. Historically, myths of trolls and fearsome outlaws spurred travellers speedily along the highland routes, and Kerlingarfjöll remained unexplored until last century. Today, increasing numbers make use of long, bumpy roads to reach this remote range. What awaits is a hiker's paradise: geysers and hot springs, glaciers and dazzling, autumnal-hued rhyolite mountains.

Borgarfjörður Eystri & Seyðisfjörður

11 A tale of two east-side fjords. Stunning Seyðisfjörður garners most of the attention – it's only 27 (sealed) kilometres from the Ring Road, and it welcomes the weekly ferry from Europe into its mountain-lined, waterfall-studded embrace. Beautiful Borgarfjörður Eystri is 70km from the Ring Road, many of them bumpy and unsealed. Its selling points are understated: puffins, hidden elves, rugged rhyolite peaks. They both have natural splendour in spades.

Seyðisfjörður

JORDAN LYE / GETTY IMAGES ©

Jaipur, Rajasthan

CAPITAL
New Delhi

POPULATION
1.2 billion

AREA
3.3 million sq km

OFFICIAL LANGUAGES
Hindi, English

India

India bristles with a mind-stirring mix of landscapes and cultural traditions. Your journey through this intoxicating country will blaze in your memory long after you've left its shores.

From the snow-dusted mountains of the far north to the sun-washed beaches of the deep south, India's dramatic terrain is breathtaking. Along with abundant natural beauties, exquisitely carved temples rise out of deserts and crumbling old fortresses peer over plunging ravines. Aficionados of the great outdoors can scout for big jungle cats on wildlife safaris, paddle in the waters of one of many beautiful beaches, take blood-pumping treks high in the Himalaya, or simply inhale pine-scented air on meditative forest walks.

Spirituality is the common thread that weaves its way through the complex tapestry that is contemporary India. The multitude of sacred sites and time-honoured rituals are testament to the country's long, colourful and sometimes tumultuous religious history. And then there are the festivals! India hosts some of the world's most spectacular devotional celebrations – from city parades celebrating auspicious events on the religious calendar to simple harvest fairs that pay homage to a locally worshipped deity.

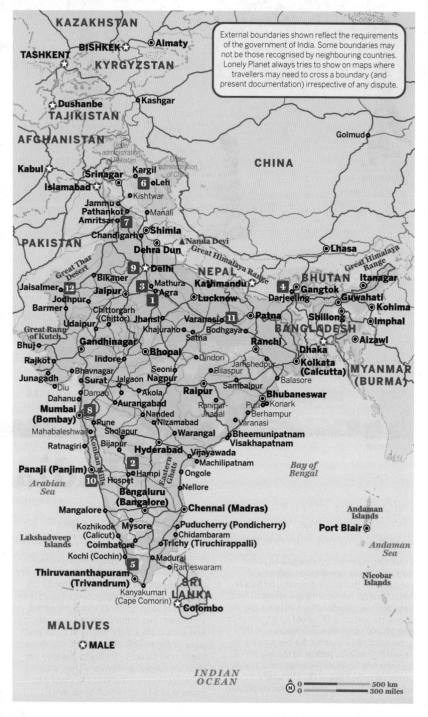

External boundaries shown reflect the requirements of the government of India. Some boundaries may not be those recognised by neighbouring countries. Lonely Planet always tries to show on maps where travellers may need to cross a boundary (and present documentation) irrespective of any dispute.

KAZAKHSTAN

TASHKENT   BISHKEK   Almaty

KYRGYZSTAN

Dushanbe   Kashgar

TAJIKISTAN

AFGHANISTAN

Under administration of Pakistan

CHINA

Golmud

Kabul   Srinagar   Kargil   **6** Leh
Islamabad   Jammu   Kishtwar
PAKISTAN   Pathankot   Manali
Amritsar   **7**
Chandigarh   Shimla
Dehra Dun   ▲ Nanda Devi   Lhasa
Great Himalaya Range

Great Thar Desert
Bikaner   **9** Delhi   NEPAL   BHUTAN   Itanagar
Jaisalmer   **12**   Jaipur   **3** Mathura   Kathmandu   **4** Gangtok   Guwahati
Jodhpur   Agra   Lucknow   Darjeeling   Shillong   Kohima
Barmer   **1**
Chittorgarh   Jhansi   Varanasi   **11** Patna   BANGLADESH   Imphal
(Chittor)   Khajuraho   Bodhgaya   Aizawl
Udaipur   Satna   Ranchi
Great Rann   Gandhinagar   Bhopal   Dindori   Dhaka
of Kutch   Indore   Jamshedpur   Kolkata
Bhuj   Seoni   Bilaspur   (Calcutta)   MYANMAR
Rajkot   Bhavnagar   Nagpur   Sambalpur   Balasore   (BURMA)
Junagadh   Surat   Jalgaon   Akola   Raipur
Diu   Daman   Aurangabad   Ranipur-   Puri   Konark
Dahanu   Nanded   Jharial   Berhampur
Mumbai   **8**   Pune   Nizamabad   Varanasi
(Bombay)   Sholapur   Warangal   Bheemunipatnam
Mahabaleshwar   Bijapur   Visakhapatnam
Ratnagiri   Hyderabad   Vijayawada
2   Machilipatnam   Bay of
Panaji (Panjim)   Hampi   Ongole   Bengal   Andaman
10   Hospet   Nellore   Islands
Arabian   Bengaluru   Port Blair
Sea   (Bangalore)
Mangalore   Chennai (Madras)   Andaman
Kozhikode   Mysore   Puducherry (Pondicherry)   Sea
(Calicut)   Coimbatore   Chidambaram
Kochi (Cochin)   Trichy (Tiruchirappalli)   Nicobar
5   Madurai   Islands
Thiruvananthapuram   Rameswaram
(Trivandrum)   SRI
Kanyakumari   LANKA
(Cape Comorin)   Colombo

MALDIVES

☪ MALE

INDIAN OCEAN

0 ___ 500 km
0 ___ 300 miles

India's
Top Experiences

Taj Mahal

1 Don't let fears of tour buses or touts or hordes of visitors get you thinking you can skip Agra's Taj Mahal – you can't. Even on a crowded, hot day, this world wonder is still the 'Crown of Palaces', a monument to love whose very walls seem to resound with the Emperor Shah Jahan's adoration of his beloved Mumtaz Mahal, the 'Gem of the Palace'. The marble mausoleum – inlaid with calligraphy, precious and semiprecious stones and intricate flower designs representing eternal paradise – is the world's most poetic parting.

Dreamy Hampi

2 The surreal boulder-scape of Hampi was once the glorious and cosmopolitan Vijayanagar, capital of a powerful Hindu empire. Still glorious in ruins, its temples and royal structures combine sublimely with the terrain: giant rocks balance on skinny pedestals near an ancient elephant garage; temples tuck into crevices between boulders; and wicker coracles float by rice paddies and bathing buffaloes near a gargantuan bathtub for a queen. Watching the sunset cast a rosy glow over the dreamy landscape, you might just forget what planet you're on.

Fantastic Festivals

3 India knows festivals, and it has been perfecting the parade for a few millennia. Holi is one of North India's most ecstatic festivals; Hindus celebrate the beginning of spring according to the lunar calendar by throwing coloured water and *gulal* (powder) at anyone within range. Bonfires the night before symbolise the demise of demoness Holika. Mathura is one of Hinduism's seven sacred cities and attracts floods of pilgrims, particularly during Janmastami (Krishna's birthday) in August/September; and Holi in February/March.

Cuppa in a Hill Station

4 The valleys, deserts and palm-lined beaches are all well and good, but it can get hot down there. India's princes and British colonials long used cool mountain towns like Darjeeling as refuges from the heat, and today the hill stations still have lush forests and crisp mountain air. So curl up under a blanket with a steaming cup of local tea and watch mountain birds swooping over hillsides, clouds passing over undulating hills of bulbous tea trees and village kids running through mountain fog and wildflowers.

if India were 100 people

72 would be Indo-Aryan
25 would be Dravidian
3 would be Mongoloid and other

belief systems
(% of population)

80 Hindu
14 Muslim
2 Christian
2 Sikh
1 Buddhist
1 Other

population per sq km

INDIA   CHINA   USA

≈ 30 people

Backwaters of Kerala

5 It's unusual to find a place as gorgeous as Kerala's backwaters: 900km of interconnected rivers, lakes and lagoons lined with tropical flora. And if you do, there likely won't be a way to experience it that's as peaceful and intimate as a few days on a teak-and-palm-thatch houseboat. Float along the water – maybe as the sun sets behind the palms, maybe while eating to-die-for Keralan seafood, maybe as you fall asleep under a twinkling sky – and forget about life on land for a while.

Himalayan Mountains & Monasteries

6 Up north, where the air is cool and crisp, quaint hill stations give way to snow-topped peaks. Here, the cultural influences came not via coasts but via mountain passes. Tibetan Buddhism thrives, and multilayered monasteries emerge from the forest or steep cliffs as vividly and poetically as the sun rises over the Ladakh plateau. Prayer flags blow in the wind, the sound of monks chanting reverberates in meditation halls, and locals bring offerings, all in the shadow of the mighty Himalaya.

Amritsar's Golden Temple

7 The Sikhs' holiest of shrines, the Golden Temple is a magical place. Seeming to float atop a glistening pool named for the 'nectar of immortality', the temple is a gorgeous structure, made even more so by its extreme goldness (the lotus-shaped dome is

Saris

Widely worn by Indian women, the elegant sari comes in a single piece and is tucked and pleated into place without the need for pins or buttons. Worn with the sari is the choli (tight-fitting blouse) and a drawstring petticoat. The palloo is the part of the sari draped over the shoulder. Also commonly worn is the salwar kameez, a traditional dresslike tunic and trouser combination accompanied by a dupatta (long scarf). Saris and salwar kameez come in a fantastic range of fabrics, colours and designs.

Food & Drink

Dahl While the staple of preference divides north and south, the whole of India is united in its love for dhal (curried lentils or pulses). You may encounter up to 60 different pulses.

Meat Although India probably has more vegetarians than the rest of the world combined, it still has an extensive repertoire of carnivorous fare. Chicken, lamb and mutton (sometimes actually goat) are the mainstays; religious taboos make beef forbidden to devout Hindus and pork to Muslims.

Rice is a common staple, especially in South India. Long-grain white rice varieties are the most popular, served hot with just about any 'wet' cooked dish.

Roti The generic term for Indian-style bread, the mainstay in the north. Roti is a name used interchangeably with chapati to describe the most common variety, the unleavened round bread made with whole-wheat flour and cooked on a *tawa* (hotplate).

Spices Christopher Columbus was actually searching for the black pepper of Kerala's Malabar Coast when he stumbled upon America. The region still grows the finest quality of the world's favourite spice, and it's integral to savoury Indian dishes.

6

Bridge to Stakna Gompa, Ladakh

gilded in the real thing). Even when crowded with pilgrims, the temple is peaceful, with birds singing outside and the sacred waters gently lapping against the godly abode.

Mumbai's Architecture

8 Mumbai has always absorbed everything in its midst and made it its own. The architectural result is a heady mix of buildings with countless influences. The art deco and modern towers give the city its cool, but it's the eclectic Victorian-era structures – the neo-Gothic, Indo-Saracenic and Gothic hodgepodge – that have come to define Mumbai. All those spires, gables, arches and onion domes, set off by palm trees and banyans, are fitting ornaments for this city.

Delhi

9 India's capital has had several incarnations over the last few thousand years, which partly explains why there's so much going on here. The big lures are the atmospheric ruins on every corner (the remains of

When to Go

LOW SEASON
(Apr–Jun)

➡ April is hot; May and June are scorching. Competitive hotel prices.

➡ From June, the monsoon sweeps from south to north, bringing humidity.

➡ Beat the heat in the cool hills.

SHOULDER
(Jul–Nov)

➡ Passes to Ladakh and the Himalaya open July to September.

➡ Monsoon rain persists till September.

➡ The southeast coast and southern Kerala see heavy rain from October to early December.

HIGH SEASON
(Dec–Mar)

➡ Pleasant weather; warm days, cool nights. Peak prices.

➡ December and January bring chilly nights in the north.

➡ Temperatures climb steadily from February.

seven historical cities) and the crumbling splendour of Old Delhi with the majestic Jama Masjid, Red Fort and other monuments of the historic Mughal capital. Plus, brilliant museums, spectacular food and Chandni Chowk – a 400-year-old bazaar designed by Shah Jahan's daughter, Jahanara.

Getting Around

Air Flights to most major centres and state capitals; cheap flights with budget airlines.

Bus Buses go everywhere; some destinations are served 24 hours but longer routes may have just one or two buses a day (typically early morning or afternoon/evening).

Train Frequent services to most destinations; inexpensive tickets available even on sleeper trains.

Goan Beaches

10 There might be no better place in the world to be lazy than on one of Goa's spectacular beaches. With palm-tree groves on one side of the white sands and gently lapping waves on the other, the best of the beaches live up to your image of a tropical paradise. But it's not an undiscovered one: the sands are also peppered with fellow travellers and beach-shack restaurants. Goa's treasures are

for social creatures and fans of creature comforts who like their seafood fresh and their holidays easy.

Holy Varanasi

11 Everyone in Varanasi seems to be dying or praying or hustling or cremating someone or swimming or laundering or washing buffaloes in the city's sewage-saturated Ganges. The goddess river will clean away your sins and help you escape from that tedious life-and-death cycle – and Varanasi is the place to take a sacred dip. So take a deep breath, put on a big smile for the ever-present touts, go to the holy water and get your karma in order.

Jaisalmer's Desert Mirage

12 Rising like a sandcastle from the deserts of Rajasthan, the 'Land of Kings', Jaisalmer's 12th-century citadel looks more like something from a dream than reality. The enormous golden sandstone fort, with its crenellated ramparts and undulating towers, is a fantastical structure, even while camouflaged against the desert sand. Inside, an ornate royal palace, fairytale *havelis* (traditional residences), intricately carved Jain temples and narrow lanes conspire to create the world's best place to get lost.

Best on Film

Fire (1996), *Earth* (1998) and *Water* (2005) The Deepa Mehta–directed trilogy was popular abroad, but controversial in India.

Pyaasa (Thirst; 1957) and Kaagaz Ke Phool (Paper Flowers; 1959) Two bittersweet films directed by and starring film legend Guru Dutt.

Gandhi (1982) The classic.

Best in Print

Midnight's Children (Salman Rushdie; 1980) Allegory about Independence and Partition.

The Guide and **The Painter of Signs** (RK Narayan; 1958, 1976) Classic novels set in the fictional town of Malgudi.

White Tiger (Aravind Adiga; 2008) Booker-winning novel about class struggle in globalised India.

Banks of the Ganges River, Varanasi

BRENT WINEBRENNER / GETTY IMAGES ©

Ubud rice terraces, Bali

CAPITAL
Jakarta

POPULATION
251 million

AREA
1.9 million sq km

OFFICIAL LANGUAGE
Bahasa Indonesia

Indonesia

From the western tip of Sumatra to the eastern edge of Papua, Indonesia offers endless exploration and infinite diversity. This unique land may well be the last great adventure on Earth.

Indonesia defines adventure: the only limitation is how many of its 17,000 islands you can reach before your visa expires. Following the equator, Indonesia stretches between Malaysia and Australia in one long intoxicating sweep. The nation's natural diversity is staggering, alluring and inspiring, from the snow-capped peaks in Papua, sandalwood forests in Sumba, dense jungle in Borneo and impossibly green rice paddies in Bali and Java. Indonesian reefs are a diver's fantasy while the surf breaks above are the best anywhere.

But even as the diversity on land and sea run like a traveller's fantasy playlist, it's the mash-up of people and cultures that's the most appealing. Bali justifiably leads off, but there are also Papua's stone-age folk, the many cultures of Flores, the artisans of Java, mall-rats of Jakarta and much more. Whether it's a dreamy remote beach, an orang-utan encounter or a Bali all-nighter, Indonesia scores.

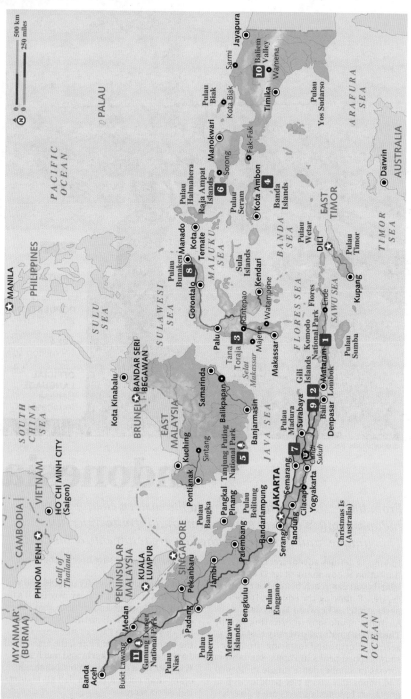

Indonesia's
Top Experiences

Komodo National Park

1 Recently declared one of the New Seven Wonders of Nature, Indonesia's best known national park comprises several islands and some of the country's richest waters within its 1817 sq km. Expect hulking mountainous islands blanketed in savannah, laced with trails and patrolled by the world's largest lizard – the komodo dragon. That's the big draw here, and it's easy to spot them, but there's also big nature beneath the water's surface where kaleidoscopic bait balls draw big pelagics like sharks and mantas in numbers you just won't see anywhere else in Indonesia.

Gili Islands

2 One of Indonesia's greatest joys is hopping on a fast boat from busy Bali and arriving on one the irresistible Gili Islands. Think sugar-white sand, bathtub-warm, turquoise waters and wonderful beach bungalows just begging you to extend your stay. Not to mention the coral reefs – which haven't looked this good in years and are teeming with sharks, rays and turtles. Add in the dining and nightlife on Gili Trawangan, and you understand why long time Gili lovers call these islands Never Never Land.

Gili Trawangan, Gili Islands

CARLINA TETERIS / GETTY IMAGES ©

Tana Toraja

3 Life revolves around death in this countryside of rice terraces, boat-shaped roofs and doe-eyed buffalo. Tana Torajan funeral ceremonies last days, and involve countless animal sacrifices for the upper classes. The festivities start with bet-heavy bull fights then lead into days of prayer, feasting and dances. At the end, the deceased is brought to their resting place. This could be carved into a cliff-face and fronted by their own wooden effigy, in a cave where relatives can visit the bones, or in hanging graves suspended from cave edges.

if Indonesia were 100 people

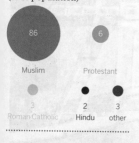

41 would be Javanese
15 would be Sundanese
3 would be Madurese
41 would be other

belief systems

(% of population)

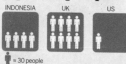

86 Muslim
6 Protestant
3 Roman Catholic
2 Hindu
3 other

population per sq km

INDONESIA   UK   US

≈ 30 people

Banda Islands

4 Here is a rich and intoxicating cocktail of history, culture and raw natural beauty. The Banda Islands – a remote archipelago draped in jungle and spice trees, fringed with white sand, surrounded by clear blue seas and pristine reefs – kick-started colonisation and helped shape the modern world. Fly to the capital – Bandaneira – from Ambon, stroll the wide avenues, admire late colonial relics, then charter a boat to the outer islands, where village life is warm and easy, and stress peels from your soul by the second.

Tanjung Puting National Park

5 *African Queen* meets *National Geographic* in this ever-popular national park, where you can not only get up close and personal with Asia's largest ape, the orang-utan, but also cruise the jungle in high style aboard your own private houseboat. The typically three-day journey takes you on a round trip up the Sungai Sekonyer to Camp Leakey, with stops at several orang-utan feeding stations and plenty of impromptu wildlife spotting. The experience manages to be authentic adventure travel, and is open to anyone.

Raja Ampat Islands

6 The remote, still-being-discovered Raja Ampat Islands off Papua's northwest tip are a diver's dream. Raja Ampat is home to the greatest diversity of marine life on the planet, from giant manta rays and epaulette sharks that use their fins to 'walk' on the sea floor, to myriad multi-coloured nudibranches ('sea slugs'), fantastic pristine coral, and every size, shape

Orang-Utans

Orang-utans, the world's largest arboreal mammal, once swung through the forest canopy throughout all of Southeast Asia but are now found only in Sumatra and Borneo. Researchers fear that the few that do remain will not survive the continued loss of habitat to logging and agriculture.

While orang-utans are extremely intelligent animals, their way of life isn't compatible with a shrinking forest. Orang-utans are mostly vegetarians; they get big and strong (some males weigh up to 90kg) from a diet that would make a Californian hippie proud: fruit, shoots, leaves, nuts and tree bark, which they grind up with their powerful jaws and teeth. They occasionally also eat insects, eggs and small mammals.

The two classic places to view orang-utans in Indonesia are Bukit Lawang on Sumatra and Tanjung Puting National Park on Kalimantan.

Food & Drink

Babi guling Spit-roast pig stuffed with chilli, turmeric, garlic and ginger.

Gado gado Very popular dish of steamed bean sprouts and various vegetables, served with a spicy peanut sauce.

Ketoprak Noodles, bean sprouts and tofu with soy and peanut sauce.

Krupuk Shrimp with cassava flour, or fish flakes with rice dough, cut into slices and fried to a crisp.

Nasi campur The national dish – steamed rice topped with a little bit of everything (some vegetables, some meat, a bit of fish, a *krupuk* or two).

Nasi goreng Fried rice.

Sate Small pieces of various types of meat grilled on a skewer and served with peanut sauce.

DENNIS WALTON / GETTY IMAGES ©

Cliff tombs and effigies, Tana Toraja

and hue of fish you can imagine. The snorkelling is great too, and the above-water scenery is just as unique.

Candi Sukuh

7 There are grander temples and larger monuments scattered across Indonesia but Candi Sukuh is something else. Perched halfway up a volcano in central Java, this remarkable temple enjoys a spectacular position overlooking the Solo plain. So many of the carvings here display signs of a fertility cult that the temple has been dubbed the 'erotic' temple. Though constructed in the 15th century, stylistically the sculptures and carvings appear to hark back to a much earlier time.

Pulau Bunaken

8 You know those gardens that seem to have hundreds of plant species artistically thriving together in small decorative plots? Now imagine that done with coral in every colour from black and white to intense purples. Next cover it all in clear water teeming with iridescent fish, some in thick schools fluttering like sprinkles of sunlight. The water around Pulau Bunaken is more beautiful than you

When to Go

HIGH SEASON
(Jul & Aug)

➡ Tourist numbers surge, from Bali to Sulawesi and beyond.

➡ Rates can spike by 50%.

➡ Dry season except in Maluku and Papua, which are rainy.

SHOULDER
(May, Jun & Sep)

➡ Dry season outside Maluku & Papua.

➡ Best weather in Java, Bali and Lombok (dry, not so humid).

➡ You can travel more spontaneously.

LOW SEASON
(Oct–Apr)

➡ Wet season in Java, Bali and Lombok.

➡ Dry season (best for diving) in Maluku and Papua.

➡ Easy to find last-minute deals (except at Christmas and New Years).

could imagine and yet it gets better: turtles the size of armchairs, reef sharks and, if you're lucky, dolphins and dugongs that swim casually through the scene.

Bali

9 Impossibly green rice terraces, pulse-pounding surf, enchanting Hindu temple ceremonies, mesmerising dance perform-ances, ribbons of beaches, charming people: there are as many images of Bali as there are flowers on the ubiquitous frangipani trees. The artistic swirl of Ubud is a counterpoint to misty treks amid the volcanoes. Mellow beach towns like Amed, Lovi-na and Pemuteran are found right round the coast, and just offshore is the laid-back idyll of Nusa Lembongan.

Best on Film

Cowboys in Paradise (2009) Controversial documentary that made headlines for its unflinching portrait of real-life gigolos in Bali.

Gie (2005) The story of Soe Hok Gie, an ethnic Chinese antidictatorship activist.It was submitted for consideration in the Best Foreign Film category of the Academy Awards.

Best in Print

Rimbaud in Java (Jamie James; 2011) Recreates poet Arthur Rimbaud's Java escape in 1876.

Four Corners (Kira Salak; 2001) The author ventures to remotest Papua and New Guinea.

Stranger in the Forest (Eric Hansen; 1988) Possibly the first non-local to walk across Borneo.

Krakatoa – The Day the World Exploded (Simon Winchester; 2003) History, geology and politics, centred on the 1883 eruption.

Getting Around

Air The domestic-flight network is growing, but schedules and rate are in a constant state of flux.

Boat Sumatra, Java, Bali and Nusa Tenggara are connected by ferries that run daily or several times a week.

Bus There's a wide variety of bus services, with everything from air-con de-luxe buses that speed across the major islands to *trek* (trucks) with wooden seats that rumble along remote dirt roads.

Car & Motorcycle Both cars and motorcycles can be readily hired. Hiring a van with driver is also common.

Baliem Valley

10 Trekking in Papua's Baliem Valley takes you into the world of the Dani, a mountain people whose traditional culture still stands proud despite changes wrought by Indonesian government and Christian missionaries. You'll sleep in their villages of grass-roofed huts, climb narrow jungle trails, traverse panoramic open hillsides, cross raging rivers by wob-bly hanging footbridges, and be charmed by the locals' smiles. Tip for those bridges: don't look at the water, but do look where you're putting your feet!

Gunung Leuser National Park

11 This vast slab of steamy tropical jungle draped across the mountains and valleys of northern Sumatra is filled with cheeping, squeaking, growling animal life. It's a naturalist's and adventure traveller's fantasy. Sitting pretty beside a chocolate coloured river, the village of Ketambe is a relaxing place to rest up for a few days. More importantly, it makes a great base camp for multiday hiking expeditions in search of howling gibbons, lethargic orangutans and maybe even a tiger or two.

Dani man, Baliem Valley

KARL LEHMANN / GETTY IMAGES ©

Market stall, Shiraz

CAPITAL
Tehran

POPULATION
79.9 million

AREA
1.6 million sq km

OFFICIAL LANGUAGE
Persian

Iran

If travel is most rewarding when it surprises, then Iran, with its bazaars, mighty deserts and sublime architecture, might just be the most rewarding destination on Earth.

Before you come to Iran, you might be thinking the main reasons to visit are because it's a bit adventurous and there's a lot to see from the years when Persia was a great world power. At some levels you'd be right.

Iran's sights will put you in the footsteps of some of history's most outstanding figures. And certainly you won't find yourself crowded out of any sights, which is fun.

The highlights, together with the atmospheric teahouses, bustling bazaars, deserts punctuated by historic oases and rugged mountain ranges, give Iran more than its fair share of fantastic places to see. But to think of Iran only in terms of 'sights' is to miss the real story.

If you like people, you'll like Iran. The Iranians, a nation made up of numerous ethnic groups and influenced over thousands of years by Greek, Arab, Turkic and Mongol occupiers, are endlessly welcoming and eager to show off and explain their intricate culture.

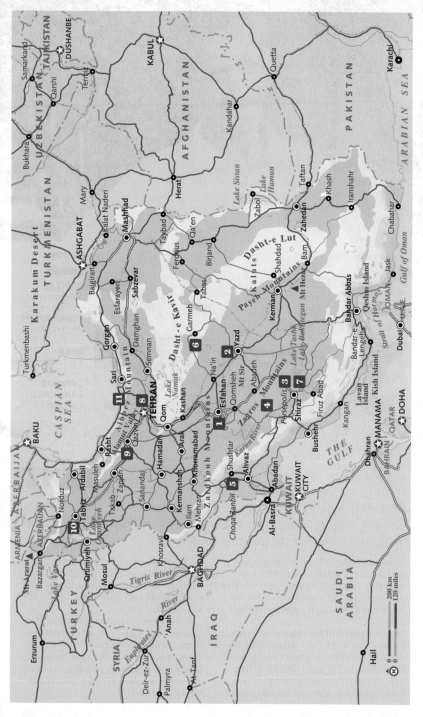

Iran's
Top Experiences

Esfahan

1 There are moments in travel that will long stay with you, and your first sight of Esfahan's majestic Naqsh-e Jahan (Imam) Square is one of them. For this square is home to arguably the most majestic collection of buildings in the Islamic world: the perfectly proportioned blue-tiled dome of the Masjed-e Shah, the supremely elegant Masjed-e Sheikh Lotfollah and the indulgent and lavishly decorated Ali Qapu Palace. Robert Byron ranked '...Isfahan among those rarer places, like Athens or Rome, which are the common refreshment of humanity'.And as the Persian proverb says: 'Esfahan is half of the world'.

Yazd

2 Few places have adapted to their environment as well as the desert city of Yazd. It's a gem of winding lanes, blue-tiled domes, soaring minarets, covered bazaars, and fine old courtyard homes topped by *badgirs* (windtowers) and watered by ingenious *qanats* (underground water channels). Several of these homes have been restored and converted into marvellously evocative traditional hotels and teahouses.

Masjed-e Sheikh Lotfollah, Esfahan

TUNART / GETTY IMAGES ©

Ancient Persepolis

3 The artistic harmony of the monumental stair-cases, imposing gateways and exquisite reliefs leaves you in little doubt that its prime Persepolis was at the centre of the known world. Built by kings Darius and Xerxes as the ceremonial capital of the Achaemenid empire, a visit to the World Heritage–listed ruins of the city also testifies to Alexander the Great's merciless destruction of that empire.

Nomads of the Zagros

4 About 2 million Iranians from several different ethnic groups still live a no-madic existence, travelling with their goats in spring and autumn in search of pasture. Qashqa'i and Bakhtiyari nomads spend the summer months in the Zagros Mountains, before heading down to the coast for the winter. You can get a taste of nomad life on a day trip from Shiraz, or stay with the Khamseh (and eat their delicious hand-made yoghurt) in the hills above Bavanat .

if Iran were 100 people

61 would be Persian
16 would be Azari
10 would be Kurdish
6 would be Lor
2 would be Turkmen & other Turkic groups
5 would be other

belief systems
(% of population)

90
Shia Muslim

9
Sunni Muslim

1
other

population per sq km

IRAN   UK   USA

♦ ≈ 16 people

Choqa Zanbil

5 Even if you don't like ancient ruins, the great bulk, semidesert isolation and fascinating back story make the Choqa Zanbil ziggurat one of the most impressive historical sites in a region full of them. Built by the Elamites in the 13th century BC, it was 'lost' under the sands in the 7th century BC and only rediscovered during a 1935 aerial survey by a British oil company. Now excavated, some of the bricks look as if they came out of the kiln last week.

Desert Homestays

6 The welcome is rarely warmer than in the vast, empty silence of Iran's two great deserts. Garmeh is the oasis village of your dreams, with a crumbling castle, swaying date palms and the sound of spring water. It's the sort of place you come for one night and stay four. Nearby Farahzad and tiny Toudeshk Cho, between Esfahan and Na'in, also offer memorable desert-style family homestays; think beds on the floor, basic bathrooms and fresh, delicious home-cooked food.

Persian Carpets

The best-known Iranian cultural export, the Persian carpet, is far more than just a floor covering to an Iranian. A Persian carpet is a display of wealth, an investment, an integral aspect of religious and cultural festivals, and part of everyday life.

In general, the designs are classified as either 'tribal' or 'city' carpets. Tribal designs vary greatly depending on their origin, but are typically less ornate. City carpets are the classic Persian rugs, usually highly ornate floral designs around one or more medallions. Usually the name of a carpet indicates where it was made or where the design originated.

Iran's bazaars are home to a dizzying array of Persian carpets and kilims. The bazaars in Esfahan, Shiraz and Tehran are the best places to buy and the experience of shopping, haggling and eventually buying is a memorable part of travelling in Iran.

Food & Drink

Almost every meal in Iran is accompanied by *nun* (bread) and/or *berenj* (rice). Most main-dish options will be some sort of kabab.

Bakhtiyari kabab Lamb chops and chicken, the king of kababs.

Barbari Crisp and salty like like Turkish bread.

Chelo kabab Any kind of kabab served with *chelo* (boiled or steamed rice); the default option will be *kubide* (ground meat) if you don't specify.

Juje kabab Grilled chicken pieces marinated in somaq.

Lavash A flat, thin *nun*, commonly eaten at breakfast.

Sangak Long, thick bread baked on a bed of stones to give it its characteristic dimpled appearance.

Taftun Crisp *nun* with a ribbed surface.

KAMRAN JEBREILI / GETTY IMAGES ©

Qashqa'i wedding ceremony

The Poets of Shiraz

7 Iranians like to say that even in the poorest home you'll find two books: a Quran and the poetry of Hafez. It's appropriate for a country whose most celebrated sons are poets, and where almost every person can quote their favourite millennium-old man of words. In Shiraz, the city of nightingales and gardens, the tombs of Hafez and Sa'di draw pilgrims from around the country. Join them as they linger over tea, reciting the works of their heroes.

Tehran Cafes & Galleries

8 Bustling Tehran can be intimidating but it does have its appeal. Beyond the museums and palaces are a range of hip cafes and contemporary art galleries that provide an entree into a side of life you otherwise only hear about. Sit over coffee for a while and you'll end up in conversation, or wander through the galleries and theatre in and around Park-e Honar Mandan.

When to Go

HIGH SEASON
(Mar-May)

➡ Ideal temperatures in most of Iran.

➡ Prices are highest and crowds biggest during No Ruz (21 March to 3 April), especially at Esfahan, Shiraz, Yazd and the Persian Gulf coast.

➡ Prices in hotels go up in April.

SHOULDER
(Jun-Oct)

➡ Warmer weather in June means fewer travellers.

➡ September and especially October temperatures more moderate than summer and prices slightly lower than March to May.

LOW SEASON
(Nov-Feb)

➡ Extreme cold, especially in the northeast and west, during winter (November to February).

➡ Mountain roads can be impassable.

➡ Hotel prices are discounted by 10% to 50%.

Hiking among the Castles of the Assassins

9 The fabled Alamut Valley offers a tempting invitation to hike, explore and reflect among the fabled Castles of the Assassins. Nestled on widely spread rocky knolls and pinnacles lie the shattered remnants of more than 50 ruined fortresses that were once home to the medieval world's most feared religious cult. Choose a day hike from Qazvin or more extensive wanderings from Gazor Khan – a full, mule-accompanied trans-Alborz crossing to the Caspian hinterland.

Best on Film

A Time for Drunken Horses (2000) Bahman Ghobadi's look at Kurdish orphans and smugglers on the Iraqi border.

Children of Heaven (1997) Majid Majidi's tale of two poor children losing a pair of shoes.

Offside (2006) Jafar Panahi's story of women spectators banned from watching football.

Taste of Cherry (1997) Abbas Kairostami looks at the taboo subject of suicide.

Best in Print

All the Shah's Men (Stephen Kinzer) Page-turning true story of the CIA's 1953 coup in Iran.

Journey of the Magi (Paul William Roberts) Thought-provoking journey 'in search of the birth of Jesus'.

Neither East Nor West (Christiane Bird) American woman's account of her travels in Iran.

The Valleys of the Assassins: and Other Persian Travels (Freya Stark) A classic travelogue – challenging perceptions and illuminating reality.

Getting Around

Air Domestic air fares in Iran are low and flights on most routes are frequent.

Bus More than 20 bus companies offer thousands of services on buses that are cheap, comfortable and frequent.

Metro The Tehran Metro is growing and Mashhad's first Metro line is operating

Minibus Minibuses are often used for shorter distances linking larger cities and towns to surrounding villages. Sometimes they're an alternative to the bus, but usually there's no choice; just take whatever is going your way.

Train Travelling by train is an inexpensive way to get around Iran and meet Iranians.

Bazaar Shopping

10 In the age of the superstore, most Iranians continue to rely on these mazes of covered lanes, *madrasehs* and caravanserais for much of their shopping. Tehran, Esfahan, Shiraz and Kashan all have atmospheric bazaars where you can browse beneath domed ceilings, dodge motorcycles and stop in tiny teahouses for a hot brew and *qalyan* (water pipe). But perhaps the greatest bazaar is the World Heritage–listed Bazar-e Tabriz, once among the most important trading centres on the Silk Road.

Skiing the Alborz Mountains

11 Think Iran and you're unlikely to think skiing, but there are more than 20 ski fields in the country. Most of the action is conveniently concentrated around Tehran. The Dizin and Shemshak resorts are the pick, with steep downhills and plenty of untracked powder to keep skiers of all levels interested. Chalets and ski passes are inexpensive compared with Western countries, and the slopes are more gender-equal than most of Iran – expect to see exposed female hair.

Ruins of Alamut Castle, near Qazvin

SIMON RICHMOND / GETTY IMAGES ©

Rabban Hormizd Monastery, Al-Kosh

CAPITAL
Baghdad

POPULATION
31.9 million

AREA
438,317 sq km

**OFFICIAL
LANGUAGES**
Arabic,
Kurdish

Iraq

One of the cradles of civilisation, Iraq has, despite its recent troubles and persistent bad press, a wealth of human and cultural riches to reveal.

Torn between its glorious past as the cradle of civilisation and the turmoil of its recent bloody history, Iraq is a country of contradictions. It is the birthplace of writing and the legendary home of the Garden of Eden, Hanging Gardens of Babylon and the Epic of Gilgamesh. But it is also a place of unimaginable horrors.

Since the 2003 US-led invasion, Iraq has been caught in a cycle of violence. The country has since intermittently hovered on the cusp of a new beginning. Even so,

with the exception of Iraqi Kurdistan, much of Iraq remains too dangerous for independent travellers. The future is far from certain, but with its rich history and warm hospitality, Iraq could become one of the great travel destinations of the Middle East, *insha' Allah*.

Iraqi Kurdistan's slogan, 'The Other Iraq', could not be more fitting. This is the Iraq you don't see in the news. It's a safe and tranquil oasis with happening cities, soaring mountains and welcoming people.

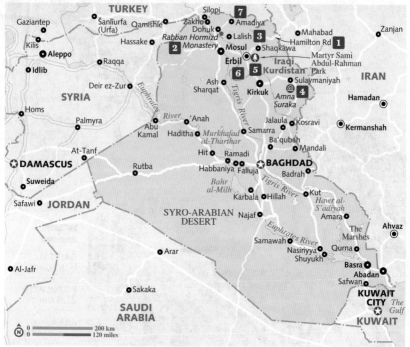

Iraq's
Top Experiences

Travelling Hamilton Road

1 Be awed by the mountain grandeur as you travel the impressive Hamilton Road that passes through the northeast corner of Iraqi Kurdistan, an unheralded area of beauty marked by cascading waterfalls, soaring snow-capped mountains, deep gorges cut by raging rivers, rolling green hills and lush valleys. Gali Ali Beg Canyon, a Grand Canyon equivalent for the Middle East, extends 12km between the Korak and Bradost mountains and is cut by two rivers that form to create the Great Zab River.

Rabban Hormizd Monastery

2 Melting like a chameleon into the cliff face is the 7th-century Rabban Hormizd Monastery. The large complex is still occupied by a handful of Chaldean Monks and as such a large chunk of it is out of bounds, but you can visit the chapel, pay your respects at the tomb of Abba Gabriel Darnbo, who did much to revitalise the monastery after it was largely abandoned in the 19th century, and explore the web of tunnels, caves and shrines that lead off from the back of the chapel. The surrounding cliffs are also full of little caves, some of which were once used to house shrines.

Lalish

3 Hidden in a deep, green valley, Lalish is the most sacred place on earth for practitioners of the Yazidi faith. At least once in their lifetime, each Yazidi must make a pilgrimage to Lalish, where their chief deity Malak Taus – the peacock angel – first landed. Some also believe that Noah's ark came to rest here. The focal point of Lalish is the Sanctuary, a temple topped by two large pyramids. The entrance is guarded by a stone relief of a black snake slithering into a hole in the wall, which some believe symbolises a snake that used its body to plug a leak in Noah's ark.

Amna Suraka

4 The Amna Suraka, Kurdish for Red Security, was once a house of unspeakable horrors. Under Saddam Hussein's regime, this imposing red building served as the northern headquarters of the notorious Iraqi Intelligence Service, or the Mukhabarat. Thousands of people, mainly Kurds, were imprisoned and tortured here. Many more simply vanished. In 1991 the Kurdish Peshmerga attacked and liberated the prison. In 2003 Hero Ibrahim Ahmed, wife of Iraqi President Jalal Talabani, spearheaded a plan to turn the building into the country's first war-crimes museum. The Amna Suraka now stands out as the most impressive museum in Iraq.

Martyr Sami Abdul-Rahman Park

5 Also known as Erbil Park, Martyr Sami Abdul-Rahman Park is one of the most beautiful urban spaces in Iraq. This oasis of fountains, lakes and gardens was built over what was previously a military base for Saddam Hussein's feared 5th Corps Army. On Fridays the park is packed with young couples, families enjoying picnics and lots and lots of boisterous wedding parties. The large lake in the centre of the park rents swan-shaped paddleboats and speedboat rides. Nearby is a huge children's playground, and off to one side are football pitches and a skateboard/BMX park.

if Iraq were 100 people

77 would be Arab
18 would be Kurdish
5 would be Turkoman, Assyrian or other

belief systems
(% of population)

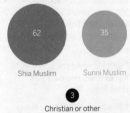

62 Shia Muslim
35 Sunni Muslim
3 Christian or other

population per sq km

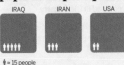

IRAQ   IRAN   USA

♦ = 15 people

When to Go

MAR

➡ Join the locals in welcoming in the Kurdish New Year with bonfires, picnics and dancing.

APR

➡ Snow-dusted mountains, flower-covered valleys, Iraqi Kurdistan looks good right now!

OCT

➡ Goodbye summer heat, hello autumnal colours and the first snowfall in the mountains.

Who are the Yazidis?

The Yazidis is a misunderstood, long-persecuted Kurdish sect that practises Yazidism, a religion that is an amalgam of Islam, Christianity, Judaism and Zoroastrian. There are about 500,000 Yazidis in the world, most in Iraqi Kurdistan. Most speak Kurdish Kurmanji.

The Yazidis believe a supreme god created the universe with seven angels, the chief among them Malak Taus, the peacock angel. He fell from grace but was later pardoned, leading many people to unfairly label Yazidis as 'devil worshippers'. Yazidis regard themselves as descendents of Adam, not Eve. Similar to Muslims, Yazidis pray five times a day.

Yazidis believe they will be reincarnated until they reach soul purity to enter heaven. They have two holy books, the Mishefa Res (black book) and the Kitab al-Jilwa (Book of Revelation).

Food & Drink

Baba ghanoog Purée of grilled aubergines (eggplants) with tahina and olive oil.

Fattoosh Toasted khobz, tomatoes, onions and mint leaves, sometimes served with a smattering of tangy pomegranate syrup.

Felafel Mashed chickpeas and spices rolled into balls and deep-fried.

İskender kebaps Döner kebab on a bed of pide bread with a side serving of yogurt.

Quzi-sham A biryani-like dish covered in fried pastry.

Tea Usually taken sweet and without milk.

Qaysari Bazaar, Erbil

Erbil's Shopping Malls

6 One of the oldest continuously inhabited cities in the world, Erbil is today the fastest-growing city in Iraq, with dozens of glossy shopping malls, amusement parks, five-star hotels, glass office blocks and a flash new airport. The hyper-glossy, hyper-huge Family Mall even contains an ice-skating rink – not to mention a 9D cinema (that's, well, we've no idea really). Clearly Erbil thinks itself the new Dubai and with the energy on the streets and the money to back it all up, who's to say it's not.

Amadiya

7 Like a village in the clouds, Amadiya – or Amedi – is built on a high plateau 1200m above sea level. The village setting is fabulously picturesque, surrounded by magnificent mountains and endless green valleys. A gate is all that is left of the once high citadel walls. The most visible landmark is the 30m high minaret of Amadiya Mosque. It's about 400 years old and pockmarked with bullet holes from the Kurdish Civil War.

Getting Around

Air Iraqi Airways flies several domestic routes, but it is so unreliable it's not worth it.

Bus Iraq's bus transport network is very poor. The few routes that exist are crowded and unsafe.

Taxi Taxis are the main mode of public transport in Iraq. In cities they are cheap and plentiful. For intercity travel within Iraqi Kurdistan, you have two choices: private taxi or cheaper, shared taxi. Shared taxis depart and arrive from a city 'garage', or large parking lot; drivers will be standing outside their vehicle, yelling the name of their destination. Shared taxis leave when they are full.

Doolin, County Clare

CAPITAL
Dublin

POPULATION
4.8 million

AREA
70,273 sq km

OFFICIAL LANGUAGES
English, Irish

Ireland

A small island with a big reputation, helped along by a timeless, age-caressed landscape and a fascinating, friendly people, whose lyrical nature is expressed in the warmth of their welcome.

You don't have to look far to find the postcard-perfect Ireland: it exists along the peninsulas of the southwest, the brooding loneliness of Connemara and the dramatic wildness of County Donegal. You'll find it in the lakelands of Counties Leitrim and Roscommon and the undulating hills of the southeast. Ireland has modernised dramatically, but some things never change. Brave the raging Atlantic on a crossing to Skellig Michael or spend a summer's evening in the yard of a thatched-cottage pub and you'll experience an Ireland that has changed little in generations, and is likely the Ireland you most came to see.

Ireland's history and culture present themselves everywhere: from the breathtaking monuments of prehistoric Ireland at Brú na Bóinne to a traditional music session in a west-Ireland pub.

Céad míle fáilte – a hundred thousand welcomes. It seems excessive, but in Ireland, excess is encouraged.

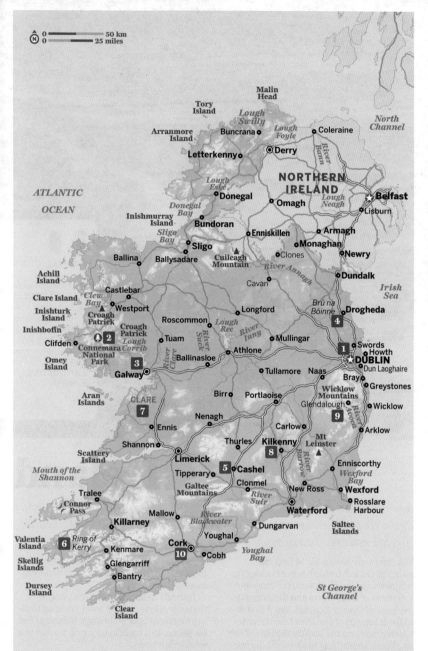

Ireland's
Top Experiences

Dublin

1 Ireland's capital and largest city by some stretch is the main gateway into the country, but it has enough attractions to keep visitors mesmerised for at least a few days. From world-class museums and entertainment to superb dining and top-grade hotels, Dublin has all the baubles of a major international metropolis. But the real clinchers are Dubliners themselves, who are friendlier, more easy-going and welcoming than the burghers of virtually any other European capital. And it's the home of Guinness.

Connemara, County Galway

2 A filigreed coast of tiny coves and beaches is the Connemara Peninsula's beautiful border with the wild waters of the Atlantic. Wandering characterful roads brings you from one village to another, each with trad pubs and restaurants serving seafood chowder cooked from recipes that are family secrets. Inland, the scenic drama is even greater. In fantastically desolate valleys, green hills, yellow wildflowers and wild streams reflecting the blue sky provide elemental beauty. Rambles take you far from others, back to a simpler time.

Bachelor's Walk, O'Connell Bridge and River Liffey, Dublin

Galway City

3 One word to describe Galway city? Craic! Ireland's liveliest city literally hums through the night at music-filled pubs where you can hear three old guys playing spoons and fiddles, or a hot, young up-and-coming band. Join the locals as they bounce from place to place, never knowing what fun lies ahead but certain of the possibility. Add in local bounty such as the famous oysters and nearby adventure in the Connemara Peninsula and the Aran Islands, and the fun never ends.

if Ireland were 100 people

85 would be Irish
10 would be other white
2 would be Asian
1 would be black
2 would be mixed and other

belief systems

(% of population)

85 Roman Catholic
3 Church of Ireland
1 Muslim
3 other Christian
8 other or none

population per sq km

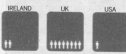

IRELAND   UK   USA

♟ ≈ 32 people

Brú na Bóinne, County Meath

4 Looking at once ancient and yet eerily futuristic, Newgrange's immense, round, white-stone walls topped by a grass dome is one of the most extraordinary sights you'll ever see. Part of the vast Neolithic necropolis Brú na Bóinne (the Boyne Palace), it contains Ireland's finest Stone Age passage tomb, predating the pyramids by some six centuries. Most extraordinary of all is the tomb's precise alignment with the sun at the time of the winter solstice.

Rock of Cashel, County Tipperary

5 Soaring up from the green Tipperary pastures, this ancient fortress takes your breath away at first sight. The seat of kings and churchmen who ruled over the region for more than a thousand years, it rivalled Tara as a centre of power in Ireland for 400 years. Entered through the 15th-century Hall of the Vicars Choral, its impervious walls guard an awesome enclosure with a complete round tower, a 13th-century Gothic cathedral and the most magnificent 12th-century Romanesque chapel in Ireland.

Ring of Kerry

6 Driving around the Ring of Kerry is an unforgettable experience in itself, but you don't need to limit yourself to the main route. Along this 179km loop around the Iveragh Peninsula there are countless opportunities for detours. Near Killorglin, it's a short

The Book of Kells

More than half a million Dublin visitors stop in each year to see Trinity College's top show-stopper, the world-famous *Book of Kells*. This illuminated manuscript, dating from around AD 800 and therefore one of the oldest books in the world, was probably produced by monks at St Colmcille's Monastery on the remote island of Iona. Repeated looting by marauding Vikings forced the monks to flee to the temporary safety of Kells, County Meath, in AD 806, along with their masterpiece. Around 850 years later, the book was brought to the college for safekeeping and has remained here since.

If it were merely words, the *Book of Kells* would simply be a very old book – it's the extensive and amazingly complex illustrations that make it so wonderful.

Food & Drink

Meat and seafood Irish meals are usually meat-based, with beef, lamb and pork common options. Seafood, long neglected, is widely available in restaurants and is often excellent, especially in the west.

Potatoes However much we'd like to disprove it, potatoes are still paramount here. The mash dishes colcannon and champ (with cabbage and spring onion, respectively) are two of the tastiest recipes in the country.

Soda bread The most famous Irish bread, and one of the signature tastes of Ireland. Irish flour is soft and doesn't take well to yeast as a raising agent, so 19th-century Irish bakers leavened their bread with bicarbonate of soda. Combined with buttermilk, it's superbly tasty, and is often on the breakfast menus at B&Bs.

Stout While Guinness is synonymous with stout the world over, few outside Ireland realise that there are two other major producers competing for the favour of the Irish drinker: Murphy's and Beamish & Crawford, both based in Cork city.

Cliffs of Moher, County Clare

hop up to the beautiful, little-known Cromane Peninsula. Between Portmagee and Waterville, you can explore the Skellig Ring. The peninsula's interior offers mesmerising mountain views. And that's just for starters. Wherever your travels take you, remember to charge your camera battery!

County Clare

7 Bathed in the golden glow of the late-afternoon sun, the iconic Cliffs of Moher are but one of the splendours of County Clare. From a boat bobbing below, the towering stone faces have a jaw-dropping beauty that's enlivened by scores of sea birds, including cute little puffins. Down south in Loop Head, pillars of rock towering above the sea have abandoned stone cottages whose very existence is inexplicable. All along the coast are little villages like trad-session-filled Ennistymon and the surfer mecca of Lahinch.

When to Go

HIGH SEASON (Jun–mid-Sep)

➡ Weather at its best.

➡ Accommodation rates at their highest (especially in August).

➡ Tourist peak in Dublin, Kerry, southern and western coasts.

SHOULDER (Easter to end May, mid-Sep to end Oct)

➡ Weather often good, sun and rain in May. 'Indian summers' and often warm in September.

➡ Summer crowds and accommodation rates drop off.

LOW SEASON (Nov–Feb)

➡ Reduced opening hours from October to Easter; some destinations shut.

➡ Cold and wet weather throughout the country; fog can reduce visibility.

➡ Big city attractions operate as normal.

Kilkenny City

8 From its regal castle to its soaring medieval cathedral, Kilkenny exudes a permanence and culture that have made it an unmissable stop on journeys to the south and west. Its namesake county boasts scores of artisans and craftspeople and you can browse their wares at Kilkenny's classy shops and boutiques. Chefs eschew Dublin in order to be close to the source of Kilkenny's wonderful produce and you can enjoy the local brewery's namesake brew at scores of delightful pubs.

Best on Film

The Wind That Shakes the Barley (2006) Two brothers from County Cork are divided by the Irish War of Independence and the Civil War. Winner of the Palm d'Or.

My Left Foot (1989) Daniel Day-Lewis portrays Christy Brown, an Irishman with cerebral palsy who overcame extreme adversity to become a well-known writer and artist.

The Magdalene Sisters (2002) The tough story of the brutal treatment of young girls sent to infamous industrial schools.

Best in Print

Dubliners (James Joyce; 1914) A collection of short stories still as poignant and relevant today as when they were written.

Paddy Clarke Ha Ha Ha (Roddy Doyle; 1993) Wonderful portrait of a 10-year-old boy's trials that was made into a popular film.

The Gathering (Anne Enright; 2007) Powerful account of alcoholism and domestic abuse in an Irish family.

Getting Around

Boat Ireland's offshore islands are all served by boat, including the Aran and Skellig Islands to the west, the Saltee Islands to the southeast, and Tory and Rathlin Islands to the north.

Bus An extensive network of public and private buses makes them the most cost-effective way to get around, with service to and from most inhabited area.

Car The most convenient way to explore Ireland's every nook and cranny. Cars can be hired in every major town and city; drive on the left.

Train A limited network links Dublin to all major urban centres, including Belfast in Northern Ireland. Expensive if you're on a budget.

Glendalough, County Wicklow

9 St Kevin knew a thing or two about magical locations. When he chose a remote cave on a glacial lake nestled at the base of a forested valley as his monastic retreat, he inadvertently founded a settlement that would later prove to be one of Ireland's most dynamic universities and, in our time, one of the country's most beautiful ruined sites. The remains of the settlement (including an intact round tower), coupled with the stunning scenery, are unforgettable.

Cork City

10 The Republic's second city is second only in terms of size – in every other respect it will bear no competition. A tidy, compact city centre is home to an enticing collection of art galleries, museums and – most especially – places to eat. From cheap cafes to top-end gourmet restaurants, Cork City excels, although it's hardly a surprise given the county's exceptional foodie reputation. At the heart of it is the simply wonderful English Market, a covered produce market that is an attraction unto itself.

English Market, Cork City

TRISH PUNCH / GETTY IMAGES ©

Dome of the Rock, Temple Mount, Jerusalem

CAPITALS
Jerusalem
Ramallah

POPULATION
12.1 million

AREA
26,990 sq km

OFFICIAL LANGUAGES
Hebrew, Arabic

Israel & the Palestinian Territories

At the intersection of Asia, Europe and Africa, the region of Israel and the Palestinian Territories has been a meeting place of cultures, empires and religions since history began.

The Holy Land, cradle of Judaism and Christianity and sacred to Muslims and Baha'is, offers visitors the opportunity to immerse themselves in the richness and variety of their own religious traditions and to discover the beliefs of other faiths.

Human beings have lived in Israel and the Palestinian Territories since long before recorded history, and thanks to the painstaking work of archaeologists, you can explore and ponder what they left behind. After you've admired the 10,000-year-old mud-brick relics of Jericho,

you might find inspiration in Jerusalem's City of David, which dates from the time of Kings David and Solomon.

Distances are short, so you can relax on a Mediterranean beach one day, spend the next floating in the Dead Sea and the day after that scuba diving in the Red Sea.

In 2012 the Palestinian Territories were elevated to a 'non-member observer state' by the United Nations but as yet a resolution of the Israeli-Palestinian conflict remains only a vague hope.

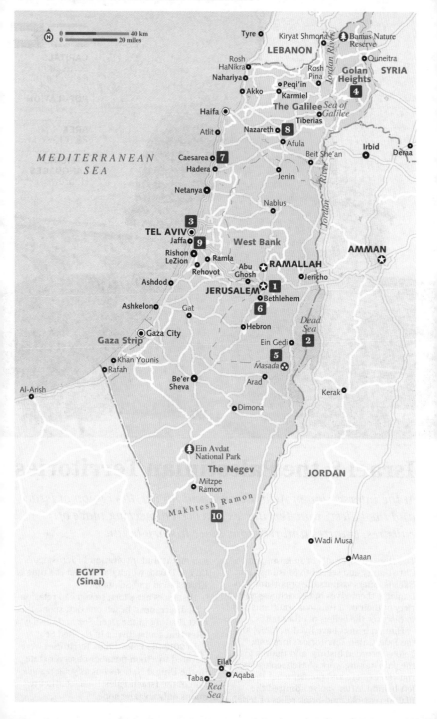

Tyre

Kiryat Shmona

Banias Nature Reserve

LEBANON

Quneitra

Rosh HaNikra

Rosh Pina

Golan Heights

SYRIA

Nahariya

Peqi'in

4

Akko

Karmiel

The Galilee

Sea of Galilee

Haifa

Tiberias

Atlit

Nazareth **8**

Irbid

Dera'a

7

Caesarea

Afula

Beit She'an

Hadera

Jenin

M E D I T E R R A N E A N

S E A

Netanya

Nablus

3

TEL AVIV

West Bank

Jaffa **9**

AMMAN

Rishon LeZion

Ramla

Abu Ghosh

RAMALLAH

Rehovot

Jericho

Ashdod

JERUSALEM **1**

Ashkelon

Gat

Bethlehem

6

Gaza Strip

Gaza City

Hebron

Dead Sea

Khan Younis

Ein Gedi

2

Rafah

5

Masada

Al-Arish

Be'er Sheva

Arad

Kerak

Dimona

Ein Avdat National Park

The Negev

JORDAN

Mitzpe Ramon

Makhtesh Ramon

10

Wadi Musa

Maan

EGYPT (Sinai)

Eilat

Taba

Aqaba

Red Sea

0   40 km
0   20 miles

Israel & the Palestinian Territories'
Top Experiences

Dome of the Rock

1 The first sight of the Dome of the Rock – its gold cap shimmering above a mystical turquoise-hued octagonal base – never fails to take one's breath away. Perhaps that's what the architects had in mind more than 1300 years ago when they set to work on this impossibly gorgeous building. The dome covers a slab of stone sacred to both the Muslim and Jewish faiths. The best view is from the Mount of Olives, but don't miss the chance to see it up close by taking an early morning walk up to the Temple Mount. The interior of the Dome is not open to non-Muslims.

The Dead Sea

2 You pass a sign reading 'Sea Level' and then keep driving downhill, eventually catching glimpses of the Dead Sea's cobalt-blue waters, outlined by snow-white salt deposits, reddish-tan cliffs and tufts of dark-green vegetation. At the oasis of Ein Gedi you can hike through unique desert habitats to crystal-clear pools and tumbling waterfalls before climbing to the Judean Desert plateau above – or heading down to the seashore for a briny, invigorating dip. To the south around Mt Sodom, outdoor options include adventure cycling along dry riverbeds.

Tel Aviv Beaches

3 Just over 100 years ago, Tel Aviv was little more than sand dunes. Today it's a sprawling cosmopolitan city bursting with bars, bistros and boutiques, but the beach is still the epicentre of life. Here, sunbathers bronze their bodies, while the more athletic swim, surf and play intense games of *matkot* (beach racquetball). Each beach along the coast of Tel Aviv has its own character and personality – sporty, party, family, alternative, gay-friendly or religious – all against the deep-blue backdrop of the Mediterranean.

if Israel were 100 people

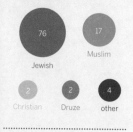

55 would be Israel-born Jewish
14 would be Europe/America/Oceania-born Jewish
4 would be Africa-born Jewish
2 would be Asia-born Jewish
25 would be non-Jewish (mostly Arab)

belief systems
(% of population)

76 Jewish
17 Muslim
2 Christian
2 Druze
4 other

population per sq km

ISRAEL
WEST BANK & GAZA
USA

≈ 32 people

Golan Heights

4 From towering Nimrod Fortress, the 'Galilee Panhandle' spreads out before you like a topographical map, but turn around and the looming flanks of Mt Hermon, snow-capped well into spring, dwarf even this Crusader-era stronghold. Hikers can take on the alpine peaks of Mt Hermon, or follow the cliff-lined wadis of the Banias and Yehudiya Nature Reserves on their way to the Jordan River and the Sea of Galilee. The Golan's basalt soils are ideal for growing grapes, so the local boutique wines are some of Israel's finest.

Masada

5 The Romans had just destroyed Jerusalem when about a thousand Jewish Zealots took refuge on a remote mesa overlooking the Dead Sea. As you peer down from their towering redoubt, you can still see the eight encircling Roman camps, connected by a siege wall, making it easy to imagine the dramatic, tragic events that unfolded here in early 73 CE. Eventually the Romans built a ramp and breached the walls, but all they found were a handful of survivors – everyone else had committed suicide rather than submit to slavery.

Old City, Bethlehem

6 For nearly two millennia Christian pilgrims have been making their way to the birthplace of Jesus and for just as long the people of Bethlehem have been feeding them in their restaurants and housing them in their inns. Bethlehem's Old City still retains the mystique of antiquity, almost unchanged

Jerusalem Syndrome

Each year tens of thousands of tourists descend on Jerusalem to walk in the footsteps of the prophets, and a handful come away from the journey thinking they are the prophets. This medically recognised ailment, called Jerusalem Syndrome, occurs when visitors become overwhelmed by the metaphysical significance of the Holy City and come to the conclusion that they are biblical characters or that the Apocalypse is near.

The ailment was first documented in the 1930s by Jerusalem psychiatrist Dr Heinz Herman, who identified, for example, an English Christian woman who was certain that Christ's Second Coming was imminent and regularly climbed Mt Scopus to welcome Him back to earth with a cup of tea.

Doctors estimate that Jerusalem Syndrome affects between 50 and 200 people per year, and although many have a recorded history of mental aberration, about a quarter of recorded cases have no previous psychiatric record.

Food & Drink

Amba Iraqi-style mango chutney.

Bourekas Flaky Balkan pastries filled with Bulgarian cheese, spinach or mushrooms.

Challah Braided bread traditionally eaten by Jews on the Sabbath.

Cholent A heavy meat and potato stew simmered overnight and served for Sabbath lunch.

Labneh Thick, creamy yoghurt cheese, often smothered in olive oil and sprinkled with zaatar.

Sabich A pita pocket filled with fried eggplant, boiled potato, hard-boiled egg, tahina, amba and freshly chopped vegies.

Schug Yemenite hot chili paste.

Zaatar A spice blend that includes hyssop, sumac and sesame seeds.

through the generations. Get a feel for it by wandering up Star St, where you can haggle for keepsakes and savour the flavours of its myriad snack stalls.

Caesarea

7 Built on an exposed section of the eastern Mediterranean with heavy surf pounding it for half the year, Caesarea never really stood a chance. Within a few centuries of its creation the awesome port built by Herod was nothing more than a storm-battered stretch of dunes covering an ancient urban fabric. Archaeologists have since uncovered most of it and in doing so have patched together Caesarea's once-glorious history. Perch yourself on the edge of the sea and visualise the faded past.

Nazareth

8 The village where Jesus grew up has also grown up and is now a bustling Arab city. In the Old City, narrow alleyways are graced with churches commemorating the Annunciation and other New Testament

When to Go

HIGH SEASON
(Jul & Aug)

➡ Warm in Jerusalem, muggy in Tel Aviv, infernal in Eilat, Tiberias, Dead Sea.

➡ Hotels prices spike and rooms are scarce.

➡ Jewish holidays of Passover, Rosh HaShana and Sukkot are also high season.

SHOULDER
(Oct, Nov & Mar–Jun)

➡ Sometimes rainy but more often warm and sunny.

➡ Spring wildflowers make March and April ideal for hiking.

➡ Tourist numbers spike during the week-long Jewish holidays of Passover and Sukkot.

LOW SEASON
(Dec–Feb)

➡ Chilly or downright cold in the north, especially at higher elevations.

➡ Popular time to head to the warmth of Eilat and the Dead Sea.

events, and with Ottoman-era mansions. A new generation of restaurants has made Nazareth a star in Israel's gastronomic firmament. Alongside delicious old-time specialities, served with traditional Arab hospitality, you can sample East–West 'fusion' dishes – fresh local herbs with artichoke hearts, or wild Galilean pine nuts with chopped beef.

Old Jaffa

9 While neighbouring Tel Aviv is only beginning its second century, Jaffa, with its ancient white fortress walls, has some 4000 years behind it. Jaffa's history reads like a who's who of conquerors – the Greeks,

Getting Around

Bus Almost every town and village has a bus service at least a few times a day, though from mid-afternoon on Friday until Saturday after dark, most intercity buses don't run at all. In East Jerusalem and the West Bank, a number of small, Arab-run bus companies provide public transport. Unlike their counterparts in Israel, they operate right through the weekend.

Car Having your own wheels lets you travel at your own pace and – if necessary – cover a lot of ground in a short amount of time. The condition of most Israeli roads is quite good (though a visible minority of Israeli drivers can be politely described as erratic). Note that most Israeli rental agencies forbid you to take their cars into the Palestinian Territories.

Sherut (Shared Taxi) These vehicles, often 13-seat minivans, operate on a fixed route for a fixed price, like a bus except that they don't have fixed stops If you don't know the fare, ask your fellow passengers. On the West Bank, shared taxis are plentiful and can take the form of chugging old Mercedes cars as well as minibuses. Sheruts are generally quicker than buses.

Romans, Crusaders, Napoleon, Ottomans and British all used this Mediterranean port, once the gateway to the Middle East. Now a mix of Arab and Jewish neighbourhoods, Jaffa is a great place to smoke a nargileh pipe, haggle for antiques in the flea market or take a cycling trip along the redeveloped coastline.

Makhtesh Ramon

10 Standing on the edge of Makhtesh Ramon

you can witness millions of years of evolution beneath your feet and barely imagine that this barren landscape was once a sea. Freezing cold at night, but baking during the day, the makhtesh, or crater as it's commonly known, is a place of extremes. The multicoloured rock formations of the Negev Highlands go on for as far as the eye can see and you can't help but wonder how such a small country can be home to such a vast secret.

Best on Film

Paradise Now (2005) Directed by Nazareth-born, Netherlands-based Hany Abu-Assad; puts a human face on Palestinian suicide bombers.

Precious Life (2010) Explores the relationships formed during a Gaza baby's medical treatment in Israel.

Waltz With Bashir (2008) Haunting, personal look at the 1982 Lebanon War.

West Bank Story (2005) A spoof on the musical *West Side Story*.

Best in Print

Secret Life of Saeed the Pesoptimist (Emile Habibi; 1974) A brilliant tragicomic tale dealing with the difficulties facing Palestinians who became Israeli citizens after 1948.

The Lover (AB Yehoshua; 1977) Set against the backdrop of the 1973 Yom Kippur War.

The Yellow Wing (David Grossman; 1987) A critical look at Israel's occupation of the Palestinian Territories.

SOREN HERBST / GETTY IMAGES ©

Cinque Terre

| CAPITAL |
| Rome |
| POPULATION |
| 61.5 million |
| AREA |
| 301,340 sq km |
| OFFICIAL LANGUAGE |
| Italian |

Italy

Italy is the ultimate dream date: impossibly good-looking, impeccably cultured and obscenely good in the kitchen. Endlessly inspiring and naturally flirtatious, it will leave you swooning.

Italians really do know how to live well. Ever since the Etruscans came, liked what they saw and decided to stay and party, the locals have embraced the finer things in life. Here, family, faith, friendship, food and wine reign supreme, contributing to the famous Italian *dolce vita* (sweet life).

Travellers have been falling under Italy's spell ever since the days of the 18th-century Grand Tour, enticed by its sun-kissed landscape, delectable cuisine and extraordinary art. This is the home of gently rolling Tuscan hills and postcard-perfect coastlines; the place where simple dishes such as pizza and pasta attain culinary perfection. It's where Michelangelo shocked the establishment with his humanist sculptures and Caravaggio shocked everyone else with his criminal highjinks and darkly atmospheric paintings.

So make like Julius Caesar. Come and see – you're sure to be conquered. If you get it right, travelling in the *bel paese* (beautiful country) is one of those rare experiences than cannot be overrated.

Italy's
Top Experiences

Virtuoso Venice

1 Imagine the audacity of people deciding to build a city of marble palaces on a lagoon. As you step through the portals of the Basilica di San Marco you may catch a glimpse of what it might have been like for a humble medieval labourer gazing upon those glittering gold mosaic domes for the first time. It's not such a stretch – seeing the millions of tiny gilt *tesserae* (hand-cut glazed tiles) fuse into a singular heavenly vision can make every leap of human imagination since the 12th century seem comparatively minor.

Ghostly Pompeii

2 Nothing piques human curiosity quite like a mass catastrophe and few can beat the ruins of Pompeii, a once-thriving Roman town frozen in time 2000 years ago in the midst of its death throes. Wander through Roman streets, snooping around the forum, the erotically frescoed brothel, the 5000-seat theatre and the sumptuous Villa dei Misteri, and ponder Pliny the Younger's terrifying account of the tragedy: 'Darkness came on again, again ashes, thick and heavy. We got up repeatedly to shake these off; otherwise we would have been buried and crushed by the weight'.

ED NORTON / GETTY IMAGES ©

GLENN BEANLAND / GETTY IMAGES ©

Eternal Rome

3 Once *caput mundi* (capital of the world), Rome was legendarily spawned by a wolf-suckled wild boy, grew to be Western Europe's first superpower, became the spiritual centrepiece of the Christian world, and is now the repository of over two and a half thousand years of art and architecture. From the Pantheon and the Colosseum to Michelangelo's Sistine Chapel, there's simply too much to see in one visit. So, do as others have done before you: toss a coin into the Trevi Fountain and promise to return.

Roman Forum, Rome

Touring Tuscany

4. Italy's most romanticised region, Tuscany was tailor-made for aesthetes. According to Unesco, Florence contains 'the greatest concentration of universally renowned works of art in the world', from Brunelleschi's *Duomo* to Masaccio's *Cappella Brancacci* frescoes. Beyond its museums and flawless Renaissance streetscapes sprawls an undulating wonderland of regional delights, from the Gothic majesty of Siena, to the Manhattan-esque skyline of San Gimignano, to the vine-laced hills of Italy's most famous wine region, Chianti.

if Italy were 100 people

93 would be Italian
4 would be Albanian and Eastern European
1 would be North African
2 would be other

belief systems
(% of population)

91 — Roman Catholics
1 — other
6 — none
2 — Muslim

population per sq km

ITALY   FRANCE   USA

† ≈ 30 people

Tackling the Dolomites

5. Scour the globe and you'll find plenty of taller, bigger and more geologically volatile mountains, but few can match the romance of the pink-hued, granite Dolomites. Maybe it's their harsh, jagged summits, the vibrant skirts of spring wildflowers or the rich cache of Ladin legends. Then again, it could just be the magnetic draw of money, style and glamour at Italy's most fabled ski resort, Cortina d'Ampezzo. Whatever the reason, this tiny pocket of northern Italy takes seductiveness to dizzying heights.

Living Luxe on Lago di Como

6. If it's good enough for George Clooney, well then it's good enough for mere mortals. Nestled in the shadow of the snow-covered Rhaetian Alps, dazzling Lago di Como is the most spectacular of the Lombard lakes, its vain Liberty-style villas home to movie moguls, fashion royalty and Arab sheikhs. Surrounded on all sides by lush greenery, the lake's siren calls include the gardens of Villa Melzi d'Eril, Villa Carlotta and Villa Balbianello, which blush pink with camellias, azaleas and rhododendrons in April and May.

Amalfi Coast

7. Italy's most celebrated coastline is a bewitching blend of superlative beauty and gripping geology: coastal mountains plunge into milky blue sea in a prime-time vertical scene of precipitous crags, sun-bleached villages and lush forests. While some may argue that the peninsula's most beautiful coast is Liguria's Cinque Terre or

Calcio: Italy's Other Religion

Catholicism may be Italy's official faith, but the true religion is *calcio* (football). On any given weekend from September to May, Italian *tifosi* (football fans) are at the *stadio* (stadium), glued to the TV, or checking the score on their mobile phone. Come Monday, they'll be dissecting the match by the office water cooler.

Like politics and fashion, football is in the very DNA of Italian culture. Indeed, they sometimes even converge. Silvio Berlusconi first found fame as the owner of AC Milan and cleverly named his political party after a well-worn football chant. Fashion royalty Dolce & Gabbana declared football players 'the new male icons', using five of Italy's hottest on-field stars to launch its 2010 underwear collection. It's no coincidence that in Italian *tifoso* means both 'football fan' and 'typhus patient'. Nothing quite stirs Italian blood like a good (or a bad) game; nine months after Italy's 2006 World Cup victory against France, hospitals in northern Italy reported a baby boom.

Food & Drink

Arancini Deep-fried rice balls stuffed with *ragù* (meat sauce), tomato and vegetables.

Caffè Join the locals for a morning cappuccino or post-lunch espresso, both taken standing at a bar.

Gelato Popular ice-cream flavours include *fragola* (strawberry), *nocciola* (hazelnut) and *stracciatella* (milk with chocolate shavings).

Pizza Two varieties: Roman, with a thin crispy base; and Neapolitan, with a higher, more doughy base. The best are always prepared in a *forno a legna* (wood-fired oven).

Wine Ranges from big-name reds such as Piedmont's Barolo to light whites from Sardinia and sparkling prosecco from the Veneto.

Lago di Carezza, Dolomites

Calabria's Costa Viola, it was the Amalfi Coast that American writer John Steinbeck described as a 'dream place that isn't quite real when you are there and...beckoningly real after you have gone'.

Italian Riviera

8 For the sinful inhabitants of Monterosso, Vernazza, Corniglia, Manarola and Riomaggiore – the five villages of the Cinque Terre – penance involved a lengthy and arduous hike up the vertiginous cliffside to the local village sanctuary to appeal for forgiveness. Scale the same trails today, through terraced vineyards and hillsides smothered in *macchia* (shrubbery) and, as the heavenly views unfurl, it's hard to think of a more benign punishment.

Sardinian Shores

9 The English language fails to accurately describe the varied blue, green and, in the deepest shadows, purple hues of Sardinia's seas. While models, ministers and permatanned celebrities wine, dine and sail along the glossy Costa Smeralda, much of

When to Go

HIGH SEASON
(Jul–Aug)

➡ Queues at sights and on the road, especially in August.

➡ Prices also rocket for Christmas, New Year and Easter.

➡ Late December to March is high season in the Alps and Dolomites.

SHOULDER
(Apr–Jun & Sep–Oct)

➡ Good deals on accommodation, especially in the south.

➡ Spring is best for festivals, flowers and local produce.

➡ Autumn provides warm weather and the grape harvest.

LOW SEASON
(Nov–Mar)

➡ Prices up to 30% less than in high season.

➡ Many sights and hotels closed in coastal and mountainous areas.

➡ A good period for cultural events in large cities.

Sardinia remains a wild, raw playground. Slather on that sunscreen and explore the island's rugged coastal beauty, from the tumbledown boulders of Santa Teresa di Gallura and the wind-chiselled cliff face of the Golfo di Orosei, to the windswept beauty of the Costa Verde's dune-backed beaches.

Savouring Emilia-Romagna

10 They don't call Bologna 'la grassa' (the fat one) for nothing. Many of Italy's classics call this city home, from mortadella and meat-stuffed tortellini, to its trademark *tagliatelle al ragù*. Shop for produce in the deli-packed Quadrilatero, and side-trip-it to the city of Modena for world-famous

aged balsamic vinegar. Just leave room for a trip to Parma, hometown of parmigiano reggiano cheese and the incomparable prosciutto di Parma. Wherever you plunge your fork, toast with a glass or three of the region's renowned Lambrusco or sauvignon blanc.

Scaling Mount Etna

11 Known to the Greeks as the 'column that holds up the sky', Mt Etna is not only Europe's largest volcano, it's one of the world's most active. The ancients believed the giant Tifone (Typhoon) lived in its crater and lit the sky with spectacular pyrotechnics. At 3329m it literally towers above

Sicily's Ionian coast. Whether you tackle it on foot or on a guided 4WD tour, scaling this time bomb rewards with towering views and the secret thrill of having come cheek-to-cheek with a towering threat.

Baroque Lecce

12 There's baroque, and then there's *barocco leccese* (Lecce baroque), the hyperextravagant spin-off defining many Puglian towns. Making it all possible was the local stone, so soft that craftspeople crowded facades with swirling designs, gargoyles and strange zoomorphic figures. Queen of the crop is Lecce's Basilica di Santa Croce.

Best on Film

Ladri di biciclette (The Bicycle Thief; Vittorio De Sica, 1948) A doomed father attempts to provide for his son without resorting to crime in war-ravaged Rome.

Cinema Paradiso (Giuseppe Tornatore, 1988) A director returns to Sicily and rediscovers his true loves: the girl next door and the movies.

Il postino (The Postman; Michael Radford, 1994) Exiled poet Pablo Neruda brings poetry and passion to a drowsy Italian isle and a misfit postman.

Best in Print

The Italians (Luigi Barzini) A revealing look at Italian culture beyond the well-worn clichés.

Gomorrah (Roberto Saviano) Fascinating, disturbing exposé of the power of the Campanian Camorra.

The Pursuit of Italy (David Gilmour) Interesting insights into Italy's past and present.

Parmigiano-reggiano cheese

DANITA DELIMONT / GETTY IMAGES ©

CAPITAL
Kingston

POPULATION
2.9 million

AREA
10,991 sq km

OFFICIAL LANGUAGE
English

Port Antonio

Jamaica

Jamaica is a powerfully beautiful country, packed with extremes: experience flat beaches twinned to green mountains, electrifying Kingston and relaxed resorts, sweet reggae and slack dancehall.

Jamaica, at first blush, is the Caribbean island many know best thanks to its relentless exposure – its music, dreadlocks, dancehall and beaches.

But did you know there are Chinese Jamaicans and Jewish Jamaicans and white Jamaicans who speak patois as fluently as downtown Kingston yardies? Jamaica, perhaps more than any other Caribbean nation, also keeps one foot rooted in Africa. From the evolution of African folk music into reggae, or the shifting of African spice rubs into delicious jerk, it's rewarding to see how the Jamaican cultural story retains its original voice whilst adapting it to the setting – and of course, rhythms – of the Caribbean.

Understand the above and you can better appreciate the good, red Jamaican soil; the respect Jamaicans have for life and nature; and the meaning 'One Love' has in a place like the Kingston ghettoes. To know Jamaica, experience it. As locals say, 'Rockstone a river naah know sun hot'. That's patois for 'experience brings knowledge,' and so much more so on an island that can express such simple proverbs so beautifully.

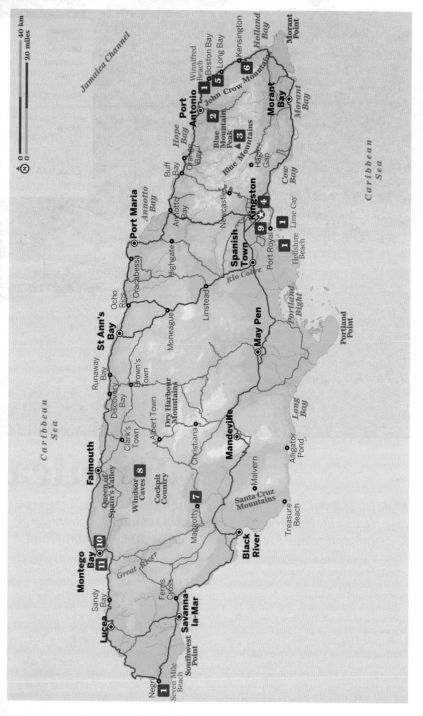

40 km
20 miles

Jamaica Channel

Caribbean Sea

Caribbean Sea

Morant Point

Holland Bay

Kensington
Long Bay
Winnifred Beach
Boston Bay
1
5 John Crow Mountain **6**

Port Antonio
2
Blue Mountain Peak **3**
Blue Mountains
Hagley Gap

Hope Bay
Orange Bay
Newcastle

Morant Bay
Morant Bay

Buff Bay

Cow Bay

Port Maria
Annotto Bay
Annotto Bay

Kingston **4**
Port Royal
9 **1**
Lime Cay
Spanish Town **1**
Hellshire Beach

Oracabessa
Highgate
Rio Cobre

Ocho Rios
Linstead

St Ann's Bay
Runaway Bay
Discovery Bay
Brown's Town
Moneague

Portland Bight

Portland Point

May Pen

Clark's Town
Albert Town
Dry Harbour Mountains
Christiana
Mandeville

Long Bay

Alligator Pond

Falmouth
Queen of Spain's Valley
Windsor Caves **8**
Cockpit Country
7
Maggotty
Malvern

Santa Cruz Mountains

Treasure Beach

Montego Bay
10
11
Great River

Lucea
Sandy Bay
Ferris Cross
Savanna-la-Mar

Black River

Southwest Point
Seven Mile Beach
Negril **1**

Jamaica's
Top Experiences

Best Beaches

1 Jamaica's beach experiences are as varied as the island's topography. The tiny, delicate Lime Cay, only reachable by boat from Port Royal, is perfect for snorkeling and picnics. Hellshire Beach heaves with Kingstonians and reverberates with loud music, its wooden shacks doing a roaring trade in fried fish. The north coast's Winnifred Beach draws the locals with its azure waters and weekend parties, while Negril's Seven Mile Beach (Long Beach) is criss-crossed by jet-ski riders, and its long crescent of white sand lined with the bodies of sun worshippers.

Rafting the Rio Grande

2 No less a celebrity then Errol Flynn started the habit of sending discerning tourists on romantic, moonlit bamboo rafting trips through the Rio Grande Valley, from Berridale to Rafter's Rest at St Margaret's Bay. These days the experience isn't quite as exclusive as it was when Mr Flynn was running the show – the Rio Grande rafting trips are actually quite affordable as Jamaican tourism activities go – but if the moon is full, you can still pole onto the waters, which turn silver and unspeakably romantic.

DOUG PEARSON / GETTY IMAGES ©

Climbing Blue Mountain Peak

3 A night hike to reach Jamaica's highest point by sunrise, your path lit by the sparks of myriad fireflies, is an experience unlike any other. As you climb, the vegetation becomes less and less tropical, until you're hiking amid stunted trees draped with old man's beard (lichen) and giant ferns. In the pre-dawn cold at the summit, you wait in rapt silence as the first rays of the sun wash over the densely forested mountain peaks all around you, illuminating the distant coffee plantations and Cuba beyond.

if Jamaica were 100 people

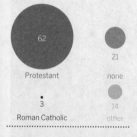

91 would black
6 would mixed
3 would other

belief systems

(% of population)

62 Protestant
21 none
3 Roman Catholic
14 other

population per sq km

JAMAICA USA UK

≈ 30 people

Kingston Nightlife

4 Whether you're attending a nightclub or a street dance, expect a sweaty, lively, no-holds-barred event. Dress up to the nines and follow the locals' lead. At a street dance, two giant speakers are placed facing each other, the street pounding with the bass, while nightclubs provide a similar indoor experience. Expect to be pulled into the melee as the locals will want to see how well you can dance, and bump and grind the best you can; the dancing will be some of the most explicit you'll ever see.

Boston Bay

5 The best experiences in Jamaica are extremely sensory affairs, but Boston Bay may be the only one that is more defined by smell than sight or sound. Well, smell and taste: Boston Bay is the supposed birthplace of jerk, the spice rub that is Jamaica's most famous contribution to the culinary arts. The turnoff to Boston Bay (itself a lovely beach) is lined with jerk stalls that produce smoked meats that redefine what heat and sweet can do as complementary gastronomic qualities. In plain English: it tastes freaking amazing.

Reach Falls

6 On Jamaica's east coast, past stretches of jungle and beach that are completely off the radar of most tourists, you'll find, up in the hills, one of Jamaica's most beautiful waterfalls – and this is an island with a lot of beautiful waterfalls. Hire a guide (you'll need one, trust us) and clamber up slippery rocks, over neon-green moss and into cool mountain pools of the freshest spring water. In some areas you can dive under watery tunnels and

Rastafarianism

A faith rather than a church, Rastafarianism has no official doctrine and is composed of a core of social and spiritual tenets, developed by charismatic Rastafarian leader Leonard Percival Howell, whose 'Twenty-One Points' say the African race was one of God's chosen races, one of the Twelve Tribes of Israel descended from the Hebrews and displaced.

Not all Rastafarians wear dreads, and others do not smoke ganja (although many believe that ganja provides a line of communication with God). All adherents, however, accept that Africa is the black race's spiritual home, to which they are destined to return.

Rastafarianism evolved as an expression of poor, black Jamaicans seeking fulfillment in the 1930s, a period of growing nationalism and economic and political upheaval.

Food & Drink

Breadkinds A catchall term for starchy sides, from plantains and yam to pancake-shaped cassava bread (bammy) and johnnycakes (fried dumplings).

Jerk Jamaica's most well-known dish, jerk is actually a cooking method: smother food in a tongue-searing marinade, then smoke over a wood fire.

Patties Baked shells filled with spicy beef, vegetables and whatever else folks desire. Cheap and filling.

Rum Clear and light white rums, flavored rums, brain-bashing overproof rums (rum over 151 proof), deep dark rums, and the rare amber nectar of the finest premium rums.

Saltfish & Ackee Jamaica's national dish, and a delicious breakfast besides. Ackee is a fleshy, somewhat bland fruit; saltfish is, well, salted fish. When mixed together they're delicious, somewhat resembling scrambled eggs.

PICK FI KINS / GETTY IMAGES ©

through blizzards of snowy-white cascading foam.

Appleton Rum Estate

7 Red Stripe is the alcohol everyone associates with Jamaica, but you may find that rum, the local spirit, provides a more diverse boozing experience. We're not saying Appleton produces the best rum on the island, but it is by far the most commonly available, bottled as several different varieties, and you can sample all these examples of the firewater at the Appleton Rum Estate in the Central Highlands. A lot of rum is served, so don't expect to accomplish much else on one of these day trips!

When to Go

HIGH SEASON
(Dec–Mar)

➡ Expect sunny, warm days, especially on the coast. Little rainfall, except in Port Antonio and the northeast.

➡ At night it can become chilly, particularly in the mountains.

SHOULDER
(Apr & May)

➡ Good time to visit; weather is still pretty dry (again, except in Port Antonio).

➡ Rates drop for accommodations.

➡ Far fewer tourists, especially in the big resorts/cruise ports.

LOW SEASON
(Jun–Nov)

➡ Sporadic heavy rainfall across the island, except the south coast.

➡ Heavy storms, including hurricanes.

➡ Many of Jamaica's best festivals happen in midsummer.

Spelunking Windsor Caves

8 The Cockpit Country of the island's interior is some of the most rugged terrain throughout the Caribbean, a series of jungle-clad round hills intersected by powerfully deep and sheer valleys. The rains gather in these mountains and the water percolates through the rocks, creating a Swiss cheese of sinkholes and caves. Windsor is one of the most dramatic and accessible, although the latter is a very relative term when used to describe this cathedral of fantastic rock formations. Oh, and there are bats. Lots of bats.

Playing Pirates at Port Royal

9 The sleepy fishing village of Port Royal only hints at past glories that made it pirate capital of the Caribbean and 'the wickedest city on Earth.' Stroll in the footsteps of pirate Sir Henry Morgan along the battlements of Fort Charles, still lined with cannons to repel the invaders; become disorientated inside the Giddy House artillery store, tipped at a jaunty angle; or admire the treasures in the Maritime Museum, rescued from the deep after two thirds of the town sank beneath the waves in the monstrous 1692 earthquake.

Best on Film

Life and Debt (2001) A powerful documentary on the impact of globalization on the Jamaican economy.

The Harder They Come (1972) A classic rags-to-rude *bwai* (rude boy) story of country boy turned Kingston criminal. One of the best soundtracks in film history.

Smile Orange (1976) A hilarious tale of a waiter hustling tourists at Jamaican resorts.

Best in Print

Lionheart Gal (1986) A lively short-story collection that reveals much about patois and the lives of women.

White Witch of Rose Hall (1928) Herbert de Lisser's classic gothic horror, set in colonial Jamaica.

Getting Around

Air There are four domestic airports, with scheduled services between Kingston and Montego Bay, and air-taxi services covering the other routes.

Bus The island's extensive transportation network links virtually every village and comprises several options, ranging from standard public buses to 'coasters' (private minibuses) and 'route taxis' (communal taxis). Taking public transportation is terrifically inexpensive.

Car Exploring by rental car can be a truly liberating experience, but make no mistake: driving in Jamaica can be a nightmare. Taxis and minibuses are a serious menace and don't be surprised if police stop you and ask for a little bribe or search your car extensively for even a trace of ganja.

Reggae Sumfest

10 If there's any cultural trend that defines Jamaica to the rest of the world, it's reggae music – quite literally the soundtrack of the island. And there is no bigger celebration of the island's 'riddims' then Reggae Sumfest, held in Montego Bay in the middle of the broiling Jamaican summer. To be fair, the ocean breezes do cool things down, but you'll still be sweating – from the fires spewing out of homemade aerosol flamethrowers (that means a song is good), the throbbing mass of bodies and the nonstop dancing.

Diving Montego Bay

11 You might find the resorts of Montego Bay to be crowded with people, but wait till you dive in the surrounding waters. They're crowded with multicolored fish and swaying sponges. For all the tropical pastels and cool blue hues, this is a subdued seascape, a silent and delicate marine ecosystem that is one of the island's unique natural resources. The best sea walls are to be found at The Point, while more advanced divers should explore the ominous Widowmakers Cave.

David 'Dread' Hinds of Jamaican reggae band Steel Pulse

ANTHONY PIDGEON / GETTY IMAGES ©

Stairway to Adashino Nembutsu-ji, Kyoto

CAPITAL
Tokyo

POPULATION
127.3 million

AREA
377,915 sq km

OFFICIAL LANGUAGE
Japanese

Japan

Japan is a world apart – a cultural Galápagos where a unique civilisation blossomed, and thrives today in delicious contrasts of traditional and modern.

Japan hits the travel sweet spot. It's unique enough to give you regular doses of 'Wow!' without any downside. Indeed, travelling in Japan is remarkably comfortable, even with the language barrier thrown in – but it's never familiar. Staying in a *ryokan* (traditional Japanese inn) is marvellously different from staying in a chain hotel. Soaking naked in an *onsen* (hot spring) with a bunch of strangers might be a little odd at first, but it is beyond relaxing. Sitting in a robe on tatami mats eating raw fish and mountain vegetables may not be how you dine back home, but it is unforgettably delicious.

Perhaps more than any country on earth, Japan makes you think. It was never extensively missionised or colonised. It practises an ancient animist/pantheist religion while pushing the boundaries of modern technology. It is a country where tens of millions of people can cram into crowded cities without ever losing their temper. And while you explore Japan, you will regularly find yourself awed by how the Japanese do things.

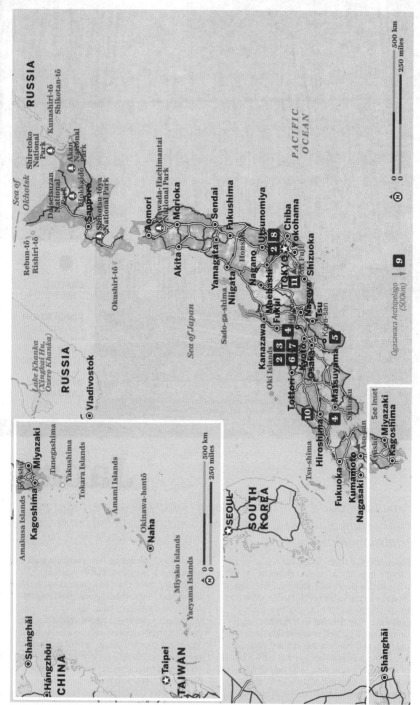

Japan's
Top Experiences

Onsen

1 There's nothing like lowering yourself into the tub at a classic Japanese onsen (natural hot spring bath). You can feel the muscles in your back relax and the 'ahhh' that you emit is just a simple way of saying 'Damn, I'm glad I came to Japan!' If you're lucky, the tub is outside and there's a nice stream running nearby. The Japanese have turned the simple act of bathing into a folk religion and the country is dotted with temples and shrines to this most relaxing of faiths.

Cherry-Blossom Viewing

2 If you think of the Japanese as sober, staid and serious people, join them under a cherry tree laden with blossoms in the springtime. It's as if the cherries release a kind of narcotic that reduces inhibitions. They'll drench you in sake and beer, stuff you with snacks, pull out portable karaoke and perhaps even get up and dance. Japan is a happy place when the cherry blossoms are out, and you're more than welcome to join the party. Two of the best places to join in the fun are Tokyo's Ueno-kōen and Kyoto's Maruyama-kōe

Ishikawajima park, Tokyo

2

KOSEI SAITO / GETTY IMAGES ©

Kyoto Temples & Gardens

3 With more than 1000 temples to choose from, you're spoiled for choice in Kyoto. Spend your time finding one that suits your taste. If you like things gaudy and grand, you'll love the retina-burning splendour of Kinkaku-ji. If you prefer wabi-sabi to rococo, you'll find the tranquillity of Hōnen-in or Shōren-in more to your liking. And don't forget that temples are where you'll find the best gardens: some of them are at Ginkaku-ji, Ryōan-ji and Tōfuku-ji. Kinkaku-ji.

Kinkaku-ji, Kyoto

Castles

4 Japan's castles have about as much in common with their European counterparts as kimonos have with Western dinner dresses. Their graceful contours belie the grim military realities behind their construction. Towering above the plains, they seem designed more to please the eye than to protect their lords. If you have an interest in the world of samurai, shōguns and military history, you'll love Japan's castles. Now that the castle at Himeji is under wraps, try the one at Matsuyama or Hikone.

if Japan were 100 people

13 would be aged 0-14
10 would be aged 15-24
38 would be aged 25-54
14 would be aged 55-64
25 would be aged 65+

belief systems

(% of population)

90
Shinto, Buddhist or both combined

8 other

2 Christian

population per sq km

JAPAN   USA   UK

= 30 people

Oku-no-in at Kōya-san

5 Riding the funicular up to the sacred Buddhist monastic complex of Kōya-san, you almost feel like you're ascending to another world. The place is permeated with a kind of august spiritual grandeur, and nowhere is this feeling stronger than in the vast Oku-no-in cemetery. Trails weave their way among towering cryptomeria trees and by the time you arrive at the main hall, the sudden appearance of a Buddha would seem like the most natural thing in the world.

Arashiyama's Bamboo Grove

6 Western Kyoto is home to one of the most magical places in all of Japan: the famed bamboo grove in Arashiyama. The visual effect of the seemingly infinite stalks of bamboo is quite different from any forest we've ever encountered – there's a palpable presence to the place that is utterly impossible to capture in pictures, but don't let that stop you from trying. If you've seen Crouching Tiger, Hidden Dragon, you'll have some idea of what this place is about.

Kyoto's Geisha Dances

7 It can't be stressed enough: if you find yourself in Kyoto when the geisha dances are on – usually in the spring – do everything in your power to see one. It's hard to think of a more colourful, charming and diverting stage spectacle. You might find that the whole thing takes on the appearance of a particularly vivid dream. When the

Staying in a Ryokan

Simply put, ryokan are traditional Japanese inns.

But this simple explanation doesn't do justice to ryokan. A high-end ryokan is the last word in relaxation. The buildings themselves employ traditional Japanese architecture in which the whole structure is organic, made entirely of natural materials such as wood, earth, paper, grass, bamboo and stone.

Nature comes into the ryokan in the form of the Japanese garden, which you can often see from the privacy of your room. But the service is what sets ryokan apart from even the best hotels. At a good ryokan, you will be assigned a personal maid.

If you can do it, we strongly recommend staying in a high-end ryokan for at least one night.

Food & Drink

Birru The quality of Japanese beer is generally excellent and the most popular type is light lager.

Okonomiyaki Various forms of batter and cabbage cakes cooked on a griddle.

Sake Most Japanese still consider sake to be the national drink, and it makes the perfect accompaniment to traditional Japanese food.

Shabu-shabu Thin slices of beef and vegetables cooked in a light broth, then dipped in a variety of special sesame-seed and citrus-based sauces.

Shōchū A distilled spirit made from a variety of raw materials, including potato and barley.

Tonkatsu A deep-fried breaded pork cutlet that is served with a special sauce, usually as part of a set meal (*tonkatsu teishoku*).

Unagi Eel is an expensive and popular delicacy in Japan.

Yakitori Skewers of charcoal-grilled chicken and vegetables.

curtain falls after the final burst of colour and song, the geisha might continue to dance in your mind for hours afterwards.

Shopping in Tokyo

8 If you want to see some incredible shops, you've got to come to a country that's been running a multibillion-dollar trade surplus for the last several decades. If it's available to humanity, you can buy it in Japan. Whether it's ¥10,000 (US$100) melons or curios from ¥100 shops (where everything goes for about US$1), you'll be amazed at the sheer variety of the goods on offer in Tokyo. No trip to Tokyo would be complete without a visit to Tsukiji Fish Market, the largest of its kind in the world.

Ogasawara Archipelago

9 This Pacific island chain, located some 1000km south of Tokyo, is one of Japan's best-kept secrets. Inhabited only within the last 180 years, these subtropical

When to Go

HIGH SEASON
(Apr & May, Aug)

➡ Flights are pricey around the Golden Week (early May), O-Bon (mid-August) and New Year.

➡ Honshū cities are busy in the cherry blossom (late March to early April) and autumn foliage (November) seasons.

SHOULDER
(Jun & Jul, Sep–Dec)

➡ June and July is rainy season in most of Japan (except Hokkaidō) – it doesn't rain every day but it can be pretty humid.

➡ Autumn (September to mid-December) is usually cool and clear.

LOW SEASON
(Jan–Mar)

➡ Winter is cool or cold in most of Honshū, but it's fine for travel.

➡ Be ready for snow in the mountains.

islands boast white-sand beaches, warm blue waters and dozens of rare plant and animal species. Divers and snorkellers can swim with dolphins, mantas and sea turtles. Hiking, kayaking, stargazing, and whale-watching and are also on the bill. The catch? The most accessible main island of Chichi-jima is a 25½-hour ferry ride from Tokyo.

Hiroshima

10 Seeing the city's leafy boulevards, it's hard to picture Hiroshima as the devastated victim of an atomic bomb. It's not until you walk through the Peace

Getting Around

Air Air services in Japan are extensive, reliable and safe.

Boat Japan is an island nation and there are many ferry services between islands and between ports on the same island. Ferries can be an excellent way of getting from one place to another and for seeing parts of Japan you might otherwise miss.

Bus Japan has a comprehensive network of long-distance buses. These 'highway buses' are nowhere near as fast as the shinkansen (Japan's famed bullet trains) but the fares are comparable with those of normal futsū (local) trains.

Train Japanese rail services are among the best in the world: they are fast, frequent, clean and comfortable.

Memorial Museum that the terrible reality becomes clear – the displays of battered personal effects say it all. But outside the quiet of the Peace Memorial Park, energetic Hiroshima rolls on. A visit here is a heartbreaking, important history lesson, but the modern city and its people ensure that's not the only memory you leave with.

Mt Fuji

11 Even from a distance Mt Fuji will take your breath away. Close up,

the perfectly symmetrical cone of Japan's highest peak is nothing short of awesome. Dawn from the summit? Pure magic. Fuji-san is Japan's most revered and timeless attraction. Hundreds of thousands of people climb it every year, continuing a centuries-old tradition of pilgrimages up this sacred volcano. Those who'd rather search for picture-perfect views from the less daunting peaks nearby can follow in the steps of Japan's most famous painters and poets.

Best on Film

Lost in Translation (2003) One of the few foreign films that manages to capture some of Japan's reality without condescending clichés.

Miyazaki Anime Director Miyazaki Hayao's animated films are classics. Start with My Neighbor Totoro (1988) or Castle in the Sky (1986).

Best in Print

A Japanese Mirror: Heroes & Villains of Japanese Culture (Ian Buruma; 1984) A look into the Japanese psyche by one of the world's most astute commentators on Japan.

The Anatomy of Dependence (Takeo Doi; 1971) A Japanese psychologist examines Japanese culture.

The Chrysanthemum & the Sword (Ruth Benedict; 1946) Groundbreaking work on Japanese culture.

The Wages of Guilt: Memories of War in Germany and Japan (Ian Buruma; 1994) A fascinating comparison of postwar Japan and Germany.

NYOMAN SUNDRA / GETTY IMAGES ©

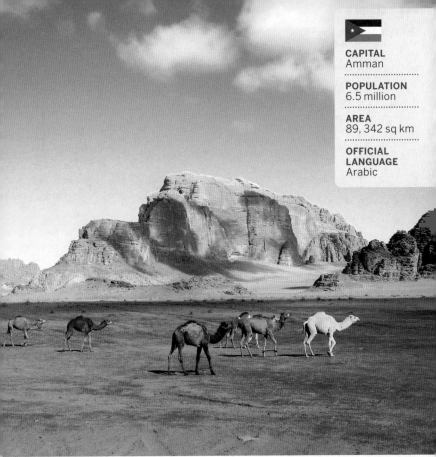

CAPITAL
Amman

POPULATION
6.5 million

AREA
89, 342 sq km

OFFICIAL LANGUAGE
Arabic

Wadi Rum

Jordan

At the crossroads of history for more than 2000 years, the kingdom of Jordan is a treasure trove of world-class heritage sites and spectacular desert scenery.

Jordan has welcomed high volumes of visitors since camel caravans plied the legendary King's Highway transporting frankincense in exchange for spices. Nabataean tradesmen, Roman legionnaires, Muslim armies and zealous Crusaders have all passed through the land we now call Jordan, leaving spectacular monuments behind. In turn, these monuments have provoked a modern wave of visitors who, since the early 19th century, have been fascinated to discover this potent past or who have gone in search of the origins of their faith.

Thanks to its diversity and small size, Jordan repays even the shortest visit with world-class sights and activities. Petra, the ancient Nabataean city locked in the heart of Jordan's sandstone escarpments, is the jewel in the crown of the country's many antiquities, but it is far from the only reason to visit. Apart from the many other spectacular historical and biblical sites, the country offers striking desert landscapes, a salty sea at the lowest point on earth, and rural towns that keep continuity with the traditions of the past.

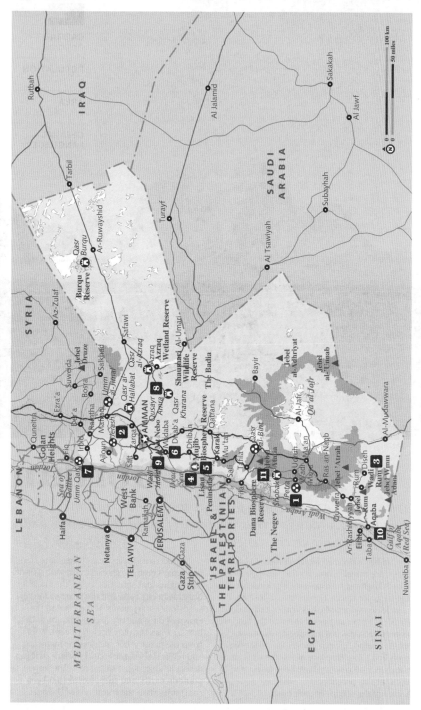

Jordan's
Top Experiences

Petra

1 Ever since the Swiss explorer Jean Louis Burckhardt rediscovered this spectacular site in 1812, the ancient Nabataean city of Petra has been drawing the crowds – and with good reason. This is without doubt Jordan's most treasured attraction and when the sun sets over the honeycombed landscape of tombs, carved facades, pillars and golden sandstone cliffs, it's a hard-hearted visitor who is left unaffected by its magic. Allow a couple of days to do the site justice and to visit the main monuments at optimum times of the day.

Ruins of Empire

2 For a country so small in size, Jordan punches well above its weight in world-class monuments, boasting some of the finest Roman ruins outside Rome. Most countries would be pleased to have attractions like the Citadel or the Roman Theatre in Amman, but these pale into insignificance compared with the superbly preserved ruins at Jerash. Visit during a chariot race when commentary from a red-plumed centurion will help bring this ancient outpost of Rome alive.

Treasury, Petra

1

Lawrence's Desert

3 It wasn't just the sublime vista of Wadi Rum, with its burnished sandstone cliffs and vivid-coloured dunes, that impressed Lawrence of Arabia as he paced on camel back through the land of the Bedouin. He was also impressed by the stoicism of the people who endured hardships associated with a life in the desert. Today, it's possible to get a glimpse of that traditional way of life, albeit with a few more creature comforts, by staying in one of the Bedouin camps scattered across this desert wilderness.

if Jordan were 100 people

98 would be Arab
1 would be Circassian
1 would be Armenian

....

belief systems
(% of population)

92 — Sunni Muslim
6 — Christian
2 — other

....

population per sq km

JORDAN   ISRAEL   UK

👤 ≈ 35 people

The Dead Sea Experience

4 Floating in the Dead Sea is one of the world's great natural experiences. Floating is the right word for it: with an eye-stingingly high salt content it is virtually impossible to swim in the viscous waters of a sea that is 415m below 'sea level'. The experience is usually accompanied by a mud bath, a bake in the sun and a health-giving spa treatment at one of the modern pleasure palaces lined up along the Dead Sea's shores.

Miraculous Mujib

5 Fresh water is in short supply in Jordan and it has already become an issue of intense political importance in dialogue with neighbouring states. Various projects, such as the 'Red to Dead' Sea Canal and a pipeline from Wadi Rum's aquifers to Amman, are being explored with ever-greater urgency. That's one reason why the miraculous springs of Mujib Biosphere Reserve are a highlight. The other reason is that the water flows through a spectacular wadi into a series of heavenly pools – paradise for the adventure-seeking traveller.

Madaba's Handmade History

6 For centuries, Madaba, at the head of the ancient King's Highway, has been a crossroad for caravans transporting goods, legions of armies pushing the borders of their empires, and pilgrims driven by faith in search of the Promised Land. To this day the town, with its museums, churches, craft workshops and

In Search of Sodom

The words 'Sodom and Gomorrah' bring dens of iniquity to mind. The Book of Genesis (Gen 19:24–25), responsible for the wicked reputation of these two towns, describes how the last straw occurred when local Sodomites demanded to have sex with angels sent by God. In response, 'the Lord rained upon Sodom and upon Gomorrah brimstone and fire... and he overthrew those cities...'

Whatever the cause of their demise (collapsing soil or a major earthquake are two possibilities), archaeologists have long speculated about the location of these sinful cities. Many archaeologists favour the southern shore of the Dead Sea. Others, the Bronze Age site of Babh adh-Dhra, on the edge of Wadi Karak. This town was destroyed in 2300 BC, but intriguingly holds the remains of 20,000 tombs containing an estimated half a million bodies – making it odds-on favourite for Sodom. Both Babh adh-Dhra and the nearby site of Numeira, believed to be Gomorrah, are covered in a 30cm-deep layer of ash, suggesting these cities ended in a great blaze.

Food & Drink

Fuul medames Fava-bean dish drizzled with fresh-pressed olive oil; served with unleavened Arabic bread, sour cream, local salty white cheese and a sprinkling of *zaatar* (thyme and other herbs).

Kunafa Addictive dessert of shredded dough and cream cheese, smothered in syrup.

Maqlubbeh Pyramid of steaming rice garnished with cardamom and sultanas; topped with slivers of onion, meat, cauliflower and fresh herbs.

Marrameeya Sage-based herbal tea, especially delicious at Dana.

Mensaf Bedouin dish of lamb, rice and pine nuts, combined with yogurt and liquid fat from the cooked meat.

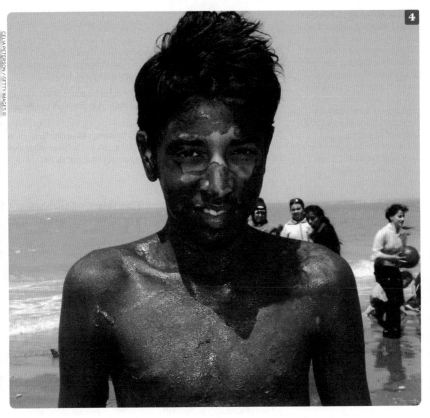

markets, retains the marks of those cultural exchanges. Perhaps the best evidence of this rich past is Madaba's magnificent collection of mosaics, a heritage con-

tinued through the town's unique mosaic school.

Blooming Beautiful

7 Carpets of scarlet poppies strewn across the

desert, ribbons of oleander in the wadis, the surprise flutter of velvet petals on a black iris along the King's Highway; Jordan is home to some of the region's most magnificent floral displays. For a truly sublime show, visit the Roman ruins of Umm Qais in the far north of the country on a sunny afternoon in April: armfuls of knee-high daisies and thistles, yellow hollyhocks and pink mallow compete for warmth between fallen masonry.

Exploring the Desert Castles

8 The plains of eastern Jordan are home to the iconic 'desert castles', a collection of early Umayyad

When to Go

HIGH SEASON (Mar–May)

➡ Perfect weather throughout, with warm days and cool nights.

➡ Northern Jordan is blanketed in wildflowers in April.

➡ Book rooms in advance in main tourist areas and expect higher rates.

SHOULDER (Sep–Feb)

➡ The best time to visit the Red Sea; prices in and around Aqaba rise accordingly.

➡ Bitter nights in the desert and even rain or snow curtail many activities such as camping.

LOW SEASON (Jun–Aug)

➡ The desert in the middle of summer is extreme. Temperatures throughout Jordan can be stifling.

➡ Prices are at their best but many places close in the low season.

pleasure palaces, bathhouses and hunting lodges that are strikingly incongruous with their barren surroundings. While visiting Jordan's eastern frontier requires some planning, this region is full of surprises, including Qusayr Amra's saucy frescos, Lawrence's winter redoubt at Azraq, a last refuge of the Arabian oryx at Shaumari Wildlife Reserve and an unlikely lake in the desert at Burqu.

Wadi Jadid

9 There's nothing new about Wadi Jadid ('New Valley' in Arabic). This undisturbed valley in the middle of nowhere typifies all that is constant in rural Jordanian life. In fact the valley would be entirely unremarkable were it not for the clusters of ancient Bronze Age dolmen that dot the terraced hillsides. Heaved into place between 5000 and 3000 BC, these impressive stone monuments are worth the effort it takes to locate them.

Best on Film

A Dangerous Man: Lawrence after Arabia (1991) Starring a young Ralph Fiennes.

Indiana Jones and the Last Crusade (1989) Harrison Ford in Petra caper.

Lawrence of Arabia (1962) David Lean's classic.

Best in Print

Heroine of the Desert (Donya al-Nahi, 2006) Reuniting children with their mothers.

Married to a Bedouin (M van Geldermalsen, 2006) Bringing a family up in Petra.

Walking the Bible (Bruce Feiler, 2005) Biblical locations.

Getting Around

Bus Public minibuses are the most common form of public transport. They normally only leave when full, so a wait is inevitable, especially in rural areas. The larger air-con tourist buses offer speedy and reliable service.

Car Jordan is an easy country to drive in (with the exception of Amman) and there are some spectacular routes linking the high ground with the Jordan Valley below sea level.

Taxi Yellow private taxis work like ordinary taxis and can be chartered for the day. White service taxis run along set routes within and between many towns Shared by more than one passenger, they usually have writing and numbers (in Arabic) showing their route.

Diving with Damsels

10 It's no secret that the Red Sea is home to some of the most spectacular underwater seascapes in the world. Jordan's Red Sea shoreline along the Gulf of Aqaba is admittedly short, but this comparatively unexploited stretch of water encompasses pristine reefs, crumbling wrecks and kaleidoscopic coral gardens. Snorkelling and diving among damsel fish, turtles and seahorses is an unforgettable experience easily arranged with dive centres in and around the seaside city of Aqaba.

The King's Highway

11 It may not be the path of literal kings, but the King's Highway follows some pretty big footsteps. These include those of the Nabataeans (their fabled city of Petra lies at the end of the King's Highway), the Romans (whose military outpost at Umm ar-Rasas is a Unesco World Heritage site) and the Crusaders (their Karak and Shobak castles are highlights in their own right). Smaller footsteps include those taken by Salome in her Dance of the Seven Veils at the desolate hilltop of Mukawir.

Qasr Kharana

FRIEDRICH SCHMIDT / GETTY IMAGES ©

CAPITAL
Astana

POPULATION
17.7 million

AREA
2.7 million sq km

OFFICIAL LANGUAGES
Kazakh, Russian

Kazakhstan

Today Kazakhstan's expanse of Eurasian steppe offers one of the last great undiscovered frontiers of travel with some home comforts and mod cons.

The world's ninth-biggest country is the most economically advanced of the 'stans', thanks to its abundant reserves of oil and most other valuable minerals. This means generally better standards of accommodation, restaurants and transport than elsewhere in Central Asia. The biggest city, Almaty, is almost reminiscent of Europe with its leafy avenues, chic cafes, glossy shopping centres and hedonistic nightlife. The capital Astana, on the windswept northern steppe, has been transformed into a 21st-century showpiece with a profusion of bold futuristic architecture. But it's beyond the cities that you'll find the greatest travel adventures, whether hiking in the high mountains and green valleys of the Tian Shan, searching for wildlife on the lake-dotted steppe, enjoying home-spun hospitality in village guesthouses, or jolting across the western deserts to remote underground mosques.

Kazakhstan's
Top Experiences

Almaty

1 Kazakhstan's economic success is most palpable here in its biggest city, where you could almost believe you are in Europe, such are the numbers of international shops and Mercedes, Audis and BMWs negotiating the peak-hour jams. This leafy city, with a backdrop of the snow-capped Zailiysky Alatau, has always been one of the most charming Russian creations in Central Asia. No one even seems bothered that Almaty has been replaced as Kazakhstan's capital.

Aksu-Zhabagyly Nature Reserve

2 This beautiful 1319-sq-km patch of valleys and mountains climbing to the Kyrgyz and Uzbek borders is the longest established (1926) and one of the easiest visited of Kazakhstan's nature reserves. The reserve, at the west end of the Talassky Alatau range, stretches from the edge of the steppe at 1200m up to 4239m at Pik Sayram. You may spot ibex, argali sheep, red marmots, eagles, various vultures – and bears (most likely in spring).

Astana

3 The country's spectacular new capital has risen fast from the northern steppe and is already a showpiece for 21st-century Kazakhstan. It is scheduled to go on rising and spreading into a city of over a million people by 2030. Its skyline grows more fantastical by the year as landmark buildings in a variety of Asian, Western, Soviet and wacky futuristic styles, sprout on vast acreage south of the Ishim River.

Turkistan

4 Here stands Kazakhstan's greatest architectural monument and its most important site of pilgrimage. The mausoleum of the first great Turkic Muslim holy man, Kozha Akhmed Yasaui, was built by Timur in the late 14th century on a grand scale comparable with his magnificent

Khan Shatyr, Astana

creations in Samarkand. Turkistan has no rivals in Kazakhstan for man-made beauty. It's an easy day trip from Shymkent.

Mangistau

5 The stony deserts of Mangistau, the region of which Aktau is capital, stretch 400km east to the border with Uzbekistan. This labyrinth of dramatic canyons, weirdly eroded, multicoloured rock outcrops, surprising lakes, mysterious underground mosques and ancient necropolises is only beginning to be explored, even by archaeologists. The underground mosques may have originated as cave hermitages for ascetics who retreated to the deserts.

Altay Mountains

6 In the far eastern corner of Kazakhstan the magnificent Altay Mountains spread across the borders to Russia, China and Mongolia. To visit you need to plan well ahead to obtain a border-zone permit, but the hassle of getting to this region is certainly worth it. Rolling meadows, snow-covered peaks, forested hillsides, glaciers, pristine lakes and rivers, and villages with Kazakh horsemen riding by make for scenery of epic proportions. Twin-headed Mt Belukha, a 4506m peak on the Kazakh–Russian border, has many mystical associations.

if Kazakhstan were 100 people

63 would be Kazakh
24 would be Russian
3 would be Uzbek
2 would be Ukrainian
8 would be other

belief systems
(% of population)

70 Muslim

24 Russian Orthodox

3 atheist

2 other Christian

1 other

When to Go

MID-APR–EARLY JUN

➡ The steppe and hills blossom and migrating birds flock in.

MAY–SEP

➡ The weather is perfect; from July it's hiking season.

NOV–APR

➡ It's cold, but skiers enjoy Central Asia's best facilities at Chimbulak.

population per sq km

KAZAKHSTAN RUSSIA USA

👤 ≈ 3 people

Abay, Cultural Icon

Writer, translator and educator Abay (Ibrahim) Kunanbaev (1845–1904) was born in the Shyngystau hills south of Semey. He studied at both a medressa and a Russian school. His later translations of Russian and other foreign literature into Kazakh, and his public readings of them, as well as his own work such as the philosophical Forty-One Black Words, were the beginning of Kazakh as a literary language and helped to broaden Kazakhs' horizons.

Abay valued Kazakh traditions but was also pro-Russian. 'Study Russian culture and art – it is the key to life,' he wrote. In Soviet times Abay's reputation had Moscow's stamp of approval, and his Russophile writings were enshrined. Today he remains the number one Kazakh cultural icon

Food & Drink

Apples Kazakhstan is reckoned to be the original source of apples.

Baursaki Fried dough balls or triangles, not unlike heavy doughnuts.

Beshbarmak Kazakh national dish; chunks of long-boiled mutton or beef served atop flat squares of pasta with onions and sometimes potatoes.

Horsemeat *Kazy*, *shuzhuk* and *karta* are all types of horsemeat sausage, in horse-intestine casing.

Kuurdak A fatty stew of potatoes, meat and offal from a horse, sheep or cow.

Kymyz Fermented mare's milk is a popular drink. It's mildly alcoholic with a sour, slightly fizzy taste.

Plov Kazakhs make a sweet *plov* (pilaf) with dried apricots, raisins and prunes.

Shubat Fermented camel's milk.

TONY WHEELER / GETTY IMAGES ©

Aralsk

7 Ponder boats marooned in the desert at Aralsk, miles from the shore of the Aral Sea, on which Aralsk was once an important fishing port. Today a large part of the sea is gone, victim of Soviet irrigation schemes that diverted its water sources, and pushed the shoreline 60km from Aralsk. If you want to witness this environmental disaster firsthand, Aralsk is easier to visit, and more interesting, than similarly defunct ports in Uzbekistan. Nor is everything quite so gloomy here: efforts to save part of the sea are succeeding.

The Baykonur Cosmodrome

8 A 6717-sq-km area of semidesert about 250km northwest of Kyzylorda has been the launch site for all Soviet- and Russian-manned space flights since Yury Gagarin, the first human in space, was lobbed up from here in 1961. Since the collapse of the USSR, Kazakhstan has leased the cosmodrome and town to Russia until 2050. Baykonur today has nine launch complexes and sends up astronauts from many countries.

Getting Around

Air A good network of domestic flights links cities all around Kazakhstan and fares are reasonable.

Bus With a few exceptions, intercity bus services are poor and getting worse. For longer trips trains are generally more comfortable.

Taxi For many intercity, trips taxis offer a much faster alternative to buses and minibuses

Train Trains serve all cities and many smaller places. They're a good way to experience Kazakhstan's terrain, vast size and people.

Wildebeest and zebras, Masai Mara National Reserve

CAPITAL
Nairobi

POPULATION
44 million

AREA
580,367 sq km

OFFICIAL LANGUAGES
English, Swahili

Kenya

Kenya is the Africa you always dreamed of. This is a land of vast savannahs, immense herds of wildlife and peoples with proud traditions on the soil where human beings were born.

When you think of Africa, you're probably thinking of Kenya: the lone acacia tree, the snow-capped mountain, the harsh deserts, the palm-fringed coastline, the great Rift Valley, the dense forests – they're all here.

Peopling this epic landscape, adding depth and resonance to Kenya's age-old story, are some of Africa's best-known peoples. The Maasai, the Samburu, the Turkana, the Swahili, the Kikuyu: these are the peoples whose histories and lives tell the story of the struggle to maintain traditions as the modern world crowds in, the daily fight for survival, the ancient tension between those who farm and those who roam.

Then, of course, there's the wildlife. From the Masai Mara to Tsavo, this is a country of vivid experiences – elephants wallowing in swamps in the shadow of Mt Kilimanjaro, the massed millions of pink flamingos, the landscape suddenly fallen silent and brought to attention by the arrival of an as-yet-unseen predator. Africa is the last great wilderness where these creatures survive.

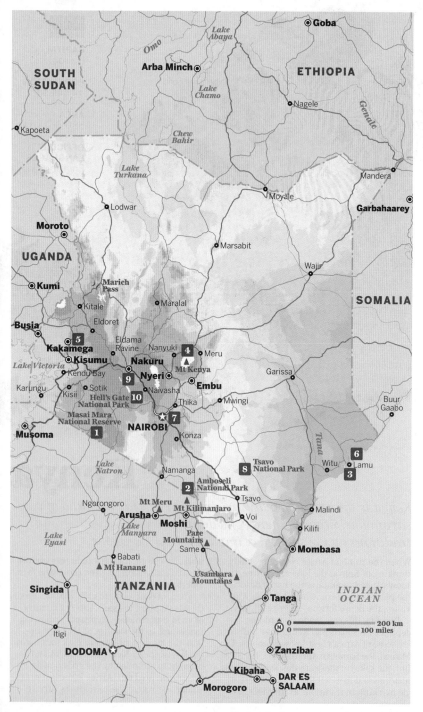

Kenya's
Top Experiences

Wildlife Migration, Masai Mara

1 Studded with flat-top acacia trees, the rolling savannahs of the Masai Mara National Reserve support some of the highest concentrations of wildlife on the planet, and provide the stage on which the legendary wildebeest migration is played out. From August, the Mara's plains are flooded with literally millions of these ungainly animals, along with herds of zebras, elephants and giraffes. Trailing this veritable walking buffet are prides of lions, solitary cheetahs and packs of laughing hyenas. Yes, come August in the Mara, it's most definitely *game on*.

Elephants of Amboseli National Park

2 There's possibly no better place in the world to watch elephants than Amboseli National Park in the country's south. A big part of the appeal is the setting – Africa's highest mountain, the snowcapped Mt Kilimanjaro, is the backdrop for seemingly every picture you'll take here. Just as significant, Amboseli was spared the worst of Kenya's poaching crisis and these elephants are remarkably tolerant of human presence (allowing you to get really close).

Wandering Lamu's Backstreets

3 Lamu is surely the most evocative destination on the Kenyan coast. With no cars around, the best way to get to know this graceful town is by wandering its backstreets, admiring the grand old Swahili doors, peeking into hidden courtyards bursting with unexpected colours, slipping into an easy chair and sipping on fruit juices, and accepting all invitations to stop and shoot the breeze (chat). Do all this, and the backstreets of Lamu will become a place you'll dream of forever.

if Kenya were 100 people

42 would be aged 0-14
19 would be aged 15-24
32 would be aged 25-54
4 would be aged 55-64
3 would be aged 65+

belief systems
(% of population)

82 Christian
11 Muslim
2 Traditionalists
5 other or none

population per sq km

KENYA   SOUTH AFRICA   UK

↑ ≈ 40 people

Hiking Mt Kenya

4 Mt Kenya is the country's highest peak and Africa's second highest. Located in the heart of the country and in the hearts of the Kikuyu people, this is not a mountain to be admired from afar. The Kikuyu tribe keeps its doors open to the face of the sacred mountain, and some still come to its lower slopes to offer prayers and the foreskins of their young men. Besides being venerated by the Kikuyu, Mt Kenya has the rare honour of being both a Unesco World Heritage site and a Unesco Biosphere Reserve.

Kakamega Forest

5 Paths lace the Kakamega Forest and offer a rare opportunity to ditch the safari 4WD and stretch your legs. This ancient forest is home to an astounding 330 bird species, 400 butterfly species and seven different primate species. But like most rainforests, the trees themselves are the chief attraction here, and in the forest gloom you'll stumble upon the botanical equivalent of beauty and the beast: delicate orchids and parasitic figs that strangle their hosts as they climb towards the light.

Dhow to Takwa

6 Set sail with the monsoon winds on a creaky dhow: the sleepy Swahili ruins of Takwa are your goal. To get there you must plot a course between the Seven Isles of Eryaya and navigate the narrow maze of mangroves. On the way, swim and snorkel with brightly coloured fish and eat coconut rice as ghost crabs play at your feet. Never does the Kenyan coast feel more romantic than when seen through the eyes of a

Christian the Lion

When Joy Adamson wrote *Born Free* on her experience raising an orphaned lion cub, few predicted the book would spend 13 weeks at the top of the *New York Times* bestseller list and go on to inspire a film that would become a worldwide hit.

It was the success of Elsa's rehabilitation that inspired John Rendall and Ace Bourke to have their own lion, Christian, in the hope that he too could be returned to the wild. Christian was originally brought from Harrods department store and lived in a London basement below their furniture shop. On learning that Christian had been successfully acclimatised, the boys returned to Kenya and their reunion with Christian was filmed for a 1971 documentary.

More than 30 years later, edited footage of this reunion went viral on YouTube and is estimated that it has now been viewed by more than 60 million people. It's a real tearjerker, especially the part when Christian first recognises his old friends and comes bounding down a rocky slope and literally leaps into their arms, almost knocking the boys off their feet in 150kg of furry, lion love.

Food & Drink

The Kenyan culinary tradition has generally emphasised feeding the masses as efficiently as possible, with little room for flair or innovation. Most meals are centred on *ugali*, a thick, doughlike mass made from boiled grains cooked into a porridge until it sets hard, then served up in flat (and rather dense) slabs.

Kenyans are enthusiastic carnivores and their unofficial national dish, *nyama choma* (barbecued meat), is a red-blooded, hands-on affair. Goat is the most common meat, but you'll see chicken, beef and some game animals.

Chai is the national obsession and, as in India, the tea, milk and masses of sugar are stewed for ages and the result is milky and very sweet. Spiced masala chai with cardamom and cinnamon is very pleasant and rejuvenating.

Kikuyu people

dhow trip around the Lamu archipelago.

Nairobi

7 Nairobi's reputation precedes it, and not always in the most enticing way. And yet Nairobi is an essential (and very often immensely enjoyable) element of the Kenyan experience. No other city in the world can boast a national park (which is home to four of the Big Five) within sight of city skyscrapers, the chance to feed orphaned baby elephants, immerse yourself in the place that inspired *Out of Africa* and visit an outstanding national museum all in a single day.

Lions at Tsavo National Park

8 The two Tsavo (East and West) National Parks are wilderness experiences par excellence: vast and dramatic landscapes where wildlife lurks in the undergrowth. All of Africa's charismatic megafauna are present here, but it's the cats – leopards, lions and

When to Go

HIGH SEASON
(Jan, Feb & Jun–Oct)

➡ Wildebeest in the Mara migrate from June to October.

➡ January and February offer hot, dry weather good for wildlife watching.

➡ Sky-high lodge prices. Book well in advance.

SHOULDER
(Nov & Dec)

➡ Short rains fall in October and November.

➡ Prices at most lodges and parks drop on 1 November, but advance reservations are still required.

LOW SEASON
(Mar–May)

➡ Long rains mean accommodation is much quieter and prices are low, but wildlife is harder to spot and mosquitoes are rife.

cheetahs – who bring this ecosystem to life. Against a backdrop of red soils, volcanic outcrops and sweeping savannah plains, these lions of legend (it was here that the man-eaters of Tsavo once struck fear into the hearts of locals) laze about in the shade, waiting for the right moment to pounce.

Lake Nakuru National Park

9 Another of Kenya's world-class parks, this is dominated by one of the Rift Valley's most beautiful lakes. The waters of lake Nakaru are lined on one side by an abrupt escarpment and the shoreline is at times

given colour and texture by massed flamingos and pelicans. But Lake Nakuru is also a wildlife haven for land-borne mammals, home as it is to lions, leopards, the highly endangered Roth-schild's giraffes, zebras, buffaloes, various primate species and Kenya's most easily spotted rhinos. No wonder it's regularly ranked among Kenya's top five parks.

Hell's Gate National Park

10 It's one thing to watch Africa's megafauna from the safety of your safari vehicle, quite another entirely to do so on foot or from astride a bicycle. Hell's Gate National Park – a dramatic volcanic landscape of red cliffs, otherworldly rocky outcrops and deep canyons in the heart of Kenya's Rift Valley – may lack preda-tors, but this chance to experience the African wild at close quarters certainly gives most people frissons of excitement. By placing you in the landscape, Hell's Gate heightens the senses, bringing alive the African wild like nowhere else in Kenya.

Getting Around

Bus Kenya has an extensive network of long- and short-haul bus routes, with particularly good coverage of the areas around Nairobi, the coast and the western regions. Buses are considerably cheaper than taking the train or fly-ing, and as a rule services are frequent, fast and often quite comfortable.

Car Having your own vehicle is a great way to see the country at your own pace. Just remember though that the biggest hazard on Kenyan roads is simply the other vehicles on them, and driving defensively is essential.

Matatu Local matatus are the main means of getting around for local people, and any reasonably sized city or town will have plenty of services covering every major road and suburb. Matatus leave when full and the fares are fixed.

Best on Film

Kibera Kid (2006) This short film, set in the Kibera slum, was written and directed by Nathan Collett. It tells the story of 12-year-old Otieno, an orphan living with a gang of thieves, who must make a choice between gang life and redemption. Featur-ing a cast of children, all of whom live in Kibera, the film played at film festivals worldwide.

Best in Print

A Primate's Memoir: Love, Death and Baboons in East Af-rica (Robert M Sapolsky) Funny, poignant account by a young primatologist in Kenya.

Dreams in a Time of War (Ngũgĩ wa Thiong'o) Kenya's premier writer looks back at his early life.

No Man's Land: An Investigative Journey Through Kenya and Tanzania (George Monbiot) The modern struggle of the region's nomadic tribes.

The Flame Trees of Thika (Elspeth Huxley) A marvellously told colonial memoir.

Greater flamingos

GALLO IMAGES · MICHAEL POLIZA / GETTY IMAGES ©

WWII artillery on Tarawa island

Kiribati

A tiny speck of islands in the Pacific, Kiribati still maintains traditional ways. Nothing happens too fast here, so wind down, relax and enjoy living on island time.

CAPITAL
Tarawa

POPULATION
103,248

AREA
811 sq km

OFFICIAL LANGUAGES
I-Kiribati, English

Curving its way above and below the equator, the Republic of Kiribati encompasses the Gilbert, Phoenix and Line Islands. Measured by land size Kiribati is a tiny nation of just over 811 sq km, but its 33 atolls span a huge 3.5 million sq km of the Pacific. Most atolls surround turquoise lagoons and barely rise above the surrounding ocean, so it's rare to be out of the sight and sound of the sea.

Kiribati's recent colonial and WWII history (the islands were occupied by the Japanese in 1942) has had little impact on the outer islands, where the people subsist on coconuts, breadfruit and fish as they have done for centuries. Even on the main island, Tarawa, most locals live in traditional raised thatched huts. Western influence is increasing, though, in the form of cars, bars, movies and the Internet, and inevitably there's an escalating urban drift from the outer islands to Tarawa.

The I-Kiribati, people of the islands, are friendly but laconic – expect a bold 'mauri' (hello) as you pass.

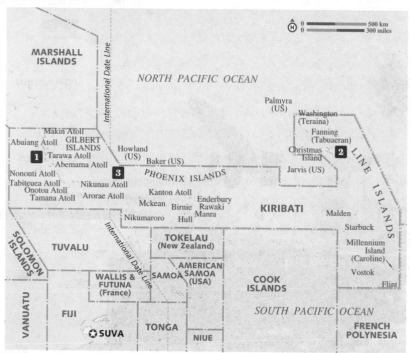

Kiribati's
Top Experiences

WWII Guns

1 On South Tarawa, Betio retains a sobering collection of eight-inch guns, bunkers and a machine-gun command post left over from WWII. In 1943, 20,000 US marines stormed Betio's beaches and routed the occupying Japanese. There's also a cemetery and a moving memorial.

Food & Drink

Breadfruit Along with the coconut, this is an island staple.

Fish & seafood Local fish dishes are abundant. Most other foods are imported from Australia.

Kaokioki Kiribati's famed local brew is tapped from coconut palms and fermented.

Christmas Island

2 Christmas Island is a paradise for visiting sportfishers and one of Kiribati's biggest tourist draws. Fly fishing is the most popular activity on Christmas Island, the endless flats of which hold enormous bonefish. Diving on Christmas Island is also outstanding. Almost all dives are done in the two coral-rich channels flanking Cook Island, where the reef drops off sharply.

Outer Gilbert Islands

3 For that castaway feeling, head to the outer Gilbert islands where you can experience traditional I-Kiribati life, and it's rare to find more than a few trucks and some motorbikes. The islands are pristine and packaged Western products are a rarity. People live off fishing and coconuts, and occasionally earn revenue by selling salted clams or copra.

When to Go

DEC–FEB

➡ Dry season and Christmas high season, though weather is still hot.

JUN–SEP

➡ A second dry season corresponding to the northern hemisphere summer.

MAR–MAY & SEP–NOV

➡ There are two rainy seasons, though cyclones are rare.

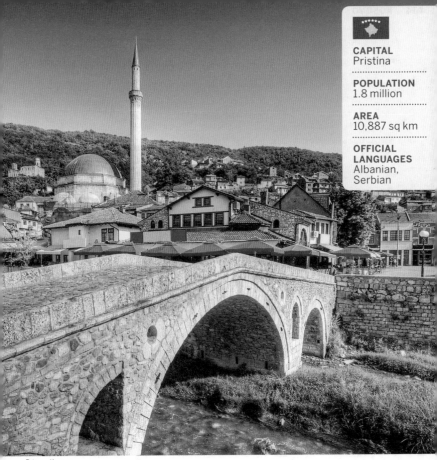

Prizren, Kosovo

CAPITAL
Pristina

POPULATION
1.8 million

AREA
10,887 sq km

OFFICIAL LANGUAGES
Albanian, Serbian

Kosovo

It may be Europe's newest country, but Kosovo's long and dramatic history can be witnessed at every turn in elegant Ottoman towns and little-visited mountain vistas.

Kosovo is contested territory. Populated predominately by Albanians, it is considered holy ground by minority Serbs. The Kosovar Albanians declared independence in 2008, a move hotly disputed by some and still not universally recognised, leading to tensions between Albanian and Serbian locals.

Far from being the dangerous or depressing place most people imagine, Kosovo is a fascinating land at the heart of the Balkans and one of the last corners of Eastern Europe where tourism has yet to take off.

Barbs of its past are impossible to miss: roads are dotted with memorials to those killed in inter-ethnic tension in 1999, while NATO forces still guard Serbian monasteries. But with independence has come a degree of stability, and Kosovo is now the latest word in getting off the beaten track in the Balkans. Visitors will be rewarded with welcoming smiles, terracotta-roofed old quarters, remote 13th-century domed Orthodox monasteries and poppy-splashed hillside meadows, which they will likely have all to themselves.

Kosovo's
Top Experiences

Pristina

1 Pristina's lively bazaar district – a maze of narrow, twisting streets – is home to many of the city's sights including the Ethnographic Museum, the 15th-century Carshi Mosque and the Sultan Mehmet Fatih Mosque, built by its namesake around 1461.

Food & Drink

Byrek Pastry with cheese or meat.

Duvĕc Baked meat and vegetables.

Fli Flaky pastry pie with honey.

Kos Goat's-milk yoghurt.

Raki Locally made spirit, usually made from grapes.

Vranac Red wine from the Rahovec region of Kosovo.

Prizren

2 Picturesque Prizren is Kosovo's second city and it shines with post-independence euphoria. The charming mosque-filled old town is well worth a wander. Prizren's 15th-century Ottoman bridge has been superbly restored. Nearby is Sinan Pasha Mosque (1561), which renovations are resurrecting as a central landmark in Prizren. Have a peek at the nonfunctioning Gazi Mehmed Pasha Baths nearby as well.

Visoki Dečani Monastery

3 The imposing white-washed monastery is located in a beautiful spot beneath the mountains and surrounded by a forest of pine and chestnut trees. Serbian monks live here in total isolation from the local community, and they get on with the serious business of making delicious wines, cheeses and honey and restoring the monastery's fabulous icons and frescoes.

When to Go

DEC–APR

➡ The skiing's good in these months.

JUN

➡ The Shqip Film Fest brings short films to Peja.

AUG

➡ It's a sweat-free summer as temperatures hover around 25°C.

Kuwait Towers

CAPITAL
Kuwait City

POPULATION
2.7 million

AREA
17,818 sq km

OFFICIAL LANGUAGE
Arabic

Kuwait

Long an oasis in the parched desert, Kuwait is now at the vanguard of political change and cultural development in the Gulf.

Kuwait, in the cradle of one of the most ancient and most contested corners of the world, is best described as a city state. For centuries Kuwait City has been like a magnet, attracting Bedouin people from the interior in search of a sea breeze and escape from recurring drought. Today the metropolis is still an oasis in a land of desert plains, but rather more of the cultural and culinary kind. Excellent museums, a corniche of combed beaches and lively res-

taurants, malls and souqs mark the Kuwait City experience.

Outside the capital there are few attractions other than coastal resorts. Oil excavation dominates the flat desert plains and there are few distinctive geographical features. That said, there is always something to see in a desert, with a bit of patience and an eye for detail; when it comes to the ritual camping expedition, Kuwaitis have plenty of both.

Kuwait's
Top Experiences

Scientific Center Aquarium

1 Housed in a sail-shaped building on the corniche, the mesmerising aquarium is the largest in the Middle East. The intertidal display, with waves washing in at eye level, is home to black-spotted sweetlips and the ingenious mudskipper.

Food & Drink

Alcohol Not available nor permissable.

Baked fish Blended with coriander, turmeric, red pepper and cardamom.

Gulf prawns Available late autumn and early winter.

Hamour or pomfret Fish stuffed with herbs and onions.

Tareq Rajab Museum

2 Housed in the basement of a large villa, this museum should not be missed. It was assembled as a private collection of Islamic art by Kuwait's first minister of antiquities and his British wife. In this Aladdin's cave of beautiful items there are superbly presented pieces from around the Muslim world, including the Arabic manuscripts that give the collection its importance.

Kuwait Towers

3 Kuwait's most famous landmark, the Kuwait Towers, with their distinctive blue-green 'sequins', are worth a visit for the prospect of sea and city that they afford. Opened in 1979, the largest of the three towers rises to a height of 187m, and houses a two-level revolving observation deck, gift shop and cafe. The lower globe on the largest tower stores around one million gallons of water.

When to Go

NOV–JAN

➡ Experience the relief of cool evenings after the burning heat of summer.

FEB

➡ Pick up a bargain in Kuwait's Halla Shopping Festival.

FEB–MAR

➡ During spring, the desert is laced in a gossamer of lime green.

Yurt camp, Lake Song-Köl, Naryn province

CAPITAL
Bishkek

POPULATION
5.5 million

AREA
199,951 sq km

OFFICIAL LANGUAGES
Kyrgyz, Russian

Kyrgyzstan

A half-forgotten land of mountain valleys, glittering lakes and felt yurts, Kyrgyzstan is a dream for DIY adventurers, eco tourists and wannabe nomads.

Kyrgyzstan is a nation defined by its topography: joyously unspoilt mountainscapes, stark craggy ridges, and rolling summer pastures (*jailoos*) are brought to life by semi-nomadic, yurt-dwelling shepherd cultures. Add to this natural beauty a well-developed network of homestays and the recent introduction of visa-free travel, and it's easy to see why Kyrgyzstan is rapidly becoming the gateway of choice for Western travellers in Central Asia. As can be expected in a country where the vast majority of attractions are rural and high altitude, the timing of your visit is crucial. Summer is ideal with hikes and roads generally accessible. Midsummer also sees Kazakh and Russian tourists converge on the beaches of never-freezing Lake Issyk-Köl. From October to May, much rural accommodation closes down and the yurts that add such character to the alpine vistas are stashed away. So think twice about a winter visit unless you've come to ski.

KAZAKHSTAN

Muyunkum
Desert

BISHKEK
Kara-Balta ● Tokmak
Taraz ◉ **8**
● Talas **3**
Balykchy
Ala-Archa
Canyon **2**
Toktogul
Lake Song-Köl
Tashkömür
4
● Arslanbob
At-Bashy
Tashkent ◉
UZBEKISTAN
● Jalal-Abad
◉ Osh
7
Sary Tash ●
Isfana ●
FAN
MOUNTAINS
Dushanbe ✪
Koh-i
Somoni
Pyanj
TAJIKISTAN

Cholpon-Ata **Karakol**
▲ Khan
Tengri
5
Lake Issyk-Köl **6**
Barskoön
1
Naryn
▲ Pobedy

Torugart
Pass
Irkeshtam
Pass

CHINA

N 0 ___ 200 km
0 ___ 100 miles

Kyrgyzstan's
Top Experiences

Horse Treks

1 Horse treks offer a not-to-be-missed chance to see the Kyrgyz countryside at its best. Kyrgyzstan is the best place in Central Asia to saddle up and join the nomads on the high pastures. Community Based Tourism offices throughout the country can organise horse hire by the hour or day. Shepherds Way is a professional local company, run by a former shepherding family, organising horse treks into the mountains behind Barskoön. The horses often give the impression they're only a hoof-beat away from reverting to their wild roots and galloping off but novice riders are seldom given unruly horses if they make their concerns known.

Lake Song-Köl

2 Distantly ringed by a saw-toothed horizon of peaks, the wide open landscapes of Song-Köl create a giant stage for constant performances of symphonic cloudscapes. Almost 20km across, and fronted by lush summer pastures, the lake's colour changes magically from tropical turquoise to brooding indigo in seconds as the sun flashes or the storms scud by in a vast meteorological theatre. It's a sublime place to watch the sun come up or to gaze into a cold, crystal-clear night sky heavy with countless stars.

Ala-Archa Canyon

3 Trek in the Ala-Archa Valley, the very grand, rugged but accessible gorge south of Bishkek. Here you can sit by a waterfall all day, hike to a glacier (and ski on it, even in summer) or trek on to the region's highest peaks. Most of the canyon is part of a state nature park, and foreigners must pay an entrance fee.

Arslanbob

4 The Babash-Ata Mountains form an impressive wall of snow-sprinkled crags behind the elevated 'oasis' of Arslanbob. Ethnically Uzbek and religiously conservative, the very large village sprawls almost invisibly along a network of tree-shaded lanes, and is surrounded by a vast tract of blossoming woodland that constitutes the world's

Horses grazing in pasture, Lake Song-Köl, Naryn province

largest walnut grove. According to local legend, the grove's seed-nuts were a miraculous gift from the Prophet Mohammad to a modest gardener who he had charged with finding paradise on earth.

Lake Issyk-Köl

5 Hemmed in by mountains, the bizarrely unfreezable Lake Issyk-Köl is the country's premier attraction. A combination of extreme depth, thermal activity and mild salinity ensures the lake never freezes; its moderating effect on the climate, plus abundant rainfall, have made it an oasis through the centuries. Scores of streams pour into the lake but none escape her. Over 170km long, 70km across and the second-largest alpine lake in the world, Issyk-Köl is a force of nature and she knows it.

Ala-Köl Lake

6 Breathtaking scenery, steaming hot pools and the first glimpse of the secret Ala-Köl lake make for great trekking. Probably the most popular destination from Karakol is a spartan hot spring development called Altyn Arashan (Golden Spa), set in a postcard-perfect alpine valley at 3000m, with 4260m Pik Palatka looming at its southern end. Much of the area is a botanical research area called the Arashan State Nature Reserve and is home to about 20 snow leopards and a handful of bears.

if Kyrgyzstan were 100 people

65 would be Kyrgyz
14 would be Uzbek
12 would be Russian
9 would be other

belief systems
(% of population)

75 Muslim
20 Russian Orthodox
5 other

When to Go

MAY–JUN

➡ Flowers bloom and tourist numbers are low; higher mountains may be snow-bound.

MID-JUL–EARLY SEP

➡ Ideal for treks; accommodation heavily booked; cities stiflingly hot.

MAR

➡ Rural accommodation closed; trekking areas inaccessible; good for skiing.

population per sq km

KYRGYZSTAN   KAZAKHSTAN   USA

† = 3 people

Home Sweet Yurt

Nothing gets the nomadic blood racing through your veins like lying awake in a yurt at night under a heavy pile of blankets wondering if wolves will come.

Yurts are the archetypal shepherd shelters – circular homes made of multilayered felt stretched around a collapsable wooden frame. The outer felt layer is coated in waterproof sheep fat, the innermost lined with woven grass matting to block the wind. Long woollen strips secure the walls and poles.

The interior is richly decorated with textiles, wall coverings and ornately worked chests. Floors are lined with thick felt and covered with bright carpets.

The central wheel-like *tunduk* that supports the roof is none other than the design depicted in the middle of Kyrgyzstan's national flag.

Food & Drink

Ashlyanfu Cold rice-noodles, jelly, vinegar and eggs.

Boorsok: Empty ravioli-sized fried dough-parcels to dunk in drinks or cream.

Bozo Thick, fizzy drink made from boiled fermented millet or other grains.

Jarma and maksym Fermented barley drinks, made with yeast and yoghurt.

Kesme Thick noodle soup with small bits of potato, vegetable and meat.

Kurut Small, very hard balls of tart, dried yoghurt; a favourite snack.

Kymys Fermented mare's milk; the national drink.

Laghman Mildly spicy, fat noodles generally served in soup

Mampar Tomato-based meat stew with gnocchi-like pasta pieces.

Vendor at Osh's bazaar

Osh

7 For centuries Silk Road traders have haggled their way from one stall to the next in Osh's bazaar, one that locals claim is older than Rome. Osh is Kyrgyzstan's second-biggest city and the administrative centre of the huge, populous province that engulfs the Fergana Valley on the Kyrgyzstan side. The thunderous daily bazaar is one of Central Asia's best, teeming with Uzbeks, Kyrgyz and Tajiks dealing in everything from traditional hats and knives to pirated cassettes and horseshoes.

Bishkek

8 The green, quiet and laid-back Kyrgyz capital seems to be the perfect introduction to the mountain republic. The entire downtown area feels like one big park, with trees sprouting from every crack in the concrete. The Kyrgyz Ala-Too range creates a magnificent backdrop and their glacial melt pours through the city centre in gurgling troughs. The low-rise Soviet-era buildings and the odd Lenin or Frunze statue lend the city a quaint historical time-warp ambience.

Getting Around

Bus Only a handful of routes employ full-size buses, but minibuses, some scheduled, others departing when full, wait for passengers at most bus stations, as do shared taxis.

Car & Motorcycle Self-drive car rental is a new concept but there are two local agencies in Bishkek. It is possible to rent Yamaha-600 trail motorbikes but they don't come cheap.

Taxi Agency or CBT-arranged drivers generally cost around double since they must cover the probability of returning empty, but such options are still worth considering for complex routes with multiple or overnight stops, and you'll often get a better vehicle (not necessarily English-speaking drivers, though).

Vang Vieng

CAPITAL
Vientiane

POPULATION
6.7 million

AREA
236,800 sq km

OFFICIAL LANGUAGE
Lao

Laos

Laos, long a forgotten backwater, combines some of the best elements of Southeast Asia in one bite-sized destination.

Pockets of pristine environment, a kaleidoscope of diverse cultures and quite possibly the most chilled-out people on earth have earned Laos cult status among travellers. Imagine a country where your pulse slows, smiles are genuine and the locals are still curious about you.

Village life is refreshingly simple, and even in Vientiane it's hard to believe this sort of languid riverfront life exists in a capital city. Magical Luang Prabang bears witness to hundreds of saffron-robed monks gliding through the streets in search of alms; it's one of the region's iconic images.

Away from the cities, it's easy to make a quick detour off the beaten track and end up in a fairytale landscape with jagged limestone cliffs, brooding jungle and the snaking Mekong River as a backdrop. Community-based trekking combines these natural attractions with a village homestay. The Lao people are wonderfully welcoming hosts and there is no better way to get to know their culture than by sharing their lives.

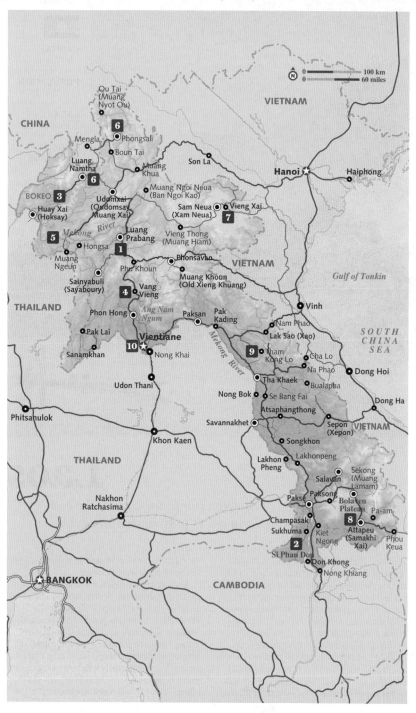

Laos'
Top Experiences

Luang Prabang

1 Hemmed in by the Mekong and Khan rivers, this timeless city of temples is a travel editor's dream: it is rich in royal history, home to saffron-clad monks, and combines stunning river views and world-class French cuisine with the best boutique accommodation in Southeast Asia. Hire a bike and explore the tropical peninsula's backstreets, take a cooking class, go on an elephant trek or just ease back with a restful massage at one of the many affordable spas. Prepare to adjust your timetable and stay in Luang Prabang a little longer than planned.

Si Phan Don

2 Legends don't happen by accident. Laos' hammock-flopping mecca has been catering to weary travellers for years. While these tropical islands bounded by the waters of the Mekong are best-known as a happy haven for catatonic sun worshippers, more active souls are also spoilt for choice. Between tubing and cycling through paddy fields, grab a kayak or fish with the locals, then round off your day with a sunset boat trip to see the rare Irrawaddy dolphin.

STEVE OGLE / GETTY IMAGES ©

The Gibbon Experience

3 Whiz hundreds of feet above the forest floor attached to a zipline. These brilliantly engineered cables, some more than 500m long, span forest valleys in the lush Bokeo Nature Reserve (habitat of the black-crested gibbon and Asiatic tiger). Your money goes toward protecting the eponymous endangered primate, and your guides are former poachers turned rangers. Zip into and bed down in high treehouses by night, listening to the call of the wild. This is Laos' premier wildlife and adrenalin high.

if Laos were 100 people

55 would be Lao
11 would be Khmu (Mon-Khmer)
8 would be Hmong

3 would be Chinese
3 would be Vietnamese
20 would be ethnic minorities

belief systems
(% of population)

50 — Buddhist
45 — Animist
2 — Christian
3 — other

population per sq km

LAOS   THAILAND   USA

= 7 people

Vang Vieng

4 The riverine jewel in Laos' karst country, Vang Vieng sits under soaring cliffs beside the flowing Nam Song and has an easy, outdoorsy vibe. Since the party crowd moved on in 2012, tranquility reigns again with more family-oriented visitors dropping in to soak up such well-organised activities as hot-air ballooning, trekking, caving and climbing. And don't forget the main draw: tubing. As budget guesthouses and fast-food joints wind down, smarter boutique hotels and delicious restaurants are blossoming in their wake. There's never been a better time to visit.

River Trips

5 River trips are a major feature of travel through Laos. One of the most popular connects Luang Prabang and Huay Xai, the gateway to the Golden Triangle, via Pak Beng. From local boats to luxury cruises, there are options to suit every budget, including floating through sleepy Si Phan Don in the far south. Beyond the Mekong, many important feeder rivers, such as the Nam Ou and Nam Tha, connect places as diverse as Nong Khiaw and Hat Sa (for Phongsali).

Trekking & Homestays

6 Laos is famous for its wide range of community-based treks, many of which include a traditional homestay for a night or more. Trekking is possible all over the country, but northern Laos is one of the most popular areas.

Ho Chi Minh Trail

The infamous Ho Chi Minh Trail is a complex network of dirt paths and gravel roads running parallel to the Laos–Vietnam border. The trail's heaviest use occurred between 1966 and 1971 when more than 600,000 North Vietnamese Army (NVA) troops – along with provisions and 500,000 tonnes of trucks, tanks, weapons and ordnance – passed along the route in direct violation of the 1962 Geneva Accords.

NVA engineering battalions worked on building roads, bridges and defence installations, and methods to hide the trails from the air were simple but ingenious. Bridges were built just below the water level and branches were tied together to hide wide roads.

Today the most accessible points are at Ban Dong, east of Sepon, and the village of Pa-am in Attapeu Province, which sits almost right on the main thoroughfare. Elsewhere you'll need to get way out into the sticks and get locals to guide you.

Food & Drink

Đạm màhk hung A salad of shredded green papaya mixed with garlic, lime juice, fish sauce, sometimes tomatoes, palm sugar, land crab or dried shrimp and chillies.

Fĕr Rice noodles in a broth with vegetables and meat, with fish sauce, lime juice, dried chillies, mint leaves, basil or hot chilli sauce.

Kòw nĕeo Sticky rice served in a small basket. Take a small amount of rice and, using one hand, work it into a ball before dipping it into the food.

Láhp Spicy salad of minced beef, pork, duck, fish or chicken, mixed with fish sauce, small shallots, mint leaves, lime juice, roasted ground rice and lots and lots of chillies.

Lòw-lów Lao liquor or rice whisky, though officially illegal, is popular in the lowlands. It's usually taken neat and offered as a welcoming gesture.

Akha women, Luang Namtha

Trekking around Phongsali is considered some of the most authentic in Laos and involves the chance to stay with the colourful Akha people. Luang Namtha is the most accessible base for ecotreks in the Nam Ha NPA, one of the best known trekking spots in the Mekong region.

When to Go

HIGH SEASON
(Nov–Mar)

➡ Pleasant temperatures in much of Laos, although cold in the mountains. It's the best all-round time to visit.

➡ Book ahead for accommodation in the peak Christmas and New Year period.

SHOULDER
(Jul & Aug)

➡ Wet in most parts of Laos with high humidity, but the landscapes are emerald green.

➡ Popular time for European tourists to visit.

LOW SEASON
(Apr–Jun & Sep–Oct)

➡ April and May brings the hot season to Laos when the thermostat hits 40°C.

➡ September and October can be very wet, with some incredible cloud formations.

Vieng Xai Caves

7 This is history writ large in stone. An area of outstanding natural beauty, Vieng Xai was home to the Pathet Lao communist leadership during the US bombing campaign of 1964–73. Beyond the breathtaking beauty of the natural caves, it is the superb audio tour that really brings the experience to life. When the bombers buzz overhead to a soundtrack of Jimi Hendrix, you'll find yourself ducking for cover in the Red Prince's lush garden.

Bolaven Plateau

8 The air is a little cooler, the waterfalls a little taller and the coffee a little

ANDREA PISTOLESI / GETTY IMAGES ©

richer on this forest-clad protuberance rising high above the floodplains of the Mekong. Write your own motorcycle diary along the lonely highways of the plateau, continuing on into the remote southeastern provinces abutting Vietnam. Or chill out for a few days in Tat Lo, a waterfall-studded backpacker hideaway on the plateau's escarpment. Looking for adventure? Trek to distant minority villages or get nose-to-nose with the jungle on ziplines in Dong Hua Sao NPA.

Best on Film

The Rocket (2013) The story of a young Lao boy blamed for bringing bad luck to his family. To win back the trust of the family he builds a giant firework to enter the annual Rocket Festival. Set against a backdrop of war, this film has won awards at the Tribeca and Berlin Film Festivals. Shot on location in Laos, it was written and directed by Kim Mordaunt and stars former street kid Sitthiphon Disamoe as Ahlo.

Best in Print

Ant Egg Soup (Natacha Du Pont de Bie; 2004) Subtitled *The Adventures of a Food Tourist in Laos;* the author samples some local delicacies (including some that aren't suitable for a delicate stomach) and includes both recipes and sketches to punctuate the story.

The Coroner's Lunch (Colin Cotterill; 2004) Delve into the delightful world of Dr Siri, full-time national coroner in the 1970s and part-time super sleuth. Try this first instalment and then seek out the other seven titles in the series.

Getting Around

Bicycle The stunning roads and light, relatively slow traffic in most towns and on most highways make Laos arguably the best country for cycling in Southeast Asia.

Boat More than 4600km of navigable rivers are the highways and byways of traditional Laos, and it's worth doing at least one river excursion while you're here. The Mekong is the longest and most important route and is navigable year-round between Luang Prabang in the north and Savannakhet in the south.

Car & Motorcycle Driving in Laos is easier than it looks. The road infrastructure is pretty basic, but outside of the large centres there are so few vehicles that it's a doddle compared to Vietnam, China or Thailand.

Tham Kong Lo

9 Imagine your deepest nightmare: the snaggle-toothed mouth of a river cave beneath a towering limestone mountain, the boatman in his rickety longtail taking you into the heart of darkness. Puttering beneath the cathedral-high ceiling of stalactites in this extraordinary 7.5km underworld in remote Khammuan Province is an awesome experience. You'll be very glad to see the light at the other end!

Vientiane

10 Could this low-slung, Mekong-bound belle be Southeast Asia's most languid capital? The cracked streets are bordered by tamarind trees and the narrow alleys choke on French villas, Chinese shophouses and glittering wats. The city brews a heady mix of street vendors, monks, fine Gallic cuisine, boutique hotels and a healthy edge that sees visitors taking spas and turning their time to yoga and cycling. It may not have Luang Prabang's good looks, but Vientiane has a vibrant, friendly charm all of its own.

Patuxai, Vientiane

DIDIER MARTI / GETTY IMAGES ©

Blackheads' House, Rīga

CAPITAL
Riga

POPULATION
2.2 million

AREA
64,589 sq km

OFFICIAL LANGUAGE
Latvian

Latvia

If you've an appetite for Europe's lesser-known lights, a taste of Latvian life with its full-voiced choirs and art nouveau architecture should stimulate the senses.

Tucked between Estonia to the north and Lithuania to the south, Latvia is the meat in the Baltic sandwich, the savoury middle, loaded with colourful fixings. Thick greens take the form of Gauja Valley pine forests peppered with castle ruins. Onion-domed Orthodox cathedrals cross the land from salty Liepāja to gritty Daugavpils. Cheesy Russian pop blares along the beach in Jūrmala. And spicy Rīga adds an extra zing as the country's cosmopolitan nexus, and unofficial capital of the entire Baltic region.

Latvians often wax poetic about their country, calling it 'the land that sings'. It seems to be in the genes; locals are blessed with unusually pleasant voices, and their canon of traditional tunes is the power source for their indomitable spirit. Latvians literally sang for their freedom from the USSR in a series of dramatic protests known as the 'Singing Revolution', and today the nation holds the Song and Dance Festival every five years, which unites thousands upon thousands of singers from across the land in splendid harmony.

Latvia's
Top Experiences

Rīga's Art Nouveau Architecture

1 More than 750 buildings in Rīga (more than any other city in Europe) boast the flamboyant and haunting art nouveau style; and the number continues to grow as myriad restoration projects get underway. In Rīga, the most noted art nouveau architect was Mikhail Eisenstein, who flexed his artistic muscles on Alberta iela. Look out for facades with screaming masks and horrible goblins, doors decorated with Medusa-like heads and reliefs showing a mishmash of nightmarish images, peacocks and bare-breasted heroines.

Cape Kolka

2 A journey to enchantingly desolate and hauntingly beautiful Cape Kolka (Kolkasrags) feels like a trip to the end of the earth. During Soviet times the entire peninsula was zoned off as a high-security military base, strictly out of bounds to civilians. The region's development was subsequently stunted and today the string of desolate coastal villages has a distinctly anachronistic feel – as though they've been locked away in a time capsule.

Rundāle Palace

3 Built for Baron Ernst Johann Biron (1690–1772), Duke of Courland, between 1736 and 1740, Rundāle Palace is a monument to 18th-century aristocratic ostentatiousness, and rural Latvia's primo architectural highlight. During the greater part of his reign, Ernst Johann lived at his main palace in Jelgava (now used as a university) and summered in Rundāle. The palace has been used in several different capacities between being a royal residence and a museum, including as a hospital for wounded soldiers during WWI. The palace became a museum in the 1970s when a team of historians dug out the plans of the original palace layout and began the lengthy restoration process.

Liepāja

4. Founded by the Livonian Order in the 13th century, Latvia's third-largest city wasn't a big hit until Tsar Alexander III deepened the harbour and built a gargantuan naval port at the end of the 1800s. For years the industrial town earned its spot on the map as the home of the first Baltic fleet of Russian submarines, but after WWII the Soviets occupied what was left of the bombed-out burg and turned it into a strategic military base. Liepāja is often called 'the place where wind is born', but the city's rough-around-the-edges vibe is undoubtedly its biggest draw.

Jūrmala

5. The Baltic's version of the French Riviera, Jūrmala (pronounced yoor-muh-lah) is a long string of townships with stately wooden beach estates belonging to Russian oil tycoons and their trophy wives. Even during the height of communism, Jūrmala was always a place to 'sea' and be seen. Wealthy fashionistas would flaunt their couture beachwear while worshipping the sun between spa treatments. On summer weekends, vehicles clog the roads when jetsetters and day-tripping Rīgans flock to the resort town for some serious fun in the sun.

Old Rīga

6. The heart of the city is a fairy-tale kingdom of winding, wobbly lanes and gingerbread trim that beats to the sound of a bumpin'

if Latvia were 100 people

61 would be Latvian
26 would be Russian
4 would be Belarusian

2 would be Ukrainian
2 would be Polish
5 would be other

belief systems
(% of population)

23 Roman Catholic

20 Lutheran

17 Orthodox Christian

40 other or none

population per sq km

LATVIA   LITHUANIA   RUSSIA

♦ ≈ 9 people

When to Go

JUN

➡ The all-night solstice rings in warmer months. Locals flock to their coastal cottages.

SEP

➡ The cool September air blows through as the last of the warm weather comes to an end.

DEC–JAN

➡ Holiday time in the birthplace of the Christmas tree. Temperatures are frigid.

Oh Christmas Tree

Rīga's Blackheads' House was known for its wild parties; it was, after all, a clubhouse for unmarried merchants. On a cold Christmas Eve in 1510, the squad of bachelors, full of holiday spirit (and other spirits, so to speak), hauled a great pine tree up to their clubhouse and smothered it with flowers. At the end of the evening, they burned the tree to the ground in an impressive blaze. From then on, decorating the 'Christmas tree' became an annual tradition, which eventually spread across the globe (as you probably know, the burning part never really caught on).

An octagonal commemorative plaque, inlaid in cobbled Rātslaukums, marks the spot where the original tree stood.

Food & Drink

Alus For such a tiny nation there's definitely no shortage of *alus* (beer) – each major town has its own brew. You can't go wrong with Užavas (Ventspils' contribution).

Black Balzām The jet-black, 45%-proof concoction is a secret recipe of more than a dozen fairy-tale ingredients including oak bark, wormwood and linden blossoms. Try mixing it with a glass of cola to take the edge off.

Kvass Single-handedly responsible for the decline of Coca Cola at the turn of the 21st century, Kvass is a beloved beverage made from fermented rye bread. It's surprisingly popular with kids!

Mushrooms Mushroom-picking takes the country by storm during the first showers of autumn.

Smoked fish Dozens of fish shacks dot the Kurzeme coast – look for the veritable smoke signals rising above the tree line. Grab 'em to go; they make the perfect afternoon snack.

Turaida Museum Reserve, Sigulda, Gauja National Park

discotheque. The curving cobbled streets of Rīga's medieval core are best explored at random. Once you're sufficiently lost amid the tangle of gabled roofs, church spires and crooked alleyways, you will begin to uncover a stunning, World Heritage–listed realm of sky-scraping cathedrals, gaping city squares and crumbling castle walls.

Sigulda

7 With a name that sounds like a mythical ogress, it comes as no surprise that Sigulda is an enchanting spot with delightful surprises tucked behind every dappled tree. Locals proudly call their town the 'Switzerland of Latvia', but if you're expecting the majesty of a mountainous snow-capped realm, you'll be rather disappointed. Instead, Sigulda mixes its own brew of scenic trails, extreme sports and 800-year-old castles steeped in legends.

Pāvilosta

8 This sleepy beach burg casually pulls off a chilled-out California surfer vibe despite its location on the black Baltic Sea. Summer days are filled with windsurfing, kiteboarding, surfing and sailing interspersed with beach naps and beers.

Getting Around

Bus Buses are much more convenient than trains if you're travelling beyond the capital's clutch of suburban rail lines.

Car Driving is on the right-hand side. Headlights must be on at all times. The number of automatic cars in Latvia is limited. Rental companies usually allow you to drive in all three Baltic countries, but not beyond.

Train Most Latvians live in the large suburban ring around Rīga, thus the city's network of commuter trains makes it easy for tourists to reach day-tripping destinations.

Baalbek

CAPITAL
Beirut

POPULATION
4.1 million

AREA
10,400 sq km

OFFICIAL LANGUAGE
Arabic

Lebanon

Lebanon is one of the most vibrant and most complicated societies on earth, grafted onto one of the Middle East's most beautiful regions.

Its name is a byword for conflict but Lebanon, the original land of milk and honey, is a friendly, welcoming and culturally rich country with one slipper in the Arab world and one Jimmy Choo planted firmly in the West. Its mosaic of peoples has coexisted here for centuries, often at war, more often at peace. It's home to a bubbling-hot nightlife in Beirut, a notorious Hezbollah (Party of God) headquarters in backwater Baalbek, a fistful of flash ski resorts, and a dozen cramped Palestinian refugee camps.

Hike the Qadisha Valley and it's hard to imagine that a conflict has ever existed here; wander past the pockmarked shell of Beirut's Holiday Inn and you'll wonder if there will ever be lasting peace. Lebanon is chaotic and fascinating – scarred by decades of civil war, invasions and terrorist attacks, yet blessed with mountain vistas, ancient ruins and a people who are resilient, indomitable and renowned for their hospitality. Heed travel warnings but don't miss the compelling and confusing wonders of Lebanon.

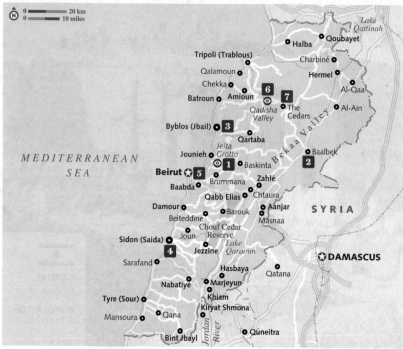

Lebanon's
Top Experiences

Jeita Grotto

1 Marvel at Jeita Grotto's glittering forest of stalactites and stalagmites. Undoubtedly one of Lebanon's greatest natural wonders and biggest tourist attractions, this stunning cave system is not to be missed, and is open every day in July and August. Extending around 6km back into the mountains, the caves were used as an ammunition store during the civil war, and their lower strata are flooded each winter. The incredible upper cavern, though, stays open all year, and can be explored on foot. Strategic lighting showcases the stalactites and stalagmites in all their crystalline glory.

Baalbek

2 Explore the haunting ruins of Baalbek. Known as Heliopolis or 'Sun City' of the ancient world, Baalbek's stupendous ruins comprise the most impressive ancient site in Lebanon and are arguably the best preserved in the Middle East. Their temples, built on an extravagant scale that outshone anything in Rome, have enjoyed a stellar reputation throughout the centuries, yet still manage to maintain the appealing air of an undiscovered wonder. This is largely due to their position in the quiet, bucolic town of Baalbek, which only really comes to life each July with the arrival of the famous annual Baalbek Festival.

Byblos

3 Wander through seaside ruins and celebrate a Mediterranean sunset in pretty Byblos. A fishing port with a plethora of ancient remains and some interesting fishy fossils, Byblos is one of the highlights of the entire Middle Eastern Mediterranean coast. The medieval town has a charming souq near the ruins, and the harbour is lined with a string of good restaurants. The site of the ancient ruins is entered through the restored 12th-century Crusader castle that dominates the sturdy 25m-thick city ramparts (which date from the 3rd and 2nd millennia BC).

Carpenter's market stall, Sidon

Old Sidon

4 Delve into the traditional, atmospheric souqs of Old Sidon. This fascinating labyrinth of vaulted souqs, tiny alleyways and medieval remnants stretches out behind the buildings fronting the harbour. Officially, there are 60 listed historic sights here, many in ruins, although renovation work is ongoing. In the souqs you'll find craftspeople plying the same trades their ancestors did for centuries. There are plenty of opportunities to pick up the local fragrant orange-blossom water (good in both sweet and savoury cooking, or as a cordial for summer drinks) and *sanioura*, a light, crumbly, shortcake-like biscuit.

Beirut

5 Drink and be merry in the cooler-than-cool cafes and dive bars of Beirut's Hamra and Gemmayzeh districts. The nation's capital is a fabulous place of glitz, glamour, restaurants and beach clubs – if, that is, you're one of the lucky ones. While the city centre is filled with suave sophistication, the outskirts of town comprise some of the most deprived Palestinian refugee camps. If you're looking for the real East-meets-West so talked about in the Middle East, this is precisely where it's at. Crowded and ancient, beautiful and blighted, hot and heady, home to Prada and Palestinians, Beirut is many things at once, but all, without doubt, compelling.

if Lebanon were 100 people

95 would be Arab
4 would be Armenian
1 would be other

belief systems
(% of population)

60 Muslim   39 Christian   1 other

When to Go

DEC–APR
➡ Skiing – and après-ski parties – in the mountains.

MAY–SEP
➡ The perfect time to go hiking along wild trails and through cedar forests.

JUL–AUG
➡ Jazz, poetry and theatre at Baalbek's famous arts festival bring the ancient Roman ruins to life.

population per sq km

LEBANON   SYRIA   ISRAEL

👤 ≈ 120 people

Lebanon's Cedars

The most famous of the world's several species of cedar tree are the cedars of Lebanon, mentioned in the Old Testament, and once covering great swathes of the Mt Lebanon Range.

Jerusalem's original Temple of Solomon was made from this cedar wood, and the ancient Phoenicians, also, found it appealing for its fragrance and durability. Such a long history of deforestation, however, has meant that today just a few pockets of cedars remain in Lebanon – despite the tree appearing proudly on the nation's flag.

The best places to view the remaining cedars of Lebanon are either at the Chouf Cedar Reserve, or at the small grove at the Cedars ski resort in the north of the country.

Food & Drink

Arak Aniseed-flavoured liquor, best served with water and ice.

Felafel Deep-fried balls of chickpea paste and/or fava beans.

Kibbeh Finely ground meat croquettes with cracked wheat.

Kofta Mincemeat with parsley and spices grilled on a skewer.

Mezze Small dishes usually served as starters, often including the three staples of hummus, *muttabal* (aubergine dip) and *tabbouleh* (parsley, tomato and bulgur wheat salad).

Shwarma Thin slices of marinated meat garnished with fresh vegetables, pickles and *tahina* (sesame-seed paste), wrapped in pita bread.

Warak arish Stuffed vine leaves (also known as *wara anaib*).

Zaatar A blend of Middle Eastern herbs, sesame seeds and salt, used as a condiment on meats, vegetables, rice and bread.

Qadisha Valley

6 Hike past rock-cut monasteries and gushing waterfalls in the scenic Qadisha Valley, a Unesco World Heritage site home to ancient monasteries and hermits' dwellings, and teeming with wildlife. The trip up to the pretty town of Bcharré takes you through some of the most beautiful scenery in Lebanon. The road winds along mountainous slopes, offering spectacular views of the valley. With plentiful opportunities for hiking quiet valley trails or scaling bleak mountain wastes, this is the perfect antidote to all that's frivolous in Beirut.

The Cedars

7 One of Lebanon's most attractive ski resorts, the Cedars is also Lebanon's oldest and most European in feel. The village takes its name from one of the country's few remaining groves of cedar trees, which stands on the right-hand side of the road as you head up towards the ski lifts. A few of these slow-growing trees are thought to be approaching 1500 years old, The ski season takes place in the resort from around December to April, depending on snow conditions; there are great off-season discounts if you're here in summer for the hiking.

Getting Around

Bus Buses travel between Beirut and all of Lebanon's major towns. In and around Beirut and the coastal strip, the bus, minibus and taxi network is extensive, cheap and fairly reliable.

Car To fully explore the hinterland of the country (especially around the Qadisha Valley, Bekaa Valley and the south) it's well worth hiring a car or negotiating a private taxi to avoid waiting for hours for a bus. You need to be a competent driver with very steady nerves to contemplate driving in Lebanon, since there are few rules of the road.

CAPITAL
Maseru

POPULATION
1.9 million

AREA
30,355 sq km

OFFICIAL LANGUAGES
Sesotho, English

Lesotho

Tiny Lesotho is Africa's 'Kingdom in the Sky', home to traditional Basotho culture where herdboys tend their sheep on steep hillsides and horsemen wrapped in blankets ride mountain passes.

Lesotho (Le- soo -too) is a vastly underrated travel destination. It's beautiful, culturally rich, safe, cheap and easily accessible from Durban and Johannesburg. The hiking and trekking is world class and the national parks' infrastructure continues to improve.

The 1000m-high 'lowlands' are the scene of low-key Lesotho life, with good craft shopping around Teyateyaneng and Maseru. But be sure to head to the valleys and mountains, where streams traverse an ancient dinosaur playground.

South Africa is just a mountain pass or two away, but Lesotho's towering peaks and isolated valleys, and the pride of the Basotho in their identity, have served to insulate Lesotho's culture from that of its larger neighbour. For anyone seeking adventure, wilderness, a laid-back pace and the chance to get acquainted with people living traditional lifestyles, Lesotho is a magical destination.

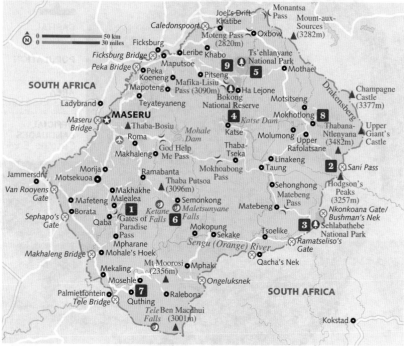

Lesotho's
Top Experiences

Semonkong Lodge

1 Semonkong Lodge is a model of community tourism place. It has an excellent restaurant, and offers village tours, a pub crawl on donkey-back, hiking and pony trekking. Just outside Malealea is the Gates of Paradise Pass. A plaque announces 'Wayfarer – pause and look upon a Gateway of Paradise'. This says it all – about the region, village and the lodge. The breathtaking mountains feature caves with San paintings, and you can enjoy a pony trek or hike.

Hiking Sani Top

2 Sani Top sits atop steep Sani Pass, the only dependable (albeit winding) road into Lesotho through the uKhahlamba-Drakensberg mountain range in KwaZulu-Natal. It offers stupendous views on clear days and unlimited hiking possibilities. From the Sani Top Chalet there are several day walks, including a long and arduous trek to Thabana-Ntlenyana (3482m), the highest peak in Southern Africa. A guide is advisable.

Sehlabathebe National Park

3 Lesotho's most under-visited national park is remote, rugged and beautiful. The rolling grasslands, wildflowers and silence provide a sense of complete isolation, which is the case, apart from the prolific birdlife (including the bearded vulture) and the odd rhebok. Hiking (and horse riding from Sani Top or the Drakensbergs) is the main way to explore the waterfalls and surrounds, and fishing is possible in the park's dams and rivers. You'll need to bring all your food to the park, and be well prepared for the changing elements. This is a summer-rainfall area, and thick mist, potentially hazardous to hikers, is common. The winters are clear but it gets cold at night, with occasional light snowfalls.

Katse Dam

4 Katse is the site of Africa's highest dam (1993m). Katse Dam's lake is serene, ringed by steep, green hillsides; even if you're

not impressed by engineering feats, the area makes for a relaxing pause.

Ts'ehlanyane National Park

5 Deep in the rugged Maluti Mountains, this 5600-hectare national park protects a beautiful, high-altitude, 5600-hectare patch of rugged wilderness, including one of Lesotho's only stands of indigenous forest. This underrated and underused place is about as far away from it all as you can get and is perfect for hiking. In addition to day walks, there is a challenging 39km hiking trail that goes from Ts'ehlanyane southwest to Bokong Nature Reserve through some of Lesotho's most dramatic terrain.

Waterfalls

6 The Maletsunyane Falls are a 90-minute walk from Semonkong (Place of Smoke). They are more than 200m high and are at their most spectacular in summer. For a thrilling descent, you can try abseiling. The remote 122m-high Ketane Falls are an exciting day trip (30km one way) from Semonkong, or a four-day return horse ride from Malealea Lodge.

Quthing

7 Quthing, the southernmost town in Lesotho, often known as Moyeni (Place of the Wind) was established in 1877, abandoned three years later and then rebuilt at the present site. About 1.5km off the highway, 5km west of Quthing, is the intriguing Masitise Cave House Museum,

if Lesotho were 100 people

33 would be aged 0-14
20 would be aged 15-24
36 would be aged 25-54
6 would be aged 55-64
5 would be aged 65+

belief systems
(% of population)

80 — Christian

20 — indigenous beliefs

When to Go

JUN–AUG

➡ Hit the slopes in Southern Africa and catch quality international ski competitions.

SEP

➡ Celebrate Lesotho culture at the renowned Morija Arts & Cultural Festival.

DEC–JAN

➡ Feel the full force of Maletsunyane, the magnificent waterfall near Semonkong.

population per sq km

LESOTHO   SOUTH AFRICA   USA

🚶 ≈ 11 people

Culture Basotho–Style

Traditional Basotho culture is flourishing, and colourful celebrations marking milestones, such as birth, puberty, marriage and death, are a central part of village life. While hiking you may see the *lekolulo*, a flutelike instrument played by herd boys; the *thomo*, a stringed instrument played by women; and the *se-tolo-tolo*, a stringed instrument played with the mouth by men.

Cattle hold an important position in daily life, both as sacrificial animals and symbols of wealth. Crop cultivation and weather are also central, and form the heart of many traditions.

The Basotho believe in a Supreme Being and place a great deal of emphasis on balimo (ancestors), who act as intermediaries between people and the capricious forces of nature and the spirit world. Evil is a constant danger, caused by boloi (witchcraft; witches can be either male or female) and thkolosi (small, maliciously playful beings, similar to the Xhosa's tokoloshe). If you're being bothered by these forces, head to the nearest ngaka – a learned man, part sorcerer and part doctor – who can combat them.

Basotho are traditionally buried in a sitting position, facing the rising sun and ready to leap up when called.

Food & Drink

The diet of Basotho people is fairly simple, with many familes keeping livestock and growing greens, corn and wheat.

Joala Traditional sorghum beer – a white flag flying in a village means that it's available.

Morogo Leafy greens, usually wild spinach, boiled, seasoned and served with pap.

built into a San rock shelter in 1866 by Reverend Ellenberger. Quthing's other claim to fame is a proliferation of dinosaur footprints.

Mokhotlong

8 Mokhotlong (Place of the Bald Ibis) is 270km from Maseru and is the first major town north of Sani Pass and has a Wild West feel to it. There's not much to do other than watch life go by, with the locals on their horses, sporting Basotho blankets. However, the Senqu (Orange) River – Lesotho's main waterway – has its source near Mokhotlong, and the town makes a good base for walks.

Pony Trekking

9 Pony trekking is one of Lesotho's top drawcards. It's done on sure-footed Basotho ponies, the result of crossbreeding between short Javanese horses and European full mounts. Advance booking is recommended, and no prior riding experience is necessary. Whatever your experience level, expect to be sore after a day in the saddle. For overnight treks, you'll need to bring food (stock up in Maseru), a sleeping bag and warm, waterproof clothing. You can arrange pony trekking at many places, including Ts'ehlanyane National Park

Getting Around

Air It's possible to fly to Lesotho from South Africa,

Bike The mountainous terrain means Lesotho is only for the physically fit.

Bus A good network of buses and minibus taxis (known locally as just 'taxis') covers most of the country. Minibus taxis serve the major towns, and many smaller towns. Buses, slightly cheaper and somewhat slower, serve the major towns. There are no classes, and service is decidedly no-frills

Local woman, Tubmanburg

CAPITAL
Monrovia

POPULATION
3.99 million

AREA
111,369 sq km

**OFFICIAL
LANGUAGE**
English

Liberia

Founded by freed slaves and emerging from the devastation of civil war, Liberia is a country rich with natural beauty that is getting back on its feet.

Long a byword for child soldiers and civil war, Liberia is emerging from the ashes. This is a country getting back on its feet, but one thing hasn't changed: Liberia is blessed with extraordinary natural beauty, its coast lined with splendid beaches and its interior awash in rainforest. Founded by freed slaves from America in the 19th century and inhabited by traditional groups famous for their artistic traditions and secret societies, Liberia's complicated cultural mix hasn't always worked.

It wasn't long ago that Liberians talked with nostalgia of 'normal days'. Now, over a decade since the war ended, 'normal days' are back in this gorgeous green land.

Today you can visit Monrovia, exploring the relics of Liberia's rich history and the American influence that still shapes it. Sapo National Park is one of the most stunning patches of rainforest in West Africa, while the sands of pretty Robertsport are shingled with fishing canoes and huge granite gems.

Liberia's
Top Experiences

Monrovia

1 A splendid African capital brimming with elegant stores and faces, a party city, a war zone marred by bullet holes and a broken-hearted city struggling to climb to its feet. See the architectural ghosts of Monrovia's past and the uniformed school-children of its future.

Harper

2 A town blessed with southern American architecture and an end-of-the-line feel. Reachable after two days on some of Liberia's worst roads, deliquescent, small-town Harper feels like the prize at the end of a long treasure hunt. The capital of the once-autonomous Maryland state, this gem is shingled with decaying ruins that hint at its former grandeur.

Sapo National Park

3 Explore the habitat of the endangered pygmy hippo, camping beneath the forest canopy and listening to the sounds of the rainforest at Liberia's only national park. It is a lush 1808-sq-km tract of rainforest containing some of West Africa's last remaining primary rainforest, as well as forest elephants, pygmy hippos, chimpanzees, antelopes and other wildlife.

Food & Drink

Rice and spicy meat sauces or fish stews are popular. Palm butter with fish and potato greens are two favourites. Other popular dishes include palava sauce (made with plato leaf, dried fish or meat and palm oil) and *jollof rice* (rice and vegetables with meat or fish). American food is popular in Monrovia. Club beer is the local brew.

When to Go

JAN–MAY

➜ This is the hot, dry season, so head to the beaches. The mercury can easily top 32°C.

JUN–OCT

➜ Spectacular storms and impressive surf, but country roads are impassable.

OCT–DEC

➜ A touch of harmattan breeze from the Sahel occasionally cools the air.

Leptis Magna

CAPITAL
Tripoli

POPULATION
6 million

AREA
1.8 million sq km

OFFICIAL LANGUAGE
Arabic

Libya

Libya, a realm of stunning coastline, dramatic Greek and Roman ruins and the majesty of the Sahara remains poised to become a travel hotspot.

Libya is a classic North African destination and its primary appeal derives from its position as an ancient crossroads of civilisations – these civilisations bequeathed to the Libyan coast some of the finest Roman and Greek ruins in existence, among them Leptis Magna, Cyrene and Sabratha. This is also one of the best places in Africa to experience the Sahara Desert, from seas of sand the size of Switzerland and sheltering palm-fringed lakes (the Ubari Sand Sea) to remote massifs adorned with prehistoric rock art (the Jebel Acacus), labyrinthine caravan towns (Ghadames) and an isolated black-as-black volcano (Wawa al-Namus) in the desert's heart.

However, the upheaval caused by Libya's democratic revolution in 2011–12 continues, meaning the future is still uncertain. That said, Libya's tourism and transport infrastructure are excellent, so once peace returns fully to the country, expect it to be one of the hottest travel destinations on the continent.

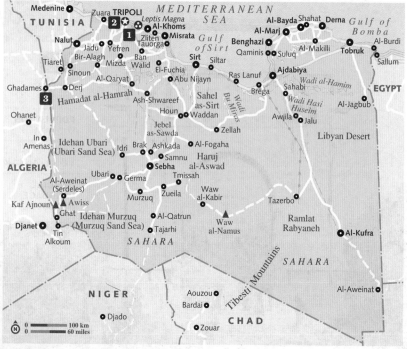

Libya's
Top Experiences

Leptis Magna

1 Leptis Magna was once the largest and greatest Roman city in Africa. Because no modern city was later built on the site and it was constructed of sturdy limestone, Leptis is that rare ancient city where sufficient traces remain to imagine the city in its heyday.

Food & Drink

Shwarma (strips of sliced meat in a pocket of bread) is widely available as a street snack. Couscous and chicken are common in Tripolitania and the Fezzan. While in Libya, be sure to eat at Tripoli's fish market, where you choose your own fish and seafood which is then cooked for you at a neighbouring restaurant.

Tripoli

2 Set on one of North Africa's best natural harbours, Tripoli exudes a distinctive Mediterranean charm infused with a decidedly Arabic-Islamic flavour. Its rich mosaic of historical influences – from Roman ruins and artefacts to the Ottoman-era medina – will leave few travellers disappointed. The city's most recognisable landmark is the castle, Al-Saraya al-Hamra.

Ghadames

3 The Unesco World Heritage–listed old city of Ghadames is everything you imagine a desert oasis to be – abundant palm groves, a labyrinthine old town, and an unhurried pace of life unchanged for centuries. Old Ghadames is another world of covered alleyways, whitewashed houses and extensive palm gardens.

When to Go

OCT–NOV & MAR–APR

➡ Libya is at its best, with clear skies and mild temperatures.

OCT–NOV

➡ Surprisingly cool, and night-time temperatures in the Sahara routinely drop below zero.

MID-MAY–SEP

➡ Summer; temperatures can be fiercely hot.

Vaduz Castle, Vaduz

Liechtenstein

With a history and monarchy as story-book as its melodious mountain scenery, rich old Liechtenstein puts a whole new perspective on 'doing a country'.

If Liechtenstein didn't exist, someone would have invented it. A tiny mountain principality governed by an iron-willed monarch in the heart of 21st-century Europe, it certainly has novelty value. Only 25km long by 12km wide (at its broadest point) – just larger than Manhattan – Liechtenstein doesn't have an international airport, and access from Switzerland is by local bus. However, the country is a rich banking state and, we are told, the world's largest exporter of false teeth.

Most blaze through Liechtenstein en route to Switzerland, stopping only for snapshots of the castle and a souvenir passport stamp. That's a shame, as the country has an overwhelming amount of natural beauty for its size. Strike out into the Alpine wilderness beyond Vaduz and, suddenly, this landlocked sliver of a micronation no longer seems quite so small.

CAPITAL
Vaduz

POPULATION
37,009

AREA
160 sq km

OFFICIAL LANGUAGE
German

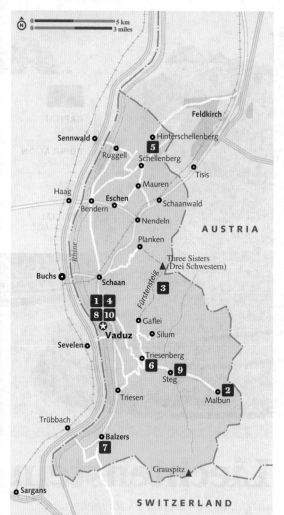

the 1600m-high resort of Malbun feels – in the nicest possible sense – like the edge of the earth. Although rather limited in scope – the runs are mostly novice with a few intermediate and cross-country runs thrown in for good measure – the skiing is inexpensive for this part of the world and it does offer some bragging rights. Indeed, older British royals such as Prince Charles learnt to ski here.

Fürstensteig

3 There are 400km of hiking trails in Liechtenstein, along with loads of well-marked cycling routes (look for signs with a cycling symbol; distances and directions will also be included). The most famous hiking trail is the Fürstensteig, a rite of passage for nearly every Liechtensteiner. You must be fit and not suffer from vertigo, as in places the path is narrow, reinforced with rope handholds and/or falls away to a sheer drop.

Drei Länder Tour

4 Liechtenstein may be little, but its location on the border to Austria and Switzerland makes it easy to pedal across borders by bike in a day. One of the most scenic and memorable rides is the 59km Drei Länder Tour (Three Countries Tour), which leads from Vaduz to the medieval town of Feldkirch in Austria. The route heads on to Illspitz and along the Rhine to Buchs in Switzerland, dominated by its 13th-century castle, Schloss Werdenberg, before heading back to Vaduz.

Liechtenstein's
Top Experiences

Vaduz Castle

1 Although the castle is not open to the public, the exterior graces many a photograph and it is worth the climb up the hill. At the top, there's a magnificent vista of Vaduz, with a spectacular mountain backdrop. There's also a network of walking trails along the ridge. For a peek inside the castle grounds, arrive on 15 August, Liechtenstein's National Day, when the prince invites the entire country over.

Malbun

2 Liechtenstein's one and only ski resort,

Hinterschellenberg

5 Hinterschellenberg briefly entered the stream of world history when about 500 Russian soldiers who had fought on the German side in WWII crossed the border in search of asylum in 1945. They remained for about two-and-a-half years, after which most made for Argentina. Liechtenstein was the only country not to cede to the Soviet Union's demands that such soldiers (considered traitors) be extradited to the USSR – which generally meant death. A memorial about 100m from the Austrian border marks the event.

Walsermuseum

6 Triesenberg's star attraction is this museum, telling the intriguing story of the Walsers and containing some curious carvings out of twisted tree trunks and branches. The Walsers were a German-speaking 'tribe' from the Valais (Wallis in German) that emigrated across Europe in the 13th century and settled in many places, including Liechtenstein, where they still speak their own dialect. Ask at the museum about visiting the nearby Walserhaus (Hag 19), a 400-year-old house furnished in 19th century fashion.

Burg Gutenberg

7 Balzers' most visible icon is this now state-owned, hilltop 13th-century castle, which only opens for concerts. It cuts a striking figure on the horizon and boasts many nice strolls

if Liechtenstein were 100 people

66 would be Liechtensteiner
34 would be other

belief systems
(% of population)

77 Roman Catholic

4 Russian Orthodox

1 Old Believer

18 other or none

population per sq km

LIECHTENSTEIN   SWITZERLAND   AUSTRIA

 ≈ 10 people

When to Go

AUGUST

➜ Come on the 15th and celebrate the country's national holiday.

DEC–MAR

➜ Bounce down snow-covered pistes at its singular ski resort.

MAY–SEP

➜ Hike to your heart's content, up, up and away from the busloads of stamp-clutching tourists.

Liechtenstein Trivia

➡ Did you know Liechtenstein is the sixth smallest country in the world?

➡ It's still governed by an iron-willed monarch who lives in a gothic castle on a hill.

➡ It really is the world's largest producer of false teeth.

➡ Liechtenstein is the only country in the world named after the people who purchased it.

➡ In its last military engagement in 1866, none of its 80 soldiers was killed. In fact, 81 returned, including a new Italian 'friend'. The army was disbanded soon afterwards.

➡ Low business taxes means around 75,000 firms, many of them so-called 'letter box companies', with nominal head offices, are registered here – about twice the number of the principality's inhabitants.

➡ Liechtenstein is Europe's fourth-smallest nation (only the Vatican, Monaco and San Marino are smaller).

Food & Drink

Liechtenstein's cuisine is influenced by its neighbours, Austria to the east and Switzerland to the west.

Beer Liechtenstein breweries produce high-quality lagers, wheat beers and ales.

Käsknöpfle Tiny cheese-flavoured flour dumplings.

Ribel A semolina dish served with sugar and fruit compote or jam.

Wine Tastings are available at many of Liechtenstein's wineries.

RICHARD FAIRLESS / GETTY IMAGES ©

in the vicinity. The area was settled as early as the Neolithic period and Roman elements have been found in the castle foundations.

Vaduz

8 Vaduz is a postage-stamp-sized city with a postcard-perfect backdrop. Crouching at the foot of forested mountains, hugging the banks of the Rhine and crowned by a turreted castle, its location is visually stunning. The centre itself is curiously modern and sterile, with its mix of tax-free luxury-goods stores and cube-shaped concrete buildings. Yet just a few minutes' walk brings you to traces of the quaint village that existed just 50 years ago, as well as quiet vineyards where the Alps seem that bit closer.

Väluna Valley

9 Väluna Valley is Liechtenstein's main cross-country skiing area with 15km of classic and skating track, including a 3km stretch that is illuminated at night. The trailheads start at Steg.

Postmuseum, Vaduz

10 Liechtenstein once made a packet producing souvenir stamps for enthusiasts, but that market has been hit by the rise of email. Here you'll find all national stamps issued since 1912.

Getting Around

Air Liechtenstein doesn't have any airports due to its very small size.

Bicycle You can rent bikes and pick up maps at the tourist information office in Vaduz.

Bus A public bus connects Switzerland and Austria. Within Liechtenstein buses travel more or less hourly from Vaduz to Malbun every day.

Train International connections make it easy to travel to Liechtenstein by rail.

Old Town, Vilnius

CAPITAL
Vilnius

POPULATION
3.5 million

AREA
65,300 sq km

OFFICIAL LANGUAGE
Lithuanian

Lithuania

Lithuania is a country full of surprises, natural and man-made, where a colourful history has been moulded by raw pagan roots fused with Catholic fervour.

A great little all-rounder, Lithuania has much to offer. Mother Nature has sprinkled a good dose of fairy dust over this enigmatic region. White sandy beaches edge the Curonian Spit, an enchanting pig-tail of land dangling off the country's western rump, and deep, magical forests guard twinkling lakes.

But you'll find that humans have left their stamp too, in undeniably weird and wonderful ways. Those with a passion for baroque architecture, ancient castles and archaeological treasures will find plenty in Vilnius, the capital, and beyond. There are sculpture parks and interactive museums for travellers wishing to delve into Lithuania's traumatic recent history; modern art spaces and exhibitions, and all-night clubbing in the cities and on the coast for those requiring something less cerebral. Throw in a whirlwind of great restaurants, beer gardens and bars, and you have urban entertainment aplenty. Combine with Lithuania's pagan roots, boundless energy and rebellious spirit, and you're in for a heck of a ride.

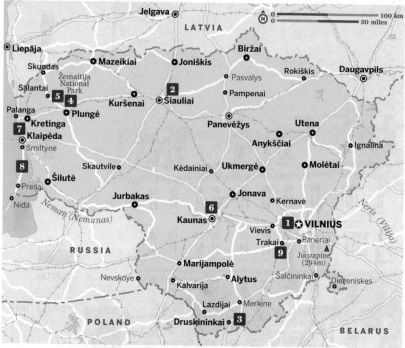

Lithuania's
Top Experiences

Vilnius

1 Explore beautiful baroque Vilnius with its cobbled streets, skyline of church spires, and bars and bistros. The baroque bombshell of the Baltics, Vilnius is a city of immense allure. As beautiful as it is bizarre, it easily tops the country's best-attraction bill, drawing tourists with a charm and golden glow that makes one wish for long, midsummer evenings every day of the year. At its heart is Europe's largest baroque Old Town, added to Unesco World Heritage list in 1994.

Hill of Crosses

2 Hear the wind sigh between the thousands of crosses on the eerie Hill of Crosses, Lithuania's most awe-inspiring sight, near Šiauliai. The sound of the myriad tiny crosses tinkling in the breeze, festooned upon the thousands of larger crosses which appear to grow on the hillock, is eerie. Legend says the tradition of planting crosses began in the 14th century. The crosses were bulldozed by the Soviets, but each night people crept past soldiers to plant more.

Grūtas Sculpture Park

3 Visit Lithuania's communist past at the Grūtas sculpture park, 8km west of the southern spa town of Druskininkai. This is a cross between kitschy entertainment and an attempt at education about life in Soviet times. The sprawling grounds, designed to look like a concentration camp, contain the entire communist pantheon – statues of Lenin, Stalin and Marx, interspersed with buildings containing exhibits on the Soviet oppression of Lithuania.

Žemaitija National Park

4 This 200-sq-km park, a magical landscape of lake and forest, is as mysterious as it is beautiful, and it's easy to see why it is enshrined in fables of devils, ghosts and buried treasure. The draw here is two-fold. You can swim, boat and bike around at your leisure, as well as pay a visit to one of the country's newest and

JOHN FREEMAN / GETTY IMAGES ©

most bizarre attractions: a museum to the Cold War, housed in what was once a Soviet nuclear missile base.

Orvydas Garden

5 One of the most unusual sights in all of Lithuania is this rock and sculpture garden. The carvings were originally created for the village cemetery in nearby Salantai but were brought to the Orvydas homestead after then Soviet leader Nikita Khrushchev turned his wrath on religious objects in the 1960s. Today, visitors can walk through the lovely farmstead gardens admiring literally hundreds of statues, carvings, busts and just plain oddities. It's an experience as awe-inspiring as it is confounding, but one that will linger long in the memory.

Museum of Devils

6 Marvel at the Horned One in many guises at the Kaunas Museum of Devils. What started as a peculiar collection of devil figurines by eccentric Antanas Žmuidzinavičius (1876–1966) has turned into a superb exploration of the devil's role in mythology around the world. Amid the wood carvings, masks and clay figurines, you can spot a woven bespectacled devil with guitar, colourful Santeria devil from Cuba, and satanic figures of Hitler and Stalin, formed from tree roots and performing a deadly dance.

Klaipėda

7 Lithuania's main port is the gateway to the Curonian Spit, but it has

if Lithuania were 100 people

84 would be Lithuanian
7 would be Polish
6 would be Russian
1 would be Belarusian
2 would be other

belief systems
(% of population)

77 Roman Catholic

4 Russian Orthodox

1 Old Believer

18 other or none

population per sq km

LITHUANIA   LATVIA   RUSSIA

≈ 9 people

When to Go

APR

➤ Some of the world's best jazz performers are at the Kaunas International Jazz Festival.

JUN & JUL

➤ The loveliest time to explore the forests and sand dunes of the Curonian Spit.

SEP

➤ Vilnius City Days, a celebration of the capital with street theatre, music and fashion.

Haggle for Amber

The Baltic States, and Lithuania in particular, are synonymous with amber, known as 'Baltic gold'. The Baltic Sea is a particularly rich source of amber gathering and the hardened tree sap has been used to make jewellery for millennia.

While amber is primarily yellow, colours can vary in shade from white to pale yellow, to orange, to what appears to be black. The rarest are blue, violet and green specimens. The value of an amber piece also depends on the texture of the item, whether there are 'inclusions' within the stone, such as embedded plants or insects, and the quality of workmanship.

There's no shortage of amber outlets in Lithuania and if you're not sure whether you're being offered the real thing, the simplest way to tell real amber from glass, plastic and other fakes is the smell test: if you rub a piece of amber vigorously, it will release the smell of pine.

Food & Drink

Alus Beer The most widely drunk alcoholic beverage; pretty good stuff at that.

Blyneliai Pancakes can be served sweet or savoury and eaten at any time during the day; look for Varskečiai, stuffed with sweet curd.

Cepelinai Parcels of potato dough stuffed with cheese, meat or mushrooms.

Mushrooms Mushroom picking is especially popular in late August and September, when the forests are studded with dozens of different varieties.

Šaltibarščiai This cold beetroot summer soup is arguably the country's signature dish; served with a plate of boiled potatoes on the side.

Turaida castle. Trakai

enough attractions of its own to warrant lingering. Inside the atmospheric torch-lit tunnels of what remains of the town's old moat-protected castle, the exhibits here tell the castle's story through a wealth of period objects and black-and-white photos of the town during WWII.

Curonian Spit

8 Breathe the pure air in the fragrant pine forests and high sand dunes of the enchanting Curonian Spit. This magical sliver of land, divided equally between Lithuania and Russia's Kaliningrad region, hosts some of Europe's most precious sand dunes and a menagerie of elk, deer and avian wildlife, with more than half its surface covered by pine forest. The Lithuania side is divided into two regions: Smiltynė village and Neringa.

Trakai

9 Wander through wonderful Trakai, home of the Karaite people and a stunning island castle. Explore the picturesque red-brick castle, Karaite culture, quaint wooden houses and pretty lakeside location. The Karaite people are named after the term kara, which means 'to study the scriptures' in both Hebrew and Arabic.

Getting Around

Car & Motorcycle Lithuanian roads are generally very good and driving (on the right) is easy.

Bus The national bus network is extensive, linking all the major cities to each other and the smaller towns to their regional hubs.

Train Whether you take the bus or the train depends very much on the route. For common journeys the train is often more comfortable and better value than the bus. For other routes, the opposite might be true.

Palais Grand-Ducal, Luxembourg City

CAPITAL
Luxembourg City

POPULATION
514,862

AREA
2586 sq km

OFFICIAL LANGUAGES
Luxembourgish, French, German

Luxembourg

The Grand Duchy of Luxembourg is famed for its banks but visually is mostly an undulating series of pretty wooded hills dotted with castle villages.

Which European nation, just 84km long, rates among the world's three richest countries? Remarkably the answer is Luxembourg. That's some achievement given its wholesale destruction during WWII, a sad history remembered in war museums across the country. The country's economic miracle started with steel but is now based particularly on banking – Belgians joke that visitors only go there to get their money out.

But don't leave Luxembourg to the bankers and Eurocrats. The capital has a fairy-tale quality to its Unesco-listed historic core, dramatically perched on a once-impregnable cliff top. Beyond, you'll rapidly find yourself in rolling part-forested hills where a string of beguiling villages each form attractive huddles beneath medieval castles. Then there's all the fun of the fizz in Moselle wine country and some loveable walks to take in the pretty micro-gorges of Müllerthal. All in all, this little country has plenty of surprises.

Constitution, the gardens in the gorge and the tiny knot of old town lanes behind the Palace (Palais Grand-Ducal). Buzzing Place Guillaume II, surveyed by the neo-classical Hôtel de Ville is the city's heart.

Musée National d'Histoire Militaire

2 Of all the many WWII museums commemorating the Battle of the Ardennes, Diekirch's Musée National d'Histoire Militaire is the most comprehensive and visual. What was once a brewery building 200m north of the town centre, is now packed full of WWII equipment, vehicles and memorabilia. Numerous well-executed mannequin scenes illustrate the suffering and hardships of the battles fought in the thick snows of Christmas 1944.

Moselle Valley

3 Welcome to one of Europe's smallest wine regions. The wide Moselle River forms the border with Germany, its steeply rising hillside banks covered with seemingly endless vineyards. In summer the scene turns a beautiful emerald green and the slopes are so neatly clipped they look combed. All along the riverside from Schengen to Wasserbillig you'll find a succession of villages and winery towns on both the Luxembourg and German sides. While none are visually outstanding, scenes are picturesque north of Ahn and above old Wellenstein village.

Château de Vianden

4 Palace, citadel or fortified cathedral? At first glance it's hard to tell

Luxembourg's
Top Experiences

Chemin de la Corniche

1 This pedestrian promenade has been hailed as 'Europe's most beautiful balcony'. It winds along the course of the 17th-century city ramparts with views across the river canyon towards the hefty fortifica-tions of the Wenzelsmauer (Wenceslas Wall). Across Rue Sigefroi, the rampart-top walk continues along Blvd Victor Thorn to the Dräi Tier (Triple Gate) tower. Much of Luxembourg's charm is gained from strolling the Chemin de la Corniche, the former ramparts around Place de la

Machtum, Moselle Valley

just what it is that towers so grandly amid the mists and wooded hills above historic little Vianden. In fact it's a vast slate-roofed castle complex whose impregnable white stone walls glow golden in the evening's floodlights, creating one of Luxembourg's most photogenic scenes. The famed château is entered through a modern exhibition hall, portcullis gate and up stairs into a vaulted hall full of pikes and armour. The crypt and Room 10 display plans and models of the castle's various incarnations, the 13th-century chapel is unusual for its central pit and some later rooms are furnished in medieval style. The kitchen is especially impressive. The Arend Room shows photos of celebrity visitors from Mikhail Gorbachev to John Malkovich. The appealingly vaulted, barrel-strewn Keller bar opens occasionally for jazz concerts.

Musée d'Histoire de la Ville de Luxembourg

5 The remarkably engrossing and interactive Luxembourg City History Museum hides within a series of 17th-century houses, including a former 'holiday home' of the Bishop of Orval. A lovely garden and open terrace offers great views.

if Luxembourg were 100 people

63 would be Luxembourger
13 would be Portugese
5 would be French
14 would be other EU
5 would be other

belief systems
(% of population)

87 Roman Catholic   13 other

population per sq km

LUXEMBOURG   BELGIUM   FRANCE

👤 ≈ 30 people

When to Go

MAY–AUG

➡ The sunniest months.

FEB–MAR

➡ The country symbolically burns the spirit of winter on the first weekend after Carnival.

NOV–FEB

➡ Weather is usually cold and wet and some attractions close.

Luxembourg's Royals

Dutch monarchs wore a second crown as Grand Dukes of Luxembourg from 1815 until 1890. When Dutch King William III died, his only surviving offspring became the Netherlands' Queen Wilhelmina. However, by Luxembourg's then-unreformed Salic Laws, its crown could not pass to a woman. Thus Adolph of Nassau took over as duke. His descendants rule to this day. In 1907, changes to the hereditary rules allowed Marie Adélaïde to become grand duchess, but perceptions of her pro-German stance in WWI meant she was persuaded to abdicate after the war. Thus, remarkably, the Grand Duchy put its royal family up for referendum in 1919. The result was a resounding 'yes' and Marie Adélaïde's younger sister Charlotte took the throne. The current Grand Duke Henri met his wife Maria Teresa, then a Cuban-born commoner, while at university in Geneva. Although they live in a castle (the 1911 Château Colmar-Berg), their kids were sent to ordinary schools, and it's quite possible to bump into a prince at the movies or to see the grand duchess out shopping. But they remain much respected, and Crown Prince Guillaume's wedding was THE national event of 2012.

Food & Drink

Judd mat gaardebounen The national dish, smoked pork in a creamy sauce with broad beans and potato chunks.

Liewekniddelen mat sauerkraut Liver meatballs with sauerkraut.

Wine The Moselle Valley produces excellent sparkling wines, fruity Rivaners, lush Pinot Blancs and balanced Rieslings.

Schiessentümpel cascade, Müllerthal

Château de Bourscheid

6 Viewed from the N27 or from the CR438 8km north of Ettelbrück, this splendid castle ruin is surely the nation's most dramatic. As you get closer, the degree of degradation is much clearer but it's still very interesting to clamber about the wall stubs. Admission includes a remarkably extensive 90-minute audio guide and there's a trio of somewhat odd 'visuella' slide presentations to ponder en route. Don't miss climbing the rather squat 12th-century square keep for classic turret-framed views over the forested river bend below.

Müllerthal

7 Perfect real estate for hobbits and pixies, Müllerthal's most intriguing corners are cut with narrow, mossy ravines, crystal-clear creeks and strange rock formations. The highlights of hiking these well-signposted trails are squeezing through shoulder-wide micro-gorges, crossing trickling streams with mossy banks and passing distinctively eroded sandstone formations. To reach these hidden corners you'll need to hike into the sighing woodlands west of historic Echternach, a curious town of Roman ghosts and waving-handkerchief dances.

Getting Around

Bike Cycling is a good alternative for seeing Luxembourg City and visiting the wine route.

Bus & Train Luxembourg's excellent public transport system is one ticket fits all, with buses and trains sharing the same ticketing system. Buses run to most of the main sights.

Car Luxembourg has some of the cheapest petrol in Western Europe and cars are an easy way to get around.

Church of St Paul

CAPITAL
Macau

POPULATION
583,003

AREA
28.2 sq km

**OFFICIAL
LANGUAGE**
Cantonese

Macau

The last outpost of the Portuguese empire, Macau still has a tangible Mediterranean feel. Nevertheless, Chinese culture shines through in this city state located at the mouth of the Pearl River.

The Chinese people have stood up and they're off to Macau. Chairman Mao (who coined the first half of that sentence) must be spinning in his glass coffin. Mainlanders can't get enough of this once Portuguese-administered backwater-turned-gambling-megaresort.

Such has been its explosive growth since 2002 that it is commonplace to refer to Macau as the Vegas of the East. It might be more appropriate to put that the other way round, since Macau has eclipsed its American rival in gambling income.

And there are many other things that Macau does better. Beyond the gaming halls, it offers cobblestoned streets punctuated with Chinese temples and baroque churches, pockets of (natural) greenery, a historic centre of Unesco World Heritage status and balmy beaches.

Macau's history has also created a one-of-a-kind cuisine that celebrates the marriage of European, Latin American, African and Asian flavours.

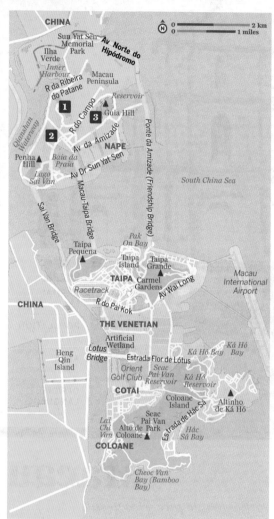

CHINA

Sun Yat Sen Memorial Park

Av Norte do Hipódromo

Ilha Verde

Inner Harbour

Macau Peninsula

R da Ribeira do Patane

Reservoir

R do Campo

Guia Hill

Qianshan Waterway

Av da Amizade

NAPE

Penha Hill

Báia da Praia

Av Dr Sun Yat Sen

Lago Sai Van

Sai Van Bridge

Macau-Taipa Bridge

Ponte da Amizade (Friendship Bridge)

South China Sea

Pak On Bay

Taipa Pequena

Taipa Island

Taipa Grande

TAIPA

Carmel Gardens

Av Wai Long

Racetrack

R do Pai Kok

Macau International Airport

CHINA

THE VENETIAN

Artificial Wetland

Lotus Bridge

Heng Qin Island

Estrada Flor de Lótus

Orient Golf Club

Seac Pai Van Reservoir

Ká Hó Bay

Ká Hó Bay

Ká Hó Reservoir

COTAI

Coloane Island

Altinho de Ká Hó

Estrada de Hác Sá

Laí Chi Van

Seac Pai Van Park

Alto de Coloane

Hác Sá Bay

COLOANE

Cheoc Van Bay (Bamboo Bay)

0   2 km
0   1 miles
N

When to Go

MAR–MAY

➡ Celebrate the arts, a sea goddess and a dragon as mist hangs over the harbour.

JUN–SEP

➡ Days in the shade of temples and dragon boats; nights aglow with fireworks.

OCT–FEB

➡ Music and Grand Prix in a high-octane run-up to Christmas and New Year.

Food & Drink

Chicken Try the Macanese speciality, *galinha africana* (African chicken), made with coconut, garlic and chillies.

Portuguese food Popular dishes include *salada de bacalhau* (dried salted cod salad), *arroz de pato* (rice with duck confit) and *leitão assado no forno* (roast suckling pig).

Seafood *Casquinha* (stuffed crab) is a favourite.

St Lazarus District

2 Stroll through this lovely neighbourhood of quiet houses and cobbled streets. Artists, designers and independents have set up shop here recently.

Guia Fort

3 As the highest point on the Macau Peninsula, this fort affords panoramic views of the city and, on a clear day, across to China. At the top you'll find a lighthouse, built in 1865 and the oldest on the China coast, and the lovely Chapel of Our Lady of Guia, built in 1622 and retaining almost 100% of its original features.

Macau's
Top Experiences

Church of St Paul

1 A gateway to nowhere in the middle of the city is all that remains of the Church of St Paul, considered by some to be the greatest monument to Christianity in Asia. The church was designed by an Italian Jesuit and built in 1602 by Japanese Christian exiles and Chinese craftsmen. In 1835 a fire destroyed everything except the facade. Like much of Macau's colonial architecture, its European appearance belies the fascinating mix of influences (in this case Chinese, Japanese, Indochinese) that contributed to its aesthetics.

Church of Sveti Jovan at Kaneo

CAPITAL
Skopje

POPULATION
2.1 million

AREA
25,713 sq km

OFFICIAL LANGUAGES
Macedonian, Albanian

Macedonia

Deep in the Balkan countryside, among slate-roofed villages, road-side cafes, lake panoramas and watermelon stalls, you find the soul of Macedonia

Macedonia (Македонија) is hard to beat. Part Balkan and part Mediterranean, and offering impressive ancient sites and buzzing modern nightlife, the country packs in much more action, activities and natural beauty than would seem possible for a place its size.

Easygoing Skopje remains one of Europe's more unusual capitals, where constant urban renewal has made the city a continuous work in progress. With its hip cafes, restaurants, bars and clubs frequented by a large student population, Skopje is also emerging on the region's entertainment scene.

In summer try hiking, mountain biking and climbing in remote mountains, some concealing medieval monasteries. Visit Ohrid, noted for its summer festival, sublime Byzantine churches and a large lake. Winter offers skiing at resorts such as Mavrovo, and food-and-grog festivities in the villages. Meeting the locals and partaking in the country's living culture can be as memorable and rewarding as seeing the sights.

Macedonia's
Top Experiences

Church of Sveti Jovan

1 Gaze out over Ohrid from the Church of Sveti Jovan at Kaneo, immaculately set on a bluff above Lake Ohrid. This stunning 13th-century church on a cliff over the lake has pride of place in Macedonia's most important historic town. It is possibly Macedonia's most photographed structure. Peer down into the azure waters and you'll see why medieval monks found spiritual inspiration here. The small church has original frescoes behind the altar.

Skopje

2 Dive into historic but still-changing Skopje, a friendly, quintessentially Balkan capital. Skopje is among Europe's most entertaining and eclectic small capital cities. While a government construction spree has sparked controversy in recent years, Skopje's abundance of statuary, bridges, museums and other structures has visitors' cameras snapping like never before and has defined the ever-changing city. Yet plenty survives from earlier times – Skopje's Ottoman- and Byzantine-era wonders include the 15th-century Kameni Most (Stone Bridge), Čaršija (old Turkish bazaar) and Sveti Spas Church, with its ornate, hand-carved iconostasis. And, with its bars, clubs and galleries, the city has modern culture too.

Zrze Monastery

3 Soak up the serenity at clifftop Zrze Monastery, with sweeping views of the Pelagonian Plain and priceless Byzantine artworks. Some 26km northwest of Prilep, towards Makedonski Brod, the 14th-century Monastery of the Holy Transfiguration rises like a revelation from a clifftop. The monastery's tranquil position around a spacious lawn, with views over the outstretched Pelagonian Plain, is stunning. At dawn, a low-lying fog sometimes shrouds the plain in marble. Its 17th-century Church of Saints Peter and Paul contains important frescoes and icons.

View from Kameni Most (Stone Bridge), Skopje

Heraclea Lyncestis

4 Heraclea Lyncestis, 1km south of Bitola, is among Macedonia's best archaeological sites. Founded by Philip II of Macedon, Heraclea became commercially significant before the Romans conquered in 168 BC. In the 4th century Heraclea became an episcopal seat, but it was sacked by Goths and then Slavs. You can see the Roman baths, portico and amphitheatre, and the striking Early Christian basilica and episcopal palace ruins, with beautiful, well-preserved floor mosaics. They're unique in depicting endemic trees and animals.

Mariovo

5 If there's one place in Macedonia that still connotes mystery, it's Mariovo. The southern-border badlands region hums with the disconcerting energy of another time, still resonating in its rugged mountains, deep river-canyons and strange plateaus dotted with deserted villages. For centuries, the 25 Mariovo villages were wealthy sheep-herding centres. They are now abandoned, yet hiking or touring the area by car and admiring the faded beauty of traditional Macedonian architecture is still a great pleasure.

if Macedonia were 100 people

64 would be Macedonian
25 would be Albanian
4 would be Turkish
3 would be Roma
4 would be other

belief systems
(% of population)

65 — Macedonian Orthodox
33 — Muslim
2 — other

When to Go

JUN–AUG
➡ Enjoy Ohrid's Summer Festival and dive into its 300m-deep lake.

SEP & OCT
➡ Partake in Skopje's Beer Fest, Jazz Festival and harvest celebrations.

DEC–FEB
➡ Ski Mavrovo and indulge in Macedonia's holiday carnivals.

population per sq km

MACEDONIA   ALBANIA   UK

≈ 20 people

Tikveš Wine Region

Macedonia's winery heartland, Tikveš has produced wine since the 4th century BC. It features rolling vineyards, lakes, caves and mountains, plus archaeological sites and churches.

It's especially beautiful at dusk, when the fading sunlight suffuses soft hills laden with millions of grapes. Tikveš' local grapes generally retain an ideal sugar concentration (17% to 26%).

Tikveš Winery is southeastern Europe's biggest winery (established 1885) and offers tours and tastings of some of their 29 wines. Kavadarci Wine Carnival is a costumed parade with public wine tastings held in September

Nearby Lake Tikveš is surrounded by scrubland and stark cliffs, dotted with medieval hermitage frescos and circled by eagles and hawks.

Food & Drink

Ajvar Sweet red-pepper sauce; accompanies meats and cheeses.

Bekonegs Not terribly traditional, but you will see this mangled rendition of 'bacon and eggs' on Macedonian breakfast menus.

Rakija Grape-based firewater, useful for toasts (and cleaning cuts and windows!).

Skopsko and Dab lagers Macedonia's favourite brews.

Šopska salata Tomatoes, onions and cucumbers topped with flaky *sirenje* (white cheese).

Uvijač Rolled chicken or pork wrapped in bacon and filled with melted yellow cheese.

Vranec and Temjanika Macedonia's favourite red- and white-wine varietals.

Pelister National Park, Bitola

Bitola

6 Enjoy the old-world ambience of Bitola and hike in nearby Pelister National Park. With elegant buildings and beautiful people, elevated Bitola (660m) has a sophistication inherited from its Ottoman days as the 'City of Consuls'. Its colourful 18th- and 19th-century townhouses, Turkish mosques and cafe culture make it Macedonia's most intriguing and liveable major town. An essential experience is sipping a coffee and people-watching along the pedestrianised Širok Sokak.

Mavrovo

7 Ski Mavrovo, Macedonia's premier and biggest winter resort. This domain, comprising 730 sq km of birch and pine forest, boasts more than just skiing with gorges, karst fields and waterfalls, plus Macedonia's highest peak, Mt Korab (2764m). The rarefied air and stunning vistas are great year-round. Located up a winding road southwest of Gostivar, Mavrovo lies near Sveti Jovan Bigorski Monastery and Galičnik, famous for its traditional village wedding.

Getting Around

Bus Buses in Skopje serve most domestic destinations. Larger buses are new and air-conditioned; *kombi* (minibuses) are usually not.

Car Cars must carry replacement bulbs, two warning triangles and a first-aid kit (available at big petrol stations). From 15 November to 15 March snow tyres must be used (otherwise you can be fined), and chains should be carried on-board too.

Taxi Taxis are relatively inexpensive and can be preferable for international travel.

Train Major rail lines travel to the Serbian and Greek borders. Smaller train lines do exist.

CAPITAL
Antananarivo

POPULATION
22.6 million

AREA
587,041 sq km

OFFICIAL LANGUAGES
French
Malagasy

Ring-tailed lemurs, Réserve Privée de Berenty

Madagascar

Lemurs, baobabs, rainforest, beaches, desert, trekking and diving: Madagascar is a dream destination for nature and outdoor lovers, and half the fun is getting to all these incredible attractions.

Madagascar is unique: 5% of all known animal and plant species can be found here, and here alone. The remarkable fauna and flora is matched by epic landscapes of an incredible diversity: you can go from rainforest to desert in just 300km. Few places on earth offer such an intense kaleidoscope of nature.

With 5000km of coastline, 450km of barrier reef and 250 islands, no stay in Madagascar would be complete without a few days on the island's shores. Divers will revel in the choice of sites, from underwater 'cathedrals' to shipwrecks, and will relish the chance to see rays, whale sharks, reef sharks and many other kinds of sharks. Snorkellers will be awed by the sheer grace of turtles and marvel at the rainbow of colours displayed by corals and fish.

There is much history to discover, too, from the 12 sacred hills of Antananarivo to the pirate cemetery of Ile Sainte Marie and the vestige of Madagascar's industrial revolution in Mantasoa.

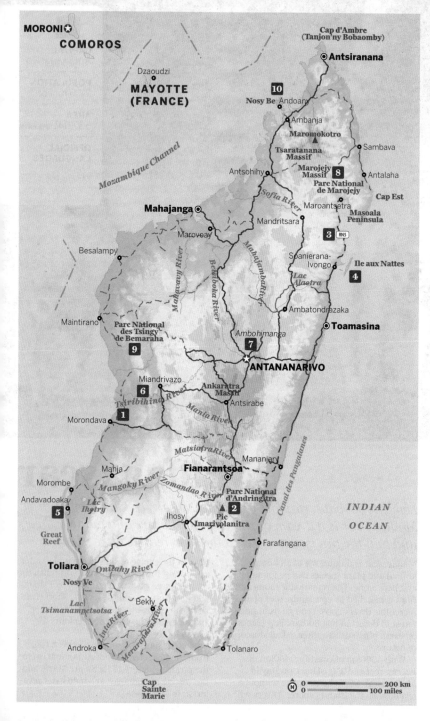

MORONI ✦
COMOROS

Cap d'Ambre
(Tanjon'ny Bobaomby)

Dzaoudzi ○

● Antsiranana

MAYOTTE
(FRANCE)

10

Nosy Be ● Andoany

○ Ambanja

▲ **Maromokotro**

**Tsaratanana
Massif**

Mozambique Channel

Antsohihy ●

**Marojejy
Massif**   **8**

○ Sambava

Antalaha ○

**Parc National
de Marojejy**

Cap Est

Sofia River

Maroantsetra ○

**Masoala
Peninsula**

Mahajanga ◉

Mandritsara ●

Marovoay ●

3 RN5

Mahavavy River

Betsiboka River

Mahajamba River

Soanierana-
Ivongo ●

Ile aux Nattes

4

Besalampy ●

Lac
Alaotra

Maintirano ●

**Parc National
des Tsingy
de Bemaraha**

9

Ambatondrazaka ●

◉ **Toamasina**

Ambohimanga

7

Miandrivazo ●

★ **ANTANANARIVO**

6

**Ankaratra
Massif**

Tsiribihina River

Antsirabe ●

1

Manra River

Morondava ●

Matsiatra River

Mahja ●

Fianarantsoa

Mananjary ●

Morombe ●

Mangoky River

Zomandao River

Andavadoaka ●

Lac
Ihotry

**Parc National
d'Andringitra**

5

Ihosy ●

2

▲ **Pic
Imarivolanitra**

**INDIAN
OCEAN**

**Great
Reef**

Farafangana ○

Canal des Pangalanes

Toliara ◉

Onilahy River

Nosy Ve

Lac
Tsimanampetsotsa

Linta River

Bekily ●

Meraraquisa River

Androka ●

Tolanaro ○

**Cap
Sainte
Marie**

Ⓝ 0 _____ 200 km
    0 _____ 100 miles

Madagascar's
Top Experiences

Sunset at Allée des Baobabs

1 Few things say Madagascar more than this small stretch of the RN8 between Morondava and Belo-sur-Tsiribihina. Lined with majestic baobabs, it comes into its own at sunset and sunrise when the trees cast their long shadows on the red sand and the sky lights up with orange and purple hues. In addition to the Allée, you'll find plenty more baobabs across southern and western Madagascar. Some can live for up to a thousand years and reach epic proportions.

Parc National d'Andringitra

2 With more than 100km of trails, a majestic mountain range, three challenging peaks and epic landscapes, this national park is a trekker's paradise. For the crème de la crème, follow the two-day Imarivolanitra Trail, which takes you from one side of the park to the other via its summit, lush valleys and some natural swimming pools, and enjoy a couple of nights under the stars. Don't let a lack of forward planning stop you: hire everything you need at the park office, from guides to cooks, porters and even camping equipment.

Tackle the Infamous RN5

3 If you revel in the idea of a road challenge, this is it. It may be a route nationale, but make no mistake, the 240km stretch between Maroantsetra and Soanierana-Ivongo is no road. It is a track, a quagmire, an obstacle course, a river in places, a mountain in others, but not a road. Semantics aside, travellers who complete the journey will have anecdotes to last them a lifetime. Mananara, halfway through the trip, is also one of the few places in Madagascar where you're likely to see an aye-aye (lemur).

if Madagascar were 100 people

70 would live in rural areas
30 would live in urban areas

belief systems
(% of population)

indigenous 52
Christian 41
Muslim 7

population per sq km

MADAGASCAR SOUTH AFRICA UK

≈ 33 people

Ile aux Nattes

4 If you've been dreaming of tropical island paradise, Ile aux Nattes is that dream come true. Standing at the tip of Ile Sainte Marie, a short pirogue ride away or a leisurely walk at low tide, this is the place to come and do absolutely nothing. Nestle in a hammock at Chez Sika, laze on the beach and swim. And when you've had enough, cross over to Sainte Marie and zoom across the island on a motorbike.

Diving & Snorkelling at Andavadoaka

5 Madagascar boasts the world's fifth largest coral reef, 450km of fringing, patch, and barrier reefs from Andavadoaka in the north to Itampolo in the south. The pearl of the barrier is Andavadoaka, where work with local communities and a marine conservation area have kept the reef in top shape. Divers who make it all the way here will be rewarded with stunning corals and abundant fish. Other spots that will blow you away are the 'cathedrals' at Ifaty and Mangily and the serene village of Ambola.

Tsiribihina River

6 Taking a trip down the Tsiribihina means disconnecting completely from everything: for two and a half days, there are no cars, no roads, and there's no mobile coverage. It is an experience of utter relaxation, with little more to do than admire the landscape, take in local life, chat to your guide, sing by the campfire and marvel at the

Shiver me timbers

In the late 17th and 18th centuries Ile Sainte Marie was the headquarters of the world's pirates, who enjoyed its proximity to maritime trade routes, its protected harbour (a great place to hide), its abundant fruit, and its women. Legendary brigands such as William Kidd once brought their boats here for repairs, and set up house on Ile aux Forbans, near Ambodifotatra.

At one point the pirate population topped 1000. Today the remains of several pirate ships still lie within a few metres of the surface in the Baie des Forbans, including Kidd's *Adventure*, and Captain Condent's famous *Fiery Dragon*, while the skull and crossbones can be seen engraved at the nearby pirate cemetery.

Food & Drink

Noodles The most common alternative to the staple rice is a steaming bowl of *mi sao* (fried noodles with vegetables or meat) or a satisfying *soupe chinoise* (clear noodle soup with fish, chicken or vegetables).

Ravitoto This well-loved Malagasy dish, is a mix of fried beef or pork with shredded cassava leaves and coconut milk; truly delicious.

Rice Eating rice three times a day is so ingrained in Malagasy culture that people sometimes claim they can't sleep if they haven't eaten rice that day. In fact, the verb 'to eat' in Malagasy, *mihinam-bary*, literally means 'to eat rice'.

Romazava A beef stew in a ginger-flavoured broth; it contains *brêdes mafana*, a green leaf reminiscent of Indian saag in taste that will make your tongue and lips tingle thanks to its anaesthetic properties!

Seafood Seafood features prominently on the menu. Prices are so low that all but the tightest budgets can gorge themselves on fish, crayfish, lobster and even tiny oysters.

Ile aux Nattes, off Ile Sainte Marie

night sky. For the real deal, hop on a wooden pirogue; for a little more comfort and conviviality, board a *chaland* (motorised barge).

Ambohimanga

7 This is Madagascar's only cultural site on Unesco's World Heritage list, and with good reason:

Ambohimanga was the seat of King Andrianampoinimerina, the Merina sovereign who decided to unify the warring tribes of the island so that his kingdom would have no frontier but the sea. The cultural significance of the site goes beyond history: Ambohimanga is revered as a sacred site by the Malagasy, who come here to invoke royal spirits and request their protection and good fortune.

Parc National de Marojejy

8 With its pristine mountainous rainforest, thick root-filled jungle and waterfalls, Marojejy is a primordial place, where the 'angel of the forest', the

When to Go

HIGH SEASON
(Jul–Oct)

➡ July and August are especially busy because of European school holidays.

➡ It's winter – balmy temperatures by day and cool nights.

➡ There's also a spike of high-season activity at Christmas/New Year.

SHOULDER
(Apr, May, Nov, Dec)

➡ Pleasant temperatures and fewer visitors.

➡ Some attractions have started closing or haven't quite reopened because of the rain.

LOW SEASON
(Jan–Mar)

➡ Cyclone season, the east coast is particularly vulnerable but all coastal areas are susceptible.

➡ Rainy season everywhere – many areas inaccessible.

➡ Discounts available in hotels.

endemic silky sifaka, inhabits misty mountains, and spectacular views of the Marojejy Massif open up through the canopy. A superb trail crescendos through the landscape, climaxing with a tough climb to the summit (2132m). Marojejy permits also provide entry to the remote and beautiful Réserve Spéciale d'Anjanaharibe-Sud, where travellers will be rewarded with the wail of the indri.

Getting Around

Air Flying within Madagascar can be a huge time-saver considering the distances and state of the roads. Unfortunately, most domestic routes are between Tana and the provinces, with few direct routes between provinces.

Boat Engineless pirogues or *lakanas* (dugout canoes), whether on rivers or the sea, are the primary means of local transport where roads disappear.

Car Madagascar is huge; the roads are bad and travel times long. It takes 24 hours of solid driving from Antananarivo (Tana) to Diego Suarez (Antsiranana), 18 to Tuléar (Toliara), 16 to Morondava and so on. Be realistic about how much ground you want to cover or you'll spend every other day in the confines of a vehicle.

Tsingy de Bemaraha

9 There is nothing else on earth quite like the jagged limestone pinnacles of Parc National des Tsingy de Bemaraha. A Unesco World Heritage site, the serrated, surreal-looking peaks and boulders are a geological work of art, the result of millennia of water and wind erosion. Just as remarkable is the excellent infrastructure the national park has put in place to explore this natural wonder: via *ferrata* (fixed-cable routes), rope bridges and ladders, with circuits combining forests, caves, pirogue trips and even abseiling.

Nosy Be

10 The 'big island' is a dream destination: you could spend two weeks here and in the surrounding islands and still feel like you haven't had enough. It's not just the world-class diving and snorkelling, the turquoise sea, the exquisitely soft light and arresting views: you can also visit spice plantations, explore miles of inland trails, see fabulous wildlife in the marine and nature reserves, feast on an abundance of seafood and sail to dozens of small islands.

Best on Film

Madagascar Narrated by Sir David Attenborough, this is an inspirational introduction to the island. It features the iconic fauna and flora, as well as its more obscure specimens, in fascinating detail and stunning images.

Quand les Étoiles Rencontrent la Mer (When the Stars Meet the Sea) Directed by the Malagasy Raymond Rajaonarivelo, this is the story of a young boy born during a solar eclipse.

Best in Print

Hainteny: The Traditional Poetry of Madagascar (Leonard Fox) Translations of beautiful Merina poems charting love, revenge and sexuality

Over the Lip of the World: Among the Storytellers of Madagascar (Colleen J McElroy) A journey through Malagasy oral traditions and myths.

Voices from Madagascar: An Anthology of Contemporary Francophone Literature (edited by Jacques Bourgeacq and Liliane Ramarosoa) Contains Malagasy writing in French and English.

DANITA DELIMONT / GETTY IMAGES ©

Lake Malawi, Usisya

CAPITAL
Lilongwe

POPULATION
17.3 million

AREA
118,484 sq km

OFFICIAL LANGUAGE
English

Malawi

Malawi is firmly back on the map with restocked parks throughout the country, reintroduced lions, world-class safari lodges and excellent tour operators.

Malawi has been historically overlooked in the table of epic safari destinations. That was until Majete Wildlife Reserve was thoroughly restocked and a lion reintroduction program began there in 2012. The country now has its 'Big Five' again, added to which are new world-class boutique hotels and luxury safari lodges; it's easy to see then why travel editors are salivating over Africa's next *big* destination.

Slicing through the landscape in a trough formed by the Great Rift Valley is Lake Malawi; a shimmering mass of glittering water swarming with colourful cichlid fish. Whether it's diving, snorkelling, kayaking or chilling on its desert islands, the lake is unforgettable.

In Malawi's deep south are the dramatic peaks of Mt Mulanje and Zomba Plateau; both are a trekker's dream, with mist-cowled forests. Head further north and you'll witness the beauty of Nyika Plateau, its grasslands reminiscent of the Scottish Highlands. In short, there's something for everyone here.

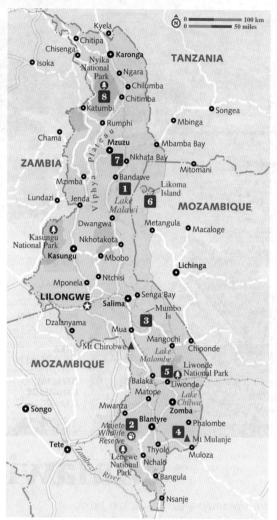

Malawi's
Top Experiences

Lake Malawi

1 The emerald jewel in Malawi's crown is undoubtedly its interior sea, Lake Malawi. Fringed by golden beaches, the 'calendar lake' – so-called because it measures 365 miles long and 52 miles wide – offers travellers an underwater paradise to swim among brilliantly coloured cichlid fish and desert islands to escape to. The resorts of Chintheche Strip, Nkhata Bay and Cape Maclear also offer a spectrum of great accommodation and activities such as kayaking and windsurfing to ensure you can make the best of it.

Majete Wildlife Reserve

2 Deep in the heartland of southern Malawi lies one of the country's most exciting reserves, thanks to its massively reinvigorated wildlife population, fenced perimeter, finessed infrastructure and a determined antipoaching program. It's official: Malawi finally has the Big Five again, since lions were introduced into Majete in 2012, joining the ranks of leopards, buffaloes, elephants and rhino. Stay at the blissfully comfortable Mkulumadzi Lodge for up-close animal encounters, and track their newly ensconced lion pride on a game drive.

Mumbo Island

3 Kayak to Mumbo Island across bottle-green Lake Malawi. Just a short stretch from Cape Maclear lies a mystery of a desert island cloaked in thick jungle, ballasted by giant boulders and fringed by turquoise water so greeny-blue that it looks as if it's leapt from an ad campaign. Accommodation here is simple and that's half the charm; and yes, those are 1.5m monitor lizards swimming across the perfect little inlet, and yup, that screech is a pair of resident fish eagles.

Mt Mulanje

4 Scramble up the twisted peaks of Mt Mulanje to admire the astounding views. A huge hulk of twisted granite rising majestically from the surrounding plains, Mt Mulanje towers over 3000m high. All over the mountain are dense green valleys and rivers that drop from sheer cliffs to form dazzling waterfalls. The locals call it the 'Island in the Sky' and on

Elephants, Liwonde National Park

misty days the mountain is shrouded in a cotton-wool haze, and its highest peaks burst through the cloud to touch the heavens.

Liwonde National Park

5 Spot hippos and crocs on the Shire River in Liwonde National Park, or get up close to elephants. This park spills over with elephants, hippos, water buffaloes and crocs. It's a comparatively small reserve set in dry savannah and forest over 584 sq km, and you can walk, drive and putter along the serene Shire River to make the best of it. Lions were reintroduced in 2013, following which, cheetahs and hyenas are also being added to the carnivore's league table.

Likoma Island

6 Escape to dreamy beaches and Malawi's finest boutique hotel, and explore traditional villages and the magnificent cathedral on Likoma Island. The 17-sq-km Likoma is a dream of turquoise waters and desert-island bliss, boasting outstanding views to nearby Mozambique. About 6000 people make their home here, and the island's relative isolation from the rest of Malawi has allowed the locals to maintain their reserved culture. It's absolutely worth the effort to get here.

Nkhata Bay

7 With its fishing boats, vivid market and guesthouses perched on cliffs overlooking glittering Lake Malawi, pretty Nkhata Bay

if Malawi were 100 people

33 would be Chewa
18 would be Lomwe
14 would be Yao
12 would be Ngoni
8 would be Tumbuka
15 would be other

belief systems
(% of population)

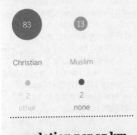

83 — Christian
13 — Muslim
2 — other
2 — none

population per sq km

MALAWI TANZANIA SOUTH AFRICA

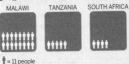

♀ ≈ 11 people

When to Go

MAY–MID-NOV
➡ The dry season is the best time to visit.

MAY–JUL
➡ National parks like Nyika are a blaze of wild flowers.

OCT–NOV
➡ Wildlife viewing is at its peak, though temperatures can be uncomfortably hot.

The Boy Who Harnessed the Wind

When the drought of 2001 brought famine, William Kamkwamba's parents could no longer afford the annual fees and the 14-year-old was forced from school. Self-educating at his old primary school, one book in particular spoke to him; it was about electricity generation through windmills.

A light-bulb moment flashed. Exhausted from his work in the fields every day, William picked around for scrap and painstakingly began his creation; a four-bladed windmill. Soon neighbours were coming to see him to charge their phones on his windmill.

When news of William's invention spread, people from across the globe offered to help him. He was shortly re-enrolled in college and travelling to America to visit windfarms, and has since been mentoring kids on how to create their own independent electricity sources. *The Boy Who Harnessed The Wind* (William Kamkwamba and Bryan Mealer) is his amazing story.

Food & Drink

The staple diet for most Malawians is *nshima*, a thick, doughy maize porridge that's bland but very filling. It's eaten with the hands and always accompanied by beans or vegetables and a hot relish, and sometimes meat or fish.

Fish is particularly good in Malawi, and *chambo*, the popular breamlike variety, and *kampango*, a lake fish similar to catfish, are both popular.

Traditional beer of the region is made from maize. Malawi's local lager is called Kuche Kuche but most travellers (and many Malawians) prefer the beer produced by Carlsberg at its Blantyre brewery. The most popular brew is Carlsberg 'green' (lager).

Horse riding, Nyika National Park

feels distinctly Caribbean. There are loads of activities to enjoy before you hammock flop, be it snorkelling, diving, fish-eagle feeding, kayaking or forest walks. On the southern side of Nkhata Bay, Chikale Beach is a popular spot for swimming and lazing on the sand. Snorkelling equipment is free for guests at most of the lodges.

Nyika National Park

8 Burnt amber by the afternoon sun, Nyika's highland grass flickers with the stripes of zebras and is punctuated by glittering boulders. Towering 2500m

above sea level, 3200-sq-km Nyika National Park is enigmatic; one moment its rolling grasslands resemble the Yorkshire Dales, then an antelope leaps across the car bonnet and you know you're in Africa. There are plenty of zebras, bushbucks, roan antelopes and elephants; more than 400 species of birds have been recorded. After the wet season the landscape bursts into life in a blaze of wildflowers. You can take a game drive, explore on a mountain bike or horse, or ramble through the hills on foot.

Getting Around

Air There are regular flights between Lilongwe and Blantyre, plus twin-prop planes to various domestic safari parks as well as Likoma Island.

Boat The *Ilala* ferry chugs passengers and cargo up and down Lake Malawi once a week in each direction. Travelling between Monkey Bay in the south and Chilumba in the north, it makes 12 stops at lakeside villages and towns in between. The whole trip, from one end of the line to the other, takes about three days.

Bus There are express bus services operating between Blantyre and Lilongwe twice a day. Country commuter buses cover the lakeshore route. There are also local minibus services which operate on a fill-up-and-go basis.

Kota Kinabalu, Sabah

Malaysia

Malaysia offers steamy jungles packed with wildlife, beautiful beaches, idyllic islands, culinary sensations and multi-ethnic cultures.

Malaysia is like two countries in one, cleaved in half by the South China Sea. The multicultural peninsula flaunts Malay, Chinese and Indian influences, while Borneo hosts a wild jungle of orang-utans, granite peaks and remote tribes. Throughout these two regions is an impressive variety of microcosms ranging from the space-age high-rises of Kuala Lumpur to the smiling longhouse villages of Sarawak.

And then there's the food. Malaysia (particularly along the peninsular west coast) has one of the best assortments of cuisines in the world. Start with Chinese-Malay 'Nonya' fare, move on to Indian curries, Chinese buffets, Malay food stalls and even impressive Western food.

Yet despite all the pockets of ethnicities, religions, landscapes and the sometimes-great distances between them, the beauty of Malaysia lies in the fusion of it all into a country that is one of the safest, most stable, diverse but manageable in all of Southeast Asia.

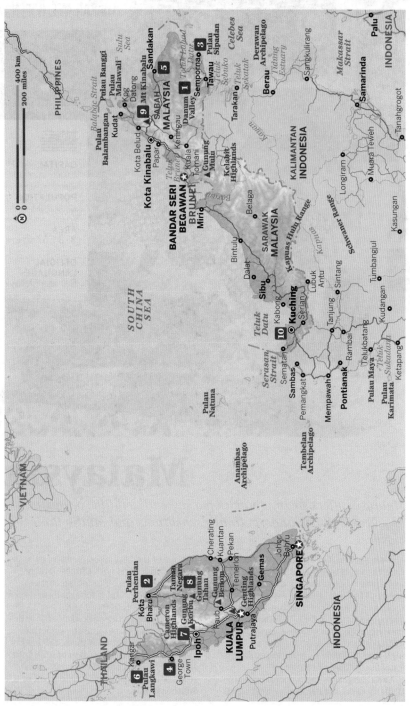

Malaysia's
Top Experiences

Jungle Treks in the Danum Valley, Sabah

1 'Walk quickly', our guide tells us. 'Fire ants.' Once again we wonder: is this really fun? But it is. Trekking in the Danum Valley is one of the most stirring experiences in Borneo – walking through a forest that is older than humanity. And while this is no open African savannah, and spotting animals can be difficult in the brush, the wildlife we see is all the more amazing for that: iridescent flying lizards, curious frogs, emerald pit vipers and, peering out with its headlight eyes, an adorable slow loris.

Pulau Perhentian, Terengganu

2 Though eastern Peninsular Malaysia has several islands offering unparalleled underwater activities, Pulau Perhentian wins when it comes to attracting snorkellers. Perhaps it's the water itself: clear and ethereally blue. Or the huge variety of marine life: sharks, tropical fish, turtles and nesting urchins. Living coral beds lie close to shore, and on most days you won't have to swim much further than the jetty at Long Beach before finding yourself inside a rainbow cloud of fish of all shapes and sizes.

Diving on Pulau Sipadan

3 Sometimes it seems as if the world's most colourful marine life – from the commonplace to utterly alien fish, molluscs and reptiles, creatures that seem to have swum through every slice of the colour wheel – considers the seawall of Sipadan to be prime real estate. They live here, play here, hunt here and eat here, and you, lucky thing, may dance an underwater ballet with them. For any diver, from the amateur to seasoned veterans like Jacques Cousteau, Sipadan is the ultimate underwater adventure.

if Malaysia were 100 people

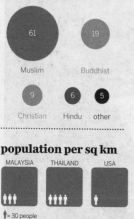

50 would be Malay
24 would be Chinese
11 would be indigenous
7 would be Indian
8 would be other

belief systems
(% of population)

61 Muslim
19 Buddhist
9 Christian
6 Hindu
5 other

population per sq km

MALAYSIA THAILAND USA

≈ 30 people

George Town's Colonial District, Penang

4 Once abandoned by locals and seemingly forgotten by tourists, George Town has emerged as one of the region's hottest destinations in the last couple of years. The 2008 Unesco World Heritage declaration sparked a frenzy of cultural preservation, and the city's charismatic shophouses have been turned into house museums, boutique hotels and chic restaurants. Aggressive drivers aside, it's also one of the best cities in Southeast Asia to explore on foot.

Sepilok Orang-Utan Rehabilitation Centre, Sabah

5 There is no primate quite like the orangutan. These great apes are a stirring combination: brawn and grace; raw power and gentle restraint; cuteness. And behind their sparkling eyes lie deep reserves of what we can only call wisdom and, sometimes, sadness. All these complicated observations occur at the Sepilok Orang-Utan Rehabilitation Centre – one of only four orang-utan sanctuaries in the world – where visitors can see the apes from an often crowded viewing platform, the highlight of many a Sabah trip.

Indulgence on Pulau Langkawi, Kedah

6 Pulau Langkawi ain't called the Jewel of Kedah for nothing, and its white-sand beaches, isolated resorts, acclaimed diving and pristine jungles live up to the metaphor. Cheap booze (Langkawi is duty-

The Peranakans

One of Peninsular Malaysia's most celebrated cultures is that of the Peranakans, descendants of Chinese immigrants who, from the 16th century onwards, settled in Singapore, Melaka and Penang. While these arrivals often married Malay women, others imported their wives from China; all of them like to refer to themselves as Straits-born or Straits Chinese to distinguish themselves from later arrivals from China.

The Peranakans took the religion of the Chinese, but the customs, language and dress of the Malays. The Peranakans were often wealthy traders who could afford to indulge their passion for sumptuous furnishings, jewellery and brocades. Today they are most famous for their delicious fusion cooking that's best experienced in Melaka.

Food & Drink

Breakfast *Nasi lemak* (coconut rice served with a variety of accompaniments), *roti canai* (Indian flat bread), *won ton mee* (egg noodles and wontons), dim sum or rice congee (savoury rice porridge).

Barbecue Fish, lobster, prawns, squid, cockles and stingray. Point to it then watch it get slathered in sambal and grilled in a banana leaf.

Dessert Malaysians drink their sweets via sugared fruit juices, sweetened condensed milk in hot beverages and scary looking icy concoctions like *cendol* and ABC (shave ice covered in coconut cream, jellies, beans and other crazy stuff).

Noodles Fried or in soup. The best include *char kway teow* (fried noodles with egg, soy sauce, chilli and a variety of additions), laksa, *curry mee* (curry noodles), *Hokkein mee* (fried noodles with chicken, pork and other additions) and *won ton mee*.

Rice *Nasi campur* is a lunch favourite of rice and a buffet of toppings.

3

RINHARD DIRSCHERL / GETTY IMAGES ©

Green sea turtle, Sipadan

free) and a decent restaurant and bar scene provide just the hint of a party vibe, while a glut of kid-friendly activities make it a great destination for families. But it's not just a holiday island; off-the-beaten-track-type exploration will reveal that Pulau Langkawi has managed to retain its endearing kampung soul.

When to Go

HIGH SEASON
(Dec–Feb)

➡ End-of-year school holidays followed by Chinese New Year push up prices. Book transport and hotels in advance.

➡ Monsoon season for the east coast of Peninsula Malaysia and western Sarawak.

SHOULDER
(Jul–Nov)

➡ July to August, vie with visitors escaping the heat of the Gulf States.

➡ The end of Ramadan (Hari Raya) also sees increased travel activity in the region.

LOW SEASON
(Mar–Jun)

➡ Avoid the worst of the rains and humidity; there's also the chance to enjoy places without the crush of fellow tourists.

Cameron Highlands, Perak

7 Misty mountains, gumboots, Tudor-themed architecture, scones, strawberries and tea plantations all converge in this distinctly un-Southeast Asian destination. Activities such as self-guided hiking, nature trekking and agricultural tourism make this one of Malaysia's most worthwhile active destinations. It also represents a clever escape within a vacation, as the elevation means that the weather in the Cameron Highlands tends to stay cool year-round.

Taman Negara, Pahang

8 To visit Taman Negara is to step back in time and experience the land as it was in primeval times. Inside this shadowy, nigh-impenetrable jungle, ancient trees with gargantuan buttressed root systems dwarf luminescent fungi, orchids, and flora rare and beautiful. Making their home within are elephants, tigers and leopards, as well as smaller wonders such as flying squirrels, lizards, monkeys, deer, tapirs and serpents of all sorts.

Best on Film

Entrapment (1999) The climax of this Sean Connery and Catherine Zeta-Jones thriller takes place at KL's Petronas Towers.

Septet (2004) Chinese boy falls for Malay girl in Yasmin Ahmad's romantic comedy.

Best in Print

Malaysia at Random (Editions Didier Millet; 2010) Quirky compendium of facts and anecdotes.

Malaysia Bagus! (Sharon Cheah; 2012) Engaging travelogue with stories from all of Malaysia's states plus Singapore.

The Garden of Evening Mists (Tan Twan Eng; 2012) Horticultural intrigue in the Malaysian highlands.

The Harmony Silk Factory (Tash Aw; 2005) Set deep in the heart of Peninsular Malaysia partly during WWII and won the 2005 Whitbread First Novel award.

Urban Odysseys (ed Janet Tay & Eric Forbes; 2009) Short stories that capture KL's multifaceted cultural flavour.

Getting Around

Air Fly between major destinations in Peninsular Malaysia and Sabah and Sarawak on Malaysian Borneo.

Boat There are no services connecting Peninsular Malaysia with Malaysian Borneo, but local boats and ferries run to offshore islands.

Bus Bus travel is economical and generally comfortable.

Car Driving in Malaysia is fanastic compared with most Asian countries, but cities can be confusing and difficult to navigate.

Train While the train is comfortable and economical, there are basically only two lines and services are slow.

Mt Kinabalu, Sabah

9 It is the abode of the spirits, the highest mountain in Malaysia, one of the most dominant geographic features in North Borneo, the bone-shaking trek that has worn out countless challengers. Mt Kinabalu is all this as well as one of the most popular tourist attractions in Borneo. Don't worry – you will still have moments of utter freedom, breathing in the only alpine air in Sabah and, if you're lucky, enjoying a horizon that stretches to the Philippines.

Kuching, Sarawak

10 Borneo's most sophisticated and stylish city, Kuching brings together a kaleidoscope of cultures, crafts and cuisines. The bustling markets amply reward visitors with a penchant for ambling, but the city's biggest draw is what's nearby: some of Sarawak's finest natural sites. You can spot semiwild orang-utans or search out a giant Rafflesia flower, look for proboscis monkeys and wild crocs on a sundown cruise in the South China Sea, and then dine on superfresh seafood or crunchy midin fern tips.

Proboscis monkey, Bako National Park, Sarawak

ALICE REECE / GETTY IMAGES ©

CAPITAL
Male

POPULATION
393,988

AREA
298 sq km

OFFICIAL LANGUAGE
Dhivehi

Maldives

Unrivalled luxury, stunning white-sand beaches and an amazing underwater world make the Maldives an obvious choice for a holiday of a lifetime.

The Maldives is home to perhaps the best beaches in the world; they're on almost every one of the country's nearly 1200 islands and are so consistently perfect that it's hard not to become blasé about them.

While some beaches may boast softer granules than others, the basic fact remains: you'll find this whiter-than-white powder sand and luminous cyan-blue water almost nowhere else on earth. This fact alone is enough to bring nearly a million people a year to this tiny and otherwise little-known Indian Ocean paradise.

Every resort in the Maldives is its own private island, and with over 100 to choose from the only problem is selecting where to stay. There's choice beyond the luxurious five- and six-star resorts. Other islands cater for families, for divers, for those on a (relative) budget, and anyone wanting a tranquil, remote and back-to-nature experience.

Ihavandhippolhu Atoll
Dhidhdhoo

North Thiladhunmathee Atoll

Kulhuduffushi
South Thiladhunmathee Atoll

Maamakunudhoo Atoll

North Miladhunmadulu Atoll

Funadhoo
South Miladhunmadulu Atoll
Noonu Atoll   **6**

Ugoofaaru
North Maalhosmadulu Atoll

Manadhoo

INDIAN OCEAN

Naifaru

South Maalhosmadulu Atoll

Faadhippolhu Atoll

Eydhafushi

Goidhoo Atoll

North Male Atoll

Rasdhoo Atoll   **2**

Thulusdhoo

✪**MALE**   **1**   **3**

Ari Atoll
5   **7**

South Male Atoll

Mahibadhoo

Felidhoo Atoll
Felidhoo

North Nilandhoo Atoll
Magoodhoo

Mulaku Atoll

South Nilandhoo Atoll

Muli

Kudahuvadhoo

Kolhumadulu Atoll

Veymandhoo

Hadhdhunmathee Atoll

Hithadhoo

INDIAN OCEAN

North Huvadhoo Atoll

Viligili

Thinadhoo
South Huvadhoo Atoll

Foammulah Atoll   Fuamulaku

Hithadhoo   Addu Atoll
Gan   **4**   **7**

0   100 km
0   60 miles
Ⓝ

Maldives
Top Experiences

Male

1 The Maldivian capital is definitely the best place to get to know locals and see what makes them tick. The brightly painted houses, crowded markets and teashops where you can chat to locals and share plates of delicious 'short eats' are just some of the highlights of this fascinating capital city – and they perfectly complement the resort experience.

Breakfast with the Hammers

2 Hammerhead sharks, definitely one of the weirdest-looking creatures in the sea (and that's saying something), can be seen in abundance in Maldivian waters – if you know where to look for them. There are few more thrilling experiences than a dawn dive, descending free fall into the deep blue to 30m, before suddenly coming upon a huge school of hungry hammerhead sharks waiting to be fed. The best place to do this is at the world-famous Hammerhead Point (aka Rasdhoo Madivaru) in Rasdhoo Atoll.

Take a Seaplane

3 Few destinations can claim that the mode of transport in which travellers arrive is one of the highlights of their trip, but that's because there are few places in the world where you need seaplanes to reach your hotel. The main port is at Male International Airport, where these zippy Twin Otters function like taxis in a country with no roads. Taking off from the water is an unforgettable experience, as is observing the spectacular coral atolls, blue lagoons and tiny desert islands from above.

Snorkel in Addu

4 When El Niño devastated the marine life of the Maldives and bleached the corals in 1998, the only area of the country to escape was the most southern atoll, Addu. While the coral all over the country is recovering impressively, here the corals are absolutely spectacular, including huge staghorn corals that didn't survive elsewhere in the Maldives. Anyone who snorkels or dives here will be in awe of the strength and variety of colour, particularly off the island of Gan.

Ari Atoll

Swim with a Whale Shark

5 The largest fish in the world, the whale shark is prevalent in Maldivian waters, especially in the south of Ari Atoll and during a full moon when the currents between the atolls are at their strongest. Swimming with one of these gentle giants is an incredible experience – they average almost 10m in length – and it's also totally safe, as despite their immense size, whale sharks feed only on plankton.

Visit an Inhabited Island

6 If you want to see the 'real' Maldives, try spending a few nights on an inhabited island in one of the new guesthouses, a million miles from the spa and infinity pool of your resort. These are most prevalent in the atolls near the capital, although they can be found as far away as Noonu Atoll. Here you can see colourful local life, try islander food and take in a traditional part of the world few people get to see.

if the Maldives were 100 people

65 would work in services
24 would work in secondary industries
11 would work in agriculture

belief systems
(% of population)

100

Sunni Muslim

population per sq km

MALDIVES   INDIA   UK

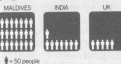

♟ = 50 people

When to Go

HIGH SEASON
(Dec–Feb)

➤ The Maldives enjoys its best weather.

➤ Expect little rain, low humidity and blue skies.

➤ Christmas and New Year involve huge price hikes and often minimum stays of 10-days or more

SHOULDER
(Mar–Apr)

➤ Great weather continues until the end of April, when the weather is at its hottest.

➤ Surf season begins in March and continues until October.

➤ Prices jump during Easter.

LOW SEASON
(May–Nov)

➤ Storms and rain more likely, but weather warm and resorts at their cheapest.

➤ Prices rise in August for European summer holidays

➤ Marine life more varied on the western side of atolls.

Bodu Beru Performance

The cultural highlight of almost any trip to the Maldives is seeing an incredible dance and drum performance known as *bodu beru*, which means 'big drum' in Dhivehi.

These traditional all-male performances are a thrilling experience. Dancers begin with a slow, nonchalant swaying and swinging of the arms, and become more animated as the tempo increases, finishing in a rhythmic frenzy.

There are four to six drummers in an ensemble and the sound has strong African influences. Witnessing it can be a fantastic experience, as the dancing becomes more and more frenetic as the night goes on.

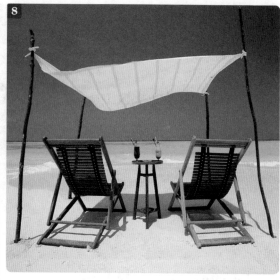

SAKIS PAPADOPOULOS / GETTY IMAGES ©

Food & Drink

Beer In Male it's all nonalcoholic, even if it doesn't look it. For those gasping for the real thing, you'll need to cross the lagoon to the airport island where alcoholic beer is widely available.

Bis hulavuu A pastry made from eggs, sugar and ghee and served cold. You may well be invited to try some if you visit an inhabited island.

Coffee Maldivians love their coffee. You can get very good espresso, latte or cappuccino anywhere in Male, as well as at most resorts and guesthouses.

Kavaabu Small deep-fried dough balls with tuna, mashed potato, pepper and lime – a very popular 'short eat'.

Short eats A selection of finger food such as *fihunu mas* (fish pieces with chilli coating), *gulha* (fried dough balls filled with fish and spices), *keemia* (fried fish rolls in batter) and *kuli boakiba* (spicy fish cakes).

Learn to Dive

7 You simply have to get beneath the water's surface in the Maldives; the corals, tropical fish, sharks, turtles and rays all make up an unforgettably alien world, which is best experienced by diving. The Maldives boasts excellent safety standards, modern equipment, passionate and experienced dive schools and the water is so warm many people don't even bother diving in a wetsuit. Some of the top diving sites can be found around Addu Atoll and Ari Atoll.

Be a (Luxurious) Castaway

8 Nearly every resort offers some variation on this theme: you and your partner or family are given a picnic basket (in the most luxurious resorts it may be a full meal set up for you by staff) and dropped off on an uninhabited, pristine island by dhoni. The crew then jump back on the boat and leave you to your own devices on a white-powder beach surrounded by a turquoise lagoon. Explore the island, dine on great food, sunbathe and swim – this is the modern castaway experience.

Getting Around

Air There are six airports in the country, all of which are linked to the capital by regular flights.

Boat The Nasheed government introduced a public ferry network in 2010, and while it's not without its faults, all the inhabited islands in the Maldives are now connected by ferry to at least somewhere else, even if it is just a couple of times a week.

Seaplane The use of seaplanes means that almost every corner of the country can be reached by air. All seaplane transfers are made during daylight hours, and offer staggering views of the atolls, islands, reefs and lagoons.

Ceremony, Dogon Country

CAPITAL
Bamako

POPULATION
16.4 million

AREA
1.2 million sq km

OFFICIAL LANGUAGE
French

Mali

Like an exquisite sandcastle formed in a harsh desert landscape, Mali is blessed with an extraordinary amount of beauty, wonders, talents and knowledge.

Few countries in Wesy Africa can boast such an array of sights, from fabled Timbuktu to riverside mosques that seem to spring from a child's imagination. Yet for now, its landscapes, monuments, mosques and music bars are off-limits, sealed from tourists by a conflict that is threatening the culture of this remarkable country.

The beating heart of Mali is Bamako, where Ngoni and Kora musicians play to crowds of dancing Malians. Further west, Fula women strap their belongings to donkeys, forming caravans worthy of beauty pageants as they make their way across the *hamada* (dry, dusty scrubland). And in the northeast, the writings of venerable African civilisations remain locked in the beautiful libraries of Timbuktu.

Adding considerable depth to these attractions is Mali's illustrious history, a story of ancient gold-rich empires along the Sahara's southern fringe. And just as rich and deep is Mali's world-famous musical soundtrack, a beguiling playlist of soulful desert blues, ancient griot tunes and frenetic dance rhythms.

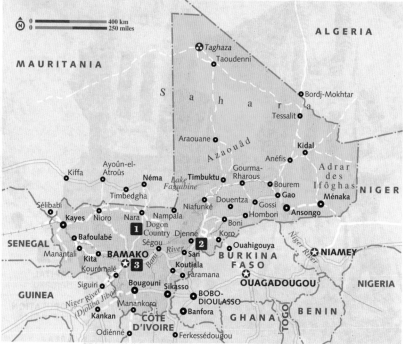

Mali's
Top Experiences

Dogon Country

1 Rose-coloured villages, big blue skies, sacred crocodiles and sandstone cliffs make up Mali's Dogon Country. Houses cling to the massive escarpment of the Falaise de Bandiagara. But more than this, a journey through Dogon Country takes you through a fascinating animist culture with complex traditions and cosmology.

Djenné

2 This Unesco World Heritage–listed old town is one of West Africa's oldest towns. Its incomparable mosque is like a fairy-tale apparition and provides the backdrop to Djenné's huge, lively and colourful Monday market. Stay after the traders and other tourists have gone and you'll share the labyrinthine streets with the locals.

Bamako

3 It's a city that grows on you and we don't just mean the pollution. Bamako today is sprawling and gritty, and can be a charmless place if you let the streets full of people, cars, buzzing flocks of *mobylettes* (mopeds) and clouds of pollution get to you. Yet, expats who live here often end up loving its great restaurants and music from some of Africa's biggest stars.

Food & Drink

Bissap/djablani Juice brewed from hibiscus petals.

Capitaine Nile Perch; a species of freshwater fish.

Castel Malian beer.

When to Go

NOV–JAN
➡ Best time to visit.
➡ Fine weather.
➡ Sufficient water levels on the Niger.

JUL–AUG
➡ Mali is wettest.
➡ Rainy season runs from June to September.

APR–JUN
➡ Temperatures exceed 40°C.
➡ September and October are also extremely hot.

Valletta

CAPITAL
Valletta

POPULATION
411,277

AREA
316 sq km

**OFFICIAL
LANGUAGES**
Maltese, English

Malta

Malta is like nowhere else. Here you'll find great prehistoric temples, fossil-studded cliffs, glittering hidden coves, thrilling diving opportunities and a history of remarkable intensity.

Despite being made up of three tiny islands on the southern edge of Europe, Malta groans under the weight of its rich history and fascinating cultural influences. As a melting pot of Mediterranean culture, Malta merits far deeper exploration than is often given to it by the package crowds whose first priority is hitting the beach.

From ancient stone temples and historic Arabic connections (listen carefully to the local language) to Sicilian-inspired cuisine and an oddly 1950s British atmosphere, Malta will almost certainly surprise you. Valletta and the Three Cities are famed for their grand churches, elegant palaces and honey-coloured limestone fortifications, while nearby Sliema and St Julian are packed with restaurants and bars. And don't forget little Gozo to the northwest – a pretty, rural island where the pace of life is that much slower. It's the perfect chill-out spot with the dramatic Dwejra coastline.

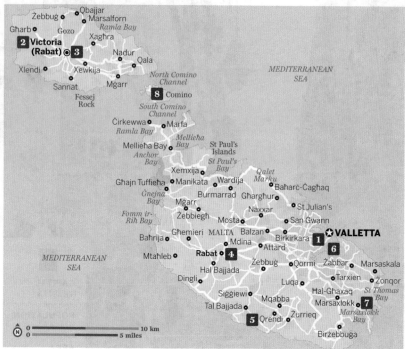

Malta's
Top Experiences

Valletta

1 Malta's capital is a remarkable city. It's the size of a small town – easy to explore on foot, and laid out in a harmonious grid formation. The tall, gracious houses are distinctive for their wood-and-glass balconies, which give them a top-heavy look. The hills mean some of the roads are so steep they have to be stepped, and the roller-coaster streetscape allows mesmerising views along the straight, narrow lanes and out to sea.

Dwejra

2 The coastline of Dwejra, in Gozo, features some astoundingly beautiful rock formations that have been sculpted by the wind and sea. From here you can take a boat trip through the Azure Window, an arch of rock that forms a doorway to the open sea. There's also the Inland Sea, which is a wonderful place to swim and snorkel when the sea is calm. Close to the coast, the great chunk of Fungus Rock rears from the piercing blue Mediterranean.

Victoria

3 The Il-Kastell of Victoria is an evocative place to wander – this tiny medina (walled city) almost seems to grow out of its rocky outcrop. It was built after a particularly devastating raid on the island, when almost every Gozitan was carried off to slavery; there was a time when the entire population of around 3000 used to sleep here at night. Sweeping sea views can be enjoyed from its battlements.

Mdina & Rabat

4 Malta's tiny historic capital is a walled city perched on a hilltop, filled with honey-coloured buildings. A treasure trove of museums, artefacts and churches, it's also appealingly mysterious at night, when everything's closed and the city is dimly lit and empty. Wander around after most people have left and you'll understand why it's known as the 'Silent City'. Mdina adjoins Rabat, itself a lovely town with some fascinating sights, many of them underground.

Azure Window, Gozo

Ħaġar Qim & Mnajdra Temples

5 These mysterious megalithic temples were built between 3600 BC and 3000 BC and are the oldest freestanding stone structures in the world, predating the pyramids of Egypt by more than 500 years. Their purpose is the subject of much debate, but their location is undoubtedly evocative: high up on the edge of coastal cliffs that are carpeted by wild flowers in spring, and with magnificent views out to sea and over to the distant islet of Filfla.

Vittoriosa's Backstreets

6 Vittoriosa – known locally as Birgu, its name before the Great Siege of 1565 – is the most fascinating of the Three Cities. This petite town, perched on its small lip of land, has stunning views all around it and perfectly preserved ancient streets within. It was the original home of the Knights of St John, but it's no museum – this is a living, breathing city with a strong sense of community. You're in luck if you've timed your visit to see Birgu by Candlelight in October.

if Malta were 100 people

95 would live in urban areas
5 would live in rural areas

belief systems
(% of population)

98
Christian

2
other

population per sq km

MALTA   GOZO   ITALY

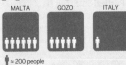

♦ ≈ 200 people

When to Go

HIGH SEASON
(Jun–Aug)

➡ Many resort hotels are booked solid and beaches are busy.

➡ Daytime temperatures in July and August can reach more than 35°C.

➡ This is also the main season for festas (feast days).

SHOULDER
(Apr–Jun, Sep–Oct)

➡ Warm and sunny, with the occasional rainfall or hot and humid wind.

➡ The sea is warmer in autumn than in spring.

➡ Holy Week is a wonderful time to be in Malta.

LOW SEASON
(Nov–Feb)

➡ Temperatures in November and December average from 12°C to 18°C.

➡ January and February are the coldest months.

➡ Christmas to New Year is a mini-high season.

Religion

Around 95% of Maltese are Catholic, and in some ways Roman Catholicism has an even stronger hold in Malta than in Italy. Church ceremonies are sombre affairs, full of tradition and reverence. Still, christenings, first communions, weddings and funerals continue to be celebrated in church, and the most important event in the calendar is the annual parish *festa* (feast day).

Each village has a *festa* honouring its patron saint. In the days leading up to the *festa*, families flock to the churches to give thanks. The streets are illuminated and the festivities culminate in a huge procession, complete with fireworks, marching brass bands and a lifesized statue of the patron saint.

Festa season runs from May to September.

Food & Drink

Braġioli These 'beef olives' are a thin slice of beef wrapped around a stuffing of breadcrumbs, chopped bacon, hard-boiled egg and parsley, then braised in a red wine sauce.

Fenek The favourite Maltese dish is rabbit – whether fried in olive oil, roasted, stewed, served with spaghetti or baked in a pie.

Ftira Bread baked in a flat disc and traditionally stuffed with a mixture of tomatoes, olives, capers and anchovies.

Ġbejniet Small, hard, white cheese traditionally made from unpasteurised sheep's or goat's milk.

Kinnie The brand name of a local soft drink, flavoured with bitter oranges and aromatic herbs.

Pastizzi Small parcels of flaky pastry filled with ricotta cheese or mushy peas. They're available in most bars or from a *pastizzerija* (usually a hole-in-the-wall takeaway or kiosk).

ALEX HARE / GETTY IMAGES ©

Marsaxlokk waterfront

Sunday Lunch in Marsaxlokk

7 It gets packed every Sunday at the small coastal town of Marsaxlokk. Locals and tourists throng to visit the buzzing fish market, where you can buy all manner of sea bounty, from colourful rock fish to baby sharks. The harbour bobs with colourful fishing boats painted with the eye of Osiris – a tradition that's thought to hark back to the Phoenician era. The seafront, lined with fish restaurants, is a great place for a long lazy lunch – a favourite activity of locals as well as visitors.

Comino

8 This small, rocky island has a beautiful coastline and an eclectic history, having served as a hermit's hideaway, a cholera isolation zone and a prison camp. Today it attracts huge numbers of visitors to its Blue Lagoon. This serene sea pool is so blue that it looks like an over-saturated image – if you manage to see it without the crowds, it's breathtaking. Comino is an equally beautiful place to walk, with easy paths around the island leading up to the 17th-century watchtower and around the coast to the island's only hotel.

Getting Around

Boat Regular water taxis run the short distance between Valletta and Sliema, and Valletta and the Three Cities. Larger car ferries shuttle between northern Malta and Gozo (see www.gozochannel.com).

Bus The popular bus network covers the country; routes generally operate from 5.30am to 11pm. See www.publictransport.com.mt for route and timetable information.

Car Considering the low rental rates it may make economic sense to hire a car, but beware that the Maltese drive in a way that can be politely described as 'after the Italian style'.

Bikini Atoll

Marshall Islands

This expanse of slender, flat coral atolls is so surrounded by tropical sea that anywhere at any time you can see, hear, smell and feel salt air and water.

A thousand or so coral islands make up the Republic of the Marshall Islands (RMI). Living on these narrow strips of land between ocean and lagoon, the Marshallese are expert fishers and navigators, having long been reliant on the sea.

Local faces reflect the islands' history. In the late 1700s, after 2000 years of isolation, these Micronesian islands were variously visited, settled, colonised or occupied by British, Russians, Germans, Japanese and Americans (at first by missionaries, later by defence forces). Today the more developed atolls have a sense of all these influences, with well-stocked stores carrying international groceries, restaurants serving the food of several nations, and basketball courts on many street corners. On the quieter backstreets the Marshallese continue to live in family compounds, surrounded by flowers.

The RMI's charm lies in its outer islands, which still retain the pristine feel of a Pacific paradise.

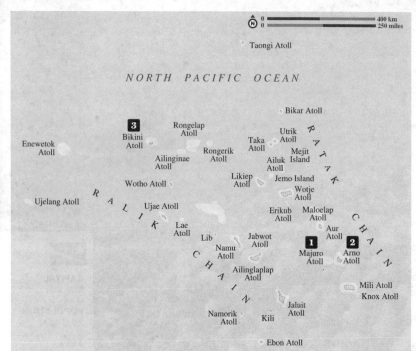

NORTH PACIFIC OCEAN

Marshall Islands'
Top Experiences

Laura

1 If the heady pace of Marshall Island life is getting too much, take a very pleasant drive along the palm-lined road to Laura. Found at the far western end of Majuro Atoll, Laura is famed for its quiet beaches. Pick up a picnic and spend the day lolling on the gorgeous white-sand beach and snorkelling on the shallow reef.

Arno Atoll

2 The Longar area in Arno is famed for its 'love school' where young women were once taught how to perfect their sexual techniques. The waters off Longar Point are known for superb deep-sea fishing, and yellowfin tuna, marlin, mahi-mahi and sailfish abound.

Bikini Atoll

3 Thanks to its ominous nuclear history, Bikini – the site of the first peacetime explosion of the atomic bomb – is one of Micronesia's premier dive spots. A highlight is the USS *Saratoga*, the world's only diveable aircraft carrier, which still holds racks of bombs. Bikini is a great spot for diving with sharks – spotting a silvertip on the wrecks is not uncommon.

Food & Drink

Coconut Drinking ice-cold coconut juice is a great way to beat the heat.

Coconut crab The largest land-living arthropod in the world is also considered a delicacy.

Pandanus fruit Snack on boiled, sweet pandanus fruit – just watch out for the hairy insides!

When to Go

JUL

➡ Fishermen's Day, held on the first Friday of the month, attracts competitive fishers.

SEP–NOV

➡ On Majuro the daily temperature is around 27°C; rains can be a blessing.

DEC–AUG

➡ The dry season in the south.

Grand-Rivière

Martinique

Southern Martinique has great beaches, fishing villages and lots of activities to keep you busy, while the north, with its mountains and botanical gardens, is perfect for hikers and nature lovers.

A slice of Gallic culture in the Caribbean, Martinique is an overseas *département* of France. While it's noticeably more tropical than the mainland, there's no denying the very French rhythm of life here. This is great for Francophiles, although it can also give rise to Martinique's – at times – distinctly un-Caribbean air.

Volcanic in origin, the island is a mountainous stunner crowned by the still-smoldering Mont Pelée, which wiped out Martinique's former capital of St-Pierre in

1902. Long luscious beaches, great diving and giant mountains covered in tropical forests are the main attractions here.

Far more developed than much of the Caribbean, Martinique suffers from un-controlled urban sprawl in some places, particularly in and around the busy capital, Fort-de-France. Those wanting to avoid the modern world's encroachment should head to the beautiful beaches of the south or to the mountains of the island's remote north.

CAPITAL
Fort-de-France

POPULATION
405,000

AREA
1100 sq km

OFFICIAL LANGUAGE
French

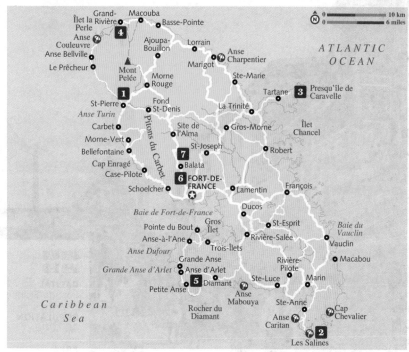

Martinique's
Top Experiences

St-Pierre

1 It's hard to believe that St-Pierre was once the most cosmopolitan city in the Caribbean. The one-time capital of Martinique was wiped out in just 10 minutes in 1902 by the towering and still-active Mont Pelée, 7km away. Though a shadow of its former self, St-Pierre is an attractive and interesting place to wander. There are many blackened ruins throughout the city, some of which are little more than foundations, while others remain partially intact. Many of the surviving stone walls have been incorporated into the town's reconstruction. Even 'newer' buildings have a period character, with shuttered doors and wrought-iron balconies.

Les Salines

2 At the undeveloped southern tip of the island, Les Salines is probably Martinique's finest beach. The gorgeous long stretch of golden sand attracts scantily clad French tourists and local families alike on weekends and holidays. While it's big enough to accommodate everyone without feeling crowded, it might be necessary to pick a direction and keep walking along the beach until the crowds thin. Les Salines gets its name from Étang des Salines, the large salt pond that backs it. There are showers and food vans near the center of the beach, and about 500m further south you'll find snack shops.

Presqu'île de Caravelle

3 This charming peninsula has some gorgeous stretches of beach and a wild and untamed feel in parts. A gently twisting road with spectacular views runs through sugarcane fields to the peninsula's main village, Tartane, and then on to Baie du Galion. On the north side of the peninsula are a couple of protected beaches: the long, sandy Plage de Tartane fronts the village, and the gently shelving, palm-fringed beach of Anse l'Étang is one of the island's nicest and is a good, uncrowded place to surf. Both beaches have plenty of restaurants; Plage de Tartane also has a fish market.

Hiking the northern coast

4 Grand-Rivière is an unspoiled fishing village scenically tucked beneath coastal cliffs at the northern tip of Martinique. While there's no road around the tip of the island, there is a 20km hiking trail leading to Anse Couleuvre on the northwest coast. The trailhead begins on the road opposite the quaint two-story *mairie* (town hall), just up from the beach. It's a moderately difficult walk, so you might want to join one of the guided hikes.

Anse d'Arlet

5 Anse d'Arlet is perhaps the most charming fishing village in southern Martinique; it retains an undiscovered feel, as there's just one small guesthouse here and (for the moment) very little else. There's a handsome coastal road crowned by an 18th-century Roman Catholic church whose doors open almost directly onto the beautiful beach, and the entire scene is framed with steep, verdant hills. Even if you're not staying here, make a trip to enjoy the sleepy village atmosphere and stellar beach.

Route de la Trace

6 The Route de la Trace (N3) winds up into the mountains north from Fort-de-France. It's a beautiful

if Martinique were 100 people

90 would be African and mixed
5 would be white
5 would be East Indian, Lebanese or Chinese

belief systems
(% of population)

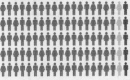

85	11	•
Roman Catholic	Protestant	Hindu

•	●
1	2
Muslim	other

population per sq km

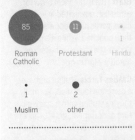

MARTINIQUE   BARBADOS   FRANCE

🚶 ≈ 115 people

When to Go

DEC–MAY

➡ The high season coincides with the dry months. The island is often crowded with French holidaymakers and hotel costs are at a premium.

JUN–NOV

➡ The rainy season, with heavy showers most days. September is the wettest month; September and August are prone to hurricanes.

DEC

➡ Music festivals are held in Fort-de-France (guitar festival in even-numbered years, jazz in odd-numbered years).

Mont Pelée Eruption

At the end of the 19th century, St-Pierre – then the capital of Martinique – was a flourishing port city. It was so cosmopolitan that it was dubbed the 'Little Paris of the West Indies.' Mont Pelée, the island's highest mountain at 1397m, was just a scenic backdrop to the city.

In the spring of 1902, sulfurous steam vents on Mont Pelée began emitting gases, and a crater lake started to fill with boiling water. Authorities dismissed it all as the normal cycle of the volcano, which had experienced harmless periods of activity in the past.

On May 8, 1902, in the most devastating natural disaster in Caribbean history, Mont Pelée exploded into a glowing burst of superheated gas and burning ash. St-Pierre was laid to waste within minutes; of its 30,000 inhabitants, there were just three surivivors.

Food & Drink

Acras A universally popular hors d'oeuvre in Martinique, *acras* are fish, seafood or vegetables tempura. *Acras de morue* (cod) and *crevettes* (shrimp) are the most common and are both delicious.

Blaff This is the local term for white fish marinated in lime juice, garlic and peppers and then poached. While it's popular across the Caribbean, its true home is Martinique.

Crabes farcis Stuffed crabs are a common local dish. Normally they're stuffed with a spicy mixture of crabmeat, garlic, shallots and parsley, and cooked in their shells.

Ti-punch Short for petit punch; this ubiquitous and strong cocktail is the normal *apéro* (aperitif) in Martinique. It's a mix of rum, lime and cane syrup – but mainly rum.

Banana flower, Jardin de Balata

drive through a lush rainforest of tall tree ferns, anthurium-covered hillsides and thick clumps of roadside bamboo. The road passes along the eastern flanks of the volcanic mountain peaks of the Pitons du Carbet. Several well-marked hiking trails lead from the Route de la Trace into the rainforest and up to the peaks. The road follows a route cut by the Jesuits in the 17th century: the Trace de Jésuites.

Jardin de Balata

7 The excellent Jardin de Balata, a mature botanical garden in a rainforest setting, is one of Martinique's best attractions and will please anyone with even a passing interest in botany. The hour-long walk around the garden is clearly marked, and a series of tree walks will keep kids interested. There are some fantastic views from here down to the coast. After the garden, the road winds up into the mountains and reaches an elevation of 600m before dropping down to Site de l'Alma, where a river runs through a lush gorge. There are picnic tables and a couple of short trails into the rainforest.

Getting Around

Boat A regular *vedette* (ferry) between Martinique's main resort areas and Fort-de-France provides a nice alternative to dealing with heavy bus and car traffic; it also allows you to avoid the hassles of city parking and is quicker to boot.

Bus Although there are some larger public buses, most buses are minivans marked 'TC' (for *taxis collectifs*) on top. Destinations are marked on the vans. Traveling by bus is best for shorter distances – and for visitors with a lot of extra time in their itinerary.

Car Renting a car is the most reliable form of transportation in Martinique. Car rental is a breeze, rates are low and the road network is excellent.

Hiking the dunes, Adrar region

CAPITAL
Nouakchott

POPULATION
3.4 million

AREA
1 million sq km

OFFICIAL LANGUAGE
Arabic

Mauritania

A seemingly endless realm of Saharan sands, lapped by the Atlantic, Mauritania is a bridge between North Africa and sub-Saharan regions.

If West Africa is a playground for overlanders, then Mauritania often seems to be little more than a transit between the better-known attractions of Marrakesh, Dakar or Bamako. As the safest trans-Saharan route for overlanders, Mauritania has long been regarded as a waystation en route from Europe to West Africa. That's a shame because Mauritania has some tremendous secrets to reveal.

Just as impressive as the cultural diversity is some of the continent's grandest scenery. The Adrar region offers epic sand dunes, eye-popping plateaus and Africa's biggest monolith. The Tagânt has similar charms, and both hide ancient caravan towns – Chinguetti, Ouadâne and Oualâta. The World Heritage feast continues along the coast at Parc National du Banc d'Arguin, which attracts millions of migratory birds and is a renowned birdwatching site.

If you just breeze through, you'll miss out on a truly incredible country. No one in Mauritania is in a rush, and you shouldn't be either.

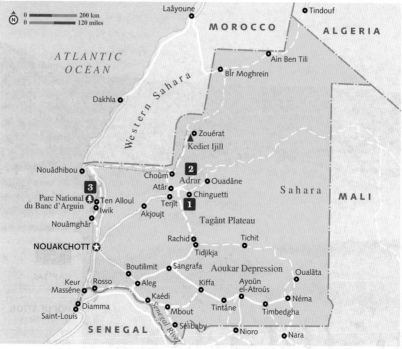

Mauritania's
Top Experiences

Chinguetti

1 Chinguetti is shrouded with a historic aura. It was once famous for its Islamic scholars, and was the ancient capital of the Moors; some of the buildings date from the 13th century. The highlight of any visit is a wander through the labyrinthine lanes of Le Ksar (Old Town).

Adrar

2 Experience the magic of the Sahara and sleep beneath the star-studded skies at the saffron dunes in the Adrar, the undoubted jewel in Mauritania's crown. It's epic Saharan country, and shows the great desert in all its variety: the ancient Saharan towns, mighty sand dunes that look sculpted by an artist, vast rocky plateaus and mellow oases fringed with date palms.

Parc National du
Banc d'Arguin

3 This World Heritage–listed park is an important breeding ground for birds migrating between Europe and southern Africa, and is one of the best bird-watching sites on the entire continent. It extends 200km north from Cape Timiris and 235km south of Nouâdhibou. The ideal way to approach the birds is by traditional fishing boat, best organised from the village of Iwik.

Food & Drink

Méchoui Traditional nomads' feast where an entire lamb is roasted over a fire and stuffed with cooked rice.

Tea Invariably strong, sweet and endlessly decanted. It's polite to accept the first three glasses offered.

Zrig Unsweetened curdled goat or camel milk.

When to Go

NOV–MAR

➡ The most pleasant months to visit the desert, although nights can be cold.

JUN–AUG

➡ The *rifi* (hot winds) send temperatures soaring to 45°C and above.

JUL–SEP

➡ The short rainy season in Nouakchott can be prone to flooding after downpours.

Le Morne Brabant

Mauritius

CAPITAL
Port Louis

POPULATION
1.3 million

AREA
2040 sq km

**OFFICIAL
LANGUAGES**
French, English

*Prediction for your arrival: it's a sunny, 29°C in the air and
water. Soon you're lazing on a white-sand beach with a tropical
fruit juice in hand – the best cure for winter blues.*

Mark Twain once wrote that 'Mauritius was
made first and then heaven, heaven being
copied after Mauritius'. For the most part,
it's true: Mauritius is rightly famed for its
sapphire waters, powder-white beaches and
luxury resorts. But there's so much more to
Mauritius than the beach when it comes to
attractions. There's bird-watching and hiking in the forested and mountainous interior
or world-class diving and snorkelling. Or
there are boat trips to near-perfect islets and
excursions to fabulous botanical gardens and
colonial plantation houses. Either way, the
possibilities can seem endless. And the real
Mauritius – a hot curry of different cultures,
traffic and quiet fishing villages – is never
far away.

Ultimately, Mauritius is the kind of place
that rewards even the smallest attempts at
exploration. So, if your biggest discovery is
the beach butler service at your hotel, then
you'll need to plan a second visit!

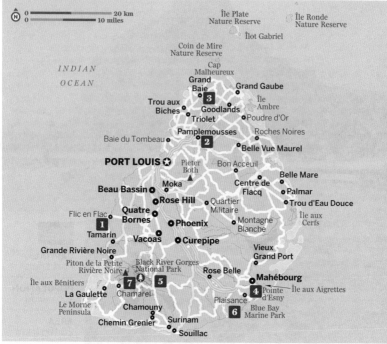

INDIAN
OCEAN

Île Plate
Nature Reserve
Île Ronde
Nature Reserve
Îlot Gabriel

Coin de Mire
Nature Reserve

Cap
Malheureux
Grand
Baie **3**
Grand Gaube
Trou aux
Biches
Goodlands
Île
Ambre
Triolet
Poudre d'Or
Baie du Tombeau
Pamplemousses **2**
Roches Noires
Belle Vue Maurel

PORT LOUIS
Pieter
Both
Bon Acceuil
Belle Mare
Moka
Beau Bassin
Centre de
Flacq
Palmar
Rose Hill
Quartier
Militaire
Trou d'Eau Douce
Flic en Flac **1**
Quatre
Bornes
Phoenix
Montagne
Blanche
Île aux
Cerfs
Tamarin
Vacoas
Curepipe
Grande Rivière Noire
Vieux
Grand Port
Piton de la Petite
Rivière Noire
Black River Gorges
National Park
Rose Belle
Mahébourg
Île aux Béniters
7 **5**
Île aux Aigrettes
La Gaulette
Chamarel
4 Pointe
d'Esny
Le Morne
Peninsula
Chamouny
Plaisance
6
Blue Bay
Marine Park
Chemin Grenier
Surinam
Souillac

Mauritius'
Top Experiences

Diving & Dolphins

1 Some of the Indian
Ocean's best dives are
found off the west coast
of Mauritius. The archi-
tecture of the underwater
rock formations and the
substantial schools of fish
make the waters off Flic en
Flac in particular a world-
class dive destination. The
best sites are the walls and
drop-offs on the edge of
the turquoise lagoon and
La Cathédrale, near Flic en
Flac, is simply marvellous.
To the south, off Tamarin,
swim with dolphins out in
the open water.

Gardens &
Great Houses

2 Mauritius' interior
is, for the most part,
steep and rugged, but it
does shelter some excep-
tional sites. First on many
travellers' lists are the vast
botanical gardens at Pam-
plemousses; the giant lily
pads have to be seen to be
believed. Not far away are
two of the finest remnants
of colonial plantation architecture in existence – the
Chateau Labourdonnais
just north of the gardens,
and Eureka, in Moka.

Seafood by
the Beach

3 The day's catch fresh
to your table, with your
toes buried in the sand. It's
something we all dream
about but it's a very real
possibility on just about any
beach or resort in Mauritius.

Lobster, octopus, grilled
fish, calamari – they're all
staples of the Indian Ocean
table. If you can't decide, all
are regular inhabitants of
your standard seafood platter; try one in Grand Baie.
Best of all, the rich stew of
sauces and cultural influences adds flavour, from
Indian curries to red Creole
sauces.

Chambres &
Tables d'Hôtes

4 Whether along the
west coast or in Pointe
d'Esny or the quiet high-
lands of Rodrigues, staying
in *chambre d'hôte* (family-
run guesthouses) is a wonderful way to learn about
local life. Rooms are often
simple, but the warmth

Hindu pilgrimage idols, Maha Shivaratree festival

and personal nature of the welcome you'll receive and the nightly table d'hôte (meal served at a *chambre d'hôte*) where the guests and hosts gather together for a traditional meal, make for the kind of experience that you'll remember long after the luxury resorts have faded in your memory.

Hindu & Creole Festivals

5 Hindu festivals are a wonderful way to liven up your visit to Mauritius. The biggest festival of all, in February or March,

is the 500,000-strong Hindu pilgrimage to the sacred lake of Grand Bassin. March is also the month of colourful Holi festivities, October means Divali, and Teemeedee in December or January is all about fire-walking wherever Hindus are found. For celebrations of Creole culture, October is particularly exuberant in Rodrigues,

Southeastern Mauritius

6 Choosing your favourite beach on Mauritius is like trying to pick a flavour

if Mauritius were 100 people

68 would be Indo-Mauritian
27 would be Creole
3 would be Sino-Mauritian
2 would be Franco-Mauritian

belief systems
(% of population)

48 Hindu
24 Roman Catholic
17 Muslim
9 Other Christian
2 Other

population per sq km

MAURITIUS   TANZANIA   uk

👤 ≈ 50 people

When to Go

JAN–FEB

➡ Peak cyclone months, with cyclones possible until April.

➡ Some resorts offer discounted packages.

➡ Cheaper airfares.

NOV–APR

➡ High season with a Christmas–New Year peak, although other factors (French school holidays) can also cause spikes.

➡ Hindu festivals and cultural events in December/January.

MAY–NOV

➡ Although Mauritius enjoys a typically tropical climate with year-round heat, the cooler winter, such as it is, runs from May to November.

Dead as a Dodo

Illustrations from the logbooks of the first ships to reach Mauritius show hundreds of plump flightless birds running down to the beach to investigate the newcomers. Lacking natural predators, these giant relatives of the pigeon were easy prey for hungry sailors, who named the bird dodo, meaning 'stupid'. It took just 30 years for sailors and their pets and pests to drive the dodo to extinction; the last confirmed sighting was in the 1660s.

In 1865 local schoolteacher George Clark discovered a dodo skeleton in a marshy area on the site of what is now the international airport. The skeleton was reassembled by scientists in Edinburgh, and has formed the basis of all subsequent dodo reconstructions, one of which is on display in the Natural History Museum in Port Louis.

NARVIKK / GETTY IMAGES ©

Food & Drink

Meat Steaks can be terrific here, especially those from South Africa. Creole sausages are distinctive and are often cooked in a red Creole sauce.

Seafood The mainstay of all the different cuisines on the island. Prawns (crevettes) and octopus (ourite) are highlights; octopus appears in salads, cooked in saffron, or in a curry. The fish of the day is nearly always a good order.

Street food Dhal puri (lentil dhal served in a chapati pancake) and boulettes (tiny steamed Chinese dumplings) are fantastic.

Tables d'hôte The eating equivalent of a family-run guesthouse, where diners often eat at a communal table and can enjoy a range of traditional dishes spread over a number of courses. If you don't eat at a table d'hôte in Mauritius, you've missed an essential part of its gastronomic culture.

of ice cream – they're all so good! The eastern and southeastern shores are quieter than those elsewhere, particularly the beaches at Pointe d'Esny and Belle Mare, and they're close to the forests of Vallée de Ferney and the offshore Île aux Aigrettes. The latter, with its endangered bird species, giant tortoises and low-slung ebony forests, is like stepping ashore on Mauritius before human beings came and tamed the landscape.

Black River Gorges & Chamarel

7 Some of the most dramatic scenery on Mauritius is found in the southwest. The thick forests of Black River Gorges National Park shelter fantastic and endangered birdlife that has been saved from the fate of the dodo, quite apart from the exceptional views from along the myriad hiking trails. After a morning's hiking, lunch just has to be in Chamarel, home to a series of superb restaurants and a well-regarded rum distillery nestled in the hills.

Getting Around

Air Pricey but efficient. Most convenient services are between Mauritius and Rodrigues.

Boat Fast, reliable but quite expensive.

Bus Very cheap. Getting around by public transport is possible but sometimes complicated and rather slow.

Car Outside cities, renting a car gives flexibility and convenience. Cars can be hired in major towns and at the airports. Drive on the left.

Taxi In some cases hiring a taxi is a great way to explore an area, especially if you can share costs with other travellers.

El Castillo, Chichén Itzá

CAPITAL
Mexico City

POPULATION
118.8 million

AREA
1.9 million sq km

OFFICIAL LANGUAGE
Spanish

Mexico

Jungles, deserts; teeming cities, one-street pueblos; fiesta fireworks, Frida's angst: Mexico conjures up so many contradictory images, but no preconceptions will ever live up to the reality.

From the southern jungles to the smoking, snowcapped volcanoes and the cactus-dotted northern deserts, all surrounded by 10,000km of coast strung with sandy beaches and wildlife-rich lagoons, Mexico is an endless adventure for the senses. Take it easy by lying on a beach, dining alfresco or strolling the streets of some pretty town, or get out and snorkel warm Caribbean reefs, hike mountain cloud forests or take a boat in search of dolphins or whales.

At the heart of your Mexican experience will be the Mexican people. A superdiverse crew, they're justly renowned for their love of color and frequent fiestas. You will rarely find Mexicans less than courteous; they're often positively charming. They are fiercely proud of Mexico, their one-of-a-kind homeland with all its variety, tight-knit family networks, beautiful-ugly cities, deep-rooted traditions, unique agave-based liquors and sensationally tasty, chili-laden food. It doesn't take long to understand why.

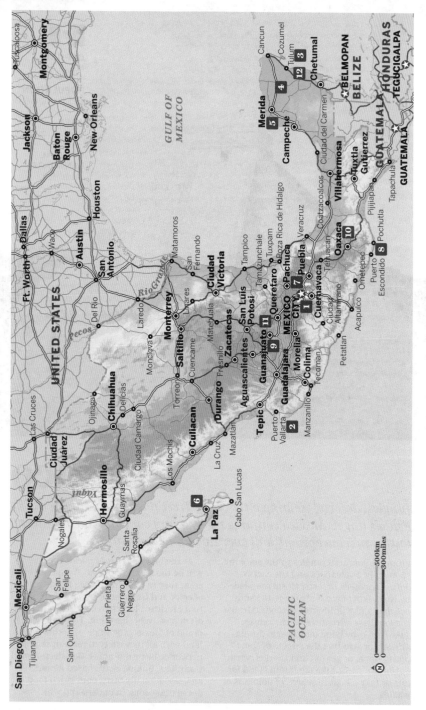

Mexico's
Top Experiences

Mexico City

1 To fully appreciate the quintessential Mexico City experience, you've got to embrace its time-honored traditions. You may find yourself on a gondola gliding through the ancient canals of Xochimilco, or knocking back tequilas in old cantinas once frequented by Mexican revolutionaries. Perhaps it's the simple pleasure of munching on street eats (insects, anyone?) or gazing upon the Aztec sun stone and other superb relics from Mexico's pre-Hispanic past at the world-class Museo Nacional de Antropología.

Puerto Vallarta

2 Tucked between jungle-clad mountains and North America's second-largest bay, Mexico's most appealing Pacific resort combines its dazzling setting with a fun-loving atmosphere that welcomes everyone from foodies and shopping devotees to outdoors enthusiasts and the international gay and lesbian community. And if you travel an hour out of town you can be basking on a secluded beach, horseback riding in the Sierra Madre, whale-watching, diving or reeling in a giant fish worthy of a tall tale at happy hour.

Palacio de Bellas Artes, Mexico City

1

STOCKCAM / GETTY IMAGES ©

Tulum

3 Take a world-famous Maya ruin, plonk it down beside the achingly white sands and turquoise-blue waters of the Caribbean and you've got the rightly popular Tulum. There are accommodations here for all budgets, from beachside shacks to top-end resorts, plus some fantastic restaurants and so many attractions in the surrounding area that it's no wonder many people come for a few days and find themselves still here, months later.

Chichén Itzá

4 Sure, it's on every tour-bus itinerary and you're never going to have the place to yourself, but there's a reason why this Maya site was declared one of the new Seven Wonders of the World – it is simply spectacular. From the imposing, monolithic El Castillo pyramid (where the shadow of the plumed serpent god Kukulcán creeps down the staircase during the spring and autumn equinoxes) to the Sacred Cenote and curiously designed El Caracol, you don't have to be an archaeologist to have an amazing time here.

if Mexico were 100 people

30 would have predominantly indigenous ancestry
9 would have predominantly European ancestry
61 would have mixed ancestry

belief systems

(% of population)

85 — Roman Catholic

8 — Pentecostal, Jehovah's Witnesses & other Evangelical

5 — none

2 — other

population per sq km

MEXICO   GUATEMALA   USA

♦ ≈ 15 people

Marvelous Mérida

5 The cultural capital of the Yucatán Peninsula, this large but manageable city has a beautifully maintained colonial heart, a wealth of museums and galleries and some of the best food in the region. Just out of town are wildlife reserves, graceful *haciendas* (estates) and jungle-shrouded cenotes to swim in. A little further afield, the little-visited Maya sites along the Ruta Puuc allow you to step back in time without being jostled by tour groups.

Isla Espíritu Santo

6 As if snorkeling with gentle whale sharks isn't enough, this unique Sea of Cortez island offers unparalleled diving, camping under a canopy of stunning stars, and kayaking along myriad azure bays with marvelous pastel cliffs. There's even a sea-lion colony. Espíritu Santo is spectacular in every way, thanks mainly to its unique geography. Pink sandstone here has been eroded by wind and waves into fingerlike protrusions, each harboring a beautiful cove.

The Pyramids of Teotihuacán

7 Once among Mesoamerica's greatest cities, Teotihuacán, just an hour out of Mexico City, is a popular day trip from the capital. The awesomely massive Pirámide del Sol (Pyramid of the Sun) and Pirámide de la Luna (Pyramid of the Moon) dominate the remains of the metropolis. Even centuries after its collapse in the 8th century AD, Teotihuacán remained a pilgrimage site for Aztec royalty.

Day of the Dead

Perhaps no other festival reveals more about Mexican spirituality than Día de Muertos (Day of the Dead), the happy-sad remembrance of departed loved ones at the beginning of November.

Today Muertos is a national phenomenon, with people everywhere cleaning graves and decorating them with flowers, holding graveyard vigils and building elaborate altars to welcome back their loved ones. For the *mestizo* (mixed-ancestry) majority, it's more of a popular folk festival and family occasion.

Sugar skulls, chocolate coffins and toy skeletons are sold in markets everywhere, both as Muertos gifts for children and graveyard decorations; this tradition derives in great measure from the work of artist José Guadalupe Posada (1852–1913), renowned for his satirical figures of a skeletal Death cheerfully engaging in everyday life, working, dancing, courting, drinking and riding horses into battle.

Food & Drink

Elotes Freshly steamed or grilled corn on the cob, usually coated in mayonnaise and often sprinkled with chili powder.

Enchiladas Lightly fried tortillas filled with chicken, cheese or eggs, and covered in a chili sauce.

Quesadillas A tortilla folded in half with a filling of cheese and/or other ingredients.

Tacos The quintessential culinary fare in Mexico can be made of any cooked meat, fish or vegetable wrapped in a tortilla, with a dash of salsa, onion and cilantro.

Tamales Made with masa mixed with lard, stuffed with stewed meat, fish or vegetables, and steamed in corn husks or banana leaf.

Tequila The Champagne of Mexico.

Oaxaca Coast

8 After a few days on this 550km sequence of sandy Pacific beaches, you'll be so relaxed you may not be able to leave. Head for the surf mecca and fishing port of Puerto Escondido, the low-key resort of Bahías de Huatulco, or the ultra-laid-back hangouts of Zipolite, San Agustinillo or Mazunte. Soak up the sun, eat good food, imbibe in easygoing beach bars, and when the mood takes you, have a surf or snorkel, or board a boat to spot turtles, dolphins, whales, crocs or birdlife.

Guanajuato

9 The glorious World Heritage–listed city of Guanajuato packs a huge amount into its narrow valley. This former mining town (now a colorful university city) is a feast of plazas, fun museums, opulent colonial mansions and pastel-hued houses. Snake your way along pedestrian alleyways, people-watch in the squares, mingle with marvelous mariachi groups, or party heartily at *estudiantinas* (traditional street parties).

When to Go

HIGH SEASON
(Dec–Apr)

➡ The driest months bring winter escapees from colder countries.

➡ Christmas and Easter are holidays, with transportation and coastal accommodations very busy.

SHOULDER
(Jul & Aug)

➡ Vacation time for many Mexicans and foreigners. Hot almost everywhere, and very wet on the Pacific coast.

LOW SEASON
(May, Jun, Sep–Nov)

➡ May & June see peak temperatures in many areas.

➡ September is the heart of the hurricane season, which brings heavy rains on the Gulf and Pacific coasts.

The underground tunnels – the town's major transport routes – make for a particularly quirky way to get around.

Oaxaca City

10 This highly individual southern city basks in bright upland light and captivates the visitor with gorgeous handicrafts, frequent fiestas and handsome colonial architecture. A uniquely savory cuisine is served at restaurants and market stalls. Oaxaca's Day of the Dead celebrations are among the most vibrant in Mexico, when homes, cemeteries and some public buildings are decorated with fantastically crafted *altares de muertos* (altars of the dead).

Best on Film

Amores Perros (Love's a Bitch; 2000) Gritty groundbreaker that set director Alejandro González Iñárritu and actor Gael García Bernal on the path to stardom.

Heli (2013) Amat Escalante won the Cannes best-director garland for this tale of a young couple caught up in the drugs war.

Y Tu Mamá También (And Your Mother Too; 2001) Classic 'growing up' road movie about two privileged Mexico City teenagers.

Best in Print

El Narco Author Ioan Grillo spent more than a decade covering the drugs war in some of the most dangerous territories.

God's Middle Finger Richard Grant investigates the narco-riddled Sierra Madre Occidental (called Bandit Roads in the UK).

Pedro Páramo The ultimate Mexican novel, by Juan Rulfo.

Under the Volcano British consul drinks himself to death in Malcolm Lowry's 1938 classic.

Getting Around

Air Over 60 cities are served by domestic flights, which are well worth considering for longer intercity trips. Fares vary widely depending on the airline and how far in advance you pay.

Bus Mexico's efficient, comfortable and reasonably priced intercity bus network is generally the best option for moving around the country: on average you pay about M$1 per kilometer on 1st-class buses, covering around 75km per hour. Services are frequent on main routes.

Car & Motorcycle A convenient option giving maximum independence: roads are serviceable, with speeds generally slower than north of the border or in Europe. Rental rates are reasonable and include basic insurance. Drive on the right.

San Miguel de Allende

11 After a hard morning of hitting the shops, churches and galleries along the cobblestone colonial streets of San Miguel de Allende, there's nothing better than enjoying a luxurious respite at one of the thermal pools outside town – one of the most relaxing experiences in the region. After your soak, head to the nearby Santuario de Atotonilco, a fascinating magnet for Mexican pilgrims.

The Riviera Maya

12 Stretching from the jet-setting, spring-breaking funfest of Cancún to the backwaters of the Sian Ka'an Biosphere Reserve, the Riviera gets a bad rap, mostly thanks to Cancún. Elsewhere, however, there are multiple opportunities to kick back without getting trampled, from little beachside fishing villages to cosmopolitan hot spots. And with water this blue, it's easy to overlook the excesses and let yourself be seduced by the dreamy tropical surrounds.

Painted ceramic skulls, Oaxaca City

MARGIE POLITZER / GETTY IMAGES ©

Pohnpei

Micronesia

The four unique states of Kosrae, Pohnpei, Chuuk and Yap have distinct cultures, traditions and identities as colourful and diverse as the multitudes of coral formations that live in their fringing reefs.

Known collectively as the Federated States of Micronesia (FSM), these four states are otherwise unrelated, and travellers looking to experience a variety of lifestyles are in luck.

Kosrea is a Pacific paradise and arguably FSM's most beautiful island. Its people are true believers, and here everything shuts down on Sunday and full focus is given to vibrant all-singing, all-dancing church ceremonies (with a relaxed island twist).

Pohnpei is home to mysterious ancient ruins and a plethora of lush landforms, and retains a system of chiefs and clan titles – a distinct style of governance that still exerts significant social and political influence.

Chuuk is renowned for its wreck diving, and while it is just coming to terms with international tourism, the uncompromising nature of the Chuukese holds firm.

Last, but not least, Yap is a fiercly traditional state retaining a true island spirit. Its people retain their architecture, customs, religions and gigantic stone money – it's an eternally fascinating place.

Micronesia's
Top Experiences

Lelu Ruins

1 Lelu Island, connected to the larger island of Kosrae by a causeway, is where a massive walled city was built between the 13th and 14th centuries for Kosraean royalty. Lelu's ruins are hidden behind thick tropical vegetation, in the kind of isolated setting you might imagine trekking hours through dense jungle to find. You can still see the dwelling compounds of the high chiefs, two royal burial mounds, a few sacred compounds and numerous large walls, built from huge hexagonal basalt logs stacked like a log cabin.

Nan Madol

2 An important political, social and religious centre built during the Saudeleur dynasty, Nan Madol was a place for ritual activity and the homes of royalty. Comprising 92 artificial islets, it's built on tidal flats and reef off Pohnpei.

Yap Island

3 Yap Proper's main island features the tiny capital, Colonia, which wraps around Chamorro Bay, offering sea views almost everywhere. Walk to the stone-money bank in the nearby village of Balabat, or visit the Ethnic Art Village, which does a great job of celebrating and preserving indigenous art. Up north, Bechiyal is a friendly beachside village with Yap's oldest *faluw* (men's house).

Food & Drink

Pohnpeian dog A traditional feast food, but the casual visitor is unlikely to come across it.

Sakau Local potently narcotic kava drink made from the roots of pepper shrubs.

When to Go

YEAR ROUND

➡ Temperatures hover around 27°C for all islands.

➡ Pohnpei gets as much as 10,000mm rainfall annually, making it one of the rainiest places on earth.

➡ A little less humid from December to June.

St George Chapel, Tiraspol

Moldova

Long-forgotten and little-known, Moldova struggles to throw off its post-communist trappings and reputation as one of the poorest nations in Europe.

Only vaguely known in Europe and all but anonymous to the rest of the world, Moldova remains a mysterious and misunderstood land: part Romanian, part Russian, all Soviet. Once at the very edge of the USSR, Moldova has gone it alone since the early '90s. Independence has been economically painful and Moldova has been racked by civil war between the central government and the secessionist Russian-speaking region known as Transdniestr, which continues to exist as a state within a state today.

Moldova gets a tiny number of tourists and isn't particularly well set up for travellers, but this is one of its greatest charms. Its out-of-the-way aspect makes travel in Moldova a challenge and an adventure, but the unhurried and timeless way of life, where there is always time to chat in the shade of summer's fruit trees, are part of its appeal.

Sights may be few and far between in the gently undulating landscape, but look no further for adventure: this is Eastern Europe's last unknown land.

CAPITAL
Chişinău

POPULATION
3.6 million

AREA
33,851 sq km

OFFICIAL LANGUAGE
Moldovan

Moldova's
Top Experiences

Chişinău

1 Though razed to the ground by WWII and a terrible 1940 earthquake, Chişinău has arguably never lost its cosmopolitan soul or charm, despite the best efforts of the Soviet authorities who oversaw the rebuilding of the city.

Food & Drink

Brânză Slightly sour sheep's milk cheese.

Mămăligă A cornmeal porridge with a breadlike consistency.

Muşchi de vacă Cutlet of beef.

Sarma Cabbage-wrapped minced meat or pilau rice packages.

Wine Cricova, Mileştii Mici and Cojuşna wineries and others offer the most fulfilling and inexpensive wine tours in the world.

Wine Cellars

2 Cricova is arguably the best known of Moldova's vineyards. Its underground wine kingdom, 15km north of Chişinău, is one of Europe's biggest. Some 60km of the 120km-long underground limestone tunnels – dating from the 15th century – are lined wall-to-wall with bottles. While Cricova has the hype, Mileştii Mici, housed in a limestone mine, is the largest cellar in Europe with over 200km of tunnels.

Orheiul Vechi

3 Detox at the fantastic Orheiul Vechi monastery complex. This is unquestionably Moldova's most fantastic and picturesque sight, drawing visitors from around the globe. The complex is carved into a massive limestone cliff in a wild, rocky, remote spot. The Cave Monastery, inside a cliff overlooking the gently meandering Răut River, was dug by Orthodox monks in the 13th century.

When to Go

JUN
➡ Parks and restaurant terraces fill with freed students, and the weather is warm.

JUL
➡ High season hits its peak with hiking, wine tours and camping all in full operation.

OCT
➡ The excellent Wine Festival is on the second Sunday in October.

Musée Océanographique de Monaco

Monaco

It might be the world's second-smallest country, but what it lacks in size it makes up for in attitude. Glitzy, glam and screaming hedonism, Monaco is truly beguiling.

CAPITAL
Monaco

POPULATION
30,500

AREA
2 sq km

OFFICIAL LANGUAGE
French

Your first glimpse of this pocket-sized principality, squeezed into just 2 sq km, might make your heart sink: after all the gorgeous medieval hilltop villages, glittering beaches and secluded peninsulas of the surrounding area, Monaco's concrete high-rises and astronomic prices come as a shock. But Monaco is captivating. The world's second-smallest state (a smidgen bigger than the Vatican), it is as famous for its tax-haven status as for its glittering casino, sports scene (Formula One, world-famous circus festival and tennis open) and a royal family on a par with British royals for best gossip fodder. For visitors, it just means an exciting trip: from an evening at the stunning casino, to a visit to the excellent Musée Océanographique, to a spot of celebrity/royalty spotting, Monaco is a fun day out on the Riviera.

In terms of practicalities, Monaco is a sovereign state, but has no border control. Most visit Monaco as a day trip from Nice, just a 20-minute train ride away.

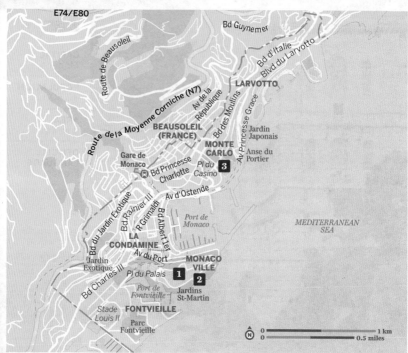

Monaco's
Top Experiences

Le Rocher

1 Monaco Ville, also called Le Rocher, thrusts skywards on a pistol-shaped rock. It's this strategic location overlooking the sea that became the stronghold of the Grimaldi dynasty. Built as a fortress in the 13th century, the palace is now the private residence of the Grimaldi ruling family.

Food & Drink

Given Monaco's location, its cuisine is influenced by French and Italian styles, and seafood features heavily. Local specialities include *stocafi* (cod in tomato sauce), *socca* (crêpes made from chickpea flour), *barbagiuan* (deep-fried pastries stuffed with spinach and leek) and *fougasse* (a sweet pastry decorated with almonds and other nuts).

Musée Océanographique de Monaco

2 Stuck dramatically to the edge of a cliff since 1910, this world-renowned museum is a stunner. Its centrepiece is its aquarium, with a 6m-deep lagoon where sharks and marine predators are separated from colourful tropical fish by a coral reef. Pay a visit to the rooftop terrace for sweeping views of Monaco and the Med.

Casino de Monte Carlo

3 Living out your James Bond fantasies doesn't get any better than at Monte Carlo's monumental, richly decorated showpiece, the 1910-built casino. The European Rooms have poker/slot machines, French roulette and *trente et quarante* (a card game), while the Private Rooms offer baccarat, blackjack, craps and American roulette.

When to Go

JAN

➜ The International Circus Festival showcases heart-stopping acts from around the globe.

APR

➜ Players and fans love the spectacle of the Monte-Carlo Masters, an annual tennis tournament.

MAY

➜ Jet-setters descend for the Grand Prix, one of Formula One's most iconic races.

Arkhangai

CAPITAL
Ulaanbaatar

POPULATION
2.9 million

AREA
1.6 million sq km

OFFICIAL LANGUAGE
Khalkha Mongol

Mongolia

Mongolia is an unspoiled wonder, a land where sand dunes sing, horses roam wild and nomadic herders greet strangers with open doors. Keep your itinerary loose and expect the unexpected.

Mongolia. The word alone stirs up visions of nomadic herders, thundering horses and, of course, the warrior-emperor Genghis Khan. The Mongols conquered half the known world in the 13th century and while their empire is long gone, visitors are still drawn to this magical land.

Mongolians know they live in a unique country. Ask anyone and they will probably start gushing about the vast steppes, rugged mountains and clear lakes. Just as appealing is Mongolia's nomadic culture, still going strong in the 21st century. The chance to sleep in a ger, help herd the sheep and milk a cow is one of the ultimate 'back to basics' experiences, made possible only because of the tremendous hospitality that exists here.

There are few countries in the world, however, with such a stark difference between the rural and urban populations. While nomadic Mongols live the simple life, their cousins in Ulaanbaatar are lurching head-long into the future. The capital is changing at a dizzying pace as Mongolia rushes to be part of the global community.

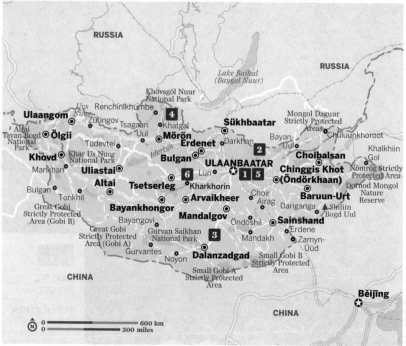

Mongolia's
Top Experiences

Naadam Festival

1 Mongolians love their naadam. With two or three days of serious wrestling, horse racing and archery action, who wouldn't? While 'naadam' literally means games, the celebration is much more than that. It's all about fun, getting together with friends and relatives, eating a lot of *khuushuur* (mutton pancakes) and emptying a vodka bottle or two. The most traditional festivals happen in small towns, where every member of the community is somehow involved. By comparison, the naadam in Ulaanbaatar feels less like a community festival and more like a big sporting event, with huge crowds and plenty of associated concerts and theatre events.

Staying in a Ger

2 Of all the experiences you are likely to have in Mongolia, the most memorable will be your visits to gers. From the outside, gers look like simple tents, but step inside and you'll be surprised by the amount of furnishings and modern appliances a nomadic family can have. There are beds, tables, chairs, dressers, a stove and often a TV and radio. Visitors are always welcome inside a ger and you don't even need to knock (Mongolians never do). Instead, when approaching a ger, call out 'Nokhoi khor', which means 'Hold the dog'. Tourist ger camps are dotted across the country – for an experience close to the city, join urban-weary Ulaanbaatarites in the Terelj Area; at 1600m, the region is cool and the alpine scenery magnificent.

Gobi Desert

3 The idea of going to the Gobi for a vacation would probably have Marco Polo turning in his grave. The Venetian traveller, and others like him, dreaded crossing this harsh landscape. Thankfully, travel facilities have improved in the past 800 years, and it's now possible to make a reasonably comfortable visit. There are shaggy camels to ride and dinosaur fossils to dig up, but the real highlight is the scenic Khongoryn

1

THOMAS L KELLY / GETTY IMAGES ©

Wrestlers, Naadam Festival

Els – towering sand dunes that whistle when raked by high winds.

Khövsgöl Nuur

4 The natural highlight of Mongolia is Khövsgöl Nuur, a 136km-long lake set on the southernmost fringe of Siberia. For Mongolians the lake is a deeply spiritual place, home to powerful *nagas* (water spirits) and a source of inspiration for shamans that live there. For foreigners Khövsgöl is a place for adventure, with horse riding, fishing, kayak- ing, trekking and mountain biking a few of the possibili- ties. Hard-core adventurers can even embark on a 15- day trek around its glorious shoreline.

Ulaanbaatar

5 Mongolia is said to be the least-densely popu- lated country on the planet. You would have a hard time believing that if you only visited its capital. The crush of people, cars and develop- ment in Ulaanbaatar can be overwhelming and exciting all at once. Beyond the

if Mongolia were 100 people

👤👤👤👤👤👤👤👤👤👤👤👤👤👤👤👤👤👤👤👤
👤👤👤👤👤👤👤👤👤👤👤👤👤👤👤👤👤👤👤👤
👤👤👤👤👤👤👤👤👤👤👤👤👤👤👤👤👤👤👤👤
👤👤👤👤👤👤👤👤👤👤👤👤👤👤👤👤👤👤👤👤
👤👤👤👤👤👤👤👤👤👤👤👤👤👤👤👤👤👤👤👤

95 would be Mongol (mostly Khalkh)
5 would be Turkic (mostly Kazakh)

belief systems
(% of population)

53
Buddhist

3
Muslim

2
Christian

3
Shamanist

39
other or none

population per sq km

MONGOLIA   RUSSIA   USA

👤 ≈ 2 people

When to Go

HIGH SEASON
(Jun–Aug)

➡ Expect hot, dry weather in June and July.

➡ Late July and August are warm but expect rain.

➡ Book flights and accommodation in advance, especially around Naadam.

SHOULDER
(May & Sep)

➡ Some ger camps may be closed.

➡ Weather can be changeable so plan for a cold snap.

➡ Fewer tourists at this time.

LOW SEASON
(Oct–Apr)

➡ Some ger camps and guesthouses close; some hotels offer discounts.

➡ Frigid in December and January. Winds and dust storms in March and April.

➡ Activities such as dog sledding, ice skating and skiing.

Trans-Mongolian Railway

The Trans-Mongolian Railway is a segment of the vast network of track that links Beijing and Moscow, a crucial piece of the world's longest continuous rail route. For rail enthusiasts, a journey along the Trans-Siberian Railway is the railroad equivalent of climbing Mt Everest.

The idea of building a rail route between Moscow and Vladivostok was hatched in the mid-19th century, but the section across Mongolia was only completed in 1956.

When riding the rails, make sure to travel as the locals do – bring loads of salami, bread and pickles, and a deck of cards or chessboard. Also bring a good phrasebook so that you can communicate with your cabin mates and new-found friends.

Food & Drink

Buuz Steamed dumplings filled with mutton and sometimes slivers of onion or garlic.

Khorkhog A dish made by placing hot stones from an open fire into a pot or urn with chopped mutton and water. The container is then sealed and left on the fire.

Makh The classic Mongolian dinner staple consists of boiled sheep bits (bones, fat, various organs and the head) with some sliced potato, served in a plastic bucket.

Shölte khool Literally, soup with food – a meal involving hot broth, pasta slivers, boiled mutton and a few potato chunks.

Süütei tsai Milk tea with salt. The taste varies by region; in Bayan-Ölgii it may even include a dollop of butter.

Tsagaan idee Literally 'white foods': yogurt, milk, delicious fresh cream, cheese and fermented milk drinks.

A temple at Erdene Zuu Khiid, Kharkhorin

heady nightlife, chic cafes and Hummers, the city has a peaceful side, too. Turn a prayer wheel at Gandan Khiid, saunter across Sükhbaatar Sq and climb up Zaisan Memorial to take a break from this bewildering place.

Erdene Zuu Khiid

6 The time-worn Buddhist monasteries (khiid) that dot the landscape are the most immediate window on Mongolia's spiritual roots. Lamas young and old sit quietly in the pews, carrying on the legacy of a religion brought here from Tibet centuries ago. The laypeople that visit the monasteries pay homage with the spin of a prayer wheel and whispered mantras. As well as a place of pilgrimage, the monasteries are also rare slices of tangible history, filled with precious Buddhist icons, Sutras and the delicate paintings that grace their ancient walls. Founded in 1586 by Altai Khaan, Erdene Zuu (Hundred Treasures) was the first Buddhist monastery in Mongolia. It once had between 60 and 100 temples and, at its peak, up to 1000 monks in residence.

Getting Around

Air Mongolia relies heavily on air transport. It has 46 functioning airports, although only 14 of those have paved airstrips. Seats can be difficult to get in summer, especially in the July tourist peak and in late August as students return to college.

Bicycle For adventurous bikers, Mongolia offers an amazing cycling experience. The vast, open steppes make for rough travel but if properly equipped there is nothing stopping you from travelling pretty much anywhere.

Bus Large buses make a daily run to most cities. Towns in the far west such as Khovd, Bayan-Ölgii and Uvs are served by minivans that run every other day.

Sveti Stefan

Montenegro

Montenegro, Crna Gora, Black Mountain: the very name conjures up images of romance and drama – and this fascinating land doesn't disappoint on either front.

CAPITAL
Podgorica

POPULATION
653, 474

AREA
13,812 sq km

OFFICIAL LANGUAGE
Montenegrin

Imagine a place with sapphire beaches as spectacular as Croatia's, rugged peaks as dramatic as Switzerland's, canyons nearly as deep as Colorado's, palazzos as elegant as Venice's and towns as old as Greece's and then wrap it up in a Mediterranean climate and squish it into an area two-thirds the size of Wales and you start to get a picture of Montenegro.

There's not a lot of it – barely 100km from tip to toe – but Montenegro's coast is quite extraordinary. Mountains jut sharply from

crystal-clear waters in such a way that the word 'looming' is unavoidable. As if that wasn't picturesque enough, ancient walled towns cling to the rocks and dip their feet in the water like they're the ones on holiday.

But when the beaches fill up with Eastern European sunseekers, intrepid travellers can easily sidestep the hordes in the rugged mountains of Durmitor and Prokletije, the primeval forest of Biogradska Gora or in the many towns and villages where ordinary Montenegrins go about their daily lives.

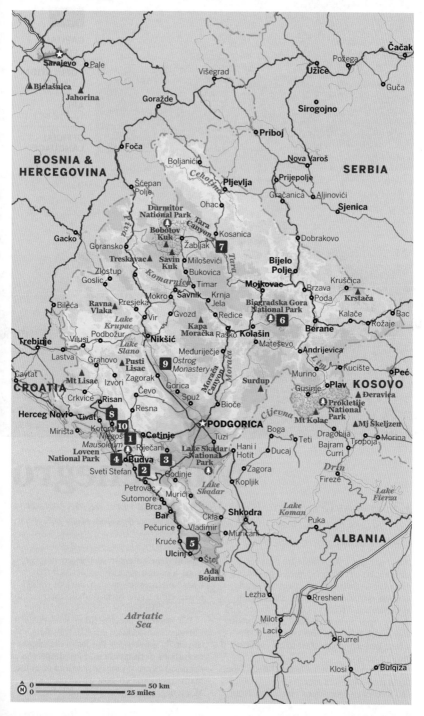

Montenegro's
Top Experiences

Njegoš Mausoleum

1 Once upon a time there was a Black Mountain. And on top of that mountain there was a tomb guarded by two granite giantesses. And inside the tomb, under a canopy of gold, there rests a great hero, lying in the arms of a giant eagle... This fairy-tale location in Lovćen National Park is the final resting place for the very real 19th-century Vladika (bishop-prince) Petar II Petrović Njegoš. The simple but affecting structure and monumental statuary do little to distract from the remarkable views over all of Old Montenegro.

Sveti Stefan

2 The postcard-perfect walled island village of Sveti Stefan is a wonder to behold. It's a little slice of Mediterranean heaven, with oleanders, pines and olive trees peeking between the terracotta roofs of pink stone dwellings. Content yourself with the views though, as access to the island is limited to guests of the exclusive resort that owns it. Laze on the beach, take a stroll through the woods to Pržno, and go crazy taking photographs – it's hard to get a bad shot.

ALAN COPSON / GETTY IMAGES ©

Rijeka Crnojevića

3 Clinging to the banks of the Crnojević River, this little village was a favourite of Montenegro's ruling Petrović-Njegoš dynasty, and some of the relatively humble stone houses were once royal dwellings. A picturesque stone bridge spans the river and a marble promenade extends along one bank, providing a launching point for boat and kayak tours heading towards Lake Skadar. The peace and quiet is just as appealing today, but the village now also has one of Montenegro's best seafood restaurants.

if Montenegro were 100 people

45 would be Montenegrin
29 would be Serbian
9 would be Bosniak
5 would be Albanian
12 would be other

belief systems
(% of population)

72 Orthodox
19 Muslim
3 Catholic
6 other or none

population per sq km

MONTENEGRO   SERBIA   UK

👤 ≈ 12 people

Stari Grad, Budva

4 Budva's walled Old Town is simply gorgeous, rising from the Adriatic like a miniature, less-frantic Dubrovnik. There's an atmosphere of romance and a typically Mediterranean love of life on every corner. While away the hours exploring the labyrinth of narrow cobbled streets, visiting tiny churches and charming galleries, drinking in al fresco cafe-bars, snacking on pizza slices, and being inspired by the sea views from the Citadela. When it's time to relax, there's a beach on either side.

Ulcinj

5 There's a special buzz to Ulcinj, Montenegro's southernmost town – an indefinable excitement that's particularly apparent on summer nights, when the beachfront thrums with Eastern-tinged pop and a constant parade of holidaymakers. Looking up to the skyline, minarets compete with an oversized socialist sculpture and the imposing walls of the Old Town, set high up on the cliff. Continuing along the coast, rocky coves give way to the long sandy expanses of Velika Plaža (Big Beach) and the clothing-optional island, Ada Bojana.

Biogradska Gora National Park

6 Nestled within the folds of the Bjelasica Mountains, Biogradska Gora has such a peaceful, solitary, untouched-by-the-world feel to it that you might not want to leave. The national park's showcase is pretty Lake Biograd,

Rocking Rambo

If anyone doubts the relevance of Eurovision they should travel through Montenegro. Montenegrins love their local pop, particularly a power ballad or a cheesy ditty played loud and accompanied by a thumping techno beat. Rambo Amadeus is Montenegro's answer to Frank Zappa. He's been releasing albums since the late '80s, flirting with styles as diverse as turbofolk and hip hop. In 2012 he created one of the more memorable Eurovision Song Contest moments, performing his song *Euro Neuro* backed by a wooden 'Trojan donkey' and breakdancers. The lyrics ('monetary breakdance, give me time to refinance') included such inspired rants as 'I don't like snobbism, nationalism, puritanism. I am different organism. My heroism is pacifism, altruism. I enjoy bicyclism, liberalism, tourism, nudism…'.

Food & Drink

Loosen your belt, you're in for a treat. Eating in Montenegro is an extremely pleasurable experience.

Most of the food is local, fresh and organic, and hence very seasonal. Despite its small size, Montenegro has at least three distinct regional styles: the food of the old Montenegrin heartland including *pršut* (smoke-dried ham), *sir* (cheese) and freshwater fish such as eel (*jegulja*), bleak (*ukljeva*) and carp (*krap*); mountain food that is traditionally more stodgy, meaty and Serb-influenced; and coastal cuisine, which is indistinguishable from Dalmatian cuisine with lots of grilled seafood, garlic, olive oil and Italian-style dishes.

The domestic wine is eminently drinkable and usually the cheapest thing on the menu. *Vranac* is the indigenous red grape, producing excellent, full-bodied wines and traditionally aged in walnut rather than oak barrels. Locally produced whites include chardonnay, sauvignon blanc and the native *krstač*.

but further enchantments await on the hiking tracks through one of Europe's most significant remaining tracts of virgin forest. This green world is quite unlike the rocky terrain that characterises most of the country's mountains, and in autumn it kicks up its heels and turns on a colourful show.

When to Go

HIGH SEASON
(Jul–Aug)

➡ The warmest, driest, busiest and most expensive time to visit.

➡ Accommodation should be booked well in advance; some places enforce three-day minimum stays.

SHOULDER
(May–Jun & Sep–Oct)

➡ The best time to come, with plenty of sunshine and average water temperatures over 20°C.

➡ Some beach bars and restaurants are closed and activities can be harder to arrange.

LOW SEASON
(Dec–Mar)

➡ The ski season kicks in, with peak prices in Kolašin and Žabljak.

➡ Many hotels, restaurants and bars on the coast close their doors and prices plummet.

Rafting the Tara River

7 It's hard to get a decent view of the beautiful Tara Canyon – its tree-lined walls, up to 1300m high, tend to get in the way. The effect is most impressive from the water, which goes some way to explaining why rafting is one of the country's most popular tourist activities. You'll hit a few rapids but outside of April and May it's a relatively gentle experience, gliding over crystalline waters through a landscape untouched by human hands.

Kotor

8 Time-travel back to a Europe of moated walled towns with shadowy lanes and stone churches on every square. It may not be as impressive as Dubrovnik's or as shiny as Budva's, but Kotor's Stari Grad (Old Town) feels much more lived in and ever-so dramatic. The way it seems to grow out of the sheer grey mountains surrounding it adds a thrill of foreboding to the experience, as if they could at any point choose to squeeze the little town in a rocky embrace.

Ostrog Monastery

9 No photo can do justice to the wonder that is Ostrog Monastery. Set in

Best on Film

Casino Royale (2006) James Bond plays poker in a casino in Montenegro; suspend your disbelief, the Montenegro scenes were actually filmed in Italy and the Czech Republic.

The Battle of Neretva (1969) Featuring a stellar cast including Yul Brynner and Orson Welles, this movie garnered an Academy Award nomination. It's set and filmed across the border in Bosnia, but director Veljko Bulajić was born in (what is now) Montenegro.

Best in Print

Montenegro: A Novel (Starling Lawrence; 1997) An entertaining tale of politics, bloodshed and romance set at the dawn of the 20th century.

Realm of the Black Mountain (Elizabeth Roberts; 2007) An interesting and detailed dissection of Montenegro's history.

The Son (Andrej Nikolaidis; 2011) Set in Ulcinj over the course of a single night, this novel won a European Union Prize for Literature.

Getting Around

Bus Buses link all major towns and are affordable, reliable and reasonably comfortable.

Car While you can get to most places by bus, hiring a car will give you freedom to explore some of Montenegro's scenic back roads. Some of these are extremely narrow and cling to the sides of canyons, so it may not suit the inexperienced or faint-hearted.

Train Trains are cheap but the network is limited and the carriages are old and can get hot. The main line links Bar, Virpazar, Podgorica, Kolašin, Mojkovac and Bijelo Polje, and there's a second line from Podgorica to Danilovgrad and Nikšić.

a seemingly sheer mountain wall, it's impossible to frame a photo to reveal its great height without reducing the luminous white monastery to little more than a speck. Orthodox Christians consider this Montenegro's holiest site and, whether you're a believer or not, it's an affecting place. The complex includes several stone churches, but none are more atmospheric than the cave chapels of the Upper Monastery, their rock walls covered in centuries-old frescoes.

The Kotor–Lovćen Road

10 One of the great highlights of Montenegro is the simple joy of travelling along its many scenic routes. The back road connecting Kotor with Cetinje is one of the very best – looping up and up, and providing ever more jaw-dropping views of the Bay of Kotor and the Adriatic Sea beyond. Any white-knuckle moments caused by the narrowness of the road and its sheer drops are compensated by vistas of lavender-grey mountains and glassy green water.

PAUL WHITFIELD / GETTY IMAGES ©

Sahara Desert

CAPITAL
Rabat

POPULATION
32.6 million

AREA
446,550 sq km

OFFICIAL LANGUAGE
Moroccan Arabic

Morocco

Morocco is an exotic gateway to Africa; its mountains, desert and coast are populated by Berbers and nomads, and its ancient medina lanes lead to souqs and riads.

From Saharan dunes to the peaks of the High Atlas, Morocco could have been tailor-made for travellers. Lyrical landscapes carpet this sublime slice of North Africa like the richly coloured and patterned rugs you'll lust after in the souqs. The mountains offer simple, breathtaking pleasures: night skies glistening in the thin air, or views over a fluffy cloudbank. On lower ground there are rugged coastlines, waterfalls and caves in forested hills, and the mighty desert. The varied terrain may inform your dreams, but it shapes the very lives of Morocco's Berbers, Arabs and Saharawis.

The trick to travelling in Morocco is to leave enough time to watch the world go by with the locals when there's so much else to fit in: hiking up North Africa's highest peak, camel trekking, shopping in the souqs, getting lost in the medina, and sweating in the hammam. Between the activities, you can sleep in the famous riads, relax on panoramic terraces and grand squares, and mop up tajines flavoured with saffron and argan.

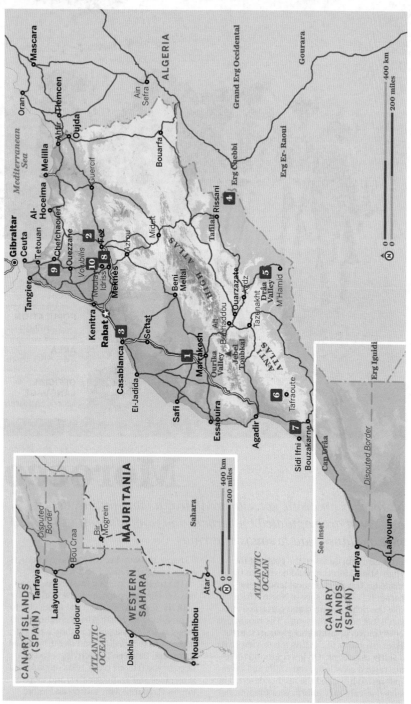

Morocco's
Top Experiences

Djemaa el-Fna

1 Even the best circuses can't compare to the madcap, Unesco-acclaimed *halqa* (street theatre) in Marrakesh's main square. By day, 'La Place' draws crowds with astrologers, snake-charmers, acrobats and dentists with jars of pulled teeth. Around sunset, 100 restaurant stalls kick off the world's most raucous grilling competition. 'I teach Jamie Oliver everything he knows!' brags a chef. 'We're number one...literally!' jokes the cook at stall number one. After dinner, Djemaa music jam sessions get underway – audience participation is always encouraged, and spare change ensures encores.

Fez Medina

2 The Fez medina is the maze to end all mazes. Don't be surprised if you get so lost you have to end up paying a small boy to take you back to familiar ground. But don't be afraid, because getting lost is half the point: blindly follow alleys into hidden squares and souqs, with the constant thrill of discovery. Treat it as an adventure, follow the flow of people to take you back to main thoroughfares, and experience the excitement of never quite knowing what's around the next corner.

Musicians playing at Djemaa el-Fna, Marrakesh

DOUG MCKINLAY / GETTY IMAGES ©

Casablanca's Architectural Heritage

3 If anyone tells you there's nothing to see in Casablanca except the Hassan II Mosque, they haven't looked up. Dating from the early 20th century when Casa was the jewel of the French colonies, a wealth of Mauresque and art-deco buildings can be found in the downtown areas, with rounded corners, tumbling friezes of flowers and curved wrought-iron balconies. Some buildings have been cared for while others are neglected; a walking tour showcases most of them.

if Morocco were 100 people

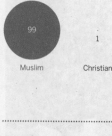

27 would be aged 0-14 years
18 would be aged 15-24 years
42 would be aged 25-54 years
7 would be aged 55-64 years
6 would be aged 65+

belief systems
(% of population)

99 Muslim
1 Christian

population per sq km

MOROCCO   ALGERIA   UK

≈ 15 people

Camel Trek in the Sahara

4 When you pictured yourself dashing into the sunset on your trusty steed, you probably didn't imagine there'd be quite so much lurching involved. Don't worry: no one is exactly graceful clambering onto a saddled hump, and the side-to-side sway of a dromedary in motion only comes naturally to Saharawis, belly dancers and genies. The rest of us novices cling on comically, knock-kneed and white-knuckled, until safely over the first dune. But as rose-gold sands of Erg Chebbi rise to meet fading violet-blue Saharan skies, grips on the reins go slack with wonder – and by moonrise, Timbuktu seems totally doable.

Drâa Valley Kasbah Trail

5 Roads now allow safe, speedy passage through the final stretches of ancient caravan routes from Mali to Marrakesh, but beyond the rocky gorges glimpsed through car windows lies the Drâa Valley of desert-traders' dreams. The palms and cool mud-brick castles of Tamegroute, Zagora, Timidarte and Agdz must once have seemed like mirages after two months in the Sahara. Fortifications that housed gold-laden caravans are now open to overnight guests, who wake to fresh boufeggou dates, bread baked in rooftop ovens, and this realisation: speed is overrated.

Tafraoute

6 The Anti Atlas' main town, Tafraoute has a jumble of pink houses

On Location

Morocco has built a reputation as a stunning movie backdrop, easily stealing scenes in such dubious cinematic achievements as *Sex and the City II*, *Prince of Persia*, *Alexander*, *Ishtar*, *Troy* and *Sahara*. But while there's much to cringe about in Morocco's IMDB filmography, the country had golden moments on the silver screen in Hitchcock's *The Man Who Knew Too Much*, Orson Welles' *Othello* and David Lean's *Lawrence of Arabia*.

Morocco has certainly proved its versatility: it stunt-doubled for Somalia in Ridley Scott's *Black Hawk Down*, Tibet in Martin Scorsese's *Kundun*, and Lebanon in Stephen Gaghan's *Syriana*, and *Inception's* Kenyan dreamscape was actually Tangier. Morocco also stole the show right out from under John Malkovich by playing itself in Bernardo Bertolucci's *The Sheltering Sky*, and untrained local actors Mohamed Akhzam and Boubker Ait El Caid held their own with Cate Blanchett and Brad Pitt in the 2006 Oscar-nominated *Babel*.

Food & Drink

B'stilla Parcel of layered filo pastry, stuffed with pigeon or chicken, nuts and cinnamon.

Couscous Slow-steamed hand-rolled semolina, served with a light broth and meat or vegetables. Usually the centrepiece of a meal.

Harira Classic thick soup with onion, lentil, chickpeas, tomato and lamb.

Khoobz Traditional Moroccan bread, baked in communal wood-fired ovens.

Mint Tea Morocco's famed 'Berber whiskey': gunpowder tea steeped in bunches of fresh mint and enough sugar to dissolve your teeth.

Tajine Slow-cooked stew in a conical-topped earthenware dish. Classic varieties include chicken with olives and lemon, *kefta* (meatballs), and beef with prunes and almonds.

and market streets with extraordinary surroundings. The Ameln Valley is dotted with *palmeraies* (palm groves) and Berber villages, and the looming mountains stage a twice-daily, ochre- and-amber light show. With a relatively undeveloped tourist industry despite the region's many charms, it's a wonderful base for activities including mountain biking and seeking out prehis- toric rock carvings. As if the granite cliffs and oases weren't scenic enough, a Belgian artist applied his paint brush to some local boulders – with surreal results.

Sidi Ifni

7 This formerly Spanish seaside town, a camel ride from the Sahara, is every bit as dilapidated, breezy and magical as well-trodden Essaouira. You can walk to the stone arches at Legzira Plage, or just explore the blue-and- white backstreets of one of southern Morocco's most alluring hang-outs. The best time to appreciate the art-deco relics – more reminiscent of Cuba than Casa – is sunset, when the

When to Go

HIGH SEASON (Nov–Mar)

➡ Spring and autumn are the most popular times to visit.

➡ Accommodation prices are highest.

➡ Marrakesh and the south are popular at Christmas and New Year.

SHOULDER (Apr & Oct)

➡ Spring sandstorms in the Sahara and rain persists in the north.

➡ Popular elsewhere.

➡ Accommodation prices and demand jump around Easter.

LOW SEASON (May–Sep)

➡ Discounts in accommodation and souqs.

➡ Domestic tourism keeps prices high on the coast.

Atlantic winds bend the palms and fill the air with a cooling sea mist.

Moulay Idriss

8 This holy town cresting two hills is a white-washed gem. For years foreigners were barred from spending the night here, but recently there's been a mini-boom in local families opening their homes up as guest houses, allowing you to get away from the nearby cities. Tour groups only ever stop here for an hour during the day, so catching the sunset over town and watching the locals promenade from the cafes on the main square are real treats.

Best on Film

A Thousand Months (2003) Faouzi Bensaïdi's family-history epic won the 2003 Cannes Film Festival Premier Regard

Casanegra (2010) Nour-Eddine Lakhmari's Oscar contender for Best Foreign Film focuses on youth in Casablanca thinking fast and growing up faster as they confront the darker aspects of life in the White City.

La Grand Villa (2010) Tracks one couple's cultural and personal adjustments after relocating from Paris to Casablanca.

Marock (2005) Leila Marrakchi's film about a Muslim girl and Jewish boy who fall in love won Un Certain Regard at Cannes.

Best in Print

Dreams of Trespass: Tales of a Harem Girlhood Fatima Mernissi's memoirs of 1940s Fez blend with other women's stories.

The Sacred Night Tahar Ben Jelloun's tale of a Marrakesh girl raised as a boy won France's Prix Goncourt.

Getting Around

Air Royal Air Maroc is the national carrier, serving Tangier, Nador, Oujda, Fez, Casablanca, Er-Rachidia, Marrakesh, Essaouira, Agadir, Laâyoune and Dakhla.

Bus The cheapest and most efficient way to travel around the country, buses are generally safe, although drivers often leave a little to be desired.

Grand Taxi The elderly Mercedes vehicles you'll see on Moroccan roads and gathered near bus stations are shared taxis. The Ziz and Drâa Valleys, the Tizi n'Test and the Rif Mountains are good to visit in a taxi.

Train Morocco's excellent train network is one of Africa's best, linking most of the main centres. There are two main lines: Tangier down to Marrakesh via Rabat and Casablanca, and Oujda or Nador in the northeast down to Marrakesh, passing Fez and Meknès.

Chefchaouen Medina

9 Tear yourself away from the laid-back joints on the square to explore one of the best medinas in Morocco. Climb up cobbled streets to discover tiny blue-washed lanes, massive studded doors and all the trappings of medina life: women in Riffian pompom hats selling vegetables on street corners; the hammam; the communal oven; and the mosque. Emerge at the top at Ras el-Maa to watch the sunset over the medina.

Volubilis

10 The long grasp of Roman North Africa stretches back to grab you at Volubilis, with its triumphal arches and dazzling array of mosaics. The setting, in the rolling countryside just north of the Middle Atlas, is superb. History continues to play out in the landscape here as well – turn your head from the Roman olive press to nearby Moulay Idriss, where presses still continue to produce some of the finest olive oil in the country.

MICHELE FALZONE / GETTY IMAGES ©

Old colonial arches, Maputo

CAPITAL
Maputo

POPULATION
24.1 million

AREA
799,380 sq km

OFFICIAL LANGUAGE
Portuguese

Mozambique

A mix of Swahili, Indian, Portuguese and African influences, overlooked Mozambique is diverse in its cultural palette and natural attractions.

Mozambique's star is on the rise. After two decades of peace, the economy is growing. Glitzy high-rises and lively street cafes compete for attention with remote island archipelagos and a steadily increasing population of wild animals. A new bridge over the Zambezi River links north and south for the first time. Yet, despite the development, centuries-old rhythms still dominate and the country moves to its own beat.

Yet this enigmatic southeast African country embraced by the Indian Ocean is well off most travellers' maps. Still, it has much to offer those who venture here. Canny travellers are venturing in to discover long, dune-fringed beaches, turquoise waters glittering with shoals of colourful fish, well-preserved corals, remote archipelagos in the north, pounding surf in the south.

Discovering these attractions is not always easy, but it is unfailingly rewarding. Bring along some patience, some endurance for long bus rides, a sense of adventure, and jump in for the journey of a lifetime.

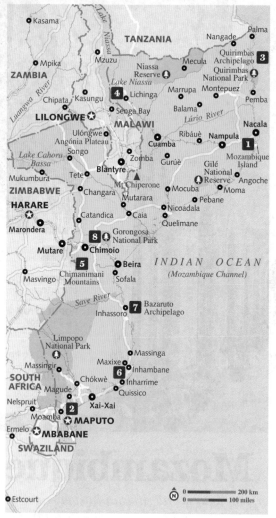

Maputo

2 Get to know Maputo, with its lively sidewalk cafes and many museums. Boasting Mediterranean-style architecture, flame-tree-lined avenues, sidewalk cafes and waterside setting, Maputo is easily one of Africa's most attractive capitals. Galabiyya garbed men gather in doorways to chat, while colourfully clad women hawk seafood and spices at the massive Municipal Market and banana vendors loll on their carts in the shade.

Quirimbas Archipelago

3 Explore the Quirimbas Archipelago, including magical Ibo, with its silver-smiths, fort and crumbling mansions. The archipelago consists of about two dozen islands and islets strewn along the 400km stretch of coastline between Pemba and the Rovuma River. Some are waterless and uninhabited, while others have histories as long as the archipelago itself. Throughout, the archipelago's natural beauty is astounding, with searingly white patches of soft sand surrounded by brilliant turquoise and azure waters alternating with greener, vegetated islands.

Lake Niassa

4 Relax along the ruggedly beautiful shoreline of Lake Niassa (Lago Niassa). The Mozambican side of the lake is beautiful and, in contrast to the Malawian side, almost completely undeveloped. It sees a small but steady stream of adventure travellers and is an excellent destination for anyone wanting to get off the beaten track. The main area for exploring is the coast between Metangula

Mozambique's
Top Experiences

Mozambique Island

1 Discover enchanting Mozambique Island (Ilha de Moçambique), with its time-warp atmosphere and cobbled streets. The crescent-shaped island measures only 3km in length and barely 500m in width at its widest section.

Yet it has played a larger-than-life role in East African coastal life over the centuries, and today is one of the region's most fascinating destinations – part slowly reawakening ghost town, part lively fishing community. It's also a picturesque and exceptionally pleasant place to wander around.

and Cóbuè, with a succession of narrow beaches backed by mountains and steep hills rising up directly from the lakeshore.

Hiking the Chimanimani Mountains

5 Silhouetted against the horizon on the Zimbabwe border southwest of Chimoio are these mountains, with Mt Binga (2436m), Mozambique's highest peak, rising up on their eastern edge. The mountains are beautiful and exceptionally biodiverse, with vegetation ranging from lowland tropical forests and miombo woodland to evergreen forests and afro-alpine grasslands. Much of the range is encompassed by the Chimanimani National Reserve.

Inhambane

6 With its serene waterside setting, tree-lined avenues, faded colonial-style architecture and mixture of Arabic, Indian and African influences, Inhambane is one of Mozambique's most charming towns and well worth a visit. It has a history that reaches back at least 10 centuries, making it one of the oldest settlements along the coast. Today Inhambane is the gateway to a fine collection of beaches, including Tofo and Barra.

Bazaruto Archipelago

7 Delight in the clear, turquoise waters filled with colourful fish, and opportunities for sailing, diving, snorkelling and birding. It

if Mozambique were 100 people

25 would speak Emakhuwa
11 would speak Portuguese
10 would speak Xichangana
50 would speak other Mozambican languages
4 would speak another language

belief systems
(% of population)

Catholic	Zionist Christian	Evangelical Pentecostal
28	16	11

Muslim	other	none
18	8	19

population per sq km

MOZAMBIQUE SOUTH AFRICA TANZANIA

👤 ≈ 6 people

When to Go

MAY–OCT/NOV
➡ Cooler, dry weather makes this the ideal time to visit.

DEC–MAR
➡ Rainy season can bring washed-out roads and occasional flooding in the south and centre.

HOLIDAYS
➡ In South African school holidays (Christmas, Easter, August) southern resorts fill up.

Traditional Religions & Healers

Traditional religions based on animist beliefs are widespread in Mozambique. The spirits of ancestors are often regarded to have significant powers over the destiny of living people. In connection with these beliefs, there are many sacred sites, such as forests, rivers, lakes and mountains, that play important roles in the lives of local communities.

Closely intertwined with traditional religions is the practice of traditional medicine, which is found throughout the country, sometimes in combination with Western medical treatment. *Curandeiros* (traditional healers) are respected and highly sought-after. In addition to *curandeiros*, you may encounter *profetas* (spirit mediums or diviners) and *feticeiros* (witch doctors).

Food & Drink

Chamusas Samosas; triangular wedges of fried pastry, filled with meat or vegetables.

Frango grelhado Grilled chicken. Cheap and easy to find; usually served with chips or rice.

Galinha á Zambeziana Chicken with a sauce of lime juice, garlic, pepper and piri-piri. Popular in Quelimane and Zambézia provinces.

Matapa Cassava leaves cooked in a peanut sauce, often with prawns or other additions.

Peixe grelhada Grilled fish, often served with rice or chips.

Prego Thin steak sandwich.

Rissois de camarão Similar to *chamusas* but semicircular, and with a shrimp filling.

Xima or Upshwa A maize- or cassava-based staple or rice, served with a sauce of beans, vegetables or fish.

Elephants, Gorongosa National Park

makes a fine upmarket holiday destination if you're looking for the quintessential Indian Ocean getaway. The archipelago consists of five main islands: Bazaruto, Benguera, Magaruque, Santa Carolina and tiny Bangué. Since 1971 much of the archipelago has been protected as Bazaruto National Park.

Gorongosa National Park

8 Watch wildlife and enjoy fine birdwatching at Gorongosa National Park, which was gazetted in 1960 and soon made headlines as one of southern Africa's premier wildlife parks. It was renowned for its large prides of lions, as well as for its elephants, hippos, buffaloes and rhinos. During the 1980s and early 1990s, poachers brought an end to this abundance but rehabilitation work began in 1995, and in 1998 Gorongosa reopened to visitors.

Getting Around

Bus Direct services connect all major towns at least daily, although vehicle maintenance and driving standards leave much to be desired.

Car & Motorcycle A South African or international drivers licence is required to drive in Mozambique. *Gasolina* (petrol) is scarce off main roads, especially in the north. *Gasóleo* (diesel) supplies are more reliable.

Chapa The main form of local transport is the *chapa*, the name given to any public transport that runs within a town or between towns. The most comfortable seat is in the front, next to the window, though you'll have to make arrangements early and sometimes pay more.

Train The only passenger train regularly used by tourists is the slow line between Nampula and Cuamba. If you have the time, it's one of southern Africa's great journeys.

Shwedagon Paya, Yangon

CAPITAL
Nay Pyi Taw

POPULATION
55.7 million

AREA
676,578 sq km

OFFICIAL LANGUAGE
Burmese

Myanmar (Burma)

Now is the moment to visit this extraordinary land, scattered with gilded pagodas, where the traditional ways of Asia endure and areas that were previously off-limits are opening up.

Turn back the clock in this time-warped country that's a world apart from the rest of Southeast Asia.

Travelling in Myanmar is a chance to swap the hubbub and electronic demands of modern life for the calm of gilded temples and ancient monasteries.

Enjoy slowly unfolding journeys through serene landscapes including meandering rivers, lush jungles, ethnic minority villages and pristine palm-fringed beaches.

Democracy champion Aung San Suu Kyi is free from house arrest and the tourism boycott has been lifted.

Myanmar remains a troubled land and it's up to you to decide whether to visit or not. Keep in mind that the long-suffering people are gentle, humorous, engaging, considerate, inquisitive and passionate; they want to play a part in the world and to know what you make of their world. Come with your mind open and you'll leave with your heart full.

Myanmar's
Top Experiences

Shwedagon Paya

1 Is there a more stunning monument to religion in Southeast Asia? We don't think so. In fact, the sheer size and mystical aura of Yangon's gilded masterpiece may even cause you to question your inner atheist. But it's not all about quiet contemplation: Shwedagon Paya is equal parts religious pilgrimage and amusement park, and your visit may coincide with a noisy ordination ceremony or fantastic fortune-telling session. If you're looking for one reason to linger in Yangon (Rangoon) before heading upcountry, this is it.

Inle Lake

2 Virtually every visitor to Myanmar makes it here at some point, but Inle Lake is so awe-inspiring that everybody comes away with a different experience. If you're counting days, you'll most likely be hitting the hotspots: water-bound temples, shore-bound markets and floating gardens. If you have more time, consider exploring the more remote corners of the lake. Either way, the cool weather, friendly folk and that placid pool of ink-like water are bound to find a permanent place in your memory.

Bagan

3 More than 3000 Buddhist temples are scattered across the plains of Bagan, site of the first Burmese kingdom. Dating to between the 11th and 13th centuries, the majority of the temples have been renovated, as Bagan remains an active religious site. Yes, there are tour buses and crowds at the most popular sunset-viewing spots, but they can be avoided. Pedal off on a bike and have your own adventure amid the not-so-ruined temples, or float over the temple tops in a hot-air balloon.

Pyin Oo Lwin

4 A one-off curiosity, Pyin Oo Lwin (once called Maymo) makes a great escape from hectic and humid Mandalay. It was once the British summer capital, and has many colonial-era buildings and a lovely botanical garden. The local taxis are colourful horse-drawn wagons, while an increasing number of restaurants make it one of the best provincial cities in Myanmar to eat in.

CLAUDE LETIEN / GETTY IMAGES ©

Mrauk U

5 The temples, monasteries, former palace, and ruined city walls of the former Rakhine capital of Mrauk U continue to paint a picture of what an amazing place this town must have been at its zenith in the 16th century. And best of all, with giant structures such as the Dukkanthein Paya and Kothaung Paya sharing real estate with rural villages and emerald-green rice fields, Mrauk U emerges as much more than a museum piece.

Mawlamyine

6 A virtual time capsule, the former capital of British Burma, Mawlamyine, has changed shockingly little since the colonial era, and its busy harbour, antique buildings, hill-top temples and imposing churches fool visitors into believing that Kipling and Orwell never left town. Even if you're not interested in history, the attractions surrounding Mawlamyine, with destinations ranging from tropical islands to deep caves, not to mention the area's unique

if Myanmar (Burma) were 100 people

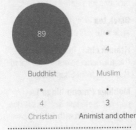

68 would be Bamar
9 would be Shan
7 would be Kayin (Karen)
4 would be Rakhaing
3 would be Chinese
2 would be Indian
2 would be Mon
5 would be other

belief systems
(% of population)

89 — Buddhist
4 — Muslim
4 — Christian
3 — Animist and other

When to Go

HIGH SEASON
(Dec–Feb)

➡ Rains least (if at all, in some places) and is not so hot.

➡ Book accommodation and transport well ahead for this busy travel season.

SHOULDER
(Oct–Nov, Mar–Apr)

➡ March to May Yangon often reaches 104°F (40°C). Hotter around Bagan and Mandalay.

➡ Cooler in the hill towns of Shan State.

➡ All transport booked solid during Thingyan in April.

LOW SEASON
(May–Sep)

➡ The southwest monsoon starts mid-May and peaks July to September.

➡ Rain can make roads impassable anywhere (especially in the delta region).

population per sq km

MYANMAR   USA   UK

🧍 ≈ 15 people

Burma or Myanmar?

What to call the Republic of the Union of Myanmar (the country's official name as of 2011) has been a political flashpoint since 1989. That was the year in which the military junta dumped Burma, the name commonly used since the mid-19th century, into the rubbish bin, along with a slew of other British colonial-era place names such as Rangoon, Pagan, Bassein and Arakan.

The UN recognises Myanmar as the nation's official name; Myanmar is more inclusive than Burma for a population that isn't by any means 100% Burman. However, nearly all opposition groups (including the NLD), many ethnic groups and several key nations including the USA and UK refer to it as Burma. As Aung San Suu Kyi told us in 2010, 'I prefer Burma because the name was changed without any reference to the will of the people.'

Food & Drink

Ăthouq Light, tart and spicy salads made with raw vegetables or fruit tossed with lime juice, onions, peanuts, roasted chickpea powder and chillies. A common one is *leq-p'eq thouq*, which includes fermented tea leaves.

Black tea Brewed in the Indian style with lots of milk and sugar.

Htamin chin Literally sour rice, this turmeric-coloured rice salad also hails from Shan State.

Mohinga ('moun-hinga') A popular breakfast dish this is rice noodles served with fish soup and as many other ingredients as there are cooks.

Shan khauk-swe Shan-style noodle soup; thin wheat noodles in a light broth with meat or tofu, available across the country but most common in Mandalay and Shan State.

Novice Buddhist nuns collecting alms, Hsipaw

Mon culture, are strong draws, yet like the city itself, see few visitors.

Myeik Archipelago

7 Spanning more than 800 islands, only two of which can claim any sort of accommodation, and many boasting virtually untouched, white-sand beaches and some of the region's best dive sites, it's hard to believe that a place such as this still exists in mainland Southeast Asia. And although accessing the area remains time-consuming and expensive, those who can afford the investment will be among the handful of people who can

claim witness to one of the final frontiers in Southeast Asian tourism, not to mention a beach junkie's fantasy destination.

Hsipaw

8 Attractive, laid-back Hsipaw is ideally placed for quick, easy hikes into fascinating Shan and Palaung villages, as well as more strenuous ones to barely visited hamlets. The surrounding area feels far less discovered than the treks available around Kalaw. Hsipaw itself is a historic town with a royal past and an area known as 'Little Bagan', full of ancient stupas.

Getting Around

Bus Frequent; reliable services and generally privately owned; overnight trips save on accommodation.

Boat Chance to interact with locals and pleasant sightseeing, but slow and only covers certain destinations.

Car Total flexibility but can be expensive; for some destinations you need a government-approved guide and driver.

Train More interaction with locals and countryside views but also uncomfortable, slow and frequently delayed.

Himba woman harvesting resin

CAPITAL
Windhoek

POPULATION
2.2 million

AREA
824,292 sq km

OFFICIAL LANGUAGE
English

Namibia

Namibia posesses some of the most stunning landscapes in Africa, and a trip through the country is one of the great road adventures.

Natural wonders such as that mighty gash in the earth at Fish River Canyon and the wildlife utopia of Etosha National Park enthral, but it's the lonely desert roads, where mighty slabs of granite rise out of swirling desert sands, that will sear themselves in your mind. It's like a coffee-table book come to life as sand dunes in the world's oldest desert meet the crashing rollers along the wild Atlantic coast. Among all this is a German legacy, evident in the cuisine and art nouveau architecture of Lüderitz or Swakopmund and in festivals such as Windhoek's legendary Oktoberfest.

Namibia is also the headquarters of adventure activities in the region, so whether you're a dreamer or love hearing the crunch of earth under your boots, travel in Namibia will stay with you long after the desert vistas fade.

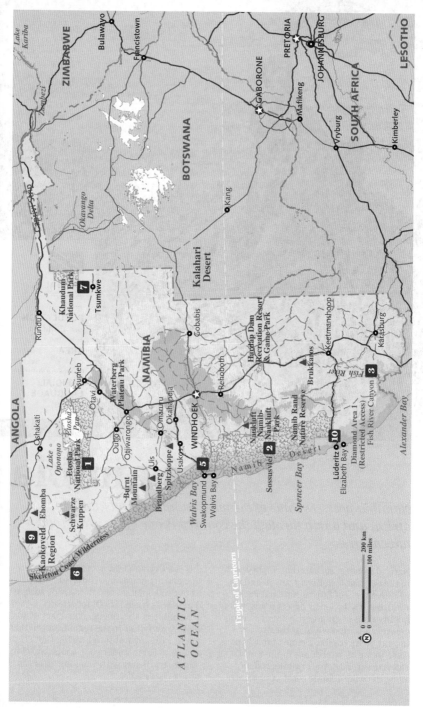

ATLANTIC
OCEAN

Tropic of Capricorn

ANGOLA

ZIMBABWE

Lake
Kariba

Zambezi

Caprivi Strip

Bulawayo

Francistown

PRETORIA

JOHANNESBURG

GABORONE

Mafikeng

SOUTH AFRICA

LESOTHO

Vryburg

Kimberley

BOTSWANA

Okavango
Delta

Kang

Kalahari
Desert

Rundu

Khaudum
National Park

Tsumkwe **7**

NAMIBIA

Gobabis

Hardap Dam
Recreation Resort
& Game Park

Keetmanshoop

Karasburg

Tsumeb

Waterberg
Plateau Park

Otavi

Rehoboth

Brukkaros

Fish River

Fish River Canyon **3**

Oshakati

Lake
Oponono

Etosha
National Park **1**

Etosha Pan

Outjo

Otjiwarongo

Omaruru

Okahandja

WINDHOEK

Naukluft
Namib-
Naukluft
Park

Namib Rand
Nature Reserve

Diamond Area 1
(Restricted Access)

Alexander Bay

Burnt
Mountain

Brandberg

Uis

Spitzkoppe

Usakos **5**

Sossusvlei **2**

Desert

Lüderitz **10**

Elizabeth Bay

Ehomba

Schwarze
Kuppen

Swakopmund

Walvis Bay

Walvis Bay

Namib

Spencer Bay

Kaokoveld
Region **9**

Skeleton Coast Wilderness **6**

200 km
100 miles

N

Namibia's
Top Experiences

Etosha National Park

1 There are few places in Southern Africa that can compete with the wildlife prospects in extraordinary Etosha National Park. A network of waterholes dispersed among the bush and grasslands surrounding the pan – a blindingly white, flat, saline desert that stretches into the horizon – attracts enormous congregations of animals. A single waterhole can render thousands of sightings over the course of a day – Etosha is simply one of the best places on the planet for watching wildlife.

Sossusvlei

2 Towering red dunes of incredibly fine sand that feels soft when it trickles through your fingers and changes indelibly with the light, Sossusvlei is an astounding place, especially given that the sands originated in the Kalahari millions of years ago. The Sossusvlei valley is dotted with hulking dunes and interspersed with unearthly dry vleis (low, open landscapes), and clambering up the face of these constantly moving giants is a uniquely Namibian experience. When you survey the seemingly endless swath of nothingness that surrounds you it feels as though time itself has slowed.

PETER TEN BROECKE / GETTY IMAGES ©

Fish River Canyon

3 Nowhere else in Africa will you find anything quite like Fish River Canyon. This enormous gash in the surface of the planet in the south of Namibia is an almost implausible landscape, however the numbers don't lie: the canyon measures 160km in length and up to 27km in width, and the dramatic inner canyon reaches a depth of 550m. Seen most clearly in the morning, Fish River Canyon is desolate, immense and seemingly carved into the earth by a master builder. The exposed rock and lack of plant life is quite startling

and trying to take pictures is soon replaced with thoughtful reflection and a quiet sense of awe. Its rounded edges and sharp corners create a symphony in stone of gigantic and imposing proportions. The best way to appreciate the enormous scope of the canyon is to embark on a monumental five-day hike that traverses half the length of the canyon, and ultimately tests the limits of your physical and mental endurance. Your reward, however, will be the chance to tackle one of Namibia's and, indeed, one of Africa's, greatest natural wonders.

Camping out on Safari

4 There's nothing quite like it for sharpening your senses and heightening your awareness of Africa. Sleeping under the stars is a soulful experience and the antithesis of the modern world's clamour – an infinity of stars, the crackle of the campfire, the immensity of the African night. But it's not for the faint-hearted, with the not-so-distant roar of a lion, and the knowledge that only flimsy canvas separates you from an angry hippo.

Swakopmund

5 Easily Namibia's finest urban scene, swanky Swakopmund is a feast of German art nouveau architecture, with its seaside promenades, half-timbered homes and colonial-era buildings. Stuck out on the South Atlantic coast and surrounded by desert, it feels like a movie set. Let loose on a skydive, horse ride or sandboard down a 300m dune because you are

The Caprivi Strip

The Caprivi Strip's notably odd shape is a story in itself. When Germany laid claim to British-administered Zanzibar in 1890 Britain objected and, in the end, Britain kept Zanzibar. But Germany was offered a vast strip of land from the British-administered Bechuanaland protectorate (now Botswana). Named the Caprivi Strip, this vital tract of land provided Germany with access to the Zambezi River.

For the Germans, the motivation for this swap was to ultimately create a colonial empire that spanned from the south Atlantic Coast to Tanganyika (now Tanzania) and the Indian Ocean. Unfortunately for them, the British colonisation of Rhodesia stopped the Germans well upstream of Victoria Falls, which proved a considerable barrier to navigation on the Zambezi.

Food & Drink

Traditional Namibian food consists of a few staples, the most common of which is *oshifima*, a doughlike paste made from millet, and usually served with a stew of vegetables or meat. Other common dishes include *oshiwambo*, a rather tasty combination of spinach and beef, and *mealie pap*, a basic porridge.

Local brews include *oshikundu* (beer made from millet), *mataku* (watermelon wine), *tambo* (fermented millet and sugar) or *mushokolo* (a beer made from a small local seed) and *walende*, which is distilled from the makalani palm and tastes similar to vodka. All of these concoctions, except walende, are brewed in the morning and drunk the same day, and they're all dirt cheap.For more conventional palates, Namibia is awash with locally brewed lagers. The most popular drop is the light and refreshing Windhoek Lager, but the brewery also produces Tafel Lager, the stronger and more bitter Windhoek Export, and the slightly rough Windhoek Special.

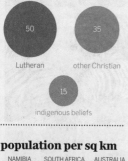

if Namibia were 100 people

60 would speak Afrikaans
32 would speak German
7 would speak English
1 would speak an indigenous language

belief systems
(% of population)

50 Lutheran
35 other Christian
15 indigenous beliefs

population per sq km

NAMIBIA   SOUTH AFRICA   AUSTRALIA

≈ 3 people

in the adventure capital of the region. 'Swakop' pulls off the backpacker scene and the clinking-wine-glass set equally, so you'll find your niche here.

Skeleton Coast

6 Travel in this part of Namibia, a treacherous stretch of the coast where many ships have become graveyards, is the stuff of road-journey dreams. It's a murky region with rocky and sandy coastal shallows, where rolling fogs and swirling sandstorms encapsulate its ghostly, isolated and untamed feel. The Skeleton Coast is among the most remote and inaccessible areas in the vast country of Namibia. And it's here in this wilderness that you can put your favourite music on, sit back and let reality meet your imagination.

The San People

7 In Namibia opportunities exist to interact with the San people – the original inhabitants of Southern Africa whose presence stretches back as much as 20,000 years. Lying at the edge of the Kalahari, Otjozondjupa is part of the traditional homeland of the Ju/'hoansi San. In Tsumkwe you can arrange everything from bush walks to hunting safaris.

Adventure Activities

8 Namibia is fast becoming the headquarters of adventure sports in the region. If you want to jump

When to Go

MAY–OCT

➡ Best time of the year for wildlife viewing.

JUN–AUG

➡ Swakopmund and Walvis Bay are subject to miserable sandstorm conditions.

SEP–OCT

➡ Windhoek comes alive with festivals that include arts events and Oktoberfest.

out of a plane, hurtle down the face of a sand dune in the world's oldest desert, or live out your Lawrence of Arabia–inspired fantasies on the back of a camel, you're in the right place. A uniquely African activity is black rhino tracking – on foot – through wild bushland with a couple of trackers, a guide and a lot of caution.

The Himba/ Herero

9 The rich culture of Namibia is best experienced in the varied communities of its Herero

population (numbering approximately 120,000), of which the Himba of the Kaokoveld are a subgroup. The characteristic Herero women's dress is derived from that of Victorian-era German missionaries and consists of an enormous crinoline worn over a series of petticoats, with a horn-shaped hat or headdress. In contrast, Himba women are famous for smearing themselves with a fragrant mixture of ochre, butter and bush herbs, which dyes their skin a burnt-orange hue.

Getting Around

Air Air Namibia has an extensive network of local flights operating out of Eros Airport, Windhoek.

Bus Public buses do serve the main towns, but they won't take you to the country's major sights.

Car By far the best way to experience Namibia is by hiring a car. There is an excellent infrastructure of sealed roads and in more remote locations there are well-maintained gravel and even salt roads.

Train Trans-Namib Railways connects some major towns, but trains are extremely slow.

Lüderitz

10 Namibia is a country that defies African stereotypes and this is perhaps nowhere more true than in the historic colonial town of Lüderitz. Straddling the icy South Atlantic and the blazing-hot Namib Desert, this mini-Deutschland is seemingly stuck in a time warp. After walking its streets, and sitting down to a plate of sausages and sauerkraut with an authentic Weiss beer, you'll survey the German art nouveau architecture, check the map again and shake your head in disbelief.

Best on Film

Beyond Borders (2003) Angelina Jolie starred in this drama about Ethiopian famine in 1984. Parts of the movie were shot in Namibia.

Mad Max: Fury Road (due 2015) The filming of the on-again-off-again fourth Mad Max movie was moved to Namibia, after unexpected rain turned the Australian desert location into a very un–Mad Max carpet of flowers.

Namibia: The Struggle for Liberation (2007) The story of Namibia's first president, Sam Nujoma.

Best in Print

Born of the Sun (Joseph Diescho; 1988) A largely autobiographical novel describing the protagonist's early life in a tribal village and his coming of age. It then follows his path through the South African mines and his ultimate political awakening.

The Sheltering Desert (Henno Martin; 1956) Records two years spent by the geologist author and his friend Hermann Korn avoiding internment as prisoners of war during WWII.

Berg St, Lüderitz

DANITA DELIMONT / GETTY IMAGES ©

Anibare Bay

CAPITAL
None
....
POPULATION
9434
....
AREA
21 sq km
....
OFFICIAL LANGUAGE
Nauruan

Nauru

Nauru's beauty can be glimpsed along its coast: seabirds swoop over green cliffs, aqua reigns along wild-ocean vistas and sunsets are nothing short of spectacular.

While the coast is beautiful – with opportunities to swim and snorkel, or watch a fiery sunset over coconut trees and salt brush – head to the island's interior and you'll find deforestation from phosphate mining and an eerie landscape of limestone pinnacles. The exposed rock reflects the sun's rays and chases away the clouds so there's lots of sunshine but frequent periods of drought.

Meanwhile, the wealth accrued from mining, followed by the poverty once the stores were depleted, have brought the country to near collapse. During the phosphate boom in the 1980s, Nauru was the second-richest country in the world in terms of per capita income; 30 years later the estimated average income is US$2500 per year. Freight deliveries are rare and employment scarcer. For the past decade Australia's controversial offshore refugee processsing centre has been a major contributor to development on Nauru.

Perhaps tourism, once thought unneeded, could help Nauru get back on its feet. Transport and hospitality services are thin on the ground but smiles are plentiful.

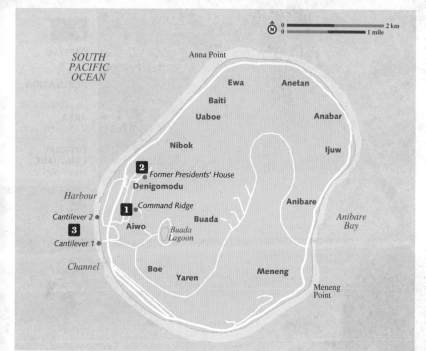

Nauru's
Top Experiences

Command Ridge

1 Nauru's highest point, where the Japanese kept watch in the 1940s, still holds some rusted WWII guns, including two large rotating six-barrel weapons that once fired 40kg shells. There's also a communications bunker, which you can enter if you have a torch or lantern.

Food & Drink

Black noddy bird This bird with the notable strange cry is a local delicacy.

Demangi The island's take on fermented toddy, made from coconut palm sap.

Seafood Catch your own marlin, yellow-fin tuna, barracuda and more with the island's fishermen, for a fresh seafood barbecue.

Former Presidents' House

2 Check out the view from the ruins of the once-splendid former Presidents' House, burned down in 2001 by a local mob who were furious at the government's mismanagement of funds. It might make you take the opportunity to ponder any potential lessons on the exploitation of finite natural resources.

Cantilevers

3 The first shipment of 2000 tonnes of phosphate left Nauru in 1907. By 1908 vast industrial architecture began to be installed. Between the world wars, the first of two huge cantilevers was built on the coast, enabling phosphate to be loaded onto ships more efficiently. After WWII demand for phosphate rose and by the 1960s a second cantilever was in operation.

When to Go

NOV–FEB
➡ Rainiest time of year.
➡ Highest number of days over 32°C.

MAR–OCT
➡ Best time to visit.
➡ Average coastal sea temperature is over 28°C.

YEAR-ROUND
➡ Hot and humid with an average temperature of 25°C.

Ama Dablam

CAPITAL
Kathmandu

POPULATION
30.4 million

AREA
147,181 sq km

**OFFICIAL
LANGUAGE**
Nepali

Nepal

Wedged between the high wall of the Himalaya and the steamy jungles of the Indian plains, Nepal is a land of snowy peaks and Sherpas, yaks and yetis, monasteries and mantras.

Ever since Nepal first opened its borders to outsiders in the 1950s, this tiny mountain nation has had an irresistible mystical allure for travellers. Today, legions of trekkers are drawn to the Himalaya's most iconic and accessible hiking, some of the world's best, with rugged trails to Everest, the Annapurnas and beyond. Nowhere else can you trek for days or even weeks in incredible mountain scenery, secure in the knowledge that a hot meal, cosy lodge and warm slice of apple pie await you at the end of the day. Nepal is nirvana for mountain lovers.

Other travellers prefer to see Nepal at a more gentle pace, admiring the peaks over a gin and tonic from a Himalayan viewpoint, strolling through the temple-lined medieval city squares of Kathmandu, Patan and Bhaktapur, and joining Buddhist pilgrims on a spiritual stroll around centuries-old stupas and temples that lie scattered across the Kathmandu Valley.

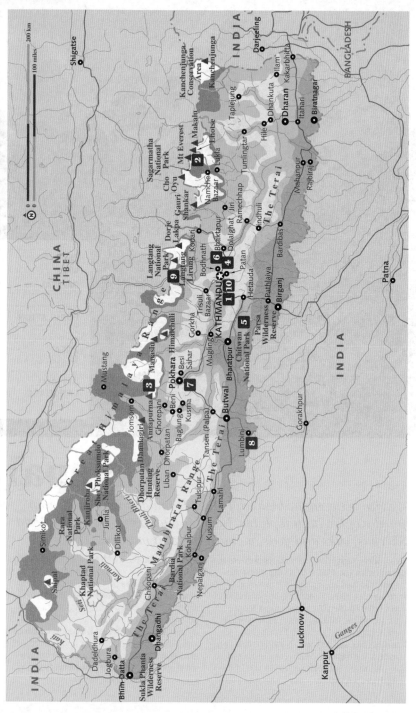

Nepal's
Top Experiences

Kathmandu's Durbar Square

1 The historic centre of old Kathmandu is an open-air architectural museum of magnificent medieval temples, pagodas, pavilions and shrines. Once occupied by Nepal's cloistered royal family and still home to the Kumari, Kathmandu's very own living goddess, Durbar Sq is very much the sacred heart of the city and the backdrop to several spec-tacular festivals. For the best approach to the square, wander through the hidden backstreet courtyards and temples of the surrounding warren-like old town.

Everest Base Camp Trek

2 Topping many people's travel bucket list is this two-week-long trek to the base of the world's highest, and most hyped, mountain. The actual views of the mountain are partial at best but the surrounding Himalayan peaks are truly awesome, and the half-hour you spend watching the alpenglow ascend beautiful Pumori or Ama Dablam peaks is worth all the altitude headaches you will doubtless suffer. The crowds can be thick in October but the welcome at the Sherpa lodges is as warm as the fresh apple pie that is served.

Annapurna Circuit Trek

3 This 19-day hike around the 8091m Annapurna massif is Nepal's most popular trek, and it's easy to see why. The lodges are comfortable, the mountain scenery is superb, the crossing of the 5416m Thorung La provides a physical challenge and the sense of journey from lowland to Trans-Himalayan plateau is immensely satisfying. Our best tip is to take your time and explore the spectacular side trips, particularly around Manang. Road construction may have eaten away at the western sections around Jomsom, but some spectacular alternative footpaths continue to avoid the road.

Bhaktapur & the Kathmandu Valley

4 The Kathmandu Valley boasts the world's densest collection of World Heritage Sites. Of the valley's three former cities, all Unesco sites, medieval Bhaktapur is easily the most intact and is bursting with temples, pagodas and ornate pools. Winding backstreets of traditional red-brick buildings lead onto squares used by locals for drying corn and making pottery. The traffic-free streets offer fabulous scope for exploration on foot. For the full experience, stay overnight in a guesthouse or attend one of the city's fantastic festivals.

Elephant Safari, Chitwan National Park

5 In the 'other Nepal', down in the humid plains, Chitwan is one of Asia's best wildlife-viewing spots and the place to don your safari togs, clamber atop a lumbering elephant and head into the dawn mist in search of rhinos and tigers. There's plenty to keep you busy here, from joining the elephants at bath time to visiting local Tharu villages, and the brave can even take a guided walk through the jungle, surrounded by the hoots and roars of the forest.

Bodhnath Stupa

6 The village of Bodhnath is the centre of Nepal's Tibetan community and home to Asia's largest stupa, a spectacular white

if Nepal were 100 people

16 would be Chhetri
13 would be Brahman-Hill
7 would be Magar
7 would be Tharu
57 would be other

belief systems

(% of population)

81 Hindu
9 Buddhist
4 Muslim
3 Kirant
1 Christian
2 other

population per sq km

NEPAL   INDIA   USA

↑ ≈ 30 people

Gurkhas

Every year hundreds of young men from across Nepal come to Pokhara to put themselves through the rigorous selection process to become a Gurkha soldier.

Prospective recruits must perform a series of backbreaking physical tasks, including a 5km uphill run carrying 25kg of rocks in a traditional doko basket. Only the most physically fit and mentally dedicated individuals make it through – it is not unheard of for recruits to keep on running with broken bones in their determination to get selected.

Identified by their curved khukuri knives, Gurkhas are still considered one of the toughest fighting forces in the world. British Gurkhas have carried out peacekeeping missions in Afghanistan, Bosnia and Sierra Leone, and Gurkha soldiers also form elite units of the Indian Army, the Singapore Police Force and the personal bodyguard of the sultan of Brunei.

Food & Drink

Beer Local brands include Gorkha, Everest and Kathmandu Beer. Tuborg (Danish), Carlsberg (Danish) and San Miguel (Spanish) are brewed in Nepal under licence.

Daal bhaat tarkari Lentil soup, rice and curried vegetables. If you are lucky it will be spiced up with *achar* (pickles) and maybe some *chapati* (unleavened Indian bread), *dahi* (curd or yoghurt) or *papad* (pappadam – crispy fried lentil-flour pancake).

Juju dhau Anyone who visits Bhaktapur should try the *juju dhau* (king of curds), wonderfully creamy thick yoghurt.

Momos Meat-or vegetable-filled dumplings.

Sikarni A popular traditional dessert of whipped yoghurt with cinnamon, nuts and dried fruit.

CRAIG FERGUSON / GETTY IMAGES ©

dome and spire that draws pilgrims from hundreds of kilometres away. Equally fascinating are the surrounding streets, bustling with monks with shaved heads and maroon robes, and lined with Tibetan monasteries and shops selling prayer wheels and incense. Come at dusk and join the Tibetan pilgrims as they light butter lamps and walk around the stupa on their daily *kora* (ritual circumambulation).

Views from Pokhara

7 Nepal's second-biggest tourist town may lack the historical depth of Kathmandu, but it more than makes up for this with a seductively laid-back vibe and one of the country's most spectacular locations. The dawn views of Machhapuchhare and Annapurna, mirrored in the calm waters of Phewa Tal or seen from the town's hilltop viewpoints, are simply unforgettable. Take them in on a trek, from the saddle of a mountain bike or from a paraglider.

When to Go

HIGH SEASON (Oct–Nov)

➡ Clear skies and warm days make autumn the peak season. Thousands of people hit the trails in the Everest and Annapurna regions and accommodation in Kathmandu gets booked up as prices peak.

SHOULDER (Mar–Apr)

➡ The second-best time to visit brings warm weather and spectacular springtime rhododendron blooms.

LOW SEASON (Jun–Sep)

➡ The monsoon rains bring landslides and clouds obscure mountain views, though hefty hotel discounts are common. Rain and leeches deter most trekkers, but this is a popular time to travel overland to Tibet.

Lumbini – Birthplace of the Buddha

8 A pilgrimage to the birthplace of the Buddha ranks as one of the subcontinent's great spiritual journeys. You can visit the exact spot where Siddhartha Gautama was born 2500 years ago, rediscovered only a century or so ago, and then tour the multinational collection of temples built by neighbouring Buddhist nations. But perhaps the most powerful thing to do is simply find a quiet spot, and a book on Buddhism, and meditate on the nature of existence. Travel experiences don't get much more profound than that.

Langtang Trekking

9 If you have only a week but want to get a taste of Nepali-style trekking, it's hard to beat the Langtang region, which borders Tibet. The scenery ranges from steep hillsides of bamboo and rhododendrons to sprawling yak pastures and finally an alpine cul de sac framed by 7000m peaks. You can even get fresh yak-cheese toasted sandwiches along the way. There are also plenty of trekking add-ons here, including walks to the sacred lakes of Gosainkund and through the charming traditional villages of the Tamang Heritage Trail.

Getting Around

Getting around in Nepal can be a challenging business. Because of the terrain, the weather conditions and the condition of vehicles, few trips go exactly according to plan. Nepali ingenuity will usually get you to your destination in the end, but build plenty of time into your itinerary and treat the delays and mishaps as part of the rich tapestry that is Nepal. And bring lots of snacks.

Walking is still the most common method of getting from A to B in Nepal, particularly in the mountains where there are no roads and few airstrips. Elsewhere, people get around on buses, jeeps, motorcycles, trains and planes that seem to be held together more by faith than mechanical integrity.

The wise traveller avoids going anywhere during major festivals when buses, flights and hotels are booked solid.

Nepal's Fantastic Festivals

10 Nepal has so many spectacular festivals that any visit is almost certain to coincide with one. Celebrations range from masked dances designed to exorcise bad demons to epic bouts of tug-of-war. For a full-on medieval experience, time your travel with one of the slightly mad chariot processions, when hundreds of enthusiastic devotees drag tottering 20m-tall chariots through the crowded city streets of Kathmandu and Patan.

Best on Film

Everest (1998; David Breashears) Imax film shot during the disastrous 1997 climbing season.

Himalaya (1999; Eric Valli) Stunningly shot in Dolpo; also released as *Caravan*.

Best in Print

Arresting God in Kathmandu (Samrat Upadhyay) Nine short stories from the first Nepali writer to be published in English.

Little Princes (Connor Grennan) Moving and inspiring account of volunteering in a Nepali orphanage.

Snake Lake (Jeff Greenwald) Memoir of family loss set against Nepal's political revolution.

The Snow Leopard (Peter Matthiessen) Classic and profound account of a trek to Dolpo.

Tiji Festival, Lo Manthang

GRANT DIXON / GETTY IMAGES ©

Delft

| CAPITAL |
| Amsterdam |
| POPULATION |
| 16.8 million |
| AREA |
| 41,543 sq km |
| OFFICIAL LANGUAGE |
| Dutch |

The Netherlands

Discover the many secrets of this gently beautiful country and its masterpieces, canal towns and windmills. Revel in the welcoming yet wry culture at a cafe, then bike past fields of tulips.

Great Dutch artists Rembrandt, Vermeer and Van Gogh have spanned the centuries, and touring the Netherlands you'll see why. Discover clichés such as tulips and windmills, or stroll canals in the midst of 17th-century splendour in beautiful small towns such as Leiden and Delft. Of course, enticing Amsterdam's phenomenal and diverse nightlife is world-famous, from its throbbing clubs to quaint brown cafes.

The locals live on bicycles and you can too. Almost every train station has a shop to rent a bike – you'll soon be off on the ubiquitous bike paths, wherever your mood takes you.

Finally there's the Dutch themselves. Warm, friendly and funny, you'll have a hard time being alone in a cafe as someone will soon strike up a conversation, and usually in English. Revel in Amsterdam, don't miss exquisite Maastricht or pulsing Rotterdam, and pick a passel of small towns to add contrast. It's a very big small country.

The Netherlands'
Top Experiences

Wandering Amsterdam's Canals

1 Amsterdam has more canals than Venice, and getting on the water is one of the best ways to feel the pulse of the city. Catch the vibe by sitting canalside and watching boats glide by: myriad cafes seem purpose-built for this sport. Or you could stroll along the canals and check out some of the city's 3300 houseboats. Better yet, hop on a tour boat and cruise the curved passages. From this angle, you'll understand why Unesco named the 400-year-old waterways a World Heritage site.

Admiring Dutch Masterpieces

2 The Netherlands has produced a helluva lot of famous artists. In Amsterdam, the Van Gogh Museum hangs the world's largest collection by tortured native son Vincent. Vermeer's *Kitchen Maid*, Rembrandt's *Night Watch* and other Golden Age masterpieces fill the mighty Rijksmuseum, while the Stedelijk Museum shows Mondrian, de Kooning and other homeboys among its edgy modern stock. Outside the capital, the Frans Hals Museum collects the painter's works in Haarlem, and the Mauritshuis unfurls a who's who of Dutch masters in Den Haag.

Rijksmuseum, Amsterdam

MERTEN SNIJDERS / GETTY IMAGES ©

Day Tripping to Delft

3 The Netherlands has no shortage of evocative old towns. Haarlem, Leiden and Utrecht are just some of the more well known. With their old canals lined with buildings whose human-scaled architecture is nothing but characterful, these towns bring the beauty of the Golden Age into the modern age. But one old canal town shines above the rest: Delft. Even if you're not staying here, an afternoon spent along its canals, churches, museums and just sitting in a cafe soaking it all in is essential time spent.

if the Netherlands were 100 people

81 would be Dutch
5 would be European
3 would be Indonesian

2 would be Turkish
2 would be Moroccan
7 would be other

belief systems

(% of population)

25 Roman Catholic
15 Protestant
5 Muslim
4 other
51 none

population per sq km

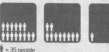

NETHERLANDS   BELGIUM   USA

♦ ≈ 35 people

Best Park in the Netherlands

4 A vast swathe of beautiful land that was once private hunting ground, Hoge Veluwe National Park combines forests, sand dunes, marshes and ponds. It's a bucolic escape from the densely packed cities and you can easily spend a day here just luxuriating in nature. But wait, there's more! At the park's centre, the Kröller-Müller Museum is one of the nation's best. Its Van Gogh collection rivals that of the namesake museum in Amsterdam, plus there is a stunning sculpture garden.

Revelling in Maastricht

5 The city where Europe's common currency began has been a meeting place for centuries. The Romans built underground forts here that you can still explore, and every generation since has left its mark. But 2000 years of history, monuments, ruins, churches and museums aside, where Maastricht really shines is in how it embraces the moment. Few places in the Netherlands have such a densely packed collection of alluring cafes great and small, filled with people enjoying every minute of life along with good food and drink.

Enjoying Cheesy Delights

6 Whether it is cubed or melted, sliced on a sandwich or shaved onto a salad, you cannot escape Dutch cheese. Names like Gouda and Edam inspire more notions of curdled milk than images of the municipalities that spawned them. And forget the bland stuff

By the Numbers

The Dutch have a great love of detail. Statistics on the most trivial subjects make the paper and somewhere down the line this feeds mountains of bureaucracy.

Secondly, the Dutch are the tallest people in the world, averaging 1.81m for men and 1.68m for women. Copious intake of milk proteins, smaller families and superior prenatal care are cited as likely causes. Whatever the reason, the Dutch keep growing, as do their doorways!

Last but not least, the Dutch are famously thrifty with their money – and they often don't know what to think of this. In one breath they might joke about how copper wire was invented by two Dutchmen fighting over a penny, and in the next, tell you that they don't like being called cheap.

Food & Drink

Beer While the big names like Heineken are ubiquitous, small brewers like Gulpen, Haarlem's Jopen, Bavaria, Drie Ringen, Leeuw and Utrecht are the best.

Erwtensoep Pea soup rich with onions, carrots, smoked sausage and bacon. Ideally a spoon stuck upright in the pot should remain standing (not served in summer).

Gouda The tastiest varieties have strong, complex flavours and are best enjoyed with a bottle of wine or two.

Indonesian The most famous dish is *rijsttafel* (rice table): an array of spicy savoury dishes such as braised beef, pork satay and ribs served with white rice.

Kroketten Croquettes are dough balls with various fillings that are crumbed and deep-fried; the variety called *bitterballen* are a popular brown cafe snack served with mustard.

Vlaamse frites The iconic French fries smothered in mayonnaise or myriad other gooey sauces.

REZA ESTAKHRIAN / GETTY IMAGES ©

you find in the supermarket, Dutch cheese comes in a vast range of styles and flavours. Start with the caraway-seed-infused variety. Next consider one of the aged goudas that is crystallised like a fine parmesan and is best had with a touch of mustard – perhaps from the cheese market in Gouda itself.

When to Go

HIGH SEASON
(Jun–Aug)

➡ Everything is open.

➡ The odds of balmy weather to enjoy a cafe or a countryside bike ride are best – but not assured.

➡ Crowds fill the famous museums.

➡ Prices peak, book ahead.

SHOULDER
(Apr, May, Sep & Oct)

➡ Most sights open and few crowds.

➡ Prices moderate, only book popular places in Amsterdam.

➡ Weather mixes the good with wet and cold. Bring warm clothes for outdoors.

LOW SEASON
(Nov–Mar)

➡ Many sights outside of major cities closed.

➡ It may just be you and a masterpiece at a famous museum.

➡ Weather cold and/ or wet, biking is only for the hardy.

➡ Deals abound.

Island Charms on Texel

7 The vast Waddenzee region, where northwest Europe almost imperceptibly melts into the sea, is recognized by Unesco as a World Heritage Site. These tidal mudflats with their hypnotic charm are punctuated by a string of offshore islands. The largest, Texel, offers endless walks on beautiful beaches, almost limitless activities and a stark beauty you can appreciate on land or on a wildlife-spotting boat trip. And when you're ready for a pause, it has inspired places to stay and some very fine food – you won't believe the smoked fish.

Savouring Amsterdam's Brown Cafes

8 It means convivial but not quite. It also means friendly but still not quite. Snug, cosy and good-humoured all apply as well. Kind of. *Gezelligheid* is the uniquely Dutch trait that is best experienced in one of the country's famous brown cafes. Named for their aged, tobacco-stained walls or just plain oldness, these small bars are filled with good cheer. It takes little time, on even your first visit, to be drawn into the cheery warmth and welcome of their *gezelligheid*.

Best on Film

Oorlogswinter (directed by Martin Koolhoven; 2008) Voted by Dutch critics as the top film of 2008. A young boy's integrity and loyalty is tested when he decides to help the Dutch Resistance shelter a downed British pilot.

Zwartboek (directed by Paul Verhoeven; 2006) This action-packed story explores some of the less heroic aspects of the Dutch Resistance in WWII. It launched the career of today's hottest Dutch actor, Carice van Houten.

Best in Print

Netherland (Joseph O'Neill; 2008) When a Dutch man faces the breakdown of his marriage in post–9/11 New York, memories of the Netherlands, cricket and a mysterious friendship complicate his life, yet repair his spirit, in this comically dark novel.

The Diary of Anne Frank (Anne Frank; 1952) A moving account of a young girl's thoughts and yearnings while in hiding from the Nazis in Amsterdam. The book has been translated into 60 languages.

Getting Around

Bicycle One of the best reasons to visit is to ride bikes. Short- and long-distance bike routes lace the country and you are often pedalling through beautiful areas. All but the smallest train stations have bike shops to rent bikes as do most towns and all cities.

Boat Ferries connect the mainland with the five Frisian Islands. Passenger ferries span the Westerschelde in the south of Zeeland. Many more minor services provide links across the myriad of Dutch canals and waterways.

Train Service is fast, distances are short and trains are frequent. Buying tickets is sometimes a challenge but once aboard, the rides can be lovely; in the spring trains in and around Leiden pass through gorgeous bulbfields.

Cycling the Countryside

9 Grab a bike and go. You can rent them anywhere and no nation on earth is better suited for cycling. Not only is it flat but there are thousands of kilometres of bike lanes and paths linking virtually every part of the country, no matter how small. For a classic day trip, head out from Rotterdam to Kinderdijk to see the heritage-listed windmills – kept here in operating condition – then enjoy the scenery from a different angle on the fast ferry back into town.

Rotterdam's Dramatic New Look

10 Unlike many European cities that emerged from the ashes of WWII with hastily reconstructed city centres, Rotterdam pursued a different path from the start. Its architecture is striking rather than functional and it has a rarity for Europe: an identifiable skyline. The world's best architects compete here for commissions that result in artful – often daring – designs. The Erasmusbrug, a birdlike bridge, is a city icon and is surrounded by buildings that are both bold and beautiful to contemplate.

Cube houses, Rotterdam

ALLAN BAXTER / GETTY IMAGES © / ARCHITECT: PIET BLOM

Tjibaou Cultural Centre, Noumea

CAPITAL
Noumea

POPULATION
264,000

AREA
18,575 sq km

OFFICIAL LANGUAGES
French, Melanesian-Polynesian dialects

New Caledonia

Dazzling – yes, New Caledonia is dazzling. Its lagoon surrounds it with every colour of blue. So the light and the space delight your senses.

The prestigious listing of the lagoon as a World Heritage site in 2008 has brought the people together to celebrate and protect it, from village level through to the government.

New Caledonia isn't just a tropical playground. There's a charming mix of French and Melanesian: warm hospitality sitting beside European elegance, gourmet food beneath palm trees, sand, resorts, bungalows, concrete, bamboo. Long gorgeous beaches are backed by cafes and bars, with horizons that display tiny islets to attract day trippers. Be lured into kayaks, rock climb, sail, dive into a world of corals, canyons, caves and heritage shipwrecks, go whale watching or snorkelling, or relax on the warm sands of a deserted isle. Natural wonders and manmade delights are at your fingertips.

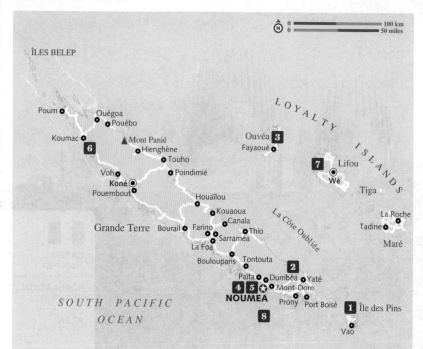

New Caledonia's
Top Experiences

Île des Pins

1 A tranquil paradise of turquoise bays, white-sand beaches and tropical vegetation, Île des Pins (Isle of Pines) is also a haunting place where dark caves hide in the forest and the bush invades the crumbling ruins of a convict prison. The Kuniés, as the island's inhabitants are known, have kept alive the tradition of sailing pirogues, and you'll see these ancient craft gliding elegantly across the calm lagoon.

Grande Terre's
Far South

2 The far south feels like a remote wilderness. The vast, empty region is characterised by its hardy scrub vegetation and red soil, and offers a wide range of activities including hiking, kayaking, abseiling and mountain biking. If you are looking for a bit of action and adventure, head to the far south. If you're looking for a peaceful, isolated spot by a river, head to the far south.

Ouvéa

3 Think 25km of long perfect white beach backed with grass and wild tropical flowers. Look further out, over an exquisite lagoon stretching as far as you can see. Add a chain of tiny islets, the Pléiades. Sound unreal? Nope. It's just Ouvéa. Admire the coral reefs, lunching on freshly caught fish then feeding a nearby shark colony.

Noumea

4 With its cheerful multi-ethnic community, New Caledonia's cosmopolitan capital is both sophisticated and uncomplicated, classy and casual. The relaxed city sits on a large peninsula, surrounded by picturesque bays, and offers visitors a variety of experiences. Diners can eat out at sassy French restaurants hidden in the Latin Quarter, dine at bold water-fronting bistros or grab a bargain meal from a nocturnal van in a car park. Meanwhile, shopaholics can blow their savings on the latest Parisian fashions or go bargain hunting for imported Asian textiles.

Baie d'Oro, Île des Pins

Nightlife in Noumea

5 Dance till the early hours at an over-water disco in Noumea – it's fun, bright and as close to the water as you can get without getting wet. The nightlife mostly happens naturally: the buzz along Baie des Citrons as young people and music fill the bars and spill across to the beach; the slightly older group that park their cars along the Anse Vata foreshore and make the most of the heavenly nights and music drifting or beating across the bay.

Grande Terre's Northwest Coast

6 Drive up to the wild northwest coast of the Grande Terre and don a cowboy attitude for a night at a farmstay. Much of the northwest coast and its rolling plains are taken up by cattle ranches so it makes more sense to head inland for horse trekking or staying on a Caldoche farm or in a Kanak homestay. Head to Koné and around for guided horse treks into the foothills or to the summits of the central mountain range.

Scuba Diving

7 Dive in at any of the World Heritage–listed lagoon's terrific sites off Grande Terre, or try the Loyalty Islands where Lifou has a number of signature sites. Here you can go diving

if New Caledonia were 100 people

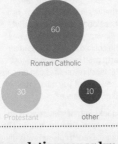

44 would be Melanesian (Kanak)
34 would be European
9 would be Wallisian and Futunian
13 would be other

belief systems
(% of population)

60
Roman Catholic

30
Protestant

10
other

population per sq km

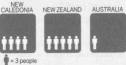

NEW CALEDONIA   NEW ZEALAND   AUSTRALIA

≈ 3 people

When to Go

APR–MAY

➡ Fresh from the heat and rains, the country is sparkling again.

JULY

➡ It may be too cool for beach-goers, but that bodes well for hikers.

OCT–NOV

➡ Catch life on the islands before folk head off on their annual summer vacation.

Kanak Grande Case

The *grande case* (chief's hut) is one of the strongest symbols of the Kanak community. It was traditionally home to the chief. Nowadays the *grande case* is the political centre of the district where the chief, who inherits his position, gathers with the village representatives to discuss the running of the community and affairs they want discussed in parliament.

Where possible, the *grande case* is built on a knoll above the rest of the village. The central pillar, an immense tree trunk, is erected first. It will support the entire *case* and symbolises the chief. A stone hearth is laid between the central pillar and the entrance which is via a low doorway flanked by carved posts.

Inside, the walls and ceiling are lined with wooden posts or beams, lashed to the frame with strong vines, all of which lean against the central pillar to symbolise the clan's close link to the chief. Finally, the roof is topped with a *flèche faîtière*, a carved wooden spear that becomes home to ancestral spirits.

Food & Drink

Bougna The Melanesian speciality – yam, sweet potato, taro, other vegetables and meat, fish or seafood covered in coconut milk, wrapped in banana leaves and cooked on hot stones in an earth oven for two hours. Most Melanesian-run *gîtes* can prepare a *bougna* but you must order 24 hours in advance.

Snacks Eateries where you can really appreciate the flare and flavour of French cuisine: everything is prepared with delicious sauces and marinades. Take the simple sandwich. It's a very long, crusty baguette with leg ham dripping out the sides, or perhaps a home-made terrine stacked inside.

Phare Amédée lighthouse, Amédée Islet

around unique cliff faces and sheltered coral massifs, such as the Shoji and Gorgones reefs. Night dives are also a great way to explore the amazing underwater world

Islands off Noumea

8 The waters around Noumea are sprinkled with beautiful islets. Most are marine reserves and the clear waters surrounding them are great for snorkelling. Amédée Islet, about 20km south of Noumea, is famous for its tall white lighthouse, Phare Amédée, which was built in France, shipped out in pieces, and assembled on the postcard island in 1865. Climb up its spiral staircase to a narrow shelf with 360-degree views. Île aux Canards and Îlot Maître are the cutest postcard-perfect poppets of islets. You can see them just a swim out from Anse Vata, sitting 2km and 1km offshore. Kite surfing is extremely popular on Îlot Maître.

Getting Around

Air New Caledonia's domestic airline is Air Calédonie which flies out of Magenta domestic airport in Noumea to Koné, Koumac, Loyalty Islands and Île des Pins.

Bicycle You have to be pretty eager to cycle round 400km-long Grande Terre. However, Ouvéa and Île des Pins are ideal for cycling. Bikes can be transported on the *Betico* and *Havannah* ferries.

Boat The *Betico*, a fast passenger ferry, sails from Noumea to Île des Pins and between the Loyalty Islands. The MV *Havannah*, a cargo boat, travels from Noumea to Lifou via Maré.

Bus Nearly every town on Grande Terre is connected to the capital by bus, all leaving from Noumea's old *gare routière*.

Mitre Peak, Milford Sound

CAPITAL
Wellington

POPULATION
4.4 million

AREA
267, 710 sq km

OFFICIAL LANGUAGE
Maori, English

New Zealand

Plucked straight from a film set or a coffee-table book of picture-perfect scenery, New Zealand is jaw-droppingly gorgeous. 'Wow!' will escape from your lips at least once a day.

New Zealand is bigger than the UK with one-fourteenth the population. Filling in the gaps are the sublime forests, mountains, lakes, beaches and fiords that have made NZ one of the best hiking (locals call it 'tramping') destinations on the planet. Tackle one of nine epic 'Great Walks' or just spend a few dreamy hours wandering through some easily accessible wilderness.

NZ chefs find inspiration in new-world culinary oceans, especially the Pacific with its abundant seafood. Thirsty? NZ's cool-climate wineries have been collecting wine-award trophies for decades now, but the country's booming craft-beer scene also deserves your serious scrutiny. And with coffee culture firmly entrenched, you can usually find a decent double-shot. See how Maori culture impresses itself on contemporary Kiwi life: across NZ you can hear Maori language, watch traditional Maori song, dance and usually a blood-curdling haka (war dance), visit *marae* (meeting houses) or join in a hangi (Maori feast).

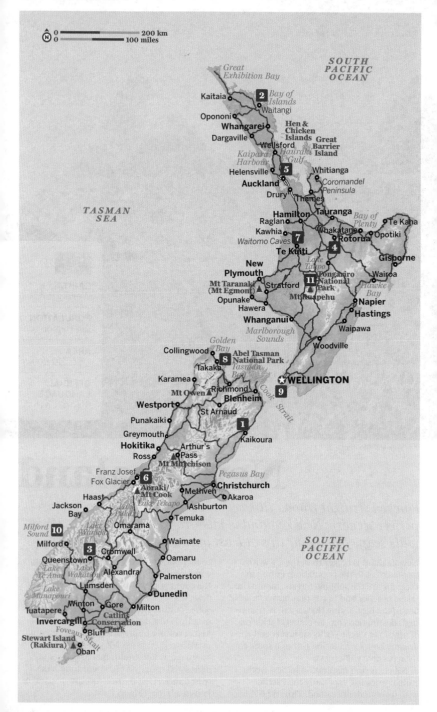

New Zealand's
Top Experiences

Kaikoura

1 First settled by Maori with their keen nose for seafood, Kaikoura is a pretty peninsula town backed by the snowcapped peaks of the Seaward Kaikoura Range. There are few places in the world with so much wildlife around: whales, dolphins, NZ fur seals, penguins, shearwaters, petrels and wandering albatross all stop by or make this area home. When it comes to 'seafood and eat it', crayfish is still king, but on fishing tours you can try other edible wonders of the deep.

Bay of Islands

2 Turquoise waters lapping in pretty bays, dolphins frolicking at the bows of boats, pods of orcas gliding gracefully by: chances are these are the kind of images that drew you to New Zealand in the first place, and the Bay of Islands will deliver them so well. Whether you're a hardened sea dog or a confirmed landlubber, there are myriad options to tempt you out on the water to explore the 150-odd islands that dot this beautiful bay, from subtropical diving to kayaking or sailing.

School of dusky dolphins, Kaikoura

KIM WESTERSKOV / GETTY IMAGES ©

Queenstown

3 Queenstown may be renowned as the birthplace of bungy jumping, but there's more to NZ's adventure hub than leaping off a bridge attached to a giant rubber band. Against the jagged indigo profile of the Remarkables mountain range, travellers can spend days skiing, hiking or mountain biking, before dining in cosmopolitan restaurants or partying in some of NZ's best bars. Next-day options include hang gliding, kayaking or river rafting, or a detour to Arrowtown or Glenorchy.

Skyline Luge track, Ben Lomond Scenic Reserve, Queenstown

Geothermal Rotorua

4 The first thing you'll notice about Rotorua is the sulphur smell – this geothermal hot spot whiffs like old socks. But as the locals point out, volcanic by-products are what everyone is here to see: gushing geysers, bubbling mud, steaming cracks in the ground, boiling pools of mineral-rich water... Rotorua is unique, There are some fairly commercial local businesses, but you don't have to spend a fortune – there are plenty of affordable volcanic encounters to be had in parks, Maori villages or just along the roadside.

if New Zealand were 100 people

69 would be European
14 would be Maori
9 would be Asian
7 would be Pacific Islanders
1 would be other

where they live
(% of New Zealanders)

63 North Island
20 South Island
10 Australia
5 rest of the world
2 travelling

population per sq km

NEW ZEALAND
AUSTRALIA
USA

≈ 3 people

Auckland Harbour & the Hauraki Gulf

5 The island-studded Hauraki Gulf is Auckland's aquatic playground, sheltering its harbour and east-coast bays and providing ample excuse for the City of Sails' pleasure fleet to breeze into action. Despite the maritime traffic, the gulf has resident pods of whales and dolphins. Rangitoto is an icon of the city, its near-perfect volcanic cone the backdrop for many a tourist snapshot. Yet it's Waiheke, with beautiful beaches, acclaimed wineries and upmarket eateries, that is Auckland's most popular island escape.

Franz Josef & Fox Glaciers

6 The spectacular glaciers of Franz Josef and Fox are remarkable for many reasons, including their rates of accumulation and descent, and their proximity to both the loftiest peaks of the Southern Alps and the Tasman Sea around 10km away. Several short walks meander towards the glaciers' fractured faces (close enough for you to feel insignificant!), or you can take a guided hike on the ice. The ultimate encounter is on a scenic flight, which often also provides grandstand views of Mt Cook, Westland forest and a seemingly endless ocean.

Waitomo Caves

7 Waitomo is a must-see: an astonishing maze of subterranean caves, canyons and rivers perforating the northern King Country limestone. The name Waitomo comes from *wai* (water) and *tomo* (hole) Black-water rafting is the big lure here (like white-water rafting but through a dark

Pounamu

Maoris consider *pounamu* (greenstone, or jade or nephrite) to be a culturally invaluable raw material. It's found predominantly on the west coast of the South Island – Maoris called the island *Te Wahi Pounamu* (The Place of Greenstone) or *Te Wai Pounamu* (The Water of Greenstone).

One of the most popular Maori *pounamu* motifs is the *hei tiki*, the name of which literally means 'hanging human form'. They are tiny, stylised Maori figures worn on a leather string or chain around the neck. They've got great *mana* (power), but they also serve as fertility symbols.

Traditionally, pounamu is bought as a gift for another person, not for yourself.

Food & Drink

If you haven't been down to your local liquor store in the last decade, you might have missed the phenomenon that is New Zealand wine: a pristine environment, abundant sunshine, volcanic soils and passionate wine-makers have been busy bottling world-beating cool-climate drops.

Gibbston Valley Negotiate a tasty pathway through the vineyards of this meandering river valley near Queenstown.

Hawke's Bay One of NZ's oldest and most established wine areas is still one of the country's best.

Marlborough The country's biggest and best wine region keeps on turning out superb sauvignon blanc.

Martinborough A small-but-sweet day-trip from Wellington: easy cycling and easy-drinking pinot noir.

Waiheke Island Auckland's favourite weekend playground has a hot, dry microclimate: perfect for Bordeaux-style reds and rosés.

Champagne Pool, Wai-O-Tapu, Rotorua

cave), plus glowworm grottoes, underground abseiling and more stalactites and stalagmites than you'll ever see in one place again. Above ground, Waitomo township is a quaint collaboration of businesses: a pub, a cafe, a holiday park and some decent B&Bs. But don't linger in the sunlight – it's party time downstairs!

Abel Tasman National Park

8 Here's nature at its most seductive: lush green hills fringed with golden sandy coves, slipping gently into warm shallows before meeting a crystal-clear sea of cerulean blue. Abel Tasman National Park is the quintessential postcard paradise, where you can put yourself in the picture assuming an endless number of poses: tramping, kayaking, swimming, sunbathing, or even makin' whoopee in the woods. This sweet-as corner of NZ raises the bar and keeps it there.

When to Go

HIGH SEASON
(Dec–Feb)

➜ Summer: busy beaches, outdoor activities, festivals, sporting events.

➜ Big-city accommodation prices rise.

➜ High season in the ski towns is winter (Jun-Aug).

SHOULDER
(Mar–Apr)

➜ Prime travelling time: fine weather, short queues, kids in school, warm ocean.

➜ Long evenings to sip Kiwi wines and craft beers.

➜ Spring (Sep-Nov) is shoulder season too.

LOW SEASON
(May–Aug)

➜ Head for the Southern Alps for some brilliant skiing.

➜ No crowds, good accommodation deals and a seat in any restaurant.

➜ Warm-weather beach towns might be half asleep.

Wellington

9 Voted the 'coolest little capital in the world' by Lonely Planet in 2011, windy Wellington lives up to the mantle by keeping things fresh and dynamic. It's long famed for a vibrant arts and music scene, fuelled by excellent espresso and more restaurants per head than New York, but a host of craft-beer bars have now elbowed in on the action. Edgy yet sociable, colourful yet often dressed in black, Wellington is big on the unexpected and unconventional. Erratic weather only adds to the excitement.

Best on Film

Once Were Warriors (1994) Lee Tamahore's harrowing tale of an urban Maori family and the reality of domestic violence in New Zealand.

Sione's Wedding (2006) A feel-good comedy with the second-biggest local takings of any NZ film.

The Lord of the Rings trilogy (2001–03) A fantasy trilogy following a hobbit's quest, filmed in New Zealand.

The Piano (1993) A romantic drama set during the mid-19th century on the west coast of New Zealand, about a mute pianist and her daughter.

Best in Print

The Bone People (1988) Keri Hulme's Man Booker Prize–winning novel.

The Carpathians (1988) The last novel by popular author Janet Frame.

The Luminaries (2013) Eleanor Catton.

Under the Mountain (1979) Maurice Gee's much-loved children's fantasy novel.

Getting Around

Air Those who have limited time to get between NZ's attractions can make the most of a widespread network of intra- and inter-island flights.

Bus Bus travel in NZ is relatively easy and well organised, with services transporting you to the far reaches of both islands (including the start/end of various walking tracks), but it can be expensive, tedious and time-consuming.

Car & Motorcycle The best way to explore NZ in depth is to have your own wheels. It's easy to hire cars and campervans at good rates. Scanning the map you might think that driving from A to B won't take long, but remember that many of the roads here are two-lane country byways, so always allow plenty of time to get wherever you're going.

Train NZ train travel is about the journey, not about getting anywhere in a hurry.

Milford Sound

10 Fingers crossed you'll be lucky enough to see Milford Sound on a clear, sunny day. That's when the world-beating collage of waterfalls, verdant cliffs and peaks, and dark cobalt waters is at its best. More likely though is the classic Fiordland combination of mist and drizzle, with the iconic profile of Mitre Peak revealed slowly through shimmering sheets of precipitation.

Tongariro Alpine Crossing

11 At the centre of the North Island, Tongariro National Park presents an alien landscape of alpine desert punctuated by three smoking and smouldering volcanoes. This track offers the perfect taste of what the park has to offer – it's for these reasons that it's often rated as one of the world's best single-day wilderness walks.

Wellington Cable Car

OLIVER STREWE / GETTY IMAGES ©

Caribbean beach

CAPITAL
Managua

POPULATION
5.8 million

AREA
130,370 sq km

OFFICIAL LANGUAGE
Spanish

Nicaragua

Affable Nicaragua embraces travelers with offerings of volcanic landscapes, colonial architecture, sensational beaches and pristine forests that range from breathtaking to downright incredible.

There are few destinations with such beauty that are as undeveloped as Nicaragua. Before you know it, you've dropped off the tourist trail and into a world of majestic mountains, cooperative farms, wetlands thronged with wildlife and empty jungle-clad beaches. Forge on and discover remote indigenous communities, overgrown pre-Columbian ruins and untouched rainforests.

Nicaragua's diverse geography is perfect for exhilarating outdoor adventures. There are no signs, no crowds and no holding back.

From the crystalline Caribbean to the pounding Pacific, Nicaragua's beaches also deliver the goods. The big barrels of Rivas are revered in surfing circles while the clear waters of the Corn Islands are superb for snorkeling.

Nicaragua is not all action – its colonial splendor comes in two distinct, but equally appealing, flavors: the elegant streetscapes of Granada, Nicaragua's best-preserved colonial town, have an architectural grace, while less polished León is a vibrant city too busy to feel like a museum.

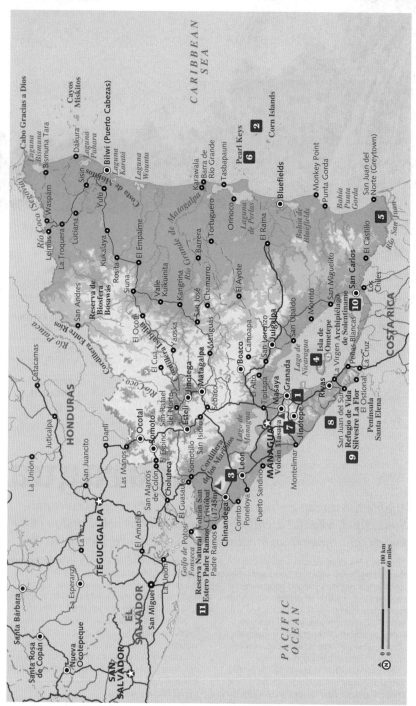

Nicaragua's
Top Experiences

Granada

1 Granada is a town of immense and palpable magnetism. At the heart of the city's charms are the picture-perfect cobblestone streets, polychromatic colonial homes and churches, and a lilting air that brings the city's spirited past into present-day tight focus. Most trips here begin and end on foot, and simply dawdling from gallery to restaurant to colonial church can take up the better part of a day. From there, you can head off to explore the myriad wild areas, islands, volcanoes and artisan villages nearby.

Little Corn Island

2 With no cars and no noise, just white-sand beaches and secluded coves mixing it with the crystal-clear Caribbean, Little Corn Island is the paramount place to take a break from the big city. There is plenty to keep you occupied during the day, including diving with hammerhead sharks and through underground caves, kitesurfing the stiff breeze and scrambling over jungle-covered headlands. And there's just enough to do at night, too. Add some great food to the mix and it's no surprise that many travelers find it so hard to leave.

Catedral de Granada

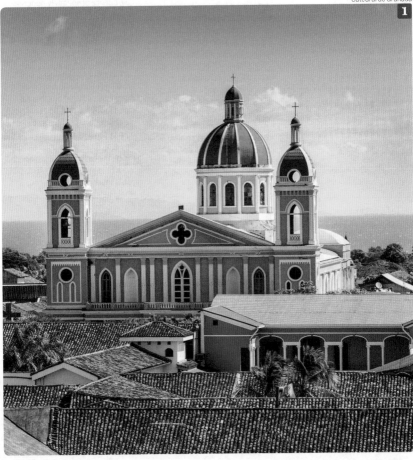

León

3 A royal city with revolutionary undercurrents, León both enchants and baffles. Within the city, you'll find an artsy, slightly edgy vibe originally fueled by the Sandinista revolution and now by the university and a 120-horsepower party scene. Come sunrise, you can spend a good day exploring the Catedral, museums and downtown area, before heading out to honeyblonde beaches, volcanoes and Old West cowboy towns.

Isla de Ometepe

4 Lago de Nicaragua's beloved centerpiece, Isla de Ometepe has it all: twin volcanoes, lush hillsides cut by walking tracks, archaeological remains, ziplines, monkeys and birdlife, waterfalls, lapping waves at your doorstep, and a laid-back island air that keeps travelers in the know as they make their way through this lost paradise found again. At the heart of the island's charms are the cool hostels, camping areas and peaced-out traveler scenes. Custom-fit your experience from high-end luxury lodges to groovy-groupie hippie huts.

Río San Juan

5 Once favored by pirates and prospectors as a path to riches, today the Río San Juan is exalted by nature lovers. All along the river, scores of birds nest on branches overhanging its slow surging waters while its lower reaches are dominated by the Reserva Biológica Indio-Maíz, a near impenetrable jungle that shelters jaguars and troupes of noisy monkeys. The only artificial attraction along the river's entire length is the grand Spanish fort over the rapids at El Castillo.

Pearl Keys

6 As you approach the dozen tiny islands ringed by snow-white sand and brilliant Caribbean waters that make up the Pearl Keys, you will enter the realms of the ultimate shipwreck fantasy. Fortunately, you'll be marooned with a capable Creole guide that will cook up a spectacular seafood meal and source ice-cold beers from a mysterious supply, leaving you more time to swim, snorkel, spot sea turtles, or just lie back in your hammock and take in the idyllic panoramic views.

Coffee Country

A visit to Nicaragua's coffee zone is about more than just sipping plenty of joe. It's about getting out and seeing where it all comes from.

More fiercely traded than any global commodity other than oil, black coffee makes up half of Nicaragua's exports and is the jittery engine upon which its economy turns. In 1999 coffee prices dropped below production costs. This prompted many of Nicaragua's farmers to try different methods of coffee production, including fair trade, which is now the fastest-growing segment of the coffee market. These growers may only make around US$2 per day, but in a desperately poor region where electricity and running water are luxuries, a more reliable price for their coffee means three meals a day – plus the chance to plan for the future.

You can visit Nicaragua's coffee-growing regions and hike among the bushes shaded by ethereal cloud forest, or pick ripe cherries alongside your hosts in a community farming cooperative. And why stop there when you can follow the beans to the roasting plant and learn to identify flavors. After this, you'll savor your morning cup in a whole new way.

if Nicaragua were 100 people

69 would identify as mestizo
17 would identify as white
9 would identify as black
5 would identify as indigenous

belief systems
(% of population)

59	23
Roman Catholic	Protestant
15	3
none	other

population per sq km

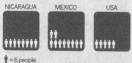

NICARAGUA   MEXICO   USA

♦ ≈ 6 people

Food & Drink

Baho Steamed beef, plantains and yucca.

Beer Local beers include Toña and Victoria, both light pilsners.

Flor de Caña The national rum.

Gallo pinto This dish of mixed rice and beans is a staple.

Nacatamles Banana-leaf packed with cornmeal and other goodness.

Quesillo Mozzarella and onions wrapped in a tortilla and topped with sour cream.

Rondón Coconut seafood stew served in the Caribbean.

JANE SWEENEY / GETTY IMAGES ©

Volcán Masaya

7 Hovering above the artisan villages of Nicaragua's Central Plateau, the smoldering Volcán Masaya and its surrounding national park are a highlight not to be missed by volcanophiles, nature lovers and adventure seekers alike. This is one of the region's most active volcanoes, and it's pretty exciting to see the sulfurous columns of gas billow toward the sky as you relish the million-dollar views. Fun short treks take you to lava caves and butterfly gardens. Come sunset, an eerie bat tour tops off your adventure.

Surfing near San Juan del Sur

8 Nicaragua sparked into international stardom on the wake of tanned-and-toned surfer dudes and dudettes. And the surfing scene north and south of regional hub San Juan del Sur remains cooled-back, reefed-out, soulful and downright brilliant. The stars of the scene are the long rideable waves that fit the bill for

When to Go

HIGH SEASON
(Dec–Apr)

➡ Prices increase by up to 25% in popular tourist spots.

➡ Make reservations in advance for beach-side accommodations.

➡ Hot, sunny and dry conditions throughout the country.

SHOULDER
(Nov)

➡ Rains ease throughout the Pacific but Caribbean still wet.

➡ Cool weather and green countryside make for best the trekking season.

➡ Coffee harvest in the northern region.

LOW SEASON
(May–Oct)

➡ Heavy rains make some roads in rural areas difficult to pass and mountain hiking trails slippery.

➡ Biggest swell on Pacific side pulls a crowd to the best breaks.

surfers of all abilities, but the chillaxed surf camps, beach parties and cool breezes add to the vibe, making a beach vacation here work for everybody in your crew.

Turtles at La Flor

9 Head to Nicaragua's southern Pacific coast between July and January to witness sea turtles by the thousands come to shore to lay their eggs at Refugio de Vida Silvestre La Flor. There's a decent beach here, as well, but the highlight is a night tour (generally from nearby San Juan del Sur), where, if you're lucky, you'll see a leatherback or olive ridley mama come to shore to lay her eggs at the end of

Best on Film

Carla's Song (1996) British bus driver falls for Nicaraguan dancer in exile in romantic drama with a political edge.

La Yuma (2009) Portrays the challenges facing a female boxer from Managua.

Palabras Magicas (2012) Modern Nicaragua, seen through the lens of a young filmmaker.

Walker (1987) Biopic of a megalomaniac with music by the late, great Joe Strummer.

Best in Print

Blood of Brothers (Stephen Kinzer; 1991) Fascinating account of revolution and war.

The Country Beneath My Skin (Gioconda Belli; 2000) Autobiography by revolutionary poet.

The Jaguar Smile (Salman Rushdie; 1987) Looks at the Sandinistas during the revolution.

Tycoon's War (Stephen Dando-Collins; 2009) Documents the epic battle between imperialists Vanderbilt and Walker.

Getting Around

Bicycle Long-distance cyclists praise Nicaragua's smooth, paved roads and wide shoulders. Bicycles are the most common form of private transport in the country and drivers are used to seeing them everywhere. However, the lax enforcement of speed limits and drink-driving legislation is an issue.

Boat Many destinations are accessible only, or most easily, by boat. Public *pangas* (small motorboat) are much more expensive than road transport.

Bus Bus service in Nicaragua is excellent if basic.

Car Driving is a wonderful way to see Pacific and central Nicaragua, but the roads on the Caribbean side are, for the most part, terrible

one of nature's most inspiring and remarkable journeys.

Islas Solentiname

10 Visit the Islas Solentiname in order to experience the magic of this remote jungle-covered archipelago where a community of exceptionally talented artists live and work among the wild animals that are their inspiration. It's a place where an enlightened priest inspired a village to construct a handsome church alive with the sounds of nature and shooting stars illuminate the speckled night sky. Even having been there, you'll struggle to believe it's real.

Reserva Natural Estero Padre Ramos

11 The Reserva Natural Estero Padre Ramos is a vast nature reserve located in the far northwestern corner of Nicaragua. The largest remaining mangrove forest in Central America, the reserve is home to ocelots, alligators and a universe's worth of birds. While this is a wild corner of Nicaragua, basic tourist services will get you into the spider-webbing mangrove forest, to the beaches where sea turtles lay their eggs and good surf dominates, and into local communities.

PICTUREGARDEN / GETTY IMAGES ©

Grand Mosque, Niamey

CAPITAL
Niamey

POPULATION
16.9 million

AREA
1.2 million sq km

OFFICIAL LANGUAGE
French

Niger

Niger is dominated by two of Africa's most iconic natural features, the Niger River in the southwest and the Sahara in the north.

Niger is perhaps West Africa's most unfairly ignored country. True, Niger only seems to make the news for its Tuareg rebellion, its uranium mines, famine and – incredibly in 2008 – for its ongoing slavery problem, but if you make the effort to visit this desert republic, you'll find a warm and generous Muslim population and some superb tout-free West African travel. Life here can be unrelentingly tough, but Niger's diverse peoples bear these difficult times with remarkable dignity.

Sadly, for the time being the country's greatest attractions, the Ténéré Desert and the Aïr Mountains are out of bounds due to

the ongoing Tuareg rebellion against the government, but the fascinating trans-Saharan trade-route town of Agadez is still accessible, as well as a bevy of attractions in the peaceful south: the ancient sultanate of Zinder, the fantastic Parc Regional du W, West Africa's last herd of wild giraffe at Kouré and the impossibly romantic Sunday market of Ayorou. Add to this the laidback but cosmopolitan capital of Niamey and a trip down the mighty Niger River in a dugout *pirogue* (traditional canoe), and you've got yourself a West African adventure that can cheerfully rival any other in this book.

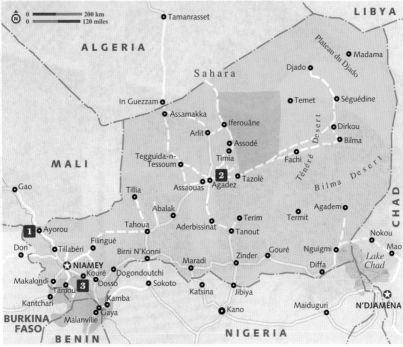

Niger's
Top Experiences

Ayorou

1 On the River Niger's banks just 24km south of the Malian frontier, this otherwise sleepy town is renowned for its Sunday market. Head to the livestock portion and witness camels, cattle, mules, sheep and goats overrunning the place, along with their fascinating nomadic owners.

Food and Drink

Bière Niger National beer.

Brochettes Kebabs, usually chicken, and beef.

Grilled fish A standard restaurant dish, particularly capitaine, or Nile perch.

Riz sauce Rice with sauce.

Tuareg Thirst-quenching tea.

Agadez

2 Once Niger's tourism capital, Agadez has fallen on decidedly hard times since the Tuareg rebellion reignited in 2007. Yet while the airport no longer sees scheduled flights and many restaurants and hotels are closed due to lack of travellers, the city remains open and this is a fascinating time to see an ancient Saharan trade town without the tour groups and touts.

Kouré

3 An absolute must on even the shortest trip to Niger is a half-day trip to Kouré, home to West Africa's last remaining giraffe herd, who quietly munch acacia trees and patrol the baking soils around dusty Kouré. The elegant long-necked beasts are rather tame and you can expect to get very close to them.

When to Go

OCT–FEB

➡ The best time to visit, as temperatures are at their coolest and rainfall is nonexistent.

MAR–JUN

➡ The hottest part of the year, with April daytime temperatures reaching 45°C (113°F) or more.

MAY–SEP

➡ Rains dampen the south, with August being the wettest time.

Abuja National Mosque

CAPITAL
Abuja

POPULATION
174.5 million

AREA
923,768 sq km

**OFFICIAL
LANGUAGE**
English

Nigeria

*Nigeria may well be West Africa's most exciting country, but with
the sensory overload of its largest city, Lagos, and reputation as a
difficult destination, it's often overlooked by travellers.*

Nigeria is a pulsating powerhouse: as the most populous nation on the continent it dominates the region economically and culturally, spreading the fruits of its rapid development throughout Africa with fury. Lagos, Nigeria's main city, is bursting at the seams: with burgeoning technology and telecommunications industries, posh restaurants and clubs, and an absolutely exploding music and arts scene, this megacity is the face of modern Africa. In villages and towns outside Gidi (as Lagosians call

their city), you may often feel as if you're a lone explorer getting a glimpse of the raw edges of the world.

Immersing yourself in the deep and layered cultures, histories, and surroundings – from the ancient Muslim cities of the north to the river deltas, from Yoruba kingdoms and spiritual shrines to the legacy of tribal conflict and the slave ports, and among simply stunning natural environments – provides a worthy antidote to a sometimes exhausting journey.

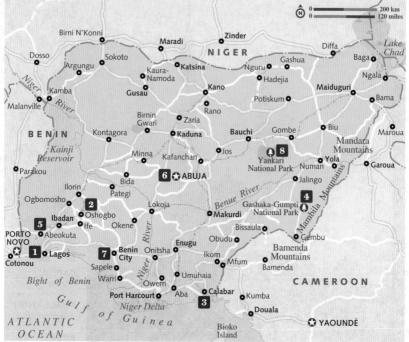

Nigeria's
Top Experiences

Lagos

1 Lagos is the newly moneyed, fastest growing and largest African city on the continent. It has wall-to-wall people, bumper-to-bumper cars, noise and pollution beyond belief, an intimidating crime rate, and maxed-out public utilities. Thanks to an influx of oil money, it has an exploding arts and music scene that will keep you engaged far past dawn. If you're headed to Nigeria, you'll have no choice but to jump right into the madness here.

Oshogbo

2 Learn about the traditional arts and ancient spiritual shrines in Oshogbo, the centre of Yoruba culture.

It was at the forefront of an explosion of contemporary art in the 1960s, and still contains several thriving galleries. Oshogbo is also home to the Osun Sacred Forest, an important shrine to the ancient Yoruba religion, and a major drawcard for visitors. At the start of August, the Osun Oshogbo Festival attracts thousands to celebrate the river goddess Osun, who legendarily founded the city.

Calabar

3 Take in colonial history and cutting-edge conservation in the easygoing old river port, Calabar. Few travellers fail to enjoy Calabar, the capital of the verdant Cross River state.

Its port has historically made the town a prosperous place – Calabar was one of Nigeria's biggest slave ports, and later a major exporter of palm oil. Even its name seems the picture of an equatorial trading post. It's one of the most rewarding Nigerian cities for visitors, with a good museum and two excellent primate conservation centres.

Gashaka-Gumti National Park

4 Head into the real wilds to explore, Gashaka-Gumti National Park, a newly reorganised mountain-meets-savannah national park. Nigeria's largest national park is also the most remote and least-

explored part of the country. Its 6700-sq-km area contains rolling hills, savannah, montane forest – as wild and spectacular a corner of Africa as you could wish for. It also is one of West Africa's most important primate habitats, as well as supporting lions, elephants, hippos and buffaloes. The park is open year-round, although access is easiest during the dry season (December to March).

Abeokuta

5 Abeokuta is well known as the birthplace of many famous Nigerians, notably former president Obasanjo and musician Fela Kuti. The founding site of Abeokuta, the famed Olumo Rock, has a rich history and great spiritual significance. You'll see shrines, sacred trees, the elderly women of the god of thunder, tribal war-time hideouts, and ultimately, at the top, an astonishing view of the city.

Abuja

6 Nigeria's made-to-measure capital, Abuja was founded during the boom years of the 1970s. After the divisive Biafran war, the decision was made to move the capital from Lagos to the ethnically neutral centre of the country. Clean, quiet and with a good electricity supply, sometimes Abuja hardly feels like Nigeria at all. It's a good place to catch your breath and do some visa shopping

if Nigeria were 100 people

29 would be Hausa and Fulani
21 would be Yoruba
18 would be Igbo
10 would be Ijaw
22 would be other ethnic groups

belief systems
(% of population)

50 Muslim   40 Christian

10

indigenous beliefs

population per sq km

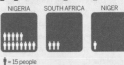

NIGERIA   SOUTH AFRICA   NIGER

👤 ≈ 15 people

When to Go

OCT–JAN
➡ Your best bet for dry weather.

DEC–JAN
➡ Lots of events and festivals; also the busiest (and most expensive) time of year.

JUN–AUG
➡ Nigeria's rainy season and usually quite wet, but not necessary to avoid.

Fela Kuti: Music is The Weapon

The impact of Fela Anikulapo Kuti's music in Nigeria, and worldwide, cannot be overstated. Fela Kuti (1938–97) was Africa's musical genius, the creator of Afrobeat – a genre combining traditional African highlife, jazz, James Brown funk grooves and Latin rhythms into a unique mix that is wholly his own – and a revolutionary.

Fela's politically inflammatory songs laid bare the corruption, violence and greed of the ruling regimes in his country and beyond. He was arrested over 100 times by the Nigerian government, and ultimately 1000 soldiers invaded Fela's living and performing compound that he shared with his 27 wives – sending nearly all of the inhabitants to the hospital, or worse.

Despite the death of his own mother due to the siege, Fela never stopped fighting the powers of imperialism, colonialism and racism with – as the legend himself put it – music as his weapon. Due to the recent re-release of his music worldwide and, interestingly, a Broadway musical based on his life, Fela's legacy is now enjoying renewed attention and a reinvigorated profile in Nigeria. The Lagos government even donated money to launch the new Kalakuta Museum and Felabration is celebrated each year around his birthday on 15 October.

Wedding, Benin City

Benin City

7 Benin City, which served as the capital of the Benin Kingdom, starting in the 15th century, gave rise to one of the first African art forms to be accepted internationally – the Benin brasses. Today the city is the centre of Nigeria's rubber trade, and a sprawling metropolis.

Yankari National Park

8 Yankari, 225km east of Jos, is Nigeria's best-known national park for observing wildlife. The park still holds reasonable numbers of buffaloes, waterbucks, bushbucks, hippos and plenty of baboons. The biggest draw is the 300-strong population of elephants – a few lions also survive there. The birdwatching is excellent too. Yankari's other attraction is the Wikki Warm Spring near the park campground. The crystal-clear water is a constant 31°C, forming a lake 200m long and 10m wide. Bring your swimming gear – the spring is a real highlight.

Food & Drink

Nigerians like their food *chop* (hot and starchy). The classic dish is a fiery pepper stew with a little meat or fish and accompanied by starch – usually pounded yam or cassava (*garri, eba*, or the slightly sour *fufu*). Another popular dish is *jollof* – peppery rice cooked with palm oil and tomato. Cutlery isn't generally used. As in most of Africa, you only eat with your right hand.

Getting Around

Air Internal flights are a quick way of getting around Nigeria.

Car & Motorcycle Nigeria's road system is good, but the smooth, sealed roads allow Nigerians to exercise their latent talents as rally drivers and accident rates are high. The only real road rule is survival of the fittest.

Minibus Each town has at least one motor park serving as the main transport depot full of minibuses and bush taxis.

Motorcycle-Taxi The quickest way to get around town is on the back of a motorcycle-taxi called an *okada* (achaba in the north).

Train There are still old rail lines in Nigeria, but no services are currently available. A project to relaunch the national railway service, starting in 2009, has stalled.

Arirang Mass Games, Mayday Stadium, Pyongyang

CAPITAL
Pyongyang

POPULATION
24.7 million

AREA
120,538 sq km

OFFICIAL
LANGUAGE
Korean

North Korea

Most people form their opinions of North Korea from news reports and James Bond movies, but there's more to the Democratic People's Republic than military parades and stand-offs with the UN.

No country in the world provokes a similar reaction to North Korea. Now on its third hereditary ruler, this nominally communist state and by-product of the Cold War has defied all expectation and survived a quarter of a century since perestroika dismantled the rest of the once-vast Soviet empire.

Most people don't even know that it's possible to travel here, and indeed the compromises required to do so are significant. You'll be accompanied by two government minders at all times and only hear a one-sided account of history. Those who can't accept this might be better off staying away – but those who can will have a fascinating trip into another, unsettling world.

With your official minders, you can roam mountain resorts and ancient capitals, though the main attractions remain the bombastic iconography of the North Korean regime and the surreal existence of ordinary people in this troubled, autocratic state.

North Korea's
Top Experiences

Mass Games

1 Visit Pyongyang between August and October to see the incredible Mass Games, a gymnastic spectacle featuring more than 100,000 participants in a dazzling display of coordinated political sloganising, gymnastics, dance, music and drama.

Pyongyang

2 Your guides will be falling over themselves to show you the monuments, towers, statues and buildings that glorify Kim Il-sung, Kim Jong-il and the Juche idea. While these are all impressive, if surreal, the real delights of Pyongyang are to be had in the quieter moments when you can get surprising glimpses of a semblence of normality, like locals having picnics and playing music.

Paekdusan

3 One of the most stunning sights on the Korean peninsula, Paekdusan (Mt Paekdu; 2744m) is the highest mountain in the country and an amazing geological phenomenon (it's an extinct volcano now containing a crater lake at its centre). It is made all the more magical by the mythology that surrounds the lake, both ancient and modern.

Food & Drink

Kimchi Traditional side dish made of fermented seasoned vegetables.

Naengmyeon Cold kudzu-flour or buckwheat noodles.

Soju Local firewater – strong stuff!

Taedonggang A pleasant locally produced lager.

When to Go

FEB

➜ The country is empty and celebrations to mark the birth of Kim Jong-il are impressive.

APR & MAY

➜ Clear skies, a lack of humidity and few visitors make this a great time to tour North Korea.

AUG–OCT

➜ The greatest show on earth, the incredible Mass Games at May Day Stadium.

Giant's Causeway, County Antrim

CAPITAL
Belfast

POPULATION
1.81 million

AREA
13,843 sq km

OFFICIAL LANGUAGES
English, Irish

Northern Ireland

From the breathtaking geological wonders of the north coast to the gritty murals of Belfast, Northern Ireland is full of a dramatic beauty that beckons to the traveller.

Once a byword for trouble, Northern Ireland has finally taken its place as one of the loveliest corners of the island. Emerging from nearly four decades of sectarian conflict, it now has as much to offer as any of Ireland's tourist havens.

The regional capital, Belfast, has shrugged off its bomb-scarred past and reinvented itself as one of the most exciting and dynamic cities in Britain – of which Northern Ireland remains a firm part. You can explore the tensions as they're expressed today on a tour of the iconic neighbourhoods of West Belfast or in the province's second city, Derry (or Londonderry), which is leading the north's cultural revival.

And it wouldn't be Ireland if it didn't have its fair share of stunning landscapes: from the Antrim Coast and its world-famous Giant's Causeway to the mountains of Mourne in south County Down.

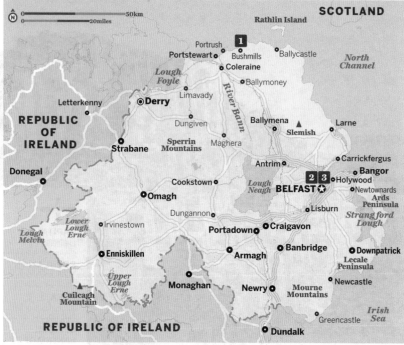

Northern Ireland's
Top Experiences

Causeway Coastal Walk

1 Put on your walking boots and set off along one of Ireland's finest coastal walks, which stretches for 16 scenic kilometres between the swaying rope bridge of Carrick-a-Rede and the geological flourish of the Giant's Causeway.

Food & Drink

Perhaps the most feared Irish speciality is the fry – the heart attack on a plate that is the second part of so many B&B deals. Who can say no to a plate of fried bacon, sausages, black pudding, white pudding, eggs and tomatoes? For the famous Ulster version, common throughout the North, simply add *fadge* (potato bread).

Black Taxi Tour, Belfast

2 No trip to Northern Ireland is complete without visiting the Republican and Loyalist murals of Belfast's Falls and Shankhill districts. Belfast's black taxi tours are justifiably famous because they provide that context, with drivers who are both insightful and darkly humorous without making light of a serious and often tragic situation.

Titanic Belfast

3 The construction of the world's most famous ocean liner is celebrated in high-tech, multimedia glory at this wonderful museum. Not only can you explore virtually every detail of the *Titanic's* construction – including a simulated 'fly-through' of the ship from keel to bridge – but you can experience the industrial bustle that was Belfast's shipyards at the turn of the 20th century.

When to Go

JUN–SEP

➜ Weather at its best but accommodation rates also at their highest.

APR–MAY & SEP–OCT

➜ Summer crowds drop off and weather remains good.

NOV–FEB

➜ Cold and wet weather; many attractions have reduced opening hours.

CAPITAL
Saipan

POPULATION
51,483

AREA
464 sq km

**OFFICIAL
LANGUAGES**
English,
Chamorro

Northern Marianas

*The Northern Marianas can seem like a package-tour nightmare.
But show a little curiosity and you'll be rewarded with turquoise
waters, white sands, and fine diving and snorkeling.*

The Northern Mariana Islands, officially the
Commonwealth of the Northern Mariana
Islands (CNMI) is currently undergoing massive change as its fiscally challenged capital
Saipan painfully comes to terms with the
loss of its lucrative Japanese tour market.
But travel trends come and go; the charm
of the islands endures. It's therefore your
mission, should you accept it, to seek out the
best of the CNMI.

Floating in American accents, Japanese
tourists and convenience stores, the Northern Marianas capital of Saipan is a package-
tour favourite. Get beyond the main island
and you'll find a less-cluttered version of
paradise where turquoise waters and white
beaches are livened up by an upsurging
Chamorro culture.

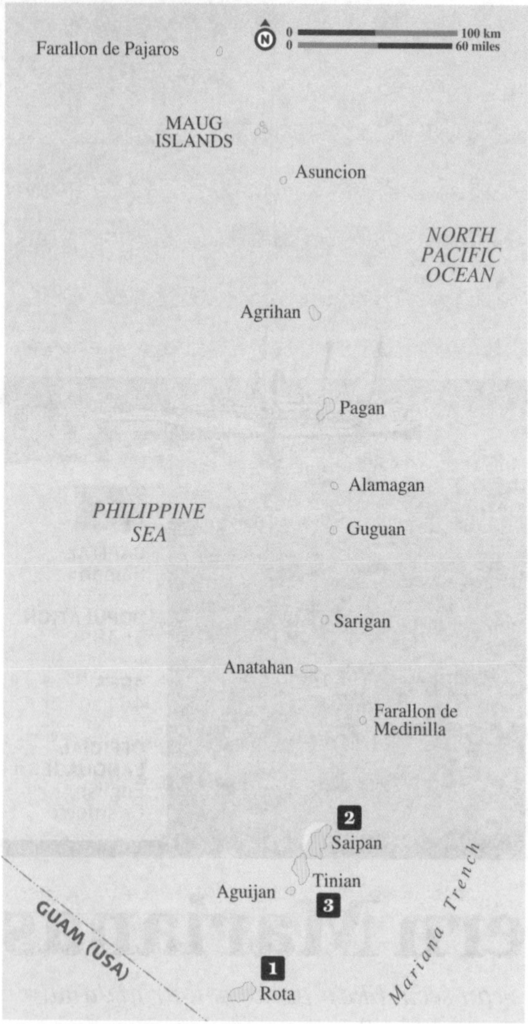

Farallon de Pajaros

MAUG
ISLANDS

Asuncion

NORTH
PACIFIC
OCEAN

Agrihan

Pagan

Alamagan

Guguan

PHILIPPINE
SEA

Sarigan

Anatahan

Farallon de
Medinilla

2 Saipan

Aguijan   Tinian

3

GUAM (USA)

1 Rota

Mariana Trench

0 ____ 100 km
0 ____ 60 miles

When to Go

DEC–MAR

➡ Best time to visit.

➡ The dry season, with slightly lower humidity.

JUL–OCT

➡ Rainy season.

OCT–NOV

➡ The most probable months for typhoons.

Food & Drink

The indigenous Chamorro food is a rich mix of Spanish, Filipino and Pacific dishes. The best Chamorro food is generally found at village fiestas.

Northern Marianas'
Top Experiences

Rota

1 The jewel in the Northern Marianas island chain is beautiful Rota. Actually, Rota is the Diamond Tiara of the Marianas, an island punctuated by a hilly interior, small farms, good spring water, enough deer to maintain a hunting season and fiery orange sunsets that light the evening skies. And a more friendly place you'd be hard-pressed to find.

The Grotto

2 Among divers in the Northern Marianas, Saipan is famous for this unique diving spot, a collapsed limestone cavern with a pool of cobalt-blue seawater filled by three underwater passageways. Once, locals who wanted to swim in the Grotto had to shimmy down a rope, but there are now steep concrete stairs down to the water. Tiny stalactites drip from above and massive spiderwebs hanging overhead make interesting photographs if caught in the right light.

Tinian

3 Tinian is a peaceful one-village island just 5km south of Saipan. It's an attractive place with ancient *latte* stones (upright posts that are the most visible remains of early Chamorro culture), ranch land with grazing cattle, secluded sandy beaches, scenic vistas and some lovely crumbling architecture.

Northern lights, Troms county

CAPITAL
Oslo

POPULATION
5.1 million

AREA
323,802 sq km

OFFICIAL LANGUAGE
Norwegian

Norway

Norway is a once-in-a-lifetime destination and the essence of its appeal is remarkably simple: this is one of the most beautiful countries on earth.

The drama of Norway's natural world is difficult to overstate. Impossibly steep-sided fjords of extraordinary beauty cut gashes from a jagged coastline deep into the interior. The fjords' fame is wholly merited, but this is also a land of glaciers, grand and glorious, snaking down from icefields that rank among Europe's largest. Elsewhere, the mountainous terrain of Norway's interior resembles the ramparts of so many natural fortresses, and yields to rocky coastal islands that rise improbably from the waters like

apparitions. And then, of course, there's the primeval appeal of the Arctic...

The counterpoint to so much natural beauty is found in the country's vibrant cultural life, which celebrates local traditions and draws in the best from around the world. Norwegian cities are cosmopolitan and brimfull of architecture that showcases the famous Scandinavian flair for design through the ages. At the same time, a busy calendar of festivals, many of international renown, are worth planning your trip around.

Magdalenefjord

Kvitøya
Storøya
Nordaustlandet

Erik Eriksenstretet

Svalbard **4**

Kong Karls
Land

Prins
Karls
Forlandet

Svenskøya

Barentsøya

Longyearbyen

Edgeøya

Spitsbergen

Storfjorden

Olgastretet

0 — 200 km
0 — 100 miles

0 — 200 km
0 — 100 miles

NORWEGIAN
SEA

Nordkapp
Kjøllefjord
Honningsvåg
Hammerfest   Båtsfjord   Vardø
Repvåg   Vadsø
Hasvik   Lakselv

Alta   Kirkenes

Tromsø **10**   Karasjok

Andenes   Skibotn
Finnsnes   Kautokeino

RUSSIA

Lofoten
Islands **3** **Harstad**
Svolvær   FINLAND
Narvik
Henningsvær
Å   Kiruna

Bodø
Ørnes   Fauske

Mo i Rana
Sandnessjøen
Mosjøen
Brønnøysund

Oulu

Namsos   SWEDEN
Steinkjer Grong
Trondheim **6**
Kristiansund   Stjørdal
Molde   Østersund
Ålesund **1** Åndalsnes   Røros
Geiranger Dombås
Florø   Trysil
Øvre ▲ Galdhøpiggen
Førde Ardal **7** **Lillehammer**   **Tampere**
Sognefjorden
Myrdal   Elverum
Bergen **Voss**
2 *Eidfjord* **5**   **Hamar**
Odda   Rødholt   Kongsvinger Turku
Leirvik   **HELSINKI**
OSLO **8**
Notodden   Uppsala   **TALLINN**
9   Moss
Stavanger Larvik Halden   ESTONIA
Egersund   Risør
Arendal   **STOCKHOLM**
Flekkefjord   Grimstad
Mandal **Kristiansand**
Hirtshals
Göteborg   LATVIA
Hanstholm
Frederikshavn

DENMARK **Aalborg**   **RĪGA**

Norway's
Top Experiences

Geirangerfjord

1 The 20km chug along Geirangerfjord, a Unesco World Heritage site, must rank as the world's loveliest ferry journey. Long-abandoned farmsteads still cling to the fjord's near-sheer cliffs while ice-cold cascades tumble, twist and gush down to emerald-green waters. Depart from Geiranger and enjoy the calm as you leave this small, heaving port, or hop aboard at altogether quieter Hellesylt. Prime your camera, grab a top-deck open-air seat and enjoy what's literally the only way to travel Norway's secluded reaches.

Bryggen, Bergen

2 Set amid a picturesque and very Norwegian coastal landscape of fjords and mountains, Bergen lays a strong claim to being one of Europe's most beautiful cities. A celebrated history of seafaring trade down through the centuries has bequeathed to the city the stunning (and Unesco World Heritage–listed) waterfront district of Bryggen, an archaic tangle of wooden buildings. A signpost to a history at once prosperous and tumultuous, the titled and colourful wooden warehouse buildings of Bryggen now shelter the chic boutiques and traditional restaurants for which the city is famous.

JOHN FREEMAN / GETTY IMAGES ©

Lofoten Islands

3 Few visitors forget their first sighting of the Lofoten Islands, laid out in summer greens and yellows, their razor-sharp peaks poking dark against a clear, cobalt sky. In the pure, exhilarating air, there's a constant tang of salt and, in the villages, more than a whiff of cod, that giant of the seas whose annual migration brings wealth. A hiker's dream and nowadays linked by bridges, the islands are simple to hop between, whether by bus, car or – ideally – bicycle.

Svalbard

4 The subpolar archipelago of Svalbard is a true place of the heart. Deliciously remote and yet surprisingly accessible, Svalbard is Europe's most evocative slice of the polar north and one of the continent's last great wilderness areas. Shapely peaks, massive icefields (60% of Svalbard is covered by glaciers) and heartbreakingly beautiful fjords provide the backdrop for a rich array of Arctic wildlife (including around one-sixth of the world's polar bears, which outnumber people here), and for summer and winter activities that get you out amid the ringing silence of the snows.

Oslo–Bergen Railway

5 Often cited as one of the world's most beautiful rail journeys, the Oslo–Bergen rail line is an opportunity to sample some of Norway's best scenery. After passing through the forests of southern Norway, it climbs up onto the horizonless beauty of the Hardangervidda Plateau and then continues down through the pretty country around Voss and on into Bergen. En route it passes within touching distance of the fjords and connects (at Myrdal) with the incredibly steep branch line down to the fjord country that fans out from Flåm.

Kystriksveien Coastal Route

6 The lightly-trafficked coastal route through Nordland is for those with leisure to savour its staggering beauty. You might well not have time for the full 650km but a sample is

Northern Lights

The aurora borealis, or northern lights, are caused by streams of charged particles from the sun, called the solar wind, which are directed by the earth's magnetic field towards the polar regions.

Visible in Norway throughout the long night of the Arctic winter from October to March, they dance across the sky in green or white curtains of light, shifting in intensity and taking on forms that seem to spring from a child's vivid imagination. While there's no guarantee that the northern lights will appear at any given time, if you are lucky enough to see them, it's an experience that will live with you forever.

Food & Drink

Aquavit The national drink, aquavit (or *akevitt*) is a potent dose of Norwegian culture made from potatoes and caraway liquor. Although the latter is an essential ingredient, modern distilleries augment the spicy flavour with any combination of orange, coriander (cilantro), anise, fennel, sugar and salt.

Cheese Norwegian cheeses have come to international attention as a result of the mild but tasty Jarlsberg, a white cheese first produced in 1860 on the Jarlsberg estate in Tønsberg.

Potatoes These feature prominently in nearly every Norwegian meal.

Reindeer Roast reindeer (*reinsdyrstek*) is something every non-vegetarian visitor to Norway should try at least once.

Salmon Where other Norwegian foods may quickly empty your wallet without adequate compensation for taste, salmon (*laks*) remains blissfully cheap, although this applies only to farmed salmon; wild salmon is considerably more expensive.

Specialities Whale steak (*hvalbiff*) or cod tongue are good if-you-dare choices for the culinary explorer.

if Norway were 100 people

94 would be Norwegian
4 would be other European
2 would be other

belief systems
(% of population)

82 Church of Norway
4 other Christian
2 Roman Catholic
2 Muslim
10 other

population per sq km

NORWAY   SWEDEN   UK

👤 ≈ 8 people

JOHAN SJÖLANDER / GETTY IMAGES ©

all but mandatory if you're progressing northwards. It's not one to be rushed. The frequent ferry hops offer compulsory, built-in breaks and stunning seascapes, while both inland glaciers and accessible offshore islands – such as Vega, famous for its eider ducks, or Lovund, home to 200,000 puffins – are seductive diversions. Longer, yes, more expensive, yes. But if you have time to spare, this is the ideal place to enjoy some solitary spendour.

Hiking the Jotunheimen

7 The high country of central Norway ranks among Europe's premier summer destinations. Although there are numerous national parks criss-crossed by well-maintained hiking trails, it's Jotunheimen National Park, whose name translates as 'Home of the Giants', that rises above all others. With 60 glaciers and 275 summits over 2000m, Jotunheimen is exceptionally beautiful and

When to Go

HIGH SEASON
(mid-Jun–mid-Aug)

➡ Accommodation and transport often booked out in advance

➡ Accommodation prices at their lowest

➡ No guarantees with the weather - can be warm and sunny or cool and rainy

SHOULDER
(May–mid-Jun & mid-Aug-Sep)

➡ A good time to travel, with generally mild, clear weather and fewer crowds

➡ Accommodation prices can be high, except on weekends

➡ Book accommodation well ahead for festivals

LOW SEASON
(Oct–Apr)

➡ Can be bitterly cold

➡ Many attractions are closed

➡ March is considered high season in Svalbard

➡ Accommodation prices high, except on weekends

home to iconic trails such as Besseggen, Hurrungane and those in the shadow of Galdhøpiggen, Norway's highest peak. Jotunheimen's proximity to the fjords further enhances its appeal.

Oslo

8 Oslo is already bursting at the seams with museums and top-notch art galleries, but now it's got itself a brand-new, glacier-white opera house that could make even Sydney envious. This is only the start of a project that will transform the city's waterfront over the next decade and in the process make Oslo one of the most happening cities in Scandinavia.

Best on Film

Kon-Tiki (2012) Oscar-nominated depiction of Thor Heyerdahl's epic 1947 raft expedition from Peru to the Polynesian islands.

Max Manus (2009) Big-budget movie that depicts the eponymous Norwegian Resistance fighter.

The Bothersome Man (2006) An absurdist fable set in a loveless and claustrophobic IKEA-world.

The Kautokeino Rebellion (2008) Recreates the 1852 Sami uprising in Kautokeino with a soundtrack dominated by Sami musician Mari Boine Persen.

Best in Print

Isles of the North (Ian Mitchell; 2011) A boat journey into the fjords, with musings on Norway's place among modern nations.

Sophie's World (Jostein Gaarder; 1991) Bestselling novel that explores the history of philosophy – good for teens and adults alike.

The Half Brother (Lars Saabye Christensen; 2001) Nordic Prize–winning novel tracing four generations of a Norwegian family.

Getting Around

Air Due to the time and distances involved in overland travel, even budget travellers may want to consider a segment or two by air.

Boat Norway's excellent system of ferries connects otherwise inaccessible, isolated communities with an extensive network of car ferries criss-crossing the fjords; express boats link the country's offshore islands to the mainland.

Bus Buses on Norway's extensive long-distance bus network are comfortable and make a habit of running on time.

Car Norwegian car hire is costly and geared mainly to the business traveller. Road tunnels make travel around (and through) Norway's mountains easy.

Pulpit Rock

9 As lookouts go, Preikestolen (Pulpit Rock) has few peers. Perched atop an almost perfectly sheer cliff that juts out more than 600m above the waters of gorgeous Lysefjord, Pulpit Rock is one of Norway's signature images and most eye-catching areas. It's the sort of place where you'll barely be able to look as travellers dangle far more than seems advisable over the precipice, even as you find yourself drawn inexorably towards the edge. The hike to reach it takes two hours and involves a full-day trip from Stavanger.

Tromsø

10 Tromsø, a cool 400km north of the Arctic Circle, is northern Norway's most significant city with, among other superlatives, the world's northernmost cathedral, brewery and botanic garden. Its busy clubs and pubs owe much to the university (another northernmost) and its students. In summer, Tromsø is a base for round-the-clock, 24-hour daylight activity. Once the first snows fall, the locals slip on their skis or snowshoes, head out of town and gaze skywards for a glimpse of the northern lights.

Oslo Opera House

8

JOHN FREEMAN / GETTY IMAGES © / ARCHITECT: SNØHETTA

Grand Mosque, Muscat

CAPITAL	
Muscat	
POPULATION	
3.2 million	
AREA	
309,500 sq km	
OFFICIAL LANGUAGE	
Arabic	

Oman

Oman is the obvious choice for those seeking out the modern face of Arabia while still wanting to sense its ancient soul.

The sultanate of Oman could be the Arabian Peninsula's most rewarding destination. More accessible than Saudi Arabia, safer than Yemen and more traditional than the Gulf emirates, Oman nonetheless has plenty to rival these countries' attractions and more. A stirring past that combines the great sweep of Bedouin history with a proud seafaring tradition has bequeathed to the country some extraordinary forts and other traditional architecture. And Mutrah Souq in Muscat is a fantasy of an Arabian bazaar come to life, with glittering gold and clouds of incense. But it's Oman's diverse natural beauty that is the main drawcard. Here you'll find beautiful beaches, the jagged ramparts of mountain ranges and the perfectly sculpted sands of the fabled Empty Quarter.

Oman is an understated presence among the glitzy states of the Gulf. What it does boast, with its rich heritage and embracing society, is a strong sense of identity, a pride in an ancient frankincense-trading past and confidence in a highly educated future.

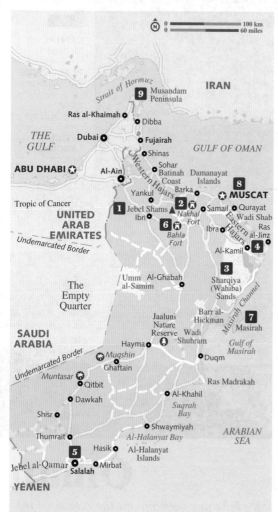

structure, the towers and entranceway of this fort were constructed during the reign of Imam Said bin Sultan in 1834. There are excellent views of the Batinah plain from the ramparts, and the *majlis* (seating area) on the top 'storey' of the fort makes a cool place to enjoy the tranquillity. The windows are perfectly aligned to catch the breeze, even in summer.

Sharqiya Sands

3 Put your driving and navigational skills to the test in Sharqiya Sands, an auburn sea of dunes. A destination in their own right, or a diversion between Sur and Muscat, these beautiful dunes, formerly known as Wahiba Sands, could keep visitors occupied for days. Home to the Bedu, the sands offer visitors a glimpse of a traditional way of life that is fast disappearing. The Bedu specialise in raising camels for racing and regular camel races take place throughout the region from mid-October to mid-April.

Ras al-Jinz

4 Attend the night-time drama of labour and delivery in Ras al-Jinz (Ras al-Junayz), an important nesting site for the endangered green turtle. Over 20,000 females return annually to the beach here at the easternmost point of the Arabian Peninsula in order to lay eggs. Oman has an important role to play in the conservation of this endangered species and takes the responsibility seriously, with strict penalties for harming turtles or their eggs.

Oman's
Top Experiences

Jebel Shams

1 Oman's highest mountain, Jebel Shams (Mountain of the Sun; 3075m), is best known not for its peak, but for the view into the spectacularly deep Wadi Ghul lying alongside it. The straight-sided Wadi Ghul is deemed the Grand Canyon of Arabia as it fissures abruptly between the flat canyon rims, exposing vertical cliffs of 1000m and more. Until recently, there was nothing between the nervous driver and a plunge into the abyss.

Nakhal Fort

2 Built on the foundations of a pre-Islamic

Salalah

5 Explore subtropical Salalah, a region famed for gold, frankincense and myrrh. The capital of the Dhofar region, it is a colourful, subtropical city that owes much of its character to Oman's former territories in East Africa. Flying into Salalah from Muscat, especially during the *khareef*, it is hard to imagine that Oman's first and second cities share the same continent. From mid-June to mid-August, monsoon clouds bring constant drizzle to the area and the stubble of Salalah's surrounding jebel is transformed into an oasis of misty pastures.

Bahla Fort

6 After two decades of restoration, be one of the first to visit Bahla Fort, a Unesco World Heritage site. A remarkable set of battlements is noticeable at every turn in the road, running impressively along the wadi and making Bahla one of the most comprehensive walled cities in the world. These walls extend for several kilometres and are said to have been designed 600 years ago by a woman.

Masirah

7 With a rocky interior of palm oases and gorgeous rim of sandy beaches, Masirah is the typical desert island. Flamingos, herons and oyster-catchers patrol the coast by day, and armies of ghost crabs march ashore at night. Home to a rare shell, the Eloise, and large turtle-nesting sites, the island is justifiably fabled as a naturalist's paradise. Expats

if Oman were 100 people

31 would be aged 0-14
20 would be aged 15-24
42 would be aged 25-54
4 would be aged 55-64
3 would be aged 65+

belief systems
(% of population)

75 Ibadhi Muslim   25 other

population per sq km

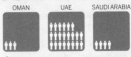

OMAN   UAE   SAUDI ARABIA

👤 = 3 people

When to Go

JAN & FEB

➡ Muscat Festival brings cultural shows and shopping to the capital.

JUL & AUG

➡ Salalah Tourism Festival celebrates the rainy season in southern Oman with shows and shopping.

NOV–MAR

➡ Cooler air and fresh winds herald the high season for tourism.

Rosewater

If you are lucky enough to find yourself in the small village of Al-Ayn on Jebel Akhdar in April, then you will be sure to have your nose assailed by the redolent Jebel Akhdar rose. These beautiful briars are cultivated not for the flower but for the aroma. For hundreds of years, the rose petals have been harvested here to produce rosewater (*attar* in Arabic) – that all-important post-dinner courtesy, sprinkled on the hands of guests from slender, silver vessels.

While the exact production of the precious perfume is a family secret, anyone on Jebel Akhdar will tell you the petals are not boiled, but steamed over a fire with an arrangement of apparatus that brings to mind home chemistry sets. However the alchemy is not, apparently, in the process of evaporation, but in the practice of picking. If you see people dancing through the roses before dawn, chances are they are not calling on the genies of the jebel to assist the blooms, but plucking petals when the dew still lies on the bushes and the oil is at its most intense.

Food & Drink

Alcohol Available at hotels and tourist-oriented restaurants.

Coffee Laced with cardamon and served with dates; an essential part of Omani hospitality.

Halwa Gelatinous sugar or date-syrup confection.

Harees Steamed wheat and boiled meat.

Lobster Local, clawless crayfish.

Shuwa Marinated lamb cooked in an underground oven.

Tap water Safe to drink but most folk drink bottled water.

stationed here affectionately termed it 'Fantasy Island'.

Mutrah Souq

8 Bargain for copper pots and gold bangles in labyrinthine Mutrah Souq. Many people come to Mutrah Corniche just to visit the souq, which retains the chaotic interest of a traditional Arab market albeit housed under modern timber roofing. There are some good antique shops selling a mixture of Indian and Omani artefacts among the usual textile, hardware and gold shops.

Musandam Peninsula

9 Separated from the rest of Oman by the east coast of the UAE, and guarding the southern side of the strategically important Strait of Hormuz, the Musandam Peninsula is dubbed the 'Norway of Arabia' for its beautiful khors, small villages and dramatic, mountain-hugging roads. Accessible but isolated in character, this beautiful peninsula with its cultural eccentricities is well worth a visit.

Getting Around

Bus Intercity buses run daily to/from most of the main provincial towns. Buses are usually on time, comfortable and safe. It is worth making reservations for longer journeys.

Car Road signs are written in English (albeit with inconsistent spelling), as well as in Arabic, and helpful brown tourist signs signal many sites of interest.

Taxi Oman has a comprehensive system of cheap but rather slow long-distance shared taxis (painted orange and white) and microbuses. Oman's shared taxis and microbuses do not wait until they are full to leave. Instead, drivers pick up and drop off extra passengers along the way.

Lahore Fort (Shahi Qila), Lahore

Pakistan

CAPITAL
Islamabad

POPULATION
193.2 million

AREA
796,095 sq km

OFFICIAL LANGUAGES
Urdu
English

Pakistan has been on the brink of being tourism's 'next big thing' for more years than we care to remember.

It's a destination that has so much to offer visitors, from some of the highest and most spectacular mountains in the world to the architectural glories of the Mughal empire, and cultural riches ranging from ancient ruins to musical mystics. But would-be visitors are frequently scared off by Pakistan's reputation for lawlessness and political instability.

Is this reputation deserved? Well, yes, and no. Parts of the country have problems with crime and insurgency, other parts are warm and welcoming; it all depends where you go. The challenge for travellers is knowing where one part ends and the other begins. Nevertheless, equipped with some local knowledge, it isn't hard to avoid the troubles and immerse yourself in a mesmerising world of desert forts, carpet-weavers and djinns.

Although conservative, Pakistanis are by nature welcoming and hospitable, and visitors are met with genuine interest and enthusiasm. Travellers who see beyond the headlines and take time to explore almost always rate Pakistan as one of their top travel destinations.

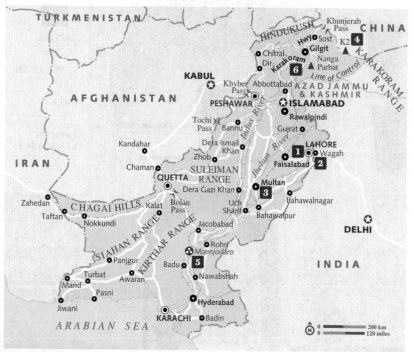

Pakistan's
Top Experiences

Lahore Fort (Shahi Qila)

1 Built, damaged, demolished, rebuilt and restored several times before being given its current form by Emperor Akbar in 1566, the Mughal fort is the star attraction of Lahore's Old City. It has an appealing 'abandoned' atmosphere (when not packed with visitors) and although it's not as elaborate as most of India's premier forts, it's still a fabulous place to wander around. The Shish Mahal (Palace of Mirrors), built for the empress and her court, is decorated with mirrors set into the stucco interior. Also breathtaking is the Naulakha marble pavilion, which is lavishly decorated with *pietra dura* – mosaics of tiny jewels arranged into intricate floral motifs. As you pass through the Alamgiri Gate, picture the incredible spectacle of the royal household parading by on elephants.

Border-Closing Ceremony, Wagah

2 Whether or not you're going to India, it's worth making a special trip to the border to watch the amazing closing-of-the-border (flag-lowering) ceremony that takes place each day. The wonderfully outlandish ceremony has been performed daily since it was first enacted in 1948. This flag-lowering, gate-closing spectacle is a curious fusion of orderly colonial-style pomp, comical Monty Pythonesque moves and dead serious national rivalry. There's copious goose-stepping, snorting, stomping and killer glares that rouse thunderous applause from the audience, who zealously egg on their soldiers by repeatedly chanting 'Pakistan zindabad!' (Long live Pakistan!). So popular is this event that grandstands have been specially constructed to accommodate the patriotic throngs that flock here. If you've got time, see it from both sides of the fence, as the objective of each side's soldiers is to out-march, out-salute and out-shout each other (if you're crossing the border you'll only get to see it from the Indian side).

K2, Karakoram Range, Kashmir

Multan's Sufi Shrines

3 From the 9th century onward, Multan has been a major Islamic centre and that heritage lives on today. Over the centuries it has attracted more mystics and holy men than perhaps anywhere else on the subcontinent and today is dominated by their awe-inspiring shrines, tombs and mosques. The mausoleum of Sheikh Rukn-i-Alam, with its stunning blue-and-turquoise tiled exterior, is a particular masterpiece.

K2

4 It might be lacking a couple of hundred metres (8611m, compared with Everest's 8850m) and it might not even have a proper name, but K2 must never be underestimated. The world's second-highest peak, standing sentinel over the Pakistan–China border, is treacherous; climbers have around a one-in-four chance of not making it back down alive. As only the most experienced must ever dare to attempt K2, try an alternative adventure. Trek in to Concordia, a glacial confluence surrounded by four of the world's 14 8000m-plus peaks, to admire from a close-yet safe distance.

Moenjodaro

5 Ramble amongst the World Heritage–listed ruins here and experience the traces of what would have been a bustling Indus

if Pakistan were 100 people

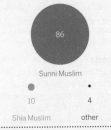

45 would be Punjabi
15 would be Pashtun
14 would be Sindhi
8 would be Muhajirs
18 would be other

belief systems
(% of population)

86
Sunni Muslim

10
Shia Muslim

4
other

population per sq km

PAKISTAN   INDIA   IRAN

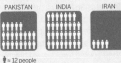

👤 ≈ 12 people

When to Go

OCT–FEB

➡ The weather is generally cool; this is the best time to visit Punjab, Sindh & Balochistan.

MAR–JUN

➡ Weather heats up at this time.

➡ The trekking season begins in late April.

JUL–SEP

➡ Monsoon season hits; avoid the south but this can be a good time to go north.

Kabbadi

A combination of wrestling, rugby and tag, kabbadi comes from the state of Punjab. Two teams, each of 12 members, are separated by a line in the middle of a 12.5m-by-10m arena. One team sends a 'raider' to the other side; he has to keep uttering the phrase 'kabaddi kabaddi' and touch as many members of the opposing team as possible without taking a second breath, and must return to his part of the field in the same breath. The defending side must protect themselves and attempt to force the invader to either touch the ground and/or take a second breath. Kabaddi has been famous in the subcontinent for centuries with major 'houses' dominating the scene and competing in national and international competitions.

Food & Drink

Meat Gosht (meat) eaten in Pakistan is usually mutton or chicken, or sometimes beef (gay ka gosht). Seafood and fish (machlee) are most common in Karachi, although some restaurants in Lahore and Islamabad offer a commendable selection. Pork is taboo for Muslims.

Roti This unleavened round bread is most often cooked in a tandoor (clay oven) in Pakistan and is usually larger than its Indian equivalent.

Sweets Pakistan has a positively lip-smacking assortment of colourful mithai (sweets). Some sweet shops produce their works of art right on the spot – look for jalebis, the orange-coloured whorls of deep-fried batter dunked in sticky sugar syrup.

Tea Pakistan is awash with tea (chai), usually 'milky tea' of equal parts water, leaves, sugar and milk brought to a raging boil and often poured from a great height.

Jeep ride to Fairy Meadows, Karakoram Highway

Valley metropolis in 2500 BC. The 250-hectare complex of excavated assembly halls, baths and houses gives a sense of a complex, sophisticated culture lost to time.

Travelling the Karakoram Highway

6 Humans have been inching along the Indus Valley for millennia, using this Silk Road strand to spread goods and ideologies between East and West. Goodness knows why – it's such difficult terrain to traverse. But traverse it they did and, finally, in 1986 some master-engineering saw it modernised: the 1200km Karakoram Highway was unveiled, linking Islamabad to Kashgar in China via the Karakorams, Himalaya and Hindu Kush ranges. It's a flabbergasting drive. There are potholes, landslides and vertical drops; there are old trucks done up like Christmas squeezing and wheezing along; there are roadblocks and bandits. But it'll be the drive of your life.

Getting Around

Air Wait until you get to Pakistan to buy domestic tickets, as they can be up to 30% cheaper than tickets purchased outside the country. The national airline connects the major centres including Islamabad, Karachi and Lahore.

Bus Getting around by bus isn't always terribly comfortable but it's undeniably cheap. There are numerous bus companies and some towns have more than one depot, which can create confusion.

Car It's common and surprisingly economical to hire a car with a driver – shop around to get the best deal.

Train Long-distance services are often crowded, so sleepers in 1st and air-con class should be booked ahead, to a maximum of 14 and 30 days respectively. Women may book female-only compartments.

CAPITAL
Melekeok

POPULATION
21,186

AREA
459 sq km

OFFICIAL LANGUAGES
Palauan, English

Rock Islands

Palau

You don't have to get wet to enjoy Palau, but it helps. This tiny island country in the western Pacific Ocean is one of the world's most spectacular diving and snorkelling destinations.

Most tourists who come to the Republic of Palau like to spend their time underwater. This is among the world's most spectacular diving and snorkelling destinations, featuring coral reefs, blue holes, WWII wrecks, hidden caves and tunnels, more than 60 vertical drop-offs, and an astonishing spectrum of coral, fish and rare sea creatures. There are also some outright miracles of evolution: giant clams that weigh a quarter of a ton, for example, and a lake teeming with 21 million softly pulsating, stingless jellyfish.

On land the republic embraces Micronesia's richest flora and fauna: exotic birds fly, crocodiles slip through the swamps and orchids sprout profusely in backyards.

The Palauan archipelago encompasses the polyglot state of Koror; the marvellous Rock Islands; Micronesia's second-largest island, Babeldaob (the land that Pacific Standard Time forgot); Peleliu, once war-ravaged, now just ravishing; tranquil, tiny Angaur; the coral atolls of Kayangel and Ngeruangel; and the remote South-West Islands.

SOUTH-WEST ISLANDS

Main Palau Islands (600km)

Ngeruangel

Sonsorol Islands (Sonsorol & Fana)

Pulo Anna

Merir

Kayangel

Tobi Helen

Kossol Reef

0   100 km
0   60 miles

Kossol Passage

PHILIPPINE SEA

☆ MELEKEOK

Babeldaob Island

Arakabesang

Malakal Koror

Ulong Auluptagel

1 2 ROCK ISLANDS

Urukthapel

NORTH PACIFIC OCEAN

70 Islands (Ngerukuid)

Neco Island

Eil Malk

Ngemelis

Ngerchong

Carp Island (Ngercheu)

Ngesebus

Peleliu

3

Angaur

South-West Islands (600km, see inset)

Ⓝ 0   20 km
0   12 miles

When to Go

DEC–MAR

➡ High season for Japanese and Korean visitors. More reliable manta and grey reef shark sightings.

APR–MAY & SEP–NOV

➡ Strong winds from July to October may make some dives inaccessible.

JUN–AUG

➡ The wettest months, with heavy thunderstorms in June.

Food & Drink

Palau's cuisine has absorbed influences from Japan, Korea, the Philippines and the USA. You're in luck if you have a seafood fetish – sushi and sashimi are popular, and mangrove crabs and shellfish are common. But the food can be quirky, too; fruit-bat pie is on many menus (they say it tastes like chicken).

to follow the path of the sun. Floating among these flimsy pink creatures – which expand and contract like so many pulsating brains – is like exploring the atmosphere of an alien world.

Palau's Top Experiences

Rock Islands

1 Comprising over 200 mushroom-shaped limestone islets undercut by erosion, the Rock Islands (known locally as Chalbacheb) are the crown jewels of Micronesia. Totally covered with green jungle, they dot the waters for a 32km stretch and are the reason why most travellers come to Palau.

Jellyfish Lake

2 The Rock Islands hold about 80 marine salt lakes, and snorkelling in Jellyfish Lake is an absolute must. It's filled with millions of harmless transparent jellyfish that swim en masse

Peleliu

3 Peleliu is peaceful and laid-back. There's not much to do here aside from walking and diving, and that's entirely the charm. It's a lovely little place, and that's why it's so hard to imagine it torn apart by war. Yet during 1944 Peleliu was the site of one of the bloodiest battles of WWII. Although the island is only 13 sq km, in two months more than 15,000 men were killed here.

Archipiélago de San Blás

CAPITAL
Panama City

POPULATION
3.6 million

AREA
75,420 sq km

OFFICIAL LANGUAGE
Spanish

Panama

From deserted islands and clear turquoise seas to the coffee farms and cloud forests of Chiriquí, Panama can be as chilled out or as thrilling as you wish.

Consider Panama a place of discovery: explore the ruins of Spanish forts on the Caribbean coast or boat deep into indigenous territories in a dugout canoe. There are plenty of beaches to choose from, too, from relaxed Caribbean hang-outs to Pacific surf.

For an urban turn, Panama City – culturally diverse, driven, rough-edged yet sophisticated – is one of Latin America's most vibrant and outward-looking capitals. The dazzling blue coastline and shimmering skyscrapers say Miami, though many joke that you hear more English spoken in Panama. Pedal the coastal green space, explore the historic Casco or attend an avant-garde performance and you will realize this tropical city isn't just about salsa – that's just the backbeat.

In the last century, Panama was defined by the canal; what lies just beyond may define it for the next. The canal expansion spells growth and even more glitz, but for now you can still pick an empty islet, live out your castaway fantasies and play *Survivor* for a day. Panama is as urbane or as wild as you want it to be.

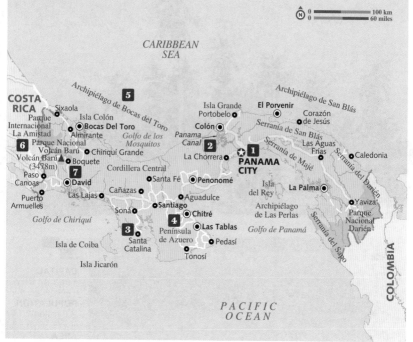

Panama's
Top Experiences

Panama City

1 Panama City is elemental Latin America: think *ceviche* (marinated seafood), casinos and stacked skylines. For this city of nearly one million, transformation is in the air: a new coastal green space, an anticipated biodiversity museum soon to open and a subway system under construction. Sure, the traffic resembles a boa constrictor digesting one megalithic meal, but its appeal persists. People are real here and nature is never far away. Beauty lives in the skewed rhythms, incongruous visions and fiery sunsets.

Panama Canal

2 One of the world's greatest shortcuts, the canal cuts right through the continental divide, linking the Atlantic and Pacific Oceans. And it's worth marveling at. Just as stunning as the hulking steel container ships passing through the locks are the legions of creatures watching from the jungle fringes. Two visitors centers offer viewing platforms and museums that showcase the construction and its expansion. There's also worthwhile boat and kayak trips on the waterway. Or you can book a partial transit and squeeze through the locks yourself.

Santa Catalina

3 This surf village is all small town, with just one paved road. Here, nature is a delight and 'resort' is still a foreign word. The biggest draws are the world-class waves that roll in year-round (but peak in February and March). The town is also the launching pad for excursions and diving trips into the wildlife-rich Parque Nacional Coiba, an island journey that may be heavy in logistics but worth every dogged effort.

Península de Azuero

4 Sweet landscapes of sculpted hills, lonely beaches and crashing surf feed the growing buzz about this rural peninsula. Yet the strongest impression is one of tradition. Spanish culture has deep roots here, evident in the charm of tiled colonials, country hospitality, religious festivals and elaborate

2

Miraflores locks, Panama Canal

polleras. Playa Venao has emerged as a major surf destination, while the more remote Playa Cambutal is still the wild beach of your dreams.

Archipiélago de Bocas del Toro

5 No wonder this Caribbean island chain is Panama's number one vacation spot. It's all good, say the locals. Pedal to the beach on a cruiser bike, hum to improvised calypso on Isla Bastimentos, and laze over dinner in a thatched hut on the waterfront. Lodgings range from cheap digs to stunning jungle lodges and luxury resorts. Surfers hit

the breaks, but there's also snorkeling with dazzling corals and oversized starfish or volunteering to help nesting sea turtles.

Parque Nacional Volcán Barú

6 Panama's only volcano dominates the misty Chiriquí highlands. At 3478m it's also the highest point in the country. Enthusiasts can make the steep and usually muddy predawn climb for the reward of viewing both the Atlantic and Pacific Oceans at the same time. Another, perhaps saner, option is the Sendero Los Quetzales, a stunning trail that traverses the park,

if Panama were 100 people

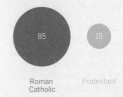

70 would be mestizo
14 would be Amerindian and mixed
10 would be white
6 would be Amerindian

belief systems
(% of population)

85 Roman Catholic

15 Protestant

population per sq km

PANAMA   USA   COSTA RICA

👤 ≈ 15 people

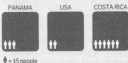

When to Go

HIGH SEASON
(mid-Dec–mid-Apr)

➡ Pacific-side dry season.

➡ Little rain in Panama City and elsewhere south of the continental divide.

HIGH SEASON PEAK (Holidays)

➡ Includes November festivals, Christmas and New Year plus Easter holidays.

➡ Hotel rates may be up to double that of normal rates.

LOW SEASON
(mid-Apr–mid-Dec)

➡ Rainy season in most of the country.

➡ Rain is sporadic: many destinations can still be enjoyed.

Obsession for Ocelots

Ocelots are nocturnal, elusive and native to Panama. When researchers and wildlife photographers had trouble capturing these cats in Panama's dense rainforest, they turned not to science but to Calvin Klein. Christian Ziegler, a photographer working on assignment for *National Geographic*, remembers, 'After hearing a claim from the San Diego Zoo, I bought Calvin Klein's Obsession when passing through duty-free.' The scent, which contains pheromones that appeal to both humans and animals, was sprayed on a tree.

The result? The ocelots rubbed up against bark doused in the scent. But, according to Ziegler, the attraction proved fleeting.

Congo dancers, Panama City

Food & Drink

Panama's national dish is *sancocho* (chicken-and-vegetable stew). *Ropa vieja* (literally 'old clothes'), a spicy shredded beef combination served over rice, is another common and tasty dish. Rice and beans are a staple in Panama and are usually served with *patacones* (fried green plantains), a small cabbage salad and meat. Seafood is inexpensive and abundant, including *ceviche* (marinated raw fish). More adventurous palates should try *pulpo al carbon* (grilled octopus). Fresh tropical juices and coconut water (known as *pipa*) are sold on the street. Don't miss regional specialties like *tortilla de maíz* (fried cornmeal cake), Caribbean coconut rice and bottled D'Elida's hot pepper sauce.

The national alcoholic drink is made of *seco*, milk and ice. *Seco*, like rum, is distilled from sugarcane, and popular in the countryside. Popular in the central provinces, *vino de palma* is fermented sap extracted from the trunk of a palm tree.

crosses over the Río Caldera and provides the chance to see exotic orchids, tapir and resplendent quetzals.

Boquete

7 Equal parts adventure hub and mountain retreat, Boquete is a magnet for expats, retirees and travelers of all stripes. Bird-watchers come for a glimpse of the resplendent quetzal, while adventurers come to climb a mountain, ride a zip line or raft the white water. But what really moves this small town is the principal crop of the world: coffee. Coffee farms dot the countryside, with tours showing the process from leaf to cup.

Festivals

8 A window into the country's wilder side, Panama's many festivals also reveal the breadth of cultures in this small country. From Caribbean Congo celebrations in Portobelo to the vibrant folkloric traditions of the Península de Azuero, the three-day Kuna stomp that is Nogagope or Panama City's open-air jazz festival, all of Panama loves a good rum-soaked time.

Getting Around

Air Domestic flights depart Panama City from Aeropuerto Albrook and arrive in destinations throughout the country.

Bus Most cities have a bus terminal with frequent regional departures and connections to Panama City and Costa Rica.

Car Rentals are not cheap but roads are generally in good condition. Some areas, including Panama City and many rural areas, are very poorly signposted.

Train Mostly a novelty, but goes between Panama City and Colón.

Tribal men, Mt Hagen Show

Papua New Guinea

Coral-ringed beaches, smouldering volcanoes and rainforest-covered mountains meet traditional villages and tropical islands in a remote and unforgettable adventure getaway.

CAPITAL
Port Moresby

POPULATION
6.4 million

AREA
462,840 sq km

OFFICIAL LANGUAGES
Tok Pisin, English, Hiri Motu

The striking natural beauty and myriad complex cultures in Papua New Guinea offer some riveting and truly life-affirming experiences – along with some challenging, frontier-style travel. Highland cultures, wild festivals, world-class diving, the notorious Kokoda Track and a relative dearth of tourists make this one of the Pacific's most intriguing destinations.

PNG is a megadiverse region, owing much of its diversity to its topography. The mountainous terrain has spawned diversity in two ways: isolated highlands are often home to unique fauna and flora found nowhere else, while within any one mountain range you will find different species as you go higher.

Slip beneath the surface to find an incredible underwater world and a wealth of WWII wreck dives. For a glimpse into PNG's fascinating tribal cultures, head to the Highlands or to the remote, untrammelled island provinces and Trobriand Islands. Just don't expect a lazy island resort holiday – PNG is a true travel experience.

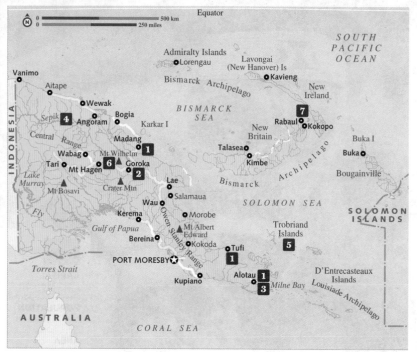

Papua New Guinea's
Top Experiences

Diving PNG

1 PNG ranks among the best destinations on Planet Scuba, with an irresistible menu of underwater treasures: luscious reefs festooned with huge sea fans; warm waters teeming with bizarre, rainbow-coloured critters; eerie drop-offs that tumble into the abyss; and a host of atmospheric WWII wrecks – not to mention the thrill of diving uncrowded sites. Among the best diving can be found at Madang, Loloata Island, Tufi and Milne Bay. A handful of beautifully set dive resorts provide the idyllic gateway to your undersea adventure. To reach even more remote and pristine environments, sign on to a live-aboard vessel.

Highland Festivals

2 Rio's Carnaval has nothing on the magnificent pageantry of a Highland festival. PNG's biggest fests, such as the Goroka Show in mid-September, are pure sensory overload, with massive feather headdresses, rustling grass skirts and evocative face and body paint adorning enormous numbers of participants – over 100 tribal groups at last count – from all across the Highlands. *Singsing* groups perform traditional songs and dances in this pride-filled extravaganza. The thrill of coming face to face with such uplifting traditional cultures is indescribable and well worth planning a trip around.

Milne Bay

3 At the eastern edge of the mainland, Milne Bay is a landscape of remarkable beauty. You'll find scattered islands, coral reefs, lovely palm-fringed beaches, hidden waterfalls, meandering rivers and steep-sided rainforest covered mountains plunging to the sea. The opportunity for adventure is staggering, with great birdwatching, bushwalking and island- and village-hopping. Alotau is the gateway to it all, and also host of the colourful Canoe Festival.

Sepik River

4 Besieged on all sides by thick jungle and shrouded in mist, the mighty Sepik wanders across northwestern PNG

PETER HENDRIE / GETTY IMAGES ©

like a lazy brown snake full of food. The river is the region's lifeblood, home to a string of villages rich in artistic tradition and cultural treasures. Here you can hire a crocodile-headed canoe and thread the seasonal waterways from one village to the next, sleeping in stilt homes and exploring the towering *haus tambarans* (spirit houses).

Trobriand Islands

5 Anthropologists have long been fascinated with the remote and isolated Trobriand Islands. Here you'll find a remarkably intact Polynesian culture, with unique traditions – based on a strict matrilineal society – and a distinct cosmology. The Trobrians are well known for its colourfully painted yam houses, wild harvest festival and celebratory cricket matches (complete with singing and dancing).

Mt Wilhelm Trek

6 The craggy ridges of the Bismarck Range culminate with the wind-scoured peak of Mt Wilhelm,

if Papua New Guinea were 100 people

87 would live in a rural area
13 would live in an urban area

belief systems
(% of population)

69 Protestant

27 Roman Catholic

3 indigenous religions

1 Baha'i

population per sq km

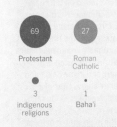

PNG   AUSTRALIA   USA

👤 ≈ 3 people

When to Go

HIGH SEASON
(May–Oct)

➡ Bigger crowds at big-name festivals and higher accommodation prices.

➡ Generally cooler, drier weather, but rainier in Milne Bay.

➡ Best time to hike the Kokoda Track.

SHOULDER
(Apr & Nov)

➡ Generally hot and humid, but with increasingly unpredictable rain patterns.

➡ Fewer visitors and cheaper accommodation.

LOW SEASON
(Dec–Mar)

➡ The wet season for much of PNG.

➡ Mild weather, less rain in Milne Bay.

➡ Heavy rains, washed-out roads in the Highlands.

➡ Best surfing off the north coast and islands.

Kokoda Track

It's muddy and gruelling, with maddeningly steep uphill scrambles followed by slippery, bone-jarring descents. Treacherous river crossings ensure feet don't stay dry for long, while the humidity wreaks havoc on even the best-prepared trekkers. Why walk the 96km Kokoda Track? To follow in the footsteps of giants, recalling the great men who fought and died on this hellish, mountainous stretch.

The WWII Kokoda campaign began in late 1942 when invading Japanese forces used the track in an attempt to take Port Moresby. They were eventually defeated by Australian (and later US) forces. Crossing the Owen Stanley Range has now become a pilgrimage for many Australians, a chance to pay their respects by sharing some of the trials of the men who fought and died here. In recent years, there has been an average of some 4000 trekkers (95% of them Australian) who gritted their teeth and tackled the mountains.

Food & Drink

Apart from the wonderful seafood found on the coast, the traditional PNG diet consists largely of bland, starchy vegetables. In the Highlands it will probably be *kaukau* (sweet potato); on the islands, it's taro or yam; and in the Sepik and other swampy areas of PNG, *saksak* (sago) is all the rage. Rice is universally popular. Pigs are the main source of meat protein, although they are generally saved for feasts. A legacy of WWII is the prevalence and popularity of canned meat and fish. Remarkably, locals prefer tinned fish to fresh fish, and whole supermarket aisles are devoted to bully beef.

View of Mt Tavurvur from Little Pigeon Island

the tallest mountain in Oceania. A predawn start has trekkers clambering up its rocky slopes so that they see the mainland's north and south coasts before the clouds roll in. If this isn't challenging enough, rugged types might want to measure their mettle against the infamous Black Cat Trail.

Rabaul

7 One of the prettiest towns in the South Pacific was devastated by Mt Tavurvur, which erupted in 1994 and buried much of Rabaul under volcanic ash. Today you can wander through the abandoned, apocalyptic streets of this once-thriving community, and take in adventures further afield. Highlights include a visit to Matupit Island, with its village of megapode egg-hunters; diving in wreck-strewn Simpson Harbour; and peering back in time at eerie WWII bunkers hidden in the hillsides. There are great views to be had, particularly from atop the volcanoes looming over town.

Getting Around

Air PNG is heavily reliant on air transport to connect its isolated and scattered population, with several local airlines offering scheduled flights.

Boat Passenger ferries operate on the northern coast and from the mainland to the island provinces with scheduled, if slightly erratic, services. Smaller trade boats also ply the coast, supplying trade stores and acting as ferries.

Car & Motorcycle Driving yourself around PNG is not really a viable way of travelling because the country only has one road – the Highlands Hwy.

Local Transport PMV (public motor vehicle) is the generic term for any public transport, be it a dilapidated minibus, a pick-up truck or even a boat.

Jesuit Mission, Trinidad

CAPITAL
Asunción

POPULATION
6.6 million

AREA
406,752 sq km

OFFICIAL LANGUAGES
Spanish, Guaraní

Paraguay

Little-visited and little-known, landlocked Paraguay is a country surrounded by South America's 'big boys', but there's a warm welcome and much to experience here.

Paraguay is a country much misunderstood. Despite its location at the heart of the continent, it is all too often passed over by travelers who wrongly assume that a lack of 'mega-attractions' means there's nothing to see. Instead, it's ideal for those keen to get off the gringo trail for a truly authentic South American experience.

Paraguay is a country of remarkable contrasts: it is rustic and sophisticated, extremely poor and obscenely wealthy; it boasts exotic natural reserves and massive human-made dams; it is a place where horses and carts pull up beside luxury automobiles, artisans' workshops abut glitzy shopping centers, and Jesuit ruins in rural villages lie just kilometers from sophisticated colonial towns. The steamy subtropical Atlantic Forest of the east is a stark contrast to the dry, spiny wilderness of the Chaco, location of the isolated Mennonite colonies.

While Paraguayans are more used to visits from their bordering neighbors, they are relaxed, kind and welcoming to anyone.

Paraguay's
Top Experiences

The Chaco

1 Spot wildlife, including jaguars, sleep under the stars and enjoy the absence of humanity in the Chaco, Paraguay's vast western plain. Occupying more than 60% of the country, less than 3% of the population lives here, including three Mennonite colonies.

Food & Drink

Asado Grilled slabs of beef and pork; a focal point of social events.

Chipa guasú Hot maize pudding with cheese and onion.

Empanadas Pasties stuffed with chicken, cheese and ham, beef or other fillings.

Sooyo Thick soup of ground meat, often with a floating poached egg.

Jesuit Missions

2 Explore the picturesque remnants of the Jesuit Missions, one of the world's least-visited Unesco sites. Set atop a lush green hill 28km northeast of Encarnación, Trinidad is Paraguay's best-preserved Jesuit *reducción*. Jesús, 12km north, is a nearly complete reconstruction of the Jesuit mission that was interrupted by the Jesuits' expulsion in 1767.

Carnavale

3 Visit Encarnación in late January and February for Paraguay's biggest party. Carnaval Paraguayan-style might not be as famous as Rio's, but if you are young and looking for a wild party, then you may find it more fun. Plenty of bare flesh, loud music and obligatory crowd involvement all make for a mad night out – it's surprisingly infectious and not to be missed.

When to Go

FEB

➜ Let loose during Carnaval season in Encarnación. Warm, tropical climate.

JUL–AUG

➜ Pleasant winter climate makes it the best time to visit the Chaco.

DEC

➜ Follow the pilgrims to the Caacupé basilica on the Día de la Virgen.

CAPITAL
Lima

POPULATION
29.9 million

AREA
1.3 million sq km

OFFICIAL LANGUAGES
Spanish, Aymara, Quechua

Woman weaving, Pisac, The Sacred Valley

Peru

Peru startles with its variety – parched coastal desert, jagged Andean peaks, lush Amazon rainforest. Its rich culture runs the gamut from sophisticated Lima to mist-shrouded ancient ruins.

A visit to South America isn't complete without a pilgrimage to the glorious Inca citadel of Machu Picchu, but, the truth is, this feted site is just a flash in a 5000-year history of peoples. Walk through the dusted remnants of a vast ancient city at Chan Chan, the largest pre-Columbian ruins in all the Americas. Fly over the puzzling geoglyphs etched into the arid earth at Nazca. Or venture into the rugged wilds that hem the stalwart fortress of Kuelap. Lima's great museums, with priceless ceramics, gold and some of the finest textiles in the world, reveal in full detail the sophistication, skill and passion of these lost civilizations. Visit remote communities and see how old ways live on. Peru is as complex as its most intricate weavings. Festivals mix ancient pageantry with stomping brass bands. The urban vanguard beams with artistry and innovation. Trails mark the way from dense jungle to glacial peaks. Immerse yourself in Peru and leave a little closer to the past.

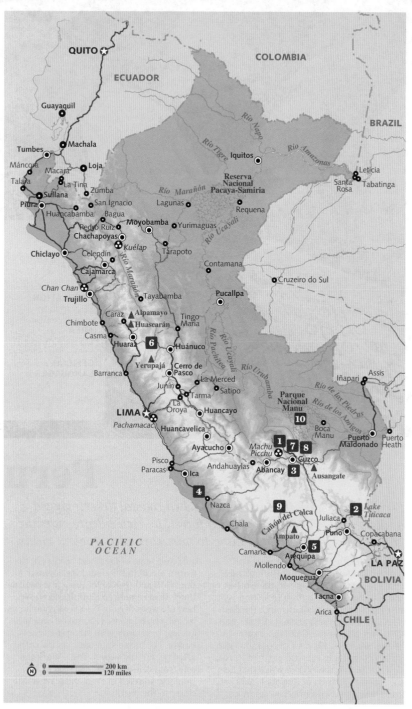

Peru's
Top Experiences

Machu Picchu

1 A fantastic Inca citadel lost to the world until its rediscovery in the early 20th century, Machu Picchu stands as a ruin among ruins. With its emerald terraces, backed by steep peaks and Andean ridges that echo on the horizon, the sight simply surpasses the imagination. Beautiful it is. This marvel of engineering has withstood six centuries of earthquakes, foreign inva-sion and howling weather. Discover it for yourself, wander through its stone temples, and scale the dizzying heights of Wayna Picchu.

Floating Reed Islands, Lake Titicaca

2 Less a lake than a high-land ocean, the Titicaca area is home to fantastical sights, but none more so than the surreal floating islands crafted entirely of tightly woven *totora* reeds. Centuries ago, the Uros people constructed the Islas Uros in order to escape more aggressive mainland ethnicities, such as the Incas. The reeds require near-constant renovation and are also used to build thatched homes, elegant boats and even archways and children's swing sets. See this wonder for yourself with a homestay.

Cuzco

3 With ancient cobblestone streets, grandiose baroque churches and the remnants of Inca temples with centuries-old carvings, no city looms larger in Andean history than Cuzco, a city that has been inhabited continuously since pre-Hispanic times. Once the capital of the Inca empire, tourist-thronged Cuzco also serves as the gateway to Machu Picchu. Mystic, commercial and chaotic, this unique city is still a stunner. Where else would you find ornately dressed women walking their llamas on leashes, a museum for magical plants, and the wildest nightlife in the high Andes?

Nazca Lines

4 Made by aliens? Laid out by prehistoric balloonists? Conceived as a giant astronomical chart? No two evaluations of Southern Peru's giant geoglyphs, communally known as the Nazca Lines, are ever the same. The mysteries have been drawing in outsiders since the 1940s when German archaeologist Maria Reiche devoted half her life to studying them. But neither Reiche nor subsequent archaeologists have been able to fully crack the code. The lines remain unfathomed, enigmatic and loaded with historic intrigue, inspiring awe in all who pass.

Colonial Arequipa

5 Peru's second-largest metropolis bridges the gap between Cuzco's Inca glories and Lima's clamorous modernity. With dazzling baroque-*mestizo* architecture hewn out of the local white *sillar* rock, Arequipa is a Spanish colonial city that hasn't strayed far from its original conception. Its ethereal natural setting, amid snoozing volcanoes and the high *pampa*, is complemented by a 400-year-old monastery, a huge cathedral and some interesting Peruvian fusion cuisine eloquently showcased in traditional *picanterías* (spicy restaurants).

Chavín de Huántar

6 The Unesco recognized ruins of Chavín de Huántar were once a righteous ceremonial center. Today, the ex-

Indigenous Peru

While Peru's social order has been indelibly stamped by Spanish custom, its soul remains squarely indigenous. According to the country's census bureau, this crinkled piece of the South American Andes harbors 52 different ethnicities, 13 distinct linguistic families and 1786 native communities. In fact, almost half of Peru's population of more than 29 million identifies as Amerindian. Together, these groups account for an infinite number of rituals, artistic traditions and ways of life – a cultural legacy that is as rich as it is long-running.

Food & Drink

Peru has long been a place where the concept of 'fusion' was a part of everyday cooking. Over the course of the last 400 years, Andean stews mingled with Asian stir-fry techniques, and Spanish rice dishes absorbed flavors from the Amazon, producing the country's famed *criollo* (creole) cooking. In the past decade, a generation of experimental young innovators has pushed this local fare to gastronomic heights.

Peru, once a country where important guests were treated to French meals and Scotch whisky, is now a place where high-end restaurants spotlight deft interpretations of Andean favorites, including quinoa and *cuy* (guinea pig). The dining scene has blossomed. And tourism outfits have swept in to incorporate a culinary something as part of every tour.

The foodie fever has infected Peruvians at every level, in no small part due to mediagenic celebrity chef Gastón Acurio, whose culinary skill and business acumen have given him rock-star status.

The short of it is that you will never go hungry in Peru: from humble spots in Moyobamba to trendy boîtes in Miraflores, this is a country devoted to keeping the human palate entertained.

if Peru were 100 people

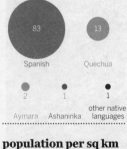

45 would be Amerindian
37 would be mestizo
15 would be white
3 would be other

languages spoken
(% of population)

83 Spanish
13 Quechua
2 Aymara
1 Ashaninka
1 other native languages

population per sq km

PERU   USA   BOLIVIA

♀ ≈ 2 people

BOB WICKHAM / GETTY IMAGES ©

Monasterio de Santa Catalina, Arequipa

ceptional feat of engineering, dating between 1200 BC and 800 BC, features striking temple-like structures above ground and a labyrinthine complex of underground corridors, ducts and chambers that invite clambering through. Nearby, the outstanding Museo Nacional de Chavín, home to the lion's share of the intricate and horrifyingly carved tenon heads that once embellished Chavín's walls, helps piece together the enigma.

The Sacred Valley

7 Ragtag Andean villages, crumbling Inca military outposts and agricultural terraces used since time immemorial are linked by the Río Urubamba as it curves and widens, coursing through the Sacred Valley. A strategic location between Cuzco and Machu Picchu makes this picturesque destination an ideal base to explore the area's famed markets and ruins. Accommodations range from inviting inns to top resorts, and

When to Go

HIGH SEASON
(Jun–Aug)

➡ Dry season in the Andean highlands and eastern rainforest.

➡ Best time for festivals and highland sports, including treks.

➡ Busiest time due to northern hemisphere holidays.

SHOULDER
(Mar–May & Sep–Nov)

➡ Spring and autumn weather in the highlands.

➡ Ideal for less-crowded visits.

➡ September to November for good rainforest trekking.

LOW SEASON
(Dec–Feb)

➡ Rainy season in the highlands.

➡ The Inca Trail closes during February for clean up.

➡ High season for the coast and beach activities.

➡ Rainy in the Amazon.

adventure options include horseback riding, rafting and treks that take you through remote weaving and agricultural villages.

The Inca Trail

8 The continent's most famous pedestrian roadway, the Inca Trail snakes 43km, up stone steps and through thick cloud forest mists. A true pilgrimage, the four- to five-day trek ends at the famous Intipunku – or Sun Gate – where trekkers get their first glimpse of the extravagant ruins at Machu Picchu. While there are countless ancient roads all over Peru, the Inca Trail, with its mix of majestic views, stagger-

ing mountain passes and clusters of ruins, remains the favorite of travelers.

Cañón del Colca

9 It's deep, very deep, but the Colca Canyon is about far more than mere statistics. In an area colonized by pre-Inca, Inca and Spanish civilizations, the culture here is as alluring as the endless trekking possibilities. Stretching 100km from end to end and plunging over 3400m at its deepest part, the canyon has been embellished with terraced agricultural fields, pastoral villages, Spanish colonial churches and pre-Inca ruins.

Getting Around

Air Domestic flight schedules and prices change frequently. New airlines open every year, as those with poor safety records close. Most big cities are served by modern jets, while smaller towns are served by propeller aircraft.

Bus Buses are the usual form of transportation for most Peruvians and many travelers. Fares are cheap and services are frequent on the major long-distance routes, but buses are of varying quality. Remote rural routes are often served by older, worn-out vehicles. Seats at the back yield a bumpier ride.

Train The privatized rail system, PeruRail, has daily services between Cuzco and Aguas Calientes, aka Machu Picchu Pueblo, and services between Cuzco and Puno on the shores of Lake Titicaca three times a week.

Parque Nacional Manu

10 Traverse three climatic zones from rearing Andean mountains to mist-swathed cloud forest on the lower slopes en route to the bowels of the jungle in Parque Nacional Manu. This has long been Peru's best-protected wilderness, brimming with fabled jungle creatures such as the anaconda, tapir, jaguars, and thousands of feasting macaws festooning clay licks with their colors. In this deep forest, tribespeople live as they have for centuries, with barely any contact with the outside world.

Red-and-green macaws, Parque Nacional Manu

MICHAEL SEWELL VISUAL PURSUIT / GETTY IMAGES ©

Ifugao rice terrace, Bangaan

CAPITAL
Manila

POPULATION
105.7 million

AREA
300,000 sq km

OFFICIAL LANGUAGES
Tagalog, English

Philippines

The Philippines is defined by its emerald rice fields, teeming megacities, graffiti-splashed jeepneys, smouldering volcanoes, fuzzy water buffaloes and smiling, happy-go-lucky people.

Just when you thought you had Asia figured out, you get to the Philippines. Instead of monks you have priests; instead of túk-túk you have tricycles; instead of *pho* you have *adobo*. At first glance the Philippines will disarm you more than charm you, but peel back the country's skin and there are treasures to be found aplenty. For starters, you can swim with whale sharks, scale volcanoes, explore desert islands, gawk at ancient emerald-green rice terraces, submerge at world-class dive sites and venture into rainforests to visit remote hill tribes.

Beyond its obvious physical assets, the Philippines possesses a quirky streak that takes a bit longer to appreciate. There are secret potions and healing lotions, guys named Bong and girls named Bing, grinning hustlers, deafening cock farms, wheezing bangkas (outrigger boats), crooked politicians, fuzzy carabao (water buffalo), graffiti-splashed jeepneys and cheap beer to enjoy as you take it all in.

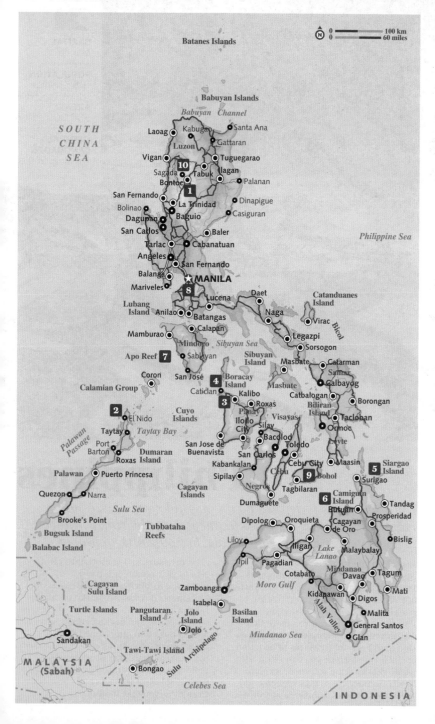

Philippines'
Top Experiences

Ifugao Rice Terraces

1 It's easy to look at a map of North Luzon and assume the Cordillera is all untamed wilderness. And yes – there's rugged jungle. But what really strikes a visitor to Banaue, Batad and the other towns of Ifugao is how cultivated the mountains are. Even the sheerest cliffs possess little patches of ground that have been tilled into rice paddies. Take all those patches together and you get a veritable blanket of upland-tilled goodness, an unending landscape of hills rounded into rice-producing lumps of emerald.

Bacuit Archipelago

2 Cruising through the labyrinthine Bacuit Archipelago of northern Palawan, past secluded beaches, pristine lagoons and rocky islets, is an experience not to be missed. Only a short bangka ride from the easygoing coastal town of El Nido, Bacuit Bay presents a thrilling mixture of imposing limestone escarpments, palm-tree-lined white-sand beaches and coral reefs. Overnight island-hopping trips in the bay or further north through the Linapacan Strait toward Coron offer an opportunity to bed down in remote fishing villages where the daily catch is grilled for dinner.

Big Lagoon, Miniloc Island

CHIQUREL ARNAUD / HEMIS.FR / GETTY IMAGES ©

Fiesta Time

3 The Philippines just isn't the Philippines without the colourful festivals, or fiestas, that rage across the country throughout the year. Even the tiniest little barangay (village) holds at least one annually. The granddaddy of them all is the Ati-Atihan Festival in Kalibo. At Bacolod's MassKara Festival and Marinduque's Moriones Festival, mischievous masked men stir the masses into a dancing frenzy. The Easter crucifixion ceremony in San Fernando produces a more macabre tableau, with Catholic devotees being physically nailed to crosses.

if the Philippines were 100 people

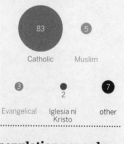

28 would be Tagalog   34 would be other
13 would be Cebuano
9 would be Ilocano
8 would be Bisaya
8 would be Hiligaynon Ilonggo

belief systems

(% of population)

83 Catholic
5 Muslim
3 Evangelical
2 Iglesia ni Kristo
7 other

population per sq km

PHILIPPINES   CHINA   SINGAPORE

✝ ≈ 140 people

Boracay

4 It wasn't that long ago that Boracay was a sleepy, almost unknown backwater. Oh, how times have changed. The world has discovered Boracay, elevating the diminutive island into a serious player in the pantheon of Southeast Asian party beaches. Yet for all that's changed, Boracay remains generally mellower than the likes of Kuta Beach or Ko Samui. And solace can still be found, in particular at the southern end of Boracay's signature White Beach, where the spirit of the old Boracay lives on.

Surfing Siargao

5 A chill-out vibe and friendly breaks for both experts and novices make this island an important player in the Philippine surfing scene. The picturesque pavilion at Cloud Nine is the community and tourism hub, but waves abound elsewhere; head to the tranquil village of Burgos in the north for an undeveloped experience or charter a bangka to seldom-visited spots. At the end of the day, regardless of your skills, nothing beats exchanging exaggerated tales of your exploits, a beachfront sundowner in your hand while you stare out at the waves rolling in.

Climbing Camiguin

6 From the northern coastline of mainland Mindanao, the rough-hewn landscape of volcanic Camiguin is camouflaged by its lush silhouette. To truly grasp this island's inspiring topography, veer into the interior on roadways that carve through dense forests and culminate in rocky path-

Karaoke

Many Westerners would sooner have their wisdom teeth removed without anaesthetic than spend an evening listening to inebriated amateurs pay homage to Celine Dion and Julio Iglesias. But when Filipinos want to unwind, they often do it with karaoke – or 'videoke' as it's known here.

Filipinos are unabashed about belting out a tune, whenever and wherever, alone or in company. They pursue the craft without a hint of irony, which means that criticising or making fun of someone's performance is decidedly taboo, and may even provoke violence.

With all that videoke going on it can be awfully hard to find peace and quiet in certain tourist hot spots. Places run by foreigners tend to be less videoke-friendly.

Food & Drink

Adobo Filipino national dish – pork, chicken or just about any meat stewed in vinegar and garlic.

Balút A boiled duck egg containing a partially developed embryo, sometimes with tiny feathers.

Halo-halo A glass packed with fruit preserves, sweet corn, young coconut and various tropical delights topped with milky crushed ice, a dollop of crème caramel and a scoop of ice cream.

Kare-kare Oxtail and vegetables cooked in peanut sauce.

Lechón Suckling pig roasted on a spit; it's de rigueur at Filipino celebrations.

Pinakbét Vegetarian dish of pumpkin, beans, eggplant and okra seasoned with garlic, onions, ginger, tomatoes and shrimp paste.

Sinigáng Any meat or seafood boiled in a sour, tamarind-flavoured soup.

Tuba A strong palm wine extracted from coconut flowers.

MassKara Festival, Bacolod

ways that trail further up into the highlands. Made for DIY adventurers, Camiguin's peaks and valleys offer streams for scrambling, mountains for scaling, canyons for rappelling and pools at the base of thundering waterfalls in which to wash off the day's exertions.

Apo Reef

7 It takes a special spot to stand out amid the Philippines' myriad dive sites. Apo Reef is such a spot. A protected, mostly sunken atoll off the west coast of Mindoro, Apo offers divers – and snorkellers – a smorgasbord of underwater splendour and marine life. On some dives you might lose track of how many sharks, rays and sea turtles you spot. Rogue tuna, wrasses and huge schools of jacks patrol deeper waters, while in the shallows eels, turtles and an array of macro (small marine) life crowd around the dazzling coral reefs.

When to Go

HIGH SEASON
(Dec–Apr)

➡ High season is dry season for most of the country; December to February are the coolest and most pleasant months to visit.

➡ Many resorts triple rates around New Year and before Easter.

SHOULDER
(May & Nov)

➡ Rising May temperatures herald the onset of the rainy season around Manila and elsewhere in the country.

➡ November sees high-season rates start to kick in at resorts.

LOW SEASON
(Jun–Oct)

➡ Wet season; accommodation prices drop by up to 30% in resort areas.

➡ Passing typhoons can cause days of torrential rain.

➡ Eastern seaboard is usually dry, but still may be susceptible to typhoons.

Manila's Nightlife

8 You name it, it's there. That about sums up Manila nightlife. From the bongo-infused hipster hang-outs of Quezon City, to Malate's live-music bars, to the chichi nightclubs of Makati and the new Resorts World, action beckons at all hours. On any given night, open-air 'restobars' are packed with beer-swilling punters until well past midnight, while karaoke bars and Filipino live music clubs bust out the tunes. On weekends, stir-crazy expats and cadres of cashed-up Makati kids keep the clubs thumping until well past dawn. Looking for something different? The drag show at Club Mwah! is classic.

Best on Film

Imelda (2004) Fascinating look into the psyche of Imelda Marcos.

Kubrador (2006) Top actress Gina Pareño stars in this film about an illegal numbers game.

Serbis (2008) Critically acclaimed film about a family-run porn-movie house in Angeles.

Best in Print

Pacific Rims: Beermen Ballin' in Flip-Flops and the Philippines' Unlikely Love Affair with Basketball (Rafe Bartholomew) As riotous as the title implies.

Playing with Water – Passion and Solitude on a Philippine Island (James Hamilton-Paterson) This timeless account of life on a remote islet sheds much light on Philippine culture.

The Tessaract (Alex Garland, 1999) A thrilling romp through Manila's dark side, this was the second novel penned by the author of the 1996 cult backpacker hit, *The Beach*.

Getting Around

Air Domestic airlines PAL and low-cost carrier Cebu Pacific serve most main cities out of Manila and/or Cebu.

Boat The islands of the Philippines are linked by an incredible network of ferry routes and prices are generally affordable. Ferries usually take the form of motorised outriggers (known locally as bangka), speedy 'fastcraft' vessels, car ferries (dubbed RORO, or 'roll-on-roll-off' ferries) and, for long-haul journeys, vast multidecked ships.

Bus & Minivan Philippine buses come in all shapes, and depots are dotted throughout towns and the countryside. Minivans are a lot quicker than buses but they are also more expensive and more cramped.

Local Transport In the Visayan islands and northern Mindanao, *habal-habal* are motorcycle taxis with extended seats. Jeepneys – modified army jeeps left behind by the Americans after WWII – are the main urban transport in most cities. They run on set routes.

Bohol Interior

9 It may all seem a bit touristy, but no visit to Bohol is complete without an inland detour to visit the iconic Chocolate Hills and cute bug-eyed tarsiers. Get there at dusk for the memorable sight of the grassy hillocks spanning out to the misty horizon. Search for tarsiers in the wild on night safaris, or head to the tarsier sanctuary where you are guaranteed to see these lovable primates.

Sagada

10 The tribes of the Cordillera of North Luzon all seem to have impressive burial practices. The hanging coffins of Sagada are stacked into niches cut into rocky cliffs, shelved like old books sitting in silent elevation over the jungle valleys. Sagada itself is one of the few traditionally 'backpacker' towns in North Luzon, with a gentle, friendly budget-traveller vibe that's hard not to love.

Makati district, Manila

HOLGER METTE / GETTY IMAGES ©

CAPITAL
Adamstown

POPULATION
65

AREA
4.5 sq km

OFFICIAL
LANGUAGES
English,
Pitkern

Stephen's lorikeet, Henderson Island

Pitcairn Island

As the smallest territory in the world and one of the most remote destinations on earth, Pitcairn Island feels both claustrophobic and wildly exhilarating.

What's rarely mentioned about Pitcairn Island, between the infamous *Bounty* story and the 2004 sexual assault trials gossip, is that it's a place of incredible natural beauty. As the smallest territory in the world and one of the most remote destinations on earth, Pitcairn Island feels both claustrophobic and wildly exhilarating. The island's 4.5 sq km surface is almost entirely sloped and has landscapes that vary from desolate rock cliffs to lush tropical hillsides.

Yet it's the 65 or so residents, descended from the *Bounty* mutineers, who make the place famous. If you can find a way to get here, spend time hiking and meeting the locals, you'll quickly understand why these Anglo-Polynesians are proud to call Pitcairn home and preserve their unique heritage.

The archipelago also consists of two atolls plus Henderson Island – a raised coral island with a virtually untouched environment and endemic birdlife.

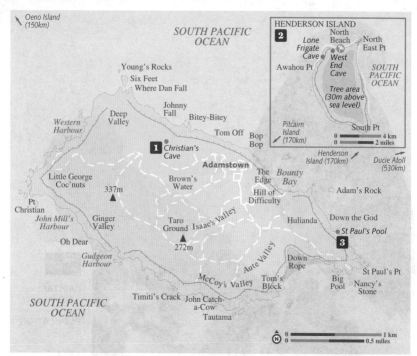

Pitcairn Island's
Top Experiences

Christian's Cave

1 Climb the precipice to Christian's Cave and imagine, as you gaze over Adamstown, what must have gone through Fletcher Christian's head as he sat there hundreds of years ago. You can eat, drink and get to know the locals at Christian's Cafe.

Henderson Island

2 Visit uninhabited Henderson Island, 170km northeast of Pitcairn Island and the largest island of the Pitcairn group. The island is populated by four species of endemic land birds – the flightless and fearless Henderson rail, the colourful Stephen's lorikeet, the territorial Henderson fruit dove and the Henderson warbler. Because of its pristine condition and rare birdlife, the island was declared a Unesco World Heritage site in 1988.

St Paul's Pool

3 Take a cool dip in the electric blue, glass-clear waters of St Paul's Pool, a stunning, cathedral-like rock formation encircling a sea-fed pool.

Food & Drink

Breadfruit Typically eaten unripe and roasted till charred on an open fire; its flavour is somewhere between a potato and a chestnut.

Drink Have a tipple with the locals at Christian's Cafe on Friday nights.

Honey Local Pitcairn honey is said to be the world's purest.

When to Go

YEAR ROUND

➡ Humidity ranges from 60–100%.

➡ Warm weather for most of the year.

OCT–APR

➡ Average summer temperatures range from 20–30°C.

APR–OCT

➡ The dry season.

➡ Slightly cooler temperatures than during summer.

Stary Rynek (Old Market Square), Poznań

CAPITAL
Warsaw

POPULATION
38.4 million

AREA
312,685 sq km

OFFICIAL LANGUAGE
Polish

Poland

Chic medieval hot spots like Kraków and Gdańsk vie with energetic Warsaw for your urban attention. Outside the cities, forests, rivers, lakes and hills beckon for some fresh-air fun.

If they were handing out prizes for 'most eventful history', Poland would be sure to get a medal. The nation has spent centuries at the pointy end of history, grappling with war and invasion. Nothing, however, has succeeded in suppressing the Poles' strong cultural identity. As a result, centres such as bustling Warsaw and cultured Kraków exude a sophisticated energy that's a heady mix of old and new.

Away from the cities, Poland offers a diverse range of experiences, from swimming on its Baltic Sea beaches to skiing or hiking in its magnificent mountains. Everywhere in between are towns and cities dotted with ruined castles, picturesque squares, colourful houses and historic churches.

Although prices are slowly rising as its economy gathers momentum, Poland is still good value for travellers year-round. As the Polish people work on combining their national identity with their place in Europe, it's a fascinating time to visit this beautiful country.

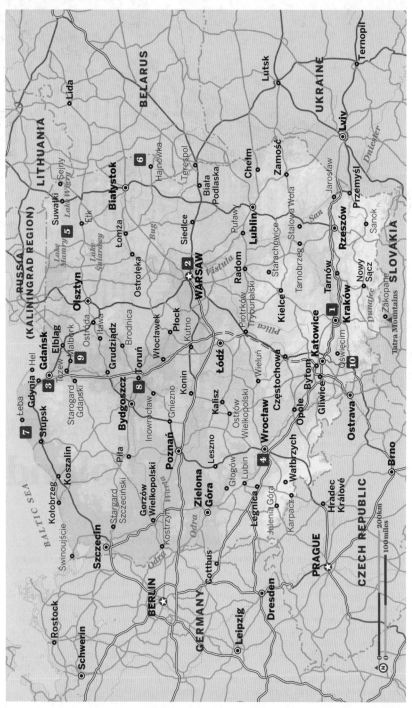

Poland's
Top Experiences

Stately Kraków

1 A unique atmosphere wafts through the attractive streets and squares of this former royal capital, with its heady blend of history and harmonious architecture. From the vast Rynek Główny, Europe's largest medieval market square, to the magnificent Wawel Castle on a hill above the Old Town, every part of the city is fascinating. Add to that the former Jewish district of Kazimierz and its scintillating nightlife (and then contrast it with the communist-era concrete structures of Nowa Huta) and it's easy to see why Kraków is Poland's most unmissable destination.

Warsaw's Palaces

2 Images of elegant palaces don't immediately come to mind when thinking of Poland's capital. After all, the city was flattened by the Germans in WWII. But that's where Warsaw really surprises. From Łazienki Park's lovely 'Palace on the Water' to stately Wilanów Palace, a veritable Varsovian version of Versailles on the city's outskirts, Warsaw sports an elegant side that people rarely see. And if size really does matter, there's that gargantuan Palace of Culture & Science right in the centre.

Wawel Castle, Kraków

MARTIN DIMITROV / GETTY IMAGES ©

Gdańsk

3 Colossal red-brick churches peer down on slender merchants' townhouses, wedged ornately between palaces that line wide, ancient thoroughfares and crooked medieval lanes. A cosmopolitan residue of art and artefact left behind by a rich maritime and trading past packs whole museums, and tourists from around the world compete with amber stalls and street performers for cobblestone space. This is Gdańsk, a Baltic seaport and Poland's metropolis of the north. It was once part of the Hanseatic League, but now it's in a league of its own.

if Poland were 100 people

15 would be aged 0-14
12 would be aged 15-24
44 would be aged 25-54
15 would be aged 55-64
14 would be aged 65+

belief systems
(% of population)

90
Roman Catholic

1
Eastern Orthodox

1
Protestant

8
other

population per sq km

POLAND	UK	RUSSIA

≈ 8 people

Wrocław

4 Throughout its turbulent history, this city on the Odra River – the former German city of Breslau – has taken everything invaders could throw at it, and survived. Badly damaged in WWII, it was artfully rebuilt around its beautiful main square, with an intriguing complex of buildings at its centre. Another attraction is the Panorama of Racławice, a vast 19th-century painting hung about the walls of a circular building. Beyond historical gems, however, Wrocław has a vibrant nightlife, with plenty of dining and drinking options throughout the narrow streets of its lively Old Town.

Great Masurian Lakes

5 Sip a cocktail on the deck of a luxury yacht, take a dip, or don a lifejacket, grab your paddle and slide off into a watery adventure on one of the interconnected lakes that make up this mecca for Polish sailing and water-sports fans. Away from the water, head for one of the region's buzzing resorts, where the slap and jangle of masts competes with the clinking of glasses and the murmur of boat talk. In winter, when the lakes freeze over, cross-country skis replace water skis on the steel-hard surface.

Białowieża Forest

6 That bison on the label of a bottle of Żubr beer starts to make a lot more sense once you've visited this little piece of pristine wood on the Belarus border. The Białowieża National Park holds one of Europe's last vestiges of primeval forest, which you

A Phoenix from the Flames

Warsaw's German occupiers razed the city at the end of WWII – only about 15% of it was left standing.

So complete was the destruction that there were even suggestions that the capital should be moved elsewhere, but instead it was decided that parts would be rebuilt.

The most valuable historic monuments were restored to their previous appearance based on original drawings and photographs. Between 1949 and 1963 work was concentrated on the Old Town, aiming to return it to its 17th- and 18th-century appearance – today not a single building in the area looks less than 200 years old.

So complete was the restoration that Unesco granted the Old Town World Heritage status in 1980.

Food & Drink

Beer Good, cold and inexpensive. Often served in colourful beer gardens.

Bigos A thick sauerkraut and meat stew.

Bread *Chleb* (bread) means more than sustenance to Poles. It's a symbol of good fortune; some older people kiss a piece of bread if they drop it on the ground. Traditional Polish bread is made with rye.

Pierogi Dumplings stuffed with filling.

Placki ziemniaczane Potato pancakes with a meaty sauce.

Soup Hearty examples include *żurek* (sour soup with sausage and hard-boiled egg) and *barszcz* (red beetroot soup).

Sweets *Szarlotka* (apple cake with cream), or the weighty *sernik* (baked cheesecake).

Vodka Try it plain, or ask for *myśliwska* (juniper-berry flavoured), *wiśniówka* (with cherries) or *żubrówka* (flavoured with bison grass).

Beach at Świnoujście

can visit in the company of a guide. Nearby there's a small reserve with another survivor from a bygone era: the once-mighty European bison.

Baltic Beaches

7 The season may be brief and the sea one of Europe's nippiest, but if you're looking for a dose of sand, there are few better destinations than the Baltic's cream-white beaches. Many people come for the strands along one of the coastal resorts, be it hedonistic Darłówko, genteel Świnoujście or the spa town of Kołobrzeg; others opt to flee the masses and head out instead for the shifting dunes of the Słowiński National Park, where the Baltic's constant bluster sculpts mountains of sifted grains.

Gothic Toruń

8 While many of northern Poland's towns went up in a puff of red-brick dust in WWII's end game, Toruń miraculously escaped intact, leaving today's visitors a

When to Go

HIGH SEASON (May–Sep)	**SHOULDER** (Mar & Apr, Oct)	**LOW SEASON** (Nov–Feb)
➡ Expect sunny skies in June and July, but prepare for rain.	➡ Some attractions may be closed or have shorter hours.	➡ Snow in the mountains brings skiers to mountain resorts.
➡ Museums, national parks and other attractions are open for business.	➡ April and October are cool, but expect some sunny days.	➡ The week between Christmas and New Year can be crowded.
➡ Prepare for crowds, especially at weekends.	➡ Easter weekend can be very crowded; book in advance.	➡ Museums and castles in smaller towns may be closed.

WITOLD SKRYPCZAK / GETTY IMAGES ©

magnificently preserved, walled Gothic city by the swirling Vistula. Wander through the old town crammed with museums, churches, grand mansions and squares, and when you're all in, perk up with a peppery gingerbread cookie, Toruń's signature snack. Another treat is the city's Copernicus connections – Poland's most illustrious astronomer allegedly first saw the light of day in one of Toruń's Gothic townhouses.

Malbork Castle

9 Medieval monster mother ship of the Teutonic order, Gothic blockbuster Malbork Castle is a mountain of bricks held together by a lake of mortar. It was home to the all-powerful order's grand master and later to visiting Polish monarchs. They have all now left the stage of history, but not even the shells of WWII could dismantle this baby. If you came to Poland to see castles, this is what you came to see; catch it just before dusk when the slanting sunlight burns the bricks kiln-crimson.

Auschwitz-Birkenau

10 This former ex-termination camp, established by the German military occupiers in 1941, is a grim reminder of a part of history's greatest genocide, the killing of more than a million people here in the pursuit of Nazi ideology. Now it's a museum and memorial to the victims. Beyond the infamous 'Arbeit Macht Frei' sign at the entrance to Auschwitz are surviving prison blocks that house exhibitions as shocking as they are informative. Not far away, the former Birkenau camp holds the remnants of the gas chambers used for mass murder. Visiting the complex is an unsettling but deeply moving experience.

Best on Film

Amator (Krzysztof Kieślowski) Early Kieślowski effort on self-censorship under communism.

Katyń (Andrzej Wajda) Moving depiction of the WWII massacre.

The Pianist (Roman Polański) Oscar-winning film about life in Warsaw's WWII Jewish ghetto.

Best in Print

God's Playground: A History of Poland (Norman Davies) Highly readable two-volume set on 1000 years of Polish history.

Survival in Auschwitz (Primo Levi) Classic of Holocaust literature that hasn't lost a drop of impact.

The Painted Bird (Jerzy Kosiński) Page-turner on the travails of an orphan boy on the run during WWII.

The Polish Officer (Alan Furst) Gripping spy novel set in Poland on the eve of WWII.

Getting Around

Bus Buses can be useful on short routes and through the southern mountains, but usually trains are quicker and more comfortable, and private minibuses are quicker and more direct.

Car & Motorcycle Major international car-rental companies have offices in larger cities and at airports. Prices are comparable to rental in Western Europe. Car theft is a problem in Poland, so consider paying for guarded parking.

Train Trains will be your main means of transport, especially for long distances. They are cheap, reliable and rarely overcrowded. Most trains offer two classes: 2nd (*druga klasa*) and 1st (*pierwsza klasa*), which is 50% more expensive.

WITOLD SKRYPCZAK / GETTY IMAGES ©

CAPITAL
Lisbon

POPULATION
10.8 million

AREA
92,090 sq km

OFFICIAL LANGUAGE
Portuguese

Praia da Dona Ana, Algarve

Portugal

Medieval castles, cobblestone villages, captivating cities and golden beaches: the Portugal experience can be many things. History, great food and idyllic scenery are just the beginning...

Celts, Romans, Visigoths, Moors and Christians all left their mark on the Iberian peninsula nation. Here, you can gaze upon 20,000-year-old stone carvings in the Vila Nova de Foz Côa, watch the sunset over mysterious megaliths outside Évora or lose yourself in the elaborate corridors of Unesco World Heritage sites in Tomar, Belém, Alcobaça or Batalha. You can pack an itinerary visiting palaces set above mist-covered woodlands, craggy clifftop castles and stunningly preserved medieval town centres.

Outside the cities, Portugal's beauty unfolds in all its startling variety. You can go hiking amid the granite peaks of Parque Nacional da Peneda-Gerês or take in the pristine scenery and historic villages of the little-explored Beiras. More than 800km of coast offers a multitude of places to soak up the splendour. Gaze out over dramatic end-of-the-world cliffs, surf stellar breaks off dune-covered beaches or laze peacefully on sandy islands fronting calm blue seas.

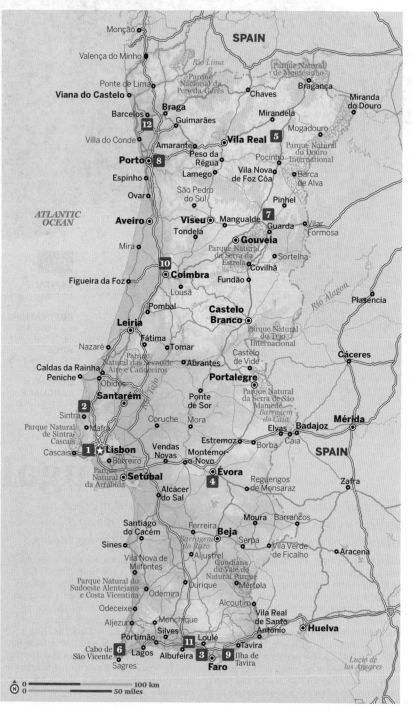

Portugal's

Top Experiences

Lisbon

1 Lisbon's Alfama district, with its labyrinthine alleyways, hidden courtyards and curving shadow-filled lanes, is a magical place in which to lose all sense of direction and delve into the soul of the city. You'll pass breadbox-sized grocers, brilliantly tiled buildings and cosy taverns filled with easygoing chatter, accompanied by the scent of chargrilled sardines and the mournful rhythms of fado drifting in the breeze. Round a bend and catch sight of steeply pitched rooftops leading down to the glittering Tejo, and you know you're hooked.

Sintra

2 Less than an hour by train from the capital, Sintra feels like another world. Like a page torn from a fairy tale, Sintra is a quaint village sprinkled with stone-walled taverns and with a whitewashed palace looming over town. Forested hillsides form the backdrop to the storybook setting, with imposing castles, mystical gardens, strange mansions and centuries-old monasteries hidden among the woodlands. The fog that sweeps in by night adds another layer of mystery, and cool evenings are best spent fireside in one of Sintra's many charming B&Bs.

Street musician sings fado, Lisbon

1

HOLGER LEUE / GETTY IMAGES ©

Parque Natural da Ria Formosa

3 This special spot feels like it's in the middle of wilderness, yet it's right off the Algarvian coast. Enclosing a vast area of *sapais* (marshes), *salinas* (salt pans), creeks and dune islands, the protected lagoon system stretches for an incredible 60km and encompasses 18,000 hectares. And it's all accessible from various towns, including Faro and Olhão – have a boat drop you at a deserted beach, or amble along the nature trail among the precious wetland birdlife.

Historic Évora

4 The Queen of the Alentejo and one of Portugal's most beautifully preserved medieval towns, Évora is an enchanting place to spend several days delving into the past. Inside the 14th-century walls, Évora's narrow, winding lanes lead to striking architectural works: an elaborate medieval cathedral and cloisters, Roman ruins and a picturesque town square. Historic and aesthetic virtues aside, Évora is also a lively university town, and its many attractive restaurants serve up excellent, hearty Alentejan cuisine.

Douro Wine Country

5 The exquisite Alto Douro wine country is the oldest demarcated wine region on earth. Its steeply terraced hills, stitched together with craggy vines that have produced luscious wines for centuries, loom on both sides of the sinuous Rio Douro. Whether you get here by driving the impossibly scenic back roads, or catch a train or boat from Porto, take the time to hike, cruise and taste. Countless vintners receive guests for tours, tastings and overnight stays.

Cabo de São Vicente

6 There's something thrilling about standing at Europe's most southwestern edge, a headland of barren cliffs to which Portuguese sailors bid a nervous farewell as they sailed past, venturing into the unknown during Portugal's golden years of exploration. The windswept cape is redolent of history – if you squint hard (really hard), you'll see

Saudade: the Portuguese Blues

The Portuguese psyche is a complicated thing, particularly when it comes to not easily translatable concepts like *saudade*. In its purest form, *saudade* is the nostalgic, often deeply melancholic longing for something: a person, a place or just about anything that's no longer obtainable. *Saudade* is deeply connected to this seafaring nation's history and remains deeply intertwined with Portuguese identity. The elusive emotion has played a starring role in some of Portugal's great works of art – in film, literature and, most importantly, music. Scholars are unable to pinpoint exactly when the term 'saudade' first arose. Some trace it back to the grand voyages during the Age of Discoveries, when sailors, captains and explorers spent many months out at sea, and gave voice to the longing for the lives they left behind.

Food & Drink

Bifana A bread roll served with a slice of fried pork inside. They're best in the Alentejo.

Francesinha Porto's favourite hangover snack is a thick open-faced sandwich covered in melted cheese.

Grilled chicken Rotisserie chicken is an art form in Portugal. Spice it up with *piri-piri* (hot sauce).

Marzipan In the Algarve, this very sweet, almond-infused confection is a local favourite.

Pastel de nata Custard tart, ideally served warm and dusted with cinnamon.

Tinned fish Sardines, mackerel and tuna served with bread, olives and other accompaniments are the latest snack craze in Lisbon.

Travesseira A rolled puff pastry filled with almond-and-egg-yolk custard. Find them in Sintra.

if Portugal were 100 people

60 would work in services
28 would work in industry
12 would work in agriculture

belief systems
(% of population)

85 Roman Catholic
9 other
4 no religion
2 other Christian

population per sq km

PORTUGAL   USA   UK

≈ 30 people

Igreja do Carmo's *azulejos* (hand-painted tiles), Porto

the ghost of Vasco da Gama sailing past. These days, a fortress and lighthouse perch on the cape. A new museum beautifully highlights Portugal's maritime navigation history.

Villages of the Beiras

7 From schist-walled communities spilling down terraced hillsides to spiky-edged sentinels that once guarded the eastern border against Spanish incursions, the inland Beiras are filled with picturesque and historical villages: Piódão, Trancoso, Sortelha, Monsanto... Today mostly devoid of residents but not yet overwhelmed by mass tourism, they are some of the country's most peaceful and appealing destinations. String a few together into the perfect road trip.

Porto

8 It would be hard to dream up a more romantic city than Portugal's second largest. Laced with narrow pedestrian laneways, it is blessed with countless baroque churches, epic theatres and sprawling plazas. Its

When to Go

HIGH SEASON
(Jul–Aug)

➡ Accommodation prices increase by 30%.

➡ Expect big crowds in the Algarve and coastal areas.

➡ Sweltering temperatures are common.

SHOULDER
(May, Jun & Sep)

➡ Wildflowers and mild days are ideal for hikes and outdoor activities.

➡ Lively festivals take place in June.

➡ Crowds and prices are average.

LOW SEASON
(Dec–Mar)

➡ Shorter, rainier days with freezing temperatures in the interior.

➡ Lower prices, fewer crowds.

➡ Attractions keep shorter opening hours.

Ribeira district – a Unesco World Heritage site – is just a short walk across a landmark bridge from centuries-old port wineries in Vila Nova de Gaia, where you can sip the world's best port.

Ilha de Tavira

9 This place has the lot for sun-seekers, beach bums, nature lovers (and naturists): mile after mile of golden beach (think sand, sand, sand, as far as the eye can see), a designated nudist area, transport via miniature train, busy restaurants and a campground. To top it off, it's part of the protected Parque Natural da Ria Formosa.

Coimbra

10 Portugal's atmospheric college town, Coimbra rises steeply from the Rio Mondego to a medieval quarter housing one of Europe's oldest universities. Students roam the narrow streets clad in black

Getting Around

Bus Cheaper and slower than trains. Useful for more remote villages that aren't serviced by trains. Infrequent service on weekends.

Car Useful for visiting small villages, national parks and other regions with minimal public transport. Cars can be hired in major towns and cities. Drive on the right.

Train Extremely affordable, with a decent network between major towns from north to south.

capes, while strolling fado musicians give free concerts beneath the Moorish town gate. Kids can keep busy at Portugal dos Pequenitos, a theme park with miniature versions of Portuguese monuments.

The Algarve

11 Sunseekers have much to celebrate when it comes to beaches. On Portugal's south coast, the Algarve has a varied coastline. There are sandy islands reachable only by boat, dramatic cliff-backed shores, rarely visited beaches and people-packed sands near buzzing nightlife. Days are spent playing in the waves, taking long ocean-

front strolls and surfing memorable breaks.

Barcelos Market

12 The Minho is famous for its sprawling outdoor markets, but the largest, oldest and most celebrated is the Feira de Barcelos, held every Thursday in this ancient town on the banks of the Rio Cávado. Most outsiders come for the yellow-dotted louça de Barcelos ceramics and the gaudy figurines, while rural villagers are more interested in buying the scrawny chickens, or browsing hand-embroidered linen, woven baskets and hand-carved ox yokes.

Portuguese cockerel figurines, Feira de Barcelos, Minho

ALAN COPSON / GETTY IMAGES ©

CAPITAL	San Juan
POPULATION	3.6 million
AREA	13,790 sq km
OFFICIAL LANGUAGES	Spanish, English

Playa Flamenco, Culebra

Puerto Rico

Puerto Rico is the fodder of many a Caribbean daydream for good reason: this natural jewel box can satisfy the lethargic beach bum, the sunrise rainforest explorer and the budding big-wave surfer.

Golden sand, swashbuckling history and wildly diverse terrain make the sun-washed backyard of the United States a place fittingly hyped as the 'Island of Enchantment.' It's the Caribbean's only island where you can catch a wave before breakfast, hike a rainforest after lunch and race to the beat of a high-gloss, cosmopolitan city after dark.

Between blinking casinos and chirping frogs, Puerto Rico is also a land of dynamic contrasts, where the breezy gate of the Caribbean is bedeviled by the hustle of contemporary America. While modern conveniences make it simple for travelers, the condo-lined concrete jungle might seem a bit too close to home. A quick visit for Puerto Rico's beaches, historic forts and craps tables will quicken a visitor's pulse, but the island's singular essence only reveals itself to those who go deeper, exploring the misty crags of the central mountains and crumbling facades of the island's remote corners.

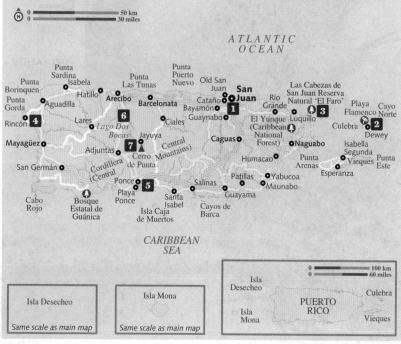

Puerto Rico's
Top Experiences

Old San Juan

1 Modern America started here. Well, almost. Established in 1521, San Juan is the second-oldest European-founded settlement in the Americas and the oldest under US jurisdiction. Even those limited to a quick visit find it easy to fall under the beguiling spell of Old San Juan's cobblestone streets, pastel-painted colonial buildings and grand fortresses. From the ramparts of El Morro, the allure of this place is evident in every direction – from the labyrinth of crooked streets to the endless sparkle of the Atlantic. By day, lose yourself in historical stories of blood and bombast; by night, float along in crowds of giggling tourists and rowdy locals.

Playa Flamenco

2 Stretching for a mile around a sheltered, horseshoe- shaped bay, Playa Flamenco is not just Culebra's best beach; it is also generally regarded as the finest in Puerto Rico, and quite possibly the whole Caribbean. In fact, certain discerning travel writers have suggested that it is among the top 10 in the world. While individual musings may sound trite, there is no denying that this gentle arc of white sand and crystal surf is something special. Backed by low scrub rather than craning palms, and equipped with basic amenities, Flamenco is the only public beach on the island. It is also the only place where you are allowed to camp.

Las Cabezas de San Juan Reserva Natural 'El Faro'

3 The diverse ecosystem of this reserve, a 316-acre nodule of land on Puerto Rico's extreme northeast tip, makes a quick day trip from the high rises of San Juan's urban core and highlights the island's ecological richness at every turn. After a quick, informative trip through the visitors center, travelers begin the compact tour of the flora and fauna. The sea grass waves alongside mangrove forest and coral-protected lagoons, while giant iguanas scuttle from underfoot and crabs scurry along the rocky shores. Adding historical value is Puerto Rico's oldest lighthouse.

Parque de Bombas, Ponce

Surfing at Rincón

4 In winter, the cold weather brings righteous swells to the island's surfing capital of Rincón, where some of the most consistent, varied and exciting surf locations in the Caribbean can be found. And while the swells attract would-be pros, beginners can paddle out to tamer breaks nearby. At sunset, crowds of locals and visitors replenish themselves with inexpensive eats and ice-cold beer while they mingle in beach bars and around bonfires on the sand.

Ponce

5 Strolling around the sparkling fountains in the central square and narrow streets of the city's historic center evokes the stately spirit of Puerto Rico's past. The city has an easygoing spirit, with businesses that open late and close early, couples who spend breezy evenings 2 miles south at the shoreline. Clusters of restaurants and cafes draw families for open-air dinners on the weekend. After the kids go to bed, the drinks flow and the area jumps with a booming mix of reggaetón and salsa.

if Puerto Rico were 100 people

76 would be white
7 would be black
4 would be mixed
13 would be other

belief systems
(% of population)

85

15

Roman Catholic   Protestant/other

population per sq km

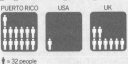

PUERTO RICO   USA   UK

♦ ≈ 32 people

When to Go

HIGH SEASON
(mid-Dec–mid-Apr & Jul)

➡ Crowds escaping the frosty US mainland in winter see hotels rates go up and seasonal attractions come to life.

➡ In July, local families create a second high season, filling beach towns.

SHOULDER
(Sep–Nov & mid-Apr–May)

➡ Puerto Rico's tourist infrastructure takes a breather to regroup during shoulder season, though there isn't a significant fluctuation in prices or services.

LOW SEASON
(Jun–Nov)

➡ Apart from July, things get pretty lethargic during hurricane season. Some resorts offer discounted packages but prices at small hotels don't drop precipitously.

A Movable Feast

Cheap, cheerful and indisputably Puerto Rican, *friquitines* (also known as *quioscos*, *kioskos* or just plain food stalls) offer some of the island's best cheap snacks. Running the gamut from smoky holes-in-the-wall to mobile trucks that park on the roadside, these kiosks offer fast food that is invariably homemade, locally sourced and tasty.

The island's most famous cluster of permanent *friquitines* (more than 60 or so in all) lines the beachfront at Luquillo. Other more movable feasts operate at weekends in places such as Piñones near San Juan and Boquerón on the west coast, although you can come across them almost anywhere.

Food & Drink

Brazo gitano The 'Gypsy's Arm' is a huge cake roll, filled with fresh, mashed fruit and sweet cheese.

Chuletas can-can The house dish at the peerless Restaurante La Guardarraya – a deep-fried bone-in pork chop – is worth going well out of your way for.

Lechón asado Smoky, spit-roasted suckling pig is sold at roadside trucks and is a taste of heaven.

Mofongo A plantain crust encases seafood or steak in this signature dish.

Piña colada A creamy mix of pineapple juice and coconut cream, sometimes the base of a rum drink.

Sorullitos de maíz Deep-fried corn-meal fritters make an excellent bar snack.

Ron The national drink (rum). Though the headquarters of Bacardi are outside San Juan, Puerto Ricans drink locally made Don Q or Castillo.

Cordillera Central

Kayaking on Lago Dos Bocas

6 Hidden in the lush vegetation of the central mountains, the calm waters of Lago Dos Bocas allow an experience for kayakers that's entirely more serene than bobbing along on the waves of the open sea. You'll first spy the lake along Rte 143 near the mountain town of Utuado, where travelers can rent boats from little lakeside restaurants. It's an ideal situation – after you work up an appetite with a few hours of paddling, enjoy a feast of freshly caught fish from the lake.

Fresh Coffee in the Central Mountains

7 Puerto Rico's legendary coffee plantations offer caffeine junkies a rare opportunity. Here, you can sip a steaming cup of rich, fresh coffee while looking over the rolling hills and quiet valleys where the beans are grown, roasted and brewed. The winding Ruta Panorámica, a white-knuckled scenic route through the mountains, takes travelers past one picturesque plantation after the next, through the village of Jayuya, in the heart of coffee country.

Getting Around

Air The bulk of Puerto Rico's domestic air traffic links San Juan to the islands of Culebra and Vieques.

Boat Passenger ferries run three to four times daily from Fajardo to Vieques and Culebra.

Car Good highways link San Juan to just about every other major point, with a drive of less than two hours. Do not take a rental car on the ferry to Vieques or Culebra, as it will void the contract with your rental agent.

Públicos *Públicos* – large vans that pick up and drop off passengers with great frequency and little haste – run between a few of the major cities, but it's a very slow (although cheap) way to travel.

Al-Biddar Tower, Doha

CAPITAL
Doha

POPULATION
2.1 million

AREA
11,586 sq km

OFFICIAL LANGUAGE
Arabic

Qatar

Combining Bedouin heritage with modern elegance and luxury, Qatar offers an excellent introduction to the Arab world.

Ask the Qataris, Bedouin roots notwith-standing, what they are most proud of and they will undoubtedly say Doha. And indeed you can see why: the modern capital with its spectacular tapering towers, elegant corniche and extravagant malls, makes Doha arguably the finest stop over in the Gulf.

But there's more to Qatar than a shopping spree. The whole country, with its heritage souqs, world-class Museum of Islamic Art, and lyrical sand dunes, provides travellers the perfect first step into the Middle East but without the tensions often associated with the region.

The success of this booming nation is more than just skin deep. Rapid economic expansion, barely slowed by the global recession, international sports tournaments, and Education City: these are some of the many hallmarks of Qatar's sophistication. Chances are, if you spend a night in the vibrant city of Doha, you'll be lobbying the relatives to stay a whole lot longer in Qatar.

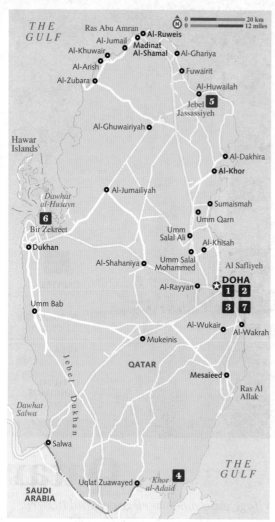

THE GULF

Ras Abu Amran
Al-Ruweis
Al-Jumail
Madinat
Al-Khuwair
Al-Shamal
Al-Ghariya
Al-Arish
Al-Zubara
Fuwairit
Al-Huwailah
Jebel
Jassassiyeh
Al-Ghuwairiyah

Hawar Islands

Dawhat al-Husayn

Al-Dakhira
Al-Khor
Al-Jumailiyah
Sumaismah
Umm Qarn
Bir Zekreet
Umm Salal Ali
Al-Khisah
Dukhan
Umm Salal Mohammed
Al Safliyeh
Al-Shahaniya
DOHA
Al-Rayyan
Umm Bab
Al-Wukair
Al-Wakrah
Mukeinis
QATAR
Jebel Dukhan
Mesaieed
Ras Al Allak
Dawhat Salwa
Salwa
THE GULF
SAUDI ARABIA
Uqlat Zuawayed
Khor al-Adaid

0 — 20 km
0 — 12 miles

Qatar's
Top Experiences

Doha

1 Step into the future by walking along Al-Corniche, Doha's über-modern seafront. The highlight of Doha is unquestionably the corniche. Doha Bay was carefully constructed with landfill to make an attractive crescent, along which runs shaded footpaths and cycling tracks. One great way to gain an introduction to the city is to begin at the Ras Abu Abboud St Flyover at the southeastern end of the corniche and either walk or drive around to the Sheraton Doha Hotel & Resort, looking out for the prominent landmarks.

Museum of Islamic Art

2 Rising from its own purpose-built island and set in an extensive landscape of lawns and ornamental trees, this is a monument of a museum. It was designed by the renowned architect IM Pei (architect of the Louvre pyramid) and is shaped like a postmodern fortress with minimal windows (to cut down on energy use) and a 'virtual' moat. The museum houses the largest collection of Islamic art in the world, collected from three continents. Exquisite textiles, ceramics, enamel work and glass are showcased conceptually: a single motif, for example, is illustrated in the weave of a carpet, in a ceramic floor tile or adapted in a piece of gold jewellery in neighbouring display cases. This is the kind of museum that is so rich in treasure that it rewards short, intense visits.

Souq Waqif

3 Step into the past in the cardamon-scented alleyways of Souq Waqif. This is a wonderful place to explore, shop, have dinner or simply idle time away in one of the many attractive cafes. There has been a souq on this site for centuries – this was the spot where Bedu once brought sheep, goats and wool to trade. It grew into a scruffy warren of concrete alleyways by the end of the last century and at one point was almost condemned for demolition. The entire market area has since been cleverly redeveloped to look like a 19th-century souq, with mud-rendered shops and exposed timber beams and some beautifully

restored original Qatari buildings.

Khor al-Adaid

4 Take a dune for a pillow and the stars for a blanket at beautiful Khor al-Adaid. This beautiful 'inland sea', near the border with Saudi Arabia is Qatar's major natural attraction. Often described as a sea or a lake, the *khor* is in fact a creek surrounded by silvery crescents of sand (known as *barchan*). All sand dunes look wonderful in the late afternoon sun, but those of Khor al-Adaid take on an almost mystical quality under a full moon when the *sabkha* (salt flats) sparkle in the gaps between the sand. This is also the perfect spot for star-gazing.

Rock Carvings of Jebel Jassassiyeh

5 It's probably fair to say that the petroglyphs of northern Qatar have been seen by very few visitors. Until very recently their whereabouts was all but a secret and only those in the know with a 4WD could find them. So what are these elusive petroglyphs? In an unpromising piece of desert known as Jebel Jassassiyeh, are remarkable ancient rock carvings – over 900 strewn across 580 sites. Some are said to depict aerial views of boats, which is interesting given that in an utterly flat country, on a usually flat sea, there would have been no opportunity for people to gain an aerial view of anything.

if Qatar were 100 people

40 would be Arab
18 would be Indian
18 would be Pakistani
10 would be Iranian
14 would be other

belief systems
(% of population)

78 Muslim
8 Christian
14 other

population per sq km

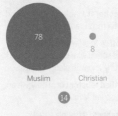

QATAR   UAE   USA

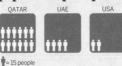

♦ ≈ 15 people

When to Go

NOV–MAR

➡ Enjoy a break from the intense heat and humidity of summer.

APR

➡ Cheer on the favourite at the Emir's Cup event – camel racing at its best.

JUN

➡ Watch the grand prix of power boat racing slice up the waters of Doha Bay.

Bonding Beads

Sit in a coffeehouse in Qatar, be present at a business meeting or watch a party of *sheesha* (water pipe used to smoke tobacco) smokers and you will notice a common activity: twirling a set of beads between thumb and forefinger, or flicking the entire set of 33, 66 or 99 beads around the wrist. At a party or wedding, they may even be whirling them overhead like a rattle.

The beads could be pearl or jade; bought in the local souq, or collected bead by bead and at great cost from around the world. Qataris favour amber *misbah* (prayer bead).

Men have carried *misbah* since the early days of Islam to help in the contemplation of God. A user usually rolls each bead while reciting the names or attributes of Allah.

While many continue to use the beads for religious purposes, prayer beads in Qatar have become a social item. If you let them function like a piece of intuited discourse, as well as talisman and storyteller, comforter and companion, you'll find you are holding the ultimate symbol of male bonding.

Food & Drink

Alcohol Available only in top-end hotel restaurants and bars.

Coffee Traditionally served pale and spiked with cardamon; or dark, strong and with plenty of sugar.

Grilled lobster Local crayfish are a popular favourite.

Khabees Dates in a variety of sizes, colours and states of ripeness.

Makbus Rice and spices with chicken, lamb or fish in a rich sauce.

Tap water Safe to drink although most people stick to bottled water.

Young Qatari with falcon

AMOS CHAPPLE / GETTY IMAGES ©

Bir Zekreet

6 There's not much in the way of altitude in Qatar, which only serves to exaggerate the little escarpment on the northwest coast of the peninsula, near Dukhan. The limestone escarpment of Bir Zekreet is like a geography lesson in desert formations, as the wind has whittled away softer sedimentary rock, exposing pillars and a large mushroom of limestone. The surrounding beaches are full of empty oyster shells with rich mother-of-pearl interiors and other assorted bivalves. The shallow waters are quiet and peaceful.

Falcon Souq

7 This fascinating new souq, next to Souq Waqif, is worth a visit just to see the kind of paraphernalia involved in falconry. All kinds of equipment, such as *burkha* (hoods) and *hubara* (feathers), are on sale. During falcon season (October to March) you will also see dozens of peregrines and other falcons patiently aperch their stands. The best part of the experience is seeing young Qataris buying their first falcon under the eyes of an uncle or grandfather, keen to hand down the family heritage of bird-handling skills.

Getting Around

Car If you're driving around Doha, you'll discover that roundabouts are very common, treated like camel-race tracks and often redundant in practice. A 4WD is essential for those wanting to explore the interior in greater depth or wishing to camp on a remote beach.

Taxi The easiest way to catch a taxi is to ask your hotel to arrange one, although technically you can wave one down from the side of the road. To visit most sights outside Doha, it's better to hire a car or arrange transport with a tour company as it usually works out considerably cheaper and it saves long waits for return transport.

Corvin Castle, Hunedoara

CAPITAL
Bucharest

POPULATION
21.8 million

AREA
238,391 sq km

OFFICIAL LANGUAGE
Romanian

Romania

Fortified churches and painted monasteries stand regally amid a pristine landscape. In the cities, former Saxon settlements such as Sibiu and Braşov ooze charm, while vibrant Bucharest is all energy.

Beautiful and beguiling, Romania's rural landscape remains relatively untouched by the country's urban evolution. It's a land of aesthetically stirring hand-ploughed fields, sheep-instigated traffic jams, and lots and lots of homemade plum brandy. The Carpathian Mountains offer uncrowded hiking and skiing, while Transylvania's Saxon towns are time-warp strolling grounds for Gothic architecture, Austro-Hungarian legacies and, naturally, plenty of Vlad Ţepeş–inspired 'Dracula' shtick. Fish – and the birds that chomp them – thrive in the Danube Delta, bucolic Maramureş has the 'Merry Cemetery', and Unesco-listed painted monasteries dot southern Bucovina. And, for the record, the big cities are a blast too.

Romania's
Top Experiences

Painted Monasteries of Bucovina

1 Tucked in the Carpathian foothills, the Unesco-listed painted monasteries of Bucovina proudly show off Romania's unique, Latin-flavoured Orthodox tradition. The churches are at one with their natural surroundings and the dizzying kaleidoscope of colours and intricate details in the frescoes bring to life everything from biblical stories to the 15th-century siege of Constantinople. The monasteries, including Humor, Sucevița and Voroneț, are the genius of Moldavian Prince Stephen the Great, who was later canonised for his works.

Hiking in the Carpathians

2 Dense primeval forests that leap straight from the pages of a Brothers Grimm story, with bears, wolves, lynx and boar, rugged mountain plateaus, well-marked trails and a network of cabins en route to keep you warm. Hiking is the best way to absorb this vibrant landscape of forests and rolling pastureland. There are also some terrific guides to lead you to the best that Romania has to offer.

Bran Castle

3 Perched on a rocky bluff in Transylvania, in a mass of turrets and castellations, Bran Castle overlooks a desolate mountain pass swirling with mist and dense forest. Its spectral exterior is like a composite of every horror film you've ever seen, but don't expect to be scared. Inside, Bran is anything but spooky, with its white walls and geranium-filled courtyard. Legend has it Vlad the Impaler (the inspiration for Count Dracula) was briefly imprisoned here.

Palace of Parliament, Bucharest

4 Depending on your point of view, this modern colossus is either a mind-blowing testament to the waste and folly of dictatorship or an awe-inspiring showcase of Romanian

Humor Monastery, Bucovina region

materials and craftsmanship, albeit applied to sinister ends. We think it's a bit of both, but whatever emotions the 'House of the People' happens to elicit, the sheer scale of Romania's entry into the 'World's Largest Buildings' competition – on par with the Taj Mahal or the Pentagon – must be seen to be believed.

Sibiu

5 Bursting with exhibitions and nightlife, tasteful Sibiu instantly dazzles with its maze of old cobbled streets winding into lustrously coloured baroque squares. By day the tapping of guildsmen – for which this Romanian city is famous – still fills the streets; by night this old charmer is aglow with sidewalk cafes and authentic subterranean restaurants where you can tuck into your goulash by candlelight. Almost every month, Sibiu, a former European Capital of Culture, hosts some kind of event, be it a film, rock or folk fest.

if Romania were 100 people

🚹🚹🚹🚹🚹🚹🚹🚹🚹🚹🚹🚹🚹🚹🚹🚹🚹🚹🚹🚹
🚹🚹🚹🚹🚹🚹🚹🚹🚹🚹🚹🚹🚹🚹🚹🚹🚹🚹🚹🚹
🚹🚹🚹🚹🚹🚹🚹🚹🚹🚹🚹🚹🚹🚹🚹🚹🚹🚹🚹🚹
🚹🚹🚹🚹🚹🚹🚹🚹🚹🚹🚹🚹🚹🚹🚹🚹🚹🚹🚹🚹
🚹🚹🚹🚹🚹🚹🚹🚹🚹🚹🚹🚹🚹🚹🚹🚹🚹🚹🚹🚹

83 would be Romanian
6 would be Hungarian
3 would be Roma
8 would be other

belief systems
(% of population)

86 — Eastern Orthodox
8 — Protestant
5 — Roman Catholic
1 — other

population per sq km

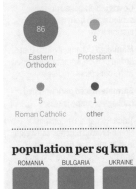

ROMANIA   BULGARIA   UKRAINE

🚹 ≈ 15 people

When to Go

HIGH SEASON
(Jun–Aug)

➜ Sunny weather, but temperatures can get oppressively hot.

➜ Locals head for the Black Sea; Mamaia is packed.

➜ Castles, museums, water parks and spas open and in high gear.

SHOULDER
(Apr–May & Sep–Oct)

➜ Some attractions are closed or have shorter hours.

➜ Trees in full blossom by April; later in higher elevations.

➜ Birdwatching in the Danube Delta at its best in late May.

LOW SEASON
(Nov–Mar)

➜ Ski season runs from mid-December to early March.

➜ Romantic cities such as Braşov and Sibiu look great in coats of snow.

➜ Attractions in smaller towns shut down or open only on weekends.

The Dracula Myth

Love it or loathe it, visit Romania and you can't ignore the omnipresence of Dracula; from mugs to T-shirts, and bat and blood-themed menus to vampire-costumed waiters.

Fifteenth-century prince Vlad Țepeș is often credited with being Dracula. His princely father, Vlad III, was called Vlad Dracul. Dracul(a) actually means 'son of the house of Dracul', which itself translates as 'devil' or 'dragon'. Add to this diabolical moniker the fact that Vlad used to impale his victims – from which you get his other surname: Țepeș (Impaler) – and it's easy to see why Dracula's creator, Irishman Bram Stoker, tapped into his bloodline.

Stoker's literary Dracula, by contrast, was a bloodsucking vampire – an undead corpse reliant on the blood of the living to sustain his own immortality. But who would have thought this would almost single-handedly spawn a literary genre?

Food & Drink

Ciorbă Sour soup that's a mainstay of the Romanian diet and a powerful hangover remedy.

Covrigi Oven-baked pretzels served warm from windows all around town.

Mămăligă Cornmeal mush that's boiled or fried, sometimes topped with sour cream or cheese.

Sarmale Spiced pork wrapped in cabbage or grape leaves.

Țuică Romanian moonshine. Home-brewed batches can weigh in at as much as 60% alcohol, and the wallop can be fast and furious. Classic *țuică* is usually distilled from plums – purists say only plums – but we've seen other fruits, like apricots and pears, employed to this nefarious end.

European bee-eaters

Wildlife in the Danube Delta

6 After flowing some 2800km across the European continent, the mighty Danube River passes through a vast expanse of remote wetland in eastern Romania – the delta – before finally emptying into the Black Sea. Under international environmental protection, the region has developed into a sanctuary for fish and fowl of all stripe and colour. Birders, in particular, will thrill to the prospect of glimpsing species such as the roller, white-tailed eagle, great white egret, mute and whooper swans, falcon, and even a bee-eater or two.

Wooden Churches of Maramureș

7 Rising from forested hillsides like dark needles, the exquisite wooden churches of Maramureș, in northern Romania, are both austere and beautiful, with roofs of shingle and weather-beaten Gothic-style steeples. Inside, you'll discover rich interiors painted with biblical frescoes, some of which date back to the 14th century. On Sundays villagers wear traditional dress for church, and attending a service is a special treat.

Getting Around

Air Given the distances and poor state of the roads, flying between cities is a feasible option if time is a primary concern.

Bus A mix of buses, minibuses and 'maxitaxis' form the backbone of the Romanian national transport system. If you understand the system, you can move around regions and even across the country easily and cheaply.

Car Roads are generally crowded and in poor condition. The country has only a few short stretches of *autostrada* (motorway), meaning that most of your travel will be along two-lane *drum național* (national highways) or *drum județean* (secondary roads).

Hermitage Pavilion, Catherine Park, Pushkin

CAPITAL
Moscow

POPULATION
142.5 million

AREA
17.1 million sq km

OFFICIAL LANGUAGE
Russian

Russia

From beautiful Lake Baikal to St Petersburg's gilded palaces, Russia is so blessed with cultural and natural treasures that it would take a lifetime to experience them all.

For centuries the world has wondered about Russia. The country has been reported as a land of unbelievable riches and indescribable poverty, cruel tyrants and great minds, generous hospitality and meddlesome bureaucracy, beautiful ballets and industrial monstrosities, pious faith and unbridled hedonism.

These eternal Russian truths coexist in equally diverse landscapes of icy tundra and sunkissed beaches, dense silver-birch forests, deep, mysterious lakes, snowcapped mountains and swaying grassland steppes. Factor in ancient fortresses, luxurious palaces, swirly-spired churches and lost-in-time wooden villages and you'll begin to see why Russia is simply amazing.

Two decades on from the demise of the Soviet Union, an economically and politically resurgent Russia is a brash, exciting and fascinating place to visit.

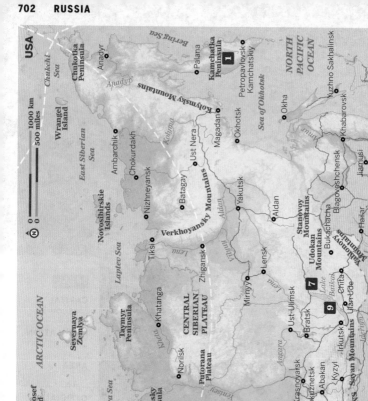
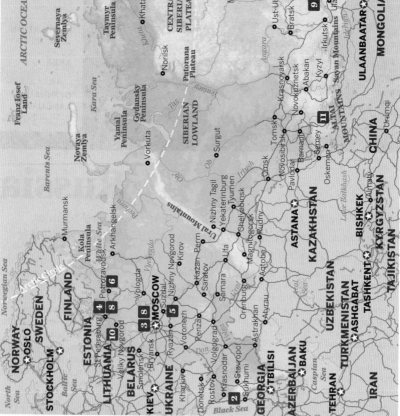

Russia's
Top Experiences

Kamchatka

1 It seems almost trite to describe Kamchatka as majestic. To many Kamchatka is, quite simply, the most beautiful place in the world. It's Yellowstone and Rotorua and Patagonia rolled into one, and it teems with wildlife free to frolic in one of the world's great remaining wildernesses. Traditionally the domain of well-heeled tourists who can afford helicopter rides to view its trademark volcanoes, geysers and salmon-devouring bears, Kamchatka has finally loosened up a bit for the independent traveller. Now if only they could fix that weather...

Exploring the Black Sea

2 The serene Black Sea coast has long been a favourite of Russian holiday makers for its seaside towns, easy-going ambience and magnificent inland scenery in the nearby Caucasus mountains. The gateway to it all is Sochi, a vibrant city reinventing itself as a first-rate international resort and host of the 2014 Winter Olympics. The looming peaks of nearby Krasnaya Polyana make a superb destination for ski lovers, while there's great hiking in the Agura Valley.

Walking Across Red Square

3 Stepping onto Red Square never ceases to inspire: the tall towers and imposing walls of the Kremlin, the playful jumble of patterns and colours adorning St Basil's Cathedral, the majestic red bricks of the State History Museum and the elaborate edifice of GUM, all encircling a vast stretch of cobblestones. Individually they are impressive, but the ensemble is electrifying. Come at night to see the square empty of crowds and the buildings awash with lights.

The Hermitage

4 Standing proudly at the end of Nevsky prospekt, Russia's most famous palace houses its most famous museum. Little can prepare most visitors for the scale of the exhibits, nor for their quality, comprising an almost unrivalled history of Western art, including a staggering number of Rembrandts, Rubens, Picassos and Matisses. There are superb antiquities, sculpture and jewellery on display. If that's not enough, then simply content yourself with wandering through the private apartments of the Romanovs, for whom the Winter Palace was home until 1917.

if Russia were 100 people

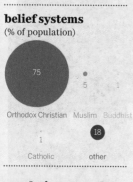

80 would be Russian
4 would be Tatar
2 would be Ukrainian
1 would be Bashkir
1 would be Chuvash
12 would be other

belief systems
(% of population)

75 Orthodox Christian
5 Muslim
1 Buddhist
1 Catholic
18 other

population per sq km

RUSSIA   UK   USA

👤 ≈ 8 people

Suzdal's Idyll

5 Ding-dong ring the bells of a few dozen churches as you ride your bike through the streets of Suzdal, lined with wooden cottages and lush gardens. This is Russia as it would have been, if not for the devastating 20th century – unpretentious, pious and very laid-back. Some of the best religious architecture is scattered around, but you can just as well spend all day lying in the grass and watching the river flow before repairing to a banya for the sweet torture of heat, cold and birch twigs.

Kizhi

6 Old buildings made from logs may not usually be synonymous with 'heart-stopping excitement', but Kizhi's collection of wooden masterpieces is enough to spike the blood pressure of those weary of even the most glorious architecture. The first glimpse of the heavenly Transfiguration Church, viewed from the approaching hydrofoil, causes such a ripple that the boat practically bounces: is it... it is! Up close, the church is a miracle of design and construct: legend has it that the unnamed builder destroyed his axe upon its completion, correctly assuming that its glory could not be matched.

Hiking the Great Baikal Trail

7 Already one of Russia's most successful environmental projects, the Great Baikal Trail has the ambitious aim of encircling Lake Baikal with marked hiking trails. That's still a long way from being achieved, but

Pushkin: Poet of Passion

Born in 1799, the son of nobility with a dollop of African blood in his lineage, Alexander Pushkin grew up in the French-speaking high society of St Petersburg. A child of his time, the Romantic Age, Pushkin was obsessed with obsessions – war, male honour, and beautiful and unattainable women.

Pushkin wrote everything from classical odes and sonnets to short stories, plays and fairy tales. He is best loved for his poems in verse, *The Bronze Horseman* and *Eugene Onegin*, in which he nearly answers that eternal question – why do Russians (like to) suffer so much? Politically, he was a hot potato and the tsars exiled him from St Petersburg three times

In 1837, Pushkin was mortally wounded in a duel fought over the honour of his wife, the Russian beauty Natalia Goncharova. He lay dying for two days while all of St Petersburg came to pay homage, dramatically directing taxi drivers, 'To Pushkin!' For a riveting account of the duel and the events that preceded it, read Serena Vitale's Pushkin's Button.

Food & Drink

Bliny Pancakes served with *ikra* (caviar) or *tvorog* (cottage cheese).

Kvas A refreshing, beerlike drink, or the red berry juice mix mors.

Pelmeni Dumplings stuffed with meat and eaten with sour cream and vinegar.

Salads A wide variety usually slathered in mayonnaise, including the chopped potato one called Olivier.

Soups Try lemony, meat solyanka or hearty fish ukha.

Vodka The quintessential Russian tipple.

Zakuski Appetisers such as olives, bliny with mushrooms, caviar and salads.

FRANZ MARC FREI / GETTY IMAGES ©

where trails have been etched into the landscape, donning boots for a trek along Baikal's shores is all the rage. Whichever section you choose, Baikal's gob-smacking vistas and the tough going will leave you breathless as you pass through virgin taiga, along isolated beaches and through cold, flowing rivers.

Going to the Ballet

8 What could be more Russian than a night at the ballet, dressed to the nines? St Petersburg's famed Mariinsky Theatre and the Bolshoi Ballet in Moscow both offer the ultimate in classical ballet or operatic experiences. The Bolshoi Theatre is where Tchaikovsky's *Swan Lake* premiered (to bad reviews) in 1877. An evening here is one of Moscow's most romantic options. Both the ballet and opera companies perform a range of Russian and foreign works. Productions take place on the main stage, now back in operation after a multiyear renovation, and on the smaller New Stage.

When to Go

HIGH SEASON (Jun–Sep)

➡ Protect against disease-carrying ticks.

➡ Book all forms of transport in advance.

➡ Prices can rise in St Petersburg, particularly during White Nights in June and July.

SHOULDER (May & Oct)

➡ Late spring and early autumn see the country bathed in the fresh greenery or russet shades of the seasons.

LOW SEASON (Nov–Apr)

➡ Snow falls and temperatures plummet, creating the wintery Russia of the imagination.

➡ Best time for skiing (although resorts charge higher prices) and visiting museums and galleries.

Olkhon Island

9 Sacred of the sacred to the shamanist western Buryats, who attach a legend or fable to every rock, cape and hillock, enchanted Olkhon sits halfway up Lake Baikal's western shore. It's obvious why the gods and other beings from the Mongol Geser epic chose to dwell on this eerily moving island, though today it's more likely to be a bunch of backpackers you meet emerging from a cave. The island's landscapes are spellbinding, Baikal's waters lap balmiest on its western shore and if you're after some Siberia-inspired meditation, there's no better spot.

Best on Film

Moscow Doesn't Believe in Tears (1980) Directed by Vladimir Menshov, this film charts the course of three provincial gals who make Moscow their home from the 1950s to the 1970s.

The Cranes Are Flying (1957) Mikhail Kalatozov's tragic WWII drama illuminated the sacrifices made by Russians during the Great Patriotic War.

The Last Station (2009) Based on the novel by Jay Parini, this film is about the last year of Leo Tolstoy's life.

Best in Print

Doctor Zhivago (Boris Pasternak) A richly philosophical novel spanning events from the dying days of tsarist Russia to the birth of the Soviet Union, offering personal insights into the revolution and the Russian Civil War along the way.

Moscow Noir Fourteen short stories by contemporary authors.

The Master and Margarita Mikhail Bulgakov's satirical masterpiece.

Getting Around

Air Flights can be delayed, often for hours and with no or little explanation. Small town airports offer facilities similar to the average bus shelter.

Boat One of the most pleasant ways of travelling around Russia is by river. You can do this either by taking a cruise, or by using scheduled river passenger services.

Bus Long-distance buses tend to complement rather than compete with the rail network. They generally serve areas with no railway or routes on which trains are slow, infrequent or overloaded.

Train Trains are generally comfortable and, depending on the class of travel, relatively inexpensive for the distances covered.

Veliky Novgorod's Kremlin

10 In the town that considers itself Russia's birthplace stands one of the country's most impressive and picturesque stone fortresses. Within the kremlin's grounds rise up the Byzantine 11th-century Cathedral of St Sophia and a 300-tonne sculpture celebrating 1000 years of Russian history. Climb the Kokui Tower for an overview of the complex, then enter the Novgorod State United Museum to see one of Russia's best collections of iconographic art.

Exploring the Altai

11 Misty mountain passes, standing stone idols, tranquil lakes and empty roads that stretch on forever. Welcome to the Altai Republic, Russia's supreme natural paradise. You can travel for hours here without seeing another soul – unless you count the wild horses and goats. From snow-capped peaks to the lunar landscapes of Kosh-Agach, desolation has never been quite so appealing. But be warned – the Altai and its mysteries possess a magnetic pull, drawing travellers back year after year.

Towers and domes of the Cathedral of St Sophia

TIM MAKINS / GETTY IMAGES ©

Mountain gorillas

CAPITAL
Kigali

POPULATION
12 million

AREA
26,338 sq km

OFFICIAL LANGUAGES
Kinyarwanda
French
English

Rwanda

While the scars still run deep, Rwanda has done a remarkable job of healing its wounds and turning towards the future with a surprising measure of optimism.

Mention Rwanda to anyone with a small measure of geopolitical conscience, and they'll no doubt recall images of the horrific genocide that brutalised this tiny country in 1994 when, in the span of just three months, nearly one million Tutsis and moderate Hutus were systematically butchered. But since those dark days a miraculous transformation has been wrought and today the country is one of ethnic unity and relative political stability, and a new-found air of optimism pervades the country.

Tourism is once again a key contributor to the economy and the industry's brightest star is the chance to track rare mountain gorillas through bamboo forests in the shadow of the Virunga volcanoes. Of course, 'Le Pays des Mille Collines' (the Land of a Thousand Hills) isn't all monkey business: Rwanda is a lush country of endless mountains and stunning scenery. The shores of Lake Kivu conceal some of Africa's best inland beaches, while Parc National Nyungwe Forest protects extensive tracts of montane rainforest.

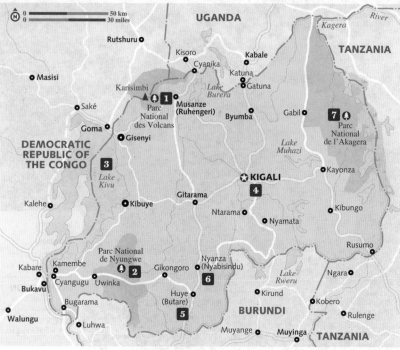

Rwanda's
Top Experiences

Parc National des Volcans

1 Volcanoes National Park, which runs along Rwanda's border with the Democratic Republic of Congo and Uganda, is home to the Rwandan section of the Virungas. Comprised of five volcanoes – the highest, Karisimbi, is more than 4500m – the Virungas are one of the most beautiful sights in both Rwanda and the whole of Africa. As if this wasn't enough of a drawcard, the bamboo- and rainforest-covered slopes of these volcanoes are also home to some of the last remaining sanctuaries of the endangered eastern mountain gorilla (*Gorilla beringei beringei*).

Parc National de Nyungwe

2 With no fewer than 13 species of primates, a rich tapestry of birdlife and a degree of biodiversity seldom found elsewhere, Nyungwe Forest National Park has been identified as one of Africa's most important conservation areas. The vast forest is home to habituated families of chimpanzees and a huge troop of colobus monkeys made up of more than 400 individuals. Whether hiking through this equatorial rainforest in search of our evolutionary kin or just in search of a waterfall, Nyungwe is guaranteed to bring out your inner Tarzan.

Lake Kivu

3 Land-locked Rwanda may be a long way from the ocean, but that doesn't mean you can't have a beach holiday here. On the contrary, Rwanda's eastern border with Democratic Republic of Congo runs the entire length of Lake Kivu. The best places to take in the lake's charms are at either Gisenyi in the north or Kibuye further south. Gisenyi has the better beaches and much of the lake's frontage here is lined with landscaped villas, plush hotels and private clubs. Kibuye has not caught on as a tourist destination for sun and sand in the same way that Gisenyi has, but enjoys a stunning location, spread across a series of hills jutting into Lake Kivu.

Kigali Memorial Centre

4 The Kigali Memorial Centre is a must for all visitors to Rwanda wanting to learn more about how it was that the world watched as a genocide unfolded in this tiny, landlocked country. More than a memorial for Kigali, more than a memorial for Rwanda and its tragedy, this is a memorial for all of us, marking the Rwandan genocide and many more around the world that never should have come to pass. Downstairs is dedicated to the Rwandan genocide; the informative tour includes background on the divisive colonial experience in Rwanda and the steady build-up to the genocide. Exhibits are professionally presented and include short video clips in French and English.

Huye (Batare)

5 The outstanding National Museum of Rwanda, the finest museum in the country, was given to the city of Huye (Batare) as a gift from Belgium in 1989 to commemorate 25 years of independence. While the building itself is certainly one of the most beautiful structures in the city, the museum wins top marks for having one of the best ethnological and archaeological collections in the entire region.

Nyanza (Nyabisindu)

6 In 1899, Mwami Musinga Yuhi V established Rwanda's first permanent royal capital in Nyanza. Today a large thatched hut, his traditional palace (well, actually a very good replica

if Rwanda were 100 people

84 would be Hutu (Bantu)
15 would be Tutsi (Hamitic)
1 would be Twa (Pygmy)

belief systems
(% of population)

56	25	11
Roman Catholic	Protestant	Adventist
5	1	2
Muslim	indigenous beliefs	none

When to Go

MID-MAY–SEP

➡ Trekking is more pleasant when rains ease during the 'long dry'.

JUN

➡ Baby gorillas are named during the Kwita Izina ceremony.

MID-MAR– MID-MAY

➡ Although it's often wet during the 'long rains', travel is still possible.

population per sq km

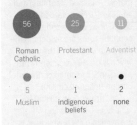

RWANDA   SOUTH AFRICA   DEMOCRATIC REPUBLIC OF THE CONGO

🧍 ≈ 11 people

Kwita Izina

In traditional Rwandan culture, the birth of a child is a momentous event that is celebrated with a tremendous amount of fanfare. The birth is marked by the presentation of the new infant to the general public, who then proceed to suggest round after round of possible names. After careful consideration, the proud parents select one for their newborn, and celebrate the naming with copious amounts of dining, drinking and dancing.

Gorillas in Rwanda are often awarded the same level of respect and admiration as humans, which is why it's only fitting they should be named in a similar manner. Since June 2005, the annual Kwita Izina (Gorilla Naming Ceremony) has been a countrywide event that is increasingly drawing a larger share of the spotlight.

Food & Drink

In the rural areas of Rwanda, food is very similar to that in other East African countries. Popular meats include *tilapia* (Nile perch), goat, chicken and beef *brochettes* (kebabs), though the bulk of most meals are based on *ugali* (maize meal), *matoke* (mashed plantains) and so-called 'Irish potatoes'. In the cities, however, Rwanda's francophone roots are evident in the *plat du jour* (plate of the day), which is usually excellently prepared and presented continental Europe–inspired cuisine.

Soft drinks (sodas) and the local beers, Primus and Mulzig, are available everywhere, as is the local firewater, *konyagi*. (a white spirit made from sugar cane). A pleasant, nonalcoholic alternative is the purplish juice from the tree tomato (tamarillo), which is a sweet and tasty concoction that somewhat defies explanation.

Defassa waterbuck

of it) and the first home built by his son and successor Mutara III Rudahigwa have been restored and form the Rukari Ancient History Museum. After visiting Belgium and seeing the stately homes there, Mutara concluded his own home wasn't up to scratch and had a second, and altogether grander, palace built on nearby Rwesero Hill, although he died before its completion. Today, this new palace serves as the Rwesero Art Museum, housing mostly contemporary paintings and stylistic sculptures on themes dealing with the genocide, unity and brotherhood.

Parc National de L'Akagera

7 Have a Rwandan-style safari experience in this up-and-coming game park. For more than a decade, Akagera was something of a vegetarian safari, given that most four-legged animals were taking an extended holiday in neighbouring Tanzania. While the once grand herds that characterised Akagera are a fraction of their original numbers, populations are noticeably on the rise. And, even if you don't come across too many wild animals, it's very likely that you won't come across too many other wildlife-viewing drivers.

Getting Around

Air There are domestic flights from Kigali to Gisenyi (on Lake Kivu's shores) and Kmembe.

Bus Privately run buses cover the entire country and have scheduled departure times. Tickets are brought in advance from a ticket office which is usually (although not always) the point of departure. You will also find plenty of well-maintained, modern minibuses serving all the main routes.

Car Rwanda has a reasonable road system, for the most part due to its small size and a large dose of foreign assistance. The only major unsealed roads are those running alongside the shore of Lake Kivu and some smaller stretches around the country.

Sopoaga Falls, 'Upolu

CAPITAL
Apia

POPULATION
195,476

AREA
2831 sq km

OFFICIAL LANGUAGE
Samoan

Samoa

Anchored at the heart of Polynesia, Samoa rises languidly from the sea, draped in jungle, dotted with flower-filled villages and surrounded by iridescent lagoons.

This tiny nation's proud history spans more than 3000 years and its people were the first Polynesians to reclaim independence following European colonisation. As such, Samoans have firmly held on to their customs.

Village life is still the norm here, and traditional governance and communal ownership carry much legal weight. The result is sweet, safe and gentle; a trip to Samoa is like sipping the world's purest water on a warm day.

If your ideal for a South Pacific holiday involves spa treatments and jet skis, Samoa may not be for you. What Samoa excels in is affordable, unpretentious beachside accommodation, friendly people and a peace and quiet rare in this world.

It's easy to get around, everyone speaks English and political stability is almost guaranteed.

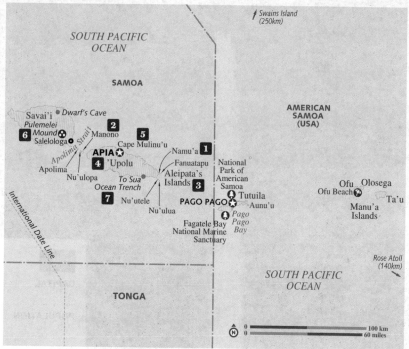

SAMOA

Samoa's
Top Experiences

Namu'a Island

1 Namu'a is only a short boat ride from Mutiatele, but once you're on this tiny private island you'll feel like 'Upolu is light years away (even though it's clearly visible across the strait). Do a circumnavigation of the shoreline (low tide only), clamber up the steep central peak and snorkel the surrounding reef. *Fale* (beach huts) are open, basic and right on the beach – there's no electricity so everything is lit by oil lamps at night. Meals are mostly local style (think fried fish and cassava for dinner, and spam and eggs for breakfast). Park your car at the shop and your resort will come to pick you up.

Manono

2 If you'd like to temporarily escape engine noise and village dogs, the small island of Manono offers a tranquil option. Canines and cars have been banished, and the only things that might snap you out of a tropical reverie are occasional blasts from stereos and the tour groups that periodically clog the island's main trail. It's obligatory for visitors to do the 1½-hour circumnavigation of the island via the path that wends its way between the ocean and people's houses. They're friendly sorts here, so expect to be greeted with a cheery 'malo' a dozen or so times.

Aleipata's beaches

3 At the southeastern end of 'Upolu, Aleipata district has a reef system that's making a good comeback after being pummelled by the 2009 tsunami. It already has surprisingly good snorkelling, and the beaches here are some of the most spellbindingly beautiful you're likely to find anywhere in the world. Check out the area's submerged beauty by walking in off the spectacular white beach at Lalomanu. If you're lucky you might spot a turtle, but beware of currents.

Apia

4 Few people come to a Pacific paradise to hang around in a small city

KYLE ROTHENBORG / GETTY IMAGES ©

with not much in the way of beaches. That's a shame as Apia can be a lot of fun – and its position makes it a handy base to explore all parts of 'Upolu. It's the only place in Samoa big enough to have a decent selection of eateries, bars and entertainment, but it's still small enough that within a week you'll be recognising people on the street.

Cape Mulinu'u

5 At Cape Mulinu'u you'll find the beautiful outlook of Fafa O Sauai'i, which was considered one of Samoa's most sacred spots in pre-Christian times. Don't pass up a swim in the large rock pool, where you don't even have to enter the water to watch fish dart around the colourful corals at the base of the rocks. Across

the road are a star mound, Vaatausili Cave and the Via Sua Toto (the 'Blood Well' – named after the warrior Tupa'ilevaililigi, who threw his enemies' severed heads in here).

Pulemelei Mound

6 Polynesia's largest ancient structure is the intriguing, pyramidal Pulemelei Mound, marked on some maps as Tia Seu Ancient Mound. It measures 61m by 50m at its base and rises to a height of more than 12m. It's a stirring place, with views from its stony summit both to the ocean and into thick, primordial jungle. On sunny days, colourful butterflies swarm across it and birds swoop overhead. The surrounding

if Samoa were 100 people

34 would be aged 0-14
20 would be aged 15-24
35 would be aged 25-54
6 would be aged 55-64
5 would be aged 65+

belief systems
(% of population)

60	19	13
Protestant	Roman Catholic	Mormon
1	5	2
Worship Centre	other Christian	other

population per sq km

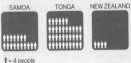

SAMOA   TONGA   NEW ZEALAND

ᵼ ≈ 4 people

When to Go

DEC–JAN
➡ Peak holiday period when Samoans living abroad visit home.

MAY–OCT
➡ Dry season and festival time.

NOV–APR
➡ Wet weather and cyclone season.

It's Just Not Cricket

Kirikiti is a unique South Pacific version of the English game of cricket, and is a great example of how an imported idea has been adapted to suit Samoan needs. The willow bat became a three-sided club of a size that would make any warlord happy, and the ball was fashioned out of rubber.

And the rules? Well, there can be any number of players in a Samoan team, which means a game can continue for days, or weeks, at a time. As the batsman swings at every ball, the leader of the opposite team jumps up and down and blows his whistle in a syncopated rhythm. The rest of the team gyrates, clapping hands in rhythmic harmony, at the same time watching for an opportunity to catch out the rival. Only when all the batsmen of the opposing team have been dismissed does the other team get its chance.

It's energetic, exuberant and lots of fun.

Food & Drink

Umu Traditional Samoan hot-stone ovens are built above ground and used to cook bread-fruit, fish, *palusami* and more.

Oka Tender chunks of raw fish are marinated in lime juice, mixed with vegetables and topped with coconut cream.

Palusami Calorie bombs of coconut cream wrapped in young taro leaves and cooked in a stone oven. Find it at the market in Apia.

Fish & chips Found on every menu. We thought the best was at Seafood Gourmet in Apia.

Koko Samoa-strong coffee-like beverage made with hot water and ground Samoan cacao.

Vailima One of the best beers in the Pacific. A crisp and refreshing lager.

MICHAEL BYRNE / GETTY IMAGES ©

area is presumably covered in house sites and other important archaeological finds but, for now, everything is covered in jungle. Unfortunately it's very difficult to visit Pulemelei Mound as it's located on disputed land. As such, there's no sign and no upkeep – the path to the site and the mound itself are becoming very overgrown.

To Sua Ocean Trench

7 Not so much 'trenches' as two sinkhole-like depressions with sheer rock walls decorated in greenery – a magical aquamarine pool swishes, linked to both, at the bottom. You can swim under a broad arch of rock from the larger pool, serenaded by droplets of water hitting the surface, to the second large opening to the sky. The pool is fed by the waves surging through an unswimmable underwater passageway. The pools are accessed by a sturdy wooden ladder. Once you've descended the 20-odd metres into the crystalline waters of this fairy grotto, there's a most serene sense of being removed from the world.

Getting Around

Boat The ferry from Mulifanua Wharf is the only option for travel between 'Upolu and Savai'i. Small boats leave from Cape Fatuosofia for Manono.

Bus Travelling by public bus in Samoa is an experience that shouldn't be missed. The buses are vibrantly painted (look out for the Bon Jovi–themed one), wooden-seated vehicles that blast Samoan pop music. Services operate completely at the drivers' whims.

Car Getting around by car in Samoa is quite straightforward. The coastal roads on both main islands are sealed and the general condition of most other main roads is also pretty good.

Castello della Cesta

San Marino

This landlocked micronation offers spectacular views from its location atop Mount Titano, a dozen kilometres from the Adriatic Coast.

San Marino has been an independent republic since AD 301 when a Croatian stone-cutter built a church atop a windswept bluff here. Of the world's 193 independent countries, San Marino is the fifth smallest and – arguably – the most curious. How it exists at all is something of an enigma. A sole survivor of Italy's once powerful city-state network, the micronation clung on long after the more powerful kingdoms of Genoa and Venice folded. And still it clings, secure in its status as the world's oldest surviving sovereign state and its oldest republic.

The country is made up of nine settlements. Città di San Marino, the medieval settlement on the slopes of 750m-high Mount Titano that was added to the Unesco World Heritage list in 2008, attracts two million annual visitors. Its highlights are its picturesque views, its atmospheric streets, and a stash of rather bizarre museums dedicated to vampires, torture, wax dummies and strange facts.

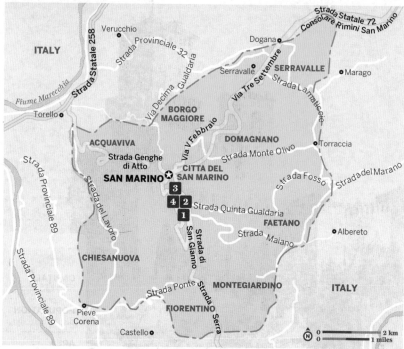

San Marino's
Top Experiences

Castello della Cesta

1 Dominating the skyline and offering superb views towards Rimini and the coast, this castle dates from the 13th century and sits atop 750m Monte Titano. Today you can walk its ramparts and peep into a small museum devoted to medieval armaments.The

admission price also includes entry to the Castello della Guaita, the older of San Marino's castles, dating from the 11th century. It was still being used as a prison until as recently as 1975.

Museo delle Curiosità

2 Overtly curious visitors or Trivial Pursuit addicts can brush up on their knowledge at this museum, a shrine to throwaway facts.

Piazza della Libertà

3 The neo-Gothic Palazzo Pubblico overlooks Piazza della Libertà, where a half-hourly changing of the guard is held from May to September.

Museo di Stato

4 San Marino's best museum by far is this well-laid-out state museum, with exhibitions about art, history, furniture and culture.

Food & Drink

Cheese Tuck into a plate of sliced beef, rocket and *parmigiano*.

Wine Sample a full-bodied Brugneto red or savour a delicate Tessano red, both made from grapes grown on San Marino's steeply terraced vineyards. Other locally produced wines include Biancale, a dry white, and Oro dei Goti, a sweet dessert wine.

When to Go

APR–JUN

➡ Spring is best for festivals, flowers and local produce.

JUL–AUG

➡ Queues at big sights and on the road, especially in August.

SEP–OCT

➡ Autumn provides warm weather and the grape harvest.

Banana Beach, Príncipe

São Tomé & Príncipe

This nation is full of beauty: rainforests blanket rolling hills and backdrop spellbinding beaches, tropical birds circle stark volcanic rock formations and aquatic life patrols immaculate shores.

If you adore quietude, take a trip to São Tomé and Príncipe, Africa's second-smallest country. These two tiny volcanic bumps anchored off the Gabonese coast easily win the hearts of foreigners with their Portuguese-Creole flavour and relaxed vibes, and it won't take too long before you're infected with the pervasive *leve leve* (which loosely means 'take it easy') mood.

The sublime laid-back tempo is enhanced by a wealth of natural attractions: miles of perfect palm-fringed beaches, huge swaths of emerald rainforest, soaring volcanic peaks and mellow fishing villages. The birdlife is excellent, and endemic plants (especially orchids) are plentiful. In season, turtle- and whale-watching opportunities abound.

This two-island nation has its cultural gems as well, with a surprising number of heritage buildings dating back to the colonial era. Tourism is still low-key and is being developed in a controlled, ecologically mindful way. No tacky resorts, just a number of locally run, enticing, nature-oriented lodges.

CAPITAL
São Tomé

POPULATION
186,817

AREA
964 sq km

OFFICIAL LANGUAGE
Portuguese

Príncipe (150km; see inset)

Príncipe (150km; see inset)

When to Go

YEAR ROUND

➜ An island of microclimates; with areas of cloudy and rainy skies and areas of sun.

MAR–MAY

➜ Daily rains generally yield to blue skies and hot temperatures for beach goers.

JUN–SEP

➜ Best time of year to visit, hikers prefer the cool, dry air and cloudy skies.

Food & Drink

Calulu Traditional stew made with more than 20 different plants and that can take hours to prepare.

Con-con Fish grilled and served with baked breadfruit.

Fish or meat Served with beans, rice or plantains.

Palm wine Freshly gathered from the trees, this is a local favourite.

São Tomé & Príncipe's
Top Experiences

São Tomé Town

1 Wander amid the colonial buildings of this charming capital town. There's a bustling market, a few quality dining options, a budding arts scene, a collection of fading pastel colonial buildings, and plenty of activities on its doorstep.

Roça São João

2 Expats and tourists get a misty look in their eyes when they talk about this colonial-era plantation building that has been turned into a cultural and ecotourism centre and guesthouse. It also sets up biking and hiking trips from the *roça* as well as various workshops.

Príncipe

3 Close your eyes. Just imagine: a dramatic landscape of jutting volcanic mountains covered mostly by dense forest; perfect beaches with astonishingly clear water; old plantation estates from colonial times; and warm greetings from friendly locals at every turn. Príncipe is the perfect place to shift into low gear, but action-seekers won't get bored, as the island also offers excellent hiking and diving options. The picture-perfect Banana Beach, made famous by a Bacardi ad, really is as spectacular as the photos look.

Al-Masjid al-Haram, Mecca

CAPITAL
Riyadh

POPULATION
26.9 million

AREA
2.1 million sq km

**OFFICIAL
LANGUAGE**
Arabic

Saudi Arabia

The birthplace and spiritual home of Islam, Saudi Arabia is as rich in attractions as it is in stirring symbolism.

If you are not a Muslim pilgrim performing the hajj, or an expat working in the oil industry, Saudi Arabia is one of the most difficult places on earth to visit. For those travellers who do get in, rock-hewn Madain Saleh is the Arabian peninsula's greatest archaeological treasure. Other wonders abound, from the echoes of TE Lawrence along the Hejaz Railway to the mudbrick ruins of Dir'aiyah. Jeddah, gateway to the holy cities of Mecca and Medina, has an enchanting old city made of coral, while the Red Sea coast has world-class diving without the crowds. Elsewhere, this is a land of astonishing natural beauty, particularly the plunging landscapes of the Asir Mountains in the Kingdom's southwest.

Best of all, there are few places left that can be said to represent the last frontier of tourism. Whether you're an expat or a pilgrim, Saudi Arabia is one of them.

Saudi Arabia's
Top Experiences

Madain Saleh

1 Extraordinary Madain Saleh is home to 131 enigmatic tombs which combine elements of Greco-Roman architecture with Nabataean and Babylonian imagery. Recent excavations have also revealed the foundations of unprepossessing houses and a market area for traders and caravans. Look out for elegant gynosphinxes: spirit guardians with women's heads, lions' bodies and wings adorning the corners of pediments.

Old Jeddah

2 A converging point for pilgrims and traders for centuries, Jeddah, the country's commercial capital, is the most easygoing city in the Kingdom, not to mention its most beguiling. The Al-Balad district, the heart of Old Jeddah, is a nostalgic testament to the bygone days of old Jeddah, with beautiful coral architecture casting some welcome shade over the bustling souqs beneath. Do as Saudi Arabians do and take a walk along the 35km-long corniche – students sit stooped over books, while families share picnics and men gather to gossip and cut commercial deals. Look out for the famous sculptures that line the wide pedestrian areas for 30km north from the port. Among the highlights are four bronzes by British sculptor Henry Moore, as well as work by Spaniard Joan Miró, Finnish artist Eila Hiltunen and Frenchman César Baldaccini.

Taif

3 Escape the summer heat like a Gulf Arab and head for the hills of Taif. In summer Taif can seem like a breath of fresh air, and compared to humid Jeddah it truly is. At 1700m above sea level, its gentle, temperate climate is its biggest attraction, and in summer Taif becomes the Kingdom's unofficial capital. With wide, tree-lined streets, traditional architecture, a lively souq and beautiful surrounding scenery, it's not hard to see why even the king relocates here. Taif is known for the cultivation of roses and fruit such as honey-sweet figs,

STILL WORKS / GETTY IMAGES ©

grapes, prickly pear and pomegranates. Over 3000 gardens are said to grace Taif and its surrounds.

Jebel Soudah

4 Enjoy the clear mountain air and exceptional scenery around Jebel Soudah. Located close to the summit of the Kingdom's highest peak, Jebel Soudah (2910m), about 22km west of Abha, this is the place to come for precipitous cliffs, deep valleys and mountaintops disappearing behind the clouds. There's no better way to enjoy the views than taking the As-Sawdah Cable Car. It drops down off the escarpment to the traditional mudbrick village of Rejal Al-Maa, with wonderful views to accompany you all the way, including stone villages, ter-

raced fields, juniper forests off in the distance and even the occasional defensive watchtower.

Dir'aiyah

5 Wander the mud-brick ruins of Dir'aiyah, a Unesco site and birthplace of modern Saudi Arabia. The ancestral home of the Al-Saud family and the birthplace of the Saudi-Wahhabi union, the historic site Old Dir'aiyah makes a welcome escape from the frenzy of Riyadh. This is one of the most evocative places in the Kingdom and its Unesco-supervised reconstruction saw it gain World Heritage status in 2010. Yet it is almost always deserted – most of the town was abandoned during the 20th century.

if Saudi Arabia were 100 people

90 would be Arab
10 would be Afro-Asian

crude oil production
(million barrels per day)

12	11	10
Saudi Arabia	USA	Russia
4	4	50
China	Canada	Rest of World

population per sq km

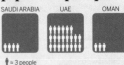

SAUDI ARABIA   UAE   OMAN

👤 ≈ 3 people

When to Go

NOV–MAR

➡ Cooler temperatures make daytime weather bearable and nights surprisingly chilly.

APR–OCT

➡ Temperatures above 40°C, high humidity along the coast; Ramadan; April sandstorms.

YEAR-ROUND

➡ Red Sea diving has excellent visibility all year, but in summer morning dives are best.

Jubba

Jubba is rightly famed for its impressive petroglyphs (rock carvings) of prehistoric animals and is arguably the premier pre-Islamic site in Saudi. The finest carvings date from around 5500 BC, when much of this area was an inland lake and local inhabitants carved game animals drawn to the waters. Elegant rock-cut ibex and oryx abound and there are also significant inscriptions in Thamudic (a pre-Arabic alphabet) dating to 1000 BC. In 1879 intrepid British explorer Lady Anne Blunt described Jubba as 'one of the most curious places in the world, and to my mind, one of the most beautiful'.

The huge site covers 39 sq km and among the enigmatic stone circles are crude carvings of camels and other domesticated animals dating from AD 300. The closest carvings to Jubba are 3km away.

Food & Drink

Fuul Mashed fava beans served with olive oil and often eaten for breakfast.

Baby camel Among the tenderest of Saudi meats, it's a particular specialty of Jeddah and the Hejaz.

Khouzi A Bedouin dish of lamb stuffed with rice, nuts, onions, sultanas, spices, eggs and a whole chicken.

Mezze Truly one of the joys of Arab cooking and similar in conception to Spanish tapas, with infinite possibilities.

Red Sea seafood Fresh and varied and at its best when slow-cooked over coals or baked in the oven; try *samak mashwi* (fish basted in a date puree and barbecued over hot coals).

Shwarma Ubiquitous kebab- or souvlaki-style pita sandwich stuffed with meat.

CHRIS MELLOR / GETTY IMAGES ©

Hejaz Railway

6 The Hejaz Railway cuts across northwestern Arabia with abandoned and evocative stations, substations and garrison forts, many of which remain. The line opened in 1908, stretching over 1000 miles through largely desert terrain; a planned extension to Mecca was never built. During the First World War, TE Lawrence helped to orchestrate the Arab Revolt, harnessing the hostility of the local Bedouin to drive out the Turks. They attacked and sabotaged the railway, which ceased to run after 1918.

Diving in the Red Sea, Yanbu

7 Dive the dazzling depths of Saudi's Red Sea and spot sharks, sea turtles and stunning coral reefs at Yanbu. With its port, refineries and petrochemical plants, this is hardly the Kingdom's most attractive spot. But it's a different story beneath the surface (of the sea, that is), as Yanbu is one of Saudi's premier diving locations. The waters of Saudi's Red Sea are teeming with wildlife, and include five species of marine turtle. Whales and dolphins are also present in the Red Sea and the Gulf.

Getting Around

Bus The buses are comfortable, air-conditioned and clean. Unaccompanied foreign women can travel on domestic buses with their *iqama* (residence permit) if an expat, or with a passport and visa if a tourist. The front seats are generally unofficially reserved for 'families' including sole women, and the back half for men.

Car & Motorcycle Despite its impressive public transport system, Saudi Arabia remains a country that glorifies the private car (the shiny 4WD is king). Roads are generally sealed and well maintained. Motorcycles are rare and generally considered a vehicle of the rural poor.

CAPITAL
Edinburgh

POPULATION
5.2 million

AREA
78,722 sq km

OFFICIAL LANGUAGES
English, Gaelic, Lallans

Trotternish Ridge, Isle of Skye

Scotland

Like a fine single malt, Scotland is a connoisseur's delight – a blend of stunning scenery and sophisticated cities, salt-tanged sea air and dark peaty waters, outdoor adventure and deep history.

Scotland harbours some of the largest areas of wilderness left in Western Europe, a wildlife haven where you can see golden eagles soar above the lochs and mountains of the northern Highlands, spot otters tumbling in the kelp along the shores of the Outer Hebrides, and watch minke whales breach through shoals of mackerel off the coast of Mull.

It's also a land with a rich, multilayered history, a place where every corner of the landscape is steeped in the past – a deserted croft on an island shore, a moor that was once a battlefield, a beach where Vikings hauled their boats ashore, or a cave that once sheltered Bonnie Prince Charlie.

Respect for top-quality local produce means that you can feast on fresh seafood mere hours after it was caught, with beef, venison and organic vegetables that were raised just a few miles away from your table. Then top it all off with a dram of single malt whisky – rich, evocative and complex, the true taste of Scotland.

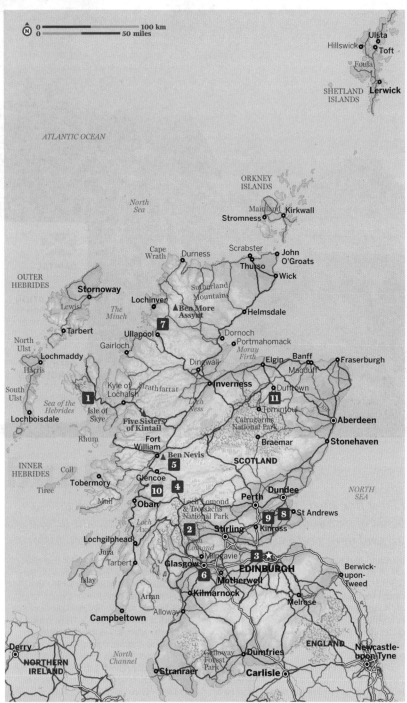

Scotland's
Top Experiences

Isle of Skye

1 In a country famous for stunning scenery, the Isle of Skye takes top prize. From the craggy peaks of the Cuillins and the bizarre pinnacles of the Old Man of Storr and Quiraing to the spectacular sea cliffs of Neist Point, there's a photo opportunity at almost every turn. Walkers can share the landscape with red deer and golden eagles, while puffins nest of the clifftops and whales and dolphins play offshore. At day's end you can refuel in convivial pubs and top seafood restaurants.

Loch Lomond

2 Despite being less than an hour's drive from the bustle and sprawl of Glasgow, the bonnie banks and bonnie braes of Loch Lomond (immortalised in the words of one of Scotland's best-known songs) comprise one of the most scenic parts of the country. It's mainland Britain's largest lake and, after Loch Ness, perhaps the most famous of Scotland's lochs. At the heart of Scotland's first national park, the loch begins as a broad, island-peppered lake in the south, its shores clothed in bluebell woods, narrowing in the north to a fjordlike trench ringed by 900m-high mountains.

Edinburgh

3 Edinburgh is a city that begs to be explored. From the vaults and wynds (narrow lanes) that riddle the Old Town to the urban villages of Stockbridge and Cramond, it's filled with quirky, come-hither nooks that tempt you to walk just a little bit further. As well as sightseeing there are top shops, world-class restaurants and a bacchanalia of bars to enjoy. This is a city of pub crawls and impromptu music sessions, mad-for-it clubbing, overindulgence, late nights and wanders home through cobbled streets at dawn.

if Scotland were 100 people

98 would be white
1 would be South Asian
1 would be other

belief systems

(% of population)

43 Church of Scotland
28 Non-Religious
16 Roman Catholic
7 other Christian
6 other

population per sq km

SCOTLAND   IRELAND   US

= 30 people

Walking the West Highland Way

4 The best way to really get inside Scotland's landscapes is to walk them. Despite the wind, midges and drizzle, walking here is a pleasure, with numerous short- and long-distance trails, hills and mountains begging to be tramped. Top of the wish list for many hikers is the 95-mile West Highland Way from Milngavie (near Glasgow) to Fort William, a challenging weeklong walk through some of the country's finest scenery, finishing in the shadow of its highest peak, Ben Nevis.

Climbing Ben Nevis

5 The allure of Britain's highest peak is strong – around 100,000 people a year set off up the summit trail, though not all make it to the top. Nevertheless, the highest Munro of them all is within the reach of anyone who's reasonably fit. Treat Ben Nevis with respect and your reward (weather permitting) will be a truly magnificent view and a great sense of achievement.

Glasgow

6 Scotland's biggest city lacks Edinburgh's classical beauty, but more than makes up for it with a barrelful of things to do and a warmth and energy that leave every visitor impressed. Edgy and contemporary, it's a great spot to browse art galleries and – despite the deep-fried-Mars Bar reputation – Scotland's best place to dine out. Add to this what is perhaps Britain's best pub culture and one of the world's best live-music scenes, and the only thing to do is live it.

The Dreaded Midge

Be prepared for an encounter with the dreaded midge. These tiny, blood-sucking flies appear in huge swarms in summer, and can completely ruin a holiday. They proliferate from late May to mid-September, but especially mid-June to mid-August. To combat them, cover up, particularly in the evening and, most importantly, use a reliable insect repellent..

Food & Drink

10 single malts:

Ardbeg (Islay) The 10-year-old from this noble distillery is a byword for excellence. Peaty but well balanced.

Bowmore (Islay) Smoke, peat and salty sea air – a classic Islay malt. One of the few distilleries that still malts its own barley.

Bruichladdich (Islay) A visitor-friendly distillery with a quirky, innovative approach – famous for very peaty special releases such as Moine Mhor.

Glendronach (Speyside) Only sherry casks are used here, so the creamy, spicy result tastes like grandma's Christmas trifle.

Highland Park (Orkney) Full and rounded, with heather, honey, malt and peat.

Isle of Arran (Arran) One of the newest of Scotland's distilleries, offering a lightish, flavoursome malt with flowery, fruity notes.

Macallan (Speyside) The king of Speyside malts, with sherry and bourbon finishes.

Springbank (Campbeltown) Complex flavours – sherry, citrus, pear drops, peat – with a salty tang.

Talisker (Skye) Brooding, heavily peaty nose balanced by a satisfying sweetness from this lord of the isles.

The Balvenie (Speyside) Rich and honeyed, this Speysider is liquid gold for those with a sweet tooth.

CHRIS HEPBURN / GETTY IMAGES ©

Northwest Highlands

7 The Highlands abound in breathtaking views, but the far northwest is truly awe-inspiring. The coastal road from Durness and Kyle of Lochalsh offers jaw-dropping scenes at every turn: the rugged mountains of Assynt, the desolate beauty of Torridon and the remote cliffs of Cape Wrath. Add in warm Highland hospitality found in classic rural pubs to make this an unforgettable corner of the country.

Golf

8 The Scots invented the game of golf and Scotland is still revered as its spiritual home by hackers and champions alike. Links courses are the classic experience here – bumpy coastal affairs where the rough is heather and machair and the main enemy is the wind, which can make a disaster of a promising round in an instant. St Andrews is golf's headquarters, and an alluring destination for anyone who loves the sport.

When to Go

HIGH SEASON (Jul–Aug)

➡ Accommodation prices 10–20% higher (book in advance if possible).

➡ Warmest time of year, but often wet.

➡ Midges at their worst in Highlands and islands.

SHOULDER (May–Jun & Sep)

➡ Wildflowers and rhododendrons bloom in May and June.

➡ Statistically, best chance of dry weather, minus midges.

➡ June evenings have daylight till 11pm.

LOW SEASON (Oct–Apr)

➡ Rural attractions and accommodation often closed.

➡ Snow on hills November to March.

➡ Gets dark at 4pm in December.

Perthshire – Big Tree Country

9 Blue-grey lochs reflect the changing moods of the weather, swaths of noble woodland clothe the hills; majestic glens scythe their way into remote wilderness, and salmon leap upriver to the place of their birth. In Perthshire, the heart of the country, picturesque towns bloom with flowers, distilleries emit tempting malty odours and sheep graze in impossibly green meadows. There's a feeling of the bounty of nature that no other place in Scotland can replicate.

Glen Coe

10 Scotland's most famous glen combines those two essential

Best on Film

The Maggie Classic 1950s Ealing comedy about the crew of a puffer on the west coast of Scotland.

Tutti Frutti Iconic 1980s TV series about a fading rock band's last tour, with Robbie Coltrane and Emma Thompson.

Best in Print

Adrift in Caledonia (Nick Thorpe) An insightful tale of hitchhiking around Scotland on a variety of vessels.

Mountaineering in Scotland (WH Murray) Classic account of hiking in Scotland in the 1930s, when just getting to Glen Coe was an adventure in itself.

Raw Spirit (Iain Banks) An enjoyable jaunt around Scotland in search of the perfect whisky.

The Poor Had No Lawyers (Andy Wightman) A fascinating analysis of who owns land in Scotland and how they got it.

Getting Around

Bicycle Scotland is a compact country, and travelling around by bicycle is a perfectly feasible proposition if you have the time.

Bus Buses are usually the cheapest way to get around, but also the slowest. The network covers most of the country, however in remote areas services are more geared to the needs of locals and may not be well timed for visitors.

Car Particularly good for the areas not covered by the rail network, including the Highlands and the Southern Uplands.

Train With a discount pass, trains can be competitive; they're also quicker than bus travel and often take you through beautiful scenery.

qualities of Highlands landscape: dramatic scenery and deep history. The peacefulness and beauty of this valley today belie the fact that it was the scene of a ruthless 17th-century massacre, when the local MacDonalds were murdered by the Campbell clan. Some of the glen's finest walks – to the Lost Valley, for example – follow the routes used by the clanspeople trying to flee their attackers, and where many perished in the snow.

Whisky

11 Scotland's national drink – from the Gaelic *uisge bagh*, meaning 'water of life' – has been distilled here for more than 500 years. More than 100 distilleries are still in operation, producing hundreds of varieties of single malt; learning to distinguish the smoky, peaty whiskies of Islay from, say, the flowery, sherried malts of Speyside has become a hugely popular pastime. Many distilleries offer guided tours, rounded off with a tasting session. Dufftown, in the heart of Speyside whisky territory, is a good place to start ticking off the local varieties.

LEON HARRIS / GETTY IMAGES ©

African Renaissance Monument, Dakar

Senegal

Skimming any holiday brochure about Senegal, you'll sooner or later stumble across the term teranga, meaning 'hospitality'. Senegal takes great pride in being the 'Land of Teranga'.

Senegal may be one of West Africa's most stable countries, but stability equates to anything but dullness: the capital, Dakar, is a dizzying, street-hustler-rich introduction to the country. Perched on the tip of a peninsula, elegance meets chaos, noise, vibrant markets and glittering nightlife, while nearby Île de Gorée and the beaches of Yoff and N'Gor tap to slow, lazy beats.

In northern Senegal, the enigmatic capital of Saint-Louis, a Unesco World Heritage site, tempts with colonial architecture and proximity to luscious national parks. Along the Petite Côte and Cap Skiring, wide strips of beaches beckon and the broad deltas of the Casamance River reveal hundreds of bird species, from the gleaming wings of tiny kingfishers to the proud poise of pink flamingos.

Whether you want to mingle with the trendsetters of urban Africa or be alone with your thoughts and the sounds of nature, you'll find your place in Senegal.

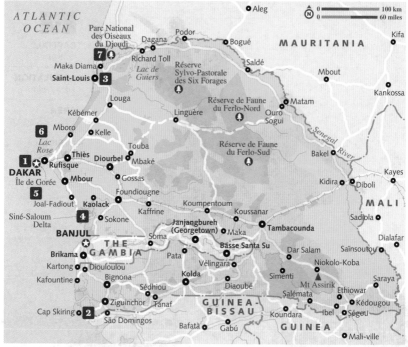

Senegal's
Top Experiences

Dakar

1 Hit West Africa's trendiest nightlife venues and swing your hips to *mbalax*, the mix of Cuban beats and traditional drumming that forms the heart and soul of the Senegalese music scene. Relax with a lazy day at the beach and feast on fresh-off-the-boat seafood, or explore the workshops of Senegal's most promising artists at the Village des Arts. Finally, climb up one of Dakar's 'breasts' to contemplate the controversial, socialist-style African Renaissance Monument and take in sweeping views across the city. Once a tiny settlement in the south of the Cap Vert peninsula, Dakar now spreads almost across its entire triangle, and keeps growing.

Cap Skiring

2 Weave your way via tiny villages to Senegal's best beaches on Cap Skiring and kick back for a day of doing absolutely nothing. The beaches at Cap Skiring are some of the finest in West Africa and, better still, they are usually empty. Most *campements* (guesthouses) and hotels are on the beach; many hotels offer a mix of activities like kayaking, quad hire and fishing trips. With its lush tropical landscapes, watered by the graceful, winding Casamance River, and the unique culture of the Diola, this area seems far from Dakar and its surroundings, in every sense.

Saint-Louis

3 Wander in the footsteps of history in West Africa's first French settlement, Saint-Louis. With its crumbling colonial architecture, horse-drawn carts and peaceful ambience, Saint-Louis has a unique historical charm – so much so that it's been a Unesco World Heritage site since 2000. The old town centre sits on an island in the Senegal River, but the city sprawls into Sor on the mainland, and onto the Langue de Barbarie, where you'll find the lively fishing community of Guet N'Dar. The island is reached via the Pont Faidherbe, the 500m-long bridge designed by Gustav Eiffel and a feat of 19th-century engineering.

MAISANT LUDOVIC / GETTY IMAGES ©

Siné-Saloum Delta

4 The 150km Petite Côte stretches south from Dakar and is one of Senegal's best beach areas. Where the Siné and Saloum Rivers meet the tidal waters of the Atlantic Ocean, the coast is broken into a stunning area of mangrove swamps, lagoons, forests and sand islands. It forms part of the magnificent 180-sq-km Siné-Saloum Delta. Ndangane is a thriving traveller centre along the coast, from where you can take a *pirogue* (traditional canoe) to almost any point in the delta.

Île de Gorée

5 Ruled in succession by the Portuguese, Dutch, English and French, the historical, Unesco-designated

Île de Gorée is enveloped by an almost eerie calm. There are no sealed roads and no cars on this island, just narrow alleyways with trailing bougainvilleas and colonial brick buildings with wrought-iron balconies – it's a living, visual masterpiece. But Gorée's calm is not so much romantic as meditative, as the ancient, elegant buildings bear witness to the island's role in the Atlantic slave trade.

Lac Rose

6 Float on the salt-heavy Lac Rose and snap otherworldly pics of the pink water contrasted with the bright blue sky. Also known as Lac Retba, this shallow lagoon surrounded by dunes is a popular day-trip destination for *dakarois* and tourists

if Senegal were 100 people

42 would be Wolof
24 would be Pular
15 would be Serer
4 would be Jola
15 would be other

belief systems
(% of population)

94 Muslim

5 Christian

1 indigenous beliefs

population per sq km

SENEGAL GUINEA-BISSAU SOUTH AFRICA

⬆ ≈ 8 people

When to Go

NOV–FEB

➡ Senegal's main tourist season is dry and cool.

DEC & MAR–JUN

➡ This is when most music festivals are held, including the Saint-Louis Jazz Festival (early May).

JUL–LATE SEP

➡ Rainy, humid season, but hotels reduce prices by up to 40%.

Senegalese Culture

'A man with a mouth is never lost' goes a popular Wolof saying. Indeed, conversation is the key to local culture, and the key to conversation is a great sense of humour. The Senegalese love talking and teasing, and the better you slide into the conversational game, the easier you'll get around.

Personal life stories in Senegal tend to be brewed from a mix of traditional values, global influences, Muslim faith and family integration. More than 90% of the population is Muslim, and many of them belong to one of the Sufi brotherhoods that dominate religious life in Senegal. The most important brotherhood is that of the Mourides.

Food & Drink

Ataaya A punchy, bittersweet brew made from fistfuls of green tea leaves and lots of sugar.

Bissap A purple drink made of water, sugar and hibiscus leaves.

Bouyi Sweet, thick juice made from the fruits of the baobab tree.

Corossol Thick, white juice made from the fruits of the soursop tree.

Mafé Platter of rice covered with a thick, smooth groundnut (peanut) sauce with fried meat and vegetables.

Pastries The French legacy has left the Senegalese with a taste for croissants and pastries.

Tiéboudienne Senegal's national dish: rice cooked in a thick tomato sauce and served with fried fish and vegetables.

Yassa poulet Grilled chicken marinated in a thick onion-and-lemon sauce. Occasionally chicken is replaced by fish or meat, in which case it's called *yassa poisson* (fish) or *yassa boeuf* (beef).

DOELAN YANN / GETTY IMAGES ©

Pelicans

alike, all coming to enjoy the calm and catch the lake's magic trick – the subtle pink shimmer that sometimes colours its waves. The spectacle is caused by the water's high salt content, which is 10 times that of your regular ocean. It's a beautiful sight but can only be enjoyed when the light is right. Your best chance is in the dry season, when the sun is high. But even if nature refuses to put on her show, a day out here is still enjoyable. You can swim in the lake, buoyed by the salt, or check out the small-scale salt-collecting industry on its shores. And up until the demise of the famous Dakar Rally, Lac Rose is where the Sahara drivers would arrive and celebrate their victories or drown their woes.

Parc National des Oiseaux du Djoudj

7 With almost 300 species of bird, this 16,000-hectare park is one of the most important bird sanctuaries in the world. Flamingos, pelicans and waders are most plentiful, and large numbers of migrating birds travel here in November. The park is best explored by *pirogue*.

Getting Around

Bus *Cars mourides* (large buses, financed by the Mouride brotherhood) connect major towns in Senegal. Book ahead of travel.

Taxi The quickest (though still uncomfortable) way of getting around the country is by *sept-place* (shared seven-seater) taxi – battered Peugeots that negotiate even the most ragged routes. Slightly cheaper but infinitely less reliable are the minibuses (Ndiaga Ndiaye or *grand car*), carrying around 40 people. Vehicles leave from the *gare routière* when they're full, and they fill up quickest in the morning, before 8am. Taxi prices are theoretically fixed, though they're steadily increasing as petrol prices rise. There's an extra, negotiable charge for luggage (10% to 20% of the bill).

Zlatibor

CAPITAL
Belgrade

POPULATION
7.2 million

AREA
77,474 sq km

**OFFICIAL
LANGUAGE**
Serbian

Serbia

Serbia's long history of multiculturalism and intellectual thought, rich folklore and thriving art and music scenes make it a must-see in the Balkans.

During the 1990s Serbia went from being the powerhouse of Yugoslavia to the bully of the Balkans. But reputations can be re-made as quickly as they may be lost. Everything you never heard about Serbia is true: it is warm, welcoming and a hell of a lot of fun. Today, the Serbs' sense of industry, creativity and initiative sees their homeland resuming a pivotal role in the region.

Exuding a feisty mix of élan and *inat* (Serbian trait of rebellious defiance), this country doesn't do 'mild': Belgrade is one of the world's wildest party destinations, Novi Sad hosts the rockingly hedonistic EXIT music festival, and even its hospitality is emphatic – expect to be greeted with *rakija* and a hearty three-kiss hello.

While political correctness is about as commonplace as a nonsmoking bar, Serbia is nevertheless a cultural crucible: there's the art nouveau town of Subotica, bohemian Niš, and the minaret-studded Novi Pazar, which nudges some of the most sacred sites in Serbian Orthodoxy.

Serbia's
Top Experiences

Belgrade

1 Outspoken, adventur-ous and audacious, Belgrade (Београд) is no 'pretty' capital, but its gritty exuberance makes it one of the most happening cities in Europe. While it hurtles towards a brighter future, its chaotic past unfolds before your eyes: socialist blocks are squeezed between art nouveau masterpieces, and remnants of the Habsburg legacy contrast with Ot-toman relics. It is here the Sava River meets the Dan-ube (Dunav), contemplative parkland nudges hectic urban sprawl, and old-world culture gives way to new-world nightlife.

Novi Pazar

2 Ponder the exotic cultural fusions of Turkish-toned Novi Pazar, the cultural centre of the Raška/Sandžak region, with a large Muslim population. Turkish coffee, cuisine and customs abound, yet some idyllic Orthodox sights are in the vicinity: this was the heartland of the Serbian medieval state. The Old Town is lined with cafes and shops peddling Turkish goods, while just across the Raška River are cafes and restaurants. Attempts to restore the ruined hammam (Turkish bath) have failed, leaving it at the mercy of coffee-drinking men and picnickers.

Subotica

3 Goggle at splendid sur-prises bursting from the Vojvodinian plains, such as the art nouveau treas-ures of Subotica. Sugar-spun art nouveau marvels, a laid-back populace and a delicious sprinkling of Serbian and Hungarian flavours make this a quaint town. Most sights are along the pedestrian strip of Kor-zo or on the main square, Trg Republike. Home to more than 25 ethnic groups, six languages and the best of Hungarian and Serbian traditions, Vojvodina's (Војводина) pancake plains mask a diversity unheard of in the rest of the country.

Republic Square in Belgrade

EXIT Festival, Novi Sad

4 Home to the epic EXIT Festival, Novi Sad's Petrovaradin Fortress is stormed by thousands of revellers each year. The first festival in 2000 lasted 100 days and galvanised a generation of young Serbs against the Milošević regime, who 'exited' himself just weeks after the event. The festival has been attended by an annual tally of about 200,000 merrymakers from around the world. Witness the laid-back town morph into the state of EXIT every July.

Drvengrad

5 Escape reality in the fantastic village of Drvengrad, built by

director Emir Kusturica for indie drama *Life is a Miracle*. Quirky, colourful flourishes give the village a fantastical feel: the Stanley Kubrick cinema shows Kusturica's films, there's a life-size statue of Johnny Depp, and Bruce Lee St is home to a restaurant where you can sip 'Che Guevara biorevolution juice' and goggle at prime panoramas. Drvengrad hosts the international Küstendorf Film and Music Festival each January.

Skiing & Hiking, Zlatibor

6 Ski, hike or just take in the mountain air in the magical villages of Zlatibor. A romantic region of gentle mountains, traditions and hospitality, the Zlatibor

if Serbia were 100 people

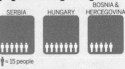

83 would be Serb
2 would be Bosniak
4 would be Hungarian
2 would be Romany
9 would be other

belief systems
(% of population)

85
Serbian Orthodox

5
Catholic

3
Muslim

1
Protestant

6
other

population per sq km

SERBIA   HUNGARY   BOSNIA & HERCEGOVINA

👤 ≈ 15 people

When to Go

HIGH SEASON (Apr)

➡ Watch winter melt away with a scenic ride on the nostalgic Šargan 8 railway.

SHOULDER (Jul & Aug)

➡ Rock out at Novi Sad's EXIT, go wild at Guča and get jazzy at Nišville.

LOW SEASON (Dec–Mar)

➡ Head to Kopaonik and Zlatibor for alpine adventure.

Madness, Made in Serbia

On the surface, the Dragačevo Trumpet Assembly (an annual gathering of brass musicians) sounds harmless; nerdily endearing even. But band camp this ain't: it is, however, the most boisterous music festival in all of Europe, if not the world.

Known as 'Guča', after the western Serbian village that has hosted it each August since 1961, the six-day debauch is hedonism at its most rambunctious: tens of thousands of beer-and-brass-addled visitors dance wild kola through the streets, gorging on spit-meat and slapping dinar on the sweaty foreheads of the (mostly Roma) trubači performers. The music itself is relentless and frenzy-fast; even Miles Davis confessed, 'I didn't know you could play trumpet that way.' Sleep is a dubious proposition, but bring a tent anyway.

Food & Drink

Burek Flaky meat, cheese or vegetable pie eaten with yoghurt.

Ćevapčići The ubiquitous skinless sausage.

Kajmak Along the lines of a salty clotted cream, this dairy delight is lashed on to everything from bread to burgers.

Karađorđeva šnicla Similar to chicken Kiev, but with veal or pork and lashings of kajmak and tartar.

Pasulj prebranac The Serbian take on baked beans, just fatter and porkier.

Rakija Distilled spirit most commonly made from plums.

Svadbarski kupus Sauerkraut and hunks of smoked pork slow-cooked in giant clay pots.

Urnebes Creamy, spicy peppers-'n'-cheese spread.

Church of Our Lady & King's Church, Studenica Monastery

region encompasses the Tara and Šargan mountains in the north and the Murtenica hills bordering BiH. The town centre (tržni centar) has everything you could need, but not far beyond are quaint villages where locals are oblivious to ski-bunny shenanigans. Zlatibor's slopes are mild. Major skiing hills are Tornik (the highest peak in Zlatibor at 1496m) and Obudovica.

Studenica Monastery

7 One of the most sacred sites in Serbia, Studenica was established in the 1190s by founder of the Serbian empire (and future saint) Stefan Nemanja and developed by his sons Vukan, Stefan and Rastko (St Sava). Active monastic life was cultivated by Sava and continues today, though this thriving little community doesn't mind visitors. Two well-preserved churches lie within impressive white-marble walls. Bogorodičina Crkva (Church of Our Lady), a royal funeral church, contains Stefan's tomb. Smaller Kraljeva Crkva (King's Church) houses the acclaimed Birth of the Virgin fresco and other masterpieces.

Getting Around

Bicycle Bicycle paths are improving in larger cities. Vojvodina is relatively flat, but main roads make for dull days. Mountainous regions such as Zlatibor offer mountain biking in summer months. Picturesque winding roads come with the downside of narrow shoulders.

Bus Services are extensive, though outside major hubs sporadic connections may leave you in the lurch for a few hours. In southern Serbia particularly, you may have to double back to larger towns.

Train Generally trains aren't as regular and reliable as buses, and can be murderously slow.

Anse Source d'Argent

<table>
<tr><td>CAPITAL
Port Louis</td></tr>
<tr><td>POPULATION
90,846</td></tr>
<tr><td>AREA
455 sq km</td></tr>
<tr><td>OFFICIAL LANGUAGES
Creole
English
Italian</td></tr>
</table>

Seychelles

Welcome to paradise. It may be a much-abused cliché, but the sandy, turquoise-rimmed islands that make up the Seychelles come as close to living up to this claim as anywhere on the planet.

Close your eyes and imagine: you're lazing on a talcum-powder beach lapped by topaz waters and backed by lush hills and big glacis boulders. Brochure material? No, just routine in the Seychelles. Many think the eye-catching images of turquoise seas and shimmering white sands are digitally enhanced but, once here, they realise the pictures barely do them justice.

With such a dreamlike setting, the Seychelles is unsurprisingly a choice place for newlyweds. But for those looking for more

than a suntan or romance, this archipelago offers a number of high-energy distractions. There are jungle and coastal walks, boat excursions, and diving and snorkelling to keep you buzzing, as well marine parks and natural reserves filled with endemic species.

The Seychelles is also more affordable than you think. On top of ultra-luxurious options, the country has plenty of self-catering facilities and family-run guesthouses. So if you are suffering from visions of tropical paradise, here is your medicine.

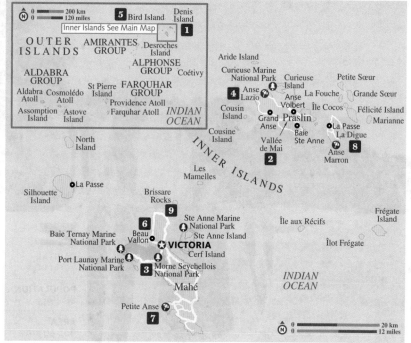

Seychelles'
Top Experiences

Denis

1 You land on a strip of coral by the sea. There's a white-sand beach lapped by luxuriously warm waters, a shimmering lagoon with every hue from lapis lazuli to turquoise, and palm and casuarina trees leaning over the shore. If working on your suntan ceases to do it for you, there are nature walks along scenic pathways as well as fishing, snorkelling and diving trips. Wildlife lovers will love it here too; Denis is a sanctuary for giant tortoises, magpie robins, paradise flycatchers and Seychelles warblers.

Valleé de Mai

2 If you can tear yourself away from the beach, Valleé de Mai is a paradise of a different kind. Inscribed by Unesco on its World Heritage list, and home to the rare and singularly beautiful coco de mer palms and a host of other endemic plants, walking in the valley is an immersion into a lush tropical forest, surrounded by birdsong. Lose yourself along the quiet hiking trails that meander through this verdant wilderness.

Morne Seychellois National Park

3 In their quest for the perfect beach, many travellers are oblivious to the fact that there's a splendid national park on Mahé, so they miss out on fantastic experiences. Take a guided hike through dense forest, coastal mangroves and rugged mountains and you'll soon believe that the world and its clamour belong to another planet. While exploring, you'll come across rare species of birds, reptiles and plants, not to mention breathtaking views.

Anse Lazio

4 On the north of Praslin Island, Anse Lazio is a prime example of just why Seychelles has become one of the most alluring destinations in the Indian Ocean. The beach here is near perfect, with golden sands, granite boulders at either end, palm trees and unbearably beautiful turquoise waters. Ideal for hours spent lying on the beach, snorkelling, or eating in one of the beachfront restaurants, it's the sort of place you'll never want to leave.

Tropical rainforest, Valleé de Mai, Praslin

Bird Island

5 The ultimate destination for ecotourism and bird-watching. Hundreds of thousands of sooty terns, fairy terns and common noddies descend en masse between May and October to nest on this coral island, just 95km south of Mahé. Now is your chance to reenact a scene from Alfred Hitchcock's *The Birds*! You only have to sit outside on your veranda and birds will come to land on your head. The island is also home to Esmeralda, the world's largest tortoise.

Beau Vallon

6 A long, brilliant-white arc of sand laced by palms and takamaka trees, Beau Vallon beach is the most popular in Mahé. The water is deep enough for swimming, and there is also some great diving and snokelling in the bay nearby. The beach may be quite built-up by Seychelles standards, but it's still quiet and idyllic compared to other tropical destinations. The seaside ambience, with fishermen selling fresh fish late in the afternoon in the shade of takamaka trees, adds a dash of life.

Anse Intendance

7 Mahé's west coast is exquisite on the eyes, and its beaches and coastal scenery are naturally the star attractions. One such jewel, Anse Intendance, is famous for its hypnotically dramatic sunset; as the sky deepens to

if the Seychelles were 100 people

92 would speak Creole
5 would speak English
3 would speak other languages

belief systems
(% of population)

82 Roman Catholic
8 Protestant
2 Hindu

1 Muslim
6 Other
1 None

population per sq km

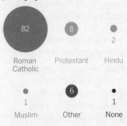

SEYCHELLES   MADAGASCAR   UK

= 40 people

When to Go

DEC–MAR

➡ The trade winds bring, warmer, wetter air streams from the northeast. Accommodation can be hard to find during December & January.

APR– MAY & OCT–NOV

➡ The 'turnaround' periods, which are normally calm and windless, are ideal for travelling.

JUN–SEP

➡ The southeast trade winds usher in cooler, drier weather, but it can be quite windy. Peak travel time (due to northern hemisphere summer holidays).

Wildlife

Giant tortoises are now found only in the Seychelles and the Galápagos Islands. The French and English wiped out the tortoises from all over the Seychelles except for the island of Aldabra, where happily more than 100,000 still survive. Many have been brought to the central islands, where they munch their way around hotel gardens, and there is also a free-roaming colony on Curieuse Island.

The Seychelles are also renowned for their bird-life, and every island seems to be inhabited by some rare species including magpie robins, Seychelles warblers, paradise flycatchers black parrots, bare-legged scops owls and Seychelles kestrels.

Food & Drink

Bat curry Known as *civet de chauve souris*, this is a local delicacy.

Beer Seybrew, the local brand of beer, is sold everywhere. Eku, another locally produced beer, is a bit harder to find.

Fish Fish, fish, fish! And rice. This is the most common combination (*pwason ek diri* in Creole patois) in the Seychelles, served ultra-fresh so it melts in your mouth. You'll devour *bourgeois*, *capitaine*, shark, *job*, parrotfish, caranx, grouper and tuna, among others.

Fruit The Seychelles are dripping with tropical fruits, including mango, banana, breadfruit, papaya, coconut, grapefruit, pineapple and carambole. Mixed with spices, they make wonderful accompaniments, such as the flavourful *chatini* (chutney).

Juice Along with coconut water, freshly squeezed juices are amongst the most delicious, natural and thirst-quenching drinks you will try in the islands.

RAINER VON BRANDIS / GETTY IMAGES ©

orange, the granite boulders that frame the beach glow with muted copper tones and form the perfect backdrop for a romantic stroll.

La Digue

8 Remember that tropical paradise that appears in countless adverts and glossy travel brochures? Here it's the real thing, with jade-green waters, bewitching bays studded with heart-palpitatingly gorgeous beaches, and green hills cloaked with tangled jungle. As if that weren't enough, La Digue is ideally situated as a springboard to surrounding islands, including Félicité, Grande Sœur and the fairy-tale Île Cocos.

Diving with Sharks

9 Discerning divers have long known of the Seychelles' claim to being one of the Indian Ocean's most rewarding dive destinations. We like it especially for its variety of sealife, and the unmistakeable cachet of swimming with whale sharks and massive rays off Mahé. There are wreck dives and mind-blowing fish off Brissare Rocks, but nothing beats the frission of getting up close and personal with the whale sharks who frequent the area.

Getting Around

Air Seychelles' only international airport is on Mahé. There are around 25 scheduled flights per day between Mahé and Praslin.

Bicycle This is the pricipal form of transport on La Digue; you can also rent cycles on Praslin, but Mahé is too hilly for casual cycling.

Boat Travel by boat is very easy between Mahé, Praslin and La Digue, with regular and efficient ferry services.

Bus If you've got time, you don't really need to rent a car to visit the islands: Mahé and Prasiln both have extensive bus services.

Car If you want to be controller of your own destiny, your best bet is to rent a car. Most of the roads on Mahé and Praslin are sealed and in good shape.

Fisherman, River No 2 Beach

CAPITAL
Freetown

POPULATION
5.6 million

AREA
71,740 sq km

OFFICIAL LANGUAGE
English

Sierra Leone

Sierra Leone is a country on the upswing and the resilient, friendly people have set about rebuilding their nation. Today there's much to discover, with scarcely another tourist in sight.

West Africa's secret beach destination rises from the soft waters of the Atlantic, dressed in sun-stained hues, rainforest green and the red, red roads of the north. Sierra Leone: the land so-named because it's shaped like a mountain lion. Sweet Salone, the locals say.

In Freetown, colourful stilted houses recall the days when freed slaves from the Caribbean were resettled upon these shores. Some landed on the peninsula, blanketed with sands as white and soft as cotton wool.

In the north, the Loma Mountains form the highest point west of Cameroon. Further east, streams cut national parks and mangrove swamps swathe rainforest that shelter endangered species like the shy pygmy hippo.

The curtains have been drawn on the painful past, and it's time for a new act in Sierra Leone. Join the island-hoppers and sun-seekers, swim in the clear blue waters, explore the archipelagos and crack open fresh lobster in the shade of skinny palms and rope-strung hammocks.

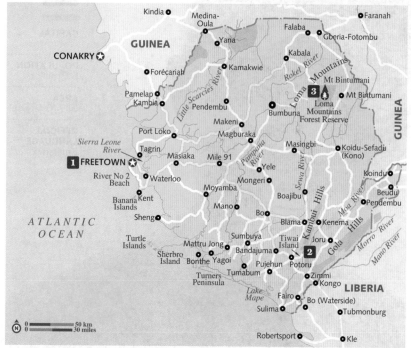

Sierra Leone's
Top Experiences

Freetown Beaches

1 Freetown's tongue stretches out along the coast, kissing beaches lined with tall, elegant palms and iced with sand that's white as snow. River No 2 shot to fame after the Bounty chocolate bar ad was filmed here, and the sugary white sands don't disappoint.

Food & Drink

Every town has at least one *cookery* (basic eating house) serving *chop* (meals).

Fry fry Simple sandwiches.

Plasas Sauce of pounded potato or cassava leaves and palm oil.

Poyo Palm wine; light and fruity.

Star Top-selling beer.

Street food Fried chicken, roasted corn, chicken kebabs.

Tiwai Island

2 'Big Island', in the Mende language, certainly packs a punch when it comes to its primate population. Set on the Moa River, the entire island is run as a conservation research project. There are more than 700 different plant species, 11 species of primates – including Diana monkeys and chimpanzees – 135 bird species, plus otters, sea turtles and the endangered, elusive pygmy hippopotamus.

Mt Bintumani

3 Also known as Loma Mansa, the breathy King of the Mountains, 1945m-high Mt Bintumani is West Africa's highest peak – until you hit Cameroon. The mountain range is rich in highland birds and mammal species, including duikers, colobus monkeys, leopards and snakes. It's worth the four-to-five day adventure; the summit looks out over most of West Africa, veiled by soft cool mist.

When to Go

NOV–JUN

➡ The dry season brings mild, dusty harmattan winds from December until February.

APRIL

➡ The average daytime temperature is 32°C.

JUN–NOV

➡ The rainy season sees spectacular storms and up to 3200mm of precipitation.

Merlion statue, Marina Bay

CAPITAL
Singapore

POPULATION
5.5 million

AREA
697 sq km

OFFICIAL LANGUAGES
Mandarin, English, Tamil, Malay

Singapore

This perennial stopover city is constantly reinventing itself as a destination in its own right, jostling for the position of top dog among Asia's – even the world's – best cities.

One of Asia's success stories, tiny little Singapore's GDP consistently ranks it as one of the wealthiest countries in the world. Along with that wealth comes a rich culture borne of a multiracial population. Get lost in the mad swirl of skyscrapers in the central business district (CBD), be transfixed by the Bolly beats in the streets of ramshackle Little India, hike a dense patch of rainforest in Bukit Timah, or just give yourself up to the air-conditioned retail mayhem of Orchard Rd. There's something for everyone here.

It's affluent, high tech and occasionally a little snobbish, but Singapore's great leveller is the hawker centre, the ubiquitous and raucous food markets where everyone mucks in together to indulge the local mania for cheap eating and drinking. In short, Singapore makes for a perfect pit stop to recover from the rough-and-tumble of the rest of Southeast Asia.

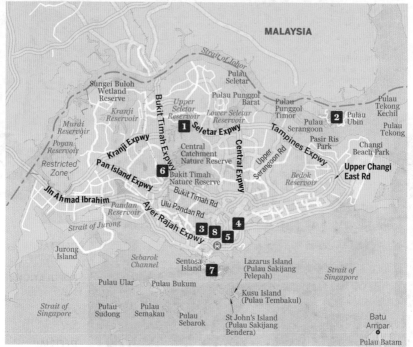

Singapore's
Top Experiences

Singapore Zoo & Night Safari

1 Let's put it out there: this is possibly the world's best zoo. The open-air enclosures allow for both freedom for the animals to roam and unobstructed visitor views. The Singapore Zoo is one of the few places outside of Borneo or Sumatra where you can stand under trees with orangutans a few feet above your head, or where mouse deer and lemurs scamper across your path. As evening closes in, the Night Safari next door uses open-concept enclosures to get visitors up close and personal with nocturnal creatures such as leopards, free-ranging deer and Malayan tigers.

Pulau Ubin

2 Singapore's very own rustic island getaway offers a glimpse at the *kampong* (village) life that was a big part of Singapore as recently as the 1960s. By hopping aboard a chugging bumboat from Changi, visitors can experience Pulau Ubin's old-growth mangrove swamps, then cycle past tin-roof shacks or rampage along a cross-country mountain bike trail and end the day with a seafood meal. If the great outdoors is not your thing, you can take a cooking class instead. If the easy island life gets you in, you can always stay a night or three at the local resort.

Botanic Gardens

3 Singapore's Botanic Gardens make a welcome escape from the bustle of city life. At the tail end of Orchard Rd, this sprawling oasis is a great place to take a picnic and people-watch. Or stroll through the orchid gardens, looking out for Vanda Miss Joaquim, Singapore's national flower. The Singapore Symphony Orchestra gives free monthly performances at the pavilion.

Little India

4 The most atmospheric of Singapore's historic quarters is as close as it gets to Singapore of the old chaotic days. Experience it with the masses on the

CHRISTOPHER CHAN / GETTY IMAGES ©

Orang-utans, Singapore Zoo

weekends when it gets packed to the gills with Indian workers wanting a slice of home. The five-foot ways of the shophouses spill over with aromatic spices and colourful products. The trendy set are drawn to cool little bars and if you have insomnia, simply head to Mustafa Centre for shopping: buy an iPad at 3am before heading for a *teh tarik* and a *roti prata*.

Baba House

5 This (free!) living museum is one of the best-preserved Peranakan heritage homes found in Singapore, and offers a glimpse into the Chinese-Malay hybrid culture of Singapore's Baba-Nonya minority. The stunningly restored Chinese mansion – complete with period furnishing – recreates a wonderful window into the life of a wealthy Peranakan family c 1928. Fact-filled and entertaining 90-minute guided tours run twice a week and need to be booked in advance.

Bukit Timah Nature Reserve

6 Hiking in sunny, humid Singapore? Why not? The country's British forefathers, Sir Stamford Raffles and William Farquhar, were great naturalists, and Singapore has a surprising number of green pockets. Hike the trails at Bukit Timah Nature Reserve, where a cacophony of insects, roving monkeys and lush canopy hark back to a time when Singapore was mostly wilderness. Also check out the Southern

if Singapore were 100 people

77 would be Chinese
14 would be Malay
8 would be Indian
1 would be other

belief systems
(% of population)

34 Buddhist
14 Muslim
11 Taoist

5 Hindu
18 Christian
18 other/none

population per sq km

SINGAPORE   HONG KONG   INDONESIA

♦ ≈ 125 people

When to Go

JAN–FEB

➡ Chinese New Year and Chingay are the events to catch.

APR–MAY

➡ Lots of events and just before the local school holidays start.

DEC

➡ The northeast monsoons bring lashing rains, but they also cool Singapore down.

Singlish

While Singapore's official languages are Malay, Mandarin, Tamil and English, its unofficial *lingua franca* is Singlish. Essentially an English dialect mixed with Hokkien, Malay and Tamil, it's spoken in a rapid, staccato fashion, with sentences polished off with innumerable but essentially meaningless exclamatory words – *lah* is the most common, but you'll also hear *mah, lor, meh, leh, hor* and several others.

Other trademarks include a long stress on the last syllable of phrases, while words ending in consonants are often syncopated and vowels distorted. What is Perak Rd to you may well be Pera Roh to your Chinese-speaking taxi driver. Verb tenses? Forget them. Past, present and future are indicated instead by time indicators, so in Singlish it's 'I go tomorrow' or 'I go yesterday'.

Food & Drink

Carrot cake Squares of radish-flour cake stir-fried with bean sprouts, chili sauce and salted radish.

Char kway teow Flat rice noodles wok-fried with bean sprouts, cockles, prawns and Chinese sausage in dark soy sauce and chilli sauce.

Hainanese chicken rice Tender poached chicken served on a bed of fragrant rice (cooked in chicken stock) with garlic chilli sauce.

Murtabak Pan-fried pancake stuffed with spiced mince meat (chicken, beef or mutton), garlic, egg and onion.

Nasi padang Steamed white rice served with a choice of meats, vegetables and curries.

Roti prata Fried flatbread typically served with curry.

Tiger beer While not the national drink, Singapore's local brew is a pale lager that goes down a treat.

ION Orchard shopping mall

Ridges, a 9km stretch of trails across shaded parks, hills and the stunning leaf-like suspended walkways of the Alexandra Link.

Sentosa Island

7 The world-class resort island of Sentosa may look gaudy from the outside, but the opening of Resorts World means Singapore's playground now has something for everyone. Parents can let their kids go nuts at Universal Studios, then in the evenings live the high-roller life at the casino. Or you can lose the shirt off your back in a different way: by kicking back on the beach, cocktail in hand.

Orchard Road

8 With every brand imaginable and over 20 malls packed into this 2.5km strip, you can shop till you drop, pick yourself up, and continue shopping some more. What was once a dusty road lined with spice plantations and orchards is now a torrent of blockbuster malls, department stores and speciality shops; enough to burn out the toughest shopaholics. It's retail therapy at its decadent best. When you've stashed your purchases back at the hotel, duck out to Emerald Hill for its Peranakan architecture and happy-hour bar specials.

Getting Around

Bus Goes everywhere the trains do and more. Great for views. Operates from 6am till midnight, with some night buses from the city.

MRT Local subway. Most convenient way to get around. Operates 6am till midnight.

Taxi Fairly cheap if you're used to NYC or London prices. Flag one on the street or at taxi stands. Good luck getting one on rainy days. Don't be surprised by hefty surcharges during peak hours and from midnight to 6am.

Mountain stream, the High Tatras

Slovakia

A land of real spirit, where folk traditions have survived the domination of foreign rulers and where a plethora of castles and chateaux pay testament to untold wars and civil conflicts.

Going strong after two decades as an independent state following the breakup of Czechoslovakia, Slovakia out-trumps the Czechs for ancient castles, and boasts nature far wilder than its western neighbours. It savours wine over beer and, in its bashful heartland amid mountains and forests, cradles an entrancing folk culture most European nations have lost.

Slovakia's small size is possibly its biggest attraction. You can hike woodsy waterfall-filled gorges one day and yodel from peaks soaring more than 2500m the next. Dinky capital Bratislava is awash with quirky museums and backed by thick forests. With its rabbit-warren Old Town, it might just win the world prize for most cafes per city resident.

Don't leave without heading east, where fortresses tower over tradition-rich medieval towns such as Levoča or Bardejov and hiking trails lace the hills.

Strike up a conversation at a bar and you'll find an intelligent, engaging and friendly person at the other end. Down a *slivovica* (firewaterlike plum brandy) and drink a toast for us – *nazdravie*!

Slovakia's
Top Experiences

The High Tatras

1 The High Tatras, the tallest range in the Carpathian Mountains, tower over most of Eastern Europe. Some 25 peaks measure above 2500m. The massif is only 25km wide and 78km long, but photo opportunities are enough to get you fantasising about a *National Geographic* career – pristine snowfields, ultramarine mountain lakes, crashing waterfalls, undulating pine forests and shimmering alpine meadows.

Bratislava

2 Proximity to nature gives Slovakia's capital its strongest flavouring. The Danube wends through town and cycle paths through its verdant flood plain, then there's ski runs and vineyards to amble among. The charming Starý Mesto (Old Town) is the place to start appreciating Bratislava. Stroll narrow pedestrian streets of pastel 18th-century buildings or sample the nigh-on ubiquitous sidewalk cafes under the watchful gaze of the city castle, harking back to medieval times. Done with the old? In with the new: the city boasts intriguing Socialist-era architecture worth checking out and one of Eastern Europe's most spectacular modern art spaces. Contrasts like this are all part of Bratislava's allure.

Spiš Castle

3 Heralding from at least as early as the 13th century, Spiš Castle and its vast complex of ruins crown a ridge above Spišské Podhradie. Its claim to fame as one of Europe's largest castle complexes will certainly seem accurate as you explore. Highlights include the climb up the central tower for spectacular panoramic views across the Spiš region. Be sure to climb the steep spiral staircase of the central tower for great views, and imagine yourself as a patrolling medieval guard as you traipse around this colossal fortress's outer walls. Can it really be that big? Indeed, Spiš Castle seemingly rambles on

THOMAS STANKIEWICZ / GETTY IMAGES ©

Painted wooden houses, Čičmany

forever. If the reconstructed ruins are this impressive, imagine what the fortress was once like.

Traditional Villages

4 If you've seen a brochure or postcard of Slovakia, you've probably seen a photograph of Čičmany; dark log homes painted with white geometric patterns fill this traditional village. Vlkolínec is a folksy mountain village and a Unesco-noted national treasure. The pastel paint and steep roofs on the 45 traditional plastered log cabins are remarkably well maintained. It's easy to imagine a *vlk* (wolf) wandering through this wooded mountainside settlement arranged along a small stream.

This is still a living village – if just barely. Of the approximately 40 residents, almost half are schoolchildren.

Wooden Churches

5 Seek out iconic, Unesco-listed wooden churches in isolated far-east Slovakia, such as Hervatov or Ladomirová. Travelling east from Bardejov, you come to a crossroads of Western and Eastern Christianity. From the 17th to the 19th centuries, nearly 300 dark-wood, onion-domed churches were erected hereabouts. Of the 40-odd remaining, eight have been recognised by Unesco. A handful celebrate Roman Catholic or Protestant faiths, but most belong to the Eastern rites of Greek

if Slovakia were 100 people

81 would be Slovak
9 would be Hungarian
2 would be Roma
8 would be other

belief systems
(% of population)

62 Roman Catholic
8 Protestant
4 Greek Catholic
13 other
13 none

population per sq km

SLOVAKIA   USA   CZECH REPUBLIC

👤 ≈ 8 people

When to Go

SEP
→ Fewer crowds but clement weather. Wine season means it's time for alcohol-themed festivities.

JUN & JUL
→ Festivals abound across the country, the High Tatras hiking trails are all open

JAN & FEB
→ Peak ski season in the mountains, but many other sights are closed.

Slovakia's Musical Hertiage

Slovakia has a surprisingly rich classical music pedigree.

The career of Franz Liszt began in the De Pauli Palace in Ventúska street in Old Town Bratislava.

Ludwig van Beethoven lived in Hlohovec, north of Bratislava, gave concerts in the capital and even dedicated a sonata (Piano Opus 78) to Therese Brunsvik, member of one of the most influential city families at that time.

Hungarian composer Béla Bartók also lived for a time in Bratislava (then Pressburg).

Trinity Square, Banská Štiavnica

Food & Drink

Baked duck/goose Served in *lokše* (potato pancakes) and stewed cabbage.

Fruit firewater Homemade or store-bought liquor, made from berries and pitted fruits, such as *borovička* (from juniper) and *slivovica* (from plums).

Halušky Mini-dumplings in cabbage or *bryndza* sauce topped with bacon.

Kapustnica Thick sauerkraut and meat soup, often with chorizo or mushrooms.

Pirohy Pocket-shaped dumplings stuffed with *bryndza* or smoked meat.

Sheep's cheese *Bryndza* is sharp, soft and spreadable; *oštiepok* is solid and ball-shaped; *žinčina* ois a traditional sheep's-whey drink (like sour milk).

Sulance Walnut- or poppy-seed-topped dumplings.

Vývar Chicken or beef broth served with *sližiky*, thin pasta strips, or liver dumplings.

Catholicism and Orthodoxy. Typically they honour the Holy Trinity with three domes, three architectural sections and three doors on the icon screen. Richly painted icons and venerated representations of Christ and the saints decorate the iconostases and invariably every inch of the churches' interiors have also been hand-painted. These can be quite a sight, but it's not easy to get inside.

Banská Štiavnica

6 A time-trapped medieval delight, Banská Štiavnica enjoyed a 16th-century heyday as an internationally renowned architectural showcase and grew to become the old Hungarian Kingdom's third-largest city. As the minerals ran out and mines closed, progress stopped. Meandering among the steeply terraced hillsides now you'll see many of the same Old Town burghers' houses, churches and alleys. Unesco recognised the town in 1972. At a fraction of its peak population today, the town is primarily a holiday destination with numerous mining-related attractions and two castles facing each other across the steep valley.

Getting Around

Air There are only domestic flights on weekdays, between Bratislava and Košice.

Bus Towns all have good bus systems; villages have infrequent service. Bratislava also has trams and trolleybuses. Read timetables carefully; fewer buses operate on weekends and holidays.

Car Car hire is available in Bratislava and Košice primarily.

Train Train is the way to travel in Slovakia; most tourist destinations are off the main Bratislava–Košice line.

Piran

CAPITAL
Ljubljana

POPULATION
1.99 million

AREA
20,273 sq km

OFFICIAL LANGUAGE
Slovenian

Slovenia

Snow-capped peaks, turquoise-green rivers and an Adriatic coastline inspired by Venice. Throughout Slovenia, a culinary and cultural sophistication hides behind a rural, rustic charm.

It's a pint-sized place, with a surface area of just more than 20,000 sq km and two million people. But 'good things come in small packages', and never was that old chestnut more appropriate than in describing Slovenia. The country has everything from beaches, snowcapped mountains, hills awash in grape vines and wide plains blanketed in sunflowers to Gothic churches, baroque palaces and art nouveau buildings. Its incredible diversity of climates brings warm Mediterranean breezes up to the foothills of the Alps, where it can still snow in summer.

The capital, Ljubljana, is a culturally rich city that values livability and sustainability over unfettered growth. This sensitivity towards the environment extends to rural and lesser-developed parts of the country as well. With more than half of its total area covered in forest, Slovenia really is one of the 'greenest' countries in the world.

Slovenia's
Top Experiences

Ljubljana

1 Slovenia's capital city strikes that perfect yet elusive balance between size and quality of life. It's big enough to be interesting, yet small enough to walk – or better yet, bike – across at a leisurely pace. The term 'jewel box' gets tossed around all too frequently to describe attractive smaller cities, but in Ljubljana's case the words are apt. What better way to describe architect Jože Plečnik's wondrously decorative pillars, obelisks and orbs that seem to top every bridge, fountain and lamp post?

Piran

2 Venice in Slovenia? Of course! That busy merchant empire left its mark up and down the Adriatic coast, and Slovenia was lucky to end up with the best-preserved medieval Venetian port outside Venice, or possibly anywhere. It's true that Piran attracts tourist numbers on a near-Venetian scale, but the beautiful setting means it's never less than a constant delight. Eat fresh seafood on the harbour, then get lost wandering the narrow streets and end up for drinks and people-watching in a glorious central square.

Lake Bled

3 Bled, Slovenia's biggest tourist draw, looks like it came off the drawing board of a gifted architect or interior designer. Start with a crystal-clear blue lake, add a tiny island over here, top it with an impossibly cute church, and then put a dramatic, cliffside castle over there. Now add some Alpine peaks to the backdrop. Voila! It really is that lovely, but Bled is more than just good looks. There's a raucous adventure scene too, with diving, cycling and rafting among other active pursuits.

Postojna Cave System

4 The caves at Postojna are Slovenia's biggest subterranean attraction. The entrance might look like nothing, but when you get whisked 4km underground on a train and only then start exploring, you begin to get a sense of the scale. The caverns are a seemingly endless parade of crystal

PHILIP GAME / GETTY IMAGES ©

fancies – from frilly chandeliers and dripping spaghetti formations, to paper-thin sheets and stupendous stalagmites. A theatrical experience in silent stone.

Predjama Castle

5 Two things Slovenia seems to specialise in: castles and caves. The country is dotted with both, but a castle in a cave? That's something special. Few fortresses have a setting as grand as this, wedged halfway up a cliff face at the foot of a valley. The location has a story behind it that's

equally dramatic: Slovenia's 'Robin Hood', Erazem Lueger, apparently taunted besieging troops here by pelting them with fresh cherries that he collected via a secret passage. He came to a swift and rather embarrassing end after being betrayed.

Crossing the Vršič Pass

6 Making your way – whether by car or bike – across this mindbogglingly scenic Alpine pass, as it zigzags through peaks and promontories, it's hard not to think of those poor

if Slovenia were 100 people

👤👤👤👤👤👤👤👤👤👤👤👤👤👤👤👤👤👤👤👤
👤👤👤👤👤👤👤👤👤👤👤👤👤👤👤👤👤👤👤👤
👤👤👤👤👤👤👤👤👤👤👤👤👤👤👤👤👤👤👤👤
👤👤👤👤👤👤👤👤👤👤👤👤👤👤👤👤👤👤👤👤
👤👤👤👤👤👤👤👤👤👤👤👤👤👤👤👤👤👤👤👤

83 would be Slovenes
2 would be Serbs
2 would be Croats
1 would be Bosniaks
12 would be other

belief systems
(% of population)

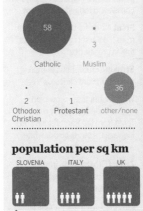

58 — Catholic

3 — Muslim

2 — Othodox Christian

1 — Protestant

36 — other/none

population per sq km

SLOVENIA | ITALY | UK

👤 ≈ 50 people

When to Go

HIGH SEASON
(Jun–Aug)

➜ Mostly sunny with occasional rain.

➜ Crowds in Ljubljana and the coast.

➜ Museums and other attractions open for business.

➜ Best time for hikes.

SHOULDER (Apr & May, Sep & Oct)

➜ Sunny, dry September is a great time for climbing Mt Triglav.

➜ Lower tariffs are in effect at many hotels.

➜ Rafting is great by late May; swimming is over by October.

LOW SEASON
(Nov–Mar)

➜ Ski season runs from mid-December to March or April.

➜ Christmas through New Year can be crowded.

➜ Attractions in smaller towns may close or have limited hours.

The Hayrack: A National Icon

Few things are as Slovenian as the *kozolec*, the hayrack seen almost everywhere in the country. Because the Alpine ground can be damp, wheat and hay are hung from racks, allowing the wind to do the drying faster and more efficiently.

Until the late 19th century, the *kozolec* was just another tool to make a farmer's work easier. But when artist Ivan Grohar made it the centrepiece of many of his impressionist paintings, the *kozolec* became as much a part of the cultural landscape as the physical one. Today it's virtually a national icon.

There are many different types of Slovenian hayracks: single ones standing alone or 'goat hayracks' with sloped 'lean-to' roofs, parallel and stretched ones and double *toplarji* (hayracks), often with roofs and storage areas on top – deserving subjects of an artist's eye.

Food & Drink

Potica A kind of nut roll eaten at teatime or as a dessert.

Prekmurska gibanica A rich concoction of pastry filled with poppy seeds, walnuts, apples, and cheese and topped with cream.

Pršut Air-dried, thinly sliced ham from the Karst region not unlike Italian prosciutto.

Štruklji Scrumptious dumplings made with curd cheese.

Wine Distinctively Slovenian tipples include peppery red Teran from the Karst region and Malvazija, a straw-colour white wine from the coast.

Žganci Groats made from barley or corn but usually *ajda* (buckwheat).

Žlikrofi Ravioli-like parcels filled with cheese, bacon and chives.

Kayakers, Soča river

Russian POWs who built the road during WWI. They're given their due, and the passage is now called the Ruska cesta (Russian Road), but talk about hard work. This summer-only roadway links Kranjska Gora with Bovec, 50km to the southwest.

Mt Triglav

7 Nothing quite says 'I'm a Slovene' like climbing to the top of the country's tallest mountain. Indeed, for Slovenes, it's practically stamped in their passports once they've made the trek. The good news for the rest of us is that Mt Triglav is a challenging but accessible peak that just about anyone in decent shape can summit with an experienced guide. There are several popular approaches, each with its own attractions and degrees of difficulty. Whichever path you choose, the reward is the same: sheer exhilaration.

River Adventures

8 Rarely does a river beckon to be rafted as convincingly as Slovenia's Soča. Maybe it's that piercing sky-blue-bordering-on-green colour of the water, or the river's refreshing froth and foam as it tumbles down the mountains. Even if you're not the rafting type, you'll soon find yourself slipping on a wetsuit for that exhilarating ride of the summer. Several outfitters in Bovec and Kobarid specialise in guided rafting trips. For the more intrepid, there's always canyoning.

Getting Around

Air Slovenia has no scheduled domestic flights.

Bicycle Cycling is a popular way of getting around. Larger towns and cities have dedicated bicycle lanes and traffic lights.

Bus A range of bus companies serve the country, but prices are uniform.

Train Travelling by train is about 35% cheaper than going by bus.

CAPITAL
Honiara

POPULATION
597,248

AREA
27,540 sq km

OFFICIAL LANGUAGE
Melanesian Pijin

Solomon Islands

For those seeking an authentic Melanesian experience or an off-the-beaten-track destination, the Solomons are hard to beat.

From WWII relics scattered in the jungle to leaf-hut villages where traditional culture is alive, the Solomon Islands has so much on offer.

Then there's the visual appeal, with scenery reminiscent of a Discovery Channel documentary: volcanic islands that jut up dramatically from the cobalt-blue ocean, croc-infested mangroves, huge lagoons, tropical islets and emerald forests.

Don't expect white-sand beaches, ritzy resorts and wild nightlife – the Solomon Islands is not a beach-holiday destination. With only a smattering of traditional guesthouses and comfortable hideaways, it's tailor-made for ecotourists.

For outdoorsy types, lots of action-packed experiences can easily be organised: climb an extinct volcano, surf uncrowded waves, snorkel pristine reefs or kayak across a lagoon. Beneath the ocean's surface, unbeatable diving adventures await.

The best part is, there'll be no crowds to mar the experience.

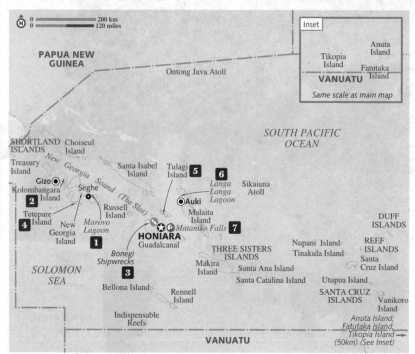

Solomon Islands'
Top Experiences

Marovo Lagoon

1 Marovo Lagoon is the world's finest double-barrier-enclosed lagoon, bordered by the large New Georgia and Vangunu Islands on one side and a double line of long barrier islands on the other. It contains hundreds of beautiful small islands, most of which are covered by coconut palms and rainforest, and surrounded by coral. Here you can visit laid-back villages and explore *tambu* (sacred) sites, picnic on deserted islands, take a lagoon tour, meet master carvers, dive in fish soup, kayak across the lagoon or take a walk through the rainforest or up awesome summits. Don't expect paradise on earth, though. Truly idyllic stretches of sand are almost nonexistent.

Kolombangara

2 A perfect cone-shaped volcano that rises to 1770m, Kolombangara looms majestically on the horizon northeast of Ghizo Island. It's a scenic two-day hike to the top and back if you are fit and have the energy. It rises from a 1km-wide coastal plain through flat-topped ridges and increasingly steep escarpments to the rugged crater rim of Mt Veve. For history buffs, there are WWII Japanese relics scattered around the island. Vila Point was an important WWII Japanese base and you can still see guns in the bush.

Bonegi Shipwrecks

3 About 12km west from Honiara, Bonegi is music to the ears of divers and snorkellers. Two large Japanese freighters sank just offshore on the night of 13 November 1942, and make for a magnificent playground for scuba divers, who call them Bonegi I and Bonegi II. As the upper works of Bonegi II break the surface, it can also be snorkelled. There's also a black-sand beach that is suitable for a picnic. Just past the Bonegi II site, there's a bush track that heads inland and runs about 400m to a well-preserved US Sherman tank called *Jezebel*.

JAMES MORGAN / GETTY IMAGES ©

Tetepare Island

4 This large rainforest island is one of the Solomons' conservation jewels and a dream come true for ecotourists. The Tetepare Descendants' Association, which manages the island, welcomes visitors in its simple yet genuinely ecofriendly leafhouses. There are plans to build another two bungalows with private facilities. What makes this place extra special is the host of environmental activities available, including snorkelling with dugongs, spotting crocodiles, birdwatching and turtle-tagging.

Diving Tulagi

5 A must for wreck enthusiasts, Tulagi has superb sunken WWII shipwrecks, including the monster-sized *USS Kanawha*, a 150m-long oil tanker that sits upright, and the *USS Aaron Ward*, a 106m-long US Navy destroyer noted for its arsenal of big guns. The catch? They lie deep, very deep (the *Kanawha* in 45m and the *Aaron Ward* in 65m) and are accessible to experienced divers only. There are also awesome reef dives, such as Twin Tunnels, which features two chimneys that start on the top of a reef in about 12m. And there's Manta Passage, near Maravagi, with regular sightings of huge manta rays.

if the Solomon Islands were 100 people

95 would be Melanesian
3 would be Polynesian
1 would be Micronesian
1 would be other

belief systems
(% of population)

Church of Melanesia	South Seas Evangelical	Seventh-Day Adventist
33	17	11

Roman Catholic	other Christian	other or none
19	17	3

population per sq km

SOLOMAN ISLANDS	AUSTRALIA	PAPUA NEW GUINEA

⬤ ≈ 3 people

When to Go

DEC–MAR

➡ Intervals of calm weather broken by storms makes for good reef breaks and diving.

JUN–SEP

➡ Mild weather (but rough seas); good for hiking, less ideal for diving. Great festivity time.

APR–MAY & OCT–NOV

➡ The shoulder seasons are relatively dry and aren't a bad time to visit.

Clan Loyalties

Solomon Islanders' obligations to their clan and village bigman (chief) are eternal and enduring, whether they live in the same village all their lives or move to another country. As in most Melanesian cultures, the *wantok* system is observed here. All islanders are born with a set of obligations to their *wantok*, but they're also endowed with privileges that only *wantok* receive. For most Melanesian villagers it's an egalitarian way of sharing the community assets. There's no social security system and very few people are in paid employment, but the clan provides economic support and a strong sense of identity.

Melanesian culture is deeply rooted in ancestor worship, magic and oral traditions. Villagers often refer to their traditional ways, beliefs and land ownership as *kastom*; it's bound up in the Melanesian systems of lore and culture.

Food & Drink

Beer The local brand of beer in the Solomon Islands is Solbrew. Smaller places may be BYO.

Central Market The country's bubbling principal food market is in Honiara and has a huge selection of fresh produce, especially fruits and vegetables, which come from outlying villages along the northern coast and from Savo island. A fish market is located at the back.

Restaurants A wide variety of cuisines are available in Honiara's restaurants, from French to Japanese, Chinese and Western foods.

Seafood Fish and seafood, including lobster, is fresh and abundant throughout the islands.

Tipping Tipping is not required or expected in the Solomons.

HOLGER LEUE / GETTY IMAGES ©

Busu Village, Langa Langa Lagoon

Langa Langa Lagoon

6 Langa Langa Lagoon is indisputedly one of Malaita's highlights. Extending from 7km to 32km south of Auki, the lagoon is famous for its artificial islands built of stones and dead corals. It's also a strong centre for traditional activities, especially shell-money making and shipbuilding. One proviso: 'lagoon' is a bit misleading. If it has recently rained, waters may be more chocolate than bright turquoise, and you won't find stunning beaches to sun yourself on. People come here for the laid-back tempo of life and the magical setting.

Mataniko Falls

7 One of the star attractions in Honiara's hinterlands is Mataniko Falls, which features a spectacular thundering of water down a cliff straight into a canyon below. The hike starts in Lelei village with a steep ascent followed by an easier stretch amid undulating hills. Then you'll tackle a gruelling descent on a slippery mud path to reach the little canyon where the Mataniko flows.

Getting Around

Air Solomon Airlines services the country's 20-odd airstrips. The main tourist gateways are serviced daily from Honiara.

Boat Outboard-powered dinghies are the most common means of transport in the Solomons. Passenger boats also ply routes between major islands.

Bus Public minibuses are found only in Honiara. Elsewhere, people pile into open-backed trucks or tractor-drawn trailers.

Car The country has around 1300km of generally dreadful roads. International driving permits are accepted, as are most driving licences.

Las Geel rock paintings

CAPITAL
Mogadishu

POPULATION
10.3 million

AREA
637,657 sq km

OFFICIAL LANGUAGES
Somali, Arabic

Somalia & Somaliland

A nation troubled and torn asunder, Somalia remains a no-go zone, but for its northernmost secessionist province of Somaliland.

Somalia proper may be set to emerge from decades of torment and trauma that brought it to international attention – most notably as a country beset by famine and militias – but like Puntland (a neighbouring, semi-autonomous state that has been self-governing since 1998), the haunt of pirates and smugglers, Mogadishu and parts thereabouts remain firm no-go zones for all Westerners. Yet the self-proclaimed Republic of Somaliland has risen from the ashes by restoring law and order within its boundaries.

Somaliland, proudly 'independent' since 1991, is now slowly emerging as a potential destination for adventurous travellers. Admire remarkable rock paintings, feel the pulse of the fast-growing capital, walk along deserted beaches, visit market towns and be awed by stunning landscapes – wherever you go, you'll feel like a pioneer. Its tourist infrastructure is still embryonic but it's this sense of pushing Africa's secret door ajar that makes Somaliland one of the most weirdly fascinating countries you could hope to visit.

The self-proclaimed Republic of Somaliland is currently an internationally unrecognised but de facto sovereign state.

When to Go

DEC–MAR

➡ Best weather; very little rain and cool temperatures.

APR–SEP

➡ Rain in April, May and September makes travel tough. July and August are oppressively hot.

OCT & NOV

➡ Weather is mixed, but temperatures make shoulder season a good travel time.

Food & Drink

Goat and camel meat are popular dishes in Somaliland. The standard breakfast throughout the country is fried liver with onions and *loxox*, a flat bread similar to the Ethiopian *injera* accompanied by honey, sugar and tea. Rice and noodles are also common staples. Tea is the favourite drink.

Somalia & Somaliland's
Top Experiences

Hargeisa

1 You'll never forget your first impression of Hargeisa, which still bears the scars of the civil war that destroyed the country in the past decades. The streets are abuzz with good-value hotels, restaurants and markets...but no alcohol, and absolutely no nightlife.

Las Geel

2 Is this Africa's best-kept secret? About 50km from Hargeisa, Las Geel features one of the most impressive collections of ancient rock art in Africa. The poignant paintings, typical Somali landscape of dry plains covered in acacia shrub, spectacular granite outcrops and total lack of crowds make for an eerie, unforgettable ambience.

Berbera

3 Nurse a soft drink, feast on fresh fish and relax on deserted beaches in Berbera. The name alone sounds impossibly exotic, conjuring up images of tropical ports. The reality is a little more prosaic; today this shady town consists mostly of crumbling buildings. There's great potential, though, with superb beaches and a relaxed atmosphere.

Table Mountain Aerial Cableway, Cape Town

CAPITAL
Pretoria

POPULATION
48.6 million

AREA
1.2 million sq km

OFFICIAL
LANGUAGES
Zulu, Xhosa,
Afrikaans,
English, Sepedi,
Setswana,
Sesotho,
Xitsonga, Swati,
Tshivenda,
Ndebele

South Africa

*An astonishingly diverse region fused by its prolific wildlife,
breathtaking landscapes and remnants of ancient culture, South
Africa will etch itself onto your heart.*

When Archbishop Desmond Tutu called
South Africa the 'Rainbow Nation', his words
described the very essence of what makes
this country extraordinary. Certainly, the
blend of peoples and cultures that his oft-
used moniker referred to is instantly evident,
but the country's diversity stretches far beyond its people.

Without straying beyond South Africa's
borders you can sleep under the stars in a
desert or hike to snow-capped peaks. The
hills of Zululand and the Wild Coast provide
a bucolic antidote to the bustle of large cities like Johannesburg and Durban. Wildlife
watching ranges from remote safari walks to
up-close encounters with waddling penguins.

Variety continues in the cuisine, with
delicate West Coast seafood, hearty Karoo
meat feasts, fragrant Cape Malay stews and
spicy Durban curries. And southwest of it
all sits Cape Town, where gourmands, art
lovers, thrill seekers and beach babes come
together to sip, surf and sunbathe in beautiful surrounds.

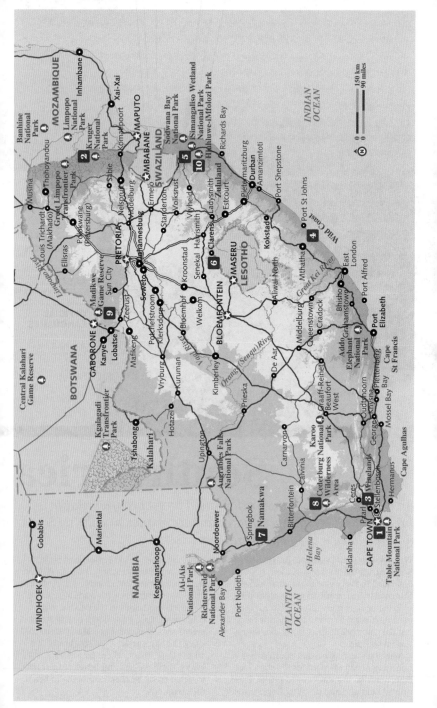

South Africa's
Top Experiences

Table Mountain

1 Whether you take the easy way up in a revolving cable car, or put in the leg work on the climb, attaining the summit of Table Mountain is a Capetonian rite of passage. Weather permitting, your rewards are a panoramic view across the peninsula and a chance to experience the park's incredible biodiversity. Schedule time for a hike – the park's 24,500 hectares have routes to suit all levels of fitness and ambition, from gentle fynbos-spotting ambles to the five-day, four-night Hoerikwaggo Trail.

Kruger National Park

2 One of South Africa's great wilderness experiences and the mightiest of all the country's national parks, a trip here will sear itself into your mind. Its accessibility, numbers and variety of wildlife, staggering size and range of activities make Kruger unique and compelling. From wilderness trails and bush walks to mountain biking and remote 4WD trails, there are myriad opportunities to enjoy both the wild and the wildlife. Kruger is simply one of the best places to see animals – big and small – in Southern Africa.

Giraffe, Kruger National Park

BOTAFOGO / GETTY IMAGES ©

Sipping in the Winelands

3 Whitewashed Cape Dutch architecture dots the landscape of rolling hills and neat rows of vines. This is the quintessential Cape, where the world-class wines are the icing on a picture-perfect cake. Stellenbosch, Franschhoek and Paarl, the area's wine-tasting towns, boast some of the oldest, largest and prettiest wine estates on the continent. But this is not the province's only wine region; head to Tulbagh for sparkling wines, Route 62 for robust reds and port, or the heights of the Cederberg for crisp sauvignon blancs.

if South Africa were 100 people

79 would be black
9 would be white
9 would be coloured
3 would be Indian/Asian

belief systems
(% of population)

80 Christian
2 Muslim
1 Hindu
17 other/none

population per sq km

SOUTH AFRICA   LESOTHO   SWAZILAND

≈ 10 people

Wild Coast Walks

4 The hauntingly beautiful Wild Coast is aptly named. With its rugged cliffs plunging into the sea, remote beaches, Xhosa villages, and history of shipwrecks and stranded sailors, it's a region ideally explored on foot. From the Great Kei River near East London to Port St Johns, pathways hug the shoreline, snaking across denuded hillsides and gorges, and overlooking massive southern right whales and dolphins in the turquoise blue seas. Power down in rustic accommodation or overnight with families in traditionally designed rondavels (round huts with conical roofs).

iSimangaliso Wetland Park

5 Its name, which means 'miracle' or 'wonder', is fitting. The iSimangaliso Wetland Park, a Unesco World Heritage site, stretches for 220 glorious kilometres, from the Mozambique border to Maphelane, at the southern end of Lake St Lucia. The 328,000-hectare park protects five distinct ecosystems, with everything from offshore reefs and beaches, to lakes, wetlands, woodlands and coastal forests. It's nature's playground, offering wildlife drives, hikes, cycling and swimming, plus extraordinary animals: loggerhead and leatherback turtles, whales and dolphins, rhinos, antelopes, zebras and hippos galore.

Clarens

6 The odd international star popping in for a lungful of fresh mountain air gives this well-heeled town an air of celebrity. Filled with galleries, antiques, classy restaurants and adventure

Nelson Mandela

Nelson Rolihlahla Mandela, one of the millennium's greatest leaders, was once vilified by South Africa's ruling whites and sentenced to life imprisonment. On his release 27 years later, he called for reconciliation.

Mandela, son of a Xhosa chief, was born on 18 July 1918. After university, he headed to Johannesburg, where he soon became immersed in politics. During the 1950s, Mandela was at the forefront of the ANC's civil disobedience campaigns. In 1964 Mandela stood trial for sabotage and fomenting revolution. He was sentenced to life imprisonment, and spent the next 18 years in Robben Island prison, before being moved to the mainland. Throughout his incarceration, Mandela refused to compromise his political beliefs.

In 1994, four years after his release, Mandela became the first freely elected president of South Africa. He stepped down in 1997, although he continued to be revered as an elder statesman until his death on 5 December 2013.

Food & Drink

Atchar Cape Malay pickle of fruits and vegetables, flavoured with garlic, onion and curry.

Chakalaka sauce Spicy tomato-based sauce seasoned with onions, peri peri, green peppers and curry.

Kingklip Excellent firm-fleshed fish, usually pan-fried.

Koeksuster Plaited doughnut dripping in honey.

Malva Delicious sponge dessert; sometimes called vinegar pudding.

Melktert Rich, custardlike tart made with milk, eggs, flour and cinnamon.

Pap & sous Maize porridge with a tomato and onion sauce or meat gravy

Venison Often springbok, but could be kudu, warthog, blesbok or other game

Vetkoek Deep-fried dough ball sometimes stuffed with mince.

3

Vineyard, Stellenbosch

activities in the surrounding countryside, there's something appealing for most visitors. There is money here, sure, but the town is laid-back and perfect for an evening stroll. With pubs to drop into for a drink and bookshops to browse, Clarens is the best place in the Free State to simply wind down.

Namakwa Wildflowers

7 Namakwa is one of South Africa's forgotten corners, stretching up the west coast towards Namibia. Crossing the remote region to reach Port Nolloth's refreshing Atlantic vistas, after hundreds of kilometres on empty roads, is wonderful throughout the year. In spring, there's the added bonus of the wildflower bloom, which turns Namakwa's rocky expanses into a technicolour carpet. You could spend days travelling through multicoloured fields, stopping at Namaqua National Park and Goegap Nature Reserve – both dedicated to wildflower watching.

When to Go

HIGH SEASON
(Dec–Mar)

➡ Peak times are around Christmas, New Year and Easter.

➡ Prices rise steeply.

➡ Accommodation in national parks and the coast books up months in advance.

➡ Tourist areas and roads busy.

SHOULDER
(Apr–May, Oct–Nov)

➡ There is a school holiday from late September to early October.

➡ Sunny spring and autumn weather in much of the country.

➡ Optimum wildlife-watching conditions begin in autumn.

LOW SEASON
(Jun–Sep)

➡ Winter is ideal for wildlife-watching.

➡ There is a school holiday from late June to mid-July.

➡ Prices sometimes reflect this holiday; otherwise they are low, with discounts and packages.

Hiking & Stargazing in the Cederberg

8 By day the clear blue skies provide an arresting contrast to the fiery orange peaks of the craggy Cederberg; by night the Milky Way shines so brightly you can almost read by its light. The Cederberg is the promised land for stargazers, for hikers and rock climbers seeking an otherworldy landscape, and for those simply in search of silent nights. Tackle the challenging Wolfberg Arch hike, the shorter walk to the Maltese Cross, or the three-day Wupperthal trail, visiting remote and forgotten mission villages en route.

Madikwe Game Reserve

9 One of the country's most exclusive reserves on this scale, Madikwe occupies 760 sq km of bushveld, savannah grassland and riverine forest. There's

Best on Film

District 9 In Peter Jackson's film giant alien 'prawns' overrun Jo'burg.

Invictus Clint Eastwood's film covers the 1995 Rugby World Cup.

Best in Print

50 People Who Stuffed Up South Africa (Alexander Parker) History's great villains.

Karoo Plainsong (Barbara Mutch) Apartheid-era drama.

Khayelitsha (Steven Otter) White journalist lives in the township.

My Traitor's Heart (Rian Malan) Journalist's hard-hitting memoirs.

Reports Before Daybreak (Brent Meersman) Novel about the '80s.

Zoo City (Lauren Beukes) Jo'burg crime thriller.

Getting Around

Air Domestic fares aren't cheap. Keep costs down by booking online months before travelling.

Bicycle As long as you are fit enough to handle the hills, South Africa offers some rewarding cycling opportunities. It has scenic and diverse terrain, abundant campsites, and numerous quiet roads.

Bus A good network of buses, of varying reliability and comfort, links major cities

Car South Africa is one of the world's great countries for a road trip. Away from the main bus and train routes, having your own wheels is the best way to get around.

a good chance of spotting some of the Big Five, as guides share radio updates about where they've spotted, say, a pride of lions or a bull elephant. The 20 lodges are experiences in themselves, from an ecolodge to five-star options that blend creature comforts into the wilderness. Visits to Madikwe are on an all-inclusive basis, allowing you to relax once you're through the gates.

Hluhluwe-iMfolozi Park

10 Sometimes overshadowed by Kruger National Park, Hluhluwe-iMfolozi is nonetheless one of South Africa's best known and most evocative parks. Stunningly beautiful, it features a variety of landscapes, from mountains with wildflowers to savannah, and, of course, it teems with wildlife – the Big Five and other amazing creatures. Hluhluwei-Mfolozi can be visited at any time – there's always something happening and plenty to see, from elephants munching Marula trees to impala, zebra, wildebeest and baby giraffes. Great wildlife drives, accommodation and scenery ensure a memorable experience.

On the trail to Wolfberg Arch, Cederberg Wilderness Area

ARIADNE VAN ZANDBERGEN / GETTY IMAGES ©

Lanterns, Samgwangsa Temple, Busan

CAPITAL
Seoul

POPULATION
49 million

AREA
99,720 sq km

OFFICIAL LANGUAGE
Korean

South Korea

The Republic of Korea offers the traveller a dazzling range of experiences, beguiling landscapes and 5000 years of culture and history.

The blue and red circle at the heart of the South Korean flag neatly symbolises the fluid mix of ancient and modern aspects of the country officially called the Republic of Korea (ROK). South Korea is a dream destination for the traveller, an engaging, welcoming place where the benefits of a fully industrialised, high-tech nation are balanced alongside a reverence for tradition and the ways of old Asia.

South Korea's compact size and superb transport infrastructure mean that tranquil-lity is achievable within an hour of the urban sprawl. Hike to the peaks of craggy mountains enclosed by densely forested national parks. Sail to remote islands, where farming and fishing folk welcome you into their homes. Sample the serenity of a Buddhist temple retreat. But rest assured – the ROK knows how to rock. There's almost always a festival or event on, and friendly Koreans are happy to share their culture. If nothing else, your tastebuds will be tingling at the discovery of one of Asia's most delicious cuisines.

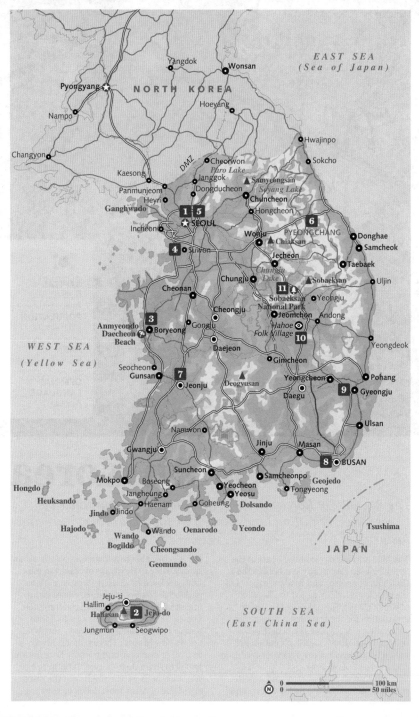

South Korea's
Top Experiences

Changdeokgung

1 The 'Palace of Illustrious Virtue' was built in the early 15th century as a secondary palace to Gyeongbukgung. These days this Unesco World Heritage–listed property in Seoul exceeds Gyeongbukgung in beauty and grace – partly because so many of its buildings were actually lived in by members of the royal family well into the 20th century. The most charming section is the Huwon, a 'secret garden' that is a royal horticultural idyll. Book well ahead to snag one of the limited tickets to view this special palace on the moonlight tours held during full-moon nights in the warm months.

Hiking around Jeju-do

2 The frequently dramatic volcanic landscape of Jeju-do, the largest of South Korea's many islands, is best seen on foot. Climbing to the summit of Hallasan, the country's highest peak, is very achievable and, in good weather, provides spectacular views. The Jeju Olle Trail is a network of 26 half- to one-day hiking routes that meander around the island's coast, part of the hinterland and three other islands. Spending a day following all or part of a trail is a wonderful way to soak up Jeju's unique charms.

Secret Garden, Changdeokgung

NKF PHOTOGRAPHY / GETTY IMAGES ©

Boryeong Mud Festival

3 Every July, thousands of people converge on the unsuspecting (but fully welcoming) town of Boryeong and proceed to jump into gigantic vats of mud. The official line is that the local mud has restorative properties but one look around and it's clear that no one really cares for much except having a slippery sloshin' messy good time. Mud aside, this foreigner-friendly and very high-profile festival also features concerts, raves and fireworks. A tip: don't wear anything you want to keep!

if South Korea were 100 people

83 would live in urban areas
17 would live in rural areas

belief systems

(% of population)

Christian 32
Buddhist 24
other 1
none 43

population per sq km

KOREA   UK   USA

▮ = 32 people

Suwon's Hwaseong Fortress

4 Built as an act of filial devotion and heavily damaged during the early-20th-century colonisation period and then the Korean War, the restoration of this Unesco World Heritage site began in the 1970s and is now almost finished. A detailed 1801 record of its construction has allowed the 5.52km-long wall and the Hwaseong Haenggung (a palace for the king to stay in during his visits to Suwon) to be rebuilt with great historical accuracy. A walk around the wall takes you through four grand gates.

Cheong-gye-cheon

5 A raised highway was demolished and the dug up ground revealed this long-buried stream. The effort has transformed Seoul's centre, creating a riverside park and walking course that provides a calm respite from the surrounding commercial hubbub. Public art is dotted along the banks of the stream and many events are held here, including a spectacular lantern festival in November, when thousands of giant glowing paper and paint sculptures are floated in the water. There's also a good museum where you can learn about the history of the Cheon-gye-cheon.

Skiing, Pyeongchang County

6 Pyeongchang won its third bid to host the Winter Olympics. In 2018 the Games will be held at the Alpensia and Yongpyong ski resorts, as well as the Gangneung coastal area. Located near each other, Alpensia and Yongpyong have dozens of runs, including slopes for families and beginners, views

Jeju's Free Divers

Jeju is famous in Korea for the hardy *haenyeo* (women free divers). Statues celebrate them all along the coast and it's not uncommon to spot the real deal on the seashore or bobbing in the ocean.

For centuries, Jeju women have been engaged in free diving to gather seaweed, shellfish, sea cucumbers, spiky black sea urchins and octopus. Working as cooperatives and sharing their catch, they use low-tech gear and no oxygen tanks. Until recently they didn't wear wetsuits, either, despite diving for long hours in all weather. They can hold their breath underwater for up to two minutes and reach a depth of 20m.

With around 5000 *haenyeo* on Jeju (down from 30,000 in the 1950s), it's a dying profession. However, a school in Hallim has been helping to preserve the legacy by teaching anyone who wants to learn the *haenyeo*'s free-diving skills.

Brenda Paik-Sunoo's book *Moon Tides: Jeju Island Grannies of the Sea* and the 2004 movie *My Mother the Mermaid* both provide more insights into the lives of *haenyeo*.

Food & Drink

Barbecue The emphasis of these restaurants is on the quality of the meat and the marinade. Diners cook their own meat on the grill at each table.

Gamjatang A spicy peasant soup with meaty bones and potatoes.

Hoe Raw fish extremely popular in coastal towns.

Jeongsik A spread of banquet dishes all served at once: fish, meat, soup, dubu jjigae, rice, noodles, shellfish and sides.

Kimchi A pickling method to preserve vegetables, most commonly Chinese cabbage.

Samgyetang Ginseng chicken soup, infused with jujube, ginger and other herbs.

of the East Sea (Sea of Japan) on clear days, as well as some spanking-new accommodation and leisure facilities.

Jeonju Hanok Maeul

7 Jeonju's version of a traditional village is arguably more impressive than Seoul's. The slate-roof houses are home to traditional arts: artisans craft fans, hand-made paper and brew *soju* (local vodka). Foodies will be pleased that the birthplace of *bibimbap* (rice, egg, meat and vegies with chilli sauce) offers the definitive version of this dish. If you decide to stay (and you will), you'll find plenty of traditional guesthouses, where visitors sleep on a *yo* (padded quilt) in an *ondol* (underfloor heating) room. In keeping with the theme, there's even one run by the grandson of King Gojong.

Busan

8 Busan has everything you could love without Seoul's congestion. Mountains, beaches, street food and seafood galore make this one of the most underrated cities in the region. If you like your squid wriggling fresh and your *soju* (local vodka) served up in a tent bar, Busan should be top of your list. The region-leading Busan International Film Festival has a new centrepiece in the Busan Cinema Centre, an architecturally dazzling structure with the biggest screen in the

When to Go

HIGH SEASON
(Jun–Sep)

➡ Be prepared for sweltering heat and a very heavy rainy season through July across the peninsula.

SHOULDER
(May, Oct)

➡ Late spring and early autumn see the country bathed in the fresh greenery or russet shades of the seasons.

LOW SEASON
(Nov–Apr)

➡ Snow falls and temperatures plummet. Best time for skiing and visiting museums and galleries.

country. It's another example of this southern port's take-no-prisoners pluck.

Bulguk-sa

9 It's hard to choose just one stand-out treasure in and around magnificent Gyeongju, but this Unesco World Cultural Heritage Site is most likely to take the honour, not least as it contains no fewer than seven Korean 'national treasures' within its walls. The high point of Shilla architecture, this incredibly sophisticated yet wonderfully subtle temple complex is a monument to the skill of its craftsmen, with its internal pagodas, its external bridges and the gorgeous, undulating scenery surrounding it.

Best on Film

In Another Country (2012) Hong Sang-soo, director of award winning Hahaha, casts Isabelle Huppert as three different women whose stories intersect in the seaside resort of Mohang.

The Host (2006) Seoul-based classic monster movie which juggles humour, poignancy and heart-stopping action.

Best in Print

Korea (Simon Winchester, 1988) Winchester travels from Jeju-do to Seoul.

Meeting Mr Kim (Jennifer Barclay, 2008) Based on Barclay's experiences in 2000, this is an amusing read with fresh insights.

Please Look After Mum (Shin Kyung-sook, 2011) Emotional drama ensues as a family searches for their mother after she goes missing on the Seoul subway.

Three Generations (Yom Sang-seop, 2005) First published in newspaper serialisations in the 1930s, this novel focuses on a family's travails under colonisation.

Getting Around

Boat Korea has an extensive network of ferries that connects hundreds of offshore islands to each other and to the mainland.

Bus Long-distance buses whiz to every nook and cranny of the country, every 15 minutes between major cities and towns, and at least hourly to small towns, villages, temples and national and provincial parks. The buses don't usually run on a regular timetable and times vary throughout the day. Terminals have staff on hand to ensure that everyone boards the right bus, so help is always available.

Train South Korea has an excellent train network. Trains are clean, comfortable and punctual, and are the best option for long-distance travel. Just about every station has a sign in Korean and English.

Hahoe Folk Village

10 The closest thing Korea has to a time machine, charming Hahoe Folk Village, some way from Andong, is a truly wonderful experience for anyone wanting to get a sense of how Korea looked, felt, sounded and smelled before the 20th century rolled over it and changed the country forever. Over two hundred people live here, maintaining traditional ways, and even inviting people to spend the night in their *minbak* (private homes with rooms for rent). For a slice of old Korea, Hahoe should be top of your list.

Templestay, Guin-sa

11 A bell rings and you wake at 3.30am to prepare for a morning meditation session. Breakfast is an austere meal, taken in silence so you can contemplate the ache in your bones from bowing 108 times in front of a Buddha image. Later, you'll have more meditation time to contemplate the surrender of your body and mind in the search for inner peace. A Templestay is the perfect antidote to fast-paced modern Korea, and the impressive complex of Guin-sa is perfect in how it sequesters you in the fortress-like compound.

Buddha statue, Bulguk-sa Temple

WIBOWO RUSLI / GETTY IMAGES ©

Jia village, near Boma National Park

CAPITAL
Juba

POPULATION
11.1 million

AREA
644,329 sq km

OFFICIAL LANGUAGES
English, Arabic

South Sudan

On 9 July 2011 Africa's largest country, Sudan, split into two and with that South Sudan, the world's newest country, was born.

The birthing process of the world's newest country was a violent and bloody one. For decades the people of South Sudan have known little but war as they fought for independence from the north – and potential visitors should know that fighting between the new government and various rebel groups continues today in many parts of the country.

Today South Sudan is one of the poorest, least-developed and most little-known nations on the planet, but the very fact that South Sudan remains such an unknown is the thing that is likely to attract the first intrepid visitors here. And once they arrive they will be amazed by a wealth of tribal groups and excited by national parks packed with vast numbers of large mammals.

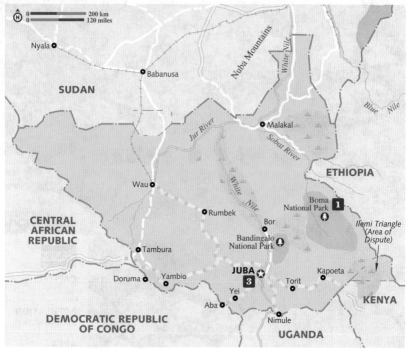

South Sudan's
Top Experiences

Boma National Park

1 This vast wilderness is home to huge quantities of wildlife including migrating herds of over a million antelope. In addition there are thought to be over 8000 elephants, 8900 buffalo and 2800 ostriches as well as lions, leopards, giraffe, hippos and numerous other species.

Tribal People

2 Possibly no other corner of Africa has such a wide diversity of tribal peoples, many of whom continue to live a largely traditional lifestyle. There are numerous ethnic groups speaking around 60 languages. Indigenous traditional beliefs are widespread and even though Christianity has made inroads it's still very much a minority religion that's often overlaid with traditional beliefs and customs.

Juba

3 The capital is a bustling boom town with busy markets and the resting place of John Garang de Mabior (or Dr John, as he's known locally), a South Sudan rebel and former First Vice-President of Sudan, who was instrumental in ending the civil war.

Food & Drink

Asida Porridge made from sorghum and served with a meaty sauce or vegetables.

White Bull A local beer.

Beans, corn, grains and peanuts Grown during the rainy season, primarily by women.

When to Go

JAN–MAR

➡ When a million white-eared kob make one of the world's largest migrations in Boma National Park.

APR–SEP

➡ The rainy season with hot and humid temperatures.

NOV–FEB

➡ Winter offers perfect temperatures and clear skies.

Park Güell, Barcelona

CAPITAL
Madrid

POPULATION
47.4 million

AREA
505,370 sq km

OFFICIAL LANGUAGE
Castilian Spanish

Spain

Passionate, sophisticated and devoted to living the good life, Spain is at once a stereotype come to life and a country more diverse than you ever imagined.

Spanish landscapes stir the soul, from the jagged Pyrenees and wildly beautiful cliffs of the Atlantic northwest to charming Mediterranean coves, while astonishing architecture spans the ages at seemingly every turn. Spain's cities march to a beguiling beat, rushing headlong into the 21st century even as timeless villages serve as beautiful signposts to Old Spain. And then there's one of Europe's most celebrated (and varied) gastronomic scenes

of seafood, paella, tapas and fine wines. But, above all, Spain lives very much in the present. Perhaps you'll sense it along a crowded after-midnight street when it seems all the world has come out to play. Or maybe that moment will come when a flamenco performer touches something deep in your soul. Or in a wild fiesta or an afternoon siesta. Whenever it happens, you'll find yourself nodding in recognition: *this* is Spain.

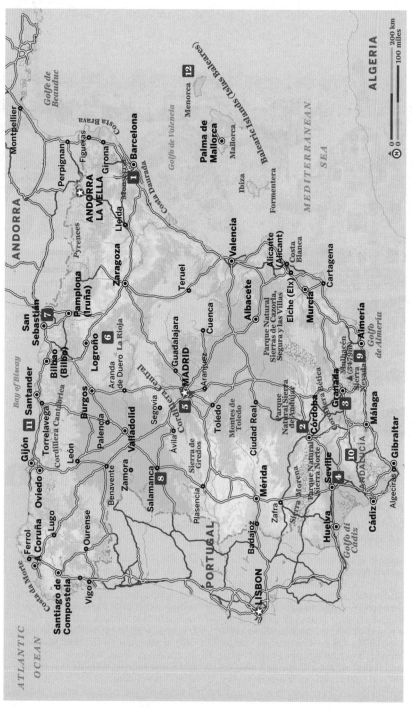

Spain's
Top Experiences

La Sagrada Família

1 One of Spain's top sights, the Modernista brainchild of Antoni Gaudí remains a work in progress more than 80 years after its creator's death. Fanciful and profound, inspired by nature and barely restrained by a Gothic style, Barcelona's quirky temple soars skyward with an almost playful majesty. The improbable angles and departures from architectural convention will have you shaking your head in disbelief, but the detail of the decorative flourishes on the Passion Facade, Nativity Facade and elsewhere are worth studying for hours.

Mezquita

2 A church that became a mosque before reverting to a church, Córdoba's Mezquita charts the evolution of western and Islamic architecture over a 1000-year trajectory. Its most innovative features include some early horseshoe arches, an intricate mihrab, and a veritable 'forest' of 856 columns, many of them recycled from Roman ruins. The sheer scale of the Mezquita reflects Córdoba's erstwhile power as the most cultured city in 10th-century Europe. It was also inspiration for even greater buildings to come, most notably in Seville and Granada.

VISIONS OF OUR LAND / GETTY IMAGES ©

1

Alhambra

3 The palace complex of Granada's Alhambra is close to architectural perfection. From afar, the Alhambra's red fortress towers dominate the Granada skyline, set against a backdrop of the Sierra Nevada's snowcapped peaks. Up close, the Alhambra's perfectly proportioned Generalife gardens complement the exquisite detail of the Palacios Nazaríes. Put simply, this is Spain's most beautiful monument.

ROBIN SMITH / GETTY IMAGES ©

Easter in Seville

4. Return to Spain's medieval Christian roots and join Seville's masses for the dramatic Easter celebration of Semana Santa. Religious fraternities parade elaborate *pasos* (figures) of Christ and the Virgin Mary around the city to the emotive acclaim of the populace; the most prestigious procession is the *madrugada* (early hours) of Good Friday. Seen for the first time, it's an unforgettable experience, an exotic and utterly compelling fusion of pageantry, solemnity and deep religious faith.

if Spain were 100 people

74 would speak Castilian Spanish
17 would speak Catalan
7 would speak Galician
2 would speak Basque

....

belief systems
(% of population)

94 Roman Catholic

6 other (mostly Islam)

....

population per sq km

SPAIN   USA   UK

🚶 ≈ 30 people

Madrid Nightlife

5. Madrid is not the only European city with nightlife, but few others can match its intensity and street clamour. As Ernest Hemingway said, 'Nobody goes to bed in Madrid until they have killed the night'. There are wall-to-wall bars, small clubs, live venues, cocktail bars and mega-clubs beloved by A-list celebrities all across the city, with unimaginable variety to suit all tastes. But it's in Huertas, Malasaña, Chueca and La Latina that you'll really understand what we're talking about.

La Rioja Wine Country

6. La Rioja is the sort of place where you could spend weeks meandering along quiet roads in search of the finest drop. Bodegas offering wine tastings and picturesque villages that shelter excellent wine museums are the mainstay in this region. The Frank Gehry–designed Hotel Marqués de Riscal, close to Elciego, has been likened to Bilbao's Guggenheim in architectural scale and ambition, and it has become the elite centre for wine tourism in the region.

Pintxos in San Sebastián

7. Chefs here have turned bar snacks into an art form. Sometimes called 'high cuisine in miniature', *pintxos* (Basque tapas) are piles of flavour often mounted on a slice of baguette. On stepping into any bar in central San Sebastián, the choice lined up along the counter will leave first-time visitors gasping. In short, this is Spain's most memor-

Camino de Santiago

'The door is open to all, to sick and healthy, not only to Catholics but also to pagans, Jews, heretics and vagabonds.' So go the words of a 13th-century poem describing the Camino. Eight hundred years later these words still ring true. The Camino de Santiago (Way of St James) originated as a medieval pilgrimage and, for more than 1000 years, people have taken up the Camino's age-old symbols – the scallop shell and staff – and set off on the adventure of a lifetime to the tomb of St James the Apostle, in Santiago de Compostela, in the Iberian Peninsula's far northwest.

Today this magnificent long-distance walk, spanning 783km of Spain's north from Roncesvalles, on the border with France, to Santiago de Compostela in Galicia, attracts walkers of all backgrounds and ages, from countries across the world. And no wonder: its list of assets (culture, history, nature) is impressive, as are its accolades. Not only is it the Council of Europe's first Cultural Route and a Unesco World Heritage site but, for pilgrims, it's a pilgrimage equal to visiting Jerusalem.

Food & Drink

Cured meats Wafer-thin slices of chorizo, lomo, salchichón and jamón serrano appear on most Spanish tables.

Olive oil Spain is the world's largest producer of olive oil.

Paella This signature rice dish comes in infinite varieties, although Valencia is its true home.

Tapas These bite-sized morsels range from uncomplicated Spanish staples to pure gastronomic innovation.

Wine Spain has the largest area of wine cultivation in the world. La Rioja and Ribera del Duero are the best-known wine-growing regions.

able eating experience. Although the atmosphere is always casual, the serious business of experimenting with taste combinations (a Basque trademark) ensures that it just keeps getting better.

Renaissance Salamanca

8 Luminous when floodlit, the elegant central square of Salamanca, the Plaza Mayor, is possibly the most attractive in all of Spain. It is just one of many high-lights in a city which has few peers in the country when it comes to architectural splendour. Salamanca is home to one of Europe's oldest and most prestigious universities, so student revelry also lights up the nights. It's this combination of grandeur and energy that makes so many people call Salamanca their favourite city in Spain.

Sierra Nevada & Las Alpujarras

9 Dominated by the Mulhacén, mainland Spain's highest peak, the Sierra Nevada is a stunning backdrop to the warm city of Granada. Skiing and hiking can be mixed with exploration of the fascinating Las Alpujarras,

When to Go

HIGH SEASON
(Jun–Aug, public holidays)

➡ Accommodation books out and prices increase by up to 50%.

➡ Expect warm, dry and sunny weather; more humid in coastal areas.

SHOULDER
(Mar–May, Sep & Oct)

➡ A good time to travel with mild, clear weather and fewer crowds.

➡ Local festivals can send prices soaring.

LOW SEASON
(Nov–Feb)

➡ Cold in central Spain; rain in the north and northwest.

➡ Mild temperatures in Andalucía and the Mediterranean coast.

➡ This is high season in ski resorts.

arguably Andalucía's most engaging collection of *pueblos blancos* (white villages). Among the last outposts of Moorish settlement on Spanish soil, these hamlets resemble North Africa, oasis-like and set amid woodlands and deep ravines.

Flamenco in Andalucía

10 Who needs rock 'n' roll? Like all great anguished music, flamenco has the power to lift you out of the doldrums and stir your soul. It's as if by sharing in the pain of innumerable generations of dispossessed misfits you open a door to a secret world of musical

Best on Film

¡Bienvenido, Mr Marshall! (1952) A small town sets out to impress American visitors in this cornerstone of Spanish cinema.

Jamón, jamón (1992) Bigas Luna's ribald comedy in which legs of ham perform a vital role.

Todo sobre mi madre (1999) Winner of a Best Foreign Language Oscar, this is one of Pedro Almodovar's more serious movies.

Volver (2006) Almodovar returns to more comedic territory with Penelope Cruz and Carmen Maura.

Best in Print

A Handbook for Travellers (Richard Ford) This 1845 classic is witty and informative.

A Pilgrim in Spain (Christopher Howse) Amusing reflections from a veteran Spain-watcher.

Everything but the Squeal (John Barlow) A fun guide to northern Spain's food culture.

Ghosts of Spain (Giles Tremlett) An account of modern Spain and the hangover from its past.

Getting Around

Boat Ferries and hydrofoils link the mainland (La Península) with the Balearic Islands and Spain's North African enclaves of Ceuta and Melilla.

Bus There are few places in Spain where buses don't go. Numerous companies provide bus links, from local routes between villages to fast intercity connections. It is often cheaper to travel by bus than by train, particularly on long-haul runs, but also less comfortable.

Train Renfe is the excellent national train system that runs most of the services in Spain. A handful of small private railway lines also operate. Reservations are recommended for long-distance trips.

ghosts and ancient Andalucian spirits. On the other side of the coin, flamenco culture can also be surprisingly jolly, jokey and tongue-in-cheek. There's only one real proviso: you have to hear it live.

Asturian Coast

11 According to one count, the emerald-green northern Spanish region of Asturias boasts more than 600 beaches. The beauty of many of these frequently wild and unspoiled stretches is utterly breathtaking. Even better, the villages of the coast and hinterland are among the prettiest anywhere along

the Spanish shoreline, and the food served in this part of the country is famous throughout Spain.

Beaches of Menorca

12 At a time when the Spanish Mediterranean has become a byword for mass tourism, Menorca is just a little bit different. Saved from the worst effects of overdevelopment, most of the island is a Unesco Biosphere Reserve with 216km of coastline and beaches that defy description. Some assert that reaching them by sea is the height of pleasure, but happening upon them from the interior brings equal joy.

Flamenco dancer, Seville, Andalucía

ANDREA PISTOLESI / GETTY IMAGES ©

Railway travel, Sri Lanka highlands

Sri Lanka

Endless beaches, timeless ruins, welcoming people, oodles of elephants, killer surf, cheap prices, fun trains, famous tea, flavourful food – need we go on?

Sri Lanka's attributes are many. Few places have as many Unesco World Heritage sites (eight) packed into such a small area. Its 2000-plus years of culture can be discovered at ancient sites filled with mystery.

When you're ready to escape the tropical climate of the coast and lowlands, head for the hills, which are verdant, virescent and virally infectious with allure. Impossibly green tea plantations and rainforested peaks beckon walkers, trekkers or just those who want to see it on a spectacular train ride.

And then there are the beaches. Dazzlingly white and all so often untrod, they ring the island so that no matter where you go, you'll be near a sandy gem.

Find a favourite beach to call your own, meditate in a 2000-year-old temple, try to keep count of the little dishes that come with your rice and curry. Stroll past colonial gems in Colombo and then hit some epic surf. Sri Lanka is spectacular, it's affordable and it's still mostly uncrowded. Now is the best time to discover it.

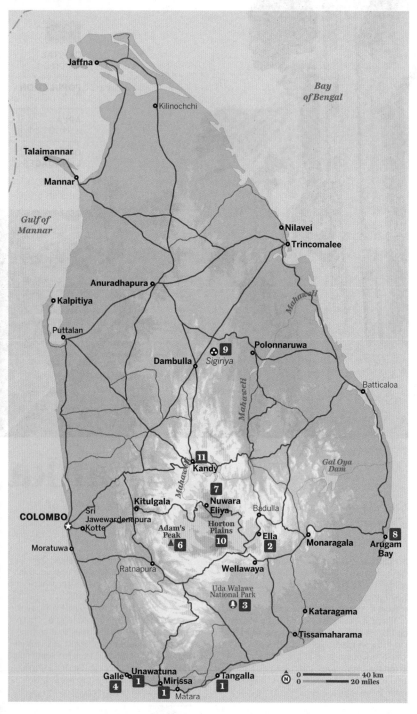

Sri Lanka's
Top Experiences

Stunning Beaches

1 There are long, golden-specked ones, there are dainty ones with soft white sand, there are wind- and wave-battered ones, and ones without a footstep for miles. Some have a slowly, slowly vibe and some have a lively party vibe, but whichever you choose, the beaches of Sri Lanka really are every bit as gorgeous as you've heard. Favourites include Tangalla, Unawatuna and Mirissa. We guarantee that after you've returned home, every time you sit in rush-hour traffic on a wet and cold Monday morning, an image of palm trees and azure Sri Lankan waters will float into your mind!

Travelling by Train

2 Sometimes there's no way to get a seat on the slow but oh-so-popular train to Ella, but with a prime standing-room-only spot looking out at a rolling carpet of tea, who cares? Outside, the colourful silk saris of Tamil tea pickers stand out in the sea of green; inside, you may get a shy welcome via a smile. At stations, vendors hustle treats, including some amazing corn and chilli fritters sold wrapped in somebody's old homework paper. Munching one of these while the scenery creaks past? Sublime.

Uda Walawe National Park

3 This huge chunk of savannah grassland centred on the Uda Walawe reservoir is the closest Sri Lanka gets to East Africa. There are herds of buffalo (although some of these are domesticated!), sambar deer, crocodiles, masses of birds, and Indian elephants – and we don't just mean a few elephants. We mean hundreds of the big-nosed creatures. In fact, we'd go so far as to say that for elephants, Uda Walawe is equal to, or even better than, many of the famous East African national parks.

if Sri Lanka were 100 people

75 would be Sinhalese
9 would be Sri Lankan Moors
4 would be Indian Tamil
11 would be Sri Lankan Tamil
1 would be other

belief systems
(% of population)

70 Buddhist
10 Muslim
13 Hindu
7 Christian

population per sq km

SRI LANKA   US   UK

≈ 30 people

Galle Fort

4 Man and nature have joined forces in Galle Fort to produce an architectural work of art. The Dutch built the streets and buildings, the Sri Lankans added the colour and style, and then nature got busy covering it in a gentle layer of tropical vegetation, humidity and salty air. The result is an enchanting old town that has recently become home to dozens of art galleries, quirky shops, and boutique cafes and guesthouses. For tourists, it's without doubt the number-one urban attraction in the country.

Ayurveda

5 If you start to feel the burden of the centuries while in Sri Lanka, you might appreciate an irony while you feel the tensions melt out of your body in an Ayurvedic sauna: the design is more than 2500 years old. Ayurveda is an ancient practice and its devotees claim enormous benefits from its therapies and treatments. Herbs, spices, oils and more are used on and in the body to produce balance. Some people go on multiweek regimens in clinics, others enjoy a pampering afternoon at a luxury spa.

Adam's Peak

6 For over a thousand years, pilgrims have trudged by candlelight up Adam's Peak (Sri Pada) to stand in the footprints of the Buddha, breathe the air where Adam first set foot on earth, and see the place where the butterflies go to die. Today tourists join the throngs of local pilgrims and, as you stand in the predawn light atop this perfect pinnacle of rock and watch the sun crawl above

What's in a Name?

Changing the country's name from Ceylon to Sri Lanka in 1972 caused considerable confusion for foreigners. However, for the Sinhalese it has always been known as Lanka and for the Tamils as Ilankai; the *Ramayana*, too, describes the abduction of Sita by the king of Lanka.

The Romans knew the island as Taprobane and Muslim traders talked of Serendib, meaning 'Island of Jewels' in Arabic. The word Serendib became the root of the word 'serendipity' – the art of making happy and unexpected discoveries. The Portuguese somehow twisted Sinhaladvipa (Island of the Sinhalese) into Ceilão. In turn, the Dutch altered this to Ceylan and the British to Ceylon.

In 1972 'Lanka' was restored, with the addition of 'Sri', a respectful title.

Food & Drink

With an island as rich in spices and ingredients as Sri Lanka, it's no surprise its foods burst with a panoply of flavours. Celebrating food is part of the culture and people spend many hours producing extraordinary dishes that are a key part of everyday life.

Hoppers These bowl-shaped pancakes are a joy to behold. Skilled cooks artfully use rice flour to create these delicate bowls. Crispy and wafer-thin, they are the ideal venue for all manner of savoury fillings.

Kotthu Rotti There is no one way to make this favourite national dish. You start with some rotti and chop it up before it goes in the frying pan; after that, what's best added to the mix is endlessly debated.

Short eats A traveller's best friend at lunch, these ubiquitous snacks are sold across the country in dizzying variety. Typically deep-fried and sold at stands, stalls or from street vendors, short eats can be samosas, crispy patties, stuffed rolls and more.

7

Tea Plantation, Nuwara Eliya, Hill Country

waves of mountains, the sense of magic remains as bewitching as it must have been for Adam himself.

Tea Plantations

7 It wasn't really all that long ago that Sri Lanka's Hill Country was largely a wild and ragged sweep of jungle-clad mountains, but then along came the British and they felt in need of a nice cup of tea. So they chopped down all the jungle and turned the Hill Country into one giant tea estate, and you know what? The result is mighty pretty! Sri Lankan tea is now famous across the world, and visiting a tea estate and seeing how the world's favourite cuppa is produced is absolutely fascinating .

When to Go

HIGH SEASON
(Dec–Mar)

➡ The Hill Country plus west- and south-coast beaches are busiest – and driest.

➡ The Maha monsoon season (October to January) keeps the East, North and Ancient Cities wet.

SHOULDER
(Apr & Sep–Nov)

➡ April and September offer the best odds for good weather countrywide.

➡ New Year's celebrations in mid-April cause transport to fill beyond capacity.

LOW SEASON
(May–Aug)

➡ The Yala monsoon season (May to August) brings rain to the south and west coasts.

➡ The weather in the North and East is best.

➡ Prices nationwide are at their nadir.

Surfing at Arugam Bay

8 The heart of Sri Lanka's nascent surf scene, the long right break at the southern end of Arugam Bay is considered Sri Lanka's best. From April to September you'll find surfers riding the waves; stragglers catch the random good days as late as November. Throughout

GAVIN HELLER / GETTY IMAGES ©

the year you can revel in the surfer vibe: there are board-rental and ding-repair joints plus plenty of laid-back, cheap hangouts offering a bed on the beach. And if you need solitude, there are fine breaks at nearby Lighthouse and Okanda.

Sigiriya Rock

9 If it was just the rolling gardens at the base of Sigiriya, they would still be a highlight. Ponds and little man-made rivulets put the water in these water gardens and offer a serene idyll amid the sweltering countryside. But look up and catch your jaw as you ponder this 370m rock that erupts out of the landscape. Etched with art and surmounted by ruins,

Best on Film

Bridge on the River Kwai David Lean's 1957 British-American WWII, Oscar-winning film was mostly shot in Sri Lanka.

Hot Spots: Sri Lanka The 2008 BBC documentary details the country's history of ethnic tensions.

Sri Lanka's Killing Fields A 2011 report by the UK's Channel Four that examines events in the final months of the war.

Best in Print

Monkfish Moon Nine short stories, by Booker Prize–nominated Romesh Gunesekera, provide a diverse glimpse of Sri Lanka's ethnic conflict.

Running in the Family A comic and reflective memoir by Michael Ondaatje of his Colombo family in the 1940s.

The Foundations of Paradise Features places remarkably like Adam's Peak and Sigiriya. Arthur C Clarke wrote 2001: A Space Odyssey and lived in Sri Lanka.

Getting Around

Bus Buses go everywhere often and cheaply. There are two kinds of bus: Central Transport Board (CTB) buses, usually the default buses with no air-con; and private buses, usually more comfortable and faster than other bus services. Vehicles range from late-model Japanese coaches to ancient minibuses.

Car Hire cars with drivers are popular and affordable. This option is more expensive than buses and trains, but is efficient, flexible and comfortable.

Train Trains are less convenient than buses but more fun and almost always more relaxed. There are some beautiful routes and tickets are cheap. Travel in 1st class is comfortable, but 2nd and 3rd classes are often crowded and uncomfortable. Train destinations are limited and travel is slow.

Sigiriya is an awesome mystery, one that the wonderful new museum tries to dissect. The climb to the top is a wearying and worthy endeavour.

Horton Plains & World's End

10 The wild, windswept Horton Plains, high, high up in Sri Lanka's Hill Country, are utterly unexpected in this country of tropical greens and blues, but they are far from unwelcome. You'll need to wrap up warm for the dawn hike across these bleak moorlands – it's one of the most enjoyable walks in the country. And then, suddenly,

out of the mist comes the end of the world and a view over what seems like half of Sri Lanka.

Kandy

11 Kandy is the cultural capital of the island and home to the Temple of the Sacred Tooth Relic, said to contain a tooth of the Buddha himself. For the Sinhalese this is the holiest spot on the island, but for tourists Kandy offers a pleasing old quarter, a pretty central lake, a clutch of museums and, in the surrounding vicinity, some beautiful botanical gardens.

MARGIE POLITZER / GETTY IMAGES ©

Nisbet Beach, Nevis

St Kitts & Nevis

Near-perfect packages. The two-island nation combines beaches with beauteous mountains, activities to engage your body and rich history to engage your mind.

Driving around the northern reaches of St Kitts, you pass mile after mile of sugar cane gone wild. The once all-encompassing lifeblood of the nation is no more and the huge plantations have been abandoned. Meanwhile beaches across the island rattle with the percussion of construction as a new economy based on tourism takes hold. Even the train once used for hauling cane now hauls tourists. But if change is coming fast to this classic eastern Caribbean island, it is managing to retain its essential qualities: a laid-back culture given to loud, boisterous celebration and an utter contempt for stress. Nevis is much the same albeit in a package that's almost impossibly alluring. Circum-navigating the island on a two-hour drive is one of life's meandering pleasures.

But if the pair offer much that's similar, they differ in the details. St Kitts is the larger and feels that way, but Nevis is a neater package, anchored by a single volcanic mountain buttressed by a handful of beaches and a tiny capital, Charlestown.

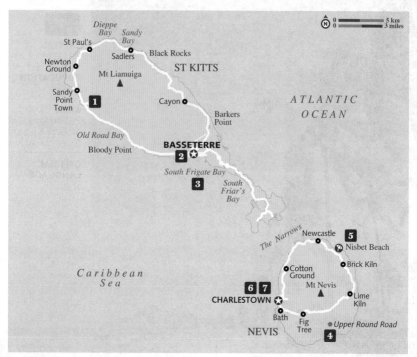

St Kitts & Nevis'
Top Experiences

Brimstone Hill Fortress

1 St Kitts' historical highlight was made a Unesco World Heritage site in 1999 for being an exceptionally well-preserved example of 17th- and 18th-century military architecture. Far larger than you'd think, this vast old military stronghold was built by the British with slave labor and offers insight into the violent and tumultuous past of the former Caribbean colonies. After a fire swept through Basseterre in 1867, some of the fort structures were partially dismantled and the stones used to rebuild the capital. In the 1960s major restoration was undertaken, and much of the fortress has

been returned to its earlier grandeur. Queen Elizabeth II inaugurated it as a national park during her visit to St Kitts in October 1985.

Basseterre

2 Basseterre (pronounced 'bass-tear') was founded more than 380 years ago as the first French town in the Caribbean. The name combines the French words 'basse' and 'terre,' which roughly translates as lowlands. Leaving behind the cruise-ship terminal at Port Zante plunges you headlong into a vibrant mix of local commerce, history and culture. Nothing in the capital has been overly gussied up, which means that surprises abound. Take time to pick out the surviv-

ing colonial buildings with their wide porches and nod to folks lounging on their stoops, Carib in hand.

South Frigate Bay

3 Frigate Bay, located 3 miles southeast of Basseterre, is an isthmus dividing the calm Caribbean side and the rougher Atlantic side, which is dominated by the massive Marriott resort. This is also the center for condo development on St Kitts, and you know you're getting close by the blight of jewelry-store billboards lining the road. The area has some good restaurants, but the key draws are the funky beach bars along South Frigate Bay beach, dubbed 'The Strip'. This is as happening as nightlife gets on St Kitts.

Upper Round Road

4 Originally built in the late 1600s, this road once linked the sugar estates, cane fields and villages surrounding Mt Nevis. Today, it travels 9 miles from Golden Rock Inn in the east to Nisbet Plantation Beach Club in the north, past farms, orchards, gardens and rainforest. Along the way, sample fresh fruit and observe monkeys and butterflies. Budget about five hours for the entire trek or you can walk in shorter sections.

Nisbet Beach

5 Backed by the eponymous plantation resort, this is perhaps the loveliest strand on Nevis, with palm-lined powdery white sand, crystal-clear water and great views across to St Kitts. The perfect place to spend the day.

Communal Barbecue

6 Nevis is a tight-knit community. Just how tight is in evidence every Friday and Saturday night, when upbeat cookouts draw

if St Kitts & Nevis were 100 people

22 would be aged 0-14
16 would be aged 15-24
45 would be aged 25-54
9 would be aged 55-64
8 would be aged 65+

land use
(% of land)

19

arable

1

permanent crops

80

other

When to Go

NOV–DEC

➡ The best time to visit, price- and weather-wise.

➡ Winter days average a temperature of 81°F (27°C).

➡ Starting in mid-December, Carnival is the biggest yearly event on St Kitts.

FEB–JUN

➡ The driest months.

➡ The four-day St Kitts Music Festival in June brings together top-name performers from throughout the Caribbean.

JUL–NOV

➡ The hurricane (and rainy) season

➡ For over 30 years between July and August, Nevis' main event has been Culturama.

population per sq km

ST KITTS & NEVIS

TRINIDAD & TOBAGO

USA

👤 ≈ 8 people

Monkey See, Monkey Do

Mischievous vervet monkeys were brought to St Kitts and Nevis by French settlers from Africa and have since flourished so well that they outnumber humans two to one. Traveling in packs of up to 30, they can be spotted in the rainforest and on St Kitts' southeast peninsula. They may look cute but residents consider them a major pest because they raid fruit and vegetable crops and destroy birds' nests. A biomedical research facility on St Kitts uses the monkeys for experiments in their research for a cure for Parkinson's disease and to do preclinical testing of a new dengue-fever vaccine.

Food & Drink

Brinley Gold Rum Locally blended rum comes in such flavors as vanilla, coffee, mango, coconut and lime. The shop in Port Zante does tastings.

Cane Spirit Rothschild More commonly known as CSR, this locally distilled libation is made from pure fermented cane juice and is best enjoyed on the rocks mixed with grapefruit-flavored Ting soda.

Carib Locally brewed lager.

Conch Served curried, marinated or soused (boiled).

Pelau Also known as 'cook-up,' this dish is the Kittitian version of paella: a tasty but messy blend of rice, meat, saltfish, vegetables and pigeon peas.

Pepperpot A stew made with any imaginable combination of meats and veggies.

Stewed saltfish Official national dish; served with spicy plantains, coconut dumplings and seasoned breadfruit.

Children's carnival, Charlestown, Nevis

locals into the streets for barbecued chicken and ribs, gossip and music. The biggest is hosted by the Water Department on Pump St, near Charlestown.

Charlestown

7 The ferry from St Kitts docks right in the pint-size center of Charlestown, Nevis' cute little capital, where banks and businesses coexist with tourist facilities and gingerbread Victorians. It's a fun spot for a stroll and is rarely overcrowded as large cruise ships bypass Nevis. Tourist tat is refreshingly limited. The greater Charlestown area can be readily explored on foot. Just a 15-minute jaunt north of the center will put you on lovely Pinney's Beach. Charlestown is also the starting point of the Nevis Heritage Trail, which links 25 sites of historical importance throughout the island, including churches, sugar estates, military installations and natural sites.

Getting Around

Boat Several passenger ferries shuttle between Basseterre and Charlestown. The trip takes about 45 minutes and is both a pleasant and scenic way to travel.

Bus Buses on both islands can resemble minivan taxis, so check the front plate to be sure. An 'H' means private bus and a 'T' means taxi (an 'R' is a rental car and a 'P' or 'PA' is a resident's car).

Car & Motorcycle Foreigners must purchase a visitor driver's license, which is valid for 90 days. Rental companies will issue you one when you fill out your contracts, and a license on one island is good for the other.

Taxi Taxis meet scheduled flights on both islands. Taxi island tours on both islands cost around US$80. A three-hour half-island tour costs US$60.

PETER PHIPP / GETTY IMAGES ©

Anse Chastanet, Soufrière

St Lucia

CAPITAL
Castries

POPULATION
162,781

AREA
616 sq km

OFFICIAL LANGUAGE
English

The colour wheel is simple on St Lucia: rich green for the tropical land, pure white for the ring of beaches and brilliant blue for the surrounding sea.

Rising like an emerald tooth from the Caribbean Sea, St Lucia definitely grabs your attention. While it fits the image of a glam honeymoon spot, this mountainous island has more to offer than sensuous beaches flanked by sybaritic lodgings.

Diving, snorkeling, sailing and kitesurfing are fabulous. On land there's no better ecofriendly way to experience the rainforest-choked interior than on foot, on horseback or suspended from a zip line. Wildlife lovers will get a buzz, too. Whales, dolphins, turtles and endemic birds can easily be approached, with the added thrill of a grandiose setting. Near Soufrière, the awesomely photogenic Pitons rise from the waves like pyramids of volcanic stone.

Bar the island's northeast, where most tourist facilities are concentrated, the rest of St Lucia is definitely a back-to-nature haven, making it possible to find a deserted bay, secluded waterfall, character-filled fishing community or odd colonial-style plantation.

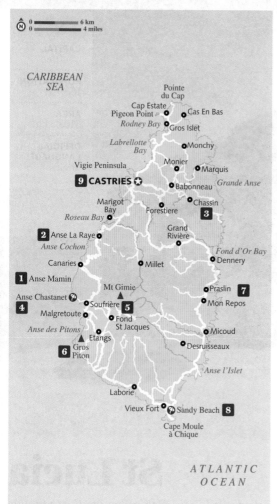

CARIBBEAN
SEA

CASTRIES

ATLANTIC
OCEAN

St Lucia's
Top Experiences

Anse Mamin

1 This dreamy enclave of golden sand edges a gently curved cove immediately north of Anse Chastanet. It's accessible by a 10-minute coastal walk or by water taxi from Anse Chastanet. Mountain biking is available, and there's a beachfront restaurant.

Anse La Raye

2 Heading south along the coast from Marigot Bay, the winding road snakes its way through the tiny village of Anse La Raye. The smattering of colorful buildings is typical of every St Lucian fishing community, and the village itself gives a good insight into the daily lives of the locals. On a Friday night Anse La Raye wakes up big time. 'Seafood Friday' has become one of the highlights for St Lucians and in-the-know tourists. Street stalls sell fish of every variety at unbeatable prices. The party gets a bit wild and goes most of the night. It will definitely be memorable, filled with food, refreshments (expect plenty of rum and beer) and dance.

Rain Forest Sky Rides

3 Why not see the beautiful rainforest from a Tarzan perspective? In the hamlet of Chassin, 30 minutes east of Rodney Bay, is an ecofriendly outfit that has set up 11 zip lines in the trees. For the less adventurous, it offers a 1½-hour aerial 'tram' ride over the canopy. A tour guide provides insight into the local flora and fauna.

Anse Chastanet

4 Stretched out in front of the resort of the same name, Anse Chastanet could be the quintessential St Lucian beach experience. Though only a mile or so from Soufrière, it feels like a lost tropical world. The sheltered bay is protected by high cliffs, with towering palms on the shore. The sparkling ash-gray beach is great for a dip and the snorkeling just offshore is some of the best on the island.

Soufrière

5 If one town were to be the heart and soul of St Lucia, it would have to be Soufrière. Its attractions include a slew of colonial-era edifices scattered in the center and a bustling seafront. The landscape surrounding the town is little

PAUL BAGGALEY / GETTY IMAGES ©

short of breathtaking. The sky-scraping towers of rock known as the Pitons stand guard over the town. Jutting from the sea, covered in vegetation and ending in a summit that looks other-worldly, these iconic St Lucian landmarks are the pride of Soufrière. A few fin strokes from the shore unveil a magical underwater world, pocketed with healthy reefs and teeming with sea life.

Gros Piton

6 If you have time for only one walk during your stay, choose the Gros Piton (2617ft) climb, because it's the most scenic. Starting from the hamlet of Fond Gens Libres, you walk almost all the way through a thick jungle, with lots of interesting fauna and flora.

Approximately halfway the path goes past a lookout that affords fantastic vistas of Petit Piton and the ocean. The final section is very steep, but the reward is a tremendous view of south-ern St Lucia and the densely forested mountains of the interior.

East Coast Fishing Villages

7 What a difference a few miles can make! A 30-minute drive from Castries transports you to yet another world, along the Atlantic-battered east coast, where you can experience St Lucia from a different perspective. In both landscape and charac-ter, this region is distinct. It feels very Creole and laid-back. While this coast lacks

if St Lucia were 100 people

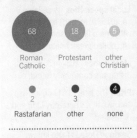

83 would be black
12 would be mixed
2 would be East Indian
3 would be other

belief systems
(% of population)

68 Roman Catholic
18 Protestant
5 other Christian

2 Rastafarian
3 other
4 none

When to Go

DEC–MARCH
➡ Winter season is most popular time to visit with very un-winter weather (average 27°C).

JUL
➡ Summer is quiet and hot with the July temperatures averaging 29°C.

JUN–OCT
➡ Hurricane season, expect more rain this time of year and maybe the odd storm.

population per sq km

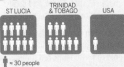

ST LUCIA   TRINIDAD & TOBAGO   USA

👤 ≈ 30 people

St Lucian Culture

St Lucians are generally laid-back, friendly people influenced by a mix of their English, French, African and Caribbean origins. For instance, if you walk into the Catholic cathedral in Castries, you'll find a building of French design, an interior richly painted in bright African-inspired colors, portraits of a Black Madonna and child, and church services delivered in English.

Approximately 85% of the population are of pure African ancestry. The predominantly African heritage can be seen in the strong family ties that St Lucians hold and the survival of many traditional customs and superstitions. *Obeah* (Vodou) is still held in equal measures of respect and fear in places like Anse La Raye.

The local snakeman is visited by islanders for his medicinal powers. One such muscular remedy he uses involves massaging the thick fat of the boa constrictor on aching limbs.

The musical sounds of the Caribbean are alive in St Lucia – calypso, reggae and dancehall all play an important role in the lives of locals.

Food & Drink

Local specialties Try callaloo soup, *lambi* (conch) and saltfish with green fig (seasoned salt cod and boiled green banana).

Meat dishes Chicken and pork dishes are commonly found.

Piton The beer of St Lucia; crisp and sweet, it's perfectly light and refreshing.

Seafood Dorado (also known as mahi mahi), kingfish, marlin, snapper, lobster, crab and shellfish feature high on the menu.

St Lucian rum The island's sole distillery produces white rums, gold rums and flavored rums.

Street market, Castries

the beaches of the west, it makes up for it with lovely bays backed by spectacular cliffs, a rocky shoreline pounded by thundering surf, and a handful of picturesque fishing towns.

Sandy Beach

8 At the southern tip of the island, Sandy Beach is a beautiful strand of white sand that always has a stiff breeze, The combination of constant strong breezes, protected areas with calm water, and a lack of obstacles make the bay of Anse de Sables a world-class destination for kitesurfers and windsurfers. It's also suitable for swim-

ming on a calm day. Best of all, it's never crowded.

Castries

9 Walking along the crowded streets of Castries, you are bombarded with the kinetics of a city that is bustling with life. The throbbing heart of the city is the market area, with the locals scurrying to fetch their wares and sell their goods. Castries' setting couldn't be more photogenic. Think massive cruise ships anchored in a sheltered bay, with the soaring Morne Fortune (2795ft) as the backdrop. Come with maximum overdraft – if you love shopping you've come to the right place

Getting Around

Bus Service is via privately owned minivans. They're a cheap way to get around and they're frequent between main towns.

Car & Motorcycle You'll find the best rates for rentals on the internet. Nearly all car-rental agencies offer unlimited mileage. If you're planning an extensive tour of the island, it's advisable to hire a 4WD.

Taxi Available at the airports, the harbor and in front of major hotels. Taxis aren't metered but adhere to standard fares.

Tobago Cays

CAPITAL
Kingstown

POPULATION
103,220

AREA
389 sq km

OFFICIAL LANGUAGE
English

St Vincent & the Grenadines

Caribbean fantasies converge on this collection of 32 islands at the south end of the Leeward Islands.

Just the name St Vincent and the Grenadines (SVG) evokes visions of exotic, idyllic island life. Imagine an island chain in the heart of the Caribbean Sea, uncluttered by tourist exploitation; with white-sand beaches on deserted islands, sky-blue water gently lapping the shore and barely a soul around.

Once you get off the big island, with its traffic, hustle and noise, and out into the Grenadines, everything changes. There are 31 Grenadines, each one more tranquil than the next and each begging to be explored. Beaches stretch out before you, the pace of life slows to a crawl and the desire to go home vanishes.

These islands have enchanted sailors for centuries, and continue to do so. Whether you have your own vessel, are happy to hitch a ride or take one of the new ferries, the island-hopping opportunities are irresistible.

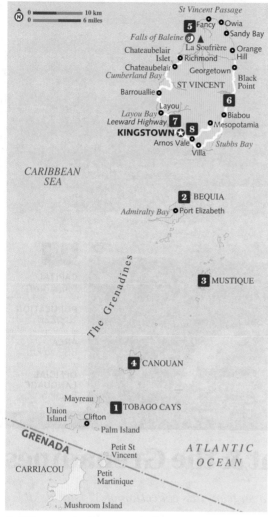

Bequia

2 Striking a balance between remoteness, accessibility, development and affordability – Bequia (pronounced 'beck-way') is the most perfect island in the whole Grenadines. Stunning beaches dotting the shoreline, accommodations to fit most budgets and a slow pace of life all help to create an environment that is utterly unforgettable. There are fine restaurants to dine in, shops that retain their local integrity and enough golden sand and blue water to keep everybody blissful.

Mustique

3 What can you say about Mustique other than 'Wow!'? First, take an island that is nearly unfathomably beautiful, with stunning beaches and everything else you expect to find in paradise, then add to the mix accommodations that defy description or affordability. With prices that exclude all but the super-rich, film stars and burnt-out musicians, this island is the exclusive playground of the uberaffluent. The private island is run by the Mustique Company, who assures guests that this paradise remains a privileged retreat. At least by night that is, as anyone can day-trip here and rub shoulders with someone notorious and end up on the cover of *Hello* or *People*. Well, it's possible.

St Vincent & the Grenadines'
Top Experiences

Tobago Cays

1 Ask anyone who's been to SVG what their highlight was and you're bound to hear all about the Tobago Cays. These five small islands offer some of the Caribbean's best diving and snorkeling. Free of any sort of development, the islands sit firmly in a national park and are only accessible via boat on a day trip from one of the Grenadines. And what a day trip it can be – the snorkeling is world class and the white-sand beaches look like a strip of blinding snow. Underwater, sea turtles and parrot fish are just the start of the myriad species you'll see. The coral is gorgeous.

Canouan

4 Canouan (pronounced 'cahn-oo-ahn') is an interesting place, both historically and aesthetically. This stunningly beautiful hook-shaped island has some of the most brilliant beaches in the entire Grenadines chain, and some of the most

secluded hideaways too. In sharp contrast, however, it is also home to one of the biggest resort developments in the region, leaving the island with a split personality.

Falls of Baleine

5 It's the stuff of tropical fantasies: a 60ft waterfall crashes down a fern-dappled rock in a silvery arc into a lovely wide freshwater pool below. The gorgeous Falls of Baleine, at the isolated northwestern tip of the island, are accessible only by boat. A few minutes' walk from the beach where your boat anchors, listen for the cascade amidst the rainforest.

Windward Highway

6 The windward (east) coast of St Vincent is a mix of wave-lashed shoreline, quiet bays and small towns. As it's away from the tourism that dominates the southern coast of the island, it's a fine place to visit for those wanting to experience a more sedate version of St Vincent. The black-sand beaches meld into the banana plantations and the lush vegetation grows up into the hilly interior. Humble villages pop up from time to time, filled

if St Vincent & the Grenadines were 100 people

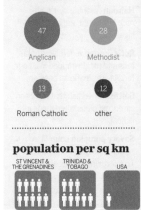

66 would be black
19 would be mixed
6 would be East Indian
4 would be European
2 would be Carib Amerindian
3 would be other

belief systems
(% of population)

47 Anglican

28 Methodist

13 Roman Catholic

12 other

population per sq km

ST VINCENT & THE GRENADINES

TRINIDAD & TOBAGO

USA

≈ 30 people

When to Go

YEAR ROUND

➡ The climate varies between the islands, as the Grenadines to the south are slightly drier and marginally warmer than St Vincent.

JAN–MAY

➡ The dry season in St Vincent.

➡ Apr is the driest month, rain averages only six days.

➡ The average high temperature in January is 29°C (85°F), while the low is 22°C (72°F).

JUL

➡ The wettest month, rain falls for an average of 26 days.

➡ The average high is 30°C (86°F), while the nightly low is 24°C (76°F).

Caribbean Rhythms

Music is the cultural lifeblood of St Vincent. The infectious Caribbean rhythms permeate the air and are inescapable wherever you go. Musical preference is divided along generational lines. Aging Rastas groove to the mellow jams of the old-school reggae icons. The younger generations are enchanted by the frenetic beats of modern dancehall and imported hip-hop. Everywhere, though, you'll hear the latest Caribbean rhythms of soca, steelpan and whatever latest variation of calypso has caught fire.

Original to SVG is Big Drum, a music style based on the namesake instrument (usually made from an old rum keg) and having a calypso beat mixed with satirical lyrics performed by a 'chantwell', a lead female singer. Wild costumes are part of the show.

Food & Drink

Callaloo A spinachlike vegetable used in soups and stews. Many vitamins!

Fresh produce St Vincent produces top quality and delicious fruits and vegetables.

Hairoun (pronounced 'highrone') The light and tasty local lager.

Rotis Curried vegetables, potatoes and meat wrapped in a flour tortilla are a national passion.

Saltfish Dried fish that has been cured, delicious when made into fishcakes.

Savory pumpkin soup More squash-like than the American Thanksgiving staple; often like a rich stew.

Seafood Lobster, shrimp, conch and fish are all popular and readily available.

Banana farm, Kingstown

with down-to-earth locals and ramshackle buildings.

Leeward Highway

7 The Leeward Hwy runs north of Kingstown along St Vincent's west coast for 25 miles. Offering some lovely scenery, the road climbs into the mountains as it leaves Kingstown, then winds through the hillside and back down to deeply cut coastal valleys that open to coconut plantations, fishing villages and bays lined with black-sand beaches.

Kingstown

8 Rough cobblestone streets, arched stone doorways and covered walkways conjure up a Caribbean of banana boats and colonial rule. The city of Kingstown heaves and swells with a pulsing local community that bustles through its narrow streets and alleyways. Steep hills surround the town, amplifying the sounds of car horns, street vendors and the music filtering through the crowd.

Getting Around

Air With the fast ferry service, internal flights are less important.

Bus Buses are a good way to get around St Vincent. The buses themselves are little more than minivans that are often jammed full.

Ferry The main islands of SVG are well linked by boats, especially the excellent new Jaden Sun fast ferry, which puts Union Island within two hours of leaving St Vincent.

Fishing Boat You can usually find someone who will get you between islands in the Grenadines. Usually this will be on a small, open fishing boat with room for at best four people with minimal luggage. The rides can be quite exciting and should not undertaken in rough seas.

Taxi Taxis are abundant on most islands and affordable for shorter trips. Agree on a fare before departure.

CAPITAL
Khartoum

POPULATION
34.8 million

AREA
1.9 million sq km

OFFICIAL LANGUAGE
Arabic, English

Pyramid, Royal City

Sudan

There is no country on earth that travellers are as apprehensive to visit as they are pained to leave. The Sudanese are as diverse as they are mysterious, as generous as they are welcoming.

Wake at the break of day under the golden pyramids of godlike kings of old; traverse a searing desert to the place where two Nile rivers become one and watch a million blood red fish swarm through gardens of coral. Whichever way you look at it, there's just no denying that among Sudan's sweeping hills of sand lie treasures the rest of the world are only just beginning to understand.

Until July 2011 Sudan was the biggest country in Africa, but now, with South Sudan having broken away to form a new nation, maps of Africa are being redrawn. This redefining of national boundaries is making for huge changes, geographically, politically, financially and culturally, for the Sudanese. But for a traveller some things never change; Sudanese hospitality remains second to none, and for most people, travelling through Sudan is such an eye-opening and rewarding experience that many come away saying that Sudan was their favourite country in Africa.

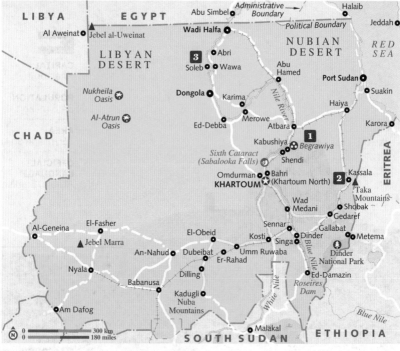

Sudan's
Top Experiences

Begrawiya

1 Seemingly lost under the folds of giant apricot-coloured dunes, this ancient royal cemetery, with its clusters of narrow pyramids blanketing the sandswept hills, is one of the most spectacular sights in Sudan – and the best thing is that you'll probably have the place largely to yourself. Some of the tombs' antechambers contain well-preserved hieroglyphics.

Kassala

2 Kassala is where half the tribes of northern Sudan seem to meet. Its huge souqs are an ethnic mosaic of colours, smells, noises and experiences. At the base of the mountains is the Khatmiyah Mosque, centre of the Khatmiyah Sufi sect. It's a lovely mudbrick building; after exploring have a little scramble around the bizarre peaks of the Taka Mountains.

Soleb

3 A little south of Abri, the wonderfully evocative Egyptian temple of Soleb is the highlight of this part of Sudan. It's not just that this enormous temple is visually stunning, but getting to it is a right rollicking adventure. In the tiny east-coast village of Wawa you'll need to find the boat man and putter across a beautiful stretch of the Nile; a walk through the palm groves will lead you to the temple.

Food & Drink

Coffee Often infused with cinnamon and cardamom.

Fuul Stewed brown beans, a traditional breakfast complete with cheese, egg, salad and flatbread.

Shai Sweet black tea.

When to Go

NOV–FEB
➜ Winter offers perfect temperatures and clear skies.

SEP–OCT
➜ Catch the camel races in Kassala.

NOV
➜ The European Film Festival is held in Khartoum.

Creole women, Paramaribo

CAPITAL
Paramaribo

POPULATION
566,846

AREA
163,800 sq km

OFFICIAL
LANGUAGES
Dutch, Sranan
Tongo

Suriname

Suriname is a warm, dense convergence of rivers that thumps with the lively rhythm of ethnic diversity.

From Paramaribo, the country's effervescent Dutch-colonial capital, to the fathomless jungles of the interior, you will get a genuine welcome to this tiny country – whether from the descendants of escaped African slaves, Dutch and British colonialists, Indian, Indonesian and Chinese indentured laborers or indigenous Amerindians.

You get the best of both worlds here: a city that is chock-full of restaurants, shopping venues and night spots and an untamed jungle utterly away from modern development.

It's not easy to get around this river-heavy, forest-dense country, and the mix of languages can make it hard to communicate, sometimes even for Dutch speakers. Don't forget that a meeting of culinary traditions means the food here is as spicy and rich as the country itself.

Suriname's
Top Experiences

Upper Suriname River

1 This is Suriname's cultural grab bag, where you can stay in river lodges on stunning white-sand beaches amid the jungle and get a glimpse into the neighboring Maroon or Amerindian villages. All locally run, the lodges hope to create a sustainable future for these remote communities that would otherwise rely on the logging and hunting industries.

Paramaribo

2 Amsterdam meets the Wild West in Paramaribo, the most vivacious capital in the Guianas. Black-and-white colonial Dutch buildings line grassy squares, wafts of spices escape from Indian roti shops, while Maroon artists sell colorful paintings outside somber Dutch forts.

Raleighvallen

3 Raleighvallen (Raleigh Falls) is a low, long staircase of cascading water on the upper Coppename River, about two hours upriver from the nearest Maroon village. Resident wildlife include free-swinging spider monkeys, electric eels and a spectacular blood-orange bird.

Food & Drink

Hagelslag Dutch-style chocolate sprinkles to go on toast for breakfast.

Parbo The local beer is quite good; it's customary to share a *djogo* (1L bottle) among friends.

Pom Creole creation using grated tayer root, shredded chicken, onion and spices baked into a casserole.

When to Go

FEB–APR
➡ The first dry season is slightly cooler than the second, and the best time to visit.

AUG–NOV
➡ The second dry season is a bit busier and hotter than the first.

DEC–JAN
➡ Paramaribo is known for its explosive New Year's Eve celebrations.

Umhlanga (Reed) dance

CAPITAL
Mbabane

POPULATION
1.4 million

AREA
17,364 sq km

OFFICIAL LANGUAGES
English, siSwati

Swaziland

Ancient traditions are inherent in everyday life in this tiny mountain kingdom, where local festivals provide a rich counterpoint to the activities and wildlife spotting on offer.

In short: big things come in small packages. The intriguing kingdom of Swaziland is diminutive, but boasts a huge checklist for any visitor. Wildlife watching? Adrenalin-boosting activities like rafting and mountain biking? Lively and colourful local culture? Tick. Tick. Tick. Plus there are superb walking trails, stunning mountain and flatland scenery, and excellent, high-quality handicrafts.

Presiding over this is King Mswati III, the last remaining absolute monarch in Africa.

The monarchy has its critics but, combined with the Swazis' distinguished history of resistance to the Boers, the British and the Zulus, it has fostered a strong sense of national pride. This is exemplified in its national festivals: the Incwala ceremony and the Umhlanga (Reed) dance.

An excellent road system makes Swaziland a pleasure to navigate. Many make a flying visit on their way to Kruger National Park, but it's worth lingering here if you get the chance.

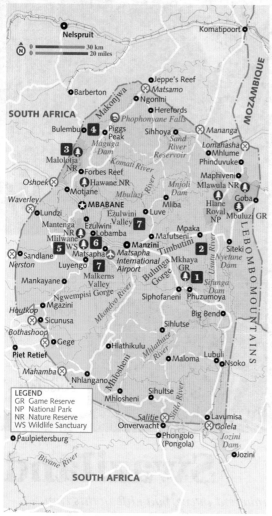

Swaziland's
Top Experiences

Mkhaya Game Reserve

1 Top of the conservation pops, Swaziland's stunning Mkhaya private reserve was established in 1979 to save the pure Nguni breed of cattle from extinction. It's known, however, for its reservation of both the black and white rhino population. The reserve is staffed entirely by Swazis from neighbouring communities who run an extremely effective anti-poaching unit. That's not all: roan and sable antelopes, tsessebis and elephants roam the reserve. A bird hide, too, gives you an opportunity to get up close and personal with rare species. The reserve's name comes from the *mkhaya* (knob-thorn) tree, which abounds here. You can't visit or stay in the reserve without booking in advance. While day tours can be arranged, it's ideal to stay for at least one night.

Rafting the Usutu River

2 One of Swaziland's highlights is whitewater rafting on the Great Usutu River, shooting the rapids or drifting downriver through stunning gorges. In sections, you'll encounter Grade IV rapids, which aren't for the faint-hearted, although even first-timers with a sense of adventure should handle the day easily. Trips run from the Ezulwini Valley.

Malolotja Nature Reserve

3 The beautiful Malolotja Nature Reserve is a true wilderness area, rugged and for the most part unspoiled. The terrain ranges from mountainous and high-altitude grassland to forest and lower-lying bushveld, all with streams and cut by three rivers, including the Komati River. It's an excellent walking destination, and an ornithologist's paradise, with over 280 species of birds. Wildflowers and rare plants are added attractions; several are found only in this part of Africa. Basic brochures outlining the hiking trails are available for free at the restaurant/reception. These days, many visit the park for the Malolotja Canopy Tour, where you can 'glide' your way across Malolotja's stunning, lush tree canopy on adrenalin-pumping zip-lines.

Hippos, Mlilwane Wildlife Sanctuary

Mlilwane Wildlife Sanctuary

4 Cycle or meander in the Mlilwane Wildlife Sanctuary and relax in its bargain lodges. This beautiful and tranquil sanctuary was created in the 1950s by conservationist Ted Reilly and was Swaziland's first protected area. Mlilwane means 'Little Fire', named after the many fires started by lightning strikes here. While it doesn't have the drama or vastness of some South African parks, it's easily accessible and worth a visit. Its terrain is dominated by the precipitous Nyonyane (Little Bird) peak. There are some fine walks in the area. Animals include zebras, giraffes, warthogs, antelopes, crocodiles, hippos and a variety of birds, including black eagles.

Bulembu

5 The historic town of Bulembu was built in 1936 for the former Havelock asbestos mine. Following the mine's closure, the 10,000 workers left, and by 2003 Bulembu was a ghost town. Several years ago the town's new investors started a community tourism project, bringing the town back to life – thousands of deserted corrugated-iron houses and many art deco buildings are being renovated. Stunning hikes in the area include the highest mountain in Swaziland, Emlembe Peak (1863m).

Lobamba

6 Lobamba is the heart of Swaziland's Royal

if Swaziland were 100 people

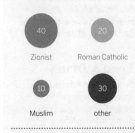

37 would be aged 0-14
22 would be aged 15-24
33 would be aged 25-54
4 would be aged 55-64
4 would be aged 65+

belief systems
(% of population)

40 Zionist
20 Roman Catholic
10 Muslim
30 other

When to Go

JAN–APR

➡ Hot weather; lush vegetation and full rivers provide perfect photographic backdrops.

FEB–MAR

➡ Buganu season – enjoy home-brew marula palm wine in rural Swaziland.

MAY–SEP

➡ Cooler days and winter foliage make for wonderful wildlife viewing in the low veld.

population per sq km

SWAZILAND   SOUTH AFRICA   MOZAMBIQUE

👤 ≈ 10 people

Swazi Ceremonies

Colourful ceremonies (and traditional dress, which is still commonly worn) underline the Swazis' unique identity.

The Incwala ceremony is held sometime between late December and early January. It's Swaziland's most sacred ceremony, celebrating the New Year and the first fruits of the harvest in rituals of thanksgiving, prayer, atonement and reverence for the king. As part of the festivities, the king grants his people the right to consume his harvest, and rains are expected to follow the ceremony.

The Umhlanga (Reed Dance) is a great spectacle in August or September, performed by unmarried girls who collect reeds for the repair and maintenance of the royal palace. It is something like a week-long debutante ball for marriageable young Swazi women and is a showcase of potential wives for the king. On the sixth day they perform the reed dance and carry the reeds they have collected to the queen mother. Princesses wear red feathers in their hair.

Buganu Festival is another 'first fruits' festival, taking place in February and celebrating the marula fruit. The women gather the fruit and ferment a brew (known as *buganu*; it packs a punch). Locals – mainly males – gather to drink and celebrate.

Food & Drink

Swaziland isn't a gourmet's paradise, but you won't eat too badly. There's a good range of places to eat in Mbabane and the tourist areas of the Malkerns and Ezulwini Valleys, with international dishes. Portuguese cuisine, including seafood, can often be found. In more remote areas, African staples such as stew and *pap* (also known as mealie meal) are common.

Beehive hut, Ezulwini Valley

Valley. The British-built royal palace, the Embo State Palace, isn't open to visitors, and photos aren't allowed. Swazi kings now live in the Lozitha State House, about 10km from Lobamba. The National Museum has some interesting displays on Swazi culture; the ticket price also allows you to enter the memorial to King Sobhuza II, the most revered of Swazi kings. Next to the museum is the parliament, which is sometimes open to visitors.

Ezulwini & Malkerns Valleys

7 Revel in a royal experience in the regal heartland of Swaziland and splurge on some handicrafts in the Ezulwini and Malkerns Valleys. The pretty valleys begin just outside Mbabane and extend east and south, incorporating the royal domain of Lobamba village. The valleys boast excellent accommodation and activities, and have a well-earned reputation for their craft centres and markets.

Getting Around

Bus Manzini has the main international bus station for transport to Johannesburg, Durban and Mozambique. Less frequent departures are in Mbabane for the northern destinations of Gauteng and Mpumalanga (South Africa). There are infrequent (but cheap) domestic buses; most depart and terminate at the main stop in the centre of Mbabane. Generally you'll find minibus taxis are the best domestic public transport.

Car Hiring a car will allow you to cover much of the country in a few days. If you have hired your car in South Africa, ensure that you have the written agreement from the rental company to enter Swaziland.

Taxi Minibus taxis leave when full; these are plentiful, run almost everywhere and stop often. There are also nonshared (private hire) taxis in some of the larger towns.

Skärhamn on Tjörn island, Bohuslän coast

Sweden

Frozen wastelands, cosy cottages, virgin forest, rocky islands, reindeer herders and Viking lore – Sweden has all that and mad style, too.

As progressive and civilised as it may be, Sweden is a wild place. Its scenery ranges from barren moonscapes and impenetrable forests in the far north to sunny beaches and lush farmland further south. Its short summers and long winters mean that people cling to every last speck of sunshine on a late August evening – crayfish parties on seaside decks can stretch into the wee hours. In winter locals rely on candlelight and *glögg* to warm their spirits.

But lovers of the outdoors will thrive here in any season: winter sees skiing and dogsledding and aurora borealis, while the warmer months invite long hikes, sunbathing and swimming, canoeing and cycling under the midnight sun – you name it, if it's fun and can be done outdoors, you'll find it here. For less rugged types, there's always restaurant and nightclub hopping and museum perusing in cosmopolitan Stockholm, lively Göteborg and beyond.

CAPITAL
Stockholm

POPULATION
9.6 million

AREA
450,295 sq km

OFFICIAL LANGUAGE
Swedish

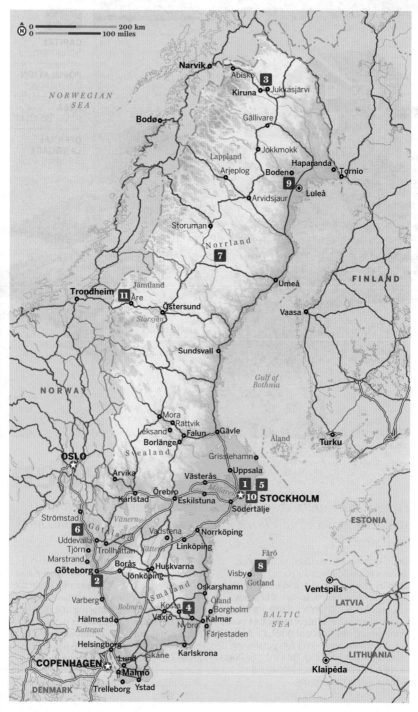

N
0   200 km
0   100 miles

NORWEGIAN SEA

Narvik
Abisko
3
Kiruna   Jukkasjärvi

Bodø
Gällivare

Jokkmokk
Lappland
Arjeplog
Haparanda
Boden   Tornio
9
Luleå

Arvidsjaur

Storuman
Norrland
7

Jämtland
Trondheim
11
Åre
Östersund
Umeå
FINLAND

Storsjön
Vaasa

Sundsvall

Gulf of Bothnia

NORWAY

Mora
Rättvik
Leksand   Falun
Borlänge
Gävle
Åland
Turku
Swealand

Arvika
Grisslehamn
Västerås   Uppsala
Mälaren
Karlstad   Örebro   **1**   **5**
Eskilstuna   **10**   **STOCKHOLM**
Strömstad   Södertälje
ESTONIA
6
Vadstena   Norrköping
Uddevalla
Tjörn   Trollhättan
Linköping
Färö
Marstrand   Borås
Huskvarna
Visby   **8**
Göteborg
2   Jönköping
Gotland
Varberg
Oskarshamn
Ventspils
Småland
Bolmen
Öland
LATVIA
Kosta   Borgholm
Halmstad   **4**
Växjö   Kalmar
BALTIC SEA
Kattegat
Nybro
Helsingborg
Färjestaden
Lund   *Skåne*
Karlskrona
COPENHAGEN
LITHUANIA
Malmö
Klaipėda
DENMARK
Trelleborg   Ystad

Sweden's
Top Experiences

Stockholm

1 The nation's capital city calls itself 'beauty on water', and it certainly doesn't disappoint in the looks department. Stockholm's many glittering waterways reflect slanted northern light onto spice-hued buildings, and the crooked cobblestone streets of Gamla Stan are magic to wander through. Besides its aesthetic virtues, Stockholm also has top-notch museums, first-class dining and all the shopping anyone could ask for. Its clean and efficient public transport and multilingual locals make the city a cinch to navigate, and at the end of the day you can collapse in a cushy designer hotel.

Göteborg

2 Göteborg is a city of contrasts, with slick museums, raw industrial landscapes, pleasant parks, can-do designers and cutting-edge food. Try delectable shrimp and fish – straight off the boat or at one of the city's five Michelin-rated restaurants. There's the thrill-packed chaos of Sweden's largest theme park, the cultured quiet of its many museums, and you can't leave without window-shopping in Haga and Linné. For a unique way of getting there, jump on a boat and navigate the 190km-length of the Göta Canal.

Gamla Stan, Stockholm

DESEO / GETTY IMAGES ©

Northern Delights

3 The twin phenomena that have made the north of Sweden so famous are both found beyond the Arctic Circle. No other natural spectacle compares to the aurora borealis – the shape-shifting lights that dance across the night sky during the Arctic winter (October to March). The Icehotel, humble igloo turned ice palace, takes its inspiration from the changeable nature of the northern lights, and is re-created in a slightly different form every winter.

SWEDEN

Kingdom of Crystal

4 In the Glasriket (Kingdom of Crystal) a rich mix of skill and brawn combine to produce stunning (and often practical) works of art. Watch local glass-blowers spin bubbles of molten crystal into fantastic creatures, bowls, vases and sculptures. Choose something for the mantelpiece or try blowing for yourself at the well-stocked centres in Kosta and Orrefors. For history on the 500-year-old industry there's Småland Museums in Växjo, and for the ultimate finish enjoy a cocktail at Kjell Engman's bar at the Kosta Boda Art Hotel.

if Sweden were 100 people

89 would be Swedish
3 would be Finn & Sami (Lapp)
1 would be Yugoslav
1 would be Iranian
6 would be other

belief systems
(% of population)

87 Lutheran
13 other

population per sq km

SWEDEN NORWAY UK

🚶 ≈ 8 people

Stockholm Archipelago

5 Scattered between the city and the open Baltic Sea, this archipelago is a mesmerising wonderland of small rocky isles, some no more than seagull launch-pads, others studded with deep forests and fields of wildflowers. All are within easy striking distance of the city, with regular ferry services and a number of organised tours for easy island-hopping. Hostels, camping grounds and more upmarket slumber options make overnighting a good option, as does the growing number of excellent restaurants.

Bohuslän Coast

6 Caught between sky and sea, the coast of Bohuslän is raw and starkly beautiful, its skerries thick with birds and its villages brightly painted specks among the rocks. Choose from myriad quaint seaside bolt-holes. Film star Ingrid Bergman loved pretty Fjällbacka, the bargain-hunting Norwegians flock to Strömstad, and every sailor knows Tjörn is the place to be in August for the round-island regatta. For a real taste of Swedish summer, spread your beach blanket on a smooth rock and tuck into a bag of peel-and-eat shrimp.

Inlandsbanan

7 Take a journey through the middle of Norrland along this historic train line (summer only), which passes by small mining towns, deep green forests, herds of reindeer and, if you're lucky, the occasional moose along the way. Built during the 1930s and rendered obsolete by 1992, the line has more than enough charm and historical appeal to make up for its lack of speed – you'll have plenty of time to contemplate the

Astrid Lindgren

Astrid Lindgren (1907–2002), one of Sweden's most famous and beloved authors, is best known for her fictional rebel, the infamous Pippi Longstocking. In a postwar world of silenced children and rigid gender roles, Pippi was bold, subversive and deliciously empowering. She didn't care for beauty creams, she was financially independent and she could even outlift the strongest man in the world, Mighty Adolf.

The character herself first found life in 1941 when Lindgren's pneumonia-struck daughter, Karin, asked her mother for a story about 'Pippi Longstocking'. The curious name inspired Lindgren to spin a stream of tales about the original wild child, which became an instant hit with Karin and her friends.

While recovering from a sprained ankle in 1944, Lindgren finally put her tales to paper and sent them to a publisher. Rejected but undefeated, she sent a second story to another publisher and scooped second prize in a girls' story competition. The following year, a revamped Pippi manuscript grabbed top honours in another competition, while her story Bill Bergson Master Detective shared first prize in 1946.

Food & Drink

Köttbullar och potatis Meatballs and mashed potatoes, served with *lingonsylt* (lingonberry jam).

Gravlax Cured salmon.

Sill & strömming Herring, eaten smoked, fried or pickled and often accompanied by capers, mustard and onion.

Toast skagen Toast with bleak roe, crème fraiche and chopped red onion.

Brännvin Sweden's trademark spirit, also called aquavit and drunk as *snaps* (vodka).

Fårö

landscape of central Norrland, in other words. It's a beautiful, oddball means of transport, best suited to those for whom adventure trumps efficiency.

Gotland & Fårö

8 Merchants in the 12th and 13th centuries dotted the beautiful island of Gotland with fabulous churches. Today, Gotland's lovely ruins, remote beaches, idyllic bike- and horse-riding paths, peculiar rock formations, excellent restaurants and rousing summer nightlife attract visitors from all over the world. The event of the season is Medieval Week, which brings Visby's old town alive with costumes, re-enactments and markets. Film buffs and nature lovers will want to head north to visit Ingmar Bergman's stomping ground of Fårö.

Gammelstad

9 Sweden is home to an abundance of Unesco World Heritage–recognised treasures. Whether you're keen on untamed nature or humankind's mark upon it,

When to Go

HIGH SEASON (mid-Jun–Aug)

➡ Season starts at Midsummer; expect warm weather and most sights and accommodation to be open.

➡ Some restaurants and shops close in August as Swedes take their own holidays.

SHOULDER (Sep–Oct)

➡ Weather is still good, even if there's no one around to enjoy it.

➡ Many tourist spots are closed, but you'll have the rest all to yourself.

➡ Hotel rates return to normal but drop at weekends.

LOW SEASON (Dec–Mar)

➡ Highlights include outdoor adventures, the northern lights and holiday markets.

➡ Book accommodation and winter activities in advance.

➡ Many campsites and hostels close for the winter.

you'll find plenty to explore here. A fine example is Gammelstad church town near Luleå – the largest in Sweden, and the medieval centre of northern Sweden. Features of the town include the stone Nederluleå church (built in 1492), which has a reredos worthy of a cathedral and choir stalls for a whole consistory, and the 424 wooden houses where the rural pioneers stayed overnight on their weekend pilgrimages.

Vasamuseet

10 Sweden is filled with great museums, but Vasamuseet in Stockholm

is unique: a purpose-built preservation and display case for an ancient sunken battleship. The ship was the pride of the Swedish Crown when it set out in August 1628, but pride quickly turned to embarrassment when the top-heavy ship tipped and sank to the bottom of Saltsjön, where it would wait 300 years for rescue. The museum explains – in fascinating multimedia – how it was found, retrieved and restored, why it sank in the first place, and what it all means to the Swedish people.

Getting Around

Air Flying domestic is expensive on full-price tickets, but substantial discounts are available with internet booking or various concession fares.

Bus You can travel by bus on any of the 24 good-value and extensive regional bus networks or on national long-distance routes.

Car Sweden has good roads and the excellent E-class motorways rarely have traffic jams.

Train Sweden has an extensive and reliable railway network, and trains are much faster than buses. Many destinations in the northern half of the country, however, cannot be reached by train alone.

Winter Sports in Åre

11 Winter sports in Lapland are a major draw. To go cross-country skiing, just grab a pair of skis and step outside; for downhill sports, be it heliskiing or snowboarding, Åre is your best bet. Few pastimes are as enjoyable as rushing across the Arctic wasteland pulled by a team of dogs, the sled crunching through crisp snow – but if you want something with a motor, you can test your driving (and racing) skills on the frozen lakes instead.

Best on Film

Let the Right One In (2008) An excellent, stylish, restrained take on the horror-film genre that gets at what it's like to be a lonely preteen in a cold, hostile world.

Lilya 4-Ever (2002) A grim tale of human trafficking.

Songs from the Second Floor (2000) Roy Andersson's bleak meditation on modern humanity.

The Seventh Seal (1957) Ingmar Bergman pits man against Death in a cosmic chess game.

Best in Print

Evil (Jan Guillou; 1981) Semi-autobiographical tale of violence at a boys' boarding school.

Faceless Killers (Henning Mankell; 1997) Henning Mankell's detective series, with Kurt Wallander, starts here.

The Girl with the Dragon Tattoo (Stieg Larsson; 2008) The Millennium Trilogy has been a global phenomenon.

The Emigrants (Vilhem Moberg; 1949) Swedish emigrants in the nineteenth century.

Vasamuseet, Stockholm

ANDERS BLOMQVIST / GETTY IMAGES ©

Guarda, Graubünden

CAPITAL
Bern

POPULATION
8 million

AREA
41,277 sq km

OFFICIAL LANGUAGES
German, French, Italian & Romansch

Switzerland

Look past the silk-smooth chocolate, cuckoo clocks and yodelling – contemporary Switzerland, land of four languages, is all about epic journeys and sublime experiences.

This country begs outdoor escapades with its larger-than-life canvas of hallucinatory landscapes, so grab your boots, leap on board, toot the bike bell and let your spirits rip. Skiing and snowboarding in the winter wonderlands of Graubünden, Bernese Oberland and Central Switzerland are obvious choices. Hiking and biking trails abound in both glacier-encrusted mountain areas and lower down along lost valleys, mythical lakeshores and pea-green vines. Travels are mapped by mountain villages with timber storage barns and chalet farmsteads brightened with red.

The perfect antidote is a surprise set of cities: the capital Bern with its medieval Old Town and world-class modern art, deeply Germanic Basel and its bold architecture, shopping-chic Geneva astraddle Europe's largest lake, tycoon-magnet Zug (play millionaire over a slice of liqueur-soaked cherry cake) and uber-cool Zürich with its rooftop bars and atypical Swiss street grit.

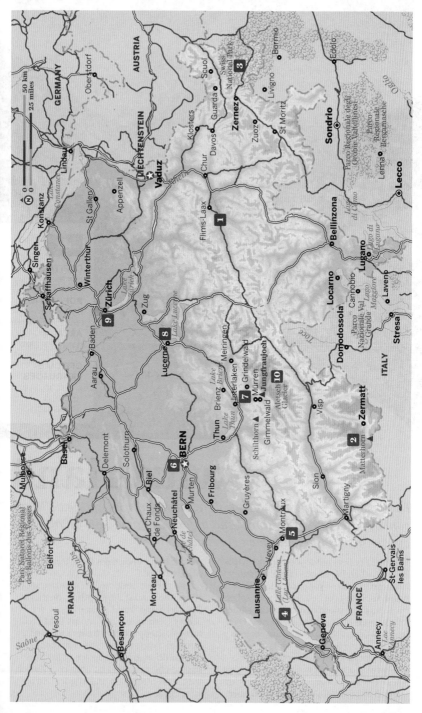

Switzerland's
Top Experiences

The Glacier Express

1 It's one of the world's most famous train rides, linking two of Switzerland's glitziest Alpine resorts. Hop aboard the iconic red train with floor-to-ceiling windows in Zermatt, sit back, and savour shot after cinematic shot of green peaks, glistening Alpine lakes, glacial ravines and other hallucinatory natural landscapes. Pulled by steam engine when it first puffed out of the station in 1930, the Glacier Express traverses 91 tunnels and 291 bridges on its famous journey to St Moritz. The icing on the cake: lunch in the vintage restaurant car.

Matterhorn

2 No mountain has more pulling power, more natural magnetism than this charismatic peak – a precocious beauty from birth who demands to be admired, ogled and repeatedly photographed at sunset, sunrise, in different seasons and from every last infuriating angle. And there is no finer place to pander to Matterhorn's every last topographic need than Zermatt, one of Europe's most highly desirable Alpine resorts, in fashion with the skiing, climbing, hiking and hip hobnobbing set since the 19th century. Darling, you'll love it.

IRIS KUERSCHNER / GETTY IMAGES ©

Hiking in the Swiss National Park

3 No country in Europe is more synonymous with magnificent and mighty hiking than Switzerland, and its high-altitude national park with eagle-dotted skies is the place to do it. Follow trails through flower-strewn meadows to piercing blue lakes, knife-edge ravines, rocky outcrops and Alpine huts where shepherds make summertime cheese with cows' milk, fresh that morning from the bell-clad herd. Nature gone wild and on the rampage, this is a rare and privileged glimpse of Switzerland before the dawn of tourism.

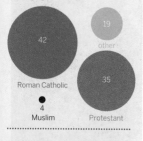

if Switzerland was 100 people

64 would speak German
20 would speak French
8 would speak another language
7 would speak Italian
1 would speak Romansch

belief systems
(% of population)

42 Roman Catholic
19 other
35 Protestant
4 Muslim

population per sq km

SWITZERLAND   USA   UK

⋔ ≈ 32 people

Europe's Largest Lake

4 The emerald vines marching uphill in perfect unison from the shores of Lake Geneva in Lavaux are staggering. But the urban viewpoint from which to admire Europe's largest lake is Geneva, French-speaking Switzerland's most cosmopolitan city where canary-yellow *mouettes* (seagulls) ferry locals across the water and Mont Blanc peeps in on the action. Strolling Old Town streets, savouring a vibrant cafe society and making the odd dash beneath its iconic pencil fountain is what life's about for the 180 nationalities living here.

Romance in Montreux

5 As if one of the world's most mythical jazz festivals with open-air concerts on the shore of Lake Geneva is not enough, Montreux has a castle to add to the French-style romance. From the lakeside town, a flower-framed footpath follows the water south to Château de Chillon. Historic, sumptuous and among Switzerland's oldest, this magnificent stone château built by the Savoys in the 13th century is everything a castle should be.

Capital Bern

6 Medieval cobbled streets, arcaded boutiques, a dancing clock and folk figures prettily frolicking in fountains since the 16th century: Switzerland's capital city, Bern, just does not fit in with the quintessential 'capital city' image at all. Indeed, few even realise this small town is even the capital, situated in the flat, unassuming, middle bit of the country (hence the

Cow Fighting

It might sound like a load of bull, but cow fights known as the *Combats de Reines* (*Kuhkämpfe* in German) are serious stuff in Val d'Hérens, organised to decide which beast is most suited to lead the herd to summer pastures. These Moo-Hammad Ali wannabes charge, lock horns then try to force each other backwards. The winner, or herd's 'queen', can be worth Sfr20,000. Contests take place on selected Sundays from late March to May and from August to September. Combatants rarely get hurt so visitors shouldn't find the competition distressing. There is a grand final in Aproz (a 10-minute postal bus ride west of Sion) in May on Ascension Day, and the last meeting of the season is held at Martigny's Foire du Valais in early October.

Food & Drink

Fondue The main French contribution to the Swiss table, a pot of gooey melted cheese is placed in the centre of the table and kept on a slow burn while diners dip in cubes of crusty bread using slender two-pronged fondue forks. The classic fondue mix in Switzerland is equal amounts of Emmental and Gruyère cheese, grated and melted with white wine and a shot of kirsch (cherry-flavoured liquor).

Raclette A half-crescent slab of the cheese is screwed onto a specially designed 'rack oven' that melts the top flat side. As it melts, cheese is scraped onto plates for immediate consumption with boiled potatoes, cold meats and pickled onions or gherkins.

Rösti A shredded, oven-crisped potato bake, perhaps topped with a fried egg.

Zuger Kirschtorte Cherry cake made from pastry, biscuit, almond paste and butter cream, all infused with cherry liqueur.

HANS GEORG EIBEN / GETTY IMAGES ©

Zytglogge (clock tower), Bern

region's name, Mittelland). Yet its very unexpectedness, cemented by the new millennium hills of Renzo Piano's Zentrum Paul Klee, is precisely its charm.

Epic Outdoors

7 No trio is more immortalised in mountaineering legend than Switzerland's 'big three' – Eiger (Ogre), Mönch (Monk) and Jungfrau (Virgin) – peaks that soar to the sky above the traditional 19th-century resort of gorgeous old Grindelwald. And whether you choose to schuss around on skis, shoot down Europe's longest toboggan run on the back of an old-fashioned sledge, bungee-jump in the Gletscherschlucht or ride the train up to Europe's highest station at 3454m, your heart will thump. James Bond, eat your heart out.

Lakeside Lucerne

8 Strolling across medieval bridges is the charm of this irresistible Romeo in Central Switzerland. Throw sparkling lake vistas, an alfresco cafe life,

When to Go

HIGH SEASON (Jul–Aug, Dec–Apr)	**SHOULDER** (Apr–Jun & Sep)	**LOW SEASON** (Oct–Mar)
➡ In July and August walkers and cyclists hit high-altitude trails.	➡ Look for accommodation deals in ski resorts.	➡ Mountain resorts go into snooze mode.
➡ Christmas and New Year see lots of activity on the slopes.	➡ Spring is idyllic with warm temperatures, flowers and local produce.	➡ Prices are up to 50% less than in high season.
➡ Late December to early April is high season in ski resorts.	➡ Watch the grape harvest in autumn.	➡ Sights and restaurants are open fewer days and shorter hours.

candy-coloured architecture and Victorian curiosities into the cooking pot and, yes, lakeside Lucerne could well be the start of a very beautiful love affair. With the town under your belt, step back to savour the ensemble from a wider perspective: views across the lake of green hillsides, meadows and hidden lake resorts from atop Mt Pilatus, Mt Rigi or Stanserhorn will not disappoint.

Zürich Lifestyle

9 One of Europe's most liveable cities, Zürich is an ode to urban renovation. It's also hip (this is where Google employees shoot down a slide to lunch). With

Best on Film

Breathless (1960) New wave classic by Swiss avant-garde filmmaker Jean-Luc Godard.

Home (2008) By a motorway, by Geneva director Ursula Meier.

Journey of Hope (1991) Oscar-winning tale of a Kurdish family seeking a better life in Switzerland.

The Kite Runner (2007) Film adaption of Khaled Hosseini's novel by Oscar-winning Swiss-German director Marc Forster.

The Pledge (2001) Love-it-or-loathe-it adaption of Friedrich Dürrenmatt's *Das Versprechen*.

Best in Print

Swiss Watching (Diccon Bewes) Amusing, astute portrait of the land of milk and money.

The Alpine Set in Switzerland (Lindsay Greatwood) Anecdotes of Charlie Chaplin, Graham Greene and other celebs living in swanky Switzerland.

The Swiss Cookbook (Betty Bossi) Culinary culture by canton/region.

Getting Around

Switzerland's fully integrated public transport system is among the world's most efficient. However, travel within Switzerland is expensive and visitors planning to use public transport on inter-city routes should consider investing in a Swiss travel pass.

Boat All the larger lakes are serviced by steamers operated by Swiss Federal Railways (SBB/CFF/FFS), or allied private companies for which national travel passes are valid.

Bus Yellow Post Buses supplement the rail network, following postal routes and linking towns to the less accessible mountain regions.

Train All major train stations are connected to each other by hourly departures, at least between 6am and midnight, and most long-distance trains have a dining car.

enough of a rough edge to resemble Berlin at times, Zürich means drinking in waterfront bars, dancing until dawn, shopping for recycled fashion accessories and boogying with the best of them at Europe's largest street party, the city's wild and wacky August Street Parade.

Aletsch Glacier

10 One of the world's natural marvels, this mesmerising glacier of gargantuan proportions in the Upper Valais is tantamount to a 23km long, five-lane highway powering between mountain peaks at altitude. Its ice is glacial-blue and 900m thick at its deepest point. The view of Aletsch from Jungfraujoch will make your heart sing, but for the hardcore adrenalin surge nothing beats getting up close: hike between crevasses with a mountain guide from Riederalp, or ski above it on snowy pistes in Bettmeralp.

TRAVELSTOCK44 / LOOK-FOTO / GETTY IMAGES ©

Crac des Chevaliers before it sustained damage

CAPITAL
Damascus

POPULATION
22.5 million

AREA
185,180 sq km

OFFICIAL LANGUAGE
Arabic

Syria

Due to a civil war that has dominated the news headlines and traumatised a nation, Syria has been off-limits for several years. But travellers to this gateway to the Middle East remember a time when Syria was famed for its culture and hospitality.

At the time of writing, you can't go: if you can, you shouldn't. Peaceful protests against the Assad regime that began in early 2011 have evolved into a chaotic and multi-faceted civil war spanning much of the country. There's violent conflict around Aleppo in the rebel-held north, Homs in central Syria and also around Damascus in the government stronghold of the south. Although organisations such as the UN and the Arab League have attempted to broker peace, events remain unpredictable.

As a result, how long this will continue is impossible to guess. When it ends, the wealth of historic sites, from Palmyra in the desert to the crusader castles like Crac des Chevaliers, within sight of the Mediterranean, will lure us back and the gracious hospitality of Syrians will warm us to their country.

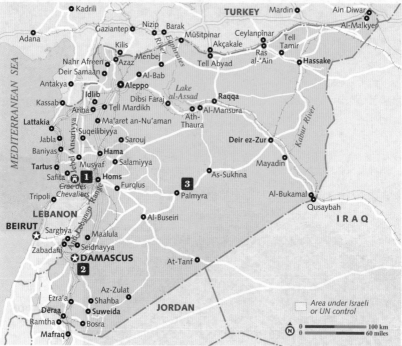

Syria's
Top Experiences

Crac des Chevaliers

1 Added to Unesco's World Heritage list in 2006, this crusader castle comprises two distinct parts: the outside wall with its 13 towers and main entrance; and the inside wall and central construction, built on a rocky platform. A moat dug out of the rock separates the two walls. The castle has been damaged by bombing during the civil war.

Damascus

2 Legend has it that on a journey from Mecca, the Prophet Mohammed cast his gaze upon Damascus but refused to enter the city because he wanted to enter paradise only once – when he died. In this city of legend, which vies for the title of the world's oldest continually inhabited city. Damascus is a place of storytellers and of souqs, home to an Old City whose architecture traces millennia of history.

Palmyra

3 The rose-gold ancient ruins of Palmyra are one of the premier ancient sites in the Middle East. Rising out of the desert of central Syria and flanked by an expansive oasis, Palmyra was once a stop on trading routes, long before the arrival of Romans in Syria. It flourished under the control of the Roman Empire in the first century AD. Today, its sunsets are as beautiful as ever.

Food & Drink

Tabbouleh and fattoush Two of the most well-known Syrian salads. Both use mint, lemon juice and olive oil for flavour, and contain cucumber and tomato.

Shay na'ana Mint tea, the essential complement to Syrian hospitality.

When to Go

MAR–APR

➡ Spring along the coast and then in the hills, which are carpeted with flowers.

JUN–JUL

➡ Scorching in the desert but magical on the Mediterranean.

SEP–OCT

➡ Autumn brings rich light and lower temperatures. Perfect.

Snorkelling in the waters of Manihi

CAPITAL	Pape'ete
POPULATION	277,293
AREA	4167 sq km
OFFICIAL LANGUAGES	French, Reo Maohi (Tahitian)

Tahiti & the French Polynesia

Sculpted by sky-piercing, moss-green peaks and lined with vivid turquoise lagoons, sultry French Polynesia is a place to take it slow and experience warm, laid-back island chic.

Just the name Tahiti conjures up centuries of legend and lifetimes of daydreams. Its 18th-century reputation as a wanton playground of flower-bedecked Polynesians in an Eden-like setting has morphed into a 21st-century image of a chic honeymoon haven. But there's more to the country than cocktails on the terrace of your over-water bungalow.

When you're not idling in the scent of gardenias, letting your cares drift away, try hiking up a waterfall valley, paddling out on a turquoise lagoon or diving through

sharky passes. While the resorts make headlines, the country's unsung heroes are the impressive collection of family pensions that range from rickety rooms in someone's home to luxurious boutique-style bungalows on private islets.

From the vast lagoons of the Tuamotu atolls, to the culturally intense Marquesas Islands and the scenic mountainscapes of the Society Islands (Tahiti, Mo'orea, Ra'iatea, Taha'a, Bora Bora and Maupiti), French Polynesia's 118 islands provide enough diversity and surprises for several voyages.

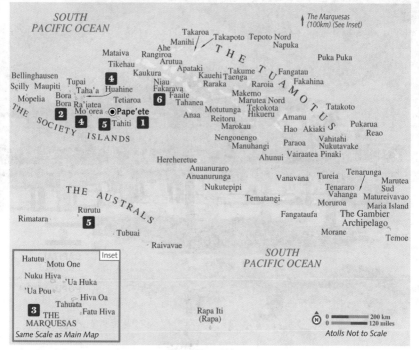

Tahiti & the French Polynesia's
Top Experiences

Polynesian Culture

1 Gentle, unpretentiously sophisticated yet fiery, the Polynesian culture is as seductive as it is soothing. Sit back with a cold Hinano under a warm dome of stars to enjoy ukulele riffs or perhaps just the sound of the surf – free days are best spent picnicking on fish and taro by the water. During the annual Heiva festival the country goes full tilt: the best dancers wear little more than palm fronds and have warp-speed wiggling hips; outrigger-canoe racing ignites the lagoons; and traditional sports such as coconut husking go pro. Held at various venues in and near Pape'ete, Heiva lasts about four weeks from late June to late July and is so impressive that it's almost worth timing your trip around it.

Bora Bora

2 As the plane begins to descend, a magical scene comes into view: a perfect Morse-code ring of *motu* (small islets), generously mop-topped with palms, separating the indigo of the ocean from the crisp palette of lagoon blues. Bora Bora is a hot favourite for honeymooners – but we feel certain you didn't come all this way merely to crack open a bottle of champagne. Hiking, diving, snorkelling and other adventure options are all readily available.

The Marquesas

3 Whether you believe in legends or not, this archipelago looks like something from the pages of a fairy tale. Think snaggle-toothed volcanic peaks, deep ravines, majestic waterfalls, secretive bays, and forests that could hold their own in a BBC documentary. The Marquesas also offer plenty of sites dating from pre-European times. Hiking, horse riding and diving will keep you busy. If you're short on time, book a cruise aboard the *Aranui*, a cargo boat and passenger vessel that serves the six inhabited islands of the archipelago.

Tahitian dancing

Marae

4 Marae are impressive religious sites built from basalt blocks placed side by side and piled up. In pre-European times, they represented the equivalent of temples, and were places of worship, burial and human sacrifice. The most important marae in French Polynesia is Marae Taputapuatea on Ra'iatea, which has been extensively restored. Huahine and Mo'orea also have a slew of well-maintained marae. These archaeological sites are shrouded with a palpable aura and make for mind-boggling open-air museums.

Whale-watching

5 You put your snorkel gear on, slip into the water and when the bubbles clear and your eyes adjust, before you is a truly massive creature: a humpback whale. French Polynesia is an important breeding ground for humpback whales, which migrate to Polynesian waters between July and October. It's one of the best places in the world to see these magnificent creatures. They

if French Polynesia were 100 people

👤👤👤👤👤👤👤👤👤👤👤👤👤👤👤👤👤👤👤👤
👤👤👤👤👤👤👤👤👤👤👤👤👤👤👤👤👤👤👤👤
👤👤👤👤👤👤👤👤👤👤👤👤👤👤👤👤👤👤👤👤
👤👤👤👤👤👤👤👤👤👤👤👤👤👤👤👤👤👤👤👤
👤👤👤👤👤👤👤👤👤👤👤👤👤👤👤👤👤👤👤👤

78 would be Polynesian
12 would be Chinese
6 would be local French
4 would be metropolitan French

belief systems
(% of population)

54 — Protestant
30 — Roman Catholic
10 — other
6 — none

population per sq km

FRENCH POLYNESIA | USA | FRANCE

👤 = 30 people

When to Go

HIGH SEASON
(Jun–Aug, Dec & Jan)

➡ June to August usually the coolest and driest months.

➡ December and January plenty of sun and cooling showers.

➡ Europeans, Americans and locals on holiday; book early.

SHOULDER
(Feb, May & Sep)

➡ February is one of the hottest months, May and September are mild.

➡ Prices same as low season.

➡ Flights and accommodation can be hard to find; book in advance.

LOW SEASON
(Mar, Apr, Oct & Nov)

➡ March and April are hot and rainy.

➡ Pleasant in October and November.

➡ Watch for frequent school holidays when interisland flights can be hard to book.

Cinematic Mutiny

The story of the famous uprising aboard the *Bounty* has been embellished by big-budget filmmakers three times in 50 years. If another version is ever made, audiences could be forgiven for having a mutiny of their own.

In 1935, *Mutiny on the Bounty* starred Charles Laughton as Captain Bligh and Clark Gable as Fletcher Christian. Very little of this film was shot on Tahiti.

With the same title, Lewis Milestone's 1962 version offered Trevor Howard as Bligh and Marlon Brando as Christian and was filmed on Tahiti and Bora Bora.

Finally, shot mostly on Mo'orea, *The Bounty*, released in 1984, starred Anthony Hopkins as Bligh and Mel Gibson as the more-handsome-than-ever Christian.

Food & Drink

Beer Wash everything down with a cold Hinano.

Chow mein This fried noodle dish is one of numerous Chinese specialities available.

Cocktails Try mai tai, made with rum, fruit juices and coconut liqueur.

Fish Features prominently in Tahitian cuisine. *Poisson cru* (raw fish in coconut milk) is the most popular local dish. It can also be served grilled, fried or poached. It's usually tuna, bonito, wahoo, mahi mahi, parrotfish or jackfish.

Ma'a Tahiti Traditional Tahitian food. It's a mix of starchy taro and *uru* (breadfruit), raw or cooked fish, fatty pork, coconut milk and a few scattered vegetables.

Po'e Baked, mashed fruit mixed with starch and doused with coconut milk.

Steaks Lamb and beef from New Zealand!

Wine Good French wines and one local wine, Vin de Tahiti.

Blacktip reef shark and diver, Mo'orea

can be observed caring for new calves and engaging in elaborate mating rituals. The best areas to spot them are Mo'orea, Tahiti and Rurutu, where operators organise whale-watching trips.

Diving & Snorkelling

6 French Polynesia is one of the richest realms in the South Pacific. Its warm, tropical waters hold some of the greatest varieties of sea life found in the region. Dream of encountering the beasts? You can mingle with grey reef sharks, manta rays, bottlenose dolphins and hammerhead sharks. Prefer smaller, technicolour critters? You'll spot loads of reef species, including stingrays, snappers and jacks. The lagoons also cater to avid snorkellers, with gin-clear waters and a smattering of healthy coral gardens around. For a true sense of wilderness and frontier diving, head to Fakarava, one of the most fascinating atolls in the Tuamotus.

Getting Around

Air Air Tahiti flies to 47 islands in all five of the major island groups, but flight frequencies ebb and flow with the seasons.

Bicycle This is an ideal region to explore by bike. Distances are manageable, the coast roads are generally flat, traffic is light (outside Pape'ete) and bikes are accepted on all the interisland ferries.

Boat Ferry travel isn't as easy as you'd hope. A number of companies shuttle back and forth between Tahiti and Mo'orea each day; other routes between the islands are less frequent. In the other archipelagos travel by boat is more difficult.

Bus There is not much of a public transportation system; Tahiti is the only island where public transport is an option. The old *le trucks* have now been almost entirely replaced by a more modern fleet of air-con buses.

STEPHEN FRINK / GETTY IMAGES ©

Chinese night market, Taipei

CAPITAL
Taipei

POPULATION
23.3 million

AREA
35,980 sq km

**OFFICIAL
LANGUAGES**
Mandarin
Taiwanese

Taiwan

*With its all-round adventure landscape, heritage-rich capital,
diverse folk traditions and feted night market scene, Taiwan
offers a continent-sized travel list for one green island.*

Famed for centuries as Ilha Formosa (Beautiful Isle), in Taiwan you can criss-cross mountains on colonial-era hiking trails, cycle a lone highway with the blue Pacific on one side and green volcanic arcs on the other or climb to the summit of Yushan, Taiwan's 3952m alpine roof.

To fuel all of this adventure, Taiwan offers the gamut of Chinese cuisines, as well as the best Japanese outside Tokyo, and a full-house of local specialities from Hakka stir-fries and Taipei beef noodles to aboriginal-style barbecued wild boar.

Taiwan will feed your soul, too: the island is heir to the entire Chinese tradition of Buddhism, Taoism, Confucianism and that amorphous collection of deities and demons worshipped as folk faith. But over the centuries the people have blended their way to a unique and tolerant religious culture. In doing so, the Taiwanese have created Asia's most vibrant democracy, and liberal society, with a raucous free press, gender equality and respect for human rights and increasingly animal rights as well.

Taiwan's
Top Experiences

Hiking the High Mountains

1 Don't forget your boots because two-thirds of Taiwan's terrain is mountainous – and what mountains they are. Hundreds soar above 3000m, and well-established hiking routes run everywhere. These are the real deal (no shops, no restaurants) and on remote trails you might find yourself alone for several days. Everyone wants to tackle Yushan, the highest peak in Northeast Asia, and the second highest, Snow Mountain, is a more scenic climb and leads to O'Holy Ridge, a five-day walk on an exposed ridgeline that never drops below 3000m.

Taroko Gorge

2 Taiwan's top tourist draw is a walk-in Chinese painting. Rising above the froth of the blue-green Liwu River, the marble walls (yes, marble!) of Taroko Gorge swirl with the colours of a master's palette. Add grey mist, lush vegetation and waterfalls seemingly tumbling down from heaven, and you truly have a classic landscape. Walk along the Swallow Grotto to see the gorge at its most sublime or brave the Jhuilu Old Trail, a vertigo-inducing path 500m above the canyon floor.

National Palace Museum

3 By a pure accident of history, Taiwan houses the greatest collection of Chinese art in the world. With ancient pottery, bronzes and jade, Ming vases, Song landscape paintings and calligraphy even a foreign eye can appreciate, Taipei's National Palace Museum isn't merely a must-visit, it's a must-repeat-visit. Why? Out of the nearly 700,000 pieces in the museum's collection – pieces spanning every Chinese dynasty – only a tiny fraction is ever on display at the one time.

Cycling the East Coast

4 Cycling fever has taken over the island, and the unspoiled and sparsely populated east coast has emerged as the top destina-

Temple and waterfall, Silver Stream Cave

tion for multiday trips. Like the sea? Then ride Highway 11, with its stunning coastline, beaches, fishing harbours and funky art villages. Love the mountains? Try the Rift Valley, bounded on each side by lush green ranges. On both routes there are enough roadside cafes, campgrounds, homestays and hot springs to ensure your cycling trip won't be an exercise in logistics.

Temple Treasures

5 There are 15,000 official temples in Taiwan, three times the number of 30 years ago. Still the focus of local culture, temples play the role of community centres as much as houses of worship. Both Tainan and Lukang boast a wealth of old buildings, from understated Confucius temples to Matsu temples rich in examples of southern folk decorative arts. But if you can only visit one temple in Taiwan, head to Bao'an Temple in Taipei, a showcase of traditional design, rites and festivities.

if Taiwan were 100 people

84 would be Taiwanese & Hakka
14 would be mainland Chinese
2 would be indigenous

belief systems
(% of population)

31	24	15
folk religions	Buddhist	Taoist

3	2	25
Protestant	I-Kuan Taoist	other or not religious

population per sq km

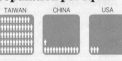

| TAIWAN | CHINA | USA |

🚶 ≈ 11 people

When to Go

HIGH SEASON
(Jul & Aug)

➜ Accommodation costs increase 30% to 50% in tourist areas.

➜ Saturday nights (year-round) and Chinese New Year also see increases.

SHOULDER
(Sep, Oct & Apr–Jun)

➜ Good discounts on hotels midweek.

➜ Crowds at major sights on weekends.

➜ Best time to visit outer islands.

➜ Peak time for Chinese tour groups from March to May.

LOW SEASON
(Nov–Mar)

➜ Few crowds except during January and Chinese New Year.

➜ Best discounts on accommodation at major tourist sights (up to 50%).

➜ High season for hot spring hotels.

Divine Power of the Mother

New temples are almost always established as a branch (or daughter) of a larger and more famous mother temple. This involves a rather fascinating process called *fēnxiāng* (spirit division).

In this practice, representatives from the newly built temple go to the elder one to obtain incense ash or statues. By doing so they bring back a little of the *líng* (divine efficacy) of the original temple deity to their own humble house of worship.

Periodically representatives from the daughter temple must return to the mother to renew or add power to the *líng* of their statue. At the mother temple they once again scoop out incense ash to place in the incense burner of their own temple.

Food & Drink

Chòu dòufu (Stinky tofu) Classic Taiwanese snack.

Fó tiào qiáng ('Buddha Jumps Over the Wall') A stew of seafood, chicken, duck and pork simmered in a jar of rice wine. Allegedly the dish is so tasty that even the Buddha – a vegetarian, of course – would hop over a wall to get a taste.

Gāoliáng jiǔ (Kaoliang liquor) Made from fermented sorghum.

Kèjiā xiǎo chǎo Stir-fried cuttlefish with leeks, tofu and pork.

Kézǎi tāng Clear oyster soup with ginger.

Tiěbǎn shānzhūròu Fatty wild boar grilled, sliced, and grilled again with onions and wild greens.

Xiǎoyú huāshēng Fish stir-fry with peanuts and pickled vegetables.

Zhà shūcài bǐng Fried, salty balls made from local mushrooms and flour.

Lanterns, Pingxi

Hot Springs

6 Formed by the collision of two major tectonic plates, Taiwan's surface has plenty of fissures and an abundance of hot springs. The waters are considered effective for everything from soothing muscles to conceiving male offspring (we can only vouch for the former). Nature lovers heading to hot springs in Beitou and Taian will find them a double happiness: stone, wood and marble are in these days, as are mountain views. And if you're willing to walk in, many pristine wild springs still lie deep in the valleys, such as Lisong Hot Spring.

Lantern Festival

7 One of the oldest of the lunar events, the Lantern Festival celebrates the end of the New Year's festivities. The focus, of course, is light, and everywhere streets and riversides are lined with luminous glowing lanterns, while giant neon and laser displays fill public squares. Making the mundane surreal and the commonplace magical, the little mountain village of Pingxi takes simple paper lanterns and releases them en masse into the night sky. There are few sights more mesmerising.

Getting Around

Bus Routes connect most north, south and west coast towns, cities and major tourist sights. There are fewer routes on the east coast.

Car or Scooter Useful for touring at your own pace, staying at B&Bs, and exploring national parks and Taiwan's scenic backcountry. Rentals are widely available. Drive on the right.

Train Trains service the north and both coasts; High Speed Rail down the west serves the main cities. Four small tourism branch lines extend into the interior.

CAPITAL
Dushanbe

POPULATION
7.9 million

AREA
143,100 sq km

OFFICIAL LANGUAGE
Tajik

Tajikistan

Tajikistan's awesomely dramatic highland landscapes are testing playgrounds for hardy climbers, trekkers and adventure travellers.

Tajikistan is the only Central Asian republic to have so far suffered from civil war, and surrounded by Turkic-speaking 'stans', the only one where Persian is spoken. In a lofty mountain cul-de-sac at the furthest corner of the former Soviet domain, it still regards tourists as relative novelties. But this is not to say it doesn't have a great deal to offer.

Aside from bustling Silk Road towns and colourful bazaars, Tajikistan's main pull is the Pamir Mountains, a high-altitude plateau of intensely blue lakes, Kyrgyz yurts and roll-ing valleys that has impressed everyone from Marco Polo to Francis Younghusband.

The people are enormously hospitable but little English is spoken and transport is irregular. Tajikistan's tourism potential is further restricted by long winters and infuri-ating border closures. But the marvels of the Wakhan Valley, the starkly beautiful 'Roof of the World' Pamirs and the breathtaking lakes and pinnacles of the Fan Mountains all make Tajikistan arguably Central Asia's most exciting destination.

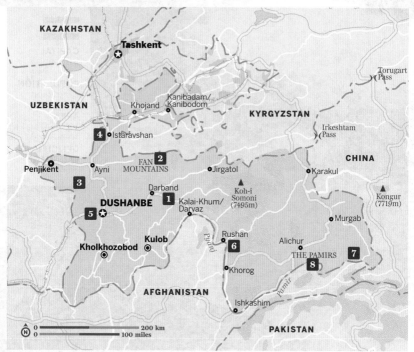

Tajikistan's
Top Experiences

Pamir Highway

1 The Pamir Highway is one of the world's great road trips, offering views of jaw-dropping high-altitude lakes and fine community-based homestays. The section from Khorog to Osh was built by Soviet military engineers between 1931 and 1934 to facilitate troops, transport and provisioning to one of the remotest outposts of the Soviet empire. Off-limits to travellers until recently, the extremely remote high-altitude road takes you through Tibetan-style high plateau scenery occasionally populated by yurts and yaks and studded with deep-blue lakes.

Fan Mountains

2 The austere but beautiful Fannsky Gory (Russian for Fan Mountains), studded with dozens of turquoise lakes and high mountain vistas, are one of Central Asia's most popular trekking and climbing destinations. They're easily accessible from Penjikent or Samarkand, and if you don't have time for a trek, a great way to get a taste of the Fans is to make a day or overnight trip from Penjikent to the Marguzor Lakes.

Iskander-Kul

3 Take in Iskander-Kul, a lovely lake on the slopes of the Fan Mountains and a great place to relax or go hiking. This gem at the southeastern end of the range is accessible to nontrekkers. The lakeside *turbaza* (Soviet-era holiday camp) is rundown but enjoys a lovely spot, with a great lakeside picnic area. Bring food and warm clothes as the lake is at an elevation of 2195m. You can enjoy great views of the main lake and smaller black Zmeinoe (Snake) Lake behind.

Istaravshan

4 Istaravshan has a small historical core that is one of the best preserved old towns in Tajikistan. Its gently intriguing maze of lanes hides a handful of mosques and madrasas, while its vast, colourful

Ayni Opera & Ballet Theatre, Dushanbe

central bazaar is a town unto itself. On a clear day, the views from Mug Teppe, the city's grassy, flat-topped former fortress hill, show off the city's mountain horizon to great advantage.

Dushanbe

5 With a cool backdrop of mountains, lazy tree-lined avenues and pastel-hued neoclassical buildings, Dushanbe is Central Asia's best-looking capital. The wide, tree-lined *prospekt* (avenue) Rudaki is the city's focus, with its neoclassical facades owing more to St Petersburg than inner Asia. A walk from north to south along Rudaki offers an excellent introduction to the city.

Jizeu Valley

6 The Jizeu (Jisev, Geisev) Valley offers idyllic scenes around a series of seasonally over-flowing, treelined riverlakes. The prettiest lakes are bracketed by two halves of the tiny traditional hamlet of Jizeu (pronounced Jee-sao) which has a wonderful, timeless feel. There's no road, and the access footpath starts with a remarkable 'cable car' – a wooden contraption that dangles on twin wires and is hand-wound to take up to four people across the gushing river.

Wakhan Valley

7 The remote and beautiful Wakhan Valley bordering Afghanistan offers

if Tajikistan were 100 people

80 would be Tajik
15 would be Uzbek
1 would be Russian
1 would be Kyrgyz
3 would be other

belief systems
(% of population)

85 — Sunni Muslim
5 — Shia Muslim
10 — other

When to Go

MID-JUN–SEP

➡ The cities sizzle, but this is the only viable time for high Pamir treks.

APR–MAY

➡ Mild in the lowlands; heavy showers cause landslides blocking mountain roads.

NOV–FEB

➡ Temperatures in the Pamirs drop to between -20°C and -45°C.

population per sq km

TAJIKISTAN   UZBEKISTAN   KYRGYSTAN

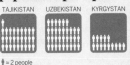

➡ ≈ 2 people

Pamiri Homes

From outside, a traditional *hune-uni chid* (Pamiri house) looks like a poor, low-slung, mud-stone box. Inside things look very different. Guests are received in the large, five-pillared room with raised areas around four sides. The most distinctive feature is the wooden ceiling built in four concentric squares, each rotated 45 degrees then topped with a skylight which provides most of the illumination. Each ceiling level represents one of the elements: earth, fire, air and water. Carpets line the walls and mattresses take the place of furniture. Amid panels of photographs, pride of place almost inevitably goes to a portrait of the Aga Khan.

HIMAGINE / GETTY IMAGES ©

Food & Drink

Beer Both Hissar and Dushanbe brew their own beer, though bottled Russian imports like the Baltika range are most common.

Borj A meat and grain mix that resembles savoury porridge.

Chakka Also known as yakka; curd mixed with herbs, typically served with flat bread.

Kurutob Tajikistan's contribution to vegetarian cuisine; a popular lunch dish made of fatir bread morsels layered with onion, tomato, parsley and coriander and doused in a yoghurt-based sauce.

Oshi siyo halav A unique herb soup.

Shir chai A popular breakfast drink in the Pamirs, shir chai is somewhere between milk tea and Tibetan butter tea.

Tuhum barak A tasty egg-filled ravioli coated with sesame-seed oil.

Silk Road forts, Buddhist ruins and towering valley walls that open regularly for glimpses of the spectacular snowbound Hindu Kush. The Tajik half of the remote Wakhan Valley, shared with Afghanistan, is a fantastic trip, either en route to Murgab or as a loop returning via the Gunt or Shokh Dara Valleys. The many side valleys reveal views of the 7000m peaks of the Hindu Kush, marking the border with Pakistan, and there's a thrill knowing that Marco Polo travelled here in 1274.

Yurtstays

8 In remote and desolately beautiful locations including the Gumbezkul Valley, Rang-kul and other places in the Pamirs, a homestay can give you an authentic feel for a way of life that has remained unchanged for countless years but which may not persist for much longer. In its simplicity, austerity and oneness with the landscape, domestic animals and the hardy residents of the mountains, it is an experience not to be missed.

Getting Around

Air Domestic flights are limited to Dushanbe–Khojand and the spectacular but notoriously unreliable Dushanbe–Khorog service.

Bus & Minibus The bus/minibus network is limited, though the new Asia Express bus company plans to expand.

Shared Taxi For now shared taxis are the only public transport between Dushanbe and Penjikent or Khojand, while shared 4WDs are the main link to Khorog and Murgab. Travellers commonly organise themselves into groups to rent chauffeured 4WD vehicles in the Pamirs or for chartering a whole shared taxi/vehicle so that they can stop more frequently en route.

Trekking Mt Kilimanjaro

Tanzania

Wildlife galore, idyllic beaches, snow-capped Kilimanjaro, moss-covered ruins, friendly people, fascinating cultures – Tanzania has all this and more wrapped up in one adventurous package.

Tanzania is *the* land of safaris, with wildebeest stampeding across the plains, hippos jostling for space in rivers, elephants kicking up the dust and chimpanzees swinging through the treetops. Wherever you go in the country, there are unparalleled opportunities to experience wildlife.

But it's not just the wildlife that enchants visitors. Tanzania's magical Indian Ocean coastline is also magical, with its tranquil islands, long beaches and sleepy villages steeped in centuries of Swahili culture. Coconut palms sway in the breeze, dhows glide by on the horizon, and colourful fish flit past spectacular corals in the turquoise waters.

More than anything, though, it is Tanzania's people that make a visit to the country so memorable, with their characteristic warmth and politeness, and the dignity and beauty of their cultures. Chances are you will want to come back for more, to which most Tanzanians would say *'karibu tena'* (welcome again).

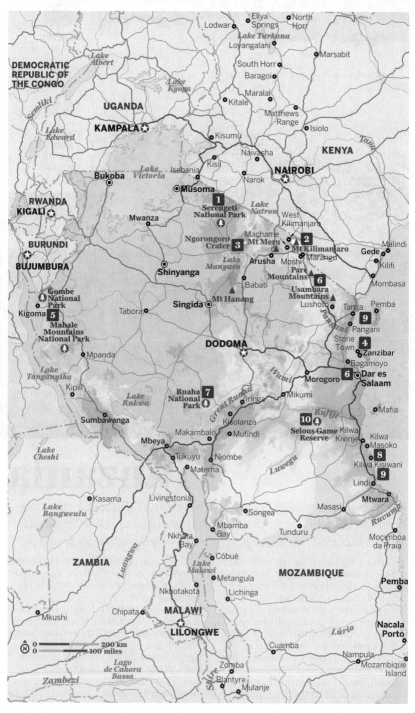

Tanzania's
Top Experiences

Serengeti National Park

1 The pounding hooves draw closer. Suddenly, thousands of wildebeest stampede by in a cloud of dust as one of East Africa's greatest natural dramas plays itself out on the Serengeti plains. In this most superlative of East African parks, time seems to have stood still. A lion sits majestically on a rock, giraffes stride gracefully into the sunset, crocodiles bask on the riverbanks and secretary birds gaze quizzically at you from the roadside. The wildlife-watching is outstanding at any time of year. Just be sure to allow enough time to appreciate all the Serengeti has to offer.

Mt Kilimanjaro

2 It's difficult to resist the allure of climbing Africa's highest peak, with its snow-capped summit and views over the surrounding plains. Hundreds of trekkers do this climb each year, with a main requirement for success being adequate time for acclimatisation. But there are also other rewarding ways to experience the mountain. Take a day hike on the lush lower slopes, spend time learning about local Chagga culture or sip a sundowner from one of the many nearby vantage points with the mountain as a backdrop.

Cheetahs, Serengeti National Park

FRANZ ABERHAM / GETTY IMAGES ©

Ngorongoro Crater

3 If you get a day without cloud cover, Ngorongoro's magic starts while you're still up on the rim, with the chill air and sublime views over the enormous crater. The descent takes you down to a wide plain cloaked in hues of blue and green. If you're lucky enough to find a quiet spot, it's easy to imagine primeval Africa, with an almost constant parade of animals against a quintessential East African backdrop. Go as early in the day as possible to maximise viewing time and to take advantage of the morning light.

if Tanzania were 100 people

74 would be rural
26 would be urban

belief systems
(% of population)

35 Muslim
34 indigenous belief
30 Christian
1 other

population per sq km

TANZANIA   KENYA   UK

≈ 45 people

Zanzibar's Stone Town

4 Whether it's your first visit or your 50th, Zanzibar's Stone Town never loses its touch of the exotic. First, you'll see the skyline, with the spires of St Joseph's Cathedral and the Old Fort. Then, wander through narrow alleyways that reveal surprises at every turn. Linger at dusty shops scented with cloves, watch as men wearing white robelike *kanzu* play the game bao. Admire intricate henna designs on the hands of women in their *bui-bui* (black cover-all). Island rhythms quickly take over as mainland life slips away.

Chimpanzee Tracking

5 Chimpanzee tracking can be hard work: climbing up steep, muddy paths, stumbling over twisted roots, making your way through dense vegetation. But in an instant the sweat is all forgotten, as chimpanzees become visible in a clearing ahead. Tanzania's remote western parks – Mahale Mountains and Gombe – are among the best places anywhere to get close to our primate cousins. Combine chimpanzee tracking with a safari in Katavi National Park or exploration of the Lake Tanganyika shoreline for an unforgettable adventure far off the beaten track.

Local Life

6 Wildlife galore, a snow-covered peak, fantastic beaches and Swahili ruins pale beside Tanzania's most fascinating resource – its people. Local culture is accessible and diverse: hunt up cultural tourism programs to pound

Ngoma

The drum is the most essential element in Tanzania's traditional music. The same word (*ngoma*) is used for both dance and drumming, illustrating the intimate relationship between the two, and many dances can only be performed to the beat of a particular type of drum. Some dances, notably those of the Sukuma, also make use of other accessories, including live snakes and other animals. The Maasai leave everything behind in their famous dancing, which is accompanied only by chants and often also by jumping.

Food & Drink

Ugali is the Tanzanian national dish. This thick, doughlike mass varies in flavour and consistency depending on the flours used and the cooking. In general, good *ugali* should be neither too dry nor too sticky. It's usually served with a sauce containing meat, fish, beans or greens. Rice and *ndizi* (cooked plantains) are other staples.

Mishikaki (marinated, grilled meat kebabs) and *nyama choma* (seasoned roasted meat) are widely available. Along the coast and near lakes, there's plenty of seafood, often grilled or cooked in coconut milk or curry-style.

Some Tanzanians start their day with *uji*, a thin, sweet porridge made from bean, millet or other flour. *Vitambua* (small rice cakes resembling tiny, thick pancakes) are another morning treat. On Zanzibar, try *mkate wa kumimina*, a bread made from a batter similar to that used for making *vitambua*. Another Zanzibari treat is *urojo*, a filling, delicious soup with *kachori* (spicy potatoes), mango, limes, coconut, cassava chips, salad and sometimes *pili-pili* (hot pepper).

Tanzania's array of beers includes the local Safari and Kilimanjaro labels. Finding a beer is no problem, but finding a cold one can be a challenge.

Maasai men

grain with the Meru, sing with the Maasai, learn about the burial traditions of the Pare and experience a local market day with the Arusha. Hike past Sambaa villages in the Usambaras and watch a Makonde woodcarver at work in Dar es Salaam. Wherever you go, Tanzania's rich cultures are fascinating to discover.

When to Go

HIGH SEASON
(Jun-Aug)

➡ Weather is cooler and dry.

➡ Hotels in popular areas are full.

➡ Animal-spotting is easiest, as foliage is sparse and animals congregate around dwindling water sources.

SHOULDER
(Sep-Feb)

➡ Weather is hot, especially December through to February.

➡ From late October, the short rains (*mvuli*) fall and the *kusi* (seasonal trade wind from the southeast) blows.

➡ High-season prices from mid-December to mid-January.

LOW SEASON
(Mar-May)

➡ Heavy rains make secondary roads muddy and some areas inaccessible.

➡ It seldom rains all day, every day. Landscapes are lush and green.

➡ Some hotels close; others offer discounts.

Elephants in Ruaha National Park

7 Rugged, baobab-studded Ruaha National Park, together with surrounding conservation areas, is home to one of Tanzania's largest elephant populations. An ideal spot to watch for the giant pachyderms is along the lovely Great Ruaha River at sunrise or sundown, when they make their way down to the banks for a snack or a swim in the company of hippos, antelopes and over 400 different types of birds. Combine a visit here with a journey through the southern highlands for an unforgettable Tanzania tour.

Ruins & Rock Art

8 Tanzania offers a wealth of attractions for history buffs. Among the most impressive of the many coastal ruins are those at Kilwa Kisiwani – a Unesco World Heritage site harking back to the days of sultans and far-flung trade routes linking inland gold fields with Persia, India and China. Standing in the restored Great Mosque, you can almost hear the whispers of bygone centuries. Inland, armed with a sense of adventure and a taste for rugged travel, head for the enigmatic Kondoa Rock-Art Sites, spread throughout Central Tanzania's Irangi hills.

Best on Film

Africa – The Serengeti (1994) A stunning IMAX documentary by George Casey, narrated by James Earl Jones.

Tumaini (Beatrix Mugishagwe; 2005) The story of a Tanzanian family devastated by AIDS.

As Old as My Tongue (Andy Jones; 2006) A portrait of world music legend, Bi Kidude.

Best in Print

My Life (Shaaban Robert; 1949) The autobiography of a man who is considered the country's national poet; he was almost single-handedly responsible for the development of a modern Swahili prose style.

The Gunny Sack (MG Vassanji; 1989) An exploration of Tanzania's rich ethnic mix through several generations of an immigrant Indian family.

The Worlds of a Maasai Warrior – An Autobiography (Tepilit Ole Saitoti; 1985) A glimpse into Maasai life and culture.

Getting Around

Bus Travelling by bus is an inevitable part of the Tanzania experience for most visitors. Prices are reasonable for the distances covered, and there's often no other way to reach many destinations. Book in advance for popular routes.

Dalla-Dalla Local routes are serviced by poorly maintained and overcrowded *dalla-dallas* (minibuses) and, in rural areas, pick-up trucks or old 4WDs. Accidents are frequent.

Train For those with plenty of time, train travel offers a good view of the countryside and local life. Breakdowns and long delays (up to 24 hours or more) are common.

Beaches

9 With over 1000km of Indian Ocean coastline, exotic archipelagos and inland lakes, you'll be spoiled for choice when it comes to Tanzania's beaches. Zanzibar's beaches are more developed, but stunning, with blindingly white sand, the obligatory palm trees and rewarding diving. For something less crowded, head to Pemba, with its idyllic coves, or the mainland near Pangani. To really get away from it all, try the far south, between Kilwa Masoko and the Mozambique border, or inland along the Lake Tanganyika shoreline.

Boat Safari in Selous Game Reserve

10 A highlight of a visit to the vast Selous Game Reserve is floating along the Rufiji River on a boat safari. As you glide past borassus palms, slumbering hippos and cavorting elephants, don't forget to watch also for the many smaller attractions along the river banks. These include majestic African fish eagles, stately Goliath herons and tiny white-fronted bee-eaters – all part of nature's daily drama in Africa's largest wildlife reserve.

Mnemba Island

CHRISTIAN ASLUND / GETTY IMAGES ©

Erawan waterfall, Kanchanaburi

Thailand

Friendly and fun-loving, exotic and tropical, cultured and historic, Thailand radiates a golden hue from its gaudy temples and tropical beaches to the ever-comforting Thai smile.

Lustrous Thailand radiates a hospitality that makes it one of the most accessibly exotic destinations on earth. Its natural landscape is part of the allure: the blonde beaches are lapped at by cerulean seas, while the northern mountains cascade into the misty horizon. In between are emerald-coloured rice fields and busy, prosperous cities built around sacred temples. It is a bountiful land where the markets are piled high with pyramids of colourful fruits and the *rót khēn* (vendor cart) is an integral piece of a city's infrastructure.

You'll suffer few travelling hardships, save for a few pushy touts, in this land of comfort and convenience. Bangkok reigns as an Asian superstar, Chiang Mai excels in liveability and the tropical islands are up all night to party. It is relatively cheap to hop around by plane and the kingdom provides a gateway to everywhere else in the region. Though the fiery curries and simple stir-fries might delay your departure.

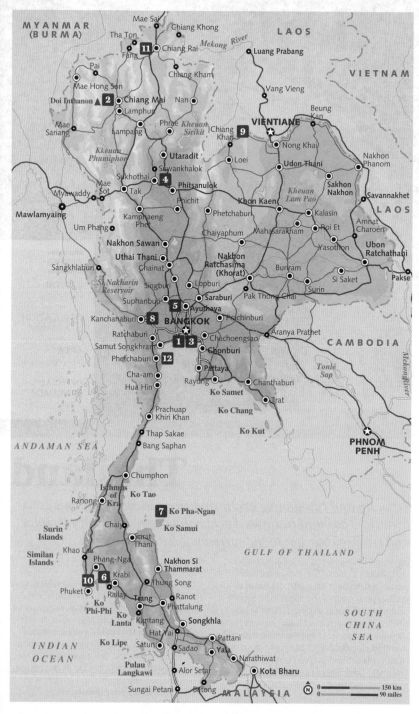

Thailand's
Top Experiences

Chatuchak Weekend Market, Bangkok

1 In a city obsessed with commerce, Chatuchak takes the prize as Bangkok's biggest, baddest market, and is yet another reason to plan your visit to the city around a weekend. Silks and sneakers, fighting fish and fluffy puppies, not to mention some pretty good food – if it can be sold in Bangkok, you'll find it here. Come early and be prepared for some serious collective bargaining as half of Bangkok squeezes into the market's narrow lanes.

Chiang Mai

2 The cultural capital of the north, Chiang Mai is beloved by culture geeks, temple-spotters and families. The old city is jam-packed with temples born during the once-independent Lanna kingdom. Cooking schools teach visitors the art of Thai food. The scenic country-side boasts jungle treks, elephant encounters and minority villages. And the city enjoys fantastic dining thanks to imports like Japanese sushi and Burmese curries, as well as homegrown northern specialities and vegetarian fare.

FEARGUS COONEY / GETTY IMAGES ©

Bangkok Nightlife

3 The nightlife scene in today's Bangkok touches on all points from trashy to classy, with a distinct emphasis on unpretentious Thai-style fun. Start your night in a bar perched on a skyscraper, throw in a few roadside beers, and finish up at a basement-level music pub; in Bangkok, a night out is whatever you want it to be.

View of Wat Phra Kaew, Bangkok

Sukhothai Historical Park

4 Step back 800 years in time at Thailand's most impressive historical park. Explore the ruins of this former capital by bicycle; wind leisurely through the crumbling temples, graceful Buddha statues and fish-filled ponds. Worthwhile museums and good-value accommodation round out the package. Despite its popularity, Sukhothai rarely feels crowded, but for something off the beaten track, head to Si Satchanalai-Chaliang Historical Park, where you might be the only one scaling an ancient stairway.

if Thailand were 100 people

75 would be Thai
14 would be Chinese
11 would be other

belief systems
(% of population)

94 Buddhist
5 Muslim
1 Christian

population per sq km

THAILAND   USA   UK

♟ ≈ 32 people

Ayuthaya

5 A once vibrant, glittering capital packed with hundreds of temples, Ayuthaya today only hints at its erstwhile glory. Cycle around the brick-and-stucco ruins, which form part of a Unesco World Heritage site, and try to imagine how the city must have looked in its prime, when it greeted merchants from around the globe. On the outskirts of the city sit several more attractions, including an enormous handicraft centre, and the most eclectic royal palace you'll ever see.

Railay

6 At the tip of the Krabi peninsula are some of Thailand's most famous natural features: the soaring limestone karsts of Railay, anchored in the ocean. The beaches are sugar-white and the forested interior is traversed by foot traffic, not cars. No traffic jams, no transport hassles. Visitors come and go by long-tail boats. Come to lounge, swim, dive or rock climb. Beginners can learn basic skills, and some stay long enough to get good enough to do a free solo on a pinnacle then tumble harmlessly into a cobalt sea.

Ko Pha-Ngan

7 Famous for its sloppy, techno-fuelled Full Moon parties, Ko Pha-Ngan has graduated from a sleepy bohemian island to an Asian Ibiza. Comfort seekers have an alternative to Ko Samui thanks to a bevy of boutique bungalows. And on the northern and eastern coasts, the ascetic hammock hangers can still escape enough of the modern life to feel like castaways. Just offshore is Sail Rock, one of the gulf's best dive sites.

The Nickname Game

At birth Thai babies are given auspicious first names, often bestowed by the family patriarch or matriarch. These poetic names are then relegated to bureaucratic forms and name cards, while the child is introduced to everyone else by a one-syllable nickname.

Thai nicknames are usually playful and can be inspired by the child's appearance (Moo, meaning 'pig', if he/+she is chubby) or a favourite pastime (Toon, short for 'cartoon' for avid TV-watchers). Girls will typically be named Lek or Noi (both of which mean 'small').

Some parents even go so far as imprinting their interests on their children's names: Golf (as in the sport) and Benz (as in the car).

Food & Drink

Beer Domestic brands (Singha, Chang, Leo) and foreign-licensed labels (Heineken, Asahi, San Miguel) are all largely indistinguishable in terms of taste and quality.

Đôm yam Sour Thai soup is a feeble description of this mouth-puckeringly tart and intensely spicy herbal broth.

Kôw pàt Fried rice; garnish it with ground chillies, sugar, fish sauce and a touch of lime.

Kôw soy Soup that combines flat egg-and-wheat noodles in a spice-laden, coconut milk–based broth.

Nám pŏn-lá-mái Fruit juices, served with a touch of sugar and salt and a whole lot of ice.

Pàt gàprow gài Fiery stir-fry of chicken, chillies, garlic and fresh basil.

Pàt tai Thin rice noodles fried with egg, tofu and shrimp, seasoned with fish sauce, tamarind and dried chili.

Pàt pàk kanáh Stir-fried Chinese greens, often fried with a meat (upon request), served over rice; simple but delicious.

Kanchanaburi

8 Walks on the wild side are the main reason to visit Kanchanaburi, where dragon-scaled limestone mountains gaze down upon dense jungle. Trek past silvery waterfalls and rushing rivers in search of elusive tigers and gibbons, then spend the night at a homestay organised through an ethnic group. Once you've explored this western province's wartime past – the infamous Bridge Over the River Kwai is here – hold on tight to experience the growing number of adventure activities, which include ziplining, kayaking and elephant riding.

Mekong River

9 From the historic timber shophouses of Chiang Khan to the waterfalls of Pha Taem National Park, northeast Thailand's glorious arc of the Mekong River offers an incomparable smorgasbord of culture and beauty. Chase the meandering river aboard a rickety bus, long-tail boat or even a

When to Go

HIGH SEASON
(Nov–Mar)

➡ A cool and dry season follows the monsoons, meaning the landscape is lush and temperatures are comfortable.

➡ Western Christmas and New Year's holidays bring crowds and rates increase 50% at the beaches.

SHOULDER
(Apr–Jun, Sep & Oct)

➡ Hot and dry (April to June)

➡ Beaches aren't crowded and the ocean provides the air-con.

➡ September and October are ideal for the north and the gulf coast.

LOW SEASON
(Jul–Oct)

➡ Monsoon season can range from afternoon showers to major flooding.

➡ Some islands shut down and boat service is limited during stormy weather.

bicycle. View the cross-pollination of Thai-Lao culture in local fishing villages, Nong Khai's bizarre sculpture park, prehistoric rock paintings in Ubon Ratchathani, holy temples and elephant villages. Those who follow this little-visited trail will be rewarded with true traveller's tales.

Phuket

10 An international beach resort, Phuket is an easy-peasy destination for all ages. You can fly in from Bangkok (or directly from China), and then retreat into a five-star resort or arty boutique hotel for a trouble-free tropical vacation. There are slinky stretches of sand, hedonistic party pits and all the mod-cons needed for 21st-century rest and recreation. Plus there are day trips to mangrove forests, monkey-rescue centres and a ton of watersports, from diving to surfing.

Chiang Rai Province

11 The days of the Golden Triangle opium trade are over, but Chiang Rai still packs intrigue in the form of fresh-air fun, such as trekking and self-guided exploration. It's also a great destination for unique cultural experiences, ranging from a visit to an Akha village to a stay at the Yunnanese hamlet of Mae Salong. From the Mekong River to the mountains, Chiang Rai is arguably Thailand's most beautiful province, and if you've set your sights further, it's also a convenient gateway to Myanmar and Laos.

Phetchaburi

12 A delightful mix of culture and nature combine in this provincial capital, a close and quiet alternative to the hectic streets of Bangkok. Explore an antique hilltop palace, sacred cave shrines and bustling temples. Wander the old shophouse neighbourhood filled with do-it-yourself businesses run by Thai aunties and grannies. Then head off to the wilds of Kaeng Krachan National Park to spot wild gibbons and exotic birds. Phetchaburi is also a smart layover for travellers returning from the south.

Best on Film

36 (Nawapol Thamrongrattanarit; 2012) Indie love affair remembered through 36 static camera set-ups.

Boundary (Nontawat Numbenchapol; 2013) Examines the military conflict at Khao Phra Wihan on the Thai–Cambodian border from the point of view of a Thai soldier.

Paradoxocracy (Pen-ek Ratanaruang; 2013) Traces the country's political history from the 1932 revolution to today.

Best in Print

Lai Chiwit (Many Lives; Kukrit Pramoj) A collection of short stories.

Monsoon Country (Pira Sudham) Brilliantly captures the northeast's struggles against nature and nurture.

Pisat, Evil Spirits (Seni Saowaphong) Deals with conflicts between the old and new generations.

Wat Rong Khun, Chiang Rai

KYLIE McLAUGHLIN / GETTY IMAGES ©

CAPITAL
Lhasa

POPULATION
5.6 million

AREA
2.5 million sq km

**OFFICIAL
LANGUAGES**
Tibetan
Chinese

Tibet's stark landscape

Tibet

Tibet is simply one of Asia's most remarkable places, offering fabulous monasteries, high-altitude treks, stunning mountain views and one of the most likeable peoples you will ever meet.

For many people, the highlights of Tibet will be of a spiritual nature – magnificent monasteries, prayer halls of chanting monks and remote cliffside retreats. Tibet's pilgrims are an essential part of this appeal, from the local grannies mumbling mantras and swinging their prayer wheels in temples heavy with the intoxicating aroma of juniper incense and yak butter, to the hard-core walking or even prostrating around Mt Kailash. Tibet has a level of devotion and faith that seems to belong to an earlier age.

For travellers nonplussed by Tibet's religious significance, the big draw is likely to be the elemental beauty of the highest plateau on earth. Geography here is on a humbling scale, from the world's highest peaks to lakes that look like inland seas and every view is lit with spectacular mountain light. Your trip will take you past glittering turquoise lakes, across huge plains dotted with grazing yaks and nomad's tents and over high passes draped with colourful prayer flags. The scope for adventure is limitless.

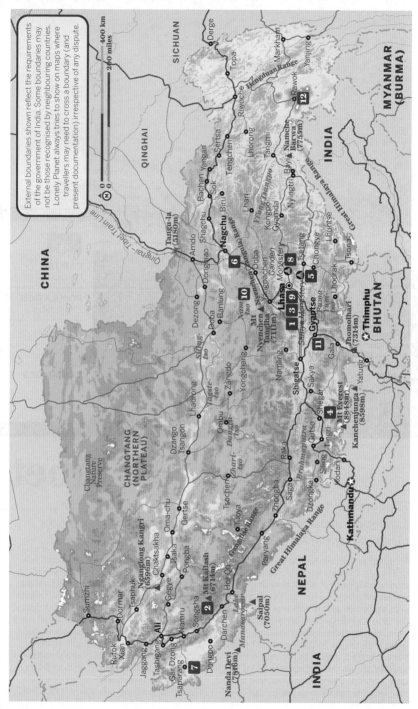

External boundaries shown reflect the requirements of the government of India. Some boundaries may not be those recognised by neighbouring countries. Lonely Planet always tries to show on maps where travellers may need to cross a boundary (and present documentation) irrespective of any dispute.

400 km
200 miles

CHINA

QINGHAI

SICHUAN

MYANMAR (BURMA)

INDIA

NEPAL

BHUTAN

Kathmandu

Thimphu

CHANGTANG (NORTHERN PLATEAU)

Changtang Nature Preserve

Qinghai-Tibet Train Line

Tanggu-la (5180m)

Nagchu

Lhasa

Gyantse

Shigatse

Mt Kailash (6714m)

Mt Everest (8848m)

Kanchenjunga (8598m)

Nanda Devi (7816m)

Jhomolhari (7314m)

Namche Barwa (7755m)

Nyenchen Tanglha (7111m)

Saipal (7050m)

Manasarovar

Tibet's
Top Experiences

Potala Palace

1 There are moments in travel that will long stay with you – and your first view of the iconic Potala Palace is one such moment. Even surrounded by a sea of Chinese development, the towering, mysterious building dominates Lhasa; it's simply hard to take your eyes off the thing. A visit to the former home of the Dalai Lamas is a spiralling descent past gold-tombed chapels, reception rooms and prayer halls into the bowels of a medieval castle. It's nothing less than the concentrated spiritual and material wealth of a nation.

Mt Kailash, Western Tibet

2 Worshipped by more than a billion Buddhists and Hindus, Asia's most sacred mountain rises from the Barkha plain like a giant four-sided 6714m chörten. Throw in the stunning nearby Lake Manasarovar and a basin that forms the source of four of Asia's greatest rivers, and who's to say this place really isn't the centre of the world? Travel here to one of the world's most beautiful and remote corners brings an added bonus: the three-day pilgrim path around the mountain erases the sins of a lifetime.

SHUO YANG / GETTY IMAGES ©

Jokhang Temple, Lhasa

3 The atmosphere of hushed awe is what hits you first as you inch through the dark, medieval passageways of the Jokhang. Queues of wide-eyed pilgrims shuffle up and down the stairways, past medieval doorways and millennium-old murals, pausing briefly to top up the hundreds of butter lamps that flicker in the gloom. It's the beating spiritual heart of Tibet. Welcome to the 14th century.

View of Mt Everest

4 Don't tell the Nepal Tourism Board, but Tibet has easily the best views of the world's most famous mountain. While two-week-long trekking routes on the Nepal side offer up only occasional fleeting glimpses of the peak, the view of Mt Everest's unobstructed north face framed in the prayer flags of Rongphu Monastery or from a tent at the Base Camp will stop you in your tracks.

Samye Monastery

5 Tibet's first monastery is a heavily symbolic collection of chapels, chörtens and shrines arranged around a medieval Tibetan-, Chinese- and Indian-style temple called the Ütse. The 1200-year-old site is where Guru Rinpoche battled demons to introduce Buddhism to Tibet and where the future course of Tibetan Buddhism was sealed in a great debate. The location on the desert-like banks of the Yarlung Tsangpo is also superb.

Riding the Rail to Lhasa

6 For all its faults, China's railway to Tibet (the world's highest) is an engineering wonder and a delightful way to reach the holy city. Pull up a window seat to view huge salt lakes, plains dotted with yaks and herders' tents, and hundreds of miles of desolate nothing, as you inch slowly up onto the high plateau. Peaking at 5072m may send you diving for the piped oxygen, but it's still a classic rail trip.

Guge Kingdom, Western Tibet

7 The spectacular lost kingdom of Guge at Tsaparang is quite unlike anything you'll see in central Tibet; it feels more like Ladakh than Lhasa. There comes a point when you are lowering yourself down a hidden sandstone staircase or crawling through an interconnected cave complex that you stop and think:

Mandalas

The mandala (*kyilkhor*, literally 'circle') is more than a beautiful artistic creation, it's also a three-dimensional meditational map. What on the surface appears to be a plain two-dimensional design emerges, with the right visual approach, as a three-dimensional picture. Mandalas can take the form of paintings, patterns of sand, three-dimensional models or even whole monastic structures, as at Samye. In the case of the two-dimensional mandala, the correct visual approach can be achieved only through meditation. One ritual calls for the adept to visualise 722 deities with enough clarity to be able to see the whites of their eyes and hold this visualisation for four hours.

The painstakingly created sand mandalas also perform the duty of illustrating the impermanence of life (they are generally swept away after a few days).

Food & Drink

Momos You don't have to look far to find these small dumplings filled with meat or vegetables or both. They are normally steamed but can be fried and are pretty good.

Thugpa This is a noodle soup made with meat or vegetables or both. Variations on the theme include *hipthuk* (squares of noodles and yak meat in a soup) and *thenthuk* (more noodles). Glass noodles known as *phing* are also sometimes used.

Tsampa This is a kind of dough made with roasted-barley flour and yak butter mixed with water, tea or beer – something wet. Tibetans skilfully knead and mix the paste by hand into dough-like balls, which is not as easy as it looks!

Yak-butter tea This is the local beverage that every traveller ends up trying at least once. Some people prefer to call it 'soup', others liken it to brewed socks and sump oil. However you describe it, your first mouthful is the signal that you have finally reached Tibet.

where Tibetans live (%)

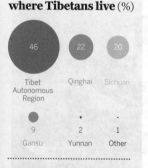

Tibet Autonomous Region	Qinghai	Sichuan
46	22	20

Gansu	Yunnan	Other
9	2	1

population per sq km

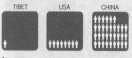

TIBET	USA	CHINA

↑ ≈ 5 people

*reliable population statistics unavailable for Tibet

CHRISTOPHER PILLITZ / GETTY IMAGES ©

Monks chanting, Jokhang Temple

'This is incredible!' What's really amazing is that you'll likely have the half-forgotten ruins to yourself. Rank this as one of Asia's great travel secrets.

Ganden–Samye Trek

8 Tibet is one of those places you really should experience at the pace of one foot in front of the other. This classic four-day trek between two of Tibet's best monasteries takes you past herders' camps, high alpine lakes and a Guru Rinpoche hermitage, as well as over three 5000m-plus passes. Hire a horse for a wonderful wilderness trek.

Sera & Drepung Monasteries, Lhasa

9 Lhasa's great religious institutions of Sera and Drepung are more than just monasteries – they are self- contained towns. A web of whitewashed alleyways climbs past medieval kitchens, printing presses and colleges to reach giant

When to Go

HIGH SEASON (May–Sep)	**SHOULDER** (Mar–Apr, Oct–Nov)	**LOW SEASON** (Dec–Feb)
➡ The warmest weather makes travel, trekking and transport easiest.	➡ The slightly colder weather means fewer travellers and a better range of 4WDs.	➡ Very few people visit Tibet in winter, so you'll have the place largely to yourself.
➡ Prices are at their highest.	➡ Prices are slightly cheaper than during the high season.	➡ Hotel prices are discounted by up to 50%, but some restaurants close.
➡ The 1 May and 1 October national holidays bring the biggest crowds.		

prayer halls full of chanting, tea-sipping red-robed monks. Don't miss the afternoon debating, an extravagant spectator sport of Buddhist dialectics and hand slapping.

Nam-tso

10 Just a few hours north of Lhasa, spectacular Nam-tso epitomises the dramatic but harsh scenery of northern Tibet. This deep blue lake is fringed by prayer flag–draped hills, craggy cliffs and nesting migratory birds, all framed by a horizon of 7000m peaks. It's cold, increasingly developed and devastatingly beautiful.

Best on Film

Kundun (1997) Martin Scorsese's beautifully shot depiction of the life of the Dalai Lama.

Vajra Sky Over Tibet (2006) John Powers' Buddhist-inspired cinematic pilgrimage to the principal sites of central Tibet.

When the Dragon Swallowed the Sun (2010) Explores the increasingly tense debate inside Tibet's exile community on how best to deal with China, featuring music by Damien Rice and Thom Yorke.

Best in Print

Fire Under the Snow (Palden Gyatso; 1997) A moving autobiography of a Buddhist monk imprisoned in Tibet for 33 years.

Tears of Blood (Mary Craig; 1992) A riveting and distressing account of the Tibetan experience since the Chinese takeover.

The Open Road: The Global Journey of the Fourteenth Dalai Lama (Pico Iyer; 2008) An engaging look at the warmth and contradictions of the 14th Dalai Lama.

Getting There & Around

Tours & Permits To board a plane or train to Tibet you need a Tibet Tourism Bureau permit, and to get this you must book a guide for your entire trip and pre-arrange transport for trips outside of Lhasa. Travel outside Lhasa requires additional permits, arranged in advance by your tour company so you need to decide your itinerary beforehand. Tour companies need 10 to 14 days to arrange permits and post you the TTB permit (the original permit is required if flying). From Nepal you need to travel on a short-term group visa, which can make it tricky to continue into the rest of China.

Transport 4WD rental is the most common form of transport, since most local public transport is officially off limits. While some areas are still a patchwork of rough roads most of the main highways are now paved. Airports are springing up on the plateau and the railway line is extending beyond Lhasa. Long-distance cyclists are an increasingly frequent sight on the roads in Tibet. It's currently no possible however to cycle anywhere in Tibet independently. You must sign up to a 'tour', which essentially means being followed by a support vehicle and guide.

Gyantse Kumbum

11 The giant chörten at Gyantse is unique in the Himalayas. As you spiral around and up the snail shell–shaped building, you pass dozens of alcoves full of serene painted buddhas, bloodthirsty demons and unrivalled Tibetan art. Finally you pop out onto the golden eaves for fabulous views of Gyantse fort and old town.

Ngan-tso & Rawok-tso

12 Tibet is not short on spectacular, remote, turquoise-blue lakes. Of these, none surpasses the crystal-clear waters, sandy beaches and snowcapped peaks of these twin lakes near Rawok. Stay overnight at a hotel on stilts above the lake and explore nearby glaciers during the day.

Prayer flags above Drepung Monastery

MERTEN SNIJDERS / GETTY IMAGES ©

Independence Plaza, Lomé

CAPITAL
Lomé

POPULATION
7.3 million

AREA
56,785 sq km

OFFICIAL LANGUAGE
French

Togo

With its palm-fringed beaches, verdant hills and savannah, and approximately 40 ethnic groups, Togo crams a whole lot of Africa into a surprisingly small space.

For those fond of travelling off the beaten track, Togo will prove a rewarding destination. It offers a great diversity of landscapes, from the lakes and palm-fringed beaches along the Atlantic coastline to the rolling forested hills in the centre. As you head further north, the landscape leaves its mantle of lush forest green for the light green and yellowy tinges of savannah land. The cherry on top is Lomé, the low-key yet elegant capital, with its large avenues, tasty restaurants and throbbing nightlife – not to mention the splendid beaches on its doorstep. Togo is also an excellent playground for hikers – there's no better ecofriendly way to experience the country's savage beauty than on foot.

Another highlight is the culture. Togo is a melting pot. The fortified compounds of Koutammakou are a reminder that the country's ethnically diverse population didn't always get along. Nowadays, however, voodoo, Muslim, Christian and traditional festivals crowd the calendar and are often colourful celebrations for all.

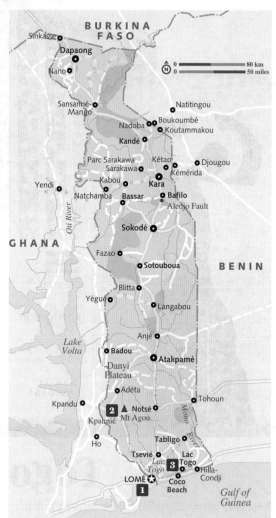

NOV–FEB

➡ The best time to visit, with pleasant temperatures perfect for outdoor activities.

MID-JUL–MID-SEP

➡ There's a dry spell in the south, which makes transport less challenging.

MAR & APR

➡ The hottest period throughout the country is best avoided.

Food and Drink

Djenkoumé A pâte made with cornflour cooked with spices and served with fried chicken and guinea fowl.

Fufu Cooked and puréed yam served with vegetables and meat.

Pâte A dough-like substance made of corn, manioc or yam; base of many Togolese dishes.

Tchoukoutou Fermented millet.

Togo's
Top Experiences

Lomé

1 Once dubbed 'the Pearl of West Africa', Togo's coastal capital, with its tasty *maquis* (informal street-side eateries), colourful markets and palm-fringed boulevards, has a charm that is unique among West African capitals,

Hiking in Kpalmié

2 Hike through cocoa and coffee plantations and luxuriant forests bristling with life, on the way up Togo's highest peak, Mt Agou (986m). Small terraced mountain villages pepper the slopes and provide fabulous views of the

area – on a clear day, you can see Lake Volta in Ghana. Alternatively, the area around Mt Kouto (710m) is another walking heaven, with forested hills, waterfalls and myriad butterflies in the early morning.

Lac Togo

3 Lac Togo is an inland lagoon stretching all the way from Lomé to Aného. Enjoy a blissful swim in the croc- and bug-free lake, or get a ride in a *pirogue* (traditional canoe) to Togoville, the former seat of the Mlapa dynasty and Togo's historical centre of voodoo.

Heilala Festival, Nuku'alofa, Tongatapu island

CAPITAL
Nuku'alofa

POPULATION
106,322

AREA
747 sq km

OFFICIAL LANGUAGE
Tongan, English

Tonga

Think lush, reef-fringed islands with sandy foreshores that virtually glow in the tropical sunshine. In Tonga you'll need to slow down to the pace of local island life.

Say goodbye to tourist hype – you're now in the Kingdom of Tonga. This 'never colonised' Polynesian kingdom is unique in its approach to tourism. This is a country that survives on international aid and remittances sent from Tongans living overseas. You may get the impression that most Tongans would prefer visitors to donate their dollars and not leave the airport; expats seem determined to build a tourist industry, but most of the locals just don't seem to care. In some ways, this is incredibly refreshing and in others incredibly frustrating. You won't have to try to gain a cultural experience – it's all around!

There's no doubting the natural beauty of Tonga. Travellers choose the pace of their adventure here, mixing sun-and-sand holidays, swimming with humpback whales, hiking in tropical rainforests or just lying on the beach and experiencing Tongan time. Throw away any preconceived ideas, slow down to the pace of local life, and you'll love the place. Expect too much and you'll likely leave frustrated.

Sea Kayaking

2 The best way to see the aquamarine waterways and remote sandy islands of Tonga's Vava'u and Ha'apai groups is to take to the water on a guided multiday kayak tour. There's plenty on offer, from single-day trips to 13-day packages, giving you the opportunity to see paradise, get a bit of exercise, and meet smiling villagers on outer islands that are usually next to impossible to get to. There's plenty of time for swimming, snorkelling, and, if you're lucky, paddling not too far away from massive humpback whales.

Tonga's Stonehenge

3 While Europeans could barely sail out of their backyards until the 1500s, the great Polynesian migration that populated the Pacific took place around 3000 years ago. Tonga's Ha'amonga 'a Maui Trilithon – South Pacific's equivalent of Stonehenge – is one of ancient Polynesia's most intriguing historical monuments. Archaeologists and oral history credit its construction to Tu'itatui, the 11th Tu'i Tonga. The structure consists of three large coralline stones, each weighing about 40 tonnes, arranged into a trilithic gate.

Tonga's
Top Experiences

Whale Watching

1 Tonga is an important breeding ground for humpback whales, which migrate to its warm waters between June and October; it's one of the few places in the world where you can swim with these magnificent creatures. They can be seen raising young in the calm reef-protected waters and engaging in elaborate mating rituals where the males 'sing'. There are whale-watching and whale-swim tour operators in all of Tonga's island groups, but the best operate in the waters around the beautiful Ha'apai islands.

'Eua Hiking

4 Drag yourself away from the beach to go hiking in the tropical rainforest of 'Eua National Park. Wildlife watchers will find that 'Eua has a lively bird population, the star of which is the *koki*, or red shining parrot. Others include *ngongo* (noddies), white-tailed *tavake* (tropic birds) and *pekapeka-tae* (swiftlets). The *peka* (fruit bat) is also commonly seen.

Humpback whale, Vava'u group

Royal Tonga

5 Nuku'alofa, on Tongatapu island is the kingdom's seat of government and the home of the royal family. While it may not fulfil a vision of Pacific paradise, Tonga's capital and 'big smoke' is the place to do a little royal-family watching. The 1867 Royal Palace is not open to visitors but you can get a good view from the waterfront area. You might have more luck spotting members of the royal family at a Sunday service at the Centenary Chapel.

Oholei Beach Feast

6 To experience the best cultural entertainment on Tongatapu, head to the Oholei Beach Resort's Feast and Show. The evening starts with entertainment on sandy Oholei Beach, followed by a tasty Tongan feast, including suckling pig roasted on a spit. The highlight though is the dancing in open-topped Hina Cave, enthusiastically performed and culminating in a captivating fire dance. It's held every Wednesday and Friday night.

if Tonga were 100 people

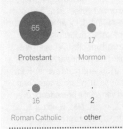

37 would be aged 0-14
19 would be aged 15-24
33 would be aged 25-54
5 would be aged 55-64
6 would be aged 65+

belief systems
(% of population)

65 Protestant

17 Mormon

16 Roman Catholic

2 other

population per sq km

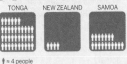

TONGA   NEW ZEALAND   SAMOA

✝ ≈ 4 people

When to Go

HIGH SEASON
(Jun–Sep)

➡ The dry season with pleasant temperatures, lower humidity and little rain.

➡ Yachties head across the South Pacific.

➡ Whales are in the region.

SHOULDER
(Apr–May & Oct–Nov)

➡ This is the period between the dry and wet seasons.

➡ Everything is open but not so many visitors around.

➡ Yachties starting to arrive in May, mostly gone by late October.

LOW SEASON
(Dec–Mar)

➡ Expect hot temperatures and high humidity.

➡ Yachties are gone. It's cyclone season.

➡ Planes are packed December to January as overseas-based islanders return to see their families.

Fakaleiti

One of the most distinctive features of Tongan culture are *fakaleiti*, a modern continuation of an ancient Polynesian tradition, known as *fa'afafine* in Samoa and *mahu* or *rae rae* in French Polynesia.

The term *fakaleiti* is made up of the prefix *faka-* (in the manner of) and *-leiti* from the English word lady. Traditionally, if a Tongan woman had too many sons and not enough daughters she would need one of the sons to assist with 'women's work' such as cooking and housecleaning. This child would then be brought up as a daughter. These days, becoming a *fakaleiti* can also be a lifestyle choice. There is little stigma attached it, and they mix easily with the rest of society, often being admired for their style. On Tongatapu, the Tonga Leitis' Association is an active group – note that members prefer to call themselves simply *leiti* (ladies).

Food & Drink

Being an island nation, Tonga is surrounded by the sea and Tongans will eat just about anything that comes out of it, from shellfish to shark to sea turtle. *'Ota 'ika*, raw fish in coconut milk, is an island-wide favourite. Pigs are prized possessions and roam the streets along with chickens. For feasts, smaller pigs are roasted on spits over open fires while bigger ones are cooked in *umu* (underground ovens). Root crops such as taro, sweet potato and yams take precedence over other vegetables, which are much harder to produce. Tropical fruits are everywhere, with coconuts, bananas and papaya available year-round. Summer is the season for mango, pineapple, passionfruit and guava.

Tongan men drink kava, made from pepper roots, as a social activity.

Tin Can Island

7 Remote Niuafo'ou, about 100km west of Niuatoputapu, resembles a doughnut floating in the sea. It is a collapsed volcanic cone thought to have once topped 1300m in height. It is also known as 'Tin Can Island' and is legendary for its former postal service. In days of old, mail was sealed in a biscuit tin and tossed overboard from a passing supply ship, where a strong swimmer from the island would retrieve it. This continued until 1931, when the mail swimmer was taken by a shark!

Diving & Snorkelling

8 Like most places in the South Pacific, Tonga's islands are surrounded by warm tropical waters, fringed by coral reefs and home to an underwater wonderland. Crusty wrecks, sea walls, caves and hard and soft coral abound, providing home to thousands of species of fish. There are good dive sites and professional operators in the Vava'u and Ha'apai groups, but some of Tonga's finest diving can be found at the sea walls off 'Eua island, including the legendary Cathedral Cave.

Getting Around

Air Flying is by far the easiest, fastest and most comfortable way to get around Tonga's many islands. Chathams Pacific operates all domestic flights in Tonga.

Boat Interisland ferries sail between Tongatapu and the main island groups and are a good way to get around if you have plenty of time.

Bus Buses run on Tongatapu, and in a more limited capacity on Vava'u and its causeway-linked islands.

Car & Taxi Rental cars and taxis are available on Tongatapu and Vava'u. Locals drive very slowly on the left-hand side of the road.

Carnival

| CAPITAL |
| Port of Spain |
| POPULATION |
| 1.2 million |
| AREA |
| 5128 sq km |
| OFFICIAL LANGUAGE |
| English |

Trinidad & Tobago

Get ready for calypso, cricket and Carnival parties when you hit these twin Caribbean islands that are better known for birdwatching than beaches.

Trinidad and Tobago are an exercise in beautiful contradiction. In Trinidad, pristine mangrove swamps and rainforested hills sit side by side with smoke-belching oil refineries and ugly industrial estates. Tobago has everything you'd expect from a Caribbean island, with palm trees and white sand aplenty, yet it's relatively unchanged by the tourist industry. Combined, this twin-island republic offers unparalleled birdwatching; first-class diving; luxuriant rainforests prime for hiking, waterfall swimming and cycling;

and electric nightlife, with the fabulous Carnival easily the biggest and best of the region's annual blowouts.

Gritty capital Port of Spain is a great place to lime with the locals, catch up with the latest soca tunes, and see a game of cricket, and it's only a short trip to the wildlife and waterfalls of the Northern Range of beaches of Maracas Bay. But don't expect anyone to hold your hand. Tourism tends to be low on the priority list, so it's up to you to take a deep breath, jump in and enjoy the mix.

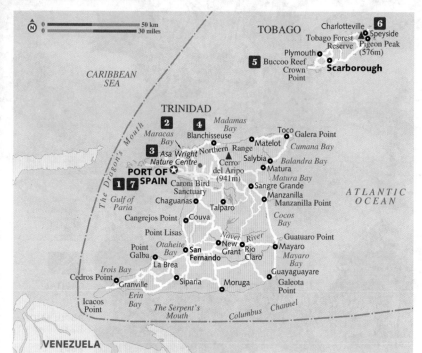

Trinidad & Tobago's
Top Experiences

Port of Spain's Carnival

1 Trinidad's Carnival, held in February or March each year (dates and location change) is considered by many to be the best in the Caribbean. Originally brought to Trinidad by French planters, and soon co-opted by African slaves as a means of satirizing colonial authority, Carnival has its roots in both West African music and mythology and European masked balls. Lavish pre-Carnival fetes and Calypso tents light up Port of Spain before the big event, then, on Carnival Monday, the wild all-night street parades begin with bands 'playing mas' to thousands of revellers.

Maracas Bay

2 Maracas Bay, on Trinidad's north coast, has the island's most popular beach. The broad, white-sand stretch, thick with palm trees contrasting against the backdrop of verdant mountains, remains an irresistible lure for both locals and travelers. Despite the curving headland, the sand is often pounded by waves that serve up good body-surfing. There are lifeguards, changing rooms, showers, picnic shelters and huts selling cold beers and shark and bake. On weekends the beach gets pretty crowded, but during the week it can feel almost deserted. It's an easy 40-minute drive from Port of Spain.

Asa Wright Nature Centre

3 For every tourist lying on the beach, there will be one staring skyward through a pair of binoculars as Trinidad and Tobago is the best place in the Caribbean for birdwatching. A former cocoa and coffee plantation transformed into an 80-hectare nature reserve, the Asa Wright Nature Centre blows the minds of twitchers, and makes a worthwhile trip even if you can't tell a parrot from a parakeet. Species found at the center include blue-crowned motmots, chestnut woodpeckers, channel-billed toucans, blue-headed parrots, 14 species of hummingbird and numerous raptors.

Paria Bay, Trinidad

Blanchisseuse

4 The tiny village of Blanchisseuse, on Trinidad's north coast, makes a great base for hiking, especially to Paria Bay. The trailhead starts just past the suspension bridge that spans the Marianne River, just before the end of the North Coast Rd. The hike winds through the forest, over the Jordan River to the spectacular and completely undeveloped Paria Beach. Further inland is Paria Falls, where you're greeted with a clear, refreshing bathing pool.

Buccoo Reef

5 Stretching offshore between Pigeon Point and Buccoo Bay, Tobago, the extensive Buccoo Reef was designated as a marine park in 1973 and a Ramsar site in 2006. The fringing reef boasts five reef flats separated by deep channels. The sheer array of flora and fauna – dazzling sponges, hard corals and tropical fish – makes marine biologists giddy. Glass-bottom-boat reef tours are an accessible way to explore Tobago's underwater treasure.

if Trinidad & Tobago were 100 people

40 would be Indian (South Asian)
38 would be African
21 would be mixed
1 would be other

belief systems
(% of population)

| 26 | 26 | 22 |
| Roman Catholic | Protestant | Hindu |

| 6 | 6 | 14 |
| Muslim | other Christian | other or none |

population per sq km

TRINIDAD & TOBAGO   USA   VENEZUELA

👤 ≈ 30 people

When to Go

HIGH SEASON
(Feb & Mar)

➡ People fleeing the northern winter arrive in droves and prices peak.

➡ This is the region's driest time.

➡ Hordes of people arrive for Carnival.

SHOULDER
(Apr–Jun & Oct–Dec)

➡ The weather is good, rains are moderate.

➡ Warm temperatures elsewhere reduce visitor numbers.

➡ Affordable rates at hotels.

LOW SEASON
(Jul–Sep)

➡ Rainy season (June to November); odds of being caught are small, but tropical storms are like clockwork.

➡ Room prices can be half or less than in high season.

Scarlet Ibis

The scarlet ibis is the national bird of Trinidad and Tobago – quite an honor since the islands have more species of birds than anywhere else in the Caribbean. The Caroni Bird Sanctuary on Trinidad's west coast, 14km south of Port of Spain, is the roosting site for thousands of these majestic birds. At sunset the birds fly in to roost in the swamp's mangroves, giving the trees the appearance of being abloom with brilliant scarlet blossoms. Even if you're not an avid birdwatcher, the sight of the ibis flying over the swamp, glowing almost fluorescent red in the final rays of the evening sun, is not to be missed.

Long, flat-bottomed motorboats, some holding up to 30 passengers, pass slowly through the swamp's channels. To avoid disturbing the birds, the boats keep a fair distance from the roosting sites, so bring a pair of binoculars. Expect to also see herons and egrets, predominant among the swamp's 150 bird species. Note that during summer very few ibis are sighted, but the trip is still worthwhile.

Food & Drink

Callaloo The leaves of the dasheen tuber cooked up with pumpkin, okra and plenty of seasoning.

Carib and Stag The national beers – always served beastly cold.

Doubles Curried *channa* (chickpeas) in a soft-fried *bara* bread.

Roti A split-pea-infused flatbread wrapped around curried meat and vegetables.

Shark and bake Seasoned shark steaks, topped with salad and local sauces and served in a floaty fried bake.

Traditional decorations, Speyside

Speyside

6 The small fishing village of Speyside on Tobago fronts Tyrrel's Bay, and attracts divers and birders. It's the jumping-off point for excursions to uninhabited islands, including Little Tobago and St Giles Island. Also known as Bird of Paradise Island, Little Tobago was the site of a cotton plantation during the late 1800s. In 1909, Englishman Sir William Ingram imported 50 greater birds of paradise from the Aru Islands, off New Guinea, and established a sanctuary to protect them.

Cricket at Queen's Park Oval

7 As with other islands of the West Indies, cricket is more than just a sport in Trinidad and Tobago, it's a cultural obsession. The sport was introduced by the British in the 19th century and during the 1970s and '80s the fearsome West Indian team was the best in the world. Retired batting star Brian Lara hails from Trinidad. Seeing an international match at Port of Spain's Queen's Park Oval is an experience with 25,000 noisy spectators packing the stands.

Getting Around

Air Caribbean Airlines operates the 20-minute flight between Trinidad and Tobago.

Boat Fast catamaran ferries make the trip between Queen's Wharf in Port of Spain, Trinidad, and the main ferry dock in Scarborough, Tobago, two to four times daily.

Bus & Taxi Buses offer travelers an inexpensive way to get around, especially on longer cross-island trips, but can be infrequent and unreliable. For shorter distances, travelers are better off taking maxi-taxis or route taxis, which run on set routes.

Car Driving offers flexibility and cars can be rented on both islands. Drive on the left-hand side of the road.

Sidi Bou Saïd

CAPITAL
Tunis

POPULATION
10.8 million

AREA
163,610 sq km

OFFICIAL LANGUAGE
Arabic

Tunisia

From the sands of the Sahara to golden-hued beaches, tangled Tunis alleys to scattered Roman ruins, Tunisia is a country that intrigues and charms at every turn.

It's but a slim wedge of North Africa's vast expanse, but Tunisia has enough history, cultural diversity and extremes of landscape to fill a country many times its size. With a sand-fringed, jasmine-scented coast, it's a destination usually equated with Mediterranean sun holidays. But get beyond the beaches and you'll find stunning Roman sites, forested hinterland, Saharan dunes and mountain oases, all of which can be experienced in a few days.

The country's tourist sector has struggled mightily since the historic Jasmine Revolution of 2011. Isolated incidents of instability grab international headlines, but it's essentially business as usual. Tunis, the capital, continues to offer an enthralling mix of tradition and modernity, Islamic serenity and seaside hedonism. Surprisingly, while much of the tourist industry founders, there's a number of new guesthouses and small hotels popping up throughout the country. Now, more than ever, Tunisians will welcome you with open arms.

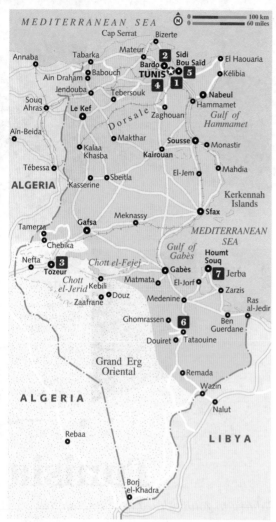

Bardo Museum

2 Take in the splendour of Roman Africa, the mysteries of Carthage and the elegance of Islamic decoration all in one museum at Tunis' Bardo. The country's top museum has a magnificent, must-see collection that provides a vibrant vision of ancient North African life. The original, glorious Husseinite palace now connects with a stark and dramatic contemporary addition, doubling exhibition space. Highlights are a huge stash of incredibly well-preserved Roman mosaics, rare Phoenician artifacts and early Islamic ceramics.

Tozeur

3 Sip mint tea in the cool of an enchanting *palmeraie* in Tozeur, a bustling southern oasis. Tozeur makes an excellent base for longer forays into the surrounding area, including the mesmerising Chott el-Jerid, Tunisia's largest salt lake, and the mountain oases to the north. Bounded on one side by an enormous *palmeraie* and with the desolate snow-white expanse of salt on the other, the town feels at once both far-flung and urban and lively. It's easy to spend a few days here occupied by the labyrinthine old quarter, Ouled el-Hadef, and the cool, winding paths of the *palmeraie*.

Tunisia's
Top Experiences

Sidi Bou Saïd

1 Kick back in this gorgeous village with its nonstop views of the intensely blue Gulf of Tunis. Thirty minutes up the TGM line from Tunis, Sidi Bou Saïd has to be one of the prettiest spots in Tunisia, if not the whole of the Mediter-ranean. With cascading bougainvillea, bright-blue window grills, narrow, steep cobbled streets and jaw-dropping glimpses of azure coast, it's a tour-bus favourite, but it wears its popularity surprisingly well. Come for a swim at its little bayside beach, or take tea at one of the historic cafes.

Tunis

4 Tunis is a fabulous introduction to the wildly divergent layers that make up modern Tunisia. The medina's organic tangle of markets, squares, mosques and shuttered town houses is surrounded by the straight, colonial lines of

KEREN SU / GETTY IMAGES ©

the Ville Nouvelle. Discover cave-like souqs selling everything from shoes to *shisha* (hookah) pipes, historic palaces and ancient hammams (traditional bathhouses). For beach outings, interesting shops and nighttime fun, join the young and well-to-do in the gorgeous northern suburbs.

Carthage

5 You'll have to use a bit of historical sixth sense to imagine this Punic and Roman site in its former glory, as the ruins are scant and scattered over a wide area, but they include impressive Roman baths, houses, cisterns, basilicas and streets. The Carthage Museum backs up imaginings of the site's former glories with material finds,

including such wonders as monumental statuary, mosaics and extraordinary everyday stuff, including razors and kohl pots. The Byrsa Quarter, an excavated quarter of the Punic city, once home to 400,000 people and surrounded by 13m-high walls, is also in the grounds of the museum.

Tataouine

6 While the name is evocative to *Star Wars* fans, the town of Tataouine is more a base for exploring the ruined hilltop *ksar* (fortified stronghold) than a destination in itself. The wonderful Festival of the Ksour in April uses the courtyards of the town for music, dance and other festivities. The best sites are quite a way from town, but can be easily

if Tunisia were 100 people

98 would be Arab
1 would be European
1 would be Jewish and other

age structure (years)
(% of population)

population per sq km

↑ ≈ 3 people

When to Go

MAR–MAY
➜ Explore Roman ruins and hike the wildflower-strewn countryside.

JUN–SEP
➜ Balmy beach frolics and music festivals.

NOV–JAN
➜ The Saharan south's high season.

Star Wars on Location

Tunisia's most famous screen role was providing the otherworldly architecture and desertscapes that gave the *Star Wars* series such a powerful visual identity.

Sidi Driss Hotel Used for interior shots of the Lars family home.

Ong Jemal Darth Maul's lookout in *The Phantom Menace*.

Sidi Bouhlel Nicknamed Star Wars Canyon, this has seen plenty of action.

Ksar Haddada A location for the Mos Espa slave quarters.

La Grande Dune This stood in for the Star Wars Dune Sea.

Chott el-Jerid Here, in the first film, Luke contemplated two suns while standing soulfully at the edge of a crater, peering over these vast, dry salt flats.

Food & Drink

Tunisians love spicy food, and it's almost impossible to encounter a meal that doesn't involve harissa, a fiery chilli paste. Fresh produce is plentiful and salads form part of most meals. The most popular are *salade tunisienne*, a tomato, onions and cucumber mix, topped with tuna, and *salade mechuoia*, a smoky, room-temperature capsicum stew.

Couscous is ubiquitous and served with lamb kebabs, legumes and vegetables, or, Tunisian-style, with fish. Baguettes are a daily staple, along with *tabouna*, the traditional flat Berber bread. Traditional pastries combine Ottoman and Sicilian techniques and flavours.

Street food here is an absolute treat. Tuck into *brik* (deep-fried, crispy pastry pockets filled with egg and meat, prawns or tuna), *lablabi* (chickpea soup) or huge sandwiches stuffed with tuna, egg, harissa and, often enough, fries.

reached by chartering a taxi, or, with luck, patience and a knack for timing, by taking local transport. Don't miss the beautiful Ksar Ouled Soltane, 22km southeast of Tataouine, where the *ghorfas* (ancient grain stores) rise a dizzying four storeys, reached by precarious dream-sequence staircases, and overlook desert-scrub hills.

Jerba

7 The island of Jerba has an intoxicating mixture of sandy beaches, desert heat and wonderfully idiosyncratic architecture. Berber culture is dominant – as the women wrapped in cream-striped textiles, topped with straw hats attest – while a Jewish community, once integral to the island's ethnic make-up, retains a small presence. To the classically inclined, the mere mention of the island's name conjures images of Homer's *Land of the Lotus Eaters*, a place so seductive that it's impossible to leave. The visitors that flock to the luxury hotels along beautiful Sidi Mahres beach appear to understand.

Getting Around

Air Domestic flights to Jerba, Tozeur, Sfax, Gabes, Gafsa and Tabarka are operated by Tunisair subsidiary Tunisair Express.

Boat There is a 24-hour car ferry between El-Jorf and the island of Jerba. There are ferries from Sfax to the Kerkennah Islands.

Bus Frequency for large towns can be up to half-hourly. The buses run pretty much to schedule, and they're fast, usually comfortable and inexpensive. Local buses go to all but the most remote villages.

Train The rail network isn't extensive, but it's efficient enough, cheap and comfortable.

Blue Mosque, İstanbul

CAPITAL
Ankara

POPULATION
80.7 million

AREA
783,562 sq km

OFFICIAL LANGUAGE
Turkish

Turkey

Turkey boasts a rich history, some of the best cuisine you will ever taste, one of the world's greatest cities, and scenery from white-sand beaches to soaring mountains.

While many Turks see their country as European, Turkey packs in as many towering minarets and spice-trading bazaars as its Middle Eastern neighbours. This bridge between continents has absorbed the best of Europe and Asia. Travellers can enjoy historical hot spots, mountain outposts, expansive steppes and *caravanserai*-loads of the exotic, without forgoing comfy beds and buses.

Despite its reputation as a continental meeting point, Turkey can't be pigeon-holed. Cappadocia, a dreamscape dotted with rock formations, is unlike anywhere else on the planet. Likewise, spots like Mt Nemrut, littered with giant stone heads, and Olympos, where Lycian ruins peek from the undergrowth, are quintessentially Turkish mixtures of natural splendour and ancient remains.

The beaches and mountains offer enough activities to impress the fussiest Ottoman sultan. Worldly pleasures include the many historic hotels, the meze to savour on panoramic terraces and, of course, Turkey's famous kebaps.

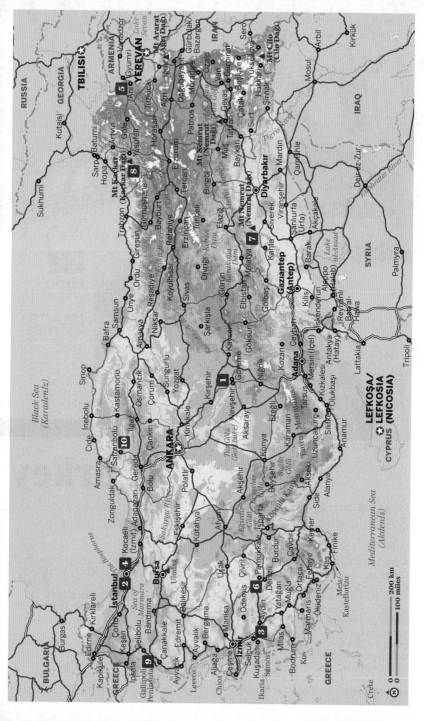

Turkey's
Top Experiences

Cappadocia

1 The hard-set honeycomb landscape looks sculpted by a swarm of genius bees. The rock columns, pyramids, mushrooms and even a few shaped like camels were formed, alongside the area's valleys of cascading white cliffs, when Mt Erciyes erupted. Humans have also left their mark here, in the form of frescoes in colourful Byzantine churches or in the bowels of complex underground cities. These days, Cappadocia is all about good times: fine wine, fine food and five-star caves; trail rides, valley hikes and hot-air ballooning. There's enough to keep you buzzing for days.

İstanbul

2 In İstanbul, you can board a commuter ferry and flit between Europe and Asia in under an hour. Every day, a flotilla takes locals up the Bosphorus and over the Sea of Marmara, sounding sonorous horns as it goes. Morning services share the waterways with diminutive fishing boats and massive container ships, all accompanied by flocks of shrieking seagulls. At sunset, the tapering minarets and Byzantine domes of the Old City are thrown into relief against a dusky pink sky – the city's most magical sight.

APRIOTT / GETTY IMAGES ©

Ephesus

3 Undoubtedly the most famous of Turkey's ancient sites, and considered the best-preserved ruins in the Mediterranean, Ephesus is a powerful reminder of Greek artistry and Roman architectural prowess. A stroll along the marble-coated Curetes Way provides myriad photo opportunities, but the true pièce de résistance is the Terraced Houses complex, offering incredible insight into the daily lives of the city's elite through vivid frescoes and sophisticated mosaics. Much of the city is yet to be unearthed.

if Turkey were 100 people

70 would be Turkish
20 would be Kurdish
10 would be other

belief systems
(% of population)

80
Muslim

19
Alevi Müslim

1
other

population per sq km

TURKEY   USA   UK

≈ 30 people

Aya Sofya

4 Even in mighty İstanbul, nothing beats the Church of the Divine Wisdom, which was the greatest church in Christendom, until the Ottomans took Constantinople. Emperor Justinian had it built in the 6th century as part of his mission to restore the greatness of the Roman Empire. Gazing up at the floating dome, it's hard to believe this fresco-covered marvel didn't single-handedly revive Rome's fortunes. Entering the ancient interior, covered in mosaics and messages left by generations of rulers, leaves an impression that few buildings in the world can equal.

Ani

5 Ani is a truly exceptional site. Historically intriguing, culturally compelling and scenically magical, this ghost city floating in a sea of grass looks like a movie set. Lying in blissful isolation right at the Armenian border, the site exudes an eerie ambience. Before it was deserted in 1239 after a Mongol invasion, Ani was a thriving city and a capital of both the Urartian and Armenian kingdoms. The ruins include several notable churches, as well as a cathedral built between 987 and 1010.

Pamukkale

6 Famed for its intricate series of travertines (calcite shelves) and crowned by the ruined Roman and Byzantine spa city of Hierapolis, the 'Cotton Castle' – a bleach-white mirage by day and alien ski slope by night – is one of the most unusual treasures

Hamams

After a long day's sightseeing, few things could be better than relaxing in a *hamam* (Turkish bath). The ritual is invariably the same. First, you'll be shown to a cubicle where you can undress, store your clothes and wrap the provided *peştamal* (cloth) around you. Then an attendant will lead you through to the hot room, where you sit and sweat for a while.

It's cheapest to bring soap and a towel and wash yourself. The hot room is ringed with individual basins, which you can fill from the taps above, before sluicing the water over yourself with a plastic scoop. It's most enjoyable to let an attendant do it for you, dousing you with warm water and scrubbing you with a coarse cloth mitten. You'll be lathered with a sudsy swab, rinsed off and shampooed. When all this is complete, you'll likely be offered a massage.

Food & Drink

Ayran This refreshing drink is made by whipping yoghurt with water and salt; it's the traditional accompaniment to kebaps.

Meat Kebaps (meat grilled on a skewer) and *köfte* (meatballs) are undoubtedly national dishes. They come in many forms, and are often named after their place of origin.

Mezes Mezes aren't just a type of dish, they're a whole eating experience. If you eat in a local household, your host may put out a few lovingly prepared dishes for guests to nibble on before the main course is served. Mezes are usually vegetable-based, though seafood dishes can also feature.

Tea Drinking *çay* (tea) is the national pastime, and the country's cup of choice is made with leaves from the Black Sea region. Sugar cubes are the only accompaniment and you'll find these are needed to counter the effects of long brewing.

in Turkey. Gingerly tiptoe through the crystal travertines and, when you reach the top, reward yourself with a refreshing dunk in Hierapolis' Antique Pool amid toppled marble columns and dramatic friezes.

Mt Nemrut (Nemrut Dağı)

7 One man's megalomania echoes across the centuries atop the exposed and rugged summit of Nemrut Dağı. A gently emerging sunrise coaxes stark shadows from the mountain's giant sculpted heads, and as dawn breaks, the finer details of the immense landscape below are gradually added. Huddling against the chill of a new morning, a warming glass of çay could not be more welcome. And when your time on the summit is complete, don't miss the graceful Roman bridge crossing the nearby Cendere River.

Kaçkar Mountains (Kaçkar Dağları)

8 Rippling along between the Black Sea coast and the Çoruh River, the Kaçkars rise to almost 4000m, affording superb hiking in

When to Go

HIGH SEASON (Jun–Aug)

➡ Prices and temperature highest. Expect crowds, book ahead. Turkish school holidays mid-June to mid-September. (İstanbul's high season is April, May, September and October.)

SHOULDER (May & Sep)

➡ Fewer crowds. Most businesses are open; prices are lower. Warm temperatures. (İstanbul's shoulder season is June to August.)

LOW SEASON (Oct–Apr)

➡ October is autumn and spring starts in April. Accommodations in tourist areas may close or offer discounts. (İstanbul's low season is November to March.)

summer. Spending a few days crossing the *yaylalar* (mountain pastures) between mountain hamlets such as Olgunlar and Ayder is one of Turkey's top trekking experiences, and the lower slopes offer cultural encounters. The local Hemşin people are a welcoming bunch, serving their beloved, fondue-like *muhlama* (cornmeal cooked in butter) in villages with Ottoman bridges and Georgian churches.

Gallipoli (Gelibolu) Peninsula

9 The narrow stretch of land guarding the entrance to the much-contested Dardanelles is a beautiful area, where

Best on Film

Vizontele Black comedy about the first family to get a TV in a small town.

Polluting Paradise A village's heartbreaking struggle to stop a waste site.

Once Upon a Time in Anatolia A murder mystery that rambles across the Turkish landmass, directed by Nuri Bilge Ceylan.

Filler ve Çimen Tells the stories of desperate characters.

....

Best in Print

Istanbul: Memories of a City In this memoir, Nobel Prize–winner Orhan Pamuk details the history of the great city and his family connections to it.

Birds Without Wings (Louis de Bernières) A lyrical epic backgrounded by the events of early 20th century Turkey.

The Bastard of İstanbul (Elif Şafak) A coming-of age saga bristling with eccentric family members.

Getting Around

Air Turkey is well connected by air throughout the country, although note that many flights go via the major hubs of İstanbul or Ankara.

Bus Turkey's intercity bus system is as good as any you'll find, with modern, comfortable coaches crossing the country at all hours and for very reasonable prices. On the journey, you'll be treated to hot drinks and snacks, plus liberal sprinklings of the Turks' beloved *kolonya* (lemon cologne).

Dolmuşes As well as providing transport within cities and towns, dolmuşes (minibuses) run between places; you'll usually use them to travel between small towns and villages.

pine trees roll across hills above Eceabat's backpacker hang-outs and Kilitbahir's castle. Touring the peaceful countryside is a poignant experience for many: memorials and cemeteries mark the spots where young men from far away fought and died in gruelling conditions. The passionate guides do a good job of evoking the futility and tragedy of the Gallipoli campaign, one of WWI's worst episodes

Safranbolu

10 Listed for eternal preservation by Unesco in 1994, Safranbolu is Turkey's prime example of an Ottoman town brought back to life. Domestic tourists descend here full of sentiment in order to stay in half-timbered houses that seem torn from the pages of a children's storybook. And the magic doesn't end there. Sweets and saffron vendors line the cobblestone alleyways, and artisans and cobblers ply their centuries-old trades beneath medieval mosques. When the summer storms light up the night sky, the fantasy is complete.

Anzac Cove, Gallipoli

Mausoleum of Sultan Sanjar, Merv

CAPITAL
Ashgabat

POPULATION
5.1 million

AREA
488, 100 sq km

OFFICIAL LANGUAGE
Turkmen

Turkmenistan

Isolated and long dominated by an eccentric president, Turkmenistan is one of the oddest corners of Central Asia yet boasts its own distinctive attractions.

By far the most mysterious and unexplored of Central Asia's 'stans, Turkmenistan became famous for the truly bizarre dictatorship of Saparmyrat Niyazov, who ruled as 'Turkmenbashi' ('leader of the Turkmen') until his death in 2006 and covered this little-known desert republic with golden statues of himself.

The result is a fascinating fiefdom of oddball sights and quirky historical remains. But it is also far more than the totalitarian theme park it's often portrayed as; Turkmen-istan is an ancient land of great spirituality, tradition and natural beauty.

The fabled cities of Merv and Konye-Urgench inspire visions of caravans plodding along the ancient Silk Road, while the stark and haunting beauty of the Karakum desert and other quirky natural phenomena are less expected but equally mesmerising sights. The full Turkmen experience is ultimately about mingling with the warm and fascinating Turkmen themselves, whose hospitality is the stuff of legend.

Turkmenistan's
Top Experiences

Konye-Urgench

1 The ancient minarets, mausoleums and palaces of Konye-Urgench stand testament to the former glories of the Khorezmshah empire. The sacred Nejameddin Kubra Mausoleum, near the middle of town, is the holiest part of Konye-Urgench.

Food & Drink

Chal Sour, fermented camel's milk that is served for breakfast.

Çörek A round and flat bread that is especially delicious when fresh from the oven.

Shashlyk A type of shish kebab and a staple dish across Turkmenistan, shashlyk is considered at its best when cooked over the branches of a saxaul tree.

Darvaza Gas Craters

2 Darvaza Gas Craters are a vision of hell amid the incredible lunar landscapes of the Karakum desert. Apparently the result of Soviet-era gas exploration in the 1950s, the three craters are artificial. One has been set alight and blazes with an incredible strength that's visible from miles away. The other two craters contain bubbling mud and water.

Ashgabat

3 The extraordinary Turkmen capital is laden with marble palaces, golden statues and fountains and is home to the wonderfully chaotic Tolkuchka Bazaar. With its lavish marble palaces, gleaming gold domes and vast expanses of manicured parkland, Ashgabat ('the city of love' in Arabic) has reinvented itself as a showcase city for the newly independent republic.

When to Go

APR–JUN

➡ Bright sunshine and cool temperatures provide the best climate for travel.

SEP–NOV

➡ The fierce summer heat gradually cools and the winter approaches.

DEC

➡ Wrap up warm, expect to see snow in the desert and very few other travellers!

Point Grace, Providenciales

Turks & Caicos

With some of the whitest beaches, the clearest waters and the most varied marine life in the Caribbean, Turks and Caicos will thrill anyone who likes to spend time in or by the water.

The Turks and where? That's the reaction most people have when you mention these tropical isles. Like all great Shangri-Las, this one is hidden just under the radar. Be glad that it is, as this tropical dream is the deserted Caribbean destination you've been looking for. And the best part – it's only 90 minutes by plane from Miami.

So why would you want to go there? How about white-sand beaches, clear blue water and a climate that defines divine. Secluded bays and islands where you'll see more wild donkeys than other travelers. Historic towns and villages where life creeps along at a sedate pace.

Divers and beach aficionados will rejoice: clear warm waters teem with marine life, yet are devoid of crashing waves. Islands like Grand Turk – set in a time long since past, with its dilapidated buildings, salt ponds and narrow lanes – contrast with the ever expanding Providenciales. While development is on the rise, all one has to do is catch a boat to the next island over and the solace of solitude returns.

CAPITAL
Cockburn Town

POPULATION
49,070

AREA
948 sq km

OFFICIAL LANGUAGE
English

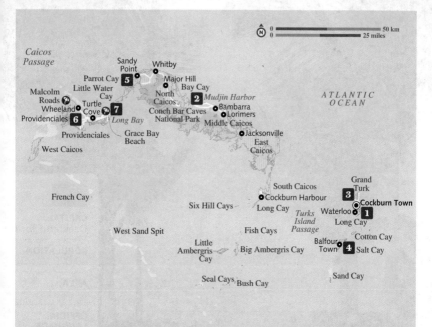

Turks & Caicos'
Top Experiences

Historic Cockburn Town

1 For a taste of the old Caribbean, look no further. Without knowing beforehand, you'd be hard pressed to guess that this sleepy place is the capital city of the Turks and Caicos. What it lacks in polish and sophistication it more than makes up for in rustic charm. The town itself comprises two parallel streets that are interconnected with narrow laneways. Brightly painted, colonial-era houses line the tiny streets and former salt-storage sheds hark back to a bygone era of dusty roads and donkey-filled streets. It's hard not to be enchanted by the whitewashed stone walls, traditional streetlamps and creaking old buildings.

Mudjin Harbor

2 The aim of the game on Middle Caicos is to relax – but if you're keen to get the blood flowing, there are a few options worth checking out. Five miles west of Bambarra Beach, directly in front of Blue Horizon Resort, is Mudjin Harbor – the rocky shore rears up to form a bit of rare elevation. Walking along the clifftop you'll be surprised to see a staircase appear out of nowhere, leading into the earth. Take it down through the cave and emerge on a secluded cliff-lined beach – this is one of the best beach entrances anywhere in the Caribbean. Looking seaward you'll be entertained by the waves crashing into the offshore rocks in spectacular fashion.

Grand Turk

3 Happily lacking the modern development that has enveloped Provo, Grand Turk is a step back in time. At just 6½ miles long, this dot amid the sea is a sparsely populated, brush-covered paradise. Where salt was once the main industry, tourism has taken over and you are blessed with a slew of charming guesthouses to choose from. Beaches rim the land and calm blue water invites you in for a refreshing swim. Diving is the main reason to come to Grand Turk – where the fish are plentiful and the reef pristine. Diving operators will take you snorkeling if you're not a diver, and run courses if you want to learn.

Courthouse, Cockburn Town, Grand Turk Island

Salt Cay

4 If you can't quite envision what the Turks would have been like in the 19th century, take a trip to Salt Cay. Like stepping into a time machine, this picturesque island is the sort of hideaway that you search your whole life to discover. A few dusty roads interconnect the handful of structures, and donkeys wander aimlessly through the streets intermixed with friendly locals. While the land is quiet, the sea surrounding the island is awash with life. Turtles, eagle rays and the majestic humpback whale all frequent the waters.

Parrot Cay

5 For true indulgence, Parrot Cay is definitely the best hotel in the Turks and Caicos, and one of the very best in the Caribbean. On its own eponymous private island, Parrot Cay is part resort with its infinity pool, water sports, diving school and superb restaurants, and part spa, with a firm emphasis on healthy treatments, yoga and 'wellness.' Of course, if you need to ask about the price, you probably can't afford it, but if you're looking for a once-in-a-lifetime splurge or you happen to be a Wall Street banker, then this is the place for you.

if the Turks & Caicos were 100 people

88 would be black
8 would be white
2 would be mixed
1 would be East Indian
1 would be other

belief systems
(% of population)

36 Baptist

12 Church of God

25 other Protestant

11 Roman Catholic

2 Jehovah's Witnesses

14 other

population per sq km

TURKS & CAICOS

HAITI

BAHAMAS

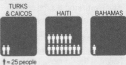
♱ ≈ 25 people

When to Go

JAN–APR

➡ The islands' high season, when the weather is normally dry and warm.

JUL–AUG

➡ Come for the Grand Turk Game Fishing Tournament, or the Annual Music & Cultural Festival, the islands' biggest party.

NOV

➡ Blow a conch shell or just head for the tasting tent at the Turks & Caicos Conch Festival.

JoJo: A National Treasure

Since the mid 1980s a 7ft bottle-nosed male dolphin called JoJo has cruised the waters off of Provo and North Caicos. When he first appeared, he was shy and limited his human contact to following or playing in the bow waves of boats. He soon turned gregarious and has become an active participant whenever people are in the water.

JoJo is now so popular that he has been named a national treasure by the Ministry of Natural Resources. This treasure is protected through the JoJo Dolphins Project. In addition to looking out for JoJo, it educates and raises awareness of issues affecting the ocean.

For more wildlife spotting, note that Salt Cay could very well be one of the best places on earth to see humpback whales – by the thousands. Every winter the gentle giants make their annual pilgrimage to the warm seas of the Caribbean to mate and give birth. From the sandy shores of Salt Cay you can watch the majestic beauties of the sea saunter past from February to March. They are plain to see from the beach but you can also get among it on a whale-watching trip or dive trip organized from either Grand Turk or Salt Cay.

Parasailing, Grace Bay Beach, Providenciales

Providenciales

6 Providenciales, or Provo as it's known locally, is the tourism capital of the Turks and Caicos. It's home to a busy international airport, some fairly rampant development and its crowning glory, miles of beautiful white-sand beaches along its northern coast. It's a great place for those wanting to enjoy cosmopolitan pursuits: you can shop in Provo's many malls, eat in its great restaurants and enjoy cocktails on the beach.

Grace Bay Beach

7 The biggest attraction on the island of Providenciales is this world-famous stretch of sand, notably long and beautiful even by Caribbean standards. This stunning stretch of snow-white sand is perfect for relaxing, swimming and evening up your sunburn. Though it's dotted with hotels and resorts, its sheer size means that finding your own square of paradise is a snap.

Food & Drink

Conch This grilled gastropod remains the dish of choice across the islands, and rigorous controls on the fishing industry mean that its numbers are not declining here.

Lobster Don't miss tasting the fresh lobster during your stay – traditionally served in a butter sauce with lime, it's the culinary highlight of the country.

Turk's Head The local beer is a great way to cool down in the height of the Caribbean afternoon.

Getting Around

Air Air Turks & Caicos flies from Providenciales to Grand Turk, North Caicos, Middle Caicos, South Caicos and Salt Cay daily. It also flies from Grand Turk to Salt Cay daily.

Bicycle Cycling is cheap, convenient and fun. Bicycles are complimentary for guests at many hotels or can be rented at concessions.

Boat TCI Ferry Service is a small passenger-ferry operation taking people from the Leeward Marina on Providenciales to North Caicos. A ferry runs biweekly trips from Grand Turk to Salt Cay.

Car Taxis get expensive in the long run so renting a car makes sense if you plan to explore Provo or Grand Turk.

Taxi Taxis are available on all the inhabited islands. Most are minivans. They're a good bet for touring, and most taxi drivers double as guides.

CAPITAL
Funafuti

POPULATION
10,698

AREA
26 sq km

OFFICIAL
LANGUAGES
Tuvaluan, English

Tepuka Island

Tuvalu

Approaching Tuvalu by plane, after miles of dull ocean, a dazzling smear of turquoise appears, ringed with coral and studded with palm-topped islets – a vulnerable Pacific paradise.

The landmass of Fongafale, Tuvalu's main island, is so startlingly narrow that as the plane nears the airstrip it seems as if it's about to tip into the ocean.

Unfortunately, environmental concerns have focused international attention on Tuvalu. As an atoll nation, the major long-term ecological threat to Tuvalu comes from global warming and rising sea levels. As well as shoreline erosion, water bubbles up through the porous coral on which the islands are based, and causes widespread salt contamination of areas used to grow staple crops. Over the past few years, king tides – the biggest swells of the year – have been higher than ever. If sea levels continue to rise as predicted, the islands could be wiped off the face of the earth.

What will happen to the population if Tuvalu does start to go under? New Zealand currently accepts 75 migrants a year and has said it will absorb Tuvalu's population if it comes to that.

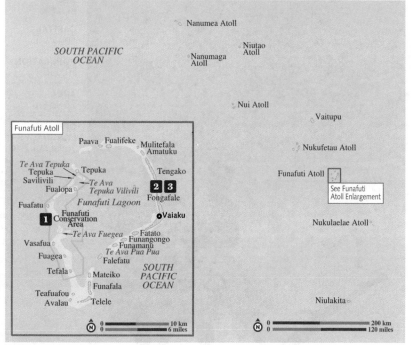

Tuvalu's
Top Experiences

Funafuti Conservation Area

1 Realise the desert-island fantasies of your wildest dreams by exploring the clear waters and palm-covered islets of the stunning Funafuti Conservation Area, a half-hour boat ride across the lagoon.

Te Ano

2 While in Tuvalu, try to watch, or better still join in, a game of Tuvalu's unique sport, *te ano*. Almost completely incomprehensible to a first-timer, it's great fun and one of the few games that men and women play together. It's played with two balls made from pandanus leaves. A popular place for playing is the runway at Fongafale's airstrip!

Fongafale

3 Fongafale is Tuvalu's answer to a metropolis, the seat of government, and the largest islet in Funafuti Atoll. Funafuti's must-sees include Funafala Islet to the south, which is lined with talcum-powder beaches and has basic accommodation right by the water. You can also take in a performance of Tuvalu's national dance, *fatele*.

Food & Drink

Staples of the Tuvaluan diet include coconut, seafood, taro and breadfruit. Most restaurants sell cheap, filling plates of Chinese-style food. Restaurants sometimes suffer from shortages when shipments don't arrive. Thursday to Saturday is party night on Fongafale, when the old timers go to 'twists' (discos) and the youngsters go 'clubbing'.

When to Go

MAY–OCT

➡ Winds are light and from the southeast (trade winds), tempering the tropical climate.

NOV–FEB

➡ The wettest season, with brief but heavy showers and hot, humid conditions.

FEB–APR

➡ Cyclone season, though Tuvalu is considered just outside the tropical cyclone belt.

Queen Elizabeth National Park

CAPITAL
Kampala

POPULATION
34.8 million

AREA
241,038 sq km

OFFICIAL
LANGUAGE
English

Uganda

This petite nation punches well above its weight in terms of nature. Its lush forests reverberate with life and their canopies shield hundreds of bird and mammal species, including half the planet's mountain gorillas.

Emerging from the shadows of its dark history, a new dawn of tourism has risen in Uganda, polishing a glint back into the 'pearl of Africa'. Travellers are streaming in to explore what is basically the best of everything the continent has to offer.

For a relatively small country, there's a lot that's big about the place. It's home to the tallest mountain range in Africa, the world's longest river and the continent's largest lake. And with half the remaining mountain gorillas residing here, and the Big Five to be ticked off, wildlife watching is huge.

While anti-gay sentiments have cast a shadow on the otherwise positive tourism picture, and tensions continue to simmer with the Karamojong in the northeast, Uganda remains one of the safest destinations in Africa. Other than watching out for the odd hippo at your campsite, there's no more to worry about here than in most other countries.

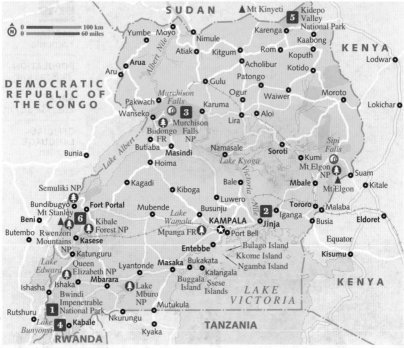

Uganda's
Top Experiences

Bwindi Impenetrable National Park

1 Home to almost half of the world's surviving mountain gorillas, the World Heritage–listed Bwindi Impenetrable National Park is one of Africa's most famous. Set over 331 sq km of improbably steep mountain rainforest, the park is home to an estimated 360 gorillas: undoubtedly Uganda's biggest tourist drawcard. The Impenetrable Forest, as it's also known, has an incredible biodiversity of flora and fauna. Its 120 species of mammal is more than any of Uganda's other national parks, though sightings are less common because of the dense forest. For birdwatch-

ers it's one of the most exciting destinations in the country, with almost 360 species.

Nile River, Jinja

2 Famous as the source of the Nile River, Jinja has emerged as the adrenaline capital of East Africa. Here you can get your fix of white-water rafting, kayaking, quad biking, mountain biking, horseback riding and bungee jumping. The town has a lush location and is the major market centre for eastern Uganda.

Murchison Falls National Park

3 Uganda's largest national park is one of its very best. Animals are in plentiful supply and

it's home to the raging Murchison Falls. The falls were once described as the most spectacular thing to happen to the Nile along its 6700km length; here the 50m-wide river is squeezed through a 6m gap and it shoots through this narrow gorge with explosive force. A three-hour trip from the park headquarters up to the base of the falls and is the highlight of the park for most visitors. There are abundant hippos, crocodiles and buffaloes and birds along the route. The halfway mark takes you 500m from the base of the falls, which provides splendid views, but to get a true sense of its power and might you'll have to head to the Top of the Falls walk.

Mountain gorillas, Bwindi Impenetrable National Park

Lake Bunyonyi

4 Lake Bunyonyi ('place of many little birds') is undoubtedly the loveliest lake in Uganda. Its contorted shore encircles 29 islands, and the steep surrounding hillsides are intensively terraced, almost like parts of Nepal. A magical place, especially with a morning mist rising off the placid waters, it has supplanted the Ssese Islands as the place for travellers to chill out on their way through Uganda. All guesthouses can arrange boat trips on the lake, either in motorboats or dugout canoes, which is still how most locals get about. And it's one of the few places in Uganda where you can swim, with no crocodiles, hippos or bilharzia, so go ahead and jump in.

Kidepo Valley National Park

5 This lost valley in the extreme northeast, along the Sudanese border, has the most stunning scenery of any protected area in Uganda. The rolling, short-grass savannah of the 1442-sq-km Kidepo Valley National Park is ringed by mountains and cut by rocky ridges. Kidepo is most notable for harbouring a number of animals found nowhere else in Uganda, including cheetahs, bat-eared foxes, aardwolves, caracal, greater and lesser kudus. There are also large concentrations of elephants, zebras, buffaloes, bushbuck, giraffes, lions, jackals, leopard, hyenas and Nile crocodiles. The bird checklist is fast approaching

if Uganda were 100 people

17 would be Baganda
10 would be Banyankole
8 would be Basoga
7 would be Bakiga
58 would be other

belief systems
(% of population)

42	42
Roman Catholic	Protestant

12	3	1
Muslim	other	none

population per sq km

DEMOCRATIC REPUBLIC
UGANDA   OF THE CONGO   KENYA

🧍 = 11 people

When to Go

JUN–SEP

➡ The best bet weather-wise; not too hot and with minimal rainfall.

JAN–FEB

➡ Perfect climate to head for the hills to climb the Rwenzoris or Mt Elgon.

OCT–NOV

➡ Can be rainy, but fewer travellers means gorilla permits are much easier to obtain.

Gorilla Tracking

Hanging out with mountain gorillas is a genuine once-in-a-lifetime experience and one of the most thrilling wildlife encounters in the world.

There are theoretically 64 daily permits available to track gorillas in Bwindi Impenetrable National Park. Permits cost US$500 and are booked through the Uganda Wildlife Authority (UWA) office in Kampala.

Once you join a tracking group, the chances of finding the gorillas are almost guaranteed. But, since the terrain in Bwindi Impenetrable National Park is mountainous and heavily forested, it can take anywhere from 30 minutes to five hours to reach them.

Walking sticks or a porter are a very good idea. Of the 28 gorilla groups living in Bwindi, nine have been habituated to be visited by tourists, with permits issued for different parts of the park. Buhoma is the most popular due to it having the most permits and best tourist facilities. Nkuringo in the southwest is also stunning, while permits are also available to Ruhija and Rushaga.

Food & Drink

Local food is much the same as elsewhere in the region, except in Uganda ugali (a food staple usually made from maize flour) is called posho, and is far less popular than matoke (mashed plantains). Rice, cassava and potatoes are also common starches. One uniquely Ugandan food is the rolex, a chapatti rolled around an omelette.

Popular local beers include the light Bell Beer, infamous for its 'Great night, good morning!' ad-jingle and stronger Nile Special. Waragi (millet-based alcohol) is the local hard stuff and tastes a little like gin, so it's best with a splash of tonic.

DANITA DELIMONT / GETTY IMAGES ©

500 species (second among the national parks only to the larger Queen Elizabeth National Park).

Rwenzori Mountains

6 Back in Uganda's heyday, the Rwenzoris were as popular with travellers as Mt Kilimanjaro and Mt Kenya, but this is definitely a more demanding expedition. The Rwenzoris have a well-deserved reputation for being very wet and muddy, with trails that are often slippery and steep. There are treks available to suit all levels and needs, from one-day jaunts in the forest to 10-day treks with technical climbs. The six-day treks are about the standard. The best times to trek are from late December to mid-March and from mid-June to mid-August, when there's less rain. Guides, who are compulsory even if you've conquered the seven summits, are on perpetual standby so you can book in the morning and leave the same day. Walking trails and huts are in pretty good shape and there are wooden pathways over the bogs and bridges over the larger rivers; all this lessens the impact of walkers on the fragile environment.

Getting Around

Bus & Minibus Uganda is the land of shared minibuses (called taxis or occasionally matatus), and except for long distances, these are the most common vehicles between towns. Except for very short distances, you're better off in a standard bus or half-sized 'coaster'. Fares are similar to minibuses (usually a little less), they're safer in a crash and they travel faster due to less-frequent stops.

Car Hiring a 4WD is the best way to get around Uganda. Most people hire a driver, but it's becoming more common for tourists to get around the national parks on their own, especially those experienced at bush driving and self-sufficient with repairs.

Kyevo-Pecherska Lavra, Kyiv

CAPITAL
Kyiv

POPULATION
44.6 million

AREA
603,550 sq km

OFFICIAL
LANGUAGE
Ukrainian

Ukraine

Big, diverse and largely undiscovered, Ukraine is one of Europe's last genuine travel frontiers, a poor nation rich in colourful tradition, warm-hearted people and off-the-map experiences.

Ukraine is big. In fact it's Europe's biggest country (not counting Russia, which isn't entirely in Europe) and packs a lot of diversity into its borders. You can be clambering around the Carpathians in search of Hutsul festivities, sipping Eastern Europe's best coffee in sophisticated Lviv and partying on Odessa's beaches, all in a few days.

A diverse landscape obviously throws up a whole bunch of outdoorsy activities. How about mountain biking or hill walking in the Carpathians, bird spotting in the Danube Delta or water sports on the Kyiv Sea? Many

Ukrainians love nothing more than wandering their country's vast forests, foraging for berries and mushrooms or picnicking by a meandering river.

History is all around you wherever you go in this vast land, whether it be among the Gothic churches of Lviv, the Stalinist facades of Kyiv, the remnants of the once-animated Jewish culture of West Ukraine or the more recent Soviet high-rises just about anywhere. After the latest political turmoils, this divided nation faces an uncertain future but its people share one thing: a talent for survival.

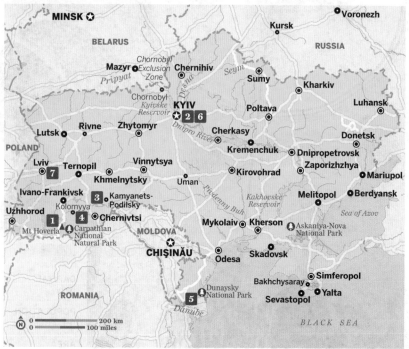

Ukraine's
Top Experiences

Carpathian Landscapes

1 By and large Ukraine is as flat as a topographically challenged blin (pancake), which makes its bumpy bits all the more special. Ukraine's slice of the Carpathian arc barely reaches over 2000m, but its soothing wooded slopes, rough stony trails, flower-filled upland pastures and wide, snaking valleys make this prime hiking, biking and skiing territory. Needless to say, the Carpathians are home to Ukraine's highest peak, 2061m Mt Hoverla, a fairly easy trek from nearby villages, as well as several ski resorts.

Kyevo-Pecherska Lavra, Kyiv

2 Discover the mysteries of Eastern Orthodoxy and descend into catacombs to see mummies of much-revered saints on an excursion to the holy of holies for all eastern Slavs. Founded as a cave monastery in 1051, the lavra is packed with golden-domed churches, baroque edifices and orchards. Religious ceremonies take place in lavishly decorated, icon-filled interiors, accompanied by beautiful choir singing and attended by flocks of pilgrims and monks. Obscure museums in the grounds are dedicated to Scythian gold and micro-miniatures and decorative arts.

Kamyanets-Podilsky

3 Ringed by the dramatic gorge of the Smotrych River, there are few more eye-pleasing spots in Ukraine than this Podillyan town. A stroll from the new bridge takes you through the cobbled quarters of this once-divided community, past beautifully renovated churches, crumbling palaces and forgotten pieces of the once beefy defences, to the town's impossibly picturesque fortress, surely one of the highlights of any visit to Ukraine. The best thing? Outside high season you may have the place entirely to yourself.

Pine forest, Carpathians

Kolomyya

4 With its traveller-friendly places to stay, two fascinating museums and effortless access to the surrounding forested hills, Kolomyya is one of the best bases from which to scale the heights of the Carpathian Mountains. The town's central Pysanky Museum, housed in a giant Easter egg, is the obvious highlight, but aimless wandering also bears fruit in the shape of some twirling Art Nouveau architecture from the town's Austro-Hungarian days.

Danube Delta Biosphere Reserve

5 Europe's largest wetland is located in Ukraine's far southwest where the Danube dumps water and silt into the Black Sea. Few make the effort to reach this far-flung wedge of fertile territory, but those who do are rewarded with astoundingly beautiful scenery, colourful birdlife, and serene evenings in drowsy Vylkovo, fancifully nicknamed the 'Ukrainian Venice' thanks to its network of canals.

if Ukraine were 100 people

77 would be Ukrainian
17 would be Russian
6 would be other

belief systems
(% of population)

50 — Ukrainian Orthodox (Kyiv Patriarchate)

26 — Ukrainian Orthodox (Moscow Patriarchate)

7 — Ukrainian Autocephalous Orthodox

8 — Greek Catholic

9 — other

population per sq km

UKRAINE   USA   UK

♦ ≈ 30 people

When to Go

HIGH SEASON
(Jul–Aug)

➡ Expect stifling heat, humidity and heavy thunderstorms.

➡ Accommodation rates rise in Crimea but fall in the Carpathians.

➡ Cities empty as people head for the coast and country.

SHOULDER
(May–Jun, Sep–Oct)

➡ Dodge the extreme temperatures of summer or winter.

➡ Spring can be chilly, but it's a pleasant time to be in blossoming Kyiv.

➡ Visit Crimea in autumn and avoid the summer crowds.

LOW SEASON
(Nov–Apr)

➡ Expect temperatures below zero, heavy snowfalls and hard frosts.

➡ The Carpathians skiing season runs November to March.

➡ Book ahead for New Year and early January.

A Midsummer Night's Dream

It involves fire, water, dancing, fortune-telling and strong overtones of sex. No wonder the Soviets tried to quash the festival of Ivan Kupala, a pagan midsummer celebration. Indeed, leaders since the Middle Ages have tried to outlaw it.

To ancient pre-Christians, Kupala was the god of love and fertility, and young people would choose a marriage partner on this midsummer eve. Today's rituals vary, but typically involve folk singing and a maypole-style dance performed by young women wearing white gowns and floral wreaths. Later, young couples dance around a bonfire. Couples also jump over small fires holding hands. Whether they maintain their grip is a test of whether their love will last.

A good spot to join Kupala celebrations is Pyrohovo in Kyiv, or head to the countryside for more traditional rituals.

Food & Drink

Borsch The Ukrainian national soup, which is made with beetroot, pork fat and herbs. There's also an aromatic 'green' variety, based on sorrel.

Kasha Sometimes translated as 'porridge', but usually turns out to be buckwheat swimming in milk and served for breakfast.

Salo Basically raw pig fat, cut into slices and eaten with bread or added to soups and other dishes. Look out for the 'Ukrainian Snickers bar' – salo in chocolate.

Varenyky Similar to Polish *pierogi* – pasta pockets filled with everything from mashed potato to sour cherries.

Vodka Also known in Ukraine as horilka, it accompanies every celebration, red-letter day and get-together – in copious amounts.

Ancient wooden church house

Pyrohovo Museum of Folk Architecture, Kyiv

6 This large chunk of countryside just outside Kyiv is filled with traditional wooden architecture representing all parts of the country. Whole churches, windmills, shops and houses were brought here from their original villages, providing a wonderful backdrop for folk festivals, which frequently take place on the grounds. Here Transcarpathia is walking distance from the Poltava region, although it might require a bit of footwork.

Lviv's Historical Centre

7 Lviv is the beating cultural heart of Ukraine, and the main square, pl Rynok, is the bustling heart of Lviv. Plonked in the middle is the huge *ratusha* (town hall), around which mill clutches of camera-toting tourists and quick-footed locals. The aroma of freshly milled coffee beans wafts across the square from the city's legendary coffeehouses, and summer tables tumble out across the Habsburg-era cobbles as old Soviet-era trams rumble past. Take a seat, order a coffee and take it all in.

Getting Around

Bus Buses serve every city and small town, but are best for short trips (three hours or less), as vehicles are generally small, old and overcrowded.

Car Unless you're used to developing-world driving conditions, getting behind the wheel in Ukraine is not recommended. The roads are Europe's worst and there's an unofficial highway code that only local drivers understand.

Taxi Travelling by taxi anywhere in the ex-USSR can be a decidedly unenjoyable experience for foreigners, so if there's a bus or tram going to your destination, take it.

Burj Khalifa towering above traditional buildings of Dubai

CAPITAL
Abu Dhabi

POPULATION
5.5 million

AREA
83, 600 sq km

OFFICIAL LANGUAGE
Arabic

United Arab Emirates

There's more to the Emirates than 21st-century glitz and glam, with cultures solidly rooted in Islam and generations of Bedouin heritage.

For most people, the United Arab Emirates (UAE) means just one place: Dubai, the sci-fi-esque city of iconic skyscrapers, palm-shaped islands, city-sized malls, indoor ski slopes and palatial beach resorts. But guess what? Beyond the glitter awaits a diverse mosaic of six more emirates, each with its own character and allure.

An hour's drive south, oil-rich Abu Dhabi, the country's capital, is quickly gaining a reputation as a hub of culture, sport and leisure. Beyond its borders looms the vast Al Gharbia desert, whose magical silence is interrupted only by the whisper of shifting dunes rolling towards Saudi Arabia.

North of Dubai, Sharjah has the country's best museums, while tiny Ajman and Umm Al Quwain provide glimpses of life in the pre-oil days, and Ras Al Khaimah is busy building up its tourism infrastructure. For the best swimming and diving, head to the emirate of Fujairah and frolic in the crystal clear and warm waters of the Gulf of Oman.

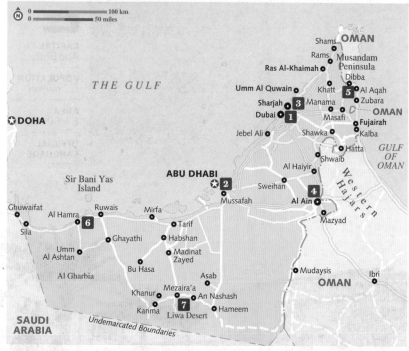

United Arab Emirates'
Top Experiences

Dubai

1 With space-age skyscrapers sprouting across an endless desert hemmed in by a coastline etched with palm-shaped archipelagos, Dubai is a 21st-century Middle Eastern Shangri-la powered by un-flinching ambition and can-do spirit. The motto: if you can think of it, it shall be done. The world's tallest building? Check. Skiing in the desert? Check. Islands shaped like the entire world? Check. Dubai is an exciting place to visit, with lovely beaches, sophisticated restaurants and bars, world-class shopping, ultra-luxe hotels, and awe-inspiring architecture, including the Burj Khalifa, the world's tallest building.

Sheikh Zayed Grand Mosque, Abu Dhabi

2 This snowy white mosque in Abu Dhabi – conceived by Sheikh Zayed himself – can accommodate up to 40,000 worshippers. More than 80 marble domes dance on its roofline, which is held aloft by over 1000 pillars and punctuated by four 107m-high minarets. The interior is a made-to-impress mix of marble, gold, semi-precious stones, crystals and ceramics. It's home to the world's largest Persian carpet (which took 2000 craftsmen two years to complete) and seven massive gold-plated crystal chandeliers.

Sharjah

3 Sharjah doesn't dazzle with glitz but with culture and got the Unesco nod back in 1998 when it was declared Arab Capital of Culture; and deservedly so. Once you have penetrated the traffic-clogged outskirts of town, the historic old town is easy to navigate on foot. Sharjah's Heritage Area is part of an ambitious long-term redevelopment project called Heart of Sharjah, scheduled for completion in 2025. It aims to restore historic buildings and turn them into hotels, museums, shops and restaurants while preserving the feel of the pre-oil days.

JOHN HARPER / GETTY IMAGES ©

Al Ain Oasis

4 Lose yourself in the labyrinth of Al Ain's shady date-palm oasis. A marked route leads through its 3000 acres, an atmospheric journey along shaded walkways and cultivated plots irrigated by a traditional *falaj* (an underground system of tunnels). There are nearly 150,000 date palms here, along with mango, almond, banana and fig trees. Keep an eye out for the ruins of an ancient fortress and a mosque as well as date storage containers.

Al Aqah

5 In Fujairah, Al Aqah is known for having the eastern coast's best beaches, which are flanked by high-end hotels. This

is prime snorkelling and diving territory, and even beginners can have a satisfying experience thanks to Snoopy Island, named by some clever soul who thought the shape of this rocky outcrop about 100m offshore resembled the *Peanuts* cartoon character sleeping atop his doghouse. Unfortunately, the 2008/09 red tide killed off much of the coral, but the waters here still teem with all sorts of colourful critters including, if you're lucky, green sea turtles and (harmless) black-tip reef sharks.

Jazirat Al Hamra Fishing Village

6 For an authentic glimpse of the pre-oil era, poke around this deli-

if the UAE were 100 people

19 would be Emerati
23 would be other Arab and Iranian
50 would be South Asian
8 would be other expatriates

belief systems
(% of population)

96 Muslim   4 Other

When to Go

NOV–MAR

➡ Moderate temps, higher room rates, major festivals, good camping.

MAR–MAY & OCT

➡ Hot days, balmy nights, good for beach vacations, desert camping.

JUN–SEP

➡ Hot and humid, steep hotel discounts, best time for diving.

population per sq km

UAE   SAUDI ARABIA   OMAN

⋔ ≈ 3 people

Camel Racing

Camel racing is not only a popular spectator sport but is deeply rooted in the Emirati soul and originally practised only at weddings and special events. These days it's big business with races held on modern, custom-built 6km- to 10km-long tracks between October and early April.

Pure-bred camels begin daily training sessions when they're about two years old. The local Mahaliyat breed, Omaniyat camels from Oman, Sudaniyat from Sudan and interbred Muhajanat are the most common breeds used in competition. Over 100 animals participate in a typical race, each outfitted with 'robo-jockeys' since the use of child jockeys was outlawed in 2005. Owners race alongside the camels in SUVs on a separate track, giving commands by remote.

Food & Drink

Strangely, restaurants serving authentic Emirati food are scarce. If you do get a chance, try these typical dishes, and don't miss out on the succulent local dates!

Balaleet Vermicelli blends with sugar syrup, saffron, rosewater and sauteed onions in this rich breakfast staple.

Fareed Mutton-flavoured broth with bread; popular at Ramadan.

Hareis Ground wheat and lamb slow-cooked until creamy (an bit like porridge); sometimes called the 'national dish'.

Khuzi Stuffed whole roasted lamb on a bed of spiced rice.

Madrooba Salt-cured fish (*maleh*) or chicken mixed with raw bread dough until thick.

Makbus A casserole of spice-laced rice and meat (usually lamb) or fish garnished with nuts, raisins and fried onions.

ciously spooky ghost town, one of the oldest and best preserved coastal villages in the UAE. First settled in the 14th century, its people subsisted mostly on fishing and pearling until they suddenly picked up and left in 1968. A stroll among this cluster of coral stone houses, wind towers, mosques, schools and shops is at its most atmospheric at sundown.

Liwa Desert

7 Approximately 250km south of Abu Dhabi, the Liwa Desert is a 150km arc of villages and farms hugging the edge of Saudi Arabia's Empty Quarter (Rub'al-Khali), which truly lives up to its name: only the odd roaming camel or small verdant oasis magnifies just how spectacular this endless landscape of undulating sand dunes, shimmering in shades of gold, apricot and cinnamon, really is. This is the Arabia described by explorer Sir Wilfred Thesiger. Once you visit, you'll understand why the Liwa has a special place in the hearts of nationals who come here to get back to their roots and take in the arid splendour of this glorious landscape.

Getting Around

Bus A growing fleet of public buses makes inter-emirate travel increasingly convenient.

Car Having your own wheels is a great way to see the UAE, allowing you to get off the major highways and to stop as you please. Well-maintained multilane highways link the cities, often lit along their entire length. For off-road driving, you need a 4WD.

Taxi Taxis are cheap, metered and ubiquitous and – given the dearth of public transportation in some emirates – often the only way of getting around. Most drivers can also be hired by the hour.

CAPITAL	Washington, DC
POPULATION	316.4 million
AREA	9.8 million sq km
OFFICIAL LANGUAGE	English

Golden Gate Bridge, San Francisco

United States of America

The great American experience is about so many things: bluegrass and beaches, snow-covered peaks and redwood forests, restaurant-loving cities and big open skies.

America is the birthplace of LA, Las Vegas, Chicago, Miami, Boston and New York City – each a brimming metropolis whose name alone conjures a million different notions of culture, cuisine and entertainment. Look more closely, and the American quilt unfurls in all its surprising variety: the eclectic music scene of Austin, the easygoing charms of antebellum Savannah, the ecoconsciousness of free-spirited Portland, the magnificent waterfront of San Francisco, and the captivating old quarters of New Orleans, still rising up from its waterlogged ashes.

This is a country of road trips and great open skies, where four million miles of highways lead past red-rock deserts, below towering mountain peaks, and across fertile wheat fields that roll off toward the horizon. The sun-bleached hillsides of the Great Plains, the lush rainforests of the Pacific Northwest and the scenic country lanes of New England are a few fine starting points for the great American road trip.

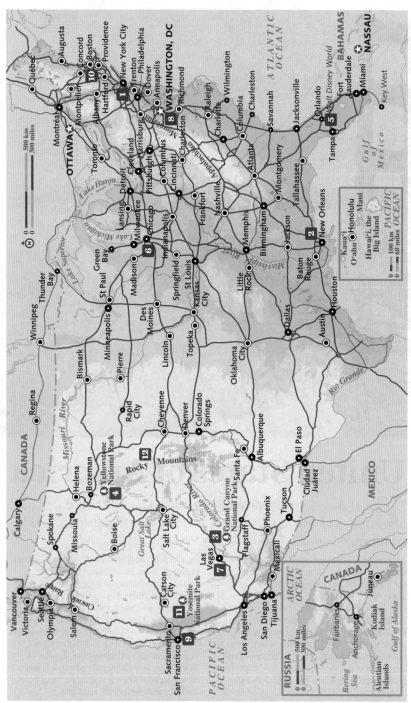

United States of America's
Top Experiences

New York City

1 Home to striving artists, hedge fund moguls and immigrants from every corner of the globe, New York City is constantly reinventing itself. It remains one of the world centers of fashion, theater, food, music, publishing, advertising and finance. A staggering number of museums, parks and ethnic neighborhoods are scattered through the five boroughs. Do as every New Yorker does: hit the streets. Every block reflects the character and history of this dizzying kaleidoscope, and on even a short walk you can cross continents.

New Orleans

2 Reborn after devastating Hurricane Katrina in 2005, New Orleans is back. Caribbean-colonial architecture, Creole cuisine and a riotous air of celebration seem more alluring than ever in the Big Easy. Nights out are spent catching Dixieland jazz, blues and rock amid bouncing live music joints, and the city's riotous annual Mardi Gras and Jazz Fest are famous the world over. 'Nola' is a food-loving town that celebrates its myriad culinary influences. Feast on soft-shelled crab before hitting the bar scene on Frenchman St.

Empire State building, Manhattan skyline

Grand Canyon

3 You've seen it on film, heard about it from all and sundry who've made the trip. Is it worth the hype? The answer is a resounding yes. The Grand Canyon is vast and nearly incomprehensible in age – it took 6 million years for the canyon to form and some rocks exposed along its walls are 2 billion years old. Peer over the edge and you'll confront the great power and mystery of this earth we live on. Once you see it, no other natural phenomenon quite compares.

Yellowstone National Park

4 Stunning natural beauty, amazing geology and some of the best wildlife watching in North America: these are just a few reasons why Yellowstone has such star power among the world's national parks. Divided into five distinct regions, this place is huge and you could spend many days exploring the park's wonders. Highlights include massive geysers, waterfalls, fossil forests, mountains, scenic overlooks and gurgling mud pools – with some 1100 miles of hiking trails the best way to take it all in.

if USA were 100 people

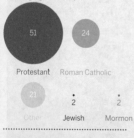

65 would be white
15 would be Hispanic
13 would be African American
4 would be Asian American
3 would be other

belief systems

(% of population)

51 Protestant
24 Roman Catholic
21 Other
2 Jewish
2 Mormon

population per sq mile

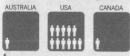

AUSTRALIA   USA   CANADA

= 11 people

Walt Disney World

5 Want to set the bar high? Call yourself 'the happiest place on earth'. Walt Disney World does, and then pulls out all the stops to deliver the exhilarating sensation that you are the most important character in the show. Despite all the frantic rides, entertainment and nostalgia, the magic is watching your own child swell with belief after they have made Goofy laugh, been curtsied to by Cinderella, guarded the galaxy with Buzz Lightyear and battled Darth Maul like your very own Jedi knight.

Chicago

6 The Windy City will blow you away with its cloud-scraping architecture, lakefront beaches and world-class museums. But its true mojo is its blend of high culture and earthy pleasures. Is there another city that dresses its Picasso sculpture in local sports team gear? Where residents queue for hot dogs in equal measure to North America's top restaurant? Winters are brutal, but come summer, Chicago fetes the warm days with food and music festivals.

Las Vegas

7 Sin City is a neon-fueled ride through the nerve center of American strike-it-rich fantasies. See billionaires' names gleam from the marquees of luxury hotels. Hear a raucous soundscape of slot machines, clinking martini glasses and the hypnotic beats of DJs spinning till dawn. Sip cocktails under palm trees and play blackjack by the pool. Visit Paris, the Wild West and a tropical island, all in one night. It's all here and it's open 24 hours,

Route 66

Whether you seek to explore retro Americana or simply want captivating scenery far from the crowds, Route 66 will take you there. The winding journey passes some of the USA's greatest attractions – the Grand Canyon, the Mississippi River, Arizona's Painted Desert and Petrified Forest National Park, and, at road's end, the Pacific beaches of sun-kissed Southern California.

Culturally, Route 66 is an eye-opener. Discard your preconceptions and unearth the joys of what some dismissively term 'flyover' states. Mingle with farmers in Illinois and country-and-western stars in Missouri. Hear the legends of cowboys and Indians in Oklahoma. Visit Native American tribal nations and contemporary pueblos across the Southwest. Then follow the trails of miners and desperados deep into the Old West.

Food & Drink

Breakfast From a giant stack of buttermilk pancakes at a vintage diner to lavish Sunday brunches, Americans love their eggs and bacon, their waffles and hash browns, and their big glasses of fresh-squeezed orange juice. Most of all, they love a steaming cup of morning coffee with unlimited refills.

Lunch An American worker's lunch hour often affords only a sandwich, burger or hearty salad. The formal 'business lunch' is more common in big cities like New York. While you'll spot diners drinking a beer or a glass of wine with lunch, the days of the socially acceptable 'three martini lunch' are long gone.

Dinner Early in the evening, Americans settle in to a weeknight dinner, which, given the workload of many families, might be takeout or prepackaged meals in a microwave. Some families still cook a traditional Sunday night dinner, when relatives and friends gather for a big feast.

Morning Glory Pool, Norris Geyser Basin

all for the price of a poker chip (and a little luck).

National Mall

8 Nearly 2 miles long and lined with iconic monuments and hallowed marble buildings, the National Mall is the epicenter of Washington, DC's political and cultural life. For exploring American history, there's no better place to ruminate, whether tracing your hand along the Vietnam War Memorial or ascending the steps of Lincoln Memorial, where Martin Luther King Jr gave his famous 'I Have a Dream' speech.

San Francisco

9 If you've ever wondered where the envelope goes when it's pushed, here's your answer. Psychedelic drugs, newfangled technology, gay liberation, green ventures and free speech all became mainstream long ago in San Francisco. Amid the clatter of trams and thick fog that sweeps in by night, the diverse hill and valley neighborhoods of San Francisco invite long days of wandering, with great indie shops,

When to Go

HIGH SEASON
(Jun–Aug)

➡ Warm days across the country, with generally high temperatures.

➡ Busiest season, with big crowds and higher prices.

➡ In ski resort areas, January to March is high season.

SHOULDER
(Oct & Apr–May)

➡ Milder temperatures, fewer crowds.

➡ Spring flowers (April); fiery autumn colors (October) in many parts.

LOW SEASON
(Nov–Mar)

➡ Wintery days, with snowfall in the north, and heavier rains in some regions.

➡ Lowest prices for accommodations (aside from ski resorts and warmer getaway destinations).

world-class restaurants and bohemian nightlife.

Boston & Cape Cod

10 Start by tracing the footsteps of early Tea Partiers like Paul Revere and Sam Adams on Boston's famed Freedom Trail. After following the road through American revolutionary history, go romp around the campus of Harvard University and do a little rabble-rousing yourself at one of the city's historic pubs. Then cool off by hitting the beaches of the Cape Cod National Seashore, hopping on a whale-watching cruise or getting lost in the wild dunes of Provincetown.

Best on Film

Annie Hall (1977) Woody Allen's brilliant romantic comedy, with New York City playing a starring role.

Godfather (1972–90) Famed trilogy that looks at American society through immigrants and organized crime.

North by Northwest (1959) Alfred Hitchcock thriller with Cary Grant on the run across America.

Singin' in the Rain (1952) Among the best in the era of musicals, with an exuberant Gene Kelly and a timeless score.

Best in Print

Beloved (1987) Toni Morrison's searing Pulitzer Prize–winning novel set during the post–Civil War years.

Huckleberry Finn (1884) Mark Twain's moving tale of journey and self-discovery.

On the Road (1957) Jack Kerouac on post–WWII America.

The Great Gatsby (1925) F Scott Fitzgerald's powerful Jazz Age novel.

Getting Around

Air The domestic air system is extensive and reliable, with dozens of competing airlines, hundreds of airports and thousands of flights daily.

Car For maximum flexibility and convenience, and to explore rural America, a car is essential. Although petrol prices are high, you can often score fairly inexpensive rentals.

Bus To save money, travel by bus, particularly between major towns and cities. As a rule, buses are reliable, cleanish and comfortable, with airconditioning, barely reclining seats, lavatories and no smoking.

Train Compared with other modes of travel, trains are rarely the quickest, cheapest, timeliest or most convenient option, but they turn the journey into a relaxing, social and scenic all-American experience.

Yosemite National Park

11 Yosemite's iconic glacier-carved valley never fails to get the heart racing, even when it's bumper-to-bumper in summer. In springtime, get drenched by the spray of its thundering snowmelt waterfalls and twirl singing to the Sound of Music in high-country meadows awash with wildflowers. The scenery of Yosemite is intoxicating, with dizzying rock walls and formations, and ancient giant sequoia trees. If you look for it, you'll find solitude and space in the 1169 sq miles of development-free wilderness.

Rocky Mountains

12 The Rockies are home to the highest peaks in the lower 48 states. Craggy peaks, raging rivers, age-old canyons and national parks set the scene. Go skiing and snowboarding down pristine, powdery slopes in the winter, hike and mountain bike amid spring wildflowers or feel the rush of white water on sun-drenched summer afternoons.

Cape Cod

JEFF GREENBERG / GETTY IMAGES ©

Carnaval, Montevideo

CAPITAL
Montevideo

POPULATION
3.3 million

AREA
176,215 sq km

OFFICIAL LANGUAGE
Spanish

Uruguay

Uruguay is a backpacker's dream. Travelers come for the wild, surf-pounded beaches, for celeb-spotting at Punta and the history-soaked smugglers' port of Colonia.

Wedged like a grape between Brazil's gargantuan thumb and Argentina's long forefinger, South America's smallest Spanish-speaking country has always been an underdog. Bypassed by the Spanish for its lack of mineral wealth, batted about like a ping-pong ball at the whim of its more powerful neighbors and neglected by many modern-day travelers, Uruguay remains a delightfully low-key, hospitable place where visitors can melt into the background – whether caught in a cow-and-gaucho traffic jam on a dirt road to nowhere or strolling with *mate*-toting locals along Montevideo's beachfront.

Short-term visitors will find plenty to keep them busy in cosmopolitan Montevideo, picturesque Colonia and party-till-you-drop Punta del Este. But if you've got time, dig a little deeper. Go wildlife-watching along the Atlantic coast, hot-spring-hopping up the Río Uruguay, or horseback riding under the big sky of Uruguay's vast interior, where fields spread out like oceans dotted with little cow and eucalyptus islands.

Uruguay's
Top Experiences

Montevideo's Carnaval

1 If you thought Brazil was South America's only Carnaval capital, think again! *Montevideanos* cut loose in a big way every February, with music and dance filling the air for a solid month. Not to be missed is the early-February Desfile de las Llamadas, a two-night parade of *comparsas* (neighborhood Carnaval societies) through the streets of Palermo and Barrio Sur districts. *Comparsas* are made up of *negros* (persons of African descent) and *lubolos* (whites who paint their faces black for Carnaval, a long-standing Uruguayan tradition). Neighborhood rivalries play themselves out as wave after wave of dancers whirl to the electrifying rhythms of traditional Afro-Uruguayan *candombe* drumming, beaten on drums of three different pitches.

Punta del Diablo

2 Once a sleepy fishing village, Punta del Diablo has long since become a prime summer getaway for Uruguayans and Argentines, and the epicenter of Uruguay's backpacker beach scene. During the day you can rent surfboards or horses along the town's main beach, or trek an hour north to Parque Nacional Santa Teresa. In the evening there are sunsets to watch, spontaneous bonfires and drum sessions to drop in on... you get the idea.

Salto

3 Built near the falls where the Rio Uruguay makes its 'big jump' (Salto Grande), Salto is Uruguay's second-largest city and the most northerly crossing point to Argentina. It's a relaxed place with some 19th-century architecture and a pretty riverfront. But the main reason people come here is to soak their weary traveling muscles in the thermal baths.

Colonia del Sacramento

4 On the east bank of the Rio de la Plata, Colonia is an irresistibly picturesque town enshrined as a Unesco World Heritage site. Its Barrio Histórico, an irregular

RICHARD I'ANSON / GETTY IMAGES ©

colonial-era nucleus of narrow cobbled streets, occupies a small peninsula jutting into the river. Pretty rows of sycamores offer protection from the summer heat, and the riverfront provides a venue for spectacular sunsets. Visitors sunbathe on the 18th-century town wall, or bounce through the cobblestoned streets in a vintage car.

Punta del Este

5 Punta del Este – with its many beaches, elegant seaside homes, yacht harbor, high-rise apartment buildings, pricey hotels and glitzy restaurants – is one of South America's most glamorous resorts and easily the most expensive place in Uruguay. Celebrity-watchers have a full-time job here. Punta is teeming with big names, and local gossipmongers keep regular tabs on who's been sighted where. Surrounding towns caught up in the whole Punta mystique include the famed club zone of La Barra to the east and Punta Ballena to the west.

Estancias

6 *Estancias*, the giant farms of Uruguay's interior, are a national cultural icon. The Uruguayan Ministry of Tourism has designated 'Estancia Turística' as a distinct lodging category, and dozens of such places have opened their doors to tourists. The granddaddy of Uruguayan tourist *estancias* is San Pedro de Timote, 14km up a dirt road from the town of Cerro Colorado,

if Uruguay were 100 people

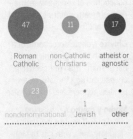

88 would be white
8 would be mestizo
4 would be black

belief systems
(% of population)

47 Roman Catholic
11 non-Catholic Christians
17 atheist or agnostic
23 nondenominational
1 Jewish
1 other

population per sq km

URUGUAY   ARGENTINA   BRAZIL

✝ ≈ 1 person

When to Go

FEB
➡ Street theater and drumming consume Montevideo during Carnaval celebrations.

MAR
➡ Enjoy Tacuarembó's gaucho festival, plus warm water on Uruguay's beaches.

OCT
➡ Soak in a hot spring near Salto or channel Carlos Gardel at Montevideo's annual tango festival.

Oxo Cubes

In 1865, the Liebig Extract of Meat Company located its pioneer South American plant southwest of downtown Fray Bentos. Looking at the abandoned factory today, you'd never guess that its signature product, the Oxo beef cube, once touched millions of lives on every continent. Oxo cubes sustained WWI soldiers in the trenches, Jules Verne sang their praises in his book *Around the Moon*, Stanley took them on his search for Livingstone, Scott and Hillary took them to Antarctica and Everest. More than 25,000 people from more than 60 countries worked here, and at its peak the factory was exporting nearly 150 different products, using every part of the cow except its moo.

Food & Drink

Asado Uruguay's national gastronomic obsession, a mixed grill cooked over a wood fire, featuring various cuts of beef and pork, chorizo, *morcilla* (blood sausage) and more.

Buñuelos de Algas Savory seaweed fritters, a specialty along the coast of Rocha.

Chajá A terrifyingly sweet concoction of sponge cake, meringue, cream and fruit, invented in Paysandú.

Chivito A cholesterol bomb of a steak sandwich piled high with bacon, ham, fried or boiled egg, cheese, lettuce, tomato, olives, pickles, peppers and mayonnaise.

Medio y medio A refreshing blend of half white wine, half sparkling wine, with ties to Montevideo's historic Café Roldós.

Ñoquis The same plump potato dumplings the Italians call gnocchi, traditionally served on the 29th of the month.

Sea lions, Cabo Polonio

amid 253 hectares of rolling cattle country. It is greatly enhanced by the complex of historic structures: a gracious white chapel, a courtyard with soaring palm trees, a library with gorgeous tilework, and a circular stone corral. Common areas feature parquet wood floors, big fireplaces, comfy leather armchairs, two pools and a sauna.

Cabo Polonio

7 Lose yourself in the sand dunes and survey the sea lions from atop the lighthouse at Cabo Polonio.

Cabo Polonio is one of Uruguay's wildest areas and home to its second-biggest sea-lion colony, near one of Uruguay's most rustic coastal villages nestled in sand dunes. Below the lighthouse, southern sea lions and South American fur seals frolic on the rocks every month except February. You can also spot southern right whales from late August to early October, penguins on the beach in July, and the odd southern elephant seal between January and March on nearby Isla de la Raza.

Getting Around

Air If you really need to get somewhere in a hurry, internal charter flights are available.

Bus Uruguayan buses and roads are well maintained and bus travel in Uruguay is a lot less painful than in many parts of the world. To get your choice of seat, buy tickets in advance from the terminal. Local buses are cheap but often slow and crowded.

Car & motorcycle Due to the excellent bus network, not many people use independent transport to get around Uruguay.

Taxis Taxis are so cheap they're hard to resist. Meters are always out of whack, so drivers consult a photocopied chart to calculate the fare.

Shah-i-Zinda, Samarkand

CAPITAL
Tashkent

POPULATION
28.7 million

AREA
447,400 sq km

OFFICIAL LANGUAGE
Uzbek

Uzbekistan

A Silk Road destination of the highest order, Uzbekistan is a centre of culture, trade and architecture that has drawn travellers for centuries.

Central Asia's cradle of culture for more than two millennia, Uzbekistan is proudly home to a spellbinding arsenal of architecture and ancient cities, all infused with the bloody, fascinating history of the Silk Road. Any romantic who has daydreamed of travelling the Golden Road to Samarkand or the desert tracks to Bukhara will have their sights firmly set on Uzbekistan.

As the cultural and historic heart of Central Asia, Uzbekistan is home to Islamic architecture of floating turquoise domes and towering minarets that rank among the region's greatest sights. And amid these treasures everyday life goes on: in the foreground bearded old men with stripy cloaks haggle over melons in the bazaar or savour a pot of green tea beside a kebab stand.

Despite being a harshly governed police state, Uzbekistan remains an extremely friendly country where hospitality remains an essential element of daily life.

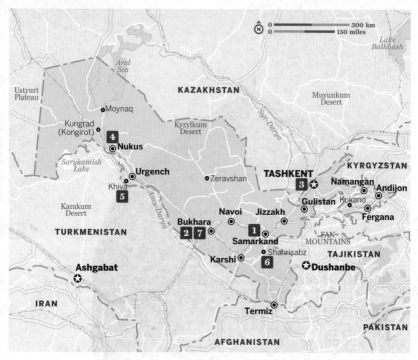

Uzbekistan's
Top Experiences

Samarkand

1 The breathtaking Registan leads a formidable cast of larger-than-life Timurid architectural gems in Samarkand. James Elroy Flecker's 1913 poem *The Golden Journey to Samarkand* evokes the romance of Uzbekistan's most glorious city. No name is so evocative of the Silk Road as Samarkand. Once your eye locks onto the domes and minarets, the sublime monuments of Timur, the bazaar and the city's long, rich history indeed work some kind of magic. If you're short on time, see the Registan, Gur-e-Amir, Bibi-Khanym Mosque and Shah-i-Zinda.

Bukhara

2 Bukhara is an exquisitely preserved holy city boasting stunning 15th-century medressas, awesome B&Bs and fascinating history. Central Asia's holiest city, Bukhara has buildings spanning a thousand years, and a thoroughly lived-in old centre that probably hasn't changed much in centuries. It is one of the best places in Central Asia for a glimpse of pre-Russian Turkestan. Most of the centre is an architectural preserve. Lyabi-Hauz, a plaza built around a pool in 1620 is the most peaceful and interesting spot in town

Tashkent Museums

3 Some of the museums in the capital city of Tashkent amount to quirky cultural gems. The History Museum of the People of Uzbekistan is a must-stop for anyone looking for a primer on the history of Turkestan from ancient times to the present. The 2nd floor has Zoroastrian and Buddhist artefacts, including several 1st- to 4th-century Buddhas and Buddha fragments from the Fayoz-Tepe area near Termiz. On the 3rd floor English placards walk you through the Russian conquests of the khanates and emirates.

BRUNO MORANDI / GETTY IMAGES ©

Savitsky Karakalpakstan Art Museum, Nukus

4 Central Asia's greatest art collection is in Nukus' Savitsky Karakalpakstan Art Museum. In fact, this is one of the most remarkable art collections in the former Soviet Union. The museum owns some 90,000 pieces – including more than 15,000 paintings – only a fraction of which are actually on display. About half of the paintings were brought here in Soviet times by renegade artist and ethnographer Igor Savitsky. Many of the early-20th- century Russian paintings did not conform to Soviet Realism, but found protection in these isolated backwaters

Khiva

5 Khiva, the last independent khanate, appears frozen in time amid the desert. Khiva's name, redolent of slave caravans, barbaric cruelty and terrible journeys across deserts infested with wild tribesmen, struck fear into all but the boldest 19th-century hearts. Nowadays it's a mere 35km southwest of Urgench, past cotton bushes and fruit trees. The historic heart of Khiva has been so well preserved that it's often criticised as lifeless – a 'museum city'. Still, you have to admit that it's one helluva museum.

Shakhrisabz

6 Shakhrisabz is a small, un-Russified town south of Samarkand, across the hills in the Kashkadarya

if Uzbekistan were 100 people

80 would be Uzbek
6 would be Russian
5 would be Tajik
3 would be Kazakh
6 would be other

belief systems
(% of population)

88 Muslim
9 Eastern Orthodox
3 other

When to Go

MARCH–MAY & SEP–NOV

➡ Mild and rainy in spring, and some light frosts in autumn.

JUN–AUG

➡ Summer is long, hot and dry.

DEC–FEB

➡ Winter weather is unstable, with snow and temperatures below freezing.

population per sq km

UZBEKISTAN   KAZAKHSTAN   TURKMENISTAN

≈ 4 people

The Arts

Traditional art, music and architecture – evolving over centuries – were placed in a neat little box for preservation following the Soviet creation of the Uzbek SSR. Somehow, in the years to follow, two major centres of progressive art were still allowed to develop: Igor Savitsky's collection of lost art from the 1930s, stashed away in Nukus' Savitsky Karakalpakstan Art Museum, and the life stories told inside the late Mark Weil's legendary Ilkhom Theatre in Tashkent.

When it comes to music, Uzbeks love Turkish pop, and their own music reflects that. The country's most famous singer is President Karimov's politician/socialite/business mogul/Harvard alumni/pop star daughter Gulnara, better known to some by her stage name, Googoosha. Googoosha steals some of the thunder from more accomplished artists, such as classical Uzbek pop artist Dado, the ever-changing girl band Setanho (erstwhile Setora) and grizzled '90s rockers Bolalar.

Food & Drink

Apricot Pits A local favourite; they're cooked in ash and the shells are cracked by the vendor before they reach the market.

Dimlama Meat, potatoes, onions and vegetables braised slowly in a little fat and their own juices. It is also called bosma.

Halim Porridge of boiled meat and wheat.

Katyk A thin yoghurt drink that comes plain but can be sweetened if you have some sugar or jam handy.

Kurut Small balls of tart, dried yoghurt.

Plov Delicious conglomeration of rice, vegetables and meat bits swimming in lamb fat and oil.

Bazaar in Bukhara

CAROL ADAM / GETTY IMAGES ©

province. The town is a pleasant Uzbek backwater – until you start bumping into the ruins dotted around its backstreets and the megalomaniac ghosts of a wholly different place materialise. This is Timur's hometown, and once upon a time it probably put Samarkand itself in the shade. It's worth a visit just to check out the great man's roots.

Uzbek Crafts

7 Uzbekistan's crafts are exemplified by silk in Margilon, ceramics in Rishton, and everything under the sun in Bukhara. If you've been travelling along the Silk Road seeking answers to where, in fact, this highly touted fabric comes from, Margilon, and its Yodgorlik Silk Factory, should be your ground zero. Uzbekistan is the world's third-largest silk producer, and Margilon is the traditional centre of the industry. Rishton, near the Kyrgyzstan border, is famous for the ubiquitous cobalt and green pottery fashioned from its fine clay. About 90% of the ceramics you see in souvenir stores across Uzbekistan originates here – most of it handmade.

Getting Around

Air Most routes along the tourist trail are well served by domestic flights to and from Tashkent.

Shared Taxi Shared taxis ply all the main intercity routes and also congregate at most border points. They leave when full from set locations – usually from near bus stations – and run all day and often through the night.

Train The most comfortable and safest method of intercity transport, though not usually the fastest. However, express (skorostnoy, or 'high-speed') trains between Tashkent, Samarkand and Bukhara, with airplane-style seating, are not much slower than a shared taxi and a lot more comfortable.

CAPITAL
Port Vila

POPULATION
261,565

LAND AREA
12,189 sq km

OFFICIAL LANGUAGES
Bislama, English, French

Local women, Tanna

Vanuatu

Tropical weather brings light and life to sandy beaches and azure waters. Throughout the islands, strong communities show off their country's attributes to a soundtrack of drumming and dance.

Where else can you jump from a coral- and tropical fish–filled blue hole into a 4WD truck to watch an active volcano spit out lava high above you? Contrasts like these make Vanuatu a country well worth taking the time to explore. The ni-Van take life in smiling strides, and as you adjust to their early mornings and dark evenings, you'll wonder why you've ever lived life in a rush.

It's all thatched-roof accommodation in the outer islands but glitzy resorts abound on Efate and Santo. These islands also boast great roads, giving you round-island access on Efate and smooth access to stunning beaches and blue holes on Santo. Add to that scented balmy breezes and several best-in-the-world experiences that few people know about: a luxury liner shipwrecked in clear waters, gigantic banyan trees, pounding waterfalls, an ancient living culture with extraordinary ceremonies and picture-perfect beaches.

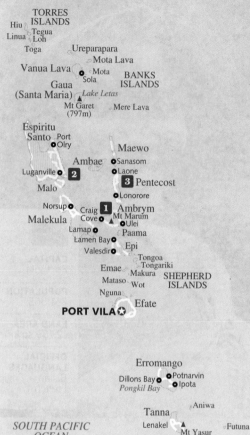

When to Go

SEP & OCT

➡ Expect pleasant, warm weather. Popular during the Australian school holidays.

NOV–APR

➡ Cyclone season, so it's possible to get excellent deals on accommodation in Vanuatu.

MAY & JUN

➡ The tropical heat dips in the cool season. Life is gearing up again after the cyclone season.

Food & Drink

Kava Mildly hallucinogenic drink made from the roots of a type of pepper plant. Offen consumed in ceremonies or to welcome visitors.

Laplap Vanuatu's national dish is made by grating manioc, taro roots or yams into a doughy paste.

Nalot A dish made from roasted taro, banana or breadfruit mixed with coconut cream.

Vanuatu's
Top Experiences

Volcanic Highs

1 Camp near Mt Marum, an active volcano, while surrounded by the jungle, cane forests, lava beds and ash plains on Ambrym. Fit travellers with a guide can climb to the caldera of Mt Marum or its smoking twin, Mt Benbow.

Underwater Adventure

2 With its luxury-liner wreck and expansive underwater American dumping ground from WWII, scuba divers (and snorkellers) love Vanuatu's Santo, especially the dive sites off Luganville.

Pentecost Land Diving

3 At the beginning of each year the stages are selected, the towers painstakingly built from local timbers and the vines carefully chosen. Then, during the *naghol* (land diving) season (April until June), the jumping begins. This is bungee jumping Vanuatu style – and it's what started the bungee phenomenon worldwide. There are several levels to dive from, with the youngest boys (and the occasional game tourist) usually leaping from the lowest rung.

St Peter's Basilica

CAPITAL
Vatican City

POPULATION
839

AREA
0.44 sq km

OFFICIAL LANGUAGES
Latin, Italian

Vatican City

The Vatican, at a mere 0.44 sq km, may be the world's smallest sovereign state, but it boasts some of Italy's most celebrated masterpieces.

Ensconced in the centre of the Italian capital Rome and enshrined in a bevy of sacrosanct traditions and rituals, the Vatican City is one of those rare places that must be visited to be believed. This is the seat of the Catholic Church, ruled with absolute authority by the Pope, who lives in a palace with over a thousand rooms and is protected by a hundred single Swiss men in ceremonious red, yellow and blue costume.

The city was established by the 1929 Lateran Treaty, and is the modern vestige of the Papal States, the fiefdom that ruled Rome and much of central Italy until the Italian reunification in 1861. The Vatican's association with Christianity dates to the 1st century, when St Peter was crucified in Nero's Circus. To commemorate this, the emperor Constantine commissioned a basilica to be built on the site where the saint was buried.

The glory of St Peter's Basilica, however, is only the beginning of the wealth of treasures that await deep inside the bowels of the Vatican Museums.

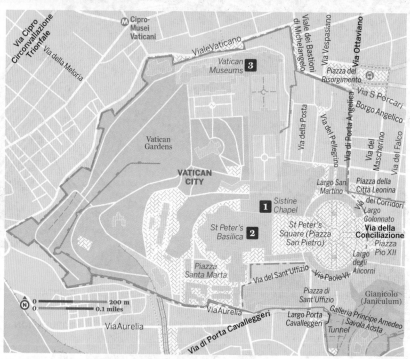

Vatican City's
Top Experiences

Sistine Chapel

1 The jewel in the Vatican crown, the Sistine Chapel is home to two of the world's most famous works of art – Michelangelo's frescos and his *Last Judgement*. Gazing heavenwards at the cinematic ceiling frescoes is an unforgettable experience. See God pointing his finger at Adam and pinch yourself that you're looking at the original painting, not a dime-a-dozen poster copy.

St Peter's Basilica

2 In a city of outstanding churches, none can hold a candle to St Peter's Basilica, Italy's largest, richest and most spectacular church. A monument to centuries of artistic genius, it contains some magnificent works of art, including three of Italy's most celebrated masterpieces: Michelangelo's *Pietà*, his breathtaking dome and Bernini's *baldachin* (canopy) over the papal altar.

Vatican Museums

3 With some 7km of exhibitions and more masterpieces than many countries, this vast musem complex, housed in the 5.5 hectare Palazzo Apostolico Vaticano, contains one of the world's greatest art collections. You'll never manage to cover the whole collection in one go – it's said that if you spend one minute on every exhibit, it would take you 12 years to see everything.

Food & Drink

Eat Roman pasta such as creamy carbonara (egg yolk, parmesan and bacon; and fiery alla matriciana (tomato, bacon and chilli).

Drink Local wines such as Frascati and Torre Ercolana.

When to Go

HIGH SEASON
(Jul & Aug)

➜ Summertime is hot and busy – make plans well in advance.

SHOULDER
(Apr–Jun)

➜ Spring is the best time to go; prices are lower and the weather is warm.

WEDNESDAYS
(Sep–Jun)

➜ The pope addresses his flock at the Vatican at 11am every Wednesday.

Salto Ángel (Angel Falls)

Venezuela

'La Tierra de Gracia' (Land of Grace), as Christopher Columbus called Venezuela in 1498, is nothing if not strangely beautiful and beautifully strange.

CAPITAL
Caracas

POPULATION
28.8 million

AREA
912.050 sq km

OFFICIAL LANGUAGE
Spanish

While other South American countries are romanticized for the tango, Machu Picchu or Carnaval, Venezuela's international reputation swirls around oil and the next international beauty-pageant winner. But through the rhetorical looking glass lies a little-known secret: Venezuela can be shockingly gorgeous and, though criminally undervisited, offers more to travelers than even the most intrepid explorers are aware.

The sixth-largest country in South America boasts Andean peaks; the longest stretch of Caribbean coastline to be found in any single nation; tranquil offshore islands set amid turquoise seas; wetlands teeming with caimans, capybaras, piranhas and anacondas; the steamy Amazon; and rolling savanna punctuated by flat-topped mountains called *tepuis*. Those seeking adventure will find hiking, snorkeling, scuba diving, kitesurfing, windsurfing, paragliding and more. Even better, Venezuela is relatively compact – no thrill is discouragingly too far from the next.

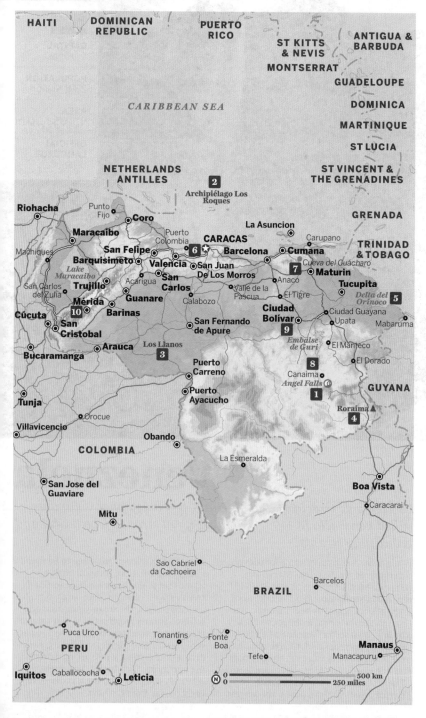

HAITI

DOMINICAN
REPUBLIC

PUERTO
RICO

ST KITTS
& NEVIS

ANTIGUA &
BARBUDA

MONTSERRAT

GUADELOUPE

CARIBBEAN SEA

DOMINICA

MARTINIQUE

ST LUCIA

NETHERLANDS
ANTILLES

2

Archipiélago Los
Roques

ST VINCENT &
THE GRENADINES

GRENADA

Riohacha

Punto
Fijo

Coro

La Asuncion

Carupano

TRINIDAD
& TOBAGO

Maracaibo

Puerto
Colombia

CARACAS

Barcelona

Cumana

Cueva del Guácharo

Machiques

San Felipe

6

Maturin

Barquisimeto

Valencia

San Juan

Anaco

Tucupita

Lake
Maracaibo

San

De Los Morros

Valle de la

El Tigre

7

Delta del
Orinoco

5

San Carlos
del Zulia

Acarigua

Carlos

Pascua

Trujillo

Calabozo

Ciudad Guayana

Mérida

10

Guanare

Ciudad

Upata

Mabaruma

Cúcuta

Barinas

Bolívar

9

San

San Fernando

El Manteco

Cristobal

de Apure

Embalse

Arauca

de Guri

El Dorado

Bucaramanga

Los Llanos

3

Puerto

8

Canaima

GUYANA

Tunja

Orocue

Carreno

Angel Falls

1

Villavicencio

Puerto

Roraima

Ayacucho

4

Obando

COLOMBIA

La Esmeralda

San Jose del
Guaviare

Boa Vista

Caracarai

Mitu

Sao Cabriel
da Cachoeira

Barcelos

BRAZIL

Puca Urco

Tonantins

Fonte
Boa

PERU

Manaus

Tefe

Manacapuru

Iquitos

Caballococha

Leticia

N 0   500 km
   0 250 miles

Venezuela's
Top Experiences

Salto Ángel (Angel Falls)

1 Fly over a surreal landscape of flat-topped *tepuis* to Venezuela's Parque Nacional Canaima, and touch down alongside the pink-tinted cascades of Canaima lagoon. Your next step is a five-hour river journey through lush jungle. From the Mirador Laime, witness the cascade of Salto Ángel, the world's tallest waterfall, as it thunders 979m from the plateau of Auyantepui. Swim while gazing up at the water flow, and then sleep in a hammock camp, serenaded by the evening jungle.

Archipiélago Los Roques

2 Island-hopping is the primary activity on Los Roques, a group of nearly 300 shimmering, sandy islands that lie in aquamarine waters some 160km due north of Caracas. It's pricier here than on the mainland because everything is imported, but for those who love undeveloped beaches, snorkeling and diving, the trip is worth every bolívar. There are no high-rise hotels and you can walk barefoot on Gran Roque's sand streets. The whole archipelago, complete with the surrounding waters (2211 sq km), was made a national park in 1972.

Los Llanos

3 One of Venezuela's best destinations is the wildlife-rich Los Llanos, an immense savanna plain south of the Andes that's also the home of Venezuela's cowboys and the twangy harp music of *joropo* (traditional music of Los Llanos). With Venezuela's greatest repository of wildlife found here, you'll be flat-out dazzled by caimans, capybaras, piranhas, anacondas and anteaters, plus an enormous variety of birds. In the rainy season, the land is half-flooded and animals are dispersed but still visible everywhere. The dry months (mid-November to April) are the high season, with a greater concentration of animals clustered near water sources.

Roraima

4 A stately table mountain towering into churning clouds, Roraima (2810m) lures hikers and nature-lovers looking for Venezuela at its natural and rugged best. Unexplored until 1884, and studied extensively by botanists ever since, the stark landscape contains strange rock formations and graceful arches, ribbon waterfalls, glittering quartz deposits and carnivorous plants. The frequent mist only accentuates the otherworldly feel.

Orinoco Delta

5 Roaring howler monkeys welcome the dawn. Piranhas clamp onto anything that bleeds. Screaming clouds of parrots gather at dusk, and weaving bats gobble insects under the blush of a million stars. For wildlife-viewing on the water's edge, it's hard to outshine the Orinoco Delta. A deep-green labyrinth of islands, channels and mangrove swamps engulfing nearly 30,000 sq km – the size of Belgium – this is one of the world's great river deltas and a mesmerizing region to explore.

Puerto Colombia

6 Puerto Colombia's beachside location makes it one of the major backpacker hangouts in Venezuela. In this attractive and laid-back colonial village packed with *posadas* and restaurants, most folks spend their days on the beach and evenings sipping *guarapita* (cane alcohol mixed with passion-fruit juice and lots of sugar) down on the

Chocolate Coast

The production of Venezuela's world-famous cocoa is most heavily concentrated around Chuao and along the coast of Parque Nacional Henri Pittier, home to the most rare and sought-after variety, *criollo*. Chocolatiers the world over seek out its virtually bitter-free, delicate taste, and you'll find broad swaths of red-scorched cocoa drying in the sun at plantations in the area. Representing only 5% to 10% of the world's cocoa production, *criollo* is considered a delicacy among cocoa varieties, and you can seek it out on a day trip to Chuao, where locals peddle everything from hot chocolate to chocolate ice-cream to chocolate liqueurs – a real sweet treat.

Food & Drink

Arepa A grilled corn pancake stuffed with cheese, beef or other fillings – ubiquitous fast food, and often eaten for breakfast.

Cachapa A larger, flat corn pancake, served with cheese and/or ham.

Casabe Huge, flat bread made from yucca; a staple in indigenous communities.

Coffee Aromatic espresso shots of homegrown liquid heaven, served in little plastic cups at the *panadería* (bakery).

Empanada Deep-fried cornmeal turnover stuffed with various fillings.

Hallaca Maize dough with chopped meat and vegetables, wrapped in banana leaves and steamed; like a Mexican tamale.

Pabellón criollo The Venezuelan national dish of shredded beef, black beans, rice, cheese and fried plantains.

Polar beer If there was a national beverage, it would be these icy minibottles of brew.

Quesilla Caramel custard.

if Venezuela were 100 people

33 would be Caracas
24 would be Maracaibo
19 would be Valencia
13 would live in Barquisimeto
11 would live in Maracay

belief systems

(% of population)

96 Roman Catholic   2 Protestant   2 other

population per sq km

VENEZUELA   MEXICO   UK

≈ 30 people

MORALES / GETTY IMAGES ©

Hato Piñero, Los Llanos

waterfront, where drumming circles rev up on weekends.

Cueva del Guácharo

7 Venezuela's longest and most magnificent cave

has 10.2km of caverns. It's inhabited by the shrieking *guácharo* (oilbird), which lives in total darkness and leaves the cave only at night in search of food. *Guácha-* *ros* have a radar location system (similar to bats) and huge whiskers that enable them to navigate in the dark. From August to December, the population in the cave is estimated at 10,000 and occasionally up to 15,000. Within its maze of stalactites and stalagmites, the cave also shelters crabs, fish and fast-moving rodents.

Canaima

8 The closest popula- tion center to Salto Ángel, Canaima is a remote indigenous village that hosts and dispatches a huge number of tourists. Although it's a base to reach Venezuela's number-one natural attraction, Canaima

When to Go

HIGH SEASON (Dec–Mar)

➡ The country vacations during Christmas (until mid-January), Carnaval and Holy Week. Transportation is busy, hotels fill quickly.

➡ Dry season runs roughly November to April.

SHOULDER (May–Oct)

➡ Salto Ángel (Angel Falls) and the Gran Sabana waterfalls gush, swollen with rainy season flow.

LOW SEASON (Oct–Nov)

➡ Low season brings some of the best prices before the Christmas and New Year holidays.

is truly gorgeous as well. The Laguna de Canaima sits at the heart of everything, a broad blue expanse framed by a palm-tree beach, a dramatic series of seven picture-postcard cascades and a backdrop of anvil-like *tepuis*. Most tours to Salto Ángel include a short boat trip and hike that allows you to walk behind some of the falls and get the backstage experience of the hammering curtains of water. Their color is a curious pink, caused by the high level of tannins from decomposed plants and trees.

Best on Film

Secuestro Express (2005) Takes a cold look at crime, poverty, violence, drugs and class relations in the capital. It broke all box-office records for a national production.

Huelepega (1999) A bleak portrayal of Caracas street children using genuine street youth, not actors.

Amaneció de golpe (1999) 'A Coup at Daybreak' is the story of how former president Hugo Chávez burst onto the political scene.

Best in Print

El falso cuaderno de Narciso Espejo (The False Notebook of Narciso Espejo; Guillermo Meneses; 1952) A groundbreaking experimental novel from the middle of the 20th century.

País portátil (Portable Country; Adriano González León; 1968) A powerful magical-realism novel, which contrasts rural Venezuela with the urban juggernaut of Caracas.

Socialist Dreams and Beauty Queens: A Couchsurfer's Memoir of Venezuela (Jamie Maslin; 2011) Fun travel lit – part memoir, part political thesis.

Getting Around

Boat Venezuela has a number of islands, but only Isla de Margarita is serviced by regular scheduled boats and ferries. The Río Orinoco is the country's major inland waterway. The river is navigable from its mouth up to Puerto Ayacucho, with limited scheduled passenger service.

Bus As there is no passenger-train service, almost all traveling is done by bus. Buses are generally fast, efficient and affordable and run regularly day and night between major population centers. Many short-distance regional routes are served by *por puestos* (literally 'by the seat') – a cross between a bus and a taxi.

Car Outside of Caracas, traveling by car can be a comfortable way of getting around.

Ciudad Bolívar

9 The proud capital of Venezuela's largest state, Ciudad Bolívar has an illustrious history as a center of the independence struggle, and wears its status proudly. The Casco Histórico (historic center) is one of the country's finest – a gorgeous ensemble of brightly painted colonial buildings, shady squares and the fine Paseo Orinoco – overlooking the country's greatest river. Travelers on their way through to Salto Ángel are usually glad to have made a stopover here.

Mérida

10 The adventure-sports capital of Venezuela, Mérida (elevation 1600m) is an affluent Andean city with a youthful energy and a robust arts scene. It has an unhurried, friendly and cultured atmosphere derived from the massive university and outdoor sports presence. Active visitors will be spoiled for choice, with myriad options for hiking, canyoning, rafting, mountain biking and paragliding. The city is also the major jumping-off point for wildlife-viewing trips to Los Llanos.

Casco Histórico, Ciudad Bolívar

JANE SWEENEY / GETTY IMAGES ©

Rice fields near Sapa

CAPITAL
Hanoi

POPULATION
92.5 million

AREA
331,210 sq km

OFFICIAL
LANGUAGE
Vietnamese

Vietnam

Astonishingly exotic and utterly compelling, Vietnam is a country of breathtaking natural beauty with an incredible heritage that quickly becomes addictive.

Unforgettable experiences are everywhere in Vietnam. There's the sublime: gazing over a surreal seascape of limestone islands from the deck of a Chinese junk in Halong Bay. The ridiculous: taking 10 minutes just to cross the street through a tsunami of motorbikes in Hanoi. The inspirational: exploring the world's most spectacular cave systems in Phong Nha-Ke Bang National Park. The comical: watching a moped loaded with honking pigs weave a wobbly route along a country lane. And the contemplative: witnessing a solitary grave in a cemetery of tens of thousands of war victims.

You'll witness children riding buffalo, see the impossibly intricate textiles of hill-tribe communities and taste the super-fresh and subtle flavours of Vietnamese cuisine.

The nation is a budget traveller's dream, with inexpensive transport, outstanding street food, good-value accommodation and *bia hoi* – perhaps the world's cheapest beer.

This is a dynamic nation on the move. Prepare yourself for the ride of your life.

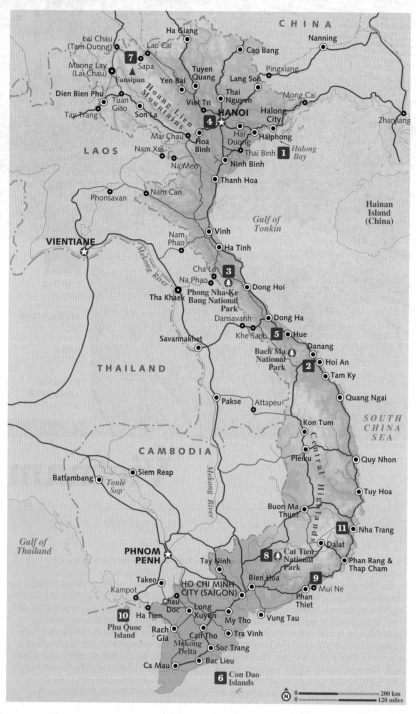

Vietnam's
Top Experiences

Halong Bay

1 Halong Bay's stunning combination of karst limestone peaks and sheltered, shimmering seas is one of Vietnam's top tourist draws, but with more than 2000 islands there's plenty of scenery to go around. Designated a World Heritage site in 1994, this mystical landscape of limestone islets is often compared to Guilin in China or Krabi in southern Thailand. In reality, it is more spectacular. Book an overnight cruise and make time for your own special moments on this wonder – rising early for an ethereal misty dawn, or piloting a kayak into grottoes and lagoons.

Hoi An

2 Vietnam's most cosmopolitan and civilised town, this beautiful, ancient port is bursting with gourmet Vietnamese restaurants, hip bars and cafes, quirky boutiques and expert tailors. Immerse yourself in history in the warren-like lanes of the Old Town, shop till you drop, tour the temples and pagodas, and dine like an emperor on a peasant's budget (and learn to cook like the locals). Then hit glorious An Bang Beach, wander along the riverside and bike the back roads. Whether you've as little as a day or as long as a month in the town, it'll be time well spent.

FOTOTRAV / GETTY IMAGES ©

Phong Nha-Ke Bang National Park

3 Picture jungle-crowned limestone hills, rainforest, turquoise streams and traditional villages. Then throw in the globe's most impressive cave systems – river-created Phong Nha Cave, the ethereal beauty of Paradise Cave and the cathedral-like chambers of Son Doong, the world's largest cave – and you can see why Phong Nha-Ke Bang is Vietnam's most rewarding national park to explore. It's a great place to really experience rural Vietnam at its most majestic.

if Vietnam were 100 people

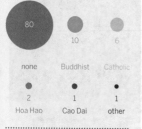

86 would be Kinh (Vietnamese)
3 would be Thai and Muong   2 would be Tay
2 would be Khmer Krom (ethnic Khmer)
1 would be Hoa (ethnic Chinese)
6 would be other

belief systems
(% of population)

80 — none
10 — Buddhist
6 — Catholic
2 — Hoa Hao
1 — Cao Dai
1 — other

population per sq km

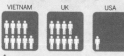

VIETNAM   UK   USA

≈ 30 people

Hanoi Old Quarter

4 Get agreeably lost in the city's centuries-old Old Quarter, a frantic commercial labyrinth where echoes of the past are filtered and framed by a thoroughly 21st-century energy. Discover Vietnam's culinary flavours and aromas at street level, perched on a tiny chair eating iconic Hanoi dishes like *pho bo*, *bun cha* and *banh cuon*. Later at night, join the socialising throngs enjoying refreshingly crisp *bia hoi* at makeshift street-corner bars.

Hue

5 The capital of the nation for 150 years in the 19th and early 20th centuries, Hue is perhaps the easiest Vietnamese city to love. Its situation on the banks of the Perfume River is sublime, its complex cuisine is justifiably famous and its streets are relatively traffic free. And that's without the majesty of the Hue Citadel, its royal residences and elegant temples, formidable walled defences and gateways. On the city's fringes are some of Vietnam's most impressive pagodas and royal tombs, many in wonderful natural settings.

Con Dao Islands

6 The furious energy that characterises Vietnamese cities can be intoxicating, but when you need an urban detox these idyllic tropical islands make the perfect escape. Once hell on earth for a generation of political prisoners, Con Dao is now a heavenly destination of remote beaches, pristine dive sites and diverse nature (including nesting turtles). It's a wonderful place to explore by bike in search of that dream beach, while the

Gone Underground

In 1966 the USA began a massive aerial and artillery bombardment of North Vietnam. Just north of the Demilitarised Zone (DMZ), the villagers of Vinh Moc found themselves living in one of the most heavily bombed and shelled strips of land on the planet. Small family shelters could not withstand this onslaught and villagers either fled or began tunnelling by hand and with simple tools into the red-clay earth.

The Viet Cong (VC) found it useful to have a base here and encouraged villagers to stay. After 18 months of tunnelling, an enormous complex was established, creating new homes on three levels from 12m to 23m below ground, plus meeting rooms and even a maternity unit (17 babies were born underground). Whole families lived here, their longest sojourn lasting 10 days and 10 nights.

Food & Drink

Banh Xeo This giant crispy, chewy rice crepe is made in 12- or 14-inch skillets or woks and amply filled with pork, shrimp, mung beans and bean sprouts.

Bun Bo Hue This punchy rice-noodle soup with beef and pork exemplifies the central Vietnamese proclivity for spicy food.

Bun Cha This street favourite features barbecued sliced pork or pork patties served with thin rice vermicelli, a heap of fresh herbs and green vegetables, and a bowl of lightly sweetened *nuoc mam*.

Com Hen Room temperature rice is served with the flesh of tiny clams, their cooking broth, and myriad garnishes.

Pho Bo A culinary highlight of the north is *pho bo* (beef noodle soup). A good pho hinges on the broth, which is made from beef bones boiled for hours in water with shallot, ginger, fish sauce, black cardamom, star anise and cassia.

4

KIM SCHANDORFF / GETTY IMAGES ©

Mobile hat shop, Hanoi

main settlement of Con Son is one of Vietnam's most charming towns.

Sapa & the Tonkinese Alps

7 Dubbed the Tonkinese Alps by the French, the spectacular Hoang Lien Mountains soar skywards along the rugged, uncompromising edges of northwest Vietnam towards the Chinese border. Shape-shifting banks of cloud and mist ebb and flow in this mountainous area, parting teasingly to reveal a glimpse of Fansipan, Vietnam's highest peak. From the sinuous and spidery ridges, rice terraces cascade down into river valleys, home for several centuries to ethnic minority villages of H'mong, Red Dzao and Giay peoples.

When to Go

HIGH SEASON (Jul–Aug)

➡ Prices increase by up to 50% on the coast; book hotels well in advance.

➡ All of Vietnam, except the far north, is hot and humid, with the summer monsoon bringing downpours.

SHOULDER (Dec–Mar)

➡ During the Tet festival, the whole country is on the move and prices rise.

➡ North of Nha Trang can get cool. In the south, clear skies and sunshine are the norm.

LOW SEASON (Apr–Jun, Sep–Nov)

➡ Perhaps the best time to tour the whole nation.

➡ Typhoons can lash the central and northern coastline until November.

Cat Tien National Park

8 One of the most accessible and impressive protected areas in Vietnam, Cat Tien lies conveniently midway between Ho Chi Minh City and Dalat. Set on a bend in the Dong Nai River, there is something vaguely *Apocalypse Now* about arriving here. Popular activities include trekking, cycling and wildlife-spotting. The park is home to the Dao Tien Endangered Primate Species Centre, where gibbons and langurs are coaxed back into their natural environment. The Wild Gibbon Trek is a must: one of the wildlife highlights of Vietnam.

Mui Ne

9 Perhaps the adrenaline epicentre of Vietnam, the beach resort of Mui Ne is a kitesurfing capital with world-class wind and conditions, and excellent schools for professional training. For those who prefer dry land, sandboarding and golf are popular alternatives.

Best on Film

Apocalypse Now (1979) The American War depicted as an epic 'heart of darkness' adventure.

Cyclo (*Xich Lo*; 1995) Visually stunning masterpiece that cuts to the core of HCMC's underworld.

Platoon (1986) Based on the first-hand experiences of the director, it follows idealistic volunteer Charlie Sheen to 'Nam.

The Deer Hunter (1978) Examines the emotional breakdown suffered by small-town servicemen.

Best in Print

The Quiet American (Graham Greene) Classic novel set in the 1950s as the French empire is collapsing.

The Sorrow of War (Bao Ninh) The North Vietnamese perspective, retold in novel form via flashbacks that tie the story together.

Vietnam: Rising Dragon (Bill Hayton) A candid assessment of the nation and one of the most up-to-date sources available.

Getting Around

Train Reasonably priced and comfortable enough if you get an air-conditioned carriage (or sleeper on overnight routes). There are no real express trains.

Plane Very cheap if you book ahead (often less than the equivalent bus fare) and the network is pretty comprehensive. However cancellations are common.

Car Very useful for travelling at your own pace or for visiting regions with minimal public transport. Rental cars always come with a driver.

Bus On the main highways services are quite good, although it's not a particularly relaxing way to travel. In the sticks things deteriorate rapidly. Open-tour buses are very inexpensive and worth considering.

The resort itself has more than 20km of palm-fringed beachfront that stretches invitingly along the shores of the South China Sea. From guesthouses to boutique resorts, designer bars to fine-value spas, Mui Ne has a broad appeal.

Phu Quoc Island

10 Lapped by azure waters and edged with the kind of white-sand beaches that make sun seekers sink to their weak knees, Phu Quoc is ideal for slipping into low gear, reaching for a seaside cocktail and toasting a blood-orange sun as it dips into the sea. And if you want to notch it up a gear, grab a motorbike and hit the red-dirt roads to your heart's content: the island is the size of Singapore.

Nha Trang

11 Nha Trang must boast one of the finest municipal beaches in Asia, a breathtaking strip of fine, golden sand lapped by the balmy waters of the South China Sea. But there's much more to the town than beach appeal, with river and island boat trips, ancient Cham towers to explore, natural mud-bath spas and a great dining scene.

PETER UNGER / GETTY IMAGES ©

RMS Rhone shipwreck dive

Virgin Islands, US & British

Consistently balmy weather, ridiculously white sand shores, diving and snorkeling, and calypso-wafting beach bars: the US and British Virgin Islands have the tropical thing down.

CAPITAL
Charlotte
Amalie (USVI),
Road Town (BVI)

POPULATION
104,737 (USVI)
31,912 (BVI)

AREA
1910 sq km
(USVI)
151 sq km (BVI)

**OFFICIAL
LANGUAGE**
English

Although considered one archipelago, the Virgin Islands are divided between two countries: the British Virgin Islands (BVI) and the United States Virgin Islands (USVI).With more than 90 little landmasses bobbing in a triangular patch of sea, steady trade winds, calm currents and hundreds of protected bays, it's easy to see how the Virgins became a tropical fantasyland.

The US Virgins hold the lion's share of population and development. St Thomas has more resorts and water sports than you can shake a beach towel at and the largest Virgin, St Croix, pleases divers and drinkers with extraordinary scuba sites and rum factories.

The British Virgins are officially territories of Her Majesty's land, but aside from plates of fish and chips, there's little that's overtly British.

Believe it or not, a day will come during your Virgin stay when you decide enough with the beach lounging. Then it's time to snorkel with turtles and spotted eagle rays, dive to explore a 19th-century shipwreck, hike to petroglyphs and sugar-mill ruins and kayak through a bioluminescent bay.

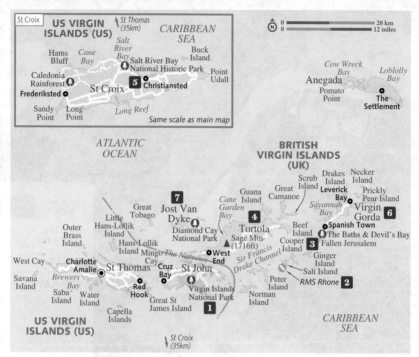

US & British Virgin Islands'
Top Experiences

Hiking in the Virgin Islands National Park

1 This national park, with its gnarled trees and spiky cacti spilling over the edges, covers some three-quarters of St John. Aside from awesome snorkeling, feral donkeys and eco-camps, the park's greatest gift to visitors is its hiking. Dozens of trails wind through the wild terrain, taking trekkers to cliff-top overlooks, petroglyphs and sugar-mill ruins. Several lead to beaches prime for swimming with turtles and spotted eagle rays. The paths are short and easy for the most part, so that any reasonably fit hiker can walk them and reap the rewards.

Diving the RMS Rhone

2 The *RMS Rhone* is one of the most famous shipwreck dives in the Caribbean. The twin-masted vessel – a Royal Mail Steamer – sank off Salt Island's coast during a hurricane in 1867. Now a national park, the steamer's remains are extensive and have become an exotic habitat for marine life. Octopuses, eels and squid swim by a setting that couldn't be more classic – so classic, in fact, that Hollywood has used it as the backdrop for numerous films, including *The Deep*. Snorkelers can access the wreck, too, since the ship's stern is in shallower water.

Exploring the Out Islands

3 The BVI's remote Out Islands are a wonderful mix of uninhabited wildlife sanctuaries, luxurious hideaways for the rich and famous, and provisioning stops for sailors. With more than 30 little landmasses to choose from, there's something for every taste. Cooper Island hosts affordable cottages. Norman Island holds buried treasure and a rowdy floating bar. Countless other isles – Ginger, the Dogs, Fallen Jerusalem – offer nothing but beaches and blue sea. If you're sans yacht yourself, climb aboard a day-sailing tour to reach them.

HOLGER LEUE / GETTY IMAGES ©

Norman Island, British Virgin Islands

Beaches

4 You don't have to be hit on the head with a coconut to know beaches are a major highlight of the Virgins. Secluded beaches, family beaches, snorkeling beaches and sunset-strolling beaches edge the islands. Loblolly Bay, Flash of Beauty, Smuggler's Cove – can you see the hammocks swinging from coconut trees? Famed White Bay on Jost Van Dyke gets its name from its crazy-white sand. Tortola has so many beaches it had to start repeating names (Long Bay on the east and west).

Historic Christiansted

5 This 18th-century town is a showcase of historic preservation. The cannon-covered fortress, flanked by West Indies neoclassical buildings in gold, pink and brown, evokes the days when Christiansted was the Danish colonies' capital and the St Croix plantocracy society was awash in gold. The district abuts Kings Wharf, the commercial landing where, for more than 250 years, ships landed with slaves and set off with sugar or molasses. Today

if the Virgin Islands were 100 people

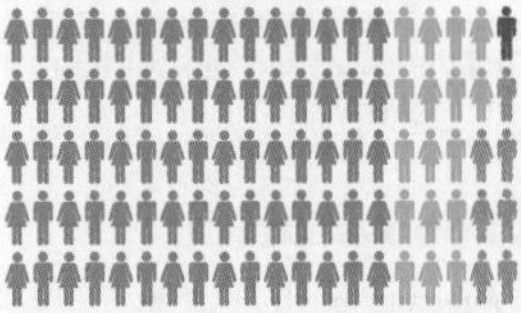

75 would speak English
17 would speak Spanish or Spanish Creole
7 would speak French or French Creole
1 would speak other languages

land vs water

(% of area)

population per sq km

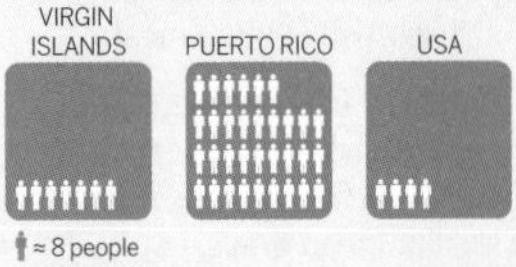

When to Go

HIGH SEASON
(Dec–Apr)

- Weather is at its best: dry and sunny, while trade winds keep humidity down.
- Accommodation prices peak (30% up on average).
- Holidays and festivals ensure a fun ambience.

SHOULDER
(May–Jul)

- Crowds and prices drop off.
- Trade winds lessen and the sea calms, so snorkeling and sailing are smoother.
- The pace is more relaxed, with a better chance to appreciate local culture.

LOW SEASON
(Aug–Nov)

- Hurricane season peaks, along with rainfall.
- Many attractions keep shorter hours.
- Some businesses close altogether (especially during September).

Poison Apples

In 1587 Sir Walter Raleigh paused at St Croix with a party of settlers on their way to North America. After the long sea voyage, the colonists were tempted by an abundance of fruit that looked like small light-green apples hanging from trees near the shore. A number of settlers ate the poisonous fruit and 'were fearfully troubled with a sudden burning in their mouths and swelling of their tongues so big that some of them could not speak.'

The colonists' nemesis was the fruit of the manchineel or 'poison apple' tree. Although the tree has been eradicated from many public areas in the Virgins, it is still around, especially on St John and less developed islands.

Because touching any part of this tree can yield caustic burns, humans must avoid the manchineel. Even rain dripping off the leaves and bark will burn if it touches your skin.

Food & Drink

Anegada lobster Hulking crustaceans grilled on the beach in converted oil drums.

Callaloo Spicy soup stirred with okra, various meats, greens and hot peppers.

Cruzan Rum St Croix's happy juice since 1760, from light white rum to banana, guava and other tropical flavors.

Fungi (*foon*-ghee) A polenta-like cornmeal cooked with okra, typically topped with fish and gravy.

Painkiller Jost Van Dyke's Soggy Dollar Bar supposedly invented this mix of rum, coconut, pineapple, orange juice and nutmeg.

Pate (*paw*-tay) Flaky fried dough pockets stuffed with spiced chicken, fish or other meat.

Roti Fiery chutney sets off the curried chicken, beef, conch or vegetable fillings in these burrito-like flat-bread wraps.

MICHAEL TUREK / GETTY IMAGES ©

it's fronted by a boardwalk of bars and dive-boat operators, with art galleries and courtyard bistros tucked into the town's laneways.

The Baths

6 The BVI's most popular tourist attraction, the Baths on Virgin Gorda are a sublime jumbled collection of sky-high granite boulders by the sea. The rocks form a series of grottoes that fill with water and shafts of kaleidoscopic sunlight. You can snorkel around the otherworldly megaliths, or take the trail through them in which you'll slosh through tidal pools, squeeze into impossibly narrow passages, and then drop out onto a sugar-sand beach.

Jost Van Dyke

7 This island, northwest of Tortola, has developed a reputation that far exceeds its mere 4 sq miles of land – and a lot of that is due to a local calypso musician named Foxy Callwood and his legendary namesake bar. Even though folks such as Keith Richards drop by for a drink, Jost remains an unspoiled oasis of green hills edged by blinding white sand. There's a small clutch of restaurants, beach bars and guesthouses, but blissfully little else.

Getting Around

Boat Frequent and inexpensive public ferries connect the main islands in the Virgins, as well as several of the smaller islands. For trips between USVI and BVI, a passport is required. If you want to do it yourself, ie operate your own boat, the major islands have marinas where you can charter sailing yachts or powerboats, either bareboat or with a crew.

Car Driving is the most convenient way to get around individual islands, as public transportation is limited and taxi fares add up in a hurry.

Plane A few commercial services fly within the Virgins, especially between St Thomas and St Croix. Other than that, you'll need to charter a plane to fly between islands.

CAPITAL
Cardiff

POPULATION
3 million

AREA
20,779 sq km

OFFICIAL LANGUAGES
Welsh, English

Llyn Ogwen, Snowdonia

Wales

The phrase 'good things come in small packages' may be a cliché, but in the case of Wales it's undeniably true.

Compact but geologically diverse, Wales offers myriad opportunities for escaping into nature. It may not be wild in the classic sense – humans have been shaping this land for millennia – but there are plenty of lonely corners to explore, lurking behind mountains, within river valleys and along surf-battered cliffs. An extensive network of paths makes Wales a hiker's paradise. Even more untamed are the islands scattered just off the coast, some of which are important wildlife sanctuaries.

Castles are an inescapable part of the Welsh landscape. They're absolutely everywhere. You could visit a different one every day for a year and still not see them all. There's also an altogether more inscrutable and far older set of stones to discover – the stone circles, dolmens and standing stones erected long before castles were ever dreamt up, before even histories were written.

Beyond the scenery and the castles, it's interactions with Welsh people that will remain in your memory the longest.

Wales'
Top Experiences

Wales Coast Path

1 Since 2012 all of Wales' famously beautiful coastal paths have been linked up in one continuous 870-mile route. Walk for two months or walk for two days – there's no rule that you have to do it all in one go. The best stretches take

in the Gower's beautiful beaches, Pembrokeshire's multicoloured cliffs and limestone arches, the remote edges of the Llŷn Peninsula and the ancient vistas of Anglesey. And if you link it up with Offa's Dyke Path, you can circle the entire country!

Snowdonia

2 The rugged northwest corner of the country has rocky mountain peaks, glacier-hewn valleys and lakes, sinuous ridges, sparkling rivers and charm-infused villages. Around Snowdon itself hordes hike to the summit and many more take the less strenuous cog railway from Llanberis. Elsewhere in Snowdonia's rugged mountains are rarely trodden areas perfect for off-the-beaten-track exploration. Glorious under the summer sun and even better under a blanket of snow, Snowdonia is one of Wales' treasures.

Conwy Castle

3 There's barely a town in Wales of any note that doesn't have a castle towering over it. None has a more symbiotic relationship with its settlement than Conwy. The castle still stretches out its enfolding arms to enclose the historic town in a stony embrace, originally designed to keep a tiny English colony safe from the populace they displaced. Even today it's an awe-inspiring sight.

Pembrokeshire

4 Famous in Britain for its beaches and coastal walks, Pembrokeshire is a small sampler of all that Wales has to offer. Pembroke has one of Britain's finest Norman castles, and there are smaller versions at nearby Tenby, Manorbier, Carew and Haverfordwest. The Preseli Hills offer upland walking and ancient standing stones. Add to that wildlife reserves, cute villages and an ancient cathedral, and all bases are covered.

Druidston Haven, Pembrokeshire

Ffestiniog & Welsh Highland Railways

5 Once you could only get views this good if you were a hunk of slate on your way to the port. These narrow-gauge train lines now shuttle passengers from Porthmadog into the mountains of Snowdonia, with the Welsh Highland Railway slicing right past Snowdon to the coast at Caernarfon. The Ffestiniog Railway heads to the former industrial heartland of Blaenau Ffestiniog, where you can delve into the slate caverns.

Brecon Beacons

6 Wales' third national park manages quite a feat – and that's to be simultaneously bleak and beautiful. Walkers will delight in its unpopulated moors and bald hills, while history buffs can seek out hill forts and barrows, and the enigmatic ruins of abbeys and castles. The towns within the park's confines are some of Wales' most endearingly idiosyncratic, including Hay-on-Wye and Abergavenny – hallowed names for book lovers and food fans respectively.

if Wales were 100 people

58 class themselves as Welsh only
7 class themselves as Welsh and British
1 class themselves as Welsh and another nationality
34 don't class themselves as Welsh

Welsh speaking
(% of population)

74 don't understand Welsh at all
19 speak Welsh
5 understand but can't speak Welsh
2 read but don't speak Welsh

population per sq km

WALES   UK   USA

♦ ≈ 3 people

When to Go

HIGH SEASON
(Jul & Aug)

➡ Weather is at its warmest; lots of festivals and events.

➡ Accommodation prices increase in coastal areas and national parks.

➡ The absolute peak is the August school holidays.

SHOULDER
(Apr–Jun & Sep–Oct)

➡ The season kicks off with Easter, in March or April.

➡ Prices peak on bank holidays.

➡ April to June are the driest months; October is one of the wettest.

LOW SEASON
(Nov–Mar)

➡ Prices rise to peak levels over Christmas and New Year.

➡ Snow can close roads, particularly in the mountains.

➡ January and February are the coldest months.

The Red Lady of Paviland

Halfway along the Gower coast is Paviland Cave, where in 1823 the Reverend William Buckland discovered a human skeleton dyed with red ochre. Due to the jewellery buried along with the bones, the good Reverend assumed the deceased was a woman. Buckland also concluded that the 'Red Lady', as the skeleton became known, must have been a Roman prostitute or witch.

Modern analysis shows that the Red Lady was actually a man who died some 29,000 years ago. Dating from before the last Ice Age, his are the oldest human remains found in the UK, and are recognised as the oldest known ritual burial in Western Europe. The Red Lady is now on display in the National Museum Cardiff.

Food & Drink

Traditionally, Welsh food was based on what could be grown locally and cheaply. This meant that oats, root vegetables, dairy products, honey and meat featured highly in most recipes. Food was hearty and wholesome but not exactly haute cuisine. The food revolution in Wales has changed that, but traditional staples still have a place here – albeit with have a contemporary twist.

Most menus will feature Welsh lamb or Welsh Black beef. On the coast try some sewin or cockles. The most traditional Welsh dish remains *cawl*, a hearty, one-pot meal of bacon, lamb, cabbage, swede and potato. Another favourite is Welsh rarebit, a kind of sophisticated cheese on toast, drizzled with a secret ingredient tasting suspiciously like beer. For breakfast, try laver bread – boiled seaweed mixed with oatmeal and served with bacon or cockles. Finish your meal with some great Welsh cheese, notably Caws Cenarth, Celtic Blue or Perl Las.

St David's Cathedral, Pembrokeshire

Carreg Cennen

7 Artfully decaying ruins in remote locations have been attracting romantic souls to Wales for hundreds of years, and it's in places like Carreg Cennen that they reach their apotheosis. The hilltop setting, within the western reaches of Brecon Beacons National Park, is bleak and barren, moody and mysterious. As you edge nearer along country lanes and the castle looms into view in the distance, it's easy to make the mental trade-in of your rental car for a fine steed, galloping bravely towards unknown danger.

St Davids

8 Some places have a presence all of their own, and that's certainly true of St Davids. Officially a city but more like a large village, the peaceful home of Wales' patron saint has attracted the spiritually minded for centuries. Whether you come seeking salvation in the surf, or hope to commune with the whales in the Celtic Deep, or whether you genuinely wish to embrace the grace of Wales' patron saint, St Davids is a strangely affecting place.

Getting Around

Bus Wales' bus services are operated by dozens of private companies. Buses are generally reasonably priced and efficient, although some have limited weekend services (or don't run at all).

Car If you want to see the more remote regions of Wales or cram in as much as possible in a short time, travelling by car or motorcycle is the easiest way to go. Rural roads are often single-track affairs with passing places only at intervals, and they can be treacherous in winter.

Train There are some fine rail journeys across Wales and a staggering number of steam and narrow-gauge railways, which offer spectacular scenery and a hypnotic, clickety-clack pace.

Old Sana'a

CAPITAL
Sana'a

POPULATION
25.3 million

AREA
527,968 sq km

OFFICIAL LANGUAGE
Arabic

Yemen

Short of the glitz of many of the Gulf states, Yemen compensates with the depth of its history and attachment to traditions and rich culture.

Yemen may be the Arabian Peninsula's poor cousin, but therein lies its charm. With none of the oil wealth of its neighbours, the country is like a time capsule preserving the traditions and texture of old Arabia.

Yemen's history reads like the retelling of a legend. To the Romans, Yemen was Arabia Felix (Happy Arabia), Gilgamesh came here seeking eternal life, Noah launched his ark from here, the Queen of Sheba once ruled the land, and there was once dazzling wealth from the frankincense trade.

This journey into the past has diverse focal points, from the Arabian Nights–aura of capital city Sana'a in the west to mud skyscrapers in the east, from stunning mountain scenery in the north to the weird and wonderful landscapes of Suqutra off the south coast.

In recent years Yemen has remained nigh-on forgotten as travel here is unfeasible – the security situation makes venturing across Yemen extremely inadvisable. Best sit tight and hope that things improve so this distinctive realm may become accessible.

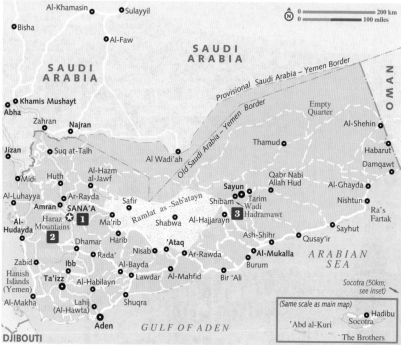

Yemen's
Top Experiences

Old Sana'a

1 Sigh over Sana'a's cake-icing-like houses and saunter through ancient alleyways created by the son of Noah. Sana'a, the world's oldest city, has many layers, colours and patterns, making it the most romantic, living, breathing Islamic city you could ever hope to find.

Haraz Mountains

2 Rising abruptly off the steamy Red Sea coastal plains, the sheer-sided Haraz Mountains have, for centuries, acted as a cultural fortress protecting the Yemeni heartland from interfering foreigners. The mountains' terraced fields and fortified villages huddle together on the most unlikely of crags.

Wadi Hadramawt

3 Wander the sandcastle cities of weird and wonderful Wadi Hadramawt, where giants once roamed and scorpions line the entrance to Hell. Hemmed in by so much sun-blasted desert, this dry river valley lined with lush oases is like another world. In an instant, sterility is replaced by fertility and ochre browns give way to disco greens.

Food & Drink

Fenugreek A bitter, livid green froth used to put a punch in a minimal broth or bean dish.

Salta A piping-hot stew containing meat broth, lentils, beans, fenugreek and coriander or other spices.

Shai This sweet tea is often served *min na'ana* (with mint).

When to Go

SEP–DEC

➡ The monsoon rains are ending, the mountains are green and the hiking superb.

NOV–FEB

➡ This is the time to hit the Tihama Red Sea coastal regions or the eastern deserts.

JUN–SEP

➡ Gale force monsoon winds can make visiting Socotra island a bit of a pain.

Devil's Pool, Livingstone Island, Victoria Falls

CAPITAL
Lusaka

POPULATION
14.2 million

AREA
752,618 sq km

OFFICIAL LANGUAGES
11 Bantu languages

Zambia

Home to an incredible diversity of wildlife, and some of Africa's best-trained guides– visitors don't just see wildlife, they get to know it.

Get out into the bush where animals, both predators and prey, wander through un-fenced camps, where night-time means swapping stories around the fire and where the human footprint is nowhere to be seen.

The rewards of travelling in Zambia are those of exploring remote, mesmerising wilderness as full of an astonishing diversity of wildlife as any part of Southern Africa. Where one day you can canoe down a wide, placid river and the next whitewater raft through the raging rapids of the Zambesi

near world-famous Victoria Falls. Though landlocked, three great rivers, the Kafue, the Luangwa and the Zambezi, flow through Zambia, defining both its geography and the rhythms of life for many of its people. For the independent traveller, however, Zambia can be a logistical challenge, because of its sheer size, dilapidated road network and upmarket resort facilities.

For those who do venture here, the rela-tive lack of crowds means an even more satisfying African journey.

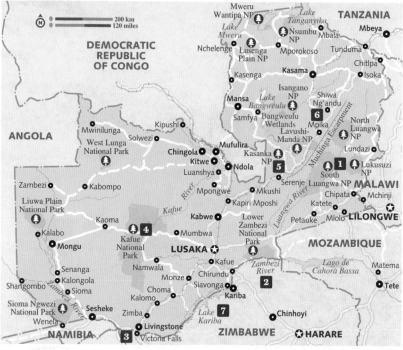

The map shows:

TANZANIA
Mweru Wantipa NP
Lake Tanganyika
Lake Mweru
Nsumbu NP
Mbeya
Mbala
Nchelenge
Lusenga Plain NP
Mporokoso
Tunduma
Chitipa
Kasama
Isoka
Kasenga
Isangano NP
Shiwa Ng'andu **6**
North Luangwa NP
Mansa
Lake Bangweulu
Bangweulu Wetlands
Mpika
Lundazi
Samfya
Lavushi-Manda NP
Kipushi
Kasanka NP
Lukusuzi NP **1**
Mwinilunga
West Lunga National Park
Solwezi
Chingola
Mufulira
Kitwe
Ndola
Serenje
South Luangwa NP **5**
MALAWI
Zambezi
Kabompo
Luanshya
Mpongwe
Mkushi
Chipata
Mchinji
Liuwa Plain National Park
Kaoma
Kafue
Kapiri Mposhi
Katete
LILONGWE
Kalabo
Kabwe
Petauke
Mlolo
Mongu
Kafue National Park **4**
Mumbwa
Lower Zambezi National Park
MOZAMBIQUE
Senanga
Namwala
LUSAKA
Kafue
Zambezi River
Lago de Cahora Bassa
Matema
Shangombo
Kalongola
Sioma
Monze
Chirundu
Siavonga
2
Tete
Sioma Ngwezi National Park
Sesheke
Choma
Kalomo
Kariba
Wenela
Zimba
Lake Kariba
Chinhoyi
NAMIBIA
Livingstone
Victoria Falls **3**
ZIMBABWE
HARARE
DEMOCRATIC REPUBLIC OF CONGO
ANGOLA
0 200 km
0 120 miles

Zambia's
Top Experiences

South Luangwa National Park

1 For scenery, variety and density of animals, accessibility and choice of accommodation, South Luangwa is the best park in Zambia and one of the most majestic in Africa. Impalas, pukus, waterbuck giraffe and buffaloes wander on the wide-open plains; leopards, of which there are many in the park, hunt in the dense woodlands; herds of elephants wade through the marshes; and hippos munch serenely on Nile cabbage in the Luangwa River. The bird life is also tremendous: about 400 species have been recorded – large birds like snake eagles, bateleurs and ground hornbills

are normally easy to spot. The quality of the park is reflected in the quality of its guides – the highest in Zambia.

Zambezi River

2 One of the best ways to see the Lower Zambezi is by canoe safari. Drifting silently past the riverbank you can get surprisingly close to birds and animals without disturbing them. Nothing beats getting eye-to-eye with a drinking buffalo, or watching dainty bushbuck tiptoe towards the river's edge. Excitement comes as you negotiate a herd of grunting hippos or hear a sudden 'plop' as a croc you hadn't even noticed slips into the water nearby.

Victoria Falls

3 Victoria Falls (*Mosi-oa-Tunya* – the 'smoke that thunders') is one of Africa's original blockbusters and although Zimbabwe and Zambia share it, Victoria Falls is a place all of its own. View it directly as a raging mile-long curtain of water, in all its glory, from a helicopter ride or peek precariously over its edge from Devil's Pools; the sheer power and force of the falls is something that simply does not disappoint. Whether you're here purely to take in the sight of a natural wonder of the world, or for a serious hit of adrenaline via rafting or bungee jumping into the Zambezi, Victoria Falls is a place where you're sure

CHRISTIAN HENRICH / GETTY IMAGES ©

Hippopotamus, South Luangwa National Park

to tick off numerous items from that bucket list.

Kafue National Park

4 This stunning park is about 200km west of Lusaka and is a real highlight of Zambia. Covering more than 22,500 sq km, it's the largest park in the country and one of the biggest in the world. This is the only major park in Zambia that's easily accessible by car. In the northern sector, the Kafue River and its main tributaries – the Lufupa and Lunga – are fantastic for boat rides to see hippos in great grunting profusion, as well as crocodiles. Away from the rivers, open *miombo* woodlands and *dambos* (grassy, swampy areas) allow you to spot animals more easily. This area is one of the best places in Zambia (maybe even in Africa) to see leopards – they are regularly spotted on night drives.

Kasanka National Park

5 One of Zambia's least-known wilderness areas and a real highlight of a visit to this part of the country is the privately managed Kasanka National Park. At just 390 sq km it's pretty small and it sees very few visitors, which is what makes it special. There are no queues of jeeps to get a look at a leopard here; instead, you'll discover great tracts of *miombo* woodland, evergreen thicket, open grassland and rivers fringed with emerald forest, all by yourself.

if Zambia were 100 people

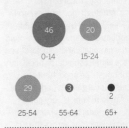

30 would speak Bemba
11 would speak Nyanja
11 would speak Tonga
24 would speak other Bantu languages
24 would speak other languages

age structure (years)
(% of population)

46 20
0-14 15-24

29 3 2
25-54 55-64 65+

When to Go

LATE MAY–EARLY OCT

➡ The dry season offers prime wildlife viewing; tourist high season.

JUN–AUG

➡ Generally dry, with cooler temperatures and sometimes frosty nights.

DEC–APR

➡ The landscape is vibrant and blooming during the rainy or 'emerald' season.

population per sq km

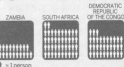

ZAMBIA SOUTH AFRICA DEMOCRATIC REPUBLIC OF THE CONGO

⬤ ≈ 1 person

Zambian Music

All of Zambia's ethnic groups have their own musical traditions. The Lozi are famous for the large drums played during the remarkable Kuomboka ceremony, while the Bemba are also renowned drummers. Other traditional musical instruments used by most groups include large wooden xylophones, often with gourds underneath the blocks for resonance, and tiny thumb pianos with keys made from flattened metal.

Contemporary Zambian musicians who have achieved some international fame include Larry Maluma, who blends traditional Zambian beats with reggae. Younger Zambians prefer reggae – both the old-school Jamaican style and the softer version popular in Southern Africa – and contemporary Zambian r'n'b and hip-hop. K'Millian is a hugely popular Zambian r'n'b artist.

Food & Drink

The staple diet for Zambians is *nshima*, a thick, doughy maize porridge that's bland but filling. It's eaten with your hands and accompanied by beans or vegetables and a hot relish, and sometimes meat or fish.

Although food isn't generally a highlight of travel in Zambia, lodges and camps in and around the national parks usually offer the highest standards of culinary options. The opportunity to taste local game is perhaps the standout; *kudu* is very good.

The local beer is Mosi. You may also come across the discarded plastic sachets of *tujilijili* (a strong home brewed alcohol). The manufacturing and importation of *tujilijili* was declared illegal in 2012. Nevertheless, a thriving business in Malawi supplies Zambian drinkers.

Stained glass windows in the chapel, Shiwa House, Shiwa Ng'andu

Shiwa Ng'andu

6 Deep in the northern Zambian wilderness sits Shiwa Ng'andu, a grand country estate and labour of love of eccentric British aristocrat Sir Stewart Gore-Brown. The estate's crowning glory is Shiwa Ng'andu manor house, which is a glorious brick mansion. Driving up to the house through farm buildings, settlements and workers' houses it almost feels like an old feudal domain: there's a whole community built around it, including a school and a hospital, and many of the people now working at Shiwa Ng'andu are the children and grandchildren of Sir Stewart's original staff.

Lake Kariba

7 Beyond Victoria Falls, the Zambezi River flows through the Batoka Gorge then enters the waters of Lake Kariba. Formed behind the massive Kariba Dam, this is one of the largest artificial lakes in Africa. The lake is enormous and spectacular with the silhouettes of jagged Zimbabwean peaks far across its shimmering waters. The Zambian side remains remote and rarely reached by visitors. For those who make it here, this remoteness is the very attraction.

Getting Around

Air The main domestic airports are at Lusaka, Livingstone, Ndola, Kitwe, Mfuwe, Kasama and Kasaba Bay. Dozens of minor airstrips cater for chartered planes.

Bus & Minibus Distances are long, buses are often slow and many roads are badly potholed, so it can exhaust even the hardiest of travellers.

Car & Motorcycle Sections of main highway can be in a pretty bad way and rapidly deteriorating. Be wary and alert at all times.

Train Domestic trains are unreliable and slow, so buses are always better. Carriage conditions range from slightly dilapidated to ready-for-scrap.

Victoria Falls

CAPITAL
Harare

POPULATION
13.7 million

AREA
390,757 sq km

OFFICIAL LANGUAGE
English

Zimbabwe

The welcomes are warm and the national parks offer some of Africa's most rewarding wildlife encounters. Zimbabwe is ready and waiting. All it's missing is you.

After a decade of political ruin, violence and economic disaster, finally some good news is coming out of Zimbabwe – tourism is back. Visitors are returning in numbers not seen since the turmoil began to spot the Big Five strut their stuff around spectacular parks, discover World Heritage–listed archaeological sites and stand in awe of a natural wonder of the world: Victoria Falls.

A journey here will take you through an attractive patchwork of landscapes, from central highveld, balancing boulders and flaming msasa trees, to laid-back towns, lush Eastern Highland mountains and a network of lifeblood rivers up north. Along the way you'll receive a friendly welcome from locals, famous for their politeness and resilience in the face of hardship.

While there may be a long way to go, sure signs of recovery continue in Zimbabwe, giving hope to this embattled nation that a new dawn will soon rise.

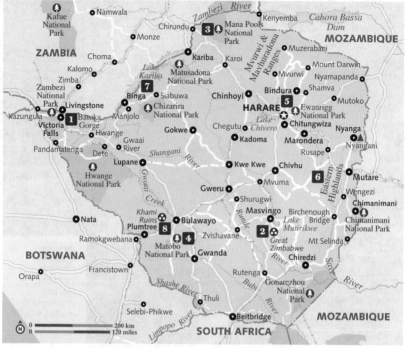

Zimbabwe's
Top Experiences

Victoria Falls

1 This is what you're here for, the mighty Victoria Falls. The 1km-long viewing path stretches along the top of the gorge, with various vantage points opening up to extraordinary front-on panoramas of the powerful curtain of water. One of the most dramatic spots is the westernmost point known as Cataract View. Another track leads to the aptly named Danger Point, where a sheer, unfenced 100m drop-off will rattle your nerves. From there, you can follow a side track for a view of the Victoria Falls Bridge.

Great Zimbabwe

2 The greatest medieval city in sub-Saharan Africa, the World Heritage listed Great Zimbabwe is one of the nation's most treasured sights. So much so, that it was named after it. This mysterious medieval city provides evidence that ancient Africa reached a level of civilisation not suspected by earlier scholars. As a religious and political capital, this city of 10,000 to 20,000 dominated a realm that stretched across eastern Zimbabwe and into modern-day Botswana, Mozambique and South Africa.

Mana Pools

3 Africa's only park (with lions) that allows unguided walking safaris. This magnificent 2200-sq-km national park is a Unesco World Heritage site, and its magic stems from its remoteness and pervading sense of the wild and natural. This is one park in Zimbabwe where you're guaranteed to see plenty of hippos, crocs, zebras and elephants, and almost guaranteed to see lions, and possibly painted dogs.

Matobo National Park

4 Home to some of the most majestic granite scenery in the world, the Matobo National Park is one of the unsung highlights of Zimbabwe. Another of Zimbabwe's Unesco World Heritage sites, the stunning and otherworldly landscape of balancing rocks, *kopjes* – giant boulders unfeasibly teetering on top

IMAGE SOURCE / GETTY IMAGES ©

Lions, Mana Pools National Park

of one another – makes it easy to understand why Matobo is considered the spiritual home of Zimbabwe. One of Zimbabwe's most breathtaking sites, the aptly named World's View takes in epic 360-degree views of the park. The peacefulness up here is immense, taking on a spiritual quality that makes it clear why it's so sacred to the Nbebele people.

Harare

5 Shop for crafts in the capital city and don't miss HIFA – Harare's International Festival of the Arts. The annual event, brings international acts alongside Zimbabwean artists. Performances include Afrobeat, funk, jazz, soul, opera, classical music, theatre and dance. The annual event, held over six days around late April or early May.

Eastern Highlands

6 This narrow strip of mountain country that makes up Manicaland isn't the Africa that normally crops up in armchair travellers' fantasies. It's a land of mountains, national parks, pine forests, botanical gardens, rivers, dams and secluded getaways. Zimbabwe's third-largest city, Mutare has a relaxed atmosphere and is a handy gateway to the Eastern Highlands or Mozambique. With its pristine wilderness, Chimanimani National Park is a hiker's paradise and shares a border with Mozambique.

if Zimbabwe were 100 people

82 would be Shona
14 would be Ndebele
2 would be other African
1 would be mixed and Asian
1 would be white

age structure (years)
(% of population)

0-14 — 39
15-24 — 22
25-54 — 31
55-64 — 4
65+ — 4

population per sq km

ZIMBABWE   SOUTH AFRICA   ZAMBIA

† ≈ 1 person

When to Go

APR–OCT
➡ Best time seasonally, with sunny days and spectacular Victoria Falls views.

NOV–APR
➡ Sporadic rain and dramatic afternoon electrical storms.

JUL–SEP
➡ Prime wildlife-viewing, good white-water rafting and canoeing on the Zambezi.

Zimbabwe in Print

Zimbabwe has produced some fine literature. The most contemporary, *Mukiwa (A White Boy in Africa)* and its sequel, *When a Crocodile Eats the Sun*, by Peter Godwin, are engrossing memoirs. Likewise, *Don't Let's Go to the Dogs Tonight – An African Childhood*, by Alexandra Fuller, is about nature and loss, and the unbreakable bond some people have with Africa.

Since independence, Zimbabwean literature has focused on the struggle to build a new society. *Harvest of Thorns*, by Shimmer Chinodya, on the Second War for Independence, won the 1992 Commonwealth Prize for Literature. Another internationally renowned writer, Chenjerai Hove, wrote the war-inspired *Bones*, the tragic *Shadows* and the humorous *Shebeen Tales*.

The country's most famous female writer is the late Yvonne Vera, known for her courageous writing on challenging issues: rape, incest and gender inequality. She won the Commonwealth Prize in 1997 for *Under the Tongue*, and the Macmillan book prize for her acclaimed 2002 novel, *The Stone Virgins*.

Food & Drink

Beer You will most commonly see lager. The domestically brewed lagers – Zambezi and Castle – are really good.

Drinks Bottled mineral water, fruit juices and soft drinks are widely available.

Sadza A white maize meal made into either porridge or something resembling mashed potato, which is eaten with your fingers with tomato-based relishes, meat and/or gravy.

Tea and coffee Both are grown in the Eastern Highlands. Cafes and restaurants in the cities serve espresso coffee from either local or imported beans.

Lake Kariba

Lake Kariba

7 Lake Kariba is the nation's Riviera where it's all about houseboats, beer, fishing and amazing sunsets. It's one of the world's largest man-made lakes, covering an area of over 5000 sq km and holding 180 billion tonnes of water. Adjoining the Matusadona National Park means it's home to plenty of wildlife, including the Big Five. There's no swimming in the lake due to big crocs and reported bilharzia. There's no better way to experience the peacefulness and beauty of Lake Kariba than by renting a houseboat.

Khami Ruins

8 Just 22km from Bulawayo, the Unesco World Heritage listed Khami Ruins may not have the grandeur of Great Zimbabwe, but it's an impressive archaeological site. The second largest stone monument built in Zimbabwe, Khami was developed between 1450 and 1650 (after Great Zimbabwe) and is spread over a 2km site in a peaceful natural setting overlooking the Khami Dam.

Getting Around

Bus Express or 'luxury' buses operate according to published timetables. However, check carefully, as most bus companies have both local ('chicken buses' for locals) and luxury coaches.

Taxi Taxis are safe and can be booked through your hotel. Most are metered and those in cities will generally travel within a 40km radius of the city. Always take a taxi at night.

Train All major train services travel at night. The most popular route is from Victoria Falls to Bulawayo. Definitely opt for 1st-class, which is cheap and comfortable and gets you a sleeping compartment.

Index

The
World

THIS BOOK

This is the first edition of Lonely Planet's *The World* guidebook. This guidebook was commissioned in Lonely Planet's London office, and produced in the Melbourne office by:

Publishing Director
Piers Pickard

Commissioning Editor
Robin Barton

Contributing Author
Will Gourlay

....

Coordinating Product Editor
Penny Cordner

Assisting Product Editors
Carolyn Bain, Paul Harding, Anne Mason, Kate Mathews, Ross Taylor, Saralinda Turner

....

Coordinating Cartographer
Wayne Murphy

Assisting Cartographers
Shahara Ahmed, Anita Banh, Jeff Cameron, Hunor Csutoros, Piotr Czajkowski, Julie Dodkins, Mick Garrett, Mark Griffiths, Corey Hutchison, David Kemp, Valentina Kremenchutskaya, Chris Lee Ack, Alison Lyall, Liam McGrellis, Chris Metzis, Anthony Phelan, Navin Sushil, Samantha Tyson, Diana Von Holdt

Coordinating Book Designer
Lauren Egan

Assisting Book Designers
Katherine Marsh, Clara Monitto, Virginia Moreno, Mazzy Prinsep, Jessica Rose, Wibowo Rusli, Wendy Wright

....

Pre-press Production
Ryan Evans

Print Production
Larissa Frost

....

Thanks
Elin Berglund, Joe Bindloss, Kate Chapman, Ruth Cosgrove, Brendan Dempsey, Helen Elfer, Samantha Forge, James Hardy, Briohny Hooper, Elizabeth Jones, Chris Love, Kate Morgan, Catherine Naghten, Darren O'Connell, Martine Power, Alison Ridgway, Dianne Schallmeiner, Luna Soo, Angela Tinson, Sam Trafford, Brana Vladisavljevic, Tasmin Waby, Tracy Whitmey, Amanda Williamson

MIX
Paper from responsible sources
FSC™ C021741

Paper in this book is certified against the Forest Stewardship Council™ standards. FSC™ promotes environmentally responsible, socially beneficial and economically viable management of the world's forests.

Published by Lonely Planet Publications Pty Ltd
ABN 36 005 607 983
1st edition – Oct 2014
ISBN 978 1 74360 065 8
© Lonely Planet 2014   Photographs © as indicated 2014
10 9 8 7 6 5 4 3 2 1
Printed in Singapore

Although the authors and Lonely Planet have taken all reasonable care in preparing this book, we make no warranty about the accuracy or completeness of its content and, to the maximum extent permitted, disclaim all liability arising from its use.